Practical Web Technologies

P.K. Yuen and V. Lau

ADDISON-WESLEY

An imprint of **Pearson Education**

London • Boston • Indianapolis • New York • Mexico City
Toronto • Sydney • Tokyo • Singapore • Hong Kong • Cape Town
New Delhi • Madrid • Paris • Amsterdam • Munich • Milan

PEARSON EDUCATION LIMITED

Head Office:
Edinburgh Gate
Harlow CM20 2JE
Tel: +44 (0)1279 623623
Fax: +44 (0)1279 431059
Website: www.pearsoned.co.uk

_____

© Pearson Education Ltd 2003

First published in Great Britain in 2003

The rights of P.K. Yuen and V. Lau to be identified as the Authors of this Work have been
asserted by them in accordance with the Copyright, Designs and Patents Act 1988.

ISBN 0 201 75076 7

British Library Cataloguing in Publication Data
A CIP catalogue record for this book can be obtained from the British Library.

Library of Congress Cataloging in Publication Data
A catalog record for this book is available from the Library of Congress.

10 9 8 7 6 5 4 3 2 1
08 07 06 05 04

Typeset by Pantek Arts Ltd, Maidstone, Kent
Printed and bound in Great Britain by Bell and Bain Ltd, Glasgow.

The Publishers' policy is to use paper manufactured from sustainable forests.

To Dan Lavin and Johan Elliash

Contents at a glance

Contents

Preface

About this book

This book combines all major practical Web technologies and covers a complete series of Web applications. It provides an instant course and a reference for Web design beginners, young professionals (Web design programmers and engineers), as well as Web practitioners. We do not attempt to cover all aspects of a particular technology or to solve every problem with a single technology. Instead, we consider Web technologies as a whole to solve problems and generate applications. The contents and materials are organized with practical implementations in mind. All major Web technologies are included and arranged into five parts and three levels of study according to their strengths, application areas, and competition with other technologies:

Basic level: HTML/XHTML, CSS, Java, ECMAScript (or JavaScript), XML, and XSLT

Intermediate: DOM (W3C Document Object Model), CGI, Perl, ASP, ASP.NET, and PHP

Advanced: MySQL (Web Databases), SSL and TLS (Web Security), WML and WMLScript (Mobile Internet)

A complete spectrum of Web applications is presented, from Web design, client and server scripting, and e-commerce to cutting-edge skills such as broadcasting live video, Web databases and SSL security. More than 400 working examples are provided. Most of them are real applications from Web industries and projects. They are presented in "cut and paste" format so that they can be used directly in other Web applications. By including over 450 illustrations and screen shots, mastering all the Web technologies step by step in a global way can be achieved smoothly.

A quick tour of the book

This book is organized into five parts containing a total of 21 chapters, as follows.

Part I covers a fundamental course of Web design. It is suitable for Web design beginners and students to design and set up functional sites on the World Wide Web with styles (CSS styles), multimedia, 2D presentation graphics, and XML/XSLT features. Step-by-step practical examples are provided throughout. We begin with a practical study of the HTML/XHTML language and quickly get into the details of the Cascading Style Sheet (CCS). With CSS styles, formatting properties such as fonts, colors, borders, alignment, background, and images can be controlled and reused in a more structured way. To enhance the functionality and put Web pages into real applications, 2D presentation graphics such as lines, graphs, shapes, bar and pie charts are introduced. Examples to display data of different stock exchange indices are provided. Multimedia is an important subject for Web page design. In addition to different multimedia types such as sound, music, video, and movie formats, we present a detailed study of media players, plugins, and how to control them within Web pages. Some advanced applications such as broadcasting live video are also included. As another dimension of Web applications, we discuss XSLT transforms step by step. With XSLT, a considerable number of XML applications can be converted to HTML/XHTML pages and displayed by Web browsers directly.

Part II is dedicated to Web programming. It is suitable for Web designers and young professionals who want to seriously enhance their career prospects. First, comprehensive mouse controls including mouse over, buttons, clicks, text, and image move with the mouse are introduced. They are the foundations of dynamic Web page design. Next, programming browser windows such as Internet Explorer (IE) and Netscape (NS) is presented with a series of real examples on browser detection, redirection, window sizing, positioning, and other controls, generating random windows, and cycling over multiple windows. To put these programming skills into practice, a number of professional techniques including single and multiple moving objects, shootings, hit and scoring, drag and drop, random flying, and catching are demonstrated. These techniques can deliver dynamic life and add eye-catching effects to a Web page and in particular are vital for many game designs on the Web.

Part III is an extension of Part II. In order to solve all browser incompatibility problems, the W3C's Document Object Model (DOM) is introduced and studied extensively. With the DOM, Web pages can be programmed across all W3C-compliant browsers including the latest IE, NS, Opera, and many more. The second half of this part is related to date and time manipulation and the controlling of email. These tools are essential for many serious online businesses. In addition to various date and time controls, dynamic clocks and calendars, applications with countdown features such as "answer question within a certain time" and "countdown to next Christmas" are exploited. Needless to say, emailing is important on the Web. Your Web site can use it to send a thank you message to your visitors, to acknowledge something, confirm an order, or deliver a receipt. From browser emails to server emailing with ASP, Perl, and PHP, we provide everything that you need to control and program them. In fact, not just text emails, but also some examples on how to generate emails with "Attachments" and "Multipurpose Internet Mail Extensions (MIME)" are illustrated step by step.

Part IV is designed for more advanced topics and is suitable for students and young professionals with some experience of HTML/XHTML and Web programming. The first half of this part concentrates on the Common Gateway Interface (CGI) and server scripting technologies such as Perl, ASP, ASP. NET, and PHP. When server pages are developed by these techniques and requested by a Web browser, HTML/XHTML documents are usually generated and returned. Since server pages are processed by a server before a browser, they open a whole new series of Web applications essential for most online businesses. This part covers in detail applications ranging from basic operations such as getting user input, using file and server storage, properties of files, folders, and drives, using and changing passwords, online guest book, and a simple e-commerce model to more dedicated applications such as online examinations and marking, reserving seats online, search engines, and ODBC databases. For ASP users, ASP objects and how to migrate to ASP.NET are also included.

The second half of this part is about Web databases. A comprehensive study of the SQL language, databases, and their applications on the Web is presented. In particular, PHP has built-in database support so that database applications are more straightforward. For Perl and ASP, database techniques known as DBI and ADO are discussed in detail. All applications are demonstrated on a popular and freely available database product, MySQL.

Part V is dedicated to a more advanced topic, namely, Web security. This part is suitable for master students and professionals. We begin with data security and move quickly on to digital cryptography. Cryptography offers message encryption so that security and protection can be established on the insecure Internet and in the Web environment. In addition to encryption/decryption, public-key cryptography, digital signatures, and Message Digest are also discussed. They can be used to generate signatures to identify who you are and to guarantee that the encrypted message is only available to those for whom it is intended. Message Digest can also be used to protect downloads against viruses and any alterations on the Web. To put these skills into practice, a freely available product, namely, GnuPG, is used to demonstrate such techniques. In order to conduct online business (e-commerce) with total security, we present a detailed discussion on the Secure Sockets Layers (SSL) and certificates. With SSL, your site can become a secure site and communicates with the HTTPS protocol. All information and traffic between a client and the site are protected. We also show you how to modify the Web server software Apache to establish a secure Web site.

As an additional topic on the Web, we discuss the Mobile Internet and Wireless Markup Language (WML). Pages developed by WML can be displayed on wireless devices such as a mobile phone. As a contrast to the Web environment, WMLScript, m-business, CGI, and databases are also included with applications.

A study map

We have tried to design the book to be flexible. A study map for the book is provided as follows:

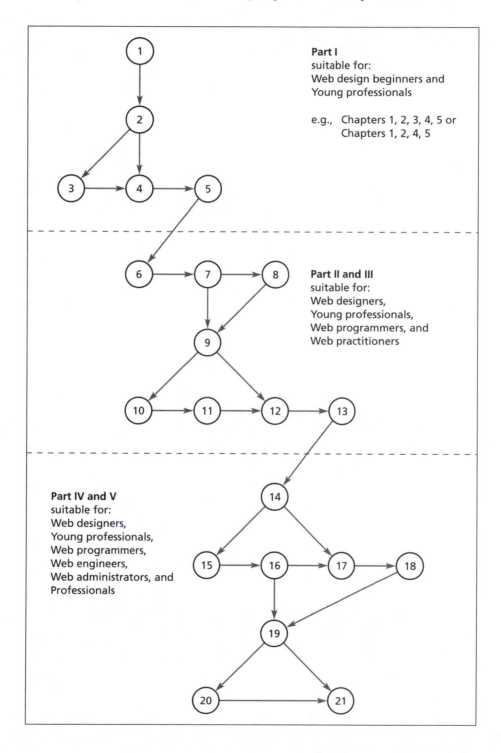

Companion Web Site

A Companion Web Site for this book can be found at www.booksites.net

Acknowledgments

One of the great joys of writing a book is to acknowledge the contributions of many individuals who have devoted tremendous efforts and long hours to this project. These include:

Sue Aikman	Daniel Akapo	Dalya Al-Quassem	Jimmy Cheng
Suet-Mui Lam	Cormac Lucas	Gautam Mitra	John Morris
Miroslav Novak	Ikenna Oliobi	Murat Uder	Lynette Van de Velde
Darren Ricks	Tai-Chuen Wong	Arthur Yuen	Charlie Yuen
Lai Ng	Ngan Po	Muna Zainalabedin	

From preparation to completion, their hard work, constructive feedback, valuable suggestions, understanding, and never-ending encouragement were crucial to making this project possible. In particular, Charlie and Tai-Chuen are contributors to this book. Charlie co-authored Chapter 4 and Tai-Chuen co-authored Chapter 5. Also, we pay tribute to the creativity and involvement of Arthur who did many of the drawings and art work for the examples.

Special thanks to the editorial team at Addison-Wesley including Simon Plumtree, Viki Williams, Tessa Fincham, and Neville Hankins for their efforts and hard work which contributed greatly to the quality of this book. It was truly a pleasure working with them.

P K Yuen
Principal Author

Part I

HTML/XHTML for instant Web

1   From HTML to XHTML and Web site design

1.1   Introduction: a practical review of XHTML

This chapter is an introduction to the Extensible Hyper Text Markup Language (XHTML) from a practical point of view, starting with simple Hyper Text Markup Language (HTML) pages and moving on quickly to XHTML documents and Web site design. You will learn how to write XHTML pages, build a functional Web site on the Internet, and get it registered on some of the most popular public search engines. Along with the Web page design, some detailed information on what happens inside the browser is also provided so that the communication and science behind the Web pages, browser, and the World Wide Web can be understood. Very little background knowledge is assumed and readers with some experience of using browsers such as Internet Explorer (IE) and Netscape (NS) should be able to complete this chapter easily.

While this chapter may not show you the whole of the subject, it should give you a solid basis for coping with more advanced stages of Web programming and technologies. Thanks to the standardization work of the World Wide Web Consortium (W3C) and many dedicated organizations and Internet engineers, Web technologies are becoming more and more stable and reliable. Many people are beginning to believe that Web applications are conquering every corner of the Internet. By following the Web standard recommended by the W3C authority, we have ensured that all examples in this chapter are XHTML compliant. They are validated as XHTML formal standard and tested on major browser software including IE5.x, IE6.+, NS4.x, NS6+, and Opera 6.+.

After covering the basic knowledge on Web configurations and how they work, this chapter will introduce some of the fundamental HTML/XHTML features such as text formatting, hyperlinks, images, and tables. These are the most basic elements that bring Web documents (or HTML files) alive. In particular, the use of images on Web pages generates a high level of visualization of documents, business logos, and commercial products. Often, they are vital for many businesses on the World Wide Web. Tables are one of the most useful tools in Web publishing: you'll find tables all over the Internet; they are often behind well-formed and structured Web pages.

Because XHTML brings strict programming style, strong discipline, and Extensible Markup Language (XML) compatibility to HTML pages, it is believed to be the next generation of HTML. Therefore in this book we generally use XHTML as our foundation for the discussion of Web technologies. Also, the discussion in this chapter will help you to understand the formal introduction to XML and XML Style Sheet Language Transformation (XSLT) in Chapter 5.

We begin by examining a sample HTML page generated by Microsoft Outlook Express. Using the simple rules and steps mentioned in section 1.2.1, HTML pages can be converted quite easily into XHTML format and put into immediate use with existing browsers such as IE or NS. Since HTML and XHTML are almost identical in practice, we generally treat all XHTML files as HTML and use the file extension ".htm."

Along with some practical examples of Web pages and the simple Cascading Style Sheet (CSS), our Web site development begins with a simple "Thank You" page for Web visitors. A page like this is handy and can be used as an error-handling page on the Internet. The "Graphical Edge" technique, using background images and transparency, is also discussed. Together with `Material Effects`, `Animated Pictures`, `Hyper Links`, and the integration of `Tables` and `Frames`, we develop a picture that every Web designer (or programmer) requires. By the end of this chapter, you will be able to have a Web site up and running and understand the basic XHTML building blocks of a Web page for World Wide Web users.

First, let's look at some basic details on Web requirements, Web configurations, and, more importantly, how the Web works.

1.1.1   Web requirements: a working browser

The basic requirement for accessing the Web is a machine (or computer) running browser software that has the ability to connect to the Internet environment and Web community. This may involve a permanent network connection, a local area network (LAN), or a personal one via a telephone line and an Internet Service Provider (ISP). A basic diagram showing how the Web works is given in Fig. 1.1.

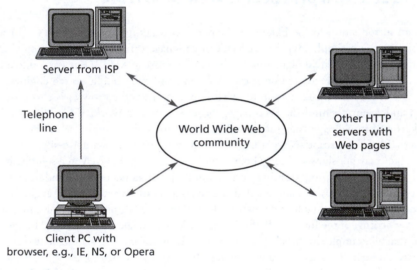

Figure 1.1 Basic Web diagram

By today's standards, with ISPs everywhere, even home-based computers are well equipped and have more than the basic Internet requirements. For the purposes of this chapter, and this book, we will assume that your machine has the basic Internet capabilities and that you have some experience in using Web browsers. Some other server requirements will be discussed when appropriate.

1.1.2   Web configurations: how the Web works

To access the Web, your computer (a Web client) will have to connect to another machine (a Web server) on the Internet via a network medium. For most home-based users, the Web server is usually a permanent machine on the Internet provided by the ISP and running server software. These systems may be a Microsoft NT system powered by the Internet Information Server (IIS) or UNIX (or LINUX) systems with Apache. Web browsers can be used to access millions of servers and get information by using the Hyper Text Transfer Protocol (HTTP). This process is sometimes called "The canonical browser–server interaction."

Typically, a Web client requests a document from a Web server through the HTTP command and a Uniform Resource Locator (URL). This occurs when the user types a Web address into the address field inside the browser. The server returns the document (usually in HTML format) and the browser displays that document in the browser window. This operation is generally referred to as *Web*.

The details of the browser–server dialog are not very important at this moment. The main task of the browser is to send the document request and the server is the machine that delivers the document. Consider the following command which you type in the address field of IE or NS:

http://www.abc.com/doc01.htm

This is one of the typical HTTP commands used to request the document doc01.htm from the www.abc.com site. A typical message that your browser will send to the server is

```
Listing: ex01-01.txt

 1:   GET /doc01.htm HTTP/1.0
 2:   Accept: www/source
 3:   Accept: text/html
 4:   Accept: image/gif
      ....
      ....
30:   Accept:
31:   User-Agent:        ((Your browser software ID))
32:   From:              ((Your Email Address ID))
34:     * a blank line *
```

For ease of reference, line numbers have been added to all listings in this book. The first line indicates which file the client wants and announces that the communication is HTTP version 1.0. This communication relies on the listed Accept elements in Multipurpose Internet Mail Extension (MIME) format. For example, in line 3, the text text/html means that the browser is expecting an HTML document in return. The blank line at the end identifies the end of the request.

The server, in this case www.abc.com, will then respond with a similar message like this:

```
Listing: ex01-02.txt

 1:   HTTP/1.0 200 OK
 2:   Date: Wednesday, 15-Oct-2003 13:04:12 GMT
 3:   Server:    ((Your Server Information))
 4:   MIME-version: 1.0
 5:   Last-modified: Monday, 13-Oct-2003 11:33:16 GMT
 6:   Content-type: text/html
 7:   Content-length: 5312
 8:       * a blank line *
 9:   <html><head><title>...</title></head><body>...((etc))
```

In line 1, the Web server agrees to use HTTP for communication and the status 200 indicates the successful completion of the whole request. After some HTTP system variables, Content-type: text/html in line 6 confirms that the document returned will indeed be an HTML document (or page). The entire HTML page will then be transmitted to the browser as illustrated in line 9. The entire dialog is specified by HTTP. The browser finally interprets this page and displays it on the screen. Again, the details of this dialog are not essential at this point.

This interaction or dialog set-up is important and considered as the foundation for all technologies between browsers and servers such as Perl, ASP, and PHP. A dialog like this will be discussed from time to time throughout this book when server technologies are introduced. At a minimum level, this dialog shows how and why a Web browser functions on the Web.

With the vast diversity of Web technologies we have today, the capabilities of browsers are far beyond the original HTML level. In order to gain a good grasp of the basic concepts, you can begin by designing some simple Web pages.

1.2   A quick start with Web pages

A Web page is a piece of information that can be displayed by the browser software. It can be as simple as displaying a single message on the screen, or as complex as a communicator for fully functional databases of large organizations shared on the Internet. The language used to compose a Web page is usually HTML, originally developed by Tim Berners-Lee and later adopted by the W3C authority. The HTML used in this chapter is simple but very practical for Web page design.

1.2.1   From HTML to XHTML

HTML is a text-based language so that it can be displayed, printed, and edited directly using your favorite editor such as Notepad on your PC. Our first HTML page is a very simple one:

```
Example: ex01-01.htm - Hello World

  1:    <html>
  2:    <body>
  3:        Hello World!
  4:    </body>
  5:    </html>
```

This will display a "Hello World!" message inside your browser. The central pillar of all HTML documents is the markup language commands (sometimes called *tag names* or *elements*).

The HTML language element <html> in line 1 asks the browser to start processing an HTML page or file. The element <body> in line 2 sets the beginning of the contents of the page. Line 3 is the message you want to display. The slash in line 4 indicates the closure of the <body> element. Line 5 denotes the closure of the HTML and hence ends the page.

Our second example is a classic one with the elements <title> and <div>:

```
Example: ex01-02.htm - A Page With Font And Size
  1:    <html>
  2:    <head>
  3:    <title>
  4:        My Second HTML Example - ex01-02.htm
  5:    </title>
  6:    </head>
  7:    <body>
  8:      <div style="font-family:arial;font-size:18pt">
  9:        Hello World!
 10:      </div>
 11:    </body>
 12:    </html>
```

The <title> elements between lines 3 and 5 will give the page a title and display it on the title bar of the browser. The <div> division elements between lines 8 and 10 state that you want to open a new division (similar to a paragraph without an additional line break) with the typeface Arial and a font size of 18pt (i.e., 18 points) displaying the "Hello World!" message. If you

- type the page into a text editor such as Notepad (without the line number of course) and
- save the page as a file with a file extension ".htm" (e.g., ex01-02.htm)

you can display the page in your favorite browser. For example, on a PC with Microsoft Windows, the browser can be activated to display the page by

- opening Windows Explorer (not the browser) and locating the file ex01-02.htm;
- double clicking the page file.

Alternatively, you can drag the file from Windows Explorer and drop it into the browser window. The result is shown in Fig. 1.2. The `style` attribute used in line 8 to specify the font and size of our message is called the CSS. The style used here is referred to as *inline* style. CSS is a very important subject on the Web. Much more information on CSS will be presented in Chapter 2.

The next example is a more interesting one: it represents a classic HTML generator. If you have Outlook Express in your system, it is quite likely that you have used it to write and send emails. Let's just write "Hello World!" in the "Outlook Express: New Mail" window with the typeface `Arial` and a font size of 18pt as shown in Fig. 1.3.

Figure 1.2 ex01-02.htm

Figure 1.3 Outlook Express

Now, if you click on the middle button Source at the bottom of the window bar (you may need to turn on the Source Edit option inside the View menu to activate this function), you will see a simple HTML page generated by Outlook Express as shown in listing ex01-03.txt.

```
Listing: ex01-03.txt

 1:    <!DOCTYPE HTML PUBLIC "-//W3C//DTD HTML 4.0 Transitional//EN">
 2:    <HTML><HEAD>
 3:    <META content="text/html; charset=windows-1252" http-equiv=Content-Type>
 4:    <META content="MSHTML 5.00.2314.1000" name=GENERATOR>
 5:    <STYLE>
 6:    </STYLE>
 7:    </HEAD>
 8:      <BODY bgColor=#ffffff>
 9:      <DIV><FONT face=Arial size=5>Hello World!</FONT>
10:    </DIV>
11:   </BODY>
12:   </HTML>
```

Apart from the document header in lines 1–4 and an empty style element `<style>` in lines 5–6, this page is very similar to our previous example. It uses `Arial` and a font size of 5 to display the "Hello World!" message. The attribute `bgColor=#ffffff` in line 8 is used to set the background color of the page to white. This HTML source code generated by Outlook Express is called the HTML 4.0 Transitional standard as indicated in the first line of the code. In many cases the document header and the `<META>` element are mainly for validation and/or information purposes. In a normal situation, the browsers will still run properly without these codes. We will discuss the importance of document headers later in Chapter 5 when XML is discussed.

HTML 4.0 Transitional is a stable version of HTML from the W3C authority, and has been adopted by a number of commercial products. This book will extend this HTML style and structure to the XHTML standard and use XHTML as a foundation for the discussions of Web technologies.

For a good starting point, you can follow these basic steps to convert HTML to XHTML structure:

- Use lower case for all elements.
- All elements should be closed (empty elements such as `<br>` should be replaced by `<br />`). This is why XHTML pages only have elements.
- Replace the HTML header `<html>` with the document header type shown in ex01-04.txt.
- All attributes should be quoted (e.g., `height="100" width="130"`).
- Stop using deprecated HTML elements such as `<font>` and replace with CSS style.

```
Listing: ex01-04.txt

1:  <?xml version="1.0" encoding="iso-8859-1"?>
2:  <!DOCTYPE html PUBLIC "-//W3C//DTD XHTML 1.0 Transitional//EN"
3:     "http://www.w3.org/TR/xhtml1/DTD/xhtml1-transitional.dtd">
4:  <html xmlns="http://www.w3.org/1999/xhtml" xml:lang="en" lang="en">
```

It is important to pay attention to the above procedures. These simple guidelines will help you to convert from an HTML to XHTML structure and lay a strong XHTML programming foundation for future practical programming on the Web.

From now on, the XHTML header (i.e., ex01-04.txt) will be used on all our Web pages. The first and the fourth line of the header are designed for XML and XML namespace so that the page will be rendered properly on dedicated XML software. Lines 2–3 are for formal declaration of the XHTML standard. In this chapter, we ignore the details, meaning, and behavior of the document header (i.e., lines 1–4) and include them as they are. In order to understand more about XHTML and use it to make our pages more colorful, we need to add more display fonts, colors, and background functionalities.

1.2.2 Adding fonts, colors, and background

Since XHTML pages ignore spaces between elements, you can write more compact code and, in many cases, this will also increase the readability of the code. Let's take a look at the following example with more control over style (i.e., fonts and their sizes).

```
Example: ex01-03.htm - A Page With Different Font Sizes

 1: <?xml version="1.0" encoding="iso-8859-1"?>
 2: <!DOCTYPE html PUBLIC "-//W3C//DTD XHTML 1.0 Transitional//EN"
 3:     "http://www.w3.org/TR/xhtml1/DTD/xhtml1-transitional.dtd">
 4: <html xmlns="http://www.w3.org/1999/xhtml" xml:lang="en" lang="en">
 5:  <head>
 6:    <title> A Page With Different Font Sizes - ex01-03.htm</title>
 7:  </head>
 8: <body>
 9: <div style="text-align:center">
10:   <span style="font-family:arial;font-size:12pt">This is Arial size=12</span><br />
11:   <span style="font-family:arial;font-size:14pt">This is Arial size=14</span><br />
12:   <span style="font-family:arial;font-size:18pt">This is Arial size=18</span><br />
13:   <span style="font-family:arial;font-size:24pt">This is Arial size=24</span><br />
14:   <span style="font-family:arial;font-size:30pt">This is Arial size=30</span><br />
15:   <span style="font-family:arial;font-size:42pt">This is Arial size=42</span><br />
16: </div>
17: </body>
18: </html>
```

The division elements `<div>` between lines 9 and 16 will generate a new paragraph to be displayed. Some Web developers may prefer to use the paragraph element `<p>` to create an additional line break instead. The division style in line 9, `style="text-align:center"`, will set the paragraph at the center of the browser window. The section element `<span>` defines a section of the document (without a new line). The font style inside the section is used to change the associated typeface and size accordingly. Finally, we use a line-break element `<br />` to generate a new line. Fig. 1.4 is a screen shot of this page.

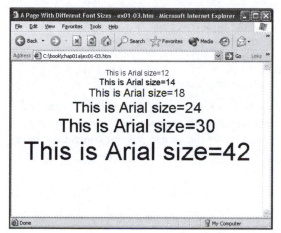

Figure 1.4 ex01-03.htm

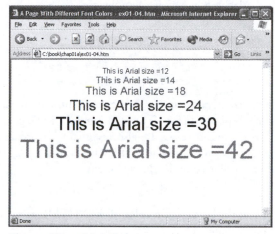

Figure 1.5 ex01-04.htm

Another useful feature of `style` is to set the `color` attribute and make color changes. This is shown in ex01-04.htm and Fig. 1.5.

Example: ex01-04.htm – A Page With Different Font Colors

```
 1: <?xml version="1.0" encoding="iso-8859-1"?>
 2: <!DOCTYPE html PUBLIC "-//W3C//DTD XHTML 1.0 Transitional//EN"
 3:     "http://www.w3.org/TR/xhtml1/DTD/xhtml1-transitional.dtd">
 4: <html xmlns="http://www.w3.org/1999/xhtml" xml:lang="en" lang="en">
 5: <head>
 6:  <title> A Page With Different Font Colors - ex01-04.htm</title>
 7: </head>
 8: <body>
 9:  <div style="text-align:center">
10:   <span style="font-family:arial;font-size:12pt;color:black">
11:   This is Arial size =12</span><br />
12:   <span style="font-family:arial;font-size:14pt;color:red">
13:   This is Arial size =14</span><br />
14:   <span style="font-family:arial;font-size:18pt;color:green">
15:   This is Arial size =18</span><br />
16:   <span style="font-family:arial;font-size:24pt;color:blue">
17:   This is Arial size =24</span><br />
18:   <span style="font-family:arial;font-size:30pt;color:black">
19:   This is Arial size =30</span><br />
20:   <span style="font-family:arial;font-size:42pt;color:fuchsia">
21:   This is Arial size =42</span><br />
22:  </div>
23: </body>
24: </html>
```

There are two simple ways to define a color value in XHTML. One is "colored by name" and the other "colored by 24-bit RGB mode." Colors in RGB mode are represented by a set of red, green, and blue color values. Each red, green, and blue is defined by an 8-bit number (hence it ranges from 0 to 255 inclusive), arranged into two hexadecimal numbers (i.e., `00-ff`). The general format for color attributes is `color="#RRGGBB"`. For example, the attribute `color="#123456"` defines a color value with `red="12"`, `green="34"`, and `blue="56"`. Since we are using two hexadecimal numbers to represent each red, green, and blue, the maximum color value is `color="#ffffff"` (i.e., white) and the minimum value is `color="#000000"` (i.e., black). Some more examples are

```
color = "#ff0000" => red=ff, green=00, blue=00 => combination is red
color = "#00ff00" => red=00, green=ff, blue=00 => combination is green
color = "#0000ff" => red=00, green=00, blue=ff => combination is blue
color = "#ffff00" => red=ff, green=ff, blue=00 => combination is yellow
color = "#ff00ff" => red=ff, green=00, blue=ff => combination is fuchsia
```

If the color values in example ex01-04.htm are replaced with the RGB value above, you will have exactly the same display as before. The total number of red, green, and blue color combinations is well over 16 million.

Background colors are also essential for many applications. One of the easiest ways to control the background color setting in XHTML is the `style="background:#cccccc"` attribute inside the `<body>` element. For example, the statement

```
<body style="background:#aaaaaa">
```

will set the background color of the XHTML page to gray. Now, let's modify the page ex01-04.htm by adding a background color:

```
Example: ex01-05.htm - A Page With Background Color:

 1: <?xml version="1.0" encoding="iso-8859-1"?>
 2: <!DOCTYPE html PUBLIC "-//W3C//DTD XHTML 1.0 Transitional//EN"
 3:     "http://www.w3.org/TR/xhtml1/DTD/xhtml1-transitional.dtd">
 4: <html xmlns="http://www.w3.org/1999/xhtml" xml:lang="en" lang="en">
 5: <head>
 6:  <title> A Page With Background Color - ex01-05.htm</title>
 7: </head>
 8: <body style="background:#aaaaaa">
 9:  <div style="text-align:center">
10:   <span style="font-family:arial;font-size:12pt;color:#000000">
11:     This is Arial size =12</span><br />
12:   <span style="font-family:arial;font-size:14pt;color:#ff0000">
13:     This is Arial size =14</span><br />
14:   <span style="font-family:arial;font-size:18pt;color:#00ff00">
15:     This is Arial size =18</span><br />
16:   <span style="font-family:arial;font-size:24pt;color:#0000ff">
17:     This is Arial size =24</span><br />
18:   <span style="font-family:arial;font-size:30pt;color:#ff00ff">
19:     This is Arial size =30</span><br />
20:   <span style="font-family:arial;font-size:42pt;color:#ffff00">
21:     <b>Arial size =42 Bold</b></span><br />
22:  </div>
23: </body>
24: </html>
```

The bold element `<b>` in line 21 is used to set the font as bold type and hence provide a stronger character effect on the screen. A screen shot of this page is shown in Fig. 1.6.

Figure 1.6 ex01-05.htm

Figure 1.7 ex01-06.htm

1.2.3   A "Thank You!" page to Web visitors

You now have everything you need to create a simple "Thank You!" Web page. This page displays a welcome message to all visitors as shown in Fig. 1.7. Since our Web site is obviously not yet fully functional, a page like this can be quite useful for visitors.

The page can be easily constructed by using `<body>`, `<div>`, `<br />` and `<b>` elements and their associated attributes.

```
Example: ex01-06.htm - A Thankyou Page

 1: <?xml version="1.0" encoding="iso-8859-1"?>
 2: <!DOCTYPE html PUBLIC "-//W3C//DTD XHTML 1.0 Transitional//EN"
 3:      "http://www.w3.org/TR/xhtml1/DTD/xhtml1-transitional.dtd">
 4: <html xmlns="http://www.w3.org/1999/xhtml" xml:lang="en" lang="en">
 5: <head>
 6:   <title> A Thankyou Page - ex01-06.htm</title>
 7: </head>
 8: <body style="background:#000044">
 9:  <div style="text-align:center">
10:   <span style="font-family:arial;font-size:42pt;color:#00ffff">
11:      <b>Welcome To</b> <br /> </span>
12:   <span style="font-family:arial;font-size:30pt;color:#ffff00">
13:      <b>My Personal Web Page</b> <br /> </span>
14:   <span style="font-family:arial;font-size:23pt;color:#ff0000">
15:      <b>www.pwt-ex.com/JohnSmith/index.htm</b> <br /> <br /> <br /> </span>
16:   <span style="font-family:arial;font-size:23pt;color:#ffff00">
17:      <b>This Web Site Will Be Available Soon !</b> <br /> </span>
18:   <span style="font-family:arial;font-size:18pt;color:#00ff00">
19:      <b>Please Contact Me Using the Following Email</b> <br /> <br /> </span>
20:   <span style="font-family:arial;font-size:14pt;color:#00ffff">
21:      <b>JohnSmith@pwt-ex.com</b> <br /> <br /> </span>
22:   <span style="font-family:arial;font-size:30pt;color:#ff0000">
23:      <b>Thank You!</b> </span>
24:  </div>
25: </body>
26: </html>
```

If you have a Web site address and some storage space on the Web site, you can put this file into storage for visitors to browse. For example, your ISP (e.g., www.pwt-ex.com) may provide you with the following personal Web site address and space (or root directory):

www.pwt-ex.com/JohnSmith   –   Web site address

`public_html`   –   Root directory for your Web site

You can upload the file (e.g., ex01-06.htm) onto the `public_html` directory of your Web site address using software such as File Transfer Protocol (FTP). Details will be presented at the end of this chapter. Your friends or other visitors can then access your page via the "http" command

http://www.pwt-ex.com/JohnSmith/ex01-06.htm

Note that if you rename the file ex01-06.htm as index.htm, visitors can normally access your page by using the command

http://www.pwt-ex.com/JohnSmith

If you have a Web site address called www.mysite.com and you have a default Web page file called index.htm or default.htm in your Web directory, then this page, and hence your site, can be browsed directly using the command

http://www.mysite.com

In practice, a "Thank You" page is sometimes very convenient for event handling such as "Error," "Sorry," "Waiting," "Alert," and "Confirm." You will notice that these types of pages are common on the Web.

In order to have a more colorful, eye-catching XHTML page, we must now integrate images into it. You will be surprised at how easily one can incorporate images into Web pages.

1.3   Using images on XHTML

Most popular browsers now support a large number of standard image formats. Two of them are introduced in this section: the "GIF" and "JPG (or JPEG)" images. They are special files used on computers to represent pictures, photos, and images. For example, the file `mypict.jpg` is a picture file called `mypict` in `jpg` format identified by the file extension `jpg`. The `gif` image files are also popular in the Web community and more details will be presented in sections 1.3.1 and 1.3.4.

Any supported images can be directly integrated into XHTML pages by using the classic image element `<img>`. Similar to the line-break element `<br>`, `<img>` is an empty element in XHTML (i.e., without an end element). You need to add "/" to close it. The best way to study the `<img>` (or `<img />`) element is to learn from examples.

1.3.1   Adding images to our pages

Suppose you have a `jpg` (or `jpeg`) image stored in a file called logo_web.jpg. This file can be easily imported into an XHTML page by using the image element `<img>` and attribute `src` (i.e., source location) as demonstrated in ex01-07.htm.

```
Example: ex01-07.htm – Using Image Element <img>

1: <?xml version="1.0" encoding="iso-8859-1"?>
2: <!DOCTYPE html PUBLIC "-//W3C//DTD XHTML 1.0 Transitional//EN"
3:     "http://www.w3.org/TR/xhtml1/DTD/xhtml1-transitional.dtd">
4: <html xmlns="http://www.w3.org/1999/xhtml" xml:lang="en" lang="en">
5: <head>
```

```
 6:    <title> Using Image Element <img> - ex01-07.htm</title>
 7:  </head>
 8:  <body style="background:#000044">
 9:   <div style="text-align:center"><br /><br />
10:    <span style="font-family:arial;font-size:22pt;color:#00ff00">
11:       <b>We Have Images!</b><br /></span>
12:    <img alt="pic" src="logo_web.jpg" /><br />
13:    <span style="font-family:arial;font-size:14pt;color:#00ffff">
14:       <b>Practical Web Technologies</b>
15:      <br /><br /></span>
16:   </div>
17:  </body>
18:  </html>
```

The key statement in this XHTML page is line 12:

```
<img alt="pic" src="logo_web.jpg" />
```

This code will ask the browser to display an image called logo_web.jpg located in the local directory. Usually, this local directory is the default directory where you store your Web page. If the image file logo_web.jpg is located inside another directory (e.g., pic.dir\logo_web.jpg), you need to modify the code to include the directory:

```
<img alt="pic" src="pic.dir\logo_web.jpg" />
```

If the picture file cannot be found, then the attribute `alt="pic"` will override execution and display the message "pic" on the screen. This attribute is compulsory to produce code to XHTML standard and reflects the strict programming discipline of XHTML.

Note that there is a difference between using directories and paths between UNIX and PC (Microsoft) environments. For UNIX users, a slash "/" is used to separate directories on a path, such as

```
usr/local/cgi-bin/public_html/default.html
```

For PC (Microsoft) systems, a back slash "\" is used instead. Since most browsers on the Web support the UNIX convention, including different versions of IE, we will use a slash throughout this book.

As we can see, the integration of images into XHTML is very simple and straightforward. Suppose we have a Web site called www.pwt-ex.com with this example ex01-07.htm in a directory book/chap01a. This page can be browsed using the following command on IE, NS, or other browsers:

```
http://www.pwt-ex.com/book/chap01a/ex01-07.htm
```

From now on, www.pwt-ex.com and /book/chapXXa are respectively the default address and directories used in this book. A screen shot of ex01-07.htm is shown in Fig. 1.8.

Let's now study another example with more images. This example involves our logo logo_web.jpg and three balloon GIF images. The balloons are arranged horizontally below the logo. Since both JPG and GIF images are supported, they can be imported into a Web page by simple `<img>` statements as shown in the example code ex01-08.htm.

```
Example: ex01-08.htm - Adding Multiple Images

 1: <?xml version="1.0" encoding="iso-8859-1"?>
 2: <!DOCTYPE html PUBLIC "-//W3C//DTD XHTML 1.0 Transitional//EN"
 3:    "http://www.w3.org/TR/xhtml1/DTD/xhtml1-transitional.dtd">
 4: <html xmlns="http://www.w3.org/1999/xhtml" xml:lang="en" lang="en">
 5: <head>
 6:   <title> Adding Multiple Images - ex01-08.htm</title>
 7: </head>
 8: <body style="background:#000044">
 9:  <div style="text-align:center"><br />
10:   <span style="font-family:times;font-size:22pt;color:#00ff00">
11:      <b>Practical Web Technologies</b><br /><br /></span>
```

```
12:    <img alt="pic" src="logo_web.jpg" width="180" height="90" /><br /><br />
13:    <img alt="pic" src="balloon.gif" />
14:    <img alt="pic" src="balloon.gif" />
15:    <img alt="pic" src="balloon.gif" /><br />
16:    <span style="font-family:times;font-size:16pt;color:#00ffff">
17:       <b>Balloon Images<br />
18:       Now I Know How To Put Images Together</b><br /></span>
19:    </div>
20:    </body>
21:    </html>
```

In line 12, the width and height attributes associated with the <img> element are used to control the size of the image. In this case, the logo picture will be stretched into the size width="180" (180 pixels) and height="90" (90 pixels). This result is shown in Fig. 1.9.

Figure 1.8 ex01-07.htm

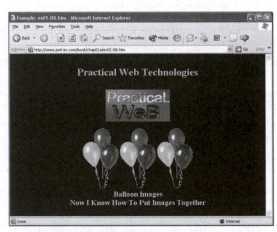

Figure 1.9 ex01-08.htm

1.3.2 Background images: edges and material effects

Many Web designers also like to use a small picture and repeatedly display it in a horizontal and/or vertical direction to form a background. This small picture can be a photo, a pattern, and/or some graphic designs. With careful arrangement, this type of background can create an eye-catching effect.

To add a background image in XHTML is very straightforward. All you need to do is to add an image file associated with the background attribute inside the <body> element. For example, the statement

```
<body style="background:url('bg_image.gif')">
```

will repeatedly insert an image bg_image.gif into the body of your page to create a background picture. Similar to the src attribute in the image element <img>, the url (i.e., the uniform resource locator) is used to locate the picture file.

Apart from a background picture, and thanks to the transparency feature, this background technique can also be used to create a "Graphical Edge" effect for Web pages. Consider the following code ex01-09.htm:

```
Example: ex01-09.htm - Generating Graphical Edges

1:  <?xml version="1.0" encoding="iso-8859-1"?>
2:  <!DOCTYPE html PUBLIC "-//W3C//DTD XHTML 1.0 Transitional//EN"
3:      "http://www.w3.org/TR/xhtml1/DTD/xhtml1-transitional.dtd">
4:  <html xmlns="http://www.w3.org/1999/xhtml" xml:lang="en" lang="en">
5:  <head>
```

```
 6:     <title> Generating Graphical Edges - ex01-09.htm</title>
 7: </head>
 8: <body style="background:url('formal.gif') repeat-x #000044">
 9:   <div style="text-align:center"><br /><br /><br /><br /><br /><br />
10:   <span style="font-family:times;font-size:20pt;color:#00ff00">
11:      <b>Practical Web Technologies</b><br /><br /></span>
12:   <img alt="pic" src="logo_web.jpg" width="180" height="90" /><br /><br />
13:   <img alt="pic" src="balloon.gif" />
14:   <img alt="pic" src="balloon.gif" />
15:   <img alt="pic" src="balloon.gif" /><br />
16:   <span style="font-family:times;font-size:16pt;color:#00ffff">
17:      <b>Balloon Images<br />
18:      I Know How To Generate Graphical Edges Now</b><br /></span>
19:   </div>
20: </body>
21: </html>
```

This example is basically the same as ex01-08.htm, with the addition of a `background` attribute to `<body>` in line 8, i.e.,

```
<body style="background:url('formal.gif') repeat-x #000044">
```

Here, the background picture formal.gif is actually a long strip of graphic design. The upper part of this strip is a graphic image and the lower part is a long strip of transparency. When the browser renders this background repeatedly in the horizontal direction (i.e., `repeat-x`), the transparency part has no effect on the page. The upper design will form a graphical edge on top of the screen. This technique has an advantage in that the size of the edge will change according to the size of the browser window (see Fig. 1.10).

Another application of this background technique is the creation of what is called a "Material Effect" for a page. A large variety of materials (or background textures) can now be found on the Internet and various Web sites. They are just small pictures (or patterns) of a given material. Some of the popular patterns commonly used on the Web are shown in Fig. 1.11.

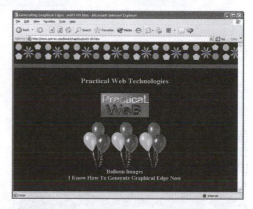

Figure 1.10 ex01-09.htm

To incorporate these effects into your Web page is very simple. Consider the page shown in ex01-10.htm:

Example: ex01-10.htm - Material Effects

```
 1: <?xml version="1.0" encoding="iso-8859-1"?>
 2: <!DOCTYPE html PUBLIC "-//W3C//DTD XHTML 1.0 Transitional//EN"
 3:      "http://www.w3.org/TR/xhtml1/DTD/xhtml1-transitional.dtd">
 4: <html xmlns="http://www.w3.org/1999/xhtml" xml:lang="en" lang="en">
 5: <head>
 6:   <title> Material Effects - ex01-10.htm</title>
 7: </head>
 8: <body style="background:url('image001.jpg')">
 9:   <div style="text-align:center"><br /><br />
10:   <span style="font-family:arial;color:#ffff00;font-size:20pt">
11:      <b>We Have Background Effects!</b><br /><br /></span>
12:   <img alt="pic" src="logo_web.jpg" /><br /><br />
13:   <span style="font-family:arial;color:#00ffff;font-size:18pt">
14:      <b>Practical Web Technologies</b>
15:      <br /><br /></span>
16:   </div>
17: </body>
18: </html>
```

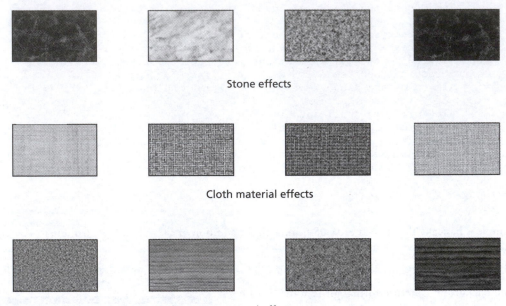

Stone effects

Cloth material effects

Wood effects

Figure 1.11 Material effect patterns

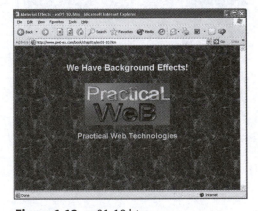

Figure 1.12 ex01-10.htm

As you can see from this example, all you have to do is to put the "Material Effect" picture file (e.g., image001.jpg) into the background attribute of the `<body>` element as illustrated in line 8. Provided the background picture file image001.jpg is in the same directory as the Web page, the browser can read the file and generate a background. A screen shot of this page is shown in Fig. 1.12.

In Fig. 1.12, the stone pattern forms a large marble background on your page creating a simple but realistic background effect. This simple but effective technique is widely used in the Web industries.

Now that you've been introduced to images and backgrounds, it's time to take a look at how animated pictures can be displayed on a Web page.

1.3.3   Animated images: cartoon animation

The fierce competition among image standards for the Web in the 1990s greatly enhanced the functionalities of image formats. One effective solution was the so-called "Graphics Interchange Format" (GIF). This image format is based on a lossless compression method called "LZW," which produces a picture that is suitable for low-bandwidth transmission. This format, particularly the "GIF89a" specification standard, provides the following functionalities for Web users:

- *Transparency*: In a "transparent GIF," one of the colors can be selected as transparent. This allows the background of the Web page to show through (as demonstrated by the previous examples).
- *Animation*: An "animated GIF" is an image file with a sequence of subimages used to produce the desired animation. A browser that supports the GIF89a standard is capable of displaying continuously all subimages or one subimage at a time.

Following the "GIF89a" specification, GIF images with animation effects are usually called "Animated GIF" and form one of the image standards on the Web. In particular, when used with dynamic motion and/or controlled movement, this feature can produce stunning effects. We will show you some simple examples in this section. More advanced techniques will be discussed in Chapter 9.

The incorporation of animated GIF pictures into an XHTML page requires no special technique. Indeed this can be achieved by using the familiar image element <img>. The following is an example of the <img> element at work:

```
Example: ex01-11.htm - 2D Animated Image

 1: <?xml version="1.0" encoding="iso-8859-1"?>
 2: <!DOCTYPE html PUBLIC "-//W3C//DTD XHTML 1.0 Transitional//EN"
 3:      "http://www.w3.org/TR/xhtml1/DTD/xhtml1-transitional.dtd">
 4: <html xmlns="http://www.w3.org/1999/xhtml" xml:lang="en" lang="en">
 5: <head>
 6:  <title>2D Animated Image - ex01-11.htm</title>
 7: </head>
 8: <body style="background:#9090ee">
 9:  <div style="text-align:center">
10:  <span style="font-family:arial;font-size:30pt;color:#00ffff">
11:      <b>Welcome To</b><br /></span>
12:  <span style="font-family:arial;font-size:23pt;color:#ffff00">
13:      <b>My Personal Web Page</b><br /><br /></span>
14:  <img alt="pic" src="line1.gif" width="550" height="8" /><br /><br />
15:  <img alt="pic" src="boom01.gif" /><br />
16:  <span style="font-family:arial;font-size:16pt;color:#00ffff">
17:   <b>Practical Web Technologies</b>
18:   <br /><br />
19:  </span>
20: </div>
21: </body>
22: </html>
```

The image (line1.gif) used in line 14 is a "Horizontal Line" type picture in red. You can use this image with attributes width and height to draw a line on your page. The animated GIF file boom01.gif is defined in line 15. This is a picture file with 16 subimages. These subimages are all GIF files with file names denoted by an01_00.gif to an01_15.gif respectively (see Fig. 1.13). The construction of the overall animated file boom01.gif is easily accomplished by the following steps:

- Draw the first image an01_00.gif (e.g., by using MS Paint).
- Erase part of the fuse in the picture and save it as an01_01.gif.
- Continue with the "deletion" picture an01_13.gif.
- Draw the "Boom" picture as an01-14.gif.
- Draw a text picture an01_15.gif.
- Use animated GIF software to combine all pictures together as a single image.
- Save (or output) this single image file as boom01.gif.

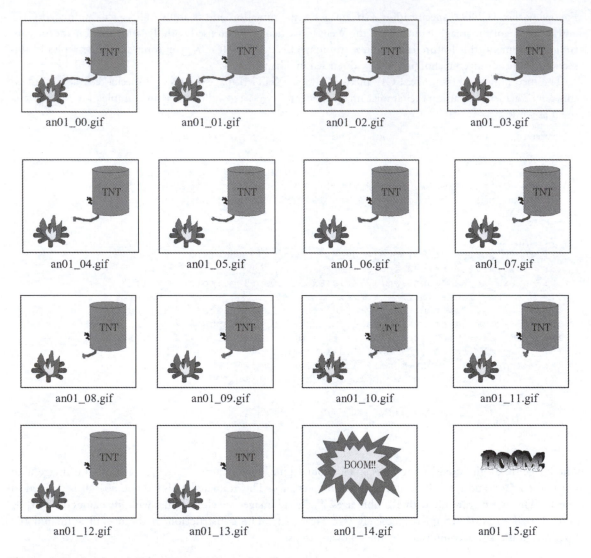

an01_00.gif   an01_01.gif   an01_02.gif   an01_03.gif

an01_04.gif   an01_05.gif   an01_06.gif   an01_07.gif

an01_08.gif   an01_09.gif   an01_10.gif   an01_11.gif

an01_12.gif   an01_13.gif   an01_14.gif   an01_15.gif

Figure 1.13 Animated GIF sequence – boom01.gif

Figure 1.14 ex01-11.htm

There are many types of animated GIF software available on the Internet. Two of the them are the GIF Construction Set from Alchemy Mindworks Inc. (www.mindworkshop.com) and GIF Animator from Ulead Systems Inc. (www.ulead.com). The software used here is GIF Animator. All these subimages are listed in Fig. 1.13 and are available individually on the Web site that accompanies this book.

One important factor in building good animated pictures is the timing control. In this example we've given subimages an01_00.gif, an01_14.gif, and an01_15.gif a longer display time. A screen shot of this animation is shown in Fig. 1.14.

1.3.4   More animated images: a 3D animated logo

The beauty of the animated GIF images is that once they are developed, they can be treated as a single picture file. The picture can be easily included in your emails, or used to produce animated effects in your Web page, without the hassle of using other Web technologies such as JavaScript, VBScript, and Java. This technique has a very important role to play in the area of small animation sequence applications such as dynamic logo design and advertising on the Internet.

In the next example, you will see how to build a realistic three-dimensional (3D) animation sequence. We start with a simple logo named "Rody" and subsequently extend it to a 3D logo with texture.

This logo can be created easily by any conventional 3D drawing package such as Cool 3D from Ulead Systems Inc. (www.ulead.com). Using this software, we can perform various types of classical 3D movements on our object, such as horizontal and vertical rotations. For the sake of discussion, we've arranged 14 different 3D positions and saved them as GIF files. These pictures are listed in Fig. 1.15.

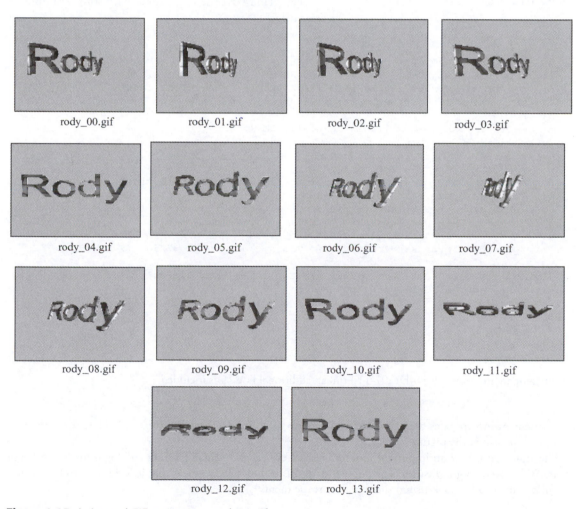

Figure 1.15 Animated GIF sequence – rody04.gif

Figure 1.16 ex01-12.htm

As mentioned above, the Cool 3D software is used to produce a single animated GIF file rody04.gif. This file is then added to ex01-11.htm to create ex01-12.htm with more animated images in one page.

If this example ex01-12.htm is run with a reasonably good machine and browser, you should see two animated pictures working simultaneously. A screen shot of this example on IE is shown in Fig. 1.16.

Another direct benefit from the transparency feature of the GIF picture is that a transparent background, in many cases, makes objects look more realistic and also makes sure that two or more files can be animated together without background (or background color) interference.

The XHTML code associated with this example is listed below:

```
Example: ex01-12.htm - 3D Animated Image

 1: <?xml version="1.0" encoding="iso-8859-1"?>
 2: <!DOCTYPE html PUBLIC "-//W3C//DTD XHTML 1.0 Transitional//EN"
 3:     "http://www.w3.org/TR/xhtml1/DTD/xhtml1-transitional.dtd">
 4: <html xmlns="http://www.w3.org/1999/xhtml" xml:lang="en" lang="en">
 5: <head>
 6:   <title>3D Animated Image - ex01-12.htm</title>
 7: </head>
 8: <body style="background:#aaaadd">
 9:   <div style="text-align:center">
10:   <span style="font-family:arial;font-size:30pt;color:#00ffff">
11:       <b>Welcome To</b><br /></span>
12:   <span style="font-family:arial;font-size:23pt;color:#ffff00">
13:       <b>My Personal Web Page</b><br /><br /></span>
14:    <img alt="pic" src="line1.gif" width="550" height="8" /><br /><br />
15:    <img alt="pic" src="rody04.gif" width="300" height="250" /><br />
16:    <img alt="pic" src="boom01.gif" /> <br />
17:   <span style="font-family:arial;font-size:16pt;color:#00ffff">
18:   <b>Practical Web Technologies</b>
19:   <br /><br />
20:   </span>
21: </div>
22: </body>
23: </html>
```

If you compare this example with ex01-11.htm, an additional line 15 is included:

```
<img alt="pic" src="rody04.gif" width="300" height="250" />
```

This statement incorporates the 3D animated logo into the page. The attributes `width` and `height` are used to control the size of the picture display.

The animated GIF is an important tool for creating eye-catching small pictures and logos for personal use or the Web advertising industries. The popularity of this technique is so great that it is difficult to find a successful commercial (or advertising) site that doesn't use them.

1.4   Hyperlinks, tables, and frames

Apart from the "http" command on the browser, the anchor element `<a>` in XHTML provides another powerful method to connect to pages and documents on other Web sites. For example, a single anchor element such as

```
<a href=http://www.othersite.com>Link To www.othersite.com</a>
```

could link (or hyperlink) your page to the site www.othersite.com. This feature can connect your page to millions of other servers or Web pages on the Internet and therefore reach a truly world-wide scale.

1.4.1   Hyperlink to the Web world

When a browser executes the following code with anchor

```
<a href="http://www.hotmail.com">Microsoft Hotmail</a>
```

it will display and underline the text "Microsoft Hotmail" on the screen. If the Web user clicks the underlined text with a mouse, the browser will invoke the hyper reference attribute `href` and perform the action http://www.hotmail.com. That is, it jumps to the home page of the "Microsoft Hotmail" and displays it on the browser screen.

If you use the attribute `target` associated with the anchor element such as

```
<a href="http://www.hotmail.com" target="_blank">Microsoft Hotmail</a>
```

then the browser will open another new browser window and use it to connect to www.hotmail.com, keeping the original browser screen unchanged.

The actions associated with `href` can be virtually anything supported by your browser, including:

- another XHTML document in a local and/or World Wide Web location;
- picture files (e.g., `gif`, `jpg`, `bmp`, or `tiff`);
- sound files (e.g., `wav`, `au`, or `aiff`);
- multimedia movie files (e.g., `mov`, `avi`, or `mpg`).

For example, when a user clicks the underlined text "Sound Of A Broken Glass" in the code

```
<a href="glass.wav">Sound Of A Broken Glass</a>
```

the `href` action is to get the sound file glass.wav and play the sound on your machine. Similar code and processes also apply to other picture and multimedia movie files. However, not all browser software supports all types of multimedia files. Multimedia and browser differences will be discussed in Chapter 4.

The following is an example of the `<a href="xxx">` element at work:

```
Example: ex01-13.htm - Hyper Links

 1: <?xml version="1.0" encoding="iso-8859-1"?>
 2: <!DOCTYPE html PUBLIC "-//W3C//DTD XHTML 1.0 Transitional//EN"
 3: "http://www.w3.org/TR/xhtml1/DTD/xhtml1-transitional.dtd">
 4: <html xmlns="http://www.w3.org/1999/xhtml" xml:lang="en" lang="en">
 5: <head>
 6:   <title> Hyper Links - ex01-13.htm</title>
 7: </head>
 8:
 9: <body style="background:#000088">
10:   <div style="text-align:center">
11:     <span style="font-family:arial;font-size:18pt;color:#ffff00"><br />
12:       <b>My Favorite Web Pages</b><br /></span>
13:     <span style="font-family:arial;font-size:16pt;color:#00ffff">
```

```
14:        <b>(Practical Web Technologies)</b><br /><br /></span>
15:      <img alt="pic" src="line1.gif" width="550" height="4" /><br /><br />
16:   </div>
17:
18:
19:   <img alt="pic" src="bullet1.gif" width="15" height="15"
20:      align="top" hspace="60" vspace="5" />
21:   <a href="http://www.pwt-ex.com" target="_blank"
22:       style="font-family:arial;font-size:16pt;color:#ffff00">
23:        <b>www.pwt-ex.com</b></a><br /><br />
24:
25:   <img alt="pic" src="bullet1.gif" width="15" height="15"
26:      align="top" hspace="60" vspace="5" />
27:   <a href="http://www.hotmail.com" target="_blank"
28:       style="font-family:arial;font-size:16pt;color:#ffff00">
29:         <b>www.hotmail.com</b></a><br /><br />
30:
31:   <img alt="pic" src="bullet1.gif" width="15" height="15"
32:      align="top" hspace="60" vspace="5" />
33:   <a href="mailto:"
34:       style="font-family:arial;font-size:16pt;color:#ffff00">
35:          <b>Send An Email To Someone</b></a><br /><br />
36:
37:   <img alt="pic" src="bullet1.gif" width="15" height="15"
38:      align="top" hspace="60" vspace="5" />
39:   <a href="file://c:" target="_blank"
40:       style="font-family:arial;font-size:16pt;color:#ffff00">
41:          <b>Files On My C Drive</b></a><br /><br />
42:
43: </body>
44: </html>
```

Figure 1.17 shows the screen shot of example ex01-13.htm.

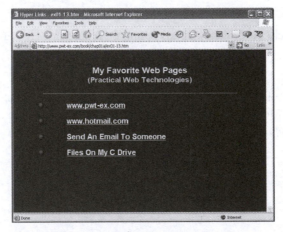

Figure 1.17 ex01-13.htm

This is a page containing four anchor elements. Let's consider them one by one in detail. The first bullet option on the screen was generated by the following XHTML code fragment:

```
19:   <img alt="pic" src="bullet1.gif" width="15" height="15"
20:      align="top" hspace="60" vspace="5" />
21:   <a href="http://www.pwt-ex.com" target="_blank"
22:       style="font-family:arial;font-size:16pt;color:#ffff00">
23:        <b>www.pwt-ex.com</b></a><br /><br />
```

First the text "www.pwt-ex.com" in line 23 is underlined by the browser. By default, the browser will underline all messages or texts bounded by the anchor element <a>. When this underlined text is clicked on using a mouse, the attribute `href="www.pwt-ex.com"` in line 21 is activated and the browser jumps to the corresponding Web site. The target attribute `target="_blank"` used in line 21 makes sure that a new browser window is opened.

Web visitors will notice a change in the shape of the mouse cursor when it runs over the underlined text. This indicates that the hyperlink is ready for a *click*.

The image file bullet1.gif used in line 19 is actually a bullet shape picture with a size of 15×15 pixels. The new image attributes `hspace` and `vspace` defined in line 20 are used to control the positions of the bullet picture. For example, `hspace="60"` sets a space of 60 pixels on both the left and right sides of the picture and `vspace="5"` sets a size of 5 pixels on both the top and bottom of the picture. They are used to make sure that the bullet is located at the proper location against the text.

If you click on the third option "Send An Email To Someone" (line 35) then the action in line 33

```
33:   <a href="mailto:"
34:       style="font-family:arial;font-size:16pt;color:#ffff00">
35:          <b>Send An Email To Someone</b></a><br /><br />
```

is activated. This "mailto" command sends a signal to the browser to launch the default email software in your system. In our case, "Microsoft Outlook Express" is activated (see Fig. 1.18). More discussion on this mail agent will be continued in Part II.

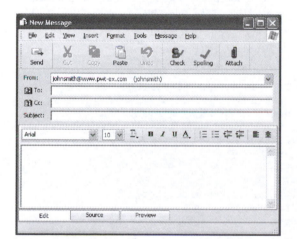

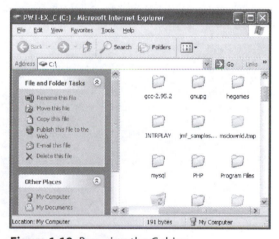

Figure 1.18 Mail agent   **Figure 1.19** Browsing the C drive

In some cases, browsers can also be used to browse all files and directories of your file system. In fact, some Web servers will even allow you to browse their file systems remotely. To demonstrate this functionality, let's click on the final option "Files On My C Drive" (line 41) in our example. This action activates the statement in line 39

```
39:   <a href="file://c:" target="_blank"
40:       style="font-family:arial;font-size:16pt;color:#ffff00">
41:          <b>File On My C Drive</b></a><br /><br />
```

and the browser will browse the whole C drive of your PC. A browsing result on our PC is shown in Fig. 1.19.

1.4.2   XHTML tables and formatting

Tables in XHTML are controlled by the element pair `<table>` and `</table>`. Between the table element pair, table rows can be defined by

`<tr></tr>` – used to defined one table row

Inside each table row, table data (or table cell) elements can be defined as

`<td></td>` – used to defined one table data

A typical table of two rows by three columns with `width="500"` and `border="2"` can be defined by the following code:

```
Listing: ex01-05.txt

1:     <table width="500" border="2">
2:       <tr>
3:        <td>Row 1 Col 1</td><td>Row 1 Col 2</td><td>Row 1 Col 3</td>
4:       </tr>
5:       <tr>
6:        <td>Row 2 Col 1</td><td>Row 2 Col 2</td><td>Row 2 Col 3</td>
7:       </tr>
8:     </table>
```

The `width` attribute in line 1 sets the width of the entire table as 500 pixels. The `border` attribute is used to set whether the table should have a border. To put this into practice, a "Shopping Note" page is developed in example ex01-14.htm.

```
Example: ex01-14.htm – XHTML Table

 1: <?xml version="1.0" encoding="iso-8859-1"?>
 2: <!DOCTYPE html PUBLIC "-//W3C//DTD XHTML 1.0 Transitional//EN"
 3: "http://www.w3.org/TR/xhtml1/DTD/xhtml1-transitional.dtd">
 4: <html xmlns="http://www.w3.org/1999/xhtml" xml:lang="en" lang="en">
 5:  <head>
 6:    <title> XHTML Table – ex01-14.htm</title>
 7:  </head>
 8: <body style="background:#444488">
 9:
10: <div align="center" style="font-family:arial;font-size:12pt">
11: <span style="font-size:23pt;color:#00ff00">
12:    <b>Shopping Note</b><br /><br /></span>
13:
14: <table width="500" border="2">
15:  <tr align="center">
16:    <td><span style="color:#ffff00"><b>Product</b></span></td>
17:    <td><span style="color:#ffff00"><b>Unit Price</b></span></td>
18:    <td><span style="color:#ffff00"><b>Quantities</b></span></td>
19:    <td><span style="color:#ffff00"><b>Sub-Total</b></span></td>
20:  </tr>
21:  <tr align="center">
22:    <td><span style="color:#00ffff"><b>CD-RW Disks</b></span></td>
23:    <td><span style="color:#00ff00"><b>0.30</b></span></td>
24:    <td><span style="color:#00ff00"><b>50</b></span></td>
25:    <td><span style="color:#ffff00"><b>15.00</b></span></td>
26:  </tr>
27:  <tr align="center">
28:    <td><span style="color:#00ffff"><b>Color Printer</b></span></td>
29:    <td><span style="color:#00ff00"><b>250</b></span></td>
```

```
30:    <td><span style="color:#00ff00"><b>1</b></span></td>
31:    <td><span style="color:#ffff00"><b>250.00</b></span></td>
32:  </tr>
33:  <tr align="center">
34:    <td><span style="color:#00ffff"><b>Printer Paper</b></span></td>
35:    <td><span style="color:#00ff00"><b>4.00 per 500</b></span></td>
36:    <td><span style="color:#00ff00"><b>5 x 500</b></span></td>
37:    <td><span style="color:#ffff00"><b>20.00</b></span></td>
38:  </tr>
39:  <tr align="center">
40:    <td><span style="color:#00ffff"><b>CD Case</b></span></td>
41:    <td><span style="color:#00ff00"><b>7.00</b></span></td>
42:    <td><span style="color:#00ff00"><b>1</b></span></td>
43:    <td><span style="color:#ffff00"><b>7.00</b></span></td>
44:  </tr>
45: </table>
46: </div>
47: </body>
48: </html>
```

This table has five rows and four columns and can be seen easily by the arrangement of the `<tr>` and `<td>` elements. Another feature of this example is that you can define an individual typeface, font size, and color for each table cell. This can help to increase the readability of a table and highlight some important items. A screen shot of this example is shown in Fig. 1.20.

If you create a table without a border (i.e., `border="0"`), the table can be used as a great tool for text alignment and integration of images. For example, the following simple code fragment can be used to construct a title page for this book with a logo:

Listing: ex01-06.txt

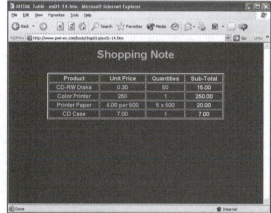

Figure 1.20 ex01-14.htm

```
1:    <table width="550" border="0">
2:      <tr>
3:        <td width="80%" align="center">
4:         <span style="font=family:arial;font-size:30pt;color:#ffff00">
5:            <b>Welcome To</b><br>
6:         <span style="font=family:arial;font-size:30pt;color:#00ffff">
7:            <b>Practical Web Technologies</b>
8:        </td><td>
9:         <img src="logo_web.jpg" width="140" height="70">
10:       </td>
11:     </tr>
12:   </table>
13:   <img src="line1.gif" width="550" height="6">
```

This simple table has one row and two columns. There is a welcome message in the first column and a logo picture logo_web.jpg in the second (see Fig. 1.21). The width attribute of the first `<td>` element in line 3

```
<td width="80%" align="center">
```

indicates that the first column of this table occupies 80% of the entire row length. This means that the book logo will have the remaining 20% of space for display. This table can be used as the header of your Web page.

Now, you can write a summary of this chapter and put the text into a new table as illustrated in the listing ex01-07.txt:

```
Listing: ex01-07.txt

 1:     <table width="500" border="0" cellspacing="10" align="center">
 2:      <tr align="left">
 3:       <td width="25">
 4:        <img alt="pic" src="bullet1.gif" width="15" height="15" /></td>
 5:       <td><span style="font-family:arial;font-size:16pt;color:#00ffff">
 6:         <b>Introduction: Building An Instant Online Web Site</b></span></td>
 7:      ... .
xx:     </table>
```

The `cellspacing` attribute in line 1

```
<table width="500" border="0" cellspacing="10" align="center">
```

sets a `space="10"` pixels for all table cells. This is used to control the spacing between the bullet and the text. The alignment attribute `align` is also included for backward compatibility with some older browsers.

The full listing of this example is given in ex01-15.htm below. Figure 1.21 shows this example at work.

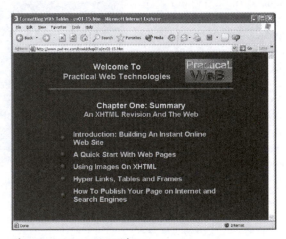

Figure 1.21 ex01-15.htm

```
Example: ex01-15.htm - Formatting With Tables

 1: <?xml version="1.0" encoding="iso-8859-1"?>
 2: <!DOCTYPE html PUBLIC "-//W3C//DTD XHTML 1.0 Transitional//EN"
 3: "http://www.w3.org/TR/xhtml1/DTD/xhtml1-transitional.dtd">
 4: <html xmlns="http://www.w3.org/1999/xhtml" xml:lang="en" lang="en">
 5: <head>
 6:   <title>Formatting With Tables - ex01-15.htm</title>
 7: </head>
 8:
 9:   <body style="background:#000088">
10:
11:    <table width="550" border="0" align="center">
12:     <tr>
13:      <td width="80%" align="center">
14:       <span style="font-family:arial;font-size:18pt;color:#ffff00">
15:        <b>Welcome To</b><br /></span>
```

```
16:            <span style="font-family:arial;font-size:18pt;color:#00ffff">
17:               <b>Practical Web Technologies</b></span>
18:          </td><td>
19:            <img alt="pic" src="logo_web.jpg" width="140" height="70" />
20:          </td>
21:          </tr>
22:        </table>
23:
24:        <div style="text-align:center">
25:         <img alt="pic" src="line1.gif" width="550" height="6" />
26:         <span style="font-family:arial;font-size:18pt;color:#ffff00">
27:            <br /><br /><b>Chapter One: Summary</b><br /></span>
28:         <span style="font-family:arial;font-size:16pt;color:#00ff00">
29:            <b>An XHTML Revision And The Web</b><br /><br /></span>
30:        </div>
31:
32:        <div style="text-align:center">
33:        <table width="500" border="0" cellspacing="10" align="center">
34:         <tr align="left">
35:            <td width="25">
36:               <img alt="pic" src="bullet1.gif" width="15" height="15" /></td>
37:            <td><span style="font-family:arial;font-size:16pt;color:#00ffff">
38:               <b>Introduction: Building An
39:                  Instant Online Web Site</b></span></td></tr>
40:         <tr align="left">
41:            <td width="25">
42:             <img alt="pic" src="bullet1.gif" width="15" height="15" /></td>
43:            <td><span style="font-family:arial;font-size:16pt;color:#00ffff">
44:               <b>A Quick Start With Web Pages</b></span></td>
45:         </tr>
46:         <tr align="left">
47:            <td width="25">
48:             <img alt="pic" src="bullet1.gif" width="15" height="15" /></td>
49:            <td><span style="font-family:arial;font-size:16pt;color:#00ffff">
50:               <b>Using Images On XHTML</b></span></td>
51:         </tr>
52:         <tr align="left">
53:            <td width="25">
54:             <img alt="pic" src="bullet1.gif" width="15" height="15" /></td>
55:            <td><span style="font-family:arial;font-size:16pt;color:#00ffff">
56:               <b>Hyper Links, Tables and Frames</b></span></td>
57:         </tr>
58:         <tr align="left">
59:            <td width="25">
60:             <img alt="pic" src="bullet1.gif" width="15" height="15" /></td>
61:            <td><span style="font-family:arial;font-size:16pt;color:#00ffff">
62:               <b>How To Publish Your Page on Internet
63:                  and Search Engines</b></span></td></tr>
64:        </table>
65:        </div>
66:        </body>
67:        </html>
```

1.4.3 A simple photo album using tables

As a practical application of XHTML tables, you can construct a simple photo album for "Wild Life." Suppose you have a collection of wild life pictures:

01_img.jpg   02_img.jpg   03_img.jpg   04_img.jpg   05_img.jpg   06_img.jpg   07_img.jpg   08_img.jpg

You want to create a Web page to display all of them. Since you may have difficulty displaying them all at the same time, one popular solution is to:

- scale down all pictures to a suitable size;
- display small pictures in a single page;
- link small pictures to their associated big pictures with an anchor element <a>.

The first step is simple and can be done by a number of graphics packages. Here, Microsoft Photo Editor was used to scale down all pictures by 75% and save them as files with prefix "s." That is, we have s01_img.jpg, ..., s08_img.jpg files in our file system.

You can use the XHTML <table> element to display all small pictures in a single page. In order to have an organized photo album, the pictures are arranged into three categories

Wild Life I: **First three files**

Butterflies: **Next two files**

Wild Life II: **Remaining files**

and a table used for each of these categories as shown in Fig. 1.22.

Figure 1.22 ex01-16.htm

Finally, the linking between small pictures and big pictures can be achieved by the <a> element. For example, the XHTML code fragment for "Wild Life I" is given in listing ex01-08.txt.

```
Listing: ex01-08.txt

1:      <table width="500" border="0" cellspacing="10">
2:       <tr align="center">
3:        <td><a href="01_img.jpg" target="_blank">
4:           <img alt="pic" src="s01_img.jpg" /></a></td>
5:        <td><a href="02_img.jpg" target="_blank">
6:           <img alt="pic" src="s02_img.jpg" /></a></td>
7:        <td><a href="03_img.jpg" target="_blank">
```

```
 8:            <img alt="pic" src="s03_img.jpg" /></a></td>
 9:         </tr>
10:       </table>
11:        <span style="font-family:arial;font-size:5;color:#ffff00">
12:           <b>Wild Life I</b> </span>
```

This is a table with three cells. The first cell, line 4, is a small picture called s01_img.jpg. This picture is displayed on the screen by

```
<img alt="pic" src="s01_img.jpg" />
```

Since this small image is entirely inside the anchor element (line 3)

```
<a href="01_img.jpg" target="_blank">
```

the hyperlink action to display the big picture 01_img.jpg is triggered by clicking on the small picture. The attribute `target ="_blank"`makes sure that the browser will open another browser window for the display.

This technique (changes from a small picture to a big picture) has been popular amongst Web developers and programmers. Many commercial Web sites and programmers generate this page using programming languages such as C/C++ or Visual Basic. Generating XHTML code using a programming language, in general, establishes an effective way to handle and maintain a large number of images. A screen shot of the big picture 01_img.jpg triggered by the small one s01_img.jpg is shown in Fig. 1.23.

A complete listing of this page appears in ex01-16.htm:

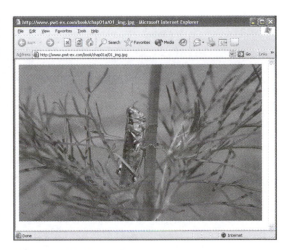

Figure 1.23 Picture 01_img.jpg

```
Example: ex01-16.htm - Small Picture Link To Big Picture

 1: <?xml version="1.0" encoding="iso-8859-1"?>
 2: <!DOCTYPE html PUBLIC "-//W3C//DTD XHTML 1.0 Transitional//EN"
 3:     "http://www.w3.org/TR/xhtml1/DTD/xhtml1-transitional.dtd">
 4: <html xmlns="http://www.w3.org/1999/xhtml" xml:lang="en" lang="en">
 5: <head>
 6:   <title> Small Picture Link To Big Picture - ex01-16.htm</title>
 7: </head>
 8:
 9: <body style="background:#888888">
10: <div style="font-family:arial;text-align:center">
11:   <span style="font-size:24pt; color:#ffff00">
12:       <b>A Simple Photo Album</b><br /></span>
13:   <span style="font-size:18pt; color:#00ff00">
14:       <b>Click Small Picture To Display Big Picture</b></span><br />
15:   <img alt="pic" src="line1.gif" width="550" height="6" /><br /><br />
16:
17:  <table width="500" border="0" align="center" cellspacing="15">
18:   <tr>
19:    <td><a href="01_img.jpg" target="_blank">
20:    <img alt="pic" src="s01_img.jpg" width="170" height="110" /></a></td>
21:    <td><a href="02_img.jpg" target="_blank">
22:    <img alt="pic" src="s02_img.jpg" width="170" height="110" /></a></td>
23:    <td><a href="03_img.jpg" target="_blank">
24:    <img alt="pic" src="s03_img.jpg" width="170" height="110" /></a></td>
```

```
25:   </tr>
26:   </table>
27:
28:   <span style="font-size:18pt;color:#ffff00">
29:     <b>Wild Life I</b></span><br /><br />
30:
31:   <table width="350" border="0" cellspacing="15" align="center">
32:    <tr align="center">
33:      <td><a href="04_img.jpg" target="_blank">
34:    <img alt="pic" src="s04_img.jpg" width="170" height="110" /></a></td>
35:      <td><a href="05_img.jpg" target="_blank">
36:    <img alt="pic" src="s05_img.jpg" width="170" height="110" /></a></td>
37:    </tr>
38:   </table>
39:
40:   <span style="font-size:18pt;color:#ffff00">
41:     <b>Butterflies</b></span><br /><br />
42:
43:   <table width="500" border="0" cellspacing="15" align="center">
44:    <tr align="center">
45:      <td><a href="06_img.jpg" target="_blank">
46:    <img alt="pic" src="s06_img.jpg" width="170" height="110" /></a></td>
47:      <td><a href="07_img.jpg" target="_blank">
48:    <img alt="pic" src="s07_img.jpg" width="170" height="110" /></a></td>
49:      <td><a href="08_img.jpg" target="_blank">
50:    <img alt="pic" src="s08_img.jpg" width="170" height="110" /></a></td>
51:    </tr>
52:   </table>
53:   <span style="font-size:18pt;color:#ffff00"><b>Wild Life II</b></span>
54:  </div>
55:  </body>
56:  </html>
```

Most computer systems such as Microsoft Windows and UNIX allow you to open windows on the screen. Can we create some windows for our Web pages? This is not an easy question to answer. One of the earliest responses from Web developers was the idea of "frames" and "iframe" (inline frame). Although these features are handy in partitioning the browser screen, they also raise questions about the structural functionalities of XML and XHTML. This is the reason why the W3C authority set up another header document called `frameset` dedicated to them. Since frame and iframe are popular in some areas, we will discuss these elements in sections 1.4.4–1.4.6.

1.4.4   Frames: windows on Web pages?

The concept of frames is very simple. If you partition a single Web page into a number of independent pages, then each independent page is a frame of the original. Naturally, one of the first operations to do with page partitions (or frames) is to assign names to each of them. This is the reason for the attribute `target=xxxx`. Since each frame can be an independent XHTML file, you may consider them as windows (or still windows) on Web pages.

Consider the following example to cut a Web page vertically into two pages:

```
Example: ex01-17.htm - Frames

1: <?xml version="1.0" encoding="UTF-8"?>
2: <!DOCTYPE html PUBLIC "-//W3C//DTD XHTML 1.0 Frameset//EN"
3:      "http://www.w3.org/TR/xhtml1/DTD/xhtml1-frameset.dtd">
4: <html xmlns="http://www.w3.org/1999/xhtml" xml:lang="en" lang="en">
5: <head>
```

```
 6:    <title>My First Frame - ex01-17.htm</title>
 7:  </head>
 8:  <frameset cols="240,*">
 9:    <frame src="ex01-17l.htm" name="left" scrolling="auto" />
10:    <frame src="ex01-17r.htm" name="right" />
11:  </frameset>
12:  </html>
```

Basically, this code cuts the page into two frames and loads the files ex01-17l.htm and ex01-17r.htm into the left and right frames for display

In lines 2–3, the keyword `frameset` is used in the header to specify that this is a frame application. In line 8, the new element `<frameset>` defines the partition of the page into frames. The attribute `cols="240,* "` indicates that the first part is from the first column to the column of 240 pixels. The remainder is the second part of the page. In line 9, the element `<frame>` is used to define the details of the first frame. This frame is called `left` and the primary XHTML file is ex01-17l.htm. The other attribute `scrolling="auto"` means that the browser can assign a scroll bar to this frame if necessary. Line 10 is the definition of another frame called `right` and with primary display XHTML file ex01-17r.htm.

The details of the left frame page (i.e., ex01-17l.htm) are listed below:

```
Example: ex01-17l.htm - The Left Frame For ex01-17.htm

 1:  <?xml version="1.0" encoding="iso-8859-1"?>
 2:  <!DOCTYPE html PUBLIC "-//W3C//DTD XHTML 1.0 Transitional//EN"
 3:        "http://www.w3.org/TR/xhtml1/DTD/xhtml1-transitional.dtd">
 4:  <html xmlns="http://www.w3.org/1999/xhtml" xml:lang="en" lang="en">
 5:  <head>
 6:    <title>The Left Frame Page of ex01-17.htm: </title>
 7:  </head>
 8:  <body style="background:#000088;font-family:arial;
 9:      font-size:16pt;text-align:center">
10:      <span style="color:#00ffff">
11:        Frame Example<br /><br /></span>
12:      <span style="color:#ffff00">
13:        Left Frame of <br />ex01-17.htm<br /><br />
14:        File Name: ex01-17l.htm</span>
15:  </body>
16:  </html>
```

This is a simple XHTML page to display some messages on the left frame of ex01-17.htm. The right frame page ex01-17r.htm for ex01-17.htm is also a very simple one:

```
Example: ex01-17r.htm - The Right Frame For ex01-17.htm

 1:  <?xml version="1.0" encoding="iso-8859-1"?>
 2:  <!DOCTYPE html PUBLIC "-//W3C//DTD XHTML 1.0 Transitional//EN"
 3:        "http://www.w3.org/TR/xhtml1/DTD/xhtml1-transitional.dtd">
 4:  <html xmlns="http://www.w3.org/1999/xhtml" xml:lang="en" lang="en">
 5:  <head>
 6:    <title>The Right Frame Page of ex01-17.htm: </title>
 7:  </head>
 8:
 9:  <body style="background:#000088;font-family:arial;
10:      font-size:16pt;text-align:center">
11:      <span style="color:#00ffff">
12:        Frame Example<br /><br /></span>
13:      <span style="color:#ffff00">
14:        Right Frame of <br />ex01-17.htm<br /><br />
15:        File Name: ex01-17r.htm</span>
16:  </body>
17:  </html>
```

If both the files ex01-17l.htm and ex01-17r.htm are available in the default Web directory, example ex01-17.htm generates a display as shown in Fig. 1.24.

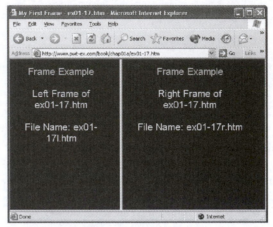

Figure 1.24 ex01-17.htm

1.4.5   A page to link all examples

One of the direct applications of the previous frame example is to build a catalog for this chapter. You can put all the major examples to the left frame and the summary of this chapter to the right. The main XHTML page now looks like the following:

```
Example: ex01-18.htm - A Page To Link All Examples

 1: <?xml version="1.0" encoding="UTF-8"?>
 2: <!DOCTYPE html PUBLIC "-//W3C//DTD XHTML 1.0 Frameset//EN"
 3:     "http://www.w3.org/TR/xhtml1/DTD/xhtml1-frameset.dtd">
 4: <html xmlns="http://www.w3.org/1999/xhtml" xml:lang="en" lang="en">
 5: <head>
 6:   <title> A Page To Link All Examples - ex01-18.htm</title>
 7: </head>
 8: <frameset cols="165,*">
 9:   <frame src="ex01-18l.htm" name="left_f" scrolling="auto" />
10:   <frame src="ex01-15.htm" name="right_f" />
11: </frameset>
12: </html>
```

This is a frameset example very similar to the previous one. Line 10 loads the summary page ex01-15.htm into the right frame. For the left frame, a new XHTML example ex01-18l.htm is used. This page incorporates all previous examples and is listed below:

```
Example: ex01-18l.htm - The Left Frame For ex01-18.htm

 1: <?xml version="1.0" encoding="iso-8859-1"?>
 2: <!DOCTYPE html PUBLIC "-//W3C//DTD XHTML 1.0 Transitional//EN"
 3:     "http://www.w3.org/TR/xhtml1/DTD/xhtml1-transitional.dtd">
 4: <html xmlns="http://www.w3.org/1999/xhtml" xml:lang="en" lang="en">
 5: <head>
 6:   <title> Left Frame For ex01-18.htm - ex01-18l.htm</title>
 7: </head>
 8:
 9: <body style="background:#000088;font-family:arial;
10:   font-size:14pt;text-align:center">
```

```
11:
12:   <span style="color:#00ffff">Chapter One<br />Examples<br />
13:   <img alt="pic" src="line1.gif" width="140" height="6"<br /></span>
14:
15:   <table align="center" style="text-align:center;font-size:10pt">
16:    <tr><td><a href="ex01-15.htm" target="right_f">
17:      <span style=";font-size:14pt;color:#00ff00">
18:       <b>Contents</b><br /></span></a></td></tr>
19:    <tr><td><a href="ex01-03.htm" target="right_f">
20:      <span style=" color:#ffff00"><b>Ex01-03.htm</b></span></a></td></tr>
21:    <tr><td><a href="ex01-04.htm" target="right_f">
22:      <span style=" color:#ffff00"><b>Ex01-04.htm</b></span></a></td></tr>
23:    <tr><td><a href="ex01-05.htm" target="right_f">
24:      <span style=" color:#ffff00"><b>Ex01-05.htm</b></span></a></td></tr>
25:    <tr><td><a href="ex01-06.htm" target="right_f">
26:      <span style=" color:#ffff00"><b>Ex01-06.htm</b></span></a></td></tr>
27:    <tr><td><a href="ex01-07.htm" target="right_f">
28:      <span style=" color:#ffff00"><b>Ex01-07.htm</b></span></a></td></tr>
29:    <tr><td><a href="ex01-08.htm" target="right_f">
30:      <span style=" color:#ffff00"><b>Ex01-08.htm</b></span></a></td></tr>
31:    <tr><td><a href="ex01-09.htm" target="right_f">
32:      <span style=" color:#ffff00"><b>Ex01-09.htm</b></span></a></td></tr>
33:    <tr><td><a href="ex01-10.htm" target="right_f">
34:      <span style=" color:#ffff00"><b>Ex01-10.htm</b></span></a></td></tr>
35:    <tr><td><a href="ex01-11.htm" target="right_f">
36:      <span style=" color:#ffff00"><b>Ex01-11.htm</b></span></a></td></tr>
37:    <tr><td><a href="ex01-12.htm" target="right_f">
38:      <span style=" color:#ffff00"><b>Ex01-12.htm</b></span></a></td></tr>
39:    <tr><td><a href="ex01-13.htm" target="right_f">
40:      <span style=" color:#ffff00"><b>Ex01-13.htm</b></span></a></td></tr>
41:    <tr><td><a href="ex01-14.htm" target="right_f">
42:      <span style=" color:#ffff00"><b>Ex01-14.htm</b></span></a></td></tr>
43:    <tr><td><a href="ex01-15.htm" target="right_f">
44:      <span style=" color:#ffff00"><b>Ex01-15.htm</b></span></a></td></tr>
45:    <tr><td><a href="ex01-16.htm" target="right_f">
46:      <span style=" color:#ffff00"><b>Ex01-16.htm</b></span></a></td></tr>
47:   </table>
48:
49:  </body>
50:  </html>
```

This is a table application and the key point of this example is the following code fragment (lines 19–20):

```
<tr><td><a href="ex01-03.htm" target="right_f">
<span style="color:#ffff00"><b>Ex01-03.htm</b></span></a></td></tr>
```

First, the browser displays the underlined text "Ex01-03.htm" on the left frame. When the user clicks on the text, the XHTML file ex01-3.htm is loaded and then displays to `target="right_f"`, which is the right frame defined by the main page (see Fig. 1.25).

You now have a Web page that links and runs all examples in this chapter.

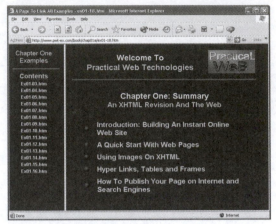

Figure 1.25 ex01-18.htm

1.4.6   Open an internal window with iframes

One of the advantages of inline frames (or iframes) is that they can be freely positioned almost anywhere inside a page. They don't need a master frame page to partition the screen (or parent frame). With a simple command format `<iframe>`, the inline frame is an XHTML element that opens an internal window anywhere to load another page.

Consider the following example ex01-19.htm:

```
Example: ex01-19.htm - IFrame

 1: <?xml version="1.0" encoding="iso-8859-1"?>
 2: <!DOCTYPE html PUBLIC "-//W3C//DTD XHTML 1.0 Transitional//EN"
 3:     "http://www.w3.org/TR/xhtml1/DTD/xhtml1-transitional.dtd">
 4: <html xmlns="http://www.w3.org/1999/xhtml" xml:lang="en" lang="en">
 5: <head>
 6:  <title>Using IFrame - ex01-19.htm</title>
 7: </head>
 8: <body style="background:#aaccaa;font-family:arial;color:#000088">
 9:  <div style="text-align:center;font-size:26pt">
10:         An Internal Window <br />For Wild Life<br />
11:    <iframe src="ex01-20.htm" align="center"
12:     width="350" height="260" scrolling="auto" />
13:  </div>
14: </body>
15: </html>
```

After the page message in line 10, we have the inline frame definition `<iframe>` (lines 11–12). This iframe has a rectangular dimension of `350x260` pixels right after the page message. Inside this box, we have another page called ex01-20.htm. This is an ordinary page to be loaded inside the iframe. The attribute `scrolling="auto"` is used to generate scroll bars if necessary. The iframe page ex01-20.htm is listed as follows:

```
Example: ex01-20.htm - A Wild Life Page For ex01-19.htm

 1: <?xml version="1.0" encoding="iso-8859-1"?>
 2: <!DOCTYPE html PUBLIC "-//W3C//DTD XHTML 1.0 Transitional//EN"
 3:     "http://www.w3.org/TR/xhtml1/DTD/xhtml1-transitional.dtd">
 4: <html xmlns="http://www.w3.org/1999/xhtml" xml:lang="en" lang="en">
 5: <head>
 6:  <title> A Page For Wild Life - ex01-20.htm</title>
 7: </head>
 8: <body style="font-family:arial;color:#000088">
```

```
 9: <table cellspacing="15">
10:  <tr><td style="font-size:14pt;font-weight:bold;text-align:center">
11:   <a href="01_img.jpg" target="_blank"><img src="s01_img.jpg" width="270"
12:    height="190" alt="pic" /><br />Grass Hopper<br /></a></td></tr>
13:  <tr><td style="font-size:14pt;font-weight:bold;text-align:center">
14:   <a href="02_img.jpg" target="_blank"><img src="s02_img.jpg" width="270"
15:    height="190" alt="pic" /><br />Peacock<br /></a></td></tr>
16:  <tr><td style="font-size:14pt;font-weight:bold;text-align:center">
17:   <a href="03_img.jpg" target="_blank"><img src="s03_img.jpg" width="270"
18:    height="190" alt="pic" /><br />Eagle I<br /></a></td></tr>
19:  <tr><td style="font-size:14pt;font-weight:bold;text-align:center">
20:   <a href="04_img.jpg" target="_blank"><img src="s04_img.jpg" width="270"
21:    height="190" alt="pic" /><br />Butterfly I<br /></a></td></tr>
22:  <tr><td style="font-size:14pt;font-weight:bold;text-align:center">
23:   <a href="05_img.jpg" target="_blank"><img src="s05_img.jpg" width="270"
24:    height="190" alt="pic" /><br />Butterfly II<br /></a></td></tr>
25:  <tr><td style="font-size:14pt;font-weight:bold;text-align:center">
26:   <a href="06_img.jpg" target="_blank"><img src="s06_img.jpg" width="270"
27:    height="190" alt="pic" /><br />Wild Duck<br /></a></td></tr>
28:  <tr><td style="font-size:14pt;font-weight:bold;text-align:center">
29:   <a href="07_img.jpg" target="_blank"><img src="s07_img.jpg" width="270"
30:    height="190" alt="pic" /><br />Eagle II<br /></a></td></tr>
31:  <tr><td style="font-size:14pt;font-weight:bold;text-align:center">
32:   <a href="08_img.jpg" target="_blank"><img src="s08_img.jpg" width="270"
33:    height="190" alt="pic" /><br />Parrot<br /></a></td></tr>
34: </table>
35: </body>
36: </html>
```

This page is a strip of eight images arranged in a vertical direction. Since they are loaded into a box window of the main page, users can use the scroll bar to see them one by one. When you click on the small picture, a bigger picture is displayed in another browser window. This is a good technique to set up an online catalog for customers. Some screen shots are shown in Figs. 1.26 and 1.27.

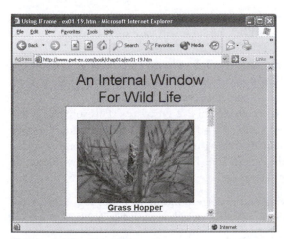

Figure 1.26 ex01-19.htm

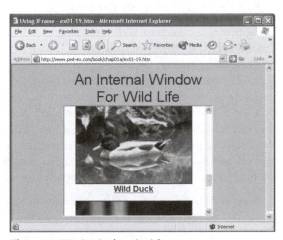

Figure 1.27 A window inside a page

1.5   Publishing your page on the Internet and search engines

1.5.1   Connecting to Web servers

Loosely speaking, a machine that runs Web server software is a Web server. This software listens to the network media and responds to any browser request. For example, Apache (http://www.apache.org) is server software freely available on most UNIX (or LINUX) and PC environments. For Microsoft Windows 98/2000/Me/NT and XP machines, the corresponding server software is IIS (i.e., Internet Information Service). Both of them are not difficult to install and use. They are not essential at this moment and will be discussed in Part IV when server technologies are introduced. The main task in this section is to show how to upload Web pages onto our Web site or server so that the pages are available for anyone on the Internet.

Before anyone can access or browse your Web pages, you need to upload your pages onto a Web server so that the canonical browser–server interaction can be performed. If you are a home-based computer user with a modem, the chances are that you already have a server provided by your ISP. In general, your ISP may provide you with the following Web server information:

- the Web server address (e.g., www.pwt-ex.com);
- a user name (or account name, e.g., johnsmith);
- a password (e.g., johnsmith);
- a Web page directory (e.g., public_html);
- a CGI scripts directory (e.g., cgi-bin);
- your Web site (URL) address (e.g., www.pwt-ex.com or www.pwt-ex.com/~JohnSmith).

Some ISPs may not provide all the information and some may give you a temporary user name and/or password to save their server access time. Contact your ISP for the data and any alternatives. For UNIX and other platform users, your system administrator should be able to provide you with the information above. Once you have the data, you can upload your Web pages and associated files onto the server using a software called File Transfer Protocol (FTP).

1.5.2   FTP uploading files

Long before browsers or Web technologies, FTP was, and still is, popular software used to download and upload files to another computer on the Internet.

Generally speaking, there are two kinds of FTP programs. One is graphics based and the other is known as "console based." Graphical FTP programs are easy to use since you can actually see and control the file transfer interactively. However, these programs are usually machine and operating system dependent.

One popular graphical FTP program used on the PC is called "AceFTP 2 Freeware." This software is free and can be downloaded from the official site: freeware.aceftp.com. With freeware, you can distribute the software to your friends provided the entire package is distributed. During the installation process, the software will ask you to obtain the registration code online from the official site. The following is a step-by-step guide on how to use the software to upload some pages onto the Web site.

Step 1: **Activate the AceFTP program by double clicking on the corresponding icon (see Fig. 1.28). Go to the** File|Connect **menu to open the "AceFTP Site Profile" window as in Fig. 1.29.**

Step 2: **To register a new server, double click on the "New Site Profile" option to open the "New Site Profile" window (see Fig. 1.30).**

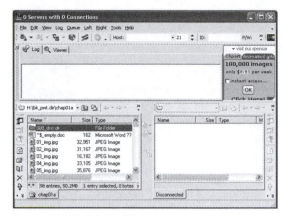

Figure 1.28 The AceFTP program

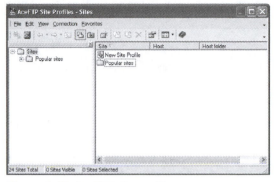

Figure 1.29 AceFTP site profile

Step 3: From this "New Site Profile" window, enter the following information as shown in Fig. 1.30:

Site name: MySite   (Any name)
Server: www.pwt-ex.com   (The server address provided by the ISP)
User ID: johnsmith   (The user name provided by the ISP)
Password: xxxxx   (The password)

Step 4: Click on the *Next* button to open another "New Site Profile" window.
From this window enter the following information as shown in Fig. 1.31:

Local folder: h:\pwt_ex.dir\chap01a   (Local directory on your PC)
Host folder: public_html/book/chap01a   (Remote directory on the server)

Figure 1.30 New Site Profile I

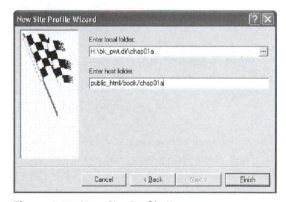

Figure 1.31 New Site Profile II

Step 5: Click on the *Finish* button to return to the "Site Profile" window with the server www.pwt-ex.com registered (see Fig. 1.32).

Step 6: Double click on the server name to open an FTP session to connect your PC and local directory to the remote server and directory (see Fig. 1.33).

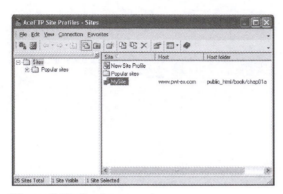

Figure 1.32 Register server

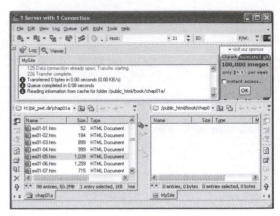

Figure 1.33 Connect local PC to server

Step 7: Now you can copy the Web pages from your PC (i.e., the left window) and paste them onto the remote Web site directory in the right window.

This operation can be done simply by mouse clicks as shown in Fig. 1.34.

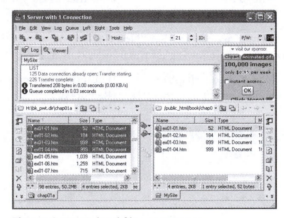

Figure 1.34 Upload files onto server

This software also allows you to create new, delete, or rename folders on both local and remote machines. Now you have some pages on your Web site www.pwt-ex.com and in your directory /book/chap01. Users on the Internet can display your page by the "http" command such as

http://www.pwt-ex.com/book/chap01a/ex01-05.htm

To use console FTP to connect to your server, all you need to do is to activate it inside a console window. For example, you can activate a DOS window, and issue the following command

ftp www.pwt-ex.com

where www.pwt-ex.com is the remote server that you want to connect to. This FTP command generates an FTP session for you to upload or download files. A typical FTP session from my desktop for file uploading is listed as follows:

```
Listing: ex01-09.txt
 1:          P:\>ftp www.pwt-ex.com
 2:          Connected to www.pwt-ex.com.
 3:          220 ProFTPD Server [www.pwt-ex.com]
 4:          User (www.pwt-ex.com(none)): JohnSmith
 5:          331 Password Required for JohnSmith.
 6:          Password:
 7:          230 User JohnSmith logged in.
 8:          ftp> cd public_html/book/chap01a
 9:          250 CWD command successful.
10:          ftp> binary
11:          200 type set to I.
12:          ftp> mput ex01-3.htm
13:          mput ex01-3.htm? y
14:          200 PORT command successful.
15:          150 Opening BINARY mode data connection for ex01-3.htm.
16:          226 Transfer complete.
17:          ftp: 507 bytes sent in 0.00Seconds 507000.00Kbytes/sec.
18:          ftp> mput balloon.gif
19:          mput balloon.gif? y
21:          150 Opening BINARY mode data connection for balloon.gif.
22:          226 Transfer complete.
23:          ftp: 4532 bytes sent in 0.05Seconds 90.64Kbytes/sec.
24:          ftp> bye
25:          221 Goodbye.
26:          P:\>
```

Line 1 is to activate the FTP program with your server address. After the user name and password in lines 4 and 6 respectively, the remote server accepts your login and provides you with an FTP session in line 7. The FTP command cd public_html is used to change the current directory to the Web page directory where all our XHTML files are based. The command in line 10, binary, is to set the FTP communication as binary mode for graphics or non-character transmissions. The file uploading command mput ex01-3.htm in line 12 uploads the XHTML file ex01-3.htm from the local machine onto the remote server. The "multiple put" command, mput, used here can accept wildcards such as "*.htm" or "*.gif." After you confirm the uploading in line 13, the FTP session will start the actual file transmission. The binary setting in line 10 is important for any picture (or non-character-based) transmission. If your FTP program is not binary mode by default, you need to set it manually. The bye command in line 24 will terminate the FTP session.

You can use the "multiple get" command mget to download files from your server or use help to see a summary of all available FTP commands. Sometimes, a graphic (or window-based) FTP program may provide you with a user-friendlier environment. Console-based FTP on the other hand is platform independent.

Once you have your Web pages uploaded, you can access them using the usual "http" command. If you have a page called index.htm (or default.htm) in the root directory such as public_html of your site, you can access this file directly using

http://www.pwt-ex.com

As another application of FTP, we consider a page that can use FTP to capture, deliver, and publish live Webcam images to Web users.

1.5.3 A simple page to publish live Webcam images

When you visit sites such as those of a safari park, university, college, school, and/or government department, the chances are that you will see a live Webcam delivering live images of animals, buildings, weather, traffic, etc. It is one of the most popular Web applications.

Suprisingly, most Webcams and their applications are, in fact, FTP based. The reason is simple: FTP establishes a link between you and the Web server. With FTP uploading, any file (including continuous live video or images) can be put onto the Web site and browsed by the Web community.

As a Web application, Webcams can use this advantage to publish live images on the Web and display them in real time. In order to do so, the following tasks are needed:

- Capture a live image and upload it onto a Web site regularly using FTP.
- Develop a Web page to display the same image again and again within a time interval.

As long as you can perform the tasks above, whether you are using a Webcam or a camera with a capture card does not matter, they are basically the same. Live pictures can transmit to Web users around the world.

To get your Webcam picture onto a Web page you should use FTP-based software. A variety of software is available to do this. Some of it is commercial packages offering live chat, stream video, and automatic Web page generation such as Webcam32 (www.webcam32.com). Some free Webcam software is also available and can be downloaded from the Internet. Two of these are Camardes (www.camarades.com) and WebcamFirst (www.webcamfirst.com).

After you have downloaded and installed the software, you may need to set up the FTP configuration. Usually it would involve your Web site address, user name, and password. A typical FTP setting on WebcamFirst to send pictures to your Web site (e.g., www.pwt-ex.com) is shown in Fig. 1.35.

Figure 1.35 A typical Webcam FTP setting

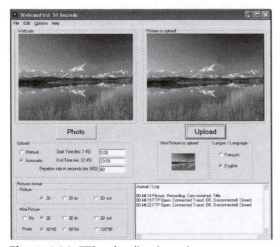

Figure 1.36 FTP uploading in action

From this figure, the captured image will be sent to the directory `webcam` of www.pwt-ex.com as a `jpg` file capture.jpg. Now, if you run the software, you will see the interaction between the capturing and uploading. A screen shot is shown in Fig. 1.36. Note that the uploading rate in this case is set to every 60 seconds.

Suppose you have two Webcams (outdoor and indoor) transmitting images to the site www.pwt-ex.com. The outdoor Webcam image is called capture.jpg and the indoor image is capture1.jpg. To write a page to display these images regularly is easy. Consider the following example:

Example: ex01-21.htm - A Webcam Page

```
 1: <?xml version="1.0" encoding="UTF-8"?>
 2: <!DOCTYPE html PUBLIC "-//W3C//DTD XHTML 1.0 Frameset//EN"
 3:      "http://www.w3.org/TR/xhtml1/DTD/xhtml1-frameset.dtd">
 4: <html xmlns="http://www.w3.org/1999/xhtml" xml:lang="en" lang="en">
 5: <head><title> A Webcam Page - ex01-21.htm</title>
 6: <meta http-equiv="refresh" content ="60">
 7: </head>
 8: <body style="text-align:center">
 9: <div><br />
10:  <table style="font-family:arial;font-size:24pt">
11:   <tr><th colspan="2">Welcome To My WebCam Site<br /><br /></th></tr>
12:   <tr><td>Out Door WebCam</td><td>In Door WebCam</td></tr>
13:   <tr><td><img src="capture.jpg"></td>
14:       <td><img src="capture1.jpg"></td></tr>
15:  </table>
16: </div>
17: </body>
18: </html>
```

This page contains 18 lines of code with one table to arrange the layout of the pictures. In lines 13–14, the two Webcam images capture.jpg and capture1.jpg are displayed by the usual image element <img>. The interesting part is the meta element used in line 6:

```
<meta http-equiv="refresh" content ="60">
```

The meta element simply asks the browser to refresh this page every 60 seconds. This way, you will have the Webcam pictures updated continuously. A screen shot of this example is shown in Fig. 1.37.

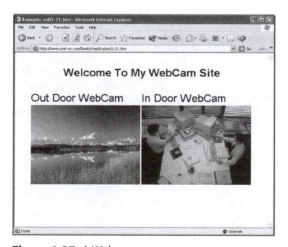

Figure 1.37 A Webcam page

Now you have a Web site up and running and also have some experience of XHTML pages. The next step is to let your friends and others know the location of your site. You can, of course, email the site address to your friends, but how about others?

1.5.4   Putting your Web site into public search engines

If you want your Web page (or Web site) to be available for a large number of visitors, one easy option would be to register it on a public search engine. Most of the public search engines are free and can be easily registered online.

One popular choice is Yahoo! at

http://www.yahoo.com

In Yahoo!, you first locate the section or category you want to register under and then activate the "Suggest a Site" option. For example, there is a site for kids in Yahoo! called Yahooligans!. If your Web site is related to young people, you are welcome to register it in the Yahooligans! search engine. Once you have registered, others can search your site with keywords.

The screen shot in Fig. 1.38 is the home page of Yahooligans! (www.yahooligans.com). In the bottom right corner, there is a "Suggest a Site" option. If you click on this option, an online registration form appears as in Fig. 1.39. Just follow the instructions on the form and most importantly make sure you have a working Web site address (i.e., http://address). Fill in the site information such as

Category:	Early learning
Title:	Young Web designer
URL:	http://www.pwt-ex.com
Description:	**Help young people (9–12) to design a funny Web page**

Finally, fill in the "Optional Information" at the bottom half of the page and then press the Submit button. It will be good practice to fill in the additional information so that the search site can contact you directly. Once you have registered your site with Yahooligans!, you can test it using their search engine. There are many search engines on the Internet and they are all similar and simple to register with online.

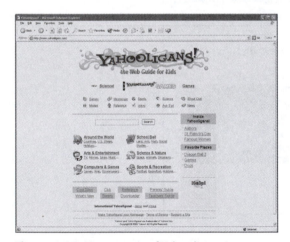

Figure 1.38 Home page of Yahooligans!

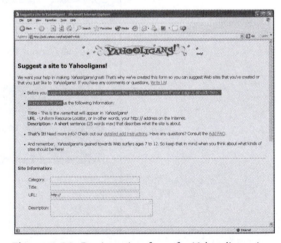

Figure 1.39 Registration form for Yahooligans!

2   Cascading Style Sheet (CSS) for Web pages

2.1   What is CSS style?

While Web site visitors demand more attractive, fast loading, and interesting sites, traditional formatting and page layout are no longer efficient enough to handle more complex design requirements. As a simple example, imagine a page with hundreds of lines and more than 50 paragraphs. Each paragraph is to be formatted by the traditional font face and size attributes. It would be an administrative nightmare to make any changes. Therefore a structural cascading mechanism is urgently needed. To rescue this reusability crisis, W3C came up with an elegant solution called the Cascading Style Sheet (CSS). It is a structure that separates formatting features from the contents of a page.

CSS works by specifying the element you want to modify, and stating how you want it to be displayed by the Web browser. For example, a typical CSS may look like this:

```
<style>
 h2 {color:red;font-family:arial;font-size:14pt}
</style>
```

This CSS defines the characteristics or style for the second-level headers (i.e., `<h2>`). In this case, the text within the element `<h2>` will be displayed using the Arial font, 14pt, and red color. More importantly, the style h2 can be cascaded over by subsequent CSS definitions.

CSS is the term used to broadly refer to several style methods of applying style elements to HTML pages. These are the inline style, internal (embedded) style, and external style sheets. A style is simply a set of formatting instructions that can be applied to a piece of text.

Styles define how to display HTML elements. The results are better font control, color management, margin control, and even the addition of special effects such as text shading. Multiple style definitions will cascade into one. This means that the first is overridden by the second, the second by the third, and so on.

2.1.1   Inline style

You have already met a number of CSS styles in Chapter 1. They are basically inline styles. You can add inline style to any "sensible" HTML elements by using the `style` attribute in the associated element. The browser will then use the inline style definitions to format only the contents of that element. The `style` attribute can contain any CSS property. Example ex02-01.htm shows how to define the style of a document body and how to change its default definitions.

Example: ex02-01.htm – Inline CSS Style

```
1: <?xml version="1.0" encoding="UTF-8"?>
2: <!DOCTYPE html PUBLIC "-//W3C//DTD XHTML 1.0 Frameset//EN"
3:     "http://www.w3.org/TR/xhtml1/DTD/xhtml1-frameset.dtd">
4: <html xmlns="http://www.w3.org/1999/xhtml" xml:lang="en" lang="en">
5: <head><title> Inline CSS Style - ex02-01.htm</title></head>
6: <body style="font-family:Times;font-weight:bold;background:#000088">
7:
8:  <div style="font-size:20pt;text-align:center;color:#00ffff">
9:   Inline CSS Style </div>
10:  <p style="font-family:arial;font-size:16pt;color:#ffff00;
11:  margin-left:20px;margin-right:20px">
12:   With CSS, we can control the margins of an element.
13:   This is a paragraph with margin-left:20px and margin-right:20px.
14:  </p>
15:
16: </body>
17: </html>
```

In this example, the `style` attribute is used within the `<body>` element (line 6). The default font and background color are now set to bold Times and color value `#000088` (dark blue) respectively. All CSS properties have to be included inside the double quotation marks of the style attribute and are separated by semi-colons.

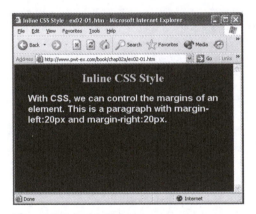

Figure 2.1 ex02-01.htm

The division element `<div>` in line 8 has all the CSS properties from `<body>` with some additional definitions. A division is similar to a paragraph but without an additional line break. Next to this division, there is a paragraph element `<p>` (line 10). This paragraph changes the default font family to "arial" and adds some margin controls. When an element has two or more of the same CSS definitions, the earlier ones will be overridden by the latest one. That is, the styles will be cascaded into one.

Notice how you can call for a font using the font's name as well as point size. In CSS, you can also use points (pt), pixels (px), percentage (%), inches (in), and centimeters (cm) to control sizing and positioning of an element. As a good design habit, always include the measurement units in your page.

A screen shot of page ex02-01.htm is shown Fig. 2.1.

2.1.2 The embedded style element `<style>`

In addition to inline style, there are also internal (or embedded) and external styles. External style is a separate file for CSS properties and will be discussed in section 2.1.3. Internal styles are usually defined within the `<style>` element. A typical example is

```
<style type="text/css">
     h2 {color:#00ffff;font-size:20pt;text-align:center}
     h4 {margin-left:70%}
     body {font-family:arial;font-size:14pt;color:#ffff00;
   background-image: url("backgr01.jpg")}
</style>
```

The browser will then read the style definitions and format the document accordingly.

A browser normally ignores unknown elements. This means that an earlier browser that does not support styles will ignore the <style> element, but the content of <style> will still be displayed on the page. It is possible to prevent an earlier browser from displaying the content by hiding it in the HTML comment symbols.

```
Example: ex02-02.htm - The Style Element <style> I

 1: <?xml version="1.0" encoding="UTF-8"?>
 2: <!DOCTYPE html PUBLIC "-//W3C//DTD XHTML 1.0 Frameset//EN"
 3: "http://www.w3.org/TR/xhtml1/DTD/xhtml1-frameset.dtd">
 4: <html xmlns="http://www.w3.org/1999/xhtml" xml:lang="en" lang="en">
 5: <head><title> The Style Element <style> I - ex02-02.htm</title></head>
 6: <style type="text/css">
 7:     h2 {color:#00ffff;font-size:20pt;text-align:center}
 8:     h4 {margin-left:70%}
 9:     p {font-family:arial;font-size:16pt;color:#ffff00;
10:         margin-left:20px;margin-right:20px}
11:     body {font-family:arial;font-size:14pt;color:#ffff00;
12:         background-image: url("backgr01.jpg")}
13: </style>
14: </head>
15: <body>
16:     <h2>Internal CSS Style</h2>
17:     <h4>This area was created by CSS margin
18:     margin-left:70% and margin-right:20%</h4>
19:      <p>With CSS, you can control text font, color, dimension, position,
20:     margin, background and much more ...</p>
21: </body>
22: </html>
```

Lines 6–13 define an internal style. This adds CSS information to a Web page. Line 7 assigns the level 2 heading with color #00ffff, font size 20pt, and text centrally aligned. Line 8 sets the left and right margins of the level 4 heading to be 70% and 20% of the element's width respectively. Line 9 defines the default font typeface "arial," font size, color value, and left and right margins of a paragraph element. The body also has a background image backgr01.jpg. This page has a screen output as shown in Fig. 2.2.

As can be seen from this example, with CSS styles you have precise control over how you would like your text to be displayed. There are also a number of CSS elements that can take a URL. In CSS, the URL should be contained within round brackets, immediately preceded by the statement URL without an equals sign as illustrated in line 12.

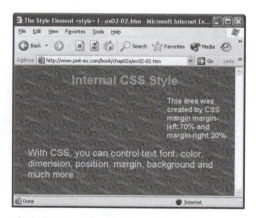

Figure 2.2 ex02-02.htm

Another useful aspect of the CSS style is the inline keyword class. This gives you ways of breaking down your style rules into very precise pieces to provide a lot of variety. You define a style class by putting a dot in front of a CSS definition. This class style can be used in almost any XHTML element with attribute class= and the unique class name.

Example ex02-03.htm defines two CSS classes. One of them is dedicated to defining a button on your browser window.

Example: ex02-03.htm - The Style Element <style> II

```
1:  <?xml version="1.0" encoding="UTF-8"?>
2:  <!DOCTYPE html PUBLIC "-//W3C//DTD XHTML 1.0 Frameset//EN"
3:  "http://www.w3.org/TR/xhtml1/DTD/xhtml1-frameset.dtd">
4:  <html xmlns="http://www.w3.org/1999/xhtml" xml:lang="en" lang="en">
5:  <head><title> The Style Element <style> II - ex02-03.htm</title></head>
6:  <style type="text/css">
7:     .txtSt {font-family:arial;color:#ffff00;font-size:20pt;
8:           font-weight:bold}
9:     .butSt {background-color:#aaffaa;font-family:arial;font-weight:bold;
10:          font-size:14pt;color:#008800;width:240px;height:30px}
11: </style>
12: </head>
13: <body style="background:#000088;text-align:center">
14: <div class="txtSt">Internal CSS Style Example II</div><br/>
15: <input type="button" class="butSt" value="CSS Style Button" />
16: </body>
17: </html>
18:
```

The screen shot is shown in Fig. 2.3. In this example, line 7 defines the CSS class with the unique name txtSt with appropriate CSS properties. Lines 9–10 define another class butSt for a button. All elements that you named class="textSt" will have the .txtSt class attributes. Similarly the <input> element that has class="butSt" will use the .butSt attributes to format the button on the Web.

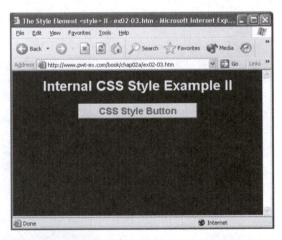

Figure 2.3 ex02-03.htm

2.1.3 External CSS style sheets

An external style sheet is ideal when the style is applied to many pages. The style information is placed in a separate document with the file extension .css. With an external style sheet, you can change the look of an entire Web site by changing the corresponding style information file. Each page must link to the style sheet using the <link> element, which usually goes within the <head> section. For example,

```
<head>
<link rel="stylesheet" type="text/css" href="ex02-04.css">
</head>
```

The browser will read the style definitions from the external CSS file ex02-04.css and format the document accordingly.

An external style sheet can be written in any text editor and should be saved with the file extension .css. You should also be sure either that this file is in the root directory with the HTML files that you intend to process or that the link is coded appropriately. An example of a style sheet file is shown below.

The following is an example of an external style sheet at work:

```
Example: ex02-04.htm - External CSS Style

 1: <?xml version="1.0" encoding="UTF-8"?>
 2: <!DOCTYPE html PUBLIC "-//W3C//DTD XHTML 1.0 Frameset//EN"
 3: "http://www.w3.org/TR/xhtml1/DTD/xhtml1-frameset.dtd">
 4: <html xmlns="http://www.w3.org/1999/xhtml" xml:lang="en" lang="en">
 5: <head><title> External CSS Style - ex02-04.htm</title></head>
 6: <link rel="stylesheet" type="text/css" href="ex02-04.css">
 7: </head>
 8: <body>
 9: <div style="text-align:center;color:#00ffff">
10:  External CSS File</div><br /><br />
11: <div>
12: This is a paragraph defined by the division element &lt;div&gt;with
13: margin-left:20% and margin-right:20%</div>
14: <hr>
15: <div>
16: This is another paragraph defined by the division element and separated
17: by a horizontal line. All CSS properties are defined in the external CSS
18: file: ex02-04.css
19: </div>
20: </body>
21: </html>
22:
```

This page includes a link (line 6) to an external style sheet called ex02-04.css. This file defines all the default formatting features used inside the page. The corresponding external CSS style sheet ex02-04.css is given next:

```
Example: ex02-04.css - External CSS File For ex02-04.htm

1: hr {color: sienna}
2: div {margin-left:20px; margin-right:20px; color:#ffff00}
3: body {background-image: url("backgr01.jpg");
4:    font-family:arial; font-size:14pt;color:#ffff00; font-weight:bold}
```

Any page containing this link adopts the styles defined in the external style sheet ex02-04.css. In this example, the horizontal rule line <hr> is changed to the color sienna. Additional margin control is added to the <div> element and the element <body> is given a different style definition. Bold "arial" and color value #ffff00 in a font size of 14 points are used as default attributes. A background image backgr01.jpg is also added to specify graphics as background images. This page has a screen output as shown in Fig. 2.4.

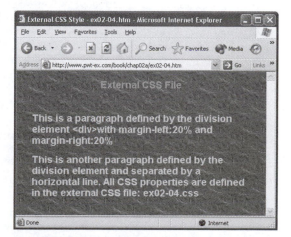

Figure 2.4 ex02-04.htm

2.1.4 Designing Web logos with CSS

Web site logos and trademarks are popular applications on the Web. You can combine inline styles, internal styles, and external style sheets in a Web page to give you maximum control. The browser will display the

Web page by first looking at inline styles, then internal styles, and whatever isn't covered in the linked external CSS style sheets. This is a powerful feature of CSS. Imagine you have a large Web site that you're controlling with a single style sheet. You may also have a page on which you want to alter some of the styles to suit a particular purpose. This can be easily achieved by combining various styles together. What you have to do is simply to place the modified styles as an internal style sheet within the Web page that you want to alter. You can also further refine individual areas within the page by adding inline styles.

The following example shows how to use an internal style with classes to define various typefaces, sizes, background colors, margin controls, and placement of objects on a Web page:

```
Example: ex02-05.htm - Web Logo Designs with CSS
 1: <?xml version="1.0" encoding="UTF-8"?>
 2: <!DOCTYPE html PUBLIC "-//W3C//DTD XHTML 1.0 Frameset//EN"
 3: "http://www.w3.org/TR/xhtml1/DTD/xhtml1-frameset.dtd">
 4: <html xmlns="http://www.w3.org/1999/xhtml" xml:lang="en" lang="en">
 5: <head><title> Web Logo Designs with CSS - ex02-05.htm</title></head>
 6: <style>
 7:    .car_Box {color:#000088;background-color:white;
 8:        width:250pt;height:80pt;
 9:        font-family:"Times New Roman";font-weight:bold}
10:    .car_L1 {color:#000088;font-size:38pt;
11:        font-weight:bold;font-family:"impact";
12:        text-align:center;margin-top:10pt}
13:    .car_L2 {color:white;background-color:#000088;
14:        font-size:16pt;font-weight:bold;
15:        text-align:center;
16:        margin-left:12pt;margin-right:12pt;
17:        font-family:"arial";
18:        letter-spacing:6pt}
19:
20:    .abc_Box {color:white; background-color:#000022;
21:        width:200pt;height:80pt;
22:        font-weight:bold;font-family:"Times New Roman";
23:        margin-top:0.3em; position:relative;
24:        top:-10%; left:52% }
25:    .abc_L1 {font-size:34pt; font-weight:bold;
26:        font-family:"Times New Roman";
27:        text-align:center; margin-top:10pt }
28:    .abc_L2 {color:#DD0000; font-size:22pt;
29:        font-family:"Times New Roman";font-weight:bold;
30:        text-align:center; margin-top:-5pt }
31:
32:    .loan_Box {color:#000088; background-color:white;
33:        width:180pt; height:80pt;
34:        font-family:"Times New Roman"; font-weight:bold }
35:    .loan_L1 {color:#000088; font-size:38pt;
36:        font-weight:bold; font-family: "impact";
37:        text-align:center }
38:    .loan_L2 {color:white; background-color:#000088;
39:        font-size:16pt; font-weight:bold;
40:        text-align:center; font-family:"arial" }
41: </style>
42:
43: <body>
44: <div style="font-family:arial; font-size:24pt; color:#008800;
45:    font-weight:bold; text-align:center" >
46:    Designing Web Logo With CSS
47: </div>
48:
```

```
49: <div class="car_Box" align="center">
50:   <div class="car_L1">Racing Sports</div>
51:   <div class="car_L2">FORMULA CARS</div>
52: </div>
53:
54: <div class="abc_Box">
55:   <div class="abc_L1">ABC.COM</div>
56:   <div class="abc_L2">Online Shopping</div>
57: </div>
58:
59: <div class="loan_Box" align="center">
60:   <div class="loan_L2">YesToAll Bank</div>
61:   <div class="loan_L1"><img src="ex02-04.gif"
62:       style="width:180pt;height:30px" alt="pic"></div>
63: </div>
64:
65: <div style="width:250px; height:80px; text-align:center;
66:   background:#0000aa;
67:      position:absolute;top:250px; left:320px">
68:      <div style="font-family:arial; font-size:14pt; text-align:center;
69:   color:#ffff00">Have A Fun Game here!</div>
70:   <div>
71:   <img src="ghost_l.gif" style="width:40px;height:40px" vspace="20"
72:   alt="pic">
73:   <img src="other.gif" style="width:140px;height:80px" alt="pic">
74:   <img src="ghost_r.gif" style="width:40px;height:40px" vspace="20"
75:   alt="pic">
76:      </div>
77: </div>
78: </body>
79: </html>
```

Various CSS classes are defined within the internal `<style>` element in lines 6–42. For example, the class `car_Box` (lines 7–9) specifies the default font typeface to be bold Times Roman. It also sets a rectangular box with dimensions 250 points by 80 points, a color value `#000088`, and a white background. Many items can be encased in boxes to produce very good effects.

The inline style within the `<div>` element in lines 44–45 is designed to temporarily override any existing CSS information that may have already been specified elsewhere. Thus the text "Designing Web Logos With CSS" will be displayed at the center in bold, 24pt, `Arial` font typeface with the color value `#008800`. This is an example of cascading in action.

Line 61 shows how to combine a class style `loan_L1` with inline style. You can also further refine the CSS element displays of individual areas within a Web page with inline styles as shown in lines 70–77. A screen shot of ex02-05.htm is shown in Fig. 2.5.

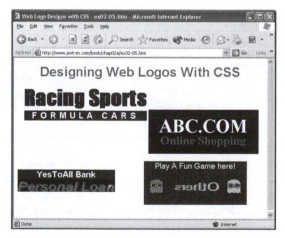

Figure 2.5 ex02-05.htm

2.2   Controlling text properties with style

CSS font properties provide a more logical set of tools to control the way texts are displayed on a Web page. They are more powerful than the FONT attribute introduced in HTML 3.x or earlier. Thus, unless backward compatibility is required, CSS properties are used throughout this book.

Some frequently used CSS properties related to font are listed in Table 2.1.

Table 2.1 Font family, size, weight, style, and color

CSS property	CSS values	NS	IE	Description	CSS version
Color	`#rrggbb` `color name`	4.+	4.+	Sets the color of the font in 24-bit red, green, blue mode	CSS1

Font	`font-family,`
	`font-size,`
	`font-style,`
	`font-weight`
		4.+	4.+	A shorthand property to set all font values	CSS1

Font family	Family name Generic family	4.+	4.+	A prioritized list of font family names	CSS1
Font size	Length – fixed % – relative	4.+	4.+	Sets the size of font	CSS1
Font style	Normal Italic Oblique	4.+	4.+	Sets the style of the font	CSS1
Font variant	Normal Small caps	4.+	4.+	Displays text in a small-caps font or normal font	CSS1
Font weight	Normal Bold Bolder Lighter	4.+	4.+	Sets the weight of the font	CSS1

CSS Level 1 (CSS1) is implemented fully in both the NS6+ and IE6+ browsers. Some other browsers such as Opera 5+ are also CSS1 compliant. Although not fully implemented, the CSS Level 2 (CSS2) specification is available via W3C. Basically the CSS2 specification not only adds to the existing CSS1 specification, but also supersedes many of its elements – in particular the additions to the font, box, and positioning elements. It is an extensive specification and takes style sheets to a new level.

2.2.1   Font family, size, weight, and color

Font family is defined by an attribute or keyword `font-family` inside a CSS definition. The general format is

```
Font-family: font_name1, font_name2, font_name3
```

where `font_name` is the name of the font available on your system. Quotation marks are used if the `font_name` contains spaces or more than one word (e.g., "Times New Roman").

It's worth pointing out that there are few truly universal fonts common to all operating systems and browsers. As a general rule, the browser does the best it can to match the requested fonts with the ones specified.

An inline CSS style example code is

```
<div style="font-family:arial, 'Times New Roman',
     'Comic Sans MS'; font-size:14pt">Hello World</div>
```

This statement tries to display the text "Hello World" with the specified font called "arial." If "arial" is not available on your system, then the font "Times New Roman" is used as a second choice.

An internal CSS style example code is

```
<style>
 h1 {font-family:Georgia, "Times New Roman", Garamond, Times, Serif }
 p {font-family: Verdana, Arial, Helvetica, Sans-serif }
 .txtSt {font-family:arial, "Times New Roman" }
</style>
```

In this example code, a new set of default font families for the level 1 heading h1, paragraph p, and the class txtSt are defined.

Font size is defined by the attribute font-size inside a CSS definition. The general format is

```
font-size: size
```

where size is a scale setting the size of the display font on the browser window. You can define sizes in basically two ways: length and percentage. Length is a fixed scale and can be specified in points (pt), pixels (px), millimeters (mm), centimeters (cm), and inches (in). The percentage size (%) represents relative font scale. As an example, the following code

```
<div style="font-size:20pt">A fixed 20pt text string</div>
<div style="font-size:150%">A relative text string (150%)</div>
```

displays the strings "A fixed 20pt text string" in 20-point font size and "A relative text string (150%)" in 150% relative to the existing font size respectively.

To use font-family and font-size together, all you have to do is to put them into a style definition separated by a semi-colon. The example code

```
<div style="font-family:arial,times;font-size:20pt">
     Hello World</div>
```

displays the text "Hello World" in 20-point "arial." All CSS style properties and values can be defined this way. You can specify as many attributes as you want, with each separated by a semi-colon.

Example Ex02-06.htm is a page illustrating various font families, sizes (both fixed and relative), and colors. Both the internal and inline CSS styles are used as you can see in the example.

```
Example: ex02-06.htm - Font Family, Size And Weight

 1: <?xml version="1.0" encoding="UTF-8"?>
 2: <!DOCTYPE html PUBLIC "-//W3C//DTD XHTML 1.0 Frameset//EN"
 3: "http://www.w3.org/TR/xhtml1/DTD/xhtml1-frameset.dtd">
 4: <html xmlns="http://www.w3.org/1999/xhtml" xml:lang="en" lang="en">
 5: <head>
 6:    <title> Font Family, Size and Weight - ex02-06.htm</title>
 7:    <style type="text/css">
 8:    h1 {font-family:'Comic Sans MS',times, font-size:20pt;color:#000088}
 9:    h2 {font-family:arial,times;font-size:200%; color:#880000 }
10:    h3 {font-size:150%;color:008800}
11:    .small {font-family:times;font-size:80%}
12:    .half {font-family:times;font-size:50%}
13:    .normal {font-family:arial,times,serif; font-size:90%}
14:    </style>
15: </head>
16:
17:    <div style="font-family:arial;font-size:20pt;font-weight:bold;
18:    text-align:center">
```

```
19:    Font family and Sizes Demo <br />(Fixed and Relative Sizes)</div>
20:
21:     <h1>A fixed text string with</br />
22:    font-family:"Comic Sans MS";font-size:20pt</h1>
23:     <h2>A relative sized text with font-family:arial;font-size:200%<br />
24:    <span class="half">and half of this size is 100%</span></h2>
25:     <h3>A text with default font and font-size:150%</h3>
26:    <span class="normal">A slightly smaller paragraph (size:90%)</span><br />
27:
28: </body>
29: </html>
```

Lines 7–14 define an internal CSS style with new CSS properties for the elements h1, h2, h3 and the classes small, half, and normal. For example, the h1 element is set to use the "Comic Sans MS" as the default font typeface, and the fixed display size of 20 points in a color with a value of #000088. Notice that "Times" is also used as a backup font in case the specified font doesn't exist on your system. "Times" is the standard default typeface for a Windows machine. Similarly the classes small, half, and normal have their own default font settings and relative display sizes. Thus the text in lines 21–22 will be displayed according to the <h1> style specified in line 8.

The division element <div> in line 17 has an inline style specifying the text to be displayed with 20-point bold Arial. A screen shot of this page is shown in Fig. 2.6.

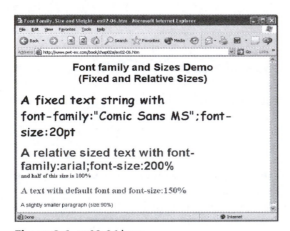

Figure 2.6 ex02-06.htm

Figure 2.7 Fonts available on a PC

Since every system may have a different set of fonts, special care should be taken when you design your Web site. There are hundreds of fonts available. As a general rule, do not try to use a lot of fonts on a page and always include a "safe" font as an option.

A complete listing of available fonts can usually be found in the font directory in your system. For a PC and a Microsoft system, the font directory is located in /windows/fonts/. Alternatively you can also obtain a full listing of all available fonts by activating the Start|Control Panel|Font icon.

Fonts can be added to, or removed from, your machine in the usual way specified by your system.

Figure 2.7 shows a screen shot of the font directory on a Windows XP system.

2.2.2   Alignment, indent, and margins

In addition to font properties, text formatting elements and margins can also be controlled using the CSS elements, Using these elements, you can specify such things as spacing between words, indentation, alignment, positions of text, and much more. Table 2.2 lists some frequently used CSS properties on margins and text alignments.

Table 2.2 Margins and alignments

CSS property	CSS values	NS	IE	Description	CSS version

`margin`	`margin-top`
	`margin-right`
	`margin-left`
	`margin-bottom`
		4.+	4.+	A shorthand property to set the margin properties in one definition	CSS1

`margin-bottom`	`auto length %`	4.+	4.+	Sets the bottom margin of an element	CSS1
`margin-left`	`auto length %`	4.+	4.+	Sets the left margin of an element	CSS1
`margin-right`	`auto length %`	4.+	4.+	Sets the right margin of an element	CSS1
`margin-top`	`auto length %`	4.+	4.+	Sets the top margin of an element	CSS1
`margin-align`	`left right` `center justify`	4.+	4.+	Aligns the text in an element	CSS1
`margin-indent`	`length %`	4.+	4.+	Indents the first line of text in an element	CSS1

CSS can take a specific unit of measurement in length. It can be in points (pt), inches (in), centimeters (cm), or a percentage (%). The left and right margins together with the division element can be used to define a text box with arbitrary length on the browser window. Consider the following example ex02-07.htm:

```
Example: ex02-07.htm - Margins and Alignments

 1: <?xml version="1.0" encoding="UTF-8"?>
 2: <!DOCTYPE html PUBLIC "-//W3C//DTD XHTML 1.0 Frameset//EN"
 3: "http://www.w3.org/TR/xhtml1/DTD/xhtml1-frameset.dtd">
 4: <html xmlns="http://www.w3.org/1999/xhtml" xml:lang="en" lang="en">
 5: <head><title>Indent Margin and Alignment - ex02-07.htm</title></head>
 6:     <style type="text/css">
 7:
 8:     .ins {font-size:14pt;font-weight:normal;text-align:left;
 9:           text-indent:1in;margin-left:5%;margin-right:50%}
10:
11:     .pts {font-size:14pt;font-weight:normal;text-align:justify;
12:           margin-left:50%;margin-right:5%}
13:
14:     .pct {font-size:14pt;font-weight:normal;text-align:left;
15:           text-indent:5%;margin-left:5%;margin-right:50%}
16:     </style>
17:
```

```
18:    <body style="font-family:arial;font-size:16pt;font-weight:bold">
19:        <div style="font-family:arial;font-size:18pt;text-align:center">
20:        Text Indent Margin and Alignment Demo</div><br />
21:
22:        <div class="ins">This is a left aligned text box defined by
23:         margin left right (5%,50%). The first line of text should be
24:        indented 1 inch from the left margin of the box.</div><br />
25:
26:        <div class="pts">This is a right aligned text box defined by
27:        margin left right (50%, 5%). All lines are justified within
28:         the text box</div><br />
29:
30:        <div class="pct">This is a left aligned text box defined by
31:        margin left right (5%, 50%). The first line of text should be
32:         indented 5% of the browser window.</div><br />
33:
34: </body>
35: </html>
36:
```

In this example, three classes `ins`, `pts`, and `pct` are defined in lines 6–16. For example, the class `ins` sets the 14pt normal text to be indented 1 inch from the left margin of the box and left aligned. The left and right margins of the box are also set to be 5% from the left edge and 50% from the right edge of the browser window respectively. Similarly for the classes `pts` and `pct`. A screen shot of this page is shown in Fig. 2.8.

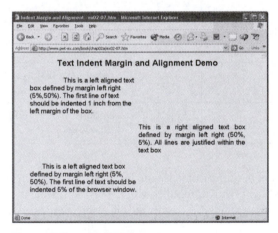

Figure 2.8 ex02-07.htm

2.2.3 Letter decoration and transformation

Letter decoration adds a decorative property (i.e., a line) to the text of the HTML element it is associated with. For example,

```
<div style="text-decoration:underline; color:#8b0000">
    Text decoration underlined</div>
```

adds a dark red line below the text "Text decoration underlined."

The `text-transform` CSS element is used to set the type of case used in the text. For example, the code

```
<div style="text-transform:lowercase">
     This text is all in lowercase</div>
```

sets all text in lower case. Table 2.3 gives some of the most frequently used CSS properties relating to `text-decoration` and `text-transform` elements.

Table 2.3 Letter decoration and transformation

CSS property	CSS values	NS	IE	Description	CSS version
text-decoration	none underline overline line-through blink	4.+	4.+	Adds decoration to text	CSS1
text-transform	none capitalize uppercase lowercase	4.+	4.+	Controls the letters in an element	CSS1

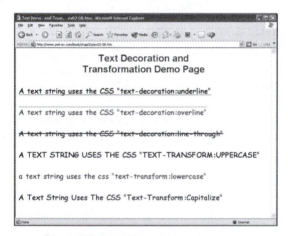

Figure 2.9 ex02-08.htm

The example program ex02-08.htm shows text-decoration and text-transform in action. The corresponding screen shot is shown in Fig. 2.09.

Example: ex02-08.htm – Letter Decoration and Transformation

```
 1: <?xml version="1.0" encoding="UTF-8"?>
 2: <!DOCTYPE html PUBLIC "-//W3C//DTD XHTML 1.0 Frameset//EN"
 3: "http://www.w3.org/TR/xhtml1/DTD/xhtml1-frameset.dtd">
 4: <html xmlns="http://www.w3.org/1999/xhtml" xml:lang="en" lang="en">
 5: <head><title>Text Decor. and Trans. – ex02-08.htm</title></head>
 6:    <style>
 7:    .bSt {font-family:'Comic Sans MS',times;font-size:18pt;
 8:         color:#000088}
 9:    </style>
10:
11: <body style="font-family:arial;font-size:24pt;font-weight:bold">
12:
13: <div style="text-align:center;color:#880000;text-align:center">
14:    Text Decoration and <br />Transformation Demo Page</div><br />
15:
16: <div class="bSt" style="text-decoration:underline;color:#000088">
17:  A text string uses the CSS "text-decoration:underline"</div><br />
18: <div class="bSt" style="text-decoration:overline;color:#008800">
```

```
19:   A text string uses the CSS "text-decoration:overline"</div><br />
20: <div class="bSt" style="text-decoration:line-through;color:#880000">
21:   A text string uses the CSS "text-decoration:line-through"</div><br />
22:
23: <div class="bSt" style="text-transform:uppercase;color:#000088">
24:   A text string uses the CSS "text-transform:uppercase"</div><br />
25: <div class="bSt" style="text-transform:lowercase;color:#008800">
26:   A text string uses the CSS "text-transform:lowercase"</div><br />
27: <div class="bSt" style="text-transform:capitalize;color:#880000">
28:   A text string uses the CSS "text-transform:capitalize"</div><br />
29:
30: </body>
31: </html>
```

In this example, only one class bSt is defined in the internal style sheet. It sets the default font family to "Comic Sans MS" and a point size of 18 and color #000088. Lines 15–27 show various effects of text decoration and text transformation.

2.2.4 Text box dimensions and spacing

With CSS, you can scale the HTML elements it is associated with to fit the specified height and width dimensions. The CSS white-space element is a powerful element that controls the way that white space and carriage returns are handled within a Web page. It allows you to add plenty of visual space to enhance the clarity of your Web pages.

Some of the most frequently used CSS properties relating to line and character spacing are given in Table 2.4. They are all CSS1 elements and therefore fully supported by both the IE6+ and NS6+ browsers.

Table 2.4 Line and character spacing

CSS property	CSS values	NS	IE	Description	CSS version
height	auto length %	6.+	4.+	Sets the height of an element	CSS1
width	auto length %	4.+	4.+	Sets the width of an element	CSS1
line-height	normal number length %	4.+	4.+	Sets the distance between lines	CSS1
white-space	normal pre nowrap	4.+	4.+	Sets how white space inside an element is handled	CSS1
letter-spacing	normal length	6.+	4.+	Increases or decreases the space between characters	CSS1
word-spacing	normal length	6.+	6.+	Increases or decreases the space between words	CSS1

These CSS properties provide you with yet more control over how your text should be displayed by the browser. For example, the CSS element `word-spacing` can be used to set the spacing distance between words on a Web page. Wide values can make your text easier to read, or achieve some visual effects. The example ex02-09.htm demonstrates some of these CSS properties.

```
Example: ex02-09.htm - Line-height, Letter and Word Spacing

 1: <?xml version="1.0" encoding="UTF-8"?>
 2: <!DOCTYPE html PUBLIC "-//W3C//DTD XHTML 1.0 Frameset//EN"
 3: "http://www.w3.org/TR/xhtml1/DTD/xhtml1-frameset.dtd">
 4: <html xmlns="http://www.w3.org/1999/xhtml" xml:lang="en" lang="en">
 5: <head><title>Line-height and Spacing - ex02-09.htm</title></head>
 6: <style>
 7:     div {font-size:14pt;color:#000088; padding:2ex;margin-left:1in;
 8:     font-weight:normal; width:6in }
 9:
10:     .line01 {line-height:150%; letter-spacing:0.2em}
11:     .line02 {line-height:200%; word-spacing:1.5em}
12: </style>
13:
14: <body>
15:
16: <div style="font-family:arial; font-size:20pt; font-weight:bold;
17:     color:#880000">CSS Line-height, Letter and Word Spacing Demo </div>
18:
19: <div>This paragraph should be leading of 100%
20: i.e., the default leading produced by the CSS line-height property.</div>
21:
22: <div class="line01">This paragraph should be leading of 150%
23: produced by the CSS line-height property. The letter-spacing
24: feature is supported in IE4 but not NS4. You should have no problem
25: if you are using NS6+</div>
26:
27: <div class="line02">This should be leading of 200% produced by the
28: CSS line-height property. Word spacing is not supported by IE4 or NS4.
29: You have no problems if you are using the latest browsers</div>
30:
31: </body>
32: </html>
```

Three CSS properties are defined within the internal CSS style sheet in lines 6–13. Line 7 has an attribute `padding:2ex` which is used to add padding (of 2ex units) equally to the top, bottom, and sides of the division element. This will add visual space to the text. Line 10 defines a class `line01` that sets the spacing of 0.2em between characters. The distance between two lines is 150% in relation to the size of the font in use. The unit em is a measure relative to the height of the current font used. The unit ex, on the other hand, refers to the relative height of a lower case "x." Line 11 is another class `line02`. It sets the distance between two lines to be 200% and the spacing distance between words is 1.5em.

An interesting element is the `<div>` element in line 16. This line has an inline style that redefines the `font-size` (20pt) and `font-weight` (bold). The browser will use this new set of CSS properties to format the text that is associated with this division element. This is an example of cascading styles in practice.

A screen shot of this example is shown in Fig. 2.10.

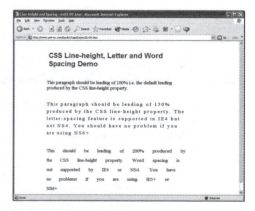

Figure 2.10 ex02-09.htm

2.3   Background and border

The background family of CSS style elements is used to set the background characteristics on your Web page. For example, you could apply some CSS background elements to highlight an area on a page, or just simply to enhance the contrasts of the display and the background. Another useful CSS element is `border`. The border properties set the display of borders around its associated CSS element. All these, together with the dimensioning and postioning CSS elements, give a variety of controls down to pixel level to help you design your pages. The dimensioning and positioning CSS elements will be discussed in more detail in section 2.4.

Some frequently used background CSS elements are shown in Table 2.5.

Table 2.5 Background CSS elements

CSS property	CSS values	NS	IE	Description
`background`	`#rrggbb`	4.+	4.+	Sets the background color or image
`background-color`	`#rrggbb` `transparent`	4.+	4.+	Sets the background color for an element, or sets it to transparent
`background-image`	`image_file_name`	4.+	4.+	Specifies the `image_file_name` as a background image
`background-repeat`	`repeat` `repeat-x` `repeat-y` `no-repeat`	4.+	4.+	Specifies how the background image is repeated
`background-atachment`	`scroll` `fixed`	4.+	4.+	Specifies background image movement when the browser window is scrolled
`background-position`	`x y` `% %` `left/center/right` `top/center/bottom`	4.+	4.+	Indicates the coordinates in which the background image first appears

Note that the `background` CSS element is the father of all the other background CSS elements, all of which share similar CSS properties for adding special background effects to your Web page. Some CSS elements like `background-repeat`, `background-attachment`, and `background-position` will not work unless the CSS element `background-image` is specified first.

Let's now have a look at the background CSS elements.

2.3.1   Background color and image

The CSS background element allows you to add a background color or image to your Web page. For example, you may like to use a dark color to set a background against light-colored paragraphs to create an effect of sidebars or offsetting text for emphasis.

The CSS element `<background-color>` takes the general format

```
<b style="background-color:#rrggbb">
     your body text here …
</b>
```

The following example ex02-10.htm shows some simple background-color effects:

```
Example: ex02-10.htm - Background Color

 1: <?xml version="1.0" encoding="UTF-8"?>
 2: <!DOCTYPE html PUBLIC "-//W3C//DTD XHTML 1.0 Frameset//EN"
 3: "http://www.w3.org/TR/xhtml1/DTD/xhtml1-frameset.dtd">
 4: <html xmlns="http://www.w3.org/1999/xhtml" xml:lang="en" lang="en">
 5: <head><title>Background Color - ex02-10.htm</title></head>
 6:
 7: <body style="background:#f0fff0">
 8:
 9: <div style="font-family:arial,times,serif; font-size:20pt;
10: font-weight:bold;text-align:center">
11:   Background Color <br />Demo</div><br />
12:
13: <div style="background-color:#00ffff;font-family:'Comic Sans MS',
14: times; font-size:20pt;color:#ff0000">
15: This text will appear in red in a small box with cyan
16: background on a larger honeydew background
17: </div><br />
18:
19: </body>
20: </html>
20
```

Line 7 sets a general background color for the whole page. With the CSS `background-color` element, you can have additional control over the background color that is associated with this element. The division element in lines 13–17 uses a different color (cyan) from that of the background (honeydew color) in order to emphasize a string of text. This page has the screen output shown in Fig. 2.11.

You can also use a small picture, a photograph, or a graphic design to form a background pattern. With the `background-image` CSS properties, your small picture is tiled repeatedly in the horizontal and/or vertical directions to form the image background. If carefully arranged, this type of background can have both an unusual and original effect.

In Chapter 1 we have already discussed adding images to the background of your Web page. This is a very straightforward process with the CSS element. The code

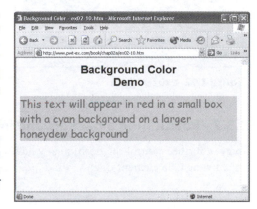

Figure 2.11 ex02-10.htm

```
<body style="background-image:url (bg_image.gif)">
```

will repeatedly insert the image bg_image.gif into the body of the page to create a background picture. Note that once this element is specified, you can further modify the behavior of the background by using the related CSS elements such as `background-repeat`, `background-attachment`, and `background-position`. These CSS elements will be discussed in section 2.3.2.

The following example shows how to create a background consisting of the image "Practical Web" logo:

```
Example: ex02-11.htm - Background Image

 1: <?xml version="1.0" encoding="UTF-8"?>
 2: <!DOCTYPE html PUBLIC "-//W3C//DTD XHTML 1.0 Frameset//EN"
 3: "http://www.w3.org/TR/xhtml1/DTD/xhtml1-frameset.dtd">
 4: <html xmlns="http://www.w3.org/1999/xhtml" xml:lang="en" lang="en">
 5: <head><title>Background Image - ex02-11.htm</title></head>
```

```
 6: <style type="text/css">
 7:    .txtSt {background-color:#000000;font-family:arial; color:ffffff;
 8:   font-size:30pt; font-weight:bold; text-align:center}
 9: </style>
10:
11: <body style="background-image: url(logo_web.jpg);
12: background-repeat:repeat">
13:
14: <br /><br />
15: <div class="txtSt">We have an image background.
16: </div>
17:
18: </body>
19: </html>
```

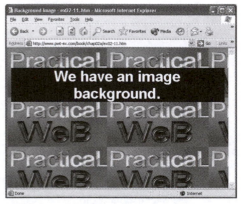

In this example, the CSS element `background-repeat:repeat` tiles the image web_logo.jpg both horizontally and vertically to create the image background. If the `background-repeat:repeat-x` is set, then the image is tiled horizontally only and can be used to create a graphical edge effect for your Web page. The `background-repeat` element is always used in conjunction with the `background-image` element and modifies the way the background image is displayed.

A screen display of this example is shown in Fig. 2.12.

More interesting examples of changing various background attributes with mouse-over (or rollover) controls can also be found in Chapter 6.

Figure 2.12 ex02-11.htm

2.3.2   Positioning a background image

You can further control the position at which a background image begins to tile on your Web page. This is all done by the CSS element `background-position`. It takes the general form

```
<body style="background-image:url (bg_image.gif)
    background-position: x y">
```

where `x y` represents the position of the image. Note that with the IE4 and NS4 browsers, tiling only happens down and to the right.

The Web page ex02-12.htm below shows an example with various backgrounds.

```
Example: ex02-12.htm - Positioning A Background Image

 1: <?xml version="1.0" encoding="UTF-8"?>
 2: <!DOCTYPE html PUBLIC "-//W3C//DTD XHTML 1.0 Frameset//EN"
 3: "http://www.w3.org/TR/xhtml1/DTD/xhtml1-frameset.dtd">
 4: <html xmlns="http://www.w3.org/1999/xhtml" xml:lang="en" lang="en">
 5: <head><title>Positioning a Background Image - ex02-12.htm</title></head>
 6:
 7: <style type="text/css">
 8:    .txtSt1 {font-family:arial; color:#ffff00;
 9:   font-size:20pt; font-weight:bold;text-indent:-50px}
10:    .txtSt2 {font-family:'Comic Sans MS'; color:#000088;
11:   font-size:20pt; font-weight:bold;text-indent:-50px}
12:    .txtSt3 {font-family:Times New Roman; color:#dd8800;
13:   font-size:20pt; font-weight:bold;text-indent:-50px}
```

```
14:
15: </style>
16:
17: <body style="background:#87ceeb;background-image: url(vstone01.gif);
18: background-repeat:repeat-y">
19:
20: <div style="font-family:arial;font-size:24pt;color:#8b0000;
21: font-weight:bold;text-align:center">Positioning A Background Image
22: <br /><br /></div>
23: <div class="txtSt1">
24: <img alt="pic" src="bullet1.gif" hspace=100 align=left>
25: The background in skyblue color<br /><br />
26: </div>
27:
28: <div class="txtSt2">
29: <img alt="pic" src="bullet1.gif" hspace=100 align=left>
30: An edge background<br /><br />
31: </div>
32:
33: <div class="txtSt3">
34: <img alt="pic" src="bullet1.gif" hspace=100 align=left>
35: You can attach a company logo here
36: <br /><br />
37: </div>
38: <img alt="pic" src="logo_web.jpg" width="180" height="90" align=right>
39:
40: </body>
41: </html>
```

In this example, the CSS background attribute `background-repeat:repeat-y` in lines 17–18 tiles the background image vstone01.gif in a vertical direction repeatedly to create an image edge background. You can also add various images to your Web page to enhance the appearance of the page.

A screen shot of example ex02-12.htm is shown in Fig. 2.13.

2.3.3 "Nailing" a background image

The CSS style element `background-attachment` allows you to control whether the background image moves when the browser window is scrolled. Similar to the `background-repeat` element, the `background-attachment` CSS element only works when the `background-image` element is set. It takes the general format

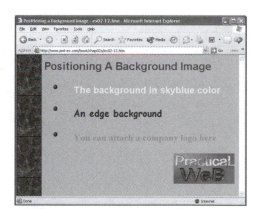

Figure 2.13 ex02-12.htm

```
<body style="background-image:url (bg_image.gif)
    background-attachment: fixed">
```

If the `background-attachment` is set to `fixed`, then the `background-image` will be fixed with respect to the viewing area and therefore not affected by any scrolling action. This has the effect of "nailing" the background image in place and may be a useful function if, for instance, you want to create a watermark feature using your own logo. Example ex02-13.htm illustrates this action.

Example: ex02-13.htm – Fixing A Background Image Position

```
 1: <?xml version="1.0" encoding="UTF-8"?>
 2: <!DOCTYPE html PUBLIC "-//W3C//DTD XHTML 1.0 Frameset//EN"
 3: "http://www.w3.org/TR/xhtml1/DTD/xhtml1-frameset.dtd">
 4: <html xmlns="http://www.w3.org/1999/xhtml" xml:lang="en" lang="en">
 5: <head><title>Positioning a Background Image - ex02-13.htm</title></head>
 6:
 7: <style type="text/css">
 8:    .txtSt1 {font-family:arial; color:#000000;
 9:    font-size:20pt; font-weight:bold}
10:    .txtSt2 {font-family:'Comic Sans MS'; color:#000088;
11:    font-size:20pt; font-weight:bold}
12:    .txtSt3 {font-family:Times New Roman; color:#dd8800;
13:    font-size:20pt; font-weight:bold}
14:
15: </style>
16:
17: <body style="background-image: url(title4.gif); background-position:center;
18: background-repeat:no-repeat;background-attachment:fixed">
19:
20: <div style="font-family:arial;font-size:24pt;color:#8b0000;
21: font-weight:bold;text-align:center">Fixing A Background Image
22: <br /><br /></div>
23: <div class="txtSt1">
24: The background-image is fixed<br /><br />
25: </div>
26:
27: <div class="txtSt2">
28: and therefore <br /><br />
29: </div>
30:
31: <div class="txtSt3">
32: will not be affected
33: <br /><br />
34: </div>
35:
36: <div class="txtSt1" style="font-size:10pt">
37: by any scrolling action<br /><br />
38: </div>
39:
40: <div class="txtSt2" style="font-size:25pt">
41: The default scroll attribute makes the background-image
43: scroll when the user scrolls the page <br /><br />
44: </div>
45:
46: </body>
47: </html>
```

In lines 17–18, the background image title4.gif is fixed at the center of the page and is unaffected by any scrolling actions. If you set background-attachment:scroll, then the scroll attribute makes the background image scroll when the user scrolls the page. The screen output of this page is shown in Fig. 2.14.

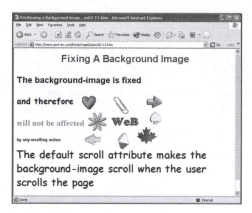

Figure 2.14 ex02-13.htm

2.3.4 Color, width, and style of element borders

One of the most powerful CSS properties is positioning. This property gives you total, pixel-level control over the location of every element on your Web page. This CSS element will be discussed in more detail in section 2.4. The remainder of this section is devoted to a discussion of the CSS border element and its associated properties.

The CSS border property sets the display of borders around the CSS element that it is associated with. Every border has three aspects: width, style, and color. These properties allow you to have full control as to how you want the borders to be displayed on the Web page.

Some frequently used CSS border elements are shown in Table 2.6.

Table 2.6 Border CSS elements

CSS property	CSS values	NS	IE	Description
border-style	none outset dashed ridge solid double dotted groove inset	4.+	4.+	Sets the style of borders
border-color	#rrggbb color name	4.+	4.+	Sets the color of border sides
border-width	length thin medium thick	4.+	4.+	Specifies the thickness of each border side
border-top	border-top-width border-style color	4.+	4.+	Sets the display values of the top border
border-right	border-right-width border-style color	4.+	4.+	Sets the display values of the right border
border-bottom	border-bottom-width border-style color	4.+	4.+	Sets the display values of the bottom border
border-left	border-left-width border-style color	4.+	4.+	Sets the display values of the left border

There are a total of nine different border styles defined in the CSS1 standard. However, only the support of the `solid` border style is required for CSS1 compliance. For example,

```
<div style="border-style:double border-color:red">
       Double bordered texts</div>
```

will create a double-line red border around "Double bordered texts." The nine different border styles are demonstrated in the example ex02-14.htm.

```
Example: ex02-14.htm - Border With CSS

 1: <?xml version="1.0" encoding="UTF-8"?>
 2: <!DOCTYPE html PUBLIC "-//W3C//DTD XHTML 1.0 Frameset//EN"
 3: "http://www.w3.org/TR/xhtml1/DTD/xhtml1-frameset.dtd">
 4: <html xmlns="http://www.w3.org/1999/xhtml" xml:lang="en" lang="en">
 5: <head><title>Borders with Styles - ex02-14.htm</title></head>
 6:    <style>
 7:    .bSt {font-family:'Comic Sans MS',times;font-size:12pt}
 8:    </style>
 9:
10: <body style="font-family:arial;font-size:20pt;font-weight:bold">
11:
12: <div style="text-align:center;color:#880000;text-align:center">
13:    Border Styles and Colors Demo Page</div><br />
14:
15: <div class="bSt" style="border-style:none;border-color:#000088">
16: The paragraph has no border style </div><br />
17:
18: <div class="bSt" style="border-style:double;border-color:#008800">
19: The paragraph has a DOUBLE border style </div><br />
20:
21: <div class="bSt" style="border-style:dashed;border-color:#ff0000">
22: The paragraph has a DASHED border style </div><br />
23:
24: <div class="bSt" style="border-style:dotted;border-color:#ffd700">
25: The paragraph has a DOTTED border style </div><br />
26:
27: <div class="bSt" style="border-style:inset;border-color:#fff4e1">
28: The paragraph has an INSET border style </div><br />
29:
30: <div class="bSt" style="border-style:outset;border-color:#ffa500">
31: The paragraph has an OUTSET border style </div><br />
32:
33: <div class="bSt" style="border-style:groove;border-color:#006400">
34: The paragraph has a GROOVE border style </div><br />
35:
36: <div class="bSt" style="border-style:ridge;border-color:#00ffff">
37: The paragraph has a RIDGE border style </div><br />
38:
39: <div class="bSt" style="border-style:solid;border-color:#0000ff">
40: The paragraph has a SOLID border style </div><br />
41:
42: </body>
43: </html>
```

In this example, the internal CSS style in lines 6–8 defines the display text properties. Lines 15–40 define all nine different `border-style` attributes. The `none` attribute is the default style. Also the support of only the `solid` style is required for CSS1 compliance. As an example, the lines 30–31

```
<div class="bSt" style="border-style:outset;border-color:#ffa500">
    The paragraph has an OUTSET border style </div><br />
```

set an orange-colored outset border. The screen shot of example ex02-14.htm is shown in Fig. 2.15.

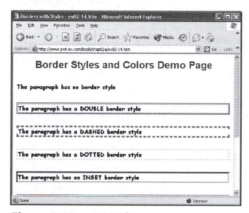

Figure 2.15 ex02-14.htm

2.4   Dimensioning and positioning of elements

Without CSS, the support for element layout is limited to images, tables, frames, and some elements' aligning attributes. This lacks advanced formatting features and event-handling functionalities. You have seen from earlier sections 2.1–2.3 that the basic idea behind the CSS styles is fairly simple. It allows you to control how your Web page should be rendered with the latest browsers. You have also seen how to control CSS properties such as the size and color of fonts, or the background color or image of a Web page in a more structural way. You can use it to format blocks of information. The CSS position element and its associated properties allow you to define exactly where your element boxes will appear. Another interesting CSS positioning attribute is the `z-index`. It provides you with a tool to create "layers" to perform some simple but effective textual effects.

CSS positioning is not restricted to just creating static Web pages where the elements are carefully positioned and laid out by the browsers. You will see in Chapter 6 that the CSS styles and properties are constantly used to combine with scripting to create dynamic HTML pages.

Some frequently used CSS positioning and its related elements are listed in Table 2.7.

Before the discussion of the CSS positioning elements, some other related elements also deserve to be mentioned. They are the CSS elements `width`, `height spacing`, and `padding`.

Table 2.7 Positioning CSS elements

CSS property	CSS values	NS	IE	Description
width	auto length %	4.+	4.+	Scales to fit the given width dimension
height	auto length %	4.+	4.+	Scales to fit the given height dimension
position	absolute relative fixed	4.+	4.+	Positioning the associated element block
top	auto length %	4.+	4.+	Sets the top edge offset of a positioned element
right	auto length %	4.+	4.+	Sets the right edge offset of a positioned element
bottom	auto length %	4.+	4.+	Sets the bottom edge offset of a positioned element
left	auto length %	4.+	4.+	Sets the left edge offset of a positioned element
z-index	auto integer	4.+	4.+	Sets the third, or depth, dimension
padding	length %	4.+	4.+	Sets the amount of padding between the border and other elements
padding-top	length %	4.+	4.+	Sets the padding to the top
padding-right	length %	4.+	4.+	Sets the padding to the right
padding-bottom	length %	4.+	4.+	Sets the padding to the bottom
padding-left	Length %	4.+	4.+	Sets the padding to the left

2.4.1 Width and height spacing

Another popular application of CSS properties is to generate a rectangular box (or element box) bounding an XHTML element. This box describes the amount of space that an element and its associated properties occupy in the layout of the document. The CSS properties width and height set the distances from the left and right edges and the top and bottom edges respectively. These CSS properties can also be applied to an individual element.

The example code

```
<div style="width:100px; height:50px; background-color:yellow">
</div>
```

defines the division element to occupy a dimension of length 50 pixels and width 100 pixels with a yellow background.

The simple example ex02-15.htm illustrates the width and height elements.

Example: ex02-15.htm – Width and Height Spacing

```
 1: <?xml version="1.0" encoding="UTF-8"?>
 2: <!DOCTYPE html PUBLIC "-//W3C//DTD XHTML 1.0 Frameset//EN"
 3: "http://www.w3.org/TR/xhtml1/DTD/xhtml1-frameset.dtd">
 4: <html xmlns="http://www.w3.org/1999/xhtml" xml:lang="en" lang="en">
 5: <head><title>Width and Height Space - ex02-15.htm</title></head>
 6:
 7: <body style="font-family:arial;font-size:14pt;color:#000000">
 8:
 9: <div style="font-family:'Comic Sans MS',times;font-size:24pt;
10:    color:#000088;font-weight:bold;text-align:center">
11: Width and Height Demo <br />
12: </div>
13:
14: <div style="color:#ffffff;position:absolute;top:0px;left:0px;
15: width:100px;height:auto;background-color:#880000">
16: <b>Width and Height Demo:</b><br />
17: You have two rectangular text areas. This one is positioned
18: at the top left hand corner (0px,0px), 100 pixels wide. The height is
19: set to auto.
20: </div><br />
21:
22: <div style="position:absolute;top:100px;left:300px;
23: width:auto;height:100px;background-color:#ffff00">
24: <b>Width and Height Demo:</b><br />
25: You have two rectangular text areas. This one is positioned
26: at (100px,300px) from the top left hand corner, 100 pixels
27: in height. The width is set to auto.
28: </div><br />
29:
30: </body>
31: </html>
```

In this example you can see that all CSS element boxes are as wide as the content areas. Lines 14–15 position the element box at the top left corner and set the element box to have a width of 100 pixels. The height of an element is normally set to auto so that the height is calculated automatically. This is the same for the second rectangular text area as shown in lines 22–23. If you need to add extra padding to an element, then you will need to use the CSS padding element. Note also that in lines 14 and 22 the CSS position element is used to control the exact position of the element box. The position element and its related properties will be discussed further in this section.

An example of this is shown in Fig. 2.16.

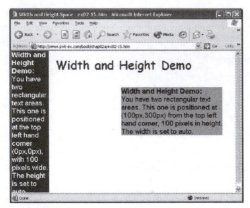

Figure 2.16 ex02-15.htm

2.4.2 Element space padding

You can generate extra space around elements by using the CSS `padding` element and its associated properties. You can control the padding spaces on a single side of the box without affecting the other sides. Adding padding to an element is not the same as adding margins to an element. Example ex02-16.htm illustrates these differences.

```
Example: ex02-16.htm - Element Padding

 1: <?xml version="1.0" encoding="UTF-8"?>
 2: <!DOCTYPE html PUBLIC "-//W3C//DTD XHTML 1.0 Frameset//EN"
 3: "http://www.w3.org/TR/xhtml1/DTD/xhtml1-frameset.dtd">
 4: <html xmlns="http://www.w3.org/1999/xhtml" xml:lang="en" lang="en">
 5: <head><title>Element Padding - ex02-16.htm</title></head>
 6:
 7: <body style="font-family:arial;font-size:14pt;color:#000000">
 8:
 9: <div style="font-family:'Comic Sans MS',times;font-size:24pt;
10:    color:#000088;font-weight:bold;text-align:center">
11: Padding Demo <br />
12: </div>
13:
14: <div style="margin:25px;color:#ffffff;position:absolute;top:50px;left:10px;
15: padding-top:20px;background-color:#880000">
16: This paragraph is indented 25 pixels from the margins. It is padded
17: only from the top by 20 pixels.
18: </div><br />
19:
20: <div style="margin:25px;position:absolute;top:150px;left:10px;
21: padding-right:5cm;background-color:#ffff00">
22: This paragraph is indented 25 pixels from the margins. It is padded
23: only from the right by 5cm.
24: </div><br />
25:
26: <div style="margin:50px;position:absolute;top:200px;left:10px;
27: padding-bottom:15pt;background-color:#ccffff">
28: This paragraph is indented 50 pixels from the margins. It is padded
29: only from the bottom by 15 point.
30: </div><br />
```

```
31:
32: <div style="margin:25px;position:absolute;top:300px;left:10px;
33: padding:1cm;background-color:#66ffcc">
34: This paragraph is indented 25 pixels from the margins. It is padded
35: on all sides by 1cm.
36: </div><br />
37: </body>
38: </html>
```

This example explores various padding settings. You can set individual padding space around the element box. For example, codes in lines 14–15 use `padding-top` to set the amount of padding space (i.e., 20 pixels) to the top of an element. A background color with value `#880000` is also used to illustrate the difference between the `margin` and `padding` properties. With `padding`, the background of the element extends into the padding. The `margin` property sets the margin distance of the element it is associated with. Under certain circumstances, it doesn't matter which one you choose. If the element has a background, however, the difference is clear.

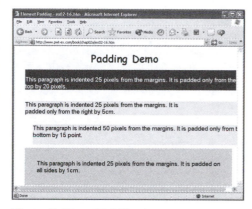

Similarly, codes in lines 20–21 and 26–27 set the amount of padding to the right and bottom of an element respectively. Lines 32–33 use `padding` to set the padding space on all sides of an element.

A screen shot of ex02-16.htm is shown in Fig. 2.17.

The next section looks at another two useful CSS positioning elements, `left` and `top`.

Figure 2.17 ex02-16.htm

2.4.3 Left and top position

You have already seen from examples ex02-15.htm and ex02-16.htm how you could position the element block on your Web page by using the CSS `left` and `top` elements. We will now look at these properties in more detail. The `left` and `top` CSS elements describe the "offset" of a positioned element's sides with respect to its element block. For example, the code fragment

```
<div style="left:100px; top:50px; padding:5px; background-color:red">
</div>
```

defines the position of the division element to be at (50px,100px) from the top left corner. It also defines a red background with a padding of 5 pixels on all sides of the element.

The example ex02-17.htm illustrates the top and left elements with some of their associated properties.

```
Example: ex02-17.htm - Left And Top Position

 1: <?xml version="1.0" encoding="UTF-8"?>
 2: <!DOCTYPE html PUBLIC "-//W3C//DTD XHTML 1.0 Frameset//EN"
 3: "http://www.w3.org/TR/xhtml1/DTD/xhtml1-frameset.dtd">
 4: <html xmlns="http://www.w3.org/1999/xhtml" xml:lang="en" lang="en">
 5: <head><title>Left and Top Position - ex02-17.htm</title></head>
 6:
 7: <body style="font-family:arial;font-size:14pt;color:#000000">
 8:
 9: <div style="font-family:'Comic Sans MS',times;font-size:24pt;
10:   color:#000088;font-weight:bold;text-align:center">
11: Left and Top Position Demo <br />
12: </div>
13:
```

```
14: <div style="border-style:double;border-color:#000000; margin:25px;
15: color:#ffffff; position:absolute;top:50px;left:10px;
16: padding:10px;background-color:#880000">
17: This paragraph is indented 25 pixels from the margins. It is positioned
18: from the top-left corner at (50px,10px) with padding 10 pixels on all
19: sides.
20: </div><br />
21: <div style="border-style:solid;border-color:blue;width:350px;
22: margin:25px;position:absolute;top:250px;left:150px;
23: padding:5px;background-color:#00ccff;z-index:-1">
24: This paragraph has width 350 pixels and is positioned from
25: the top-left corner at (250px,150px).
26: </div><br />
27:
28: <div style="border-style:solid;border-color:blue;width:350px;
29: margin:25px;position:absolute;top:200px;left:350px;
30: padding:5px;background-color:#ffff00;z-index:-2">
31: This paragraph has width 350 pixels and is positioned from
32: the top-left corner at (200px,300px).
33: </div><br />
34:
35: <div style="border-style:solid;border-color:blue;width:250px;
36: margin:25px;position:absolute;top:60%;left:-15px;
37: padding:5px;background-color:#00ff33">
38: This paragraph has width 250 pixels and is positioned from
39: the left side by a negative value.
40: </div><br />
41:
42: </body>
43: </html>
```

The `top` and `left` elements allow you to control exactly how your element blocks should appear in a Web page. With these properties, it is possible to set everything about an element, e.g., margins, borders, padding, and content, for a positioned element. All these properties will be preserved and kept with the positioned element blocks.

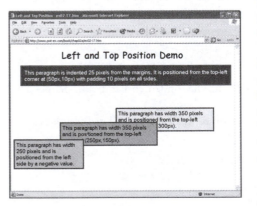

Figure 2.18 ex02-17.htm

In this example, lines 14–15 set the first element block to be displayed at a position (50px, 10px) from the top left corner. Lines 21–23 define a different top left corner position for a different element block. Note that another CSS element, `z-index`, is used in line 23. The `z-index` allows you to "stack" different element blocks together and provides you with "depth" information. This very useful element will be discussed in section 2.4.5.

It is also possible to use negative values as shown in lines 35–37. The effect of using negative values allows you to position an element outside its element block.

A screen shot of ex02-17.htm is shown in Fig. 2.18.

2.4.4   Positioning a group of elements

Web page designers have traditionally spent much of their time trying to control the layout and appearance of their Web pages. CSS addresses this need by providing the Web designers with a powerful CSS element, `position`, for positioning elements. This element, together with its associated properties, gives you total, pixel-level control over the layout of your Web pages. You can easily specify how your Web pages should be rendered by Web browsers.

The concept behind the CSS `position` element is simple. It allows you to specify exactly how element boxes should be positioned on a Web page. The position element sets its position on a page by using absolute or relative positioning values. For example, the code segment

```
<div style="position:absolute; top:20px; left:30px; width:200px;
    height:200px; background-color:yellow">
</div>
```

defines an element box of dimension width 200 pixels and height 200 pixels, with a yellow background, and is positioned absolutely to the top left corner at coordinates (20px, 30px). In the example code, if `position:absolute` is replaced by `position:relative` the element box will be positioned relative to the placement of the previous element box on the page.

As already discussed, the CSS's `top` and `left` properties are used for specifying, in pixels, the starting position of the top left corner of the element box. Its position is described relative to either the top left corner (0px, 0px) in absolute positioning, or the placement of other content in relative positioning. You have already seen from examples ex02-15.htm to ex02-17.htm how positioning works. Here is another simple one:

```
Example: ex02-18.htm - Positioning A Group Of Elements

 1: <?xml version="1.0" encoding="UTF-8"?>
 2: <!DOCTYPE html PUBLIC "-//W3C//DTD XHTML 1.0 Frameset//EN"
 3: "http://www.w3.org/TR/xhtml1/DTD/xhtml1-frameset.dtd">
 4: <html xmlns="http://www.w3.org/1999/xhtml" xml:lang="en" lang="en">
 5: <head><title>Positioning - ex02-18.htm</title></head>
 6:
 7: <style>
 8:         .bst {font-family:'Comic Sans MS',times;font-size:28pt;
 9:         color:#000088;font-weight:bold">}
10: </style>
11:
12: <body style="font-family:arial;font-size:14pt;color:#000000;
13:         background-color:#ccffcc">
14:
15: <div class="bSt" style="position:absolute;top:400px;left:25px">
16: <i>Practical Web Technology</i> <br />
17: </div>
18:
19: <div style="position:absolute;top:100px;left:10px">
20: <img alt="pic" src="logo2.gif" width="250" height="300">
21: </div>
22:
23: <div style="position:absolute; top:150px;left:400px;
24:         width:200px;height:auto">
25: You can use the element box as a convenient 'grid' for positioning
26: a block of text by leaving out the background color of the
27: element box.
28: <br /></div>
29:
30: <div style="font-size:28;position:absolute;top:30px;left:350px">
31: <b>The Positioning Demo</b></br />
32: <img alt="pic" src="hline.gif" width="300" >
33: </div>
34:
35: </body>
36: </html>
```

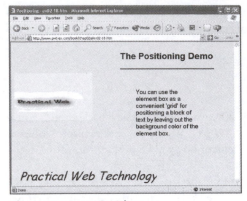

Figure 2.19 ex02-18.htm

You will notice in this example that absolute positioning is used throughout. With absolute positioning, the order of the elements in your HTML document doesn't matter: Web browsers will simply put the element boxes at their specified absolute positions. For instance, in this example, lines 15–17 define the text to be displayed at the bottom of the page while lines 19–21 position an animated image logo at the top left corner. You can also use the position element as a convenient tool to control the position of a block of texts. You do this simply by leaving out the background color of the element blocks so that the default background color of the page is used. This technique is shown in lines 23–28.

A screen shot of ex02-18.htm is shown in Fig. 2.19.

2.4.5 One element behind another

In many circumstances, you will need to maintain a stack of layers of elements. The CSS property z-index gives you the control you need to alter the way, or order, in which elements overlap each other. The z-index property takes an integer value. An element with a high z-index value is closer to the front, or top, than those with lower z-index values. You can assign any integer value, including negative, to any size of z-index. For example, a value of –1 means that the associated element will be placed behind the default text on the page. This is a useful feature in many situations. For instance, you could use this feature to set a background layer containing images so that your text can appear over it. Similarly a very high z-index value may be used if you want to be fairly certain that an element will always stay in front of everything else.

You can create some dynamic, interesting effects when the z-index property is combined with some other Web technologies. For example, you will see later in Chapter 9 how to program a moving object behind another one. Example ex02-19.htm below modifies ex02-18.htm to create some interesting "shadow" effects:

```
Example: ex02-19.htm - The Use Of CSS z-index

 1: <?xml version="1.0" encoding="UTF-8"?>
 2: <!DOCTYPE html PUBLIC "-//W3C//DTD XHTML 1.0 Frameset//EN"
 3: "http://www.w3.org/TR/xhtml1/DTD/xhtml1-frameset.dtd">
 4: <html xmlns="http://www.w3.org/1999/xhtml" xml:lang="en" lang="en">
 5: <head><title>Z-index - ex02-19.htm</title></head>
 6:
 7: <style>
 8:   .bSt1 {font-family:'Comic Sans MS',times;font-size:28pt;
 9:   color:#000088;font-weight:bold;z-index:2"}
10:
11: </style>
12:
13: <body style="font-family:arial;font-size:14pt;color:#000000;
14: background-color:#ccffcc">
15:
16: <div class="bSt1" style="position:absolute;top:380px;left:40px;
17: color:#ffff00;z-index:-1">
18: <i>Practical Web Technology</i>
19: </div>
20:
21: <div class="bSt1" style="position:absolute;top:390px;left:35px;
22: color:#00ffcc;z-index:1">
23: <i>Practical Web Technology</i>
24: </div>
```

```
25:
26: <div class="bSt1" style="position:absolute;top:400px;left:30px">
27: <i>Practical Web Technology</i>
28: </div>
29:
30: <div style="position:absolute;top:10px;left:10px">
31: <img alt="pic" src="logo_web.jpg" width="250" height="150">
32: </div>
33:
34: <div style="position:absolute;top:20px;left:20px;z-index:-1">
35: <img alt="pic" src="logo_web.jpg" width="250" height="150">
36: </div>
37:
38: <div style="position:absolute; top:300px;left:150px;
39: padding:15px;background-color:#00ffff;z-index:4">
40: This paragraph has z-index = 4.
41: <br /></div>
42:
43: <div style="position:absolute; top:260px;left:200px;
44: padding:15px;background-color:#ffcccc;z-index:3">
45: This paragraph has z-index = 3.
46: <br /></div>
47:
48: <div style="position:absolute; top:255px;left:450px;
49: padding:15px;background-color:#ff0000;z-index:2">
50: This paragraph has z-index = 2.
51: <br /></div>
52:
53: <div style="position:absolute; top:220px;left:250px;
54: padding:15px;background-color:#ffff00;z-index:-1">
55: This paragraph has z-index = -1.
56: <br /></div>
57:
58: <div style="font-size:28;position:absolute;top:30px;left:350px">
59: <b>The Z-index Demo</b></br />
60: <img alt="pic" src="hline.gif" width="250" >
61: </div>
62:
63: </body>
64: </html>
```

The code fragments in lines 16–19, 21–24, and 26–28 are almost identical. They differ only in the top left positions and their z-index values. By simply changing their (absolute) positions and their associated z-index values, you can add a third dimension to your element to create some realistic drop shadow effects. Similarly lines 34–36 add a third dimension to the logo image. The effect of various z-index values is demonstrated in lines 38–56.

A screen shot of ex02-19.htm is shown in Fig. 2.20.

The next example, ex02-20.htm, makes extensive use of absolute positioning and z-index properties. This Web page has a graphics heading built with only carefully positioned text. A screen shot of this example is shown in Fig. 2.21.

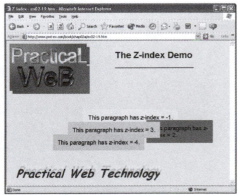

Figure 2.20 ex02-19.htm

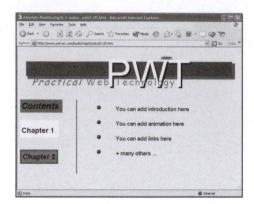

Figure 2.21 ex02-20.htm

Example Ex02-20.htm is listed below:

```
Example: ex02-20.htm - Absolute Positioning and z-index

 1: <?xml version="1.0" encoding="UTF-8"?>
 2: <!DOCTYPE html PUBLIC "-//W3C//DTD XHTML 1.0 Frameset//EN"
 3: "http://www.w3.org/TR/xhtml1/DTD/xhtml1-frameset.dtd">
 4: <html xmlns="http://www.w3.org/1999/xhtml" xml:lang="en" lang="en">
 5: <head><title>Absolute Positioning & Z-index - ex02-20.htm</title></head>
 6: <style>
 7:   .txtSt1 {font-family:arial}
 8:   .txtSt2 {font-family:'Comic Sans MS',Times;
 9:        color:#ff0000;font-size:24pt;letter-spacing:4;
10:        position:absolute;top:95px;left:50px;z-index:6}
11:   .txtSt3 {font-family:arial,Times;padding:5px;
12:        font-size:18pt;
13:        font-weight:bold;position:absolute;z-index:7}
14:   .back1 {background-color: #0000ff;position:absolute;
15:        top:50px;left:30px;width:700;height:50px;z-index:3}
16:   .back2 {background-color: #8a2be2;position:absolute;
17:        top:55px;left:35px;width:705px;height:55px;z-index:2}
18:   .back3 {background-color: #5f9ea0;position:absolute;
19:        top:50px;left:150px;width:500px;height:50px;z-index:3}
20:   #level1 {color:#ffff00;font-size:96pt;position:absolute;
21:        top:20px; left:300px;z-index:5}
22:   #level2 {color:#000000;font-size:96pt;position:absolute;
23:        top:25px; left:305px;z-index:4}
24:   .cont {font-family:arial;font-weight:bold;font-size:18pt;
25:        padding:20px 15px 10px 5px;z-index:7}
26: </style>
27:
28: <body style="font-family:arial;font-size:14pt">
29: <div id="level1"><img src="mline1.gif"
30:    style="width:220pt;height:30px;position:absolute;
31:    top:0px" alt="pic"></div>
32: <div id="level1">
33:   <p class="txtSt1">PWT</p>
34: </div>
35: <div id="level2">
36:   <p class="txtSt1">PWT</p>
37: </div>
38: <div class="back1">
39:   <h2> </h2>
```

```
40: </div>
41: <div class="back2">
42:    <h3> </h3>
43: </div>
44: <div class="txtSt2">
45:    <i><b>Practical</b></i> Web Technology</div>
46:
47: <div class="txtSt3" style="font-size:22pt;
48:    background-color:#008000;top:180px"><i>Contents</i></div>
49: <div class="txtSt3" style="background-color:#ffff00;
50:    padding: 20 15 10 5;top:250px">Chapter 1</div><br />
51: <div class="txtSt3" style="background-color:#ff0000;
52:    border-style:double;top:350px">Chapter 2</div><br />
53:
54: <div style="font-size:28;position:absolute;top:180px;left:200px">
55:    <img alt="pic" src="vline1.gif" height="250" >
56: </div>
57:
58: <div style="position:absolute;top:200px;left:220px">
59:    <img alt="pic" src="bullet1.gif" hspace=50 align=left>
60:    You can add introduction here<br />
61: </div>
62:
63: <div style="position:absolute;top:250px;left:220px">
64:    <img alt="pic" src="bullet1.gif" hspace=50 align=left>
65:    You can add animation here<br /><br />
66: </div>
67:
68: <div style="position:absolute;top:300px;left:220px">
69:    <img alt="pic" src="bullet1.gif" hspace=50 align=left>
70:    You can add links here<br /><br />
71: </div>
72:
73: <div style="position:absolute;top:350px;left:220px">
74:    <img alt="pic" src="bullet1.gif" hspace=50 align=left>
75:    + many others ...<br /><br />
76: </div>
77:
78: </body>
79: </html>
```

This example contains no additional new features. Only a careful study of the codes is needed to understand fully how this example works. Lines 29–45 show how you can build a graphical heading by using only text and style sheets. Lines 47–76 demonstrate once again various CSS properties such as padding, border, and position.

2.5   Other design techniques using the CSS style

2.5.1   Changing the cursor shape with CSS

It is sometimes useful to alter the browser's environment. For example, you may want to change the browser's cursor when the mouse passes over a given element. To change the shape of a cursor with CSS is easy: all you need is to define the style attribute with the cursor keyword. The following are the 16 frequently used cursor shapes defined in CSS1:

cursor:auto	cursor:n-resize	cursor:crossbar	cursor:se-resize
cursor:default	cursor:sw-resize	cursor:hand	cursor:s-resize
cursor:move	cursor:w-resize	cursor:e-resize	cursor:text
cursor:ne-resize	cursor:wait	cursor:nw-resize	cursor:help

Consider the following example page ex02-21.htm:

Example: ex02-21.htm – Changing Cursor Shape With CSS

```
 1: <?xml version="1.0" encoding="UTF-8"?>
 2: <!DOCTYPE html PUBLIC "-//W3C//DTD XHTML 1.0 Frameset//EN"
 3: "http://www.w3.org/TR/xhtml1/DTD/xhtml1-frameset.dtd">
 4: <html xmlns="http://www.w3.org/1999/xhtml" xml:lang="en" lang="en">
 5: <head><title>Changing Cursor Shape – ex02-21.htm</title></head>
 6: <body style="font-family:arial;font-size:18pt;background:#eeeeee">
 7:
 8: <div style="font-size:24pt;font-weight:bold;color:#00aa00;
 9:     text-align:center"><br />
10: Move the mouse over the words <br />to see the cursor change<br /><br />
11:
12: <table style="font-size:18pt;font-family:arial;color:#000000">
13: <tr>
14:   <td style="width:200px"><span style="cursor:auto">Auto</span></td>
15:   <td><span style="cursor:crosshair">Crosshair</span></td></tr>
16: <tr>
17:   <td><span style="cursor:default">Default</span></td>
18:   <td><span style="cursor:hand">Hand</span></td></tr>
19: <tr>
20:   <td><span style="cursor:move">Move</span></td>
21:   <td><span style="cursor:e-resize">e-resize</span></td></tr>
22: <tr>
23:   <td><span style="cursor:ne-resize">ne-resize</span></td>
24:   <td><span style="cursor:nw-resize">nw-resize</span></td></tr>
25: <tr>
26:   <td><span style="cursor:n-resize">n-resize</span></td>
27:   <td><span style="cursor:se-resize">se-resize</span></td></tr>
28: <tr>
29:   <td><span style="cursor:sw-resize">sw-resize</span></td>
30:   <td><span style="cursor:s-resize">s-resize</span></td></tr>
31: <tr>
32:   <td><span style="cursor:w-resize">w-resize</span></td>
33:   <td><span style="cursor:text">text</span></td></tr>
34: <tr>
35:   <td><span style="cursor:wait">wait</span></td>
36:   <td><span style="cursor:help">help</span></td></tr>
37: </table>
38: </div>
39: </body>
40: </html>
```

The 16 frequently used cursor shapes are defined in lines 14–36. The cursor shape is defined by the keyword cursor followed by its attribute. For example, line 35 defines a "wait" cursor and it changes to an hourglass when the mouse passes over the word "wait." This page has the screen shot shown in Fig. 2.22.

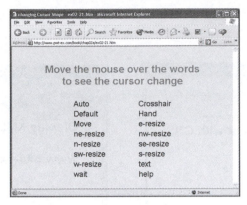

Figure 2.22 ex02-21.htm

2.5.2 Displaying XML pages with CSS

Extensible Markup Language (XML) is a meta programming language that can be used to create a data format for structured document interchange. How to display an XML page on the Web is a big issue – a whole book or more could be written on this subject alone. We will cover XML and XSLT in more detail in Chapter 5.

Consider the following example ex02-22.xml:

Example: ex02-22.xml – Display XML Document With CSS

```
1: <?xml version="1.0"?>
2: <?xml-stylesheet type="text/css" href="ex02-22.css" ?>
3:
4: <page>
5:    <contents>
6:     <myPar>Display XML Document with CSS.</myPar>
7:     <myPar>www.pwt-ex.com</myPar>
8:    </contents>
9: </page>
```

This is a simple XML page with one root element, <page>. Inside this page element, there will be a content element <contents> and one child element called myPar. By defining the XML style sheet in line 2

```
<?xml-stylesheet type="text/css" href="ex02-22.css" ?>
```

the external CSS file ex02-22.css will be called to display the XML page. The style file is shown below:

Example: ex02-22.css – External CSS File For ex02-22.xml

```
1: myPar
2: {
3:    display: inline;
4:    display: block;
5:    margin-left: 40pt;
6:    font-family:arial;
7:    font-size: 22pt;
8:    font-weight: bold;
9:    color: #000088;
10:
11:    margin-bottom: 30pt;
12:    text-align: left;
13:    line-height: 30px;
14:    text-indent: 0px;
15: }
```

This program will work on all the latest browsers including IE6+, NS6+, and Opera 6+. A screen shot of this program working in IE and NS is shown in Figs 2.23 and 2.24 respectively.

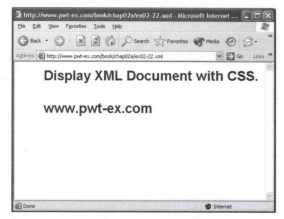

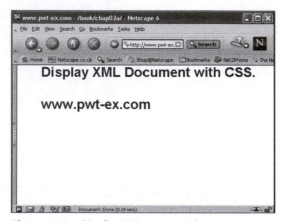

Figure 2.23 Display XML page with IE   **Figure 2.24** Display XML page with NS

2.5.3   Generating a text background with scripts

The power of scripting languages has become extremely important in the development of Web technologies. It adds programming capabilities to Web pages. In fact, scripts are indispensable tools for almost all Web programmers. In this book, we have chapters dedicated to Web programming with scripts. Even at this premature stage, we would like to show you how a simple script can be used to enhance the features of your Web pages.

The next example ex02-23.htm uses a very simple script function to generate a repeated text background on the page.

```
Example: ex02-23.htm – Generating A Text Background

 1: <?xml version="1.0" encoding="UTF-8"?>
 2: <!DOCTYPE html PUBLIC "-//W3C//DTD XHTML 1.0 Frameset//EN"
 3: "http://www.w3.org/TR/xhtml1/DTD/xhtml1-frameset.dtd">
 4: <html xmlns="http://www.w3.org/1999/xhtml" xml:lang="en" lang="en">
 5: <head>
 6: <title>Generating a Text Background – ex02-24.htm </title>
 7: </head>
 8: <script>
 9:   function display_string()
10:   {
11:     for (ii=0;ii<500;ii++)
12:     {
13:     document.write("P r a c t i c a l   W e b T e c h n o l o g i e s ")
14:
15:     }
16:   }
17:
18: </script>
19:
20: <body style="background:#000088;color:#ffff00;font-weight:bold">
21: <script>display_string()</script>
22: <div style="position:absolute;left:100px;top:100px;
23:     font-size:150pt;color:#ff0000">PWT</div>
24: </body>
25: </html>
```

To define a script, the `<script>` element is used. This Web page contains two `<script>` elements: the first one in lines 8–18 defines a script (or JavaScript) with one function, `display_string()`. This function has a for-loop which will execute the following statements 500 times (see lines 11–15):

```
document.write("P r a c t i c a l   W e b T e c h n o l o g i e s ")
```

This statement outputs the text between the quotation marks to the Web page. The space between each character would allow the browser to have a line break at any point. You can use the non-breaking space symbol ` ` as illustrated in line 13 to add more space so that the text is more readable. The second `<script>` element in line 21 executes the defined function `display_string()` and therefore a background text is created. A screen shot of this page is shown in Fig. 2.25.

Figure 2.25 ex02-23.htm

3

Graphics, fonts, and colors using Java

3.1 Beginning Java programming

3.1.1 An introduction to Java and J2SDK

Java was the first object-oriented programming language created for the Internet. It adds dynamic features to numerous, otherwise static Web pages. Since its arrival on the Internet scene in 1996, it has been a powerful programming tool for Web programmers and developers. Countless Web applications have been developed using Java, particularly in the graphics and Internet game areas. Today, even though we have more new technologies and choices on the Web, Java still remains a strong competitor in presentation (or business) graphics and multimedia for the Web community. For example, Java is still one of the best languages that provide powerful graphics libraries to create all-singing, all-dancing 2D graphics on the Web. This chapter is not an introductory text on the Java language and features. Instead, we will concentrate on how to use it to generate presentation graphics and distribute them on Web pages. With Java, incorporating graphics into XHTML documents is no longer a difficult challenge.

Java started as a language called Oak in the early 1990s. It was designed by Sun Microsystems and originally intended to be used to develop programmable applications for smart consumer electronics products. This had little success. The language was then rebranded as Java and officially released in early 1996 to the Internet community. Since then Java has taken off and enjoyed immense popularity in the area of Web programming. One reason was due to its capability to run on Web pages. Browsers can download a Java program (called a Java applet) included on a Web page and run it locally. Java applets can be used to create animations, graphics, games, and a wide range of exciting special effects.

Java is a compiled and interpreted language. When a Java source is compiled, it produces an intermediate code called `bytecode`. Bytecode instructions would allow any machine equipped with a bytecode interpreter to run the code. This feature is platform or operating system independent and sometimes is referred to "Java Run-Time Environment" (JRE) or "Java Virtual Machine" (JVM). The idea of bytecode is also used to develop the Wireless Markup Language (WML) for devices such as mobile phones. The WML and Mobile Internet will be discussed later in Chapter 21.

If you want to use Java, you need first to install a Java software development environment on your computer. A minimum Java development environment includes a "Java 2 Software Development Kit" (J2SDK) with a JRE or JVM. You need the JVM to run Java applets and applications embedded into your Web pages. The J2SDK is mainly used to develop Java programs. The J2SDK and JRE used in this chapter are `j2sdk-1_3_1_02` and `j2re-1_4_0_01`.

If you are using IE5.x and NS4.x you already have JVM installed on your machine. For Microsoft XP, IE6.+, and NS6.+, however, JRE or JVM is no longer an integral part of the package. You may download these packages free from Sun's Java Web site

http://www.javasoft.com

The site is regularly updated and is the primary source for Java technology containing tutorials, documentations, and a vast collection of Java libraries.

The J2SDK environment is basically everything you need to build Java applications and use them on your Web pages. After installation, you will have several directories (or folders) containing a large number of programs on your machine. Two of them are particularly important and will be used frequently in this chapter. They are:

javac – To activate the Java compiler.
java – To activate the Java interpretor.

The first program is used to compile Java source code (or program) into bytecode. The second one is to interpret the bytecode and run it on your machine. Both of them can be found in the `bin` directory of your J2SDK installation. One of the best ways to understand `javac` and `java` is to use them to develop a simple application. Also, if the Java program HelloWorld.java in section 3.1.2 runs successfully on your machine, it is likely that you have a proper J2SDK installation.

3.1.2 My first Java program

Once you have J2SDK installed on your machine, you can start programming Java and build Java applications on the Web. Since the J2SDK development environment has no GUI, the package and related tools are all run from the console window such as the DOS command line. This means that you start your Java tool by typing its name, file names, or any other option arguments into the console window. Let's look at the classic "Hello World" Java application program. With a plain text editor such as Notepad, you type the code as shown in the following example HelloWorld.java:

```
Example: HelloWorld.java - My First Java Program

1: class HelloWorld
2: {
3:  public static void main(String args[])
4:  {
5:  System.out.println("Hello, World!");
6:  }
7: }
```

This is a simple Java program to print a simple text to screen. Line 1 defines a class with the identity `HelloWorld`. Line 3 sets the status of the object to be `static` (i.e., unchanged), and accessible by any classes without limitation (i.e., `public`). The `println()` function or method in line 5 is then used to print a text string to the screen.

As a standard Java convention, you save your Java program file with the `.java` extension. For instance, the file in this example is called HelloWorld.java. Without this extension, the Java compiler may not be able to recognize your program. You also need to make sure that your program and the Java compiler are in the same directory, or a correct path is specified. To compile this Java program, you can use the `javac` command such as

javac HelloWorld.java

Note that the Java language is case sensitive. You need to make sure that any commands and file names are matched exactly, or they will not be recognized. If the program compiles successfully, it will create a Java bytecode file called HelloWorld.class. This file name needs to be matched. The bytecode can be executed by the interpreter `java`. Type the command

java HelloWorld

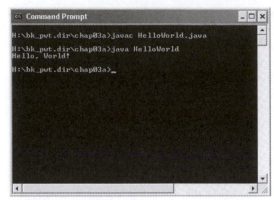

Figure 3.1 *"HelloWorld"*

and you should see the text string "Hello World" printed to your screen. A screen shot of this example is shown in Fig. 3.1.

Due to the practical nature of this book, we will not discuss the full language details of Java here. For example, we will not discuss the full aspects of object-oriented features of Java or provide the full definitions of function, method, and class. In fact, we consider functions are basically the same as methods in this chapter. In order to have a good starting point, some basic language features such as loops and conditionals are demonstrated in the next section.

3.1.3   A Java program with basic language features

Let's look at a slightly more complex Java example. The following program, AddingNumbers.java, can read a set of integers and print out the total sum.

```
Example: AddingNumbers.java - A Java Program To Add Numbers

 1: class AddingNumbers
 2: {
 3:   public static void main(String[] args)
 4:   {
 5:     int sum=0, size;
 6:     int[] intNumbers;
 7:
 8:     size = args.length;
 9:     intNumbers = new int[size];
10:
11:     if (size>0)
12:     {
13:       sum=0;
14:       for (int i=0; i<size; i++)
15:       {
16:         intNumbers[i]=Integer.parseInt(args[i]);
17:         sum = sum + intNumbers[i];
18:       }
19:     }
20:     System.out.println("The sum of " + size + " numbers is : " + sum);
21:   }
22: }
```

This program demonstrates the following language features of Java in a simple way:

- the use of variables (line 5);
- the use of arrays (lines 3 and 6);
- the `if` (conditional) statement in Java (see lines 11–19);
- the for-loop (see lines 14–18).

This program will accept a series of command arguments as input and store them into a string array called `args` (see line 3). For example, after you have compiled the program, the program can be activated by the Java interpreter as

```
java AddingNumbers 3 4 6
```

The input numbers 3, 4, and 6 will be considered as a string and stored in the element `args[0]`, `args[1]`, and `args[2]` respectively. The length of this array is `args.length`, which has the value of 3 and is assigned to the variable `size` in line 8. This variable is an integer (i.e., `int size`) and is used to specify the dimension of an array called `intNumbers` in line 9.

The conditional statement in line 11 states that if the size of the input argument is bigger than zero (i.e., `size > 0`), the process in lines 11–19 is activated to calculate the sum. The actual calculation is carried out by the for-loop (see lines 14–18). Since the input numbers are considered as strings, the `parseInt()` function in line 16 is used to convert the `i`th string `args[i]` into an integer. For example, the statement

```
intNumber[0]=Integer.parseInt(args[0]);
```

will convert the first input argument `args[0]`, which has the text "3," into an integer and store it in the integer array `intNumber[0]`.

The for-loop in lines 14–18 is simply adding together all values in the array `intNumbers[]`. The final result (i.e., `sum`) is output to the screen by the statement in line 20. A screen shot of this example is shown in Fig. 3.2.

Again, it is not feasible to show you all the language features of Java in one chapter. This program shows the language features of Java that we are going to use in the remaining sections.

Now that you have some idea about Java programming it's time to consider how to use Java on Web pages.

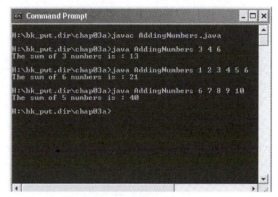

Figure 3.2 Adding numbers

3.2 Controlling fonts and colors with Java applets

Undoubtedly, one of the most popular applications of using Java is through embedding applets in HTML/XHTML pages. An applet, in general, is a small program which will run automatically when downloaded into the browser. Java applets are applet programs written in Java. Throughout this chapter, the word applet refers to a Java applet.

3.2.1 A simple Java applet

Let's convert the first Java program HelloWorld.java into an applet. Generally you need to perform the following tasks when creating any applet applications:

- Create a Java program to generate the applet application.
- Compile the source code files into bytecode or class.
- Create an HTML/XHTML page and use the applet element `<applet>` to call the class.

Consider the following Java code HelloWorldApplet.java:

```
Example: HelloWorldApplet.java - Hello World Applet

 1: import java.awt.*;
 2: import java.applet.*;
 3:
 4: public class HelloWorldApplet extends Applet
 5: {
 6:   public void paint (Graphics g)
 7:   {
 8:     g.drawString("Hello World! - My First Applet",10,10);
 9:   }
10: }
```

This Java applet is slightly longer than the HelloWorld.java program. First, in order to generate applet code and use it in a browser, two Java packages (or class libraries) are included as illustrated in lines 1 and 2. Line 1 includes the package called `java.awt` (Java Abstract Windowing Toolkit). This package provides a number of interface features such as controlling windows, creating controls, fonts, images, and drawings which, in many cases, are necessary for the integration of Java code and the associated Web page. The `java.applet` package provides the capability of generating code to be used inside a Web page. The asterisk "*" at the end means that all public classes from the named package are imported. The Java statement in line 4 will generate a class called `HelloWorldApplet` and will be executed by a Web page. Inside this class, we have a public method (see lines 6–9):

```
public void paint (Graphics g)
{
  g.drawString("Hello World! - My First Applet",10,10);
}
```

This method is supplied with a graphics object `graphics` by the local system and transfers it to the variable `g`. The function `g.drawString()` is to output the text 'Hello World! - My First Applet" to the applet window at the pixel position (10, 10) from the top left corner of the window. To call this Java applet, the following XHTML element is used:

```
<applet code="name_of_applet_class" width=m height=n> </applet>
```

where `name_of_applet_class` is the name of the applet class, and the parameters m and n define the size of the applet window. After you have compiled the Java program HelloWorldApplet.java successfully, you can use the applet element above to execute the associated bytecode (or class). Consider our first Web page ex03-01.htm to call the Java applet:

```
Example: ex03-01.htm - Hello World Applet

 1: <?xml version="1.0" encoding="UTF-8"?>
 2: <!DOCTYPE html PUBLIC "-//W3C//DTD XHTML 1.0 Frameset//EN"
 3: "http://www.w3.org/TR/xhtml1/DTD/xhtml1-frameset.dtd">
 4: <html xmlns="http://www.w3.org/1999/xhtml" xml:lang="en" lang="en">
 5: <head>
 6: <title>Hello World Applet - ex03-01.htm</title>
 7: </head>
 8: <body style="font-size:28pt; text-align:center;font-weight:bold">
 9:   Embedding Java Applet Using XHTML<br />
10: <applet code="HelloWorldApplet.class" width=200 height=50>
11: </applet>
12: </body>
13: </html>
```

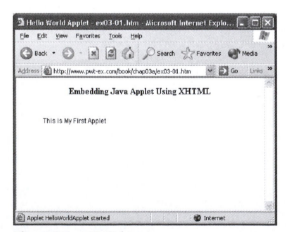

Figure 3.3 ex03-01.htm

This page will call the Java applet HelloWorldApplet.class and run the program inside the applet window. A screen shot of this example is shown in Fig. 3.3.

You now know how to include a Java applet in a Web page and display a message. The next step is to control the font and color. More importantly, we will show you how to incorporate graphics into XHTML documents.

3.2.2   A Java applet to set font and color

Unlike many other Web technologies, Java applets are not just programs that you can embed into your Web pages and run. Strictly speaking, applets are not run by the calling browsers. A Java-enabled browser passes any Java applications to the JVM or JRE and therefore Java programs will run unchanged whatever the host platform, achieving the so-called what-you-see-is-what-you-get (WYSIWYG) feature. For example, different systems such as Windows and LINUX may handle fonts and their associated font properties in a different way. If you want your Web page to have the same font, font metric, or displaying effect across different operating systems and browsers, Java may be a solution for you.

Consider the following Java program:

```
Example: Font01.java - Using Font And Color

 1: import java.awt.*;
 2: import java.applet.*;
 3:
 4: public class Font01 extends Applet
 5: {
 6:  public void paint(Graphics gg)
 7:  {
 8:     Graphics2D g = (Graphics2D) gg;
 9:
10:     g.setFont( new Font("Arial",Font.BOLD,26) );
11:     g.setColor(Color.blue);
12:
13:     g.drawString("This is Java Applet",20,60);
14:     g.drawString("Arial Font, Bold, Size:26",20,90);
15:     g.drawString("Text Color:blue",20,120);
16:  }
17: }
```

This program is similar to the `HelloWorldApplet` mentioned in section 3.2.1. The only main difference is that we have added lines 8–11 to set the displaying font and color. The statement in line 8

```
Graphics2D g = (Graphics2D) gg;
```

sets up an instance of class `Graphics2D` from the package `java.awt` so that the object variable `g` will have the capability to handle more advanced graphics. The class `Graphics2D` is, in fact, a subclass of "Graphics" containing some more advanced 2D graphics capabilities. Although it is not very important for this example, it is essential for our examples later in this chapter.

Once you have the graphics `g`, to set up the displaying font is just a simple process. For example, you can call the function `setFont()` to define a font style as demonstrated in line 10, i.e.,

```
g.setFont( new Font("Arial", Font.BOLD, 26) );
```

In this case, the default drawing font is `Arial`, bold, and a size of 26 points (1 point = 1/72 inch). In addition to the `Font.BOLD` style some other options for the font style are `Font.PLAIN` and `Font.ITALIC`. If you want to set bold and italic combinations, you can use the following:

```
Font.BOLD + Font.Italic
```

The function (or method) `g.setColor()` in line 11 is used to set the drawing color as blue. Some other color options are listed in Table 3.1.

Table 3.1 Java color constants

Color.darkGray	Color.yellow	Color.red
Color.black	Color.orange	Color.green
Color.lightGray	Color.magenta	Color.blue
Color.gray	Color.cyan	
Color.white	Color.pink	

To call this Java applet, all you need is to replace the body part (lines 8–12) of ex03-01.htm by the XHTML code fragment in ex03-01.txt and call it ex03-02.htm.

```
Listing: ex03-01.txt - XHTML Code Fragment For Example ex03-02.htm

1: <body style="font-size:18pt; text-align:center;font-weight:bold">
2:    Java Applet: Font And Color<br />
3:    <applet code="Font01.class" width=450 height=400>
4:    </applet>
5: </body>
```

A screen shot of this example in action is shown in Fig. 3.4.

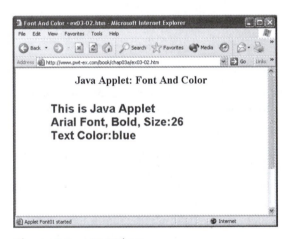

Figure 3.4 ex03-02.htm

3.2.3 Font rotation and translation

With Java, graphical objects can be manipulated easily. For example, rotation and translation can be performed on a Web page without any complications. This feature greatly enhances the functionality of XHTML documents. To translate a graphical object, you can use the function

```
translate(xpos,ypos)
```

This command will translate the origin to the coordinate position (xpos,ypos). To rotate a graphical object, the following function can be used:

```
rotate(angle_in_radian)
```

This function will rotate the coordinate system to an angle measured in radians. A positive angle value rotates the object in a anti-clockwise direction. The combination of rotation and translation, in many cases, can be used to create special effects. Consider the XHTML page ex03-03.htm:

```
Example: ex03-03.htm - Font Rotation And Translation

 1: <?xml version="1.0" encoding="UTF-8"?>
 2: <!DOCTYPE html PUBLIC "-//W3C//DTD XHTML 1.0 Frameset//EN"
 3:   "http://www.w3.org/TR/xhtml1/DTD/xhtml1-frameset.dtd">
 4: <html xmlns="http://www.w3.org/1999/xhtml" xml:lang="en" lang="en">
 5: <head>
 6:   <title>Font Rotation and Translation - ex03-03.htm</title>
 7: </head>
 8: <body style="font-size:18pt; text-align:center;font-weight:bold">
 9:   Font Rotation And Translation<br /><br />
10:   <applet code="Font02.class" width=450 height=400>
11:     <param name="text" value="....Web Technology">
12:     <param name="size" value="18">
13:   </applet>
14: </body>
15: </html>
```

This is a simple page with one applet element (lines 10–13) to call the Java program: Font02.class. The applet element also contains two parameter elements (i.e., <param>) which can be used to pass values to the Java class. For example, the first parameter element (see line 11)

```
<param name="text" value="....Web Technology">
```

specifies a parameter called text. The value of this text is "....Web Technology." The Java function

```
textV = getParameter("text");
```

can be used to identify the parameter text, get the string value, and assign the string to variable textV. The parameter in line 12 is to pass the font size 18 to the Font02.class program. The parameter element <param> provides a useful way to pass values to Java programs.

As a simple example, the program Font02.class will only translate and rotate the string to form a circle. A screen shot is shown in Fig. 3.5.

As you can see from Fig. 3.5, the string is first translated to near the center of the page and then rotates the text to give a circle. The actual Java code to do the rotation and translation is provided in the following example.

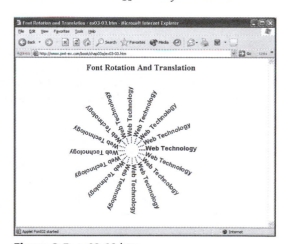

Figure 3.5 ex03-03.htm

```
Example: Font02.java - Rotation And Translation

 1: import java.awt.*;
 2: import java.applet.*;
 3:
 4: public class Font02 extends Applet
 5: {
 6:   String tmpSt, textV;
 7:   int sizeV;
 8:
 9:   public void init()
10:   {
```

```
11:      textV = getParameter("text");
12:
13:      tmpSt= getParameter("size");
14:      sizeV = Integer.parseInt(tmpSt);
15:  }
16:
17:  public void paint(Graphics gg)
18:  {
19:      int ii;
20:
21:      Graphics2D g = (Graphics2D) gg;
22:      g.setFont( new Font("Arial",Font.BOLD,sizeV) );
23:      g.setColor(Color.blue);
24:
25:      g.translate(200,200);
26:      for (ii=1;ii<=16;ii++)
27:      {
28:        g.rotate(Math.PI/8.0);
29:        g.drawString(textV,20,0);
30:      }
31:  }
32: }
```

This Java applet code contains two functions. The first function init() (i.e., initialization) will be executed after the program is loaded. The getParameter() functions in line 11–12 are used to get the text and font size from the XHTML page. Since values from the Web page are considered as strings, the Integer.parseInt() function in line 14 is employed to convert the text string into an integer.

The font size variable sizeV is used in line 22 to define the font. After setting the drawing color to blue in line 23, the function

```
g.translate(200,200)
```

is called to translate the origin to new position (200, 200). The for-loop in lines 26–30 is to rotate the text 16 times. Each rotation will be done with an angle equal to PI/8.0 radians. For each rotation, the text from the Web page is displayed. After 16 rotations, the text string is rotated 2*PI radians (i.e., 360 degrees) which is a complete circle. Now, let's see how to add colors to the circular text string.

3.2.4   A page with random colors

The color constants listed in Table 3.1 are a convenient way to specify standard colors for a drawing process. If you want to use more colors, the Color() function (or object) may be more suitable. For example, the following command will use the Color() function to set the current color as blue, which will have the same effect as the color constant Color.blue:

```
setColor( new Color(0,0,255) )
```

The Color() function takes three integers from 0 to 255, each representing the red (R), green (G), and blue (B) components. For example, Color(255,0,0) represents the red color, the same as the color constant Color.red. The combinations of all (R, G, B) components yield a total of more than 16 millions colors.

If you replace the paint() function in the Java program Font02.java by the Java code below, you will have a new Java program called Font03.java (Don't forget to change the applet name in line 4 to Font03).

```
Listing: ex03-02.txt - Java Code Fragment For Font03.java

 1:  public void paint(Graphics gg)
 2:  {
 3:      int ii;
 4:
 5:      Graphics2D g = (Graphics2D) gg;
```

```
 6:     g.setFont( new Font("Arial",Font.BOLD,sizeV) );
 7:
 8:
 9:     g.translate(200,200);
10:     for (ii=1;ii<=16;ii++)
11:     {
12:       g.rotate(Math.PI/8.0);
13:       g.setColor( new Color((int) (Math.random()*256),
14:                             (int) (Math.random()*256),
15:                             (int) (Math.random()*256)) );
16:       g.drawString(textV,20,0);
17:     }
18: }
```

If you compare this `paint()` function with the one in Font02.java, you will find that a `setColor()` statement is added in lines 13–15. The function

```
Color( (int) (Math.random()*256),
       (int) (Math.random()*256),
       (int) (Math.random()*256))
```

returns a color in terms of random red, green, and blue (i.e., RGB) mode. The mathematical function `Math.random` returns a random value between 0 and 1. The expression `(int) (Math.random()*256)` provides a random value between 0 and 255 for each RGB component. The `setColor()` function in line 13 sets the random color as the drawing color and therefore you have a random color effect.

Now, replace line 10 of ex03-03.htm by the following line and call it example ex03-04.htm:

```
10: <applet code="Font03.class" width=450 height=400>
```

This new example executes the Java program Font03.class to generate random colors on the text circle. Whenever the page is called, a new set of colors will be displayed. A screen shot of this example is shown in Fig. 3.6.

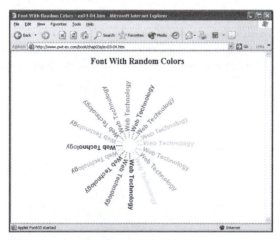

Figure 3.6 ex03-04.htm

3.2.5   Selecting color with `JColorChooser()`

When it comes to practical use, a color-choosing dialog window may be more convenient for your clients or users. Java provides a standard color chooser called `JColorChooser()` so that users from different computing platforms can have the same color controlling mechanism. This `JColorChooser()` function (or method) will open a dialog window and allow you to pick a color dynamically. By following the next example, you can develop a page to activate the `JColorChooser()` so that the text color can be changed dynamically.

First, we want to set up a color button called `ColorButton` so that the color-picking box `ColorChooser()` can be activated by a simple mouse click. To build a button in Java, you can use the code

```
public void init()
{
  ColorButton = new Button("Activate JColorChooser");
  add(ColorButton);
  ColorButton.addActionListener(this);
}
```

The `new Button()` statement creates a button called `ColorButton` with label "Activate JColorChooser." The `add()` function is used to display the created button on the Java page. In order to listen to any mouse click on this button, you need to set up the so-called action listener or the `addActionListener()` function associated with the button `ColorButton`. In general, we would like the button to be created at the beginning of our Java program and therefore all statements are put inside a function called `init()` (i.e., initialization).

When you set up an action listener function, you need to develop a function called `actionPerformed()` to handle an event such as the button click. The `actionPerformed()` function in this case is defined as

```
public void actionPerformed ( ActionEvent event)
{
 color = JColorChooser.showDialog(
          ColorChooser.this,
          "Select Your Color", color );
 if ( color == null )
    color = Color.blue;
 repaint();
}
```

When there is a click on the button `ColorButton`, this function will be activated. The `JColorChooser.showDialog()` function opens a dialog window with the title "Select Your Color." This dialog window will attach to the Java program as specified by the first argument `ColorChooser.this`. You can pick a color dynamically inside the window and the selected `color` will be returned to the variable `color`. If there is no color selected, the default color is set to be blue (i.e., `Color.blue`). The `repaint()` function causes the page to redraw so that the newly selected color will take effect immediately.

To put the discussion above into action, consider the first part of the Java program ColorChooser.java.

Example: ColorChooser.java – To Pick A Color (Part One)

```
1: import java.awt.*;
2: import javax.swing.*;
3: import java.awt.event.*;
4: import java.applet.*;
5:
6: public class ColorChooser extends Applet implements ActionListener
7: {
8:    private Button ColorButton;
9:    private Color color = Color.blue;
10:
11:   public void init()
12:   {
13:     ColorButton = new Button("Activate JColorChooser");
14:     add(ColorButton);
15:     ColorButton.addActionListener(this);
16:   }
17:
```

```
18:    public void actionPerformed( ActionEvent event)
19:    {
20:     color = JColorChooser.showDialog(
21:             ColorChooser.this,
22:             "Select Your Color", color );
23:
24:     if ( color == null )
25:         color = Color.blue;
26:     repaint();
27:    }
28:
```

In order to handle mouse clicks and events, the packages `javax.swing` and `java.awt.event` are imported as illustrated in lines 2 and 3. The statement in line 6 specifies that the Java applet that we are going to generate is called `ColorChooser`, which includes an `ActionListener`. Inside this `ColorChooser` class, two private variables are used so that the variables cannot be easily changed by other classes or functions. The first variable defines a button called `ColorButton` and the second variable specifies a color with initial value `Color.blue` (i.e., blue color).

The `init()` function is to generate the button and set up the action listener. The details of the action response function `actionPerformed()` are defined in lines 18–27.

Now, you need to construct the `paint()` function so that it will respond to the `repaint()` function call as in line 26. The `paint()` function is a simple one and is listed in the second part of this Java code:

Listing: Continuation Of The Java Program ColorChooser.java

```
29:    public void paint(Graphics gg)
30:    {
31:     Graphics2D g = (Graphics2D) gg;
32:
33:     g.setFont( new Font("Arial",Font.BOLD,26) );
34:     g.setColor(color);
35:
36:     g.drawString("This is a text message",20,80);
37:     g.drawString("You can select and change the color",20,110);
38:     g.drawString("using the Java JColorChooser",20,140);
39:    }
40: }
41:
```

This Java code contains only one function, `paint()`. This function is very similar to the function mentioned in previous examples. The main feature of this function is line 34 which is used to set the current color as the newly selected color from the `JColorChooser()` dialog window. The color of the text will be changed immediately. If you replace the body part of ex03-02.htm by the XHTML code in ex03–03.txt and call it example ex03-05.htm, you will have a Web page to call the applet and make color selections. Some screen shots are shown in Figs. 3.7–3.10.

Listing: ex03-03.txt - Code Fragment For Example ex03-05.htm

```
1: <body style="font-size:22pt; text-align:center;font-weight:bold">
2:    Select and Change Color With <br />The JColorChooser<br /><br />
3:
4:    <applet code="ColorChooser.class" width=500 height=200>
5:    </applet>
6: </body>
```

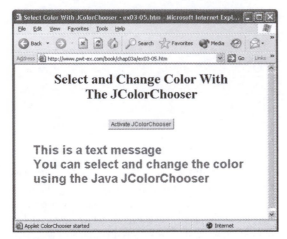

Figure 3.7 ex03-05.htm

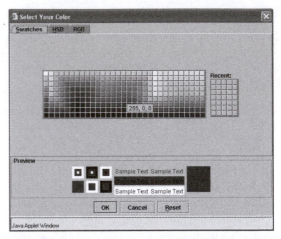

Figure 3.8 The `JColorChooser()` dialog window I (switch)

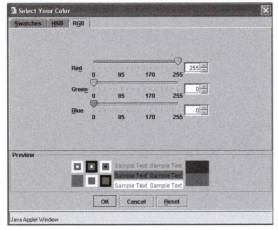

Figure 3.9 The `JColorChooser()` dialog window II (RGB)

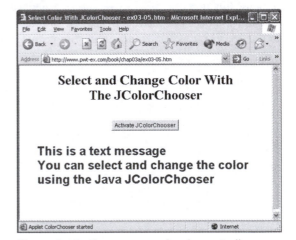

Figure 3.10 Change text color dynamically

There are three coloring methods to define a color in `JColorChooser()`. Fig. 3.8 demonstrates the so-called "Switch" method. Your mouse can pick any color inside the window and switch the color in your application. Figure 3.9 illustrates the RGB coloring method. You can use your mouse to select the color by changing the RGB value on the slide bar. After the OK button is pressed, the color of the text will be changed immediately as in Fig. 3.10.

It's now time to consider how to use graphics on Web pages.

3.3 Displaying graphics and shapes using Java

3.3.1 Lines, rectangles, and ovals on Web pages

Before Java, using graphics on Web pages was considered to be a challenge for all Web programmers. Indeed, Java still remains one of the best technologies to provide graphics capabilities on the World Wide Web. At a basic level, Java provides a set of simple functions to draw fundamental graphic shapes including lines, rectangles, and ovals on your Web pages. Some frequently used graphics functions and their calling syntax are listed below:

- `drawLine(x1,y1,x2,y2)` – Draws a line from position (x1,y1) to (x2,y2) in the applet window.
- `drawRect(x1,y1,w,h)` – Draws a rectangle at position (x1,y1) with w (i.e., width) and h (i.e., height) pixels.
- `fillRect(x1,y1,w,h)` – Same as `drawRect()` except fills rectangle with current color.
- `clearRect(x1,y1,w,h)` – Same as `drawRect()` except fills rectangle with background color.
- `drawOval(x,y,w,h)` – Draws oval in bounding rectangle of width (w) and height (h) and at position (x,y).
- `fillOval (x,y,w,h)` – Same as `drawOval()` except fills rectangle with current color.
- `drawRoundRect( x,y,w,h,arcWidth,arcHeight)` – Draws rectangle with rounded corners at position (x,y) with width w and height h. The `arcWidth` and `arcHeight` specify the oval fitted into the round corners of the rectangle.
- `fillRoundRect( x, y, w, h, arcWidth, arcHeight )` – Same as `drawRoundRect()` except fills rectangle with current color.

To show you how to draw these graphics and shapes, consider the following Java program:

```
Example: Graphics01.java - Using Java Graphics On Web Page I

 1: import java.awt.*;
 2: import java.applet.*;
 3:
 4: public class Graphics01 extends Applet
 5: {
 6:  public void paint(Graphics gg)
 7:  {
 8:     Graphics2D g = (Graphics2D) gg;
 9:
10:     g.setFont(new Font("Arial",Font.BOLD,16));
11:     g.setStroke(new BasicStroke(5));
12:
13:     g.setColor(Color.blue);
14:     g.drawRect(50,40,150,100);
15:     g.drawString("drawRect(50,60,150,100)",30,180);
16:
17:     g.setColor(Color.lightGray);
18:     g.fillRect(270,40,150,100);
19:     g.drawString("fillRect(270,40,150,100)",250,180);
20:
21:     g.setColor(Color.red);
22:     g.drawOval(50,220,150,100);
23:     g.drawString("drawOval(50,220,150,100)",30,360);
```

```
24:
25:      g.setColor(Color.magenta);
26:      g.drawRoundRect(270,220,150,100,40,60);
27:      g.drawString("drawRoundRect(270,220,150,", 250,360);
28:      g.drawString("100,40,60)",350,380);
29:   }
30: }
```

This applet code contains some simple graphic shapes including a rectangle, a filled rectangle, an oval, and a rounded rectangle. After the font setting in line 10, the statement

```
g.setStroke(new BasicStroke(5));
```

is used to set the drawing stroke (or line thickness) as 5 pixels. The statement in line 14 draws a rectangle at position (50, 60) and `width=150` and `height=100`. After that, text is printed at the bottom of the shape. Lines 17–19 draw a filled rectangle. An oval shape is drawn by the statements in lines 21–23. The statement in line 26

```
g.drawRoundRect(270,220,150,100,40,60);
```

draws a round rectangle at position (270, 220) with `width=150` and `height=100`. The round corner is in fact an oval with `width=40` and `height=60`.

To run this applet, all you need is to create an XHTML page (e.g., ex03-06.htm) with the following body part:

```
Listing: ex03-04.txt - Code Fragment For Example ex03-06.htm

1: <body style="font-size:18pt; text-align:center;font-weight:bold">
2:    Some Simple Graphics Shapes<br />Using Java <br />
3:    <applet code="Graphics01.class" width=500 height=400>
4:    </applet>
5: </body>
```

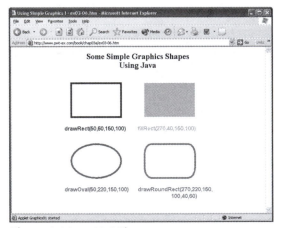

Figure 3.11 ex03-06.htm

A screen shot of this example is shown in Fig. 3.11.

A page like this for drawing some simple shapes has little practical value. To construct something more practical, let's consider the following example. Suppose you are arranging a meeting for your team via the company Internet (or intranet). Wouldn't it be good if you could make a big cross to cancel out the old date and emphasize a new meeting date? The applet code of this example is given below:

```
Example: Graphics02.java - Using Java Graphics On Web Page II

1: import java.awt.*;
2: import java.applet.*;
3:
4: public class Graphics02 extends Applet
5: {
6:  public void paint(Graphics gg)
7:  {
```

```
 8:        Graphics2D g = (Graphics2D) gg;
 9:
10:        Font txtFont = new Font("Arial",Font.BOLD,26);
11:        g.setFont(txtFont);
12:
13:        g.setColor(Color.red);
14:        g.setStroke(new BasicStroke(10));
15:        g.drawLine(20,130,280,40);
16:        g.drawLine(20,40,280,130);
17:
18:        g.setColor(Color.blue);
19:        g.drawString("CA Group Memo",20,60);
20:        g.drawString("The 10 th Meeting on",20,90);
21:        g.drawString("Wednesday 10.am, Room C110",20,120);
22:
23:        g.setColor( Color.magenta);
24:        g.fillRect(10,160,400,10);
25:        g.setColor( Color.blue);
26:
27:        g.drawString("CA Group Memo",20,220);
28:        g.drawString("The 10 th Meeting on",20,250);
29:        g.drawString("Friday 2.pm, Room C110",20,280);
30:  }
31: }
32:
```

There is no new statement in this applet when compared to the previous example. The following statements in lines 14–16 draw a big cross:

```
g.setStroke(new BasicStroke(10));
g.drawLine(20,130,280,40);
g.drawLine(20,40,280,130);
```

The first statement is to set the stroke (or thickness) of the drawing process. The next two lines draw two lines crossing each other on top of the old meeting date in lines 19–21. The fillRect() function in line 24 is used to draw a filled rectangle on the page. Since the height of this rectangle is very thin (10 pixels), the result is similar to drawing a thick line. After this line, the new meeting date is generated as shown in lines 27–29.

A page like this could be used in a variety of situations. If you have a listing and require a feature to cross out some of the records, you may need this simple graphical technique. To run this applet, all you need is to create an XHTML page (e.g., ex03-07.htm) with the following body part:

```
Listing: ex03-05.txt - Code Fragment For Example ex03-07.htm

1: <body style="font-size:18pt; text-align:center;font-weight:bold">
2: Meeting Re-Schedule<br />
3: <applet code="Graphics02.class" width=450 height=300>
4: </applet>
5: </body>
```

A screen shot of this page is shown in Fig. 3.12.

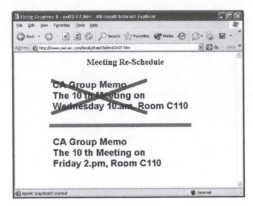

Figure 3.12 ex03-07.htm

3.3.2   Polylines and polygons using arrays

In addition to some basic graphics such as lines, rectangles, and ovals, Java also contains functions to handle polylines and polygons. In general, to draw a 2D polyline or polygon, the vertices of the polyline/polygon are first stored in two arrays. One array is for the *x*-coordinates and the other for the *y*-coordinates. For example, suppose you have a triangle with the following vertices: (-20,60), (20,60), and (0,100). You can declare two integer arrays such as xData[] and yData[] to store the corresponding coordinates:

```
int xData[] = {-20, 20, 0};
int yData[] = {60, 60, 100};
```

The elements of the arrays are

```
xData[0]= -20, xData[1]= 20, xData[2]= 0
yData[0]= 60, yData[1]= 60, yData[2]= 100
```

Once the coordinates are stored, you can use the following drawPolyline() function to draw the polyline on the screen:

```
drawPolyline( xData, yData, 3)
```

This drawPolyline() function takes three parameters. The first one is the array (i.e., xData[]) storing the *x*-coordinates of all vertices. The second is the array for the *y*-coordinates. The third parameter specifies how many points should be used from the arrays. Basically, this function draws all the lines joining the points forming a polyline.

If you want to draw the polygon, you can use the function

```
drawPolygon( xData, yData, 3)
```

This function draws the polygon by joining up all the lines including the line between the starting and end points. You can fill the polygon with the current color by issuing the function

```
fillPolygon( xData, yData, 3)
```

With Java, you can also define the polygon as an object first and then draw it as an entity. For example, you can use the following code:

```
int xData[] = {-20, 20, 0};
int yData[] = {60, 60, 100};
Polygon myPoly = new Polygon( xData, yData, 3);
drawPolygon(myPoly);
```

After the vertices in the first two lines are specified, the third line is used to define a polygon `myPoly` with `Polygon` data type. All the vertices of the polygon are defined inside the `Polygon()` function. The `drawPolygon()` function is then employed to draw the polygon as an entity.

To put all these into action, consider the Java program Graphics03.java:

Example: Graphics03.java – Polylines and Polygons

```
 1: import java.awt.*;
 2: import java.applet.*;
 3:
 4: public class Graphics03 extends Applet
 5: {
 6:  public void paint(Graphics gg)
 7:  {
 8:     Graphics2D g = (Graphics2D) gg;
 9:     int ii;
10:     int xData1[]={-20,-60,-20,20,60,20};
11:     int yData1[]={0,40,80,80,40,0};
12:
13:     // Draw a Polyline
14:     g.setStroke(new BasicStroke(5));
15:     g.setColor(Color.blue);
16:     g.translate(80,60);
17:     g.drawPolyline(xData1,yData1,6);
18:
19:     // Draw a Polygon
20:     g.translate(0,100);
21:     g.setColor(Color.red);
22:     g.fillPolygon(xData1,yData1,6);
23:
```

This is the first part of the Java program Graphics03.java. After all the vertices of the polyline are stored in arrays `xData[]` and `yData[]` as in lines 10–11, the `drawPolyline()` function is employed to draw the polyline in line 17 in the color blue. The translation in line 16 is to make sure that the polyline is located at the selected position. Next, we want to draw the same polygon below the polyline. This can be done by the simple translation `translate(0,100)`. This function will move the origin down by 100 pixels. When the `fillPolygon()` function in line 22 is executed, the polygon is drawn and filled with red color at a position below the polyline.

To demonstrate how to define the polygon data type, consider the second part of the Java program:

Listing: Continuation Of The Java Program Graphics03.java

```
24:     // Defines a new polygon
25:     int xData2[]={-20,20,0};
26:     int yData2[]={60,60,100};
27:     Polygon myPoly = new Polygon(xData2, yData2, 3);
28:
29:     // Draw Polygon with rotation and random colors
30:     g.translate(180,-10);
31:     for (ii=1;ii<=8;ii++)
32:     {
33:       g.rotate(Math.PI/4.0);
34:       g.setColor( new Color((int) (Math.random()*256),
35:                             (int) (Math.random()*256),
36:                             (int) (Math.random()*256)) );
37:
38:       g.drawPolygon(myPoly);
39:     }
40:
```

```
41:     // Draw and fill polygon with Rotation and random colors
42:     g.translate(220,0);
43:     for (ii=1;ii<=8;ii++)
44:     {
45:       g.rotate(Math.PI/4.0);
46:       g.setColor( new Color((int) (Math.random()*256),
47:                             (int) (Math.random()*256),
48:                             (int) (Math.random()*256)) );
49:
50:       g.fillPolygon(myPoly);
51:     }
52:   }
53: }
```

Lines 25–26 specify the two arrays of a polygon. Line 27 declares a polygon using the arrays xData and yData. The translation in line 30 is to move the origin to the right hand side so that the polygon will appear along with the polyline drawn previously. The for-loop and the rotation in lines 31–39 draw the polygon eight times with random colors forming a circular shape.

Lines 42–51 draw the same set of polygons with random filling colors. The translation in line 42 is used to make sure that the new polygons are drawn at the right hand side of the previous ones. To call this Java code, all you need is a Web page (e.g., ex03-08.htm) that contains the following body element:

```
Listing: ex03-06.txt - Code Fragment For Example: ex03-08.htm

1: <body style="font-size:18pt; text-align:center;font-weight:bold">
2:     Two Dimensional Polylines and Polygons<br />
3:     Using Java Graphics<br />
4:   <applet code="Graphics03.class" width=580 height=350>
5:   </applet>
6: </body>
```

This XHTML page calls the program Graphics03.class to draw some simple shapes. A screen shot of this example is shown in Fig. 3.13.

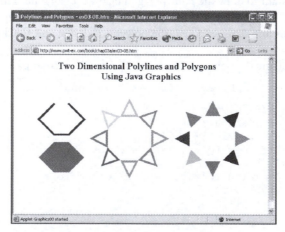

Figure 3.13 Polylines and polygons

3.3.3 Arcs, chords, and pies with Java2D shapes

Similar to the `Polygon` data type introduced in section 3.3.2, the Java package extends the idea and provides an elegant method for handling more advanced graphics, namely the graphics with Java2D shapes. The basic idea is simple and can be explained by the following processes:

- define the graphical shapes (e.g., `shape_object`);
- use the `draw()` function to draw the shape (e.g., `draw(shape_object)`); or
- use the `fill()` function to fill the shape (e.g., `fill(shape_object)`).

Shapes can be built in or user defined so that a large number of shapes and graphics can be rendered in a relatively simple way. For example, some of the frequently used Java2D shapes are

```
Line2D.Double(x1,y1, x2,y2)
Rectangle2D.Double(x1,y1,w,h)
RoundRectangle2D.Double(x1,y1,w,h,arcWidth,arcHeight)
```

The statements above define a line, a rectangle, and a rounded rectangle respectively. All parameters are the same as the `drawLine()`, `drawRect()`, and `drawRoundRect()` functions mentioned at the beginning of section 3.3. For example, the first statement defines a line from position $(x1,y1)$ to $(x2,y2)$ in double precision (i.e., high accuracy). Once you have defined the shape, you can use the `draw()` and `fill()` functions to draw and fill the shapes. For example, the following statement will draw a line from $(20,30)$ to $(100,200)$ on the screen:

```
draw(new Line2D.Double(20,30,100,200));
```

Here we are more interested in a new shape called the Java2D arc (or Arc2D). To specify an arc, you can use the function

```
Arc2D.Double(x, y, w, h, sAngle, rAngle, arc_type)
```

This function defines an arc in double precision at the position (x, y) with dimension `width=w` and `height=h` pixels. The arc starts from an angle `sAngle` (starting angle) and runs to an angle specified by `rAngle` (i.e., run angle or arc angle). All angles are measured in degrees. A positive running degree `rAngle` represents an anti-clockwise arc. Negative `rAngle` means a clockwise arc. If the parameter `w` equals `h`, the arc is a circular arc.

The `arc_type` can have three options:

- `Arc2D.OPEN` – Draws the arc as a curve.
- `Arc2D.CHORD` – Draws the arc and a line joining the end points.
- `Arc2D.PIE`   – Closes the arc with two lines from the center.

Once the arc is defined, you can use the following `draw()` function to draw the arc:

```
draw( Arc2D.Double(30,40,140,140,0,120,Arc2D.PIE) )
```

This statement draws a pie at position (30, 40), with dimension 140×140 (width × height). The starting angle is from 0 degrees with a running angle (or arc angle) of 120 degrees. The main purpose of the `draw()` function is to draw the specified object, which in this case is a pie curve.

If you want to fill the pie shape, you can issue the command

```
fill( Arc2D.Double(30,40,140,140,0,120,Arc2D.PIE) )
```

Consider the following Java program:

```
Example: Arc01.java - Arcs, Chords, And Pies

 1: import java.awt.*;
 2: import java.awt.geom.*;
 3: import java.applet.*;
 4:
 5: public class Arc01 extends Applet
 6: {
 7:  public void paint(Graphics gg)
 8:  {
 9:   Graphics2D g = (Graphics2D) gg;
10:
11:   g.setFont(new Font("Arial",Font.BOLD,16));
12:   g.setStroke(new BasicStroke(5));
13:
14:   g.setColor(Color.red);
15:   g.draw(new Arc2D.Double(30,40,140,140,40,160,Arc2D.OPEN));
16:   g.drawString("draw(new Arc2D.Double(30,40,",0,160);
17:   g.drawString("140,140,40,160,Arc2D.OPEN)",30,180);
18:
19:   g.setColor(Color.blue);
20:   g.draw(new Arc2D.Double(340,40,140,140,40,160,Arc2D.CHORD) );
21:   g.drawString("draw(new Arc2D.Double(340,40,",320,160);
22:   g.drawString("140,140,40,160,Arc2D.CHORD)",360,180);
23:
24:   g.setColor(Color.magenta);
25:   g.draw( new Arc2D.Double(30,200,140,140,40,160,Arc2D.PIE) );
26:   g.drawString("draw(new Arc2D.Double(30,200,",0,370);
27:   g.drawString("140,140,40,160,Arc2D.PIE))",30,390);
28:
29:   g.setColor( ranColor());
30:   g.fill(new Arc2D.Double(340,200,140,140,40,160,Arc2D.PIE) );
31:   g.setColor( ranColor());
32:   g.fill(new Arc2D.Double(340,200,140,140,200,60,Arc2D.PIE) );
33:   g.setColor( ranColor());
34:   g.fill(new Arc2D.Double(340,200,140,140,260,40,Arc2D.PIE) );
35:   g.setColor( ranColor());
36:   g.fill(new Arc2D.Double(340,200,140,140,300,100,Arc2D.PIE) );
37:
38:   g.drawString("Draw and fill a Completed Pie",320,370);
39:  }
40:
41:  public Color ranColor()
42:  {
43:    return(new Color((int) (Math.random()*256),
44:                     (int) (Math.random()*256),
45:                     (int) (Math.random()*256) ));
46:
47:  }
48: }
```

In order to use Java2D graphics and shapes, you will need to import the package java.awt.geom. With the explanations given previously, this Java program should be quite easy to read. Line 15 draws an open arc from the Java2D shape definition

```
Arc2D.Double(30,40,140,140,40,160,Arc2D.OPEN)
```

The `Arc2D.OPEN` arc type specifies an open arc. Similarly, line 20 draws a chord. A pie is drawn by the statement in line 25. Finally, the statements in lines 29–36 draw and fill a completed pie chart. For each part of the pie chart, a random color (i.e., `ranColor()`) is called so that the color of each pie is different.

The body part of the XHTML page to call this Java code is listed below (ex03-09.htm).

```
Listing: ex03-07.txt - Code Fragment For Example: ex03-09.htm

1: <body style="font-size:18pt; text-align:center;font-weight:bold">
2:     Graphics: Arc, Chord and Pie<br />Using Java2D Shapes <br />
3:     Using Java2D Shapes <br />
4:   <applet code="Arc01.class" width=580 height=350>
5:   </applet>
6: </body>
```

This XHTML page calls the program Arc01.class and a screen shot of this example is shown in Fig. 3.14. Before we go on to use Java for business graphics, let's consider how to use Java to draw some more general graphs.

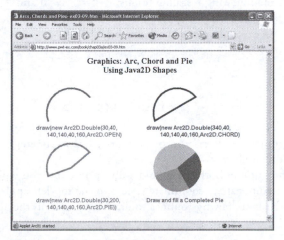

Figure 3.14 Arcs, chords, and pies

3.3.4 Controlling the applet coordinate system

Many graphical formulas or curves have the mathematical form $y = f(x)$. For example, a sine curve is a function where $f(x) = \sin(x)$. In general both the variables x and y are real numbers. A real number can be considered as a number with decimals. In terms of computations, they are represented by data of type `float` or `double`. In a normal situation, the type `double` has higher accuracy (or precision) than `float`. We will not discuss the details or definitions of `float` or `double` but simply consider them as a representation of a decimal number.

The graph of the form $y = f(x)$ is usually represented by the x, y coordinate system or $(x, f(x))$ of real numbers. However, the screen of the computer, or more precisely the applet window, is made up of pixels. Everything displayed on the applet window is referenced by the pixel coordinates. For example, the following applet code defines an applet window with dimension `width=600` by `height=400` pixels:

```
<applet code="Line01.class" width=600 height=400></applet>
```

The top left corner of the applet window is represented by the integer coordinate (0, 0). If you issue the command

```
drawString("Message at (200,30)",200,30)
```

the message is displayed at the coordinate 200 pixels to the right and 30 pixels down from the applet window. Compared to the ordinary coordinate system $(x, f(x))$, they are quite different. Up to this point, all Java graphics and drawings are based on the applet window coordinate system. In order to draw a general graph of the form $y = f(x)$ effectively on a particular area in the applet window, a conversion from the graph coordinate system to a specific applet window area is practically essential. Also, it will give full control over the applet windows including drawing on any scale and multiple displays.

In general, to draw a mathematical formula of the form $y = f(x)$ onto a physical screen or an applet window, you need a method to rescale the ranges of the x- and y-axes or (x, y) coordinates into the integer-based applet window coordinates. First, consider the one-dimensional (1D) case, and suppose the width of the applet window is from A to B. The range of the graph on the x-axis is from `minData` to `maxData`. A simple rescaling formula is

$$H(t) = \frac{((t - minData)*B + (maxData - t)*A)}{(maxData - minData)}$$

where the parameter `t` is between the values of `minData` and `maxData`. For example, suppose you have a function f(x) and the range of x is from `minData=0.0` to `maxData=3.0`. If the applet window's width is from `A=0` and `B=600` pixels, you have the following rescaling results: `H(0.0) = 0` and `H(3.0) = 600`. That is, the range of the function or data is completely mapped into the applet window's coordinates. Based on this formula, the Java function `myScale()` is developed as shown below:

```java
public double myScale(int A,int B,double minData,double maxData,double t)
{
    double rDiff;
    rDiff = maxData - minData;
    return( ((t - minData)*B + (maxData -t)*A )/rDiff );
}
```

This function takes the arguments `A`, `B`, `minData`, `maxData`, and parameter `t`. The computation result is returned as a double-precision number.

Apply the `myScale()` function in both the x- and y-directions, and you will have a general, yet simple method for converting the traditional x,y coordinate system to the top left applet window system. After the conversion, you can apply the Java drawing routines to draw the graph on the applet window. Consider the following Java code:

```
Example: Coor01.java - Controlling Coordinate Systems (Part One)

 1: import java.awt.*;
 2: import java.awt.geom.*;
 3: import java.applet.*;
 4:
 5: public class Coor01 extends Applet
 6: {
 7:
 8:   public double myScale(int A,int B,double minData,
 9:                         double maxData,double t)
10:   {
11:      double rDiff;
12:      rDiff = maxData - minData;
13:      return( ((t - minData)*B + (maxData -t)*A )/rDiff );
14:   }
15:
16:   public Color ranColor()
17:   {
18:     return(new Color((int) (Math.random()*256),
19:                      (int) (Math.random()*256),
20:                      (int) (Math.random()*256)));
21:
22:   }
23:
```

This is the first part of the program Coor01.java. This class contains one major function, `myScale()`, which is used to perform coordinate system rescaling. As you will see even at this simple stage, this function has already provided some practical applications. Consider the test driver `paint()` function below:

```
Listing: Continuation Of The Java Program Coor01.java (Part Two)

24:  double xxMax, xxMin, yyMax, yyMin;
25:  int    xxA, xxB, yyA, yyB;
26:  int    xiTmp, yiTmp, ii, noData;
27:  double xTmp, yTmp;
28:
29:  public void paint(Graphics gg)
30:  {
31:    Graphics2D g = (Graphics2D) gg;
32:
33:    // Draw a sine curve with filled rectangles
34:    noData = 24;
35:    xxA = 40; xxB = 560; yyA = 240; yyB = 40;
36:    xxMin = -0.1; xxMax = 1.2; yyMin = -1.2; yyMax = 1.2;
37:
38:    for (ii=0;ii<= noData;ii++)
39:    {
40:      xTmp = (double) ii/noData;
41:      yTmp = Math.sin(2* Math.PI * xTmp );
42:      xiTmp = (int) myScale(xxA,xxB,xxMin,xxMax,xTmp);
43:      yiTmp = (int) myScale(yyA,yyB,yyMin,yyMax,yTmp);
44:      g.setColor(ranColor());
45:      g.fillRect(xiTmp-5,yiTmp-5,10,10);
46:    }
47:    g.setFont(new Font("Arial",Font.BOLD,18));
48:    g.setColor(Color.blue);
49:    g.drawString("f(x) = sin(x)",xiTmp+10,yiTmp-20);
50:
51:    // Draw a cosine curve with filled circles
52:    for (ii=0;ii<= noData;ii++)
53:    {
54:      xTmp = (double) ii/noData;
55:      yTmp = Math.cos(2* Math.PI * xTmp);
56:      xiTmp = (int) myScale(xxA,xxB,xxMin,xxMax,xTmp);
57:      yiTmp = (int) myScale(yyA,yyB,yyMin,yyMax,yTmp);
58:      g.setColor(ranColor());
59:      g.fillOval(xiTmp-5,yiTmp-5,10,10);
60:    }
61:    g.setColor(Color.blue);
62:    g.drawString("f(x) = cos(x)",xiTmp+10,yiTmp-20);
63:  }
64: }
65:
```

This test `paint()` function draws two curves. One is the sine function and the other is the cosine function. Lines 35–36 define two bounding boxes:

```
   xxA = 40;      xxB = 560;  yyA = 240;    yyB = 40;
 xxMin = -0.1; xxMax = 1.2; yyMin = -1.2; yyMax = 1.2;
```

The first bounding box is used to specify an area in the applet window. The *x*-direction is from 40 to 560 pixels moving to the right. The *y*-direction is from 240 to 40 pixels moving upward. All graphics will be drawn inside this applet window area. The bounding box defined by xxMin, xxMax, yyMin, yyMax will be mapped into the applet window. The for-loop in lines 38–46 calculates all the positions (xTmp,yTmp) of a sine curve.

The position is then converted into the integer-based applet window coordinate (xiTmp,yiTmp) in lines 56–57. Once you have the window coordinate, the standard fillRect() function can be called to draw a filled rectangle bounding the point as illustrated in line 45. Lines 47–49 draw the text "f(x) = sin(x)" at the end of the curve. Lines 51–63 draw a cosine curve in a similar manner.

To call this applet, all you need is to write an XHTML page (e.g., ex03-10.htm) with the code

```
<applet code="Coor01.class" width=600 height=300>
</applet>
```

A screen shot of this example is shown in Fig. 3.15.

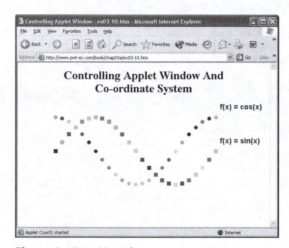

Figure 3.15 ex03-10.htm

For a more general example, let's consider how to draw a set of general data stored in arrays.

3.3.5   Drawing general data on applet windows

Suppose you have a set of data stored in arrays xxData[] and yyData[]. This data set can be drawn on the applet window by the following Java code fragment:

```
xx0 = (int) myScale(xxA,xxB,xxMin,xxMax,xxData[0]);
yy0 = (int) myScale(yyA,yyB,yyMin,yyMax,yyData[0]);
for(ii=1;ii<noData;ii++)
{
  xxTmp = (int) myScale(xxA,xxB,xxMin,xxMax,xxData[ii]);
  yyTmp = (int) myScale(yyA,yyB,yyMin,yyMax,yyData[ii]);
  Line2D.Double myLine = new Line2D.Double(xx0,yy0,xxTmp,yyTmp);
  g.draw(myLine);
  xx0 = xxTmp; yy0 = yyTmp;
}
```

The first two lines are used to convert the first data xxData[0] and yyData[0] to the position on the applet window (xx0,yy0). This point will be used as the starting point to draw a line. The for-loop will convert one by one all the consecutive points to the coordinate (xxTmp,yyTmp) on the applet window. Once you have two points, the standard Line2D.Double() function is used to define a line from (xx0,yy0) to (xxTmp,yyTmp). The draw() function draws the line on the window. After finishing one line, the end point (xxTmp,yyTmp) is assigned to the starting point (xx0,yy0) so that the for-loop can continue to draw lines until the data set is exhausted. To see this idea in action, you can develop a Java program called Lines.java. Apart from the class name, the first 23 lines of this program are the same as those in Coor01.java. The remaining coding is listed in ex03-08.txt.

```
Listing: ex03-08.txt - Code Fragment For The Java Program Lines.java

24:
25:    double[] xxData, yyData;
26:    double xxMax, xxMin, yyMax, yyMin;
27:    int xxA, xxB, yyA, yyB;
28:    int noData;
29:    int ii, xxTmp, yyTmp, xx0,yy0;
30:
31:    public void paint(Graphics gg)
32:    {
33:     Graphics2D g = (Graphics2D) gg;
34:
35:     noData=100;
36:     xxData = new double[noData];
37:     yyData = new double[noData];
38:
39:     for (ii=0;ii<noData;ii++)
40:     {
41:       xxData[ii] = Math.cos(ii* Math.PI *2 /20) * ii/20;
42:       yyData[ii] = Math.sin(ii* Math.PI *2 /20) * ii/20;
43:     }
44:
45:     Dimension d = getSize();
46:     xxA = d.width/8;
47:     xxB = 6 * xxA;
48:     yyA = d.height - d.height/8;
49:     yyB = d.height - 6 * d.height/8;
50:     xxMin = -5; xxMax = 5; yyMin = -5.4; yyMax = 5.4;
51:
```

This code fragment contains the paint() function. Lines 35–37 are used to create the arrays xxData[] and yyData[] with 100 elements. The for-loop in lines 39–43 fills the arrays with a spiral formula. In fact, a spiral is basically a circular function with an increasing radius.

Lines 45–49 define the display area in the applet window. First, the size of the applet window is retrieved by the statement d=getSize(); so the width and height of the applet window defined in the XHTML page are returned by the variables d.width and d.height. These two variables can be used to define the bounding box in the applet window. In this case, it is slightly smaller than the applet window itself. Line 50 defines the bounding box of the data set.

```
Listing: Continuation Of The Java Program Lines.java

52:     g.setColor(Color.red);
53:     g.setStroke(new BasicStroke(3));
54:     xx0 = (int) myScale(xxA,xxB,xxMin,xxMax,xxData[0]);
55:     yy0 = (int) myScale(yyA,yyB,yyMin,yyMax,yyData[0]);
56:     for(ii=1;ii<noData;ii++)
57:     {
58:       xxTmp = (int) myScale(xxA,xxB,xxMin,xxMax,xxData[ii]);
59:       yyTmp = (int) myScale(yyA,yyB,yyMin,yyMax,yyData[ii]);
60:       Line2D.Double myLine = new Line2D.Double(xx0,yy0,xxTmp,yyTmp);
61:       g.draw(myLine);
62:     xx0 = xxTmp; yy0 = yyTmp;
63:     }
64:
65:     g.setColor(Color.black);
66:     g.setStroke(new BasicStroke(1));
67:     for(ii=0;ii<noData;ii++)
68:     {
```

```
69:     xxTmp = (int) myScale(xxA,xxB,xxMin,xxMax,xxData[ii]);
70:     yyTmp = (int) myScale(yyA,yyB,yyMin,yyMax,yyData[ii]);
71:     g.drawOval(xxTmp-5,yyTmp-5,10,10);
72:   }
73:   g.setFont(new Font("Arial",Font.BOLD,18));
74:   g.setColor(Color.blue);
75:   g.drawString("A Spiral Field",xxTmp+10,yyTmp);
76: }
77: }
```

After the color and drawing stroke are set, the statements in lines 54–63 draw polylines joining all the points in the data sets xxData[] and yyData[] as described above. The for-loop in lines 67–72 draws a circle bounding each data point. Finally, a text "A Spiral Field" is displayed at the end of the spiral. If you have a page with the XHTML applet code (e.g., ex03-11.htm)

```
<applet code="Lines.class" width=600 height=300></applet>
```

you can run the applet and see a screen shot as shown in Fig. 3.16.

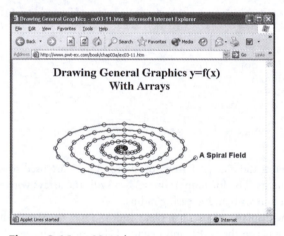

Figure 3.16 ex03-11.htm

You now have some idea about Java graphics and it's time to apply what you have learned to some real applications.

3.4   Business graphics with Java applets

3.4.1   A Java function to display indices of stock exchanges

Most scientific graphs are formula or mathematical model based. This means that graph data can be, more or less, generated or predicted with good accuracy. Business graphs, on the other hand, are more challenging. These types of graphs are more data based and full of unpredictable features. The indices of share markets, foreign exchange rates, business sales, or even daily temperatures are just some of the examples in this category. It may not be easy to find a mathematical model to fit them. The importance of business graphs is not the symmetry, smoothness, or even the beauty of the curve, it is based on real data and is an indispensable tool for decision making in the real world. For example, if business sales or production is down for three consecutive months, a careful analysis of related graphs such as supply, marketing, advertising, production costs, etc., may provide the answers and, in many cases, can help to make business decisions.

As the final part of this chapter, we are going to develop some Java programs dedicated to business graphs or graphics. At an elementary level, the basic requirements for a good Java program for business graphs are as follows:

- Multiple curves can be drawn and displayed easily.
- Data points can be highlighted so that consecutive changes on intervals are visible.
- Each curve can have a name attached to it.
- The program should be flexible.
- The program should be fully automated and user-friendly.

Suppose you have been asked to develop a Web page including a chart displaying the share indices of "Dow Jones," "Nikkei," and "Hang Seng" daily. In order to achieve flexibility and user-friendliness, the following XHTML <div> division element may be a good starting point:

Listing: ex03-09.txt - Indices For Stock Exchanges

```
 1: <div style="font-size:22pt; text-align:center;font-weight:bold">
 2:     Daily Indices Of Share Market<br />(Thursday)<br />
 3:   <applet code="Graphs02.class" width=600 height=350>
 4:     <param name="xTitle" value="Days">
 5:     <param name="yTitle" value="Index Value">
 6:     <param name="NumberOfCurve" value="3">
 7:     <param name="NumberOfData" value="4">
 8:     <param name="Data1" value="Hang Seng,10723,10733,10643,10745">
 9:     <param name="Data2" value="Nikkei,11352,11114,11218,11147">
10:     <param name="Data3" value="Dow Jones,10249,10209,10382,10176">
11:     <param name="NmberOfLabel" value="5">
12:     <param name="labelName" value="Mon,Tue,Wed,Thu,Fri">
13:   </applet>
14: </div>
```

This Web page or division element activates a Java applet called Graphs02.java (see later) showing the indices "Hang Seng," "Nikkei," and "Dow Jones" on four days of a week. The values of xTitle and yTitle in lines 4–5 are strings displayed on the *x*- and *y*-axes. The value of NumberOfCurve is 3, which means that three curves are defined and they are Data1, Data2, and Data3 representing the three different indices. The value of NumberOfData is 4 indicating that each share index contains a set of five numeric data. Consider the third curve (see line 10):

```
<param name="Data3" value="Dow Jones,10249,10209,10382,10176">
```

The first value of this curve represents the name of the curve, which in this case is "Dow Jones." The numeric data after that are the indices for Monday, Tuesday, Wednesday, and Thursday respectively. If you run this example on a browser, you will see a picture as shown in Fig. 3.17.

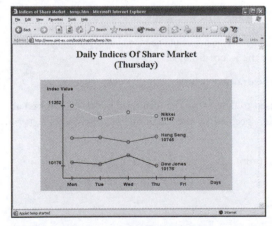

Figure 3.17 Stock exchange indices I

As you can see from Fig. 3.17, the name of each curve and current value are displayed. The five label names are displayed below the *x*-axis. Also, the maximum and minimum values of the data appear on the *y*-axis. If you replace lines 7–10 by the statement

```
<param name="NumberOfData" value="5">
<param name="Data1" value="Hang Seng,10723,10733,10643,10745,10710">
<param name="Data2" value="Nikkei,11352,11114,11218,11147,10963">
<param name="Data3" value="Dow Jones,10249,10209,10382,10176,10185">
```

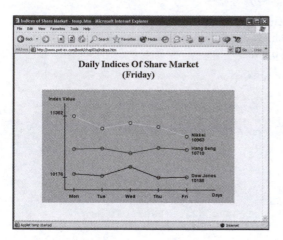

Figure 3.18 Stock exchange indices II

you will add more data to each curve. That is, the share indices for Friday are included. A screen shot of this new page is shown in Fig. 3.18.

As you will find out, the Java program to display the indices is quite flexible and can be applied to many graphical presentation applications. For example, it can be used to display daily temperature or weather data, monthly company sales, and many other applications. Another advantage of using the `<div>` element is that you can use CSS position properties to put the applet window anywhere on the Web page.

In this section, you will learn how to build this application step by step. The program is based on a Java function called `myDrawLines()` which is a modification of the Coor01.java program in section 3.3.4. This function has more general input arguments and the calling syntax is

```
Listing: ex03-10.txt - Calling Syntax Of Java Function myDrawLines()
 1: public void myDrawLines(
 2:    int xA, int xB, int yA, int yB,
 3:    double xMin, double xMax, double yMin, double yMax,
 4:    int noData, double[] xData, double[] yData, Color lineColor,
 5:    int drawType, Color typeColor, int sizeX, int sizeY,
 6:    boolean labelF, Boolean dataF String labelS,
 7:    Color labelC,int labelOx, int labelOy,
 8:    Graphics gg)
```

The arguments in line 2 define the bounding box in the applet window, line 3 specifies the bounding box of the data, and line 4 provides details about the data:

noData   – Number of data to draw.

xData[]   – Array to store the *x*-coordinates.

yData[]   – Array to store the *y*-coordinates.

lineColor – Determine the drawing color.

The arguments in line 5 are used to determine the joining type (or highlights) at each of the data points. There are four joining types available, specified by the value of the variable, drawType. The value of drawType can be one of the following:

1: Draw circles at each data point.   3: Draw rectangles.

2: Draw filled circles.   4: Draw filled rectangles.

For example, the input for the arguments in line 5, "`3,new Color(255,0,0),20,30`," draws a red rectangle with size 20 × 30 pixels bounding each data point. The final arguments in lines 7–8 determine the curve name and location offsets. Consider the input

```
true, true, "My Curve", new Color(0,0,255), 10, 20
```

The first `true` value will display a blue text "My Curve" at the end of the curve with offsets 10 pixels right and 20 pixels down. The second `true` will display the data value at the same time. A false value for the variable `labelF` means no display at all.

Now, let's take a look at the program fragment of Graphs01.java listed in ex03-11.txt.

Listing ex03-11.txt – Code Fragment For Graphs01.java

```
24:  public void myDrawLines(int xA, int xB, int yA, int yB,
25:     double xMin,double xMax, double yMin, double yMax,
26:     int noData,double[] xData, double[] yData, Color lineColor,
27:     int drawType, Color typeColor,int sizeX, int sizeY,
28:     boolean labelF, boolean dataF, String labelS,
29:     Color labelC,int labelOx, int labelOy, Graphics gg)
30:  {
31:     Graphics2D g = (Graphics2D) gg;
32:     int ii, x1,y1, halfX, halfY;
33:     double[] xDraw = new double[noData];
34:     double[] yDraw = new double[noData];
35:     double xStart, yStart;
36:
37:     // Step 1: Connecting all the data points with a line
38:     for (ii =0;ii<noData;ii++)
39:     {
40:       xDraw[ii]=myScale(xA,xB,xMin,xMax,xData[ii]);
41:       yDraw[ii]=myScale(yA,yB,yMin,yMax,yData[ii]);
42:     }
43:
44:     g.setColor(lineColor);
45:     xStart= xDraw[0];
46:     yStart =yDraw[0];
47:     for (ii=1;ii<noData;ii++)
48:     {
49:       Line2D.Double myLine = new Line2D.Double(xStart,yStart,
50:                                        xDraw[ii],yDraw[ii]);
51:       g.draw(myLine);
52:       xStart = xDraw[ii];
53:       yStart = yDraw[ii];
54:     }
55:
56:     // Step 2: Highlight each data point depending on the drawType
57:     if ((drawType > 0) &&(drawType <5) )
58:     {
59:
60:      halfX = sizeX/2;
61:      halfY = sizeY/2;
62:      for(ii=0;ii<noData;ii++)
63:      {
64:        x1 = (int) myScale(xA,xB,xMin,xMax,xData[ii]);
65:        y1 = (int) myScale(yA,yB,yMin,yMax,yData[ii]);
66:        g.setColor(typeColor);
67:        if (drawType ==1)
68:           g.drawOval(x1- halfX,y1-halfY,sizeX,sizeY);
```

```
69:        else if(drawType ==2)
70:            g.fillOval(x1- halfX,y1-halfY,sizeX,sizeY);
71:        else if (drawType ==3)
72:            g.drawRect(x1- halfX,y1-halfY,sizeX,sizeY);
73:        else if (drawType ==4)
74:            g.fillRect(x1- halfX,y1-halfY,sizeX,sizeY);
75:    }
76:    }
77:
78:    // Step 3: Display the name of the curve
79:    if (labelF == true)
80:    {
81:        x1 = (int) myScale(xA,xB,xMin,xMax,xData[noData -1]);
82:        y1 = (int) myScale(yA,yB,yMin,yMax,yData[noData -1]);
83:        g.setColor(labelC);
84:        g.drawString(labelS,x1+labelOx,y1-labelOy);
85:        if (dataF == true)
86:        {
87:            g.drawString(""+ (int) yData[noData -1],x1+labelOx,y1+15);
88:        }
89:    }
90: }
```

Apart from the class name Graphs01, the first 23 lines are the same as those in Coor01.java containing the usual myScale() function. Apart from the slightly complicated input arguments, this function is not that difficult to read. Basically, the function is divided into three parts (or steps). The first part (lines 37–54) converts all the points into the applet window coordinates xDraw[] and yDraw[] using the two bounding boxes {xA,xB,yA,yB} and {xMin,xMax,yMin,yMax}. The for-loop in lines 47–54 is used to draw a line connecting all the coordinates.

The second part (lines 56–76) is to highlight all data points. First, the data point is converted into the applet coordinate (x1,y1) as illustrated in lines 63–64. A condition if statement is used to determine what kind of connection type the user wants to apply. For example, if the drawType is 2, the statement in line 69 will be executed:

```
g.fillOval(x1- halfX,y1-halfY,sizeX,sizeY);
```

This statement draws a filled circle (or oval) at (x1-halfX,y1-halfY) position with dimensions sizeX and sizeY. The variables halfX and halfY are used to make sure that the circle is drawn with its center point at coordinates (x1,y1). A simple for-loop draws a small circle bounding each data point. The third part (lines 78–89) is to display the identity of the curve. If the value of labelF is true, the name of the curve is displayed. If the dataF variable is true, the value of the final data value will be displayed as well.

As a test driver for this function, we consider the following paint() function as the continuation of the Java program Graphs01.java.

```
Listing: Continuation Of The Java Program Graphs01.java

91:
92: public void paint(Graphics gg)
93: {
94:   Graphics2D g = (Graphics2D) gg;
95:   double xxMax, xxMin, yyMax, yyMin;
96:   int xxA, xxB, yyA, yyB, noData;
97:
98:   xxA = 20; xxB = 320; yyA = 240; yyB=40;
99:   xxMin = 0; xxMax = 6; yyMin = 100; yyMax = 500;
100:
```

```
101:    // Draw data lines with circles
102:    double[] xData={1,2,3,4,5,6};
103:    double[] yData={120,370,460,405,270,300};
104:    String curveName="myCurve01";
105:    noData = 6;
106:    g.setStroke(new BasicStroke(2));
107:    g.setFont(new Font("Arial",Font.BOLD,14));
108:    myDrawLines(xxA,xxB,yyA,yyB,xxMin,xxMax,yyMin,yyMax,
109:            noData,xData,yData,new Color(255,0,0),
110:            1,new Color(0,100,0),15,15, 34
111:            true,true,curveName,new Color(255,0,255),15,0,gg);
112:
113:    // Draw data lines with rectangle
114:    double[] x1Data={1,2,3,4,5,6,7,8,9};
115:    double[] y1Data={230,175,367,280,120,229,101,460,410};
116:    curveName="myCurve02";
117:    noData = 9;
118:    g.setStroke(new BasicStroke(2));
119:    myDrawLines(xxA,xxB,yyA,yyB,xxMin,xxMax,yyMin,yyMax,
120:            noData,x1Data,y1Data,new Color(0,0,200),
121:            3,new Color(100,0,0),15,15,
122:            true,true,curveName,new Color(255,0,255),15,0,gg);
123:  }
124: }
```

This testing function `paint()` contains two curves. After the details of the two bounding boxes in lines 98–99, the first curve is defined. This curve is called "myCurve01" with a set of six data points. The curve is drawn in red on the applet window with green circles around the points (see lines 109–110). The name and last value are displayed following the instruction as in line 111. The second curve is defined and drawn by the statements in lines 113–122. Since there is no parameter reading from the calling Web page (not yet), all you need is the following XHTML code (e.g., ex03-12.htm) to include this applet:

```
<applet code="Graphs01.class" width=600 height=300></applet>
```

You can run the applet and a screen shot of this example is shown in Fig. 3.19.

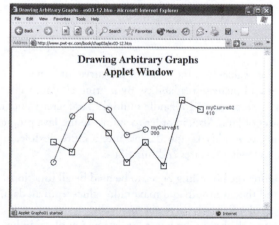

Figure 3.19 ex03-12.htm

3.4.2   Automation and more interaction with Web pages

To write a successful applet, the applet must be able to work with a Web page and take parameters from users. In the early example ex03-03.htm, you learned how to set up parameters for Java inside a Web page such as

```
<applet code="xxxx.class" width=xxx heigh=xxx>
    <param name="ParamterName01" value="ParameterValue 01">
    <param name="ParamterName02" value="ParameterValue 02">
</applet>
```

In Java, the parameters can be retrieved by the function `getParameter()`. For example, the value of `ParameterName01` can be obtained by the statement

```
parameterSt = getParameter("ParameterName01");
```

In this section, we go beyond this parameter setting and retrieval technique. As a starting point, we are going to handle parameters returned by a Web page such as ex03-13.htm below.

```
Example: ex03-13.htm - Display Daily Indices Of Stock Exchanges

 1: <?xml version="1.0" encoding="UTF-8"?>
 2: <!DOCTYPE html PUBLIC "-//W3C//DTD XHTML 1.0 Frameset//EN"
 3: "http://www.w3.org/TR/xhtml1/DTD/xhtml1-frameset.dtd">
 4: <html xmlns="http://www.w3.org/1999/xhtml" xml:lang="en" lang="en">
 5: <head><title>Indices of Share Market - ex03-13.htm</title></head>
 6: <body>
 7:  <div style="font-size:22pt; text-align:center;font-weight:bold">
 8:      Daily Indices Of Share Market<br />(Friday)<br /><br />
 9:   <applet code="Graphs02.class" width=600 height=350>
10:    <param name="xTitle" value="Days">
11:    <param name="yTitle" value="Index Value">
12:    <param name="NumberOfCurve" value="3">
13:    <param name="NumberOfData" value="4">
14:    <param name="Data1" value="Hang Seng,10723,10733,10643,10745">
15:    <param name="Data2" value="Nikkei,11352,11114,11218,11147">
16:    <param name="Data3" value="Dow Jones,10249,10209,10382,10176">
17:    <param name="NumberOfLabel" value="5">
18:    <param name="labelName" value="Mon,Tue,Wed,Thu,Fri">
19:   </applet>
20:  </div>
21: </body>
22: </html>
```

In this page, we have put all data values and the name of the curve into one `<param>`. This arrangement may save a lot of XHTML coding and increase readability. By putting all data values together as in lines 14–16, some careless data errors can be eliminated. To handle multiple parameter values of this kind, you need to use the string and substring features of Java. Also, in order to automate the Java program and make it more flexible and user-friendly, we are going to modify Graphs01.java into a more flexible, automatic, and powerful class Graphs02.java by adding the following features and functions:

- Global Variables – Define the bounding boxes to be used by all functions.
- `myFindMinMax()` – Find the minimum and maximum values from all data.
- `mySetColor()` – Set color for each curve automatically.
- `mySetFrame()` – Define the bounding boxes for data and applet window, draw the *x,y*-axes, and label them in a fully automatic way.
- `myDrawGraphs()` – Organize above and call the `myDrawLines()` function to draw all the curves.
- `myGetArgs()` – More interaction with the XHTML page and get all parameters.

With all these modifications, you will have an example one step closer to a more mature Java program. In particular, the myGetArgs() function is the main connection between your Web pages and the Java program.

Apart from the class name, the first 90 lines of Graphis02.java are the same as those in Graphs01.java containing the functions myRescale(), ranColor(), and myDrawLines(). The remaining Java coding is listed and explained step by step below:

```
Listing ex03-12.txt - Code Fragment For Graphs02.java

 91:   //Global Variables
 92:   double      xxMax, xxMin, yyMax, yyMin;
 93:   int         xxA, xxB, yyA, yyB;
 94:   int         noData,noCurve;
 95:   String[][]  tData;
 96:   String[]    labelSt;
 97:   Color[]     curveColor;
 98:   int         segNumber, baseLine;
 99:   double      minData, maxData;
100:   String      xTitle,yTitle;
101:
102:   public void myFindMinMax()
103:   {
104:    int ii,jj; double tTmp;
105:    maxData = (double) Integer.parseInt(tData[0][1]);
106:    minData = maxData;
107:    for(jj=0;jj<noCurve;jj++)
108:    {
109:     for (ii=1;ii<=noData;ii++)
110:     {
111:       tTmp= (double) Integer.parseInt(tData[jj][ii]);
112:       if (maxData < tTmp)
113:            maxData = tTmp;
114:       if (minData > tTmp)
115:            minData = tTmp;
116:    }
117:   }
118:  }
119:
120:   public void mySetColor()
121:   {
122:     int ii;
123:     curveColor= new Color[noCurve];
124:     if (noCurve == 3)
125:     {
126:      curveColor[0] = new Color(255,0,0);
127:      curveColor[1] = new Color(255,255,0);
128:      curveColor[2] = new Color(0,255,0);
129:     } else {
130:      for(ii=0;ii<noCurve;ii++)
131:      {
132:       curveColor[ii] = ranColor();
133:      }
134:     }
135:   }
136:
```

First, we have some global variables. After declaring the variables for the bounding boxes in lines 92–93, all data for the curves are stored into one 2D array of string tData[][]. The labels on the *x*-axis are stored in the array labelSt. Each curve may have a different color and therefore the color for each curve is stored in the array of color curveColor[]. The titles for the *x*- and *y*-axes are stored in variables xTitle and yTitle. The myFindMinMax() function in lines 102–118 is to look through all the data in array tData[][] to find the minimum and maximum data (i.e., minData and maxData). These two will be marked on the *y*-axis. The mySetColor() function is used to set the color for each curve automatically. In this case, if exactly three curves are displayed, the colors will be red, yellow, and green (see lines 124–129). If not, the color of each curve will be randomly picked as illustrated in lines 130–133.

Next, you need a facility to define the bounding boxes automatically. Consider the Java code below:

Listing: Continuation of Graphs02.java – The mySetFrame() Function

```
137:  public void mySetFrame(Graphics gg)
138:  {
139:    int ii;
140:    Graphics2D g = (Graphics2D) gg;
141:
142:    Dimension d = getSize();
143:    int xDiff = d.width/(segNumber*2);
144:    int yDiff = d.height/(segNumber +3);
145:    xxA = 10; xxB = d.width - 60;
146:    yyA = d.height - 40; yyB = yDiff;
147:
148:    g.setColor(new Color(200,200,200) );
149:    g.fillRect(0,0,d.width,d.height);
150:    g.setFont(new Font("Arial",Font.BOLD,14));
151:
152:    double dataDiff = (maxData - minData)/segNumber;
153:    xxMin = 0; xxMax = segNumber+1;
154:    yyMin = minData - dataDiff; yyMax = maxData + dataDiff;
155:
156:  int ix0 = (int) myScale(xxA,xxB,xxMin,xxMax,xxMin);
157:  int ix1 = (int) myScale(xxA,xxB,xxMin,xxMax,xxMax);
158:  int iy0 = (int) myScale(yyA,yyB,yyMin,yyMax,yyMin);
159:  int iy1 = (int) myScale(yyA,yyB,yyMin,yyMax,yyMax);
160:  int iMin = (int) myScale(yyA,yyB,yyMin,yyMax,minData);
161:  int iMax = (int) myScale(yyA,yyB,yyMin,yyMax,maxData);
162:      baseLine = iy0;
163:    g.setStroke(new BasicStroke(2));
164:    g.setColor(Color.blue);
165:    g.drawString(xTitle,ix1-10,iy0+20);
166:    g.drawString(yTitle,ix0+10,iy1-10);
167:    g.drawString(""+(int) minData,ix0+15,iMin-5);
168:    g.drawString(""+(int) maxData,ix0+15,iMax-5);
169:
170:    g.setColor(Color.black);
171:    g.drawLine(ix0+xDiff,iy0,ix1,iy0);
172:    g.drawLine(ix0+xDiff,iy0,ix0+xDiff,iy1);
173:    g.drawLine(ix0+xDiff-5,iMin,ix0+xDiff+5,iMin);
174:    g.drawLine(ix0+xDiff-5,iMax,ix0+xDiff+5,iMax);
175:
176:    for (ii=1;ii<=segNumber;ii++)
177:    {
178:      int xAxis = (int) myScale(xxA,xxB,xxMin,xxMax,ii);
179:      g.drawLine(xAxis,iy0-5,xAxis,iy0+5);
180:      g.drawString(labelSt[ii],xAxis-15,iy0+25);
181:    }
182:  }
183:
```

This function is to set the bounding boxes on the applet window and the data. The statement in line 142 gets the dimension of the applet window defined by the calling Web page. The width and height of the applet window are stored in the properties `d.width` and `d.height`. The bounding box on the applet window is defined in lines 145–146. Then the window is filled with a gray color. The bounding box of the data is defined in lines 152–154. The *x*- and *y*-axes are defined by the statements in lines 156–161. The statements in lines 165–168 display the titles of the *x*- and *y*-axes. The minimum and maximum data values are drawn at the same time. Lines 170–174 are used to draw the *x*- and *y*-axes. Finally, the for-loop in lines 176–182 draws all the labels on the *x*-axis.

The actual drawing function is `myDrawGraphs()` and is listed below:

Listing: Continuation of Graphs02.java - The myDrawGraphs() Function

```
184:   public void myDrawGraphs(Graphics gg)
185:   {
186:     Graphics2D g = (Graphics2D) gg;
187:     int ii,jj;
188:     double[] xData;
189:     double[] yData;
190:     String tmpSt;
191:
192:     xData = new double[noData];
193:     yData = new double[noData];
194:     for(ii=0;ii<noData;ii++)
195:     {
196:       xData[ii]=ii+1;
197:     }
198:
199:     myFindMinMax();
200:     mySetFrame(gg);
201:
202:     g.setStroke(new BasicStroke(3));
203:     for(jj=0;jj<noCurve;jj++)
204:     {
205:       tmpSt = (String) tData[jj][0];
206:       for(ii=0;ii<noData;ii++)
207:       {
208:        yData[ii]= (double) Integer.parseInt(tData[jj][ii+1]);
209:       }
210:       g.setStroke(new BasicStroke(2));
211:       g.setColor(Color.red);
212:       myDrawLines(xxA,xxB,yyA,yyB,xxMin,xxMax,yyMin,yyMax,
213:               noData,xData,yData,
214:               curveColor[jj],1,new Color(0,100,0),10,10,
215:               true,true,tmpSt,new Color(0,0,255),15,0,gg);
216:     }
217:   }
218:
```

This function declares two arrays `xData[]` and `yData[]` storing the *x*- and *y*-coordinates of each curve. The for-loop in lines 194–197 fills the array `xData[]`. After finding the minimum and maximum values of all data, the `mySetFrame()` function in line 200 is called to draw the axis and necessary labels. The double for-loop in lines 203–216 extracts the data of each curve from the array `tData[][]` into array `yData[]`. When the data of one curve are extracted, a function call to `myDrawLines()` draws the curve onto the applet window as illustrated in lines 212–215. When all the curves are drawn, all the graphs will appear on the applet window.

To get the parameters from the Web page, you use the function `myGetArgs()` listed below:

Listing: Continuation of Graphs02.java – The myGetArgs() Function

```java
219:  public void myGetArgs()
220:  {
221:   String tmpSt, tmpSt2;
222:   int ii,jj, index2, tmp2;
223:
224:    xTitle = getParameter("xTitle");
225:    yTitle = getParameter("yTitle");
226:    noCurve= Integer.parseInt(getParameter("NumberOfCurve"));
227:    noData= Integer.parseInt(getParameter("NumberOfData"));
228:    segNumber= Integer.parseInt(getParameter("NumberOfLabel"));
229:
230:    //Extracts all labels on x-axis
231:    labelSt=new String[segNumber+1];
232:    tmpSt2 = getParameter("labelName");
233:    index2=0; labelSt[0]="";
234:    for(jj=1;jj<segNumber;jj++)
235:    {
236:      tmp2 = tmpSt2.indexOf(',',index2);
237:      tmpSt = tmpSt2.substring(index2,tmp2);
238:      labelSt[jj] = tmpSt.trim();
239:      index2 = tmp2 +1;
240:    }
241:    tmp2 = tmpSt2.indexOf(',',index2);
242:    if (tmp2 > index2)
243:        tmpSt = tmpSt2.substring(index2,tmp2);
244:    else
245:        tmpSt= tmpSt2.substring(index2);
246:    labelSt[jj]= tmpSt.trim();
247:
248:    //Extract all data from each curve
249:    tData = new String[noCurve][noData+1];
250:    for (ii=1;ii<=noCurve;ii++)
251:    {
252:      tmpSt2 = getParameter("Data"+ii);
253:      index2=0;
254:      for(jj=0;jj<noData;jj++)
255:      {
256:        tmp2 = tmpSt2.indexOf(',',index2);
257:        tmpSt = tmpSt2.substring(index2,tmp2);
258:        tData[ii-1][jj] = tmpSt.trim();
259:        index2 = tmp2 +1;
260:      }
261:      tmp2 = tmpSt2.indexOf(',',index2);
262:      if (tmp2 > index2)
263:        tmpSt = tmpSt2.substring(index2,tmp2);
264:      else
265:        tmpSt= tmpSt2.substring(index2);
266:      tData[ii-1][jj]= tmpSt.trim();
267:    }
268:  }
269:
```

First, this function uses the getParameter() function to get the input data (see lines 224–228) including the strings for the *x,y*-axes titles (xTitle and yTitle), number of curves (noCurve), number of data for each curve (noData), and number of labels on the *x*-axis (segNumber). Lines 230–246 extract all labels on the *x*-axis. If you have a parameter on the Web page

```
<param name="labelName" value="Mon,Tue,Wed,Thu,Fri">
```

the string tmpSt2 in line 232 stores the entire value "Mon,Tue,Wed,Thu,Fri." Starting from index2=0, the indexOf() function used in line 236 will return the first appearance of the comma (i.e., ",") in the string tmpSt2 to tmp2. The substring() function in line 237 extracts the string between index2 and tmp2 (i.e., "Mon"). After trimming all the white spaces using the function trim() in line 238, these data are assigned to string array labelSt[]. Next, you assign the comma position as the current position and continue the for-loop in lines 234–240 until the last label. The if statement in lines 242–246 says that if the original string contains more data than required, the next data before the next comma are extracted. If the last required data are the end data of the string, the end data are extracted.

Very similar ideas are used to read all the curve data and store them into the 2D array tData[][] in lines 248–267. That is, after the double for-loop, all the data of each curve are stored in tData[][] as strings.

The final part of this Java program is quite simple and is listed below:

```
Listing: Continuation of Graphs02.java - The init() and paint() Function

270:  public void init()
271:  {
272:      myGetArgs();
273:      mySetColor();
274:  }
275:
276:  public void paint(Graphics gg)
277:  {
278:      myDrawGraphs(gg);
279:  }
280: }
```

The init() function first calls myGetArgs() to get the parameters from the Web page. It then sets up the color for each curve by a function call to mySetColor(). The paint() function simply calls the drawing function myDrawGraphs() to draw and display all curves on the applet window.

With Graphics02.java, you can now run the Web page ex03-13.htm and you should see the same result as in Fig. 3.17. If you add one more data in example ex03-13.htm as described at the beginning of section 3.4.2 and call the new example ex03-14.htm, you should see the same result as in Fig. 3.18.

In order to demonstrate the flexibility of this program Graphs02.class, we consider a Web page (ex03-15.htm) displaying a daily temperature chart for major cities. This page contains the <div> element:

```
Listing: ex03-13.txt - Web Page Fragment For Example ex03-15.htm

 1: <div style="font-size:22pt; text-align:center;font-weight:bold">
 2:      Daily Temperature Chart For<br />Major Cities<br /><br />
 3:  <applet code="Graphs02.class" width=600 height=350>
 4:     <param name="xTitle" value="Days">
 5:     <param name="yTitle" value="Temperature">
 6:     <param name="NumberOfCurve" value="4">
 7:     <param name="NumberOfData" value="7">
 8:     <param name="Data1" value="Hong Kong,31,29,33,30,31,34,32">
 9:     <param name="Data2" value="Tokyo,19,23,22,17,19,22,16">
10:     <param name="Data3" value="New York,24,21,19,22,25,19,24">
11:     <param name="Data4" value="London,14,11,16,15,10,8,11">
12:     <param name="NumberOfLabel" value="7">
13:     <param name="labelName" value="Mon,Tue,Wed,Thu,Fri,Sat,Sun">
14:  </applet>
15: </div>
```

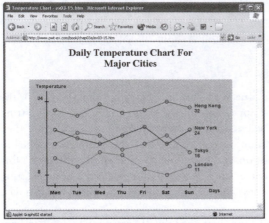

Figure 3.20 ex03-15.htm

This Web page is easy to read and a screen shot of this example is shown in Fig. 3.20. Thanks to the conditional statements in lines 241–246 and 261–265, another feature of Graphs02.class is that you can draw previous data by just changing the value of NumberOfData.

To demonstrate yet another feature of Graphs02.class, consider a chart showing the product sales of a company around the world. The <div> element of this Web page (ex03-16.htm) is listed below:

```
Listing: ex03-14.txt - Web Page Fragment For Example ex03-16.htm

 1: <div style="font-size:22pt; text-align:center;font-weight:bold">
 2:    Company Product Sales<br />Around The World<br /><br />
 3: <applet code="Graphs02.class" width=600 height=350>
 4: <param name="xTitle" value="Months">
 5: <param name="yTitle" value="Sales Millions">
 6: <param name="NumberOfCurve" value="3">
 7: <param name="NumberOfData" value="12">
 8: <param name="Data1" value="Singapore,11,19,13,6,15,19, 21,16,25,25,12,13">
 9: <param name="Data2" value="Tokyo,51,43,50,51,43, 55,41,63,55,35,72,33">
10: <param name="Data3" value="Paris,31,36,43,46,31,33,28,46,47,27, 51,23">
11: <param name="NumberOfLabel" value="12">
12: <param name="labelName" value="Jan,Feb,Mar,Apr,May,
13:    Jun,Jul,Aug,Sep,Oct,Nov,Dec">
14: </applet>
15: </div>
```

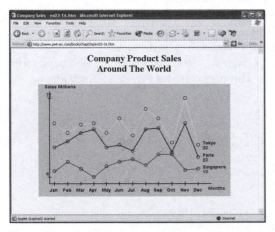

Figure 3.21 ex03-16.htm

This page is very similar to example ex03-15.htm. You may have also noticed that the curve data in lines 8–10 contain some white spaces. This example will work well on the browser since we have used the trim() function to trim off the white spaces in the myGetArgs() function (see lines 238, 246, 258, and 266 of Graphs02.java). The program will generate errors if trim() is not used. A screen shot of this example is shown in Fig. 3.21. Apart from these features, no other protection against user errors on the Web page is employed. For a more professional program, more protection coding is needed.

3.4.3 Displaying bar and pie charts

The program Graphs02.class provides a framework for building more graphics functionalities. For example, you can put bar chart and pie chart functionalities into the class by adding the bar and pie drawing routines (or functions). This arrangement will take advantage of the existing functions already in the class.

Consider the structure of the class Graphs02.java below:

- myScale()   — Mapping the *x,y*-axes into the applet window.
- ranColor()   — Generating random color.
- myDrawLines()   — A general routine to draw lines.
- Global Variables — Define bounding box parameter as global.
- myFindMinMax()   — Find the minimum and maximum data.
- mySetColor()   — Set up color for each curve.
- mySetFrame()   — Draw *x,y*-axes and associated labels.
- myDrawGraphs()   — Organize functions above to draw curves.
- myGetArgs()   — Get parameters from Web page.

A bar chart and a pie chart routine can be added after the function mySetFrame() to form a new class called Graphs03.java. To complete this new class, all you have to do is to modify the two functions myDrawGraphs() and myGetArgs() to accept the new bar and pie chart functions.

Now change the class name in Graphs02.java to Graphs03 and save it as Graphs03.java. Insert the following bar chart function myBarChart() after the function mySetFrame() (i.e., at line 183 in Graphs02.java):

Listing: ex03-15.txt – The Bar Chart Function In Graphs03.java

```
 1:  public void myBarChart(int xxA, int xxB, int yyA, int yyB,
 2:    double xxMin,double xxMax, double yyMin, double yyMax,
 3:    int noData,double[] xData, double[] yData, int baseLine,
 4:    Color barColor, boolean showText, Color textColor, Graphics gg)
 5:  {
 6:   Graphics2D g = (Graphics2D) gg;
 7:   int xi1,yi1,ii,offSet, halfOff;
 8:
 9:   g.setFont(new Font("Arial",Font.BOLD,14));
10:   for(ii=0;ii<=noData;ii++)
11:   {
12:     g.setColor(barColor);
13:     xi1 = (int) myScale(xxA,xxB,xxMin,xxMax,xData[ii]);
14:     yi1 = (int) myScale(yyA,yyB,yyMin,yyMax,yData[ii]);
15:     offSet = (xxB - xxA)/(noData *2);
16:     halfOff = offSet/2;
17:
18:     g.setPaint(
19:        new GradientPaint(xi1,yi1,ranColor(),
20:         xi1+halfOff,baseLine-yi1,ranColor(),true) );
21:
22:     Rectangle2D.Double myRect = new Rectangle2D.Double(xi1-halfOff,
23:                                  yi1,offSet,baseLine-yi1);
24:     g.fill(myRect);
25:
26:     if (showText == true)
27:     {
28:       g.setColor(textColor);
29:       g.drawString(""+ (int) yData[ii],xi1-halfOff,yi1 - 10);
30:     }
31:  }
32: }
```

This function draws a long rectangle (or bar) at each position stored in the arrays xData[] and yData[]. The *x,y*-positions are first converted to applet window coordinates (xi1,yi1) in lines 13–14. Then the width of the rectangle is calculated and stored in variable offSet (see line 15). To define the bar, you can use the Java2D rectangle shape as illustrated in lines 22–23. The variable halfOff equals half of the offset to make sure that the bar is drawn evenly along the labels. The values of the baseLine and yi1 are measured from the top of the applet window to the *x*-axis and the bar respectively. The difference between these two values is the height of the bar itself. The fill() function in line 24 draws the filled rectangle. In order to make this example more interesting, random gradient colors are used to draw each bar. The GradientPaint() function in lines 19–20 smoothly changes one color to another from one coordinate to another coordinate. Finally, if the value of the showText variable is true, the data associated with each bar are displayed at the top.

Another function called myPieChart() is also added right after the bar chart function myBarChart() to draw a complete pie on the applet window. This function is listed in ex03-16.txt.

Listing: ex03-16.txt – The Pie Chart Function In Graphs03.java

```
 1:  public void myPieChart( int noData,double[] xData,double[] yData,
 2:    boolean showText, Color textColor, Graphics gg)
 3:  {
 4:   Graphics2D g = (Graphics2D) gg;
 5:   double sum;
 6:   int ii, ang1, ang2, sizeB, sizeP, rTmp;
 7:   Color[] pieColor1, pieColor2;
 8:
 9:   pieColor1 = new Color[noData];
10:   pieColor2 = new Color[noData];
11:   g.setFont(new Font("Arial",Font.BOLD,14));
12:
13:   Dimension d = getSize();
14:   xxA = 0; xxB = d.width; yyA = d.height; yyB = 0;
15:   sizeB = (int) ( (yyA - yyB)/(noData*2) );
16:   sizeP = (int) ((yyA -yyB) * 0.9);
17:   rTmp =  (int) ((xxB-xxA) *0.4);
18:   if (sizeP > rTmp)
19:       sizeP = rTmp;
20:
21:   sum = 0.0f;
22:   for(ii=0;ii<noData;ii++)
23:   {
24:     sum = sum + yData[ii];
25:   }
26:
27:   ang1 = 20;
28:   for (ii=0;ii< noData;ii++)
29:   {
30:     pieColor1[ii] = ranColor();
31:     pieColor2[ii] = ranColor();
32:     g.setPaint( new GradientPaint(0,0,pieColor1[ii],
33:                 sizeB,sizeB,pieColor2[ii],true) );
34:     ang2 = (int) (360 * yData[ii]/sum +0.6);
35:     g.fill(new Arc2D.Double(20,20,sizeP,sizeP,ang1,ang2,Arc2D.PIE) );
36:     ang1 = ang1 + ang2;
37:
38:     if (showText == true)
39:     {
40:      int iiTmp = (int) (10000*yData[ii]/sum +1);
41:      g.fillRect((xxB-xxA)/2,ii*(sizeB+20)+20,sizeB,sizeB);
```

```
42:          g.setColor(Color.black);
43:          g.drawString(" "+labelSt[ii+1]+" - ("+ (double) iiTmp/100.0 + "% )",
44:                   (xxB-xxA)/2 + sizeB+10,ii*(sizeB+20)+35);
45:       }
46:     }
47: }
```

This function draws a complete pie using the data `xData[]` and `yData[]`. If the value of the variable `showText` is true, the text associated with each pie is displayed with the `TextColor` (see line 2). Since we don't want to draw the *x,y*-axes, the input arguments in lines 1–2 are simpler. As mentioned in section 3.3.3, the following Java2D shape function can be used to draw a pie at position (x1,y1):

```
Arc2D.Double(x1,y1,sizeX,sizeY,ang1,ang2,Arc2D.PIE)
```

where variables `sizeX` and `sizeY` are the dimensions of the box bounding the pie. The pie is drawn from angle `ang1` to angle `ang2`. In order to calculate the angles of the pie chart, each `yData[]` is converted to a percentage. The percentage can be calculated by the individual data `yData[ii]` divided by the total sum of `yData[]` data. When you multiply the percentage by 360, you have the running angle (i.e., `ang2`) of the pie as in line 34. With the starting angle `ang1`, the pie is defined and drawn in line 35. If the value of the variable `showText` is true, a rectangle (see line 41) together with the label and percentage of the pie is drawn (see lines 43–44). The color of each pie is governed by the random gradient color in lines 32–33.

To incorporate these two functions into the class and to distinguish it from the curve situation, you may need to add an integer variable `graphType` at the global variable section of the class. When the value of `graphType` is 1, the class draws lines. If `graphType` is 2 or 3, a bar chart or a pie chart is drawn. Now, consider the `myDrawGraphs()` function (see lines 184–217 of Graphs02.java). First, you may need to locate the functions `myFindMinMax()` and `mySetFrame()` and perform the following changes:

```
if ((graphType ==1)||(graphType==2))
{
  myFindMinMax();
  mySetFrame(gg);
}
```

This `if` statement makes sure that the *x,y*-axes are drawn when a curve or a bar chart is required. All you have to do next is to replace the function call to `myDrawLines()` (see lines 212–215 in Graphs02.java) according to a situation depending on the value of variable `graphType`, e.g.,

```
if (graphType ==1)
{
  myDrawLines(xxA,xxB,yyA,yyB,xxMin,xxMax,yyMin,yyMax,
       noData,xData,yData,
       curveColor[jj],1,new Color(0,100,0),10,10,
       true,true,tmpSt,new Color(0,0,255),15,0,gg);
}
if (graphType ==2)
{
  myBarChart(xxA,xxB,yyA,yyB,xxMin,xxMax,yyMin,yyMax,
       noData,xData,yData,baseLine,new Color(0,0,255),
       true,new Color(0,0,255),gg);
}
if (graphType ==3)
{
  myPieChart(noData,xData,yData,
       true,new Color(0,0,255),gg);
}
```

Finally, the function `myGetArgs()` can be modified by the following Java code:

Listing: ex03-17.txt - The myGetArgs() Function In Graphs03.java

```
 1:  public void myGetArgs()
 2:  {
 3:    String tmpSt, tmpSt2;
 4:    int    ii,jj, index2, tmp2;
 5:
 6:    graphType = Integer.parseInt(getParameter("GraphType"));
 7:    if ( (graphType>0) && (graphType <4))
 8:    {
 9:     if (graphType ==1)
10:     {
11:       noData= Integer.parseInt(getParameter("NumberOfData"));
12:       noCurve= Integer.parseInt(getParameter("NumberOfCurve"));
13:       xTitle = getParameter("xTitle");
14:       yTitle = getParameter("yTitle");
15:       segNumber= Integer.parseInt(getParameter("NumberOfLabel"));
16:     }
17:     if (graphType==2)
18:     {
19:       noData= Integer.parseInt(getParameter("NumberOfData"));
20:       noCurve = 1;
21:       xTitle = getParameter("xTitle");
22:       yTitle = getParameter("yTitle");
23:       segNumber= Integer.parseInt(getParameter("NumberOfLabel"));
24:     }
25:     if (graphType==3)
26:     {
27:       noData= Integer.parseInt(getParameter("NumberOfData"));
28:       noCurve = 1;
29:       segNumber= noData;
30:     }
31:
32:     //Extracts all labels on x-axis
33:     labelSt=new String[segNumber+1];
34:       ==== ==== ==== ==== ==== ==== ==== ====
35:       ==== ==== ==== ==== ==== ==== ==== ====
36:         The Corresponding Original Statements are here
37:       ==== ==== ==== ==== ==== ==== ==== ====
38:       ==== ==== ==== ==== ==== ==== ==== ====
39:     }
40:  }
```

First, this function gets the parameter of `GraphType` from the calling Web page and stores the value into integer variable `graphType` (see line 6). Then the parameters are read into the class according to the value and requirement of `graphType`. Lines 11–15 get the parameters for displaying the curves. Lines 17–24 and 25–30 are the requirements for displaying the bar and pie chart respectively. The remaining part starting from line 32 is the same as the corresponding statements in the `myGetArgs()` function in the Java program Graphs02.java.

For a bar chart test page, let's consider a page (e.g., ex03-17.htm) with the following `<div>` division element:

Listing: ex03-18.txt - Code Fragment For Example ex03-17.htm

```
 1: <div style="font-size:22pt; text-align:center;font-weight:bold">
 2:   Bar Chart: Company Product Sales<br />(Singapore Office)<br /><br />
 3: <applet code="Graphs03.class" width=600 height=350>
 4: <param name="GraphType" value="2">
 5: <param name="xTitle" value="Months">
 6: <param name="yTitle" value="Sales Millions">
```

```
 7: <param name="NumberOfData" value="12">
 8: <param name="Data1" value="Singapore,11,19,13,6,15,19, 21,16,25,25,12,13">
 9: <param name="NumberOfLabel" value="12">
10: <param name="labelName" value="Jan,Feb,Mar,Apr,May,
11:     Jun,Jul,Aug,Sep,Oct,Nov,Dec">
12: </applet>
13: </div>
```

At line 4 of this page, a new parameter called `GraphType` is added. The value of this parameter is 2, indicating that a bar chart is drawn. Since the format of this example is the same as previous examples, the remaining statements in this page are easy to read. A screen shot of this example is shown in Fig. 3.22.

For a pie chart testing page, consider a page (e.g., ex03-18.htm) with the following division `<div>` element:

```
Listing: ex03-19.txt - Code Fragment For Example ex03-18.htm

 1: <div style="font-size:22pt; text-align:center;font-weight:bold">
 2:     Pie Chart: Company Product Sales<br />
 3:     (First 6 Months In Singapore Office)<br /><br />
 4: <applet code="Graphs03.class" width=600 height=350>
 5:   <param name="GraphType" value="3">
 6:   <param name="NumberOfData" value="6">
 7:   <param name="Data1" value="Singapore,11,19,13,6,15,19">
 8:   <param name="labelName" value="Jan,Feb,Mar,Apr,May,Jun">
 9: </applet>
10: </div>
```

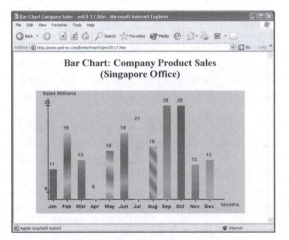

Figure 3.22 ex03-17.htm

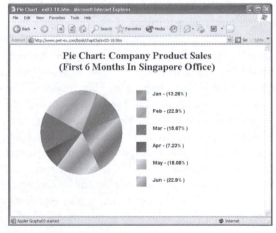

Figure 3.23 ex03-18.htm

The `GraphType` in line 5 indicates that the pie chart function is called and a complete pie is displayed according to the parameters in lines 6–8. A screen shot of this example is shown in Fig. 3.23.

Again, the Java program Graphs03.java is just a demonstration example to show how to build a more complex Java applet to incorporate some presentation graphics such as business curves, bar charts, and pie charts. The concepts and skills can be extended to develop more challenging and practical Web applications.

Java is a rich subject and capable of almost anything. Only a few practical and selected topics are presented here. For further study, readers are advised to read some dedicated texts or to visit the official site of Java (www.javasoft.com) for more tutorials, examples, libraries, and other resources.

4 Images, animations, and multimedia

4.1 Using multimedia on the Web

4.1.1 An introduction to multimedia

Together with the font, color, images, and graphics, another most exciting element on the Web is the capability to deliver multimedia functionalities for users and page designers. Live chat, video on demand, or even live video conference already exists over Web connections. On the whole, multimedia is one of the factors that makes Web browsing so impressive and popular on the Internet. Someone may even claim that the force of multimedia pushes the limits of XHTML to bring life to Web pages. We would like to stress that the force of multimedia also pushes the limits of the bandwidth (speed of the Internet) to deliver sound, video, and movie entertainment in real time.

In fact, multimedia is an ambiguous term describing many different things. Someone may define multimedia as everything but text. We would argue that the graphical display or some art writing styles of text may be considered as graphics and hence inside the definition of multimedia. We are not here to argue about the definition of multimedia in general. This chapter will focus on multimedia as the digital images, sound, video, and movie that you see, hear, and enjoy in your daily life.

You will learn about multimedia and their applications with XHTML in early sections of this chapter. Multimedia on the whole is a big and diverse subject. Improvements follow one after another – even Microsoft has to introduce many different kinds of media formats for IE and its associated media player. Together with QuickTime movies and MPEG, we have many different kinds of audio, video, and movie formats. Even a modest discussion of these formats one by one would be beyond the scope of this chapter.

To play back sound, video, and movies on a Web browser would normally require add-on software such as a "Media Player" to achieve the multimedia playback action. Some popular media players available on the Internet are:

- Windows Media Player from Microsoft
- QuickTime Player from Apple
- RealPlayer from RealNetworks
- Java Player from Sun Microsystems

This chapter begins with the Windows Media Player (WMP) from Microsoft associated with Windows systems. This means that if you are using Microsoft Windows, the default media player for IE is WMP. For example, the following XHTML code fragment would activate WMP to play back a sound and a video file:

```
<a href="glass.wav">Click Me To Play Some Sound </a>
 <a href="dropxx01.avi">Click Me To Play Video</a>
```

Since both the `wav` (sound) and the `avi` (video) files are supported by Microsoft's systems and IE, the anchor element can be used to activate WMP to play back the sound and video. We will also show you how to embed WMP into a Web page. More importantly, we will show you how to create and use the control buttons of WMP on the Web. In order to play back QuickTime movies (`mov`), the QuickTime Player, browser compatibility issues, and plugins are also discussed. The information can be used as a foundation for further studies. In the final section of this chapter, multimedia with Java is introduced. Images, animations, and multimedia applications with Java and the Java Multimedia Framework (JMF) are also presented with examples.

4.1.2 Multimedia file formats on the Web

Multimedia supports in terms of file formats were available even in the early days of the Web. In normal circumstances, if your system has the capability to play the sound or video clips via a media player, you can play back using a Web page. Browsers such as IE, NS, or Opera can activate the player to perform multimedia actions depending on the information given by file extensions or in the system registry.

A media player is a piece of software with the capability to interpret the media files to play sound and/or video on your system. Some of the most popular media players on the Web are the Windows Media Player (WMP), RealPlayer (RP), QuickTime, and Java Player. In fact, one of the most important subjects on multimedia applications over the Internet is to control the media player to play back sound and movies within Web pages.

In order to have a simple and clear discussion, we roughly characterize some common files supported and used on the Internet into four categories. They are document, image, sound, and movie. We generally consider all of them as multimedia types.

In normal circumstances, each category of file can be identified by the file extension. For our practical purposes, some frequently used and supported file formats are listed in Table 4.1.

Table 4.1 Common file types supported by browser

Document	Image	Sound	Movie
`.txt,  htm,  .xml,  .xsl`	`.gif`	`.wav`	`.mov`
`.css,  .java,  .js`	`.tiff`	`.au`	`.avi,   .wmv`
`.asp,  aspx`	`.jpg or .jpeg`	`.midi or .mid`	`.mpg or .mpeg`
`.sql,  .pl,  .php,  .wml`	`.bmp`	`.mp3`	

Each file extension defines a specific file format and indeed can be considered as an application or a technology on the Web.

Document

`.txt`	— Document contains text only
`.htm`	— Generally considered as HTML/XHTML document
`.xml`	— Extensible Markup Language
`.xsl`	— XML Stylesheet Language Transformation (XSLT) file
`.css`	— Cascading Style Sheet (CSS) file
`.js`	— ECMAScript (or JavaScript) file
`.java`	— Java program file

`.asp`	—	Active Server Page (ASP) from Microsoft
`.aspx`	—	ASP Dot NET (ASP.NET) page from Microsoft
`.sql`	—	Structured Query Language (SQL) file
`.pl`	—	Practical Extraction and Report Language (Perl) or Perl Script
`.php`	—	PHP: Hypertext Preprocessor (PHP) server page
`.wml`	—	Wireless Markup Language (WML) from Wireless Application Protocol (WAP) Forum

Image

`.gif`	—	Graphics Interchange Format (GIF) image file
`.tiff`	—	Tagged Image File Format (TIFF) image file
`.jpg` or `.jpeg`	—	Joint Photographic Expert Group (JPEG) image file

Sound

`.wav`	—	Waveform sound file from Microsoft
`.au`	—	Audio sound file from Sun Microsystems
`.mid`	—	Musical Instrument Digital Interface (MIDI) sound file
`.mp3`	—	MPEG Layer 3 sound file

Movie

`.avi`	—	Audio Video Interlace (AVI) movie file
`.wmv`	—	Windows Media Video (WMV) movie file
`.mov`	—	QuickTime Movie file from Apple
`.mpg` or `.mpeg`	—	Moving Picture Expert Group (MPEG) movie file

The document types will be discussed one by one in detail throughout this book. In fact, some of them, such as images and their applications on the Web, are covered in earlier chapters. Indeed, it is believed that by putting images on a Web page, we have established a far more interesting and colorful Web community. Image animation is the first step toward video. By integrating images together with a fixed or variable time interval, digital movies are developed. Video and movies are time-based image animations. In fact, sound and music can also be considered as a time-based animation against each sound note. By interlacing audio and video, sound video and movies are created. They are all time-based media applications.

With cameras, capture cards, and Webcams everywhere, making digital home video and movies with sound today is as easy as operating a domestic consumer product such as a hi-fi system. By finishing this chapter, you will know how to use different multimedia types (movie types), how to perform playback on your favorite browsers, and more importantly deliver them on the Web with browser and media player compatibility.

Again, multimedia is an exciting and diverse subject, but browser incompatibility appears quite often. For example, your IE and system may not support QuickTime movie (i.e., `.mov`) format without plugin software. Sometimes, plugin software can completely change the behavior of the browser and it may be difficult to change it back. Together with various formats and media player differences, confusion may arise easily even for experienced Web users. We begin with simple examples and will cover all these compatibility issues in this chapter. Let's consider some easy examples to play sound and video on Web pages.

4.2   Basic multimedia applications on the Web

4.2.1   A simple page with sound and music

One of the simplest ways to include multimedia files on Web pages is to use the anchor element <a> and let your system handle all the sound and video playback. For example, suppose you have a sound file called mu_mid.mid. The sound format and file extension are supported by your system. To play this music on your browser, all you have to do is to issue the anchor element such as

```
<a href="mu_mid.mid">click me to play some sound</a>
```

When you press the underlined text, the default player of your system will be called to play the sound file. In this case, we assume the music file mu_mid.mid is in the current directory. Otherwise you may need to specify the file's path. For many Windows systems, WMP is activated to play the sound. Again WMP is assumed as the default media player in early sections of this chapter. As long as your system supports the sound and/or music format, the anchor element will work. Also, you can put some images inside the anchor element to trigger the href action. Consider the following example:

```
Example: ex04-01.htm – My First Multimedia Page With Sound And Music

 1: <?xml version="1.0" encoding="UTF-8"?>
 2: <!DOCTYPE html
 3:       PUBLIC "-//W3C//DTD XHTML 1.0 Transitional//EN"
 4:       "http://www.w3.org/TR/xhtml1/DTD/xhtml1-transitional.dtd">
 5: <html xmlns="http://www.w3.org/1999/xhtml" xml:lang="en" lang="en">
 6: <head><title> ex04-01.htm </title></head>
 7: <style>
 8:   .txtSt {font-family:arial;font-size:18pt;color:#ffff00;
 9:          font-weight:bold;background:#000088}
10: </style>
11: <body vlink="#000088" alink="#000088" link="#000088" class="txtSt">
12:   <div align="center"><br />
13: A Simple Page To Play Sound<br />Please Click The Pic To Play<br /><br />
14:   <table class="txtSt" style="font-size:14pt">
15:    <tr>
16:     <td> <a href="mu_glass.wav"><img src="pic_glass.gif" alt="pic"
17:          width="150" height="120" /></a> </td>
18:     <td> <a href="mu_gun.wav"><img src="pic_gun.gif" alt="pic"
19:          width="150" height="120" /></a> </td>
20:     <td> <a href="mu_mid.mid"><img src="pic_music.gif" alt="pic"
21:          width="150" height="120" /></a> </td> </tr>
22:    <tr> <td> Broken Glass</td><td>Gun Shot</td><td>Midi Music</td></tr>
23:   </table>
24:   </div>
25: </body>
26: </html>
```

This is a simple page to play three sound files. They are:

- mu_glass.wav – The sound of a broken glass
- mu_gun.wav – The sound of a gun
- mu_mid.mid – The midi music

arranged by a table in lines 14–23. Each sound file will be triggered by an image. When the image is clicked, the corresponding sound or music will be activated and played by the default media player. For example, if you click the "Broken Glass picture," the WMP is activated and will play the corresponding sound file mu_glass.wav. Some screen shots of this page in action are shown in Figs 4.1 and 4.2.

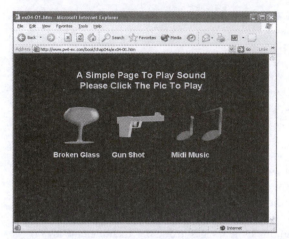

Figure 4.1 ex04-01.htm

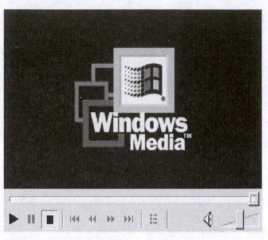

Figure 4.2 Sound Play by WMP

Using anchor `<a>` for multimedia applications is very simple. You don't need to worry about browser capability and add-on software such as plugins. As long as you have a default media player such as WMP installed and supporting the media format, your media application will run properly.

4.2.2   A simple page with video clips

Not just sound files, but also movies and video clips can be played using the same method. The next example can be used to play back some video clips using the anchor element `<a>`.

Example: ex04-02.htm - A Page With Some Video Clips

```
 1: <?xml version="1.0" encoding="UTF-8"?>
 2: <!DOCTYPE html
 3:      PUBLIC "-//W3C//DTD XHTML 1.0 Transitional//EN"
 4:      "http://www.w3.org/TR/xhtml1/DTD/xhtml1-transitional.dtd">
 5: <html xmlns="http://www.w3.org/1999/xhtml" xml:lang="en" lang="en">
 6: <head><title> ex04-02.htm </title></head>
 7: <style>
 8:  .txtSt {font-family:arial;font-size:18pt;color:#ffff00;
 9:          font-weight:bold;background:#000088}
10: </style>
11: <body vlink="#000088" alink="#000088" link="#000088" class="txtSt">
12: <div align="center"><br />
13:     A Simple Page To Play Video Clips<br />
14:     Please Click The Pic To Play<br /><br />
15: <table class="txtSt" style="font-size:14pt">
16:  <tr>
17:  <td><a href="vcd.mpg">
18:    <img src="vcd.gif" alt="pic" width="200" height="180" /></a> </td>
19:  <td><a href="dropxx1.mpg">
20:    <img src="movie01.gif" alt="pic" width="200" height="180" /></a> </td>
21:  <tr> <td>Video Logo Clip</td><td>MPEG Video Clip</td></tr>
22: </table>
23: </div>
24: </body>
25: </html>
```

This page contains two video clips: they are defined by two anchor elements in lines 17 and 19. The video clips are triggered by two images vcd.gif and movie01.gif. The images are animated GIF pictures so that some animations are achieved before the video playback. Again, when one of the pictures is clicked, the WMP is activated to play the video clip. Some screen shots of this example are shown in Figs 4.3 and 4.4.

Figure 4.3 ex04-02.htm

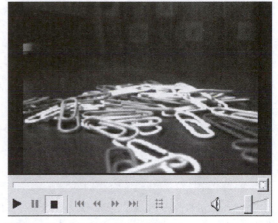

Figure 4.4 Playing a movie clip

Figure 4.4 is a movie clip of Video Compact Disc (VCD) format. A VCD is a kind of Compact Disc (CD) holding video and/or movies, using compressed MPEG-1 video. In general, its resolution is 352 × 240 (NTSC) or 352 × 288 (PAL), which is roughly comparable to VHS. Compared to VCD, the Digital Versatile Disc (DVD) provides much higher resolution (700 × 480), comparable to laserdisc (LD). Typical DVD movies use MPEG-2 compression, rather than the MPEG-1 compression used by VCDs. That means that if you have an MPEG-1 player, you can play back VCD video. If you have an MPEG-2 player, you can play back DVD movies.

In normal circumstances, using anchor element <a> will activate the media player as a separate application and may open another window. In many cases, the integrity of the page or page layout will be destroyed. Some of you may ask whether you can embed the video and/or sound inside a Web page. Or more precisely, can we control the media player within a Web page? Due to browser and system incompatibility, this is not an easy question. You will learn about the answer, solutions, and about related technologies in this chapter.

If you are using IE, one simple solution to embed video in a Web page is to use the image element <img>.

4.2.3 Embedding video with the `<img>` element

From XHTML, you have learned that `<img>` is a W3C standard element to display an image on a Web page. This element and its attributes, such as `align`, `hspace`, `vspace`, `alt`, `name`, `src`, `ismap`, `usemap`, `border`, `height`, and `width`, are supported by all browsers. In order to support video playback, Microsoft has extended the capability of `<img>` by introducing an additional attribute called `dynsrc`. This attribute is used to store the URL of the video and dedicate it for video playback. When used, it will replace the value assigned to the src attribute and use the value of `dynsrc` instead. For example, the following statement can be used to play a video clip:

```
<img src= "pic01.gif" dynsrc= "dropxx1.mpg" />
```

In this case, the video dropxx1.mpg will replace the picture pic01.gif displayed by the browser. Consider the following example:

```
Example: ex04-03.htm - Embedding Video With <img>

 1: <?xml version="1.0" encoding="UTF-8"?>
 2: <!DOCTYPE html
 3:      PUBLIC "-//W3C//DTD XHTML 1.0 Transitional//EN"
 4:       "http://www.w3.org/TR/xhtml1/DTD/xhtml1-transitional.dtd">
 5: <html xmlns="http://www.w3.org/1999/xhtml" xml:lang="en" lang="en">
 6: <head><title> ex04-03.htm </title></head>
 7: <style>
 8:    .txtSt {font-family:arial;font-size:18pt;color:#ffff00;
 9:            font-weight:bold;background:#000088}
10: </style>
11: <body class="txtSt">
12:  <div align="center"><br />
13:   Embedding Video Within Image Element &lt;img&gt;<br /><br />
14:   <img dynsrc="dropxx1.mpg" />
15:  </div>
16: </body>
17: </html>
```

This is a simple page to use `<img>` to play back video. The most important statement is line 14. If you are using IE4+, the browser will process and display the file dropxx1.mpg as a video clip. A screen shot of this page is shown in Fig. 4.5.

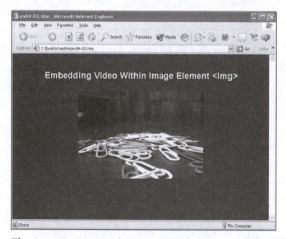

Figure 4.5 ex04-03.htm

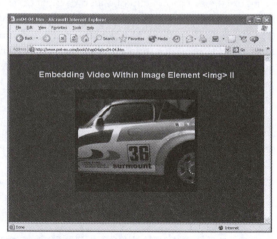

Figure 4.6 ex04–04.htm

Now, you modify line 14 of this page as

```
<img src="logo_web.jpg" dynsrc="carxx2.avi"
        alt="pic" width="350" height="300" />
```

and call the new example ex04-04.htm. The statement above embeds another movie format (carxx2.avi) supported by WMP. This example also shows that you can control the dimensions of the display by providing the `width` and `height` values. By putting an image into the `src` attribute, the browser can display this image while loading the movie. A screen shot of this example is shown in Fig. 4.6.

To embed video with `<img>`, in many cases, is handy to develop multimedia applications. However, `dynsrc` is not a standard attribute recommended by W3C. Both NS and Opera would ignore the `dynsrc` attribute and process `<img>` for image only. For NS and Opera browsers, plugins are used. Plugins (sometimes called plug-ins) are software that can be used to enhance the functionality of a browser. Plugins will be discussed later in section 4.4. For now, let's consider some more applications using WMP, particularly how to use the controlling buttons of WMP on Web pages.

4.2.4 Including objects with the `<object>` element

To include objects in Web pages is not new in HTML/XHTML. For example, `<img>` can be considered as an XHTML element to include an image object. The `<applet>` element is of course another example to include an object: namely the Java applet. According to W3C, they are specific elements that include specific objects. For example, you cannot use `<img>` to include a Java applet or vice versa. In order to develop an all-purpose mechanism for generic object inclusion, the W3C authority introduced a new element called `<object>` in HTML4. This object element can be used to include an image, applet, plugin, handler, and others in a Web page. In the truly diverse world of multimedia, it is a first step toward an all-singing and dancing element to include generic objects.

For example, suppose you have an image logo_web.jpg. You can use the following `<img>` statement to display it on a Web page:

```
<img src="logo_web.jpg" />
```

Alternatively, you can also use the object element `<object>` to display the same picture. Consider the following example:

```
Example: ex04-05.htm - Display An Image Using <object>

 1: <?xml version="1.0" encoding="UTF-8"?>
 2: <!DOCTYPE html
 3:     PUBLIC "-//W3C//DTD XHTML 1.0 Transitional//EN"
 4:     "http://www.w3.org/TR/xhtml1/DTD/xhtml1-transitional.dtd">
 5: <html xmlns="http://www.w3.org/1999/xhtml" xml:lang="en" lang="en">
 6: <head><title> ex04-05.htm </title></head>
 7: <body>
 8: <object
 9:    data="logo_web.jpg"
10:    type="image/jpeg"
11:    width="350" height="250" >
12: </object>
13: </body>
14: </html>
```

To use `<object>`, you may need to define the attributes `data` and `type` as illustrated in lines 9–10. The `data` attribute specifies the URL of the data and the `type` attribute defines the MIME type (or content type) of the data declared in the browser–server dialog. In this case, the MIME type of a JPEG image is image/jpeg.

Another application of the object element is to include a Java applet in Web pages. For example, there is a standard Java applet demo in J2SDK called Clock2.java. This program comes with the standard Java package and will display an animated clock on a page. Once you compile the program and produce a bytecode application (Clock2.class), you can use the following applet element to display the clock:

```
<applet code="Clock2.class" width="170" height="150">
</applet>
```

To display this clock using the `<object>` element, consider the following example:

```
Example: ex04-06.htm – Include Java Applet Using <object>

1: <?xml version="1.0" encoding="UTF-8"?>
2: <!DOCTYPE html
3:      PUBLIC "-//W3C//DTD XHTML 1.0 Transitional//EN"
4:      "http://www.w3.org/TR/xhtml1/DTD/xhtml1-transitional.dtd">
5: <html xmlns="http://www.w3.org/1999/xhtml" xml:lang="en" lang="en">
6: <head><title> ex04-06.htm </title></head>
7: <body>
8:   Display A Live JAVA Clock <br />
9:   Using &lt;object&gt; Element<br /><br />
10: <object
11:   data="Clock2.class"
12:   codetype="application/java-archive"
13:   classid="java:Clock2.class"
14:   width="170" height="150" >
15: </object>
16: </body>
17: </html>
```

This page inserts a Java applet into an XHTML page using `<object>`. The `data` attribute in line 11 specifies the location of the applet. In this case, the applet is a Java class (or `bytecode`) from file Clock2.class located in the local directory. By setting the `codetype` attribute in line 12, the browser can retrieve the Java application if necessary. The `classid` attribute in line 13 is used to identify the Java program Clock2.class to run.

Just like Java applet, this page runs on all browsers with Java and supporting the `<object>` element, which includes IE5+, NS4+, and Opera 5+. A screen shot of this page on IE6 is shown in Fig. 4.7. Another screen shot of this page on an older browser NS4.x is shown in Fig. 4.8. More Java, including the Java Media Framework and its multimedia applications, will be discussed later in section 4.5.

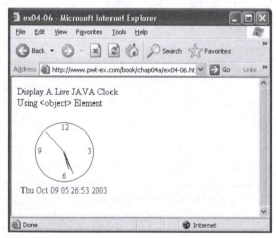

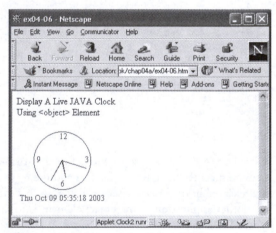

Figure 4.7 ex04-06.htm   **Figure 4.8** Using `<object>` on NS4.x

As mentioned earlier, the `classid` attribute of the `<object>` element can be used to identify the Java program to be run. In fact, this attribute can also be used to identify and include an ActiveX control in a Web page. In the next section, we will show you how to embed WMP into a Web page, particularly how to use the control buttons of WMP in your application.

4.3 Embedding and controlling WMP

4.3.1 Identifying WMP with ActiveX controls

If you are using a Windows system, chances are that you already have WMP up and running on your system for multimedia applications. There are a number of ways to activate this software. In particular, we have shown you at the beginning of this chapter how to use the anchor element `<a>` to activate WMP. In order to control WMP more effectively, you need something called ActiveX or ActiveX control.

ActiveX controls were created by Microsoft based upon the Component Object Model (COM) technology. They are a refinement of the Object Linking and Embedding (OLE) custom controls. Basically, they are programs that can be called and embedded inside another program. Any program that is a container for ActiveX controls can host them. Thus, you can employ ActiveX controls in a Web page since IE is a container. You can also employ ActiveX controls in applications such as Visual Basic since Visual Basic forms are containers.

Since ActiveX controls are specific Microsoft products, examples in this section or related to ActiveX may only work on IE and Windows platforms.

In a Windows system, ActiveX controls are identified by a unique value called class identity (`clsid`). This value is stored in the system registry. To see the `clsid`, you can use the registry editor `regedit`. For example, if you open a DOS window and type the "regedit" command, you will see the "Registry Editor" window. If you go to

```
My Computer|HKEY_LOCAL_MACHINE|SOFTWARE|Microsoft|Multimedia|MPlayer2
```

from the "registry editor" window (Fig. 4.9), you will see the following information:

```
CLSID          {22d6f312-b0f6-11d0-94ab-0080c74c7e95}
Player.Path  T:\Program Files\Windows Media Player\mplayer2.exe
```

WMP is identified by the class identity (CLSID) and the location is specified by the `Player.Path`. The `Player.Path` may be different on your system.

Figure 4.9 The "Registry Editor" window

The CLSID can help you to embed WMP into your Web pages.

4.3.2   Embedding WMP

To embed WMP into your Web page, you need to declare the CLSID and the value in the `classid` attribute with the `<object>` element. Consider the following example:

```
Example: ex04-07.htm – Embedding Windows Media Player In A Web Page

1:  <?xml version="1.0" encoding="UTF-8"?>
2:  <!DOCTYPE html
3:        PUBLIC "-//W3C//DTD XHTML 1.0 Transitional//EN"
4:        "http://www.w3.org/TR/xhtml1/DTD/xhtml1-transitional.dtd">
5:  <html xmlns="http://www.w3.org/1999/xhtml" xml:lang="en" lang="en">
6:  <head><title> ex04-07.htm </title></head>
7:  <style>
8:    .txtSt {font-family:arial;font-size:18pt;font-weight:bold}
9:  </style>
10: <body style="background:#000088;color:#ffff00;text-align:center">
11: <div class="txtSt">
12:   Embedding Windows Media Player<br />
13:   Inside A Web Page<br /><br />
14:
15:   <object
16:       classid="CLSID:22d6f312-b0f6-11d0-94ab-0080c74c7e95"
17:       type="application/x-oleobject"
18:       id="MediaPlayer1" width="320" height="240">
19:   <param name="FileName" value="mu_mid.mid" />
20:   </object>
21: </div>
22: </body>
23: </html>
```

This page can be used as a framework to embed WMP into your Web application. The important statements are in lines 16–17. In line 16, the `classid` attribute is used to identify the WMP program. The value

```
CLSID:22d6f312-b0f6-11d0-94ab-0080c74c7e95
```

Figure 4.10 Embedding WMP

will identify WMP in your system and every other Microsoft Windows system. Line 17 is the content type used by WMP. When used together, the entire WMP will be included in your Web page. The information in line 18 provides further information on how you may want to use WMP. In this case, an `id="MediaPlayer1"` is assigned to WMP.

Now, you have WMP embedded in the page. To use the player is simple: all you have to do is to assign a file for it to play. This can be done by the parameter element `<param>`. Similar to Java, the `<param>` element can be used to input a parameter into the application (i.e., WMP). The statement in line 19 assigns a music MIDI file for WMP to play. A screen shot of this example is shown in Fig. 4.10.

One of the advantages of including WMP this way is that all the controlling buttons of WMP are embedded. No extra programming or coding is needed. That means you can use the control buttons of WMP to "Stop" and/or "Play" the music.

Since WMP has the capability to play a large amount of multimedia file formats, you can change the page to perform other multimedia applications easily. For example, you can change line 19 of ex04-07.htm to

```
<param Name="FileName" Value="dropxx1.mpg" />
```

and call the new example ex04-08.htm. WMP will play back the mpeg video file dropxx1.mpg instead of playing music. A screen shot of this video playback is shown in Fig. 4.11. Can we create and control the action buttons in WMP?

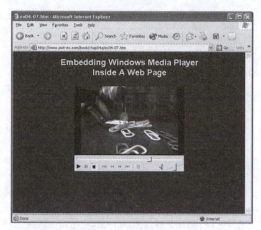

Figure 4.11 Playing MPEG video

4.3.3 Creating control buttons for WMP

In this section, we will show you how to create some control buttons for WMP. Microsoft WMP is a big object offering more than 20 functions that can be called within a Web page. As a starting point, our next WMP application can only be a simple one. It contains the following features:

- Display the WMP.
- Play back a multimedia file.
- Turn off the control buttons that come with WMP.
- Create two controlling buttons "Play" and "Stop."
- Bind the "Play" button to play a multimedia file.
- Bind the "Stop" button to stop the playback.

Consider the following example codes:

```
Example: ex04-09.htm - Creating Simple Buttons For WMP

 1: <?xml version="1.0" encoding="UTF-8"?>
 2: <!DOCTYPE html
 3:       PUBLIC "-//W3C//DTD XHTML 1.0 Transitional//EN"
 4:       "http://www.w3.org/TR/xhtml1/DTD/xhtml1-transitional.dtd">
 5: <html xmlns="http://www.w3.org/1999/xhtml" xml:lang="en" lang="en">
 6: <head><title> ex04-09.htm </title></head>
 7: <style>
 8:   .txtSt {font-family:arial;font-size:18pt;font-weight:bold}
 9:   .butSt{font-family:arial;font-size:12pt;color:#008800;
10: background-color:#ffcccc;width:160px;height:26px;font-weight:bold}
11: </style>
12: <body style="background:#000088;color:#ffff00;text-align:center">
13:
14: <div class="txtSt">
15:     Creating Simple Buttons For<br />
16:     Windows Media Player<br /><br />
```

```
17: <object
18:   classid="CLSID:22D6F312-B0F6-11D0-94AB-0080C74C7E95"
19:   type="application/x-oleobject"
20:   id="MediaPlayer1" width="320" height="240">
21: >
22:   <param name="FileName"        value="dropxx1.mpg">
23:   <param name="ShowControls"  value="false">
24:   <param name="ShowStatusBar" value="true">
25: </object><br /><br />
26:
27: <input type="button" value="Play" class="butSt"
28:   onclick="document.MediaPlayer1.Play();" name="Play" >
29: <input type="button" value="Stop" class="butSt"
30:   onclick="document.MediaPlayer1.Stop();"name="Stop" >
31: </div>
32: </body>
33: </html>
```

In fact, this example page is a modification of ex04-07.htm. First, we have added a new CSS style in line 9 called butSt. This style is used to format the "Play" and "Stop" buttons. After the usual WMP object inclusion in lines 17–20, some parameter elements <param> are used to change the properties of WMP. Line 22 assigns the video file dropxx1.mpg to be played back by the player. The statement in line 23

```
<param name="ShowControls" value="false">
```

is used to turn off all the control buttons that come with WMP. Line 24 turns on the status bar of WMP so that the button status can be shown on the screen.

After the <object> element, two buttons are defined. The first button is called "Play" which can be used to play back a multimedia file. The definition of this button is defined in lines 27–28:

```
<input type="button" value="Play" class="butSt"
  onclick="document.MediaPlayer1.Play();" name="Play" >
```

Consider the first line of this input element. The <input> and type="button" define a push button on the screen. This push button has a display value or name called "Play." The display format of this button is specified by the CSS style butSt. The second line of this statement states that when the button is pressed, the function

```
document.MediaPlayer1.Play()
```

is activated. Since MediaPlayer1 is the identity of WMP (see line 20), the keyword document.MediaPlayer1 technically identifies WMP. Finally, calling the Play() method of MediaPlayer1 ultimately activates the playback function of the player. Similarly, calling the method Stop() in line 30 will stop the playback. A screen shot of this example is shown in Fig. 4.12.

In addition to the functions (or methods) Play() and Stop(), the WMP object also contains more than 100 properties that you can use for your applications. In the following example, we are going to show you how to turn the original control buttons of WMP on or off. This can be done via the properties of the WMP object. Consider the page below:

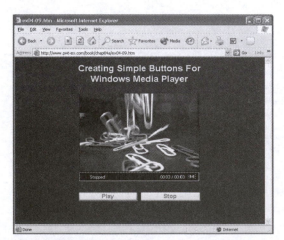

Figure 4.12 Creating buttons

Example: ex04-10.htm - Changing Properties Of Windows Media Player

```
 1: <?xml version="1.0" encoding="UTF-8"?>
 2: <!DOCTYPE html
 3:       PUBLIC "-//W3C//DTD XHTML 1.0 Transitional//EN"
 4:       "http://www.w3.org/TR/xhtml1/DTD/xhtml1-transitional.dtd">
 5: <html xmlns="http://www.w3.org/1999/xhtml" xml:lang="en" lang="en">
 6: <head><title>ex04-10.htm </title></head>
 7: <style>
 8:  .txtSt {font-family:arial;font-size:18pt;font-weight:bold}
 9:  .butSt{font-family:arial;font-size:12pt;color:#008800;
10:  background-color:#ffcccc;width:160px;height:26px;font-weight:bold}
11: </style>
12: <body style="background:#000088;color:#ffff00;text-align:center">
13:
14: <div class="txtSt">
15:     Creating Simple Buttons For<br />
16:     Windows Media Player<br /><br />
17: <object
18:   classid="CLSID:22D6F312-B0F6-11D0-94AB-0080C74C7E95"
19:   type="application/x-oleobject"
20:   id="MediaPlayer1" width="320" height="240">
21: >
22:   <param name="FileName" value="carxx2.mpg">
23:   <param name="ShowControls" value="0">
24:
25: </object><br /><br />
26:
27: <input name="Play" type="button" value="Play" class="butSt"
28:     onclick="document.MediaPlayer1.Play();">
29: <input name="Stop" type="button" value="Stop" class="butSt"
30:     onclick="document.MediaPlayer1.Stop()"> <br />
31:
32: <input name="showBut" type="button" value="Show Controls" class="butSt"
33:     onclick="document.MediaPlayer1.ShowControls = true">
34: <input name="hide" type="button" value="Hide Controls" class="butSt"
35:     onclick="document.MediaPlayer1.ShowControls = false">
36: </div>
37: </body>
38: </html>
```

This page is a modification of ex04-09.htm. Two more buttons are added along with the "Play" and "Stop." They are "Show Controls" and "Hide Controls." When the "Show Controls" button is pressed, the controls of WMP are displayed; the "Hide Controls" button hides the controls of WMP. Unlike "Play" and "Stop," the controls are activated by the following property of the WMP object (see line 33):

```
document.MediaPlayer1.ShowControls = true
```

The MediaPlayer1 keyword identifies the WMP application. When the value of the property ShowControls is set to true, the original controls of WMP will be displayed. If the value of the property is set to false, all buttons and the slide bar will be hidden from the users.

Some screen shots of this example are shown in Figs 4.13 and 4.14.

Figure 4.13 ex04-10.htm

Figure 4.14 Hiding the controls

Now you have seen some of the sound, music, and movie formats used on the Web. In fact, WMP supports a large number of media formats. An interesting one will be introduced in the next section.

4.3.4   The Windows Media Video (WMV) format

To see how many multimedia types are supported in WMP is easy. For example, you can fire up WMP and go to Tools | Options to open the "Options" window. From this window, click on the "File Types" menu, and you will see Fig. 4.15. For some earlier versions of WMP, the file type may be called "Formats."

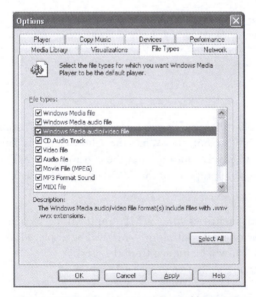

Figure 4.15 File types supported by WMP

The window contains all media file types supported by WMP. There are 12 categories which support more than 30 file extensions. Among them, there is an interesting one called "Windows Media audio/video file" (i.e., item 3). If you click on this one, you will get following description:

```
"The Windows Media audio/video file format(s) include
    files with .wmv and .wmx extensions"
```

At the time of writing, this wmv file format is formally known as "Windows Media 8 Video" file format. Why is this interesting? Well, take a look at the comparison on file sizes in Table 4.2.

Table 4.2 Movie types and size comparison

Movie types	Size	Movie types	Size	Movie types	Size
carxx2.avi	9,581 K	dropxx2.avi	7,279K	robotxx2.avi	20,758 K
carxx2.mov	1,030 K	dropxx2.mov	1,091K	robotxx2.mov	2,116 K
carxx2.mpg	421 K	dropxx2.mpg	503 K	robotxx2.mpg	835 K
carxx2.wmv	97 K	dropxx2.wmv	121 K	robotxx2.wmv	213 K

From this table, you can see that the file size of a wmv movie is about 1% of the avi counterpart. This format, in general, is less than 25% of MPEG-1 VCD format (mpg). For this size, Microsoft claims that quality video and movie can be played live on the Web with very low bandwidth connections.

The next question would be: how can we convert existing movie format to the wmv file format? To answer this question, Microsoft provides software called "Windows Media Encoder" (WME) available from the download center of www.microsoft.com.

After downloading and installing the WME, you can activate it to convert the existing file format into this wmv video type. As a simple example, let's consider how to convert an avi movie carxx2.avi into carxx2.wmv.

First, activate the WME software and click on the first option "to convert a file using the New Session Wizard" (see Fig. 4.16). You will see the "New Session Wizard" window as illustrated in Fig. 4.17.

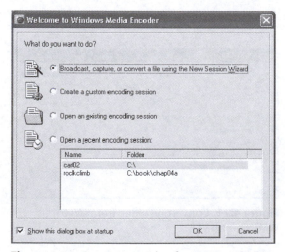

Figure 4.16 Converting video from AVI to WMV Format I

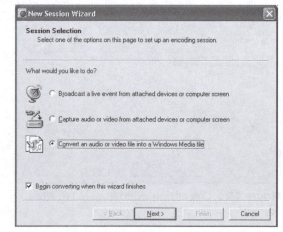

Figure 4.17 Converting video from AVI to WMV Format II

When you pick the third choice, "Convert an audio or video file into a Windows Media file," and press the Next button, you will see Fig. 4.18. From this window, you can browser the `avi` file to be converted. In this case the input file is carxx2.avi and the output file is carxx2.wmv. Now select the "File will stream from a Web server or play directly on a computer" option (see Fig. 4.19).

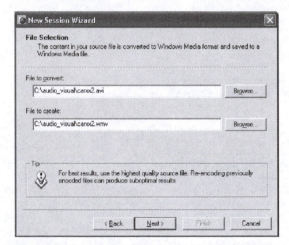

Figure 4.18 Converting video from AVI to WMP Format III

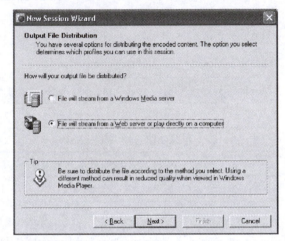

Figure 4.19 Converting video from AVI to WMV Format IV

From Fig. 4.19, select the profile you want to use. For this simple case, we will select the profile "WM8 Video for DSL/Cable Delivery (250KBps, 320x240, 30fps)" as illustrated in Fig. 4.20. Now, you can keep pressing the Next button until you reach Fig. 4.21.

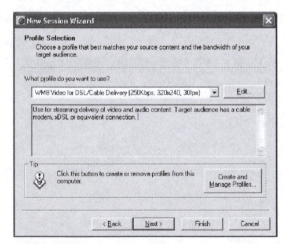

Figure 4.20 Converting video from AVI to WMV Format V

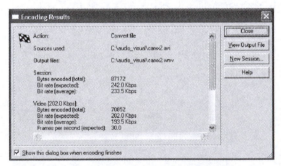

Figure 4.21 Converting video from AVI to WMV Format VI

When you press the OK button as shown in Fig. 4.21, you will see a big window where the conversion of the movie format is performed quite automatically (see Fig. 4.22). Note that the conversion will include any sound track within the original `avi` file.

As you can see from Fig. 4.22, the left window contains the input `avi` movie and the other contains the output `wmv` movie format. Now, you should have the new movie file carxx2.wmv in the directory specified in Fig. 4.18. You can play the video via the View Output button of the encoder. In this case, WMP will play back carxx2.wmv as demonstrated in Fig. 4.23.

Figure 4.22 Converting video from AVI to WMV Format 8

Figure 4.23 Playback of the video carxx2.wmv

In fact, the capability of the media encoder is more than just converting existing movie formats to `wmv`. If you have a capturing device installed on your system, such as a Webcam or a camera with a capture card, you can also use the encoder to capture the video. In this case, the video capture and conversion to `wmv` format will be performed at the same time. The encoder can use the installed capture device automatically. For example, on our system it can use an installed camera or a Web camera. The encoder uses the camera to capture live video in `wmv` format. A screen shot of the capturing is illustrated in Fig. 4.24.

In this case, the left window contains the video from the capture device and the right window contains the video output in `wmv` format. You can use ex04-10.htm to play back this captured movie robotxx2.wmv as in Fig. 4.25.

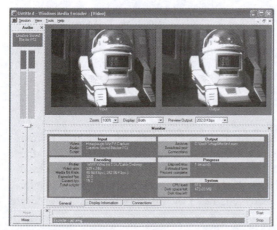

Figure 4.24 Output live video in Microsoft WMV format

Figure 4.25 Playback using WMP

Embedding WMP or ActiveX controls into Web pages is handy when you are using Microsoft systems with browsers supporting ActiveX. For other systems or browsers, another technology called "plugins" is widely used and accepted.

4.4   Using plugins for multimedia applications

4.4.1   What are plugins?

Roughly speaking, plugins (or plug-ins) are small pieces of software which can be used to enhance the capability of a browser. Plugins were created by Netscape in the early days of Web browsing to expand the functionalities of the NS. Sometimes people refer to plugins as Netscape Plugins (NS Plugins). Usually they are Dynamic Linking Library (DLL) files located in the "plugins" directory of the Netscape family of browsers. When compared to ActiveX embedding, they are similar but also have some differences. They are similar in the sense that you can use a plugin to display a video just as well as you can use an ActiveX control.

One of the big differences between ActiveX and plugins is that ActiveX controls work with programs. The primary goal of ActiveX is to distribute small programs to add some sort of functionality to the Web page. Because of that, ActiveX programs have a life apart from the Web page or browser. Also, you may need to identify the ActiveX by CLSID. On the other hand, plugins are designed to integrate more with browsers and work with data that a browser cannot handle. Once installed, you can use plugins without worrying about the CLSID value. Plugins are widely supported by all major browsers such as IE, NS, and Opera. Even WMP itself can be used as plugin software. Some other popular NS plugins are:

> ***Apple QuickTime***: This plugin lets you experience multimedia applications such as QuickTime animation, music, MIDI, audio, video, and virtual reality (VR) panoramas and objects directly in a Web page. Available for Windows 95 or later, and MacOS 8.1 or later.

> ***Adobe Acrobat Reader***: A reliable, efficient, and effective way to share information electronically. Available for LINUX, Windows 95 or later, MacOS8.1 or later, and UNIX.

> ***Macromedia Flash Player***: This lets you experience animation and entertainment on the Web and is a popular Web application for vector graphics, animation, Flash Showcase, and examples. Available for LINUX, Windows 95 or later, MacOS 8.1 or later, and UNIX versions.

> ***Shockwave by Macromedia***: This lets you experience quality interactive games, multimedia, graphics, and streaming audio on the Web. Available for Windows 95 or later, MacOS 8.1 or later.

> ***RealPlayer by RealNetworks***: This lets you play back streaming audio, music, video, animations, and multimedia presentations on the Web. Available for LINUX, Windows 95 or later, Mac OS, and UNIX versions.

These plugins can be found and downloaded from Netscape's official site (www.netscape.com). For our multimedia purposes, we only consider the following plugins:

Windows Media Player Plugin – wmpplugin.exe

Apple QuickTime – QuickTimeInstaller.exe

The WMP Plugin can be downloaded from Microsoft's official site. Readers may notice that we keep referencing the official sites of a particular Web product or service rather than providing the absolute URL address. One reason is that, in our experience, the URL address of a product changes all the time. For example, by the time you read this some of the Web sites hosting a particular product or service may have changed. Therefore, the official site is provided for reference. Users can use the search engine of the official site to search or locate the Web products or services required.

To install the plugins is simple, all you have to do is to download them from the site and run the program. In most cases, the installation program will place the necessary `.dll` files into the appropriate plugin directory. For example, if you run the program QuickTimeInstaller.exe, you will have a QuickTime player as a stand-alone program together with the QuickTime plugins. The QuickTime player and plugins support the popular media file formats given in Table 4.3.

Table 4.3 QuickTime plugins

Features	Description	File extensions	MIME type

Video	Video only and video with audio file formats	`mov` – QuickTime movie
		`avi` – Video for Windows
		`mpg` or `mpeg` – MPEG movie
			`video/quicktime`
			`video/avi`
			`video/mpeg, video/x-mpeg`

Audio	Audio-only file formats	`wav` – WAVE audio file
		`mid` – MIDI file
		`mp3` – MPEG layer 3
			`audio/wav` or `audio/x-wav`
			`audio/mid, audio/midi`
			`audio/mp3, audio/x-mp3`

The file extensions are associated with the media format and handled by the QuickTime plugins. In many cases, the QuickTime plugins will override the original system settings. This means that some of the audio/video files originally played by, say, WMP will be handled by the QuickTime plugin player after installation. For example, if you run the ex04-02.htm page with NS6.x, you will see the QuickTime plugin embedded in the browser as illustrated in Figs 4.26a and 4.26b.

Figure 4.26a Using Quicktime plugin I

Figure 4.26b Using Quicktime plugin II

One of the advantages of using plugins is that you no longer need the `classid` value to identify the program as in ActiveX. When you activate plugins with anchor `<a>`, the plugin software or media player will be embedded into the browser. Normally, the player will appear on a separate page as illustrated in Fig. 4.26b.

Now you have a plugin media player (QuickTime) up and running on your system. To fully embed this player and many others such as WMP and RealTime player into a Web page, you need a more general embedding element. This element is called `<embed>`. It is a non-standard but widely supported element to embed multimedia applications into a Web page.

4.4.2 The embed element `<embed>`

As we mentioned earlier, the embed element `<embed>` is not a W3C recommendation to embed an object. However, this element is very popular among the Web community. In particular, from simple music playback to watching an entire movie, it is used at all levels. Also, due to its popularity, almost all Web developers and major browsers support it strongly, including IE, NS, and Opera.

Let's consider an example to play back some audio in various forms. The example below will play three different kinds of music using QuickTime plugins. The first is an MPEG Layer 3 format known as MP3. The others are the `wav` and `midi` formats. As a feature of plugins, we have rescaled the plugin QuickTime player to be so small that it looks like a button. Although this is not the proper way to display the control buttons of a player, it does provide an immediate effect and the functionality of a control button. When the user presses one of the playback buttons, the associated music will be played instantly. The page code of the plugin is listed below:

```
Example: ex04-11.htm - Embedding Audio With <embed> Element

 1: <?xml version="1.0" encoding="UTF-8"?>
 2: <!DOCTYPE html
 3:     PUBLIC "-//W3C//DTD XHTML 1.0 Transitional//EN"
 4:     "http://www.w3.org/TR/xhtml1/DTD/xhtml1-transitional.dtd">
 5: <html xmlns="http://www.w3.org/1999/xhtml" xml:lang="en" lang="en">
 6: <head><title> ex04-11.htm </title></head>
 7: <style>
 8:  .txtSt {font-size:18pt;font-weight:bold;color:#ffff00;
 9:     background:#000088;font-family:arial}
10: </style>
11: <body class="txtSt"> <br />
12: <div align="center">
13:    Embedding Audio Within A Web Page<br /><br />
14:  <table style="font-size:14pt">
15:  <tr><td width="430">
16:    Using &lt;embed&gt; element, you can embed audio and/or
17:    music into your Web page. Also, by reducing the size of the media
18:    player, the player is similar to a button. </td></tr>
19:  <tr><td>  
20:      <embed src="dvd02.mp3" autostart="false" width="50" height="15"
21:       type="audio/x-mp3" /> -- MPEG Layer 3 (MP3) Music
22:  </td></tr><tr><td>  
23:      <embed src="dvd.wav" autostart="false" width="50" height="15"
24:       type="audio/wav" /> -- Wav Music
25:  </td></tr><tr><td>  
26:      <embed src="mu_mid.mid" autostart="false" width="50" height="15"
27:       type="audio/midi" /> -- Midi Music
28:  </td></tr>
29:  </table>
30:  </body>
31:  </html>
```

This page contains three sessions of music embedded in the Web page by the `<embed>`element. Lines 20–21 define the first session of music:

```
<embed src="dvd02.mp3" autostart="false" width="50" height="15"
     type="audio/x-mp3" /> -- MPEG Layer 3 (MP3) Music
```

This is a small piece of music in MP3 format. The playback will be controlled by plugin software specified by the content type audio/x-mp3. Since you only have QuickTime plugins installed at this moment, the playback will be performed by QuickTime. The `src` attribute specifies the file name storing the music. One interesting feature of this example is the dimension settings. By setting the dimensions as width="50" and `height="15"` the controls of the player will look like a button and therefore can be used as a button. The `autostart` attribute specifies that the music will not be played automatically. You must click the appropriate button to play the music.

The other two sessions of music are defined in a similar manner. A screen shot of this example running on NS6.2 is shown in Fig. 4.27.

Another interesting feature of this example is that, if you click on two pieces of music, the music will be played simultaneously. They are played independently so that it is just like mixing the music together.

The QuickTime player and its associated plugin software are famous for playing back QuickTime movies. There are a large number of movies and video in QuickTime (`.mov`) format which is supported by major film industries. Let's consider an example to play back QuickTime movies.

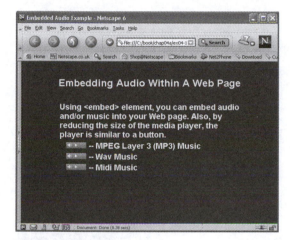

Figure 4.27 ex04-11.htm

Figure 4.28 QuickTime player

4.4.3 A page to play back movies using plugins

QuickTime movies are widely supported by the film and TV broadcasting industries. In order to get an idea of its popularity, you can activate the QuickTime player as illustrated in Fig. 4.28.

For multimedia applications, you can obviously employ this media player to play back video and/or movies on your system as a standalone program. On the other hand, you can embed the video and/or movies into a Web page using the <embed> element. Consider the following example:

```
Example: ex04-12.htm – PlayBack Movies Using Plugins

 1: <?xml version="1.0" encoding="UTF-8"?>
 2: <!DOCTYPE html
 3:      PUBLIC "-//W3C//DTD XHTML 1.0 Transitional//EN"
 4:      "http://www.w3.org/TR/xhtml1/DTD/xhtml1-transitional.dtd">
 5: <html xmlns="http://www.w3.org/1999/xhtml" xml:lang="en" lang="en">
 6: <head><title> ex04-12.htm </title></head>
 7: <style>
 8: .txtSt {font-size:18pt;font-weight:bold;color:#ffff00;
 9:      background:#000088;font-family:arial}
10: </style>
11: <body class="txtSt"> <br />
12: <div align="center">
13:     Embedding Movies Within A Web Page<br />
14:     Using &lt;embed&gt; And Plugins<br /><br />
15: <table style="font-size:14pt;text-align:center" >
16: <tr><td>
```

```
17:          <embed src="dropxx1.mov" autostart="false" width="340" height="270"
18:            type="video/quicktime" /><br />QuickTime Movie (dropxx1.mov)
19:     </td><td>  
20:          <embed src="robotxx2.mpg" autostart="false" width="340" height="270"
21:            type="video/mpeg" /><br />MPEG Movie (robotxx2.mpg)
22:     </td></tr>
23:     </table>
24:     </body>
25:     </html>
```

This is a page to play back some movies supported by the QuickTime plugins. The first movie is in QuickTime format with file extension .mov. This browser identifies the movie by the MIME type

    video/quicktime

and activates the proper plugin accordingly. The src attribute and dimension settings are very similar to the example ex04-10.htm. A screen shot of this example is shown in Fig. 4.29.

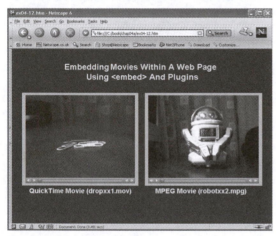

Figure 4.29 ex04-12.htm

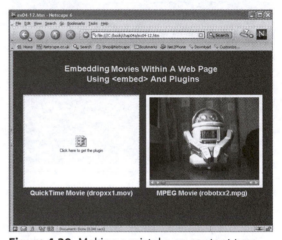

Figure 4.30 Making a mistake on content type

If you have made a mistake about the type, the page will not work properly. For example, suppose you have made a mistake in line 18 as follows:

    videa/quicktime – Spelling mistake

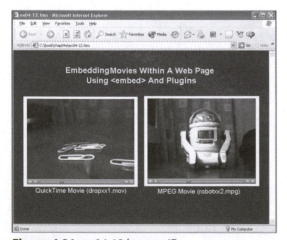

Figure 4.31 ex04-12.htm on IE

The browser can no longer recognize the type and will try to get the plugin software from the Internet. A screen shot of this situation is demonstrated in Fig. 4.30.

Since IE also supports plugins and the <embed> element, this example will run on IE without any modification. A screen shot of this example on IE is shown in Fig. 4.31.

By using the QuickTime plugin on IE, QuickTime movie (.mov) can be played on the IE family of browsers. Now, you have a system where both IE and NS can play back QuickTime movies. However, in normal circumstances, the QuickTime plugin or player cannot play back Windows Media video and/or movie format. The next question is: how can we play back Windows Media formats or wmv movies on an NS browser?

In order to play back the Windows Media Video (WMV) file on the NS family of browsers, the WMP plugin is needed. The plugin software is called, again,

Windows Media Player Plugin – wmpplugin.exe

and can be downloaded from Microsoft's official site. Once this program is run and installed, you are ready to use WMP as the plugin. The MIME type of WMP is identified by

```
application/x-mplayer2
```

By using WMP as the plugin, the Windows Media Video (wmv) file can be played on the NS family of browsers. Consider the following example:

```
Example: ex04-13.htm - Using WMP As Plugin

 1: <?xml version="1.0" encoding="UTF-8"?>
 2: <!DOCTYPE html
 3:      PUBLIC "-//W3C//DTD XHTML 1.0 Transitional//EN"
 4:      "http://www.w3.org/TR/xhtml1/DTD/xhtml1-transitional.dtd">
 5: <html xmlns="http://www.w3.org/1999/xhtml" xml:lang="en" lang="en">
 6: <head><title> ex04-13.htm </title></head>
 7: <style>
 8:  .txtSt {font-size:18pt;font-weight:bold;color:#ffff00;
 9:     background:#000088;font-family:arial}
10: </style>
11: <body class="txtSt">
12:  <div align="center">
13:     Using Windows Media Player As Plugin<br /><br />
14:
15:    <embed type="application/x-mplayer2"
16:       src="dropxx1.wmv"
17:       name="MediaPlayer2"
18:       width="300"
19:       height="270"
20:      autoStart="true"
21:       showControls="true">
22:    </embed>
23:
24: </body>
25: </html>
```

Line 15 is to identify WMP by the content type "application/x-mplayer2." The `src` attribute specifies the data source which in this case is a Windows media file called "dropxx1.wmv." After the name and dimension of the embedded object, the following two attributes are defined as true:

```
autoStart = "true "
showControls = "true"
```

The first attribute will start the playback once the statement is executed; the second is to show all the control buttons of the player. This example will run on IE and NS4.x and NS6.x. A screen shot on NS6.2 is shown in Fig. 4.32.

Figure 4.32 ex04-13.htm on NS6.2

4.4.4 Cross-browser applications with plugins

Now, you have two plugins on your system: QuickTime supports mov movie and WMP supports the wmv format. They both support others too! This may create a slightly confusing situation, in particular for beginners who have modest experience of multimedia. Which media player is used to play back what is not clear. Even more confusing is the situation that some of the mov files can be played back using WMP and some cannot.

One of the best ways to explain the situation is by example. Consider the following example which can activate WMP to play back dropxx1.wmv video. Both the type and the file extension are pointing to the right identity:

```
<embed type="application/x-mplayer2"
  src="dropxx1.wmv"
      name="MediaPlayer2"
      width="350"
      height="270"
  autoStart="true"
      showControls="true">
>
</embed>
```

In fact, this example is the main part of ex04-13.htm. If you change the movie file to dropxx1.mov and call the new example ex04-14.htm, you have a QuickTime movie. The example turns out to be:

```
Example: ex04-14.htm - Cross Browser Applications I

 1: <?xml version="1.0" encoding="UTF-8"?>
 2: <!DOCTYPE html
 3:     PUBLIC "-//W3C//DTD XHTML 1.0 Transitional//EN"
 4:     "http://www.w3.org/TR/xhtml1/DTD/xhtml1-transitional.dtd">
 5: <html xmlns="http://www.w3.org/1999/xhtml" xml:lang="en" lang="en">
 6: <head><title>ex04-14.htm</title></head>
 7: <style>
 8:   .txtSt {font-family:arial;font-size:18pt;font-weight:bold}
 9:   .butSt{font-family:arial;font-size:12pt;color:#008800;
10:   background-color:#ffcccc;width:160px;height:26px;font-weight:bold}
11: </style>
12: <body style="background:#000088;color:#ffff00;text-align:center">
13: <div class="txtSt"> <br />
14: Cross Browser Applications with Plugin I<br /><br />
15:
16:    <embed type="application/x-mplayer2"
17:        src="dropxx1.mov"
18:        name="MediaPlayer2"
19:        width="350"
20:        height="270"
21:      autoStart="true"
22:        showControls="true"
23:      >
24:    </embed>
25:
26: </div>
27: </body>
28: </html>
```

With both these plugins, you may find some interesting results as discussed below.

The IE6.x browser will activate the QuickTime player to play back the movie dropxx1.mov as illustrated in Fig. 4.33a. The NS6.2 browser activates WMP to play the movie instead (see Fig. 4.33b).

Figure 4.33a ex04-14.htm on IE6.2

Figure 4.33b ex04-14.htm on NS6.2

The reason is that IE will interpret the file extension specified in line 17 and therefore identify the QuickTime player for the playback. The NS browser, on the other hand, identifies the MIME type first and ultimately activates WMP instead. Also, the QuickTime movie in this example, dropxx1.mov, can be played by WMP so that the movie shows up on the screen correctly. If you use a QuickTime movie (.mov) that cannot be played by WMP, like the ones you download from the Internet, the IE browser will play it properly. This is because IE interprets the file extension first. The NS browser, in this case, will not play back at all since the MIME type is wrong.

In the following example, we consider another situation when IE and NS are used to play back an MPEG movie. First, the statements in lines 16–24 of ex04-14.htm are modified as

```
<embed type="application/x-mplayer2"
  src="robotxx2.mpg"
      name="MediaPlayer2"
      width="350"
      height="270"
  autoStart="true"
      showControls="true"
  >
  </embed>
```

This new example is called ex04-15.htm. For comparison, some screen shots in IE and NS of this example are shown in Figs 4.34a and 4.34b.

Since the QuickTime plugin has been installed on the system, IE will activate it to handle and play back the MPEG movie via the file extension. This arrangement will override the MIME type specification. NS, on the other hand, follows the instruction of the MIME type and uses WMP for the playback. You may ask: how can we employ WMP within IE for the playback?

Figure 4.34a ex04-15.htm on IE   **Figure 4.34b** ex04-15.htm on NS

Basically, there are two solutions. As we mentioned earlier, the QuickTime plugin has altered the system registry so that all MPEG files with mpg extension will be handled by QuickTime. One solution is to change the system registry. Another quick solution is to rename the movie file robotxx2.mpg as something that cannot be recognized by the system or IE. For example, you can modify the code fragment above as

```
<embed type="application/x-mplayer2"
  src="robotxx2mpg"
       name="MediaPlayer2"
       width="350"
       height="270"
  autoStart="true"
       showControls="true"
 >
 </embed>
```

and call this example as ex04-16.htm. Note that the source file is robotxx2mpg without any file extension. This will force the IE browser to employ the player specified in the MIME type attribute.

When talking about multimedia applications across browsers and platforms, we must say that Java is a strong competitor at every level. For example, if you want to develop a multimedia application that can run on Windows, UNIX/LINUX, and others, one of your best bets would be to use the Java Media Player and Java Media Framework (JMF).

4.5   Using the Java Media Framework (JMF) and Player

4.5.1   Installing and using JMF

In addition to the Java package J2SDK, JMF is an optional software package from Sun Microsystems dedicated to multimedia applications. The package enables audio, video, and other time-based media to be added to Java applications and applets. JMF is a powerful package containing a large number of functions such as playback, capture and stream video, or movie broadcasting.

In addition to Java, this package greatly enhances the multimedia capability of browsers across different platforms. JMF is a powerful toolkit for Web developers to design scalable multimedia applications. Basically, there are three versions of JMF:

- jmf-2.1_1a-alljava.zip – A cross-platform JMF
- jmf-2.1_1a-win.exe – The JMF Performance Pack for Windows
- jmf-2.1_1a-solaris.bin – The JMF Performance Pack for Solaris SPARC

All three packages can be downloaded from the official site of Sun Microsystems (java.sun.com or java.sun.com/products/java-media/jmf/index.html).

The cross-platform version was written entirely using the Java programming language and is designed for use on Java-capable machines. The Performance Pack for Windows is a JMF version optimized for the Windows systems. The Solaris Performance Pack is designed to run on and is optimized for the Solaris platform.

If you are using Windows, it is recommended that you download and install the Windows version. The executable program jmf-2.1_1a-win.exe is an "InstallShield" executable. That means that by double clicking on this program, JMF will be installed easily. Also, the program detects whether or not a default browser is installed and then installs JMF for its use.

If you are installing the generic version jmf-2.1_1a.zip, you may need to run the appropriate zip command such as `winzip` or `unzip` to extract JMF onto your system and directory. The JMF of this version was written using Java `bytecode` ready for Java-enabled machines.

If you install JMF yourself, you may need to set up the system variable (or environment variable) so that the JMF classes are available through the `CLASSPATH` variable. For example, if you are using a UNIX/LINUX machine, you may need to set up the environment using the following command:

```
setenv JMFHOME /home/someuser/JMF2.1.1
setenv CLASSPATH $JMFHOME/lib/jmf.jar:.:${CLASSPATH}
```

For Windows systems, you may need to set the following:

```
set JMFHOME=C:\JMF2.1.1
set CLASSPATH=%JMFHOME%\lib\jmf.jar;.;%CLASSPATH%
```

If you are using Windows, the "set" command inside a DOS window should display all environment variables on your machine. You should examine the `CLASSPATH` settings to make sure that JMF is set up correctly. Alternatively, the official site of Sun Microsystems (www.java.com) contains a utility or a page to test the JMF installation and configuration for your machine.

Bundled with JMF is a program called Java Media Studio (`JMStudio`). At a minimum level, this program can be used as a media player to play back a large number of sound, music, and movie files. It is also a good tool to convert movie formats from one form to another.

For example, you can follow the instructions below to convert an `avi` video to QuickTime movie `mov` format.

Step 1: Activate the `JMStudio` as in Fig. 4.35.
Step 2: Go to the menu File | Open File and load the `avi` file, e.g., carxx1.avi, onto the studio (Fig. 4.36).

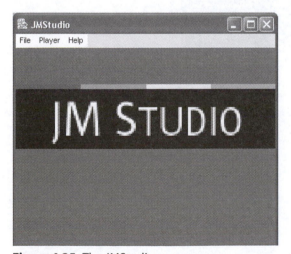

Figure 4.35 The JMStudio program

Figure 4.36 Open the AVI file

Step 3: Go to the menu File | Export to activate the "Export" window (Fig. 4.37). From the format field, select the QuickTime (mov) format. Press the Save button.

Step 4: From the "Save As" window as in Fig. 4.38, type in the QuickTime movie name (e.g., carxx2.mov).

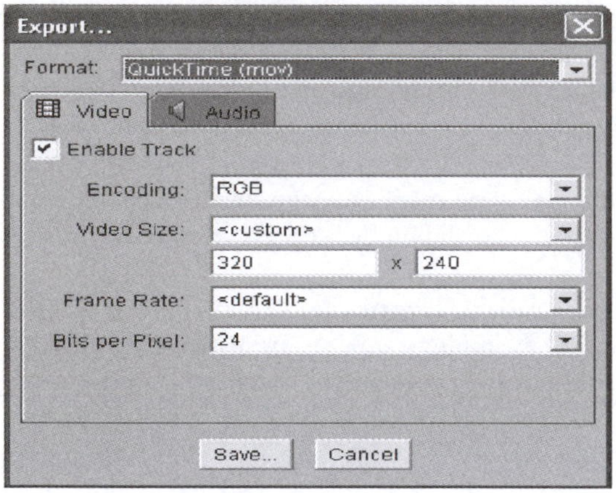

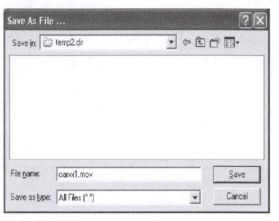

Figure 4.37 The "Export" window

Figure 4.38 Save the QuickTime movie carxx2.mov

That's it. The QuickTime movie should be saved inside the directory that you have chosen. To see the QuickTime movie carxx2.mov, you can double click on the file and activate the QuickTime player for the playback. A screenshot of the playback is shown in Fig. 4.39.

Figure 4.39 Playback the QuickTime movie

This JMStudio program is free and is an example from the JMF package. The source code of this program is called JMStudio.java and can be compiled and launched using the following commands:

```
javac JMStudio.java
java JMStudio
```

As we mentioned in the previous chapter, the command javac in the first line is used to compile a Java program. The result in this case is a program JMStudio.class. The second command java is used to launch the application (see Fig. 4.35).

Now you have some experience of using JMF and its associated player. JMF is a powerful tool for handling multimedia applications. It would be interesting if we were to embed the player into a Web page and use it for the Web community.

4.5.2   Play back sound and movies using JMF

We mentioned earlier that the JMF package was written by the Java language. Whether we use it as a stand-alone programming language or as a language on the Web, Java is a powerful tool for developing professional applications. Even in a modest form, Java supports various multimedia formats. Consider the following Java program:

```
Example: SimpleSound.java - The Java Program To Play A Simple Audio Clip

 1: import java.applet.*;
 2: import java.awt.*;
 3: import javax.swing.*;
 4:
 5: public class SimpleSound extends JApplet
 6: {
 7:     private AudioClip sound;
 8:     public void init()
 9:     {
10:         sound = getAudioClip( getDocumentBase(), "dvd02.wav" );
11:         sound.play();
12:     }
13: }
```

This is a very simple Java program to play back sound files. The program will generate a class bytecode which can be used on a Web page. The `javax.swing` package in line 3 contains an object called `AudioClip`. This object is used to define a variable `sound` in line 7. The main part of this program contains two statements only:

```
sound = getAudioClip( getDocumentBase(), "dvd02.wav" );
sound.play();
```

The first statement is to get the sound file dvd02.wav and assign it to the variable `sound`. Since the `sound` variable or object was generated by the object `AudioClip`, it contains all the properties and methods of `AudioClip`. A simple call to `sound.play()` would play back the sound file. One beauty of this example is that it will play back all sound files recognized by the Java language. You don't need to know the details and structure of the file itself.

To call this program, the following Web page is used:

```
Example: ex04-17.htm - Playback Simple Sound File Using Java Applet

 1: <?xml version="1.0" encoding="UTF-8"?>
 2: <!DOCTYPE html
 3:     PUBLIC "-//W3C//DTD XHTML 1.0 Transitional//EN"
 4:     "http://www.w3.org/TR/xhtml1/DTD/xhtml1-transitional.dtd">
 5: <html xmlns="http://www.w3.org/1999/xhtml" xml:lang="en" lang="en">
 6: <head><title> ex04-17.htm </title></head>
 7: <body>
 8: <applet code="SimpleSound.class" width="350" height="30">
 9: </applet>
10: </body>
11: </html>
```

This page uses a simple applet element `<applet>` to call the program SimpleSound.class and ultimately play back the sound file.

The Java program SimpleSound.java is a sloppy example and far from a professional standard. At a minimum level, a professional multimedia application should contain the following features:

- Play back sound file formats such as `wav`, `mid`, and `au`.
- Play back movie file formats such as `avi`, `mov`, and `mpg`.
- Contain standard controlling buttons such as Play, Stop, Forward, Backward, and a progress bar.
- Contain error detection code to handle some basic errors.

Fortunately, we don't need to develop a program of a multimedia player like this. The JMF package contains a large number of media player examples to help us. For example, the Java program SimplePlayerApplet.java from JMF is a functional media player available for immediate use. To use this program, you need to compile it using

```
javac SimplePlayerApplet.java
```

The result is a class ready to be used as an applet from a Web page. Consider the following page:

```
Example: ex04-18.htm - Embedding The JMF Player

 1: <?xml version="1.0" encoding="UTF-8"?>
 2: <!DOCTYPE html
 3:      PUBLIC "-//W3C//DTD XHTML 1.0 Transitional//EN"
 4:      "http://www.w3.org/TR/xhtml1/DTD/xhtml1-transitional.dtd">
 5: <html xmlns="http://www.w3.org/1999/xhtml" xml:lang="en" lang="en">
 6: <head><title> ex04-18.htm </title></head>
 7: <style>
 8:  .txtSt {font-family:arial;font-size:18pt;font-weight:bold}
 9:  .butSt{font-family:arial;font-size:12pt;color:#008800;
10:  background-color:#ffcccc;width:160px;height:26px;font-weight:bold}
11: </style>
12: <body style="background:#000088;color:#ffff00;text-align:center">
13: <div class="txtSt"> <br />
14:  Using The Java Media Player Applet <br />
15:  SimplePlayerApplet <br /><br />
16:
17: <applet code="SimplePlayerApplet.class"
18:      width="320"
19:      height="260"
20: >
21: <param name="file" value="dropxx1.avi" />
22: </applet>
23:
24: </div>
25: </body>
26: </html>
```

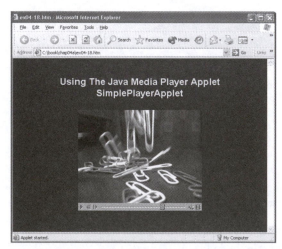

Figure 4.40 Embedding JMF Player (ex04-18.htm)

Also, this is a simple page to use the applet element to embed the SimplePlayerApplet.class in a Web page. The applet element <applet> in line 17 defines an area of dimension 320 × 260 for the player. The media file in this case is dropxx1.avi and is defined by the parameter element <param>. The Java program SimplePlayerApplet.java will get the file name from the <param> element and perform the multimedia playback. A screen shot of this example is shown in Fig. 4.40.

Putting the media file into the <param> element is a good move. In fact, you don't need to know the details of the Java program if you don't want to. Now, let's consider some examples to add more features to this media player without touching the Java code.

4.5.3   A page to select and play back movies

If you have a large number of movies, how would you deliver them on the Internet? One of the simplest and most effective methods is to display each movie as one button. When the user clicks one of the buttons, the corresponding movie will be played by the player. To develop this example, you can use the Java program SimplePlayerApplet.java in section 4.5.2 as a player.

The idea for this example is simple. Basically, one button for each movie is generated. When one of the buttons is clicked, the following statements similar to lines 17–22 of example ex04-18.htm are generated:

```
<applet code="SimplePlayerApplet.class"
   width="320"
   height="260"
>
<param name="file" value="dropxx1.avi" />
</applet>
```

If you substitute the media file dropxx1.avi in the `<param>` element with the movie of your choice, this applet code will activate the player to play back the movie you want.

Consider the page below:

Example: ex04-19.htm – A Page To Select and Play Back Movies

```
 1: <?xml version="1.0" encoding="UTF-8"?>
 2: <!DOCTYPE html
 3:      PUBLIC "-//W3C//DTD XHTML 1.0 Transitional//EN"
 4:      "http://www.w3.org/TR/xhtml1/DTD/xhtml1-transitional.dtd">
 5: <html xmlns="http://www.w3.org/1999/xhtml" xml:lang="en" lang="en">
 6: <head><title> ex04-19.htm </title></head>
 7: <style>
 8:  .txtSt {font-size:18pt;font-weight:bold;color:#ffff00;
 9:     background:#000088;font-family:arial}
10:  .butSt{font-family:arial;font-size:12pt;color:#008800;
11:  background-color:#ffcccc;width:160px;height:26px;font-weight:bold}
12: </style>
13:
14: <script>
15:  function show(ss)
16:  {
17:   llst='<applet code=SimplePlayerApplet width="320" height="270" >' +
18:    '<param name=file value="' + ss + '" /></applet> <br />' + ss
19:   document.getElementById('myId').innerHTML = llst
20:  }
21: </script>
22:
23: <body class="txtSt">
24: <div align="center">
25:    A Page To Select Movie<br /><br />
26:
27: <form name="myForm">
28:   <input type="button" value="robotxx2.avi" class="butSt"
29:       onclick="show('robotxx2.avi')" />
30:   <input type="button" value="dropxx1.mov" class="butSt"
31:       onclick="show('dropxx1.mov')" />
32: <input type="button" value="carxx2.mpg" class="butSt"
33:       onclick="show('carxx2.mpg')" />
34: </form>
35:
36: <div id="myId"></div>
37:
38: </body>
39: </html>
```

In this example, we want to play back three movies. They are robotxx2.avi, dropxx1.mov, and carxx2.mpg. Each movie is associated with one button defined in lines 28, 30, and 32. Consider the first button:

```
<input type="button" value="robotxx2.avi" class="butSt"
    onclick="show('robotxx2.avi')" />
```

This input element `<input>` with `type="button"` defines a button. This button has a display name called "robotxx2.avi" and a CSS style definition `butSt`. When this button is clicked, the function

```
show("robotxx2.avi")
```

is activated to play back the movie robotxx2.avi. The detail of this function is defined in lines 15–20:

```
function show(ss)
{
 llst='<applet code=SimplePlayerApplet width="320" height="270" >' +
  '<param name=file value="' + ss + '" /></applet> <br />' + ss
 document.getElementById('myId').innerHTML = llst
}
```

First, the movie file name robotxx2.avi is substituted into this function as variable `ss`. Inside this function, there is a string called `llst`. This string stores the details of the applet element `<applet>`. When the `ss` variable is used in the string `llst`, the entire string `llst` turns out to be:

```
<applet code="SimplePlayerApplet.class" width="320" height="270" >
<param name="file" value="robotxx2.avi" /></applet><br /> robotxx2.avi
```

This code will activate the `SimplePlayerApplet` player to play back the file robotxx2.avi. Also, the file name is displayed at the bottom at the same time. Here we have used the JavaScript or ECMAScript function to output the XHTML applet element `<applet>`. ECMAScript will be discussed further in Part II of this book. The statement in line 19

```
document.getElementById('myId').innerHTML = llst
```

outputs the XHTML string `llst` to the location identified by the attribute `id="myId"` (see line 36). Note that the `innerHTML` property is not a W3C recommendation. It can be used to send an XHTML string to a particular location and is a popular technique among the Web community. A screen shot of this example is shown in Fig. 4.41.

Figure 4.41 Select a movie

Another way to make your selection and play your favorite movie is to use the XHTML select box.

4.5.4   Select and play back movie with a select box

A select box is a small text box with a down arrow on the right hand side. When a user clicks on the down arrow, the box will be extended and contain all the available options. The user can then make a selection among the options. To generate a select box containing three movies, the following XHTML code is used:

```
<form name="myForm">
  <select name="myMovie" class="butSt">
      <option value="robotxx2.avi">robotxx2.avi</option>
      <option value="dropxx1.mov">dropxx1.mov</option>
      <option value="carxx2.mpg"> carxx2.mpg</option>
  </select>
</form>
```

The three movies, robotxx2.avi, dropxx1.mov, and carxx2.mpg, will appear as options in the box. One of the reasons we put the form element `<form>` outside of the select box is that once a selection is made, this selection can be accessed by the command

```
myForm.myMovie.value
```

With all these at hand, you can develop the Web page as follows:

```
Example: ex04-20.htm - Select and Play Back Movies With Select Box

 1: <?xml version="1.0" encoding="UTF-8"?>
 2: <!DOCTYPE html
 3:       PUBLIC "-//W3C//DTD XHTML 1.0 Transitional//EN"
 4:       "http://www.w3.org/TR/xhtml1/DTD/xhtml1-transitional.dtd">
 5: <html xmlns="http://www.w3.org/1999/xhtml" xml:lang="en" lang="en">
 6: <head><title> ex04-20.htm </title></head>
 7: <style>
 8:  .txtSt {font-size:18pt;font-weight:bold;color:#ffff00;
 9:     background:#000088;font-family:arial}
10:  .butSt{font-family:arial;font-size:12pt;color:#008800;
11:  background-color:#ffcccc;width:160px;height:26px;font-weight:bold}
12: </style>
13: <script>
14: function show(ss)
15: {
16:  llst='<applet code=SimplePlayerApplet width="320" height="270" >' +
17:      '<param name=file value="' + ss + '" /></applet> <br />' + ss
18:  document.getElementById('myId').innerHTML = llst
19: }
20: </script>
21: <body class="txtSt">
22: <div align="center">
23:     Select and Playback Movie <br />
24:     With A Select Box<br /><br />
25:
26: <form name="myForm">
27:   <select name="myMovie" class="butSt">
28:      <option value="robotxx2.mpg">robotxx2.avi</option>
29:      <option value="dropxx1.mov">dropxx1.mov</option>
30:      <option value="carxx2.mpg">carxx2.mpg</option>
31:   </select>
32:   <input type="button" value="Go" class="butSt"
33:       onclick="show(myForm.myMovie.value)" />
34: </form>
35: <div id="myId"></div>
36: </body>
37: </html>
```

This page is a modification of example ex04-19.htm to accommodate a select box. It is defined in lines 27–31. To trigger the selection, a button is generated in lines 32–33. When this button is pressed, the selection value is stored in the property

```
myForm.myMovie.value
```

By putting this value into the function

```
show(myForm.myMovie.value)
```

the applet code defined in lines 14–19 would play back the movie you have selected. A screen shot of this example at work is shown in Fig. 4.42.

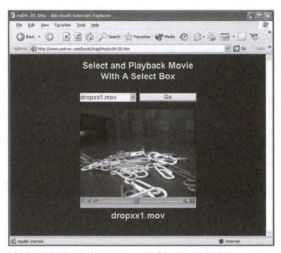

Figure 4.42 Select a movie from a select box

One interesting feature of JMF is the capability to deliver live video broadcasting, and this will be discussed next.

4.5.5 Broadcasting live video using JMF

Broadcasting live video means we want to send and receive video pictures in real time across a network or the Internet. One typical application of live video is video conferencing on the Web. Unlike a document, a picture, or a fixed length video, live video (or live stream) usually may not have a predefined duration. Downloading the entire stream before playing it, in many cases, would be impossible.

Traditional HTTP and FTP suites are based on the Transmission Control Protocol (TCP). It is a protocol designed for reliable data transmission. Among other things, when a packet is lost or corrupted, the protocol requests another transmission. This will guarantee reliable data transfer and maintain the integrity of documents, pictures, and files. Because of this and the overhead involved, TCP is not ideal for live media transmission.

Alternatively, the User Datagram Protocol (UDP) is widely used for stream media purposes. UDP is similar to TCP, is a transport protocol, and can be used for data transmission. The main difference is that UDP is not reliable. Packets or data are no longer guaranteed to reach their destination. In fact, there is no guarantee that packets or data will arrive in the order that they were transmitted. All these drawbacks are tolerable when we use it for video conferencing and transmission. Based on UDP, the Internet Engineering Task Force (IETF) has developed a protocol called the Real-Time Transport Protocol (RTP) which can be used for real-time data transmission.

JMF can use this RTP to transmit real-time data. Also, media players associated with JMF can receive the transmission via RTP.

As a simple example, let's consider a Java program provided by JMF. This program is called VideoTransmit.java and can be used to transmit live video data to a location. In order to transmit data in real time, usually three parameters are needed and they are the "Source Locator," "IP Address," and "Destination Port." The source locator is to identify the media content to send and can be any one of the following:

- A media file such as file://c:/book/chap04a/robotxx2.mov.
- A URL such as http://www.pwt-ex.com/dropxx2.mpg.
- A capture `datasource`, either "vfw://0" or "sunvideo://0/1/jpeg."

The IP address should be the usual IP address of the computer receiving the transmission. For our system, the address is 169.254.101.152. The port number can be any free port available. In this case, port 8080 is used in our example.

If you have a live camera such as a Webcam attached to your system, you can use this VideoTransmit.java program to transmit the live image to a location identified by the IP address and port. First, you need to compile it to `bytecode` using the command:

```
javac VideoTransmit.java
```

You need to install JMF properly to do that. If the compilation is successful, you will have the program VideoTransmit.class on your system. To activate the program and start the transmission, you can use

```
java VideoTransmit vfw://0 169.254.101.152 8080
```

This command starts capturing the live image from the Webcam (or any capturing device) and transmits it to the destination 169.254.101.152 via the port 8080. By default, the transmission will last only 60 seconds. You can, however, change the Java program to suit your needs. A screen shot of this command running on a DOS window is shown in Fig. 4.43.

Figure 4.43 Transmitting live video using RTP

In order to receive the broadcast, you need to activate the media player and listen to the IP address and port number with RTP. For our simple example, consider the page below:

```
Example: ex04-21.htm - Receiving Live Video Broadcasting

1: <?xml version="1.0" encoding="UTF-8"?>
2: <!DOCTYPE html
3:      PUBLIC "-//W3C//DTD XHTML 1.0 Transitional//EN"
4:      "http://www.w3.org/TR/xhtml1/DTD/xhtml1-transitional.dtd">
```

```
 5: <html xmlns="http://www.w3.org/1999/xhtml" xml:lang="en" lang="en">
 6: <head><title> ex04-21.htm </title></head>
 7: <style>
 8:   .txtSt {font-family:arial;font-size:18pt;font-weight:bold}
 9:   .butSt{font-family:arial;font-size:12pt;color:#008800;
10:   background-color:#ffcccc;width:160px;height:26px;font-weight:bold}
11: </style>
12: <body style="background:#000088;color:#ffff00;text-align:center">
13: <div class="txtSt"> <br />
14:   Receiving Live Video Broadcasting<br />
15:   Using RTP Protocol<br /><br />
16:
17: <applet code="SimplePlayerApplet.class"
18:    width="320"
19:    height="260"
20: >
21: <param name="file" value="rtp://169.254.101.152:8080/video" />
22: </applet>
23:
24: </div>
25: </body>
26: </html>
```

This is a simple page to activate one of the simple media players from JMF. The applet code activates the SimplePlayerApplet and plays back the media. The media content is specified by the parameter element <param> in line 21. Instead of providing the media file name to the program, we set up the RTP address for the value attribute. The rtp address used is

rtp://169.254.101.152:8080/video

Together with the IP address and port number, the content type is also used. A screen shot of the live transmission is shown in Fig. 4.44.

More information on RTP, live media broadcasting, and samples is available on the JMF sections of the official site java.sun.com.

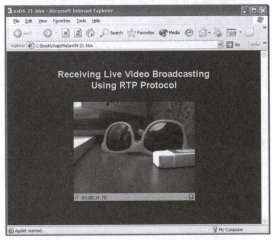

Figure 4.44 Receiving live video using RTP

5

XML and XSLT

5.1 An introduction to XML and XSLT

5.1.1 What is XML?

Extensible Markup Language (XML) is similar to XHTML and is used to develop documents or pages used on the World Wide Web. They both share the same structure and the main components of the language are elements. Unlike XHTML, which is designed for formatting and displaying a document, the main purpose of an XML page (or document) is to describe the data structure and relationships of the elements (XML elements) involved. Because of that, XML is more abstract, general, and more powerful in the sense that it is extensible. Extensible means XML has no predefined elements. In other words, you can create your own elements and attributes in an XML document. In fact, when you develop an XML page, you have no choice but to create your own elements and attributes. More interestingly, attributes can be reformulated by the relationship of child elements in a more general way.

A well-defined (or well-formed) XML document conforms to the following XML rules:

- Must begin with XML declaration, e.g., `<?xml version="1.0" encoding="iso-8859-1"?>`.
- Must have one unique root element, e.g., `<root>`.
- All start tags must match end tags, e.g., `<contents></contents>`.
- XML tags are case sensitive.
- All elements must be closed.
- All elements must be properly nested.
- All attribute values must be quoted, e.g., `<contents from="www.pwt-ex.com">`.
- XML entities must be used for special characters, e.g., `&lt;`, `&gt;`, ` `.

These rules are the same as those in XHTML mentioned in Chapter 1 since XHTML documents are technically XML pages. Consider the following example:

```
Example: ex05-01.xml - My First XML Page

1: <?xml version="1.0" encoding="iso-8859-1"?>
2: <message>
3:    <contents>My First XML Page</contents>
4:    <from>www.pwt-ex.com</from>
5: </message>
```

This is a simple XML page. The first line specifies the document as XML version 1.0 with character set `Latin-1/Western European`. Basically, this is the only requirement for a well-formed XML page. Some of you may notice that this line 1 is the same as all XHTML pages in this book. The reason is simple: all XHTML pages conform to the XML standard and they are all XML well-formed documents.

The rest of the page defines a message element `<message>`. This element contains two child elements, `<contents>` and `<from>`. The values of these two elements are also defined. Unlike XHTML, all white spaces in XML are recognized. As a result, this page describes a relationship of elements `<contents>`, `<from>`, and `<message>`. Lines 2–4 can also be formulated as

```
<message>
  <contents from="www.pwt-ex.com">My First XML Page</contents>
</message>
```

In this case, the `from` attribute in ex05-01.xml is considered as an attribute of `<contents>`. You can rewrite both `contents` and `from` as attributes in the `<message>` if you prefer. Also, all names of XML elements are user defined.

Since there is no predefined element in XML, we cannot expect an ordinary browser such as IE, NS, or Opera to display the page with formatting properties. For example, if you request the document ex05-01.xml by using

http://www.pwt-ex.com/book/chap05a/ex05-01.xml

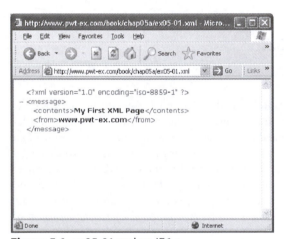

you will see Fig. 5.1 on your screen.

You may ask: if XML contains no formatting property or element, how can we display the page on the Web? Where are all those font-family, font-size, colors, images, and tables in XHTML?

The answer lies in the beauty of XML. Since the structure of XML is abstract but technically simple, XML pages can be transformed to other software or device languages relatively easy. In fact, XML has been used to create the Wireless Markup Language (WML) and display WML pages on your mobile phone. For our Web environment and Web application, we will consider how to transform XML pages into XHTML and one of the popular choices is to use XML Style Sheet Language transformation (XSLT).

Figure 5.1 ex05-01.xml on IE6.+

5.1.2   What is XSLT and how does it work?

One of the best ways to explain XSLT and to show you how it works is by example. The following is a simple XSLT example.

XHTML uses predefined elements, which can be displayed directly on a browser. The CSS for XHTML can be considered as a more structural way to organize the formatting layout so that reusability and structure are enhanced.

For XML, the style sheet is called XSL (XML Style Sheet). Since there is no predefined element in XML, traditional XHTML elements such as `<div>`, `<p>`, and `<table>` no longer have meanings. The role of XSL is more abstract and far more powerful than CSS. On the whole, XSL is a language or mechanism to describe how XML documents should be displayed.

One of the most important parts of XSL is the XSL transformation (XSLT), which can be used to transform an XML page into other formats. Consider the following example:

```
Example: ex05-02.xml - My First XML Page With XSLT

1: <?xml version="1.0"?>
2: <?xml-stylesheet type="text/xsl" href="ex05-02.xsl" ?>
3: <message>
4:   <contents>My First XML Page With XSLT</contents>
5:   <from>www.pwt-ex.com</from>
6: </message>
7:
```

If you compare this page with ex05-01.xml, you will find that the main different is in line 2. This line

```
<?xml-stylesheet type="text/xsl" href="ex05-02.xsl" ?>
```

defines a transformation method for the page. The transform is based on XSL with `text/xsl` type. The detailed XSL transformation and specifications are defined in the file ex05-02.xsl. The coding of this file is listed below:

```
Example: ex05-02.xsl – The XSLT Transformation File For ex05-02.xml

1: <?xml version="1.0" encoding="iso-8859-1"?>
2: <xsl:stylesheet version="1.0"
3:   xmlns:xsl="http://www.w3.org/1999/XSL/Transform">
4:
5: <xsl:template match="/">
6:
7:   <html xmlns="http://www.w3.org/1999/xhtml" xml:lang="en" lang="en">
8:   <head><title>My First XSLT Transform</title></head>
9:   <body style="background:#000088;color:#ffff00;font-family:arial;
10:               font-size:24pt;font-weight:bold;text-align:center">
11:   <div style="text-align:center"><br /><br />
12:     <xsl:value-of select="message/contents" /> <br /><br />
13:     <xsl:value-of select="message/from" /> <br />
14:   </div>
15: </body>
16: </html>
17:
18: </xsl:template>
19: </xsl:stylesheet>
```

Line 1 is the header for the XML page. This means that XSLT files are basically XML pages. Lines 2–3 define the header for XSLT. In this case, whoever calls this XML document will use this style sheet to transform an XML page.

Line 5 defines an XSL template. The attribute `match="/"` means that this template is used to transform the entire XML page. The actual template is defined in lines 7–16 and, in fact, is an XHTML document. The XSLT, in effect, will transform the calling document into an XHTML document and therefore can be displayed directly on a browser.

Inside the XHTML template, the interesting part is the XSL element (line 12)

```
<xsl:value-of select="message/contents" />
```

This element is to get the value of the original XML page. In this case, the value is the string under the root element `<message>` and the first child element `<contents>`. The value is "My First XML Page With XSLT" which is located at line 4 of ex05-01.xml.

When you request this XML page with

http://www.pwt-ex.com/book/chap05a/ex05-02.xml

you will see the transform in action as illustrated in Fig. 5.2. Before we continue to discuss XML and XSLT, let's consider some Document Type Definitions and schema used in XML.

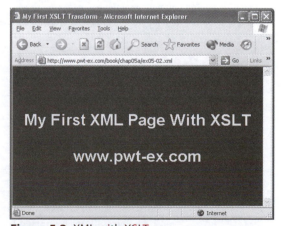

Figure 5.2 XML with XSLT

5.1.3   The Document Type Definition (DTD) used in XML

The purpose of a DTD is to define the legal building blocks of a markup language (ML). DTD is generally defined in the Standard Generalized Markup Language (SGML: ISO 8879) and used by all known MLs such as HTML, XHTML, and XML.

An XML document with correct XML syntax is said to be "Well-Formed." The document is characterized as "Valid" if it also conforms to the rules of a DTD. Usually, you declare your DTD within the DOCTYPE definition. The general DOCTYPE syntax is defined by

```
<!DOCTYPE root-element [element-declaration]>
```

This is the internal declaration of DOCTYPE. All elements used in the document should be declared inside the brackets. Consider the following example:

```
Example: ex05-03.xml - An XML Page With DTD

 1: <?xml version="1.0" encoding="iso-8859-1"?>
 2: <?xml-stylesheet type="text/xsl" href="ex05-02.xsl" ?>
 3: <!DOCTYPE
 4:   message
 5:   [
 6:     <!ELEMENT message (contents,from)>
 7:     <!ELEMENT contents (#PCDATA)>
 8:     <!ELEMENT from (#PCDATA)>
 9:   ]
10: >
11: <message>
12:    <contents>My First XML Page</contents>
13:    <from>www.pwt-ex.com</from>
14: </message>
```

Line 3 defines the declaration of the DOCTYPE. The root element of the page is also declared. Inside the element-declaration bracket (lines 6–8), three elements are defined. The first element is called `<message>` and contains two child elements, `<contents>` and `<from>`. The document type of the `<contents>` element is Parsed Character Data (PCDATA). Some frequently used building blocks or components of DTD are:

- Elements   –   The main components of both XML and XHTML.
- Tags   –   Used to mark up elements.
- Attributes –   Provide extra information about elements.
- Entities   –   Variables to define special text or characters. Some commonly used entities are:

Entity	Character
<	<
>	>
&	&
"	"
'	'
	Non-breaking-space

- PCDATA   –   The text found between the start tag and the end tag of an XML element. Elements and entities inside PCDATA will be expanded.
- CDATA   –   Text that will not be parsed by a parser.

The DTD defined in this way is called the internal DOCTYPE declaration due to the fact that all elements are declared inside the page. Alternatively, you can define the DTD as an external file. The general syntax to declare an external DOCTYPE is

```
<!DOCTYPE root-element SYSTEM "filename">
```

For example, you can define all elements in lines 6–8 of ex05-03.xml in a file called ex05-05.dtd. This file can be used by many XML pages with element `<message>` and subelements `<from>` and `<contents>` including ex05-04.xml below:

```
Example: ex05-04.xml – An XML Page Using DTDs

1: <?xml version="1.0" encoding="iso-8859-1"?>
2: <?xml-stylesheet type="text/xsl" href="ex05-02.xsl" ?>
3: <!DOCTYPE message SYSTEM "ex05-05.dtd">
4: <message>
5:    <contents>My First XML Page</contents>
6:    <from>www.pwt-ex.com</from>
7: </message>
```

By using DTD, your XML pages can have a format defined by you and describing each element of the document. Many organizations on the Web such as W3C offer software DTD validators to verify your page and issue validated certificates. W3C also offers logo(s) for validated pages (see www.w3.org). With DTD, other groups or people can interchange data with you.

```
Example: ex05-05.dtd – External DTDs For XML Pages

1:  <!ELEMENT message (contents,from)>
2:  <!ELEMENT contents (#PCDATA)>
3:  <!ELEMENT from (#PCDATA)>
```

While the DTD provides definitions for elements and attributes in XML pages, the developers recognize the following drawbacks:

- DTD is not written like XML.
- There is little or no support for data types.

To address these shortcomings, W3C created the so-called "XML Schema Definition (XSD)."

5.1.4   The XML Schema Definition (XSD)

XML Schema was originally created by Microsoft to provide data type definitions for XML pages. It became an official W3C recommendation in the middle of 2001. Similar to DTD, XSD is used to define the legal building blocks of an XML page. The main difference is that XSD is written in XML and with data types supported. Since we mainly use DTDs in this chapter, only a brief XSD discussion is provided in this section.

One of the simplest ways to understand the idea of XSD is by example. Consider the following:

```
Example: ex05-06.xml – An XML Page Using XSD

1: <?xml version="1.0" encoding="iso-8859-1"?>
2: <?xml-stylesheet type="text/xsl" href="ex05-02.xsl" ?>
3: <message
4:    xmlns:xsi="http://www.w3.org/2001/XMLSchema-instance"
5:    xsi:nonamespaceSchemaLocation="ex05-07.xsd">
6:
7: <contents>My First XML Page</contents>
8: <from>www.pwt-ex.com</from>
9: </message>
```

From this simple page, you can see that there is no DTD defined. Instead, the XSD references are embedded inside the message element `<message>`. The detailed XSDs of this page are declared in an external file called ex05-07.xsd. This file can be used by XML pages with a structure of `<message>`, `<from>`, and `<contents>` elements including ex05-06.xml. Consider the following:

```
Example: ex05-07.xsd - XSDs For XML Pages With <from> and <contents>

 1: <?xml version="1.0" encoding="iso-8859-1"?>
 2: <xs:schema xmlns:xs="http://www.w3.org/2001/XMLSchema">
 3: <xs:element name="message">
 4:   <xs:complexType>
 5:     <xs:sequence>
 6:       <xs:element name="contents" type="xs:string" />
 7:       <xs:element name="from" type="xs:string" />
 8:     </xs:sequence>
 9:   </xs:complexType>
10: </xs:element>
11: </xs:schema>
```

Line 3 specifies the element message as the root element of the page. This message element `<message>` is declared as `complexType` since it contains other elements. Inside the `<message>` element there is a sequence of elements defined. They are, obviously, the `<contents>` and `<from>`. Consider the definition of the `<contents>` element:

```
<xs:element name="contents" type="xs:string" />
```

In XSD, elements can be defined with a name and a type. The type is used to declare the data type of the element. In this case, the data type of the contents element is a string. Some frequently used XSD data types are:

```
xs:string        xs:decimal
xs:integer       xs:boolean
xs:date          xs:time
```

These data types provide a rich set of definitions for data used on XML pages. As we mentioned at the beginning of this section, only a brief discussion on XSD is provided. For more detailed information, the relevant XML Schema pages from www.w3.org are recommended.

Now, let's start to use XSLT to convert XML pages into XHTML.

5.2   Transforming XML to XHTML using XSLT

5.2.1   Basic elements in XSLT

Browsers (or user agents) support XSLT while the XSLT standard is still in a draft condition. Therefore not all browsers are fully compatible with the W3C standard recommendation. For example, IE5 was released in March 1999 and supports the working draft (WD document) of the XSLT transform at that time. However, the final release of the XSLT standard is different to the working draft and therefore IE5 is not fully W3C XSLT compatible.

In order to support the standard, it is recommended that the latest browsers such as IE6+. and NS6+. are used in this chapter.

In this section, you are going to learn more about the basic elements in XSLT and how they can be used for the transformation. Based on the official W3C recommendation, some of the basic XSLT elements are listed in Table 5.1.

Table 5.1 Basic elements in XSLT

Basic element	Description of its functionality
`xsl:apply-imports`	To apply a template from an imported style sheet
`xsl:apply-templates`	To apply a template to the current element
`xsl:attribute`	To add an attribute to the nearest containing element
`xsl:attribute-set`	To define a named set of attributes
`xsl:call-template`	To call a named template
`xsl:choose`	To choose between a number of alternatives based on conditions
`xsl:comment`	To write an XML comment
`xsl:copy`	To copy the current node without child nodes and attributes to the output
`xsl:copy-of`	To copy the current node with child nodes and attributes to the output
`xsl:decimal-format`	To define the character or string to be used when converting numbers into strings, with the format number function
`xsl:element`	To add a new element node to the output
`xsl:fallback`	To define an alternative for not implemented instructions
`xsl:for-each`	To create a loop in the output stream
`xsl:if`	To write a conditional statement
`xsl:import`	To import a style sheet
`xsl:include`	To include a style sheet
`xsl:key`	To define a key
`xsl:message`	To write a message to the output
`xsl:namespacealias`	To map one namespace to another namespace
`xsl:number`	To write a formatted number to the output
`xsl:otherwise`	To indicate what should happen when none of the `<xsl:when>` elements inside an `<xsl:choose>` element is satisfied
`xsl:output`	To control the transformed output
`xsl:param`	To define parameters
`xsl:preserve-space`	To define the handling of white space
`xsl:processing-instruction`	To write a processing instruction to the output
`xsl:sort`	To define sorting
`xsl:strip-space`	To define the handling of white space
`xsl:stylesheet`	To define the root element of the style sheet

Table 5.1 Continued

xsl:template	To define a template for output
xsl:text	To write text to the output
xsl:transform	To define the root element of the style sheet
xsl:value-of	To create a text node and insert a value into the result tree
xsl:variable	To declare a variable
xsl:when	To define a condition to be tested and perform an action if the condition is true. This element is always a child element of `<xsl:choose>`
xsl:with-param	To pass parameters to templates

To provide a full account of each of these elements is not the objective of this chapter or this book. For our practical purposes, we concentrate on application examples and some frequently used elements. Let's begin with some basic XSLT techniques to convert an XML page to XHTML.

5.2.2   Simple XSLT for XML pages

Basically, XSL or XSLT is a style sheet language that can be used to transform an XML page into other formats. It is a powerful language and has many applications on XML and related subjects. As an introduction, simple XSLTs are presented in this section to convert XML documents into XHTML. We begin with the simple elements introduced in section 5.1.

For our very first XML page, consider the following document:

Example: ex05-08.xml – XML Page With Simple XSLT

```
 1: <?xml version="1.0" encoding="ISO-8859-1"?>
 2:
 3: <street>
 4:   <profile>
 5:     <name>Charlie</name>
 6:     <job>Engineer</job>
 7:     <sex>male</sex>
 8:     <phone>123456789</phone>
 9:     <location>England</location>
10:     <address>No.10 Richmond Road, West Yorkshire, England</address>
11:      <age>20</age>
12:   </profile>
13:   <profile>
14:     <name>Peter</name>
15:     <job>Clerk</job>
16:     <sex>male</sex>
17:     <phone>223224225</phone>
18:     <age>25</age>
19:     <location>England</location>
20:     <address>No.11 Richmond Road, West Yorkshire, England</address>
21:   </profile>
22:   <profile>
23:     <name>Mary</name>
24:     <job>Secretary</job>
25:     <sex>female</sex>
```

```
26:        <phone>88834421</phone>
27:        <age>19</age>
28:        <location>England</location>
29:        <address>No.12 Richmond Road, West Yorkshire, England</address>
30:     </profile>
31: </street>
```

This is an XML page to describe a house owner in a street. Each house along the street and its owner are described as a `<profile>` element in this document. If you activate this page by the following command on IE and NS

http://www.pwt-ex.com/book/chap05a/ex05-08.xml

you will obtain Figs 5.3 and 5.4.

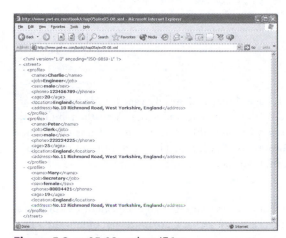

Figure 5.3 ex05-08.xml on IE6.x

Figure 5.4 ex05-08.xml on NS6.x

As you can see from these figures, XML is not displayed well in ordinary browsers such as IE and NS. In order to view and display this XML file, a simple linkage of the style sheet (XSL) to the XML page is needed. For example, you can add the statement below at the line 2 position of ex05-08.xml and call it ex05-09.xml:

```
<?xml-stylesheet type="text/xsl" href="ex05-09.xsl" ?>
```

This statement declares an XML style sheet to transform the XML to other documents. The content type of this transform is "text/xsl." The `href` attribute specifies ex05-09.xsl as the XSL transformation file with all corresponding defined styles. Again this statement needs to be at the location of line 2 of ex05-08.xml so that the browser will read it before rendering the page. Once you insert this statement into ex05-08.xml and call it example ex05-09.xml, you can develop the XSLT file for the transform. The XSLT file ex05-09.xsl is defined as follows:

```
Example: ex05-09.xsl - XSLT For ex05-09.xml

 1: <?xml version="1.0" encoding="ISO-8859-1"?>
 2: <xsl:stylesheet version="1.0"
 3:     xmlns:xsl="http://www.w3.org/1999/XSL/Transform">
 4: <xsl:template match="/">
 5: <html xmlns="http://www.w3.org/1999/xhtml" xml:lang="en" lang="en">
 6: <head><title>ex05-09.xsl</title></head>
 7: <body>
 8:     <table border="1">
 9:        <tr>
10:           <th>Name</th>
```

```
11:            <th>Job</th>
12:            <th>Sex</th>
13:            <th>Age</th>
14:            <th>Phone</th>
15:            <th>Location</th>
16:            <th>Address</th>
17:        </tr>
18:        <tr>
19:          <td><xsl:value-of select="street/profile/name"/></td>
20:          <td><xsl:value-of select="street/profile/job"/></td>
21:          <td><xsl:value-of select="street/profile/sex"/></td>
22:          <td><xsl:value-of select="street/profile/age"/></td>
23:          <td><xsl:value-of select="street/profile/phone"/></td>
24:          <td><xsl:value-of select="street/profile/location"/></td>
25:          <td><xsl:value-of select="street/profile/address"/></td>
26:        </tr>
27:    </table>
28: </body>
29: </html>
30: </xsl:template>
31: </xsl:stylesheet>
```

Line 1 of this page declares that this document is an XML page. Lines 2–3 specify that this document is an XSL to convert the calling page into a document described by the statements following. After the template in line 4, the rest of this document is, in fact, an XHTML page with one table. The first row of this table (lines 9–17) defines the heading Name, Job, Sex, Age, Phone, Location, and Address. The second row of the table is where the XML data mentioned in ex05-08.xml should fit in. Consider the first table element in line 19:

```
<xsl:value-of select="street/profile/name" />
```

This statement contains the popular "value of" XSLT element `<xsl:value-of>`. This element can obtain a value from the XML page and use it in the XSLT file. In this case, the `select` attribute will obtain the value from the `<street>`, `<profile>`, and `<name>` nodes of the XML tree. The value is in fact the owner of the house and is then output at the same location. After you have completed all the table data in lines 19–25, you have a completed XHTML document. The document is then returned to the browser for display. To activate this XML page, all you have to do is to issue the usual "http" command such as:

http://www.pwt-ex.com/book/chap05a/ex05-09.xml

provided both the XML (ex05-09.xml) and XSLT (ex05-09.xsl) files are available on the server www.pwt-ex.com and the associated directory. For local testing, you can drag (or double click) the XML file into the IE or NS browser.

Some screen shots of this example on IE 6.1 and NS6.2 are shown in Figs 5.5 and 5.6.

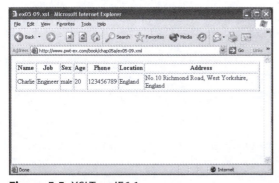

Figure 5.5 XSLT on IE6.1

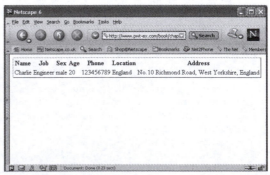

Figure 5.6 XSLT on NS6.2

Although this is a simple example, it demonstrates that XML pages can be converted into XHTML and displayed on browsers properly. Let's consider some more examples.

5.2.3   Using templates in XSLT

In the last example, there is one statement that we haven't explained in detail, i.e., the template statement in line 4:

```
<xsl:template match="/">
```

The keyword `xsl:template` in the statement notifies the user agent that it is the starting point of a template. This template is used to describe how to transform the target XML and define each display element contained in the corresponding XML.

Along with the template definition, there is a `match` attribute. This attribute is used to associate the template with an XML element. In this case, the match "/" indicates that the template applies to the entire XML document. In other words, it means that the transform scans through the root "/" of the XML source document, which matches the template arguments and specifications. One such template specification is the `select` attribute used in line 19:

```
<xsl:value-of select="street/profile/name" />
```

The syntax for the `select` attribute value is called an "XSL Pattern." It works like navigating a file system where a slash "/" selects subdirectories.

The `<xsl:value-of>` element is only good to display one value at a time. Even with all statements defined in lines 19–25, only one row of the table is displayed.

In order to display more data from the XML file, proper use of the template and the `match` attribute are required. For example, the following XSLT page ex05-10.xsl can be used to extract and display all addresses of Richmond Road. First, we modify line 2 of ex05-09.xml by

```
<?xml-stylesheet type="text/xsl" href="ex05-10.xsl" ?>
```

and call the new page ex05-10.xml. The XSLT is listed below:

```
Example: ex05-10.xsl - XSLT With Template

 1: <?xml version="1.0" encoding="ISO-8859-1"?>
 2: <xsl:stylesheet version="1.0"
 3:    xmlns:xsl="http://www.w3.org/1999/XSL/Transform">
 4:
 5:  <xsl:template match="/">
 6:   <html xmlns="http://www.w3.org/1999/xhtml" xml:lang="en" lang="en">
 7:   <head><title>ex05-10.xsl</title>
 8:    <style>
 9:     .txSt {font-family:arial;font-size:18pt;font-weight:bold}
10:    </style>
11:   </head>
12:   <body class="txSt" style="background-color:#000088;color:#ffff00">
13:    <div class="txSt" style="font-size:20pt;text-align:center">
14:      Profile Of Richmond Road <br /><br /></div>
15:
16:    <xsl:apply-templates select="//address" />
17:   </body>
18:   </html>
19:  </xsl:template>
20:
21:  <xsl:template match="address">
22:    <div style="margin-left:40pt; margin-bottom: 12pt;
23:                text-align:left; line-height: 12pt;
24:                font-family:arial; font-size:16pt" >
25:       <xsl:value-of select="." />
26:    </div>
27:  </xsl:template>
28: </xsl:stylesheet>
```

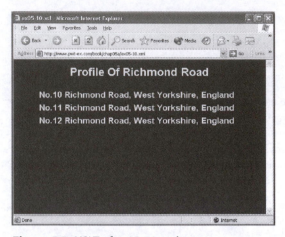

Figure 5.7 XSLT of ex05-10.xml

This XSLT file contains two templates. The first template is defined in lines 5–19 with the match attribute `match="/"`. This template applies to the entire XML document to transform it into XHTML. In line 16 of this template, there is an `apply-templates` element `<xsl:apply-templates xxx>`. This element is used to apply another template (lines 21–27) that matches the `<address>` element in the XML file. The user agent (or an XSLT-supported browser) will search the calling XML file and look for the `<address>` element for a match. If a match is found, the value will be inserted into line 22. The entire division element `<div>` will be substituted back into line 13 to compose the XHTML document. A screen shot of this example is shown in Fig. 5.7.

Now, to display the entire XML file all you need to do is to add more data fields into the second template. But first, you need to modify line 2 of ex05-10.xml by the statement

```
<?xml-stylesheet type="text/xsl" href="ex05-11.xsl" ?>
```

and call the new page ex05-11.xml. Consider the following XSLT file:

```
Example: ex05-11.xsl- - XSLT With Template II

 1: <?xml version="1.0" encoding="ISO-8859-1"?>
 2: <xsl:stylesheet version="1.0"
 3:   xmlns:xsl="http://www.w3.org/1999/XSL/Transform">
 4:
 5: <xsl:template match="/">
 6:   <html xmlns="http://www.w3.org/1999/xhtml" xml:lang="en" lang="en">
 7:   <head><title>ex05-11.xsl</title>
 8:    <style>
 9:      .txtSt {font-family:arial;font-size:14pt;font-weight:bold}
10:    </style>
11:   </head>
12:   <body class="txtSt" style="background:#000088;color:#ffff00">
13:   <div style="font-size:18pt;text-align:center">
14:       Street Profile of Richmond Road <br /><br />
15:   </div>
16:
17:      <xsl:apply-templates />
18:
19:   </body>
20:   </html>
21: </xsl:template>
22:
23: <xsl:template match="profile">
24:    Name:- <xsl:apply-templates select="name" /> <br />
25:    Job:- <xsl:apply-templates select="job" /> <br />
26:    Sex:- <xsl:apply-templates select="sex" /> <br />
27:    Address:- <xsl:apply-templates select="address" /> <br />
28:    Phone:- <xsl:apply-templates select="phone" /> <br /><br />
29: </xsl:template>
30:
31: </xsl:stylesheet>
```

Again, this XSLT file contains two templates. The first template matches the root ("/") of the XML document. The `apply-templates` element without a `select` attribute used in line 17 means that all the nodes of the XML page from the root are applied.

A second template is defined in lines 23–29. This template will apply to all nodes of the profile tree. For example, suppose the first node of the profile tree in ex05-11.xml is

```
<profile>
  <name>Charlie</name>
  <job>Engineer</job>
  <sex>male</sex>
  <phone>123456789</phone>
  <age>20</age>
  <location>England</location>
  <address>No.10 Richmond Road, West Yorkshire, England</address>
</profile>
```

This template will transform the data into

```
Name:- Charlie <br />
Job:- Engineer <br />
Sex:- M <br />
Address:- No.10 Richmond Road, West Yorkshire, England <br />
Phone:- 123456789 <br /> <br />
```

The paragraph is then inserted into the first template at line 17.

After the XSLT of all nodes, a completed XHTML document is generated to display data in the XML page. A screen shot of this example is shown in Fig. 5.8.

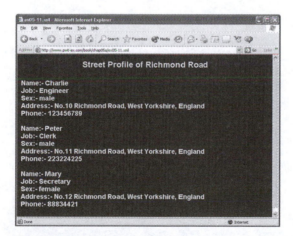

Figure 5.8 XSLT of ex05-11.xml

You now have some basic understanding of XML documents and XSL transformations. In fact, XML documents are data based and similar to a database in some ways.

5.3   Manipulating XML data with XSLT

5.3.1   Generating loops with XSLT

In this section, we consider some XSLT pages and techniques that can perform some data manipulation of an XML file. First, we will show you how to perform loops on XML data. Based on the loops, a number of basic database operations such as sorting, filtering, and query can be performed.

Another way to display the entire XML page or data is to use the `for-each` element `<xsl:foreach>`. This element has the following general form:

```
<xsl:for-each select="street/profile">
  xxx
  xxx
</xsl:for-each>
```

This statement can read all children of the `<profile>` element one by one specified by the calling XML document. To construct an example of this feature, you first modify line 2 of ex05-11.xml to call the XSLT page. The new page is called ex05-12.xml. The XSLT file ex05-12.xsl is listed below:

```
Example: ex05-12.xsl – Generating Loops

 1: <?xml version="1.0" encoding="ISO-8859-1"?>
 2: <xsl:stylesheet version="1.0"
 3: xmlns:xsl="http://www.w3.org/1999/XSL/Transform">
 4: <xsl:template match="/">
 5: <html xmlns="http://www.w3.org/1999/xhtml" xml:lang="en" lang="en">
 6: <head><title>ex05-12.xsl</title>
 7:  <style>
 8:    .txtSt {font-family:arial;font-size:19pt;font-weight:bold}
 9:  </style>
10: </head>
11: <body class="txtSt" style="color:#000088">
12:    Household Records Of Richmond Road <br />
13:    West Yorkshire <br /><br />
14:    <table border="1" style="background:#888888;
15:      color:#ffffff;font-family:arial;font-size:14pt">
16:     <tr>
17:       <th>Name</th> <th>Job</th>
18:       <th>Sex</th> <th>Age</th>
19:       <th>Phone</th> <th>Location</th> <th>Address</th>
20:     </tr>
21:     <xsl:for-each select="street/profile">
22:     <tr>
23:       <td><xsl:value-of select="name"/></td>
24:       <td><xsl:value-of select="job"/></td>
25:       <td><xsl:value-of select="sex"/></td>
26:       <td><xsl:value-of select="age"/></td>
27:       <td><xsl:value-of select="phone"/></td>
28:       <td><xsl:value-of select="location"/></td>
29:       <td><xsl:value-of select="address"/></td>
30:     </tr>
31:     </xsl:for-each>
32:    </table>
33:  </body>
34:  </html>
35: </xsl:template>
36: </xsl:stylesheet>
```

If you compare this page with ex05-09.xsl, you will find that we have inserted the `for-each` element `<xsl:for-each select=xxx>` in lines 21–31. As a result, it works like a simple for-loop to generate a series of statements between the loops. It will generate a number of table rows for the XHTML table. Also, we have added some CSS style settings in this example to show that XSLT takes care of CSS properties as well. A screen shot of this example is shown in Fig. 5.9.

Now, you have put the data into a table. The next question is: how can you a sort the data?

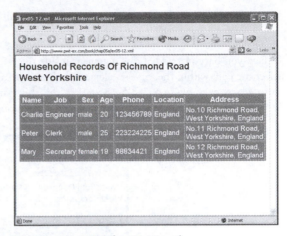

Figure 5.9 XSLT of ex05-12.xml

5.3.2 Sorting XML data with XSLT

One important feature for data manipulation is sorting. With XSLT, you will find that to sort the data within an XML document is very easy. In many cases, all you have to do is to add one sort statement into your XSLT page. Consider the following example ex05-13.xsl:

```
Example: ex05-13.xsl - Sorting Elements

 1: <?xml version="1.0" encoding="ISO-8859-1"?>
 2: <xsl:stylesheet version="1.0"
 3: xmlns:xsl="http://www.w3.org/1999/XSL/Transform">
 4: <xsl:template match="/">
 5:  <html xmlns="http://www.w3.org/1999/xhtml" xml:lang="en" lang="en">
 6:  <head><title>ex05-13.xsl</title>
 7:   <style> .txtSt {font-family:arial;font-size:19pt;font-weight:bold}
 8:   </style>
 9:  </head>
10:  <body class="txtSt" style="color:#000088">
11:     Household Records Of Richmond Road <br />
12:     West Yorkshire <br />(With Sorting On Names)<br /><br />
13:     <table border="1" style="background:#888888;
14:       color:#ffffff;font-family:arial;font-size:14pt">
15:       <tr>
16:         <th>Name</th> <th>Job</th>
17:         <th>Sex</th> <th>Age</th>
18:         <th>Phone</th> <th>Location</th>
19:         <th>Address</th>
20:       </tr>
21:       <xsl:for-each select="street/profile">
22:       <xsl:sort select="name" />
23:       <tr>
24:         <td><xsl:value-of select="name"/></td>
25:         <td><xsl:value-of select="job"/></td>
26:         <td><xsl:value-of select="sex"/></td>
27:         <td><xsl:value-of select="age"/></td>
28:         <td><xsl:value-of select="phone"/></td>
29:         <td><xsl:value-of select="location"/></td>
30:         <td><xsl:value-of select="address"/></td>
31:       </tr>
32:       </xsl:for-each>
33:     </table>
34:  </body>
35:  </html>
36: </xsl:template>
37: </xsl:stylesheet>
```

If you compare this example with ex05-12.xsl, you will find that the main difference is the statement in line 22:

```
<xsl:sort select="name" />
```

In fact, you have just added this statement inside the for-each loop described in lines 22–32. This statement will select the data within the <name> element and perform a sort. Suppose you have modified line 2 of ex05-12.xml to form a new example (e.g., ex05-13.xml) to call this transformation page. If you activate this new XML page by http://www.pwt ex.com/book/chap05a/ex05-13.xml, you will see the sort result as illustrated in Fig. 5.10.

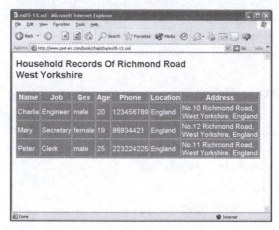

Figure 5.10 XSLT with sorting

By just using one more statement, XML data can be sorted automatically. You can use this statement to sort almost any data described in your XML pages. In general, the sort element in XSLT has the following syntax:

```
<xsl:sort    select       ="expression"
             order        ="ascending|descending"
             case-order   ="upper-first|lower-first"
             lang         ="language-code"
             data-type    ="text|number|qname"/>
```

The detailed explanation of the attributes and values is given in Table 5.2.

Table 5.2 XSLT sort element

Attribute	Value	Description
select	expression	Sort expression
order	ascending descending	Sort order; the default is "ascending"
case-order	upper-first lower-first	Upper case letters or lower case letters come first
lang	language-code	The language to use for sorting purposes
data-type	text number qname	The type of the data to be sorted (number, text, or user-defined type) and the default type is "text"

Next, we are going to show you how to perform some data filtering using XSLT pages and techniques.

5.3.3   Using XSLT filtering and query features

To be able to select and filter data is important for many data-related applications. In XSLT, some of these filtering and query features can be implemented easily. For example, you can use the `select` attribute to filter the data in an XML file. Consider the following XSLT page:

Example: ex05-14.xsl - XSLT With Filtering And Query

```
 1: <?xml version="1.0" encoding="ISO-8859-1"?>
 2: <xsl:stylesheet version="1.0"
 3: xmlns:xsl="http://www.w3.org/1999/XSL/Transform">
 4: <xsl:template match="/">
 5:  <html xmlns="http://www.w3.org/1999/xhtml" xml:lang="en" lang="en">
 6:  <head><title>ex05-14.xsl</title>
 7:   <style> .txtSt {font-family:arial;font-size:19pt;font-weight:bold}
 8:   </style>
 9:  </head>
10:  <body class="txtSt" style="color:#000088">
11:     Household Records Of Richmond Road <br />
12:     West Yorkshire <br /><br />
13:     <table border="1" style="background:#888888;
14:       color:#ffffff;font-family:arial;font-size:14pt">
15:       <tr>
16:         <th>Name</th> <th>Job</th>
17:         <th>Sex</th> <th>Age</th>
18:         <th>Phone</th> <th>Location</th>
19:         <th>Address</th>
20:       </tr>
21:       <xsl:for-each select="street/profile[name='Peter']">
22:       <tr>
23:         <td><xsl:value-of select="name"/></td>
24:         <td><xsl:value-of select="job"/></td>
25:         <td><xsl:value-of select="sex"/></td>
26:         <td><xsl:value-of select="age"/></td>
27:         <td><xsl:value-of select="phone"/></td>
28:         <td><xsl:value-of select="location"/></td>
29:         <td><xsl:value-of select="address"/></td>
30:       </tr>
31:       </xsl:for-each>
32:     </table>
33:   </body>
34:  </html>
35: </xsl:template>
36: </xsl:stylesheet>
```

As you can see from this example, you don't need to add any additional statements to perform data filtering. Instead, you can modify the `select` attribute to do the job. The statement in line 21

```
<xsl:for-each select="street/profile[name='Peter']">
```

generates a `for-each` loop and selects any data whose name is Peter at the same time. If you modify the XML page ex05-13.xml and call it ex05-14.xml to call this XSLT, you will see the selected result as illustrated in Fig. 5.11.

Another way to perform selection is to use the `if` conditional element `<xsl:if test=xxx>`. For example, the following statement can be used to pick all the names equal to "Peter":

```
<xsl:if test="name='Peter'">
    xxx xxx xxx
    xxx xxx xxx
</xsl:if>
```

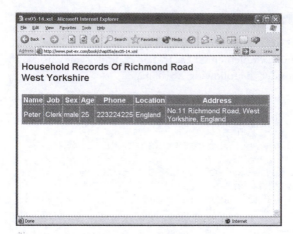

Figure 5.11 XSLT with selection

As a simple example, you can modify the second half of ex05-14.xsl (starting from line 21) as follows:

```
Listing: ex05-01.txt - Code Fragment Of ex05-15.xsl

21:         <xsl:for-each select="street/profile">
22:         <xsl:if test="name='Peter'">
23:         <tr>
24:           <td><xsl:value-of select="name"/></td>
25:           <td><xsl:value-of select="job"/></td>
26:           <td><xsl:value-of select="sex"/></td>
27:           <td><xsl:value-of select="age"/></td>
28:           <td><xsl:value-of select="phone"/></td>
29:           <td><xsl:value-of select="location"/></td>
30:           <td><xsl:value-of select="address"/></td>
31:         </tr>
32:         </xsl:if>
33:         </xsl:for-each>
34:       </table>
35:     </body>
36:     </html>
37: </xsl:template>
38: </xsl:stylesheet>
```

The if element in this example performs a selection. Only those names equal to "Peter" will get through the statements in lines 23–31. This example has the same result as example ex05-14.xsl.

Another interesting XSLT query is the combination of the choose, when, and otherwise elements. The general calling format for this query is

```
<xsl:choose>
   <xsl:when test="name='Peter'">
        xxx coding for the test xxx
   </xsl:when>
   <xsl:otherwise>
        xxx coding for the otherwise xxx
   </xsl:otherwise>
</xsl:choose>
```

This structure is often used to select some particular data for a special purpose. For a simple use of this structure, let's consider the following example:

Example: ex05-16.xsl - Using The Choose Feature

```
 1: <?xml version="1.0" encoding="ISO-8859-1"?>
 2: <xsl:stylesheet version="1.0"
 3: xmlns:xsl="http://www.w3.org/1999/XSL/Transform">
 4: <xsl:template match="/">
 5:  <html xmlns="http://www.w3.org/1999/xhtml" xml:lang="en" lang="en">
 6:  <head><title>ex05-16.xsl</title>
 7:   <style> .txtSt {font-family:arial;font-size:19pt;font-weight:bold}
 8:   </style>
 9:  </head>
10:  <body class="txtSt" style="color:#000088">
11:     Household Records Of Richmond Road <br />
12:     West Yorkshire <br /><br />
13:     <table border="1" style="background:#888888;
14:       color:#ffffff;font-family:arial;font-size:14pt">
15:      <tr>
16:        <th>Name</th> <th>Job</th>
17:        <th>Sex</th> <th>Age</th>
18:        <th>Phone</th> <th>Location</th>
19:        <th>Address</th>
20:      </tr>
21:      <xsl:for-each select="street/profile">
22:      <tr>
23:       <xsl:choose>
24:       <xsl:when test="name='Peter'">
25:        <td style="background:#ff0000;color:#ffff00">
26:           <xsl:value-of select="name"/></td>
27:        <td><xsl:value-of select="job"/></td>
28:        <td><xsl:value-of select="sex"/></td>
29:        <td><xsl:value-of select="age"/></td>
30:        <td><xsl:value-of select="phone"/></td>
31:        <td><xsl:value-of select="location"/></td>
32:        <td><xsl:value-of select="address"/></td>
33:       </xsl:when>
34:       <xsl:otherwise>
35:        <td><xsl:value-of select="name"/></td>
36:        <td><xsl:value-of select="job"/></td>
37:        <td><xsl:value-of select="sex"/></td>
38:        <td><xsl:value-of select="age"/></td>
39:        <td><xsl:value-of select="phone"/></td>
40:        <td><xsl:value-of select="location"/></td>
41:        <td><xsl:value-of select="address"/></td>
42:       </xsl:otherwise>
43:       </xsl:choose>
44:      </tr>
45:      </xsl:for-each>
46:     </table>
47:  </body>
48:  </html>
49: </xsl:template>
50: </xsl:stylesheet>
```

The choose element will take effect at line 23. The when element in line 24

```
<xsl:when test="name='Peter'">
```

will test the data for the name equal to "Peter." If there is a match, the formatting statements in lines 25–32 will be used to format the data. In this case, both the foreground and background colors of the data will be changed. If the name is not "Peter," the statements (lines 34–42) in the `otherwise` element `<xsl:otherwise>` are executed. As a result, only the record with name equal to "Peter" will change color. A screen shot of this example is shown in Fig. 5.12.

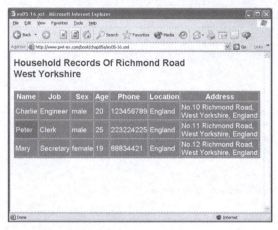

Figure 5.12 XSLT with choose

In order to use XSLT more effectively, you may need to use variables in XSLT.

5.3.4 Using variables in XSLT

You can declare a variable in XSLT by using the variable element `<xsl:variable>`. This element has the following general calling format:

```
<xsl:variable name="name" select="expression">
    xxx xxx xxx
</xsl:variable>
```

The attributes and accepted values are listed in Table 5.3.

Table 5.3 The attributes and values of the `variable` element

Attribute	Value	Description
name	name	Variable name
select	expression	Variable value

The `name` attribute is to identify the variable so the corresponding value stored in the variable can be accessed. The `select` attribute is the usual expression (select expression) and is used to obtain the value of the variable. For example, the statement below declares a variable element called `jacket`:

```
<xsl:variable name="jacket" select="'leather'" >
</xsl:variable>
```

In fact, the `select` attribute is optional. For example, the following example will define a variable with an empty string as value:

```
<xsl:variable name="jacket"> xxx xxx xxx </xsl:variable>
```

For a practical example, let's consider a menu from a restaurant. The menu consists of some dishes grouped into different categories. By using XML and XSLT, you will find that it is easier to generate line numbers for the menu item than the HTML/XHTML counterpart. Consider the XML data page for the menu:

Example: ex05-17.xml - Using XSLT Variables

```
 1: <?xml version="1.0"?>
 2: <?xml-stylesheet type="text/xsl" href="ex05-17.xsl"?>
 3: <menu>
 4:   <item>
 5:     <dishes_type>Sea Food -- $7.60</dishes_type>
 6:     <dishes>Fried Fish In Thai Style (Hot) -- With Salad</dishes>
 7:     <dishes>Fried Squid In Thai Style (Hot) -- With Salad</dishes>
 8:     <dishes>Curry Crab Thai Style (Hot) -- With Salad</dishes>
 9:   </item>
10:   <item>
11:     <dishes_type>Curry &amp; Meat -- $6.40</dishes_type>
12:     <dishes>Red Beef Curry (Hot) -- With Salad</dishes>
13:     <dishes>Green Curry Chicken (Hot) -- With Salad</dishes>
14:     <dishes>Roast Pork Curry (Hot) -- With Salad</dishes>
15:   </item>
16:   <item>
17:     <dishes_type>Rice &amp; Noodles -- $3.40</dishes_type>
18:     <dishes>Fried Rice Noodles Thai Style </dishes>
19:     <dishes>Fried Rice In Thai Style </dishes>
20:     <dishes>King Prawn Fried Rice In Thai Style</dishes>
21:   </item>
22: </menu>
```

This menu has three item elements `<item>`. Each item contains one dish-type element `<dishes_type>` and some dishes `<dishes>`. In practice, we would like to build a line number on the `<dishes>` element across the whole page to make it easier for customers to make their choices. To do that, you can use the XSLT below:

Example: ex05-17.xsl - Using Variables

```
 1: <?xml version="1.0" encoding="ISO-8859-1"?>
 2: <xsl:stylesheet version="1.0"
 3:  xmlns:xsl="http://www.w3.org/1999/XSL/Transform">
 4:
 5: <xsl:template match="/">
 6:  <html xmlns="http://www.w3.org/1999/xhtml" xml:lang="en" lang="en">
 7:  <head><title>ex05-17.xsl</title>
 8:  </head>
 9:  <body style="font-family:arial;;font-weight:bold;
10:       width:800px;height:600px;background:#000088">
11:   <div style="color:#00ff00;font-size:20pt;text-align:center" >
12:       ABC Resturant <br /> (Thai and Oriental Tastes)<br /><br />
13:    <xsl:apply-templates select="/menu/item" />
14:    <span style="font-size:16pt">
15:       All Dishes Come With Coconut Soup Of The Day<br /><br /></span>
16:   </div>
17:  </body>
18:  </html>
19: </xsl:template>
20:
```

```
21:  <xsl:template match="item">
22:    <div align="center">
23:      <table style="font-size:14pt;color:#00ffff;font-family:arial;
24:             margin-top:10px;text-align:left">
25:        <tr><td colspan="2" style="font-size:16pt;
26:             color:#ffff00;text-align:left">
27:          <xsl:apply-templates select="dishes_type" /> </td>
28:        </tr>
29:        <xsl:apply-templates select="dishes" />
30:      </table><br />
31:    </div>
32:  </xsl:template>
33:
34:  <xsl:template match="dishes" >
35:    <tr>
36:      <td width="50" style="text-align:left">
37:        <xsl:variable name="add_no">
38:          <xsl:number level="any" from="menu" />
39:        </xsl:variable>
40:        <xsl:value-of select="$add_no"/>
41:      </td>
42:      <td width="400" style="text-align:left">
43:        <xsl:value-of select="."/></td>
44:    </tr>
45:  </xsl:template>
46:
47: </xsl:stylesheet>
```

This transform has three templates. The first template is defined in lines 5–19 and specifies the framework of an XHTML page. When the user agent executes the statement in line 13

```
<xsl:apply-templates select="/menu/item"/>
```

each element `<item>` from the XML document will be processed and output as part of the XHTML page. When each `<item>` element is called, it will be formatted by the template defined in lines 21–32. Inside this template is a table. The first row of the table (lines 25–28) outputs the dish type. The statement in line 29

```
<xsl:apply-templates select="dishes" />
```

output all values of `<dishes>`. Before the output, all `<dishes>` elements are formatted by the third template defined in lines 34–45. This template is used to generate line numbers on the `<dishes>` elements. The important part of this template is in lines 37–40:

```
<xsl:variable name="add_no">
    <xsl:number level="any" from="menu" />
</xsl:variable>
<xsl:value-of select="$add_no"/>
```

First, a variable called $add_no is declared by using the variable element `<xsl:variable>`. Inside this element, an XSLT number element `<xsl:number>` is defined. The attribute `from="menu"` instructs the user agent (or capable browser) to search the `<menu>` tree for the `<dishes>` node and assign a number to it. The number is output by the `value-of` element. For example, after this template transformation, the first two dishes in the XML file ex05-17.xml turn out to be

```
<tr>
  <td width="50" style="text-align:left"> 1 </td>
  <td width="400" style="text-align:left">
    Fried Fish In Thai Style (Hot) -- With Salad </td>
</tr>
```

```
<tr>
  <td width="50" style="text-align:left"> 2 </td>
  <td width="400" style="text-align:left">
    Fried Squid In Thai Style (Hot) -- With Salad</td>
</tr>
```

When all the transformations are completed, you will have an XHTML document returned to the browser. A screen shot of this example is shown in Fig. 5.13.

Figure 5.13 Generating line numbers

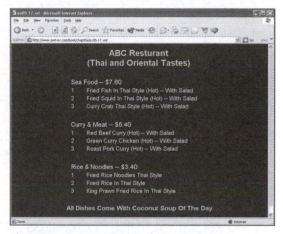

Figure 5.14 Line number for each dish type

From this figure, you can see that the line numbers of the dishes are consecutive. If you change the statement in line 38 as follows:

```
<xsl:number level="any" from="item" />
```

the line number starts from the item element and search for each `<dishes>`. In this case, there will be a recount after each `<item>`. A screen shot of this in action is shown in Fig. 5.14. However, if you change the statement to

```
<xsl:number level="any" from="dishes" />
```

all counting will be zero. This is due to the fact that there is no `<dishes>` element inside `<dishes>`. Now, let's consider some other XML techniques on the Web.

5.4 Using CSS and parser on XML documents

5.4.1 Using CSS on XML pages

CSS is considered to be an integral part of all HTML/XHTML documents and used on almost every serious page on the Web. By separating the formatting properties such as color, font, size, background, and border from the markup contents, CSS provides a structural base for all HTML/XHTML documents.

One of the interesting features of CSS is that it can be used to redefine the formatting properties of an HTML/XHTML tag. Consider the following example:

```
Example: ex05-18.htm - Redefine Formatting Properties Using CSS

 1: <?xml version="1.0" encoding="UTF-8"?>
 2: <!DOCTYPE html
 3:     PUBLIC "-//W3C//DTD XHTML 1.0 Transitional//EN"
 4:     "http://www.w3.org/TR/xhtml1/DTD/xhtml1-transitional.dtd">
 5: <html xmlns="http://www.w3.org/1999/xhtml" xml:lang="en" lang="en">
 6: <head><title>ex05-18.htm </title>
 7: <link rel="stylesheet" type="text/css" href="ex05-18.css">
 8: </head>
 9: <body>
10:    Body Text Defined By External CSS
11: <div>
12:    This is a paragraph with formatting properties
13:    margin-left :30px; margin-right:30px and margin-top:15px
14: </div>
15: <div style="margin-left:80px;margin-right:180px;color:#880088">
16:    This is another paragraph defined by the CSS properties
17:    of the previous paragraph with another margin and color.
18: </div>
19: </body>
20: </html>
```

This is an XHTML page calling an external CSS style file. The statement in line 7

```
<link rel="stylesheet" type="text/css" href="ex05-18.css">
```

specifies an external CSS file used to provide the formatting properties of this page. This CSS file is ex05-18.css and is used to redefine the formatting properties of the <body> and <div> elements. Note that the <div> element in line 15 cascades a new definition with the inline style. The detail of the CSS file is listed below:

```
Example: ex05-18.css - External CSS File For ex05-18.htm

 1: body {
 2:    color:#000088; font-family:arial;
 3:    font-size:18pt; font-weight:bold;
 4:    text-align:center; margin-top:20px;
 5: }
 6:
 7: div {
 8:    text-align:left; font-size:14pt;
 9:    color:#880000; margin-left:50px;
10:    margin-right:30px; margin-top:15pt
11: }
```

This CSS file contains the definition of two predefined elements, <body> and <div>, in all HTML/XHTML documents. The browser will use these definitions to format the contents related to <body> and <div> until the definition is overridden or cascaded by the new definition as illustrated in line 15 of ex05-18.htm. A screen shot of this example is shown in Fig. 5.15.

To use the CSS feature on XML is easy. You can define the CSS properties of XML elements and use the following statement to include the CSS file in the XML document:

```
<?xml-stylesheet type="text/css" href="ex05-19.css" ?>
```

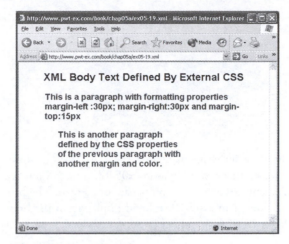

Figure 5.15 ex05-18.htm

When this statement is executed, the browser knows that the incoming file is an `xml-stylesheet` with content type `text/css`. This content type specifies an external CSS file and the attribute `href` provides the location of the file. A capable browser will read this CSS file and format the XML document for display. Consider the following example:

```
Example: ex05-19.xml - Display XML Page Using CSS I

 1:  <?xml version="1.0"?>
 2:  <?xml-stylesheet type="text/css" href="ex05-19.css" ?>
 3:  <body>
 4:      XML Body Text Defined By External CSS
 5:   <div01>
 6:      This is a paragraph with formatting properties
 7:      margin-left :30px; margin-right:30px and margin-top:15px
 8:   </div01>
 9:   <div02>
10:   This is another paragraph defined by the CSS properties
11:   of the previous paragraph with another margin and color.
12:   </div02>
13: </body>
```

This simple XML document is a modification of ex05-18.htm. Since the XML element is not predefined, we have used an element called `<body>` here. This `<body>` has nothing to do with the body element in HTML/XHTML and contains no predefined property. To generate the same output as in ex05-18.htm, an external CSS file ex05-19.css is used as illustrated in line 2. Note that the statements in lines 1 and 2 are not XML elements and they don't need the end tag. The listing of the CSS file ex05-19.css is provided below:

```
Example: ex05-19.css - External CSS File For ex05-19.xml

 1: body {
 2:    display:block;
 3:    color:#000088;       font-family:arial;
 4:    font-size:18pt;      font-weight:bold;
 5:    text-align:center; margin-top:20px
 6: }
 7:
 8: div01 {
 9:    display:block;
10:    text-align:left;    font-size:14pt;
```

```
11:    color:#880000;       margin-left:50px;
12:    margin-right:30px; margin-top:15pt
13: }
14:
15: div02 {
16:    display:block;
17:    text-align:left;      font-size:14pt;
18:    color:#880088;        margin-left:80px;
19:    margin-right:180px;   margin-top:15pt
20: }
```

This CSS file provides all definitions for elements used in the XML document ex05-19.xml. In this example, you don't need to cascade the formatting definition as in ex05-18.htm. You just redefine the definition for the second paragraph as a new element `<div02>` with properties of its own. The browser will read this CSS file and use it to format the XML document ex05-19.xml and display it on the browser screen. This displaying method is supported by the latest IE (IE6.+) and NS (NS6.+) browsers. Some screen shots of this example are shown in Figs 5.16 and 5.17.

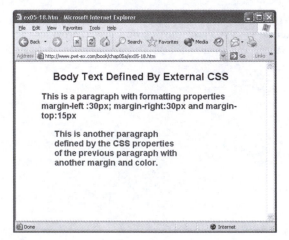

Figure 5.16 ex05-19.xml on IE

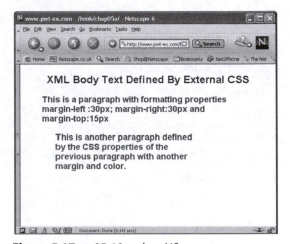

Figure 5.17 ex05-19.xml on NS

Note that the "display:block" properties are used to control the display as a paragraph. Otherwise, the next paragraph will join up to the previous one.

As you have learned from previous sections, one of the important applications of XML documents is to display and handle data information such as catalogs, menus, listings, and database output. It will be easier for an application to generate XML documents than HTML/XHTML pages. For example, suppose you have an XML output from a database containing the staff information of an insurance company. The information is organized as "name," "birth," "sex," "location," and "salary" in XML format. The XML page is listed below:

Example: ex05-20.xml - Display XML Page Using CSS II

```
1: <?xml version="1.0" encoding="ISO-8859-1"?>
2:
3: <?xml-stylesheet type="text/css" href="ex05-20.css"?>
4: <admin>
5:    <title> Staff Of ABC Insurance</title>
6:    <person>
7:      <name>Michael</name>
8:      <birth>1950-12-18</birth>
9:      <sex>M</sex>
```

```
10:        <location>London</location>
11:        <salary>30,000</salary>
12:      </person>
13:      <person>
14:        <name>Mary</name>
15:        <birth>1980-6-22</birth>
16:        <sex>F</sex>
17:        <location>Paris</location>
18:        <salary>23,000</salary>
19:      </person>
20:      <person>
21:        <name>Peter</name>
22:        <birth>1975-10-11</birth>
23:        <sex>M</sex>
24:        <location>New York</location>
25:        <salary>28,000</salary>
26:      </person>
27:      <person>
28:        <name>Sue</name>
29:        <birth>1969-1-19</birth>
30:        <sex>F</sex>
31:        <location>Paris</location>
32:        <salary>30,000</salary>
33:      </person>
34: </admin>
```

There are a number of techniques that can be used to display this XML document. Although not as sophisticated as XSLT, this XML page can be displayed using the following CSS file technique. Consider the CSS file ex05-20.css:

Example: ex05-20.css - External CSS File For ex05-20.xml

```
 1: admin {
 2:      background-color: #000088;
 3:      font-family:arial; font-weight:bold;
 4:      width: 100%; height:100%
 5: }
 6:
 7: title {
 8:      display: block;
 9:      font-size:30pt; color:#ffff00;
10:      margin-top:20pt; margin-bottom: 30pt;
11:      text-align:center
12: }
13:
14: person {
15:      display: block;
16:      margin-bottom: 10pt; margin-left: 70pt;
17: }
18:
19: name {
20:      color: #ffff00;
21:      font-size: 20pt;
22: }
23:
24: birth {
25:      color: #00ff00;
26:      font-size: 20pt;
27: }
```

```
28:
29: sex,location {
30:     color: #ffff00;
31:     margin-left: 20pt;
32:     font-size: 20pt;
33: }
34:
35: salary {
36:     color: #ffffff;
37:     margin-left: 20pt;
38:     font-size: 20pt;
39:}
```

The element `<admin>` is the root element of the XML page containing all other elements. For this element, we define the background color as `#000088` (deep blue). The 100% `width` and `height` attribute settings guarantee that the background color covers the whole page. The remaining elements are self-explanatory. In many cases, you can use one definition to define two elements as illustrated in lines 29–33. This is a simple example to display a database result using XML pages. The database fields are displayed in different colors. A proper chapter on databases and the MySQL database package will be introduced in Part IV of this book. Some screen shots of this example on IE and NS are shown in Figs 5.18 and 5.19.

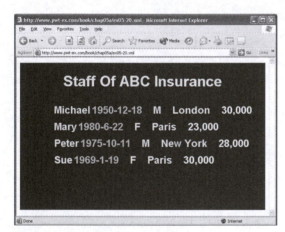

Figure 5.18 ex05-20.xml on IE

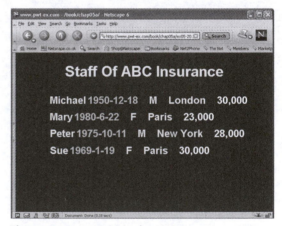

Figure 5.19 ex05-20.xml on NS

Using CSS to display XML documents is not an ideal approach to XML. The examples here show that this can be done when a simple XML page is involved. For a quick solution, the CSS approach may be handy. However, for a sophisticated solution, the use of XSLT is highly recommended.

5.4.2 Handling XML documents with parser

Since IE5.0, Microsoft has bundled the browser with an XML parser which can be used to embed and handle XML documents in an HTML/XHTML page. This means that if you are using IE 5.0 or later, you already have this XML parser installed. At a minimum level, the parser can be employed to display an XML page with XSLT.

Consider the following XML page containing information on office equipment data and insurance:

Example: ex05-21.xml - An XML Page On Office Equipment Data

```
 1: <?xml version="1.0" encoding="ISO-8859-1"?>
 2:
 3: <inventory>
 4:    <item>
 5:        <name>Computer</name>
 6:        <price>$1100</price>
 7:        <des>PC From ABC Equip. Corp.</des>
 8:        <id>Insurance Id:iv8002</id>
 9:    </item>
10:    <item>
11:        <name>Camcorder</name>
12:        <price>$400</price>
13:        <des>Camcorder From ABC Equip. Corp.</des>
14:        <id>Insurance Id:iv8003</id>
15:    </item>
16:    <item>
17:        <name>Photocopier</name>
18:        <price>$2100</price>
19:        <des>Photocopier From ABC Equip. Corp.</des>
20:        <id>Insurance Id:iv8004</id>
21:    </item>
22:    <item>
23:        <name>Notebook computer</name>
24:        <price>$1600</price>
25:        <des>Notebook Computer From ABC Equip. Cor.</des>
26:        <id>Insurance Id:iv8005</id>
27:    </item>
28:    <item>
29:        <name>Mobile PDA and Phone</name>
30:        <price>$500</price>
31:        <des>Mobile PDA with Phone From ABC Equip. Corp.</des>
32:        <id>Insurance Id:iv8006</id>
33:    </item>
34: </inventory>
32
```

This page is a general XML document containing the data of inventory and insurance information. This means that this page contains no specific display or transformation methods.

As you learned from section 5.2.2, if you insert the following statement in line 2

```
<?xml-stylesheet type="text/xsl" href="ex05-21.xsl" ?>
```

this page is handled by the XML-style sheet ex05-21.xsl and therefore can be displayed by the browser. The listing of ex05-21.xsl is shown as follows:

Example: ex05-21.xsl - XSLT Transformation For ex05-21.xml

```
 1: <?xml version="1.0" encoding="iso-8859-1"?>
 2: <xsl:stylesheet version="1.0"
 3:   xmlns:xsl="http://www.w3.org/1999/XSL/Transform">
 4:
 5: <xsl:template match="/">
 6:  <html xmlns="http://www.w3.org/1999/xhtml" xml:lang="en" lang="en">
 7:  <head><title> ex05-21.xsl </title></head>
 8:  <body style="font-family:Arial, helvetica, sans-serif; font-size:12pt;
 9:          background-color:#ffffff">
```

```
10:    <div style="font-size:20pt;font-weight:bold;text-align:center">
11:         Office Inventory and Insurance</div> <br /><br />
12:
13:    <xsl:for-each select="inventory/item">
14:      <div style="background-color:#8888ff; color:white;font-size:14pt">
15:       <span style="font-weight:bold; color:white">
16        <xsl:value-of select="name" />- <xsl:value-of select="price" /></span>
17:      </div>
18:      <div style="margin-bottom:15px;font-weight:bold">
19:          <xsl:value-of select="des" />
20:          <span style="font-style:italic;font-weight:bold;color:#880000">
21:            -- <xsl:value-of select="id"/> Fully Covered
22:          </span>
23:      </div>
24:    </xsl:for-each>
25:  </body>
26:  </html>
27:  </xsl:template>
28:  </xsl:stylesheet>
```

Alternatively, if you are using IE5.0 or later, you can develop an XHTML page to embed both ex05-21.xml and the transform file ex05-21.xsl into the XHTML page. Consider the following XHTML page:

```
Example: ex05-21.htm - Microsoft XML Parser

 1: <?xml version="1.0" encoding="UTF-8"?>
 2: <!DOCTYPE html
 3:       PUBLIC "-//W3C//DTD XHTML 1.0 Transitional//EN"
 4:       "http://www.w3.org/TR/xhtml1/DTD/xhtml1-transitional.dtd">
 5: <html xmlns="http://www.w3.org/1999/xhtml" xml:lang="en" lang="en">
 6: <head><title>ex05-21.htm </title>
 7: <body>
 8: <script>
 9:   var xml = new ActiveXObject("Microsoft.XMLDOM")
10:       xml.async = false
11:       xml.load ("ex05-21.xml")
12:
13:   var xsl = new ActiveXObject("Microsoft.XMLDOM")
14:       xsl.async = false
15:       xsl.load("ex05-21.xsl")
16:       document.write(xml.transformNode(xsl))
17: </script>
18: </body><html>
```

This is an XHTML page to call the XML parser to display an XML page. After the usual XHTML header in lines 1–7, a script block of JavaScript or ECMAScript is declared to define the XML parser. To display an XML page with XSLT, two procedures are needed. The first step is to define and load the XML page into the parser. This is the job of lines 9–11. Line 9 creates an instance of the XML parser. Line 10 turns off the asynchronization setting. Therefore the parser will not continue before the document is fully loaded successfully. Line 11 instructs the parser to load the XML document which in this case is ex05-21.xml.

The next step is to load the XSLT file which is defined in lines 13-15. When both XML and XSL files are loaded, the following statement in line 16 is used to display the XML document on the browser window:

```
document.write(xml.transformNode(xsl))
```

A screen shot of this example on IE6.x is shown in Fig. 5.20.

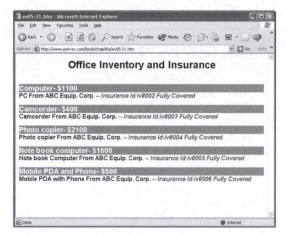

Figure 5.20 XML parser on IE

The real strength of the XML parser (Microsoft.XMLDOM) is that all elements and values of an XML page can be accessed through the Document Object Model (DOM). The DOM will be discussed in more detail in Chapters 10 and 11.

5.4.3 Accessing XML elements with parser

One of the important features of the XML parser is that elements of an XML page can be located and accessed via the DOM. The DOM is an important achievement of W3C. It provides a structure for markup languages including HTML/XHTML and XML. To see how the parser and DOM work, let's consider the following XML page:

```
Example: ex05-22.xml - Accessing XML Elements with Parser

 1: <?xml version="1.0" encoding="ISO-8859-1"?>
 2: <?xml-stylesheet type="text/css" href="ex05-20.css"?>
 3: <admin>
 4:    <person>
 5:      <name>Michael</name>
 6:      <birth>1950-12-18</birth>
 7:      <sex>M</sex>
 8:      <location>London</location>
 9:      <salary>30000</salary>
10:    </person>
11:    <person>
12:      <name>Mary</name>
13:      <birth>1980-6-22</birth>
14:      <sex>F</sex>
15:      <location>Paris</location>
16:      <salary>23000</salary>
17:    </person>
18: </admin>
```

This page contains one main element `<admin>`. Inside this `<admin>`, there are two child elements called `<person>`. Each `<person>` element also contains five child elements, namely, `<name>`, `<birth>`, `<sex>`, `<location>`, and `<salary>`.

Using the parser and DOM terms, the `<admin>` element can be accessed by the statement

```
xmlDoc.documentElement.firstChild
```

The object `xmlDoc.documentElement` represents the entire structure of the page and the first child of this page is, therefore, the `<admin>` element. Since there is only one child in this outermost level, the statement

```
xmlDoc.documentElement.lastChild
```

represents the same `<admin>` element in this case. A collection of all children of this outermost level is represented by the following statement:

```
prinodes = xmlDoc.documentElement.childNodes
```

Now, all the child nodes of the outermost level are assigned to the object `prinodes` (primary nodes). This object has two elements:

```
prinodes.item(0)
```
 – The first `<person>` element

```
prinodes.item(1)
```
 – The second `<person>` element

The `prinodes.item(0)` object represents the first `<person>` element. Data and information on this person can be collected by the statement

```
nodes = prinodes.item(0).childNodes
```

Now, all child nodes of the first `<person>` element are assigned to an object called `nodes`. Therefore, the data of the first person in ex05-22.xml are

```
nodes.item(0).text -- Michael
nodes.item(1).text -- 1950-12-18
nodes.item(2).text -- M
nodes.item(3).text -- London
nodes.item(4).text -- 30000
```

With these in mind, we can develop an XHTML page to gain access to all elements of an XML page. Consider the following XHTML page:

Example: ex05-22.htm – Accessing XML Element With Parser

```
 1: <?xml version="1.0" encoding="UTF-8"?>
 2: <!DOCTYPE html
 3:     PUBLIC "-//W3C//DTD XHTML 1.0 Transitional//EN"
 4:     "http://www.w3.org/TR/xhtml1/DTD/xhtml1-transitional.dtd">
 5: <html xmlns="http://www.w3.org/1999/xhtml" xml:lang="en" lang="en">
 6: <head><title>Example: ex05-22.htm </title>
 7: <script>
 8:    function xml_dom()
 9:    {
10:      var xmlDoc=new ActiveXObject("Microsoft.XMLDOM")
11:      xmlDoc.async="false"
12:      xmlDoc.load("ex05-22.xml")
13:
14:      prinodes=xmlDoc.documentElement.childNodes
15:      for (jj=0;jj< prinodes.length;jj++)
16:      {
17:        nodes = prinodes.item(jj).childNodes
18:        for (ii=0;ii< nodes.length -1 ;ii++)
19:        {
20:           document.write( nodes.item(ii).text + ", ")
21:        }
22:        document.write( nodes.item(ii).text)
23:        document.write("<br />")
```

```
24:     }
25:   }
26: </script>
27: <body style="background:#000088;color:#ffff00;text-align:center;
28:       font-family:arial;font-size:18pt;font-weight:bold">
29: <br />Access XML Elements With Parser<br /><br />
30:
31: <script>xml_dom()</script>
32: </body>
33: </html>
```

This is an XHTML page containing one Javascript (or ECMAScript) function called `xml_dom()`. After the usual body definition (lines 27–29), the Javascript function is called by the statement

```
<script>xml_dom()</script>
```

The detailed definition of this function is defined in lines 8–25. The first three lines of this function (lines 10–12) are to load the XML parser. After that, a collection of child nodes of the outermost level is assigned to the object `prinodes` (line 14). The number of elements inside `prinodes` is stored in the property

```
prinodes.length
```

This is a number and in this case is 2. A simple for-loop on variable `jj` to `prinodes.length` is used to gain access to all the <person> elements (lines 15–24). For each <person> element, all child nodes are assigned to the object nodes by

```
nodes = prinodes.item(jj).childNodes
```

A simple for-loop on variable `ii` to value `nodes.length` `-1` (lines 18–24) provides all data and information on the associated person in ex05-22.xml. The output statement in line 20

```
document.write( nodes.item(ii).text + ", ")
```

is to print out individual data such as name, birthday, sex, and location, depending on the item number `ii`. All the data are separated by a comma. When the last item is reached, the statement in line 22 is used to output the data without a comma. A screen shot of this example is shown in Fig. 5.21.

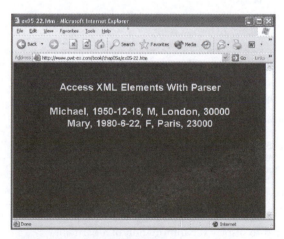

Figure 5.21 XML and parser II

When dealing with large amount of data or a large XML file, displaying all records at the same time may not be a convenient approach. For these applications, the ability to navigate data or XML elements is essential.

5.4.4   Navigating XML data using parser

In this section, we consider an example that can navigate the data in an XML file. For obvious reasons, we cannot employ a big file. For our demonstration, we consider the following XML document:

```
Example: ex05-23.xml - Navigating XML Data

 1: <?xml version="1.0" encoding="ISO-8859-1"?>
 2: <?xml-stylesheet type="text/css" href="ex05-20.css"?>
 3: <admin>
 4:    <person>
 5:      <name>Michael</name>
 6:      <birth>1950-12-18</birth>
 7:      <sex>M</sex>
 8:      <location>London</location>
 9:      <salary>30,000</salary>
10:    </person>
11:    <person>
12:      <name>Mary</name>
13:      <birth>1980-6-22</birth>
14:      <sex>F</sex>
15:      <location>Paris</location>
16:      <salary>23,000</salary>
17:    </person>
18:    <person>
19:     <name>Peter</name>
20:     <birth>1975-10-11</birth>
21:     <sex>M</sex>
22:     <location>New York</location>
23:     <salary>28,000</salary>
24:   </person>
25:   <person>
26:     <name>Sue</name>
27:     <birth>1969-1-19</birth>
28:     <sex>F</sex>
29:     <location>Paris</location>
30:     <salary>30,000</salary>
31:   </person>
32: </admin>
```

This XML file is the same as ex05-22.xml with two more pieces of data. They represent the sales team of an insurance company.

For simplicity, our navigating example contains four buttons. They are:

Next – Move to next record when pressed.

Previous – Move to previous record when pressed.

First – Move to the first record.

Last – Move to the last record.

Basically, the DOM structure of this XML document is read by the parser. By using the DOM information, a JavaScript function is developed to display the information of a particular `<person>` element. For this example, the function is

```
xml_dom_parser(item_no)
```

We can manipulate the value of the variable `item_no` to achieve the performance of the buttons. For example, when the First button is pressed, all we need to do is to call `xml_dom_parser(0)`. This will display all the information of the first `<person>` element in the XML page. When the Next button is pressed, the `item_no` is incremented by 1 and then `xml_dom_parser(item_no)` is called.

The first part of this example is listed below:

Example: ex05-23.htm - Navigating XML Data With Parser (Part One)

```
 1: <?xml version="1.0" encoding="UTF-8"?>
 2: <!DOCTYPE html
 3:     PUBLIC "-//W3C//DTD XHTML 1.0 Transitional//EN"
 4:     "http://www.w3.org/TR/xhtml1/DTD/xhtml1-transitional.dtd">
 5: <html xmlns="http://www.w3.org/1999/xhtml" xml:lang="en" lang="en">
 6: <head><title>Example: ex05-23.htm </title>
 7:
 8: <style>
 9:  .txtSt{background:#000088;color:#ffff00;
10:    font-family:arial;font-size:20pt;font-weight:bold}
11:  .buSt{background:#aaffaa;font-family:arial;font-weight:bold;
12:    font-size:14pt;color:#aa0000;width:150px;height:35px}
13: </style>
14:
15: <script>
16:   var xmlDoc=new ActiveXObject("Microsoft.XMLDOM")
17:       xmlDoc.async="false"
18:       xmlDoc.load("ex05-23.xml")
19:
20:   var prinodes=xmlDoc.documentElement.childNodes
21:   var last_no = prinodes.length -1
22:   var item_no =0
23:
24:   function xml_dom_parser(var_no)
25:   {
26:     nodes = prinodes.item(var_no).childNodes
27:     document.getElementById("name").innerText = nodes.item(0).text
28:     document.getElementById("birth").innerText = nodes.item(1).text
29:     document.getElementById("sex").innerText = nodes.item(2).text
30:     document.getElementById("location").innerText = nodes.item(3).text
31:     document.getElementById("salary").innerText = nodes.item(4).text
32:   }
33:
34:   function next() {
35:     if (item_no < prinodes.length -1) {
36:        item_no ++
37:        xml_dom_parser(item_no)
38:     }
39:   }
40:
41:   function previous() {
42:     if (item_no > 0) {
43:        item_no --
44:        xml_dom_parser(item_no)
45:     }
46:   }
47:
48:   function first_item() {
49:     item_no = 0
50:     xml_dom_parser(item_no)
```

```
51:   }
52:
53:   function last_item() {
54:     item_no = last_no
55:     xml_dom_parser(item_no)
56:   }
57: </script>
58:
```

After the XHTML header and some style definitions, this page contains a script block to define JavaScript or ECMAScript statements and functions. Lines 16–18 are used to defined the XMLDOM parser and load the XML page ex05-23.xml as data. The next three statements declare three variables. The prinodes is an object containing the collection of all <person> elements. The variable last_no in line 21 is the last item of the <person> element. The item_no variable represents the current <person> element and is initially set to 0. Putting a variable outside any function is to declare it as a global variable and available anywhere in the page.

The first JavaScript function in this page is

```
function xml_dom_parser(var_no)
```

This function will display all information inside the <person> element associated with the var_no. For example, when var_no is 2, the statement in line 26 turns out to be

```
nodes = prinodes.item(2).childNodes
```

Since the counting starts from 0, the object nodes contain a collection of all information associated with the third <person> element in ex05-23.xml. The remaining statements in lines 27–32 are used to extract the name, birthday, sex, location, and salary information for display. For example, consider the statement in line 27

```
document.getElementById("name").innerText = nodes.item(0).text
```

The keyword nodes.item(0).text contains the name of the person. This name is going to be displayed at the XHTML element location with an id attribute equal to "name." For example, if you have an XHTML element such as

```
<span id="name"></span>
```

the name will be displayed inside this element.

The next() function declared in lines 34–39 is simple. When this function is called, the item_no is incremented by 1 and then the xml_dom_parser(item_no) function is called. The remaining JavaScript functions previous(), first_item(), and last_item() are easy to understand.

The second part of this example is an XHTML document to display the result and is listed below:

```
Listing: Continuation Of The Example ex05-23.htm (Part Two)

59: <body class="txtSt" style="text-align:center">
60: <div style="text-algin:center">
61:   Staff Information Of ABC Insurance<br /><br /></div>
62:
63: <table cellspacing="10" class="txtSt" style="font-size:16pt">
64:   <tr><td width="150">Name </td>
65:       <td width="150"><span id="name"></span></td></tr>
66:   <tr><td>Birthday </td><td><span id="birth"></span></td></tr>
67:   <tr><td>Sex </td><td><span id="sex"></span></td></tr>
68:   <tr><td>Location </td><td><span id="location"></span></td></tr>
69:   <tr><td>Salary </td><td><span id="salary"></span></td></tr>
70: </table><br />
71:
```

```
72:  <input type="button" class="buSt" value="next" onclick="next()" />
73:  <input type="button" class="buSt" value="previous" onclick="previous()" />
74:          <br />
75:  <input type="button" class="buSt" value="first" onclick="first_item()" />
76:  <input type="button" class="buSt" value="last" onclick="last_item()" />
77:
78:  <script>xml_dom_parser(item_no)</script>
79:  </body>
80:  </html>
```

The first part of this listing is a table to display the result. The first row of the table is (see lines 64–65)

```
<tr><td width="150">Name </td>
    <td width="150"><span id="name"></span></td></tr>
```

The item of this row is a text name. The second item of this row contains an XHTML element:

```
<span id="name"></span>
```

This element has an id equal to "name" and therefore is ready to display anything instructed by the statement

```
document.getElementById("name").innertext = xxxxx
```

as illustrated in line 27 of this example. The remaining table elements are defined in a similar manner. The last part of this page (see lines 72–78) contains four buttons. The first button is

```
<input type="button" class="buSt" value="next" onclick="next()" />
```

This button has a value (or label) as "next." When this button is clicked, the function next() is called and moves the record to the next one. All other buttons are declared in a similar fashion.

In order to kick off the page, the statement in line 78 is used. This statement starts the page with a function called xml_dom_parser(item_no). Since the item_no is initially set to 0, the page will start by displaying the information of the first <person> element.

Some screen shots are shown in Figs 5.22–5.25.

Figure 5.22 The first <person>

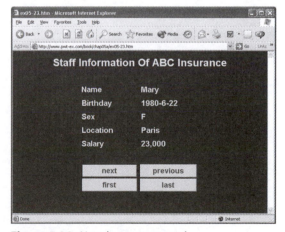

Figure 5.23 Next button pressed

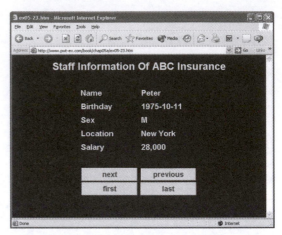

Figure 5.24 Last button pressed

Figure 5.25 Previous button pressed

Part II

Practical programming techniques for the Web I

6

Start with mouse-over control

6.1 Introduction: mouse events on the Web

Without a doubt, one of the necessary devices attached to our computer is the mouse. Indeed, from the moment you turn on your computer, you will need a mouse to help you to navigate your system. For example, you use your mouse to pick an icon, to activate a menu, and even to exit from your system. When surfing on the Web, the mouse is an absolute necessity. For HTML designers, mouse control capability is overwhelmed only by the HTML anchor element <a>. With just one mouse click, the anchor element can take you to the outside world. HTML, as a language, didn't tell us how to control a mouse for other purposes. It did, however, provide a series of events (*mouse events*) for us to use and control them indirectly. This chapter is dedicated to the discussion of mouse events. The differences among browsers and the confusion over the Document Object Model (DOM) are also discussed at the same time. This chapter presents a comprehensive discussion on "mouse-over" (or rollover) techniques together with demonstrations. We also show you how to capture the position of the mouse and to move objects (texts and images) along with the mouse. All these ideas are put together in section 6.5 to build a menu system with window style. You will see that a menu system can be implemented easily with mouse-over techniques. Some of the techniques in this chapter lead to the discussion on Web programming in later chapters.

In general we follow the W3C recommendations on mouse events. All examples will run on the latest versions of both IE and NS browsers. A majority of them will run even without the need for any browser detection codes. Along with the W3C standard, some professional techniques to deal with mouse events concerning backward compatibility are also presented. These discussions, particularly in the early sections, should provide enough background material and ideas to help you develop all-singing and dancing Web pages that are independent of browsers and versions.

What are mouse events, anyway?

6.1.1 Mouse events

Any operation that involves a mouse will generate mouse events. These events are used to trigger certain kinds of actions designed by Web programmers. In this chapter, we're going to discuss the four basic mouse operations in Table 6.1 and their corresponding mouse events.

Table 6.1 Mouse events

Operations	Events	XHTML description
Mouse movement	onmousemove	The mouse was moved within the boundary of the element
Mouse click	onclick	The mouse has been clicked
Mouse in	onmouseover	The mouse enters the bounds of an element from outside the element
Mouse out	onmouseout	The mouse was moved out of the boundary of the element

Before you can capture the mouse events and act accordingly, you need to associate each XHTML element with an identity (id). Previous HTML such as HTML4.01 defines a name attribute for elements <a>, <applet>, <frame>, <img>, and <map>. In XHTML the name attribute is deprecated and the attribute id is used instead. For backward compatibility, and to develop Web pages for all major browsers, we follow the recommendations of the W3C authority to use both the name and id, with identical values such as

```
<img alt="pic" id="pic01" name="pic01" src="pic01.jpg" />
```

An element with an id is considered as an object with its own boundary. For each action like "Move Over" or "On Click," the browsers (or capable browsers) capture the event and refer back to the element in the form of a mouse event. Web programmes may need to use some kind of programming techniques to handle these mouse events (or simply events). This idea is used to form the so-called "Document Object Model" or DOM as it is now famously known. Basically, the DOM is a structure on the Web to allow us to access Web page elements by means of other technologies.

6.1.2   DOM confusion

Unfortunately, the lack of standard implementation and cooperation amongst major browser developers creates a confusing situation regarding the DOM. For example, Web programmers, for the last few years, have had difficulties sorting out a unifying DOM structure between the IE and NS families of browsers. As a result, a detection process is usually needed and consequently two sets of coding are required in order to display Web pages correctly. One set is for the IE and the other for NS. The following is a popular browser detection code:

```
Listing: ex06-01.txt

 1:    <script language="JavaScript">
 2:    <!--
 3:    if (document.all)
 4:    {
 5:      alert("Browser: Internet Explorer Detected");
 6:      // doing all sort of things for IE.
 7:    }
 8:    else if (document.layers)
 9:    {
10:      alert("Browser: Netscape Navigator Detected");
11:      // doing all sort of things for Netscape.
12:    }
13:    else
14:    {
15:      alert("Panic: Unrecognized Browser Detected");
16:    }
17:    // -->
18:    </script>
```

This code works well for the IE family and NS4.x and previous versions. If you run this on NS 6.x, you will get the "Panic: Unrecognized Browser Detected" message. This is because NS6.x doesn't support IE's `document.all` or its own `document.layers` feature. Netscape gave up its own DOM in favor of the W3C's. Similar things are happening among IE family members. In fact, it is not just the differences in the DOM that you may need to handle, but also the "Event Model" differences.

Fortunately, you don't really need to handle these situations in great detail at this moment. Later in this chapter, we will show you how to handle browsers' differences and to write the corresponding detection codes. First let's begin with some simple mouse control programs with no or very little browser and version conflicts.

6.2 Beginning mouse over (or rollover)

6.2.1 My first mouse-over page

In this section, a mouse-over technique that will work on all major browsers and versions is introduced. Our first mouse-over (or rollover) HTML page will display a picture. This picture will change to another one when a mouse runs over it. You are bound to have seen lots of Web pages with this feature and may wonder how they do it. You may be surprised to find out that this can be done by just three lines of code:

```
Listing: ex06-02.txt

1:      <a href="#" onmouseover='document.my_img.src="rody04.gif"'>
2:         <img alt="pic" id="my_img" name="my_img" src="logo_web.jpg" />
3:      </a>
```

These lines of code may look strange. Believe it or not, they are very popular among Web professionals. Basically, this is an HTML anchor `<a>` element that includes an image. The `<img>` element is used to specify an image to be displayed on a page. Inside this element, a name called `my_img` is assigned in line 2. The image itself is a JPG picture file called `logo_web.jpg`. Our page displays this picture when first activated. When you click on this image picture, the anchor element activates the hyper reference and jumps to another page. We have put a # symbol inside the `href` attribute so that the anchor will not jump to another page. The command

```
onmouseover
```

is an intrinsic event provided by HTML/XHTML to handle a mouse-over situation. This is triggered when a mouse runs over the boundary of the element concerned. When the mouse runs over the picture, for example, the following action will be executed:

```
document.my_img.src = "rody04.gif"
```

This changes our image resource to a new file called `rody04.gif`. Since the statement has immediate effect, you will see the change of image in real time. The statement `document.my_img` is a DOM structure used to identify the XHTML element that we want to change. The interesting part is that we have used an anchor element `<a>` to trigger the `onmouseover`. This is because not all browsers support `onmouseover` on every XHTML element. However, they all support mouse events with anchor. Since the anchor element `<a>` is used here, this is an all-singing and dancing setting and will work on all major browsers and versions.

To complete this as a working Web page, you can:

- add a simple header and a basic background color `#a0a0ff`;
- set the `link`, `vlink`, and `alink` color as background color to cover the tail of `<a>`.

Example: ex06-01.htm - My First Mouse Over Page

```
1:     <?xml version="1.0" encoding="iso-8859-1"?>
2:     <!DOCTYPE html PUBLIC "-//W3C//DTD XHTML 1.0 Transitional//EN"
3:         "http://www.w3.org/TR/xhtml1/DTD/xhtml1-transitional.dtd">
4:     <html xmlns="http://www.w3.org/1999/xhtml" xml:lang="en" lang="en">
5:     <head>
6:       <title>My First Mouse Over Page - ex06-01.htm</title>
7:     </head>
8:     <body bgcolor="#a0a0ff" vlink="#a0a0ff"
9:           link="#a0a0ff" alink="#a0a0ff">
10:      <div align="center"><br /><br />
11:      <a href="#" onmouseover='document.my_img.src="rody04.gif"'>
12:        <img alt="pic" id="my_img" name="my_img" src="logo_web.jpg" />
13:      </a>
14:      </div>
15:    </body>
16:    </html>
```

This page will work on major browsers including some of their older versions. Some results are captured in Figs 6.1 and 6.2.

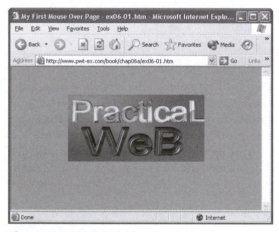

Figure 6.1 ex06–01.htm

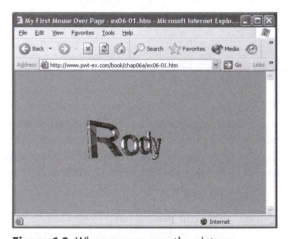

Figure 6.2 When mouse over the picture

You can add the onmouseout command as in line 13 of ex06-02.htm to change the picture back to its original when a mouse moves out.

Example: ex06-02.htm - My Mouse In And Out Page

```
1:     <?xml version="1.0" encoding="iso-8859-1"?>
2:     <!DOCTYPE html PUBLIC "-//W3C//DTD XHTML 1.0 Transitional//EN"
3:         "http://www.w3.org/TR/xhtml1/DTD/xhtml1-transitional.dtd">
4:     <html xmlns="http://www.w3.org/1999/xhtml" xml:lang="en" lang="en">
5:     <head>
6:       <title>My Mouse In and Out Page - ex06-02.htm</title>
7:     </head>
8:     <body bgcolor="#a0a0ff" vlink="#a0a0ff"
9:           link="#a0a0ff" alink="#a0a0ff">
10:      <div align="center"><br /><br />
11:      <a href="#"
12:        onmouseover='document.my_img.src="rody04.gif"'
```

```
13:            onmouseout='document.my_img.src="logo_web.jpg"'>
14:        <img alt="pic" id="my_img" name="my_img" src="logo_web.jpg" />
15:      </a>
16:      </div>
17:    </body>
18:    </html>
```

When the mouse comes out from the picture, the browser will generate an onmouseout event and the statement in line 13 will change the picture back to its original one. If you want the page to have the capability to jump to other pages, you simply add the usual hyperlink inside the href attribute in line 11.

6.2.2   Mouse events supported by browsers and versions

W3C's XHTML standard suggests global support for mouse events on almost all its elements. The latest versions of IE and NS fully implement this recommendation. Some earlier browsers such as NS4.x support very few of them. For professional Web programmers, precautions should be taken when browser differences are essential. For example, the program ex06-02.htm can be written as ex06-03.htm, making use of a more structural approach such as getElementById recommended by the W3C authority.

Example: ex06-03.htm - Mouse Over For IE4+ And N6+ Only

```
 1:    <?xml version="1.0" encoding="iso-8859-1"?>
 2:    <!DOCTYPE html PUBLIC "-//W3C//DTD XHTML 1.0 Transitional//EN"
 3:        "http://www.w3.org/TR/xhtml1/DTD/xhtml1-transitional.dtd">
 4:    <html xmlns="http://www.w3.org/1999/xhtml" xml:lang="en" lang="en">
 5:    <head>
 6:       <title> Mouse Over For IE4+ and N6+ Only - ex06-03.htm </title>
 7:    </head>
 8:    <body style="background:#a0a0ff">
 9:    <div align="center"> <br /><br />
10:     <img alt="pic" id="my_img"
11:       src="logo_web.jpg"
12:       onmouseover='document.getElementById("my_img").src="rody04.gif"'
13:       onmouseout='document.getElementById("my_img").src="logo_web.jpg"' />
14:    </div>
15:    </body>
16:    </html>
```

In this case, both onmouseover and onmouseout are included inside the image element <img>. This program will, of course, work on the latest versions of IE and NS, but fails to run on NS4.x. This is because NS4.x doesn't support mouse events inside image elements and getElementById features. The attribute id="my_img" in line 10 is for identity purposes and ready for the use of getElementById.

It is almost impossible to provide a full account of elements and attributes that support mouse events associated with all browsers and versions. For practical purposes, Table 6.2 lists some of the most popular elements and attributes.

Table 6.2 Mouse events support table

Elements		HTML and XHTML versions						Browsers and versions		
Element and attributes		**3.0**	**3.2**	**4.0**	**4.01**	**X1.0**		**IE**	**NS**	**O**
`<a href>`		–	–	✗	✗	✗		4.0+	4.0+	–
`<a name>`		–	–	✗	✗	✗		4.0+	6.0+	–
`<div>`		–	–	✗	✗	✗		4.0+	6.0+	–
`<img>`		–	–	✗	✗	✗		4.0+	6.0+	–
`<input type=button>`		–	–	✗	✗	✗		4.0+	4.0+	–
`<object>`		–	–	✗	✗	✗		5.0+	6.0+	–
`<span>`		–	–	✗	✗	✗		4.0+	6.0+	–
`<table>`		–	–	✗	✗	✗		4.0+	6.0+	–
`<td>`		–	–	✗	✗	✗		4.0+	6.0+	–
`<tr>`		–	–	✗	✗	✗		4.0+	6.0+	–

IE – Internet Explorer   4.0 – HTML V.4.0
NS – Netscape   4.01 – HTML V.4.01
O – Other browsers   X1.0 – XHTML V.1.0

From this table, you can clearly see that NS4.x does not support onmouseover events with the image element `<img>`. In fact, in the case of mouse events, NS4.x supports very few XHTML elements. If you want to write a page that is all singing and dancing, the anchor `<a href="#"..>` technique as demonstrated in example ex06-02.htm is quite useful. In the next section, we will use the same technique to develop a simple art gallery page for all major browsers with no detection code needed.

6.2.3   A simple art gallery

In this section, we consider a Web page to display a series of cyber art with browser backward compatibility. For simplicity, only one page of art with six animated contents is constructed. In order to have a tabular form, all art contents are organized into a 3×2 XHTML table and use the anchor technique merely to support earlier browsers.

The main structure of the page is a table as shown in the following code (lines 12–49):

```
Example: ex06-04.htm - A Simple Art Gallery

 1: <?xml version="1.0" encoding="iso-8859-1"?>
 2: <!DOCTYPE html PUBLIC "-//W3C//DTD XHTML 1.0 Transitional//EN"
 3:     "http://www.w3.org/TR/xhtml1/DTD/xhtml1-transitional.dtd">
 4: <html xmlns="http://www.w3.org/1999/xhtml" xml:lang="en" lang="en">
 5: <head>
 6:   <title> A Simple Art Gallery - ex06-04.htm </title>
 7: </head>
 8: <body style="background:#80bb80">
 9: <div align="center">
10: <img alt="pic" src="head.gif" />
11: <img alt="pic" src="line1.gif" width="600" height="6" />
12: <table>
```

```
13:   <tr align="center"><td width="300" height="180">
14:    <a href="#" onmouseout='document.item11.src="p_cover.gif"'
15:       onmouseover='document.item11.src="rody04.gif"'>
16:     <img alt="pic" src="p_cover.gif" width="250" height="170" border="0"
17:       id="item11" name="item11" /></a>
18:   </td><td width="300" height="180">
19:    <a href="#" onmouseout='document.item12.src="p_cover.gif"'
20:       onmouseover='document.item12.src="gasty4.gif"'>
21:    <img alt="pic" src="p_cover.gif" width="250" height="170" border="0"
22:       id="item12" name="item12" /></a>
23:   </td></tr>
24:
25:   <tr align="center"><td width="300" height="180">
26:     <a href="#" onmouseout='document.item21.src="p_cover.gif"'
27:        onmouseover='document.item21.src="boom.gif"'>
28:    <img alt="pic" src="p_cover.gif" width="250" height="170" border="0"
29:        id="item21" name="item21" /></a>
30:   </td><td width="300" height="180">
31:     <a href="#" onmouseout='document.item22.src="p_cover.gif"'
32:        onmouseover='document.item22.src="chengs.gif"'>
33:    <img alt="pic" src="p_cover.gif" width="250" height="170" border="0"
34:        id="item22" name="item22" /></a>
35:   </td></tr>
36:
37:   <tr align="center"><td width="300" height="180">
38:     <a href="#" onmouseout='document.item31.src="p_cover.gif"'
39:        onmouseover='document.item31.src="title4.gif"'>
40:    <img alt="pic" src="p_cover.gif" width="250" height="170" border="0"
41:        id="item31" name="item31" /></a>
42:  </td><td width="300" height="180">
43:     <a href="#" onMouseOut='document.item32.src="p_cover.gif"'
44:        onMouseOver='document.item32.src="pumkin.gif"'>
45:    <img alt="pic" src="p_cover.gif" width="250" height="170" border="0"
46:        id="item32" name="item32" /></a>
47:  </td></tr>
48:
49:  </table>
50:  </div>
51:  </body>
52:  </html>
```

Line 13 defines a table row with alignment at the center and table data <td> with size 300×180 pixels. Inside the table data, there is an anchor element and the usual onmouseover and onmouseout settings to trigger the events. In line 16, the image itself is defined by the <img> element with name identity item11. The second art content of the first row is defined in a very similar manner (lines 18–23). Continue to define the table row three times and you will have a 3×2 XHTML table. The collection of art here is just a set of simple animated GIF files.

Because we've added the complication of using the anchor element, this page works on earlier browsers as well as the latest ones. Recall that our initial aim of this chapter is to develop all-singing and dancing mouse-over Web pages that do not need any detection code. The results are shown in Figs 6.3 and 6.4.

Now we are beginning to understand why so many Web pages on the Internet actually use the anchor element to deal with mouse-over control. For many cases the anchor element did provide a gateway for backward compatibility. Next, you will see how to use the same technique to change the global background colors of a Web page. After that we will show you how to use a more structural approach (W3C's recommendations) to solve more complex problems.

Figure 6.3 Art gallery I

Figure 6.4 Art gallery II

6.2.4 Changing background color with mouse over

The first global settings that we want to manipulate are the global background colors. Background color is a property inside the document object and can be accessed through the classical `bgColor` value. This is an immediate process. Any value changes will result an instant update. Our next example shows background color change with mouse over. When the mouse runs over the color region, the global background color changes instantly. The original background color will be restored when the mouse moves out of the color region.

```
Example: ex06-05.htm - Changing Background Color

 1: <?xml version="1.0" encoding="iso-8859-1"?>
 2: <!DOCTYPE html PUBLIC "-//W3C//DTD XHTML 1.0 Transitional//EN"
 3:     "http://www.w3.org/TR/xhtml1/DTD/xhtml1-transitional.dtd">
 4: <html xmlns="http://www.w3.org/1999/xhtml" xml:lang="en" lang="en">
 5: <head>
 6:   <title> Changing Background Color - ex06-05.htm </title>
 7: </head>
 8: <style>
 9:   h3{font-family:arial;font-size:12pt;color:#0000ff}
10: </style>
11:
12: <body bgColor="#eeeeee">
13: <table border="4" align="center" bgColor="#cccccc">
14:  <tr><td colspan="5" align="center">
15:      <h3> Changing Background Color With Mouse Over</h3>
16:      </td></tr>
17:  <tr align="center">
18:   <td width="80" height="28">
19:    <a href="#" onmouseout='document.bgColor="#eeeeee"'
20:                onmouseover='document.bgColor="#ff0000"'>
21:    <img alt="pic" src="red.gif" width="80" height="28" border="0" />
22:  </a></td>
23:   <td width="80" height="28">
24:    <a href="#" onmouseout='document.bgColor="#eeeeee"'
25:                onmouseover='document.bgColor="#00ff00"'>
26:    <img alt="pic" src="green.gif" width="80" height="28" border="0" />
27:  </a></td>
28:   <td width="80" height="28">
```

```
29:     <a href="#" onmouseout='document.bgColor="#eeeeee"'
30:                 onmouseover='document.bgColor="#0000ff"'>
31:     <img alt="pic" src="blue.gif" width="80" height="28" border="0" />
32:   </a></td>
33:   <td width="80">
34:     <a href="#" onmouseout='document.bgColor="#eeeeee"'
35:                 onmouseover='document.bgColor="#ffff00"'>
36:   <img alt="pic" src="yellow.gif" width="80" height="28" border="0" />
37:   </a></td>
38:   <td width="80">
39:     <a href="#" onmouseout='document.bgColor="#eeeeee"'
40:                 onmouseover='document.bgColor="#ff00ff"'>
41:   <img alt="pic" src="pink.gif" width="80" height="28" border="0" />
42:     </a></td>
43:  </tr>
44:  </table>
45:  </body>
46:  </html>
```

Lines 13–44, and hence the whole program, are a table with two rows. The first row, lines 14–16, is just a header. The second row has five elements. The first element is defined by

```
18:   <td width="80" height="28">
19:     <a href="#" onmouseout='document.bgColor="#eeeeee"'
20:                 onmouseover='document.bgColor="#ff0000"'>
21:     <img alt="pic" src="red.gif"a width="80" height="28" border="0" />
22:   </a></td>
```

This is a table cell of 80×28 pixels (line 18). Inside this area is a small picture (a red color picture). The main action is in lines 19–20. When a mouse runs over this small picture, the onmouseover will set the bgColor to #ff0000 (red) as indicated in line 20. When the mouse is outside the image region, the onmouseout event (line 19) is activated and restores the global background color. Some of the screen shots are listed in Figs 6.5 and 6.6.

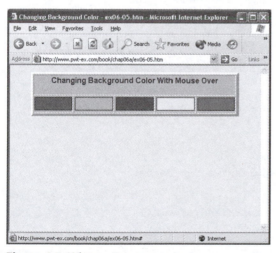

Figure 6.5 When mouse over green

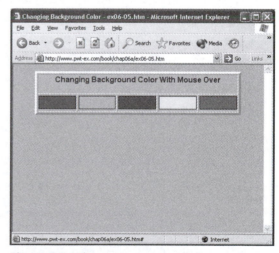

Figure 6.6 When mouse over yellow

In general Netscape's browsers are case sensitive and Microsoft's are not. If you use bgcolor instead of bgColor, this example will run on IE but not NS.

A more structural approach recommended by the W3C authority is to use getElementById and the style operator. First, you need to give the document body an id and use a CSS style such as

```
<body id="body01" style="background-color:#eeeeee">
```

This `id="body01"` identifies the body element by `getElementById` later and changes its background color attribute. You can replace lines 18–22 of the previous example by the following listing:

Listing: ex06-03.txt

```
1: <tr align="center">
2: <td style="width:80px;background-color:#ff0000"
3:   onmouseover=
4:   'document.getElementById("body01").style.backgroundColor="#ff0000"'
5:   onmouseout=
6:   'document.getElementById("body01").style.backgroundColor="#aaaaaa"'>
7: </td>
```

Line 2 is table data of size 80 pixels. The `background-color` setting will set the background color of the table data as red so that we don't need any color image here. Lines 3–6 are the main actions for the `onmouseover` and `onmouseout` commands. Finally `getElementById` and `style` are used to change the background color (lines 4 and 6). This approach provides a more structured behavior toward XHTML and Web programming. We will focus more on this approach as recommended by the W3C authority.

6.2.5   Creating background textures

We've already had some experience of textures from Chapter 1. Textures play an important role in Web page design and businesses. A good background texture always gives a good first impression to readers and provides a warm welcome to visitors or potential customers. For some business sectors, this could play a vital part in attracting new customers. Just imagine that you are a Web programmer working for a company selling a large variety of marbles or stones, or a textile company selling fabrics, or an interior design company specializing in flooring texture. You will need a dynamic background texture for your Web site to enhance your business. In the next example, a simple Web page is built to generate background textures. A table of small pictures such as stones, fabric materials, and wood is used. When a visitor runs over one of the images using a mouse, the entire background will change into the selected texture. The page has the following code:

Example: ex06-06.htm - Creating Background Texture

```
1:    <?xml version="1.0" encoding="iso-8859-1"?>
2:    <!DOCTYPE html PUBLIC "-//W3C//DTD XHTML 1.0 Transitional//EN"
3:       "http://www.w3.org/TR/xhtml1/DTD/xhtml1-transitional.dtd">
4:    <html xmlns="http://www.w3.org/1999/xhtml" xml:lang="en" lang="en">
5:    <head>
6:      <title> Creating Background Texture - ex06-06.htm </title>
7:    </head>
8:
9:    <style>
10:      h3 { font-family: Arial; font-size: 16pt;
11:          font-weight:bold; color: yellow;text-align:center}
12:      body{background-color:#448844}
13:      .td01{background:#00ffff;width:70px;height:60px}
14:      .img01{width:50px;height:50px;vertical-align:middle"}
15:    </style>
16:
17:    <body id="body01">
18:    <div align="center">
19:    <table border="3">
20:     <tr><td colspan="5" style="background:#000088">
21:        <h3>Creating Background Textures</h3></td></tr>
22:     <tr><td class="td01" align="center">
23:      <img alt="pic" class="img01" src="texture01.jpg"
24:        onmouseover=
25:        "document.getElementById('body01').background='texture01.jpg'"
26:        onmouseout="document.getElementById('body01').background=''" />
```

```
27:        </td>
28:        <td class="td01" align="center">
29:         <img alt="pic" class="img01" src="texture02.jpg"
30:          onmouseover=
31:           "document.getElementById('body01').background='texture02.jpg'"
32:           onmouseout="document.getElementById('body01').background=''" />
33:        </td>
34:        <td class="td01" align="center">
35:         <img alt="pic" class="img01" src="texture03.jpg"
36:          onmouseover=
37:           "document.getElementById('body01').background='texture03.jpg'"
38:           onmouseout="document.getElementById('body01').background=''" />
39:        </td>
40:        <td class="td01" align="center">
41:         <img alt="pic" class="img01" src="texture04.jpg"
42:          onmouseover=
43:           "document.getElementById('body01').background='texture04.jpg'"
44:           onmouseout="document.getElementById('body01').background=''" />
45:        </td>
46:        <td class="td01" align="center">
47:         <img alt="pic" class="img01" src="texture05.jpg"
48:          onmouseover=
49:           "document.getElementById('body01').background='texture05.jpg'"
50:           onmouseout="document.getElementById('body01').background=''" />
51:        </td>
52:        </body>
53:        </html>
```

After the `style` definition in lines 9–15, the key element of this page is the code fragment occupying lines 22–27:

```
22:        <td class="td01" align="center">
23:         <img alt="pic" class="img01" src="texture01.jpg"
24:          onmouseover=
25:           "document.getElementById('body01').background='texture01.jpg'"
26:           onmouseout="document.getElementById('body01').background=''" />
27:        </td>
```

Line 22 defines table data with a style class `td01` specifying color and size. Inside the table data (line 23) is an image with file name texture01.jpg. The next two lines indicate that if a mouse runs over this small picture, the browser will get the body id (i.e., `body01`) and use the image file texture01.jpg to generate the entire background texture. If the mouse runs outside the picture, the background color will be restored, as in Figs 6.7 and 6.8.

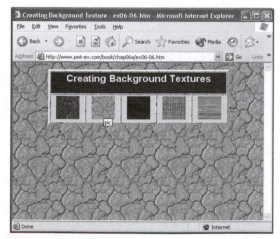

Figure 6.7 Mouse-over texture I

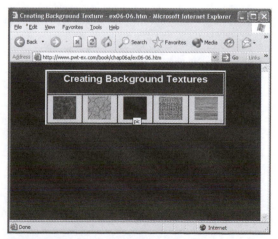

Figure 6.8 Mouse-over texture II

6.3   Changing text attributes with mouse over

6.3.1   Highlighting text with a dynamic background color

Another popular technique on the Web is to change text background color dynamically when the mouse moves over it. This is often used to highlight options or selected items so that the visitor knows what he or she is choosing. It also has the so-called "getting the attention" effect. By using style (CSS style) and the DOM structure, changing text colors (whether foreground or background) can be done in an elegant way.

Suppose you have a CSS style class called .text01 as listed in ex06-04.txt:

Listing: ex06-04.txt

```
1:     <style>
2:       .text01 {
3:         font-size:16pt;
4:         font-family:arial,sans-serif;
5:         color: green;
6:         background-color:white
7:       }
8:     </style>
```

Any attributes or properties inside this style can be accessed and changed by using the this.style operator. For example, the following code is used to change the background color when a mouse runs over it:

Listing: ex06-05.txt

```
1:   <span class="text01"
2:      onmouseover='this.style.backgroundColor="#ffaaaa"'
3:      onmouseout='this.style.backgroundColor="white"'>
4:    Practical XHTML </span>
```

Line 1 uses <span> with style class class="text01". This style contains typeface font, size, and color settings used to display the message in line 4. Since we assume mouse events are supported by the browser on the element <span>, attributes onmouseover and onmouseout are used directly in lines 2–3. The purpose of this.style is to identify this element and backgroundColor property to change the background color.

As a complete example, you can now add more items and highlight the changing background colors.

Example: ex06-07.htm – Highlight Item By Mouse Over

```
 1:  <?xml version="1.0" encoding="iso-8859-1"?>
 2:  <!DOCTYPE html PUBLIC "-//W3C//DTD XHTML 1.0 Transitional//EN"
 3:      "http://www.w3.org/TR/xhtml1/DTD/xhtml1-transitional.dtd">
 4:  <html xmlns="http://www.w3.org/1999/xhtml" xml:lang="en" lang="en">
 5:  <head>
 6:  <title> Highlight Item By Mouse Over - ex06-07.htm </title>
 7:  </head>
 8:  <style>
 9:     .text01
10:     {
11:       font-size:16pt;
12:       font-family:arial,sans-serif;
13:       color: green;
14:       background-color:white
15:     }
16:  </style>
17:  <body>
18:  <span class="text01" style="color:black">Practical Web Technologies<br />
19:  <br />   
20:  <span class="text01"
```

```
21:      onmouseover='this.style.backgroundColor="#ffaaaa"'
22:      onmouseout='this.style.backgroundColor="white"'>
23:   Practical XHTML</span><br />
24: <span class="text01"
25:      onmouseover='this.style.backgroundColor="#ffaaaa"'
26:      onmouseout='this.style.backgroundColor="white"'>   
27:   Practical Programming Techniques For The Web</span><br />
28: <span class="text01"
29:      onmouseover='this.style.backgroundColor="#ffaaaa"'
30:      onmouseout='this.style.backgroundColor="white"'>   
31:    Server CGI Techniques For Web Business</span><br />
32: <span class="text01"
33:      onmouseover='this.style.backgroundColor="#ffaaaa"'
34:      onmouseout='this.style.backgroundColor="white"'>   
35:  Web Development With DOM and DHTML</span>
36: </body>
37: </html>
```

This XHTML page will work on W3C-compatible browsers such as the latest IE and NS since they share the same DOM structure to access the CSS properties. Some of the screen displays are captured in Figs 6.9 and 6.10.

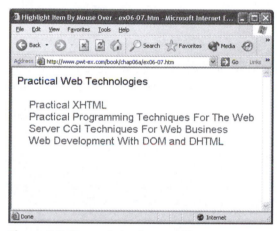

Figure 6.9 Dynamic background I

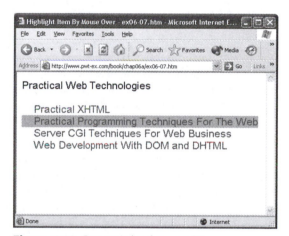

Figure 6.10 Dynamic background II

6.3.2 Changing text sizes and fonts on the fly with the style object

From the discussion above, it is clear that in order to change the properties of a CSS class, you need to find the corresponding property names in events. To access CSS styles and properties, the style object inside the browser can be used. Almost all properties in a CSS sheet can be accessed and changed via this "style" object. This is why we have the word `style` inside the `this.style.backgroundColor` statement used in our previous examples. This `style` object has a long list of properties and therefore only a simple table related to fonts and colors is given in Table 6.3.

Table 6.3 Style object properties for font size and color

CSS properties	Style object properties	Attributes
font-family	fontFamily	Specific (Arial etc.) Generic (serif etc.)
font-style	fontStyle	Normal, italic, oblique
font-size	fontSize	In absolute or relative units
font-weight	fontWeight	Normal, bold, bolder, lighter, or numeric values 100–900
color	color	Color names or #RRGGBB
background-color	backgroundColor	Color names or #RRGGBB

With this table, it should be quite easy to rewrite example ex06-04.htm to change font sizes and colors on the fly.

6.3.3   CSS class name swapping

Using the style object is a convenient way to change one or two CSS properties at one time. If you don't want to use script functions, then to change more than two CSS properties via onmouseover could be quite annoying. Don't forget that you may need to change them back to their originals when onmouseout is true. It is much better if we can have a simple way to swap two CSS class names. This can be done by the this operator and className attribute as described in the next example.

Consider the following page with five style classes. Each of them has a set of specific settings to catch the visitor's attention.

```
Example: ex06-08.htm - Swapping Class Name When Mouse Over

1:  <?xml version="1.0" encoding="iso-8859-1"?>
2:  <!DOCTYPE html PUBLIC "-//W3C//DTD XHTML 1.0 Transitional//EN"
3:      "http://www.w3.org/TR/xhtml1/DTD/xhtml1-transitional.dtd">
4:  <html xmlns="http://www.w3.org/1999/xhtml" xml:lang="en" lang="en">
5:   <head>
6:    <title>Swapping Class Name When Mouse Over - ex06-08.htm </title>
7:   </head>
8:  <style>
9:    .text01 {font-size:16pt; font-family:arial,sans-serif;color:green;}
10:
11:   .text02 {font-size:26pt; font-family:arial,sans-serif;color:red;}
12:
13:   .text03 { font-size:18pt; font-family:Times,sans-serif;color:blue;
14:       font-style: italic; background-color:#ffaaaa}
15:
16:   .text04 { font-size:18pt; font-family:Times,sans-serif;color:#ff00ff;
17:       position: relative; left: 100px }
18:
19:   .text05 { font-size:18pt; font-family:Times,sans-serif;color:#000088;
20:       position: relative; top: 20px }
21:  </style>
22:  <body>
23:   <span id="part1" class="text01" style="color:black">
24:       Practical Web Technologies<br /><br />   
25:
26:   <span class="text01"
27:       onmouseover='this.className="text02"'
```

```
28:          onmouseout='this.className="text01"'>
29:    Change To Bigger
30:  </span><br />   
31:
32:  <span class="text01"
33:        onmouseover='this.className="text03"'
34:        onmouseout='this.className="text01"'>
35:    Change To Blue and Italic
36:  </span><br />   
37:
38:  <span class="text01"
39:        onmouseover='this.className="text04"'
40:        onmouseout='this.className="text01"'>
41:    Jump To Left
42:  </span><br />   
43:
44:  <span class="text01"
45:        onmouseover='this.className="text05"'
46:        onmouseout='this.className="text01"'>
47:    Going Down!</span>
48: </body>
49: </html>
```

Between lines 8 and 21, we have five style class specifications:

- `text01` – Basic style (i.e., Arial font, size 16 pt, and green color)
- `text02` – Basic style with 26pt font size and red color
- `text03` – Basic style with italic font style and a background color
- `text04` – Basic style with different left location
- `text05` – Basic style with different top location

Next, four paragraphs are defined with `text01` as primary class names and change to other class names when a mouse passes over them. The purpose of the statement `this.className=xxx` is to swap the class and accomplish the task. Some screen shots are listed in Figs 6.11–6.14.

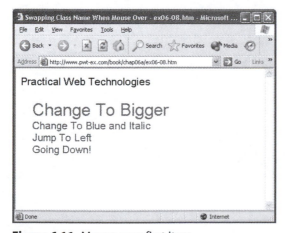

Figure 6.11 Mouse over first item

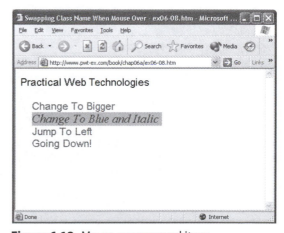

Figure 6.12 Mouse over second item

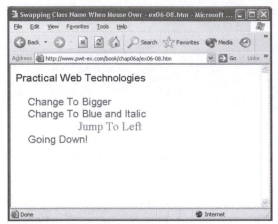

Figure 6.13 Mouse over third item

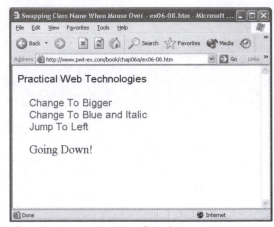

Figure 6.14 Mouse over fourth item

6.3.4   Output text with mouse over

To be able to change the texts (or messages) on the screen dynamically or, more precisely, to change the contents of an XHTML element to achieve a certain purpose is important for many applications. This feature not only can improve the look, clarity, and sophistication of a Web page, but also can be used to develop a so-called *hyper help* or *hyper explanation* system. Basically this technique starts from one thing: when a mouse runs over certain items, more information will be displayed on a specific area. For a simple example, consider the following code:

Example: ex06-09.htm - Output Text When Mouse Over

```
 1:    <?xml version="1.0" encoding="iso-8859-1"?>
 2:    <!DOCTYPE html PUBLIC "-//W3C//DTD XHTML 1.0 Transitional//EN"
 3:        "http://www.w3.org/TR/xhtml1/DTD/xhtml1-transitional.dtd">
 4:    <html xmlns="http://www.w3.org/1999/xhtml" xml:lang="en" lang="en">
 5:    <head>
 6:      <title> Output Text When Mouse Over - ex06-09.htm </title>
 7:    </head>
 8:    <style>
 9:      .text01 {font-size:48pt; font-family:arial,sans-serif;
10:             text-align:center;color: red;font-weight:bold}
11:
12:      .text02 {font-size:48pt; font-family:arial,sans-serif;
13:             text-align:right;color: green;font-weight:bold}
14:    </style>
15:    <body>
16:
17:    <span class="text01"
18:        onmouseover="this.innerHTML='Got You!'"
19:        onmouseout="this.innerHTML='Touch Here!'">
20:      Touch Here!</span>
21:
22:    <br /><br /><br /><br />
23:
24:    <div class="text02"
25:        onmouseover="this.innerHTML='Thank You!'"
26:        onmouseout="this.innerHTML='Touch Here!'">
27:      Touch Here!</div>
28:    </body>
29:    </html>
```

This page generates two paragraphs with the messages "Touch Here!" on the left and another "Touch Here!" on the right as indicated in lines 19 and 26 respectively (see Figs 6.15 and 6.16). These two messages have the CSS class names text01 and text02 in the usual way. The interesting part is line 18

```
onmouseover="this.innerHTML='Got You!'"
```

This statement is activated when a mouse runs over the first message defined in line 18. The this operator together with the property innerHTML will change the content of our first message to "Got You!" instantly. Although the keyword innerHTML is not W3C approved, it is popular and will allow XHTML elements to be embedded in the message. For <span>, you need to touch the message itself in order to make a change. For <div>, changes are made as soon as you touch the line (the whole line). As good practice, you also need to change the message back to its original form when the mouse leaves the message region.

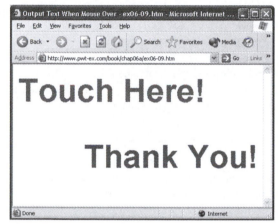

Figure 6.15 ex06-09.htm

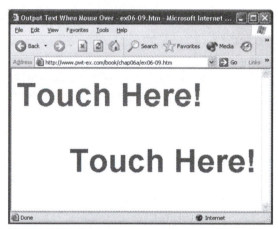

Figure 6.16 Mouse over second message

We'd like to point out again that the property innerHTML is not part of the W3C standard recommendation. However, most major browsers support this property due to its popularity in industry.

6.3.5   A simple text message board

To demonstrate the usefulness of output text in a real application, let's consider a message board technique. This technique involves a message board with some items (or menu). When a mouse runs over an item, the board will display an appropriate message. This is a very common technique in Web sites that are related to the zodiac. They usually use different table shapes and pictures to represent the twelve groups of stars. Of course we are not going to talk about the zodiac here. Instead we want to show you how to implement a simple message board. Our board has five rows and two columns arranged as shown in Fig. 6.17.

A Simple Message Board	
XHTML	Term explanation is here:-
CSS	
DOM	
W3C	

Figure 6.17 Message board diagram

The first row occupies two columns. The second row, second column is the display board itself. The board occupies four rows. These can be done by table attributes `colspan=2` and `rowspan=4` respectively. When a mouse runs over, for example, the first item "XHTML," the following message is displayed:

```
Extensible Hyper Text Markup Language:-
A Basic Language on the Web
for publishing
```

In addition, each line of the message will have a different style. For that two texture mappings covering the board are used to achieve a more realistic effect. The message board has the layout and functionalities as shown in Figs 6.18 and 6.19.

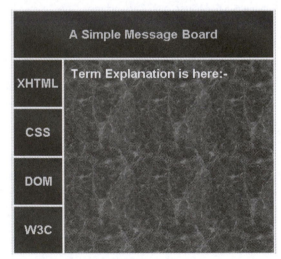

Figure 6.18 ex06-18.htm

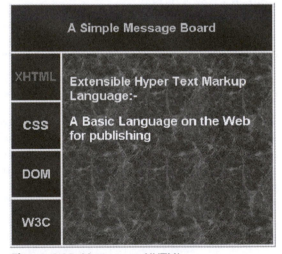

Figure 6.19 Mouse over XHTML

The following code fragment defines the first table item "XHTML":

```
Listing: ex06-06.txt

1: <tr><td style="background:url('texture03.jpg');width:80px;height:80px">
2:        <span id="htm" class="text01"
3:           onmouseover='mouse_over("htm","t_html)'
4:           onmouseout='mouse_out("htm","t_default)'>XHTML</span></td>
```

This code fragment contains two user-defined script functions to handle the mouse events. The function `mouse_over("htm," t_html)` in line 3 takes two arguments, one for the item identity and the other for the message to be displayed. The message `t_html` is a variable containing a combination of XHTML elements and is passed to the function for displaying.

The script function `mouse_over()` is defined by

Listing: ex06-07.txt

```
1:   function mouse_over(var_id, str_var)
2:    {
3:      document.getElementById(var_id).style.color="red";
4:      document.getElementById("h_2").innerHTML=str_var;
5:    }
```

Since the W3C standard strongly recommends the use of `getElementById` feature, here is an example to demonstrate how to use it for argument passing. The first statement of the function (line 3) is to get the identity of the input element (i.e., `var_id`) and to change the text color to red. The second statement in line 4 will output the string (i.e., `str_var`) to the XHTML element with an identity `h_2`. The `innerHTML` is to confirm that the output string (or `str_var`) may contain XHTML language elements.

Since the `getElementById` feature is standard, more structured, and highly recommended by the W3C authority, we will use it frequently.

Example: ex06-10.htm - A Text Message Board

```
 1: <?xml version="1.0" encoding="iso-8859-1"?>
 2: <!DOCTYPE html PUBLIC "-//W3C//DTD XHTML 1.0 Transitional//EN"
 3:     "http://www.w3.org/TR/xhtml1/DTD/xhtml1-transitional.dtd">
 4: <html xmlns="http://www.w3.org/1999/xhtml" xml:lang="en" lang="en">
 5: <head>
 6:   <title> A Text Message Board - ex06-10.htm </title>
 7: </head>
 8:
 9: <style>
10:   .text00 {font-size:16pt; font-family:arial,sans-serif;
11:     font-weight:bold; color: #00ff00;}
12:   .text01 {font-size:16pt; font-family:arial,sans-serif;
13:     font-weight:bold;color: #00ffff; }
14:   h3 {font-size:16pt; font-family:arial,sans-serif;
15:     font-weight:bold; color: #ffff00; position:relative;left:10;top:10}
16:   h4 {font-size:16pt; font-family:arial,sans-serif;
17:     font-weight:bold; color: #ffffff; position:relative;left:10;top:10}
18: </style>
19:
20: <script>
21:     t_default = "<h3><b>Term Explanation is here:- </b></h3>";
22: w_html="<h3><br /><b>Extensible Hyper Text Markup Language:- </b></h3>";
23: p_html="<h4><b>A Basic Language on the Web <br />for publishing</b></h4>";
24:     t_html = w_html + p_html;
25: w_css="<h3><br /><b>Cascading Style Sheet:- </b></h3>";
26: p_css="<h4><b>Used to define the properties of HTML elements</b></h4>";
27:     t_css = w_css + p_css;
28: w_dom="<h3><br /><b>Document Object Model:- </b></h3>";
29: p_dom="<h4><b>A Structure To Access Web Elements</b></h4>";
30:     t_dom = w_dom + p_dom;
31: w_w3c="<h3><br /><b>World Wide Web Consortium:- </b></h3>";
32: p_w3c="<h4><b>Authority To Set The Web Standard</b></h4>";
33:     t_w3c = w_w3c + p_w3c;
34:
```

```
35:  function mouse_over(var_id, str_var)
36:  {
37:    document.getElementById(var_id).style.color="red";
38:    document.getElementById("h_2").innerHTML=str_var;
39:  }
40:
41:  function mouse_out(var_id, str_var)
42:  {
43:    document.getElementById(var_id).style.color="#00ffff";
44:    document.getElementById("h_2").innerHTML=str_var;
45:  }
46: </script>
47:
48: <body style="background:#ffffff"><br />
49: <div align="center">
50: <table width="450" border="2" cellspace="5"><tbody align="center">
51:   <tr><td colspan="2"
52:       style="background:url('texture03.jpg');height:80px">
53:       <span class="text00">
54:       <b>A Simple Message Board</b></span></td></tr>
55:
56:   <tr><td style="background:url('texture03.jpg');width:80px;height:80px">
57:       <span id="htm" class="text01"
58:         onmouseover='mouse_over("htm",t_html)'
59:         onmouseout='mouse_out("htm",t_default)'>XHTML</span></td>
60:
61:     <td rowspan=4 id="h_2" style="background:url('texture01.jpg');
62:         width:350px;text-align:left;vertical-align:top">
63:       <span id="h_2">
64:         <h3>Term Explanation is here:- </b></h3></span></td></tr>
65:
66:   <tr><td style="background:url('texture03.jpg');width:80px;height:80px">
67:       <span class="text01" id="css"
68:         onmouseover='mouse_over("css",t_css)'
69:         onmouseout='mouse_out("css",t_default)'>CSS</span></td></tr>
70:
71:   <tr><td style="background:url('texture03.jpg');width:80px;height:80px">
72:       <span class="text01" id="dom"
73:         onmouseover='mouse_over("dom",t_dom)'
74:         onmouseout='mouse_out("dom",t_default)'>DOM</span></td></tr>
75:
76:   <tr><td style="background:url('texture03.jpg');width:80px;height:80px">
77:       <span class="text01" id="w3c"
78:         onmouseover='mouse_over("w3c",t_w3c)'
79:         onmouseout='mouse_out("w3c",t_default)'>W3C</span></td></tr>
80: </tbody>
81: </table></div>
82: </body>
83: </html>
```

Instead of using script functions, another alternative is to put everything inside the onmouseover and onmouseout event handlers. For example, lines 58–59 in ex06-10.htm can be replaced by ex06-08.txt.

```
Listing: ex06-08.txt

  1: onmouseover='this.style.color="red";
  2:  document.getElementById("h_2").innerHTML=t_html'
  3: onmouseout='this.style.color="#00ffff";
  4:  document.getElementById("h_2").innerHTML=t_default'>XHTML</span></td>
```

The statement in line 1 changes the element color to red, and continues to execute the statement in line 2 to display the message in the board. The semi-colon at the end of line 1 is used to separate two executable statements. The use of script functions will usually make the code clearer and can also handle more complex problems. With minimal modifications, this example can output images to form an image display board.

6.3.6   An image display board

You can use the skeleton of our previous example ex06-10.htm and convert it to an image display board (i.e., ex06-11.htm). First, you need to make a copy of ex06-10.htm and call it the ex20-11.htm. The next step is to replace lines 20–34 in ex06-10.htm by the six lines in ex06-09.txt.

```
Listing: ex06-09.txt

1: <script>
2:     t_default = "<img src='logo_web.jpg' />";
3:     t_pic1 = "<img src='title4.gif' />";
4:     t_pic2 = "<img src='chengs.gif' />";
5:     t_pic3 = "<img src='boom.gif' width='280' height='220' />";
6:     t_pic4 = "<img src='pumkin.gif' width='280' height='220' />";
```

As you can see, this listing contains one default image and four animated GIF pictures. These GIF pictures are integrated inside the string variables t_pic1 to t_pic4. To handle the picture with the mouse, you replace lines 56–59 of ex06-10.htm by the four lines in listing ex06-10.txt.

```
Listing: ex06-10.txt

1:   <tr><td background="texture03.jpg" width="80" height="80">
2:        <span id="pic1" class="text01"
3:          onmouseover='mouse_over("pic1",t_pic1)'
4:          onmouseout='mouse_out("pic1",t_default)'>Pic 1</span></td>
```

This code defines the second row and first column of the board and displays the text pic1 inside it. When a mouse runs over this text, the code in line 3 will change the color of the text to red and output the XHTML statement stored in string variable t_pic1. Since the string t_pic1 contains an image element <img> (see line 3 of ex06-09.txt), the innerHTML will render it correctly inside the display board.

To get a better layout for the image, the left and top attributes (see line 62) of ex06-10.htm are set as the center and middle respectively. If you activate the page ex06-11.htm, you will obtain Figs 6.20 and 6.21.

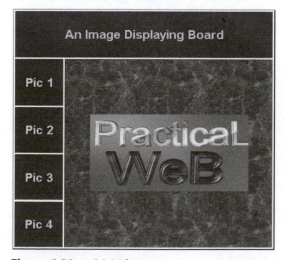

Figure 6.20 ex06-11.htm

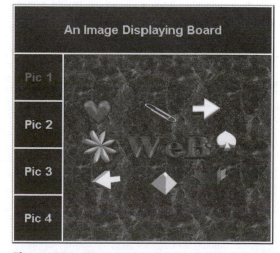

Figure 6.21 Mouse over pic1

6.4   Basic mouse clicks and position control

6.4.1   My first mouse click page

In XHTML, the first mouse click element is the anchor. Without knowledge of the mouse events, the anchor is a good practical way to implement a mouse click and provides links to the outside world. In fact anchor itself is a click event without a button. Another popular use of mouse clicks is using buttons. Buttons can be defined as an attribute inside the `<input>` element and associated with forms `<form>`. Let's consider the following "My First Mouse Click Page."

Example: ex06-12.htm - My First Mouse Click Page

```
 1: <?xml version="1.0" encoding="iso-8859-1"?>
 2: <!DOCTYPE html PUBLIC "-//W3C//DTD XHTML 1.0 Transitional//EN"
 3:      "http://www.w3.org/TR/xhtml1/DTD/xhtml1-transitional.dtd">
 4: <html xmlns="http://www.w3.org/1999/xhtml" xml:lang="en" lang="en">
 5: <head>
 6:    <title> My First Mouse Click Page - ex06-12.htm </title>
 7: </head>
 8: <style>
 9:    .text01{font-family:Arial;color:red;font-weight:bold;font-size:14pt}
10: </style>
11: <body>
12: <div class="text01" align="center"><br />My First Mouse Click Page
13: <form><br />
14: <input type="button" value="Button 1" onclick='alert("Button 1")' /> 
15: <input type="button" value="Button 2" onclick='alert("Button 2")' /> 
16: <input type="button" value="Button 3" onclick='alert("Button 3")' /> 
17: <input type="button" value="Button 4" onclick='alert("Button 4")' /> 
18: <input type="button" value="Button 5" onclick='alert("Button 5")' /> 
19: </form>
20: </div>
21: </body>
22: </html>
```

This page is very simple. After the main header in line 12, five buttons, "Button 1," "Button 2," "Button 3," "Button 4," and "Button 5," are defined. These buttons are all inside the form element `<form>` in lines 13–19. The mouse click event for each button is controlled by the `onclick` event as illustrated in line 14. For example, when a mouse click happens inside "Button 1," an alert window is triggered to display the message "Button 1" (Figs 6.22 and 6.23). The non-break space ` ` is used to separate each button. The form element `<form>` is not compulsory in the latest W3C recommendations. However, without the form declaration, some earlier browsers may not generate the buttons on the screen.

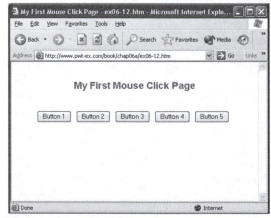

Figure 6.22 ex06-12.htm

Figure 6.23 Onclick Button 1

6.4.2   Buttons with style and a mouse click counter

Outputting the mouse click message to an alert window is useful to track down the click events. In practice, you may also want some more features. One such demand is to record and display the number of mouse clicks on certain areas (including icons and buttons). This number of hits and counting capability are vital techniques for many game designs. Suppose you have two buttons on a page. The following code (a script function) can be used to record and display how many mouse clicks occur in a particular region.

```
Listing: ex06-11.txt:

 1:    <script>
 2:    var hits1 = 0;
 3:    var hits2 = 0;
 4:
 5:    function mouse_click(but_no)
 6:    {
 7:      if (but_no == 1)
 8:      {
 9:        hits1 += 1;
10:       document.getElementById("but01").innerHTML="<h3>"+hits1+"</h3>";
11:     }
12:     if (but_no == 2)
13:     {
14:       hits2 += 1;
15:       document.getElementById("but02").innerHTML="<h3> "+hits2+"</h3>";
16:     }
17:   }
18:   </script>
```

This code fragment contains one script function inside the <script> element (lines 1–18). Lines 2–3 define two variables hits1 and hits2 to record how many times mouse clicks are involved. The function itself (line 5) requires one input argument but_no to indicate which button has been clicked. If the argument but_no equals 1, the record hits1 will be updated by 1. This is illustrated in line 9. In line 10, the output message "<h3>"+hits1+"</h3>" is sent to the field with id="but01". Since <h3> is an element with CSS style, the innerHTML is used to interpret the result. To put this function into action, consider the following example ex06-13.htm:

```
Example: ex06-13.htm - My Mouse Click And Count

 1: <?xml version="1.0" encoding="iso-8859-1"?>
 2: <!DOCTYPE html PUBLIC "-//W3C//DTD XHTML 1.0 Transitional//EN"
 3:     "http://www.w3.org/TR/xhtml1/DTD/xhtml1-transitional.dtd">
 4: <html xmlns="http://www.w3.org/1999/xhtml" xml:lang="en" lang="en">
 5: <head>
 6:     <title> My Mouse Click and Count - ex06-13.htm </title>
 7: </head>
 8: <style>
 9:     h3{ font-family:Arial;font-size:20;color:black}
10: </style>
11:
12: <script>
13: var hits1 = 0;
14: var hits2 = 0;
15: function mouse_click(but_no)
16: {
17:   if (but_no == 1)
18:   {
19:     hits1 += 1;
```

```
20:        document.getElementById("but01").innerHTML="<h3>"+hits1+"</h3>";
21:        }
22:      if (but_no == 2)
23:        {
24:        hits2 += 1;
25:        document.getElementById("but02").innerHTML="<h3>"+hits2+"</h3>";
26:        }
27:    }
28: </script>
29: <body>
30:    <div align="center"><h3><br />Mouse Click and Count<br /></h3>
31:    <input type="button"
32:     style='font-family:Arial;background-color:#ffaaaa;
33:       font-weight:bold;font-size:18pt'
34:       onmouseover='this.style.color="red"'
35:       onmouseout='this.style.color="black"'
36:       value="Button 1" onclick='mouse_click(1)' /> 
37:
38:   <input type="button"
39:     style='font-family:Arial;background-color:#aaffaa;
40:       font-weight:bold;font-size:18pt'
41:       onmouseover='this.style.color="red"'
42:       onmouseout='this.style.color="black"'
43:       value="Button 2" onclick='mouse_click(2)' /> <br /><br />
44:
45: <table cellspacing="20">
46:    <tr align="center">
47:      <td id="but01" style="background-color:#ffaaaa;
48:         width:130px;height:70px"><h3>0</h3></td>
49:      <td id="but02" style="background-color:#aaffaa;
50:         width:130px;height:70px"><h3>0</h3></td>
51:    </tr></table>
52: </div>
53: </body>
54: </html>
```

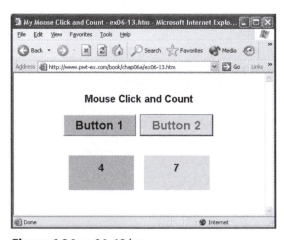

Figure 6.24 ex06–13.htm

The script function mouse_click() in ex06-11.txt is put into lines 12–28 so that it can be called inside the XHTML page. Lines 31–36 define a button ready to call the mouse_click() function. The onmouseover and onmouseout attributes of the button are used to change the button color and to highlight the text. When the button is clicked, the onclick event handler (line 36) activates the script function mouse_click(1) with the input argument 1 to indicate "Button 1" has been clicked. The counting result is sent to the table field in line 47 with an id="but01".

The main feature of this example is the two buttons defined in lines 31–43. The button technique is used here to trigger the onmouseover, onmouseout, and onclick events (see Fig. 6.24).

If you don't want to use buttons, you can design a new example to allow a mouse click and counting around a region. For example, you can replace the body part of example ex06-13.htm with the following code fragment ex06-12.txt, and call this new example ex06-14.htm.

```
Listing: ex06-12.txt - Code Fragment For ex06-14.htm

 1: <body>
 2: <div align="center"><h3><br />Mouse Click and Count<br /></h3>
 3: <br />
 4: <table cellspacing="20" border=0>
 5:  <tr align="center">
 6:   <td id="but01"
 7:      style="background-color:#ffaaaa;width:130px;height:150px"
 8:      onclick='mouse_click(1)'><h3>0</h3></td>
 9:   <td id="but02"
10:      style="background-color:#aaffaa;width:130px;height:150px"
11:      onclick='mouse_click(2)'><h3>0</h3></td>
12:    </tr></table>
13: </div>
14: </body>
```

As you can see, the `onclick` event handler (line 8) is inside the `<td>` element. If a mouse click happens inside this region, the counting will be increased and output the result to the same location. Figure 6.25 shows the screen shot of this example. Since XHTML supports `onclick` events for almost all elements, you can implement this mouse click and counting technique on various elements and shapes.

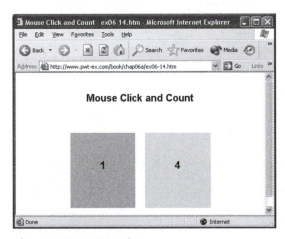

Figure 6.25 ex06-14.htm

6.4.3 Mouse positions

Mouse (or cursor) positions provide helpful information as a user interface and play a vital role in any moving object applications. To track down mouse movements, you need to understand something called "Event Model." Unfortunately, the set-up of an event model is a browser-dependent process. That means you need browser detection code. With detection, you can easily develop a mouse movement page with backward compatibility. The following page is a classic one and is popular amongst Web professionals.

```
Example: ex06-15.htm - My Mouse Positions

 1: <?xml version="1.0" encoding="iso-8859-1"?>
 2: <!DOCTYPE html PUBLIC "-//W3C//DTD XHTML 1.0 Transitional//EN"
 3:     "http://www.w3.org/TR/xhtml1/DTD/xhtml1-transitional.dtd">
 4: <html xmlns="http://www.w3.org/1999/xhtml" xml:lang="en" lang="en">
 5: <head>
 6:   <title> My Mouse Positions - ex06-15.htm </title>
 7: <script>
 8:   var tempX = 0;
```

```
 9:    var tempY = 0;
10:    var IE = document.all?true:false;
11:
12:    if (!IE) document.captureEvents(Event.MOUSEMOVE);
13:    document.onmousemove = getPosition;
14:
15:    function getPosition(e)
16:    {
17:     if (IE)
18:     { // grab the mouse x-y co-ordinates if browser is IE
19:      tempX = event.clientX;
20:      tempY = event.clientY;
21:     }
22:     else
23:     { // grab the mouse x-y co-ordinates if browser is NS
24:      tempX = e.pageX;
25:      tempY = e.pageY;
26:     }
27:
28:     if (tempX < 0){tempX = 0;}
29:     if (tempY < 0){tempY = 0;}
30:     document.mouse_f.MouseX.value = tempX;
31:     document.mouse_f.MouseY.value = tempY;
32:     return true;
33:     }
34:
35: </script>
36: </head>
37: <body>
38: <h2 style="font-family:times;font-size:16pt">My Mouse Position Page</h2>
39:
40: <form id="mouse_f" name="mouse_f">
41:  Mouse Position on X
42:  <input type="text" id="MouseX" name="MouseX" value="0" size="4" /><br />
43:  Mouse Position on Y
44:  <input type="text" id="MouseY" name="MouseY" value="0" size="4" /><br />
45: </form>
46:
47: </body>
48: </html>
```

First, a simple browser detection code in line 10 is used so that the proper mouse move event can be set in lines 12–13. The script function getPosition() captures the mouse position. By setting this getPosition() function in the mouse move event, this function is called whenever the mouse changes its position. Inside this script function, a simple conditional statement is employed to handle the browser differences. If the browser is IE, the x and y mouse coordinates from IE's event model are obtained. If the browser is NS, we get mouse coordinates from events e.pageX and e.pageY respectively. The temporary mouse positions, tempX and tempY, are assigned to the XHTML form element in lines 30–31 for display purposes (Fig. 6.26). As a result, this page captures the mouse movement and displays the mouse coordinates on a browser's screen.

If you replace lines 30 and 31 by the following code

```
document.getElementById("MouseX").value = tempX;
document.getElementById("MouseY").value = tempY;
```

(i.e., use `getElementById`), you can eliminate the use of the `form` element. This provides a clearer and a more structured understanding of the process.

With this approach, you can rewrite the body part of this example using the listing in ex06-13.txt and have a new mouse position page with style (ex06-16.htm). This page will only work on W3C standard browsers.

```
Listing: ex06-13.txt - Code Fragment For ex06-16.htm

 1: <body>
 2:
 3: <h3>My Mouse Position Page -- ex06-16.htm</h3><br />
 4: <h4>
 5: Mouse Position on X
 6: <input type="text" id="MouseX" name="MouseX" value="0"
 7:        style="font-family:arial;color:Blue;
 8:           font-size:16pt;background:#aaaaee" size="4" /><br />
 9:
10: Mouse Position on Y
11: <input type="text" id="MouseY" name="MouseY" value="0"
12:        style="font-family:arial;color:blue;
13:           font-size:16pt;background:#aaeeaa" size="4" /><br />
14: </h4>
15: </body>
```

The screen captures of ex06-15.htm and ex06-16.htm are shown in Figs 6.26 and 6.27.

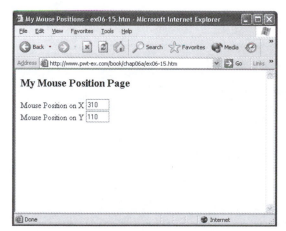

Figure 6.26 ex06-15.htm

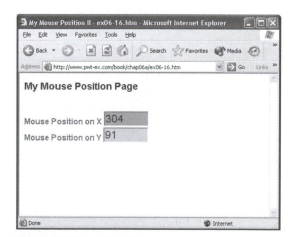

Figure 6.27 ex06-16.htm

Once you have a technique for tracking down the mouse movement, you can develop Web pages to allow texts and/or images to follow it.

6.4.4   Moving text and images with a mouse

In this section, we consider examples of simple moving objects on Web pages. Since we haven't formally introduced Dynamic XHTML (DXHTML), we will keep the discussion simple. More details on moving objects are given in Chapter 9. The idea of moving objects with a mouse is basically a two-step process.

- Capture the mouse position when the mouse moves.
- Assign the new mouse position to an object.

Capturing the mouse position can be done by techniques already discussed in section 6.4.3. In order to change the object position in real time, you need the CSS position properties and DOM interaction. As a demonstration, a simple text message "Cursor Text" is generated. This text will follow your mouse movement anywhere inside the browser screen. Consider the example ex06-17.htm below:

```
Example: ex06-17.htm - Moving Text With Mouse

 1: <?xml version="1.0" encoding="iso-8859-1"?>
 2: <!DOCTYPE html PUBLIC "-//W3C//DTD XHTML 1.0 Transitional//EN"
 3:     "http://www.w3.org/TR/xhtml1/DTD/xhtml1-transitional.dtd">
 4: <html xmlns="http://www.w3.org/1999/xhtml" xml:lang="en" lang="en">
 5:
 6: <head>
 7:   <title> Moving Text With Mouse - ex06-17.htm </title>
 8: <script>
 9:   var tempX = 0;
10:   var tempY = 0;
11:   var IE = document.all?true:false;
12:
13:   if (!IE) document.captureEvents(Event.MOUSEMOVE);
14:   document.onmousemove = cursor;
15:
16:  function cursor(e)
17:  {
18:
19:    if (IE)
20:    { // grab the mouse x-y co-ordinates if browser is IE
21:     tempX = event.clientX;
22:     tempY = event.clientY;
23:    }
24:    else
25:    { // grab the mouse x-y co-ordinates if browser is NS
26:     tempX = e.pageX;
27:     tempY = e.pageY;
28:    }
29:    document.getElementById("mov_text").style.visibility="visible";
30:    document.getElementById("mov_text").style.position="absolute";
31:    document.getElementById("mov_text").style.left=tempX+10+"px";
32:    document.getElementById("mov_text").style.top=tempY+"px";
33:  }
34:
35: </script>
36: </head>
37:
38: <style> h3{font-family:arial;font-size:12pt;color:#ff0000}</style>
39: <body>
40:
41: <h3 style="font-size:14pt;color:#0000ff">Moving Text With Mouse</h3>
```

```
42:
43: <h3 id="mov_text" style="visibility:hidden">Cursor Text</h3>
44:
45: </body>
46: </html>
```

This example is a modification of ex06-15.htm. In line 43, the text "Cursor Text" is generated using the element `<span>` and `id="mov_text"`. The initial CCS visibility setting is hidden so that it is not displayed. The next step is to set up the browser detection code and event model as described in section 6.4.3. The script function `cursor()` is called once a mouse movement is detected. The new mouse `x-y` coordinates are assigned to the variables `tempX` and `tempY` respectively. In lines 29–32, we use the DOM structure to access the CSS properties of this "mov_text" text. Line 29 is used to set the visibility of the text to visible so that the text can be displayed. Line 30 is to set the coordinate system as absolute. Line 31 assigns the new text's "left" position as the `x` coordinate of the mouse plus 10 pixels. Line 32 sets the mouse's `y` coordinate to the "top" position of the text. The script function `cursor()` is activated whenever there is a mouse movement. You now have a truly real-time Web page with a moving object (see Fig. 6.28).

If you use the XHTML image element `<img>` instead of the text, you will have a moving image along with the mouse. The first thing you need to do is to replace the body part of example ex06-17.htm (lines 39–45) with the listing in ex06-14.txt and call this example ex06-18.htm.

```
Listing: ex06-14.txt - Code Fragment For ex06-18.htm

1:   <body>
2:   <h3>Image With Mouse Movement</h3>
3:   <img id="mov_object" style="visibility:hidden" src="logo_web.jpg"
4:      width="100" height="60" />
5:   </body>
```

This code fragment defines an image object with `id="mov_object"`. Next, you replace all texts "mov_text" by this new identity "mov_object." The script function `cursor()` makes the image move along with the mouse (see Fig. 6.29).

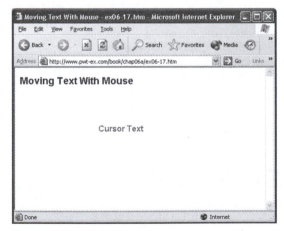

Figure 6.28 ex06-17.htm

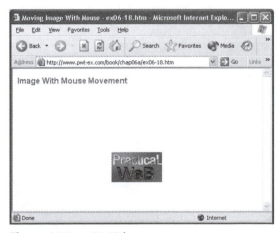

Figure 6.29 ex06-18.htm

6.5   Generating menus with mouse over

As the final section in this chapter we will show you how to use the mouse techniques that you have learned to build a menu system in window style. For simplicity, we will restrict ourselves to building a menu with just one header item. It should not be too difficult to extend this idea to more complex applications.

6.5.1   Pull-down menu (window style) using XHTML

One popular menu system used in windows is called the "Pull Down Menu." This is usually a series of menu items (or headers) on top of the application. When your mouse runs over one of the menu headers, a pull-down menu section is displayed to show more options. Since pull-down menus are essential in window programming, there are a variety of tools to help developers to build menus for their windows. In this section, only XHTML and some script functions are used to accomplish this task.

The idea and process of generating pull-down menus with XHTML is not difficult. It is a two-process application. First, you need to create the menu headers. Each header is usually a text message with CSS position, size, color, and background. The second process is to create the pull-down window of the menu. This is usually a series of text messages with similar CSS settings to the header. The pull-down action of the menu is just another simple mouse-over application. You can use the CSS visibility to do the trick. When the mouse runs over the header, you turn off the visibility of the header and turn on the visibility of the pull-down section. When the mouse moves out of the pull-down section, you reset the original visibilities. The completed listing of the XHTML code is given below:

```
Example: ex06-19.htm - Pull-Down Menu

 1: <?xml version="1.0" encoding="iso-8859-1"?>
 2: <!DOCTYPE html PUBLIC "-//W3C//DTD XHTML 1.0 Transitional//EN"
 3:     "http://www.w3.org/TR/xhtml1/DTD/xhtml1-transitional.dtd">
 4: <html xmlns="http://www.w3.org/1999/xhtml" xml:lang="en" lang="en">
 5: <head> <title> Pull-Down Menu - ex06-19.htm </title>
 6: <style>
 7:   .MenuStyle
 8:   {
 9:   border: groove 4px;padding:3;font-family:arial;text-align:left;
10:   font-size:14pt;width:120px;height:30px;background-color:#c0c0c0;
11:   position:absolute;top:25px;left:20px
12:   }
13: </style>
14:
15: <script>
16:   function showMenu()
17:   {
18:    document.getElementById("myMenu02").style.visibility="visible";
19:    document.getElementById("myMenu02").style.height="210px";
20:    document.getElementById("myMenu").style.visibility="hidden";
21:   }
22:
23:   function hideMenu()
24:   {
25:    document.getElementById("myMenu02").style.visibility="hidden";
26:    document.getElementById("myMenu").style.visibility="visible";
27:   }
28: </script>
29: </head>
30: <body>
31: <br /><br />
```

```
32:    <span id="myMenu02" class="MenuStyle" style="visibility:hidden"
33:     onmouseover="showMenu()" onmouseout="hideMenu()">
34:    <span align="center"> Edit</span><br /><hr />
35:    <span onmouseover='this.style.color="red"'
36:     onmouseout='this.style.color="black"'> Cut</span><br />
37:    <span onmouseover='this.style.color="red"'
38:     onmouseout='this.style.color="black"'> Copy</span><br />
39:    <span onmouseover='this.style.color="red"'
40:     onmouseout='this.style.color="black"'> Paste</span><br />
41:    <span onmouseover='this.style.color="red"'
42:     onmouseout='this.style.color="black"'> Spelling
43:     &gt;&gt;</span><br /><br /><hr />
44:    <span onmouseover='this.style.color="red"'
45:     onmouseout='this.style.color="black"'> Select All</span><br />
46:    </span>
47:
48:    <span id="myMenu" class="MenuStyle" style="visibility:visible"
49:    onmouseover="showMenu()" onmouseout="hideMenu()"> Edit</span><br />
50:
51: </body>
52: </html>
```

The menu header is defined in lines 48–49 with CSS style `MenuStyle` and `id="myMenu"`. This header contains just one-word, "Edit." When the mouse runs over this header, the script function `showMenu()` is called and replaces the header with its pull-down section. The pull-down section is defined in lines 32–46 containing the itemized menu choices: "Edit," "Cut," "Copy," "Paste," "Spelling," "hr" (i.e., a horizontal line), and "Select All." We use a nested `<span>` here to form a section. The master `<span>` is defined in line 32 with `id="myMenu02"`. The CSS visibility of this id is used to control the existence of this pull-down section. When the mouse moves inside any pull-down section items, the color of the text will also change to red.

This page uses two script functions `showMenu()` and `hideMenu()` to perform the task. Function `showMenu()` (see lines 16–21) is to display the pull-down section of the menu. This is just a change of the CSS visibility of the object. Since the pull-down section is longer than the menu header, you may also need to increase the height of `myMenu02` to 210 pixels to cover all items. Alternatively, you can set up another independent CSS style with a new height to accommodate the items. The function `hideMenu()` is used to restore the original CSS visibility to show the menu header.

Some screen shots of the page are shown in Figs 6.30 and 6.31.

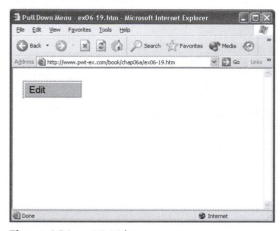

Figure 6.30 ex06-19.htm

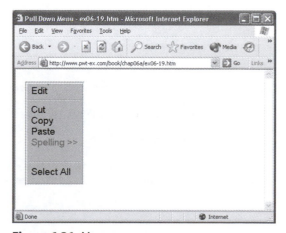

Figure 6.31 Mouse over menu

6.5.2   Generating sub-menus

The same technique can be used to generate sub-menus of a menu system. For example, you can generate a sub-menu for the "Spelling" section in the previous example by adding another section. You may want to see a pop-up sub-menu appear when the mouse runs over the "Spelling" choice. This is just like adding another nested `<span>` with a new `id="myMenu03"` and style. As a simple demonstration, we include the "Dictionary," "Oxford Learner," "Advanced Learner," "Oxford Popular," "Popular Thesaurus," "hr," and "Customize" as our sub-menu items. To complete the task, we also need to add two more script functions to control the CSS visibilities. One is called `showSub()` and the other is `hideSub()`. When the mouse runs over the sub-menu, the script functions `showMenu()` and `showSub()` are called simultaneously to display both menus at the same time. This action can be implemented by the following code fragment:

```
64 <span id="myMenu03" class="SubMenuStyle" style="visibility:hidden"
65 onmouseover="showMenu();showSub()" onmouseout="hideMenu();hideSub()">
```

With a basic understanding of mouse-over techniques and CSS style, the complete code listing (ex06-20.htm) for our sub-menu program should be self-explanatory:

```
Example: ex06-20.htm - Generating Sub-Menu

 1: <?xml version="1.0" encoding="iso-8859-1"?>
 2: <!DOCTYPE html PUBLIC "-//W3C//DTD XHTML 1.0 Transitional//EN"
 3:     "http://www.w3.org/TR/xhtml1/DTD/xhtml1-transitional.dtd">
 4: <html xmlns="http://www.w3.org/1999/xhtml" xml:lang="en" lang="en">
 5: <head>
 6:   <title> Generating Sub-Menu - ex06-20.htm </title>
 7: <style>
 8:   .MenuStyle
 9:   {
10:    border: groove 4px;padding:3;font-family:arial;text-align:left;
11:    font-size:14pt;width:120px;height:30px;background-color:#C0C0C0;
12:    position:absolute;top:25px;left:20px
13:   }
14:
15:   .SubMenuStyle
16:   {
17:    border: groove 4px;padding:3;font-family:arial;text-align:left;
18:    font-size:14pt;width:190px;height:210px;background-color:#C0C0C0;
19:    position:absolute;top:135px;left:123px
20:   }
21: </style>
22:
23: <script>
24:   function showMenu()
25:   {
26:    document.getElementById("myMenu02").style.visibility="visible";
27:    document.getElementById("myMenu02").style.height="210px";
28:    document.getElementById("myMenu").style.visibility="hidden";
29:   }
30:   function hideMenu()
31:   {
32:    document.getElementById("myMenu02").style.visibility="hidden";
33:    document.getElementById("myMenu").style.visibility="visible";
34:   }
35:
```

```
36:    function showSub()
37:    {
38:     document.getElementById("myMenu03").style.visibility="visible";
39:    }
40:
41:    function hideSub()
42:    {
43:     document.getElementById("myMenu03").style.visibility="hidden";
44:    }
45:
46: </script>
47: </head>
48:
49: <body>
50: <br /><br />
51:  <span id="myMenu02" class="MenuStyle" style="visibility:hidden"
52:    onmouseover="showMenu()" onmouseout="hideMenu()">
53:    <span align="center"> Edit</span><br /><hr>
54:    <span onmouseover='this.style.color="red"'
55:      onmouseout='this.style.color="black"'> Cut</span><br />
56:    <span onmouseover='this.style.color="red"'
57:      onmouseout='this.style.color="black"'> Copy</span><br />
58:    <span onmouseover='this.style.color="red"'
59:     onmouseout='this.style.color="black"'> Paste</span><br />
60:    <span onmouseover='this.style.color="red";showSub()'
61:     onmouseout='this.style.color="black";hideSub()'>
62:      Spelling &gt;&gt;</span><br /><br /><hr>
63:    <span onmouseover='this.style.color="red"'
64:      onmouseout='this.style.color="black"'> Select All</span><br />
65:  </span>
66:
67:
68:  <span id="myMenu03" class="SubMenuStyle" style="visibility:hidden"
69:   onmouseover="showMenu();showSub()" onmouseout="hideMenu();hideSub()">
70:  <span align="center"> Dictionary</span><br /><hr>
71:  <span onmouseover='this.style.color="red"'
72:   onmouseout='this.style.color="black"'> Oxford Pocket</span><br />
73:  <span onmouseover='this.style.color="red"'
74:   onmouseout='this.style.color="black"'> Advanced Learner</span><br />
75:  <span onmouseover='this.style.color="red"'
76:   onmouseout='this.style.color="black"'> Oxford Popular</span><br />
77:  <span onmouseover='this.style.color="red"'
78:   onmouseout='this.style.color="black"'> 
79:   Popular Thesaurus</span><br /><br /><hr>
80:  <span onmouseover='this.style.color="red"'
81:   onmouseout='this.style.color="black"'> Customize</span><br />
82:  </span>
83:
84:  <span id="myMenu" class="MenuStyle" style="visibility:visible"
85:   onmouseover="showMenu()" onmouseout="hideMenu()"> Edit</span><br />
86:
87: </body>
88: </html>
```

The screen shots of the sub-menu are shown in Figs 6.32 and 6.33.

Figure 6.32 Sub-menu

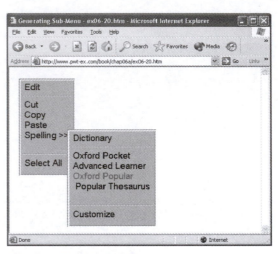

Figure 6.33 ex06-20.htm

In addition to the horizontal menu bar, this sub-menu technique can also be used to develop a full vertical menu bar as used in a number of professional Web sites.

7

Practical use of script

7.1 Web programming with scripts

7.1.1 Global programming via Internet browsers

In the mid-1990s, Netscape created LiveScript, a loosely defined scripting language for its 2.0 browser. It was designed to handle forms and images. The early versions of this language were mainly dedicated to a small group of Web designers without a compiler (Java-type compiler), or without any object-oriented programming experience. In December 1995, Netscape and Sun Microsystems (the creator of the Java language) reintroduced this language under the new name JavaScript and claimed it as a complement of both HTML and Java. Java and JavaScript are primarily programming languages for Web pages. Apart from this, they are quite different. For a number of years JavaScript suffered deeply from criticisms such as:

- It is not a compilation language.
- It exerts little discipline on code and data.
- It offers very little or no security on intellectual property.
- It lacks an IDE (Integrated Development Editor) and reliable cross-platform debugger.

Despite all these criticisms, JavaScript is by far the most popular programming language for the Web. It has the ability to "talk" directly to the browser software with simple and easy human sentences (scripts). Since all major browsers include JavaScript as an integral part, we don't need the "run time environment" to run them. JavaScript is a truly global programming language embedded in the Web browsers.

In response to the popularity of JavaScript, Microsoft released its own scripting language, VBScript (a small version of Visual Basic), which is platform dependent. In July 1996, Microsoft also released an implementation of JavaScript called "JScript" bundled together with all IE browsers. As a technology that has survived on this ever-changing Web environment for more than 10 years, JavaScript is now one of the fundamental technologies on the Web. Together with the European Computer Manufacturers Association (ECMA) standardization (later adopted by the ISO) and W3C DOM, JavaScript is considered by many Web developers as the foundation for the next generation of dynamic client-side Web applications, i.e., global programming via Internet browsers.

7.1.2 ECMAScript and the standard

The standardization of JavaScript began in conjunction with ECMA in November 1996. It adopted this standard in June 1997 and later it was adopted also by the International Organization for Standardization (ISO). This standard has been formally named "ECMA-262: ECMAScript Language Specification." The language itself is conveniently called ECMAScript.

All major browsers now support the ECMAScript released in December 1999 (http://www.ecma.ch) which includes all of the features from the earlier JavaScript version 1.2. We support the standards and adopt ECMAScript as the principal scripting language (client-side script) throughout this book.

Some ECMAScript (or JavaScript) has been used in many situations in previous chapters. They are characterized by the scripting element <script> inside a Web page. In fact, <script> is an XHTML element and would allow you to define an ECMAScript section anywhere within a Web page. Consider the following script fragment:

```
Listing: ex07-01.txt

1: <script language="JavaScript">
2:    document.write("<div>I Know Some ECMAScript (or JavaScript) Now!</div>")
3: </script>
```

This is a simple script to output an XHTML string to the browser. The <script> element in lines 1 and 3 specifies a script section (or a script block) so that the browser is able to interpret statements inside the block as scripting language. The language attribute in line 1 indicates that the scripting language is JavaScript. The only JavaScript statement inside the block is line 2. This built-in function document.write() is to output an XHTML statement back to the browser.

As ECMAScript is the standard and compatible with JavaScript, we generally use ECMAScript as the default client-side script. In order to avoid any confusion over different names and versions of the language, the following code is used to define an ECMAScript block:

```
<script> </script>
```

Since ECMAScript is an important subject on the Web and will be used heavily in this chapter, some practical language features are discussed in the next section.

7.1.3   Some language features of ECMAScript

For obvious reasons, a comprehensive tutorial on ECMAScript or full details of the language features are not feasible. For a friendly starting point and to prepare ourselves for the ECMAScript programming in this chapter and other chapters to come, some aspects of ECMAScript are provided. For our practical purposes, the following language features are considered:

- Variables – e.g., `var msg="A String"`, `n=123`, `f=1.04`, `flag=true`
- Conditionals – e.g., `if (ii < 10) {...}`
- Loops – e.g., for-loop: `for (ii=1;ii<10;ii++){...}`
- Arrays – e.g., `var myArray = new Array(12, 45, 78)`
- Functions – Built-in and user-defined functions

Also, they are the general practical aspects of many programming languages such as C, C++, and Visual Basic. In fact, we have used some of these ECMAScript features in Chapter 6, including some user-defined functions for controlling mouse events.

Unlike many other programming languages such as C and C++, ECMAScript is a loose language, particularly on variable declarations. In other words, you are free to define variables as you like without worrying about the data type and structure. Whether it is a string, integer, floating point number, or a Boolean type, you can define the variable simply using the keyword var as demonstrated in the example above. Consider the following ECMAScript code:

Listing: ex07-02.txt - Variable And Conditional Features Of ECMAScript

```
1: <script>
2:   var IE = document.all?true:false
3:     if (IE) document.write("You are using Internet Explorer")
4:     else document.write("You are not using Internet Explorer")
5: </script>
```

This code listing defines a script section and can be used on Web pages. The variable IE in line 2 is declared as the returned value of a Boolean type (true or false). Therefore, the variable IE is considered as a Boolean variable. The if statement in line 3 is a conditional feature of ECMAScript to detect the true or false status of the variable IE. In fact, this code is used on a number of occasions in Chapter 6 to detect browser type.

Another general programming feature is looping. Looping can make a series of tasks and coding more economical. Consider the following for-loop in ECMAScript:

Listing: ex07-03.txt - Using For-loop In ECMAScript

```
1: <body style="font-family:arial;font-weight:bold;text-align:center">
2: <script>
3:   var msg ="Hello World! "
4:   for (ii=14;ii<21;ii++)
5:   {
6:     document.write('<div style="font-size:' + ii + 'pt">')
7:     document.write(msg + 'Font Size = ' + ii + '</div>')
8:   }
9: </script>
10: </body>
```

First, a "Hello World!" string is declared as variable msg in line 3. Lines 4–8 define a for-loop on variable ii to run through values from 14 to 20. That is, to run the statements in lines 6–7 seven times. In this case, the following XHTML statements will be output to the browser:

```
<div style="font-size:14pt">Hello World! Font Size =14</div>
   ...        ...        ...
<div style="font-size:20pt">Hello World! Font Size =20</div>
```

In ECMAScript, the plus sign "+" is used to concatenate strings and variables. This feature will be used quite often in this book to construct XHTML statements. A screen shot of this page is shown in Fig. 7.1. As you can see, the value of the variable ii is carried through the loop. Sometimes, you don't even need to declare the variable ii before using it as demonstrated in ex07-03.txt.

ECMAScript, in fact, is an object-oriented programming language. The language comes with a number of objects so that functions or methods associated with objects can be freely called by users. For example, the built-in function document.write() is actually a method of the document object. Object-oriented

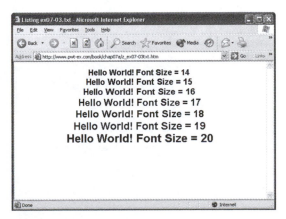

Figure 7.1 The for-loop

features greatly enhance the capabilities of ECMAScript and make it powerful and yet easy enough to be used on Web pages. For example, when you declare an array in ECMAScript, the array object is activated and the length of the array is attached. Consider the following example with an array and a user-defined function:

Listing: ex07-04.txt – Using Array And Function

```
 1: <script>
 2: function display_chap()
 3: {
 4:   var mArray=new Array(
 5:      "1: From HTML to XHTML and Web Site Design",
 6:      "2: Cascading Style Sheet (CSS) for Web Pages",
 7:      "3: Graphics, Font and Colors with Java and JavaScript",
 8:      "4: Images, Animations and Multimedia",
 9:      "5: XML and XSLT")
10:   for (ii=0;ii< mArray.length;ii++)
11:   {
12:      document.write('<div style="font-size:16pt">'+mArray[ii] + '<br />')
13:   }
14: }
15: </script>
16:
17: <body style="font-family:arial;font-weight:bold">
18: <div style="font-size:20pt;text-align:center">
19:    Practical Web Technology (Part I)
20: </div> <br />
21:   <script> display_chap() </script>
22: </body>
```

In this code fragment, we have two script sections. The first script section (lines 1–15) contains a user-defined function called display_chap(). Inside this function, we have defined an array mArray and a for-loop. The array mArray has five elements and they are all strings. Since the starting index of an array in ECMAScript is 0, the first element of mArray is (see line 5)

```
mArray[0] = "1: From HTML to XHTML and Web Site Design"
```

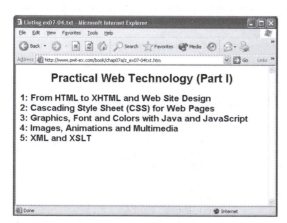

Figure 7.2 Array and user-defined function

Also, all arrays are created as an object in ECMAScript and therefore the length of the array is attached automatically. In this case, the variable mArray.length contains the value 5 representing the total length of the mArray. A simple for-loop in lines 10–13 can be used to output all elements inside mArray.

After the main message defined in lines 18–20, another script section is created at line 21. Inside this section, the function display_chap() is called to display all elements of the array. A screen shot is shown in Fig. 7.2.

You now have some ideas on the language features of ECMAScript and how to use them on Web pages. One of the great strengths of ECMAScript (or simply script) is the capability to handle a user interface and to provide window programming facilities for Web page design.

7.2 Basic boxes and controls

7.2.1 User alert and confirm boxes

Script has a set of built-in functions that can make your life a lot easier. For example, if you want to generate a user alert box, all you have to do is to call the script function `alert()`. In many cases, a user alert box can provide helpful information to prevent errors and to confirm actions. An alert box is just a small window with an OK button and a warning message (see Fig. 7.3). You can create an alert box easily with the script in ex07-05.txt.

```
Listing: ex07-05.txt

1:   <body>
2:   <script>
3:     alert("This is a user alert box! ")
4:   </script>
5:   </body>
```

In line 2, if you use

```
<script language="VBScript">
```

this program will become a VBScript program. As mentioned in the previous section, ECMAScript (or simply script) is used as a general scripting language throughout this book. ECMAScript is a standard and is nicely platform independent. Some information on VBScript will be presented in Chapter 16.

Figure 7.3 Alert box

Figure 7.4 Confirm box

Another useful box is the confirm box. This box has two buttons and can return the button values (Fig. 7.4). To create this box, a simple script as shown in ex07-06.txt is used.

```
Listing: ex07-06.txt

1:   <body>
2:   <script>
3:     var but_val=confirm("This is a confirm box!")
4:     document.write(but_val)
5:   </script>
6:   </body>
```

The variable `but_val` in line 3 is set to true if the user clicks the OK button. The Cancel button creates a false value.

Let's now look at a more practical example. We consider an advertising page on the Web to sell computers. This advertisement uses the alert box to provide more information to the potential buyer. The confirm box is used to confirm and secure the order. Consider the following example code:

```
Example: ex07-01.htm - Alert And Confirm Boxes

 1: <?xml version="1.0" encoding="iso-8859-1"?>
 2: <!DOCTYPE html PUBLIC "-//W3C//DTD XHTML 1.0 Transitional//EN"
 3:     "http://www.w3.org/TR/xhtml1/DTD/xhtml1-transitional.dtd">
 4: <html xmlns="http://www.w3.org/1999/xhtml" xml:lang="en" lang="en">
 5: <head><title>Alert and Confirm Boxes - ex07-01.htm</title></head>
 6:
 7: <script>
 8: function orderBox()
 9: {
10:  var confirmBut
11:  var msg
12:  confirmBut = confirm("Place An Order Now?")
13:  if (confirmBut == true)
14:  {
15:    msg='<span class="textSt">Thank You! <br \>' +
16:               'We will process your order immediately.</span>'
17:    document.getElementById("confirmMsg").innerHTML=msg;
18:  }
19:  else
20:  {
21:    msg='<span class="textSt">WWW.COMPUTER.COM</span>'
22:    document.getElementById("confirmMsg").innerHTML=msg;
23:
24:  }
25: }
26:
27: function alertBox()
28: {
29: alert("This computer package is 50% cheaper \nthan others in the market");
30: }
31: </script>
32:
33: <style>
34:  .headSt {font-family:arial;font-size:22pt;text-align:center;
35:     color:#ff0000;font-weight:bold}
36:  .textSt {font-family:arial;font-size:12pt;color:#000088;font-weight:bold}
37:  .butSt{font-family:arial;font-size:12pt;color:#008800;
38:     background-color:#ffcccc;width:160px;height:26px;font-weight:bold}
39: </style>
40:
41: <body style="background-color:#ccccff;text-align:center">
42:
43:    <span class="headSt">Buy This Computer Today !</span>
44:    <br /><br /><img src="line1.gif" width="420" height="6" /><br /><br />
45:
46:    <span class="textSt">Intel CPU 2000 GHZ</span><br />
47:    <span class="textSt">100 GB Hard Disk</span><br />
48:    <span class="textSt">512 MB RAM</span><br$/>
49:    <span class="textSt">21 Inch Monitor</span><br />
50:    <span class="textSt">5 Years On Site Maintenance</span><br /><br />
51:    <span class="textSt">For XXX </span>
52:
```

```
53:    <br /><br /><img src="line1.gif" width="420" height="6" /><br /><br />
54:
55:    <input class="butSt" type="button" value="More Information"
56:       onClick="alertBox()" />  
57:    <input class="butSt" type="button" value="Order"
58:       onClick="orderBox()" /><br /><br />
59:
60:    <span id="confirmMsg" class="textSt">WWW.COMPUTER.COM</span>
61:
62: </body>
63: </html>
```

After the main advertising text in lines 43–54, we define two buttons called "More Information" and "Order" in this page. The More Information button activates the script function named `alertBox()` (lines 27–31) to open an alert box to display more information about the computer package. The symbol `\n` in line 29 is used to generate a line break inside the box. This in fact is the C language style (not XHTML) but adopted by the ECMAScript language. The Order button displays the confirm box with two buttons. When the user clicks the OK button, the following message (see lines 15–16)

Thank You!

We will process your order immediately.

is displayed at the location `id=confirmMsg` as indicated in line 17. This technique is commonly used to confirm an order on the Web. Some screen shots are shown in Figs 7.5 and 7.6.

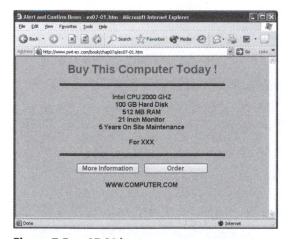

Figure 7.5 ex07-01.htm

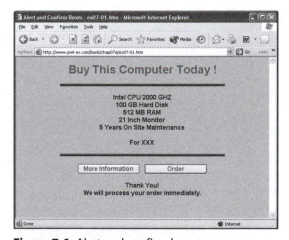

Figure 7.6 Alert and confirm boxes

7.2.2 Getting user input with prompt boxes

Alert and confirm boxes are useful for simple tasks such as displaying information and taking click actions. For more complex tasks, such as real user input (or typing input), we need something special called a prompt box. A prompt box allows you to prompt a message and read user input. The input text is then returned to the page once the OK button is clicked. The following is a typical example of a prompt box.

```
var inputName = prompt("Please Enter Your Name","John Smith");
```

The prompt() function accepts two arguments. The first argument is the prompted message "Please Enter Your Name." The second argument "John Smith" is the default message inside the input field of the prompt box. Once the OK button is clicked, the name John Smith is assigned to the variable as inputName (see Fig. 7.7). You can, of course, enter any other name in the input field.

With a prompt box, you can replace the script function orderBox() of lines 8–25 in ex07-01.htm with the listing ex07-07.txt and call the new example ex07-02.htm.

```
Listing: ex07-07.txt - Code Fragment For ex07-02.htm

 8: function orderBox()
 9: {
10:  var inputName
11:  var msg
12:  inputName = prompt("Please Enter Your Name","John Smith")
13:  if (inputName !=null && inputName !="")
14:  {
15:    msg='<span class="textSt">Thank You! ' + inputName + '<br />' +
16:              'We will process your order immediately.</span>'
17:    document.getElementById("confirmMsg").innerHTML=msg;
18:  }
19:  else
20:  {
21:    msg='<span class="textSt">WWW.COMPUTER.COM</span>'
22:    document.getElementById("confirmMsg").innerHTML=msg;
23:
24:  }
25: }
```

Once you click the OK button in the prompt box, the input name will appear just after the "Thank You!" message (line 15) as shown in Fig. 7.8.

Figure 7.7 Prompt box   **Figure 7.8** ex07-02.htm

7.2.3 Page redirection and random redirection

One of the common Web operations is to redirect the visitor to another Web page. Page redirection can be useful when you have, or change to, a new Web address. For example, once the old W3C authority site www.w3c.org had a page redirection to the new address www.w3.org.

The following is the body part of our next example (ex07-03.htm) to redirect visitors to another page immediately.

```
Listing: ex07-08.txt - Code fragement For ex07-03.htm

1: <body>
2: <script>
3:    location.href="welcome.htm"
4: </script>
5: <div>
6:   We would be surprised if you see this message.<br />
7:   This page has been redirected!
8: </div>
9: </body>
```

The simple command `location.href` in line 3 has the effect of redirecting visitors to another page. In this case, it redirects the visitor to another Web page welcome.htm. The codes in lines 5–8 should never be executed. In our next example, we show how to construct a page that can redirect visitors randomly to a list of other Web pages.

```
Example: ex07-04.htm - Random Page Re-direction

 1: <?xml version="1.0" encoding="iso-8859-1"?>
 2: <!DOCTYPE html PUBLIC "-//W3C//DTD XHTML 1.0 Transitional//EN"
 3:     "http://www.w3.org/TR/xhtml1/DTD/xhtml1-transitional.dtd">
 4: <html xmlns="http://www.w3.org/1999/xhtml" xml:lang="en" lang="en">
 5: <head><title>Random Page Re-direction - ex07-04.htm </title></head>
 6: <body>
 7:
 8: <script>
 9:   mySites=new Array("ex07-01.htm",
10:                     "ex07-02.htm",
11:                     "ex07-03.htm",
12:                     "welcome.htm")
13:   siteCount=mySites.length
14:
15:   siteNo=Math.floor(Math.random()*siteCount)
16:   window.location=mySites[siteNo]
17: </script>
18:
19: </body>
20: </html>
```

First, in lines 9–12, a new array is created to hold all the Web pages that we want to redirect to. As mentioned in section 7.1.3, each array in ECMAScript has a length property to indicate how many elements are inside it. In our example four elements ranging from 0 through 3 are defined as follows:

```
mySites[0] = ex07-01.htm    mySites[1] = ex07-02.htm
mySites[2] = ex07-03.htm    mySites[3] = welcome.htm
```

The random number generator (line 15) `Math.random()` generates a random number between 0 and 1. This number is then multiplied by `siteCount`. The integer part provides the random page number `siteNo` that we want to redirect to.

You now have a page that can redirect visitors randomly to other pages related to your friends' and/or business partners' sites. This technique is an integral part of many Web sites on the Internet.

7.2.4 Title and status bar animation

The title element `<title>` is used to specify the message in the title bar of the browser window. This message can also be represented by the property of the document object, e.g.,

```
document.title ="Practical Web Technologies"
```

At the bottom of the browser window, there is a status bar that can be used to display some useful information. The message inside this bar is a property of the window object

```
window.status="Practical Web Technologies"
```

The next example shows how to manipulate the messages in these bars and to perform simple animations. Consider the following listing ex07-05.htm:

Example: ex07-05.htm - Title & Status Bar Animation

```
 1: <?xml version="1.0" encoding="iso-8859-1"?>
 2: <!DOCTYPE html PUBLIC "-//W3C//DTD XHTML 1.0 Transitional//EN"
 3:     "http://www.w3.org/TR/xhtml1/DTD/xhtml1-transitional.dtd">
 4: <html xmlns="http://www.w3.org/1999/xhtml" xml:lang="en" lang="en">
 5: <head><title> Title & Status Bar Animation - ex07-05.htm </title></head>
 6:
 7: <body onload="animateMsg()" style="background-color:#000088">
 8: <script>
 9:
10:    var myTitle = "Practical Web Technologies ...."
11:    var i = 0
12:
13:   function animateMsg()
14:   {
15:    myTitleMsg = myTitle.substring(i,myTitle.length)+
16:        myTitle.substring(0,i)
17:    myStatusMsg = myTitle.substring(0,i) +
18:        myTitle.charAt(i).toUpperCase()+
19:        myTitle.substring(i+1,myTitle.length)
20:
21:    document.title = "Title Bar Animation: "+myTitleMsg
22:    window.status = myStatusMsg
23:
24:    if (i < myTitle.length)
25:    {
26:      i++
27:    }
28:    else
29:    {
30:      i = 0
31:    }
32:    setTimeout("animateMsg()",150)
33:   }
34: </script>
35: <span style="font-family:arial;font-size:14pt;color:#ffff00">
36: Title Bar and Status Bar Animation : ex07-05.htm
37: </body>
38: </html>
```

The main operation of this example is the script function `animateMsg()` defined in lines 13–33. First, the page uses a variable called `myTitle` to store the title message "Practical Web Technologies…." The function `animateMsg()` is then used to animate the title. In lines 15–16, we use a substring method on the string variable `myTitle`:

```
myTitleMsg = myTitle.substring(i,myTitle.length)+
    myTitle.substring(0,i)
```

The first substring returns the message starting from the *i*th character to the length of the variable. The second substring returns the message from 0 position to the *i*th character. This means that if you animate this `myTitleMsg` with the conditional statement on variable *i* as shown in lines 24–31, you will have an animated string on the title bar. The status bar animation in lines 17–19 animates, one by one, characters in the string `myTitle` to upper case. The functions `charAt(i)` and to `UpperCase()` (line 18) are standard methods associated with any string (or substring) object. A screen shot of this animated result is shown in Figs 7.9a, 7.9b, and 7.9c.

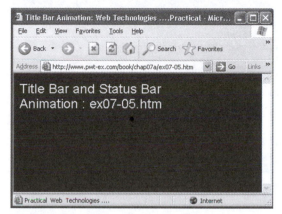

Figure 7.9b Title bar animation

Figure 7.9a Title bar and status bar Animation

Figure 7.9c Status bar animation

7.3   Detection

7.3.1   Browser detection

In many cases, it is important for Web designers to ensure that the right design goes to the right browsers. There are a number of ways to detect different browser software. For example, we have used IE's `document.all` feature in Chapter 6 to distinguish between IE and NS browsers. One easy practical statement

```
var IE = document.all?true:false
```

can do the trick. However, this statement contains no information about the identity of the browser or its version. For proper identity detection, you need to use the properties of the navigator object inside the browser. Consider the following example ex07-06.htm:

```
Example: ex07-06.htm - Browser Detection

1: <?xml version="1.0" encoding="iso-8859-1"?>
2: <!DOCTYPE html PUBLIC "-//W3C//DTD XHTML 1.0 Transitional//EN"
3:     "http://www.w3.org/TR/xhtml1/DTD/xhtml1-transitional.dtd">
4: <html xmlns="http://www.w3.org/1999/xhtml" xml:lang="en" lang="en">
5: <head><title> Browser Detection - ex07-06.htm </title></head>
6: <body style="font-family:arial;font-size:16pt;color:#000088">
7:  <script>
8:     document.write(window.navigator.appName +"<br />")
```

```
 9:    document.write(window.navigator.appVersion +"<br />")
10:  </script>
11:  </body>
12:  </html>
```

The name (or identity) of the browser is usually stored in the `appName` property of the navigator object (line 8) and the `appVersion` property carries the version number (line 9). Examples of detection results on IE and NS are shown in Figs 7.10 and 7.11 respectively. Another useful piece of information on the identity and version is the `navigator.userAgent` property. Generally speaking, detection is a process to obtain value(s) from the target object. In the next example, you will learn how to use the `navigator` together with the `screen` and `location` objects to build a fully functional detection page on browsers, systems, and Internet networks.

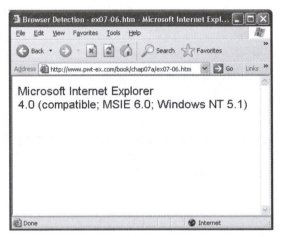

Figure 7.10 Browser detection on IE6 (ex07-06.htm)

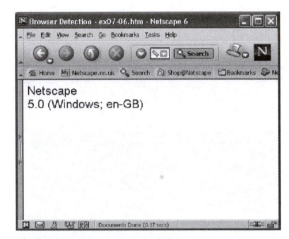

Figure 7.11 Detection on NS6

7.3.2 Browser, system, and network detection

In this section, you will write a Web page to detect different browsers, systems, and networks. This page will also demonstrate how to use buttons to set off different actions. It has three buttons and the detection results are displayed immediately on the same page. For each of these detections, you will build an XHTML table on the fly by using script. This table is represented as a string. The final process is then to output this string to a desirable area by using the `innerHTML` feature.

To build the tables, the following three script functions are created:

```
browserDet()    systemDet()    networkDet()
```

Inside each function there is a script string to incorporate the necessary table and detection elements. For example, the following code fragment ex07-09.txt is used to build the `networkDet()` function.

```
Listing: ex07-09.txt

 1:  function networkDet()
 2:  {
 3:   outputMsg = "<table width='600' class='strSt'>" +
 4:    "<tr><td style='color:#008800'>Network Detection:</td>" +
 5:      "<td width='70%'></td></tr>" +
 6:    "<tr><td>location.href</td>" +
 7:        "<td>" + location.href +"</td></tr>" +
     ... ...
     ... ...
20:    "<tr><td>location.protocol</td>" +
```

```
21:        "<td>" + location.protocol + "</td></tr>" +
22:      "</table>"
23:    document.getElementById("outId").innerHTML=outputMsg
24:    }
```

The string `outputMsg` in lines 3–22 contains an XHTML table. This string is generated on the fly to obtain the network information through the `location` object. The `innerHTML` feature (line 23) is used to output the table to an element with `id="outId"`. If you type the command

http://www.pwt-ex.com/book/chap07/ex07-07.htm?name=author#par01

on the browser's URL bar, the `location.href` in line 7 will contain the whole command. The `location.protocol` property in line 21 will have the value "`http`" as the protocol.

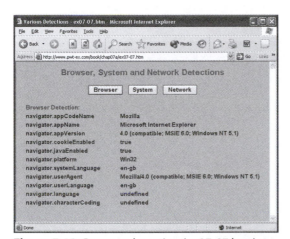

Figure 7.12 Browser detection (ex07-07.htm)

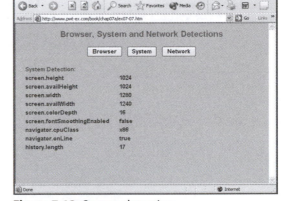

Figure 7.13 System detection

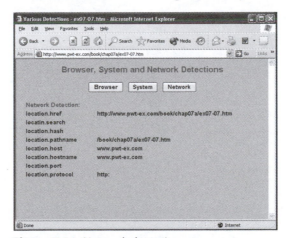

Figure 7.14 Network detection

The full listing of this program ex07-07.htm is given below. Figures 7.12–7.14 show the program at work.

```
Example: ex07-07.htm - Browser, System And Network Detection

1: <?xml version="1.0" encoding="iso-8859-1"?>
2: <!DOCTYPE html PUBLIC "-//W3C//DTD XHTML 1.0 Transitional//EN"
3:     "http://www.w3.org/TR/xhtml1/DTD/xhtml1-transitional.dtd">
4: <html xmlns="http://www.w3.org/1999/xhtml" xml:lang="en" lang="en">
5: <head><title> Various Detections - ex07-07.htm </title></head>
```

```
 6:  <style>
 7:   h1 {font-family:arial; font-size:16pt; color: red}
 8:   .strSt{font-family:arial;font-size:11pt;color:#0000ff;font-weight:bold}
 9:  </style>
10:
11:  <script>
12:   var outputMsg
13:   function browserDet()
14:   {
15:    outputMsg = "<table width='600' class='strSt'>" +
16:    "<tr><td style='color:#008800'>Browser Detection:</td>" +
17:       "<td width='60%'></td></tr>" +
18:    "<tr><td>navigator.appCodeName</td>" +
19:       "<td>" + navigator.appCodeName + "</td></tr>" +
20:    "<tr><td>navigator.appName</td>" +
21:       "<td>" + navigator.appName + "</td></tr>" +
22:    "<tr><td>navigator.appVersion</td>" +
23:       "<td>" + navigator.appVersion + "</td></tr>" +
24:    "<tr><td>navigator.cookieEnabled</td>" +
25:       "<td>" + navigator.cookieEnabled + "</td></tr>" +
26:    "<tr><td>navigator.javaEnabled</td>" +
27:       "<td>" + navigator.javaEnabled() + "</td></tr>" +
28:    "<tr><td>navigator.platform</td>" +
29:       "<td>" + navigator.platform + "</td></tr>" +
30:    "<tr><td>navigator.systemLanguage</td>" +
31:       "<td>" + navigator.systemLanguage + "</td></tr>" +
32:    "<tr><td>navigator.userAgent</td>" +
33:       "<td>" + navigator.userAgent + "</td></tr>" +
34:    "<tr><td>navigator.userLanguage</td>" +
35:       "<td>" + navigator.userLanguage + "</td></tr>" +
36:    "</table>"
37:    document.getElementById("outId").innerHTML=outputMsg
38:   }
39:
40:   function systemDet()
41:   {
42:    outputMsg = "<table width='600' class='strSt'>" +
43:    "<tr><td style='color:#008800'>System Detection:</td>" +
44:       "<td width='60%'></td></tr>" +
45:    "<tr><td>screen.height</td>" +
46:       "<td>" +screen.height +"</td></tr>" +
47:    "<tr><td>screen.availHeight</td>" +
48:       "<td>" + screen.availHeight + "</td></tr>" +
49:    "<tr><td>screen.width</td>" +
50:       "<td>" + screen.width + "</td></tr>" +
51:    "<tr><td>screen.availWidth</td>" +
52:       "<td>" + screen.availWidth + "</td></tr>" +
53:    "<tr><td>screen.colorDepth</td>" +
54:       "<td>" + screen.colorDepth + "</td></tr>" +
55:    "<tr><td>screen.fontSmoothingEnabled</td>" +
56:       "<td>" + screen.fontSmoothingEnabled + "</td></tr>" +
57:    "<tr><td>navigator.cpuClass</td>" +
58:       "<td>" + navigator.cpuClass + "</td></tr>" +
59:    "<tr><td>navigator.onLine</td>" +
60:       "<td>" + navigator.onLine + "</td></tr>" +
61:    "<tr><td>history.length</td>" +
62:       "<td>" + history.length + "</td></tr>" +
63:    "</table>"
```

```
64:    document.getElementById("outId").innerHTML=outputMsg
65:   }
66:
67:   function networkDet()
68:   {
69:    outputMsg = "<table width='600' class='strSt'>" +
70:     "<tr><td style='color:#008800'>Network Detection:</td>" +
71:       "<td width='70%'></td></tr>" +
72:     "<tr><td>location.href</td>" +
73:       "<td>" + location.href +"</td></tr>" +
74:     "<tr><td>locatin.search</td>" +
75:       "<td>" + location.search + "</td></tr>" +
76:     "<tr><td>location.hash</td>" +
77:       "<td>" + location.hash + "</td></tr>" +
78:     "<tr><td>location.pathname</td>" +
79:       "<td>" + location.pathname + "</td></tr>" +
80:     "<tr><td>location.host</td>" +
81:       "<td>" + location.host + "</td></tr>" +
82:     "<tr><td>location.hostname</td>" +
83:       "<td>" + location.hostname + "</td></tr>" +
84:     "<tr><td>location.port</td>" +
85:       "<td>" + location.port + "</td></tr>" +
86:     "<tr><td>location.protocol</td>" +
87:       "<td>" + location.protocol + "</td></tr>" +
88:     "</table>"
89:    document.getElementById("outId").innerHTML=outputMsg
90:   }
91: </script>
92: <body style="background-color:#cccccc">
93: <div align="center">
94: <h1>Browser, System and Network Detections</h1>
95:    <input type="button" class="strSt" value="Browser"
96:      onclick="browserDet()" />  
97:    <input type="button" class="strSt" value="System"
98:      onclick="systemDet()" />  
99:    <input type="button" class="strSt" value="Network"
100:      onclick="networkDet()" />
101: <br /><br /><div id="outId"></div>
102: </div>
103: </body>
104: </html>
```

Next, we will show you how to use the system and network detection results to write browser-dependent codes.

7.3.3 Conditionals depending on browser

If you just want to detect whether a visitor is using an IE browser, the code fragment ex07-10.txt is an efficient conditional:

```
Listing: ex07-10.txt

1: <body>
2: <script>
3: var IE = document.all?true:false
4: if (IE==true)
5:    document.write("You are using IE type browser")
6:   else
7:     document.write("You are not using IE type browser")
8: </script>
9: </body>
```

The `document.all` feature used in line 3 is a conditional statement to identify an IE browser. This method, however, contains no information about other browsers. For a more accurate detection, you can use the `indexOf()` command (or method) to compare the browser string and perform more specific identity detection. For example, you can use the code ex07-11.txt to detect NS6:

```
Listing: ex07-11.txt

1: <body>
2: <script>
3:    browserType = navigator.userAgent
4:    if (browserType.indexOf("Netscape6") != -1)
5:      document.write("You are using Netscape6")
6:    else
7:      document.write("You are not using Netscape6")
8:  </script>
9: </body>
```

The `indexOf()` function in line 4 is a string comparison function. This function will determine whether the keyword "Netscape6" exists inside the string variable `browserType`.

If you put in more conditionals such as `if` statements, you will have a Web page to detect various Web browsers. Consider the example code ex07-08.htm:

```
Example: ex07-08.htm - Browser Detection II

1: <?xml version="1.0" encoding="iso-8859-1"?>
2: <!DOCTYPE html PUBLIC "-//W3C//DTD XHTML 1.0 Transitional//EN"
3:     "http://www.w3.org/TR/xhtml1/DTD/xhtml1-transitional.dtd">
4: <html xmlns="http://www.w3.org/1999/xhtml" xml:lang="en" lang="en">
5: <head><title> Browser Detection II - ex07-08.htm </title></head>
6:
7: <style>h3{font-family:arial;font-size:16pt;color:#ffff00}</style>
8: <body style="background-color:#000088;text-align:center">
9:  <h3>Conditionals On Browser Version<br /><br />
10:
11: <script>
12: var outMsg="You Are Using An Unknown Browser"
13: var browserT=navigator.appName
14: var versionSt=navigator.appVersion
15: var versionN = navigator.appVersion.charAt(0)
16: if (browserT=="Microsoft Internet Explorer")
17: {
18:   if (versionSt.indexOf("MSIE 6") !=-1)
19:      outMsg="You Are Using MSIE 6.x"
20:   else if (versionSt.indexOf("MSIE 5") !=-1)
21:      outMsg="You Are Using MSIE 5.x"
22:   else if (versionN ==4)
23:      outMsg="You Are Using MS Internet Explorer 4"
24:   else if (versionN < 4)
25:      outMsg="You Are Using MS Internet Explorer 3 or Earlier"
26:   else
27:      outMsg="Please Program Me To Include This Version"
28: }else{
29:   if (browserT=="Netscape")
30:   {
31:     if (navigator.userAgent.indexOf("Netscape6") !=-1)
32:      outMsg="You Are Using Netscape 6.x"
33:     else if (versionN ==4)
34:      outMsg="You Are Using Netscape Version 4.x"
35:     else if (versionN < 4)
```

```
36:      outMsg="You Are Using Netscape Version 3.x or Earlier"
37:    else
38:      outMsg="Please Program Me To Include This Version"
39:  }
40: }
41: document.write("<h3>"+outMsg+"</h3>")
42: </script>
43: </body>
44: </html>
```

This page will detect IE and Netscape browsers along with their different versions. The command `naviga-tor.appVersion.charAt(0)` in line 15 is used to return the first character of the `appVersion`. This character (or number) normally stores the version number and helps to identify a range of versions as indicated in lines 22, 24, 33, and 35. This example also contains a message for future versions.

7.3.4 Page redirection depending on browser

If you have Web pages dedicated to some specified browsers and their versions, you can use the redirection technique discussed in section 7.2 to redirect your browser. For example, you can replace the script part (lines 11–42) in ex07-08.htm with the script code in ex07-12.txt to form a new example ex07-09.htm. This example will redirect a page depending on the browser. Figures 7.15 and 7.16 show the program at work in NS6 and NS4.x.

Figure 7.15 Browser detection on NS6

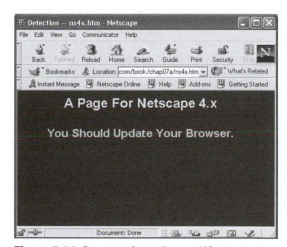

Figure 7.16 Browser detection on NS4.x

```
Listing: ex07-12.txt - Code Fragment For ex07-09.htm

 1: <script>
 2: var outMsg="You Are Using An Unknown Browser"
 3: var browserT=navigator.appName
 4: var versionSt=navigator.appVersion
 5: var versionN = navigator.appVersion.charAt(0)
 6: if (browserT=="Microsoft Internet Explorer")
 7: {
 8:  if (versionSt.indexOf("MSIE 6") !=-1)
 9:     location.href="ie6x.htm"
10:  else if (versionSt.indexOf("MSIE 5") !=-1)
11:     location.href="ie5x.htm"
12:  else if (versionN ==4)
13:     location.href="ie40.htm"
```

```
14:  else if (versionN < 4)
15:     location.href="ieless4.htm"
16:  else
17:     outMsg="Please Program Me To Include This Version"
18: }else{
19:  if (browserT=="Netscape")
20:  {
21:    if (navigator.userAgent.indexOf("Netscape6") !=-1)
22:     location.href="ns6.htm"
23:    else if (versionN ==4)
24:     location.href="ns4x.htm"
25:    else if (versionN < 4)
26:     location.href="nsless4.htm"
27:    else
28:     outMsg="Please Program Me To Include This Version"
29:  }
30: }
31: </script>
```

7.3.5 International languages and detection

In many practical applications, Web programmers may also need to detect other properties and control the browser accordingly. One such popular application is the international languages issue. XHTML uses the ISO language code (or primary code) and country code (or subcode) pair to identify a particular language and country. For example, "en-gb" represents English in Great Britain. The first two-letter code is the primary code used to specify the language and can be used with the language attribute such as lang="" in XHTML. Some language codes (and their abbreviations) are listed in Table 7.1.

Table 7.1 ISO 639 language abbreviations

en	English	nl	Dutch	ar	Arabic	ja	Japanese
fr	French	el	Greek	he	Hebrew	hi	Hindi
de	German	es	Spanish	ru	Russian	ur	Urdu
it	Italian	pt	Portuguese	zh	Chinese	sa	Sanskrit

Suppose you have two Web pages in different languages, one in French and English, the other in Japanese and English. The following simple example ex07-10.htm will detect the language and redirect the user to the appropriate site.

```
Example: ex07-10.htm - Language And Detection

 1: <?xml version="1.0" encoding="iso-8859-1"?>
 2: <!DOCTYPE html PUBLIC "-//W3C//DTD XHTML 1.0 Transitional//EN"
 3:     "http://www.w3.org/TR/xhtml1/DTD/xhtml1-transitional.dtd">
 4: <html xmlns="http://www.w3.org/1999/xhtml" xml:lang="en" lang="en">
 5: <head><title> Language and Detection - ex07-10.htm </title></head>
 6: <body style="background-color:#000088">
 7: <script>
 8:   if (navigator.appName.indexOf("Microsoft")!=-1)
 9:       languageSt=eval("navigator.systemLanguage")
10:   if (navigator.appName.indexOf("Netscape")!=-1)
11:       languageSt=eval("navigator.language")
```

```
12:
13:    if (languageSt.indexOf("ja") !=-1)
14:        location.href="japan.htm"
15:    else
16:        location.href="french.htm"
17: </script>
18: </body>
19: </html>
```

The conditional statements in lines 8–11 are used to get the language string. If the language string contains the language code "ja" (i.e., Japanese), the code in line 14 will redirect the browser to japan.htm. In all other cases it will load the French and English page called french.htm. Some screen shots of these results are shown in Figs 7.17 and 7.18.

Figure 7.17 French.htm

Figure 7.18 Japan.htm

In some cases, you may need to turn on the encoding environment of your browser to see the special country encoding (e.g., the Japanese character set). The main body code for this example, japan.htm, is listed in ex07-13.txt.

```
Listing: ex07-13.txt – Code Fragment For japan.htm

 1: <style>h3{font-family:arial;font-size:18pt;color:#ffff00}
 2:     h2{font-family:arial;font-size:18pt;color:#00ffff}
 3:     .butSt{font-family:arial;font-size:14pt;color:#008800;width:200}
 4: </style>
 5: <body style="background-color:#000088;text-align:center">
 6: <br /><br />
 7: <h3>いつもご利用ありがとうございます。<br /><br /></h3>
 8: <h2>Thank you very much for <br />
 9:    visiting our web site.<br /><br /></h2><br />
10: <h3>Language Available:</h3>
11: <input type="button" class="butSt" value="Japanese & English"
12:       onclick="location.href='japan.htm'" />
13: <input type="button" class="butSt" value="French & English"
14:       onclick="location.href='french.htm'" />
15: </body>
```

7.3.6 Controlling browser size and hostname with detection

The main advantage of detection is to be able to control and ensure that the right design goes to the right browser. Our next example shows how to detect the screen resolution and change the browser window to half of its screen size. The properties `screen.availWidth` and `screen.availHeight` are used to get the screen width and height size. Then the window resize method (or function) `window.resizeTo(width,height)` is used to resize the browser. In this example, we also use the `location.hostname` to get the host of the page. A message is displayed if the user gets this page from another provider or source (see listing ex07-11.htm).

```
Example: ex07-11.htm - Detect And Control Screen Size & Hostname

 1: <?xml version="1.0" encoding="iso-8859-1"?>
 2: <!DOCTYPE html PUBLIC "-//W3C//DTD XHTML 1.0 Transitional//EN"
 3:     "http://www.w3.org/TR/xhtml1/DTD/xhtml1-transitional.dtd">
 4: <html xmlns="http://www.w3.org/1999/xhtml" xml:lang="en" lang="en">
 5: <head><title> Screen Size & Hostname - ex07-11.htm </title></head>
 6: <body style="background-color:#000088;text-align:center;
 7:     font-family:arial;font-size:16pt;color:#ffff00">
 8: <script>
 9:  var winWidth=Math.floor(screen.availWidth 2)
10:  var winHeight=Math.floor(screen.availHeight 2)
11:     window.resizeTo(winWidth,winHeight)
12:
13:   if (location.hostname != "www.pwt-ex.com")
14:     outMsg="Please Get This Page From www.pwt-ex.com"
15:   else
16:     outMsg="This Page Is From www.pwt-ex.com"
17:
18:   document.write("<br />The Available Screen Resolution = " +
19:       screen.availWidth+" * "+ screen.availHeight)
20:   document.write("<br />The Browser Window Resize To = " +
21:       winWidth+" * "+ winHeight+"<br /><br />")
22:   document.write("The Detected Hostname is "+location.hostname)
23:   document.write("<br />"+outMsg)
24: </script>
25: </body>
26: </html>
```

The `winWidth` in line 9 is a variable used to store the integer part (`Math.floor`) of half the screen width. Together with the variable `winHeight`, you can resize the window to a desirable size as indicated in line 11. The conditional statement in line 13 is used to detect the hostname. Lines 18–23 are used to output the message on the page.

If you obtain this page from location www.pwt-ex.com, the detection code in lines 13–14 will have the screen display as shown in Fig. 7.19. If you obtain this page from any other Internet source, e.g., www.isp.com, you will have the display as shown in Fig. 7.20.

For some browser software, the function `document.write()` may output the message to a new page. This will destroy most of the original settings including the page itself and its style. In practice, programmers may like to output messages to a dedicated area (or element) and keep the same Web page settings. For keeping the page settings and delivering XHTML messages anywhere you want, you may prefer to use the non-standard feature `innerHTML` (supported by both IE and NS) to perform the task. For example, the following code fragment ex07-14.txt can be used to do the same job as in ex07-11.htm.

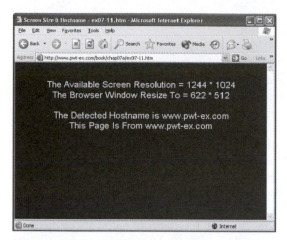

Figure 7.19 An authorized page (ex07-11.htm)

Figure 7.20 An unauthorized page

```
Listing: ex07-14.txt - Code Fragment For ex07-12.htm

 1: <body style="background-color:#000088;text-align:center;
 2:       font-family:arial;font-size:16pt;color:#ffff00">
 3: <script>
 4:  var winWidth=Math.floor(screen.availWidth/2)
 5:  var winHeight=Math.floor(screen.availHeight/2)
 6:      window.resizeTo(winWidth,winHeight)
 7:   if (location.hostname != "www.pwt-ex.com")
 8:      outMsg="Please Get This Page From www.pwt-ex.com"
 9:   else
10:      outMsg="This Page Is From www.pwt-ex.com"
11: </script><br /><br />
12:
13:   <div id="detectScnSize"></div><br />
14:   <div id="detectHost"></div>
15:
16: <script>
17:  document.getElementById("detectScnSize").innerHTML=
18:    "The Available Screen Revolution = " +
19:    screen.availWidth+ " * " + screen.availHeight +
20:    "<br />The Browser Window Resize To =" +winWidth+ " * "+ winHeight
21:  document.getElementById("detectHost").innerHTML=
22:    "The Detected Hostname is "+location.hostname+"<br />"+outMsg
23: </script>
24: </body>
```

This code fragment uses the same window resize and hostname detection (lines 4–10). After that, two division elements are created for output. Finally, the example uses the getElementById feature to locate the element and output the message as required.

Please note that two separate sets of script are used here. The order of the scripts is important. If you arrange the second set of script, lines 16–23, before line 13, you will output the message to some unknown elements.

7.4   Cookies, cookies

7.4.1   My first cookie

A cookie is a small piece of information stored on the client machine by a Web page. The Netscape browser stores its cookie in a file called `cookies.txt`. For IE systems, a whole directory (under the Windows directory) called "Cookies" is dedicated to storing cookie information. Cookies, or cookie information, can be accessed and manipulated using the script feature `document.cookie`.

The original idea of cookies was to make life easier for surfers to access their favorite Web sites. For example, when you visit a site for the first time, you may be asked to enter your name and perhaps your email address and some other information to identify yourself. The site will then place a cookie containing this information on your system. When you return the next time, the site will request information based on the cookie on your machine to determine who you are and perhaps whether you have authorization to access the site.

Cookies are an important, and yet controversial, issue on the Internet. A number of online shopping facilities use cookies to store the shopping items (i.e., the shopping trolley). Since cookie messages are unprotected and transparent to users, they create serious security issues and affect each Web user.

Let's now take a look at how a Web site (e.g., www.pwt-ex.com) can set a cookie in your local machine. Consider the example ex07-13.htm:

```
Example: ex07-13.htm - Set My First Cookie

 1: <?xml version="1.0" encoding="iso-8859-1"?>
 2: <!DOCTYPE html PUBLIC "-//W3C//DTD XHTML 1.0 Transitional//EN"
 3:      "http://www.w3.org/TR/xhtml1/DTD/xhtml1-transitional.dtd">
 4: <html xmlns="http://www.w3.org/1999/xhtml" xml:lang="en" lang="en">
 5: <head><title> Set My First Cookie - ex07-13.htm </title></head>
 6: <body style="background-color:#000088;font-family:arial;font-size:16pt;
 7:      text-align:center;color:#ffff00">
 8: <h2 style="font-size:22pt;color:#00ffff">Welcom To WWW.PWT-EX.COM</h2>
 9: <img src="line1.gif" width="450" height="6" /><br /><br />
10: <script>
11:  var expDate = new Date ()
12:  expDate.setTime(expDate.getTime() + (1000 * 60 * 60 * 24))
13:  document.cookie="Username=JohnSmith; expires="+expDate.toGMTString()
14:  document.cookie="Email=JohnSmith@isp.com; expires="+expDate.toGMTString()
15: </script><br />
16: <div> Practical Web Technologies</div>
17: <div>We Have Put Cookies In Your Machine</div>
18: </body>
19: </html>
```

If you visit this page from www.pwt-ex.com, the site will put two cookies (lines 13 and 14) in your machine, one to store the name of the user and the other to store the email address.

Basically, every cookie consists of three parts: cookie name, cookie value, and an expiry date. The cookie name and value can be any character string representing the information that you want to store. The expiry date will determine the life of the cookie. If the date is before the current time, the cookie is deleted immediately. If no expiry date is set, the cookie will be deleted soon after your Web session. Usually, this date can be set by the following procedure:

- Get the current time.
- Add a counting number in terms of a thousandth of a second.

A typical example is demonstrated in lines 11–12. The counting number `1000*60*60*24` in line 12 represents one day. If you want the cookie to last for a year, you can use the counting number `1000*60*60*24*365`.

The general format to set a cookie in a client machine is

```
document.cookie="cookieName=cookieValue; expires=expirationDate"
```

The three variables `cookieName`, `cookieValue`, and `expirationDate` are user defined. They form the basic components of a cookie. All cookie transactions between the browser and server are normally transparent to users. We deliberately put some output messages (lines 16–17) in our example to notify us (see Fig. 7.21).

Figure 7.21 ex07-13.htm

The interesting thing is that when you visit the site www.pwt-ex.com again, your browser will search for cookies from www.pwt-ex.com and return them as a string in `document.cookie`. Example ex07-14.htm shows how to design a page to read cookies.

```
Example: ex07-14.htm - Display My Cookie

 1: <?xml version="1.0" encoding="iso-8859-1"?>
 2: <!DOCTYPE html PUBLIC "-//W3C//DTD XHTML 1.0 Transitional//EN"
 3:     "http://www.w3.org/TR/xhtml1/DTD/xhtml1-transitional.dtd">
 4: <html xmlns="http://www.w3.org/1999/xhtml" xml:lang="en" lang="en">
 5: <head><title> Display My Cookie - ex07-14.htm </title></head>
 6: <body style="background-color:#000088;font-family:arial;font-size:16pt;
 7:         text-align:center;color:#ffff00">
 8: <h2 style="font-size:22pt;color:#00ffff">Welcom To WWW.PWT-EX.COM</h2>
 9: <img src="line1.gif" width="450" height="6" /><br /><br />
10: <script>
11:    if (document.cookie == "")
12:    {
13:      document.write("There Are No Cookies Here<br />")
14:      document.write("You Are New To Us. Welcome!")
15:    } else {
16:      document.write("You Have Visited Us Before <br />")
17:      document.write("Cookie Information: <br />")
18:      document.write(document.cookie)
19:    }
20: </script><br />
21: </body>
22: </html>
```

The main operation of this example is a conditional statement on `document.cookie` (lines 11–19). You know that you have a new visitor if the string is empty. If the string is not empty, you can output the cookie information as illustrated in Fig. 7.22.

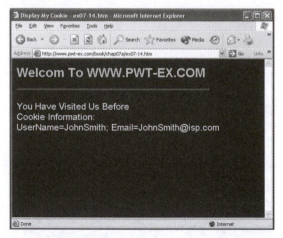

Figure 7.22 ex07-14.htm

The next section shows how to construct a Web page with counting and last visit capabilities.

7.4.2 Counting and remembering last visit with cookies

Let's see how you can develop a Web page with counting and last visit functionalities. We know from the structure of cookies that the most basic cookie controls are to set and get cookie values. You first need to develop two script functions `setCookie()` and `getCookie()`. These functions will also be used later in section 7.4.4 to build a cookie library. This page remembers every visit by someone with a last visit date and time stamp. The program code is shown in ex07-15.htm.

```
Example: ex07-15.htm - Counting And Last Visit Date And Time
 1: <?xml version="1.0" encoding="iso-8859-1"?>
 2: <!DOCTYPE html PUBLIC "-//W3C//DTD XHTML 1.0 Transitional//EN"
 3:     "http://www.w3.org/TR/xhtml1/DTD/xhtml1-transitional.dtd">
 4: <html xmlns="http://www.w3.org/1999/xhtml" xml:lang="en" lang="en">
 5: <head><title> Counting and Last Visit - ex07-15.htm </title></head>
 6: <body style="background-color:#000088;font-family:arial;font-size:16pt;
 7:       text-align:center;color:#ffff00">
 8: <h2 style="font-size:22pt;color:#00ffff">Welcom To WWW.PWT-EX.COM</h2>
 9: <img src="line1.gif" width="450" height="6" /><br /><br />
10:
11: <script>
12:   function setCookie(cookieName, cookieValue, expDate)
13:   {
14:     var cookieSt = cookieName + "=" + escape(cookieValue) +
15:       ((expDate) ? "; expires=" + expDate.toGMTString() : "")
16:     document.cookie = cookieSt
17:   }
18:
19:   function getCookie(cookieName)
20:   {
21:    var cookieItem = document.cookie.split("; ")
22:    for (i=0; i< cookieItem.length; i++) {
23:     if (cookieName == cookieItem[i].split("=")[0])
24:      return unescape(cookieItem[i].split("=")[1])
25:     }
```

```
26:     return null
27:    }
28:
29:    cTime = new Date
30:    expDate = new Date
31:    expDate.setTime(expDate.getTime() + (1000 * 60 * 60 * 24*365))
32:
33:    pCount = eval(getCookie("pageCount"))
34:    pCount++
35:    lVisit = getCookie("lastVisit")
36:    if (lVisit == null) lVisit = ""
37:
38:    setCookie("pageCount",pCount,expDate)
39:    setCookie("lastVisit",cTime,expDate)
40:
41:    document.write("You Have Visited Us "+pCount+" times.<br />")
42:    if (lVisit != "")
43:      document.write("Your Last Visit Was : <br />" + lVisit)
44:
45: </script>
46: </body>
47: </html>
```

The setCookie() function in lines 12–17 takes the cookieName, cookieValue, and expDate (expiry date) as arguments and sets the cookie accordingly. The command escape(cookieValue) at the end of line 14 is used to turn the cookieValue into an escape format so that spaces and other special characters can be handled correctly.

The getCookie()function in lines 19–27 takes one argument, namely, cookieName. This function returns the cookieValue associated with the argument. First, this function splits the entire cookie string from document.cookie into an array of cookieItem (see line 21). Then string comparison takes place to identify the cookieName (lines 22–23). If a match is found, the cookieValue will be returned as a unescape string (line 24).

The rest of the program is simple. This page will plant two cookies (the pageCount and lastVisit cookies) on the client machines. The value of the pageCount is a number to record the number of visits. The value of lastVisit is a string representing the time of last visit. We first use the getCookie() function to get the value of pageCount (line 33). This value is incremented by 1 (line 34) and then the value is put back as a cookie (line 38). You obtain the lastVisit information in line 35. Update this value with the current time and put it back as a cookie (line 39). Finally, you output the stored values pCount and lVisit to the screen (lines 41–43). In this way, both the pageCount and lastVisit cookies will be updated after each visit. Figure 7.23 shows a screen shot of ex07-15.htm.

Figure 7.23 ex07-15.htm

7.4.3 Deleting some or all of your cookies

Since the lives of cookies depend on their expiry dates, one natural way to delete them is to reset this value. For example, the line of code

```
eDate.setTime(eDate.getTime() - (1000 * 60 * 60 * 24))
```

will get yesterday's date. If you set this date on a cookie, the cookie will be deleted immediately. For example, one can use the following code ex07-16.htm to delete the pageCount cookie to restart a page count.

```
Example: ex07-16.htm - Restart Page Count

 1: <?xml version="1.0" encoding="iso-8859-1"?>
 2: <!DOCTYPE html PUBLIC "-//W3C//DTD XHTML 1.0 Transitional//EN"
 3:     "http://www.w3.org/TR/xhtml1/DTD/xhtml1-transitional.dtd">
 4: <html xmlns="http://www.w3.org/1999/xhtml" xml:lang="en" lang="en">
 5: <head><title> Re-start Page Count - ex07-16.htm </title></head>
 6: <body>
 7: <script>
 8:   cTime = new Date
 9:   expDate = new Date
10:   expDate.setTime(expDate.getTime() - (1000 * 60 * 60 * 24))
11:   document.cookie="pageCount=0; expires="+expDate
12: </script>
13: </body>
14: </html>
```

Figure 7.24 shows the result when you run ex07-16.htm to delete the pageCount cookie and then rerun the previous example ex07-15.htm to show the page count.

Figure 7.24 After restarting the counter in ex07-16.htm

The following example shows how to delete all your cookies. The page begins by displaying all your cookies. If you click the Delete button, all your cookies will be deleted.

```
Example: ex07-17.htm - Delete All Cookies

 1: <?xml version="1.0" encoding="iso-8859-1"?>
 2: <!DOCTYPE html PUBLIC "-//W3C//DTD XHTML 1.0 Transitional//EN"
 3:     "http://www.w3.org/TR/xhtml1/DTD/xhtml1-transitional.dtd">
 4: <html xmlns="http://www.w3.org/1999/xhtml" xml:lang="en" lang="en">
 5: <head><title> Delete All Cookies - ex07-17.htm </title></head>
 6: <body style="background-color:#000088;font-family:arial;font-size:14pt;
```

```
 7:            text-align:left;color:#ffff00">
 8: <h2 style="font-size:22pt;color:#00ffff">Delete All Your Cookies</h2>
 9: <img src="line1.gif" width="450" height="6" /><br /><br />
10:
11: <script>
12:  function showCookies()
13:  {
14:   if (document.cookie !="")
15:   {
16:    cookieItem = document.cookie.split("; ")
17:    document.write("You Have "+cookieItem.length+" cookies<br /><br />")
18:    for (i=0; i< cookieItem.length; i++)
19:    {
20:     document.write("Cookie Name = "+cookieItem[i].split("=")[0]+"<br />")
21:     document.write("Cookie Value = "+
22:        unescape(cookieItem[i].split("=")[1])+"<br />")
23:    }
24:   } else
25:    document.write("<br />You Have No Cookies! <br />")
26:  }
27:
28:  function delAllCookies()
29:  {
30:   if (document.cookie !="")
31:   {
32:    eDate = new Date
33:    eDate.setTime(eDate.getTime() - (1000 * 60 * 60 * 24))
34:    cookieItem = document.cookie.split("; ")
35:    for (i=0; i< cookieItem.length; i++)
36:    {
37:      document.cookie=cookieItem[i].split("=")[0]+
38:        "=; expires="+eDate.toGMTString()
39:    }
40:   }
41:  }
42: showCookies()
43: </script><br />
44: <input type="button" value="Delete Cookies"
45:    onclick="delAllCookies();location.reload()" />
46: </body>
47: </html>
```

This example consists of two script functions, showCookies() (see lines 12–26) and delAllCookies() (see lines 28–41). First, we activate the showCookies() function (line 42) to display all cookies. A button with caption "Delete Cookies" is then created in lines 44–45. If this button is pressed, the function delAllCookies() will delete all cookies. The function location.reload() in line 45 is used to reload the page. Figure 7.25 shows all your cookies, and Fig. 7.26 demonstrates the deletion process.

Figure 7.25 ex07-17.htm

Figure 7.26 After the deletion

7.4.4   Practical use of cookie functions (cookie library)

In this section, we want to group and modify some of the cookie functions to build a small cookie library. The basic functions in the library are:

- `setCookie()`   –   Set cookie information.
- `getCookie()`   –   Get cookie value by cookie name.
- `delCookie()`   –   Delete cookie by name.
- `delAllCookies()` –   Delete all cookies.

We will put these functions into a single external script file called cookie.js and use this library and its functions in later examples.

Example: cookie.js – The ECMAScript File For Cookies

```
 1: function setCookie(cookieName, cookieValue, expDate)
 2: {
 3:   if ((cookieName=="")||(cookieValue==""))
 4:   {
 5:     document.write("Error..setCookie requires Name and Value")
 6:   } else {
 7:     var cookieSt = cookieName + "=" + escape(cookieValue) +
 8:       ((expDate) ? "; expires=" + expDate.toGMTString() : "")
 9:     document.cookie = cookieSt
10:   }
11: }
12:
13: function getCookie(cookieName)
14: {
15:   if (document.cookie !=""){
16:    var cookieItem = document.cookie.split("; ")
17:    for (i=0; i< cookieItem.length; i++) {
18:     if (cookieName == cookieItem[i].split("=")[0])
19:       return unescape(cookieItem[i].split("=")[1])
20:    }
21:   }else
22:     return null
23: }
24:
```

```
25: function delCookie(cookieName)
26: {
27:  if (document.cookie != "")
28:  {
29:   eDate = new Date
30:   eDate.setTime(eDate.getTime() - (1000 * 60 * 60 * 24))
31:   document.cookie = cookieName + "=;expires="+eDate.toGMTString()
32:  }
33: }
34:
35: function delAllCookies01()
36: {
37:  if (document.cookie !="")
38:  {
39:   eDate = new Date
40:   eDate.setTime(eDate.getTime() - (1000 * 60 * 60 * 24))
41:   cookieItem = document.cookie.split("; ")
42:   for (i=0; i< cookieItem.length; i++){
43:    document.cookie=cookieItem[i].split("=")[0]+
44:      "=;expires="+eDate.toGMTString()
45:   }
46:  }
47: }
48:
49: function delAllCookies(confirmV)
50: {
51:  if (confirmV !="Confirm")
52:  {
53:    delAllCookies01()
54:  } else {
55:    if (confirm("Delete Them all?"))
56:    delAllCookies01()
57:  }
58: }
```

To build a general purpose library, you need to modify some of the previous functions slightly. The `setCookie()` (see lines 1–11) and `getCookie()` (see lines 13–23) functions are very similar to those in example ex07-15.htm. We have added some codes into the functions to protect our program. The `delCookie()` function in lines 25–33 will now take an argument, the name of the cookie, and delete that cookie accordingly. The function `delAllCookies()` in lines 49–58 calls the function `delAllCookies01()` to delete all cookies quietly. If you execute this command with a `Confirm` string, i.e., `delAllCookies("Confirm")`, a confirm box will be displayed before any deletion is executed. You will see how to use this library to solve some simple practical tasks in the next section.

Before you write any code to use the library, you will find that a testing function `showCookieTable()` at the end of the library to show all available cookies and values is useful.

```
Listing: Continuation Of The ECMAScript File cookie.js
```

```
59: function showCookieTable()
60: {
61:  var localMsg=""
62:  var cookieTable=""
63:  if (document.cookie !=""){
64:   var cookieItem = document.cookie.split("; ")
65:   for (i=0; i< cookieItem.length; i++)
66:   {
67:     localMsg=localMsg+"<tr><td width='140'>"+
68:        cookieItem[i].split("=")[0]+"</td>"+
```

```
69:              "<td width='300'>"+
70:              unescape(cookieItem[i].split("=")[1])+"</td></tr>"
71:       }
72:    cookieTable="<table>"+localMsg+"</table>"
73:    document.write(cookieTable)
74:    }else
75:      document.write("There Is No Cookie Here")
76: }
```

This function collects all cookies and formats them into an XHTML table string. A function like this may not be absolutely necessary but, in many cases, is convenient for the purpose of testing and further development.

To use the library, you need to include the line of code

```
<script src="cookie.js"></script>
```

before any function call is made. With the use of this libary, it is easy to set and display cookies. We will show you how to use them to develop an online shopping cart application later. First, let's write a Web page to test the cookie functions.

7.4.5   Manipulating cookies with library functions

As a mean of testing the library functions, we create some general information about users:

UserName	–	To store the user name
Emai	–	Email address
ShoppingId	–	Shopping identity for online shopping
Address	–	Home address
State	–	State
Country	–	Country
Tel	–	Telephone number

This information is stored as cookie names on local machines. To manipulate cookies, six buttons are created:

Set Some Cookies	–	Fill cookie information
Del Information	–	Delete information with prompt box
Del Cookies Quietly	–	Delete all information quietly
Del Cookies (Confirm)	–	Delete all information with confirm box
Show Cookies	–	Show cookie information
Reset Email	–	Reset email address with prompt box

The first button fills the cookies with user information. This is just a test example, but in real applications you should display a form for the visitor to fill in. Forms and user input will be discussed in later chapters when server technologies are introduced. If you click the first and the Show Cookies buttons, you should see the screen as shown in Fig. 7.27. The Del Information button displays a prompt box to ask you to enter the information you want to delete. If you enter "ShoppingId," the ShoppingId cookie will be deleted (see Fig. 7.28). You may need to press the Show Cookies button to see the result.

Figure 7.27 ex07-18.htm

Figure 7.28 Delete the "ShoppingId"

If you press the Del Cookies (Confirm) button and select OK in the confirm box, all your cookies will be deleted (see Fig. 7.29). Finally, if you press the Reset Email button, the current email address will appear in a prompt box for you to modify. You can change your email address as shown in Fig. 7.30 and then display the result by pressing the Show Cookies button.

Figure 7.29 Delete all cookies

Figure 7.30 Prompt for email

With the cookie library cookie.js, this page can be easily developed. The coding is given in ex07-18.htm.

Example: ex07-18.htm - A Page To Test The Cookie Library

```
1: <?xml version="1.0" encoding="iso-8859-1"?>
2: <!DOCTYPE html PUBLIC "-//W3C//DTD XHTML 1.0 Transitional//EN"
3:     "http://www.w3.org/TR/xhtml1/DTD/xhtml1-transitional.dtd">
4: <html xmlns="http://www.w3.org/1999/xhtml" xml:lang="en" lang="en">
5: <head><title> Test The Cookie Library - ex07-18.htm </title></head>
6:
7: <style>
8:   .tx01{background-color:#000088;font-family:arial;
```

```
 9:          font-size:14pt;color:#ffff00;text-align:center}
10:   .tx02{font-size:22pt;color:#00ffff}
11:   .butStyle{background-color:#aaffaa;font-family:arial;font-weight:bold;
12:          font-size:12pt;color:#008800;width:180px;height:30px}
13: </style>
14:
15: <body class="tx01" align="center">
16: <span class="tx02">Welcome To WWW.PWT-EX.COM</span><br />
17: <img src="line1.gif" width="450" height="6" /><br /><br />
18:
19: <script src="cookie.js"></script>
20: <script>
21:  function setSomeCookies()
22:  {
23:   delAllCookies()
24:   expDate = new Date
25:   expDate.setTime(expDate.getTime() + (1000 * 60 * 60 * 24*365))
26:   setCookie("UserName","John Smith Junior",expDate)
27:   setCookie("Email","JohnSmith@isp.com",expDate)
28:   setCookie("ShoppingId","0123456789",expDate)
29:   setCookie("Address","188 Sunny Road, Los Angeles",expDate)
30:   setCookie("State","California",expDate)
31:   setCookie("Country","USA",expDate)
32:   setCookie("Tel","11223344",expDate)
33:  }
34:
35:  function delInfo()
36:  {
37:   userInfo = prompt("Enter The Information To Delete")
38:   if (userInfo !="")
39:   delCookie(userInfo)
40:  }
41:
42:  function resetEmail()
43:  {
44:   expDate = new Date
45:   expDate.setTime(expDate.getTime() + (1000 * 60 * 60 * 24*365))
46:   userEmail = prompt("Enter Your Email",getCookie('Email'))
47:   if (userEmail !="")
48:   setCookie("Email",userEmail,expDate)
49:  }
50:
51:     window.resizeTo(620,550)
52:     showCookieTable()
53: </script><br />
54:
55: <input type="button" value="Set Some Cookies"
56:     class="butStyle" onclick="setSomeCookies()" />
57: <input type="button" value="Del Information"
58:     class="butStyle" onclick="delInfo()" /><br />
59:
60: <input type="button" value="Del Cookies Quietly"
61:     class="butStyle" onclick="delAllCookies()" />
62: <input type="button" value="Del Cookies (Confirm)"
63:     class="butStyle" onclick="delAllCookies('Confirm')" /><br />
64:
```

```
65: <input type="button" value="Show Cookies"
66:    class="butStyle" onclick="location.href='ex07-18.htm'" />
67: <input type="button" value="Reset Email"
68:    class="butStyle" onclick="resetEmail()" />
69: </body>
70: </html>
```

The six buttons created in lines 55–68 all have XHTML scripting features. Each button is associated with one script function. The first button function `setSomeCookies()` defined in lines 21–33 is simply a series of function calls to `setCookie()` functions. This is necessary to make sure that we have something to play with. The second button function `delInfo()` as defined in lines 35–40 will first display a prompt box (line 37) and then delete the information you want to delete. The Del Cookies Quietly and Del Cookies (Confirm) buttons are used to call the library directly. Since we have used the library function `showCookieTable()` in line 52 before any real actions, the Show Cookies button defined in lines 65–66 is just a reload of this page. Again the Reset Email button and hence the function, lines 42–49, is designed to use the prompt box to display and obtain the email address.

This example shows that implementation of the library will make a complex program more simple, efficient, and readable. This technique plays an important role in real programming practice. Let's now consider a practical example.

7.5   Implementation of an online shopping cart

One of the popular applications of cookies is to develop the so-called "Online Shopping Cart." When a customer visits a cyber store (i.e., online shopping), it is likely that he or she will go through pages and pages of products in different categories. Often, the customer may pick up some bargains but then change his or her mind later. An efficient way to store shopping items with the flexibility to add or delete through pages is to use cookies. Another main advantage is that cookie information is usually stored on a local machine containing user information. From a business point of view, cookies are excellent tools for tracing special or potential customers and targeting them for business purposes.

The main aim of this example is to show you a cut-down version of a shopping cart. More importantly, this case study demonstrates how to format a Web problem, solution techniques, and how to put client-side scripting language into practical action at the same time. The last is necessary for further study of Web technologies.

Now, let's see how XHTML features can be integrated with Web programming and used as an excellent tool for program interfacing.

7.5.1   Using XHTML as an interface

From a Web programmers' point of view, markup languages or elements in general can be considered as a programming interface. In fact, they are the interface between the Internet (or World Wide Web) and the users. In particular, when working with other Web technologies, languages such as XHTML provides a universal and excellent tool for human and machine interrogation. The first interface and control that we would like to introduce here is called the "checkbox."

A checkbox is a small box on a Web page and can be generated by the following XHTML statement:

```
<input style="height:25px;width:25px"
    type="checkbox" id="CheckBox1" name="CheckBox1" />
```

This is a 25×25 pixels box with identity "CheckBox1." When you perform a mouse click inside the box, a "tick" symbol will appear inside it. That is, you can use a mouse click to check and uncheck the box. Since there is no user input (or typing) involved, errors can be minimized.

With scripting techniques, you can check and uncheck this box by assigning a value to the variable `document.getElementById("CheckBox1").checked` such as:

```
document.getElementById("CheckBox1").checked=1 - checked
document.getElementById("CheckBox1").checked=0 - unchecked
```

This variable can also be used to test whether a box has been checked.

Our project in this section is to write a Web page to sell some computer equipment online. The items and prices are listed as follows:

```
Color Laser Printer     400
CD-RW (20x20x60)        100
Digital Camera          100
Monitor (19 inch)       170
```

Using checked boxes, the interface implementation of this page has a simple form (ex07-19.htm):

Example: ex07-19.htm - Online Shopping Cart I

```
 1: <?xml version="1.0" encoding="iso-8859-1"?>
 2: <!DOCTYPE html PUBLIC "-//W3C//DTD XHTML 1.0 Transitional//EN"
 3:     "http://www.w3.org/TR/xhtml1/DTD/xhtml1-transitional.dtd">
 4: <html xmlns="http://www.w3.org/1999/xhtml" xml:lang="en" lang="en">
 5: <head><title>Online Shopping Cart I -- ex07-19.htm</title></head>
 6: <style>
 7:   .tx01{background-color:#000088;font-family:arial;
 8:      font-size:14pt;color:#ffff00;text-align:left}
 9:   .tx02{font-size:22pt;color:#00ffff}
10:   .butStyle{background-color:#aaffaa;font-family:arial;
11:      font-size:14pt;color:#008800;width:170px;height:35px}
12: </style>
13:
14: <body class="tx01" style="text-align:center">
15: <span class="tx02">Today's Special Buy</span><br />
16: <img src="line1.gif" width="450" height="6" /><br /><br />
17:
18: <script src="cookie.js"></script>
19: <script src="online.js"></script>
20: <script>
21:   initialAll()
22:   userName = getCookie("UserName")
23:   outMsg="For: "+userName+" (Half Price!)"
24:   document.write(outMsg)
25: </script><br /><br />
26:
27: <table border="0" align="center"><tr align="center">
28:    <td width="200">Description</td><td width="120">Price (USD)</td>
29:    <td width="150">Put In <br /> Shopping Cart</td></tr>
30:   <tr align="center"><td>Color Laser Printer</td><td>400</td>
31:    <td><input style="height:25px;width:25px"
32:       type="checkbox" id="prt" name="prt" /></td></tr>
33:   <tr align="center"><td>CD-RW (20x20x60)</td><td>100</td>
34:    <td><input style="height:25px;width:25px"
35:       type="checkbox" id="cdrw" /></td></tr>
36:   <tr align="center"><td>Digital Camera</td><td>100</td>
37:    <td><input style="height:25px;width:25px"
38:       type="checkbox" id="cam" /></td></tr>
```

```
39:    <tr align="center"><td>Monitor (19 inch)</td><td>170</td>
40:      <td><input style="height:25px;width:25px"
41:          type="checkbox" id="mon" /></td></tr>
42: </table><br />
43: <input type="button" value="Shopping Cart" class="butStyle"
44:      onclick="orderItem();location.href='ex07-20.htm'" />
45: <input type="button" value="Reset Boxes" class="butStyle"
46:      onclick="resetBoxes()" />
47: </body>
48: </html>
```

Apart from the script language in lines 18–25, this page should be self-explanatory. The interface consists of one table (five rows by three columns) and two buttons. A screen shot of this example code is shown in Fig. 7.31.

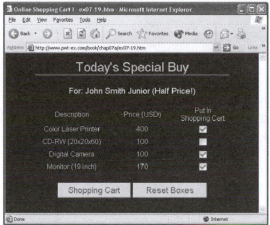

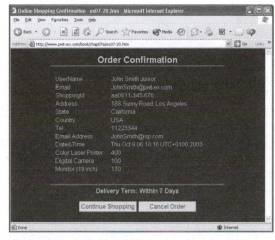

Figure 7.31 ex07-19.htm   **Figure 7.32** ex07-20.htm

In addition to the script library cookie.js, this page also uses another library called online.js (line 19). We will discuss this program file in more detail later. After the initialization code in line 21, the page tries to obtain the UserName from the local cookie. If the customer is a member of our online shopping site, the cookie name UserName should be nonzero. Our page will target this customer and offer him or her a good discount. For simplicity, our initialization code will make sure that we have a customer called "John Smith Junior." After he has picked some items from the shopping list and pressed the Shopping Cart button, the selected items will be stored as cookies. A new page ex07-20.htm needs to be activated to display the shopping cart (see Fig. 7.32).

Example: ex07-20.htm – A Page For Order Confirmation

```
 1: <?xml version="1.0" encoding="iso-8859-1"?>
 2: <!DOCTYPE html PUBLIC "-//W3C//DTD XHTML 1.0 Transitional//EN"
 3:     "http://www.w3.org/TR/xhtml1/DTD/xhtml1-transitional.dtd">
 4: <html xmlns="http://www.w3.org/1999/xhtml" xml:lang="en" lang="en">
 5: <head><title>Online Shopping Confirmation - ex07-20.htm </title></head>
 6: <style>
 7:   .tx01{background-color:#000088;font-family:arial;font-size:13pt;
 8:      font-weight:bold;color:#ffff00;text-align:left}
 9:   .tx02{font-size:18pt;color:#00ffff}
10:   .butStyle{background-color:#aaffaa;font-family:arial;font-weight:bold;
11:      font-size:12pt;color:#008800;width:160px;height:28px}
12: </style>
```

```
13:
14: <body class="tx01" style="text-align:center">
15: <script src="cookie.js"></script>
16: <script src="online.js"></script>
17:
18:    <span class="tx02">Order Confirmation</span><br />
19:    <img src="line1.gif" width="480" height="6" /><br /><br />
20:
21:    <script>showCookieTable()</script><br />
22:
23:    <img src="line1.gif" width="480" height="6" />
24:    <div class="tx01" style="color:#00ff00;text-align:center">
25:       Delivery Term: Within 7 Days</div><br />
26:
27: <input type="button" value="Continue Shopping"
28:    class="butStyle" onclick="location.href='ex07-19.htm'" />
29: <input type="button" value="Cancel Order" class="butStyle"
30:    onclick="delOrders();location.href='ex07-20.htm'" /><br />
31: </body>
32: </html>
```

The main part of this page is the library function `showCookieTable()` in line 21. As mentioned earlier, this function is used to display all cookies on the screen. We will make some improvements to this function later. If the customer clicks the Continue Shopping button (lines 27–28), this page will jump back to the previous page ex07-19.htm. If the user clicks the Cancel Order button (lines 29–30), the script function `delOrders()` in online.js is called and all shopping records are destroyed. Let's now take a look at the main program file online.js in more detail.

7.5.2 Constructing the program file

Online shopping usually involves customer information (`userInfo`), shopping items (`goodsName`), and prices (`goodsPrice`). These can be implemented in the main program online.js as arrays. Consider the first part of the main program:

```
Example: online.js - The ECMAScript For Online Shopping (Part One)

 1: userInfo=Array("UserName","Email Address",
 2:                "ShoppingId","Date&Time")
 3: userInfoLength = userInfo.length
 4:
 5: goodsName=Array("Color Laser Printer","CD-RW(20x20x60)",
 6:                "Digital Camera","Monitor (19 inch)")
 7: goodsLength=goodsName.length
 8:
 9: goodsPrice=Array(400,100,100,170)
10:
11: goodsId=Array("prt","cdrw","cam","mon")
```

The most important line of code is line 11. The `goodsId` is an array representing each of the checked boxes used in the interface (ex07-19.htm). This is the bridge between our programming and the interface. The first function in this program file is initialization `initialAll()`.

```
Listing: Continuation Of The ECMAScript online.js (Part Two)

12:
13: function initialAll()
14: {
15:   expDate = new Date
```

```
16:   expDate.setTime(expDate.getTime()+(1000 * 60 * 60 * 24*365))
17:   setCookie("UserName","John Smith Junior",expDate)
18:   setCookie("Email Address","JohnSmith@isp.com",expDate)
19:   setCookie("ShoppingId","aa0811-345-678",expDate)
20:   window.resizeTo(620,560)
21: }
22:
```

This function, as mentioned earlier, is used to make sure that the information of a customer such as name, email address, and a shopping identity is obtained. Line 20 is to resize the window so that the layout and over-all display are under control. The next part is the function resetBoxes() to uncheck all checkboxes.

Listing: Continuation Of The ECMAScript online.js (Part Three)

```
23:   function resetBoxes()
24:   {
25:    for (ii=0;ii<goodsLength;ii++)
26:    {
27:      document.getElementById(goodsId[ii]).checked=0
28:    }
29:   }
30:
```

This function is called when the Reset Boxes button in ex07-19.htm is pressed. As you can see, this function contains a simple for-loop over all shopping items and hence the checkboxes. The goodsId[ii] in line 27 is used to identify the checkbox and uncheck it. The next part is our main shopping cart function called orderItem().

Listing: Continuation Of The ECMAScript online.js (Part Four)

```
31:   function orderItem()
32:   {
33:    currentT = new Date
34:    expDate = new Date
35:
36:    expDate.setTime(expDate.getTime() +(1000 * 60 * 60 * 24*365))
37:    setCookie("Date&Time",currentT,expDate)
38:    for (ii=0;ii<goodsLength;ii++)
39:    {
40:     if (document.getElementById(goodsId[ii]).checked)
41:         setCookie(goodsName[ii],goodsPrice[ii],expDate)
42:     else delCookie(goodsName[ii])
43:    }
44:
45:   }
46:
```

When the user presses the Shopping Cart button in ex07-19.htm, this function will reset the Date&Time vari-able as in line 37. The next step (lines 38–43) is to run through a loop over each checked box. If the checkbox is checked (line 40), the item name and price are stored as cookies (line 41). If the checkbox is unchecked, the cookie is deleted in line 42. When this function returns, the page in ex07-19.htm will jump to the page ex07-20.htm to display the result. The final function in the library provides a cancellation of all items in the shopping cart.

Listing: Continuation Of The ECMAScript online.js (Part Five)

```
47:   function delOrders()
48:   {
49:    for (ii=0;ii<goodsLength;ii++)
50:    {
```

```
51:       delCookie(goodsName[ii])
52:     }
53:   }
54:
```

When the Cancel Order button is pressed, this function is called. All cookies related to `goodsName[]` will be destroyed by the for-loop defined in lines 49–52.

This working Web program on the shopping cart offers only basic operations. It is time to consider some modifications and improvements.

7.5.3   Improvements and modifications

When you finish a working program, it is good practice to write down any further ideas and thoughts that could improve your Web page. As a simple example, two improvements to page ex07-19.htm are introduced.

- The ability to trace members of our shopping site and ensure that only members can buy online.
- Always remember the items in the shopping cart.

These improvements require some modifications to our earlier page ex07-19.htm. One of the modified versions is ex07-21.htm and the body part of this page is listed in ex07-15.txt.

```
Listing: ex07-15.txt - Code Fragment Of ex07-21.htm

 1: <body class="tx01" style="text-align:center">
 2: <span class="tx02">Today's Special Buy</span><br />
 3: <img src="line1.gif" width="450" height="6" /><br /><br />
 4:
 5: <script src="cookie.js"></script>
 6: <script src="online.js"></script>
 7: <script>
 8:   var disableFlag = 0
 9:   userName = getCookie("UserName")
10:   shopId = getCookie("ShoppingId")
11:   if ((userName != null) && (shopId !=null))
12:   {
13:     outMsg="For: "+userName+" (Half Price!)"
14:   }
15:   else
16:   {
17:     outMsg="Please Set Up An Account First"
18:     disableFlag=1
19:   }
20:   document.write(outMsg)
21:   window.resizeTo(620,550)
22: </script><br /><br />
23:
24: <table border="0" align="center"><tr align="center">
25:     <td width="200">Description</td><td width="120">Price (USD)</td>
26:     <td width="150">Put To <br /> Shopping Cart</td></tr>
27:   <tr align="center"><td>Color Laser Printer</td><td>400</td>
28:     <td><input style="height:25px;width:65px"
29:           type="checkbox" id="prt" name="prt" /></td></tr>
30:   <tr align="center"><td>CD-RW (20x20x60)</td><td>100</td>
31:     <td><input style="height:25px;width:25px"
32:           type="checkbox" id="cdrw" /></td></tr>
33:   <tr align="center"><td>Digital Camera</td><td>100</td>
34:     <td><input style="height:25px;width:25px"
35:           type="checkbox" id="cam" /></td></tr>
```

```
36:    <tr align="center"><td>Monitor (19 inch)</td><td>170</td>
37:      <td><input style="height:25px;width:25px"
38:             type="checkbox" id="mon" /></td></tr>
39: </table><br />
40: <input type="button" value="Shopping Cart" class="butStyle" id="but01"
41:        onclick="orderItem();location.href='ex07-22.htm'" />
42: <input type="button" value="Reset Boxes" class="butStyle" id="but02"
43:        onclick="resetBoxes()" />
44:
45: <script>
46:    if (disableFlag ==1) disableAll()
47:    recallOrders()
48: </script>
49: </body>
```

The basic modifications are lines 8–21. First, a test is run to see whether the local system has a `UserName` and `ShoppingId` as cookies. If no such cookie exists, the system outputs a message to ask the user to set up an account first before shopping. This page sets the `disableFlag` variable to true (line 18). This `disableFlag` variable is used in line 46 to disable all checked boxes and buttons. Note that two button identities are added in lines 40 and 42, so that these buttons can be disabled too. A function `recallOrders()` is also added in line 47 to always remember the items in the shopping cart and set the checked boxes appropriately.

The program file online.js is expanded to include these two newly added functions.

Listing: ex07-16.txt - Continuation Of The ECMAScript online.js (Part Six)

```
55: function disableAll()
56: {
57:    for (ii=0;ii<goodsLength;ii++)
58:    {
59:      document.getElementById(goodsId[ii]).disabled=1
60:    }
61:    document.getElementById("but01").disabled=1
62:    document.getElementById("but02").disabled=1
63: }
64:
65:  function recallOrders()
66:  {
67:    for (ii=0;ii<goodsLength;ii++)
68:    {
69:     if (getCookie(goodsName[ii])!=null)
70:        document.getElementById(goodsId[ii]).checked=1
71:    }
72: }
73:
```

The `disableAll()` function in lines 55–63 is simply a loop to disable all checked boxes. Along with the checked boxes, a feature to disable all buttons is added so that no user actions are accepted. The second function `recallOrder()` is a loop to run through the stored cookies. If the cookie is not empty, the function sets the associated checkbox to true. Put this function into page ex07-21.htm; the page can always remember the items in the shopping cart. The disable feature of this example is illustrated in Fig. 7.33.

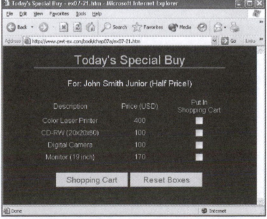

Figure 7.33 ex07-21.htm

Recall from the beginning of section 7.4 that the implementations of cookies are different for different browsers. For instance, one major difference between IE and NS on cookies is the way they store and retrieve cookie information. This may affect the displaying order on screen when calling our library function showCookieTable(). To overcome this problem, you may need to write another displaying function to show cookies in the way you want. Since we use an array to program our shopping cart, overcoming this problem is not difficult. First, you need to modify the interface page ex07-20.htm as ex07-22.htm. The body part of this example is listed below.

Listing: ex07-17.txt – Code Fragment Of ex07-22.htm

```
 1: <body class="tx01" style="text-align:center">
 2: <script src="cookie.js"></script>
 3: <script src="online.js"></script>
 4:
 5:   <span class="tx02">Order Confirmation</span><br />
 6:   <img src="line1.gif" width="480" height="6" /><br /><br />
 7:
 8:   <script> showGoodsTable() </script><br />
 9:
10:   <img src="line1.gif" width="480" height="6" />
11:   <div class="tx01" style="color:#00ff00;text-align:center">
12:      Delivery Term: Within 7 Days</div><br />
13:
14: <input type="button" value="Continue Shopping"
15:    class="butStyle" onclick="location.href='ex07-21.htm'" />
16: <input type="button" value="Cancel Order" class="butStyle"
17:    onclick="delOrders();location.href='ex07-22.htm'" /><br />
18: </body>
```

In this example, we have changed the old calling function showCookieTable() to showGoodsTable(). This function is incorporated inside our program file online.js.

Listing: ex07-18.txt – Continuation Of The ECMAScript online.js (Part Seven)

```
74: function showGoodsTable()
75: {
76:  var localMsg=""
77:  var goodsTable=""
78:
79:   for (ii=0; ii<userInfoLength; ii++)
80:   {
81:    varSt = getCookie(userInfo[ii])
82:    if (varSt !=null)
83:    {
84:     localMsg=localMsg+"<tr><td width='150' align='left'>"+
85:        userInfo[ii]+"</td>"+
86:        "<td width='300' align='left'>"+
87:        varSt+"</td></tr>"
88:    }
89:   }
90:
91:   for (ii=0; ii<goodsLength; ii++)
92:   {
93:    varSt = getCookie(goodsName[ii])
94:    if (varSt !=null)
95:    {
96:     localMsg=localMsg+"<tr><td width='150' align='left'>"+
97:        goodsName[ii]+"</td>"+
98:        "<td width='300' align='left'>"+
```

```
99:              varSt+"</td></tr>"
100:     }
101:   }
102:   goodsTable="<div align='center'><table>"+localMsg+"</table></div>"
103:   document.write(goodsTable)
104:   }
105:
```

The layout and rearrangement of orders are handled through the loops in lines 79–89 and lines 91–104. Figure 7.34 is the screen shot showing how this page works in NS6.x.

With examples ex07-17.htm, ex07-19.htm, and ex07-21.htm, we have some background knowledge (or a basic prototype) of online shopping. Online shopping and security will be discussed further in Part V of this book.

Figure 7.34 ex07-22.htm on NS

8 Controlling frames and browser window(s)

8.1 Controlling frames I

8.1.1 A classic dynamic menu with swapping frames

One of the advantages of using frames is that individual pages can be organized (or networked together) to form a larger and more complex application. A typical application (see Chapter 1, ex01-17.htm) is to divide the screen into two frames (usually left and right) or more and build a menu (or navigation bar) system. The left frame, for example, stores the menu items. When one of the menu items is pressed, a corresponding page is sent to the right frame. Many organizations use this technique to introduce their departments and a lot of businesses advertise their products in the same way on the Web. This is a static XHTML menu technique and one restriction is that you don't know much about the information of a selected menu item. In this section, we will show you how to write a Web page with a navigation bar. This page has a master frame page as given in ex08-01.htm.

```
Example: ex08-01.htm – Swapping Frames

 1: <?xml version="1.0" encoding="UTF-8"?>
 2: <!DOCTYPE html PUBLIC "-//W3C//DTD XHTML 1.0 Frameset//EN"
 3:      "http://www.w3.org/TR/xhtml1/DTD/xhtml1-frameset.dtd">
 4: <html xmlns="http://www.w3.org/1999/xhtml" xml:lang="en" lang="en">
 5: <head><title>Swapping Frames - ex08-01.htm </title></head>
 6: <frameset cols="35%,*">
 7:   <frame src="left01a.htm" id="left_f" name="left_f" />
 8:   <frame src="right01a.htm" id="right_f" name="right_f" />
 9: </frameset>
10: </html>
```

This frame page divides the screen into left and right frames with the preloaded pages left01a.htm and right01a.htm respectively. The left frame has an identity `left_f` (line 7). This identity can be used to access the frame later. The page left01a.htm is listed as follows:

```
Example: left01a.htm – The Left Frame For ex08-01.htm

 1: <?xml version="1.0" encoding="iso-8859-1"?>
 2: <!DOCTYPE html PUBLIC "-//W3C//DTD XHTML 1.0 Transitional//EN"
 3:      "http://www.w3.org/TR/xhtml1/DTD/xhtml1-transitional.dtd">
 4: <html xmlns="http://www.w3.org/1999/xhtml" xml:lang="en" lang="en">
 5: <head><title> File: left01a.htm </title>
 6: <style> .mSt{font-family:arial;font-size:16pt;
 7:          font-weight:bold;color:#ffff00}</style>
 8: <script>
 9:   function switchFrame(varV)
```

```
10:    {
11:      parent.left_f.location.href="left01"+varV+".htm"
12:      parent.right_f.location.href="right01"+varV+".htm"
13:    }
14:  </script>
15: </head>
16:
17: <body style="background:#000088;text-align:center">
18:   <div class="mSt" style="color:#00ffff">Company I<br /><br /></div>
19:   <span class="mSt" style="color:#ff00ff">Page A</span><br />
20:   <a href="javascript:switchFrame('b')" class="mSt">Page B</a><br />
21:   <a href="javascript:switchFrame('c')" class="mSt">Page C</a>
22: </body>
23: </html>
```

This page contains three items, namely, "Page A," "Page B," and "Page C" (see lines 19–21). The items "Page B" and "Page C" are hyperlinks. For example, when the underlined text "Page B" is clicked, the JavaScript function `switchFrame('b')` is called (see line 20). The argument b is substituted into variable varV in lines 9–13 and the statements

```
parent.left_f.location.href="left01"+varV+".htm"
parent.right_f.location.href="right01"+varV+".htm"
```

send the pages left01b.htm and right01b.htm to the left and right frames respectively. The file right01a.htm in the right frame is a Web page with a simple ECMAScript function.

```
Example: right01a.htm - The Right Frame For ex08-01.htm

 1: <?xml version="1.0" encoding="iso-8859-1"?>
 2: <!DOCTYPE html PUBLIC "-//W3C//DTD XHTML 1.0 Transitional//EN"
 3:      "http://www.w3.org/TR/xhtml1/DTD/xhtml1-transitional.dtd">
 4: <html xmlns="http://www.w3.org/1999/xhtml" xml:lang="en" lang="en">
 5: <head><title>File right01a.htm </title>
 6:  <style>
 7:   h3{font-family:arial;font-size:18pt;font-weight:bold}
 8:   .mSt{font-family:arial;font-size:16pt;font-weight:bold;color:#ffff00}
 9:  </style>
10:  <script>
11:   function switchFrame(varV)
12:   {
13:      parent.left_f.location.href="left01"+varV+".htm"
14:      parent.right_f.location.href="right01"+varV+".htm"
15:   }
16:  </script>
17: </head>
18:
19: <body style="background:#000088;text-align:center">
20:   <h3 style="color:#ffff00">Company I<br /><br /><br /></h3>
21:   <h3 style="color:#00ffff">This is Page A<br /><br /></h3>
22:   <br /><br /><br /><br />
23:
24: <div align="left" class="mSt" style="color:#ff00ff">A
25:   <a href="javascript:switchFrame('b')" class="mSt">B</a>
26:   <a href="javascript:switchFrame('c')" class="mSt">C</a>
27: </div>
28: </body>
29: </html>
```

The same swapping technique is employed in lines 24–27 to control the changing frames from the footnote of the right page. Some of the frame swapping actions are captured in Figs 8.1 and 8.2.

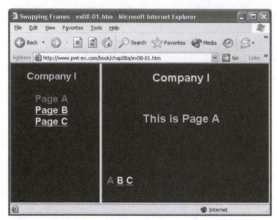

Figure 8.1 Activate Page A

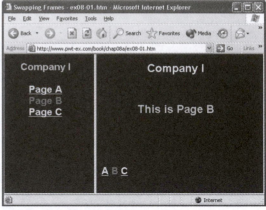

Figure 8.2 Activate Page B

This is a classic example and works even on some old browsers. The main drawback of this technique is that it contains too many files. For instance, for this example to work, you need to have the following files:

ex08-01.htm   (Master frame file)

left01a.htm   right01a.htm

left01b.htm   right01b.htm

left01c.htm   right01c.htm

In this case, one master frame file and six child frame pages are needed. You can imagine that the administrative work will soon become a nightmare if you have dozens of menu items. To solve this problem, we consider using variables in the master frame page.

8.1.2   Another approach to dynamic menu

Since the master frame file is always available, you can also store some variables to represent the status of each menu item. Child frames can access these variables and values later. The master frame file is listed in ex08-02.htm.

```
Example: ex08-02.htm – Another Approach To Swapping Frames

 1: <?xml version="1.0" encoding="UTF-8"?>
 2: <!DOCTYPE html PUBLIC "-//W3C//DTD XHTML 1.0 Frameset//EN"
 3:      "http://www.w3.org/TR/xhtml1/DTD/xhtml1-frameset.dtd">
 4: <html xmlns="http://www.w3.org/1999/xhtml" xml:lang="en" lang="en">
 5: <head><title> Another Swapping Frames – ex08-02.htm </title></head>
 6: <script>
 7:    paDisable=-1
 8:    pbDisable=0
 9:    pcDisable=0
10: </script>
11: <frameset cols="35%,*">
```

```
12:    <frame src="left02.htm" id="left_f" name="left_f" />
13:    <frame src="right02a.htm" id="right_f" name="right_f" />
14: </frameset>
15: </html>
```

This page has three new variables, `paDisable`, `pbDisable`, and `pcDisable` (lines 7–9). They represent the on and off status of the corresponding "Page A," "Page B," and "Page C" menu items in the left frame. Initially, we want the "Page A" item disabled (`paDisable=-1`) when the page is loaded. In this example, only one left frame, left02.htm, is used to hold and control the menu (line 12). Consider the left page:

```
Example: left02.htm - The Left Frame For ex08-02.htm

 1: <?xml version="1.0" encoding="iso-8859-1"?>
 2: <!DOCTYPE html PUBLIC "-//W3C//DTD XHTML 1.0 Transitional//EN"
 3:      "http://www.w3.org/TR/xhtml1/DTD/xhtml1-transitional.dtd">
 4: <html xmlns="http://www.w3.org/1999/xhtml" xml:lang="en" lang="en">
 5: <head><title>File left02a.htm: </title>
 6: <style> .mSt{font-family:arial;font-size:16pt;border:0;
 7:            background:#000088;font-weight:bold;color:#ffff00}
 8: </style>
 9:  <script src="frame01.js"></script>
10: </head>
11:
12: <body style="background:#000088;text-align:center">
13:  <div class="mSt" style="color:#00ffff">Company I<br /><br /></div>
14:  <input type="button" id="pa" onclick="resetD('a');switchFrame('a')"
15:     onmouseover="this.style.background='#008800'" value="Page A"
16:     onmouseout="this.style.background='#000088'" class="mSt" /><br />
17:  <input type="button" id="pb" onclick="resetD('b');switchFrame('b')"
18:     onmouseover="this.style.background='#008800'" value="Page B"
19:     onmouseout="this.style.background='#000088'" class="mSt" /><br />
20:  <input type="button" id="pc" onclick="resetD('c');switchFrame('c')"
21:     onmouseover="this.style.background='#008800'" value="Page C"
22:     onmouseout="this.style.background='#000088'" class="mSt" /><br />
23:
24:  <script> initialV() </script>
25: </body>
26: </html>
```

This left page is a controller and uses an external program file frame01.js to perform the dynamic frame swapping. The program file contains three functions (see line 14):

```
resetD("a") switchFrame("a") initialV()
```

The `switchFrame('a')` function is used to send a page (e.g., Page A in this case) to the right frame. The reset function `resetD('a')` sets the parent variable `paDisable` to be true. The initialization function `initialV()` in line 24 initializes all variables when this page is loaded. It also sets the status and changes the color of disabled items. Once the disable flag of an item is set, there will be no action related to that item. Also in this example, we use buttons with no borders to simulate the plain text situations. Mouse-over and mouse-out events are used to highlight menu items. When the user presses the menu item, "Page A" in line 14, the script function `resetD('a')` is called to disable the menu and to switch the frames accordingly. These changes will take effect only after the initialization function `initialV()` is called. The listing of the ECMAScript is shown below:

```
Example: frame01.js - The ECMAScript File For left02.htm

 1: function switchFrame(varV)
 2: {
 3:   parent.left_f.location.href="left02.htm"
 4:   parent.right_f.location.href="right02"+varV+".htm"
 5: }
```

```
 6: function resetD(varL)
 7: {
 8:  parent.paDisable=0
 9:  parent.pbDisable=0
10:  parent.pcDisable=0
11:  if (varL =='a') parent.paDisable=-1
12:  if (varL =='b') parent.pbDisable=-1
13:  if (varL =='c') parent.pcDisable=-1
14: }
15: function initialV()
16: {
17: document.getElementById("pa").disabled=parent.paDisable;
18: document.getElementById("pb").disabled=parent.pbDisable;
19: document.getElementById("pc").disabled=parent.pcDisable;
20: if (parent.paDisable)document.getElementById("pa").style.color="#aaaaaa"
21: if (parent.pbDisable)document.getElementById("pb").style.color="#aaaaaa"
22: if (parent.pcDisable)document.getElementById("pc").style.color="#aaaaaa"
23: }
```

Line 4 illustrates the string concatenation capability of ECMAScript in the function `switchFrame()`. In practice, you may want to substitute the actual names of the frames into a function argument. Some actions and screen shots are captured in Figs 8.3 and 8.4.

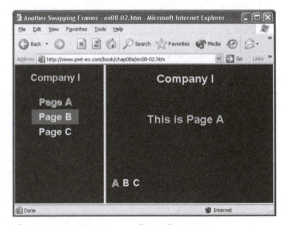

Figure 8.3 Mouse over Page B

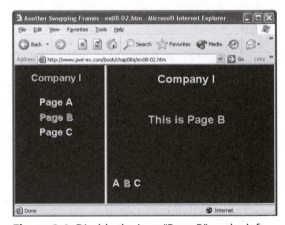

Figure 8.4 Disable the item "Page B" on the left

Similarly the right page (e.g., right02a.htm) for ex08-02.htm also uses the same program file frame01.js to control and swap the frames. Consider the right page:

```
Example: right02a.htm - The Right Frame For ex08-02.htm

 1: <?xml version="1.0" encoding="iso-8859-1"?>
 2: <!DOCTYPE html PUBLIC "-//W3C//DTD XHTML 1.0 Transitional//EN"
 3:     "http://www.w3.org/TR/xhtml1/DTD/xhtml1-transitional.dtd">
 4: <html xmlns="http://www.w3.org/1999/xhtml" xml:lang="en" lang="en">
 5: <head><title> File right02a.htm </title>
 6:  <style>
 7:   h3{font-family:arial;font-size:18pt;font-weight:bold}
 8:   .mSt{font-family:arial;font-size:16pt;border:0;
 9:        background:#000088;font-weight:bold;color:#ffff00}
10:  </style>
11:  <script src="frame01.js"></script>
```

```
12: </head>
13: <body style="background:#000088;text-align:center">
14:   <h3 style="color:#ffff00">Company I<br /><br /></h3>
15:   <h3 style="color:#00ffff">This is Page A<br /><br /></h3>
16:    <br /><br /><br /><br />
17:
18: <div align="left" class="mSt" style="color:#aaaaaa">
19:   <input type="button" value="A"
20:     disabled class="mSt" style="color:#aaaaaa" />
21:   <input type="button" value="B"
22:     onclick="resetD('b');switchFrame('b')" class="mSt" />
23:   <input type="button" value="C"
24:     onclick="resetD('c');switchFrame('c')" class="mSt" />
25: </div>
26: </body>
27: </html>
```

Again, three buttons with no borders are used in this page to simulate the plain text. When the visitor clicks one of these buttons, the same swapping technique is employed to send the corresponding frame to the right hand side (see lines 19–24). The central idea is to manipulate the variables in the parent frame.

Now, it's time to consider some housekeeping of frames. First, if you don't want your page to appear or be included inside a frame of someone's Web site, you may want to develop a page that cannot be framed.

8.1.3 A page that cannot be framed

To develop such a page is easy. You can first detect the top level of the window and then compare it to the current page (or window). If they are not equal, you can set the top level of the window as the current page. Suppose we have a master frame page as shown in ex08-03.htm.

Example: ex08-03.htm – A Page that Cannot Be Framed

```
1: <?xml version="1.0" encoding="UTF-8"?>
2: <!DOCTYPE html PUBLIC "-//W3C//DTD XHTML 1.0 Frameset//EN"
3:       "http://www.w3.org/TR/xhtml1/DTD/xhtml1-frameset.dtd">
4: <html xmlns="http://www.w3.org/1999/xhtml" xml:lang="en" lang="en">
5: <head>
6:   <title>ex08-03.htm </title>
7: </head>
8: <frameset rows="50%,*">
9:   <frame src="upper.htm"   id="upper_f"   name="upper_f" />
10:   <frame src="lower.htm"   id="lower_f"   name="lower_f" />
11: </frameset>
12: </html>
```

This master frame page calls two pages, upper.htm and lower.htm. These are allocated to the upper and lower parts of the browser screen respectively. However, if the lower page contains the statements as in lines 8–9 of lower.htm, the calling process will be interrupted.

Example: lower.htm – The Bottom Frame For ex08-03.htm

```
1: <?xml version="1.0" encoding="UTF-8"?>
2: <!DOCTYPE html PUBLIC "-//W3C//DTD XHTML 1.0 Frameset//EN"
3:       "http://www.w3.org/TR/xhtml1/DTD/xhtml1-frameset.dtd">
4: <html xmlns="http://www.w3.org/1999/xhtml" xml:lang="en" lang="en">
5: <head><title>File: lower.htm</title></head>
6: <style>h2{font-family:arial;font-size:18pt;color:#ffff00}</style>
7: <script>
8:   if (window.top.location != window.self.location)
```

```
 9:          window.top.location = window.self.location
10: </script>
11: <body style="background:#000088;text-align:center">
12: <h2>This Page Cannot Be Framed<br />File: lower.htm</h2>
13: </body>
14: </html>
```

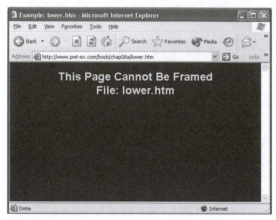

Figure 8.5 ex08-03.htm

When this page is called, the script statement in line 8 detects the top level of the window and compares it to the current window level. If they are not the same, the statement in line 9 will assign the top level as the current window. As a result, this lower.htm page will replace the master frame and therefore we have only one page on the browser screen (see Fig. 8.5).

In practice, this technique provides a way to prevent a page accidentally, or deliberately, being loaded into a frame. If you want, you can add lines 7–10 to your master frame pages to ensure that they are always on the top window level. Another housekeeping technique on frames is to make sure that a page is always enclosed inside a frame.

8.1.4 Keeping frames in order

For a successful frame application, the ordering, presentation, and interrelationship between the use of frames and Web pages are vital. In many cases, for instance, you don't want a frame page that is out of control and is not inside a frame. To keep frames under control, the same window location techniques are used. Consider a master frame page ex08-04.htm with the code fragment

```
Listing: ex08-01.txt - Code Fragment Of ex08-04.htm

1: <frameset cols="45%,*">
2:  <frame src="left04.htm" id="left_f" name="left_f" />
3:  <frame src="right04.htm" id="right_f" name="right_f" />
4: </frameset>
```

If you want the two child frame pages (left04.htm and right04.htm) always under the master frame, you can add a small piece of script code as listed in left04.htm.

```
Example: left04.htm - The Left Frame For ex08-04.htm
 1: <?xml version="1.0" encoding="UTF-8"?>
 2: <!DOCTYPE html PUBLIC "-//W3C//DTD XHTML 1.0 Frameset//EN"
 3:      "http://www.w3.org/TR/xhtml1/DTD/xhtml1-frameset.dtd">
 4: <html xmlns="http://www.w3.org/1999/xhtml" xml:lang="en" lang="en">
 5: <head><title>File: left04.htm</title></head>
 6: <style>h2{font-family:arial;font-size:18pt;color:#ffff00}</style>
 7: <script>
 8:   if (window.top.location == window.self.location)
 9:       window.top.location.href ="ex08-04.htm"
10: </script>
11: <body style="background:#000088;text-align:center">
12: <h2>This Left Page Must Be <br />In a Frame<br />File: left04.htm</h2>
13: </body>
14: </html>
```

The script statements in lines 8–9 are simple. First, we detect the window level. If the current window is the top, we assign our master frame page as the top level. This will load all child frames and pages automatically (see Fig. 8.6).

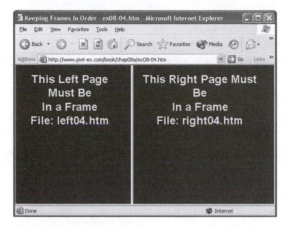

Figure 8.6 ex08-04.htm

With these housekeeping techniques, we're now ready to consider applications with more dynamic frames.

8.2   Controlling frames II

8.2.1   Creating a dynamic advertising strip with frames

You may have noticed that almost all tobacco advertisements have an additional small strip at the bottom to state something like "Smoking May Damage Your Health." In practice, an advertising strip on the Web can be anything like simple text output, animated images, and movie clips. This strip is attached to many of your pages at run time. Only one copy of the strip page is needed and it can be updated on a daily basis. As a simple example we want to add a small strip at the top of each page (dynamically). The strip is, in fact, the text message "Please Protect Wild Life!"

First, you need to collect a small library of wild life images. For each picture, a page is developed to display it. At the very top of these pages, a small piece of script is used to add the strip. For example, our first image page wild01.htm is listed below.

```
Example: wild01.htm - A Testing Wild Life Page For ex08-05.htm

 1: <?xml version="1.0" encoding="UTF-8"?>
 2: <!DOCTYPE html PUBLIC "-//W3C//DTD XHTML 1.0 Frameset//EN"
 3:      "http://www.w3.org/TR/xhtml1/DTD/xhtml1-frameset.dtd">
 4: <html xmlns="http://www.w3.org/1999/xhtml" xml:lang="en" lang="en">
 5: <head><title>File: wild01.htm </title></head>
 6: <script>
 7:   if (window.top.location == window.self.location)
 8:       window.top.location.href ="ex08-05.htm?wild01.htm"
 9: </script>
10: <body style="background:#000088;text-align:center">
11: <img src="01_img.jpg">
12: </body>
13: </html>
```

The body part of this page is a single statement to display a document containing an image, 01_img.jpg. The script (lines 7–8) is used to compare the window level. If the current window is at the top level, the following statement is executed:

```
window.top.location.href ="ex08-05.htm?wild01.htm"
```

This statement not only assigns the top window a page ex08-05.htm, but also sends an argument wild01.htm along with it. The master frame page ex08-05.htm identifies this argument and sends the page wild01.htm into a frame. The master frame page is listed in ex08-05.htm.

```
Example: ex08-05.htm - A Page To Protect Wild Life

 1: <?xml version="1.0" encoding="UTF-8"?>
 2: <!DOCTYPE html PUBLIC "-//W3C//DTD XHTML 1.0 Frameset//EN"
 3:     "http://www.w3.org/TR/xhtml1/DTD/xhtml1-frameset.dtd">
 4: <html xmlns="http://www.w3.org/1999/xhtml" xml:lang="en" lang="en">
 5: <head><title> A Page To Protect Wild Life - ex08-05.htm</title></head>
 6: <script>
 7:   window.resizeTo(800,660)
 8:   lPage="wild01.htm"
 9:   if (location.href !="")
10:   {
11:    hrefSt=location.href
12:    if (hrefSt.indexOf('?') !=-1)
13:       lPage=hrefSt.substring(hrefSt.indexOf('?')+1,hrefSt.length)
14:   }
15:   document.writeln('<frameset rows="40,*" frameborder="0" border="0" >')
16:   document.writeln('<frame src="top05.htm" name="top" id="top"'+
17:      'scrolling="no" frameborder="0" noresize="noresize" />')
18:   document.writeln('<frame src="'+lPage+'" name="low" id="low" '+
19:      'scrolling="no" frameborder="0" noresize="noresize" />')
20:   document.writeln('<\/frameset>')
21:
22: </script>
23: </html>
```

The important part of this page is lines 9–14. Remember that the location.href property carries the whole URL (or http:) input. This location string is used to test for an empty input. If this string is not empty, another test is activated to see whether this string contains any "?" symbol (line 12). If a "?" symbol is detected, the file after that symbol is copied to variable lPage (line 13). The output statements in lines 15–20 generate a dynamic frame at run time. In terms of this example, the frame setting is

```
<frameset rows="40,*" frameborder="0" border="0" >
<frame src="top05.htm" name="top" id="top"
    scrolling="no" frameborder="0" noresize="noresize" />
<frame src="wild01.htm" name="low" id="low"
    scrolling="no" frameborder="0" noresize="noresize" />
</frameset>
```

This puts the page wild01.htm into the lower part of the screen. The upper part is the strip page top05.htm. We turn off all frame attributes because we want the two frames to be fully integrated together. The strip page top05.htm is listed as follows:

```
Example: top05.htm - The Top Page For ex08-05.htm

 1: <?xml version="1.0" encoding="UTF-8"?>
 2: <!DOCTYPE html PUBLIC "-//W3C//DTD XHTML 1.0 Frameset//EN"
 3:     "http://www.w3.org/TR/xhtml1/DTD/xhtml1-frameset.dtd">
 4: <html xmlns="http://www.w3.org/1999/xhtml" xml:lang="en" lang="en">
 5: <head><title>File top05.htm </title></head>
```

```
 6: <style> .mSt{font-family:arial;font-size:14pt;height:25px}</style>
 7: <script>
 8:   if (window.top.location == window.self.location)
 9:      window.top.location.href ="ex08-05.htm"
10: </script>
11: <body style="background:#000088;color:#ffff00;text-align:center">
12: <div class="mSt">Please Protect Wild Life !</div>
13: </body>
14: </html>
```

As you can see, this is a very simple page containing one conditional `if` statement in lines 8–9. The `if` statement indicates that any direct call for this page will result in a redirection to the frame page ex08-05.htm. If you issue the command

http://www.pwt-ex.com/book/chap08a/ex08–05.htm?wild01.htm

the two pages top05.htm and wild01.htm will be combined together as one page. A screen shot of this example is shown in Fig. 8.7. To complete this example, eight wild life pages from wild01.htm through wild08.htm are prepared. The following command will display the pages top05.htm and wild06.htm together (see Fig. 8.8):

http://www.pwt-ex.com/book/chap08a/ex08-05.htm?wild06.htm

Figure 8.7 ex08-05.htm

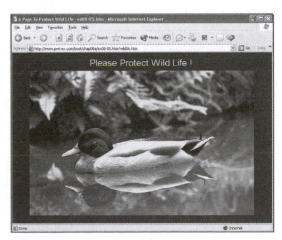

Figure 8.8 wild06.htm

The page top05.htm in this example is like an advertising strip page on top of each wild life picture and can be changed easily without touching other pages and pictures. Also, this strip page can be anything, including sound and pictures on the Web. These advantages make it a desirable technique to satisfy many advertising needs. Many commercial Web sites use similar techniques to create small frames (advertising areas) solely for advertising purposes.

8.2.2 Frame structure and access model

In example ex08-02.htm, we demonstrated how to store data in the master frame page and share them among child frames. In fact, data and (script) functions can be stored in any child frame and shared with others. Before we discuss how functions and data are shared among frames, we need to understand some basic frame structures (from a programming point of view) and how to work with them. Consider the master frame file ex08-06.htm:

Example: ex08-06.htm – Frame Structure And Access Model

```
 1: <?xml version="1.0" encoding="UTF-8"?>
 2: <!DOCTYPE html
 3:      PUBLIC "-//W3C//DTD XHTML 1.0 Frameset//EN"
 4:      "http://www.w3.org/TR/xhtml1/DTD/xhtml1-frameset.dtd">
 5: <html xmlns="http://www.w3.org/1999/xhtml" xml:lang="en" lang="en">
 6: <head>
 7:   <title> Frame Structure and Access Model - ex08-06.htm</title>
 8: </head>
 9: <script>window.resizeTo(650,500)</script>
10: <frameset cols="30%,*">
11:  <frameset rows="40%,*">
12:   <frame src="left06a.htm" id="left_fa" name="left_fa" />
13:   <frame src="left06b.htm" id="left_fb" name="left_fb" />
14:  </frameset>
15:  <frameset rows="30%,*">
16:   <frame src="right06a.htm" id="right_fa" name="right_fa" />
17:   <frame src="right06b.htm" id="right_fb" name="right_fb" />
18:  </frameset>
19: </frameset>
20: </html>
```

This file divides the screen into four parts and assigns each part to a page. The way that we order the frames is important. In this case, the frames and their associated pages are arranged as left06a.htm, left06b.htm, right06a.htm, and right06b.htm. In terms of the "Access Model," a 2 × 2 table of frames is defined and pages can be accessed via the model convention as given in Table 8.1.

Table 8.1 Frame access convention

`top.document`	–	ex08-06.htm
`top.frames[0].document`	–	left06a.htm
`top.frames[1].document`	–	left06b.htm
`top.frames[2].document`	–	right06a.htm
`top.frames[3].document`	–	right06b.htm

With this model in mind, you can now write a page, e.g., right06b.htm, to access properties of other pages through frames. Let's take a look at the listing of right06b.htm:

Example: right06b.htm – The Right Bottom Page For ex08-06.htm

```
 1: <?xml version="1.0" encoding="UTF-8"?>
 2: <!DOCTYPE html
 3:      PUBLIC "-//W3C//DTD XHTML 1.0 Transitional//EN"
 4:      "http://www.w3.org/TR/xhtml1/DTD/xhtml1-transitional.dtd">
 5: <html xmlns="http://www.w3.org/1999/xhtml" xml:lang="en" lang="en">
 6: <head><title>File: right06b.htm</title></head>
 7: <style>
 8:  h3{font-family:arial;font-size:12pt;color:#ffff00}
 9: </style>
10: <body style="background:#000088">
11:  <h3>This Is The Right Frame Second Row<br />
12:      File: right06b.htm<br /><br />
13:      Frame Access Model<br /></h3>
14:  <script>
15:   document.write("<h3>top.document.Title= "+
```

```
16:         top.document.title+"<br />")
17:
18:    document.write("top.frames[0].document.title= "+
19:        top.frames[0].document.title + "<br />")
20:    document.write("top.frames[1].document.title= "+
21:        top.frames[1].document.title + "<br />")
22:
23:    document.write("top.frames[2].document.title= "+
24:        top.frames[2].document.title + "<br />")
25:    document.write("top.frames[3].document.title= "+
26:        top.frames[3].document.title + "<br /></h3>")
27: </script>
28: </body>
29: </html>
```

This page uses the frame model to access properties of all other pages. For example, line 18 is used to print out the title of top.frames[0], i.e., the title of page left06a.htm. This page left06a.htm is listed below. The screen shot of this example is shown in Fig. 8.9.

Example: left06a.htm - The Left Top Page For ex08-06.htm

```
1: <?xml version="1.0" encoding="UTF-8"?>
2: <!DOCTYPE html PUBLIC "-//W3C//DTD XHTML 1.0 Transitional//EN"
3:        "http://www.w3.org/TR/xhtml1/DTD/xhtml1-transitional.dtd">
4: <html xmlns="http://www.w3.org/1999/xhtml" xml:lang="en" lang="en">
5: <head><title>File: left06a.htm</title></head>
6: <style> h3{font-family:arial;font-size:12pt;color:#ffff00} </style>
7: <body style="background:#000088">
8:    <h3>This Is The Left Frame First Row<br />
9:        File: left06a.htm</h3>
10: </body>
11: </html>
```

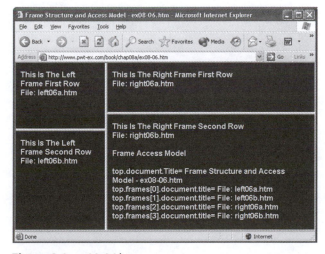

Figure 8.9 ex08-06.htm

Some browsers such as NS6 do not assign a value to the top.frames[ ] array until that particular frame is loaded. This is why we have chosen to print the output in the last frame file right06b.htm.

8.2.3   Sharing data and functions among frames

For frame applications, the ability to allow function calling, data sharing, and communication among frames presents state-of-the-art challenges to Web programmers. To address these issues, some fundamental program design concepts are needed. Examples may be the best way to demonstrate these concepts. Consider the following master frame page ex08-07.htm:

Example: ex08-07.htm – Sharing Data And Functions With Frames

```
1: <?xml version="1.0" encoding="UTF-8"?>
2: <!DOCTYPE html PUBLIC "-//W3C//DTD XHTML 1.0 Frameset//EN"
3:      "http://www.w3.org/TR/xhtml1/DTD/xhtml1-frameset.dtd">
4: <html xmlns="http://www.w3.org/1999/xhtml" xml:lang="en" lang="en">
5: <head><title> Sharing Data And Functions - ex08-07.htm </title></head>
6: <script> window.resizeTo(550,400)</script>
7: <frameset cols="30%,*">
8:   <frameset rows="70%,*">
9:     <frame src="left07a.htm" id="left_f1" name="left_f1" />
10:     <frame src="left07b.htm" id="left_f2" name="left_f2" />
11:   </frameset>
12:   <frame src="right07a.htm" id="right_f" name="right_f" />
13: </frameset>
14: </html>
```

There are three frames in this page, left07a.htm (line 9), left07b.htm (line 10), and right07a.htm (line 12). The first page, left07a.htm, contains some data, a function, and a menu:

Example: left07a.htm – The Left Page For ex08-07.htm

```
1: <?xml version="1.0" encoding="iso-8859-1"?>
2: <!DOCTYPE html PUBLIC "-//W3C//DTD XHTML 1.0 Transitional//EN"
3:      "http://www.w3.org/TR/xhtml1/DTD/xhtml1-transitional.dtd">
4: <html xmlns="http://www.w3.org/1999/xhtml" xml:lang="en" lang="en">
5: <head><title>File: left07a.htm </title>
6: <style> .mSt{font-family:arial;font-size:16pt;border:0;
7:          background:#000088;font-weight:bold;color:#ffff00}
8: </style>
9: <script>
10:  var aCount=0
11:  var bCount=0
12:  var cCount=0
13:  var pPage="Page A"
14:  var cPage="Page A"
15:  function backgroundText(varSt,varC)
16:  {
17:   top.frames[varC].document.write('<div style="font-family:arial;'+
18:     'font-size:12pt;color:#666600;position:absolute;top:0px">')
19:   for(i=0;i<40;i++)
20:     top.frames[varC].document.write(varSt)
21:   top.frames[varC].document.write("</div>")
22:  }
23: </script>
24: </head>
25:
26: <body style="background:#000088;text-align:center">
27:  <div class="mSt" style="color:#00ffff">Company I<br /><br /></div>
28:  <input type="button" onclick="pPage=cPage;cPage='Page A';
29:    parent.left_f2.location.href='left07b.htm'
30:    parent.right_f.location.href='right07a.htm'"
```

```
31:      onmouseover="this.style.background='#008800'" value="Page A"
32:      onmouseout="this.style.background='#000088'" class="mSt" /><br />
33:   <input type="button" onclick="pPage=cPage;cPage='Page B';
34:      parent.left_f2.location.href='left07b.htm'
35:      parent.right_f.location.href='right07b.htm'"
36:      onmouseover="this.style.background='#008800'" value="Page B"
37:      onmouseout="this.style.background='#000088'" class="mSt" /><br />
38:   <input type="button" onclick="pPage=cPage;cPage='Page C';
39:      parent.left_f2.location.href='left07b.htm'
40:      parent.right_f.location.href='right07c.htm'"
41:      onmouseover="this.style.background='#008800'" value="Page C"
42:      onmouseout="this.style.background='#000088'" class="mSt" /><br />
43: </body>
44: </html>
```

In this page, three buttons are used to simulate three menu items: "Page A," "Page B," and "Page C" (lines 28, 33, and 38). The corresponding pages of the items in the right frame are right07a.htm, right07b.htm, and right07c.htm respectively. When, for example, "Page A" is pressed (lines 28–32), left07b.htm and right07a.htm will be sent to the left bottom and right frames respectively (see lines 29–30). Also, when "Page A" is pressed, the following statement is executed (see line 28):

```
pPage=cPage;cPage="Page A"
```

The first part of this statement stores the current page (cPage) in the previous page variable pPage and puts the string "Page A" into the current page variable cPage. These two variables are declared in lines 13–14 and are used to remember the item that we have selected.

In lines 10–12, the three variables aCount, bCount, and cCount are defined. They are used to count the number of times that visitors have visited the frames and pages. The function backgroundText() declared in lines 15–22 is also available for the use of other frames. This function takes two arguments, varSt (a string variable) and varC (a channel variable), and generates a background text in the calling frame. Consider the right page right07a.htm:

```
Example: right07a.htm - The Right Page For ex08-07.htm

 1: <?xml version="1.0" encoding="iso-8859-1"?>
 2: <!DOCTYPE html PUBLIC "-//W3C//DTD XHTML 1.0 Transitional//EN"
 3:      "http://www.w3.org/TR/xhtml1/DTD/xhtml1-transitional.dtd">
 4: <html xmlns="http://www.w3.org/1999/xhtml" xml:lang="en" lang="en">
 5: <head><title> File : right07a.htm </title>
 6:  <style>
 7:   h3{font-family:arial;font-size:22pt;font-weight:bold;
 8:      position:absolute;top:20px;left:10px}
 9:  </style>
10:  <script>
11:     parent.left_f1.aCount++
12:     parent.left_f1.backgroundText("T h i s  i s  P a g e  A - ",2)
13:  </script>
14: </head>
15: <body style="background:#000088">
16:  <h3 style="color:#ffff00">
17:    This Is Page A<br /><br />
18:    You Have Visited Us <br />
19:    <script>document.write(parent.left_f1.aCount)</script> Times</h3>
20: </body>
21: </html>
```

When this page is loaded, it increases the counting (aCount) in the top left frame location parent.left_f1 (line 11). Next, it calls the function backgroundText() to generate a background text (line 12). The integer argument at the end of line 12 is the channel variable to specify the right frame (i.e., top.frames[2]). Finally, the script in line 19 outputs the number of visits to the screen.

The left bottom page left07b.htm is relatively simple and is listed below:

```
Example: left07b.htm - The Left Bottom Page For ex08-07.htm

 1: <?xml version="1.0" encoding="iso-8859-1"?>
 2: <!DOCTYPE html PUBLIC "-//W3C//DTD XHTML 1.0 Transitional//EN"
 3:     "http://www.w3.org/TR/xhtml1/DTD/xhtml1-transitional.dtd">
 4: <html xmlns="http://www.w3.org/1999/xhtml" xml:lang="en" lang="en">
 5: <head><title>File: left07b.htm </title></head>
 6: <body style="background:#000088;color:#ffff00;
 7:         font-size:12pt;font-family:arial;font-weight:bold">
 8: You Previously<br /> Pressed
 9: <script> document.write(parent.left_f1.pPage) </script>
10: </body>
11: </html>
```

Line 9 is the only important statement in this page. It outputs the past page variable pPage from location parent.left_f1 to the screen. Figure 8.10 shows the screen shot of this example.

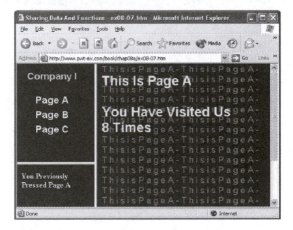

Figure 8.10 ex08-07.htm

8.2.4   Sending information to frames interactively

In this section, we consider the task of getting information from a user and sending him or her to another "appropriate" frame. Getting information from a user will normally require form element (or form interface) design. This is an independent subject and a more detailed discussion follows in Part IV. The form interface used here is a simple one. It involves some text boxes, checkboxes, and a text area. First, a master frame page is defined as in ex08-08.htm.

```
Example: ex08-08.htm - Send Data To Frame

 1: <?xml version="1.0" encoding="UTF-8"?>
 2: <!DOCTYPE html PUBLIC "-//W3C//DTD XHTML 1.0 Frameset//EN"
 3:     "http://www.w3.org/TR/xhtml1/DTD/xhtml1-frameset.dtd">
 4: <html xmlns="http://www.w3.org/1999/xhtml" xml:lang="en" lang="en">
 5: <head><title> Send Data To Frame - ex08-08.htm </title></head>
```

```
 6: <script> window.resizeTo(700,580)</script>
 7: <frameset cols="40%,*">
 8:   <frame src="left08.htm" id="left_f" name="left_f" />
 9:   <frame src="right08.htm" id="right_f" name="right_f" />
10: </frameset>
11: </html>
```

The left frame left08.htm is our form interface. The input information is sent to the right frame right08.htm. To keep the process simple, we just want to get "Name," "Email," "Favorite Browsers," and "Comments" from the user. This XHTML form interface consists of two parts: the first part is to get some text input from the user.

Example: left08.htm - The Left Page For ex08-08.htm (Part One)

```
 1: <?xml version="1.0" encoding="UTF-8"?>
 2: <!DOCTYPE html PUBLIC "-//W3C//DTD XHTML 1.0 Transitional//EN"
 3:       "http://www.w3.org/TR/xhtml1/DTD/xhtml1-transitional.dtd">
 4: <html xmlns="http://www.w3.org/1999/xhtml" xml:lang="en" lang="en">
 5: <head><title> File: left08.htm </title>
 6: <style>
 7:   .mSt{font-family:arial;font-size:12pt;font-weight:bold}
 8:   .butSt{background-color:#aaffaa;font-family:arial;font-weight:bold;
 9:       font-size:12pt;color:#ff0000;width:180px;height:30px}
10: </style>
11: </head>
12: <body style="background:#000088;color:#ffff00">
13: <div class="mSt">Please Enter Your Information<br /><br />
14:
15:   <table align="center">
16:     <tr class="mSt"><td>Name:</td>
17:       <td><input type="text" id="in1" name="in1"
18:           value="John Smith" /></td></tr>
19:     <tr class="mSt"><td>Email:</td>
20:       <td><input type="text" id="in2" name="in2"
21:           value="JohnSmith@isp.com" /></td></tr>
22:   </table><br />
23:
```

This page contains a table and some <input> elements. After the text "Name" in line 16, we have an input element in line 17. The type of the input element is text which allows a user to type in his or her name. The second input element in lines 20–21 is to get the "Email" address. The second part of this interface shows how to use checkboxes and text area to get user information.

Listing: Continuation Of The Page left08.htm (Part Two)

```
24: Favorite Browsers<br /><br />
25: <table align="center"><tr class="mSt">
26:   <td><input type="checkbox" id="br1" name="br1" checked /> IE</td>
27:   <td><input type="checkbox" id="br2" name="br2" checked /> NS</td></tr>
28:   <tr class="mSt">
29:    <td><input type="checkbox" id="br3" name="br3" /> Others</td></tr>
30: </table><br />
31:
32:   Comments<br /><br /></div><div class="mSt" align="center">
33:   <textarea rows="5" cols="30" id="com1" name="com1">
34:     I support W3C standard browsers.
35:   </textarea><br /><br />
36:   <input type="button" onclick="wPage()" value="Send Data" class="butSt" />
37: </div>
38:
```

This code fragment contains three checkboxes (lines 26–29) for some favorite browsers: namely, "IE," "NS," and "Others." The IE and NS checkboxes are initially checked. The comment section (lines 32–35) is a text area field. The size of this input field is set to five rows of 30 characters and has an initial value "I support W3C standard browsers." (line 34). In line 36, a button is used to activate a function called wPage() and send the input data to the right frame. The final part of this interface provides the definition of the function wPage().

```
Listing: Continuation Of The Page left08.htm (Part Three)

39: <script>
40:   brs = new Array(" ","IE","NS","Others")
41:   function wPage()
42:   {
43:     lMsg="Name: "+document.getElementById("in1").value+"<br />"+
44:         "Email: "+document.getElementById("in2").value+"<br />"+
45:         "Favorite Browsers: "
46:     for (i=1;i<4;i++)
47:     {
48:       var1 = "br"+i
49:       if (document.getElementById(var1).checked !=0)
50:         lMsg = lMsg + brs[i]+"  "
51:     }
52:     lMsg = lMsg +"<br /><br />Comments: <br />"+
53:       document.getElementById("com1").value
54:     top.frames[1].document.getElementById("rMsg").innerHTML=lMsg
55:   }
56:   </script>
57: </body>
58: </html>
```

When the user presses the Send Data button, the function wPage() will be called and create a local string called lMsg to capture the input data for "Name" and "Email" (lines 43–44). Next is a for-loop to check the checkboxes (lines 46–51). We detect the checkboxes one by one. If a checkbox is checked, the corresponding browser name is added to the local string lMsg. Lines 52–53 are used to add the information in the textarea to lMsg. Finally, in line 54, this lMsg is output to the right frame (i.e., top.frames[1]) as an innerHTML message to the location with an identity id=rMsg.

Compared to the left frame, the right frame right08.htm has a simpler structure.

```
Example: right08.htm - The Right Page For ex08-08.htm

 1: <?xml version="1.0" encoding="iso-8859-1"?>
 2: <!DOCTYPE html PUBLIC "-//W3C//DTD XHTML 1.0 Transitional//EN"
 3:     "http://www.w3.org/TR/xhtml1/DTD/xhtml1-transitional.dtd">
 4: <html xmlns="http://www.w3.org/1999/xhtml" xml:lang="en" lang="en">
 5: <head><title>File: right08.htm</title></head>
 6: <style>.mSt{font-family:arial;font-size:22pt;font-weight:bold}</style>
 7: <body style="background:#000088">
 8:  <div class="mSt" style="color:#00ffff;text-align:center">
 9:     Personal Information<br /><br /><br /></div>
10:  <div class="mSt" style="font-size:14pt;color:#ffff00"
11:     id="rMsg" name="rMsg">
12:  </div>
13: </body>
14: </html>
```

This page uses a division element <div> in lines 10–11 with identity rMsg to accept an incoming data string. When the user presses the Send Data button, the left page information will be sent to this division element and appear in the right page. Some screen shots of this example are presented in Figs 8.11 and 8.12.

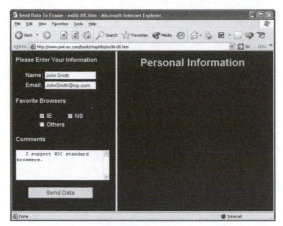

Figure 8.11 ex08-08.htm

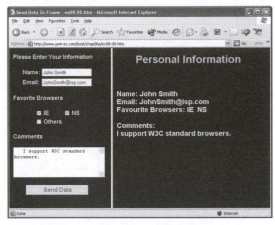

Figure 8.12 Send data to frame

8.2.5 Controlling iframes

Inline frames, or iframes, can be considered as sub-windows within an XHTML page. They have the power of frames and the flexibilities of an XHTML element. Since they are XHTML elements, you don't need to write any master frame page for them. In fact, they have attributes of both frames and elements. In the following example, we demonstrate how to embed two iframes in a page and swap them using a button. The main program (or page) has the following listing (ex08-09.htm):

```
Example: ex08-09.htm - Controlling Iframes

 1: <?xml version="1.0" encoding="iso-8859-1"?>
 2: <!DOCTYPE html PUBLIC "-//W3C//DTD XHTML 1.0 Transitional//EN"
 3:     "http://www.w3.org/TR/xhtml1/DTD/xhtml1-transitional.dtd">
 4: <html xmlns="http://www.w3.org/1999/xhtml" xml:lang="en" lang="en">
 5: <head><title> Controlling Iframes - ex08-09.htm</title></head>
 6: <style>
 7:   .butSt{background-color:#aaffaa;font-family:arial;font-weight:bold;
 8:       font-size:12pt;color:#ff0000;width:180px;height:30px}
 9: </style>
10: <script>
11: window.resizeTo(680,630)
12: swapV=0
13: function swapFrames()
14: {
15:   if (swapV ==0)
16:   {
17:     swapV=1
18:     document.getElementById("if_b").src="iframe_a.htm"
19:     document.getElementById("if_a").src="iframe_b.htm"
20:   }
21:   else
22:   {
23:     swapV=0
24:     document.getElementById("if_b").src="iframe_b.htm"
25:     document.getElementById("if_a").src="iframe_a.htm"
26:   }
27: }
28: </script>
29: <body>
```

```
30: <div align="center">
31:
32:   <iframe src="iframe_a.htm" width="250" height="410"
33:     frameborder="0" noresize="noresize" scrolling="no"
34:     id="if_a" name="if_a"></iframe>
35:
36:                  
37:
38:   <iframe src="iframe_b.htm" width="250" height="410"
39:     frameborder="0" noresize="noresize" scrolling="no"
40:     id="if_b" name="if_b"></iframe><br /><br />
41:
42:   <input class="butSt" type="button"
43:       onclick="swapFrames()" value="Swap Iframes">
44: </div>
45: </body>
46: </html>
```

The first main element of this page is lines 32–34. This is an `iframe` with some basic attributes of both frame and XHTML elements. This `iframe` includes a page called iframe_a.htm. All attributes such as border, resize, and scrolling of this frame are off simply because we want this frame to be fully integrated into the master page. Another `iframe` is defined in lines 38–40. Line 42 is a button used to swap the frames. The swap function `swapFrames()` is declared in lines 13–27 and a variable `swapV` is used to control the swapping. If the value of `swapV` is 0, you exchange the `iframe` source files; if the value is not 0, you change them back.

The `iframe` source file, e.g., iframe_a.htm, is itself a simple page and is listed below:

Example: iframe_a.htm – The Left Iframe Page For ex08-09.htm

```
 1: <?xml version="1.0" encoding="iso-8859-1"?>
 2: <!DOCTYPE html PUBLIC "-//W3C//DTD XHTML 1.0 Transitional//EN"
 3:     "http://www.w3.org/TR/xhtml1/DTD/xhtml1-transitional.dtd">
 4: <html xmlns="http://www.w3.org/1999/xhtml" xml:lang="en" lang="en">
 5: <head><title>File: iframe_a.htm </title><head>
 6: <style> .mSt{font-family:arial;font-size:16pt;border:0;
 7:             font-weight:bold;color:#ffff00}
 8: </style>
 9: <body style="background:#000088;text-align:center">
10: <div class="mSt" style="font-size:22pt;color:#00ffff">
11: IFrame A<br /><br /></div>
12:
13: <table border="0" align="center">
14:  <tr align="center">
15:    <td><img src="ace.gif" alt="pic" /></td>
16:    <td><img src="clubs.gif" alt="pic" /></td></tr>
17:
18:  <tr align="center">
19:    <td><br /><input type="button" value="Red"
20:      style="width:76px;height:35px;font-family:arial;font-size:14pt"
21:      onclick="document.body.style.backgroundColor='#aa0000'"></td>
22:    <td><br /><input type="button" value="Blue"
23:      style="width:76px;height:35px;font-family:arial;font-size:14pt"
24:      onclick="document.body.style.backgroundColor='#000088'"></td></tr>
25:
26:  <tr align="center"><td colspan=2><br />
27:    <img src="chessa.gif" alt="pic" /></td></tr>
28: </table>
29: </body>
30: </html>
```

As you can see, this is mainly a table that consists of three rows. The first row (lines 14–16) has two animated `gif` images. The second row (lines 18–24) contains two buttons used to control the background color; you can change the background color within this `iframe`. The third row contains only one animated `gif` picture. The other `iframe` file, iframe_b.htm, has a similar structure. Some of the actions on screen are captured in Figs 8.13 and 8.14.

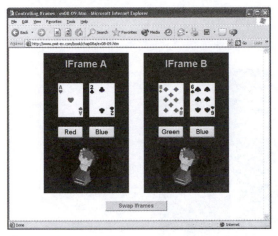

Figure 8.13 ex08-09.htm

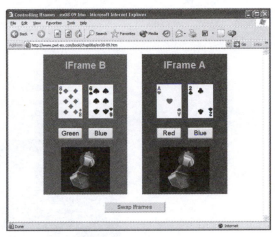

Figure 8.14 Swapping iframes

8.3   Browser window(s) I

8.3.1   Opening single and multiple new window(s)

Browsers can interpret XHTML code and display them correctly on screen. They also provide a rich source for basic windows programming without the need for or understanding the use of compilers. From plain windows to fully functional Web browsing windows, from text files, XHTML pages, audio, and images to movie clips, all of them can be controlled with little effort. For example, the code

```
<script> window.open()</script>
```

opens a new browser window (empty window) immediately. The code

```
<script> window.open("http://www.microsoft.com")</script>
```

opens a browser window and loads the corresponding Web site (www.microsoft.com) into it. Basically, you can put any supported file format (e.g., images, audio, and movie clips) into the argument. For example, the code

```
<script> window.open("01_img.jpg")</script>
```

will open a window and display a `jpg` (or JPEG) picture. To open multiple new windows, more `window.open` commands are used. Consider the example in ex08-10.htm:

```
Example: ex08-10.htm - Open Multiple Browser Windows

1: <?xml version="1.0" encoding="UTF-8"?>
2: <!DOCTYPE html PUBLIC "-//W3C//DTD XHTML 1.0 Frameset//EN"
3:      "http://www.w3.org/TR/xhtml1/DTD/xhtml1-frameset.dtd">
4: <html xmlns="http://www.w3.org/1999/xhtml" xml:lang="en" lang="en">
5: <head><title>Open Multiple Windows - ex08-10.htm </title></head>
```

```
 6: <script>
 7:    window.open("01_img.jpg")
 8:    window.open("02_img.jpg")
 9:    window.open("03_img.jpg")
10:    window.open("04_img.jpg")
11: </script>
12: <body></body>
13: </html>
```

Yes, you are right! This page opens four browser windows and displays four pictures immediately as shown in Fig. 8.15.

Figure 8.15 ex08-10.htm

Some Web sites are still practicing this technique in a nasty way by displaying many other sites without their owners' or users' consent.

8.3.2   Using the basic attributes of new window(s)

The `window.open` command used in our last example has a rich set of arguments to control the look (or skin) of the browser window. For example, the following code displays the pictures in plain window frames:

```
Example: ex08-11.htm – Browser Window With Attributes I

 1: <?xml version="1.0" encoding="UTF-8"?>
 2: <!DOCTYPE html PUBLIC "-//W3C//DTD XHTML 1.0 Frameset//EN"
 3:       "http://www.w3.org/TR/xhtml1/DTD/xhtml1-frameset.dtd">
 4: <html xmlns="http://www.w3.org/1999/xhtml" xml:lang="en" lang="en">
 5: <head><title>Browser Window Attributes I – ex08-11.htm </title></head>
 6: <script>
 7:
 8:    lookSt ="menubar=no,toolbar=no,location=no,status=no"
 9:
10:      window.open("01_img.jpg","Pic1",lookSt)
11:      window.open("02_img.jpg","Pic2",lookSt)
12:      window.open("03_img.jpg","Pic3",lookSt)
13:      window.open("04_img.jpg","Pic4",lookSt)
14: </script>
15: <body></body>
16: </html>
```

Figure 8.16 ex08-11.htm

The third argument of the `window.open` command (lines 10–13) is used to control the "look" of the window. It is a long string with attribute settings. We use a string variable `lookSt` to describe attribute settings. If you turn off the menu bar, toolbar, location, and status as demonstrated in line 8, you will have plain windows as shown in Fig. 8.16. In practice, you could use the following attributes and settings:

menu bar	**scroll bar**	**location**	**status**
toolbar	**resizable**	**copy history**	

The second argument in `window.open` represents the identity of the newly opened window. For example, you can use four different window identities, `Pic1`, `Pic2`, `Pic3`, and `Pic4`, to represent four different windows. The next example shows how to use this feature to output any XHTML-supported file to the same window.

```
Example: ex08-12.htm - Browser Window With Attributes II

 1: <?xml version="1.0" encoding="UTF-8"?>
 2: <!DOCTYPE html PUBLIC "-//W3C//DTD XHTML 1.0 Frameset//EN"
 3:       "http://www.w3.org/TR/xhtml1/DTD/xhtml1-frameset.dtd">
 4: <html xmlns="http://www.w3.org/1999/xhtml" xml:lang="en" lang="en">
 5: <head><title>Browser Window Attributes II - ex08-12.htm</title></head>
 6: <style>
 7:  .mSt{font-family:arial;font-size:14pt;font-weight:bold;color:#ffff00}
 8:  .bSt{background-color:#aaffaa;font-family:arial;font-weight:bold;
 9:       font-size:12pt;color:#ff0000;width:120px;height:30px}
10: </style>
11:
12: <script>
13:  window.resizeTo(440,380)
14:
15:  xhtmlFile = Array(7)
16:  for (i=1;i<7;i++)
17:  {
18:    xhtmlFile[i]="0"+i+"_img.jpg"
19:  }
20:
21:  function sPage()
22:  {
23:   varL = document.getElementById("sel").selectedIndex
24:   imgSt = xhtmlFile[varL +1]
25:   titleSt="MyPic"
```

```
26:    lookSt="menubar=no,toolbar=no,location=no,resizable=yes"
27:    window.open(imgSt,titleSt,lookSt)
28:    }
29: </script>
30:
31: <body style="background:#000088;text-align:center">
32: <div class="mSt">Show Picture To A Window</div>
33: <br /> <br />
34:
35: <table align="center"><tr><td>
36:    <select class="bSt" id="sel" name="sel">
37:     <option>Parrot</option>
38:     <option>Peacock</option>
39:     <option>Eagle</option>
40:     <option>Butterfly I</option>
41:     <option>Butterfly II</option>
42:     <option>Wild Duck</option>
43:     </select>   
44: </td><td>
45:    <input type="button" onclick="sPage()" value="Show Pic" class="bSt" />
46: </td></tr></table>
47:
48: </body>
49: </html>
```

Example ex08-12.htm can be used as a general program to send any XHTML-supported file to a browser window. An array `xhtmlFile` (see line 15) is used to remember all the picture files that we want to send. In this case, the picture files are 01_img.jpg, 02_img.jpg, … , 06_img.jpg as indicated in the for-loop in lines 16–18.

The main body is a simple *combo* (or *listed*) box declared in lines 36–43. Inside the box, six objects, Parrot, Peacock, …, Wild Duck, are used to associate with the image files 01_img.jpg, 02_img.jpg, … 06_img.jpg respectively. If the user picks the item "Parrot," the page displays the corresponding picture file 01_img.jpg in a separate window.

The script function `sPage()` (see lines 21–28) is executed once the Show Pic button (line 45) is pressed. The selected object in the listed box is returned by the integer variable `selectedIndex`. That is, if you select the first item, the `selectedIndex` will have the value 0. This variable is used in line 23. Since variable `selectedIndex` is an integer starting from 0, you need to add 1 to reflect the true identity of the corresponding picture file (line 24). The image string variable `imgSt` together with the title string `titleSt` (line 25) and the look string `lookSt` (line 26) is used to open a new window and display the image. Some of the screen shots are displayed in Figs 8.17 and 8.18.

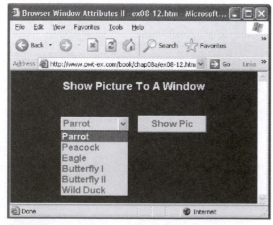

Figure 8.17 ex08-12.htm

Figure 8.18 Picture of a parrot

8.3.3 Position and size of new window(s)

In additon to the look of a new window, the third argument of the `window.open` command also contains the size and position features. The size of a new window is controlled by the `width` and `height` attributes. For example, the code

```
<script>window.open("01_img.jpg","myPic","width=700,height=450")</script>
```

will display the picture in a new window of size 700 × 450 pixels. The position of the new window is controlled by the attributes `top` and `left`. The `top` attribute is measured from the top of your monitor screen and the `left` attribute from the left. The following code places a new window at the location 100 pixels from the top and 150 pixels from the left:

```
<script>window.open("01_img.jpg","myPic","top=100,left=150")</script>
```

The next example, ex08-13.htm, is a modification of ex08-12.htm to give a full-screen display.

```
Listing: ex08-02.txt - Code Fragment For ex08-13.htm

 1: <script>
 2:   window.resizeTo(440,380)
 3:   xhtmlFile = Array(7)
 4:   for (i=1;i<7;i++)
 5:   {
 6:     xhtmlFile[i]="0"+i+"_img.jpg"
 7:   }
 8:   function sPage()
 9:   {
10:   varL = document.getElementById("sel").selectedIndex
11:   imgSt = xhtmlFile[varL +1]
12:   titleSt="MyPic"
13:
14:   sWidth=screen.availWidth
15:   sHeight=screen.availHeight
16:
17:   lookSt="menubar=no,toolbar=no,location=no,resizable=yes,"+
18:          "top=0,left=0,width="+sWidth+",height="+sHeight
19:   window.open(imgSt,titleSt,lookSt)
20:   }
21: </script>
```

In this code fragment two new variables `sWidth` and `sHeight` are added in the function `sPage()`. The variable `sWidth` is used to store the available screen width returned by the `screen.availWidth` property. Together with the `sHeight` value, all these values are then added to the end of the look string `lookSt` (line 18). We also use `top=0` and `left=0` to locate the window at the top left corner of the monitor.

8.3.4 Random positioning of a series of pictures

In this section, you will learn how to develop a page that can open a series of randomly positioned new windows. The first step is to calculate the top left corner of every new window that you create. This is done by the random method of the browser:

```
topPic=Math.floor(Math.random()*500)
leftPic=Math.floor(Math.random()*700)
```

In this case, the random area is set to be 700×500 pixels. The coding of this example is given in ex08-14.htm.

```
Example: ex08-14.htm – Random Positioning Of A Series Of Pictures
 1: <?xml version="1.0" encoding="UTF-8"?>
 2: <!DOCTYPE html PUBLIC "-//W3C//DTD XHTML 1.0 Frameset//EN"
 3:        "http://www.w3.org/TR/xhtml1/DTD/xhtml1-frameset.dtd">
 4: <html xmlns="http://www.w3.org/1999/xhtml" xml:lang="en" lang="en">
 5: <head><title>Random Positioning Of Pictures - ex08-14.htm </title></head>
 6: <style>
 7:   .mSt{font-family:arial;font-size:14pt;font-weight:bold;color:#ffff00}
 8:   .bSt{background-color:#aaffaa;font-family:arial;font-weight:bold;
 9:        font-size:12pt;color:#ff0000;width:120px;height:30px}
10: </style>
11: <script>
12:   window.resizeTo(440,380)
13:
14:   xhtmlFile = Array(7)
15:   for (i=1;i<7;i++)
16:   {
17:     xhtmlFile[i]="0"+i+"_img.jpg"
18:   }
19:
20:   function randomPic()
21:   {
22:     for (i=1;i<7;i++){
23:       topPic=Math.floor(Math.random()*500)
24:       leftPic=Math.floor(Math.random()*700)
25:
26:       imgSt=xhtmlFile[i]
27:       titleSt="Pic"+i
28:       lookSt="menubar=no,toolbar=no,location=no,resizable=yes,top="+
29:              topPic+",left="+leftPic+",width=730,height=450"
30:       window.open(imgSt,titleSt,lookSt)
31:     }
32:   }
33: </script>
34: <body style="background:#000088;text-align:center"><div class="mSt">
35:     Random Positioning Of <br />A Number Of Pictures</div><br /><br />
36: <input type="button" onclick="randomPic()" value="Show Pic" class="bSt" />
37: </body>
38: </html>
```

This example displays six images (01_img.jpg through 06_img.jpg) randomly on the screen. The title variable titleSt in line 27 guarantees that all new windows are independent. Since the variables topPic and leftPic have random values, the new window that is generated by the window.open statement in line 30 has a random position (see Figs 8.19 and 8.20).

There is no timing control code in this example, which means that all pictures are displayed on the screen instantly. The speed of the display depends only on the speed of your computer. If you want to have more control over the display speed, the script part of this example (lines 11–33) needs to be modified to incorporate timing control. A modification ex08-15.htm is given as follows:

Figure 8.19 ex08-14.htm

Figure 8.20 Random positioning of pictures

```
Listing: ex08-03.txt - Code Fragment For ex08-15.htm

 1: <script>
 2:  window.resizeTo(440,380)
 3:  xhtmlFile = Array(7)
 4:  displaySpeed=550
 5:
 6:  for (i=1;i<7;i++)
 7:  {
 8:     xhtmlFile[i]="0"+i+"_img.jpg"
 9:  }
10:  i=0
11:  function randomPic()
12:  {
13:     i++
14:     if (i < 7)
15:     {
16:       topPic=Math.floor(Math.random()*500)
17:       leftPic=Math.floor(Math.random()*700)
18:
19:       imgSt=xhtmlFile[i]
20:       titleSt="Pic"+i
21:       lookSt="menubar=no,toolbar=no,location=no,resizable=yes,top="+
22:              topPic+",left="+leftPic+",width=730,height=450"
23:       window.open(imgSt,titleSt,lookSt)
24:       setTimeout("randomPic()",displaySpeed)
25:     } else return true
26:  }
27: </script>
```

The variable i in line 10 is used to count and represent the *i*th image. The function terminates if you have already displayed six images. If the value of i is less than 7, the picture is displayed at a random position (lines 16–23). The setTimeout() function in line 24 is used to count the timing. For every displaySpeed=550 unit time (1,000 units = 1 second), the randomPic() function is recalled and continues to display the images.

8.3.5   Cycling show of a group of XHTML pages

How do you handle a "cycling show" on a group of XHTML pages? Suppose you have a group of six pages, `xhtmFile[1]`, `xhtmlFile[2]`. ..., `xhtmlFile[6]` and want to develop a show that can display all of them randomly on screen. When all six pages are displayed on the screen, all the windows (or pages) will be closed and the random cycling show can be restarted.

For simplicity, the picture files from previous examples are used in these pages. Since we want to close all the windows once all pages are on the screen, a technique to close a window is needed.

When the `window.open` command opens a new window, the system will normally return a *handle* so that references can be made later. One usage of this window handle is to close it with the `close()` method (or function). For example, the following statement opens a new window with `winHandle`:

```
<script> winHandle = window.open("http://www.microsoft.com")</script>
```

To close this window, you can use the command

```
<script> winHandle.close() </script>
```

For a more protective (or professional) style, the following statement is used:

```
<script> if (winHandle && !winHandle.closed) winHandle.close() <script>
```

Now consider the coding in ex08-16.htm:

```
Example: ex08-16.htm - A Cycling Show

 1: <?xml version="1.0" encoding="UTF-8"?>
 2: <!DOCTYPE html PUBLIC "-//W3C//DTD XHTML 1.0 Frameset//EN"
 3:     "http://www.w3.org/TR/xhtml1/DTD/xhtml1-frameset.dtd">
 4: <html xmlns="http://www.w3.org/1999/xhtml" xml:lang="en" lang="en">
 5: <head><title>Cycling Show - ex08-16.htm </title></head>
 6: <style>
 7:  .mSt{font-family:arial;font-size:14pt;font-weight:bold;color:#ffff00}
 8:  .bSt{background-color:#aaffaa;font-family:arial;font-weight:bold;
 9:      font-size:12pt;color:#ff0000;width:120px;height:30px}
10: </style>
11: <script>
12:  window.resizeTo(440,380)
13:
14:  displaySpeed=550
15:  totalFile=6
16:  displayCycle=3
17:  ranTop = 500
18:  ranLeft = 700
19:
20:  xhtmlFile = new Array(totalFile+1)
21:  winH = new Array(totalFile+1)
22:  winId= new Array(totalFile+1)
23:
24:  for (i=1;i<= totalFile;i++)
25:  {
26:    xhtmlFile[i]="0"+i+"_img.jpg"
27:    winId[i]="winId"+i
28:    winH[i]="winHandle"+i
29:  }
30:  iFile=1
31:  iCycle=1
32:
```

```
33:  function randomPic()
34:  {
35:    if (iCycle <= displayCycle)
36:    {
37:      if (iFile <=totalFile)
38:      {
39:        topPic=Math.floor(Math.random()*ranTop)
40:        leftPic=Math.floor(Math.random()*ranLeft)
41:
42:        imgSt=xhtmlFile[iFile]
43:        titleSt=winId[iFile]
44:        lookSt="menubar=no,toolbar=no,location=no,resizable=yes,top="+
45:        topPic+",left="+leftPic+",width=730,height=450"
46:        winH[iFile]=window.open(imgSt,titleSt,lookSt)
47:        iFile++
48:
49:        setTimeout("randomPic()",displaySpeed)
50:      }
51:      else
52:      {
53:        for (j=1;j<=totalFile;j++)
54:        {
55:            if (winH[j] && !winH[j].closed) winH[j].close()
56:        }
57:        iFile=1
58:        iCycle++
59:        setTimeout("randomPic()",displaySpeed)
60:      }
61:    } else {
62:
63:        iCycle=1
64:        iFile=1
65:        return
66:    }
67:  }
68: </script>
69:
70: <body style="background:#000088;text-align:center">
71: <div class="mSt">Cycling Show A Group Of 6 Pages <br />
72:    (Picture Pages) 3 Times</div><br /> <br />
73: <input type="button" onclick="randomPic()" value="Show Pic" class="bSt" />
74: </body>
75: </html>
```

The first part of this page is for parameter settings (lines 14–29). Five parameters are used to control the execution of the page.

- displaySpeed   –   Integer, to control the time interval for each display.
- totalFile   –   Integer, to indicate how many page files.
- displayCycle   –   Integer, to control how many cycles.
- ranTop   –   Integer, the maximum random range from the top.
- ranLeft   –   Integer, the maximum random range from the left.

The for-loop in lines 24–29 is used to set the `xhtmlFile[ ]` array so that all pages are in good order. The `ramdonPic()`function (lines 33–67) is a modified version of the previous example to incorporate `displayCycle` and close all window functionalities. If all pages have already been displayed on the screen, the for-loop in lines 53–56 will close them all. Finally, if the cycle reaches the `displayCyle`, the parameters `iCycle` and `iFile` (see lines 63–64) are reset so that the cycling show stops and can retart. Some screen shots are shown in Figs 8.21 and 8.22.

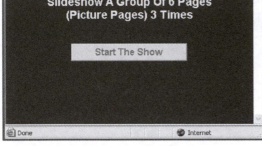

Figure 8.21 ex08-16.htm

Figure 8.22 Cycling show

8.4   Browser window(s) II

8.4.1   Locating page objects with window scrolling

When dealing with browser controls (single or multiple windows), another useful function is window scrolling. Window scrolling moves the window to particular *x,y* coordinates. Consider the command

```
<script> window.scroll(150,250)</script>
```

This moves the current window's left top corner to the location (150, 250) measured by pixels. When working with multiple windows, window handles are often used as identities. In the next example, a page is developed to control the scrolling of a strip of pictures so that only one picture can be seen at any one time. The controlling page is listed in ex08-17.htm.

```
Example: ex08-17.htm – Window Scrolling I

 1: <?xml version="1.0" encoding="UTF-8"?>
 2: <!DOCTYPE html PUBLIC "-//W3C//DTD XHTML 1.0 Frameset//EN"
 3:     "http://www.w3.org/TR/xhtml1/DTD/xhtml1-frameset.dtd">
 4: <html xmlns="http://www.w3.org/1999/xhtml" xml:lang="en" lang="en">
 5: <head><title> Window Scrolling I – ex08-17.htm </title></head>
 6: <style>
 7:  .mSt{font-family:arial;font-size:18pt;font-weight:bold;color:#00ffff}
 8:  .bSt{background-color:#aaffaa;font-family:arial;font-weight:bold;
 9:      font-size:12pt;color:#ff0000;width:248px;height:30px}
10: </style>
11:
12: <script>
13:  window.resizeTo(440,340)
```

```
14:   function scrollDown(lineLeft,lineDown)
15:   {
16:    lookSt="menubar=no,toolbar=no,location=no,status=no,scrollbars=yes,"+
17:          "resizable=no"
18:    winH=window.open("ex08-17a.htm","myWin",lookSt)
19:    winH.resizeTo(430,380)
20:    winH.focus()
21:    setTimeout("winH.scroll("+lineLeft+","+lineDown+")",1000)
22:   }
23: </script>
24:
25: <body style="background:#000088;text-align:center">
26:   <div class="mSt">Window Scrolling</div><br /><br /><br />
27:   <input type="button" onclick="scrollDown(5,80)"
28:        value="Scroll To Butterfly_I" class="bSt" /><br /><br />
29:   <input type="button" onclick="scrollDown(405,80)"
30:        value="Scroll To Butterfly_II" class="bSt" /><br /><br />
31: </body>
32: </html>
```

This page contains two buttons (lines 27–30). When the first button, Scroll To Butterfly_I, is pressed, the function `scrollDown()` with parameters 5 and 80 is called. The parameters are used to locate the coordinates (5, 80) in a child window and display them at the top left corner. This technique is often used in commercial Web sites to locate small products. The child window you are going to open is a plain one and without most of the controls (lines 16–17). After resizing the child window to 430 × 380 pixels (line 19), the `setTimeout()` function is called to execute the scrolling via the handle `winH` (i.e., `winH.scroll`).

The child window page ex08-17a.htm is given below:

Example: ex08-17a.htm – The Child Window Page For ex08-07.htm

```
 1: <?xml version="1.0" encoding="UTF-8"?>
 2: <!DOCTYPE html PUBLIC "-//W3C//DTD XHTML 1.0 Frameset//EN"
 3:        "http://www.w3.org/TR/xhtml1/DTD/xhtml1-frameset.dtd">
 4: <html xmlns="http://www.w3.org/1999/xhtml" xml:lang="en" lang="en">
 5: <head><title>File: ex08-17a.htm</title></head>
 6: <style>
 7:  .mSt{font-family:arial;font-size:18pt;font-weight:bold;color:#ffff00}
 8: </style>
 9: <body style="background:#000088;text-align:center">
10: <script>
11:  lMsg=""
12:  document.write('<pre style="color:#666600" text-align="left"><br />')
13:  for(i=0;i<=60;i++)
14:  {
15:    for (j=0;j<=5;j++)
16:    {
17:      lMsg = lMsg +"P r a c t i c a L W e B "+
18:            " T e c h n o l o g i e s "
19:    }
20:    lMsg = lMsg +"<br />"
21:  }
22:  document.write(lMsg+"</pre>")
23: </script>
24:
25: <div class="mSt" style="position:absolute;left:45px;top:100px">
26:    Butterfly_I<br /><br /><img src="s_04_img.jpg" alt="pic" /></div>
27: <div class="mSt" style="position:absolute;left:445px;top:100px">
28:    Butterfly_II<br /><br /><img src="s_05_img.jpg" alt="pic" /></div>
29: </body>
30: </html>
```

As you can see from lines 25–28, this is a page with two pictures. The first picture is located at (45, 100) and the second one at (445, 100). Note also that we have used XHTML preformat element `<pre>` to create background text in lines 12–23. Some screen shots are shown in Figs 8.23 and 8.24.

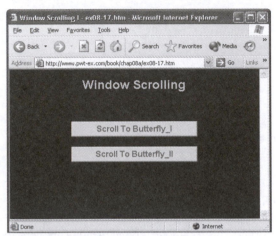

Figure 8.23 ex08-17.htm

Figure 8.24 Scrolling butterfly

8.4.2 Image transition using scrolling effects

If you want to open multiple windows and have simple animations on each of them, then the scrolling technique is a good tool. In particular, a single parent window can control all child windows. As a demonstration, you are going to develop a page for one parent with two child windows. Each child window incorporates some images and performs simple animations by using scrolling effects. The parent page (or window) has the following listing:

```
Example: ex08-18.htm - Window Scrolling II

 1: <?xml version="1.0" encoding="UTF-8"?>
 2: <!DOCTYPE html PUBLIC "-//W3C//DTD XHTML 1.0 Frameset//EN"
 3:      "http://www.w3.org/TR/xhtml1/DTD/xhtml1-frameset.dtd">
 4: <html xmlns="http://www.w3.org/1999/xhtml" xml:lang="en" lang="en">
 5: <head><title> Window Scrolling II - ex08-18.htm </title></head>
 6: <style>
 7:   .mSt{font-family:arial;font-size:18pt;font-weight:bold;color:#00ffff}
 8:   .bSt{background-color:#aaffaa;font-family:arial;font-weight:bold;
 9:        font-size:12pt;color:#ff0000;width:248px;height:30px}
10: </style>
11: <script>
12:   window.resizeTo(440,340)
13:
14:   function scrollL(lineLeft,lineDown)
15:   {
16:   lookSt="menubar=no,toolbar=no,location=no,status=no,scrollbars=yes,"+
17:          "resizable=no"
18:   winH=window.open("ex08-18a.htm","myWin1",lookSt)
19:   winH.resizeTo(350,250)
20:   winH.focus()
21:   for (i=1;i<lineLeft;i++)
22:     setTimeout("winH.scroll("+i+","+lineDown+")",400)
```

```
23:    for (i=lineLeft;i > 1;i--)
24:      setTimeout("winH.scroll("+i+","+lineDown+")",400)
25:    }
26:
27:    function scrollD(lineLeft,lineDown)
28:    {
29:    lookSt="menubar=no,toolbar=no,location=no,status=no,scrollbars=yes,"+
30:          "resizable=no"
31:    winH2=window.open("ex08-18b.htm","myWin2",lookSt)
32:    winH2.resizeTo(350,250)
33:    winH2.focus()
34:    for (i=1;i<lineDown;i++)
35:      setTimeout("winH2.scroll("+lineLeft+","+i+")",400)
36:    for (i=lineDown;i > 1;i--)
37:      setTimeout("winH2.scroll("+lineLeft+","+i+")",400)
38:    }
39: </script>
40: <body style="background:#000088;text-align:center">
41:   <div class="mSt">Image Transitions</div><br /><br /><br />
42:   <input type="button" onclick="scrollL(350,1)"
43:         value="(Window 1) - Left & Right" class="bSt" /><br /><br />
44:   <input type="button" onclick="scrollD(1,225)"
45:         value="(Window 2) - Up & Down" class="bSt" /><br /><br />
46: </body>
47: </html>
```

This main window has two buttons (lines 42–45). The first button named "(Window 1)-Left & Right" opens a child window and control the left and right motion. The second button controls the up and down movement. The script function scrollL() in lines 14–25 is the power source. Inside this function, two for-loops (lines 21–24) are used for the animations. By increasing the value of the variable i as in line 21, you will have motion moving toward the left. By decreasing the variable i as in line 23, you will have motion moving toward the right. The up and down animations are similar and listed in lines 27–38.

The body elements of the two child pages ex08-18a.htm and ex08-18b.htm are listed in ex08-04.txt and ex08-05.txt respectively.

```
Listing: ex08-04.txt - Code Fragment For ex08-18a.htm

1: <body>
2:   <div class="mSt" style="position:absolute;left:1px;top:1px">
3:     <img src="s_04_img.jpg" alt="pic" /></div>
4:   <div class="mSt" style="position:absolute;left:350px;top:1px">
5:     <img src="s_05_img.jpg" alt="pic" /></div>
6: </body>
```

This page contains two images and arranges them horizontally with the CSS positioning method. The next page contains two vertical images. Some of the results are captured in Figs 8.25 and 8.26.

```
Listing: ex08-05.txt - Code Fragment For ex08-18b.htm

1: <body>
2:   <div class="mSt" style="position:absolute;left:1px;top:1px">
3:     <img src="s_01_img.jpg" alt="pic" /></div>
4:   <div class="mSt" style="position:absolute;left:1px;top:225px">
5:     <img src="s_06_img.jpg" alt="pic" /></div>
6: </body>
```

Figure 8.25 Left and right motion

Figure 8.26 Up and down motion

8.4.3 Browser window interaction (an XHTML interpreter)

Have you ever considered writing a Web page that can understand the XHTML language, CSS, and ECMAScript? With browser window interaction, i.e., sending data from one browser window to another, an XHTML interpreter can be developed with minimal effort.

Sending data from one window to another requires the following steps:

- Open the window.
- Open a document.
- Write data to the opened document.
- Close the document.

In terms of ECMAScript, we have:

- `newH=window.open()`
- `newH.document.open()`
- `newH.document.write("Some Data Here")`
- `newH.document.close()`

For simplicity, our XHTML interpreter is a Web page (ex08-19.htm) containing a simple interface to collect data (XHTML statements). This interface consists of two text boxes and one `textarea`. The text boxes are used to collect "Name" and "Email" address whereas the `textarea` is to collect the XHTML statements. The interface part of the page is listed as follows:

Example: ex08-19.htm – An XHTML Statement Interpreter (Part One)

```
 1: <?xml version="1.0" encoding="UTF-8"?>
 2: <!DOCTYPE html PUBLIC "-//W3C//DTD XHTML 1.0 Transitional//EN"
 3:     "http://www.w3.org/TR/xhtml1/DTD/xhtml1-transitional.dtd">
 4: <html xmlns="http://www.w3.org/1999/xhtml" xml:lang="en" lang="en">
 5: <head><title>An XHTML Interpreter - ex08-19.htm</title>
 6: <style>
 7:   .mSt{font-family:arial;font-size:12pt;font-weight:bold}
 8:   .butSt{background-color:#aaffaa;font-family:arial;font-weight:bold;
 9:       font-size:12pt;color:#ff0000;width:270px;height:30px}
10:   .areaSt{background-color:#aaffaa;font-family:arial;font-weight:bold;
11:       font-size:12pt;color:#ff0000;width:550px;height:240px}
12: </style>
13: </head>
14: <body style="background:#000088;color:#ffff00">
```

```
15:
16: <div class="mSt">An XHTML Statement Interpreter<br /><br />
17:   <table align="center">
18:     <tr class="mSt"><td>Name:</td>
19:       <td><input type="text" id="in1" name="in1" class="butSt"
20:             value="John Smith" /></td></tr>
21:     <tr class="mSt"><td>Email:</td>
22:       <td><input type="text" id="in2" name="in2" class="butSt"
23:             value="JohnSmith@isp.com" /></td></tr>
24:   </table><br />
25:   Please Enter XHTML In The Box:<br /><br />
26: </div>
27:
28: <div class="mSt" align="center">
29:   <textarea class="areaSt" rows="12" cols="50" id="com1" name="com1">
30:   </textarea><br /><br />
31: <input type="button" onclick="wPage()" value="Send Data" class="butSt" />
32: <input type="button" onclick="someSt()" value="Some Data" class="butSt" />
33: </div>
34:
```

The table defined in lines 17–24 contains two text boxes and is a simple interface used to collect data Name and Email. The textarea in lines 29–30 defines an area for the user to input XHTML statements. After the textarea, two buttons are defined. The first button "Send Data" (line 31) is used to send the XHTML statements to another browser window to be interpreted. The second button is used to create some testing data in the textarea. The programming part of this example is listed below:

Listing: Continuation Of The Page ex08-19.htm (Part Two)

```
35: <script>
36:   window.resizeTo(650,650)
37:   var newH = false
38:
39:   function someSt()
40:   {
41:    butMsg ='<div align="center">\nThis is an XHTML button<br \/>\n'+
42:      '\t<input type="button" value="My Button" \/> <br \/><br \/>'
43:    imgMsg='\nI know image too<br \/>\n'+
44:      '<img src="logo_web.jpg" width="160" height="100" alt="pic" \/>'
45:    scriptMsg='\n\n<br \/><br \/>Some ECMAScript<br \/>\n<script>\n\t'+
46:      'for(i=0;i<4;i++)\n\t document.write("Practical Web Technologies'+
47:      '<br \/>")\n <\/script>\n<\/div>'
48:    lMsg = butMsg + imgMsg + scriptMsg
49:      document.getElementById("com1").value=lMsg
50:   }
51:
52:   function writeWindow(x)
53:   {
54:    bmSt='<body style="background:#000088;font-family:arial;'+
55:      'font-size:14pt;color:#ffff00;text-align:left>"'
56:    emSt='</body>'
57:    if (!newH)
58:    {
59:    newH=window.open()
60:    newH.document.open()
61:    newH.document.write(bmSt+x+emSt)
62:    newH.document.close()
63:    } else {
64:    newH.document.open()
```

```
65:       newH.document.write(bmSt+x+emSt)
66:       newH.document.close()
67:     }
68:   }
69:
70:   function wPage()
71:   {
72:     lMsg="<div>Name: "+document.getElementById("in1").value+"<br />"+
73:       "Email: "+document.getElementById("in2").value+"<br /><br />"+
74:       "Your Testing Result: <br />"+
75:     "<img src='line1.gif' width='400' height='6' alt='pic' /><br /><br />"+
76:       document.getElementById("com1").value+"</div>"
77:       writeWindow(lMsg)
78:     }
79:   </script>
80: </body>
81: </html>
```

The wPage() function (lines 70–79) is called when the user presses the Send Data button. This function collects Name, Email, and the data in the textarea. It then calls the writeWindow() function (lines 52–68) which will open a new window and send the data as an XHTML document to that window. When the user presses the second button, Some Data, the function someSt() in lines 39–50 is called. This function generates some default data including a button, an image, and some script statements for testing. Some screen shots are shown in Figs 8.27 and 8.28.

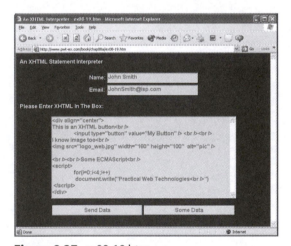

Figure 8.27 ex08-19.htm

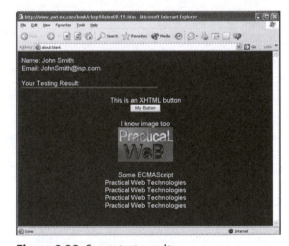

Figure 8.28 Some test results

8.4.4 Last modified property and printing a page

One of the popular document properties on the Web is the "last modified" property. This property is a string containing date and time information to remember when the page was last modified. Many Web sites use this record as a reminder as to when the page should be updated. To display this property, all you need is the code

```
<script> document.write(document.lastModified) </script>
```

Consider the following example ex08-20.htm:

```
Example: ex08-20.htm – Last Modified Property

 1: <?xml version="1.0" encoding="UTF-8"?>
 2: <!DOCTYPE html PUBLIC "-//W3C//DTD XHTML 1.0 Frameset//EN"
 3:     "http://www.w3.org/TR/xhtml1/DTD/xhtml1-frameset.dtd">
```

```
 4: <html xmlns="http://www.w3.org/1999/xhtml" xml:lang="en" lang="en">
 5: <head><title> Last Modified Property - ex08-20.htm </title></head>
 6: <style>
 7:    .mSt{font-family:arial;font-size:18pt;font-weight:bold;color:#00ffff}
 8: </style>
 9:
10: <body style="background:#000088;text-align:center">
11: <div class="mSt" style="font-size:10pt;color:#ffff00;text-align:right">
12:    Last Modified At:<br />
13:    <script> document.write(document.lastModified) </script><br /><br />
14: </div>
15: <div class="mSt" >Practical Web Technologies<br />
16:    This Page Has A Last Modified Date </div>
17: </body>
18: </html>
```

This page has the "last modified" date and time attached at the top right hand corner as indicated in lines 11–14 (see Fig. 8.29).

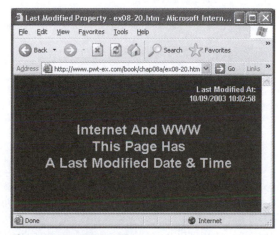

Figure 8.29 ex08-20.htm

Occasionally, you may want to control the printing of a page yourself. This is true particularly when you deal with multiple windows or a window with no menu bar available. The command to print is a method of the window object and can be activated by the coding

```
<script> window.print() </script>
```

This function calls the printing facilities of your system (operating system) and therefore is independent of the printing devices. To deal with multiple windows, the window.print() can be replaced by the window handle (e.g., newH.print()). Consider the following example:

```
Example: ex08-21.htm - Printing A Page
 1: <?xml version="1.0" encoding="UTF-8"?>
 2: <!DOCTYPE html PUBLIC "-//W3C//DTD XHTML 1.0 Frameset//EN"
 3:      "http://www.w3.org/TR/xhtml1/DTD/xhtml1-frameset.dtd">
 4: <html xmlns="http://www.w3.org/1999/xhtml" xml:lang="en" lang="en">
 5: <head><title> Printing A Page - ex08-21.htm </title></head>
 6: <style>
 7:    .mSt{font-family:arial;font-size:18pt;font-weight:bold;color:#00ffff}
 8:    .bSt{background-color:#aaffaa;font-family:arial;font-weight:bold;
 9:         font-size:12pt;color:#ff0000;width:200px;height:30px}
10: </style>
```

```
11: <body style="background:#000088;text-align:center">
12:
13: <script>
14:   window.resizeTo(400,360)
15:   lookSt="menubar=no,toolbar=no,status=no,resizable=yes,"+
16:       "scrollbars=yes,width=380,height=250"
17:
18:   newH1=window.open("s_02_img.jpg","win1",lookSt)
19:   newH2=window.open("s_06_img.jpg","win2",lookSt)
20:   newH3=window.open("s_07_img.jpg","win3",lookSt)
21:
22:   function imgPr(varL)
23:   {
24:     if (varL ==1) newH1.print()
25:     if (varL ==2) newH2.print()
26:     if (varL ==3) newH3.print()
27:   }
28: </script>
29:
30: <div class="mSt">
31:   Printing Control Page<br />Press The Button To Print<br /><br />
32: </div>
33: <input type="button" class="bSt" value="Peacock"
34:     onclick="imgPr(1)" /><br />
35: <input type="button" class="bSt" value="Wild Duck"
36:     onclick="imgPr(2)" /><br />
37: <input type="button" class="bSt" value="Eagle"
38:     onclick="imgPr(3)" />
39: </body>
40: </html>
```

After the window format string defined in line 15, three child windows are opened. Each window has a picture inside and is associated with a window handle (lines 18–20). These handles are used inside the print function imgPr() in lines 22–27 to identify the picture and print. In this case, three buttons (lines 33–38) are used to control the printing process. When the first button, Peacock, is pressed (Fig. 8.30), the function imgPr(1) is called. The argument 1 activates the first function newH1.print() in line 24. The standard print window appears as in Fig. 8.31. From this print window you can select your printer and other settings. When the Print button is pressed, the selected picture will be printed.

Figure 8.30 ex08-21.htm

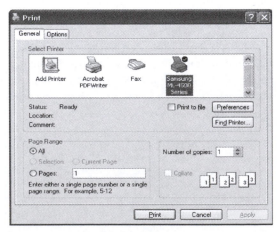

Figure 8.31 The print window

9 Programming moving objects

9.1 An introduction to moving objects

Programming moving objects on the Web is the art of combining various Web technologies. It is the first step toward the goal of creating sophisticated dynamic pages. In general, we consider an XHTML page as dynamic if its content contains dynamic programming or features. Under this broad definition, almost all examples and XHTML pages in this book are dynamic. Moving objects are certainly one of them. Some people may see the contents of this chapter more as Dynamic HTML (DHTML). Since DHTML is not a standard defined by the W3C authority or anyone else, we don't want to create yet another keyword here. Instead our discussion will concentrate on the construction of moving objects and how to program them.

The term object in this chapter represents any XHTML entity including texts and/or images displayable on a Web page. To many of us, programming moving objects is a combination, and practical use, of the

- Extensible Hyper Text Markup Language (XHTML)
- Cascading Style Sheet (CSS)
- Document Object Model (DOM)
- European Computer Manufacturers Association Script (ECMAScript)

XHTML provides a rich set of tools and methods for you to create instant documents and objects on the Web. With CSS, you can organize and manipulate the positions and properties as well as styles of an XHTML page. With the DOM, you can have a full picture of a Web page and a vital link between the scripting language and page elements. For example, you can use the DOM function `getElementById()` to access all XHTML elements. By using ECMAScript, you can access and manipulate objects and elements in a page in real time via the DOM. By combining all these technologies together, you have endless possibilities to create dynamic features on Web pages.

Before the detailed discussion on programming moving objects, a review of how to use the CSS positions is essential.

9.1.1 Positioning objects with CSS style

Along with the display, look, and formatting properties, another great strength of the CSS style is to provide position and accurate measurements on objects or entities defined on a page. For example, you can use the following CSS properties to define an object with position and dimension:

```
Listing: ex09-01.txt - Position Properties In CSS

1: <div name="myObject" id="myObject"
2:    style="position: absolute;
3:           top: 40px;
4:           left: 100px;
5:           height: 50px;
```

```
 6:            width: 200px;
 7:            font-family: arial;
 8:            font-size: 18pt;
 9:            color:#ffff00;
10:            background:#000088">
11:   This is a paragraph located at 40 pixels from the top and 100 pixels
12:   from the left.
13:   </div>
```

In this example, the division <div> element is used to define an object. In fact most XHTML elements with an identity and CSS capabilities can also be used to define an object on the Web. In this case, the object is a paragraph with its own font family, font size, color, and background color (lines 7–10). The more interesting part of this example is the position properties defined in lines 2–6. The first position property

```
position: absolute;
```

instructs the browser to use an absolute measurement for all positions inside this object. Under absolute measurement, the top left corner of the browser screen has the coordinates (0, 0). That is, top=0px (pixel) and left=0px. The statements in lines 3 and 4

```
top:40px; left:100px;
```

define a location as (40, 100) pixels from the top left corner of the browser screen. The dimension statements in lines 5 and 6

```
height:50px; width:200px;
```

specify a rectangular area 50 × 200 (height × width) for the object, and thus all other CSS properties will be restricted and applied only to this area.

Note that px is used here to specify the measurement in pixels. Other scale units such as pt (points), in (inches), and cm (centimeters) can also be used.

The CSS position and dimension properties are the basic elements to define an object. As you will see in this chapter, you can use the basic position and dimension descriptions such as top, left, height, and width to create moving objects and dynamic pages.

To help understand how to program objects, we first consider a page with fixed objects. Then the motion is just a matter of changing their positions continuously. Consider the page

```
Example: ex09-01.htm - Object Positioning

 1: <?xml version="1.0" encoding="iso-8859-1"?>
 2: <!DOCTYPE html PUBLIC "-//W3C//DTD XHTML 1.0 Transitional//EN"
 3:     "http://www.w3.org/TR/xhtml1/DTD/xhtml1-transitional.dtd">
 4: <html xmlns="http://www.w3.org/1999/xhtml" xml:lang="en" lang="en">
 5: <head><title> Object Positioning - ex09-01.htm </title></head>
 6: <body style="background:#000088;font-family:arial;font-size:28pt;
 7:   color:#ffff00;font-weight:bold;text-align:center">
 8: <div align="center">
 9:   Object Positioning with <br /> CSS Sheets</div>
10:
11:   <div name="myObj1" id="myObj1"
12:     style="position: absolute;
13:        top: 120px;
14:       left: 40px;
15:       height: 130px;
16:       width: 250px;
17:     background: #ffffff;
18:       color: #000000;
19:     font-size: 20px;
20:     font-family: Times">
21:   My first object is at<br />
22:     top: 120px <br /> left: 40px <br />
```

```
23:    height:130px <br /> width: 250px </div>
24:
25: <div name="myObj2" id="myObj2"
26:   style="position: absolute;
27:      top: 350px;
28:      left: 400px;
29:      height: 160px;
30:      width: 290px;
31:      background: #ffff00;
32:      color: #880000;
33:      font-size: 24px;
34:      font-family: Times">
35: My second object is at<br />
36: top: 350px <br /> left: 440px <br />
37: height:160px <br /> width: 290px</div>
38:
39: <div name="myObj3" id="myObj3"
40:      style="position:        absolute;
41:      top: 180px;
42:      left: 330px;
43:      height: 140px;
44:      width: 200px;
45:      background:    #aaffaa;
46:      color: #880000;
47:      font-size:     24px;
48:      font-family:    Times">
49:   My Logo<br />
50:   <img src="logo_web.jpg" alt="pic" height="90" width="140" /></div>
51:
52: </div>
53: </body>
54: </html>
```

In this page, inline CSS is used to define three styles, with independent positions and dimensions. Each style specifies an object's properties. Object 1 with identity myObj1 is a paragraph and has a starting location at coordinates (120 ,40) pixels in (top, left) format. Object 2 is similar to object 1 but with different CSS settings. Object 3 contains an image with its own dimension control. The image logo_web.jpg is first rescaled into the dimension as defined in line 50 and then the entire object is restricted by the CSS settings. A screen shot of this page is given in Fig. 9.1.

You now have some static objects. To move them is just a matter of changing their position continuously in real time.

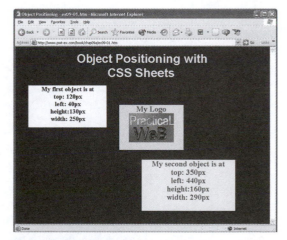

Figure 9.1 ex09-01.htm

9.1.2 Some moving texts

The central idea for moving objects is to manipulate the top and left properties of the CSS style. Due to proprietary features and various types of incompatibilities among browsers, Web programmers in the past have struggled to find a unified way to change the (top, left) coordinates of an object. Also it was no surprise to find that even different versions of the same browser could have some form of incompatibilities. Thanks to the standardization of the CSS, DOM, and W3C, it is now possible to develop more reliable and compatible Web applications as long as the standards are followed. The following example shows a page with moving texts. Since we follow standard recommendations, this page will work on all W3C-compliant browsers without the need for any detection. This page is listed in ex09-02.htm.

Example: ex09-02.htm - Some Moving Texts

```
 1: <?xml version="1.0" encoding="iso-8859-1"?>
 2: <!DOCTYPE html PUBLIC "-//W3C//DTD XHTML 1.0 Transitional//EN"
 3:     "http://www.w3.org/TR/xhtml1/DTD/xhtml1-transitional.dtd">
 4: <html xmlns="http://www.w3.org/1999/xhtml" xml:lang="en" lang="en">
 5: <head><title> Some Moving Texts - ex09-02.htm</title></head>
 6: <body style="background:#000088;font-family:arial;font-size:28pt;
 7:   color:#ffff00;font-weight:bold;text-align:center">
 8: <div align="center">Some Moving Texts <br /></div>
 9:
10:  <div name="myObj1" id="myObj1"
11:   style="position: absolute;
12:         top: 120px;
13:         left: 40px;
14:         height: 100px;
15:         width: 250px;
16:         background: #ffffff;
17:         color: #000000;
18:         font-size: 20px;
19:         font-family: Times">
20:   My first object has dimension<br />
21:   height: 100px <br /> width: 250px</div>
22:
23:  <div id="myObj2" id="myObj2"
24:   style="position: absolute;
25:         top: 280px;
26:         left: 200px;
27:         height: 100px;
28:         width: 290px;
29:         background: #ffff00;
30:         color: #880000;
31:         font-size: 24px;
32:         font-family: Times">
33:   My second object has dimension<br />
34:   height: 100px <br /> width: 290px</div>
35:
36: <script>
37: var ixDelta = 5
38: var iyDelta = 5
39: var lxPos = 0
40: var lyPos = 0
41:
42: function MoveLeft()
43: {
44:  lxPos = parseInt(document.getElementById("myObj1").style.left)+ixDelta
45:  if (lxPos >= 400 || lxPos < 0) ixDelta = ixDelta * -1
46:  document.getElementById("myObj1").style.left = lxPos + "px"
47: }
48:
49: function MoveUp()
50: {
51:  lyPos = parseInt(document.getElementById("myObj2").style.top)+iyDelta
52:  if (lyPos >= 320 || lyPos < 0) iyDelta = iyDelta * -1
53:  document.getElementById("myObj2").style.top = lyPos + "px"
```

```
54: }
55:
56: setInterval("MoveLeft();MoveUp()",50)
57: </script>
58: </body>
59: </html>
```

The two objects myObj1 and myObj2 are first defined in lines 10–34. These two paragraphs of text have independent CSS positions and settings. The script section (lines 36–57) contains two functions, MoveLeft() and MoveUp(). The first script function MoveLeft() moves the object myObj1 to the left and right. The second one moves the object myObj2 up and down. In order to make the texts move, you need to call these two functions continuously for a certain time interval. The function setInterval() in line 56 instructs the browser to call these two functions simultaneously every 50 milliseconds.

Consider the function MoveLeft() (i.e., move the object to the left and right-hand side):

```
function MoveLeft()
{
 lxPos = parseInt(document.getElementById("myObj1").style.left)+ixDelta
 if (lxPos >= 400 || lxPos < 0) ixDelta = ixDelta * -1
 document.getElementById("myObj1").style.left = lxPos + "px"
}
```

This function has only three lines. The first line is to get the left location of the object myObj1, increment by ixDelta, and assign the value to a local variable lxPos (i.e., local *x*-position). If this lxPos value is 400 or more, or alternatively less than 0, the sign of the increment ixDelta is changed so that the movement of the text changes direction. The final line of this function is to assign the value of lxPos to the left position of the object myObj1, so that new position can be updated.

According to the W3C standard, the position (top and left) and dimension (height and width) values should have a measurement unit attached to them. This is why the pixel unit "px" is added at the end of the function. Some browsers may perform the page and action correctly even without the pixel unit, but they are not W3C standard compliant. Some browsers such as NS6+ (NS6.0 and NS6.1) will not function correctly without them. Also, since the CSS value or data stored in the property document.getElementById("myObj1").style.left have a pixel unit, you need to use a function parseInt() to parse the value and convert it to an integer as illustrated in the first line of the function.

The up and down function MoveUp() in lines 49–54 also contains only three statements. The statements are similar to those discussed above. This page works on all W3C-compliant browsers and a screen shot of this page in action is shown in Fig. 9.2.

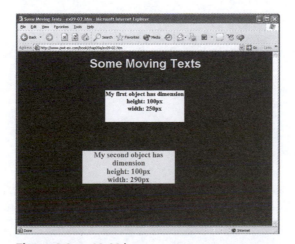

Figure 9.2 ex09-02.htm

9.1.3 **Screen depth and** `z-index`

While the top and left values define a 2D coordinate system of a Web page, you can use another CSS property called the z-index to specify the screen depth. In fact, the z-index is a stack order to determine whether an object should be in front of or behind another object. Consider the following example:

```
Example: ex09-03.htm - Screen Depth And Z-index

 1: <?xml version="1.0" encoding="iso-8859-1"?>
 2: <!DOCTYPE html PUBLIC "-//W3C//DTD XHTML 1.0 Transitional//EN"
 3:    "http:/+www*w3.org/TR/xhtml1/DTD/xhtml1-transitional.dtd">
 4: <html xmlns="http://www.w3.org/1999/xhtml" xml:lang="en" lang="en">
 5: <head><title> Screen Depth and Z-index - ex09-03.htm </title></head>
 6: <body style="background:#000088;font-family:arial;font-size:28pt;
 7:    color:#ffff00;font-weight:bold;text-align:center">
 8: <div align="center">Screen Depth and Z-index</div>
 9: <div style="font-size:18pt" id="xyPos" name="xyPos"></div>
10:
11: <div id="frontPic" name="frontPic"
12:    style="position: absolute;
13:          top: 100px;
14:          left: 140px;
15:          height: 300px;
16:          width: 140px;
17:          color: white;
18:          text-align: center;
19:          background: red;
20:          font-size:18pt;
21:          font-weight: bold;
22:          z-index: 4">
23: <b>Front Pic<br /> Z-index= 4</div>
24:
25: <div id="backPic" name="backPic"
26:    style="position: absolute;
27:          top: 100px;
28:          left: 360px;
29:          height: 300px;
30:          width: 140px;
31:          color: white;
32:          text-align: center;
33:          background: blue;
34:          font-size: 18pt;
35:          font-weight: bold;
36:          z-index: 2">
37: <b>Back Pic<br /> Z-index=2</div>
38:
39: <div id="middlePic" name="middlePic"
40:    style="position: absolute;
41:          top: 120px;
42:          left: 0px;
43:          height: 230px;
44:          width: 200;
45:          color: #ffff00;
46:          text-align: center;
47:          font-size: 20pt;
48:          font-weight: bold;
49:          z-index: 3">
50: Pumkin Head <br>Middle Pic<br><img src="pumkin.gif" alt="pic" /></div>
51:
52: <script>
53: var ixDelta = 5;
54: function MoveLeft()
```

```
55: {
56:    lxPos = parseInt(document.getElementById("middlePic").style.left)+ixDelta
57:    if (lxPos >= 400 || lxPos < 0) ixDelta = ixDelta * -1
58:    document.getElementById("xyPos").innerHTML="(top,left) = (120,"+lxPos+")"
59:    document.getElementById("middlePic").style.left = lxPos + "px"
60: }
61: setInterval ("MoveLeft()",50)
62: </script>
63: </body>
64: </html>
```

This example contains three pictures, namely, frontPic, backPic, and a moving image middlePic. Each of them has a z-index value as one of the CSS properties. A z-index value is a stack order, which means that a bigger value will be on top of smaller values just like a stack. These front and back features should be clearer if you animate the middle image middlePic by calling the script function MoveLeft() as defined in lines 54–61. This function is basically the same as that in example ex09-02.htm to move the object in the left and right directions. The image itself is an animated gif file. You will have a more realistic animation effect if you can combine animated gif with motion. The additional statement in line 58 is used to output the (top, left) coordinates to xyPos as defined in line 9. As the middle image moves, the coordinates are updated continuously. A screen shot of this page in action is shown in Fig. 9.3.

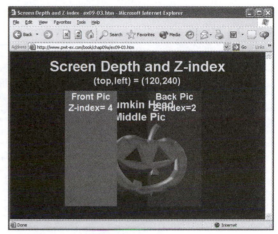

Figure 9.3 ex09-03.htm

We now have some ideas on moving objects and how to program them. In real applications, the ultimate goal is the ability to control objects with user interrogations, and to develop stunning dynamic Web pages. In fact, you may recall that Chapter 6 of this book was devoted to the discussion of mouseover control and how to program XHTML page dynamically. From mouseover techniques to the control of browser windows, they are all examples of dynamic features. These techniques can be used to advance our study of moving objects. For example, a combination of mouse techniques and moving objects is very popular. They have an important impact on a number of entertainment industries, including games on the Web. In order to advance the discussion on these subjects and be able to interface with hardware, we begin with mouse event and event handlers.

9.2 Controlling objects with event handlers

You've already encountered some examples of mouse events and mouse control in Chapter 6. These examples are just special cases of event handlers.

An event handler is basically a software tool used to handle application events that are generated normally by hardware devices such as the keyboard and mouse. For example, when a mouse runs over an object on a Web page, the browser will generate a mouse-over event. If you have the onmouseover handler installed, it will be triggered and perform appropriate actions (script statements or functions) designed by the author. An event model is the internal structure of a browser dealing with how an event handler is handled. Since events can be intercepted by handlers at any level, different event models may produce different results. This type of inconsistency could be quite difficult to find and correct. For Web programmers, special care is necessary when setting up general event handlers, as compatibility, especially backward browser compatibility, is an important issue. More details on event models are given later in section 9.3. For now, let's consider some event handlers and get ready for some action.

9.2.1   Basic event handlers

Both IE and NS provide a rich set of event handlers to cover most hardware events. Most of them are the same and follow the W3C standard. However, they all have their own extensions to include new features and to ensure some sort of backward compatibility with their own kind. The standard W3C event document is big, so even to provide a listing of all the commands and specifications is beyond the scope of this chapter. In this section, we classify some frequently used and widely supported event handlers into three categories, namely, "Mouse and Keyboard," "Document and Browser Window," and "Form-Related" event handlers. The mouse and keyboard event commands are listed in Table 9.1.

Table 9.1 Mouse and keyboard event handlers

Command	Description
onclick	The pointing device has been clicked
ondblclick	The pointing device has been double clicked
onmousedown	The pointing device button has just been pressed
onmouseup	The pointing device button has just been released
onmouseover	The pointing device enters the bounds of an element from outside the element
onmousemove	The pointing device was moved within the boundary of the element
onmouseout	The pointing device was moved out of the boundary of the element
onkeypress	A keyboard key is pressed and released for an element that has focus
onkeydown	A keyboard key is depressed for an element that has focus
onkeyup	A keyboard key is released for an element that has focus

These commands are frequently used in all aspects of Web programming. One good example is in the use of buttons such as

```
<input type="button" onclick="anotherFunction()">
```

Another example is to change an image when the mouse runs over it:

```
<img src="img01.gif" name="myImg" id="myImg"
   onmouseover='document.getElementById("myImg").src="img02.gif"' />
```

These are our old friends and used everywhere on the Web. Together with the mouse and keyboard, you also need some event commands to control how the document should be loaded and how the browser window should behave. In many cases, these event controls are used inside the body element to monitor the behavior of the browser window to see, for example, whether or when

- the browser window has been moved;
- the window/object has been resized;
- the window scroll bar position has been changed etc.

The event commands are listed in Table 9.2.

Table 9.2 Document and browser windows event handlers

Command	Description
onabort	Image downloading has been interrupted
onbeforeunload	The page is about to be unloaded from its current context
onerror	An error has occurred during the loading of external page dependencies or during the processing of a script
onload	The document or other external dependency has finished loading to the browser
onmove	The browser window has been moved
onresize	The window/object has been resized
onscroll	The window/object has been scrolled
onstop	The element's scroll bar position has been changed
onunload	The page is unloading from its current context

Other popular handlers on the Web are the form control handlers. They are used to control the effects of a form such as submission and validation (see Table 9.3).

Table 9.3 Form-related event handlers

Command	Description
onblur	The current element has lost focus (by keyboard tabbing or mouse)
onchange	The current element has lost focus (by keyboard or mouse) and the element's contents have changed
onfocus	The element has received focus
onreset	A form's Reset button has been activated
onsubmit	A form's submittal process is beginning

Again, there are many more event handlers available on both the IE and NS. For practical purposes, these built-in handlers are standard, widely used, and handy tools for many Web programming situations.

Event handlers play an essential part in any interactive programming on the Web. They are the vital links between XHTML, scripting languages, and your hardware devices to provide real-time interactions between the user and your Web page. Let's now look at some examples.

9.2.2   A page to capture and test various events

To demonstrate the idea and to put some of the handlers into action, a page is developed to show how to handle some keyboard, mouse, and browser window events. This page can also be used to test the capability of browsers on handling hardware events. Consider the page ex09-04.htm below:

```
Example: ex09-04.htm - A Page To Test Various Events

 1: <?xml version="1.0" encoding="iso-8859-1"?>
 2: <!DOCTYPE html PUBLIC "-//W3C//DTD XHTML 1.0 Transitional//EN"
 3:     "http://www.w3.org/TR/xhtml1/DTD/xhtml1-transitional.dtd">
 4: <html xmlns="http://www.w3.org/1999/xhtml" xml:lang="en" lang="en">
 5: <head><title> A Page To Test Various Events - ex09-04.htm </title></head>
 6:
 7: <body style="background:#000088;font-family:arial;font-size:28pt;
 8:     color:#ffff00;font-weight:bold;text-align:center"
 9:   onmousedown="events(1)"
10:   onmouseup="events(2)"
11:   onkeydown="events(3)"
12:   onkeyup="events(4)"
13:   ondblclick="events(5)"
14:   onresize="events(6)"
15:   onscroll="events(7)"
16: >
17: <div align="center">Basic Event Handlers</div><br />
18:   <table style="font-size:18pt"><tr><td width="200">
19:         onmousedown()</td><td width="200">onmouseup</td></tr>
20:     <tr><td>onkeydown()</td><td>onkeyup()</td></tr>
21:     <tr><td>onresize()</td><td>onscroll()</td></tr>
22:   </table><br />
23: <div style="font-size:18pt;color:#00ff00"
24:   id="eventMsg" name="eventMsg"></div><br />
25: <div style="font-size:18pt">One of the above events has
26:   been captured.The event message is displayed in green color.<br />
27:
28: <script>
29:   Msg = new Array()
30:   Msg[1]="A mouse button is down."
31:   Msg[2]="A mouse button has just been released."
32:   Msg[3]="A keyboard key has been pressed."
33:   Msg[4]="A keyboard key has been released."
34:   Msg[5]="The mouse has been double-clicked."
35:   Msg[6]="The window has been resized."
36:   Msg[7]="The window scrollbar position has been changed."
37:
38:   function events(msgId)
39:   {
40:     document.getElementById("eventMsg").innerHTML=Msg[msgId]
41:   }
42: </script>
43: </body>
44: </html>
```

You can call this page a dedicated event tester since its only real function is to trap events. In order to capture the event on the entire page, we put the handlers inside the body element. There are six of them as illustrated in lines 9–15. The first handler is

```
onmousedown="events(1)"
```

This command captures the moment when you hold down a mouse button inside the page. The event triggers the function `events()` with argument "1." This function (lines 38–41) has only one statement and that is to output the message `Msg[1]` to the location with `id="eventMsg"`. The message `Msg[1]` is defined in line 30 and you will see a message "A mouse button is down." on the screen. This mouse-down handler will be used later to catch and hold a flying object. A screen shot of this event is shown in Fig. 9.4. Some other events have also been captured and are shown in Figs 9.5–9.7.

Figure 9.4 ex09-04.htm

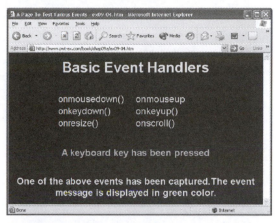

Figure 9.5 Key pressed

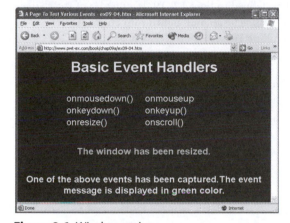

Figure 9.6 Window resize

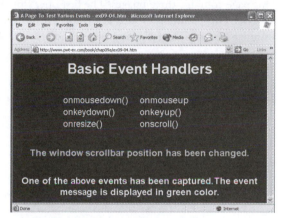

Figure 9.7 Window scroll

9.2.3 Some jumping characters

To apply handlers to moving objects, let's consider a simple example with jumping characters. This page contains three characters "W," "e," and "B," in image format. When a mouse click or a key press event occurs, some of the characters will move. Some simple controls are also added in this page so that the same event may trigger different motions. The code of this page is listed in ex09-05.htm.

```
Example: ex09-05.htm - Jumping Characters

 1: <?xml version="1.0" encoding="iso-8859-1"?>
 2: <!DOCTYPE html PUBLIC "-//W3C//DTD XHTML 1.0 Transitional//EN"
 3:     "http://www.w3.org/TR/xhtml1/DTD/xhtml1-transitional.dtd">
 4: <html xmlns="http://www.w3.org/1999/xhtml" xml:lang="en" lang="en">
 5: <head><title> Jumping Characters - ex09-05.htm </title></head>
 6:
 7: <script src="ex09-05.js"></script>
 8: <body style="background:#dddddd;font-family:arial;font-size:28pt;
 9:     color:#000088;font-weight:bold;text-align:center"
10:   onclick="selectAction()" onkeypress="selectAction()">
11:
12: <div align="center">Jumping Characters<br />
13:  <span style="font-size:18pt;color:#880000">Click Left Mouse Or
```

```
14:    <br /> Press Keyboard </span>
15:  </div>
16:
17:  <div id="char01" name="char01"
18:     style="position: absolute;top: 300px;left: 50px">
19:   <img src="sspic01.gif" alt="pic" height="130" width="130" /></div>
20:
21:  <div id="char02" name="char02"
22:     style="position: absolute;top: 330px;left: 160px">
23:   <img src="sspic02.gif" alt="pic" height="100" width="100" /></div>
24:
25:  <div id="char03" name="char03"
26:      style="position: absolute;top: 310px;left: 255px">
27:   <img src="sspic03.gif" alt="pic" height="120" width="120" /></div>
28:
29:  </body>
30:  </html>
```

This page contains three images. The first one, sspic01.gif as defined in lines 17–19, is a picture of the character "W." This picture is located at the top left position (300, 50). The second and third pictures are defined in a similar pattern. The following event handlers are defined in line 10:

```
onclick="selectAction()" onkeypress="selectAction()"
```

This statement captures any mouse click or key press event and triggers the function selectAction() as defined in an external file ex09-05.js. The listing of this file is

Example: ex09-05.js – The ECMAScript For ex09-05.htm

```
 1: function mChar03()
 2: {
 3:  var ixDelta = 20
 4:  var iyDelta = -35
 5:  lxPos = parseInt(document.getElementById("char03").style.left)+ixDelta
 6:  lyPos = parseInt(document.getElementById("char03").style.top)+iyDelta
 7:  if (lxPos >= 400 || lyPos < 10)
 8:  {
 9:    lxPos=250
10:    lyPos=310
11:  document.getElementById("char03").style.left = lxPos + "px"
12:  document.getElementById("char03").style.top = lyPos + "px"
13:  return
14:  }
15:  document.getElementById("char03").style.left = lxPos + "px"
16:  document.getElementById("char03").style.top = lyPos + "px"
17:  setTimeout("mChar03()",50)
18: }
19:
20: var ixDelta2 =-0.2
21: function mChar01()
22: {
23:  ixDelta2 = 0.2 + ixDelta2
24:
25:  lxPos = -150 * Math.cos(ixDelta2) + 200
26:  lyPos= -150* Math.sin(ixDelta2) + 300
27:
28:  if (lxPos >= 400 || lyPos > 300)
29:  {
30:    lxPos= 50
31:    lyPos=300
```

```
32:    ixDelta2 =-0.2
33:  document.getElementById("char01").style.left = lxPos + "px"
34:  document.getElementById("char01").style.top = lyPos + "px"
35:  return true
36:  }
37:  document.getElementById("char01").style.left = lxPos + "px"
38:  document.getElementById("char01").style.top = lyPos + "px"
39:  setTimeout("mChar01()",50)
40: }
41:
42: var sAction=1
43: function selectAction()
44: {
45:  if (sAction ==1){
46:        sAction = 2
47:        mChar03()
48:  } else {
49:        sAction = 1
50:        mChar01()
51:  }
52: }
```

The selectAction() function in lines 42–52 of this file is actually a controller used to decide which object should be animated. If the variable sAction equals 1, the function mChar03() is called to animate the "B" picture. Otherwise the mChar01() function is called to move the "W" picture. The swap use of the sAction allows you to have different animations every time an event occurs.

The motion inside the function mChar03() is in a straight line. By adding the following top and left values to the (top, left) coordinates of the object in each step

```
iyDelta = -35              top value

ixDelta = 20               left value
```

a constant movement is achieved and generates a straight line motion effect. The function mChar01() defined in lines 21–40 is a circular motion. The basic equations defining the motion are

```
Y = R * cos (t)            top value

X = R * sin (t)            left value
```

where variable R is the radius and t is time. In terms of programming, we have

```
ixDelta2 = 0.2 + ixDelta2                   (i.e. variable t)
lyPos= -150 * Math.sin(ixDelta2) + 300      (i.e. variable Y)
lxPos = -150 * Math.cos(ixDelta2) + 200     (i.e. variable X)
```

We have used the radius R=150 in this case. The negative values of the radius and the translation at the end of the equations are used to adjust the motion so that the picture "W" appears to jump from the front to the back. The clipping conditional statement in line 28 is to make sure that the object moves back to its original position after the jump. This function is called regularly once every 50 milliseconds to create realistic motion until one of the clipping conditions is satisfied.

Since the event handlers react quicker than the setTimeout() function, if you press two keys simultaneously you will see two characters move together. Some screen shots are given in Figs 9.8 and 9.9.

The next example shows how to select and drive multiple objects by using the mouse.

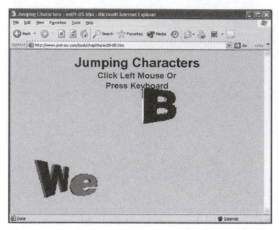

Figure 9.8 ex09-05.htm

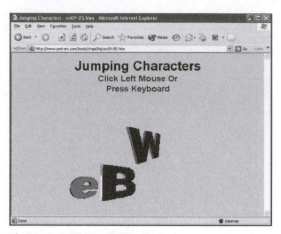

Figure 9.9 Picture "W" jumps

9.2.4   Selecting and driving objects with the mouse

Another basic technique of moving objects is to guide an object, or entity, with a mouse click. When you click your mouse, the selected object will go to your mouse point. To illustrate this technique, the images in the previous example are used as objects and some buttons are added so that a selection can be made. The XHTML interface program is listed in ex09-06.htm.

Example: ex09-06.htm - Picking And Driving Objects

```
 1: <?xml version="1.0" encoding="iso-8859-1"?>
 2: <!DOCTYPE html PUBLIC "-//W3C//DTD XHTML 1.0 Transitional//EN"
 3:    "http://www.w3.org/TR/xhtml1/DTD/xhtml1-transitional.dtd">
 4: <html xmlns="http://www.w3.org/1999/xhtml" xml:lang="en" lang="en">
 5: <head><title> Picking and Driving Objects - ex09-06.htm </title></head>
 6: <style>
 7:   .butSt{background-color:#aaffaa;font-family:arial;font-weight:bold;
 8:      font-size:16pt;color:#880000;width:180px;height:40px}</style>
 9: <script src="ex09-06.js"></script>
10: <body style="background:#dddddd;font-family:arial;font-size:28pt;
11:      color:#000088;font-weight:bold;text-align:center" >
12:
13: <div align="center">Select & Drive Objects With Mouse <br />
14:  <span style="font-size:18pt;color:#880000">Click Mouse To Drive Object
15:  <br /> Press Button To Make Selection</span></div>
16:
17: <div id="char01" name="char01"
18:     style="position: absolute;top: 300px;left: 50px">
19:     <img src="sspic01.gif" alt="pic" id="imgW" name="imgW"
20:     height="130" width="130" /></div>
21: <div id="char02" name="char02"
22:     style="position: absolute;top: 330px;left: 160px">
23:     <img src="sspic02.gif" alt="pic" id="imgE" name="imgE"
24:     height="100" width="100" /></div>
25: <div id="char03" name="char03"
26:     style="position: absolute;top: 310px;left: 255px">
27:     <img src="sspic03.gif" alt="pic" id="imgB" name="imgB"
28:     height="120" width="120" /></div>
29:
```

```
30: <input type="button" class="butSt"
31:     style="position: absolute;top:180px;left:450px"
32:     value="Move W" onclick="buttonClk(1)" />
33: <input type="button" class="butSt"
34:     style="position: absolute;top:230px;left:450px"
35:     value="Move e" onclick="buttonClk(2)" />
36: <input type="button" class="butSt"
37:     style="position: absolute;top:280px;left:450px"
38:     value="Move B" onclick="buttonClk(3)" />
39: <input type="button" class="butSt"
40:     style="position: absolute;top:330px;left:450px"
41:     value="Reset Pictures" onclick="resetPic()" />
42: </body>
43: </html>
```

The first part of this page (lines 17–28) is basically the same as that in example ex09-05.htm to define three images, "W," "e," and "B." The second part in lines 30–41 defines four buttons. The first button (lines 30–32)

```
<input type="button" class="butSt"
    style="position: absolute;top:180px;left:450px"
    value="Move W" onclick="buttonClk(1)" />
```

is located at the top left coordinate (180, 450) and has the name "Move W." When this button is pressed, the function buttonClk(1) is called and changes the selected object to "W." Therefore the motion applies to the new selected object. The second (lines 33–35) and the third buttons (lines 36–38) are defined in a similar fashion. The last button activates the function resetPic() to restore all three pictures to their original position.

If a mouse click takes place on the page, but not on the buttons, the function mouseClk() is executed to drive the selected object to the mouse point, creating a motion effect. Both buttonClk() and mouseClk() functions are defined in the external script function ex09-06.js. Before the program is listed, some screen shots are shown in Figs 9.10 and 9.11.

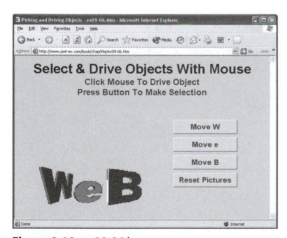

Figure 9.10 ex09-06.htm

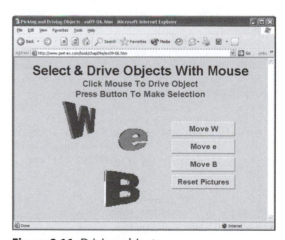

Figure 9.11 Driving objects

The external script file ex09-06.js is listed as follows:

```
Example: ex09-06.js - The ECMAScript For ex09-06.htm

1: var IE=document.all?true:false
2: if (!IE) document.captureEvents(Event.CLICK)
3: document.onclick=mouseClk
4:
5: var lxPos0=0
```

```
 6: var lyPos0=0
 7: var lxPos1=0
 8: var lyPos1=0
 9:
10: var iTDelta=0
11: var selectObj="char01"
12: var working =0
13: var objWidth=55
14: var objHeight=55
15:
16: function mAction()
17: {
18:  if (working ==0)
19:  {
20:   iTDelta = iTDelta + 0.1
21:   lxPos = (1-iTDelta) * lxPos0 + iTDelta * lxPos1 - objWidth
22:   lyPos = (1-iTDelta) * lyPos0 + iTDelta * lyPos1 - objHeight
23:
24:   if (iTDelta > 1) return true
25:
26:   document.getElementById(selectObj).style.left = lxPos + "px"
27:   document.getElementById(selectObj).style.top = lyPos + "px"
28:   setTimeout("mAction()",10)
29:  }
30: }
31:
32: function resetPic()
33: {
34:  working =1
35:   document.getElementById("char01").style.top = 300 + "px"
36:   document.getElementById("char01").style.left = 50 + "px"
37:   document.getElementById("char02").style.top = 330 + "px"
38:   document.getElementById("char02").style.left = 160 + "px"
39:   document.getElementById("char03").style.top = 310 + "px"
40:   document.getElementById("char03").style.left = 255 + "px"
41: }
42:
43: function buttonClk(objNo)
44: {
45:   working =1
46:   if (objNo ==1) selectObj="char01"
47:   if (objNo ==2) selectObj="char02"
48:   if (objNo ==3) selectObj="char03"
49: }
50:
51: function mouseClk(e)
52: {
53:  if (working ==0)
54:  {
55:
56:   lxPos0 = parseInt(document.getElementById(selectObj).style.left) +
57:           objWidth
58:   lyPos0 = parseInt(document.getElementById(selectObj).style.top) +
59:           objHeight
60:
61:   if (IE) {
62:      lxPos1 = event.clientX
63:      lyPos1 = event.clientY
```

```
64:    } else {
65:        lxPos1 = e.pageX
66:        lyPos1 = e.pageY
67:    }
68:    iTDelta = -0.1
69:    mAction()
70:    } else {
71:    working =0
72:    }
73: }
```

If any one of the first three buttons is pressed, the button click function `buttonClk()` is activated to select the target object. For example, if the Move e button is pressed, the function `buttonClk(2)` is activated and the statement in line 47 will select the "e" picture as the moving target (`selectObj`). The fourth button calls the function `resetPic()` that is defined in lines 32–41 to reset the pictures to their original positions.

One interesting point is that any button click (i.e., click the button using the mouse) is generally a mouse click and will trigger the general mouse click function `mouseClk()`. To prevent any confusion or undesirable effects from different event models (discussed later) and to guarantee the action that we want, we need to employ the variable `working` so that the function `mouseClk()` ignores the click the first time and listens to the next click event.

To make this example work, the following browser detection code (see lines 1–3) is set to listen to the mouse click event:

```
var IE=document.all?true:false
if (!IE) document.captureEvents(Event.CLICK)
document.onclick=mouseClk
```

You've seen this structure in Chapter 6 where very little explanation was given. In fact, this is an event handler with script. The first line detects whether IE is in use. The second statement is dedicated to some older browsers such as NS4.x used to capture the click event. After that, W3C standard code is used to assign the function `mouseClk()` to the `document.onclick` handler to listen to any mouse click action on the page. You can ignore the first two statements if only W3C-compliant browsers are used.

A genuine mouse click event occurring in the page will trigger the function `mouseClk()`. This function gets the starting position `lxPos0` and `lyPos0` of the selected object as shown in lines 56–59. Lines 61–67 are used to get the current mouse position and assign it as the end point. Also in this example, IE and NS browsers are assumed. Once you have the start and end points, you can call the `mAction()` function to move the object. This function uses the straight line equations

$$X = (1 - t) * X_0 + t X_1$$
$$Y = (1 - t) * Y_0 + t Y_1$$

where t is a parameter that takes values from 0 to 1. The straight line starts from the point (X_0, Y_0) and goes to (X_1, Y_1). The details of the function `mAction()` are defined in lines 16–30. In terms of programming, the straight line equation turns out to be

```
iTDelta = iTDelta + 0.1
lxPos = (1-iTDelta) * lxPos0 + iTDelta * lxPos1 - objWidth
lyPos = (1-iTDelta) * lyPos0 + iTDelta * lyPos1 - objHeight
```

It stops drawing when the parameter `iTDelta` reaches 1. Otherwise, the position of the selected object is updated to the new position `lxPos` and `lyPos` and therefore makes the object move. Finally, two more variables, `objWidth` and `objHeight`, are used to locate a point inside the selected object. This point is roughly designed but will come to the tip of the mouse.

Event handlers are quite useful and can be established without disturbing the page. In order to set up an event handler in this way, further understanding of the browsers and how they handle events is needed. This leads to our discussion on event models of browsers.

9.3   Setting up general event handlers

9.3.1   Event models of browsers

An event model is the inside structure of a browser used to handle events. Unfortunately, different browsers, such as IE and NS, in general have different event models. This section discusses such models and shows how to set up event handlers or listeners for each of them.

In normal circumstances, you don't need to consider event models in your Web page design. However, if you have a dynamic Web page and the behavior of IE and NS browsers is different and drives you mad, you may need to consider the event model structure of the browser.

IE introduced the concept of so-called *event bubbling* as the event model. This contrasts with NS4.x where events dive from the window object to the target object. From the object tree of a general page (see Fig. 9.12), you can see the event diving, or descending, structure.

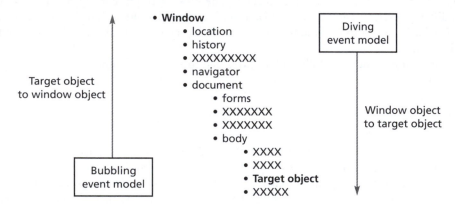

Figure 9.12 Object tree of a Web page

During event diving, the event can be intercepted and processed at any level from window to target.

An event in the IE family, on the other hand, bubbles outward from the target object to the window object, walking through all the involved objects and levels along the way. At each upward level, the object can intercept the event and process it. The order of event interception is determined by the upward order. This action is similar to a bubbling effect and the model is therefore called the "Bubbling Event Model." The target object is always first, followed by any higher level in the hierarchy. Consider again example ex09-06.htm. Any button click generates an `onclick` event starting at the target button and then traveling upward to the body and captured by the body `onclick` handler. This is typical event bubbling. To prevent the `onclick` handler inside the `<body>` from moving the picture, a detection variable is employed.

Yes, you are right! Example ex09-06.htm will perform differently on NS4.x from the theory of a diving event model. More precisely, when a button is clicked, the `mouseClk()` function runs first and drives the picture to the button position before changing the next selected picture. However, this example runs properly on NS6+, because NS6+ also supports the bubbling event model.

NS6+ has its own unique and interesting event model which combines the diving model of NS4.x and the bubbling model of IE. Events in NS6+ propagate outward from the target object to the browser window and also can be set as in the diving model. Any object in the hierarchical direction can capture the event before it reaches the other end. That is, NS6+ supports both directions and you can specify whether you want to intercept the event during its diving phase or its bubbling phase.

To demonstrate these behaviors, let's consider some simple examples.

9.3.2   A page to test event models

To test the event model of a browser is quite straightforward. The basic idea is to detect which object or level captures the first event. If the first event is captured at the target object, the event model is "Bubbling." Otherwise, the model is a "Diving" type. However, for backward compatibility and to develop an event model page to test IE5.x, NS6.x, and NS4.x, a classical technique that combines form and anchor is used. The XHTML coding of this page is

```
Example: ex09-07.htm - A Page To Test Event Model

 1: <?xml version="1.0" encoding="iso-8859-1"?>
 2: <!DOCTYPE html PUBLIC "-//W3C//DTD XHTML 1.0 Transitional//EN"
 3:     "http://www.w3.org/TR/xhtml1/DTD/xhtml1-transitional.dtd">
 4: <html xmlns="http://www.w3.org/1999/xhtml" xml:lang="en" lang="en">
 5: <head><title> A Page To Test Event Model - ex09-07.htm </title></head>
 6: <script src="ex09-07.js"></script>
 7: <body style="background:#dddddd;font-family:arial;font-size:20pt;
 8:             color:#000088;font-weight:bold">
 9: <div align="center" >Test Event Model<br /><br />
10: <form action="" id="myform" name="myform">
11:   <a href="javascript:targetClk()" style="font-family:arial;
12:     font-size:18pt;font-weight:bold" onClick="targetClk()" onmouseout=
13:     "outsideTarget()" onmouseover="insideTarget()" >Press Me</a>
14:                     <br /><br />
15:   <input type="text" id="outMsg" name="outMsg" style="font-family:arial;
16:     font-size:18pt;font-weight:bold;width:340px;height:40px"
17:     value="Please Click The Text Above" />
18: </form></div>
19: </body>
20: </html>
```

This is a form application so that the text input in lines 15–17 can be displayed correctly in some older browsers. To demonstrate a comprehensive technique, an anchor element is employed to trigger the event. The onmouseover and onmouseout event handlers are used to restrict the mouse click to occur inside the target object so that the internal operations of the browser can be tested properly. The external script file ex09-07.js mentioned in line 6 is listed as follows:

```
Example: ex09-07.js - The ECMAScript For ex09-07.htm

 1:   var IE=document.all?true:false
 2:   if (!IE) document.captureEvents(Event.CLICK)
 3:   document.onclick=mouseClk
 4:
 5:   var modelV =0           // 1 - Diving Model, 2 - Bubbling Model
 6:   var insideTar = false
 7:   var outSt = new Array()
 8:   outSt[0]="Please Click The Text Above"
 9:   outSt[1]="Diving Event Model"
10:   outSt[2]="Bubbling Event Model"
11:
12:   function mouseClk()
13:   {
14:     if (modelV ==0) modelV=1
15:     if (!insideTar) {
16:         modelV=0
17:         outputMsg(0)
18:     }
19:   }
20:
```

```
21:    function targetClk()
22:    {
23:      if (modelV ==0) {
24:              outputMsg(2)
25:              modelV =2
26:      }
27:      if (modelV ==1) outputMsg(1)
28:    }
29:
30:    function outputMsg(stV)
31:    {
32:       document.myform.outMsg.value=outSt[stV]
33:    }
34:
35:    function insideTarget()
36:    {
37:      insideTar = true
38:    }
39:    function outsideTarget()
40:    {
41:      insideTar = false
42:    }
```

The first three lines are used to set up the mouse click event. The variable modelV stores the event model of the browser. The insideTar variable together with the functions insideTarget() and outsideTarget() determines whether or not the mouse click occurs inside the target. If not, the click event is generally ignored. If a click event occurs at the target and modelV=0, the event model is a bubbling type. The outputMsg(2) function in line 24 displays the text "Bubbling Event Model" to the text area with name="outMsg". If modelV=1, this means the event is diving from the mouseClk() function to the target and therefore is a diving model. The text "Diving Event Model" is then displayed by the statement in line 27. Some screen shots of this example on NS4.x and NS6.x are shown in Figs 9.13 and 9.14.

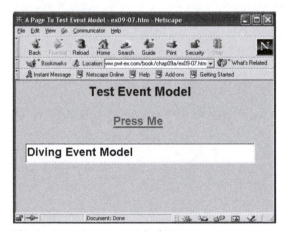

Figure 9.13 Event model of NS4.x

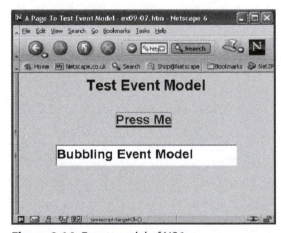

Figure 9.14 Event model of NS6.x

9.3.3   Setting up event handlers and listeners

There are a number of ways to set up event handlers. The first one, and possibly the most popular one, is to use standard handlers such as `onclick`, `onmousemove`, `onkeypress`, etc., inside an XHTML element. Another one is to use the script without any handler references in the page element. For example, the following code can be used to set up an event handler on the document body:

```
var IE=document.all?true:false
if (!IE) document.captureEvents(Event.CLICK)
document.onclick=mouseClk
```

This handler will listen to any click event on the document body and redirect the event to the function `mouseClk()`. The main characteristic of this code is that you don't need to put the standard handler `onclick="mouseClk()"` inside the body element. If you are using a W3C-compliant browser, you can ignore the first two statements. Only the statement `document.onclick= mouseClk` is needed to set up an event handler on the document body. In fact, event handlers can be set up this way on most of the XHTML elements. Thus if you have an object on a page such as

```
<div id="obj01" name="obj01"
  style="font-family:arial;font-size:18pt;font-weight:bold;
  background:#ffff00;position:absolute;top:80px;left:250px;
  width:100px;height:40px" />Obj01</div>
```

you can set up an `onclick` event handler using a simple script:

```
<script>document.getElementById("obj01").onclick = obj01Clk</script>
```

This way, you can set up event handlers entirely by using script. Again, you can see that the standardization and the efforts of W3C have made life elegantly simple: all programming can be done in one format.

Perhaps another more advanced method to set up an event handler is to use a "listener." An event listener is actually a function to listen to events and attach them to a specific action. Unfortunately, IE and NS have different event listener functions.

To set up an event listener on IE for the `obj01` example, you can use the following code:

```
objClk = document.getElementById("obj01")
objClk.attachEvent("onclick",myClk)
```

The main idea is to get an element and to attach it to an event using the event listener. The event listener function `attachEvent()` was first introduced in IE5.x to attach an element any event. In this case, the browser will listen to any `onclick` event and redirect control to the function `myClk()`. One of the strengths of the event listener is that you can attach many actions to the same event for the same object. For NS6+, the same event listener is

```
objClk = document.getElementById("obj01")
objClk.addEventListener("click", myClk, false)
```

First, you have a different function name for the listener. Second, in order to use this `addEventListener()` properly, you don't include the "on" prefix for the event names you need to use `mousemove`, `mousedown`, `keypress`, etc., instead. Finally, the listener has a third Boolean argument. This Boolean variable is used to instruct the listener which event model should be used. A `true` value signals the listener to use the diving event model and the bubbling event model otherwise. The `addEventListener()` function is a standard function recommended by W3C. In order to gain more experience and to put these into action, consider some popular and practical techniques for moving objects.

9.4   Practical techniques for moving objects

9.4.1   Moving the Pacman

The ability to control the movement of an object is vital for many entertainment industries on the Web. The techniques can be quite complicated. In order to focus on a basic level, only left, right, up, and down straight movements are considered. In terms of the keyboard, the following keys are used to trigger the actions:

"a" key – Move left   "w" key – Move up

"d" key – Move right   "s" key – Move down

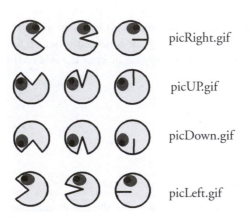

picRight.gif

picUP.gif

picDown.gif

picLeft.gif

Figure 9.15 Images for the Pacman

These keys are located on the left hand side of your keyboard and can be easily controlled by your left hand. Also, these keys exist on all kinds of keyboards including those on laptop computers. The object you are going to create is simple – the "Pacman." This object has four different faces and some simple animations. The XHTML page uses these keys to drive them. In order to do that, you need to set up some event listeners to listen to the keystroke. There will be a message box to display the movement and object selections. The animated `gif` files in Fig. 9.15 are used to create the Pacman.

The picRight.gif (picture right) is an animated `gif` file representing a sequence of actions moving to the right. Others are the sequences representing the movement in the corresponding directions. For example, when you press the "w" key, the image will change to picUp.gif and move upward. This example has two parts. By combining animated `gif` pictures with motion, some realistic motions can be achieved. The XHTML interface part is listed as follows:

```
Example: ex09-08.htm - Controlling Moving Object With Keyboard

 1: <?xml version="1.0" encoding="iso-8859-1"?>
 2: <!DOCTYPE html PUBLIC "-//W3C//DTD XHTML 1.0 Transitional//EN"
 3:     "http://www.w3.org/TR/xhtml1/DTD/xhtml1-transitional.dtd">
 4: <html xmlns="http://www.w3.org/1999/xhtml" xml:lang="en" lang="en">
 5: <head><title> Moving Object with Keyboard - ex09-08.htm </title></head>
 6: <style>
 7:   .butSt{background-color:#aaffaa;font-family:arial;font-weight:bold;
 8:       font-size:14pt;color:#880000;width:250px;height:40px}</style>
 9: <script src="ex09-08.js"></script>
10: <body style="background:#dddddd;font-family:arial;font-size:20pt;
11:     color:#000088;font-weight:bold">
12:
13: <div align="center" >Control Moving Object With Keyboard</div>
14: <img src="picRight.gif" id="obj01" name="obj01"
15:     style="font-weight:bold;position:absolute;
16:       top:80px;left:250px;width:100px;height:100px" />
17:
18: <table style="position:absolute;top:100px;left:460px;text-align:left">
19:   <tr><td class="butSt" style="text-align:center">Instructions</td></tr>
20:   <tr><td class="butSt"> Press a to move left</td></tr>
21:   <tr><td class="butSt"> Press d to move right</td></tr>
22:   <tr><td class="butSt"> Press w to move up</td></tr>
23:   <tr><td class="butSt"> Press s to move down</td></tr>
```

```
24: </table>
25:
26: <span style="font-family:arial;font-size:16pt;font-weight:bold;
27:    position:absolute;top:400px;left:100px;width:150px;height:40px">
28:    Message:</span>
29: <span id="outMsg" name="outMsg" style="font-family:arial;font-size:16pt;
30:    font-weight:bold;background:#aaaaaa;position:absolute;top:400px;
31:    left:200px;width:350px;height:70px;color:#0000ff"></span>
32: </body>
33: </html>
```

Although we have four images for the Pacman representing four movement directions, only one is displayed at any one time. After the picture, you have a table (lines 18–24) to display the movement instructions. Finally, a message area is used to display the current action of the page. Some screen shots of this page are shown in Figs 9.16 and 9.17.

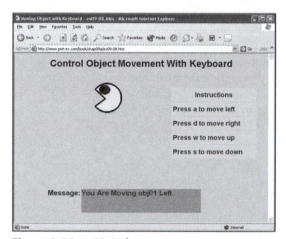

Figure 9.16 ex09-16.htm

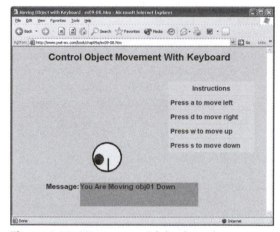

Figure 9.17 Movement with keyboard

Note that no specific or standard event handlers are used in this page. This example demonstrates that all handlers can be set up by using script. All event listeners and functions are defined inside the external script file called ex09-08.js. The first part of this file is given below.

Example: ex09-08.js – The ECMAScript For ex09-08.htm (Part One)

```
 1: var IE=document.all?true:false
 2:
 3: if (!IE)
 4: {  //Set up the Event Listener For NS (Netscape is assumed)
 5:     document.addEventListener("mousedown",mouseClk,false)
 6:     document.addEventListener("keypress",onKey,false)
 7: }else {
 8:     document.attachEvent("onmousedown",mouseClk)
 9:     document.attachEvent("onkeypress",onKey)
10: }
11:
12: function mouseClk(e)
13: {
14:    butS =""
15:    if (IE) {
16:        lxPos1 = event.clientX
```

```
17:        lyPos1 = event.clientY
18:        butV = event.button
19:        if (butV ==1) butS="Left "
20:        if (butV ==2) butS="Right "
21:    } else {
22:        lxPos1 = e.pageX
23:        lyPos1 = e.pageY
24:        butV = e.which
25:        if (butV ==1) butS="Left "
26:        if (butV ==3) butS="Right "
27:    }
28:    document.getElementById("outMsg").innerHTML= "You Have Click "+
29:        butS+" Mouse <br /> At Top Left Co-ord. ("+lyPos1+","+lxPos1+")"
30: }
31:
```

First, a detection statement is used to test the type of browser. If the NS browser is detected, we set up the event listeners with the `addEventListener()` function. Otherwise, the IE event listener function `attachEvent()` is employed. In either case, we want to listen to both the `onmousedown` and `onkeypress` events.

If a mouse-down event occurs, the `mouseClk()` (lines 12–30) function is called. This function is used to capture the mouse position when the corresponding mouse button is pressed. The information is displayed to the message box with `id="outMsg"`. Listening to the mouse down is not the main function of this page. It is here as an example to show how mouse positions and buttons can also be trapped and displayed.

The coding for the object movement is listed in the second part of the script file ex09-08.js.

Listing: Continuation Of The ECMAScript ex09-08.js (Part Two)

```
32: dirSt=""
33: selectObj = "obj01"
34: ixDelta = 10
35: iyDelta = 10
36: upBd = 20
37: lowBd = 300
38: leftBd = 20
39: rightBd = 330
40:
41: function onKey(e)
42: {
43:   if (IE) {
44:       chV = String.fromCharCode(event.keyCode)
45:   } else {
46:       chV = String.fromCharCode(e.which)
47:   }
48:   if (chV =="a") moveHor(1)
49:   if (chV =="d") moveHor(-1)
50:   if (chV =="w") moveVer(1)
51:   if (chV =="s") moveVer(-1)
52:
53:    document.getElementById("outMsg").innerHTML=
54:         "You Are Moving "+selectObj+ dirSt
55: }
56:
```

A number of global variables are defined in lines 32–39 and their explanations are as follows:

- `dirSt` – Stores the movement directions "Left," "Right," "Up," and "Down."
- `selectObj` – Stores the object identity that we are going to move.
- `ixDelta` – Specifies how far an object should move horizontally.

- `iyDelta` – Specifies how far an object should move vertically.
- `upBd` – The upper boundary for the object.
- `lowBd` – The lower boundary for the object.
- `leftBd` – The left boundary for the object.
- `rightBd` – The right boundary for the object.

If a key is pressed, the `onKey()` function is called. This function uses a variable `chV` (i.e., character variable) to store the key. The property `event.keyCode` is an IE property and `e.which` is a property of NS. They are used to store the ASCII value of the key pressed. The function `String.fromCharCode()` converts the ASCII value to the character key. For example, if the pressed key is "a," the `moveHor(1)` function is called and moves the object in the left direction. A function call to `moveHor(-1)` will move the object to the right. Similarly, the "w" and "s" keys will move the object up and down respectively using the function `moveVer()`.

The definition of the `moveHor()` and `moveVer()` functions are specified as follows:

Listing: Continuation Of The ECMAScript ex09-08.js (Part Three)

```
57: function moveHor(dirV)
58: {
59:   if (dirV ==1)
61:   {
62:     dirSt="Left"
63:     document.getElementById("obj01").src = "picLeft.gif"
64:   } else {
65:     dirSt="Right"
66:     document.getElementById("obj01").src = "picRight.gif"
67:   }
68:   xPos = parseInt(document.getElementById(selectObj).style.left)
69:   if (((xPos > leftBd )&&(dirV ==1 ))||((xPos < rightBd )&&(dirV ==-1 )))
70:   document.getElementById(selectObj).style.left=xPos -(ixDelta* dirV) +"px"
71: }
72:
73: function moveVer(dirV)
74: {
75:   if (dirV ==1)
76:   {
77:     dirSt="Up"
78:     document.getElementById("obj01").src = "picUp.gif"
79:   } else {
80:     dirSt="Down"
81:     document.getElementById("obj01").src = "picDown.gif"
82:   }
83:   yPos = parseInt(document.getElementById(selectObj).style.top)
84:   if (((yPos > upBd )&&(dirV == 1))||((yPos < lowBd )&&(dirV == -1 )))
85:   document.getElementById(selectObj).style.top =yPos -(iyDelta* dirV) +"px"
86: }
```

Consider the horizontal move function `moveHor()`. If the variable `dirV` equals 1, the direction string `dirSt` is set to "Left" and changes the moving object image to picLeft.gif so that the Pacman's mouth faces in the left direction. If the value of `dirV` is –1, the Pacman's picture is set to picRight.gif so that the mouth of the Pacman faces right. Next, we get the *x*-position of the Pacman from the statement as indicated in line 68. If the position is bigger than the left boundary and the moving direction is left, you can move the object in the left direction with a step value `ixDelta`. You can only move the object to the left when some spaces are available. Similarly, you can only move the object to the right if the position of the object is less than the right boundary (`rightBd`).

The function `moveVer()` (i.e., move vertically) is similar to `moveHor()` and will move the object up and down depending on the direction variable `dirV`.

9.4.2 A shooting game

Another popular example of moving objects is a shooting game page. To program a shooting game even at a basic level, you will need to combine a number of techniques that you've learned. Almost any game involves:

- a moving object;
- a controllable moving object (the gun);
- shooting action (firing a bullet);
- hitting the target;
- counting the number of hits;
- counting the number of misses;
- some buttons to control the progress;
- game-over criteria; and
- winning conditions.

For simplicity, we are going to use the Pacman's ghost as the moving object. The rule of the game is simple. A moving ball is the "bullet" and ready to fire. No gun is really needed. The bullet can move left and right by using the keyboard and can fire upward at will to hit the ghost. We also have a message area to show the number of hits, missed shots, and the total score. The score is the difference between the hits and the misses. If the total score is a negative number (i.e., more misses than hits), the game is over. You win the game if you have a total score of 5. You also have some buttons to control the progress of the game.

Surprisingly, the whole game can be implemented with a reasonable number of lines of coding. The page contains an XHTML interface page and an external script file. The main purpose of the interface is to design the shooting field scoreboard, and to display the instructions on how to play.

Example: ex09-09.htm – A Shooting Game

```
 1: <?xml version="1.0" encoding="iso-8859-1"?>
 2: <!DOCTYPE html PUBLIC "-//W3C//DTD XHTML 1.0 Transitional//EN"
 3:     "http://www.w3.org/TR/xhtml1/DTD/xhtml1-transitional.dtd">
 4: <html xmlns="http://www.w3.org/1999/xhtml" xml:lang="en" lang="en">
 5: <head><title> A Shooting Game - ex09-09.htm </title></head>
 6: <style>
 7:   .tx01St={font-family:arial;font-size:18pt;font-weight:bold}
 8:   .butSt{background-color:#dddddd;font-family:arial;font-weight:bold;
 9:      font-size:18pt;color:#880000;width:60px;height:40px}
10:   .butSt1{background-color:#aaffaa;font-family:arial;font-weight:bold;
11:      font-size:18pt;color:#880000;width:110px;height:40px}
12:
13: </style>
14: <body style="background:#dddddd;font-family:arial;font-size:20pt;
15:    color:#000088;font-weight:bold">
16: <div style="position:absolute;top:15px;left:250px">A Shooting Game</div>
17: <img src="line1.gif" style="position:absolute;
18:    top:50px;left:150px;width:380px;height:6px" />
19: <img src="line1.gif" style="position:absolute;
20:    top:320px;left:150px;width:380px;height:6px" />
21:
22: <table style="font-family:arial;font-size:16pt;color:#888888;
23:        position:absolute;top:100px;left:210px">
24:   <tr><td>Press "a" To Move Left</td></tr>
25:   <tr><td>Press "d" To Move Right</td></tr>
26:   <tr><td>Press "w" To Fire </td></tr>
27:   <tr><td>Total Score 5 To Win </td></tr>
28:   <tr><td>Negative Total Score - Game Over</td></tr>
29: </table>
30:
31:
32: <img src="ghost_r.gif" id="obj01" name="obj01" alt="pic"
```

```
33:    style="position:absolute;top:80px;left:250px;width:70px;height:70px" />
34:
35: <img src="bullet1.gif" id="obj00" name="obj00" alt="pic"
36:    style="position:absolute;top:340px;left:350px;width:30px;height:30px" />
37:
38: <table style="position:absolute;top:80px;left:25px">
39: <tr><td class="tx01St">Scores</td></tr>
40: <tr><td class="butSt">Hit : </td><td class="butSt">
41:      <span id="obj01Msg" name="obj01Msg">0</span></td></tr>
42: <tr><td class="butSt">Miss : </td><td class="butSt">
43:      <span id="obj02Msg" name="obj02Msg">0</span></td></tr>
44: <tr><td class="butSt">Total : </td><td class="butSt">
45:      <span id="obj03Msg" name="obj03Msg">0</span></td></tr>
46:
47: <tr><td colspan="2"><input type="button" id= "startBut" name="startBut"
48:        class="butSt1" value="Start" onclick="restart()"/></td></tr>
49: <tr><td colspan="2"><input type="button" class="butSt1" id= "stopBut"
50:        name="stopBut" value="Stop" onclick="stop()"/></td></tr>
51: </table>
52: <script src="ex09-09.js"></script>
53: </body>
54: </html>
```

After the page title in line 16, two straight red lines are used to draw the shooting area. Inside the shooting area, an XHTML table (lines 22–29) is used to display the instructions on how to play the game. They are:

- Press "a" To Move Left
- Press "d" To Move Right
- Press "w" To Fire
- Total Score 5 To Win
- Negative Total Score – Game Over

The moving object defined in lines 32–33 is a picture of a ghost (Pacman's ghost), ghost_r.gif. The ghost is designed to move right and left continuously with a different color. The gun is actually a bullet picture specified in lines 35–36. The movement of the bullet is controlled by the keyboard and "w" key will fire the bullet upward to hit the target. A table is also used to draw a scoreboard, which stores the information about the number of hits, misses, and total score. At the end of this XHTML table, two buttons are defined. The Stop button (lines 49–50) is used to suspend the game at any time. Once the game is stopped or suspended, another button (the Start button) will appear to allow the user to continue the game. Some screen shots of this page are given in Figs 9.18–9.21.

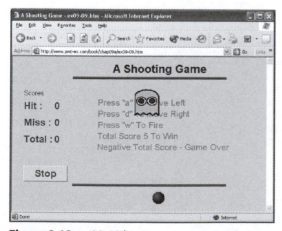

Figure 9.18 ex09-09.htm

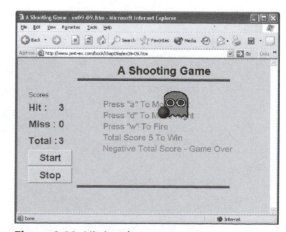

Figure 9.19 Hitting the target

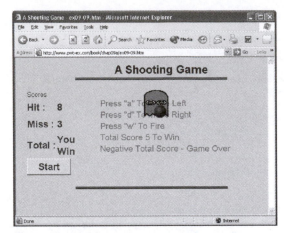

Figure 9.20 You win

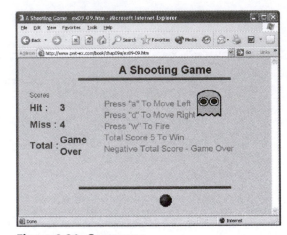

Figure 9.21 Game over

The included program file ex09-09.js is the heart of this page, providing all the functionalities for the object movements, bullet controls, firing, impact, and score counting. The first part of this file is listed as follows:

Example: ex09-09.js – The ECMAScript For ex09-09.htm (Part One)

```
 1: var IE=document.all?true:false
 2: if (!IE) {
 3:    document.addEventListener("keypress",onKey,false)
 4: }else {
 5:    document.attachEvent("onkeypress",onKey)
 6: }
 7:
 8: function onKey(e)
 9: {
10:   if (IE) {
11:      chV = String.fromCharCode(event.keyCode)
12:   } else {
13:      chV = String.fromCharCode(e.which)
14:   }
15:   if (chV =="a") moveHor(1)
16:   if (chV =="d") moveHor(-1)
17:   if (chV == "w") fireBall()
18: }
19:
20: var selectObj = "obj00"
21: var working = 1
22: document.getElementById("startBut").style.visibility="hidden"
23:
24: function resetPos()
25: {
26:   document.getElementById(selectObj).style.top = 340 +"px"
27:   document.getElementById(selectObj).style.left = 350 +"px"
28:   document.getElementById("startBut").style.visibility="visible"
29: }
30:
31: function restart()
32: {
33:  working =1
34:  resetPos()
```

```
35:    document.getElementById("startBut").style.visibility="hidden"
36: }
37:
38: function stop()
39: {
40:    working =0
41:    document.getElementById("startBut").style.visibility="visible"
42: }
43:
```

The first line of this program file is to detect the browser and then set up the event listener depending on the browser type (IE or NS). The listener will listen to any keyboard event and call the onKey() function as defined in lines 8–18. Inside this function, the String.fromCharCode() function is used to convert the keycode to a character. If the character equals "a," the function moveHor(1) is called to move the bullet to the left. The argument 1 signals the function to move the bullet to the left. If the keystroke is a "d" character, the moveHor(-1) function moves the bullet to the right. A "w" key will call the fireBall() function to fire the bullet.

After the event listener, some global variables are used to set up events and the environment. The variable selectObj="obj00" is to set the bullet object so that it corresponds to the keyboard input. We set the variable working=1 (line 21) to start the program. Whenever the program or the motion starts, the Start button is hidden to avoid some misuse of the button. The resetPos() function is to reset the position of the bullet. The restart() function (lines 31–36) is called whenever the Start button is clicked by a mouse. The stop function is used to suspend the program at any time.

The second part of the program controls the impact and the score counting.

Listing: Continuation Of The ECMAScript ex09-09.js (Part Two)

```
44: hitScore = 0
45: missScore =0
46: totalScore = 0
47:
48: widthX0 = 30
49: heightY0 = 30
50: widthX1 = 50
51: heightY1 = 50
52:
53: function hitT()
54: {
55:    xPos1 = parseInt(document.getElementById("obj01").style.left)
56:    yPos1 = parseInt(document.getElementById("obj01").style.top)
57:
58:    xPos = parseInt(document.getElementById(selectObj).style.left)
59:    yPos = parseInt(document.getElementById(selectObj).style.top)
60:
61:    if ( ((xPos1 < xPos ) && (xPos < (xPos1+widthX1)) &&
62:      ((yPos1 + heightY1) > yPos) && (yPos > yPos1)) ||
63:      ((xPos1 < (xPos+ widthX0) ) && (xPos < (xPos1+widthX1)) &&
64:      ((yPos1 + heightY1) > yPos) && (yPos > yPos1)) ||
65:      ((xPos1 < xPos ) && (xPos < (xPos1+widthX1)) &&
66:      ((yPos1 + heightY1) > (yPos+heightY0)) && ((yPos+heightY0) > yPos1)) ||
67:      ((xPos1 < (xPos+ widthX0) ) && (xPos < (xPos1+widthX1)) &&
68:      ((yPos1 + heightY1) > (yPos+heightY0)) && ((yPos+heightY0) > yPos1)) )
69:    {
70:       hitScore++
71:       document.getElementById("obj01Msg").innerHTML = hitScore
72:       totalScore = hitScore - missScore
73:       document.getElementById("obj03Msg").innerHTML = totalScore
```

```
74:        if (totalScore > 4)
75:        {
76:            document.getElementById("obj03Msg").innerHTML = "You Win"
77:            document.getElementById("startBut").style.visibility="hidden"
78:            document.getElementById("stopBut").style.visibility="hidden"
79:            stop()
80:        }
81:     return true
82: } else {
83:     return false
84: }
85: }
86:
```

Again, variables are introduced when needed. First, we set all the score variables to zero. To control the hit and impact, some collision criteria are needed. The dimensions of the bullet are widthX0=30 and heightY0=30 (pixels) and it has a rectangular shape. The dimensions of the target are widthX1=50 and heightY1=50 (pixels). The collision moment of two objects occurs when:

- the top left corner of the bullet is inside the target dimension;
- the top right corner of the bullet is inside the target dimension;
- the bottom left corner of the bullet is inside the target dimension; and
- the bottom right corner of the bullet is inside the target dimension.

This is a long conditional if statement and is illustrated in lines 61–68. Once there is an impact, the hitScore (number of hits) and the totalScore (total score) are updated. If the totalScore is 5, the player wins and the game will stop.

Another important part of the program is to control the firing of the bullet. The bullet will move left, right, and upward to hit the target.

Listing: Continuation Of The ECMAScript ex09-09.js (Part Three)

```
87:
88: ixDelta = 10
89: iyDelta = 20
90: leftBd = 200
91: rightBd = 500
92:
93: function moveHor(dirV)
94: {
95:  if (working ==1) {
96:    xPos = parseInt(document.getElementById(selectObj).style.left)
97:    if (((xPos > leftBd ) && (dirV ==1 )) ||
98:       ((xPos < rightBd ) && (dirV ==-1 )))
99:     document.getElementById(selectObj).style.left=
100:        xPos - (ixDelta* dirV)+"px"
101:  }
102: }
103:
104: function fireBall()
105: {
106:  if (working==1)
107: {
108:   xPos = parseInt(document.getElementById(selectObj).style.left)
109:   yPos = parseInt(document.getElementById(selectObj).style.top)
110:
111:   if (yPos < 20)
112:   {
```

```
113:      working = 0
114:      resetPos()
115:      missScore++
116:      document.getElementById("obj02Msg").innerHTML = missScore
117:      totalScore = hitScore - missScore
118:      if (totalScore > -1)
119:        document.getElementById("obj03Msg").innerHTML = totalScore
120:      else {
121:        document.getElementById("obj03Msg").innerHTML = "Game Over"
122:        document.getElementById("startBut").style.visibility="hidden"
123:        document.getElementById("stopBut").style.visibility="hidden"
124:      }
125:    } else {
126:       yPos = yPos - iyDelta
127:       document.getElementById(selectObj).style.top = yPos +"px"
128:       if (hitT())stop()
129:    }
130:    setTimeout("fireBall()",20)
131:  }
132: }
133:
```

The movement of the bullet cannot be less than 200 pixels from the left boundary or more than 500 pixels from the left. Also, the bullet can only move 10 pixels horizontally each time. These are the restrictions on the bullet and applied inside the function moveHor(). This function has an argument dirV to control the left or the right movement of the bullet. When dirV=1, the bullet moves to the right and when dirV=-1, it moves in the left direction.

When the "w" key is pressed, the function fireBall() is called. This function will fire the bullet and try to hit the target. If the variable working is not 1, nothing will happen. This arrangement is to make sure that the game can be stopped completely at any time.

The position of the bullet is captured by the xPos and yPos variables (lines 108–109). If yPos is less than 20 pixels, the bullet has reached the top and hence misses the target. In this case, the working variable is set to 0, which resets the bullet position and increments the missScore (the number of misses). If the missScore is negative, both the Start and Stop buttons will be hidden and the game is over. Otherwise, the missScore and totalScore are updated. If the bullet has not yet reached the top, the bullet will continue to move upward by the statements given in lines 126–127. For each step, a call to the function hitT() is needed to test whether the target is hit. The setTimeout() function in line 130 makes sure that this function will be called every 20 millitseconds and continues the movement until the bullet reaches the top or hits the target.

The final part of the program is much easier. It contains only one function, moveLeft(), used to move the target object to the left and right continuously.

Listing: Continuation Of The ECMAScript ex09-09.js (Part Four)

```
134:
135: llxPos = 0
136: iixDelta = 10
137: dirVar = 1
138: function MoveLeft()
139: {
140:  if (working ==1)
141:  {
142:   llxPos = parseInt(document.getElementById("obj01").style.left)
143:   if (llxPos < leftBd)
144:   {
145:     dirVar = 1
146:     document.getElementById("obj01").src = "ghost_r.gif"
```

```
147:    }
148:
149:    if (llxPos > rightBd )
150:    {
151:      dirVar = -1
152:      document.getElementById("obj01").src = "ghost_l.gif"
153:    }
154:      document.getElementById("obj01").style.left =
155:            (llxPos + iixDelta * dirVar) + "px"
156:  }
157: }
158: setInterval("MoveLeft()",50)
159: restart()
```

Inside the moveLeft() function, the current left position of the target is obtained by the statement in line 142. If the position is less than the left boundary (leftBd), the direction of movement is changed to the right (dirVar=1) and the target picture to ghost_r.gif. If the left position is more than the right boundary (rightBd), on the other hand, the movement changes to the opposite direction and uses the ghost_l.gif picture as the moving target. The direction dirVar and the step variable iixDelta are used to update the position of the target.

Finally, by calling this function continuously as illustrated in line 158, we have a moving target on the page. The restart() function at the end of this program activates the bullet and ready for firing. As a final remark, since there is no code to stop the left and right keys after firing, this means that you can still control the bullet to move left or right in a path to hit the target.

9.4.3   Dragging and dropping objects

Dragging is an essential technique in any window-based operating system. From organizing icons to performing some real applications, holding down the mouse button on an object and dragging it somewhere else is a daily working routine. Have you ever considered how it works? In fact, the basic procedures to implement drag and drop operations are to:

- select the object using a mouse-down event;
- move the mouse while holding the mouse down;
- change the object's position along with the mouse movement; and
- release the object when the mouse button is up.

One simple implementation of these tasks on the Web is to use onmousedown and onmouseup event handlers on the object. Defining the handlers this way means they will have effect only when the object is activated. This means that the handlers only exist when you touch the object. Therefore there is no need to pick up the object from the higher level. For this application, it may be more convenient to set up handlers at the document level (i.e., using XHTML attributes) to trap any mouse movements.

To construct an example, let's consider three objects. The first object is an information board to display which object you have picked and the position to drop the object. The second object is a logo picture and the final one is a moving object. All three objects can be dragged and dropped anywhere inside the page.

The interface part of the page is listed in ex09-10.htm.

```
Example: ex09-10.htm - Drag And Drop Objects

1: <?xml version="1.0" encoding="iso-8859-1"?>
2: <!DOCTYPE html PUBLIC "-//W3C//DTD XHTML 1.0 Transitional//EN"
3:     "http://www.w3.org/TR/xhtml1/DTD/xhtml1-transitional.dtd">
4: <html xmlns="http://www.w3.org/1999/xhtml" xml:lang="en" lang="en">
5: <head><title> Drag and Drop Objects - ex09-10.htm </title></head>
6: <body style="background:#dddddd;font-family:arial;font-size:20pt;
```

```
 7:     color:#000088;font-weight:bold">
 8: <div style="text-align:center">Drap And Drop Objects</div>
 9:
10: <table id="obj000" style="font-family:arial;font-size:18pt;color:#880000;
11:     position:absolute;top:100px;left:20px;width:300px;height:60px"
12:     onmousedown="mouseDownEvent(0)" onmouseup="mouseUpEvent()">
13:  <tr><td>Picked Object :</td>
14:      <td style="color:#000088"><span id="objPick"></span></td></tr>
15:  <tr><td>Mouse Position:</td>
16:      <td style="color:#000088"><span id="mPos"></span></td></tr>
17: </table>
18:
19: <img id="obj001" src="logo_web.jpg" alt="pic"
20:     style="position:absolute;top:60px;left:360px;width:120px;height:80px"
21:     onmousedown="mouseDownEvent(1)" onmouseup="mouseUpEvent()" />
22:
23: <img id="obj002" src="picRight_y.gif" alt="pic"
24:     style="position:absolute;top:250px;left:240px;width:60px;height:60px"
25:     onmousedown="mouseDownEvent(2)" onmouseup="mouseUpEvent()" />
26:
27: </body>
28: <script src="ex09-10.js"></script>
29: </html>
```

This page contains three objects with identities `obj000`, `obj001`, and `obj002`. The `obj000`, defined in lines 10–17, is an XHTML table to display the "Picked Object" and current "Mouse Position." The second and third objects are pictures defined with the image elements as given in lines 19 and 23. All objects are designed with drag and drop features.

The three objects have `onmousedown` and `onmouseup` standard event handlers attached to them. The first one is in line 12:

```
onmousedown = "mouseDownEvent(0)"
```

When a user touches this object and holds down the left mouse button, the function `mouseDownEvent(0)` is called with `0` as argument. The argument sets the selected object as `obj000`. If the user moves the mouse while holding down the mouse button, another mouse move event will move the selected object along with the mouse. The `onmousedown` events for the other two objects are similar; the `onmouseup` event is simply to release the selected object. All these functionalities are implemented in the external program file ex09-10.js. Before listing the program file, some screen shots of the page are shown in Figs 9.22 and 9.23.

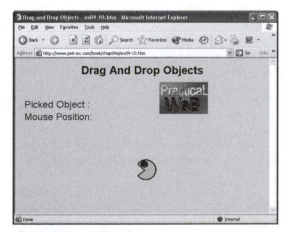

Figure 9.22 ex09-10.htm

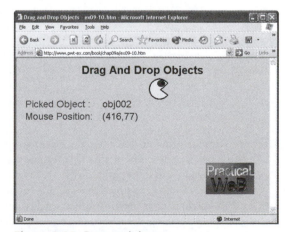

Figure 9.23 Drag and drop

The first part of this program file is listed as follows:

Example: ex09-10.js - The ECMAScript For ex09-10.htm (Part One)

```
 1: var IE = document.all?true:false
 2:
 3: llxPos = 0
 4: iixDelta = 10
 5: dirVar = 1
 6: working =1
 7: function MoveLeft()
 8: {
 9:  if (working ==1)
10:  {
11:    llxPos = parseInt(document.getElementById("obj002").style.left)
12:    if (llxPos < 200)
13:    {
14:      dirVar = 1
15:      document.getElementById("obj002").src = "picRight_y.gif"
16:    }
17:
18:    if (llxPos >= 450 )
19:    {
20:      dirVar = -1
21:      document.getElementById("obj002").src = "picLeft_g.gif"
22:    }
23:    document.getElementById("obj002").style.left =
24:          (llxPos + iixDelta * dirVar) + "px"
25:  }
26: }
27: setInterval("MoveLeft()",50)
28:
29: var selectObj = null
30: function mouseDownEvent(objId)
31: {
32:   if (objId ==2) working = 0
33:   selectObj="obj00"+objId
34:   document.getElementById("objPick").innerHTML= selectObj
35: }
36:
37: function mouseUpEvent()
38: {
39:   if (selectObj != null)
40:   {
41:    working =1
42:    selectObj = null;
43:   // document.getElementById("objPick").innerHTML= ""
44:   // document.getElementById("mPos").innerHTML= ""
45:    return(false)
46:  }
47: }
48:
```

After the familiar browser detection statement in line 1, the first function MoveLeft() is defined in lines 7–26. We have already come across this function several times. In this case, it is used to move the object obj002 to the right and left continuously.

The onmousedown event function mouseDownEvent(objId) is defined in lines 30–35. If the input argument objId equals 2, that means you have picked up the moving object obj002. In this case, we need to stop the movement by setting the variable working=0 before dragging and dropping it in another location. The string concatenation statement

```
SelectObj = "obj00" + objId
```

is a common way to construct the identity of an object. Once the identity of the selected object is known, the information is displayed to the display board. When the mouse button is released, the mouseUpEvent() is called to release the selected object and reset the information on the display board.

The main function of this example is to control the mouse movement and is listed in the second part of the program file ex09-10.js.

```
Listing: Continuation Of the ECMAScript ex09-10.js (Part Two)

49: var objW = 0
50: var objH = 0
51: function mouseMoveEvent(e)
52: {
53:   if (selectObj != null)
54:   {
55:     if (IE)
56:     {
57:       lxPos = event.clientX
58:       lyPos = event.clientY
59:     } else {
60:       lxPos = e.pageX
61:       lyPos = e.pageY
62:     }
63:     document.getElementById("mPos").innerHTML= "("+lxPos+","+lyPos+")"
64:     objW = parseInt(document.getElementById(selectObj).style.width)
65:     objH = parseInt(document.getElementById(selectObj).style.height)
66:
67:     document.getElementById(selectObj).style.left = lxPos - objW/2 +"px"
68:     document.getElementById(selectObj).style.top = lyPos - objH/2 +"px"
69:   }
70:   return(false)
71: }
72:
73: document.onmousemove=mouseMoveEvent
```

The mouseMoveEvent() function (lines 51–71) is called if even a tiny movement of the mouse is detected. This function may be called hundreds if not thousands of times even for a simple mouse operation. The implementation and operation of this function should be kept to a minimum to save system resources. Thus this function will do nothing if no object is picked. If the mouse touches an object, the position of the mouse is captured in lines 56–63. This information is displayed in the display board as usual at the top left coordinate. In order to catch the center of the selected object, we calculate its width and height as shown in lines 64–65. Finally, the center position of the selected object is updated to the new mouse position. This effect is known as "drag and drop."

9.5 Handling multiple moving objects

9.5.1 Generating multiple flying objects

One of the efficient ways to create and control multiple objects is to use an array structure. By using one variable name, an array can store a number of different things. It also allows you to manipulate them in a consistent manner. This section is dedicated to multiple moving objects and to showing you how to use an array to generate and control them on a Web page. For example, if you have a butterfly image bfly01.gif, you can display it at the (90, 240) top left position with the following XHTML statement:

```
<img id="obj1" src="bfly01.gif" alt="pic" s
  style="position:absolute;top:90px;left:240px;width:32px;height:32px" />
```

If you have 5 red butterflies (bfly01.gif), 5 blue butterflies (bfly02.gif), and 10 different locations, then one practical way to display them all is to use the array structure. To construct this example, and to use it to build a more functional application for this section, we begin with a simple interface program. This XHTML interface is listed in ex09-11.htm.

```
Example: ex09-11.htm - Display Multiple Objects

 1: <?xml version="1.0" encoding="iso-8859-1"?>
 2: <!DOCTYPE html PUBLIC "-//W3C//DTD XHTML 1.0 Transitional//EN"
 3:     "http://www.w3.org/TR/xhtml1/DTD/xhtml1-transitional.dtd">
 4: <html xmlns="http://www.w3.org/1999/xhtml" xml:lang="en" lang="en">
 5: <head><title> Display Multiple Objects - ex09-11.htm </title></head>
 6: <body style="background:#dddddd;font-family:arial;font-size:20pt;
 7:     color:#000088;font-weight:bold">
 8:
 9:  <div style="text-align:center">Generating Multiple Objects</div>
10:  <div id="buttLoc"></div>
11:  <script src="ex09-11.js"></script>
12: </body>
13: </html>
```

Basically, this page contains three statements (lines 9–11): a display text, an empty division. and an included script file. In fact, it is possible to build an entire page with script. One of the great strengths of XHTML and many other markup languages is that the language itself can be generated by other programs or techniques without too much difficulty. The external file ex09-11.js contains a script to generate 10 butterflies at 10 different locations and to display them at the element position with id="buttLoc" (butterfly location). The script file at this moment is also simple and is listed as follows:

```
Example: ex09-11.js - The ECMAScript For ex09-11.htm

 1:
 2: llX = new Array(240,380,180,410,210,440,240,380,180,440)
 3: llY = new Array(90 ,140,140,110,110,140,140,90 ,90 ,90)
 4: llSt =""
 5:
 6: for (ii=0;ii<5;ii++)
 7: {
 8:   llSt = llSt + '<img id=\"obj'+ii+'\" src=\"bfly01.gif\" alt=\"pic\" '+
 9:          'style=\"position:absolute;top:'+llY[ii]+
10:          'px;left:'+llX[ii]+'px;width:32px;height:32px\" />'
11: }
12:
13: for (ii=5;ii<10;ii++)
14: {
15:   llSt = llSt + '<img id=\"obj'+ii+'\" src=\"bfly02.gif\" alt=\"pic\" '+
16:          'style=\"position:absolute;top:'+llY[ii]+
17:          'px;left:'+llX[ii]+'px;width:32px;height:32px\" />'
18: }
19:
20: document.getElementById("buttLoc").innerHTML=llSt
21:
```

Again, a string concatenation technique is used, taking advantage of the array structure. Variables llY (local location *Y*) and llX are two arrays to hold the top and left positions of the butterflies. The for-loop in lines 6–11 is basically used to generate the XHTML image element for the display. This for-loop generates five butterflies with different locations and another for-loop in lines 13–18 generates another five blue butterflies. The statement in line 20 outputs the image string llSt (local location string) on the page at the location with id="buttLoc".

To appreciate more the combination of these techniques, let's consider adding some random flying motion to the butterflies. In order to have a realistic flying action and to keep the coding to a minimum, we add the following features:

- Assign each butterfly a flying flag to determine whether the butterfly should fly.
- To make a butterfly fly, we randomly change the top and left positions.
- The flying direction should also be randomly changed.

To put these into action, ex09-11.js is extended to form a new example. The XHTML page for this example becomes:

Example: ex09-12.htm – Handling Multiple Moving Objects

```
 1: <?xml version="1.0" encoding="iso-8859-1"?>
 2: <!DOCTYPE html PUBLIC "-//W3C//DTD XHTML 1.0 Transitional//EN"
 3:     "http://www.w3.org/TR/xhtml1/DTD/xhtml1-transitional.dtd">
 4: <html xmlns="http://www.w3.org/1999/xhtml" xml:lang="en" lang="en">
 5: <head><title> Handling Multiple Objects - ex09-12.htm </title></head>
 6: <body style="background:#dddddd;font-family:arial;font-size:20pt;
 7:     color:#000088;font-weight:bold">
 8:
 9:  <div style="text-align:center">Generating Multiple Objects</div>
10:  <div id="buttLoc"></div>
11:     <script src="ex09-11.js"></script>
12:     <script src="ex09-12.js"></script>
13: </body>
14: </html>
```

In this example, the same script file ex09-11.js is used to generate the butterflies on the page. Another script file, ex09-12.js, is dedicated to generating the flying motions and is listed below.

Example: ex09-12.js – The ECMAScript For ex09-12.htm

```
 1:
 2: var flyFlag = new Array
 3: var maxHeight = 600
 4: var maxWidth = 600
 5:
 6: for(mm=0;mm<10;mm++)
 7: {
 8:    flyFlag[mm]=true
 9: }
10:
11: function moveFlyObj()
12: {
13:   for(ii=0;ii<10;ii++)
14:   {
15:    if (flyFlag[ii]==true)
16:    {
17:     objSt = "obj"+ii
18:     mObjStyle = document.getElementById(objSt).style
19:     mObjStyle.top=change_top(parseInt(mObjStyle.top))+"px"
20:     mObjStyle.left=change_left(parseInt(mObjStyle.left))+"px"
21:    }
22:   }
23:   setTimeout("moveFlyObj()",150)
24: }
25:
```

```
26:  function chgDir()
27:  {
28:     if (Math.random() < .5) return true
29:     return false
30:  }
31:
32:  var flyStep =15
33:
34:  function change_top(vTopPos)
35:  {
36:     chgTop = Math.floor(Math.random() * flyStep)
37:     if ((chgDir() || vTopPos >= maxHeight) && vTopPos > flyStep)
38:         vTopPos -= chgTop
39:     else vTopPos += chgTop
40:
41:     return vTopPos
42:  }
43:
44:  function change_left(vLeftPos)
45:  {
46:     chgLeft = Math.floor(Math.random() * 15)
47:     if ((chgDir() || vLeftPos >= maxWidth) && vLeftPos > flyStep)
48:         vLeftPos -= chgLeft
49:     else vLeftPos += chgLeft
50:
51:     return vLeftPos
52:  }
53:
54:  moveFlyObj()
55:
```

Another array, flyFlag, is used to determine which butterfly should fly and which should not. The for-loop in lines 6–9 provides an initial flying condition for all butterflies. The variables maxHeight and maxWidth are used to restrict the flying boundary and to act as a rough guide for changing the flying direction of the butterflies.

The important function here is moveFlyObj() given in lines 11–24. This function checks the flying condition of each butterfly and makes it fly. The first two lines of this function are to get the moving object style (mObjStyle). The object style statement in line 19

```
mObjStyle.top=change_top(parseInt(mObjStyle.top))+"px"
```

calls the change_top() function to change the top position of the moving object. This new value is assigned back to the object to deliver the movement. This is a compact statement and the "px" (pixel) at the end of the code is essential to comply with the W3C standard. This is important, especially if you want the program to work on NS6+. Inside the change_top() function, we have two random functions used to obtain the new position. The effect is similar to flying. The first random function Math.random() is to get the value for the random flying (line 36):

```
chgTop = Math.floor(Math.random() * flyStep)
```

A random number (between 0 and 1) times the flyStep yields the step the butterfly should fly upward. Together with a 50% chance for the random change of flying direction issued by chgDir() in line 37, the result is random flying in the up and down directions. The left position situation is similar to that of the top and is handled by the change_left() function. Finally, there are 10 butterflies flying together to give a more realistic picture. A screen shot of this page is shown in Fig. 9.24.

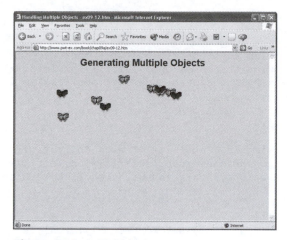

Figure 9.24 ex09-12.htm

9.5.2 Catching flying objects with the mouse

In order to catch the butterflies with the mouse, you need to set up some event handlers to control the mouse movements and picking actions. As an alternative, a mouse click is shown here instead of the drag and drop technique as described in section 9.4.3. You need to set up the following operations:

- When the mouse clicks on a butterfly, the butterfly stops flying and is locked.
- While a butterfly is locked and mouse movement detected, the butterfly moves with the mouse.
- Another mouse click releases and drops the butterfly.

We will use some of the previous coding. First, the interface page of this example is

```
Example: ex09-13.htm - Catching The Flying Butterflies

 1: <?xml version="1.0" encoding="iso-8859-1"?>
 2: <!DOCTYPE html PUBLIC "-//W3C//DTD XHTML 1.0 Transitional//EN"
 3:     "http://www.w3.org/TR/xhtml1/DTD/xhtml1-transitional.dtd">
 4: <html xmlns="http://www.w3.org/1999/xhtml" xml:lang="en" lang="en">
 5: <head><title>Catching The Flying Butterflies - ex09-13.htm</title></head>
 6: <body style="background:#eeeeee;font-family:arial;font-size:20pt;
 7:     color:#000088;font-weight:bold">
 8: <div style="position:absolute;top:20px;left:180px">
 9:       Catching Some Flying Butterflies</div>
10: <div id="buttLoc"></div>
11: <div id="infoLoc"></div>
12: <div id="boxLoc"></div>
13:    <script src="ex09-13a.js"></script>
14:    <script src="ex09-13b.js"></script>
15: </body>
16: </html>
```

This page is similar to that of ex09-12.htm but with more fields. The statement in line 10 concerns the location of the butterflies. The information on how to play will be displayed at the location specified in line 11. In order to collect the captured butterflies, we have some boxes displayed at the location given in line 12. These features are generated by the external file ex09-13a.js.

```
Example: ex09-13a.js - The ECMAScript For ex09-13.htm

 1:
 2: llX = new Array(340,480,280,510,310,540,340,480,280,540)
 3: llY = new Array(90 ,140,140,110,110,140,140,90 ,90 ,90)
 4: llSt =""
```

```
 5:
 6: for (ii=0;ii<5;ii++)
 7: {
 8:   llSt = llSt + '<img id=\"obj'+ii+'\" src=\"bfly01.gif\" alt=\"pic\" '+
 9:     'style=\"position:absolute;top:'+llY[ii]+'px;left:'+llX[ii]+
10:     'px;width:32px;height:32px;z-index:2\" onclick=\"mClick('+ii+')\" />'
11: }
12:
13: for (ii=5;ii<10;ii++)
14: {
15:   llSt = llSt + '<img id=\"obj'+ii+'\" src=\"bfly02.gif\" alt=\"pic\" '+
16:     'style=\"position:absolute;top:'+llY[ii]+'px;left:'+llX[ii]+
17:     'px;width:32px;height:32px;z-index:2\" onclick=\"mClick('+ii+')\" />'
18: }
19:
20: infoSt =""
21: infoSt = infoSt + '<table style=\"font-family:arial;font-size:16pt;'+
22:     'color:#888888;position:absolute;top:100px;left:210px;z-index:1\">'+
23:     '<tr><td>******************************</td></tr> '+
24:     '<tr><td>Click One Butterfly To Catch</td></tr> '+
25:     '<tr><td>Move Mouse To Move </td></tr> '+
26:     '<tr><td>(Don\'t Hold Down Mouse Button While Moving)</td></tr> '+
27:     '<tr><td>One More Mouse Click To Release</td></tr> '+
28:     '<tr><td>******************************</td></tr></table> '
29:
30: boxSt=""
31: boxSt = boxSt +
32:   '<img id=\"red_buf\" src=\"close_box.gif\" alt=\"pic\" style=\"'+
33:     'position:absolute;left:200px;top:290px;height:130px;width:120px;'+
34:     'background: #bbbbbb;z-index: 0\" /> '+
35:   '<div id=\"FirstPar\" style=\"position:absolute;left:200px;top:430px; '+
36:     'height:60px;width:110px;font-size:14pt;color:#aa0000;z-index:3\"> '+
37:     'Red Butt. Box</div> '+
38:   '<img id=\"red_buf\" src=\"close_box.gif\" alt=\"pic\" style=\"'+
39:     'position:absolute;left:400px;top:290px;height:130px;width:120px;'+
40:     'background: #bbbbbb;z-index: 0\" /> '+
41:   '<div id=\"FirstPar\" style=\"position:absolute;left:400px;top:430px; '+
42:     'height:60px;width:110px;font-size:14pt;color:#0000aa;z-index:3\"> '+
43:     'Blue Butt. Box</div> '
44:
45: document.getElementById("buttLoc").innerHTML=llSt
46: document.getElementById("infoLoc").innerHTML=infoSt
47: document.getElementById("boxLoc").innerHTML=boxSt
48:
```

One way to catch the butterflies is to set up event handlers on each of the butterfly objects. The for-loop in lines 6–11 is designed just for that. For example, when the loop variable $ii=0$, the for-loop in lines 6–11 turns out to be

```
<img id="obj0" src="bfly01.gif" alt="pic"
   style="position:absolute;top:90px;left:340px;
   width:32px;height:32px;z-index:2" onclick="mClick(0)" />
```

The z-index value is used so that the butterfly is captured at a suitable level. The onclick handler will trigger and handle all moving activities. All 10 butterflies are concatenated into one string and output to the screen by executing the statement in line 45.

Part III

Practical programming techniques for the Web II

10 Using the Document Object Model (DOM) I

10.1 An introduction to the DOM

10.1.1 What is the DOM?

The DOM is defined by the W3C authority as follows:

> *The Document Object Model is a platform- and language-neutral interface that will allow programs and scripts to dynamically access and update the content, structure, and style of documents. The document can be further processed and the results of that processing can be incorporated back into the presented page.*

In fact, long before the involvement of the W3C and its standardization, browsers had already introduced methods and properties that would allow alien technologies to communicate the contents of a document. This was a natural process to extend their functions and capabilities to a wider area of applications. You could imagine the excitement of a Web programmer in those early days who could change an image by using `onmouseover`, manipulate the width and height of a picture, and query the data and properties of a division `<div>` element. All these could be done with just a couple of lines of coding for Web audiences world-wide. Although the implementations were proprietary at the beginning, they did provide a solid technique to manipulate a Web page and to make it do what you want. This was the initial reason for the formation of the DOM and was very much driven by application demands.

For some early browsers such as NS4.x, the object models and the ways to store and access them were basically tied up with JavaScript. Since the JavaScript engine and its implementation were considered as a part of the browser at that time, there was no difference as to who was controlling the storage in the memory. However, this set-up turned out to be a nightmare for other technologies such as Active Server Page (ASP) and VBScript. In order to define a unified and language-independent structure, IE (or IE4.0) was the first to attempt to take the objects out of a Web page and to embed them into the browser as a data structure very much like a tree. This produced a browser that could contain information to be processed by other technologies such as JScript, VBScript, and a combination of both. The word "object" in this chapter is not just an entity in the language of XHTML but also contains properties and member functions from the concept of object-oriented programming. Naturally, the differences between IE and NS created two different DOMs.

10.1.2 DOM differences and the standard

Some ideas on the confusion regarding the DOMs were briefly mentioned at the beginning of Chapter 6. It's time to provide a clearer picture. As a simple example, consider the following page fragment:

```
Listing: ex10-01.txt - A Paragraph To Explain The DOM

1: <div id="obj1" name="obj1" style="position:absolute;top:120px;
2:        left:150px;width:390px;height:190px;background:#aaffaa">
3:   <div id="obj2" name="obj2" style="font-family:arial;font-weight:bold;
```

```
4:         font-size:14pt;color:#ff0000;text-align:left;position:relative;
5:         top:20px;left:15px;width:300px;height:160px">
6:    DOM is a language independent Application Program Interface (API) to
7:    allow scripting or other technologies to gain access to the Web page.
8:    </div>
9: </div>
```

This fragment contains two objects, obj1 and obj2. The object obj2 is a division element inside obj1 with a relative position so that any changes to the position of obj1 will result in the relative movement of obj2. If you are using NS4.x, the following code can be used to change the background color and the position of obj1:

```
<script>
   document.obj1.bgColor="Blue"
   document.obj1.top=300
   document.obj1.left=250
<script>
```

For NS4.x, the names of the element are part of the document object and therefore their properties can be accessed directly using the name method document.obj1. For the IE family, you can use the following codes to perform a similar task:

```
<script>
   document.all.obj1.style.backgroundColor="Blue"
   document.all.obj1.style.pixelTop=300
   document.all.obj1.style.pixLeft=250
<script>
```

In this case, the style operator is used to gain access to the CSS properties. The method document.all.obj1 is a classical DOM structure of IE to locate obj1 method and its related properties. This structure is still supported by the IE browser family. However, the performances of NS and IE are still not the same even in this simple case.

NS6+ doesn't support any of the above structures and will treat them as illegal statements. Instead, NS6+ supports the W3C DOM standard and the following codes are recommended for the same job:

```
<script>
   document.getElementById("obj1").style.backgroundColor="Blue"
   document.getElementById("obj1").style.top=300+"px"
   document.getElementById("obj1").style.left=250+"px"
<script>
```

Fortunately, the IE family including IE5+ and IE6+ supports the W3C standard. This means that we can now program Web pages in a more unified way with just one set of codes for all browsers that support the W3C standard. However, it is equally important to know about the various DOM differences among browsers. This will not only help you to read and understand some older pages and their behavior, but also provide you with solid knowledge to deal with backward compatibility issues. In particular, it will definitely help you to answer the following frequently asked question from your boss or customers:

Your page is great. Can you make it work for the xxx browser and version xx?

Thanks to the standardization, both the IE and NS browsers are gradually coming closer together. As a Web programmer, you can now program comfortably with just one set of standard codes using W3C's DOM recommendations. Apart from some exceptions and special cases, you no longer need to deal with the division, anchor, image, form, table, and many other elements in a proprietary way. You have the entire picture of the Web page and it is fully open to the scripting and other technologies. Whether you want to make the object move by changing the CSS top left position of an element as in the previous chapter, or to change the contents or color of a paragraph, the DOM provides you with all the answers and explanations of how it works.

More importantly, the DOM also provides a series of standard interfaces for you to access some special elements such as text boxes, radio buttons, checkboxes, select boxes, and text areas. These are vital components in Web programming and will be discussed in this chapter along with some practical applications.

The application of the DOM is far beyond those mentioned above. With the DOM, programmers can build documents, search for elements, walk through the page structures, and add, modify, or delete the elements and contents of a general page. We will cover some basic DOM techniques in this chapter. More advanced study regarding the DOM will be discussed in the next chapter. As a starting point, some basic input elements such as "Text Field," "Button," "Radio," and "Checkbox" of XHTML are introduced from the DOM's point of view. More importantly, we will show you how to control them with programming techniques via the DOM.

10.2   Controlling input elements with DOM interfaces

10.2.1 Generating text field, button, radio, and checkbox

Some of the most popular interface elements on the Web are "Text Box," "Button," "Radio Box," and "Check Box." In order to get user input and to interact with the user, these boxes are important and usually implemented by using the HTML/XHTML `<input>` element. For example, the statement

```
<input type="text" class="styleSt" value="My Text Box" />
```

is often used to generate a text field (or text box) to get text input. This text field contains some CSS properties and has an initial value as "My Text Box." You can, of course, change the value by typing something else on the page. Different type attributes would generate different input elements. Some of the most frequently used types are:

- `type="text"`   –   Generates a text field.
- `type="button"`   –   Generates a button.
- `type="radio"`   –   Generates a radio box.
- `type="checkbox"`   –   Generates a checkbox.

With the W3C DOM, these elements can be studied in a systematic way. First, consider the following page on how to generate these input elements:

```
Example: ex10-01.htm - Generating Input Boxes

 1: <?xml version="1.0" encoding="iso-8859-1"?>
 2: <!DOCTYPE html PUBLIC "-//W3C//DTD XHTML 1.0 Transitional//EN"
 3:     "http://www.w3.org/TR/xhtml1/DTD/xhtml1-transitional.dtd">
 4: <html xmlns="http://www.w3.org/1999/xhtml" xml:lang="en" lang="en">
 5: <style>
 6:   .styleSt{width:280px;height:35px;background:#aaffaa;font-family:arial;
 7:   font-weight:bold;font-size:18pt;color:#880000}</style>
 8: <head><title>Generating Input Boxes -- ex10-01.htm</title></head>
 9: <body style="background:#000088;font-family:arial;font-size:22pt;
10:     color:#ffff00;font-weight:bold;text-align:center"><br />
11:   Generating Input Boxes<br /><br />
12:
13: <table style="font-size:18pt;font-weight:bold;text-align:left">
14:  <tr><td>A Button: </td><td>
15:    <input type="button" value="This is a Button"
16:        class="styleSt" style="background:#cccccc" /></td></tr>
17:  <tr><td>A Text Box: </td><td>
18:    <input type="text" value="This is a Text Box" class="styleSt"
```

```
19:                 style="color:#000000;background:#ffffff"/></td></tr>
20:     <tr><td>A Radio Button: </td><td>
21:     <input type="radio" class="styleSt" name="radB" style="width:40px" />
22:     <input type="radio" class="styleSt" name="radB" style="width:40px" />
23:   </td></tr><tr><td>A CheckBox: </td><td>
24:     <input type="checkbox" class="styleSt" style="width:40px" />
25:     <input type="checkbox" class="styleSt" style="width:40px" /></td></tr>
26: </table>
27: </body>
28: </html>
```

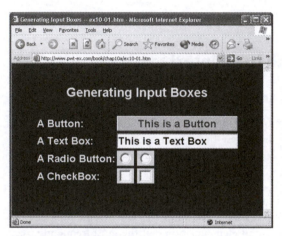

Figure 10.1 ex10-01.htm

This page is quite simple. It generates four kinds of input boxes using the <input> element. Four different input types are used: "text," "button," "radio," and "checkbox." The statements defined in lines 15 and 18 generate a button and a text field. Two radio boxes are then defined and finally two checkboxes are drawn in lines 24–25. They all have CSS properties attached to them and are organized by a table element. Note that the radio boxes (lines 21–22) have the same name="radB" so that only one selection can be picked at any time. A screen shot of this page is shown in Fig. 10.1.

XHTML as a language does not specify any implementations or procedures on how to handle these input elements after displaying them on the screen. To control these boxes and use them in our applications, we need to know:

- How to gain access to the user input such as the text in the text box.
- How to get the selection of the radio boxes.
- How to pick up values of all the checked boxes.

The answers are provided by the interfaces of the DOM.

10.2.2 The DOM interface for input elements

Prior to the W3C recommendations, the implementations on how to handle input elements beyond XHTML level were mostly proprietary. They were either inconsistent or incomplete. With the W3C DOM (www.w3.org), the DOM in general works by providing a series of interfaces to cover from top to bottom every element of the XHTML language. The interface for input elements is called "Interface HTMLInputElement" and was originally designed for the HTML. It is fully embedded and compatible with our XHTML discussions. The definition of this interface for input elements is

```
Listing: ex10-02.txt - The DOM Interface For Input Elements

1: interface HTMLInputElement : HTMLElement {
2:          attribute DOMString        defaultValue;
3:          attribute boolean          defaultChecked;
4:  readonly attribute HTMLFormElement form;
5:          attribute DOMString        accept;
6:          attribute DOMString        accessKey;
7:          attribute DOMString        align;
8:          attribute DOMString        alt;
```

```
 9:              attribute boolean          checked;
10:              attribute boolean          disabled;
11:              attribute long             maxLength;
12:              attribute DOMString        name;
13:              attribute boolean          readOnly;
14:              attribute DOMString        size;
15:              attribute DOMString        src;
16:              attribute long             tabIndex;
17:    // Modified in DOM Level 2:
18:              attribute DOMString        type;
19:              attribute DOMString        useMap;
20:              attribute DOMString        value;
21:    void                 blur();
22:    void                 focus();
23:    void                 select();
24:    void                 click();
25: };
```

Lines 2–20 are the attributes (or properties) of this interface. The remaining lines are the member functions that you can call within this interface object. The attributes are in line with the attributes defined inside the <input> element of the XHTML language. For example, you can define a disabled button using XHTML language as:

```
<input type="button" disabled onclick="myFun()" id="but" />
```

To activate this button, the `disabled` attribute defined in line 10 can be used as follows:

```
<script> document.getElementById("but").disabled=false</script>
```

In this section, we restrict our discussion to the `type` (line 18) "text," "password," "button," "radio," and "checkbox."

There is an independent interface for buttons called "Interface HTMLButtonElement" so that buttons can be defined as independent elements and to access them. The attributes of the button interface are, however, included in this input element interface. For the types concerned, we consider some frequently used properties and functions and show how to master them in a professional way.

value – (line 20) is a string variable (`DOMString` is basically a string)
  • When the type equals "Text," "Button," "File," or "Password," this represents the current contents of the element.
readOnly – (line 13) is a Boolean variable (true or false)
  • This control is read-only and only applies to type "text" or "password."
disabled – (line 10) is a Boolean variable
  • This will make the element unavailable.
checked – (line 9) is a Boolean variable
  • Mainly used when the type equals "radio" or "checkbox," this represents the current selection of the associated box.
focus() – (line 22) is a function to provide keyboard focus to the element.

The best way to demonstrate how to use these properties is to look at some practical applications.

10.2.3 Controlling text fields and buttons

Text fields and buttons are one of the most widely used interfaces in the Web programming industry. Together with radio, checkbox, select box, and text area, you have a set of handy Web programming tools. To generate and use these tools is easy, although more experience may be needed if you want to master them confidently and to put them into your applications. A good place to start is to learn some combination skills involving text fields and buttons.

In the next example, two text fields and some buttons are developed. We demonstrate how to use the `readOnly` attribute to make a text field read-only so that information cannot be modified. This technique is often used by professionals to minimize user errors. The `focus()` function is also employed to show how to move your keyboard cursor to a text field for typing purposes. One characteristic of this example is that buttons can change their names and actions.

Example: ex10-02.htm – Controlling Text Fields And Buttons (DOM)

```
 1: <?xml version="1.0" encoding="iso-8859-1"?>
 2: <!DOCTYPE html PUBLIC "-//W3C//DTD XHTML 1.0 Transitional//EN"
 3:     "http://www.w3.org/TR/xhtml1/DTD/xhtml1-transitional.dtd">
 4: <html xmlns="http://www.w3.org/1999/xhtml" xml:lang="en" lang="en">
 5: <head><title> Text Fields and Buttons I -- ex10-02.htm</title></head>
 6: <style>
 7:   .butSt{background-color:#aaaaaa;font-family:arial;font-weight:bold;
 8:       font-size:14pt;color:#aa0000;width:150px;height:35px}
 9:   .txtSt{background-color:#aaffaa;font-family:arial;font-weight:bold;
10:       font-size:16pt;color:#880000;width:300px;height:35px}
11:   .txtSt2{font-family:arial;font-weight:bold; text-align:left;
12:       font-size:14pt;color:#ffff00}
13: </style>
14: <body style="background:#000088;font-size:20pt;text-align:center"
15: class="txtSt2"><br />Simple Controls On Text Field<br /><br />
16:
17: <div class="txtSt2" style="text-align:center"><br />
18:   <span>Text Field 1: </span>
19:   <input type="text" id="myText1" name="myText1"
20:      value="This is Text Field 1" class="txtSt" /><br /><br />
21:   <span>Text Field 2: </span>
22:   <input type="text" id="myText2" name="myText2"
23:      value="This is Text Field 2" class="txtSt" /><br /><br /><br />
24:
25:   <table class="txtSt2" align="center">
26:   <tr>
27:     <td>Text1 Control<br /> Buttons</td>
28:     <td><input type="button" id="readBut1" onclick="readOnlyTxt(1)"
29:         value="ReadOnly" class="butSt" /></td>
30:     <td><input type="button" onclick="focusTxt(1)"
31:         value="Focus" class="butSt" /></td></tr>
32:   <tr>
33:     <td>Text2 Control<br /> Buttons</td>
34:     <td><input type="button" id="readBut2" onclick="readOnlyTxt(2)"
35:         value="ReadOnly" class="butSt" /></td>
36:     <td><input type="button" onclick="focusTxt(2)"
37:         value="Focus" class="butSt" /></td></tr>
38:   </table>
39: </div>
40: <script src="ex10-02.js"></script>
41: </body>
42: </html>
```

Two input elements with `type="text"` are defined in lines 18–23. These two text fields are controlled by two rows of buttons. Consider the two buttons in the first row (lines 28–31):

```
<input type="button" id="readBut1" onclick="readOnlyTxt(1)"
   value="ReadOnly" class="butSt" />

<input type="button" onclick="focusTxt(1)"
        value="Focus" class="butSt" />
```

When the first button is pressed, the function `readOnlyTxt(1)` performs the following actions:

- It sets the first text field as read-only so that no modifications can be made.
- It changes the color of the read-only text field.
- It changes the button to "Read and Write" so that the text field can be changed back again by another click.

The second button is to move the keyboard cursor into the first text field by calling the function `focusTxt(1)`. The second row of buttons (lines 33–37) is used to control the second text field in a similar fashion. Some screen shots of this example are shown in Figs 10.2 and 10.3.

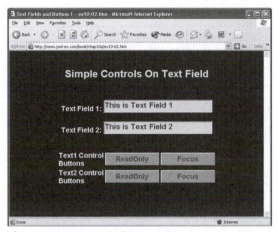

Figure 10.2 ex10-02.htm

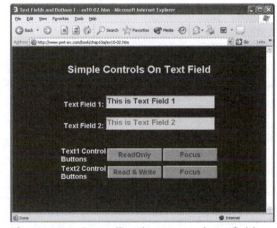

Figure 10.3 Controlling buttons and text fields

The program file for this example is ex10-02.js and listed below.

```
Example: ex10-02.js - The ECMAScript For ex10-02.htm

 1: function focusTxt(llV)
 2: {
 3:   objV = "myText"+llV
 4:   document.getElementById(objV).focus()
 5: }
 6:
 7: var readonlyV1 = 0
 8: var readonlyV2 = 0
 9:
10: function readOnlyTxt(llV)
11: {
12:  if (llV ==1) {
13:   if (readonlyV1 ==0 ) {
14:    readonlyV1 = 1
15:    objV = "myText"+llV
16:    document.getElementById(objV).readOnly = true
17:    document.getElementById(objV).style.color="#888888"
18:    document.getElementById("readBut1").value="Read & Write"
19:   } else {
20:    readonlyV1 = 0
21:    objV = "myText"+llV
22:    document.getElementById(objV).readOnly = false
23:    document.getElementById(objV).style.color="#880000"
24:    document.getElementById("readBut1").value="ReadOnly"
25:   }
```

```
26:    } else {
27:     if (readonlyV2 ==0 ) {
28:      readonlyV2 = 1
29:      objV = "myText"+llV
30:      document.getElementById(objV).readOnly = true
31:      document.getElementById(objV).style.color="#888888"
32:      document.getElementById("readBut2").value="Read & Write"
33:     } else {
34:      readonlyV2 = 0
35:      objV = "myText"+llV
36:      document.getElementById(objV).readOnly = false
37:      document.getElementById(objV).style.color="#880000"
38:      document.getElementById("readBut2").value="ReadOnly"
39:     }
40:    }
41: }
```

This listing contains two functions. The first one is focusTxt(llV). It takes an argument and the statements inside the function are

```
objV = "myText"+llV
document.getElementById(objV).focus()
```

The first statement is to compose the identity of the object. Then the focus() function is called to move the keyboard cursor to that element.

The code for the second function readOnlyTxt(llV) is longer. First, global variables readonlyV1 and readonlyV2 are used to store the current read-only status of the text fields. A zero value indicates a "Read & Write" situation and "Read Only" otherwise. If the function readOnly(llV) is called with argument llV=1, the first text field is considered and the following statements (lines 13–26) are executed:

```
if (readonlyV1 ==0 ) {
 readonlyV1 = 1
 objV = "myText"+llV
 document.getElementById(objV).readOnly = true
 document.getElementById(objV).style.color="#888888"
 document.getElementById("readBut1").value="Read & Write"
} else {
 readonlyV1 = 0
 objV = "myText"+llV
 document.getElementById(objV).readOnly = false
 document.getElementById(objV).style.color="#880000"
 document.getElementById("readBut1").value="ReadOnly"
 }
}
```

That is, if the first text field is "Read & Write," it is changed to read-only. The color of the text field and the name of the button are changed as well. If the current status of the text field is "Read Only," the statements after the else keyword are executed. In this case, the readOnly status of the text field is set to false so that user input can be accepted. The color and the name of the button are also changed at the same time.

Manipulating text attributes such as readOnly with programming techniques is popular among professionals since they are one of the important tools to eliminate unnecessary user errors.

To show how to capture data from text boxes, we consider another example: ex10-03.htm. In terms of page design and structure, this example is similar to ex10-02.htm. We also have two text fields and four buttons arranged into two rows. The first button captures the text of the first text field and outputs the data to a dedicated area. The second button is used to make the text field disappear entirely. The third and fourth buttons control the second text field. Consider the XHTML code fragment of this example below:

Listing: ex10-03.txt - Page Fragment For ex10-03.htm

```
 1:  <table class="txtSt2" align="center">
 2:   <tr>
 3:     <td>Text1 Control<br /> Buttons</td>
 4:     <td><input type="button" id="showTxt1" onclick="showTxt(1)"
 5:         value="Show Text" class="butSt"></td>
 6:     <td><input type="button" id="disappTxt1" onclick="disappTxt(1)"
 7:         value="Disappear" class="butSt"></td></tr>
 8:   <tr>
 9:     <td>Text1 Control<br /> Buttons</td>
10:     <td><input type="button" id="showTxt2" onclick="showTxt(2)"
11:         value="Show Text" class="butSt"></td>
12:     <td><input type="button" id="disappTxt2" onclick="disappTxt(2)"
13:         value="Disappear" class="butSt"></td></tr>
14:  </table><br /><br />
15:
16:   <input type="text" id="outMsg" name="outMsg" readOnly="true"
17:     value="Text Field Message" class="txtSt"/><br />
18: </div>
19: <script src="ex10-03.js"></script>
20:
```

If you replace lines 25–40 in ex10-02.htm with this fragment, you will have the XHTML code for ex10-03.htm. Basically, this fragment changes the names of the buttons and the functions associated with them. If you press the button defined in line 4, the function showTxt(1) is called to capture the text in "Text Field 1" and displays it to the message area in lines 16–17. If the second button is pressed, the function disappTxt(1) is called and makes the entire "Text Field 1" disappear. These two functions are specified in the program file ex10-03.js.

Example: ex10-03.js - The ECMAScript For ex10-03.htm

```
 1: function showTxt(llV)
 2: {
 3:   objV = "myText"+llV
 4:   document.getElementById("outMsg").value =
 5:   document.getElementById(objV).value
 6: }
 7:
 8: var disappV1 = 0
 9: var disappV2 = 0
10:
11: function disappTxt(llV)
12: {
13:  if (llV ==1) {
14:   if (disappV1 ==0 ) {
15:    disappV1 = 1
16:    objV = "myText"+llV
17:    document.getElementById("disappTxt1").value="Appear"
18:    document.getElementById(objV).style.visibility="hidden"
19:   } else {
20:    disappV1 = 0
21:    objV = "myText"+llV
22:    document.getElementById("disappTxt1").value="Disappear"
23:    document.getElementById(objV).style.visibility="visible"
24:   }
25:  } else {
26:   if (disappV2 ==0 ) {
27:    disappV2 = 1
```

```
28:     objV = "myText"+llV
29:     document.getElementById("disappTxt2").value="Appear"
30:     document.getElementById(objV).style.visibility="hidden"
31:   } else {
32:     disappV2 = 0
33:     objV = "myText"+llV
34:     document.getElementById("disappTxt2").value="Disappear"
35:     document.getElementById(objV).style.visibility="visible"
36:   }
37:   }
38: }
```

The function `showTxt()` is easy to understand. The `document.getElementById(objV).value` captures the content of the text field and the statement in line 4 displays it to the area with `id="outMsg"`. The `disappTxt()` function uses the CSS property

```
document.getElementById(objV).style.visibility="hidden"
```

to make the text field disappear (line 18). Some screen shots are shown in Figs 10.4 and 10.5.

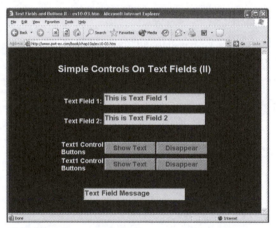

Figure 10.4 ex10-03.htm

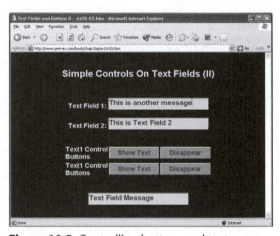

Figure 10.5 Controlling buttons and text fields (II)

You now have some hands-on experiences to handle input elements. It is time to consider a real application. The next section shows you how to change your password.

10.2.4 A page to change your password

Providing facilities to change a password is a general application on the Web. From the membership of a kids club to the Internet banking and commercial sectors, a simple and friendly facility to allow users to change their passwords regularly is considered to be a good security measure. We are not going to discuss Internet security, at least not yet, just a simple facility to allow users to change their passwords.

Even a basic facility to change a password involves the following operations. You need to

- generate a text field for the password and capture the password data;
- capture the keystroke, in particular the carriage return (ASCII value 13) so that you know the user has finished typing and further action is needed;
- generate a confirm password window at run time to allow the user to retype the password; and
- compare the password and the confirm data for a match.

To make this example more interesting, no inline event handlers are set up to capture the keystroke, event listener techniques are used instead. In order to handle the differences of the IE, NS, and some backward compatibility issues, two sets of coding are used together with a simple detection routine to detect the IE and NS browsers.

The interface part of this page is simple and is listed below:

Example: ex10-04.htm - A Page To Change Password

```
 1: <?xml version="1.0" encoding="iso-8859-1"?>
 2: <!DOCTYPE html PUBLIC "-//W3C//DTD XHTML 1.0 Transitional//EN"
 3:     "http://www.w3.org/TR/xhtml1/DTD/xhtml1-transitional.dtd">
 4: <html xmlns="http://www.w3.org/1999/xhtml" xml:lang="en" lang="en">
 5: <head><title> A Page To Change Password -- ex10-04.htm</title></head>
 6: <style>
 7:   .butSt{background-color:#aaffaa;font-family:arial;font-weight:bold;
 8:       font-size:18pt;color:#880000;width:250px;height:35px}
 9:   .txtSt{font-family:arial;font-weight:bold; text-align:left;
10:       font-size:14pt;color:#ffff00}
11: </style>
12: <body style="background:#000088">
13:
14: <table style="position:absolute;left:60px;top:50px;
15:           font-size:18pt" class="txtSt">
16:  <tr><td colspan="2" style="text-align:center">
17:     Changing Your Password<br /><br/></td></tr>
18:  <tr><td>Name:</td>
19:     <td><input type="text" id="nameSt" class="butSt" ></td></tr>
20:  <tr><td>New Password:</td>
21:     <td><input type="password" id="passSt" class="butSt"></td></tr>
22:  <tr style="visibility:hidden" id="confirm"><td>Confirm Password:</td>
23:     <td><input type="password" id="confirmSt" class="butSt" ></td></tr>
24:  <tr><td colspan="2"><br /><br />
25:     <div id="outMsg" class="txtSt"></div></td></tr>
26: </table>
27:
28: <script src="ex10-04.js"></script>
29: </body>
30: </html>
```

In this page, we use a table to accommodate text fields on "Name" (line 19), "New Password" (line 21), and "Confirm Password" (line 23). The new password and confirm password have the attribute `type="password"` so that the content will not be displayed on screen.

The "Confirm Password" element defined in line 22 has the initial CSS property `visibility:hidden` so that the entire row will not be displayed at all.

In a normal change password operation, we would like to implement the following features:

- When the user finishes typing his or her name in the "Name" field and hits the return key, the keyboard cursor will jump to the "New Password" field.
- When the user finishes typing the password and hits the return key, a "Confirm Password" text field appears and focus on this field.
- As soon as the user finishes the confirm password and hits the return key again, the new password and the confirmed one are compared to check for a match.
- The matching result is displayed in a dedicated display area defined in line 25.

Some screen shots of this example in action are shown in Figs 10.6–10.9.

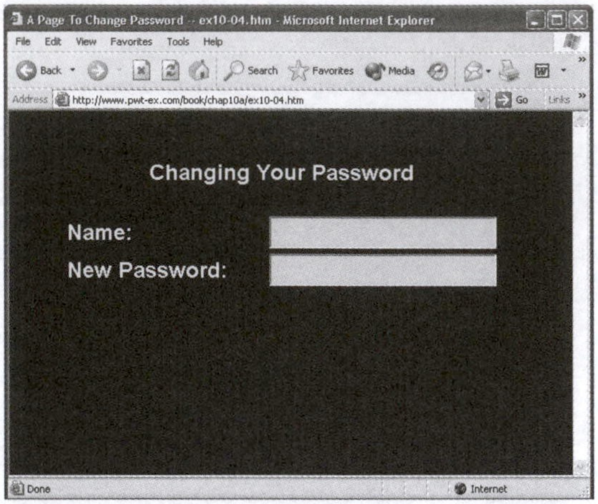

Figure 10.6 ex10-04.htm

Figure 10.7 Generating confirm password at run time

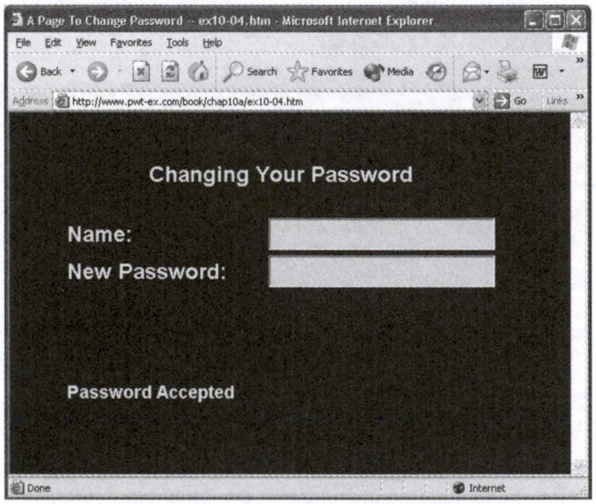

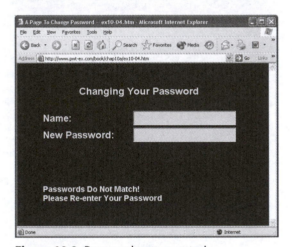

Figure 10.8 Password accepted

Figure 10.9 Password not accepted

The driving force behind the interface is the external ECMAScript ex10-04.js and the first part of this program is listed below:

```
Example: ex10-04.js - The ECMAScript For ex10-04.htm (Part One)

 1:
 2:  var IE = document.all?true:false
 3:  var objV
 4:  if (!IE)
 5:  {
 6:      objV1 = document.getElementById("nameSt")
 7:      objV1.addEventListener("keypress",proName,false)
 8:      objV2 = document.getElementById("passSt")
 9:      objV2.addEventListener("keypress",proNew,false)
10:      objV3 = document.getElementById("confirmSt")
11:      objV3.addEventListener("keypress",proConfirm,false)
12:  }else {
13:      objV1 = document.getElementById("nameSt")
14:      objV1.attachEvent("onkeypress",proName)
```

```
15:     objV2 = document.getElementById("passSt")
16:     objV2.attachEvent("onkeypress",proNew)
17:     objV3 = document.getElementById("confirmSt")
18:     objV3.attachEvent("onkeypress",proConfirm)
19:  }
20:
21:  function chkReturn(e)
22:  {
23:   if (IE) {
24:       if (escape(event.keyCode)=="13") return true
25:   } else {
26:       if (escape(e.keyCode) == "13") return true
27:       else return false
28:   }
29:  }
30:
```

This part of the program is to set up the event listeners. The first line detects the browser type. If the NS (NS6+) browser is detected, the statements in lines 6–11 are used to set up the event listeners. Similarly the execution of statements in lines 13–18 sets the listeners for IE-type browsers.

Since we need to listen to the keystrokes on the "Name," "New Password," and "Confirm Password" fields, three listeners are set. When any keystroke is detected in the "Name" field, the function proName() is called to process the name. If a carriage return key is found, the function is to move the keyboard cursor to the next field.

The function chkReturn() defined in lines 21–29 is designed to trap the carriage return key which has the ASCII value 13. This function returns a true value when ASCII 13 code is detected. Again two sets of code are used. The second part of the ECMAScript ex10-04.js contains all the process functions for the page ex10-04.htm.

```
Listing: Continuation Of The ECMAScript ex10-04.js (Part Two)

31:  function proName(e)
32:  {
33:   if (chkReturn(e)) document.getElementById("passSt").focus()
34:  }
35:
36:  function proNew(e)
37:  {
38:   if (chkReturn(e)) {
39:    document.getElementById("confirm").style.visibility="visible"
40:    document.getElementById("confirmSt").focus()
41:   }
42:  }
43:
44:  function restorePar(e)
45:  {
46:      document.getElementById("nameSt").value =""
47:      document.getElementById("passSt").value =""
48:      document.getElementById("confirmSt").value=""
49:
50:      document.getElementById("nameSt").focus()
51:      document.getElementById("confirm").style.visibility = "hidden"
52:  }
53:
54:  function proConfirm(e)
55:  {
56:   if (chkReturn(e))
57:   {
58:    ISt01 = document.getElementById("confirmSt").value
```

```
59:    ISt02 = document.getElementById("passSt").value
60:    if ( ISt01 != ISt02) {
61:     outSt = "Passwords Do Not Match! <br />"+ "Please Re-enter Your Password"
62:    } else {
63:      outSt = "Password Accepted"
64:    }
65:    document.getElementById("outMsg").innerHTML= outSt
66:    restorePar()
67:    }
68:  }
```

The first function `proName()` is simple. If the keystroke is the return key, the `focus()` function sets the cursor to the "New Password" field. The second function `proNew()` is called whenever a key event occurs inside the new password field. If the return key is detected, the statement in line 39 is executed to make the entire row with identity `id="confirm"` visible so that the "Confirm Password" field appears. The statement in line 40 is to focus on the confirm box. If the user hits the return key inside the confirm box, the `proConfirm()` function compares the password data and the data in the confirm field. If they are the same, the statement in 65 displays the message "Password Accepted." Whether you have a matched password or not, the function `restorePar()` is called to reset all the text field attributes.

10.3   Multiple checkboxes and radio boxes

10.3.1 Using multiple checkboxes

Another programming tool to get user input and associated with the HTMLinputElement interface is the checkbox. This is an ideal feature to handle multiple selections on an options list. To control them, or to detect whether the boxes have been checked, you use the property "checked" as defined by the interface in ex10-02.txt. For example, if you have a checkbox defined as

```
<input type="checkbox" id="myCheckBox">
```

you can use the following script statement to check whether the box has been checked:

```
document.getElementById("myCheckBox").checked
```

This statement returns a true value if the box has been checked. Multiple checkboxes can be set up in this way to handle multiple selections. To control and to access multiple checkboxes, let's consider the following page to collect data on your favorite browsers.

```
Example: ex10-05.htm - A Page To Collect Data On Favorite Browsers
 1: <?xml version="1.0" encoding="iso-8859-1"?>
 2: <!DOCTYPE html PUBLIC "-//W3C//DTD XHTML 1.0 Transitional//EN"
 3:      "http://www.w3.org/TR/xhtml1/DTD/xhtml1-transitional.dtd">
 4: <html xmlns="http://www.w3.org/1999/xhtml" xml:lang="en" lang="en">
 5: <style>
 6:   .styleSt{width:320px;height:35px;background:#aaffaa;font-family:arial;
 7:    font-weight:bold;font-size:14pt;color:#880000}
 8:   .tableSt{font-size:14pt;font-weight:bold;text-align:left}</style>
 9: <head><title>Your Favorite Browsers - ex10-05.htm</title></head>
10:
11: <body style="background:#000088;font-family:arial;color:#ffff00">
12:
13: <table class="tableSt" style="position:absolute;top:30px;left:60px">
14:  <tr><td colspan="2" style="text-align:center;font-size:22pt">
15:          Your Favorite Browsers<br /><br /></td></tr>
16:  <tr><td>Name: </td>
```

```
17:        <td><input type="text" value="" class="styleSt" id="nameId"
18:           style="color:#000000;background:#dddddd"/></td></tr>
19:   <tr><td>Email Address: </td>
20:        <td><input type="text" value="" class="styleSt" id="emailId"
21:           style="color:#000000;background:#dddddd"/></td></tr>
22:  </table>
23:
24:  <table class="tableSt" style="position:absolute;top:230px;left:60px">
25:   <tr><td>Internet Explorer:   </td>
26:        <td><input type="checkbox" class="styleSt" id="chk0"
27:           style="width:40px" /></td></tr>
28:   <tr><td>Netscape 6.+:  </td>
29:        <td><input type="checkbox" class="styleSt" id="chk1"
30:           style="width:40px" /></td></tr>
31:   <tr><td>Netscape Navigator:   </td>
32:        <td><input type="checkbox" class="styleSt" id="chk2"
33:           style="width:40px" /></td></tr>
34:  </table>
35:
36:  <table class="tableSt" style="position:absolute;top:230px;left:340px">
37:   <tr><td>Opera:   </td>
38:     <td><input type="checkbox" class="styleSt" id="chk3"
39:           style="width:40px" /></td></tr>
40:   <tr><td>KDE (LINUX):   </td>
41:     <td><input type="checkbox" class="styleSt" id="chk4"
42:           style="width:40px" /></td></tr>
43:   <tr><td>Others:   </td>
44:     <td><input type="checkbox" class="styleSt" id="chk5"
45:           style="width:40px" /></td></tr>
46:  </table>
47:
48:  <table class="tableSt" style="position:absolute;top:400px;left:100px"><tr>
49:   <td><input type="button" class="styleSt" style="width:200px;
50:     background:#aaaaaa" value="Reset" onclick="resetPar()"/></td>
51:   <td><input type="button" class="styleSt" value="Send" id="proDataBut"
52:     style="width:200px;background:#aaaaaa" onclick="proData()" /></td></tr>
53:   <tr><td colspan="2"><div id="outMsg" style="width:400px;height:60px">
54:     </div></td></tr>
55:  </table>
56:  </body>
57:  <script src="ex10-05.js"></script>
58:  </html>
```

This page has four tables. The first table in lines 13–22 contains two text fields to collect information for "Name" and "Email Address." The second table defined in lines 24–34 generates a column of three checkboxes with identities chk0, chk1, and chk2

```
<input type="checkbox" class="styleSt" id="chk0" style="width:40px" />
<input type="checkbox" class="styleSt" id="chk1" style="width:40px" />
<input type="checkbox" class="styleSt" id="chk2" style="width:40px" />
```

representing browser selections "Internet Explorer," "Netscape 6.+," and "Netscape Navigator." Another column of checkboxes is defined in a separate table in lines 36–46. These two columns of checkboxes are arranged side by side with position settings. Two action buttons and a display area are also defined by using a table as shown in lines 48–55.

When the Send button is clicked, all the information on "Name," "Email Address," and checked boxes is displayed in the display area. You also use the `disabled` attribute of the input interface to disable the Send button. The Reset button can be used to restore all the parameters to their original values. Some screen shots of this example are shown in Figs 10.10 and 10.11.

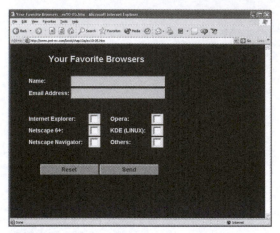

Figure 10.10 ex10-05.htm

Figure 10.11 Collecting browser data

The program part of this example is given in ex10-05.js.

Example: ex10-05.js – The ECMAScript For ex10-05.htm

```
 1:  var noChkBox=6
 2:  function resetPar()
 3:  {
 4:    document.getElementById("nameId").value=""
 5:    document.getElementById("emailId").value=""
 6:    document.getElementById("outMsg").innerHTML=""
 7:    document.getElementById("proDataBut").disabled=false
 8:    for (jj=0;jj<noChkBox;jj++)
 9:    {
10:      chkB = "chk"+jj
11:      document.getElementById(chkB).checked = false
12:    }
13:  }
14:
15:  chkArr = new Array("Internet Explorer","Netscape 6.+",
16:   "Netscape Navigator","Opera","KDE (LINUX)","Others")
17:
18:  function proData()
19:  {
20:    llSt = "Name: "+document.getElementById("nameId").value +"<br />"
21:    llSt = llSt + "Email: "+ document.getElementById("emailId").value +
22:     "<br />"+"Browsers: "
23:    for (jj=0;jj<noChkBox;jj++)
24:    {
25:      chkB = "chk"+jj
26:      if (document.getElementById(chkB).checked )
27:        llSt = llSt + chkArr[jj] + ", "
28:    }
29:    document.getElementById("outMsg").innerHTML = llSt
30:    document.getElementById("proDataBut").disabled=true
31:  }
```

The `resetPar()` function is easy to understand. The first job of this function is to clear any messages in "Name," "Email Address," and the display area. After enabling the Send button in line 7, a for-loop is executed to uncheck all the checkboxes.

In this example, no direct information is provided to link the checkboxes and their corresponding values. We need to find a way to provide it ourselves. For this purpose, an array is defined in lines 15–16, i.e.,

```
chkArr[0] = "Internet Explorer" ,…, chrArr[5]= "Others"
```

This array is employed inside the function `proData()`. After the "Name" and "Email Address" data, the for-loop in lines 23–28 is used to run through all the checkboxes. If the *jj*th checkbox is checked, the associated array element `chkArr[jj]` representing the corresponding value of the checkbox is added to the display string `llSt`. You output the display string `llSt` by executing the statement in line 29. The Send button is disabled before the end of the function.

Some people may prefer to put the selection data into the checkbox element as a value such as

```
<input type="checkbox" class="styleSt" id="chk0"
    style="width:40px" value="Internet Explorer" />
```

A simple function call to the function `getElementById("chk0").value` would return the data. Using the array as in this example has the advantage that data can be changed easily.

10.3.2 Controlling radio boxes

The checkbox may be an ideal tool to handle multiple selections. But for a multiple-choice application in which only one answer can be picked, the radio box is surely a better tool. Compared to the radio box, the checkbox has a different access scheme. Thanks to the W3C, you now have a universal technique to access them. This method is referred to as "Collection" and is an important subject for the remainder of this chapter.

As a simple application, we consider a page that allows users to pick a free gift. The coding for this example is

```
Example: ex10-06.htm – Radio Boxes

 1: <?xml version="1.0" encoding="iso-8859-1"?>
 2: <!DOCTYPE html PUBLIC "-//W3C//DTD XHTML 1.0 Transitional//EN"
 3:     "http://www.w3.org/TR/xhtml1/DTD/xhtml1-transitional.dtd">
 4: <html xmlns="http://www.w3.org/1999/xhtml" xml:lang="en" lang="en">
 5: <style>
 6:  .styleSt{width:320px;height:35px;background:#aaffaa;font-family:arial;
 7:    font-weight:bold;font-size:14pt;color:#880000}
 8:  .radSt{width:320px;height:35px;background:#aaffaa;font-family:arial;
 9:    font-weight:bold;font-size:14pt;color:#880000;width:30px;height:30px}
10:  .tableSt{font-size:14pt;font-weight:bold;text-align:left}</style>
11: <head><title>Radio Boxes – ex10-06.htm</title></head>
12: <body style="background:#000088;font-family:arial;color:#ffff00">
13: <form action="">
14: <table class="tableSt" style="position:absolute;top:30px;left:120px">
15:  <tr><td colspan="2" style="font-size:18pt;text-align:center">
16:     A Simple Example On Radio Boxes<br />
17:     Please Pick Your Free Gift<br /><br /></td>
18:  <tr><td>A Portable DVD Player:   </td><td><input type="radio"
19:     class="radSt" id="radB" name="radB" checked /></td></tr>
20:  <tr><td>A Digital Camera:   </td>
21:   <td><input type="radio" class="radSt" id="radB" name="radB" /></td></tr>
22:  <tr><td>Car Rental For One Week:   </td>
23:   <td><input type="radio" class="radSt" id="radB" name="radB" /></td></tr>
24:  <tr><td>An Air Ticket To Spain:   </td>
25:   <td><input type="radio" class="radSt" id="radB" name="radB" /></td></tr>
```

```
26:   <tr><td colspan="2"><br /><input type="button" class="styleSt"
27:     onclick="getData()" value="Send" style="width:100px"></td></tr>
28:   <tr><td colspan="2"><br /><div id="outMsg" name="outMsg"></div></td></tr>
29: </table>
30: </form>
31: </body>
32: <script>
33:   choiceArr = new Array("A Portable DVD Player","A Digital Camera",
34:     "Car Rental For One Week", "An Air Ticket To Spain")
35:
36:   function getData()
37:   {
38:    llV = document.getElementsByName("radB")
39:    for (jj=0;jj<llV.length;jj++)
40:    {
41:      if (llV.item(jj).checked) llSt = choiceArr[jj]
42:    }
43:    document.getElementById("outMsg").innerHTML = "Your Have Picked: "+ llSt
44:   }
45: </script>
46: </html>
```

The table in lines 14–29 generates four radio boxes and each of them has the exact format

```
<input type="radio" class="radSt" id="radB" name="radB" />
```

All four radio boxes have the same name, "radB." It is essential to define radio boxes with the same name so that only one box can be selected. In this example, the table and hence the radio boxes are inside a form element defined in lines 13–30. This arrangement is necessary only for some browsers that cannot interpret radio boxes as individual elements. Traditionally, input elements are embedded in the form element. More details about form structure and element collection are given in the next chapter.

Once the Send button is pressed, the function `getDate()` is called. Inside this function, there is another important function provided by the DOM called `getElementsByName(),`. The main duty of this function is to collect all elements with the same name and return them as a collection similar to an array. The statement in line 38

```
llV = document.getElementsByName("radB")
```

is used to collect all the radio boxes and return them as a collection called `llV`. The `llV.length` property contains the length of the collection and the `item()` function can be used to access the boxes. For example, `llV.item(2)` represents the third radio box and `llV.item(2).checked` represents the check status of the box. Sometimes, the `item()` function is integrated into the browser as an array structure and can be called by

```
llV[2].checked
```

The `item()` function is formally declared inside the interface specification provided by W3C's DOM. Now, the for-loop in lines 39–42 is a loop to run through all radio boxes and to detect which one is checked. The checked box data are assigned to `llSt` and output to the screen via the statement in line 43. A screen shot of this example is shown in Fig. 10.12.

10.3.3 A page to obtain personal data

One of the common applications of text fields, buttons, checkboxes, and radio boxes is as a page to obtain personal data. A simple but effective page to obtain user data is often vital to many database type applications since not many visitors would like to fill in a complicated form. The following is a simplified version of an example to collect user data for a dating agency. Based on this example, a page matching new friends or companions will be introduced at the end of this chapter. This data collection page has the display shown in Fig. 10.13.

Figure 10.12 ex10-06.htm

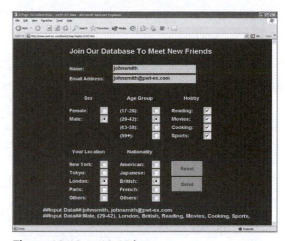

Figure 10.13 ex10-07.htm

From Fig. 10.13, you can see the following fields:

- "Name" and "Email Address" – two text fields
- "Sex" field – two radio boxes
- "Age Group" field – four radio boxes
- "Hobby" field – four checkboxes (for multiple selections)
- "Your Location" field – four radio boxes
- "Nationality" field – four radio boxes
- Two buttons named "Reset" and "Send"

One efficient way to lay out these items is to use a table. Using a table for each item has the advantage that it can be placed anywhere independently. For example, you can implement the first two text fields as one table. The "Sex" field (two radio boxes) can be implemented as another table as shown in the listing ex10-04.txt.

Listing: ex10-04.txt - A Table With Two Radio Boxes

```
 1: <table class="tableSt" style="position:absolute;top:230px;left:220px">
 2:   <tr><td colspan="2" style="text-align:center">Sex<br /><br /></td>
 3:   <tr><td style="width:120px">Female:   </td>
 4:     <td><input type="radio" class="radSt" id="sex" name="sex" /></td></tr>
 5:   <tr><td>Male:   </td>
 6:     <td><input type="radio" class="radSt" id="sex" name="sex" /></td></tr>
 7: </table>
```

This is a table with two radio boxes. The tables for "Age Group," "Hobby," "Your Location," and "Nationality" are similar and you perhaps don't want to write five similar tables in one page. Can you program them in a more professional and compact manner?

If you separate all components of the table into changeable and fixed keywords, you will find that the table in ex10-04.txt can be generated by the function `genTable()`:

```
function genTable(topV,leftV,widthV,noElV,eleArr,titleV,typeV,idV)
```

where the arguments are:

- `topV`: the top position of the table
- `leftV`: the left position of the table
- `widthV`: the width (pixel) of the text before the radio or checkbox
- `noElV`: number of radio or checkboxes

- `eleArr`: an array to store the text before the boxes
- `titleV`: the text at the top of the field
- `typeV`: 1 for radio boxes and 2 for checkboxes
- `idV`: identity of the boxes

In particular, the "Sex" table (ex10-04.txt) can be generated by

```
sexArr = new Array("Female","Male")
genTable(230,220,120,2,sexArr,"Sex",1,"sex")
```

Similarly, all other tables, "Age Group," "Hobby," "Your Location," and "Nationality," are just simple function calls to `genTable()`. More precisely, we have

```
ageArr = new Array("(17-28)","(29-42)","(43-58)","(59+)")
genTable(230,420,120,4,ageArr,"Age Group",1,"age")

hobArr = new Array("Reading","Movies","Cooking","Sports")
genTable(230,620,120,4,hobArr,"Hobby",2,"hob")
locArr = new Array("New York","Tokyo","London","Paris","Others")
genTable(450,220,120,5,locArr,"Your Location",1,"loc")

natArr = new Array("American","Japanese","British","French","Others")
genTable(450,420,120,5,natArr,"Nationality",1,"nat")
```

A general function like this is highly reusable and could be quite handy in your programming life to increase productivity.

Note that you have used `typeV=2` in the "hobby" table, indicating that checkboxes are used. The current design of the page is shown below.

```
Example: ex10-07.htm - A Page To Collect Data

 1: <?xml version="1.0" encoding="iso-8859-1"?>
 2: <!DOCTYPE html PUBLIC "-//W3C//DTD XHTML 1.0 Transitional//EN"
 3:     "http://www.w3.org/TR/xhtml1/DTD/xhtml1-transitional.dtd">
 4: <html xmlns="http://www.w3.org/1999/xhtml" xml:lang="en" lang="en">
 5: <style>
 6:  .styleSt{width:320px;height:35px;background:#aaffaa;font-family:arial;
 7:   font-weight:bold;font-size:14pt;color:#880000}
 8:  .radSt{width:320px;height:35px;background:#aaffaa;font-family:arial;
 9:   font-weight:bold;font-size:14pt;color:#880000;width:30px;height:30px}
10:  .tableSt{font-size:14pt;font-weight:bold;text-align:left}</style>
11: <head><title>A Page To Collect Data - ex10-07.htm</title></head>
12: <script src="ex10-07.js"></script>
13: <body style="background:#000088;font-family:arial;color:#ffff00">
14:
15: <table class="tableSt" style="position:absolute;top:30px;left:220px">
16:  <tr><td colspan="2" style="text-align:center;font-size:22pt">
17:     Join Our Database To Meet New Friends<br /><br /></td></tr>
18:  <tr><td>Name: </td>
19:    <td><input type="text" value="" class="styleSt" id="nameId"
20:         style="color:#000000;background:#dddddd"/></td></tr>
21:  <tr><td>Email Address: </td>
22:    <td><input type="text" value="" class="styleSt" id="emailId"
23:         style="color:#000000;background:#dddddd"/></td></tr>
24: </table>
25:
26: <script>
27:     genTable(230,220,120,2,sexArr,"Sex",1,"sex")
28:     genTable(230,420,120,4,ageArr,"Age Group",1,"age")
29:     genTable(230,620,120,4,hobArr,"Hobby",2,"hob")
```

```
30:      genTable(450,220,120,5,locArr,"Your Location",1,"loc")
31:      genTable(450,420,120,5,natArr,"Nationality",1,"nat")
32: </script>
33:
34: <table class="tableSt" style="position:absolute;top:500px;left:620px"><tr>
35:  <td><input type="button" class="styleSt" style="width:120px;height:60px;
36:    background:#aaaaaa" value="Reset" onclick="resetPar()"/></td></tr>
37:  <tr><td><input type="button" class="styleSt" value="Send" id="proDataBut"
38:    style="width:120px;height:60px;background:#aaaaaa" onclick="proData()" />
39:  </td></tr>
40: </table>
41:
42: <div id="outMsg" class="tableSt" style="position:absolute;top:690px;
43:     left:120px;font-size:16pt"></div>
44: </body>
45: </html>
```

In order to show different varieties of coding, we use the XHTML table and the `genTable()` function in this example.

The table in lines 15–24 generates the "Name" and "Email Address" text fields. The script block in lines 27–31 calls the `genTable()` function to generate "Sex," "Age Group," "Hobby," "Your Location," and "Nationality" tables. They all use radio boxes with the exception of the "Hobby" table, which uses checkboxes. The final XHTML table in lines 34–40 generates two buttons called "Reset" and "Send." There is also a display area defined by the division element in lines 42–43 so that messages can be displayed there.

The Reset button calls the function `resetPar()` (clear parameter) to clear all the text fields and boxes. The Send button calls the function `proData()` (process data) to get all the selected data and to display them in the display area. A screen shot of this example is shown in Fig. 10.13.

This example uses an ECMAScript ex10-07.js in line 12. The first part of this program is listed below.

```
Example: ex10-07.js - The ECMAScript For ex10-07.htm (Part One)

 1:    sexArr = new Array("Female","Male")
 2:    ageArr = new Array("(17-28)","(29-42)","(43-58)","(59+)")
 3:    hobArr = new Array("Reading","Movies","Cooking","Sports")
 4:    locArr = new Array("New York","Tokyo","London","Paris","Others")
 5:    natArr = new Array("American","Japanese","British","French","Others")
 6:
 7:  function genTable(topV,leftV,widthV,noElV,eleArr,titleV,typeV,idV)
 8:  {
 9:   boxType=""
10:   if ((typeV ==1)|| (typeV ==2))
11:   {
12:    tabSt= "<table class=\"tableSt\" style=\"position:absolute;top:" +
13:           topV+"px;left:"+leftV+"px\">"
14:    tabSt= tabSt + "<tr><td colspan=\"2\" style=\"text-align:center\">"+
15:           titleV+"<br /><br /></td>"
16:
17:    if (typeV ==1) boxType ="radio"
18:        else boxType ="checkbox"
19:    for(jj=0;jj<noElV;jj++)
20:    {
21:      tabSt = tabSt+ "<tr><td style=\"width:"+widthV+"px\">"+
22:        eleArr[jj]+":   </td><td><input type=\"" + boxType +
23:        "\" class=\"radSt\" name=\""+idV+"\" /></td></tr>"
24:    }
25:    tabSt = tabSt +"</table>"
26:    document.write(tabSt)
27:   }
28: }
29:
```

Lines 1–5 define the arrays for "Sex," "Age Group," "Hobby," "Your Location," and "Nationality." The function `genTable()` generates a table with radio or checkboxes. When `typeV=1`, this function produces a table with radio boxes and checkboxes when `typeV=2`. If the box type is not equal to 1 or 2, nothing will happen. The format of the generated table is very similar to the table in ex10-04.txt and is stored in the variable `tabSt` (table string). Once you know the box type, the for-loop in lines 19–24 adds all the boxes to the table string. The generated tables are then output to the page by executing the statement in line 26.

The second part of the program file contains a `resetPar()` function to clear all the data fields and prepare for the next input. The coding is listed below.

```
Listing: Continuation Of The ECMAScript ex10-07.js (Part Two)

30:   sexV = document.getElementsByName("sex")
31:   ageV = document.getElementsByName("age")
32:   hobV = document.getElementsByName("hob")
33:   locV = document.getElementsByName("loc")
34:   natV = document.getElementsByName("nat")
35:
36:   function resetPar()
37:   {
38:     document.getElementById("nameId").value=""
39:     document.getElementById("emailId").value=""
40:     document.getElementById("outMsg").innerHTML=""
41:
42:     for (jj=0;jj<sexV.length;jj++)
43:     {
44:       sexV.item(jj).checked = false
45:     }
46:     for (jj=0;jj<ageV.length;jj++)
47:     {
48:       ageV.item(jj).checked = false
49:     }
50:     for (jj=0;jj<locV.length;jj++)
51:     {
52:       locV.item(jj).checked = false
53:     }
54:     for (jj=0;jj<natV.length;jj++)
55:     {
56:       natV.item(jj).checked = false
57:     }
58:     for (jj=0;jj<hobV.length;jj++)
59:     {
60:       hobV.item(jj).checked = false
61:     }
62:
63:   }
64:
```

To clear all the boxes, the codes in lines 30–34 demonstrate a grouping technique. For example, the DOM function `getElementsByName()` is employed in line 30 to build a collection of all elements with the name=`"sex"` and store the collection in variable `sexV`. Once we have the object variable `sexV`, the for-loop (lines 42–45)

```
for (jj=0;jj<sexV.length;jj++)
{
  sexV.item(jj).checked = false
}
```

would clear all the settings of the radio boxes. A series of for-loops would uncheck all the boxes in this example. Since `sexV` is an object, `sexV.length` stores the number of radio boxes and the function `sexV.item(jj)` is a legal and efficient way to gain access to the jjth radio box. The final part of the program file contains a function `proData()` to process the data and is listed below.

```
Listing: Continuation Of The ECMAScript ex10-07.js (Part Three)
65:  function proData()
66:  {
67:    nameSt = document.getElementById("nameId").value
68:    emailSt = document.getElementById("emailId").value
69:
70:    llSt = "##Input Data##:"+nameSt+", "+emailSt+"<br /> "
71:    llSt = llSt + "##Input Data##:"
72:    for (jj=0;jj<sexV.length;jj++)
73:    {
74:      if (sexV.item(jj).checked) llSt = llSt +sexArr[jj]+", "
75:    }
76:    for (jj=0;jj<ageV.length;jj++)
77:    {
78:      if (ageV.item(jj).checked) llSt = llSt + ageArr[jj]+", "
79:    }
80:    for (jj=0;jj<locV.length;jj++)
81:    {
82:      if (locV.item(jj).checked) llSt = llSt + locArr[jj]+", "
83:    }
84:    for (jj=0;jj<natV.length;jj++)
85:    {
86:      if (natV.item(jj).checked) llSt = llSt + natArr[jj]+", "
87:    }
88:    for (jj=0;jj<hobV.length;jj++)
89:    {
90:      if (hobV.item(jj).checked) llSt = llSt + hobArr[jj]+", "
91:    }
92:
93:    document.getElementById("outMsg").innerHTML = llSt
94:  }
95:
```

When the Send button is pressed, this `proData()` function is called. After obtaining the "Name" and "Email Address" data and storing them into a string `llSt` (lines 67–71), a series of for-loops is executed to check all the boxes on the entire page. If the check status of a box is true, the associated array data is added to the string `llSt`. For example, consider the for-loop in lines 76–79:

```
for (jj=0;jj<ageV.length;jj++)
{
    if (ageV.item(jj).checked) llSt = llSt + ageArr[jj]+", "
}
```

This loop runs through all radio boxes that are associated with the age group. If the checked status of a radio box `ageV.item(jj).checked` is true, the associated data stored in the array `ageArr[jj]` are added to the string `llSt`. Since this element collection method is a W3C standard for all input elements, the checkboxes in lines 88–91 can also be collected in this way.

10.4   Select boxes and their applications

10.4.1 The DOM interface for select box

The next DOM interface that we want to talk about is the *select box interface*. It can be used to access a select box. Select box, sometimes called *combo box*, is defined in HTML/XHTML specifications as an independent element. To generate a select box, the `<select>` element is used. A typical example to generate a select box is shown in ex10-08.htm.

```
Example: ex10-08.htm - Generating A Select Box

 1: <?xml version="1.0" encoding="iso-8859-1"?>
 2: <!DOCTYPE html PUBLIC "-//W3C//DTD XHTML 1.0 Transitional//EN"
 3:     "http://www.w3.org/TR/xhtml1/DTD/xhtml1-transitional.dtd">
 4: <html xmlns="http://www.w3.org/1999/xhtml" xml:lang="en" lang="en">
 5: <style>
 6:    .selSt{width:280px;height:35px;background:#aaffaa;
 7:      font-family:arial;font-weight:bold;font-size:18pt;color:#880000}
 8: </style>
 9: <head><title>Generating A Select Box -- ex10-08.htm</title></head>
10: <body style="background:#000088;font-family:arial;font-size:22pt;
11:      color:#ffff00;font-weight:bold;text-align:center"><br />
12: Generating A Select Box<br /><br />
13:
14:   <select id="mySelectBox" name="mySelectBox" class="selSt">
15:    <option>First Option</option>
16:    <option>Second Option</option>
17:    <option>Third Option</option>
18:    <option>fourth Option</option>
19:   </select>
20:
21: </body>
22: </html>
```

The `<select>` element defined in lines 14–19 generates a select box on the screen and all the option elements `<option >` in lines 15–18 form a series of pull-down selections.

Before the W3C DOM standardization, the ways of controlling select boxes were mostly proprietary. For different browsers, you may need different techniques to gain access to the selected item. With the W3C DOM, we have a standard interface to control this box. A simplified definition of this interface is given below.

```
Listing: ex10-05.txt - DOM Interface For Select Box

 1: interface HTMLSelectElement : HTMLElement {
 2:    readonly attribute DOMString        type;
 3:             attribute long             selectedIndex;
 4:             attribute DOMString        value;
 5:    readonly attribute long length;
 6:    readonly attribute HTMLFormElement  form;
 7:    readonly attribute HTMLCollection   options;
 8:             attribute boolean          disabled;
 9:             attribute boolean          multiple;
10:             attribute DOMString        name;
11:             attribute long             size;
12:             attribute long             tabIndex;
13:    void                add(in HTMLElement element,
14:                            in HTMLElement before)
15:                                            raises(DOMException);
16:    void                remove(in long index);
17:    void                blur();
18:    void                focus();
19: };
```

Again we will not explain this interface line by line. A detailed definition of this interface is provided in the DOM document of W3C. For our practical purposes, we concentrate on the following properties and functions:

selectedIndex
- The ordinal index of the selected option, starting from 0. The value −1 is returned if no element is selected.

length
- The number of options in the select.

options
- The collection of option elements contained by this element.

void add (in HTMLElement element, in HTMLElement before)
- Add a new element to the collection of option elements for this select.

void remove (in long index)
- Remove an element from the collection of option elements for this select. Does nothing if no element has the given index.

To understand and use these features, let's consider a page to offer discount holidays on the Web using select boxes.

10.4.2 A page to offer discount holidays

A more general discussion on the structure of the DOM and its related interfaces is given in the next chapter. In this section, some basic controlling and accessing techniques that relate to the select box are discussed. Consider the following page offering special discount holidays to potential customers:

```
Example: ex10-09.htm - A Page To Offer Discount Holidays

 1: <?xml version="1.0" encoding="iso-8859-1"?>
 2: <!DOCTYPE html PUBLIC "-//W3C//DTD XHTML 1.0 Transitional//EN"
 3:     "http://www.w3.org/TR/xhtml1/DTD/xhtml1-transitional.dtd">
 4: <html xmlns="http://www.w3.org/1999/xhtml" xml:lang="en" lang="en">
 5: <style> .selSt{width:380px;height:35px;background:#aaffaa;
 6:    font-family:arial;font-weight:bold;font-size:16pt;color:#880000}</style>
 7: <head><title>Offering Discount Holidays -- ex10-09.htm</title></head>
 8: <body style="background:#000088;font-family:arial;font-size:22pt;
 9:       color:#ffff00;font-weight:bold;text-align:center"><br />
10: Special 25% Discount <br />Holiday Offer<br /><br />
11:
12: <div style="position:absolute;top:160px;left:60px;text-align:left;
13:   font-size:18pt">Holiday Packages<br />
14:    <select id="holiday" name="holiday" class="selSt">
15:     <option />London and Paris (10 Nights)
16:     <option />New York (7 Nights)
17:     <option />Los Angeles (7 Nights)
18:     <option />Rome and Italy (10 Nights)
19:     <option />Hong Kong and Thailand (10 Nights)
20:     <option>Japan and China (14 Nights)</option>
21:    </select><br /><br /><br /><br />
22:    <div id="outMsg"></div>
23: </div>
24:   <input type="button" value="Order" onclick="orderHoliday()"
25:      style="position:absolute;top:165px;left:460px;width:100px;
26:      height:60px;font-family:arial;font-size:18pt;font-weight:bold" />
27:  </body>
28:  <script>
```

```
29:  function orderHoliday()
30:  {
31:    llV = document.getElementById("holiday")
32:    selectV = llV.selectedIndex
33:    llSt = "You Have Selected The Holiday Package: "+selectV +"<br />"
34:    llSt = llSt + "Which Is:"+ llV.options.item(selectV).firstChild.data
35:    document.getElementById("outMsg").innerHTML=llSt
36:  }
37: </script>
38: </html>
```

Again, the select element `<select>` in lines 14–21 generates a select box on the page and all the option elements between lines 15 and 20 form a series of pull-down selections. Buttons, select boxes, and many other boxes can have CSS properties to enhance their look and feel. In this example, the select box has an identity `id="holiday"` which provides some special discount holiday offers to customers.

Once the Order button defined in lines 24–26 is clicked, the function `orderHoliday()` is called. To access the selected choice, all you have to do is to get hold of the property `selectedIndex`. More precisely, you have the following statement by combining the codes in lines 31–32:

```
document.getElementById("holiday").selectedIndex
```

Since the `selectedIndex` variable only reflects the position of the selection which starts from 0, its value is a number. For example, if you pick the "London and Paris (10 Nights)" option, the `selectedIndex` has a value of 0. The `selectedIndex` will have a value of 5 if you pick "Japan and China (14 Nights)." Some screen shots of this example are shown in Figs 10.14 and 10.15.

Figure 10.14 ex10-09.htm

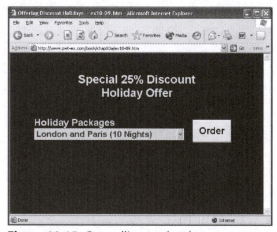

Figure 10.15 Controlling a select box

A common technique to convert the option position to the actual data is to use the array structure. For the select box, the DOM interface provides an options property for you to gain direct access to the text of the option. For example, once you have the selected number stored in `selectV` in line 32, the combination of the `firstChild.data` returns the selected data, i.e.,

```
selectV = llV.selectedIndex
llV.options.item(selectV).firstChild.data
```

Sometimes, the ability to change the options list at run time can produce an impressive effect and appeals to visitors and customers. In the next example, we show you how to change the option string at run time.

10.4.3 Controlling text area and select boxes

Text area is a handy tool to allow users to type in a long paragraph of information. Compared to the select box, text area has a relatively simple format and the interface is listed in ex10-06.txt.

```
Listing: ex10-06.txt - DOM Interface For Text Area

 1: interface HTMLTextAreaElement : HTMLElement {
 2:          attribute DOMString         defaultValue;
 3:   readonly attribute HTMLFormElement  form;
 4:          attribute DOMString         accessKey;
 5:          attribute long              cols;
 6:          attribute boolean           disabled;
 7:          attribute DOMString         name;
 8:          attribute boolean           readOnly;
 9:          attribute long              rows;
10:          attribute long              tabIndex;
11:   readonly attribute DOMString         type;
12:          attribute DOMString         value;
13:   void              blur();
14:   void              focus();
15:   void              select();
16: };
```

To define a `textarea` with XHTML, the following statement is often used:

```
<textarea id="myTxtArea" cols="60" rows="10">This is my text area
</textarea>
```

The `cols` and `rows` attributes are character based and therefore the statement above defines `textarea` with 10 rows and each row is 60 characters long. The initial value is the string "This is my text area."

To access `textarea`, the DOM property `value` in line 12 is often used. As a practical example, we look at an example to combine `textarea` with select boxes. Consider the page given below:

```
Example: ex10-10.htm - Text Area and Select Boxes

 1: <?xml version="1.0" encoding="iso-8859-1"?>
 2: <!DOCTYPE html PUBLIC "-//W3C//DTD XHTML 1.0 Transitional//EN"
 3:     "http://www.w3.org/TR/xhtml1/DTD/xhtml1-transitional.dtd">
 4: <html xmlns="http://www.w3.org/1999/xhtml" xml:lang="en" lang="en">
 5: <style>
 6:  .areaSt{background:#aaffaa;font-family:arial;font-weight:bold;
 7:     width:500px;height:200px;font-size:16pt;color:#880000;
 8:     position:absolute;left:100px;top:100px}
 9:  .butSt{background-color:#aaffaa;font-family:arial;font-weight:bold;
10:     font-size:14pt;color:#880000;width:120px;height:28px}
11: </style>
12: <head><title> Text Area and Select Boxes -- ex10-10.htm</title></head>
13: <body style="background:#000088;font-family:arial;font-size:22pt;
14:        color:#ffff00;font-weight:bold;text-align:center"><br />
15:    Generating and Controlling Text Area<br /><br />
16: <textarea cols="60", rows="9" class="areaSt" id="myTxtArea">
17:
18:    "The Document Object Model is a platform-
19:    and language-neutral interface that will
20:    allow programs and scripts to dynamically
21:    access and update the content, structure,
22:    and style of documents."
23:    (www.w3.org)
24:
```

```
25: </textarea>
26: <table style="position:absolute;left:90px;top:320px;font-size:14pt">
27:  <tr><td>Font Color:</td>
28:    <td><select onchange="changeCSS()" id="colIdx" class="butSt">
29:    <option>#880000</option><option>#008800</option>
30:    <option>#000088</option></select></td></tr>
31:  <tr><td>Bg. Color:</td>
32:    <td><select onchange="changeCSS()" id="bgIdx" class="butSt">
33:    <option>#aaffaa</option><option>#ffaaaa</option>
34:    <option>#aaaaff</option></select></td></tr>
35:  <tr><td>Font Size:</td>
36:    <td><select onchange="changeCSS()" id="sizeIdx" class="butSt">
37:    <option>16pt</option><option>12pt</option>
38:    <option>14pt</option></select></td></tr>
39:  <tr><td>Font Family:</td>
40:    <td><select onchange="changeCSS()" id="famIdx" class="butSt">
41:    <option>Arial</option><option>Times</option></select></td></tr>
42: </table>
43:
44: <table style="position:absolute;left:360px;top:330px;font-size:14pt">
45:  <tr><td colspan="2"><input type="button" class="butSt"
46:    style="background:#cccccc;color:#000000;width:200px;height:50px"
47:      onclick="resetPar()" value="Reset Parameters" /></td></tr>
48:  <tr><td colspan="2"><input type="button" class="butSt"
49:    style="background:#cccccc;color:#000000;width:200px;height:50px"
50:      onclick="txtContent()" value="Text Area Content" /></td></tr>
51: </table>
52: <div style="position:absolute;top:500px;left:30px;font-size:14pt"
53:    id="outMsg"></div>
54: </body>
55: <script src="ex10-10.js"></script>
56: </html>
```

This page contains a `textarea` (lines 16–25) of 9 rows and each row has 60 characters. The initial content of the `textarea` is the text between the tag names. After the `textarea`, we have a table containing four select boxes (lines 26–42) used to control the following properties of `textarea`:

```
Font color          Font size
Background color    Font family
```

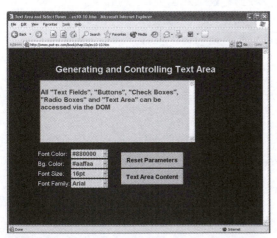

An event handler `onchange=changeCSS()` is assigned to each select box so that whenever there is a change of selection, the `changeCSS()` function is called. This makes sure that the associated change is in real time. Two buttons are also defined in lines 44–51 to reset the parameters of the select boxes and get the content of `textarea`. A screen shot of this page is shown in Fig. 10.16.

Figure 10.16 ex10-10.htm

The program file for this example is ex10-10.js and is listed as follows:

```
Example: ex10-10.js - The ECMAScript For ex10-10.htm

 1: sizeIndex = new Array(16,12,14,18)
 2: famIndex = new Array("Arial","Times")
 3: colIndex = new Array("#880000","#008800","#000088")
 4: bgIndex = new Array("#aaffaa","#ffaaaa","#aaaaff")
 5: function changeCSS()
 6: {
 7:   llSize = document.getElementById("sizeIdx").selectedIndex
 8:   llFam = document.getElementById("famIdx").selectedIndex
 9:   llCol = document.getElementById("colIdx").selectedIndex
10:   llBg = document.getElementById("bgIdx").selectedIndex
11:
12:   llV = document.getElementById("myTxtArea").style
13:   llV.fontSize = sizeIndex[llSize]+"pt"
14:   llV.color = colIndex[llCol]
15:   llV.fontFamily = famIndex[llFam]
16:   llV.background = bgIndex[llBg]
17: }
18:
19: function resetPar()
20: {
21:   document.getElementById("sizeIdx").selectedIndex= 0
22:   document.getElementById("colIdx").selectedIndex= 0
23:   document.getElementById("famIdx").selectedIndex= 0
24:   document.getElementById("bgIdx").selectedIndex= 0
25:   document.getElementById("outMsg").innerHTML= ""
26:
27:   llV = document.getElementById("myTxtArea").style
28:   llV.fontSize = "16pt"
29:   llV.color = "#880000"
30:   llV.fontFamily = "Arial"
31:   llV.background = "#aaffaa"
32: }
33:
34: function txtContent()
35: {
36:   llV = document.getElementById("myTxtArea")
37:   document.getElementById("outMsg").innerHTML=llV.value
38:
39: }
```

First, we use arrays to remember all the values for "Font Size," "Font Family," "Font Color," and "Background Color." These arrays are also used later to convert the selected option to the selection data. There is an event handler onchange="changeCSS()" installed for each of the select boxes, e.g., the first select box (lines 28–30 of ex10.10.htm):

```
<select onchange="changeCSS()" id="colIdx" class="butSt">
   <option>#880000</option>
   <option>#008800</option>
   <option>#000088</option>
</select>
```

The function changeCSS() is called if any changes of the selection are detected. The event function changeCSS() defined in ex10-10.js gets all the selected values from the select boxes (lines 7–10 of ex10-10.js) and then assigns them to the CSS property of textarea. Since the assignment of CSS is a real-time process, the change is immediate.

If the Reset Parameters button is pressed, the `resetPar()` function (lines 19–32) is called. This function first restores the `selectedIndex` of select boxes to 0 and then assigns the original value of the CSS properties back to `textarea`.

If the Text Area Content button is pressed, the function `txtContent()` gets the contents of `textarea` and displays the information to the output area specified in line 37. A screen shot of this in action is shown in Fig. 10.17.

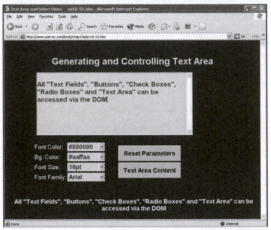

Figure 10.17 Controlling text area and select boxes

10.4.4 A page to change options at run time

In fact, both the IE and NS family of browsers allow you to change options inside a select element at run time. The basic format is simple. All you have to do is to change the `firstChild.data` property of the desired option. For example, the following statements can change the first option of the "holiday" select box to "My First Option":

```
llV = document.getElementById("holiday")
llV.options.item(0).firstChild.data = "My First Option"
```

As an application of this feature, we consider a page to give away some free gifts to customers. Suppose you have two kinds of free gifts, "Holiday Add On," and "Consumer Goods," and each catalog has its own items. The user can pick one of the radio buttons representing the associated catalog and select the gift items from a select box. The changes on the select box are transparent to the user and are in real time.

The interface part of this example is

Example: ex10-11.htm – A Page To Change Options At Run Time

```
 1:   <?xml version="1.0" encoding="iso-8859-1"?>
 2:   <!DOCTYPE html PUBLIC "-//W3C//DTD XHTML 1.0 Transitional//EN"
 3:       "http://www.w3.org/TR/xhtml1/DTD/xhtml1-transitional.dtd">
 4:   <html xmlns="http://www.w3.org/1999/xhtml" xml:lang="en" lang="en">
 5:   <style> .selSt{width:380px;height:35px;background:#aaffaa;
 6:   font-family:arial;font-weight:bold;font-size:16pt;color:#880000}</style>
 7:   <head><title> Change Options At Run Time -- ex10-11.htm</title></head>
 8:   <body style="background:#000088;font-family:arial;font-size:22pt;
 9:       color:#ffff00;font-weight:bold;text-align:center"><br />
10:   Special Promotion From www.pwt-ex.com<br/>Claim Your Free Gift
11:     <br /><br />
12:   <form action="">
13:   <table style="position:absolute;top:160px;left:60px;text-align:left;
14:    font-size:18pt">
15:    <tr><td colspan="2">Select Your Free Gift Catalog Please</td></tr>
16:    <tr><td colspan="2">Holiday Add On</td>
17:     <td><input type="radio" id="gift" name="gift" checked
18:      onclick="chgCatalog(1)" class="selSt" style="width:40px" /></td></tr>
```

```
19:    <tr><td colspan="2">Consumer Goods</td>
20:      <td><input type="radio" id="gift" name="gift"
21:       onclick="chgCatalog(2)" class="selSt" style="width:40px" /></td></tr>
22:   </table>
23:   </form>
24:
25:   <div style="position:absolute;top:300px;left:60px;text-align:left;
26:         font-size:18pt">Your Free Gift<br />
27:     <select id="freeGift" name="freeGift" class="selSt">
28:     <option>Two Nights Hotel In London</option>
29:     <option>One Week Free Car Rental</option>
30:     <option>Free Travel Insurance</option>
31:     <option>Dinner For Two</option>
32:     <option>One Free Local Excursion</option>
33:     </select><br /><br /><br />
34:     <div id="outMsg"></div>
35:   </div>
36:   <input type="button" value="Order" onclick="orderGift()"
37:       style="position:absolute;top:305px;left:460px;width:100px;
38:       height:60px;font-family:arial;font-size:18pt;font-weight:bold" />
39: </body>
40: <script src="ex10-11.js"></script>
41: </html>
42:
```

This page contains two radio boxes and one select box. The radio boxes are defined inside the table in lines 13–22. The select box is specified inside the division element in lines 25–35. Initially, the first box, "Holiday Add On," is checked so that the select box contains the following options:

- Two Nights Hotel in London
- One Week Free Car Rental
- Free Travel Insurance
- Dinner For Two
- One Free Local Excursion

Once the radio box "Consumer Goods" is clicked, the options list of the select box changes to the following list:

- Digital DVD Playero
- Digital Camera
- Postscript Printer
- DVD & RW Combo Drive
- A Handheld Computer

When a selection is picked and the Order button is pressed, the selected option is displayed in the display area. Some screen shots of this example in action are shown in Figs 10.18 and 10.19.

Figure 10.18 ex10-11.htm

Figure 10.19 Change options with radio boxes

The driving force for this example is the program file ex10-11.js listed below.

Example: ex10-11.js - The ECMAScript For ex10-11.htm

```
1:   function chgCatalog(butV)
2:   {
3:    llV = document.getElementById("freeGift")
4:    llV.length = 5
5:    llV.selectedIndex = -1
6:    if (butV ==1) {
7:     llV.options.item(0).firstChild.data = "Two Nights Hotel in London"
8:     llV.options.item(1).firstChild.data = "One Week Free Car Rental"
9:     llV.options.item(2).firstChild.data = "Free Travel Insurance"
10:    llV.options.item(3).firstChild.data = "Dinner For Two"
11:    llV.options.item(4).firstChild.data = "One Free Local Excursion"
12:    llSt = "Pick Holiday Add On!"
13:    }
14:   if (butV ==2) {
15:    llV.options.item(0).firstChild.data = "Digital DVD Player"
16:    llV.options.item(1).firstChild.data = "Digital Camera"
17:    llV.options.item(2).firstChild.data = "Postscript Laser Printer"
18:    llV.options.item(3).firstChild.data = "DVD & RW Combo Drive"
19:    llV.options.item(4).firstChild.data = "A Handheld Computer"
20:    llSt = "Pick Your Consumer Goods!"
21:    }
22:   llV.selectedIndex =0
23:   document.getElementById("outMsg").innerHTML=llSt
24:   }
25:
26:   function orderGift()
27:   {
28:    llV = document.getElementById("freeGift")
29:    selectV = llV.selectedIndex
30:    llSt = "Your Free Gift Is: "+
31:          llV.options.item(selectV).firstChild.data
32:    document.getElementById("outMsg").innerHTML=llSt
33:   }
```

This program file is in fact quite easy to understand. When the first radio box "Holiday Add On" is pressed, the `chgCatalog(butV)` function is called with `butV=1`. Since the argument `butV` is 1, the statements in lines 7–11 are executed and the options of the select box are determined accordingly. When `chgCatalog(2)` is called, the similar statements in lines 15–19 specify another new set of options for the select box. The "Pick Your Consumer Goods!" message is output to the display area at the end of this function.

When the user clicks the Order button, the function `orderGift()` is called. This function gets the selected item via the `firstChild.data` property in line 31 and outputs a message to the display area to indicate the selection.

10.4.5 Adding and deleting an option

A select box is similar to a drop-down menu. The options are mostly hidden from the user until the associated "arrow" button is clicked. In many cases this feature makes them an ideal tool to add or delete options (or items) at run time unnoticed. To allow the addition or deletion of elements on a page is another achievement of the W3C DOM. To understand this requires some knowledge of the DOM's tree and structure. However, the interface for the select element also provides two functions for you to add and delete options in an easy way. The prototypes of these two functions are

```
void add(element, before)
void remove(in long index)
```

One good way to demonstrate how to use them is by means of an example. For this purpose, we develop a page with a text field, two buttons, and one select box. The text field allows a user to type in a new option. When the Add Option button is clicked, the text will be added at the end of the select box as an additional option. When the Delete button is clicked, the option at the end of the select box will be deleted. Some screen shots of this example in action are shown in Figs 10.20 and 10.21.

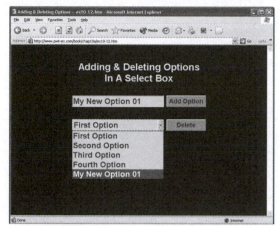

Figure 10.20 ex10-12.htm

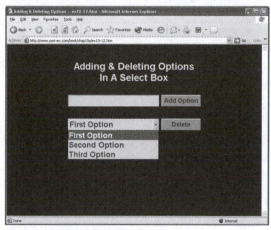

Figure 10.21 Delete some options

The construction of the text field, buttons, and select box is quite simple and is listed in the following page:

Example: ex10-12.htm – Adding & Deleting Options

```
 1: <?xml version="1.0" encoding="iso-8859-1"?>
 2: <!DOCTYPE html PUBLIC "-//W3C//DTD XHTML 1.0 Transitional//EN"
 3:     "http://www.w3.org/TR/xhtml1/DTD/xhtml1-transitional.dtd">
 4: <html xmlns="http://www.w3.org/1999/xhtml" xml:lang="en" lang="en">
 5: <style>
 6:   .selSt{width:280px;height:35px;background:#aaffaa;
 7:    font-family:arial;font-weight:bold;font-size:18pt;color:#880000}
 8:   .butSt{width:120px;height:35px;background:#aaaaaa;
 9:    font-family:arial;font-weight:bold;font-size:14pt;color:#880000}
10: </style>
11: <head><title>Adding & Deleting Options -- ex10-12.htm</title></head>
12: <body style="background:#000088;font-family:arial;font-size:22pt;
13:     color:#ffff00;font-weight:bold;text-align:center"><br />
14:   Adding & Deleting Options <br />In A Select Box<br /><br />
15:
16:   <input type="text" id="addId" class="selSt" />
17:   <input type="button" value="Add Option" class="butSt"
18:      onclick="addOption()"/><br /><br />
19:
20:   <select id="mySelectBox" name="mySelectBox" class="selSt">
21:     <option />First Option
22:     <option />Second Option
23:     <option />Third Option
24:     <option />Fourth Option
25:   </select>
26:   <input type="button" value="Delete" class="butSt" id="delId"
27:      onclick="delOption()" />
28:
29: </body>
30: <script src="ex10-12.js"></script>
31: </html>
```

A text field and a button are defined in lines 16–17. If the Add Option button is clicked, the function addOption() is called to get the text and append it to the end of the select box. The select box is defined in lines 20–24 with four options. Another button is created just after the select box. This button calls the function delOption() to delete the last option of the box. The addOption() and delOption() functions are specified in the file ex10-12.js.

```
Example: ex10-12.js - The ECMAScript For ex10-12.htm
 1:   function addOption()
 2:   {
 3:
 4:    llV = document.getElementById("mySelectBox")
 5:    if ( llV.length < 10)
 6:    {
 7:     newoption = document.createElement("option")
 8:     newoption.text = document.getElementById("AddId").value
 9:     llV.add(newoption)
10:     llV1 = document.getElementById("delId")
11:     if (!llV1.disabled) llV1.disabled = false
12:    }
13:   }
14:
15:   function delOption()
16:   {
17:    llV = document.getElementById("mySelectBox")
18:    if (llV.length > 0)
19:    {
20:      llV.remove(llV.length-1)
21:    } else {
22:      document.getElementById("delId").disabled = true
23:    }
24:   }
```

To use the add() function, you need to create an element <option> and put some information into the newly created option. This is the job of the statements in lines 7–8:

```
newoption = document.createElement("option")
newoption.text = document.getElementById("AddId").value
```

These two statements produce the following result:

```
<option> .. Some Text From The Text Field .. </option>
```

Once you have this XHTML element stored in the newoption object, the add() function can be called to add the option to the select box. The statement in line 9

```
llV.add(newoption)
```

is equivalent to putting the <option> element at the end of the select box; llV is the object identity of the select box defined in line 4:

```
llV = document.getElementById("mySelectBox")
```

The following function call puts the option element in the third position of the select box:

```
llV.add(newoption,2)
```

Whenever the Add Option button is clicked, the text in the text field is added to the select box until there are 10 options in the box. The two statements in lines 10–11 are used to detect whether the Delete button has been disabled since there are no more options in the box. If the button is disabled, the statement in line 11 turns it on again.

To delete an option in the select box is easy. All you have to do is to call the DOM function `remove()`. You first get the identity of the select box as shown in line 17 and then make the call

```
llV.remove(llV.length -1)
```

This statement removes the last option in the select box. If you keep pressing the Delete button, the options in the box will be deleted one by one until none is left and the button will be disabled. Now let's consider a practical example.

10.5   A page to match new friends

Match finding is another popular application on the Web. For either a Web page to match a handful of people in the Internet or running a dedicated dating agency, you will need a database-type finding and matching technique. For specialized commercial corporations, large databases and powerful search engines are employed. Of course this also includes a charging mechanism.

For demonstration purposes, the example in this section contains very few data and was generated by ourselves. You can add more data if you want. No formal search engine is used. We first generate some data with a database-type format and then perform some basic searching and matching techniques with the `getElementsByName()` function.

The main purpose of this example is to show how select box and the function `getElementsByName()` can be used in a practical application. More importantly, it also shows the power of element collection in a simple way. Element collection is a structural way to understand the DOM and is the gateway to a more advanced study of the so-called DOM Core. We will cover these topics in the next chapter.

10.5.1 The display and data structure of the page

For simplicity, the client data in our example are restricted to "Sex," "Age Group," "Favorite Hobby," "Location," "Nationality," and "Occupation." The matching criteria are also restricted and only the following matching specifications are imposed.

- Sex – "Female" or "Male"
- Age Groups – "(17–28)," "(29–42)," or "(43–58)"
- Favourite Hobby – "Reading," "Movies," "Cooking," or "Sports"
- Location – "Not Important," "New York," "Tokyo," "London," "Paris," or "Others"
- Nationality – "Not Important," "American," "Japanese," "British," "French," or "Others"
- Occupation – "Not Important"

The "Not Important" criterion means that you can pick that choice and accept all matching ones in that field. Note that the "Occupation" field contains only one option, "Not Important." We feel that occupation is not an important criterion for matching friends. Naturally, six select boxes are needed to perform the tasks. One display area is also specified to show the matching results. The display part of this example is listed in ex10-13.htm.

```
Example: ex10-13.htm - A Page To Match New Friends

 1: <?xml version="1.0" encoding="iso-8859-1"?>
 2: <!DOCTYPE html PUBLIC "-//W3C//DTD XHTML 1.0 Transitional//EN"
 3:     "http://www.w3.org/TR/xhtml1/DTD/xhtml1-transitional.dtd">
 4: <html xmlns="http://www.w3.org/1999/xhtml" xml:lang="en" lang="en">
 5: <head><title> A Page To Match New Friends -- ex10-13.htm</title></head>
 6: <style>
 7:    .butSt{background-color:#aaffaa;font-family:arial;font-weight:bold;
 8:       font-size:14pt;color:#880000;width:160px;height:30px}
```

```
 9:    .txtSt{background-color:#aaffaa;font-family:arial;font-weight:bold;
10:      font-size:16pt;color:#880000;textalign:left}
11: </style>
12: <body style="background:#000088;font-family:arial;font-size:22pt;
13:    color:#ffff00;font-weight:bold">
14:
15: <div style="position:absolute;top:20px;left:200px">
16:   A Page To Match New Friends</div>
17: <table border="5" style="position:absolute;top:80px;left:100px">
18:  <tr><td><textarea id="outMsg" style="width:550px;height:220px"
19:     readonly="true" cols="75" rows="10" class="txtSt">
20:     Matching Results Are Here</textarea></td></tr></table>
21:
22: <table style="position:absolute;left:60px;top:350px;font-size:14pt">
23:  <tr><td>Sex</td>
24:   <td><select id="sexIdx" class="butSt">
25:   <option>Female<option>Male</select></td></tr>
26:  <tr><td>Age Group</td>
27:   <td><select id="ageIdx" class="butSt">
28:   <option>17-28</option><option>29-42</option>
29:   <option>43-58</option></select></td></tr>
30:  <tr><td>Main Interest</td>
31:   <td><select id="hobIdx" class="butSt">
32:   <option>Reading</option><option>Movies</option>
33:   <option>Cooking</option><option>Sports</option></select></td></tr>
34: </table>
35:
36: <table style="position:absolute;left:360px;top:350px;font-size:14pt">
37:  <tr><td>Location</td>
38:    <td><select id="locIdx" class="butSt">
39:    <option>Not Important</option><option>New York</option>
40:    <option>Toyko</option><option>London</option>
41:    <option>Paris</option><option>Others</option></select></td></tr>
42:  <tr><td>Nationality</td>
43:    <td><select id="natIdx" class="butSt">
44:    <option>Not Important</option><option>American</option>
45:    <option>Japanese</option><option>British</option>
46:    <option>French</option><option>Others</option></select></td></tr>
47:  <tr><td>Occupation</td>
48:    <td><select id="occIdx" class="butSt">
49:    <option>Not Important</select></td></tr>
50: </table>
51:
52: <input type="button" onclick="findFriend()" style="position:absolute;
53:    top:470px;left:270px;width:200px;font-family:arial;font-size:14pt"
54:    value="Find New Friends" />
55:
56: <script src="ex10-13a.js"></script>
57: <script src="ex10-13b.js"></script>
58: </body>
59: </html>
```

This page uses a text area (lines 18–29) as a screen and all matching results are output to this text area. One advantage of using the text area is that it will scroll automatically if you have a long list of matching results. Also, the text area has a read-only status so that no typing is allowed.

After the display screen, we have two tables and each table consists of three select boxes. All the matching criteria are stored as options. All select boxes in the second table display "Not Important" as default. If the "Not Important" option is picked, the system will ignore all matching criteria in the box. Some screen shots of this feature in action are shown in Figs 10.22 and 10.23.

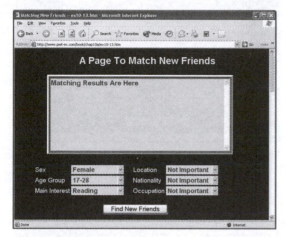

Figure 10.22 ex10-13.htm

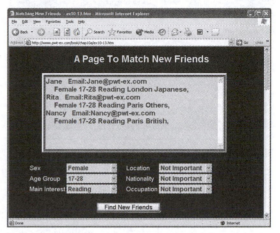

Figure 10.23 Matching results (I)

The initial settings for the matching are:

```
Sex             – Female        Location       – Not Important
Age Group       – 17–28         Nationality    – Not Important
Hobby           – Reading       Occupation     – Not Important
```

A total of 32 clients are created in this example: 16 of them are female and the other 16 are male. All client data are generated by a random number generator. Since a random method is used, you may expect a different result every time you run this page.

If you press the Find New Friends button, the search results are shown in the display area with "Name," "Email Addresses," and other information. In this case, you have four matched results (see Fig. 10.23). Based on these results, you can narrow your search further by, for example, selecting the nationality option as "Japanese":

```
Sex             – Female        Location       – Not Important
Age Group       – 17–28         Nationality    – Japanese
Hobby           – Reading       Occupation     – Not Important
```

When you press the button again, only the data with the "Japanese" option are displayed (see Fig. 10.24).

If you change the age group and press the button, then due to the small "database" you may not have a match (see Fig. 10.25). Again, since the data are generated by a random function, you may have a completely different matching result every time you run the page.

Let's now take a look at the format for the client data and see how the data are generated.

Figure 10.24 Matching results (II)

Figure 10.25 Matching results (III)

10.5.2 Generating the client data

The driving force of this example lies in the external files ex10-13a.js and ex10-13b.js. The first one is a program used to generate the data. In real applications, data should come from some external databases. However no matter what kinds of databases are used, this page will still work as long as the returned data are in a format consistent or compatible with that shown in this example. The first program file ex10-13a.js is listed as follows:

```
Example: ex10-13a.js - The ECMAScript For ex10-13.htm

 1: fArr = new Array("Katy","Anne","Jane","Rose","Pat","Barba",
 2:         "Linda","Amanda","Sue","Rita","Sota","Pam","Nancy",
 3:         "Betty","Susan","Cathy")
 4: mArr = new Array("Peter","Tom","Sam","Ban","Andy","Gary",
 5:         "Simon","Jimmy","Dan","John","Robin","Bob","Paul",
 6:         "Richard","Nick","Michael")
 7: aArr = new Array("17-28","29-42","43-58")
 8: hArr = new Array("Reading","Movies","Cooking","Sports")
 9: lArr = new Array("New York","Tokyo","London","Paris","Others")
10: nArr = new Array("American","Japanese","British","French","Others")
11:
12: noFemale=16
13: noMale = 16
14:
15: function genData()
16: {
17:   outSt = ""
18:   dV = new Array()
19:   for (jj=0;jj< noFemale;jj++)
20:   {
21:     ageV = aArr[Math.round(Math.random()*2)]
22:     hobbyV = hArr[Math.round(Math.random()*3)]
23:     locateV = lArr[Math.round(Math.random()*4)]
24:     natV = nArr[Math.round(Math.random()*4)]
25:     dV[jj] = fArr[jj] + "   Email:"+fArr[jj]+"@pwt-ex.com, "+
26:       "Female "+ageV+" "+hobbyV+" "+locateV+" "+natV+","
27:   }
28:   for (jj= noFemale;jj<(noFemale + noMale);jj++)
29:   {
30:     ageV = aArr[Math.round(Math.random()*2)]
31:     hobbyV = hArr[Math.round(Math.random()*3)]
```

```
32:     locateV = lArr[Math.round(Math.random()*4)]
33:     natV = nArr[Math.round(Math.random()*4)]
34:     dV[jj] = mArr[jj-noFemale] + "   Email:"+
35:         mArr[jj-noFemale]+"@pwt-ex.com, Male " +ageV+" "+hobbyV +
36:         " "+locateV+" "+natV+","
37:   }
38:   headSt = "<div name=\"pa\" id=\"pa\" style=\"visibility:hidden\"> "
39:   for (jj=0; jj< dV.length; jj++)
40:   {
41:    outSt = outSt +headSt +dV[jj]+"</div>"
42:   }
43:   document.write(outSt)
44: }
45:
46: genData()
```

The beginning of this program is a series of arrays used to store the options so that the actual data can be converted. They are

fArr – Female array	hArr – Hobby array	aArr – Age array
mArr – Male array	lArr – Location array	nArr – Nationality array

In this case, the array `fArr` contains 16 female names and `mArr` has 16 male names. The first for-loop in lines 19–27 is responsible for generating the information for all female data. The age group, hobby items, locations, and nationalities are generated randomly. The format of the data is specified in lines 25–26. For example, typical data may look like

Name	Email Address	Sex	Age	Hobby	Location	Nationality
Katy	Email:Katy@pwt-ex.com	Female	(17-28)	Reading	New York	British

The second for-loop is responsible for generating the data for all male names. After all female and male data are generated, 32 XHTML division elements are created in lines 38–42. A typical division element is

```
<div name="pa" id="pa" style="visibility:hidden">
   Katy    Email: Katy@pwt-ex.com, Female(17-29) Reading New York British,</div>
```

All 32 elements in this format are returned back to the page by calling the function `genData()` in line 46. The `visibility:hidden` condition is used to prevent these data from appearing on the page. When these elements are sent back to the page, you can use `getElementsByName()` to group them, to search, and to perform some database functions.

10.5.3 Searching and matching the client data

The grouping, searching, and matching functionalities are defined in another file ex10-13b.js. The first part of this file is listed as follows:

```
Example: ex10-13b.js - The ECMAScript For ex10-13.htm (Part One)

1: sexIndex = new Array("Female","Male")
2: ageIndex = new Array("17-28","29-42","43-58")
3: hobIndex = new Array("Reading","Movies","Cooking","Sports")
4: locIndex = new Array("Not Important","New York","Tokyo","London",
5:           "Paris","Others")
6: natIndex = new Array("Not Important","American","Japanese",
7:           "British","French","Others")
8:
```

```
 9: function matchSex(llV)
10: {
11:   lIdx = document.getElementById("sexIdx").selectedIndex
12:   if ( llV.indexOf(sexIndex[lIdx]) != -1) return true
13:    else return false
14: }
15:
16: function matchAge(llV)
17: {
18:   lIdx = document.getElementById("ageIdx").selectedIndex
19:   if ( llV.indexOf(ageIndex[lIdx]) != -1) return true
20:    else return false
21: }
22:
23: function matchHob(llV)
24: {
25:   lIdx = document.getElementById("hobIdx").selectedIndex
26:   if ( llV.indexOf(hobIndex[lIdx]) != -1) return true
27:   else return false
28: }
29:
30: function matchLoc(llV)
31: {
32:   lIdx = document.getElementById("locIdx").selectedIndex
33:   if (lIdx ==0) return true
34:   else {
35:     if ( llV.indexOf(locIndex[lIdx]) != -1) return true
36:     else return false
37:   }
38: }
39:
40: function matchNat(llV)
41: {
42:   lIdx = document.getElementById("natIdx").selectedIndex
43:   if (lIdx ==0) return true
44:   else {
45:     if ( llV.indexOf(natIndex[lIdx]) != -1) return true
46:     else return false
47:   }
48: }
49:
```

This file is responsible for all the matching. It begins with the matching arrays in lines 1–7:

```
sexIndex        locIndex        hobIndex
ageIndex        natIndex
```

These arrays represent the options in each group. The first matching function matchSex is responsible for matching the "Female" or "Male" option:

```
function matchSex(llV)
{
  lIdx = document.getElementById("sexIdx").selectedIndex
  if ( llV.indexOf(sexIndex[lIdx]) != -1) return true
   else return false
}
```

When client data is substituted into this function as `llV`, this function gets the selected item `selectedIndex` from the select box with `id="sexIdx"`. This value is stored in a local variable `lIdx`; `llV` contains the input testing data and `sexIndex[lIdx]` contains the selected option. Therefore, the statement

```
llV.indexOf(sexIndex[lIdx])
```

searches the input element `llV` against the picked option from the "Sex" select box. If there is no match, a value of –1 is returned, otherwise you have a match and it returns true.

All other functions

- `matchAge()` – Match the age group
- `matchHob()` – Match the hobby
- `matchLoc()` – Match the location
- `matchNat()` – Match the nationality

are defined in a similar manner. For the location and nationality functions, if the `selectedIndex` is 0, you have a "Not Important" situation and this returns true immediately to accept all matches. As mentioned before, the "Occupation" select box is not implemented.

The second part of the external file ex10-13b.js listed below controls all operations.

Listing: Continuation Of The ECMAScript ex10-13b.js (Part Two)

```
50: function resetPar()
51: {
52: document.getElementById("sexIdx").selectedIndex =0
53: document.getElementById("ageIdx").selectedIndex =0
54: document.getElementById("hobIdx").selectedIndex =0
55: document.getElementById("locIdx").selectedIndex =0
56: document.getElementById("natIdx").selectedIndex =0
57:   resultSt = "Matching Results Are Here"
58: document.getElementById("outMsg").value= resultSt
59: }
60:
61: function findFriend()
62: {
63:   matchV = 0
64:   var resultSt =""
65:   llV = document.getElementsByName("pa")
66:   for (jj=0;jj< llV.length;jj++)
67:   {
68:    llSt1 = llV.item(jj).firstChild.data
69:    if (matchSex(llSt1) && matchAge(llSt1) && matchHob(llSt1) &&
70:        matchLoc(llSt1) && matchNat(llSt1))
71:   {
72:     matchV =1
73:     lL1 = llSt1.indexOf(",")
74:     if (lL1 !=-1) {
75:      llSt1 = llSt1.substring(0,lL1) +"\n "+
76:              llSt1.substring(lL1+1,llSt1.length)
77:      resultSt = resultSt +llSt1 +"\n"
78:     }
79:    }
80:   }
81:   if (matchV ==0) resultSt = "Sorry No Match Available!"
82:   if (matchV ==-1) resultSt = "Output Result Is Here"
83:   document.getElementById("outMsg").value=resultSt
84: }
85:
86: resetPar()
```

The first function is this program file is resetPar(). It is called whenever the page is reloaded (line 86) to initialize all select boxes and default display strings.

The main function of this example is the function findFriend() defined in lines 61–84. The getElementsByName("pa") function returns a collection of all female and male data elements since they all have a name="pa". This means that the object 11V in line 65 contains a collection of 32 data. An example of these 32 data may be

```
<div name="pa" id="pa" style="visibility:hidden">
  Katy   Email: Katy@pwt-ex.com, Female (17-28) Reading New York British,</div>
<div name="pa" id="pa" style="visibility:hidden">
  Anne   Email: Anne@pwt-ex.com, Female (29-42) Sports Paris Japanese,</div>
         ... ... ...       ... ... ...
<div name="pa" id="pa" style="visibility:hidden">
  Michael Email: Michael@pwt-ex.com, Male (17-29) Movies Tokyo French,</div>
```

The firstChild.data in line 68 parses the string from the division element so that you have the text data stored as a string in 11St1. For example, the statement

```
11St1 = 11V.item(0).firstChild.data
```

contains the string

```
"Katy Email: Katy@pwt-ex.com, Female(17-28) Reading New York British,"
```

If all the matching results (lines 69–70) return true, you have a match for all criteria. This matched data are then split into two substrings at the first occurrence of the comma ",". The first substring contains the name and email address of the match and the second line contains the options. Both substrings are added to the resultant string resultSt. Finally, all matched results are output to the display area via the statement in line 83.

The getElementsByName() function provides a powerful feature on XHTML documents. A more structural study is discussed in the next chapter.

11 Using the Document Object Model (DOM) II

11.1 The object structure of the DOM

11.1.1 The DOM structure

According to the W3C authority, the DOM is designed to allow programs and scripts to dynamically access and update the contents, structures, and styles of documents. Some of these features were discussed in Chapter 10. In fact almost any elements in an HTML/XHTML document can be accessed, modified, deleted, or added by using the DOM's features. To do this, the DOM must have an internal representation of the entire page. More precisely, inside the DOM each document has a logical structure, or representation, that is very much like a tree.

For example, if an XHTML document is a big tree, then the following XHTML table in ex11-01.txt can be considered as a branch of the tree:

```
Listing: ex11-01.txt - An XHTML Table

 1: <table>
 2: <tr><td>Top Pos:</td>
 3:     <td><select onchange="changeCSS()" id="topIdx" >
 4:         <option>120px</option><option>50px</option>
 5:         <option>150px</option>
 6:         </select></td></tr>
 7: <tr><td>Left Pos:</td>
 8:     <td><select onchange="changeCSS()" id="leftIdx" >
 9:         <option>150px</option><option>40px</option>
10:         <option>200px</option><option>260px</option>
11:         </select></td></tr>
12: <tr><td>Bg. Color:</td>
13:     <td><select onchange="changeCSS()" id="bgIdx" >
14:         <option>#aaffaa</option><option>#ffaaaa</option>
15:         <option>#aaaaff</option>
16:         </select></td></tr>
17: </table>
```

This is an XHTML table which contains three rows. Each row has two cells. The first cell contains a text string and a select box is embedded in the second table cell. Furthermore, there are some options attached to each select box.

The DOM represents this table as a tree data structure of objects. The table element in line 1 is the starting node of this branch. The three table rows are the next level of the branch and can be represented as another three nodes. The table data, text strings, select boxes, and all options are organized in this way to form a sub-tree of the document. A graphical representation of this subtree is shown in Fig. 11.1.

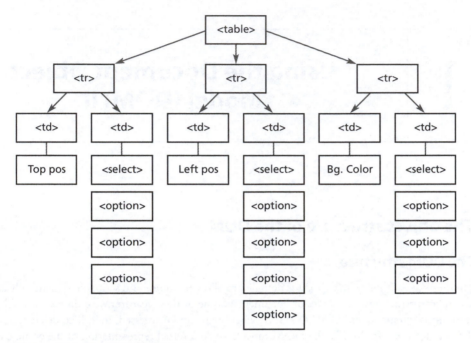

Figure 11.1 The DOM structure

Along with the data structure, all properties and related functions (if any) associated with each element are also stored and can be referenced in an object-oriented manner. Thus the modeling is based on the objects of a document (HTML/XHTML or XML) and hence is called the "Document Object Model." An object model is not just a data structure of nodes, it also represents objects, which have identities, functions, and inheritance.

For example, when you execute the command

```
localV = document.getElementById("topIdx")
```

the `getElementById()` function searches the tree and tries to find the node with the identity `"topIdx"`. When this node is found, it will return it as an object to the `localV` variable. This variable `localV` is therefore an object related to the select box in line 3 and therefore `localV.length` is legal (in terms of syntax error) to represent the number of options in the box.

One direct advantage of this tree structure is that elements can be searched, added, inserted, and deleted anywhere. Normally, each document contains one `doctype` node, one root element node, and some comments. The root element serves as the root of the element tree for the document and Fig. 11.1 is just one branch of this element tree.

At the time of writing, the W3C DOM has gone through level 1, 2, and 3 specifications, making it an ideal standard to develop applications on the Web. From basic HTML, Style, Event to Core, the standard has covered almost all aspects of Web programming and their related subjects. For example, the document "Document Object Model Style Specifications" specifies all aspects to access CSS style properties via programs or scripts. Programming interfaces are provided to demonstrate the structure, properties, functions, and calling methods. The DOM is big by any standard and keeps evolving. This may be the reason why there are still no browsers that manage to fully implement all specifications of the DOM. Sometimes the importance of backward compatibility requirements for commercial browsers makes the job even harder (if not impossible). We all want standards but also need some sort of backward compatibility at the same time!

To understand the DOM further, let's begin our structure study by investigating the function `getElementById()` in detail and look at the general picture of accessing page elements.

11.1.2 A general picture to access Web page elements

Perhaps the most popular technique of all to find an element from the DOM tree is to use the function

```
document.getElementById()
```

This is a powerful function and can locate any element within a page. An investigation of this function also reveals a general picture to search and to group elements. To have a better understanding, we start from the answers to the following questions:

- Where does this function come from?
- What is the relationship of this function to the DOM?
- How many other general access functions and methods are there in the DOM?

As discussed in Chapter 10, the DOM works by providing a number of object interfaces to be accessed and used by other programs and scripts. Some basic DOM interfaces such as input, select, and text area have also been discussed in Chapter 10. Another important DOM interface is called the "Interface HTMLDocument." This interface is closely related to HTML and hence to XHTML documents, holding a more general picture to gain access to page elements.

According to the W3C authority, the HTMLDocument is the root of the HTML (or XHTML) hierarchy and holds the entire content of the document. The header definition of this interface (or class definition) is provided as follows:

```
Listing: ex11-02.txt - The HTMLDocument Interface

 1: interface HTMLDocument : Document {
 2:           attribute DOMString          title;
 3:  readonly attribute DOMString          referrer;
 4:  readonly attribute DOMString          domain;
 5:  readonly attribute DOMString          URL;
 6:           attribute HTMLElement        body;
 7:  readonly attribute HTMLCollection     images;
 8:  readonly attribute HTMLCollection     applets;
 9:  readonly attribute HTMLCollection     links;
10:  readonly attribute HTMLCollection     forms;
11:  readonly attribute HTMLCollection     anchors;
12:           attribute DOMString          cookie;
13:  void              open();
14:  void              close();
15:  void              write(in DOMString text);
16:  void              writeln(in DOMString text);
17:  Element           getElementById(in DOMString elementId);
18:  NodeList          getElementsByName(in DOMString elementName);
19: };
```

Some people may refer to this interface as the document interface in the DOM since all properties and functions related to this interface have a prefix "document." The interface contains a number of attributes consistent with the attributes in the XHTML specifications. The attributes described here can be used to gain access and modify contents using programming techniques. The first attribute is "title" and therefore the statement

```
document.title = "My New Title"
```

can be used to change the title of the page to "My New Title." The DOMString indicates that the type of the title is just a string. Some of the attributes are classified as read-only and cannot be changed. The type of the body in line 6 is the HTMLElement and that means it will return the element as an object. For example, the statement

```
document.body.style.color = "#ff0000"
```

can be used to change the font color of the document body. Since document.body is an object, the statement document.body.style.color is legal.

The `HTMLCollection` type is similar to an array structure. It provides another powerful way to access page elements. We will discuss it in section 11.2. Line 12 is a cookie (`document.cookie`) and this has already been covered in Chapter 7.

The remaining part of this interface contains some functions (or methods) that you can use with the document object. The `document.open()` and `document.close()` functions are used to access the document stream. Some examples on how to use them have also been covered in Chapter 7. Interestingly, the important `document.write()` and `document.writeln()` functions are also declared here.

The next function is the `getElementById()` function. Since the return type is an element, the statement

```
Document.getElementById("myId").style.color="#0000ff"
```

is legal and is used here to access the element with `id="myId"` to change the CSS style color to blue. The last function `getElementsByName()` is a powerful function. It groups elements together and is particularly useful in database-related applications. This function returns a collection of nodes (or elements) with the same name. The "Matching New Friends" example of the last chapter is an example of this function. In practice, this function is quite efficient and can be used conveniently to handle a number of objects.

From a programming point of view, the following object items in the interface

```
images, applets, links, forms, anchors
```

return a collection of object elements (`HTMLCollection`) associated with them. Together with

```
getElementById() and getElementsByName()
```

we have a general picture to access page elements. Apart from the `getElementById()` function, all the others have a common feature: they are used to group elements together. This type of grouping behavior creates another dimension of applications and forms the central topic in the next section.

11.2 The collection features provided by the DOM

11.2.1 Collecting page elements by name

The `getElementsByName()` is our first function to collect and to gain access to a group of elements. We have used it in previous chapters and it is time now to study it in more detail from a data structure point of view. The formal declaration of the `getElementsByName()` function is

```
NodeList getElementsByName(DOMString elementName)
```

This function takes a string `elementName` as argument and searches the entire document. It returns a collection of elements that matches the `elementName`. To use this function, you need to understand the return type `NodeList`. The type `NodeList` is actually an object with data and functions. The definition of `NodeList` is given by the interface

```
interface NodeList {
  Node  item(in unsigned long index);
  readonly attribute unsigned long     length;
};
```

This object contains one read-only value `length` to indicate the number of returned elements in the collection. The member function `item(index)` is used to locate a specific element in the collection. This `item()` function has a return type as `Node`. This is a complicated object inside the DOM and not all browsers implement it fully. It has more than 10 properties and a number of associated functions. We are interested in two of the properties at this moment, namely, `firstChild` and `data`. The `firstChild` property is also a node and will lead us to the element itself and its related data. The data return the string of text under the element. One simple example should clarify these issues. The concept of `NodeList` and `Node` is important for the understanding of the data structure and the use of the DOM tree. We will walk through the DOM tree together later in this chapter. First, consider a simple example to use `getElementsByName()`, `NodeList`, and `Node` interfaces.

Suppose you have the Web page below:

```
Example: ex11-01.htm - Grouping Elements By Name

 1:  <?xml version="1.0" encoding="iso-8859-1"?>
 2:  <!DOCTYPE html PUBLIC "-//W3C//DTD XHTML 1.0 Transitional//EN"
 3:      "http://www.w3.org/TR/xhtml1/DTD/xhtml1-transitional.dtd">
 4:  <html xmlns="http://www.w3.org/1999/xhtml" xml:lang="en" lang="en">
 5:  <head><title>Grouping Elements By Name -- ex11-01.htm</title></head>
 6:  <style>
 7:   .butSt{background-color:#dddddd;font-family:arial;font-weight:bold;
 8:      font-size:14pt;color:#880000;width:220px;height:35px}
 9:  </style>
10:  <body style="background:#000088;font-family:arial;font-size:22pt;
11:      color:#ffff00;font-weight:bold;text-align:center">
12:   Grouping Page Elements By Name <br/>Some Blinking Paragraphs<br /><br />
13:
14:  <div name="pa" id="pa" style="color:#ffffff">This is paragraph one</div>
15:  <div name="pa" id="pa" style="color:#ffff00">This is paragraph two</div>
16:  <div name="pa" id="pa" style="color:#ff0000">This is paragraph three</div>
17:  <div name="pa" id="pa" style="color:#00ff00">This is paragraph four</div>
18:      <br /><br />
19:  <input type="button" onclick="myBlink()" class="butSt"
20:      value="Blinking Paragraphs">
21:  <input type="button" onclick="myToUpper()" class="butSt"
22:      value="To Upper Case">
23:
24:  <script src="ex11-01.js"></script>
25:  </body>
26:  </html>
```

This page contains four paragraphs as indicated in lines 14–17. They are all defined by a division element with the same name and identity, "pa." Soon after the paragraphs, there are two buttons. The first button calls the function `myBlink()` to change the color of all paragraphs randomly. The effect of this is very much like blinking. The second button is used to change all paragraphs to upper case.

This simple example shows how to use grouping to utilize the special effect "blinking." Some screen shots of this example in action are shown in Figs 11.2 and 11.3.

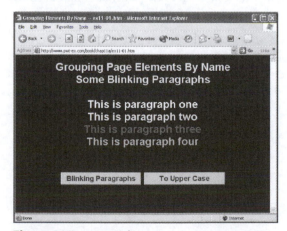

Figure 11.2 ex11-01.htm

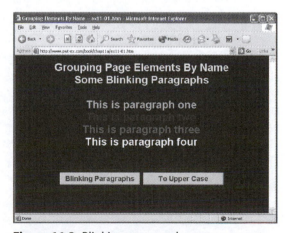

Figure 11.3 Blinking paragraphs

The external program file ex11-01.js of this example is listed below.

Example: ex11-01.js – The ECMAScript For ex11-01.htm

```
 1:
 2: colorArr = new Array("#ff0000","#00ff00","#0000ff","#ffffff","#ffff00")
 3: function myBlink()
 4: {
 5:    llV = document.getElementsByName("pa")
 6:    noPar = llV.length
 7:    for(jj=0;jj<noPar;jj++)
 8:    {
 9:     llV.item(jj).style.color=colorArr[Math.round(Math.random()*4)]
10:    }
11:    setTimeout("myBlink()",200)
12:
13: }
14:
15:  function myToUpper()
16:  {
17:   llV = document.getElementsByName("pa")
18:   noPar = llV.length
19:   for (jj=0;jj<noPar;jj++)
20:   {
21:     llSt = llV.item(jj).firstChild.data
22:     llSt = llSt.toUpperCase()
23:     llV.item(jj).firstChild.data = llSt
24:   }
25:  }
```

In line 2, an array is used to specify the color for the paragraph blinking. When the Blinking Paragraphs button is clicked, the myBlink() function is called. The first statement of this function in line 5 is

```
llV = document.getElementsByName("pa")
```

This statement collects all elements with name="pa" and returns them as a collection to variable llV. Variable llV is actually a NodeList so that the property length and function item() can be called from llV. The statement in line 6 uses llV.length to represent the number of items in the collection. The for-loop in lines 7–10 changes the color of all paragraphs randomly. The object llV.item(jj) represents the jjth object in the collection and the style.color is then legal to change the paragraph's color.

The other button activates the myToUpper() function. After the collection of elements, the string llSt in line 21

```
llSt = llV.item(jj).firstChild.data
```

stores the text data of the jjth object. The firstChild element can be considered as the first node from the object llV.item(jj) and the data return the text. Since llSt is a string, the string function toUpperCase() will change the paragraph to upper case. The resultant string is then put back into the paragraph in line 23. Grouping elements by name is a handy technique for manipulating a number of objects as well as performing some special effects.

Sometimes, the item() function is integrated into the object and works as an array structure. For example, llV.item(jj) can also be written as llV[jj].

11.2.2 Using collections provided by the DOM

Even before the W3C standard, most browsers had their own DOM and accessing methods for page elements. For example, if you declare an image element as

```
<img src="myPic.gif" alt="pic" id="myPic" name="myPic" />
```

you can access this image and change the picture by using the following statement:

```
<script>
  document.myPic.src = "myNewPic.gif"
</script>
```

Here `document.myPic` is a property of the DOM (but not the W3C DOM) and can be used to manipulate the attributes of the associated elements of some browsers. A large number of pages on the Web still use this naming access method. To group elements in these formats requires special design of element names and identities.

Since element grouping is an important subject on the Web, the W3C DOM provides a number of specially designed structures to use them. The method `document.getElementsByName()` is the first one. Another one is to use the `HTMLCollection` type provided by the DOM interface. For some important elements such as images, applets, links, forms, and anchors, W3C provides standard interfaces to group them together as a special collection. Consider the definitions in lines 7–11 of ex11-02.txt:

```
readonly attribute HTMLCollection  images;
readonly attribute HTMLCollection  applets;
readonly attribute HTMLCollection  links;
readonly attribute HTMLCollection  forms;
readonly attribute HTMLCollection  anchors;
```

For every image element used in a page, the `document.images` object is a collection of them so that we can control them more easily. The formal definition of the `HTMLCollection` is provided by the following interface:

```
interface HTMLCollection {
  readonly attribute unsigned long    length;
  Node                 item(in unsigned long index);
  Node                 namedItem(in DOMString name);
};
```

This specification is similar to `NodeList` with length and function `item()`. For example, suppose you have two image elements defined in a page such as

```
<img src="myPic01.gif" />
<img src="myPic02.gif" />
```

You can change the resource of the images to a new image, myNewPic01.gif, by executing the following statements:

```
<script> document.images.item(0).src ="myNewPic01.gif"
         document.images.item(1).src ="myNewPic01.gif" </script>
```

This grouping feature provides a convenient way of performing special effects on a wide variety of applications. As a practical example, consider a ghost that appears randomly in a pyramid. The interface part of this example is given below:

```
Example: ex11-02.htm - Grouping By Collections
 1:  <?xml version="1.0" encoding="iso-8859-1"?>
 2:  <!DOCTYPE html PUBLIC "-//W3C//DTD XHTML 1.0 Transitional//EN"
 3:      "http://www.w3.org/TR/xhtml1/DTD/xhtml1-transitional.dtd">
 4:  <html xmlns="http://www.w3.org/1999/xhtml" xml:lang="en" lang="en">
 5:  <head><title>Grouping By Collections - ex11-02.htm</title></head>
 6:  <style>
 7:   .butSt{background-color:#dddddd;font-family:arial;font-weight:bold;
 8:      font-size:14pt;color:#880000;width:220px;height:35px}
```

```
 9:  </style>
10:  <body style="background:#000088;font-family:arial;font-size:22pt;
11:     color:#ffff00;font-weight:bold;text-align:center">
12:  DOM: The Image Collection<br />Random Ghosts In A Pyramid<br /><br />
13:  <img src="cover.jpg" alt="pic" style="width:100px;height:100px" /><br />
14:  <img src="cover.jpg" alt="pic" style="width:100px;height:100px" />
15:  <img src="cover.jpg" alt="pic" style="width:100px;height:100px" /><br />
16:  <img src="cover.jpg" alt="pic" style="width:100px;height:100px" />
17:  <img src="cover.jpg" alt="pic" style="width:100px;height:100px" />
18:  <img src="cover.jpg" alt="pic" style="width:100px;height:100px" /><br />
19:  <img src="cover.jpg" alt="pic" style="width:100px;height:100px" />
20:  <img src="cover.jpg" alt="pic" style="width:100px;height:100px" />
21:  <img src="cover.jpg" alt="pic" style="width:100px;height:100px" />
22:  <img src="cover.jpg" alt="pic" style="width:100px;height:100px" />
23:         <br /><br />
24:  <input type="button" onclick="myStart()" class="butSt" value="Start">
25:  <input type="button" onclick="myStop()" class="butSt" value="Stop">
26:  </body>
27:  <script src="ex11-02.js"></script>
28:  </html>
```

Lines 13–22 define10 images arranged in a pyramid shape. All these images have an initial picture cover.jpg. When the Start button is clicked, a ghost appears in the image element randomly. When the Stop button is clicked, the ghost disappears. Without using the standard image collection technique, to perform such animation we will need some sort of special design of the image element names and identity. With the collection technique, however, putting the ghost into random locations of the pyramid is much simpler. The file ex11-02.js is the program to do this task:

Example: ex11-02.js - The ECMAScript For ex11-02.htm

```
 1:  var noImage = 9
 2:  var rImg = 0
 3:  var imgPic01 = true
 4:  var startV = true
 5:  function myImg()
 6:  {
 7:    noImg = document.images.length
 8:    document.images.item(rImg).src = "cover.jpg"
 9:    rImg = 0
10:    rImg = Math.round(Math.random()*noImage)
11:    if (startV) {
12:      if (imgPic01) {
13:        document.images.item(rImg).src = "ghost_l.gif"
14:        imgPic01 = false
15:      } else {
16:        document.images.item(rImg).src = "ghost_r.gif"
17:        imgPic01 = true
18:      }
19:      setTimeout("myImg()",300)
20:    }
21:  }
22:
23:  function myStart()
24:  {
25:    startV = true
26:    myImg()
27:  }
28:  function myStop()
29:  {
30:    startV = false
31:  }
```

The myStart() and myStop() functions are simple. When the variable startV equals true, the action starts by calling the function myImg() in line 26. The myStop() function sets the startV variable to false so that no further action is performed. The important function is myImg(). First, the document.images.length stores the number of image elements inside the page. The statement in line 10 generates a random number from 0 to noImage (number of images). If the starting variables startV and imagePic01 are true, you set the random image element's resource file as ghost_l.gif. If the imgPic01 is not true, you change to another ghost picture by providing an alternative picture file in line 16. As a result, you have two ghost pictures appearing on the pyramid. The setTimout() function in line 19 is used to control the speed of the program. Some screen shots of this example are shown in Figs 11.4 and 11.5.

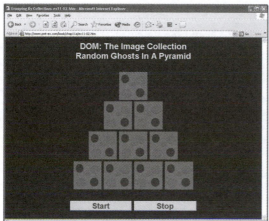

Figure 11.4 ex11-02.htm

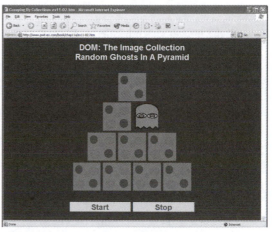

Figure 11.5 Ghost in a pyramid

Another important collection function is the document.form. Any elements declared inside the form element <form> are collected into the form collection so that you can access and control them just like using arrays. The form and its collection play a major role in the development of the Web, particularly when communication with the server is needed. A typical form element and a simple calling format may look like this:

```
<form action="myProgram.xxx" method="post">
  < .. .. some elements ..may be a button>
  < .. .. some elements ..may be a select box>
  < .. .. some elements ..may be an image>
  < .. .. some elements ..may be a checkbox>
  <input type="submit" value="Submit">
</form>
```

When the Submit button is pressed, all the data inside the form are collected and passed to the server program "myProgram.xxx." Here myProgram.xxx can be a "Program Extract Report Language" (Perl), "PHP: Hyper Preprocessor" (PHP), "Active Server Page" (ASP), or any other executable program on the server. This "client and server" communication link creates an exciting new application field on the Web, which forms the basis for database and e-commerce applications. We will discuss the server and its related database in more detail in Part IV.

To understand how forms can be used to collect page elements, let's look at an example similar to ex11-02.htm. We add a tag name <form> before the first image element as indicated in the following page fragment and call this example ex11-03.htm. This page calls a modified script program ex11-03.js which is similar to line 27 in ex11-02.htm.

```
Listing: ex11-03.txt - Page Fragment For ex11-03.htm
 1:  <form action="">
 2:  <img src="cover.jpg" alt="pic" style="width:100px;height:100px" /><br />
 3:  <img src="cover.jpg" alt="pic" style="width:100px;height:100px" />
 4:  <img src="cover.jpg" alt="pic" style="width:100px;height:100px" /><br />
 5:  <img src="cover.jpg" alt="pic" style="width:100px;height:100px" />
 6:  <img src="cover.jpg" alt="pic" style="width:100px;height:100px" />
 7:  <img src="cover.jpg" alt="pic" style="width:100px;height:100px" /><br />
 8:  <img src="cover.jpg" alt="pic" style="width:100px;height:100px" />
 9:  <img src="cover.jpg" alt="pic" style="width:100px;height:100px" />
10:  <img src="cover.jpg" alt="pic" style="width:100px;height:100px" />
11:  <img src="cover.jpg" alt="pic" style="width:100px;height:100px" />
12:  </form>
```

Now, all the images are embedded in the form collection (lines 1 to 12) and the statement

```
document.form.item(0).src or document.form[0].src
```

represents the resource or the picture file of the first image in line 2. In order to perform the same action as that in ex11-02.htm, all you have to do is to modify the function `myImg()` in ex11-02.js to use the form. The modified function `myImg()` in the program file ex11-03.js is listed as follows:

```
Listing: ex11-04.txt - The Modified myImg() Function In ex11-03.js
 1:  function myImg()
 2:  {
 3:    noImg = document.form.length
 4:    document.images.item(rImg).src = "cover.jpg"
 5:    rImg = 0
 6:    rImg = Math.round(Math.random()*noImage)
 7:    if (startV) {
 8:      if (imgPic01) {
 9:        document.form.item(rImg).src = "ghost_l.gif"
10:        imgPic01 = false
11:      } else {
12:        document.form.item(rImg).src = "ghost_r.gif"
13:        imgPic01 = true
14:      }
15:      setTimeout("myImg()",300)
16:    }
17:  }
```

By comparing this function with that listed in ex11-02.js, you can see that only a simple replacement from "images" to "form" is required to do the job. The beauty of the element collection is that complicated operations involving a group of elements can be done in a much simpler way. To demonstrate this, we modify this example into a game.

11.2.3 A page to catch random ghosts

To transform ex11-02.htm into a simple game, you use the same interface to draw the pyramid and some ghost pictures. The rules of the game are simple. When the game starts, a ghost appear randomly in the pyramid. You use the mouse to click on the ghost. If the mouse hits the ghost, the number of hits on the scoreboard will be increased by 1. Otherwise the number of misses on the scoreboard will be increased by 1. The game is over when a total of five misses is recorded. The interface part of this example is listed in ex11-04.htm.

Example: ex11-04.htm - Catch Some Ghosts

```
 1:  <?xml version="1.0" encoding="iso-8859-1"?>
 2:  <!DOCTYPE html PUBLIC "-//W3C//DTD XHTML 1.0 Transitional//EN"
 3:      "http://www.w3.org/TR/xhtml1/DTD/xhtml1-transitional.dtd">
 4:  <html xmlns="http://www.w3.org/1999/xhtml" xml:lang="en" lang="en">
 5: <head><title>Catch Some Ghosts -- ex11-04.htm</title></head>
 6:  <style>
 7:   .butSt{background-color:#dddddd;font-family:arial;font-weight:bold;
 8:       font-size:18pt;color:#880000;width:220px;height:35px}
 9:  </style>
10:  <body style="background:#000088;font-family:arial;font-size:22pt;
11:      color:#ffff00;font-weight:bold;text-align:center">
12:  Application Of Image Collection<br />Catch Random Ghosts<br /><br />
13:
14:  <div id="showPyramid"></div><br />
15:
16:  <div style="position:absolute;top:80px;left:130px;font-size:16pt">
17:     <span>No. Of Hits</span><br /><input type="text" readonly value="0"
18:         class="butSt" style="width:100px" id="hitId" /><br /><br />
19:     <span>No. Of Misses</span><br /><input type="text" readonly value="0"
20:         class="butSt" style="width:100px" id="missId"/>
21:  </div>
22:
23:  <input type="button" onclick="myStart()" class="butSt"
24:      value="Start" id="startId">
25:  <input type="button" onclick="myStop()" class="butSt" value="Stop">
26:  <br /><br /> <div id="outMsg"></div>
27:
28: </body>
29:  <script src="ex11-04.js"></script>
30:  </html>
```

To enhance the reusability of programming codes, the pyramids are generated by a program and displayed in a location with id="showPyramid" as shown in line 14. Lines 16–21 generate the scoreboard. The numbers of hits and misses are displayed inside the read-only text fields specified in lines 17–20. There are two buttons to control the process: the Start button to start the game and the Stop button to stop at any time. The game is over when a total of five misses is reached. In this case the Start button will be disabled and the color changed to gray. Some screen shots of this example are shown in Figs 11.6 and 11.7.

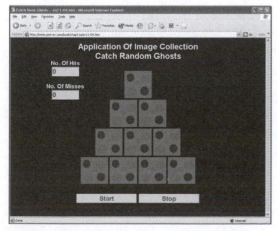

Figure 11.6 ex11-04.htm

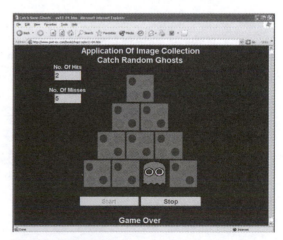

Figure 11.7 Game over

One interesting feature this example is that you can change the number of rows of the pyramid just by changing one parameter inside the program. The first part of the file ex11-04.js is responsible for generating the pyramids.

Example: ex11-04.js – The ECMAScript For ex11-04.htm (Part One)

```
 1:
 2: var noHit = 0
 3: var noMiss =0
 4: var noRows = 4
 5: var speedV = 500
 6:
 7: function initPar()
 8: {
 9:  noPic = 0
10:  noHit = 0
11:  noMiss =0
12:  lSt = ""
13:  for (jj=0;jj<noRows;jj++)
14:  {
15:   for(kk=0;kk<=jj;kk++)
16:   {
17:   lSt = lSt +"<img src=\"cover.jpg\" alt=\"pic\" "+
18:      "style=\"width:100px;height:100px\" vspace=\"3\" "+
19:      "hspace=\"3\" onclick=\"myHit("+noPic+ ")\" />"
20:   noPic++
21:   }
22:   lSt = lSt + "<br />"
23:  }
24:  document.getElementById("hitId").value = noHit
25:  document.getElementById("missId").value = noMiss
26:  document.getElementById("showPyramid").innerHTML=lSt
27: }
28: initPar()
29:
```

The function `initPar()` (initial parameter) initializes the game and generates the pyramid shapes for the ghost to appear. One benefit of generating XHTML by using an external program is that you can change the number of rows and the controlling speed. The variables in lines 4 and 5 are

```
noRows = 4 and speedV = 500
```

and any changes of these values will result in changes of the shape and/or the speed of the ghost in the pyramid. You can build some select boxes to use these properties and to add more functionality to the page. The two for-loops (lines 13–23) generate four rows of image elements. There are a total of 10 pictures in the following format:

```
<img src="cover.jpg" alt="pic" style="width:100px;height:100px"
     vspace="3" hspace="3" onclick="myHit(0)" /><br />
<img src="cover.jpg" alt="pic" style="width:100px;height:100px"
     vspace="3" hspace="3" onclick="myHit(1)" /><br />
   ...      ... ...
<img src="cover.jpg" alt="pic" style="width:100px;height:100px"
     vspace="3" hspace="3" onclick="myHit(9)" /><br />
```

Once you have defined these images, the scoreboard is initialized and the string 1st is displayed on the screen by executing the statement in line 26. The second part of this program file is listed below.

```
Listing: Continuation Of The ECMAScript ex11-04.js (Part Two)
30: var rImg = 0
31: var imgPic01 = true
32: var startV = true
33: var l1St = ""
34:
35: function myImg()
36: {
37:   if (startV) {
38:     noImg = document.images.length
39:     document.images.item(rImg).src = "cover.jpg"
40:     rImg = 0
41:     totPics = (noRows * (noRows +1))/2 -1
42:     rImg = Math.round(Math.random()* totPics)
43:     if (imgPic01) {
44:        document.images.item(rImg).src = "ghost_l.gif"
45:        imgPic01 = false
46:     } else {
47:        document.images.item(rImg).src = "ghost_r.gif"
48:        imgPic01 = true
49:     }
50:     setTimeout("myImg()",speedV)
51:   }
52: }
53:
54: function myStart()
55: {
56:   startV = true
57:   myImg()
58: }
59:
60: function myStop()
61: {
62:   startV = false
63: }
64:
```

The main function in this part is myImg() and is similar to the previous example. It generates the random appearance of the ghost. Since you have the number of rows as variable, you need to calculate how many pictures there are in total on the screen. The formulas can easily be constructed as follows:

1 row = 1 picture
2 rows = 3 pictures
3 rows = 6 pictures
k rows = $k * (k+1)/2$ pictures

This formula is used in line 41 to calculate the number of pictures in the game. This number is subsequently used to generate random appearances. The −1 at the end of line 41 indicates that you start the counting from 0. The speed variable speedV is used in line 50 to control the speed of motion. The higher the value of speedV, the faster the motion.

When the Stop button is pressed, the myStop() function is called to set the start variable startV to false so that no motion is allowed. Similarly, when the Start button is clicked, the myStart() function sets startV to true and executes the function myImg() to start the game.

The final part of the program contains some process functions to perform "hit the target" operations and is given below.

```
Listing: Continuation Of The ECMAScript ex11-04.js (Part Three)
65: function displayHit()
66: {
67:   document.getElementById("hitId").value = noHit
68:   document.getElementById("missId").value = noMiss
69:   document.getElementById("outMsg").innerHTML = llSt
70:   startV = true
71: }
72:
73: function gameOver()
74: {
75:  startV = false
76:  document.getElementById("startId").disabled=true
77:  document.getElementById("startId").style.color="#888888"
78:  document.getElementById("hitId").value = noHit
79:  document.getElementById("missId").value = noMiss
80:  document.getElementById("outMsg").innerHTML = "Game Over"
81: }
82:
83: function myHit(hitV)
84: {
85:  if (startV)
86:  {
87:   startV = false
88:   if (hitV == rImg) {
89:     llSt = "You Have Hit The Target"
90:     noHit++
91:   } else {
92:     llSt = "You Have Missed The Target"
93:     noMiss++
94:   }
95:   if ( noMiss < 5) displayHit()
96:   else gameOver()
97:  }
98: }
```

When one of the pictures is hit, the myHit(hitV) function is activated. For example, if you hit the first image in the second row, the function myHit(1) is called. Since the rImg variable stores the current position of the ghost display, a simple comparison between hitV (hit variable) and rImg can determine whether you have caught the ghost. If the target is hit, the variable noHit (number of hits) is increased by 1. The message "You Have Hit The Target" is assigned to the string variable llSt to be displayed later. Similarly, if the target is missed, the noMiss (number of misses) is increased by 1. If the total number of misses is less than 5, the function displayHit() is called to display the result. Otherwise, the function gameOver() is called to indicate that the game is now finished. In the latter situation, the value of the variable startV is set to false to stop the game. Also, the Start button is disabled and the color changed to gray immediately. The message "Game Over" is output to the display area. In this example, it can be clearly seen that the collection of page elements makes the task of Web page design, manipulation, and programming much easier.

11.2.4 Collecting page elements by tag name

To use the function `getElementsByName()`, you need to assign names to each element. This has to be done at the design level. The internal collection feature provided by the DOM only applies to a handful of elements such as images, forms, applets, etc. Another, more general, element collection feature provided by the DOM is the function `getElementsByTagName()`. Since tag names are identical to elements in the XHTML language, this function can be used to group any elements without any restrictions.

To demonstrate this function, consider a simple page with some division <div>, image <img>, and input <input> elements. Three input elements as buttons are used. If any one of the buttons is clicked, all tag names with the associated elements are collected and the number is displayed on the screen. You can input the tag name as an argument and therefore only one user function is needed in the example. This page is listed in ex11-05.htm.

```
Example: ex11-05.htm - Grouping Elements By Tag Name

 1:   <?xml version="1.0" encoding="iso-8859-1"?>
 2:   <!DOCTYPE html PUBLIC "-//W3C//DTD XHTML 1.0 Transitional//EN"
 3:        "http://www.w3.org/TR/xhtml1/DTD/xhtml1-transitional.dtd">
 4:   <html xmlns="http://www.w3.org/1999/xhtml" xml:lang="en" lang="en">
 5:   <head><title>Grouping Elements By Tag Name - ex11-05.htm</title></head>
 6:   <style>
 7:    .butSt{background-color:#dddddd;font-family:arial;font-weight:bold;
 8:         font-size:14pt;color:#880000;width:150px;height:35px}
 9:   </style>
10:   <body style="background:#000088;font-family:arial;font-size:22pt;
11:       color:#ffff00;font-weight:bold;text-align:center">
12:    Grouping Page Elements By Tag Name<br /><br />
13:
14:   <div style="color:#ffffff">This is paragraph one</div>
15:   <div style="color:#ffff00">This is paragraph two</div>
16:   <div style="color:#ff0000">This is paragraph three</div>
17:   <div style="color:#00ff00">This is paragraph four</div>
18:   <img src="picUp.gif" alt="pic" width="100" height="100" />
19:   <img src="picRight.gif" alt="pic" width="100" height="100" />
20:   <img src="picDown.gif" alt="pic" width="100" height="100" />
21:   <img src="picLeft.gif" alt="pic" width="100" height="100" />
22:      <br /><br />
23:   <input type="button" onclick="groupE('div')" class="butSt"
24:       value="Grouping div " />
25:   <input type="button" onclick="groupE('img')" class="butSt"
26:       value="Grouping Img" />
27:   <input type="button" onclick="groupE('input')" class="butSt"
28:       value="Grouping Input" />
29:   <br /><br /><div id="outMsg"></div>
30:   <script>
31:   function groupE(stV)
32:   {
33:     llSt = ""
34:     divV = document.getElementsByTagName(stV)
35:     llSt = "There are "+divV.length+" &lt;"+stV+"&gt; elements <br />"
36:     document.getElementById("outMsg").innerHTML = llSt
37:   }
38:   </script>
39:   </body>
40:   </html>
```

There are five divisions, four images, and three input elements in this page. If the first button defined in lines 23–24 is clicked, the function `groupE(div)` is called. This function executes the statement

```
divV = document.getElementsByTagName(stV)
```

with `stV="div"`. All elements with the name "div" are collected and returned as a collection to variable `divV`. This `divV` is a collection and therefore `divV.length` stores the number of items in the collection set. A string variable `11St` is constructed to show the collection on the screen. In order to display the word `<div>`, we use the expression `&lt;div&gt;` as illustrated in line 35. Some screen shots of this example are shown in Figs 11.8 and 11.9.

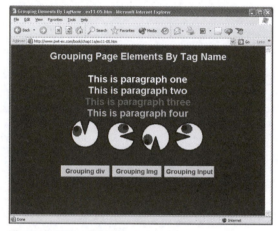

Figure 11.8 ex11-05.htm

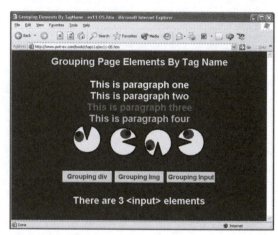

Figure 11.9 Counting the elements

11.3 The DOM Core

11.3.1 What is the DOM Core?

Supporting the standard, particularly the W3C DOM, is perhaps the most critical long-term requirement for the next generation of platform- and device-independent Web applications. The DOM has three level specifications and each level consists of different modules and documents:

W3C DOM, level 1 (two documents – September 2000):

>> DOM Level 1 Core
>> DOM Level 1 HTML

W3C DOM, level 2 (four documents – November 2000):

>> DOM Level 2 Core
>> DOM Level 2 HTML
>> DOM Level 2 Events
>> DOM Level 2 Style

W3C DOM, level 3 (two documents – September 2001):

>> DOM Level 3 Core
>> DOM Level 3 Events

Most of the documents are well over 100 pages long. At the time of writing, most browsers are still struggling to fully implement levels 1 and 2. These include IE6 and NS6.x. All DOM levels are backward compatible. You can consider level 3 as an extension of level 2 and level 2 an extension of level 1. The DOM HTML document consists of a group of specially designed interfaces dedicated to the HTML, and hence for XHTML, language. Apart from the styles and events, most of the previously discussed DOM functions belong to the DOM HTML. The DOM Style and Events documents laid down the fundamental specifications for programs and scripts to use style (CSS style) and system events.

The DOM Core document provides a crucial set of core properties and methods for reading, writing, and changing the content of documents on any devices and language platforms. The methods of the DOM Core apply equally well to HTML/XHTML and XML. These methods provide a tool not only to manipulate current HTML/XHTML Web contents, but also to set the preparatory work for future XML-based Web contents and applications.

Since the DOM Core is designed for a wide variety of platforms and languages, the structures and interfaces are a little more abstract than those you have encountered thus far. The DOM Core is also a good place to study the tree representation of the document, i.e., the DOM tree.

11.3.2 The node representation of page elements

From the viewpoint of the DOM Core, documents are represented as a hierarchy of node objects (a tree structure) and page elements are represented by nodes. Each node contains both the properties and methods as specialized interfaces. Some types of nodes may have child nodes of various types; other nodes are called leaf nodes and cannot have any child below them in the document structure. Consider the following empty XHTML skeleton:

```
Listing: ex11-05.txt - An Empty Page

1: <?xml version="1.0" encoding="iso-8859-1"?>
2: <!DOCTYPE html PUBLIC "-//W3C//DTD XHTML 1.0 Transitional//EN"
3:     "http://www.w3.org/TR/xhtml1/DTD/xhtml1-transitional.dtd">
4: <html xmlns="http://www.w3.org/1999/xhtml" xml:lang="en" lang="en">
5:   <head></head>
6:   <body>
7:   </body>
8: </html>
```

In terms of the tree notation, this document can be expressed as a tree starting from the document object collection (document node). This collection has three items and each item is a node as follows:

```
document.item(0).nodeName = !
document.item(1).nodeName = !
document.item(2).nodeName = HTML
```

The `item` method returns a node object and the `nodeName` property is used to access the name of the node. The returned `nodeName` from the tree structure is not case sensitive. Since most pages start from HTML, you have a special name called `documentElement` to represent this node, i.e.,

```
document.documentElement - <html>
```

The head and body are considered as children of HTML. Starting from `<html>`, the `<head>` element is the first child and the `<body>` element is the last child, i.e.,

```
document.documentElement.firstChild - <head>
document.documentElement.lastChild - <body>
```

If you want to print out the words "HEAD" and/or "BODY," the `nodeName` property is needed. Another useful entity of the DOM tree is the `childNodes` property. This returns a collection of all nodes under the current node or element. For example, the following statement returns a collection of all nodes or elements of a page under `<body>`:

```
document.documentElement.lastChild.childNodes
```

To see this explanation in action, let's consider the following demonstration example:

```
Example: ex11-06.htm - Node Representation Of Elements

1:   <?xml version="1.0" encoding="iso-8859-1"?>
2:   <!DOCTYPE html PUBLIC "-//W3C//DTD XHTML 1.0 Transitional//EN"
3:       "http://www.w3.org/TR/xhtml1/DTD/xhtml1-transitional.dtd">
4:   <html xmlns="http://www.w3.org/1999/xhtml" xml:lang="en" lang="en">
5:   <head><title>Node Representation of Elements-ex11-06.htm</title></head>
6:   <body style="background:#000088;font-family:arial;font-size:22pt;
7:       color:#ffff00;font-weight:bold;text-align:center">
8:   Node Representation of Elements<br /><br />
9:   <style>
10:   .butSt{background-color:#dddddd;font-family:arial;font-weight:bold;
11:       font-size:14pt;color:#880000;width:150px;height:35px}
12:  </style>
13:  <div style="color:#ffffff">This is paragraph one</div>
14:  <div style="color:#ffff00">This is paragraph two</div>
15:  <div style="color:#ff0000">This is paragraph three</div>
16:  <div style="color:#00ff00">This is paragraph four</div><br /><br />
17:  <input type="button" value="Element Tree" class="butSt"
18:      onclick="sTree()" />
19:  <div id="outMsg" style="font-size:14pt"></div>
20:  <script>
21:   function sTree()
22:   {
23:   llV = document.documentElement.lastChild.childNodes
24:   llSt = "<br />document.documentElement.lastChild.childNodes <br />"
25:   for (jj=0;jj<llV.length;jj++)
26:   {
27:     llSt = llSt +."item("+jj+").nodeName = "+
28:         llV.item(jj).nodeName+"<br />"
29:   }
30:
31:   document.getElementById("outMsg").innerHTML = llSt
32:   }
33:  </script>
34:  </body>
35:  </html>
```

Under the `<body>` element, this page contains the following:

- one text;
- two line breaks `<br />`;
- one `<style>`;
- four divisions `<div>`;
- one input `<input>`;
- one division `<div>`;
- one script `<script>`.

When the Element Tree button is clicked in line 17, the `sTree()` (i.e., show tree) function is activated to collect all elements or nodes inside `<body>` and to display them one by one. The variable in line 23

```
llV = document.documentElement.lastChild.childNodes
```

contains the collection `nodeList` of all elements under `<body>`. Therefore, you can use the property `llV.length` and method `llV.item()` to gain access to the items of the collection. In particular,

```
llV.item(jj).nodeName
```

returns the element name (or node name) of the `jj`th item in the collection. A for-loop on `jj` is used to display all items on the screen. Some screen shots are shown in Figs 11.10 and 11.11.

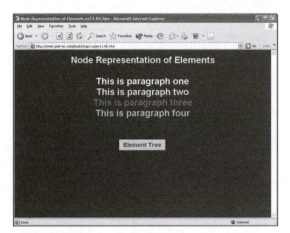

Figure 11.10 ex11-06.htm

Figure 11.11 Node representation of page elements

Once the tree is built, the contents of individual elements can be accessed, inserted, deleted, and manipulated. For example, the item number for script `<script>` is 13, the contents of which are stored in the expression

```
llV.item(13).text
```

If you put this statement into line 30 of ex11-06.htm, you will see the content text of the script. Also, from ex11-06.htm, you can see that the script is the last child of the `<body>` element. This means that the contents of the script can be displayed by the following statement:

```
document.documentElement.lastChild.lastChild.text
```

All nodes and tree representations of the page elements are part of the DOM Core specifications from W3C. Since the DOM works by providing object interfaces for applications, one direct learning approach to the DOM Core is to look at some of their interfaces.

11.4 Working with the DOM Core interfaces

11.4.1 The node interface

The node interface is the skeleton and primary data structure of the entire DOM Core. Beginning with just a single node, the whole document tree is clearly represented. For example, the `firstChild`, `lastChild`, `nodeName`, and `childNodes` objects are defined in the node interface. In fact, the node interface also contains a number of primary methods or functions such as insert, remove, replace, and append for you to manipulate a document tree.

The node interface is a big interface and if you ignore the declarations of the "NodeType," "TreePosition," and some other functions not frequently used, you will get a simplified version of the interface as listed in ex11-06.txt.

```
Listing: ex11-06.txt - DOM Core: Document Interface - Node
 1: interface Node {
 2:
 3:     readonly attribute DOMString          nodeName;
 4:              attribute DOMString          nodeValue;
 5:     readonly attribute Node              parentNode;
 6:     readonly attribute NodeList          childNodes;
 7:     readonly attribute Node              firstChild;
 8:     readonly attribute Node              lastChild;
 9:     readonly attribute Node              previousSibling;
10:     readonly attribute Node              nextSibling;
11:     readonly attribute NamedNodeMap      attributes;
12:
13:     // Modified in DOM Level 3:
14:     Node                insertBefore(in Node newChild,
15:                                     in Node refChild);
16:     // Modified in DOM Level 3:
17:     Node                replaceChild(in Node newChild,
18:                                     in Node oldChild);
19:     // Modified in DOM Level 3:
20:     Node                removeChild(in Node oldChild);
21:     Node                appendChild(in Node newChild);
22:     boolean             hasChildNodes();
23: };
```

Instead of providing definitions for every property and function of the interface, we would like to explain and show you how to use them by example. Consider the following page fragment:

```
Listing: ex11-07.txt - Page Fragment Of Example ex11-07.htm (Part One)
 1:  <body id="body" style="background:#000088;font-family:arial;
 2:    font-size:22pt;color:#ffff00;font-weight:bold;text-align:center">
 3:  DOM Core - Node Interface<br /><br />
 4:
 5:  <br />
 6:  <div style="color:#ffffff" id="id01">This is paragraph one</div>
 7:  <div style="color:#ffff00">This is paragraph two</div>
 8:  <div style="color:#ff0000">This is paragraph three</div><br /><br />
 9:  <div id="outMsg" style="font-size:14pt"></div>
10:  </body>
```

The nodeName and nodeValue represent the name and the value of the node. They are strings and can be displayed easily on the screen. Since the node is an object, you may need these two and possibly other properties to view the information of the node. For example, the following script statements return the element name and text of the division in line 6:

```
childV = document.getElementById("id01")
```

childV.nodeName   – returns the name "DIV"

childV.firstChild.nodeValue   – returns the string "This is paragraph one"

The parentNode object returns the parent of this node. Most nodes have a parent. However, if a node has just been created and not yet added to the tree, or if it has been removed from the tree, this is "null." For example, the parent of childV is <body>:

childV.parentNode.nodeName   –   returns the name "BODY"

The `childNodes` object is a collection of type `NodeList` and contains all children of the node concerned. If the node contains no children, `NodeList` has no nodes, i.e., "null."

The `firstChild` and `lastChild` objects represent the first child and the last child of the node respectively. Again, if there is no such node, "null" is returned. Example ex11-06.htm shows the behavior of these properties.

The `previousSibling` object is the node immediately preceding this node and `nextSibling` is the node immediately following the current node. If there is no such node, "null" is returned. For example,

```
childV.previousSibling.nodeName    –    returns the name "BR"

childV.nextSibling.nodeName        –    returns the name "DIV"
```

To show all these in action, we consider the remaining part of the example ex11-07.htm.

```
Listing: Continuation Of The Example ex11-07.htm (Part Two)

11: <script>
12:     llSt = 'childV = document.getElementById("id01") <br />'
13:     childV = document.getElementById("id01")
14:     llSt = llSt +"childV.nodeName= "+childV.nodeName +'<br />'
15:     llSt = llSt +"childV.firstChild.nodeValue= "+
16:             childV.firstChild.nodeValue +'<br />'
17:     llSt = llSt +"childV.parentNode.nodeName= "+
18:             childV.parentNode.nodeName +'<br />'
19:     llSt = llSt +"childV.nextSibling.nodeName= "+
20:             childV.nextSibling.nodeName +'<br />'
21:     llSt = llSt +"childV.previousSibling.nodeName= "+
22:             childV.previousSibling.nodeName +'<br />'
23:
24:  document.getElementById("outMsg").innerHTML = llSt
25: </script>
26: </html>
```

This page fragment is a script block illustrating the applications of `noName`, `nodeValue`, `parentNode`, `nextSibling`, and `previousSibling`. All these properties have a reference point defined in line 13, i.e., the division with an `id="id01"`. A screen shot of this example is shown in Fig. 11.12.

The ability to define attributes inside the node interface is a powerful feature. It provides a method to gain access and to control all attributes (if any) of an element. At the time of writing, not many browsers (including IE5.5) have managed to implement it completely. Attributes of the node interface can be considered as a collection of attributes of a node. For example, the following statements provide a complete listing of the attribute on `childV`:

Figure 11.12 ex11-07.htm

```
for (jj=0;jj< childV.attributes.length;jj++)
{
 childV.attributes.item(jj).nodeName
 childV.attributes.item(jj).nodeValue
}
```

If your browser has a proper implementation of the node interface, you should have the results

```
childV.attributes.item(0).nodeName = style
childV.attributes.item(0).nodeValue = color: rgb(255,255,255);
childV.attributes.item(1).nodeName = id
childV.attributes.item(1).nodeValue = id01
```

They represent the attribute settings of the division element given in line 6 of ex11-07.txt, i.e.

```
<div style="color:#ffffff" id="id01">This is paragraph one</div>
```

The node interface also provides a useful set of functions or methods for you to add, delete, and modify the existing DOM tree representation of a document. In order words, you can modify the structure of a document at run time by using the node functions `insertBefore()`, `removeChild()`, and `appendChild()` to insert, remove, and append page elements.

To add or insert a new element to the structure of a document, you need to know how to generate or to create a new element at run time. For this purpose, some knowledge of the document interface of the DOM Core is necessary.

11.4.2 The document interface of the DOM Core

Another interface we need to continue the discussion on the DOM Core is the document interface. This interface represents the entire HTML or XML document. It is the root of the document tree, and provides primary access to the document's data. The document interface also contains a number of methods to create objects or page elements at run time.

It is outside the scope of this book to give every detailed definition and explanation of the properties and functions inside the document interface. We concentrate only on the functions that are needed in our applications. A simplified version of the document is listed in ex11-08.txt.

```
Listing: ex11-08.txt - DOM Core: Document Interface - Document

 1:
 2: interface Document : Node {
 3:    // Modified in DOM Level 3:
 4:    readonly attribute DocumentType       doctype;
 5:    readonly attribute Element            documentElement;
 6:
 7:    Element             createElement(in DOMString tagName)
 8:
 9:    Text                createTextNode(in DOMString data);
10:    Comment             createComment(in DOMString data);
11:
12:    NodeList            getElementsByTagName(in DOMString tagname);
13:
14:    // Introduced in DOM Level 2:
15:    Element             getElementById(in DOMString elementId);
16:
17: };
```

The `doctype` attribute in line 4 returns the DTD associated with this document. A document without one will return "null."

The `documentElement` attribute allows direct access to the child node, i.e., the root element of the document. For HTML/XHTML documents, it represents the element <html>, i.e.,

```
document.documentElement – returns the node of the <html> element
```

Another frequently used shortcut to the child node is

`document.body` – returns the node of the `<body>` element

The first important function of this interface is `createElement()`. This function is often used to create an element of the type specified. For example, the statement

```
document.createElement("div")
```

creates an element pair `"<div></div>"`. Almost any XHTML element and node can be generated this way at run time. If you want to add some text to the newly created division element `<div>`, the function `createTextNode()` is needed. This function converts a text string into a node type. For example, a typical application of this function is

```
newdiv = document.createElement("div")
newText = createTextNode("This is a new text node")
newdiv.appendChild(newText)
```

After generating two new nodes from the functions of the document interface, the `appendChild()` function from the node interface is used to append the two nodes together. The resulting statement is

```
<div>This is a new text node</div>
```

This is a powerful structure and enables us to create element and insert and delete them anywhere on the DOM tree at run time.

The function `createComment()` generates a comment node with the specified string. The remaining functions `getElementsByName()` and `getElementById()` are frequently mentioned and used in the last and current chapters.

11.4.3 Inserting and deleting page elements at run time

The DOM Core provides an opportunity to modify page structure in real time. Some of these functions are listed as follows:

```
Node insertBefore(in Node newChild, in Node refChild)
Node removeChild(in Node oldChild)
Node appendChild(in Node newChild)
```

The first function allows you to insert a node (whether new or old) before a node inside the DOM tree. A typical procedure to use the `insertBefore()` function is

```
newDiv = document.createElement("div")
newText = createTextNode("This is a new text node")
newDiv.appendChild(newText)
myRefNode = document.getElementById("id01")
document.body.insertBefore(newDiv,myRefNode)
```

The first three lines together create the node `"<div>This is a new text node</div>"`. The fourth line gets the node that you want to insert just before that. The final line can be interpreted as: insert the `newDiv` node before the node `myRefNode` inside the body node collection.

The `removeChild()` function is easier to use. For example, the following statement removes the node with `id="id01"` from the body collection of the DOM tree:

```
idObj = document.getElementById("id01")
document.body.removeChild(idObj)
```

The node itself, and all subsequent subnodes if any, will be removed from the tree at the same time. Consider the following example:

```
Example: ex11-08.htm - Insert And Delete Elements At Run Time (Part One)

 1:  <?xml version="1.0" encoding="iso-8859-1"?>
 2:  <!DOCTYPE html PUBLIC "-//W3C//DTD XHTML 1.0 Transitional//EN"
 3:      "http://www.w3.org/TR/xhtml1/DTD/xhtml1-transitional.dtd">
 4:  <html xmlns="http://www.w3.org/1999/xhtml" xml:lang="en" lang="en">
 5:  <head><title>Insert and Delete at Run Time -- ex11-08.htm</title></head>
 6:  <style>
 7:   .butSt{background-color:#dddddd;font-family:arial;font-weight:bold;
 8:       font-size:14pt;color:#880000;width:150px;height:35px}
 9:  </style>
10:  <body style="background:#000088;font-family:arial;font-size:22pt;
11:      color:#ffff00;font-weight:bold;text-align:center">
12:   Inserting and Deleting Elements <br />At Run Time<br /><br />
13:
14:  <div id="id01" style="color:#ffffff">This is paragraph one</div>
15:  <div style="color:#ffff00">This is paragraph two</div>
16:  <div style="color:#ff0000">This is paragraph three</div>
17:  <div style="color:#00ff00">This is paragraph four</div>
18:  <img src="picUp.gif" alt="pic" width="100" height="100" />
19:  <img src="picRight.gif" alt="pic" width="100" height="100" />
20:  <img src="picDown.gif" alt="pic" width="100" height="100" />
21:  <img src="picLeft.gif" alt="pic" width="100" height="100" />
22:      <br /><br />
23:
24:  <input type="button" onclick="myDelApp(1)" class="butSt"
25:      value="Remove div" />
26:  <input type="button" onclick="myDelApp(2)" class="butSt"
27:      value="Remove Img" /><br />
28:  <input type="button" onclick="myAddApp(1)" class="butSt"
29:      value="Append div" />
30:  <input type="text" id="txId" class="butSt" style="width:350px;
31:      color:#008800" value="Enter Text Here"/>
32:  <br /><br /><span id="outMsg"></span>
33:
```

This code fragment is the first part of the example ex11-08.htm containing the interface part. For demonstration purposes, this page contains four division elements and four images. The divisions are defined in lines 14–17 and the images are in lines 18–21. You also have two buttons soon after the images. When the Remove div button is clicked (lines 24–25), the function myDelApp(1) is called to delete the first item of the divisions. The argument 1 in the myDelApp() function indicates that we want to delete the <div> element. On the other hand, if myDelApp(2) in lines 26–27 is called, the first image is removed.

The third and fourth input elements defined in lines 28–31 are considered as a pair. The third input is a button with the name "Append div." The fourth input element is actually a text field to allow you to type something in. Once the typing is finished and the Append div button is clicked, a node is generated and inserted at the end of the divisions.

The details of the functions myDelApp() and myAddApp() are listed in the second part of the example:

```
Listing: Continuation Of The Example ex11-08.htm (Part Two)

34:  <script>
35:  function myDelApp(stV)
36:  {
37:    objDiv = document.getElementsByTagName("div")
38:    objImg = document.getElementsByTagName("img")
39:
```

```
40:  if((stV ==1)&&(objDiv.length > 0)) document.body.removeChild(objDiv.item(0))
41:  if((stV ==2)&&(objImg.length > 0)) document.body.removeChild(objImg.item(0))
42:
43:      llSt = "There are "+objDiv.length+" &lt;div&gt; elements <br />"+
44:                "and "+objImg.length+" &lt;img&gt; elements left <br />"
45:      document.getElementById("outMsg").innerHTML = llSt
46:  }
47:
48:  function myAddApp(stV)
49:  {
50:      objDiv = document.getElementsByTagName("div")
51:      objImg = document.getElementsByTagName("img")
52:
53:      if ((stV ==1) && (objDiv.length < 6)) {
54:          newO = document.createElement("div")
55:          txtId = document.getElementById("txId")
56:          newT = document.createTextNode(txtId.value)
57:          newO.appendChild(newT)
58:          document.body.insertBefore(newO,objImg.item(0))
59:      }
60:
61:      llSt = "There are "+objDiv.length+" &lt;div&gt; elements <br />"+
62:                "and "+objImg.length+" &lt;img&gt; elements left <br />"
63:      document.getElementById("outMsg").innerHTML = llSt
64:  }
65:  </script>
66:
67:  </body>
68:  </html>
```

Inside the function myDelApp(), the statements in lines 37 and 38 are used to collect all the division and image elements and assign them to the objects objDiv and objImg. If the value of the variable stV is 1, the if statement in line 40 is executed and the function removeChild() is called to delete the selected division specified by objDiv.item(0). If the variable stV is 2, the statement in line 41 is activated and the selected image element will be deleted from the page. It is good practice to check the object length objDiv.length (see line 40) before any deletion to prevent undesirable effects or system errors.

The function myAddApp() in lines 48–64 is used to insert elements into the page. When this function is called, the following tasks are performed to insert the text before the first image element:

- Create a division element (line 54).
- Get the text from the text box (line 55).
- Create a text node with the text (line 56).
- Add the text node to the division element (line 57).
- Insert the node before the first image element (line 58).

Most XHTML elements contain attributes. In many cases, attributes are the integral part of an element. Elements such as anchor <a> and image <img> require them to function properly. The next step is to know how to generate attributes for an element at run time. Some screen shots of this example are shown in Figs 11.13 and 11.14.

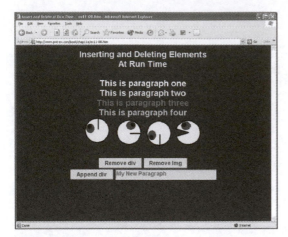

Figure 11.13 ex11-08.htm

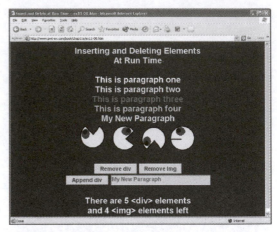

Figure 11.14 Inserting and deleting elements at run time

11.4.4 Generating and controlling attributes with the element interface

The `attributes` property (not supported by IE5.5) defined in the node interface provides a handy way to gain access to the existing attributes of a page element. However, the node interface contains very little information on how to create them in the first place. In fact, the functions to generate and control attributes at run time are embedded inside another DOM core interface called the "element interface." A simplified verion of the interface is listed in ex11-09.txt.

```
Listing: ex11-09.txt - DOM Core: Doucment Interface - Element

 1: interface Element : Node {
 2:    readonly attribute DOMString        tagName;
 3:    DOMString          getAttribute(in DOMString name);
 4:    void               setAttribute(in DOMString name,
 5:                                    in DOMString value)
 6:
 7:    void               removeAttribute(in DOMString name)
 8:
 9:    NodeList           getElementsByTagName(in DOMString name);
10:
11:    // Introduced in DOM Level 2:
12:    boolean            hasAttribute(in DOMString name);
13:
14: };
```

The function `getAttribute()` in line 3 is a general standard function to obtain attributes from elements. Again, not all browsers (including IE5.5) implement and support this function completely. For example, suppose that you have defined a division element as

```
<div id="id01" style="color:#ffffff;font-size:16pt;
     font-family:arial">This is paragraph one</div>
```

The script statements

```
objV = document.getElementById("id01")
objV.getAttribute("id")
```

return the value "id01," whereas the command

```
objV.getAttribute("style")
```

returns the CSS style settings as

```
color: rgb(255,255,255); font-size: 16pt; font-family: arial;
```

IE5.5 doesn't fully support the `getAttribute()` function and some ways to work around it are necessary. You will need IE6+ and NS6+ to display the result directly. The `setAttribute()` function is a powerful function to set the attributes of an element. One very simple use of this function is

```
objV.setAttribute("style","color:#ffff00;font-size:18pt;
      font-family:Times")
```

Since the variable `objV` represents the element with `id="id01"`, the call on the `setAttribute()` function above sets the CSS style of the division element. Obviously, you can also use the style object to set the style properties one by one. The real strength of this function is that it can set the attributes of a newly created element.

The following is a typical program fragment to generate an image at run time and insert it before an element with `id="id01"`:

```
1:  objV = document.getElementById("id01")
2:  newImg = document.createElement("img")
3:  tmpV = newImg.setAttribute("alt","pic")
4:  tmpV = newImg.setAttribute("hspace","10")
5:  tmpV = newImg.setAttribute("vspace","10")
6:  tmpV = newImg.setAttribute("src","myPic.jpg")
7:  tmpV = document.body.insertBefore(newImg,objV)
```

You create the image element `<img>` and assign the element to a variable `newImg` in line 2. In lines 3–6, the function `setAttribute()` is called to build up the attributes that are associated with `<img>`. At the end of line 6, you have an image element like this:

```
<img alt="pic" hspace="10" vspace="10" src="myPic.jpg" />
```

The final line is to insert this image element before the element with `id="id01"`. To actually use these attribute functions, let's consider an example to generate photographs online.

11.4.5 Generating images at run time

To put the `setAttribute()` function into action, we consider a simple example to generate images from your hard drive to a Web page at run time. This example uses an input element with `type="file"` to get a picture file from your hard drive and then insert it into a page as an element. A modification of this example is also discussed in section 11.5.1 to build a more practical example. That is, a page to generate an image and organize an online photo album at run time.

The interface part of this example is listed as follows:

```
Example: ex11-09.htm - Generating Images At Run Time

1:  <?xml version="1.0" encoding="iso-8859-1"?>
2:  <!DOCTYPE html PUBLIC "-//W3C//DTD XHTML 1.0 Transitional//EN"
3:      "http://www.w3.org/TR/xhtml1/DTD/xhtml1-transitional.dtd">
4:  <html xmlns="http://www.w3.org/1999/xhtml" xml:lang="en" lang="en">
5:  <head><title>Generating Images At Run Time - ex11-09.htm</title></head>
6:  <style>
7:   .butSt{background-color:#aaaaaa;font-family:arial;font-weight:bold;
8:      font-size:14pt;color:#880000;width:150px;height:35px}
9:  </style>
```

```
10:   <body style="background:#dddddd;font-family:arial;font-size:20pt;
11:      color:#000088;font-weight:bold;text-align:center">
12:    Inserting Images At Run Time<br />
13:
14:   <div id="id01" style="color:#00ff00"></div>
15:
16:   <img src="line1.gif" width="550" height="6" alt="pic" />
17:   <table align="center">
18:   <tr><td><input type="text" readonly class="butSt"
19:         style="color:#000088" value="Pic File Name" /></td>
20:     <td><input type="file" id="fileId"
21:         class="butSt" style="width:350px" /><br /></td></tr>
22:   <tr><td><input type="button" onclick="myAddPic()"
23:         class="butSt" value="Insert Pic" /></td>
24:     <td><input type="button" onclick="genBr()"
25:         class="butSt" value="Line Break" /></td></tr>
26:   </table>
27:   <script src="ex11-09.js"></script>
28:   </body>
29:   </html>
```

The division element defined in line 14 is an empty element ready to accept the images loaded from your hard drive. After the graphic line in line 16, there is a table with two rows. The first row contains two input elements. The first input element is a text to display "Pic File Name." The type of the second input element in lines 20–21 is `type=file`. This button opens a "Choose File" dialog box so you can search your local hard drive for a desirable picture. Once you have picked your picture file with a double click or opened it inside the dialog box, the file name of the picture appears inside the input field specified in lines 20–21.

The second row of the table contains two buttons. When the Insert Pic button (lines 22–23) is clicked, the `myAddPic()` function is called to load the picture into the page. All pictures are loaded adjacent to each other until the Line Break button is clicked to generate a line break.

Some screen shots of this example are shown in Figs 11.15–11.17.

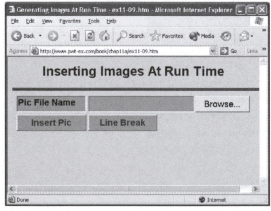

Figure 11.15 ex11-09.htm

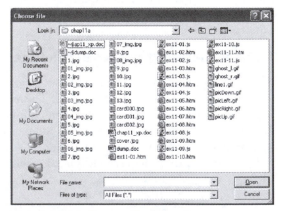

Figure 11.16 Choose file dialog box

Figure 11.17 Inserting image at run time

The external program file ex11-09.js is listed below.

Example: ex11-09.js - The ECMAScript For ex11-09.htm

```
 1:  var IE = document.all?true:false
 2:
 3:  var widthV=200
 4:  var heightV=150
 5:  var hspaceV =10
 6:  var vspaceV =10
 7:  var picV = "pic"
 8:  var objV = document.getElementById("id01")
 9:
10:  function myAddPic()
11:  {
12:    fileV = document.getElementById("fileId").value
13:    fileVV = "file://"+fileV
14:    newImg = document.createElement("img")
15:    tmpV = newImg.setAttribute("alt",picV)
16:    tmpV = newImg.setAttribute("hspace",hspaceV)
17:    tmpV = newImg.setAttribute("vspace",vspaceV)
18:
19:    if (!IE){
20:      tmpV = newImg.setAttribute("width",200)
21:      tmpV = newImg.setAttribute("height",150)
22:    }
23:
24:    tmpV = newImg.setAttribute("src",fileVV)
25:    tmpV = document.body.insertBefore(newImg,objV)
26:
27:    if (IE) {
28:      newImg.style.width=widthV+"px"
29:      newImg.style.height=heightV+"px"
30:    }
31:  }
32:
33:  function genBr()
34:  {
35:   lineBr = document.createElement("br")
36:   tmpV = document.body.insertBefore(lineBr,objV)
37:  }
38:
```

The first line is to detect whether an IE browser is used. The next couple of lines are the parameters controlling the size of the image. Initially, a dimension of 200×150 pixels is specified to display the picture. The `hspaceV` and `vspaceV` variables provide some extra spaces between each picture. The statement in line 8 declares a variable `objV` (object variable) before which all images are inserted.

Once the Insert Pic button is clicked, the `myAddPic()` function is called. First, this function gets the file name from the input field with `id="fileId"`. We add the keyword `file://` in front of the file name to indicate that the file name is from a local hard drive. The statement in line 14 generates an image element at run time, i.e., `<img />`. To control the image, we want the image element to have the following attributes:

```
<img alt="pic" hspace="10" vspace="10" width="200" height="150"
     src=file://xxxxx />
```

Lines 15–17 use the function `setAttribute()` to set `hspace` and `vspace`. Since IE (IE5.x and IE 6.01) didn't support W3C's `setAttribute()` function on width and height, a browser detection is used in lines 19–22. If the browser is not IE, we continue W3C's attribute settings and use the statement

```
document.body.insertBefore(newImg,objV)
```

and ultimately insert the newly created image element before the object `objV` with identity `id="id01"`. After this element insertion, an IE detection code is used to set the image's width and height using IE's style properties.

When the Line Break button is pressed, the function `genBr()` defined in lines 33–37 is called. This function creates a line break element, i.e., `<br />`, which is inserted before the object element `objV`.

11.5 Some DOM Core applications

11.5.1 A page to organize your photos

We will look at two DOM Core applications in this section. Our first application is a continuation of the last example, ex11-09.htm. To transform this example into a user-friendly program, we will add the following three features.

- Pictures generated on the page can be moved freely on the page when you hold down the mouse so that photos can be organized anywhere you like.
- A Gen. Page (generating page) button is added and when this button is clicked, a new page in a new window is generated. All the organized pictures are arranged in the designed positions. This page can then be saved to your local storage or hard drive so that you can view your photos at any time.
- When one of the pictures inside the generated page is clicked, the full size of the image is displayed in another window.

The interface part of this example is simple and is listed as follows:

```
Example: ex11-10.htm - A Page To Organize Your Photos

 1:  <?xml version="1.0" encoding="iso-8859-1"?>
 2:  <!DOCTYPE html PUBLIC "-//W3C//DTD XHTML 1.0 Transitional//EN"
 3:      "http://www.w3.org/TR/xhtml1/DTD/xhtml1-transitional.dtd">
 4:  <html xmlns="http://www.w3.org/1999/xhtml" xml:lang="en" lang="en">
 5:  <head><title>A Page To Organize Your Photos - ex11-10.htm</title></head>
 6:  <style>
 7:  .butSt{background-color:#dddddd;font-family:arial;font-weight:bold;
 8:      font-size:14pt;color:#880000;width:150px;height:35px}
 9:  </style>
10:  <body style="background:#bbbbbb;font-family:arial;font-size:20pt;
11:      color:#008800;font-weight:bold;text-align:center">
```

```
12:    Inserting Images At Run Time<br />
13:
14:  <table align="center"><tr>
15:  <td><input type="text" class="butSt" value="File Name:"
16:        style="color:#000088"/></td>
17:  <td><input type="file" id="fileId" class="butSt"
18:        style="width:350px" /></td></tr><tr>
19:  <td><input type="button" onclick="myAddPic()" class="butSt"
20:        value="Insert Pic" /></td>
21:  <td><input type="button" onclick="genPage()" class="butSt"
22:        value="Gen. Page" /></td></tr>
23:  </table>
24:
25:  <img src="line1.gif" width="550" height="6" alt="pic" /><br />
26:  <div id="id02" style="color:#00ff00"></div><br />
27:
28:  <script src="ex11-10.js"></script>
29:  </body>
30:  </html>
```

This interface is similar to that in ex11-09.htm. A Gen. Page button is added so that a Web page is generated and all pictures are imported into this new page. The source of this page can then be saved as an independent application and hence could be used as standalone page or reused in other applications.

To show this application in action, we start by generating five pictures as shown in Fig. 11.18. Once the pictures are loaded, they can be moved anywhere on the screen by clicking the picture and holding down the mouse button. This feature is simply a moving object application of Chapter 9. A simple positioning of the images is shown in Fig. 11.19.

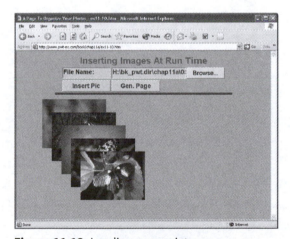

Figure 11.18 Loading some pictures

Figure 11.19 Positioning the images

When you have finished with the arrangement of the images and the Gen. Page button is clicked, a new window is opened on the screen with all the desirable images and positions embedded (see Fig. 11.20). When any of the pictures of this new page is clicked, the full size of the picture is displayed in another new window (see Fig. 11.21).

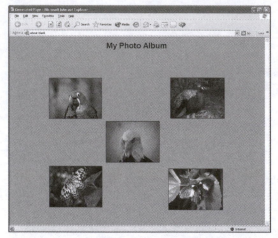

Figure 11.20 Generating new page

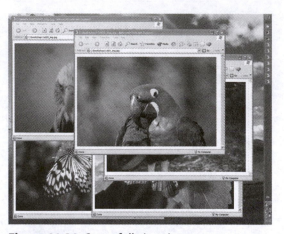

Figure 11.21 Some full-size pictures

If the XHTML code of this page is saved to your local hard drive by using the normal "View" and "Source" options, the page can then be reviewed again at any time.

The external program file ex11-10.js contains the code to control all actions. The first part of the program file is listed as follows:

Example: ex11-10.js – The ECMAScript For ex11-10.htm (Part One)

```
 1:  var IE = document.all?true:false
 2:
 3:  var widthV=200
 4:  var heightV=150
 5:  var hspaceV =10
 6:  var vspaceV =10
 7:  var picV = "pic"
 8:  var objV = document.getElementById("id02")
 9:  var noPic =0
10:
11:  function myAddPic()
12:  {
13:    noPic++
14:
15:    fileV = document.getElementById("fileId").value
16:    fileVV = "file://"+fileV
17:    newImg = document.createElement("img")
18:    tmpV = newImg.setAttribute("alt","pic")
19:    imgV = "img"+noPic
20:    tmpV = newImg.setAttribute("id",imgV)
21:    tmpV = newImg.setAttribute("hspace",hspaceV)
22:    tmpV = newImg.setAttribute("vspace",vspaceV)
23:
24:  if (!IE) {
25:    tmpV = newImg.setAttribute("width",widthV)
26:    tmpV = newImg.setAttribute("height",heightV)
27:    tmpV = newImg.setAttribute("onmousedown","mouseDownEvent("+noPic+")")
28:    tmpV = newImg.setAttribute("onmouseup","mouseUpEvent()")
29:    tmpSt="position:absolute;top:"+(100+noPic*40)+"px;left:"+
30:          (40+noPic*30)+"px"
31:    tmpV = newImg.setAttribute("style",tmpSt)
```

```
32:    }
33:      tmpV = newImg.setAttribute("src",fileVV)
34:      tmpV = document.body.insertBefore(newImg,objV)
35:
36:    if (IE) {
37:      imgObj = document.getElementById(imgV)
38:      imgObj.style.width=widthV+"px"
39:      imgObj.style.height=heightV+"px"
40:      imgObj.style.position="absolute"
41:      imgObj.style.top=(100+noPic*40) +"px"
42:      imgObj.style.left=(40+noPic*30)+"px"
43:      imgObj.attachEvent("onmousedown",mouseDownEvent)
44:      imgObj.attachEvent("onmouseup",mouseUpEvent)
45:    }
46:  }
47:
```

The first part of the program file contains one function, myAddPic(). The main purpose of this function is to generate image elements at run time. The browser detection code in line 1 is needed in order to take care of some backward compatibility issues.

From line 3 to line 22, the program is very similar to that in ex11-09.js. The aim is to create the image element <img />. Since some earlier IE browsers (including IE5.0 and IE5.5) didn't support the setAttribute() function on events such as onmousedown and onmouseup, the W3C standard statements in lines 24–32 are dedicated to the NS6+ series. That is, if the browser is not IE, the W3C standard coding (lines 25–31) is used to set the width, height, onmousedown, onmouseup, and style properties of the image element. After all the attribute settings, the image is inserted into the page by executing the statement in line 34.

If IE is detected, the alternative codes dedicated to the IE browser are executed in lines 36–45. In order to prevent a complete overlap of images, we change the top and left position of every loaded picture (see lines 29–30 and lines 41–42). Launching the onmousedown and onmouseup events (lines 43–44) guarantees that the pictures can move with the mouse. The code for controlling the picture and mouse movements is provided in the second part of the program ex11-10.js.

Listing: Continuation Of The ECMAScript ex11-10.js (Part Two)

```
48: var selectObj = null
49: var working =0
50:
51: function mouseDownEvent(objId)
52: {
53:   selectObj="img"+objId
54:   if (IE) selectObj = event.srcElement.id
55: }
56:
57: function mouseUpEvent()
58: {
59:   if (selectObj != null)
60:   {
61:     working =1
62:     selectObj = null;
63:   }
64: }
65:
66: function mouseMoveEvent(e)
67: {
68:   if (selectObj != null)
69:   {
```

```
70:     if (IE)
71:     {
72:      lxPos = event.clientX
73:      lyPos = event.clientY
74:     } else {
75:      lxPos = e.pageX
76:      lyPos = e.pageY
77:     }
78:     objW = widthV
79:     objH = heightV
80:     document.getElementById(selectObj).style.left = (lxPos - objW/2) +"px"
81:     document.getElementById(selectObj).style.top = (lyPos - objH/2) +"px"
82:     }
83:  return (false)
84: }
85:
86: document.onmousemove=mouseMoveEvent
87:
```

In fact, this part of the program is simply a cut-down version of ex09-10.js in Chapter 9. When the left mouse button is down, this event triggers the function mouseDownEvent() to get the identity of the object held by the mouse. If IE is detected, the event.srcElement (source element) returns the identity of the picture. When the mouse button is up, the function mouseUpEvent() is called to release the object. The function mouseMoveEvent() in lines 66–84 listens to every mouse movement, to capture the mouse positions and to store them in variables lxPos and lyPos. These new mouse positions are then used to move the picture.

The final part of the program contains a single function genPage(). This function is called when the Gen. Page button is pressed.

Listing: Continuation Of The ECMAScript ex11-10.js (Part Three)

```
88: function genPage()
89: {
90:     headSt = ' <?xml version="1.0" encoding="iso-8859-1"?> \n'+
91:  ' <!DOCTYPE html PUBLIC "-//W3C//DTD XHTML 1.0 Transitional//EN" \n'+
92:  ' "http://www.w3.org/TR/xhtml1/DTD/xhtml1-transitional.dtd"> \n '+
93:  '<html xmlns="http://www.w3.org/1999/xhtml" xml:lang="en" lang="en"> \n'+
94:  '<head><title>Generated Page</title></head> \n'+
95:  '<body id="body" style="background:#aaaaaa;font-family:arial;'+
96:  'font-size:22pt; \n color:#000088;font-weight:bold;text-align:center">\n'+
97:     '<div> My Photo Album</div><br />'
98:     llStV =""
99:     for (jj=1;jj<document.images.length;jj++)
100:    {
101:     tmpV = document.images.item(jj).src
102:     topV = document.images.item(jj).style.top
103:     leftV = document.images.item(jj).style.left
104:     llStV = llStV+ '<a href="'+tmpV+'" target=_blank >'+
105:     '<img src="'+tmpV+'" width="'+widthV+'" height="'+heightV+'" hspace="'+
106:      hspaceV+'" vspace="'+vspaceV+
107:     '" style="position:absolute;top:'+topV+';left:'+leftV+'" /></a> \n'
108:    }
109:    winH = window.open()
110:    winH.document.open()
111:    winH.document.write(headSt+llStV+'</body></html>')
112:    winH.document.close()
113: }
```

Inside this function, we have a string called `headSt` to store a general header for the newly created page. After the header string, a for-loop is employed to get information about the pictures already on the screen. For every image on the screen the statements in lines 101–107 are employed to generate an XHTML image element that looks like this:

```
<a href="xxPic.xx" target=_blank>
<img src="xxPic.xx" width="widthV" height="heightV"
    hspace="hspaceV" vspace="vspaceV"
    style="position:absoluate;top:topV;left:leftV" /></a>
```

All loaded images are stored as a string in variable `llStV`. The final step of the program is to perform the following tasks:

- open a new window;
- open a document for writing;
- output the strings `headSt`, `llStV`, and `"</body></html>"` to the newly created document; and
- close the document.

All these tasks can be accomplished by executing the four statements in lines 109–112.

Again the source of this new page can be saved in your local storage and reviewed at any time. For this example, the generated page looks like the following:

```
Listing: ex11-10.txt - The Generated Web Page From ex11-10.htm

 1:   <?xml version="1.0" encoding="iso-8859-1"?>
 2:   <!DOCTYPE html PUBLIC "-//W3C//DTD XHTML 1.0 Transitional//EN"
 3:    "http://www.w3.org/TR/xhtml1/DTD/xhtml1-transitional.dtd">
 4:   <html xmlns="http://www.w3.org/1999/xhtml" xml:lang="en" lang="en">
 5:  <head><title>Generated Page</title></head>
 6:  <body id="body" style="background:#aaaaaa;font-family:arial;
 7:    font-size:22pt;color:#000088;font-weight:bold;text-align:center">
 8:  <div> My Photo Album</div><br />
 9:  <a href="file:///P:/chap11a/01_img.jpg" target=_blank ><img
10:   src="file:///P:/chap11a/01_img.jpg" width="200" height="150" hspace="10"
11:   vspace="10" style="position:absolute;top:137px;left:113px" /></a>
12:  <a href="file:///P:/chap11a/03_img.jpg" target=_blank ><img
13:   src="file:///P:/chap11a/03_img.jpg" width="200" height="150" hspace="10"
14:   vspace="10" style="position:absolute;top:135px;left:456px" /></a>
15:  <a href="file:///P:/chap11a/05_img.jpg" target=_blank ><img
16:   src="file:///P:/chap11a/05_img.jpg" width="200" height="150" hspace="10"
17:   vspace="10" style="position:absolute;top:301px;left:298px" /></a>
18:  <a href="file:///P:/chap11a/06_img.jpg" target=_blank ><img
19:   src="file:///P:/chap11a/06_img.jpg" width="200" height="150" hspace="10"
20:   vspace="10" style="position:absolute;top:468px;left:115px" /></a>
21:  <a href="file:///P:/chap11a/07_img.jpg" target=_blank ><img
22:   src="file:///P:/chap11a/07_img.jpg" width="200" height="150" hspace="10"
23:    vspace="10" style="position:absolute;top:474px;left:485px" /></a>
24: </body>
25 </html>
```

This page is just a simple application of XHTML with image elements. It should be easy to read and understand. Next, we look at a more exciting interactive card game.

11.5.2 An interactive card game

In this section, we show how to use the `removeChild()` method to construct an interactive card game. This game demonstrates that even a very simple use of the function can create an interesting effect. The rules of the game are simple. Five cards are generated randomly, with one master card and four associated cards below it. The value of the master card is displayed at the top level. The values of the four associated, or guess, cards are covered and located on the right below the master card.

Based on an elimination method, a player needs to guess which one of the associated cards has a smaller value than the master card. The player needs to eliminate any three out of the four unwanted cards by clicking on each one of them in turn. A mouse click on any of the associated cards has the effect of eliminating it from the screen. As you can imagine, the `removeChild()` function is employed to remove it from the DOM tree. When the final card is clicked, the value of the card is reviewed. If the value of the card is less than the master card, a "You Win" message is displayed at the bottom. For simplicity, no fancy styles or additional features are implemented in this example. Only the bare bones of a gambling game are constructed.

The card game involves 13 cards and they are arranged as follows:

```
Picture File : 1.jpg – Heart 2
Picture File : 2.jpg – Heart 3
        *** ***   *** ***
Picture File : 12.jpg – Heart K
Picture File : 13.jpg – Heart A
```

The careful design of the file names provides a handy way to display and to compare values. Some screen shots shown in Figs 11.22 and 11.23 may be useful to help understand the discussion of the game.

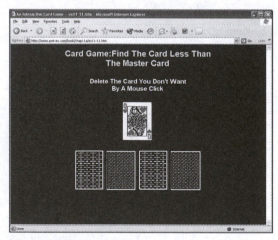

Figure 11.22 ex11-11.htm

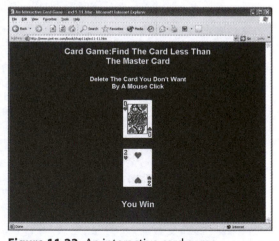

Figure 11.23 An interactive card game

The interface part of the game is listed below:

```
Example: ex11-11.htm – An Interactive Card Game

1:   <?xml version="1.0" encoding="iso-8859-1"?>
2:   <!DOCTYPE html PUBLIC "-//W3C//DTD XHTML 1.0 Transitional//EN"
3:       "http://www.w3.org/TR/xhtml1/DTD/xhtml1-transitional.dtd">
4:   <html xmlns="http://www.w3.org/1999/xhtml" xml:lang="en" lang="en">
5:   <head><title> An Interactive Card Game -- ex11-11.htm</title></head>
6:   <style>
7:   .butSt{background-color:#dddddd;font-family:arial;font-weight:bold;
8:       font-size:14pt;color:#880000;width:150px;height:35px}
```

```
 9:    </style>
10:    <body style="background:#000088;font-family:arial;font-size:20pt;
11:        color:#ffff00;font-weight:bold;text-align:center">
12:    Card Game:Find The Card Less Than <br />The Host Card<br /><br />
13:    <div id="id01" style="color:#ffffff;font-size:16pt">Delete The Card You
14:        Don't Want <br />By A Mouse Click</div><br/>
15:
16:    <img src="card000.jpg" id="cov00" name="cov00" alt="Pic 0"
17:        width="100" height="130" /><br /><br />
18:    <img src="card000.jpg" id="cId00" name="cId00" alt="Pic 1"
19:        width="100" height="130" onclick="myDelApp(0)" />
20:    <img src="card002.jpg" id="cId01" name="cId01" alt="Pic 2"
21:        width="100" height="130" onclick="myDelApp(1)" />
22:    <img src="card000.jpg" id="cId02" name="cId02" alt="Pic 3"
23:        width="100" height="130" onclick="myDelApp(2)" />
24:    <img src="card002.jpg" id="cId03" name="cId03" alt="Pic 4"
25:        width="100" height="130" onclick="myDelApp(3)" />
26:    <br /><br /><div id="outMsg"></div>
27:
28: <script src="ex11-11.js"></script>
29: </body>
30: </html>
```

This page contains five images. The first one defined in lines 16–17 is the master (or host) card and others in lines 18–25 are the associated ones. The associated cards have identities arranging from "cId00" to "cId03." If the first associated card is clicked by a mouse, the function myDelApp(0) is called to eliminate this card by removing it from the DOM tree. When the final card is clicked, the value of the card is shown and is compared to the value of the master card. If the value is bigger than the master card, the "You Lose" message is displayed at the bottom. Otherwise the "You Win" message is displayed.

The external program file ex11-11.js is listed as follows:

Example: ex11-11.js – The ECMAScript For ex11-11.htm

```
 1:    function genRan()
 2:    {
 3:     tmpV = Math.round(Math.random()*14)
 4:     while(tmpV <1 || tmpV > 13) tmpV = Math.round(Math.random()*14)
 5:     return tmpV
 6:    }
 7:
 8:    hostcard = 0
 9:    card = new Array()
10:    function getNo()
11:    {
12:      hostcard = genRan()
13:      document.getElementById("cov00").src = hostcard+".jpg"
14:      card[0] = genRan()
15:      while (hostcard == card[0]) card[0] = genRan()
16:      card[1] = genRan()
17:      while ((hostcard == card[1]) ||(card[0] == card[1])) card[1] = genRan()
18:      card[2] = genRan()
19:      while ((hostcard == card[2])||(card[0] == card[2])||
20:            (card[1]==card[2])) card[2] = genRan()
21:      card[3] = genRan()
22:      while ((hostcard == card[3])||(card[0] == card[3])||
23:            (card[1]==card[3])||(card[2]==card[3])) card[3] = genRan()
24:    }
25:    getNo()
26:
```

```
27:   function myDelApp(stV)
28:   {
29:    if (document.images.length < 3) {
30:     document.images.item(1).src = card[stV]+".jpg"
31:     if (hostcard > card[stV]) llSt = "You Win"
32:     else llSt = "You Lose"
33:     document.getElementById("outMsg").innerHTML = llSt
34:    } else {
35:     tmpV ="cId0"+stV
36:     objV = document.getElementById(tmpV)
37:     document.body.removeChild(objV)
38:    }
39:
40:  }
```

The first function `genRan()` in this program is a random number generator and returns an integer between 1 and 13. We first initialize the master card value to 0 in line 8 and define an array to hold the values of all associated cards in line 9.

One thing you need to be careful with when dealing with card games is that no card should appear twice in any circumstances. This is the job of a function called `getNo()` defined in lines 10–24. This function assigns random numbers to the cards and prevents any duplication at the same time. Note that the main focus of this demonstration example is on some basic ideas and techniques when dealing with card games. For clarity and readability, no commercial protection coding or tricks are used.

To prevent card duplication, we first generate a random value for the master card. The next step is to get another random number for the first associated card. The while–loop in line 15 is used to prevent any duplication. The statements in the while-loop can be interpreted as: while the first associated card (`card[0]`) equals the master card (`hostcard`), get another random number for `card[0]`. For every associated card, you need to employ a while-loop to compare all previous cards to avoid any duplication. That is, if duplication has occurred, the card needs to be regenerated. Since you have only four associated cards, the function `getNo()` is not too complicated to handle. After the execution of this `getNo()` function, all cards should have a unique value associated with them.

When one of the associated cards is clicked, the `myDelApp()` function is called. For example, when the second associated card is pressed, the function `myDelApp(1)` is executed and the statements in lines 35–37

```
tmpV ="cId0"+stV
objV = document.getElementById(tmpV)
document.body.removeChild(objV)
```

get the identity of the card and ultimately remove it from the DOM tree. When a card (i.e., an image) is deleted from the DOM tree, the `document.images.length` value will automatically be decreased by 1. You can use this value to detect how many images are on the screen. If this number is less than 3, as indicated in line 29, you know that only two cards, the "master" and the last associated, are left. In this case, the following statements are executed:

```
document.images.item(1).src = card[stV]+".jpg"
if (hostcard > card[stV]) llSt = "You Win"
else llSt = "You Lose"
```

Since only two cards are left, the `document.images.item(1)` object represents the last associated card. The first statement above gets the value of the card and displays it. If the value is less than the master card value (`hostcard`), the local string is assigned the "You Win" message. Otherwise the "You Lose" message is assigned. This local string `llSt` is then output to the screen by executing the statement in line 33.

12 Date and time manipulations

12.1 An introduction to date and time functions

12.1.1 Working with the date object

In Chapter 7, you learned how to use the time functions `getTime()` and `setTime()` to set and change the expiry date of a cookie. These two functions are designed to manipulate the time stores in a date object. The following is typical example code used to get the date and time of yesterday.

```
1: dateObj = new Date()
2: currentTime = dateObj.getTime()
3: yesterdayDate = currentDate - 1000*60*60*24
```

The first line is used to create a new object variable (or instance) named `dateObj` from the `date` object provided by the browser. Once we have done that, we can access all the methods of the object from the `dateObj` variable as demonstrated in line 2 (i.e., the `getTime()` function is a member of the date object). This is a great strength of the so-called object-oriented programming design. By using a dot (.) operator, object variables can call all member functions (or methods) of their parent. It took more than 10 years for the traditional structural programming world to adopt this new programming approach to fight against program corruptions. Only object variables can call member functions and therefore prevent global, and large-scale, damage to programs and/or systems.

To continue the date and time discussion, let's consider the following example ex12-01.htm:

Example: ex12-01.htm - Date And Time Functions

```
 1: <?xml version="1.0" encoding="iso-8859-1"?>
 2: <!DOCTYPE html PUBLIC "-//W3C//DTD XHTML 1.0 Transitional//EN"
 3:     "http://www.w3.org/TR/xhtml1/DTD/xhtml1-transitional.dtd">
 4: <html xmlns="http://www.w3.org/1999/xhtml" xml:lang="en" lang="en">
 5: <head><title>Date And Time Functions -- ex12-01.htm </title></head>
 6: <body style="background:#000088;text-align:center;font-family:arial">
 7: <script>
 8:   lMsg = '<div style="font-size:18pt;color:#ffff00;font-weight:bold"><br />'
 9:   lMsg = lMsg +"The Use Of getTime() and setTime() Functions<br /><br />"
10:   dateObj = new Date()
11:   currentTime = dateObj.getTime()
12:   lMsg = lMsg +"Today in milliseconds is: " +currentTime+"<br /><br />"
13:   lMsg = lMsg + "Today is: "+ dateObj +"<br />"
14:   yesterdayTime= dateObj.setTime(currentTime - 1000*60*60*24)
15:   lMsg = lMsg + "Yesterday is: "+ dateObj +"<br />"
16:   tomorrowTime = dateObj.setTime(currentTime + 1000*60*60*24)
17:   lMsg = lMsg + "Tomorrow is: "+ dateObj +"</div>"
```

```
18:    document.write(lMsg)
19: </script>
20: </body>
21: </html>
```

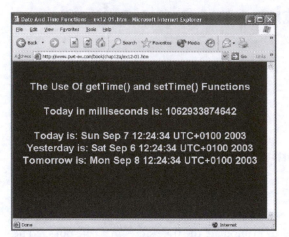

Figure 12.1 ex12-01.htm

The `getTime()` function (line 11) returns an integer value representing the number of milliseconds between midnight of the *zero time* (the first day of January 1970) and the time stores in the date object. The range of this value is approximately 285,616 years either side (positive and negative) from the zero time. Thus a negative number indicates a date prior to 1970.

By creating a new object in line 10, we have an object with an internal time string. The variable `currentTime` has a value of the local date and time in milliseconds of the date object. By subtracting `1000*60*60*24` (one day), this value is used to find the date of yesterday (line 14). You can generate and output the normal date and time of yesterday as illustrated in line 15. The same technique is used to calculate tomorrow's date and time (lines 16–17). A screen shot is shown in Fig. 12.1.

Manipulating the date and time in milliseconds is not very convenient and sometimes difficult to understand. In practice, we need to convert (or redefine) these values to a format that we are familiar with.

12.1.2 Setting date and time at creation level

By default, calling the statement `dateObj = new Date()` with no argument is equivalent to storing the current date in the variable `dateObj`. To set the date and time at the creation level, you can use the following numeric and string formats:

`new Date("Month dd, yyyy hh:mm:ss")` — **String format,**
e.g., `var dateObj=new Date("October 24, 2004 13:48:00")`

`new Date("Month dd, yyyy")` — **String format,**
e.g., `var dateObj=new Date("October 24, 2004")`

`new Date(yy,mm,dd,hh,mm,ss)` — **Numeric format,**
e.g., `var my_date=new Date(2004,09,24,13,48,00)`

`new Date(yyyy,mm,dd)` — **Numeric format,**
e.g., `var dateObj=new Date(2004,09,24)`

Since the numeric month starts from zero, the true value of 09 is actually October. The next example ex12-02.htm is used to put these settings into action.

```
Example: ex12-02.htm - Create The Date Object Variable

1: <?xml version="1.0" encoding="iso-8859-1"?>
2: <!DOCTYPE html PUBLIC "-//W3C//DTD XHTML 1.0 Transitional//EN"
3:      "http://www.w3.org/TR/xhtml1/DTD/xhtml1-transitional.dtd">
4: <html xmlns="http://www.w3.org/1999/xhtml" xml:lang="en" lang="en">
5: <head><title>Create The Date Object Variable -- ex12-02.htm</title></head>
6: <body style="background:#000088;text-align:center;font-family:arial;
7:      font-size:16pt;color:#ffff00">
8: <script>
```

```
 9:    var dateObj=new Date()
10:    document.write("<br />The Current Date and Time is<br />")
11:    document.write(dateObj+"<br /><br /><br />")
12:
13:    document.write("Some Date and Time Settings are <br /><br />")
14:    dateObj=new Date("October 24, 2003 13:48:00")
15:      document.write(dateObj+"<br />")
16:    dateObj=new Date("October 24, 2004")
17:      document.write(dateObj+"<br />")
18:    dateObj=new Date(2005,09,24,13,48,00)
19:      document.write(dateObj+"<br />")
20:    dateObj=new Date(2006,09,24)
21:      document.write(dateObj+"<br />")
22: </script>
23: </body>
24: </html>
```

If you call the date object with no argument as demonstrated in line 9, the current date and time value (as a string) is stored in the variable `dateObj`. A simple `document.write()` function call as in line 11 outputs the current date and time such as

```
Fri Oct 24 11:40:00 UTC+0100 2003
```

UTC represents Universal Coordinate Time, which is similar to GMT (Greenwich Mean Time). If you are using NS browsers, the output string is

```
Fri Oct 24 13:48:00 GMT+0100 (GMT Daylight Time) 2003
```

in GMT format. We generally refer to this string as the time string stored in the date object (or variable). Lines 14–21 illustrate some different settings for this time string. A screen shot is shown in Fig. 12.2.

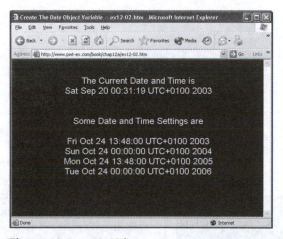

Figure 12.2 ex12-02.htm

If you don't feel comfortable with the UTC or GMT time format, you can add the function (or method) `toLocaleString()` at the end of the date object. This changes the time format in the current local default format. For example, if you are in Europe and have changed lines 9–11 in ex12-02.htm to

```
 9: var dateObj=new Date()
10: document.write("<br />The Current Date and Time is<br />")
11: document.write(dateObj.toLocaleString() +"<br /><br /><br />")
```

you will see the date and time in local format as (see ex12-02a.htm in the companion Web site)

```
The Current Date and Time is
20 September 2003 00:24:11
```

12.1.3 Basic date and time functions

Associated with each date object or object variables, there are a number of built-in functions ready for you to use. For example, the following are some of the most frequently used date functions on the Web.

- `getFullYear()` – Returns the year stored in the date object.
- `getMonth()` – Returns the month value in the date object.
- `getDate()` – Returns the day of the month.
- `getDay()` – Returns the day of the week.

From an object-oriented programming point of view, member functions of an object are usually called methods. To use these functions, let's take a look at the next example, ex12-03.htm. It gets today's date from the date object.

```
Example: ex12-03.htm - Date Functions

 1: <?xml version="1.0" encoding="iso-8859-1"?>
 2: <!DOCTYPE html PUBLIC "-//W3C//DTD XHTML 1.0 Transitional//EN"
 3:     "http://www.w3.org/TR/xhtml1/DTD/xhtml1-transitional.dtd">
 4: <html xmlns="http://www.w3.org/1999/xhtml" xml:lang="en" lang="en">
 5: <head><title>Date Functions -- ex12-03.htm </title></head>
 6: <body style="background:#000088;text-align:center;font-family:arial;
 7:     font-size:16pt;color:#ffff00">
 8: <script>
 9:   cDate = new Date()
10:   document.write("Getting Today's Date From The Date Object<br /><br />")
11:   document.write("The Day of The Week = "+cDate.getDay()+"<br />")
12:   document.write("The Date of The Month = "+cDate.getDate()+"<br />")
13:   document.write("The Current Month = "+(cDate.getMonth()+1)+"<br />")
14:   document.write("The Current Year = "+cDate.getFullYear()+"<br />")
15: </script>
16: </body>
17: </html>
```

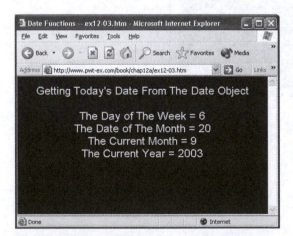

Figure 12.3 ex12-03.htm

Line 9 is used to declare a date object variable called `cDate`. This variable has all the built-in functions and properties that are associated with the object. From lines 10–14, we can see how this object variable is used to get each item of today's date.

Note that all these functions return numerical values. Since the `getMonth()` function starts from the value 0, we need to increase it by 1 (line 13) to reflect the true calendar month. A screen shot of this page is shown in Fig. 12.3.

Some older Web browsers may use the function `getYear()` instead of the `getFullYear()`. The function `getYear()` is obsolete since it can only return the value representing the difference between the stored year and 1900. For example, 1999 is returned as 99, and 2004 is returned as 104. This problem is normally referred to a "millennium bug" and special care is needed.

Compared to the date, the time functions are simpler. For each date object variable, we have the following time functions:

- `getHours()` – Returns the hours in the date object.
- `GetMinutes()` – Returns the number of minutes past the hour.
- `GetSeconds()` – Returns the number of seconds past the minute.

These functions are designed to get the local time stored in our computer. A simple demonstration of how to use them is shown in ex12-04.htm.

```
Example: ex12-04.htm - Time Functions

 1: <?xml version="1.0" encoding="iso-8859-1"?>
 2: <!DOCTYPE html PUBLIC "-//W3C//DTD XHTML 1.0 Transitional//EN"
 3:     "http://www.w3.org/TR/xhtml1/DTD/xhtml1-transitional.dtd">
 4: <html xmlns="http://www.w3.org/1999/xhtml" xml:lang="en" lang="en">
 5: <head><title>Time Functions -- ex12-04.htm </title></head>
 6: <body style="background:#000088;text-align:center;font-family:arial;
 7:     font-size:16pt;color:#ffff00">
 8: <script>
 9:  cDate = new Date()
10:  document.write("Getting Local Time From The Date Object<br /><br />")
11:  document.write("The Current Hour = "+cDate.getHours()+"<br />")
12:  document.write("The Current Minutes = "+cDate.getMinutes()+"<br />")
13:  document.write("The Current Seconds = "+cDate.getSeconds()+"<br />")
14: </script>
15: </body>
16: </html>
```

Again, we first create a date object variable (cDate) in line 9. Then we can directly call the time functions as member functions of the object. A screen shot of this page at work is shown in Fig. 12.4. If you refresh this page, you should notice the changes on "The Current Seconds" field.

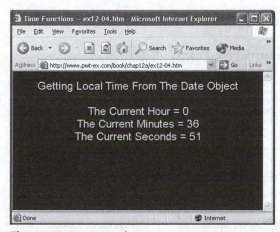

Figure 12.4 ex12-04.htm

For each `get` function, we also have a corresponding `set` function in the date object. They are:

- `setFullYear()` – Sets the year of the date object.
- `setMonth()` – Sets the month value of the date object.
- `setDate()` – Sets the day of the month.
- `setDay()` – Sets the day of the week.

- `setHours()` – Sets the hours of the date object.
- `setMinutes()` – Sets the minutes of the date object.
- `setSeconds()` – Sets the seconds of the date object.

Together with the `get` functions, they form the basic date and time functions and are embedded inside the browser. As a simple demonstration of how to use them, we have listed the script part of example ex12-05.htm in the listing ex12-01.txt.

Listing: ex12-01.txt – Code Fragment Of ex12-05.htm

```
 1: <script>
 2:  dateObj = new Date()
 3:  dateObj.setFullYear(2003)
 4:  dateObj.setMonth(11)
 5:  dateObj.setDate(31)
 6:  dateObj.setHours(0)
 7:  dateObj.setMinutes(0)
 8:  dateObj.setSeconds(0)
 9:  document.write(dateObj)
10: </script>
```

Once you have created the date object (`dateObj`) in line 2, you can set the date and time of this object individually. For example, `setMonth(11)` sets the month as December. The output statement in line 9 writes the following time string to the browser screen:

```
Wed Dec 31 00:00:00 UTC 2003
```

or the following string if you are using NS6:

```
Wed Dec 31 00:00:00 GMT+0000 (GMT Standard Time) 2003
```

Now, let's consider some applications of the date and time functions.

12.2 Static date and time on the Web

12.2.1 A page can say good morning

One simple use of time detection is to develop a Web page that can greet visitors with some voice messages depending on the time. A few seconds of voice messages such as "Good Morning" can give a warm welcome to your visitors and customers. Our next example shows how to divide the time into four sections with time-dependent text and voice messages. The structure of the page is listed below:

Display message	Timing range	Voice file
Good Morning	From 6 am To 12 am	gm.wav
Good Afternoon	From 0 pm To 5 pm	ga.wav
Good Evening	From 5 pm To 12 pm	ge.wav
Please Go To Bed	From 0 am To 6 am	gb.wav

If someone visits this page at, say, eight o'clock in the morning, the page will display the message "Good Morning" and play the sound file gm.wav.

The structure of this page is simple and can be accomplished by a series of detections on the value returned by the getHour() function. The code of this page is listed in ex12-06.htm.

Example: ex12-06.htm - A Page Can Say Good Morning

```
 1: <?xml version="1.0" encoding="iso-8859-1"?>
 2: <!DOCTYPE html PUBLIC "-//W3C//DTD XHTML 1.0 Transitional//EN"
 3:     "http://www.w3.org/TR/xhtml1/DTD/xhtml1-transitional.dtd">
 4: <html xmlns="http://www.w3.org/1999/xhtml" xml:lang="en" lang="en">
 5: <head><title>A Page Can Say Good Morning -- ex12-06.htm</title></head>
 6: <body style="background:#000088;text-align:center;font-family:arial;
 7:     font-size:16pt;color:#ffff00">
 8: <script>
 9:  cDate = new Date()
10:  cHours = cDate.getHours()
11:  lMsg = "<br />A Page Can Display And Say Something <br />"+
12:     'Depending On The Current Time<br /><br />'+cDate+
13:     '<br /><span style="color:#00ffff"><br />'
14:  sFile="ge.wav"
15:
16:  if ( cHours >= 0 && cHours < 6){
17:     lMsg = lMsg +"Now Is Very Early Morning "+
18:        "<br />Please Go To Bed!<br /><br />"
19:     sFile = "gb.wav"
20:  }
21:  if ( cHours >= 6 && cHours < 12){
22:     lMsg = lMsg +"Good Morning! <br /><br />"
23:     sFile = "gm.wav"
24:  }
25:  if ( cHours >=12 && cHours < 17){
26:     lMsg = lMsg +"Good Afternoon! <br /><br />"
27:     sFile = "ga.wav"
28:  }
29:  if ( cHours >=17 && cHours < 24){
30:     lMsg = lMsg +"Good Evening! <br /><br />"
31:     sFile = "ge.wav"
32:  }
33:
34:  lMsg = lMsg +"</span>I Can Determine The Time Now"
35:  document.write('<div>'+lMsg+'</div>')
36:  document.write('<embed src='+sFile+' hidden="true" autostart="yes" />')
37: </script>
38: </body>
39: </html
```

We use four conditional statements to detect different time periods of a day. If the hour value in the variable cHour falls into one of the time periods or zones, a message related to the time is added to the message string lMsg. A sound file corresponding to the time zone is also assigned to the variable sFile. Each of the sound files plays back a simple voice message:

gm.wav – **A voice message to say "Good Morning"**

ga.wav – **A voice message to say "Good Afternoon"**

ge.wav – **A voice message to say "Good Evening"**

gb.wav – **A voice message to say "Please Go To Bed"**

By using the date and time functions of the date object, Web pages can determine the time and act accordingly. The screen shots are shown in Figs 12.5 and 12.6.

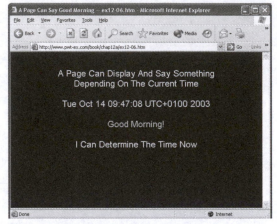

Figure 12.5 ex12-06.htm

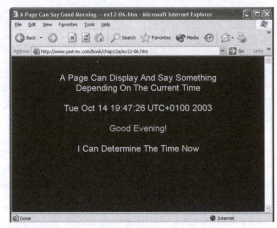

Figure 12.6 Good Evening!

12.2.2 Matching the names of weekdays and months

From the discussion in section 12.1.3, we know that all `get` functions related to the date object return numerical values. In many applications, we may need to convert some of the numeric values to commonly used names. Two such conversions frequently found on the Web are the matching of the days of a week and months of a year. By using the array structure, we can perform this matching easily. For example, the following declaration defines an array of seven elements:

```
mDay = new Array("Sunday","Monday","Tuesday",
        "Wednesday","Thursday","Friday","Saturday")
```

The index of the array can be used to match the names of the days of a week as

```
mDay[0]="Sunday", mDay[1]="Monday",..,mDay[6]="Saturday"
```

Now, let's consider an example that can display a logo together with a date string. This example uses an XHTML string to integrate a text header with date and time.

Consider the following example ex12-07.htm:

```
Example: ex12-07.htm - A Header With Date

 1: <?xml version="1.0" encoding="iso-8859-1"?>
 2: <!DOCTYPE html PUBLIC "-//W3C//DTD XHTML 1.0 Transitional//EN"
 3:     "http://www.w3.org/TR/xhtml1/DTD/xhtml1-transitional.dtd">
 4: <html xmlns="http://www.w3.org/1999/xhtml" xml:lang="en" lang="en">
 5: <head><title>A Header With Date - ex12-07.htm </title></head>
 6: <style> .mSt{font-size:16pt;color:#ffff00;font-weight:bold } </style>
 7: <body style="background:#000088;text-align:center;font-family:arial">
 8: <script src="date.js"></script>
 9: <div align="center" id="myHeader"></div>
10: <div class="mSt"><br />A Page With Logo and Today's Date.<br /><br />
11:     All Components Of The Header Are <br />
12:     Integrated As A Single String</div>
13: <script>
14:     document.getElementById("myHeader").innerHTML=disHeader()
15: </script>
16: </body>
17: </html>
```

This page includes an ECMAScript program file called date.js in line 8. This program file provides the function disHeader() to be used in line 14. Line 9 creates an initially empty division with id="myHeader" for the header. The script function disHeader() (i.e., display header) at the end of line 14 is defined in date.js. This function returns an XHTML string with header and date to the getElementById() function in line 14 and ultimately will be displayed at the location defined in line 9. The program file date.js is listed in ex12-02.txt.

```
Listing: ex12-02.txt - The ECMAScript date.js

 1: mDay = new Array("Sunday","Monday","Tuesday","Wednesday","Thursday",
 2:     "Friday","Saturday")
 3: mMonth = new Array("January","February","March","April","May","June",
 4:     "July","August","September","October","November","December")
 5:
 6: function disHeader()
 7: {
 8:   dateObj = new Date()
 9:
10:   lHeader = '<table><tr class="mSt"><td width="60%">'+
11:     '<img src="logo_web.jpg" width="160" height="80" alt="pic" /></td>'+
12:     '<td>'+mDay[dateObj.getDay()]+'<br />'+
13:     dateObj.getDate()+' '+mMonth[dateObj.getMonth()]+' '+
14:     dateObj.getFullYear()+'</td></tr></table><br />'+
15:     '<img src="line1.gif" width="450" height="6" alt="pic" /><br />'
16:     return(lHeader)
17: }
18:
```

This program file begins with two arrays mDay (match day) and mMonth (match month). These arrays are used inside the function disHeader() to display the header in lines 6–17.

When the dateObj.getDay() function in line 12 returns the numeric value, the array mDay is used to match the names of the days. The mMonth array used in line 13 is the array to match the names of the months. They represent part of an XHTML language string called lHeader declared in lines 10–15. This string technique is popular on the Web and used to build one or more local header messages. The variable lHeader is in fact just an XHTML table. This table contains a logo picture and today's date.

The disHeader() function combines all components of the header into a table string. This way, the

Figure 12.7 ex12-07.htm

header can be considered as an entity and can be printed out or handled as a single object and/or returned to the caller as demonstrated in line 16. A screen shot of this page is shown in Fig. 12.7.

12.2.3 Detecting leap years

One of the oldest problems when dealing with date and time is the detection of leap years. For example, you probably know that 2004 and 2008 are leap years; and you can hardwire the code to deal with them directly. Obviously, this is not an ideal solution and a leap year calculation (or detection) function is necessary. Also, we don't want to use the complicated rules of leap years such as:

- a leap year every four years;
- one leap year short every one hundred years; and
- more for every two thousand years etc.

One easy option is to use the built-in functions of the date object such as `getTime()` to determine the number of days in February. For example, you can develop a leap year detection function, e.g., `leapYear()`, based on `getTime()` as in the listing ex12-03.txt. In this chapter, we want to expand the file date.js into a functional date and time function library. The `leapYear()` function and many others are added at the end of the program file date.js as follows:

```
Listing: ex12-03.txt - Adding The Function leapYear() Into date.js

19:  function leapYear(iYear)
20:  {
21:    dateObj1= new Date(iYear,1,1,0,0,0)
22:    dateObj2= new Date(iYear,2,1,0,0,0)
23:    cntV1 = dateObj1.getTime()
24:    cntV2 = dateObj2.getTime()
25:    daysFeb = Math.round((cntV2-cntV1)/(1000*60*60*24))
26:    if (daysFeb != 29)
27:    {
28:       return(false)
29:    } else {
30:       return(true)
31:    }
32:  }
33:
```

This function is to determine whether the input year (`iYear`) is a leap year. First, we need a date object (i.e., `dateObj1`) to have the time string as February 1. The second date object (`dateObj2`) declared in line 22 has the time string as March 1. The difference between these two date objects in terms of the `getTime()` function represents the time units of the entire February. If this time unit is divided by (`1000*60*60*24`) as indicated in line 25, the number of days in February is obtained. To avoid any calculation confusion (floating points and integers) in some systems, you may also need to use a simple rounding method (`Math.round`) to find the number of days in February. If the number of days is 29, you know that you have a leap year and can return the value true.

To test this function, you can develop the following page (ex12-08.htm) to display some leap years.

```
Example: ex12-08.htm - Detecting Leap Years

 1: <?xml version="1.0" encoding="iso-8859-1"?>
 2: <!DOCTYPE html PUBLIC "-//W3C//DTD XHTML 1.0 Transitional//EN"
 3:     "http://www.w3.org/TR/xhtml1/DTD/xhtml1-transitional.dtd">
 4: <html xmlns="http://www.w3.org/1999/xhtml" xml:lang="en" lang="en">
 5: <head><title>Detecting Leap Years -- ex12-08.htm </title></head>
 6:
 7: <script src="date.js"></script>
 8:
 9: <body style="background:#000088;text-align:center;font-family:arial;
10:     font-size:18pt;color:#ffff00;font-weight:bold">
11:
12: <div>A Page To Display Some Leap Years <br /></div>
13: <img src="line1.gif" width="450" height="6" /><br /><br />
14:
15: <script>
16:   for (ii=2000;ii<=2010;ii++)
17:   {
18:     if (leapYear(ii))
19:       document.write(ii+' is a leap year.<br />')
20:     else
21:       document.write(ii+' is not a leap year.<br />')
22:   }
23: </script>
24: </body>
25: </html>
```

Apart from the program file date.js in line 7, the main operation of this page is the for-loop in lines16–22. If the conditional on the `leapYear()` function (see line 18) returns a true value, the output statement in line 19 is executed. If the returned value is false, the year is not a leap year and the statement in line 21 is output. A screen shot of this page is shown in Fig. 12.8.

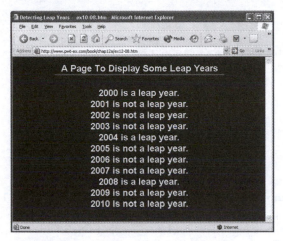

Figure 12.8 ex12-08.htm

12.2.4 Getting an input date with drop-down boxes

One of the essential techniques on the Web is to get a date from users (or customers). This can be a birthday, delivery date, pay date, or any important date that needs to be remembered. A simple efficient way to obtain this information could be important in a commercial environment. As a practical example, we are going to develop a Web page with drop-down boxes to obtain the date information.

One main advantage of using drop-down boxes is that it can minimize user errors. Three drop-down boxes representing year, month, and date are used. Users can simply pick the value inside the boxes and no additional input such as typing is needed. In this section a programming technique to change the contents of some drop-down boxes interactively is also introduced. For example, if the user selects April as the month, the drop-down box for the date will only display 30 days (from 1 to 30). Once the Submit button is pressed, the input date is displayed immediately. Our example can also handle leap years at the same time. The treatment here serves as an introduction to professional Web programming; it is neither perfect nor complete.

The structure of this page contains two files, one for the XHTML code (ex12-09.htm) and the other for programming code inside date.js. The XHTML file acts as an interface and is listed as follows:

```
Example: ex12-09.htm – Getting An Input Date With Drop-Down Boxes

 1: <?xml version="1.0" encoding="iso-8859-1"?>
 2: <!DOCTYPE html PUBLIC "-//W3C//DTD XHTML 1.0 Transitional//EN"
 3:     "http://www.w3.org/TR/xhtml1/DTD/xhtml1-transitional.dtd">
 4: <html xmlns="http://www.w3.org/1999/xhtml" xml:lang="en" lang="en">
 5: <head><title>Controlling An Input Date - ex12-09.htm </title></head>
 6: <style>
 7:   .mSt{font-size:16pt;color:#ffff00;font-weight:bold }
 8:   .bSt{font-size:14pt;color:#000088;font-weight:bold;font-family:arial;
 9:     width:150;height:30;background:#aaccaa}
10: </style>
11: <body style="background:#000088;text-align:center;font-family:arial">
12: <script src="date.js"></script>
13: <div align="center">
```

```
14:    <div id="myHead"></div><br /><br />
15:    <span class="mSt">Getting An Input Date With Drop-Down Boxes</span>
16:       <br /><br />
17:    <table border="0" cellspacing="10" class="mSt">
18:     <tr><td width="160">Year : </td>
19:        <td width="280"><span id="yearL"></span></td></tr>
20:      <tr><td>Month: </td><td><span id="monthL"></span></td></tr>
21:      <tr><td>Date : </td><td><span id="dateL"> </span></td></tr>
22:      <tr><td><input type="button" value="Get Input Date"
23:         onclick='document.getElementById("dayL").innerHTML=disInputDate()'
24:         class="bSt" /></td><td><span id="dayL"></span></td></tr>
25:    </table>
26: </div>
27: <script>
28:    document.getElementById("myHead").innerHTML=disHeader()
29:    myGetDate(1940,2020,"yearL","monthL","dateL","dayL")
30: </script>
31: </body>
32: </html>
```

Similar to earlier examples, this interface page includes the program file date.js in line 12. It contains all script functions that are needed to perform the actions. Line 14 of this interface defines a division with `id=myHead` ready for us to output a header string in line 28. Lines 17–25 define a table with four rows. Each row has an identity location for output. For example:

```
19: <span id="yearL"></span>       – Location for the "Year" drop-down box
20: <span id="monthL"></span>      – Location for the "Month" drop-down box
21: <span id="dateL"></span>       – Location for the "Date" drop-down box
24: <span id="dayL"></span>        – Location to output the date string
```

A button is created in lines 22–24 to trigger the printout of the date string `dayL`. In this example, the main controlling function is `myGetDate(1940,2020,"yearL","monthL","dateL","dayL")` in line 29. The first two arguments of this function are the start and end years. In this case, the date information between 1940 and 2020 is considered. The next four arguments are location identities specified by XHTML elements. In this case, the year drop-down box is displayed at the location where `id="yearL"` (year location). The month drop-down box is located at the element with `id="monthL"`. Finally, if the user presses the button as shown in line 22, the function `disInputDate()` returns the input date and displays it at the location defined by `id="dayL"`. Some screen shots of this page in action are shown in Figs 12.9 and Fig. 12.10.

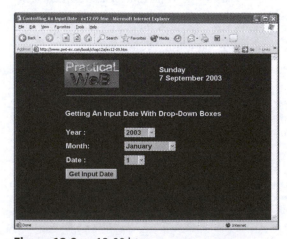

Figure 12.9 ex12-09.htm

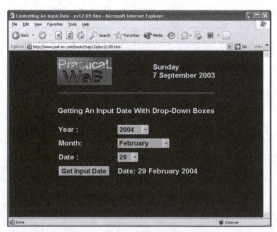

Figure 12.10 Get input date

The interesting part of this page is the ability to control the number of days corresponding to a particular month. As demonstrated in Fig. 12.10, if you pick the year 2004 (a leap year) and February, the drop-down box of the date only has 29 days (1–29). The implementations of these features are discussed below.

First, in order to simplify the variable passing, global variables are used in this example. After the global variable section, we have the main controlling function myGetDate() as follows:

```
Listing: ex12-04.txt - Adding The Function myGetDate() Into date.js
34:   gl_stYear = 1940
35:   gl_endYear = 2020
36:   gl_yearL =''
37:   gl_monthL=''
38:   gl_dateL =''
39:   gl_dayL=''
40:
41:   function myGetDate(l_stYear,l_endYear,l_yearL,l_monthL,l_dateL,l_dayL)
42:   {
43:     ldateObj = new Date()
44:     gl_stYear = l_stYear
45:     gl_endYear = l_endYear
46:     gl_yearL = l_yearL
47:     gl_monthL = l_monthL
48:     gl_dateL = l_dateL
49:     gl_dayL = l_dayL
50:     disYear()
51:     document.getElementById("gYear").selectedIndex=
52:         (ldateObj.getFullYear()-gl_stYear)
53:     disMonth()
54:     disDay()
55:   }
56:
```

Lines 34–39 define some global variables for the start and end years and display locations. The first job of this function myGetDate() is to assign the input to the global variables (lines 44–49). Line 50 is to call another function disYear(). This function generates a drop-down box at the location gl_yearL. Lines 51–52 are used to guarantee that the first year appears in the year drop-down box as the current year. The functions disMonth() and disDay() generate boxes for months and days respectively. The disYear() function has the listing

```
Listing: ex12-05.txt - Adding The Function disYear() Into date.js
57:   function disYear()
58:   {
59:   // yearSt - A String To Represent The Drop-Down Box For Year
60:     yearSt ='<select id="gYear" name="gYear" class="bSt" '+
61:       'style="width:90px" onchange="disDay()">'
62:
63:     for (ii=gl_stYear;ii<=gl_endYear;ii++)
64:     {
65:       yearSt = yearSt + '<option>'+ii+'</option>'
66:     }
67:     yearSt = yearSt + '</select>'
68:     document.getElementById(gl_yearL).innerHTML=yearSt
69:   }
70:
```

This is a drop-down box defined by the element <select> (line 60). The contents of this box are stored in the string variable yearSt. The for-loop in lines 63–66 is used to fill the year (from gl_stYear to gl_endYear) information in the box. When the contents of this drop-down box are filled, the string, yearSt, is output to the location where id=gl_yearL (line 68). We use a special event onchange in line 61 to detect the selected value of this drop-down box. If it has been changed, the function disDay() is called to recalculate the number of days corresponding to the month field automatically. This will guarantee that you have a dynamic number of days.

The next function `disMonth()` (i.e., display month) has a similar structure as `disYear()` and is listed in ex12-06.txt.

```
Listing: ex12-06.txt – Adding The Function disMonth() Into date.js
71:  function disMonth()
72:  {
73:   // monthSt - A String To Represent The Drop-Down Box For Month
74:   monthSt = '<select id="gMonth" name="gMonth" class="bSt" '+
75:            'onchange="disDay()">'
76:   for (ii=0;ii<=11;ii++)
77:   {
78:     monthSt = monthSt + '<option>'+mMonth[ii]+'</option>'
79:   }
80:   monthSt = monthSt + '</select>  '
81:   document.getElementById(gl_monthL).innerHTML=monthSt
82:  }
83:
```

The for-loop in lines 76–79 is used to add the month information to the drop-down box. The array variable `mMonth` (line 78) matches the name of the months, i.e.,

```
mMonth[0]=January, ..., mMonth[11]=December
```

Next is the function `disDay()` to show the drop-down box for the date. This function generates the box on the fly to respond to the month information.

```
Listing: ex12-07.txt – Adding The Function disDay() Into date.js
84:  function chgButMsg()
85:  {
86:   daySt = ""
87:   document.getElementById(gl_dayL).innerHTML=daySt
88:  }
89:
90:  function disDay()
91:  {
92:   noDays = 31
93:   yIndx = document.getElementById("gYear").selectedIndex
94:   mIndx = document.getElementById("gMonth").selectedIndex
95:   chgButMsg()
96:   if (mIndx ==1)
97:   {
98:     if (leapYear(yIndx+gl_stYear)) noDays = 29
99:     else noDays = 28
100:  }
101:  if ((mIndx ==3)||(mIndx ==5)||(mIndx ==8)||(mIndx ==10)) noDays = 30
102:
103:   // daySt - A String To Represent The Drop-Down Box For Date
104:   daySt = '<select id="gDate" name="gDate" class="bSt" '+
105:      'style="width:60px" onchange="chgButMsg()">'
106:
107:   for (ii=1;ii<=noDays;ii++)
108:   {
109:     daySt = daySt + '<option>'+ii+'</option>'
110:   }
111:   daySt = daySt + '</select>'
112:   document.getElementById(gl_dateL).innerHTML=daySt
113:  }
114:
```

First, we get the drop-down box values for year and month (lines 93–94) and store them in the index variables yIndx and mIndx. Then the function chgButMsg() (see line 95) is called to destroy the previous result. If the month is February (see line 96) and the year is a leap year (see line 98), we assign the number of days variable noDay as 29. Since the month index mIndx starts from zero, the statement in line 101 is used to detect

April (mIndx=3), June, September, and November (mIndx=10)

These months have 30 days. Armed with the information on number of days stored in variable noDays, you can use a for-loop in lines 107–110 to build a customized drop-down box as a string called daySt.

Finally, when the user presses the Get Input Date button (line 22 in ex12–09.htm), the following function disInputDate() is activated:

```
Listing: ex12-08.txt – Adding The Function disInputDate() Into date.js

115:   function disInputDate()
116:   {
117:     // dIndx - Store the Date From DropDown Box (Values 0-Max:31)
118:     dIndx = document.getElementById("gDate").selectedIndex
119:
120:     // mIndx - Store the Month From DropDown Box (Values 0-11)
121:     mIndx = document.getElementById("gMonth").selectedIndex
122:
123:     // yIndx - Store the Year From DropDown Box (Starting from 0)
124:     yIndx = document.getElementById("gYear").selectedIndex
125:
126:     lMsg = 'Date: '+(dIndx+1)+' '+mMonth[mIndx] +' '+(yIndx + gl_stYear)
127:     return(lMsg)
128:   }
129:
```

This function gets the year, month, and date information from the drop-down boxes (see lines 117–124). This information forms a string lMsg to be returned to the calling function in lines 126–127.

Since all selected indices from drop-down boxes start from zero, you need some adjustments in line 126 to reflect the true identity (or value) for year, month, and date.

You now have a vehicle to get a user input date. This can be used to get delivery date, payment day, customer's birthday, meeting date, appointment date, etc. As mentioned before, the main advantage of this approach is that no user typing is needed and therefore user errors are minimized.

One direct use of this structure is to build a Web page to find the day of a week from a user input date.

12.2.5 A page to find the weekday

Another simple application of drop-down boxes introduced in the previous section is to find the weekday of a given date. With the help of the program file date.js, this page is easy to construct and is listed in ex12-10.htm.

```
Example: ex12-10.htm - A Page To Find The Weekday

 1:  <?xml version="1.0" encoding="iso-8859-1"?>
 2:  <!DOCTYPE html PUBLIC "-//W3C//DTD XHTML 1.0 Transitional//EN"
 3:      "http://www.w3.org/TR/xhtml1/DTD/xhtml1-transitional.dtd">
 4:  <html xmlns="http://www.w3.org/1999/xhtml" xml:lang="en" lang="en">
 5:  <head><title>To Find The Weekday -- ex12-10.htm </title></head>
 6:  <style>
 7:    .mSt{font-size:16pt;color:#ffff00;font-weight:bold }
 8:    .bSt{font-size:14pt;color:#000088;font-weight:bold;font-family:arial;
 9:      width:150;height:30;background:#aaccaa}
10:  </style>
11:  <body style="background:#000088;text-align:center;font-family:arial">
```

```
12: <script src="date.js"></script>
13: <div align="center">
14:    <div id="myHead"></div><br /><br />
15:    <span class="mSt">Getting An Input Date With Drop-Down Boxes</span>
16:        <br /><br />
17:    <table border="0" cellspacing="10" class="mSt">
18:      <tr><td width="160">Year : </td>
19:         <td width="280"><span id="yearL"></span></td></tr>
20:      <tr><td>Month: </td><td><span id="monthL"></span></td></tr>
21:      <tr><td>Date : </td><td><span id="dateL"></span></td></tr>
22:      <tr><td><input type="button" value="Find The Day"
23:         onclick='document.getElementById("dayL").innerHTML=findDay()'
24:         class="bSt" /></td><td><span id="dayL"></span></td></tr>
25:    </table>
26: </div>
27: <script>
28:    document.getElementById("myHead").innerHTML=disHeader()
29:    myGetDate(1940,2020,"yearL","monthL","dateL","dayL")
30: </script>
31: </body>
32: </html>
```

This page is very similar to the page listed in ex12-09.htm. The only difference lies in lines 22–24. Line 22 is a button with the name "Find The Day." When the user presses this button, the function findDay() is activated in line 23. This function is used to read the year, month, and date from the drop-down boxes. It calculates the corresponding day of the week and returns it to the caller. The caller displays the returned day at the location with id=dayL. We have added this function findDay() at the end of our program file date.js.

Listing: ex12-09.txt – Adding The Function findDay() To date.js

```
130:  function findDay()
131:  {
132:   // dIndx - Store the Date From Drop-Down Box (Values 0-Max:31)
133:   dIndx = document.getElementById("gDate").selectedIndex
134:   // mIndx - Store the Month From Drop-Down Box (Values 0-11)
135:   mIndx = document.getElementById("gMonth").selectedIndex
136:   // yIndx - Store the Year From Drop-Down Box (Starting from 0)
137:   yIndx = document.getElementById("gYear").selectedIndex
138:   dateObj = new Date(yIndx+gI_stYear,mIndx,dIndx+1)
139:   return(mDay[dateObj.getDay()])
140:  }
141:
```

This function reads the year, month, and date values from the drop-down boxes (see lines 133–137). The information is used to declare a date object (dateObj) in line 138. The member function (or method) getDay() returns the day associated with the date object. Finally, the array variable mDay is used to match the names of the weekday. A screen shot of this page is shown in Fig. 12.11.

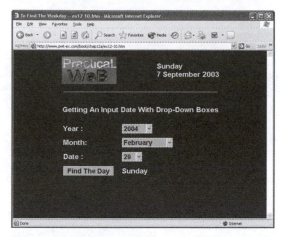

Figure 12.11 ex12-10.htm

12.3 Dynamic date and time on the Web

12.3.1 Implementation of clocks with different time formats

One simple implementation of a clock is shown in the following code:

```
Example: ex12-11.htm - Simplest Clock 01

 1: <?xml version="1.0" encoding="iso-8859-1"?>
 2: <!DOCTYPE html PUBLIC "-//W3C//DTD XHTML 1.0 Transitional//EN"
 3:     "http://www.w3.org/TR/xhtml1/DTD/xhtml1-transitional.dtd">
 4: <html xmlns="http://www.w3.org/1999/xhtml" xml:lang="en" lang="en">
 5: <head><title>Simplest Clock 01 - ex12-11.htm</title></head>
 6: <body onload="simplestClock()">
 7: <h2>A Simple Clock Implementation<h2><br />
 8: <form name="form01" action="">
 9:  <input type="text" name="clock01" id="clock01" value="cSt" size="40" />
10: </form>
11: <script>
12: function simplestClock()
13: {
14:   dateObj = new Date()
15:   document.form01.clock01.value=dateObj
16:   setTimeout("simplestClock()",1000)
17: }
18: </script>
19: </body>
20: </html>
```

This page opens a text input area with name `clock01` and an initial value `cSt` (line 9). When the page is loaded, the `onload` event defined in line 6 activates the script function `simplestClock()`. Inside this function (lines 14–16), a date object is created and the time string in the date object is output to the element with name `clock01`. The `setTimeout()` function used in line 16 is an important function. It is used to call the `simplestClock()` for every 1,000 time units (i.e., every 1 second). This way, the clock can be continuously updated. We used an old document access method (i.e., an old DOM) here. The input text in line 9 is embedded inside a form element with name `form01` (lines 8–10). This name is used to access the value of the input text (line 15). One advantage of this structure is that this page will run on almost all browsers including some older versions. However, with the absence of CSS style, this clock is not very impressive. A modified version is listed in ex12-12.htm.

Example: ex12-12.htm - Simplest Clock 02

```
 1: <?xml version="1.0" encoding="iso-8859-1"?>
 2: <!DOCTYPE html PUBLIC "-//W3C//DTD XHTML 1.0 Transitional//EN"
 3:     "http://www.w3.org/TR/xhtml1/DTD/xhtml1-transitional.dtd">
 4: <html xmlns="http://www.w3.org/1999/xhtml" xml:lang="en" lang="en">
 5: <head><title>Simplest Clock 02 - ex12-12.htm </title></head>
 6: <style>
 7:   .mSt{font-family:arial;font-size:16pt;color:#ffff00;font-weight:bold }
 8: </style>
 9: <body style="background:#000088;text-align:center" onload="Clock02()">
10:
11: <div class="mSt"><br />A Simple Clock Implementation II<br /><br /><br />
12:   <div id="clockL"></div>
13: </div>
14:
15: <script>
16: function Clock02()
17: {
18:   dateObj = new Date()
19:   document.getElementById("clockL").innerHTML=dateObj
20:   setTimeout("Clock02()",1000)
21: }
22: </script>
23: </body>
24: </html>
```

Figure 12.12 ex12-12.htm

The main characteristics of this page are the use of CSS style and the getElementById feature recommended by the W3C authority. We define a division with id="clockL" (clock location) in line 12. The getElementById in line 19 can use the identity to access this element anywhere in the document. The running of the clock is powered by the setTimeout() function in line 20. A screen shot of this page is shown in Fig. 12.12.

Sometimes, the time string stored inside a date object may be too long and not very convenient to use. With the basic member functions of the date object, we can handle some popular time formats in a nice way. The next example, ex12-13.htm, uses the built-in time functions and displays "Military Time," "Digital Time," and "Standard Time" on the screen.

Example: ex12-13.htm - Clock

```
 1: <?xml version="1.0" encoding="iso-8859-1"?>
 2: <!DOCTYPE html PUBLIC "-//W3C//DTD XHTML 1.0 Transitional//EN"
 3:     "http://www.w3.org/TR/xhtml1/DTD/xhtml1-transitional.dtd">
 4: <html xmlns="http://www.w3.org/1999/xhtml" xml:lang="en" lang="en">
 5: <head><title>Clock - ex12-13.htm</title></head>
 6: <style> .mSt{font-size:16pt;color:#ffff00;font-weight:bold } </style>
 7: <body style="background:#000088;text-align:center;font-family:arial"
 8:             onload="Clock03()">
 9: <div class="mSt" style="font-size:20pt;color:#00ffff" align="center">
10:   <br />Some Popular Time Formats<br />For A Running Clock<br /><br />
11: <table class="mSt" cellspacing="10">
```

```
12:     <tr><td>Military Time :</td><td><div id="mTimeL"></div></td></tr>
13:     <tr><td>Digital Time:</td><td> <div id="dTimeL"></div></td></tr>
14:     <tr><td>Standard Time:</td><td> <div id="sTimeL"></div></td></tr>
15:   </table>
16: </div>
17: <script>
18: function Clock03()
19: {
20:  dateObj = new Date()
21:  cHours = dateObj.getHours()
22:  cMinutes = dateObj.getMinutes()
23:  cSeconds = dateObj.getSeconds()
24:
25:  militaryTimeSt= ((cHours < 10)? '0':'')+cHours+':'+
26:  ((cMinutes < 10)? '0':'')+cMinutes
27:
28:  digitalTimeSt= ((cHours < 10)? '0':'')+cHours+':'+
29:   ((cMinutes < 10)? '0':'')+cMinutes+':'+((cSeconds < 10)? '0':'')+
30:   cSeconds
31:
32:  standardTimeSt= ((cHours==0 || cHours==12) ? '12': cHours %12)+':'+
33:  ((cMinutes < 10)? '0':'')+cMinutes+':'+((cSeconds < 10)? '0':'')+
34:  cSeconds+((cHours < 12) ? ' AM':' PM')
35:
36:  document.getElementById("mTimeL").innerHTML=militaryTimeSt
37:  document.getElementById("dTimeL").innerHTML=digitalTimeSt
38:  document.getElementById("sTimeL").innerHTML=standardTimeSt
39:  setTimeout("Clock03()",1000)
40: }
41: </script>
42: </body>
43: </html>
```

After the heading message in line 10, we create a 3 × 2 table. The first column of this table contains the messages "Military Time," "Digital Time," and "Standard Time." The second column of the table defines the locations mTimeL for the military time, dTimeL for the digital time, and sTimeL for the standard time as indicated in lines 12–14.

Inside the function Clock03() (see lines 18–40), a date object is defined in line 20 to get the current hours, minutes, and seconds (see lines 21–23). These values are used to build the required military, digital, and standard time strings. The construction of the military time string militaryTimeSt begins in line 25. If the current hour value cHours is less than 10, we add an additional character "0" to the string. After the string concatenation with cHours at the end of line 25, we have a military time format for the hour. The statement ((cHours < 10)? '0':'') is sometimes called the "Ternary" conditional operator originally from the C/C++ language.

The construction of the digital time string (see lines 28–30) is similar to the military case. Finally, the standard time string in line 32 has the expression

```
((cHours==0 || cHours==12) ? '12': cHours %12)
```

This expression can be read as follows: if cHours equals 0 or 12, return 12, otherwise return the remainder of cHours divided by 12 (i.e., cHours %12). This expression guarantees that the range of cHours lies between 0 and 12. At the end of line 34, the ternary operator is again used to determine AM or PM time.

The time strings `militaryTimeSt`, `digitalTimeSt`, and `standardTimeSt` are output to the specific locations as stated in lines 36–38. A screen shot of the page in action is shown in Fig. 12.13.

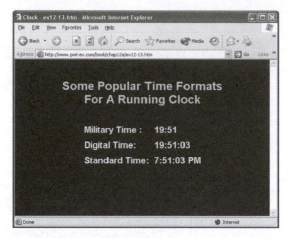

Figure 12.13 ex12-13.htm

12.3.2 A digital clock with animated images

With the image skills you have learned in previous chapters, you can build a digital clock with a more realistic scene. The clock that we are going to develop contains 11 images representing the 10 digits and one semicolon. Obviously the images will change when the clock is updated.

First, a table represented as a string to accommodate the digital clock images is needed. This string can be placed anywhere in the page using the output function `document.write()` or the `document.getElementById("location")` function. Once the clock is displayed on the screen, an image animation technique is used to update the clock. The main page of the clock is listed in ex12-14.htm.

Example: ex12–14.htm – A Digital Clock With Animated Images

```
 1: <?xml version="1.0" encoding="iso-8859-1"?>
 2: <!DOCTYPE html PUBLIC "-//W3C//DTD XHTML 1.0 Transitional//EN"
 3:     "http://www.w3.org/TR/xhtml1/DTD/xhtml1-transitional.dtd">
 4: <html xmlns="http://www.w3.org/1999/xhtml" xml:lang="en" lang="en">
 5: <head><title>A Digital Clock With Images - ex12-14.htm</title></head>
 6: <style> .mSt{font-size:16pt;color:#ffff00;font-weight:bold } </style>
 7: <script src="date.js"></script>
 8: <script src="imgclock.js"></script>
 9: <body style="background:#000088;text-align:center;font-family:arial">
10: <div align="center"><br />
11:    <div id="myHeader"></div><br /><br />
12:    <div class="mSt">
13:       A Digital Clock With Animated Images<br /><br /></div>
14:    <div id="clockL"></div>
15: </div>
16:  <script>
17:    document.getElementById("myHeader").innerHTML=disHeader()
18:    document.getElementById("clockL").innerHTML=showClock()
19:    showTime()
20:  </script>
21: </body>
22: </html>
```

This page includes two script program files, date.js and imgclock.js. The date.js program file is the same as that used in section 12.2. It provides the disHeader() function to be called in line 17 for generating the header. The statement in line 14 declares a location prepared for the clock. The showClock() function at the end of line 18 is defined inside the file imgclock.js. This function returns an XHTML language string (table) representing a clock and is displayed at the clock location. Finally, the showTime() function is used to animate the images while the clock is updated.

The first part of the ECMAScript imgclock.js is listed as follows:

```
Example: imgclock.js - The ECMAScript Clock With Animated Images (Part One)

 1: img_suf="dc.gif"
 2:
 3: function showClock()
 4: {
 5:  digits= new Array()
 6:  for (ii=0;ii<=9;ii++)
 7:  {
 8:    digits[ii]=ii+img_suf
 9:  }
10:  clockSt ="<table border=2 cellPadding=0 cellSpacing=0 width=125>"+
11:   "<tbody><tr><td align=left bgColor=#000044 width=120>"+
12:   "<img id='h1' src='0dc.gif' border='0'"+
13:       " alt='pic' width='15' height='23' />"+
14:   "<img id='h2' src='0dc.gif' border='0'"+
15:       " alt='pic' width='15' height='23' />"+
16:   "<img SRC='mdc.gif' border='0' alt='pic' width=13 height=23>"+
17:   "<img id='m1' src='0dc.gif' border='0'"+
18:       " alt='pic' width='15' height='23' />"+
19:   "<img id='m2' src='0dc.gif' border='0'"+
20:       " alt='pic' width='15' height='23' />"+
21:   "<img src='mdc.gif' border='0' alt='pic' width=13 height=23>"+
22:   "<img id='s1' src='0dc.gif' border='0'"+
23:       " alt='pic' width='15' height='23' />"+
24:   "<img id='s2' src='0dc.gif' border='0'"+
25:       " alt='pic' width='15' height='23' />"+
26:   "</td></tr></tbody></table>"
27:  return(clockSt)
28: }
29:
```

After the global variable for the image suffix img_suf in line 1, the first function showClock() defines an array to remember the images shown in Fig. 12.14. We use 10 array elements to represent each picture, i.e.,

```
digits[0]=0dc.gif,   digits[1]=1dc.gif,   ...,   digits[9]=9dc.gif
```

This is one of the techniques used to compose image source files by using script. The remaining part of this function generates a string clockSt representing a digital clock. The clock string clockSt in lines 10–26 is a string of an XHTML table. This table contains only one row and one column with eight images. Each component of hours, minutes, and seconds is represented by two images and separated by an image of the semi-colon (i.e., mdc.gif). All images have a unique identity so that updating can be performed easily. This string is returned to the caller (line 27) and can be placed anywhere on the page.

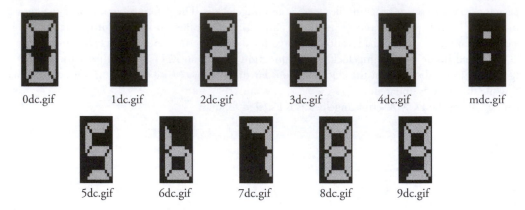

0dc.gif   1dc.gif   2dc.gif   3dc.gif   4dc.gif   mdc.gif

5dc.gif   6dc.gif   7dc.gif   8dc.gif   9dc.gif

Figure 12.14 Pictures for a digital clock

The second part of the ECMAScript imgclock.js is listed below:

```
Listing: Continuation Of The ECMAScript imgclock.js (Part Two)
30: dTime = 0
31:
32: function showTime(){
33:  now= new Date()
34:  sTime = now.getTime() + dTime
35:  now.setTime(sTime)
36:
37:  var hours = now.getHours()
38:  var minutes = now.getMinutes()
39:  var seconds = now.getSeconds()
40:
41:  document.getElementById("s1").src=digits[Math.floor(seconds/10)]
42:  document.getElementById("s2").src=digits[(seconds%10)]
43:  document.getElementById("m1").src=digits[Math.floor(minutes/10)]
44:  document.getElementById("m2").src=digits[(minutes%10)]
45:  document.getElementById("h1").src=digits[Math.floor(hours/10)]
46:  document.getElementById("h2").src=digits[(hours%10)]
47:  setTimeout("showTime()",1000)
48: }
```

Once the clock is displayed on the screen, this function can be called to update the images of the clock. First, we obtain the current time in line 33. This time can be adjusted by the variable dTime in line 34 to form a new show time variable sTime. The variable dTime is useful if we want to display the time in a different time zone.

After the show time variable sTime is set in line 35, new hours, minutes, and seconds are evaluated. These values are used to change the associated images accordingly (see lines 41–46). For example, the value in line 41

```
digits[Math.floor(seconds/10)]
```

represents the image of the tenth digit of the "seconds." This image is used to update the clock table with id="s1". The statement in line 47 guarantees that the clock is updated every second. A screen shot is shown in Fig. 12.15.

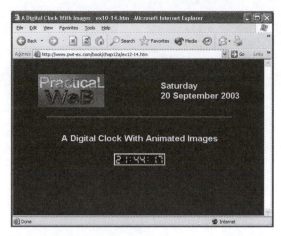

Figure 12.15 ex12-14.htm

12.3.3 A running countdown to Christmas

You must have seen a countdown somewhere on the Web and wondered how to do it. You will see in this section that the techniques involved are quite simple. We could use a countdown to the open day of a new shopping mall, a big discount day, anniversary, or a specific celebration day. Our next development shows how to write a page to perform a countdown to the next Christmas Day. This page displays the date of next Christmas first and then performs the days, hours, minutes, and seconds of the countdown. The countdown information is updated every second. If Christmas passes, the program will use the next Christmas Day and start a new countdown.

The program code of this page is in ex12-15.htm.

```
Example: ex12-15.htm - Countdown To Christmas

 1: <?xml version="1.0" encoding="iso-8859-1"?>
 2: <!DOCTYPE html PUBLIC "-//W3C//DTD XHTML 1.0 Transitional//EN"
 3:      "http://www.w3.org/TR/xhtml1/DTD/xhtml1-transitional.dtd">
 4: <html xmlns="http://www.w3.org/1999/xhtml" xml:lang="en" lang="en">
 5: <head><title>CountDown To Christmas -- ex12-15.htm</title></head>
 6: <style> .mSt{font-size:16pt;color:#ffff00;font-weight:bold } </style>
 7: <body style="background:#000088;text-align:center;font-family:arial"
 8:              onload="countXmax()">
 9: <div class="mSt" style="color:#00ffff;font-size:20pt" align="center">
10:      <br />CountDown To Next Christmas<br /><br />
11:   <span id="xmaxL" class="mSt"></span><br /><br />
12:   <table class="mSt" width="250" >
13:   <tr><td>Days</td><td><span id="dayL" class="mSt"></span></td></tr>
14:   <tr><td>Hours</td><td><span id="HoursL" class="mSt"></span></td></tr>
15:   <tr><td>Minutes</td><td><span id="MinutesL" class="mSt"></span></td></tr>
16:   <tr><td>Seconds</td><td><span id="SecondsL" class="mSt"></span></td></tr>
17:   </table>
18: </div>
19:
20: <script>
21:   mDay = new Array("Sunday","Monday","Tuesday","Wednesday","Thursday",
22:       "Friday","Saturday")
23: function countXmax()
24: {
25:   dateObj = new Date()
26:   cYear = dateObj.getFullYear()
27:   cHours = dateObj.getHours()
```

```
28:    cMinutes = dateObj.getMinutes()
29:    cSeconds = dateObj.getSeconds()
30:
31:    xmaxObj = new Date()
32:    xmaxObj.setMonth(11)
33:    xmaxObj.setDate(24)
34:    xmaxObj.setHours(23)
35:    xmaxObj.setMinutes(59)
36:    xmaxObj.setSeconds(59)
37:
38:    cTimeDiff = (xmaxObj.getTime() - dateObj.getTime())
39:    if (cTimeDiff < 0)
40:    {
41:      xmaxObj.setFullYear(cYear+1)
42:      cTimeDiff = (xmaxObj.getTime() - dateObj.getTime())
43:    }
44:    xmaxSt=mDay[xmaxObj.getDay()+1]+' December '+
45:           ' 25 '+xmaxObj.getFullYear()
46:    cDays = Math.floor(cTimeDiff/(1000*60*60*24))
47:
48:    document.getElementById("xmaxL").innerHTML=xmaxSt
49:    document.getElementById("dayL").innerHTML=cDays
50:    document.getElementById("HoursL").innerHTML= 23 - cHours
51:    document.getElementById("MinutesL").innerHTML= 59 - cMinutes
52:    document.getElementById("SecondsL").innerHTML= 60 - cSeconds
53:    setTimeout("countXmax()",1000)
54: }
55: </script>
56: </body>
57: </html>
```

Line 10 is to display the message "CountDown To Next Christmas." Line 11 is the location for the date of next Christmas. Lines 12–17 are used to construct a table for the countdown days, hours, minutes, and seconds.

Inside the script function countXmax() (see lines 23–54), a date object dateObj is defined to get the current year cYear, hours cHours, minutes cMinutes, and seconeds cSeconds. In lines 31–36, a Christmas date object xmaxObj is used to set the date and time of Christmas, i.e., "23:59:59," on December 24 of the current year.

A comparison of the time unit of Christmas against the current date and time takes place in line 38. If the time difference is negative, we know that the current Christmas Day has passed. The coding in lines 41–42 is then used to get the date of next Christmas. The time string for next Christmas is then output to the specific location specified in line 48. The cDays variable in line 46 is to store the number of days to Christmas. Once we have the value of cDays, the countdown action is a simple process as indicated in lines 49–52. A screen shot of this page at work is shown in Fig. 12.16.

Figure 12.16 ex12-15.htm

12.3.4 Countdown with animated images

To use animated images for the countdown is straightforward. All we need is to replace the countdown number with individual digits. With the digit pictures given in Fig. 12.14, we can modify the function `countXmax()` in ex12-15.htm to include animated images. This new example is called ex12-16.htm. The new `countMax()` function is listed in ex12-10.txt and a screen shot of ex12-16.htm is shown in Fig. 12.17.

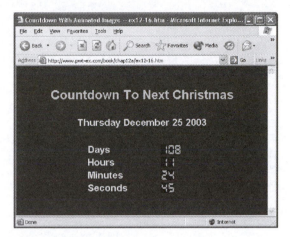

Figure 12.17 ex12-16.htm

```
Listing: ex12-10.txt - Code Fragment For ex12-16.htm

 1: function countXmax()
 2: {
 3:  dateObj = new Date()
 4:  cYear = dateObj.getFullYear()
 5:  cHours = dateObj.getHours()
 6:  cMinutes = dateObj.getMinutes()
 7:  cSeconds = dateObj.getSeconds()
 8:
 9:  xmaxObj = new Date()
10:  xmaxObj.setMonth(11)
11:  xmaxObj.setDate(24)
12:  xmaxObj.setHours(23)
13:  xmaxObj.setMinutes(59)
14:  xmaxObj.setSeconds(59)
15:
16:  cTimeDiff = (xmaxObj.getTime() - dateObj.getTime())
17:  if (cTimeDiff < 0)
18:  {
19:    xmaxObj.setFullYear(cYear+1)
20:    cTimeDiff = (xmaxObj.getTime() - dateObj.getTime())
21:  }
22:  xmaxSt=mDay[xmaxObj.getDay()+1]+' December '+
23:         ' 25 '+xmaxObj.getFullYear()
24:  cDays = Math.floor(cTimeDiff/(1000*60*60*24))
25:
26:  tmp1 = Math.floor(cDays/100)
27:  tmp = cDays - (tmp1 * 100)
28:  daySt = '<img src="'+tmp1+'dc.gif" + border="0" '+
29:             ' alt="pic" width="15" height="23" />'+
30:          '<img src="'+(Math.floor(tmp/10))+'dc.gif" + border="0" '+
```

```
31:                 ' alt="pic" width="15" height="23" />'+
32:              '<img src="'+(Math.floor(tmp % 10))+'dc.gif" + border="0" '+
33:                 ' alt="pic" width="15" height="23" />'
34:
35:  tmp = 23-cHours
36:  hourSt = '<img src="'+(Math.floor(tmp/10))+'dc.gif" + border="0" '+
37:                 ' alt="pic" width="15" height="23" />'+
38:              '<img src="'+(Math.floor(tmp % 10))+'dc.gif" + border="0" '+
39:                 ' alt="pic" width="15" height="23" />'
40:
41:  tmp = 59 - cMinutes
42:  minuteSt = '<img src="'+(Math.floor(tmp/10))+'dc.gif" + border="0" '+
43:                 ' alt="pic" width="15" height="23" />'+
44:              '<img src="'+(Math.floor(tmp % 10))+'dc.gif" + border="0" '+
45:                 ' alt="pic" width="15" height="23" />'
46:
47:  tmp = 60 - cSeconds
48:  secondSt = '<img src="'+(Math.floor(tmp/10))+'dc.gif" + border="0" '+
49:                 ' alt="pic" width="15" height="23" />'+
50:              '<img src="'+(Math.floor(tmp % 10))+'dc.gif" + border="0" '+
51:                 ' alt="pic" width="15" height="23" />'
52:
53:  document.getElementById("xmaxL").innerHTML=xmaxSt
54:  document.getElementById("dayL").innerHTML= daySt
55:  document.getElementById("HoursL").innerHTML= hourSt
56:  document.getElementById("MinutesL").innerHTML= minuteSt
57:  document.getElementById("SecondsL").innerHTML= secondSt
58:  setTimeout("countXmax()",1000)
59: }
```

This function now outputs the images rather than the numeric values. After we obtain the cDay value in line 24, a string daySt is used to get the image representation of cDay. This string is used in line 54 to return to the caller. The hours, minutes and seconds are returned in lines 55–58.

12.3.5 A question timer

Countdown timers have many applications on the Web. They provide essential timing control for slide shows, product or catalog advertisements, or even online auction sites with auction hammers. They also are an integral part of many online tests, examinations, and question-related data collections. For obvious reasons, our implementation of a question timer is a simple one. Our page displays one question at one time. The question is simple and expects a yes or no answer. The yes or no is implemented as two radio boxes so that only one answer can be checked. There is a 5 second countdown timer attached to each question. When the time is up, the page will display another question. The coding of this page is given in ex12-17.htm.

```
Example: ex12-17.htm - A Question Timer

 1: <?xml version="1.0" encoding="iso-8859-1"?>
 2: <!DOCTYPE html PUBLIC "-//W3C//DTD XHTML 1.0 Transitional//EN"
 3:     "http://www.w3.org/TR/xhtml1/DTD/xhtml1-transitional.dtd">
 4: <html xmlns="http://www.w3.org/1999/xhtml" xml:lang="en" lang="en">
 5: <head><title>A Question Timer - ex12-17.htm</title></head>
 6: <style>
 7:   .mSt{font-size:16pt;color:#ffff00;font-weight:bold }
 8:   .rbSt{width:35px;height:35px;background:#aaccaa}
 9: </style>
10: <body style="background:#000088;font-family:Arial;text-align:center"
11:               onload="countDown()" >
```

```
12:   <div class="mSt" align="center"> A Question CountDown Timer
13:     <br />Answer The Following Question Within 5 Seconds<br /><br /><br />
14:   <div id="questL" class="mSt" style="background:#008800;width:450px;
15:       height:200px"></div><br /><br /><br />
16:   <div class="mSt">Count Down :    <span class="mSt"
17:       id="countL">5</span></div>
18: </div>
19:
20: <script>
21:   cDown=6
22:   questFlag = 1
23:   disFlag = 0
24:   quest = new Array()
25:   yesNoSt = '<form><table cellspacing="25"><tr class="mSt">'+
26:    '<td><input type="radio" class="rbSt" checked id="rd01" name="rd" />'+
27:    '  Yes</td><td><input type="radio" class="rbSt" id="rd01" '+
28:    'name="rd" />  No</td></tr></table></form>'
29:
30:   quest[1]='Are We Alone In This Universe?<br /><br />'+yesNoSt
31:   quest[2]='Do You Believe World War III Is Coming?<br /><br />'+yesNoSt
32:   quest[3]='<span style="font-size:20pt"><br /><br />Thank You!</span>'
33:   questLength=3
34:
35:   function countDown()
36:   {
37:     cDown--
38:     if (disFlag == 0) {
39:       document.getElementById("questL").innerHTML="<br />"+quest[questFlag]
40:       disFlag = 1
41:       if (questFlag >= questLength) return(true)
42:     }
43:     if (cDown <= -1) {
44:         questFlag++
45:         disFlag = 0
46:         cDown = 6
47:     } else{
48:         document.getElementById("countL").innerHTML=cDown
49:     }
50:     setTimeout("countDown()",1000)
51:   }
52: </script>
53: </body>
54: </html>
```

After the message heading "Answer The Following Question Within 5 Seconds" in line 13, we create an area called questL (question location) with dimension 450×200 pixels. This area is used to place our questions. Below this question area, a countdown feature using countL is declared in line 17 to display the countdown action.

In the first part of the program (lines 21–24), we have declared the following variables:

- cDown   —   To store the countdown seconds.
- questFlag   —   To indicate which question is to be displayed.
- disFlag   —   To indicate whether the question has already been on the screen.
- quest[ ]   —   An array to store the questions.

The yes or no string variable yesNoSt in line 25 defines two radio boxes, Yes and No, so that the user can select only one of them.

The actual questions are input into lines 30–31. As a simple demonstration, only two questions are defined. Each question has the `yesNoSt` (yes or no boxes) attached at the end. The final element of the question array (`quest[3]`) is actually a "Thank You" message to mark the end of all questions.

When the function `countdown()` is activated, we decrease `cDown` by 1 (line 37) so that there are exactly 5 seconds to answer the question. If the question hasn't been displayed before (i.e., `disFlag ==0`), the statement in line 39 is used to display the question and set `disFlag` as true in line 40. If the displayed question is the last question, it stops the function and returns to the caller in line 41.

The second half of the function (lines 43–49) starts the actual countdown procedure. If the countdown is not negative (line 43), the countdown number is displayed as in line 48. If the countdown is a negative number, the next question is displayed (see line 44). In this case, you also need to reset `disFlag` as false in line 45 and assign the variable `cDown=6` so that a new countdown can be started. Some screen shots of this page in action are shown in Figs 12.18 and 12.19.

Figure 12.18 ex12-17.htm

Figure 12.19 Question timer

12.4 Generating calendars

12.4.1 Adding a month calendar to a page

Without doubt, another popular use of the date object is to generate a calendar. Since we know how to get the year, month, and date from a date object, to generate a calendar is just a formatting process. Our first aim here is to generate the current month calendar to a page. Consider the following example code ex12-18.htm:

```
Example: ex12-18.htm - A Page To Show A Month Calendar

 1: <?xml version="1.0" encoding="iso-8859-1"?>
 2: <!DOCTYPE html PUBLIC "-//W3C//DTD XHTML 1.0 Transitional//EN"
 3:     "http://www.w3.org/TR/xhtml1/DTD/xhtml1-transitional.dtd">
 4: <html xmlns="http://www.w3.org/1999/xhtml" xml:lang="en" lang="en">
 5: <head><title>A Month Calendar -- ex12-18.htm</title></head>
 6: <style> .mSt{font-size:16pt;color:#ffff00;font-weight:bold } </style>
 7: <script src="calendar.js"></script>
 8: <body style="background:#000088;text-align:center;font-family:arial">
 9:
10: <div class="mSt" style="font-size:20pt;color:#00ffff" align="center">
11:     <br />The Calendar of Current Month<br /><br />
12:     <div id="cMonthL"></div>
```

```
13:    <div id="calendarL"></div>
14: </div>
15:
16: <script>
17:  dateObj = new Date()
18:  tmpMonth = dateObj.getMonth()
19:  tmpYear = dateObj.getFullYear()
20:  document.getElementById("cMonthL").innerHTML=
21:    mMonth[tmpMonth]+" "+tmpYear
22:  document.getElementById("calendarL").innerHTML=
23:    getCalendar(tmpYear,tmpMonth)
24: </script>
25: </body>
26: </html>
```

Again, in this example XHTML is used as an interface. Line 12 defines a location for the current month (cMonthL). This location is used in lines 20–21 to output the month and year. Line 13 is our main location for the calendar. We use a script function getCalendar() (see line 23) to output the month calendar to this location. The script function returns an XHTML table and is defined in a program file called calendar.js.

Example: calendar.js - The ECMAScript For ex12-18.htm

```
 1:  mDay = new Array("Sunday","Monday","Tuesday","Wednesday","Thursday",
 2:      "Friday","Saturday")
 3:  mMonth = new Array("January","February","March","April","May","June",
 4:      "July","August","September","October","November","December")
 5:
 6:
 7:  function getCalendar(yy,mm)
 8:  {
 9:   calDay = new Array(43)
10:   for (ii=0;ii<=42;ii++) calDay[ii]=''
11:
12:   calObj = new Date(yy,mm,1,0,0,0)
13:   cal2Obj = new Date(yy,mm+1,1,0,0,0)
14:   stDays = calObj.getDay()
15:   noDays=Math.round((cal2Obj.getTime() - calObj.getTime())/(1000*60*60*24))
16:
17:   for (ii=stDays+1;ii<=noDays+stDays;ii++)
18:   {
19:     calDay[ii]=ii-stDays
20:   }
21:
22:   calSt='<table class="mSt" cellspacing="5"><tr><td>Sun</td><td>Mon</td>'+
23:     '<td>Tue</td><td>Wed</td><td>Thu</td><td>Fri</td><td>Sat</td>'
24:
25:   for(jj=0;jj<=5;jj++){
26:     calSt = calSt +"<tr align='center'>"
27:     for (ii=1;ii<=7;ii++){
28:       calSt=calSt + "<td>"+calDay[(ii+jj*7)]+"</td>"
29:     }
30:    calSt=calSt+"</tr>"
31:   }
32:   calSt=calSt+"</table>"
33:   return(calSt)
34:  }
35:
```

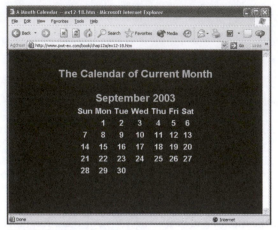

Figure 12.20 ex12-18.htm

A screen shot of this example is shown in Fig. 12.20.

There are a number of ways to implement a calendar function. Some of them may include clever tricks to manipulate the days. Our implementation is just a simple one and easy to understand. This function takes two arguments, year (yy) and month (mm).

First we need to find out the number of days noDays and the starting weekday stDays of the given month. For simplicity, we arrange all the days into six rows. Each row consists of seven days. The for-loop used in lines 17–20 is to shift the starting day of the month (stDays) to fit into the calendar array (calDay). The variable calSt (line 22) is an XHTML string (a table) representing the calendar. The double for-loops in lines 25–31 are used to fill up the month. At the end this string (calSt) returns to the caller in line 33.

12.4.2 A general page for calendars

As a more practical example, we want to build a general page for calendars. This page has a drop-down box containing years from 1998 to 2020 inclusive. When the page is loaded, the 12-month calendar of the current year is displayed. When the user picks another year from the drop-down box, the calendar changes instantly. This page uses the same getCalendar() function in the program file calendar.js. First, the interface part of this page is listed in ex12-19.htm.

```
Example: ex12-19.htm - A General Calendar Page

 1: <?xml version="1.0" encoding="iso-8859-1"?>
 2: <!DOCTYPE html PUBLIC "-//W3C//DTD XHTML 1.0 Transitional//EN"
 3:     "http:o/www.w3.org/TR/xhtml1/DTD/xhtml1-transitional.dtd">
 4: <html xmlns="http://www.w3.org/1999/xhtml" xml:lang="en" lang="en">
 5: <head><title>A General Calendar -- ex12-19.htm</title></head>
 6: <style>
 7:   .mSt{font-size:12pt;color:#ffff00;font-weight:bold }
 8:   .hSt{font-size:18pt;color:#00ffff;font-weight:bold }
 9:   .bSt{font-size:18pt;color:#000088;font-weight:bold;
10:     width:100px;height:35px;background:#aaccaa}
11: </style>
12:
13: <script src="calendar.js"></script>
14: <body style="background:#000088;text-align:center;font-family:arial">
15:
16: <div align="center">
17: <table width=800>
18:  <tr><td align="left" width="20%">
19:         <img src="logo_web.jpg" width="110" height="60" /></td>
20:      <td width="60%" align="center"><div style="font-size:64pt;
21:        color:#00ffff;font-weight:bold" id="cYearHead"></div></td>
22:      <td align="right"><div id="yearBox"></div></td>
23:  </tr></table>
24: </div>
25: <img src="line1.gif" width="800" height="6" /><br /><br />
26:
```

```
27: <div id="cCalendar"></div>
28:
29: <script>
30:   dateObj = new Date()
31:   defaultYear = dateObj.getFullYear()
32:   disCalendar(1998,2020,defaultYear,"cYearHead","yearBox","cCalendar")
33: </script>
34:
35: </body>
36: </html>
```

Lines 17–23 define a table to accommodate a header. This header contains an image (logo), a location `id="cYearHead"` (lines 20–21) to display a year string in a big font size, and a location `id="yearBox"` for a drop-down box. Line 27 defines a location `id="cCalendar"` for the actual calendar.

The main part of this page is the function `disCalendar()` (see line 32). This function takes a number of arguments. The first two represent the start and end year for which the calendar is constructed. In this case, the calendar covers the years from 1998 to 2020 inclusively. From the statements in lines 30–31, we know that the default year `defaultYear` for display is the current year. The final three arguments are for the locations to display. The year header displays in `id="cYearHead"`, the drop box displays in `id="yearBox"`, and the actual calendar displays in `id="cCalendar"`.

If the value of the drop box is changed, the calendar will change immediately. Some screen shots of the page in action are shown in Figs. 12.21 and 12.22.

Figure 12.21 ex12-19.htm

Figure 12.22 Year 2020 calendar

The function `disCalendar()` is added to the end of calendar.js and is listed in ex12-11.txt.

Listing: ex12-11.txt – Adding The Function disCalendar() In calendar.js

```
37:   gl_stYear = 2000
38:   gl_endYear = 2010
39:   gl_disYear = 2000
40:   gl_headL = ""
41:   gl_boxL = ""
42:   gl_calendarL = ""
43:
44:   function disCalendar(stYear,endYear,disYear,headL,boxL,calendarL)
45:   {
46:     gl_stYear = stYear
47:     gl_endYear = endYear
48:     gl_headL = headL
```

```
49:   gl_boxL = boxL
50:   gl_calendarL = calendarL
51:   gl_disYear = disYear
52:
53:   showYearBox()
54:   document.getElementById("gYear").selectedIndex =
55:       (gl_disYear - gl_stYear)
56:   showCalendar()
57:   }
58:
```

To simplify passing variables among functions, global variables are used to implement this function. The six global variables (see lines 37–42) represent the starting year gl_stYear, ending year gl_endYear, default display year gl_disYear, and various display locations. The first three variables have arbitrary initial values. The first part of this disCalendar() function is to fill up the global variables (lines 46–51). The showYearBox() function in line 53 is to display the year drop box. The statements in lines 54–55 set the initial value of the box. Since the selected items of the drop box start from zero, the difference in line 55 is necessary to reset the correct value. The function showCalendar() in line 56 is used to display the calendar.

The coding for the showYearBox() function is shown below.

Listing: ex12-12.txt – Adding The Function showYearBox() In calendar.js

```
59:   function showYearBox()
60:   {
61:    yearSt ='<select id="gYear" name="gYear" class="bSt" '+
62:       'onchange="chgYear()">'
63:
64:    for (ii=gl_stYear;ii<=gl_endYear;ii++){
65:      yearSt = yearSt + '<option>'+ii+'</option>'
66:    }
67:    yearSt = yearSt + '</select>'
68:    document.getElementById(gl_boxL).innerHTML=yearSt
69:   }
70:
```

This function displays the string yearSt of a drop box to the location gl_boxL in line 68. If the selected value of the box has changed, the chgYear() function is called in line 62. The chgYear() function displays the calendar to the location defined by the global variable gl_calendarL. The function chgYear() is listed as follows:

Listing: ex12-13.txt – Adding The Function chgYear() In calendar.js

```
71:   function chgYear()
72:   {
73:    gl_disYear=(document.getElementById("gYear").selectedIndex + gl_stYear)
74:    showCalendar()
75:   }
76:
```

This function gets the selected year from the drop box. Since the selected value from the box starts from zero, you need to add the starting year to reveal the true identity of the year (line 73). When you have the selected year, you can call the function showCalendar() to show the actual calendar. The listing of the function showCalendar() is given in ex12-14.txt.

Listing: ex12-14.txt – Adding The Function showCalendar() In calendar.js

```
77:   function showCalendar()
78:   {
79:    calYear = gl_disYear
80:    document.getElementById(gl_headL).innerHTML=calYear
81:
82:    cMonth= new Array("January","February","March","April","May","June",
```

```
 83:    "July","August","September","October","November","December")
 84:
 85:    calTable = '<table class="mSt" cellspacing="15">'
 86:    for (ii=0;ii<=3;ii++){
 87:     calTable = calTable + '<tr valign="top">'
 88:     for (jj=0;jj<=2;jj++){
 89:      calTable=calTable+'<td width="250" height="210" align="center">'+
 90:        '<span class="hSt">'+ (cMonth[jj+ (ii*3)])+
 91:        '</span><div id="'+cMonth[jj+(ii*3)]+'"></div>'
 92:     }
 93:     calTable = calTable + '</tr>'
 94:    }
 95:    calTable = calTable + '</table>'
 96:    document.getElementById(gl_calendarL).innerHTML=calTable
 97:
 98:    for (nn=0;nn<=11;nn++) {
 99:       document.getElementById(cMonth[nn]).innerHTML=getCalendar(calYear,nn)
100:    }
101:  }
```

Line 80 is to display the year value to the global header location `gl_headL`. The remaining part of this function is an example of a double-table (i.e., a table within a table) application. The double for-loops in lines 86–94 define a 4 × 3 table to accommodate the 12 months. This string or calendar table `calTable` is then displayed at the location `gl_calendarL` in line 96. Once this table is displayed, the for-loop in lines 98–100 is used to fill up each element of the table by a single-month calendar. This way you can have a full calendar (i.e., 12 months) on the screen. The array `cMonth` used in lines 82–83 is to make the function more independent, so that this function can be taken out as a standalone function more easily.

So far, we have presented a comprehensive discussion on client-side date and time functions and their applications on the Web. In practice, and in many cases, date and time are obtained from the server to reflect the true status of the Web site. Once the date and time information is obtained from the server, all the client-side techniques that we discussed can be applied.

12.5   Getting date and time information from server

12.5.1 Why server time?

From the canonical client–server interaction, we know that a server is basically a machine to hold XHTML (or HTML) files and send them to the browsers. In fact, the capabilities of servers are far beyond the original HTML imagination. Enhanced by various Web technologies including security, they can perform all kinds of processing, manipulations and protection checks before sending the XHTML (or HTML) files. Server technologies will be discussed in Parts IV and V. In the following sections, we will introduce some techniques that can be used to obtain the date and time information from the server. That is, to ask the server to send date and time to the browser as XHTML information. Why do we need server date and time in the first place? Well, the main advantages of using the server are:

- A server is usually a more reliable machine that is always running and has a live connection to the Internet.
- Since users or clients cannot change the date and time information of a server, the record is more reliable and can be used as solid proof of any business activities.

In fact, server time is an integral part of almost any commercial transactions and e-businesses on the Internet.

A formal discussion of server technologies is presented in Part IV. Before that two server technologies are introduced here, namely, Active Server Page (ASP) and PHP Hypertext Preprocessor (PHP). ASP was originated by Microsoft Corporation and can be found in Windows 9.x, NT, 2000, and XP server environments. ASP pages in this book will have file extension `.asp`. PHP is more platform independent and can be found in most UNIX (or LINUX) installations. PHP pages or scripts will have file extension `.php`. As a user, you need to find out what type of technologies are supported by your server (or ISP). For obvious reasons, only simple server applications involving date and time will be considered here.

In addition to the server date and time, we will also show you how to integrate them with all the techniques that you have learned in previous sections. Now, let's see how to obtain a date and time from a server using ASP.

12.5.2 Server date and time using ASP

Microsoft's ASP provides a framework for using existing scripting languages such as ECMAScript (or JScript) at the server level. An ASP script can perform a task as simple as displaying the value of a variable to one as complex as sending a Structured Query Language (SQL) statement to a complicated database structure shared among big organizations. There are two basic scripting languages used in ASP, VBScript (a small version of Visual Basic) and JScript. Since JScript is a full implementation of ECMA-262 (i.e., ECMAScript), JScript is used for our discussion here.

If your server supports ASP, you can use the following two procedures to convert all your XHTML files to ASP.

- Rename the XHTML files with extensions `.htm`, `.html`, or `.xhtml` to `.asp`.
- Copy and paste the following ASP statement to line 1 of the file:

```
<%@language="JScript" %>
```

For VBScript, users may use `<%@language="VBScript" %>` instead. Our next example is an ASP conversion of ex12-03.htm. This converted example, ex12-20.asp, is listed as follows:

```
Example: ex12-20.asp - Date Functions

 1: <%@language="JScript" %>
 2: <?xml version="1.0" encoding="iso-8859-1"?>
 3: <!DOCTYPE html PUBLIC "-//W3C//DTD XHTML 1.0 Transitional//EN"
 4:     "http://www.w3.org/TR/xhtml1/DTD/xhtml1-transitional.dtd">
 5: <html xmlns="http://www.w3.org/1999/xhtml" xml:lang="en" lang="en">
 6: <head><title>Date Functions -- ex12-20.asp</title></head>
 7: <body style="background:#000088;text-align:center;font-family:arial;
 8:     font-size:16pt;color:#ffff00">
 9: <script>
10: <% cDate = new Date() %>
11: document.write("Getting Today's Date From The Server<br /><br />")
12: document.write("The Day of The Week = "+ <%= cDate.getDay()%> +"<br />")
13: document.write("The Date of The Month = "+<%= cDate.getDate()%>+"<br />")
14: document.write("The Current Month = "+<%= (cDate.getMonth()+1)%>+"<br />")
15: document.write("The Current Year = "+<%= cDate.getFullYear()%>+"<br />")
16: </script>
17: </body>
18: </html>
```

Any statements between the ASP bracket pair `<%` and `%>` will be processed by the server before sending them back to the browser. As you can see from this example, all ASP date and time functions and commands are the same as ECMAScript. They are bracketed with the ASP element pair. The equal sign (=) used in the bracket pair in line 12

```
<%= cDate.getDay() %>
```

means print out the value of `cDate.getDay()`. That is, get the weekday from the server and output the value at the current location. We have put this page into a system that supports ASP, such as the Internet Information Server (IIS). You can issue the following command on a browser to see the result:

   http://www.pwt-ex.com/book/chap12a/ex12-20.asp

If you have the ASP program ex12-20.asp stored in the appropriate folder or location, you will see the result of this page as in Fig. 12.23.

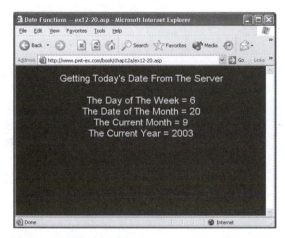

Figure 12.23 ex12-20.htm

As for curiosity, if you activate the "view source" option from the browser, you will see the source code of this page as in listing ex12-15.txt.

```
Listing: ex12-15.txt - The XHTML Page Generated By ex12-20.asp

 1: <?xml version="1.0" encoding="iso-8859-1"?>
 2: <!DOCTYPE html PUBLIC "-//W3C//DTD XHTML 1.0 Transitional//EN"
 3:     "http://www.w3.org/TR/xhtml1/DTD/xhtml1-transitional.dtd">
 4: <html xmlns="http://www.w3.org/1999/xhtml" xml:lang="en" lang="en">
 5: <head><title> Date Functions -- ex12-20.asp </title></head>
 6: <body style="background:#000088;text-align:center;font-family:arial;
 7:     font-size:16pt;color:#ffff00">
 8: <script>
 9:
10:  document.write("Getting Today's Date From The Server<br /><br />")
11:  document.write("The Day of The Week = "+ 6 +"<br />")
12:  document.write("The Date of The Month = "+20+"<br />")
13:  document.write("The Current Month = "+9+"<br />")
14:  document.write("The Current Year = "+2003+"<br />")
15: </script>
16: </body>
17: </html>
```

If you compare this page with ex12-20.asp, you can see that the server actually generates the date and time information. These values are then returned to the browser as a formatted XHTML file.

The manipulation of static date and time is easy. All you have to do is enclose the statements inside the ASP element pair `<%` and `%>`. For dynamic date and time, however, some special treatment is needed.

12.5.3 Dynamic time implementation with ASP

In order to save the resources of Internet traffic and valuable server time, and for many other practical reasons, a mechanism that keeps calling the server date and time functions is not recommended. Instead a server reference technique may be more appropriate in practice. The idea is simple: for example, you first get the server time as a reference or a starting point. The increment of the local time is then used to update this reference. This way, you have an instant dynamic clock with server time.

Consider the following example ex12-21.asp. This example is a modification of ex12-13.htm to create dynamic server time.

```
Example: ex12-21.asp - Server Clock

 1: <%@language="JScript" %>
 2: <?xml version="1.0" encoding="iso-8859-1"?>
 3: <!DOCTYPE html PUBLIC "-//W3C//DTD XHTML 1.0 Transitional//EN"
 4:     "http://www.w3.org/TR/xhtml1/DTD/xhtml1-transitional.dtd">
 5: <html xmlns="http://www.w3.org/1999/xhtml" xml:lang="en" lang="en">
 6: <head><title>Server Clock - ex12-21.asp</title></head>
 7: <style> .mSt{font-size:16pt;color:#ffff00;font-weight:bold } </style>
 8: <body style="background:#000088;text-align:center;font-family:arial"
 9:             onload="Clock03()">
10: <div class="mSt" style="font-size:20pt;color:#00ffff" align="center">
11:   <br />Some Popular Time Formats<br />For A Clock On Server<br /><br />
12: <table class="mSt" cellspacing="10">
13:   <tr><td>Military Time :</td><td><div id="mTimeL"></div></td></tr>
14:   <tr><td>Digital Time:</td><td><div id="dTimeL"></div></td></tr>
15:   <tr><td>Standard Time:</td><td><div id="sTimeL"></div></td></tr>
16: </table>
17: </div>
18: <script>
19: fdateObj = new Date()
20: <%sDate = new Date()%>
21: sgetTime = <%=sDate.getTime()%>
22: dTime = sgetTime - fdateObj.getTime()
23:
24: function Clock03()
25: {
26:  dateObj = new Date()
27:  sTime = dateObj.getTime() + dTime
28:  dateObj.setTime(sTime)
29:
30:  cHours = dateObj.getHours()
31:  cMinutes = dateObj.getMinutes()
32:  cSeconds = dateObj.getSeconds()
33:
34:  militaryTimeSt= ((cHours < 10)? '0':'')+cHours+':'+
35:  ((cMinutes < 10)? '0':'')+cMinutes
36:
37:  digitalTimeSt= ((cHours < 10)? '0':'')+cHours+':'+
38:   ((cMinutes < 10)? '0':'')+cMinutes+':'+((cSeconds < 10)? '0':'')+
39:   cSeconds
40:
41:  standardTimeSt= ((cHours==0 || cHours==12) ? '12': cHours %12)+':'+
42:  ((cMinutes < 10)? '0':'')+cMinutes+':'+((cSeconds < 10)? '0':'')+
43:  cSeconds+((cHours < 12) ? ' AM':' PM')
44:
45:  document.getElementById("mTimeL").innerHTML=militaryTimeSt
46:  document.getElementById("dTimeL").innerHTML=digitalTimeSt
```

```
47:    document.getElementById("sTimeL").innerHTML=standardTimeSt
48:    setTimeout("Clock03()",1000)
49: }
50: </script>
51: </body>
52: </html>
```

Line 19 declares a local date object and line 20 a date object on the server. The difference in the server time and local time dTime in line 22 is the reference. This reference is then used in line 27 to get the server time string sTime. The setTime() method used in line 28 is to create a date object with the server time string. This date object can then be used by any date and time functions associated with the browser as if it is a local time object. The setTimeout() method (see line 48) fires up the regular update so that the clock is moving. A screen shot of this page is shown in Fig. 12.24.

Figure 12.24 ex12-21.htm

12.5.4 Countdown with ASP

Another more practical example is the construction of a countdown page to Christmas Day using server time. This page, ex12-22.asp, has the following listing:

```
Example: ex12-22.asp - Server Countdown With Images

 1: <%@language="JScript" %>
 2: <?xml version="1.0" encoding="iso-8859-1"?>
 3: <!DOCTYPE html PUBLIC "-//W3C//DTD XHTML 1.0 Transitional//EN"
 4:      "http://www.w3.org/TR/xhtml1/DTD/xhtml1-transitional.dtd">
 5: <html xmlns="http://www.w3.org/1999/xhtml" xml:lang="en" lang="en">
 6: <head><title>Server Countdown With Images - ex12-22.asp</title></head>
 7: <style> .mSt{font-size:16pt;color:#ffff00;font-weight:bold } </style>
 8: <body style="background:#000088;text-align:center;font-family:arial"
 9:             onload="countXmax()">
10: <div class="mSt" style="color:#00ffff;font-size:20pt" align="center">
11:      <br />Countdown To Next Christmas <br />(Server Time)<br /><br />
12:   <span id="xmaxL" class="mSt"></span><br /><br />
13:   <table class="mSt" width="250" >
14:   <tr><td>Days</td><td><span id="dayL" class="mSt"></span></td></tr>
15:   <tr><td>Hours</td><td><span id="HoursL" class="mSt"></span></td></tr>
16:   <tr><td>Minutes</td><td><span id="MinutesL" class="mSt"></span></td></tr>
17:   <tr><td>Seconds</td><td><span id="SecondsL" class="mSt"></span></td></tr>
18:   </table>
19: </div>
20: <script>
21:   mDay = new Array("Sunday","Monday","Tuesday","Wednesday","Thursday",
22:       "Friday","Saturday")
23:
24: fdateObj = new Date()
25: <%sDate = new Date()%>
26: sgetTime = <%=sDate.getTime()%>
27: dTime = sgetTime - fdateObj.getTime()
28:
29:   xmaxObj = new Date()
```

```
30:   xmaxObj.setMonth(11)
31:   xmaxObj.setDate(24)
32:   xmaxObj.setHours(23)
33:   xmaxObj.setMinutes(59)
34:   xmaxObj.setSeconds(59)
35:
36:  function countXmax()
37:  {
38:
39:   dateObj = new Date()
40:   sTime = dateObj.getTime() + dTime
41:   dateObj.setTime(sTime)
42:
43:   cYear = dateObj.getFullYear()
44:   cHours = dateObj.getHours()
45:   cMinutes = dateObj.getMinutes()
46:   cSeconds = dateObj.getSeconds()
47:   cTimeDiff = (xmaxObj.getTime() - dateObj.getTime())
48:   if (cTimeDiff < 0)
49:   {
50:    xmaxObj.setFullYear(cYear+1)
51:    cTimeDiff = (xmaxObj.getTime() - dateObj.getTime())
52:   }
53:   xmaxSt=mDay[xmaxObj.getDay()+1]+' December '+
54:           ' 25 '+xmaxObj.getFullYear()
55:   cDays = Math.floor(cTimeDiff/(1000*60*60*24))
56:
57:   tmp1 = Math.floor(cDays/100)
58:   tmp = cDays - (tmp1 * 100)
59:   daySt = '<img src="'+tmp1+'dc.gif" + border="0" '+
60:             ' alt="pic" width="15" height="23" />'+
61:           '<img src="'+(Math.floor(tmp/10))+'dc.gif" + border="0" '+
62:             ' alt="pic" width="15" height="23" />'+
63:           '<img src="'+(Math.floor(tmp % 10))+'dc.gif" + border="0" '+
64:             ' alt="pic" width="15" height="23" />'
65:
66:   tmp = 23-cHours
67:   hourSt = '<img src="'+(Math.floor(tmp/10))+'dc.gif" + border="0" '+
68:              ' alt="pic" width="15" height="23" />'+
69:           '<img src="'+(Math.floor(tmp % 10))+'dc.gif" + border="0" '+
70:              ' alt="pic" width="15" height="23" />'
71:
72:   tmp = 59 - cMinutes
73:   minuteSt = '<img src="'+(Math.floor(tmp/10))+'dc.gif" + border="0" '+
74:                ' alt="pic" width="15" height="23" />'+
75:             '<img src="'+(Math.floor(tmp % 10))+'dc.gif" + border="0" '+
76:                ' alt="pic" width="15" height="23" />'
77:
78:   tmp = 60 - cSeconds
79:   secondSt = '<img src="'+(Math.floor(tmp/10))+'dc.gif" + border="0" '+
80:                ' alt="pic" width="15" height="23" />'+
81:             '<img src="'+(Math.floor(tmp % 10))+'dc.gif" + border="0" '+
82:                ' alt="pic" width="15" height="23" />'
83:
84:   document.getElementById("xmaxL").innerHTML=xmaxSt
85:   document.getElementById("dayL").innerHTML= daySt
86:   document.getElementById("HoursL").innerHTML= hourSt
```

```
87:    document.getElementById("MinutesL").innerHTML= minuteSt
88:    document.getElementById("SecondsL").innerHTML= secondSt
89:    setTimeout("countXmax()",1000)
90: }
91: </script>
92: </body>
93: </html>
```

It is not difficult to see that we have used the same reference technique here. Lines 24–27 are used to get the time reference of the server and the local client. This time difference variable (dTime) is used to create the date object with the server time string in lines 40–41. The remaining operations are the same as those in ex12-16.htm. The client-side increment of the time in line 89 has an updating effect on the server time.

Once you understand this idea, you can tackle a slightly different server technology, namely PHP Hypertext Preprocessor (PHP).

12.5.5 Server date and time using PHP

PHP is similar to ASP in that they are both server-side scripting languages. In principle, they both process a file and produce an XHTML file for the browser. The commands and how to use them, of course, are different. PHP is considered as another popular server technology on the Web based on the following two reasons:

- PHP is simple to use yet powerful enough to handle complicated problems such as databases in a surprisingly simple way.
- PHP is freely available on most platforms (from Microsoft Windows to LINUX systems).

As an introduction (and a good starting point), only PHP's date and time applications are considered here. A more formal discussion of PHP follows in Part IV.

To handle date and time information using PHP, you need to remember the following five points:

- PHP files should have the file extension .php.
- PHP statements (or commands) should be enclosed by the PHP pair <?PHP and ?>.
- PHP variables have prefix $ (such as $myVar).
- PHP uses echo as output statements such as echo("My Message").
- PHP statements terminate with a semi-colon such as echo("My Message");.

With these in mind, let's consider the following example ex12-23.php:

```
Example: ex12-23.php - Getting Date & Time Using PHP

 1: <?PHP echo"<?";?>xml version="1.0" encoding="iso-8859-1"<?PHP echo"?>";?>
 2: <!DOCTYPE html PUBLIC "-//W3C//DTD XHTML 1.0 Transitional//EN"
 3:      "http://www.w3.org/TR/xhtml1/DTD/xhtml1-transitional.dtd">
 4: <html xmlns="http://www.w3.org/1999/xhtml" xml:lang="en" lang="en">
 5: <head><title> Example: ex12-23.php </title></head>
 6: <body style="background:#000088;text-align:center;font-family:arial;
 7:      font-size:16pt;color:#ffff00">
 8: <?PHP
 9:  $today = getdate();
10:    $month = $today['month'];
11:    $mday = $today['mday'];
12:    $year = $today['year'];
13:    $hours = $today['hours'];
14:    $minutes = $today['minutes'];
15:    $seconds = $today['seconds'];
16:    $weekday = $today['weekday'];
17: ?>
```

```
18: <script>
19:    document.write("<br />Getting Today's Date Using PHP<br /><br />")
20:    document.write("The Day of The Week = <?PHP echo "$weekday"; ?> <br />")
21:    document.write("The Date of The Month = <?PHP echo "$mday"; ?> <br />")
22:    document.write("The Current Month = <?PHP echo "$month"; ?> <br />")
23:    document.write("The Current Year = <?PHP echo "$year"; ?> <br />")
24: </script>
25: </body>
26: </html>
```

As we mentioned earlier, PHP is a preprocessor with the starting element `<?` and ending with `?>`. In fact, the PHP statement

```
<?PHP echo "<?"; ?>
```

is used in line 1 to produce the necessary symbol `<?` for consistent XML coding. Likewise, we also need another one at the end of line 1.

The main PHP date and time block starts from line 8. The `getDate()` in line 9 is a PHP function used to return an array containing the date and time information. This array is assigned to variable `$today`. Therefore, `$today['month']` contains the information of the current month (see line 10). A series of variables are used to remember the date and time returned by the `getDay()` function (see lines 10–16). If you want to output the value of a variable such as `$weekday`, you can use the echo statement

```
<?PHP echo "$weekday"; ?>
```

as demonstrated in line 20. Since PHP is a preprocessor, the interpretation of the echo command is done before any ECMAScript statement from the browser. Thus you need to include the entire PHP output statement inside the double quotes of the ECMAScript (see line 20). If you put this PHP page into a system with PHP support, such as the UNIX/LINUX environment running Apache, you can use the following "http" command

http://www.pwt-ex.com/book/chap12a/ex12-23.php

to access the page and see the result. A screen shot of the page is shown in Fig. 12.25.

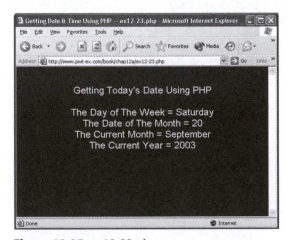

Figure 12.25 ex12-23.php

Again, if you activate the "view source" option from the browser, you will see the following XHTML coding:

```
Listing: ex12-15.txt - The Date And Time Page Generated By ex12-23.php

 1: <?xml version="1.0" encoding="iso-8859-1"?>
 2: <!DOCTYPE html PUBLIC "-//W3C//DTD XHTML 1.0 Transitional//EN"
 3:     "http://www.w3.org/TR/xhtml1/DTD/xhtml1-transitional.dtd">
 4: <html xmlns="http://www.w3.org/1999/xhtml" xml:lang="en" lang="en">
 5: <head><title> Example: ex12-23.php </title></head>
 6: <body style="background:#000088;text-align:center;font-family:arial;
 7:     font-size:16pt;color:#ffff00">
 8:
 9: <script>
10:  document.write("<br />Getting Today's Date Using PHP<br /><br />")
11:  document.write("The Day of The Week = Saturday <br />")
12:  document.write("The Date of The Month = 20 <br />")
13:  document.write("The Current Month = September <br />")
14:  document.write("The Current Year = 2003 <br />")
15: </script>
16: </body>
17: </html>
```

12.5.6 A digital clock using PHP

As another application using PHP, let's modify the digital clock in ex12-14.htm to deal with server time. The main page of this example is listed in ex12-24.php.

```
Example: ex12-24.php - A Digital Clock With Images Using PHP

 1: <?PHP echo"<?";?>xml version="1.0" encoding="iso-8859-1"<?PHP echo"?>";?>
 2: <!DOCTYPE html PUBLIC "-//W3C//DTD XHTML 1.0 Transitional//EN"
 3:     "http://www.w3.org/TR/xhtml1/DTD/xhtml1-transitional.dtd">
 4: <html xmlns="http://www.w3.org/1999/xhtml" xml:lang="en" lang="en">
 5: <head><title> Example: ex12-24.php </title></head>
 6: <style> .mSt{font-size:16pt;color:#ffff00;font-weight:bold } </style>
 7: <script src="date.js"></script>
 8: <script src="imgclock.js"></script>
 9: <body style="background:#000088;text-align:center;font-family:arial">
10: <div align="center"><br />
11:    <div id="myHeader"></div><br /><br />
12:    <div class="mSt">
13:       A Digital Clock With Images<br />(Using PHP)<br /><br /></div>
14:    <div id="clockL"></div>
15: </div>
16:  <script>
17:   fdateObj = new Date()
18:   <?PHP $uTime = mktime(); ?>
19:   sgetTime = <?PHP echo("$uTime \n"); ?>
20:   sgetTime = sgetTime * 1000
21:   dTime = sgetTime - fdateObj.getTime()
22:
23:   document.getElementById("myHeader").innerHTML=disHeader()
24:   document.getElementById("clockL").innerHTML=showClock()
25:   showTime()
26:  </script>
27: </body>
28: </html>
```

In this page, the same reference technique mentioned in the previous section is used to obtain the dynamic server time. The PHP time function `mktime()` in line 18

```
<?PHP $uTime = mktime(); ?>
```

returns the total number of seconds since January 1, 1970 (the UNIX time convention). A negative value indicates a date before the starting date. This number is assigned to a PHP variable `$uTime`. The `echo` statement in line 19 is to output the total seconds so that the ECMAScript variable `sgetTime` can have this value. Since ECMAScript time is in milliseconds, you need to multiply `sgetTime` by 1,000 to get the seconds as illustrated in line 20. Once you have done that, the reference time variable `dTime` will be calculated in line 21. The `dTime` variable is used as an adjustment to reflect the information of the server time. Since this variable is in the program file imgclock.js, no further modification of imgclock.js is needed. A screen shot of this example is shown in Fig. 12.26.

Figure 12.26 ex12-24.php

13 Practical emailing

13.1 An introduction to email and mail agents

13.1.1 Set up your mail agents

The ability to send an electronic message (email) to customers, friends, or groups of people anywhere has become a daily necessity for a computer system. Many systems can also inform the user of any incoming mail at the time when he or she logs in to the system. For example, the user will see a message such as "You have mail" in UNIX (or LINUX) systems, or be greeted by a voice message by some ISPs. In Microsoft Windows systems, a mail user agent such as Outlook Express can even allow the user to access different accounts from different ISPs. In this chapter, we are going to discuss email systems and how to program them on the Web. Basic browser emailing to server mail with ASP, PHP, and Perl is also discussed. Information on the Simple Mail Transfer Protocol (SMTP), Post Office Protocol (POP3), and Multipurpose Internet Mail Extension (MIME) is provided for practical purposes. Examples are given to show how to use them on the Web. Before you can gain access and control the email system, some basic knowledge of email messages and their agents is essential.

An email system has two fundamental components: the mail user agent (e.g., Outlook Express) and the mail transport agent (e.g., `sendmail` and `smail`). The user agent is the interface to the mail package that you use to write and read mails. The transport agent handles the actual processes of sending and receiving mails and is usually hidden from front end users. To install an email system and its associated agents from scratch is normally the job of the network administrator and your ISP. However, several simple steps to configure your email system can enhance the understanding of how email systems function on the Web.

One of the important tasks for mail delivery is to handle addresses for the sender and the recipient. For the Transmission Control Protocol/Internet Protocol (TCP/IP), or simply Internet convention, a typical email address may look like this: JohnSmith@pwt-ex.com. That is, user JohnSmith at domain name pwt-ex.com. From the sender to the recipient, the transport agent must establish a connection from the sender's domain (or machine) to a mail machine somewhere along the route to the destination and to deliver the mail. For TCP/IP networks, the SMTP is often used to establish the process of sending mails, while the POP3 is usually used for receiving mails. If a user signs up to an ISP, the ISP should provide the user with two machine names (SMTP and POP3 servers) together with other information so that the user can commission the mail agents to send or get emails. In the case of home users, for example, the typical information needed to set up the mail agents and the accounts are:

- Service provider's telephone number
- User name or account name
- Password
- Email address (e.g., JohnSmith@pwt-ex.com)
- SMTP server name (e.g., smtpmail.pwt-ex.com)
- POP3 server name (e.g., popmail.pwt-ex.com)

The first three pieces of information are used to establish the connection to the ISP using a telephone line. If you have a permanent connection, a telephone number is not needed. The user name and password will then be used again together with the remaining information to set up the mail user agent so that you can read, write, and deliver emails.

The SMTP and POP3 servers could be the same machine. As an example, let's consider how to set up the email user agent Outlook Express. First, you activate Outlook Express and go to Tools, Accounts, press Add, and select Mail to launch the "Internet Connection Wizard." After the creation of a name for your email account, you need to fill in your email address (Fig. 13.1). When you press the Next button, the Wizard will ask you for the email server names (Fig. 13.2).

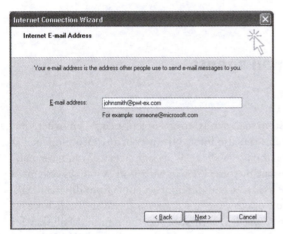

Figure 13.1 Email address   **Figure 13.2** Email servers

Another Next button takes you to the final dialog box. In this dialog box, you need to fill in your user name and password in order to gain access to your own email account (Fig. 13.3). Outlook Express is now ready to send and receive emails. Your email account will appear in Outlook Express's "Internet Account," window (Fig. 13.4).

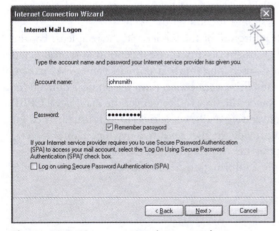

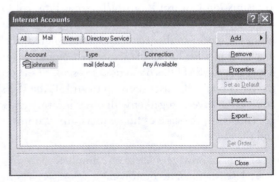

Figure 13.3 User name and password   **Figure 13.4** Email account

You follow a similar procedure to set up the mail agents on other systems. Depending on the ISP, sometimes you may also need the information called Domain Name System (DNS) to solve some naming conventions.

In order to simplify mail traffic on the Internet and to deliver email more effectively, your mail host normally uses `Mail Exchanger` to route all mails to you and other users to this machine. The use of a mail exchanger allows machines that are not connected to the Internet all the time to have mails received by a host (or service provider).

As an email user, you don't need to know much about the mail transport agents (`sendmail`, `smail`, etc.) and how they work. You need only to concentrate on the mail user agent, i.e., reads, writes, and sends emails. As a Web programmer, knowledge of how to control email and in particular program the user agent is needed. Before you can control the user agent effectively, you need to understand the basic structure and controllable components of an email.

13.1.2 Basic components of an email

An email message consists of a body and a header. The body part is usually text based and is the content of the message. The header is a chunk of information at the beginning of the message that contains information such as the sender, recipient, date, and subject. A blank line separates the header and the body parts. Many emails also include data at the end, called a *signature*, to provide further information on the sender.

The following is a typical header from a mail agent:

```
Listing: ex13-01.txt - Basic Components Of An Email

 1: X-Envelope-To: JohnSmith@pwt-ex.com
 2: Received: from sand2.global.net.uk ([195.147.246.100])
 3:    by mx2.global.net.uk with esmtp (Exim 3.03 #41)
 4:    id 143xOF-00071a-00
 5:    for JohnSmith@pwt-ex.com; Thu, 04 Dec 2003 09:30:59 +0000
 6: Received:from pa4s11a08.client.global.net.uk([195.147.91.165]helo=JohnSmith)
 7:    by sand2.global.net.uk with smtp (Exim 3.16 #1)
 8:    id 143xOZ-0002EV-00
 9:    for JohnSmith@pwt-ex.com; Thu, 04 Dec 2003 09:31:19 +0000
10: Message-ID: <000201c06031$4e6cefc0$a55b93c3@JohnSmith>
11: From: "JohnSmith" <JohnSmith@pwt-ex.com>
12: To: <JohnSmith@pwt-ex.com>
13: Subject: Hello
14: Cc: John@pwt-ex.com
15: Date: Thu, 4 Dec 2003 09:33:40 -0000
16: MIME-Version: 1.0
17: Content-Type: multipart/alternative;
18:    boundary="----=_NextPart_000_0005_01C06030.C8E32540"
19: X-Priority: 3
20: X-MSMail-Priority: Normal
21: X-Mailer: Microsoft Outlook Express 5.00.2314.1300
22: X-MimeOLE: Produced By Microsoft MimeOLE V5.00.2314.1300
23: X-Envelope-From: JohnSmith@pwt-ex.com
```

Line 1 is the `Envelope` containing the address of the recipient. The two `Received` fields (lines 2–9) are used to show which machines last relayed the email to you (or your machine). The `Received` field can have many different formats and aliases. Each intermediate machine will and can add a line to show the path of the email before reaching you. The `Message-ID` field (line 10) is a unique number used to identify your message. These are the system fields and will be handled by various email agents and systems.

The user input areas include the `From` field (line 11) that contains the identity and address of the sender. The `To` field (line 12) shows the recipient of the email. The `Subject` field (line 13) provides a description of the message. The `Cc` field (line 14) contains the identity addresses of any other users that should also have a copy of the message. Together with the email body, these are the controllable fields that we are going to use with our Web technologies.

The `Date` field (line 15) lists the date when the original email was sent. The remaining information (lines 16–23) specifies the email document type and the identity of the mail agent.

Many mail agents have built-in extensions to include some functions such as multimedia, special international language sets, encryption, and many others. Let's begin with a discussion of email control with browsers.

13.2   Basic emailing with browsers

13.2.1 Activate email client with "Mailto"

The email (or mailto: URL) capability of a browser is a powerful feature that unfortunately is underused by many Web users. One reason for its low usage may be that users are not aware of its multiple and controllable features. For example, the multiple attributes support the `cc`, `bcc`, `subject`, and `body` fields. For many applications, including the handling of user feedback, signing up for a mail list on product promotions, or newsletters and complaints, the ability to activate a mail client locally and assemble a mail message is essential and deserves more attention from Web developers.

As part of the XHTML language and script, mailto (or mailto: URL) provides a simple way to activate an email client on a system. Mailto is not an XHTML element. It is an action and can be invoked inside the anchor or form element. A simple way of using mailto: URL is given below:

```
<a href="mailto: ">Activate Email Client</a>
```

When the underlined text is pressed, the mailto action will activate the default mail client of your system. The first email example ex13-01.htm puts this statement into action.

```
Example: ex13-01.htm - Email With Mailto I

 1: <?xml version="1.0" encoding="iso-8859-1"?>
 2: <!DOCTYPE html PUBLIC "-//W3C//DTD XHTML 1.0 Transitional//EN"
 3:      "http://www.w3.org/TR/xhtml1/DTD/xhtml1-transitional.dtd">
 4: <html xmlns="http://www.w3.org/1999/xhtml" xml:lang="en" lang="en">
 5: <head><title>Email With Mailto I -- ex13-01.htm</title></head>
 6: <body style="background:#000088;text-align:center;font-family:arial">
 7:    <div ><br /><br />
 8:    <a href="mailto:" style="font-size:16pt;color:#ffff00">
 9:       <b>Activate Email Client</b>
10:    </a><br /><br /></div>
11: </body>
12: </html>
```

Line 8 launches the mail client. Since mailto is a hyper reference in XHTML, this action is independent of browsers and systems. For example, if the user browses this page with IE and clicks the underlined text in line 9, Outlook Express or Outlook appears as shown in Fig. 13.5. We use Outlook Express for demonstration purposes throughout this chapter. If you have a different default email client, the result may be different on your screen.

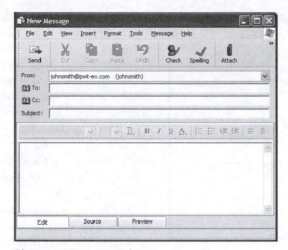

Figure 13.5 ex13-01.htm

If you have a default email account in the system, your email address will appear in the From field of the mail client. To complete the email, you may need to fill in the To and Subject fields and of course the Body before sending it out. All these requirements lead to the next question: "Can we fill in those fields inside a Web page?"

The mailto action supports a number of parameters in order to help fill in those input fields. If you want to send an email to info.abc.com, you can use

```
<a href="mailto:info@abc.com">
```

If you want to make a copy of the message to someone such as john@abc.com, you can add the cc field as:

```
<a href="mailto:info@abc.com?cc=john@abc.com">
```

The question mark before the cc is essential. You can add other properties such as bcc (blind copy), subject, and body as name/value pairs (name=value). Each name is followed by an equals sign and a value. In general the list of name/value pairs is separated from the email address by a question mark (?). Individual name/value properties are separated from each other by an ampersand (&). The following example should make the rules easy to understand:

```
<a href="mailto:info@abc.com?cc=John@abc.com&subject=Comments">
```

As a simple application, we apply the mailto and its name/value rules to develop a page to get comments from customers.

```
Example: ex13-02.htm - Email With Mailto II

 1: <;xml version="1.0" encoding="iso-8859-1"?>
 2: <!DOCTYPE html PUBLIC "-//W3C//DTD XHTML 1.0 Transitional//EN"
 3:      "http://www.w3.org/TR/xhtml1/DTD/xhtml1-transitional.dtd">
 4: <html xmlns="http://www.w3.org/1999/xhtml" xml:lang="en" lang="en">
 5: <head><title>Email With Mailto II -- ex13-02.htm</title></head>
 6: <body style="background:#000088;text-align:center;font-family:arial">
 7:   <div ><br /><br />
 8:   <a href="mailto:info@abc.com?cc=John@abc.com&subject=Comments&body=
 9:      Please Give Us Some Comments" style="font-size:16pt;color:#ffff00">
10:    <b>Click Here To Give Us<br /> Some Feedback</b>
11:   </a><br /><br /></div>
12: </body>
13: </html>
```

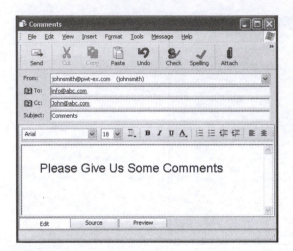

Figure 13.6 ex13-02.htm

The anchor element with mailto in line 8 is used to activate the mail client. The email addresses of the recipients, info@abc.com and cc=John@abc.com, are, of course, used here as an example. The word "Comments" is put into the subject line and finally the simple message "Please Give Us Some Comments" in the email body. This page will automatically open a new email by using the default email client and fill in the To, Subject, Cc, and Body fields. If the user is using an IE browser and the default mail client is Outlook Express, then the corresponding screen display is as shown in Fig. 13.6.

The body pair (name/value pair) in line 8 can be a message with multiple paragraphs. To generate new paragraphs this way, hexadecimal code may be needed in your message. For example, the carriage return (%0D) and line feed (%0A) codes are combined together as %0D%0A to insert a new line for Microsoft systems. Only carriage return is needed in UNIX (or LINUX) systems. Since question marks and ampersands are used as delimiters in the mailto action, hexadecimal notation should be used to prevent any confusion.

Users may need to press the Send button on Outlook Express to send the mail. For practical reasons such as integrity and consistency, you may want to embed the mail client into your Web design. So can we actually write and send emails within a Web page?

13.2.2 A feedback page

One example of using email within a Web page is to get visitors' comments or feedback. You may want to find out how visitors view and feel about your site or services. A simple feedback page usually contains the following features:

- A recipient field which contains your Web site address.
- A text area for the user to enter his or her comments.
- A Send button to send the email.

Forms and tables are usually used to implement these features. As a demonstration, the following example page ex13-03.htm is considered:

```
Example: ex13-03.htm - A Page For Feedback

 1: <?xml version="1.0" encoding="iso-8859-1"?>
 2: <!DOCTYPE html PUBLIC "-//W3C//DTD XHTML 1.0 Transitional//EN"
 3:     "http://www.w3.org/TR/xhtml1/DTD/xhtml1-transitional.dtd">
 4: <html xmlns="http://www.w3.org/1999/xhtml" xml:lang="en" lang="en">
 5: <head><title>Customer Feedback Page -- ex13-03.htm</title></head>
 6: <style>
 7:   .tx01{font-size:14pt;color:#ffff00;background:#a0a0ff;font-weight:bold}
 8:   .tx02{font-size:22pt;color:#ffff00;font-weight:bold;text-align:center}
 9:   .butSt{background-color:#aaffaa;font-family:arial;font-weight:bold;
10:       font-size:12pt;color:#008800;width:80px;height:30px}
11: </style>
12: <body style="background:#000088;text-align:center;font-family:arial">
13: <br>
14: <form name="mail" method='post' enctype="text/plain"
```

```
15:    action='mailto:info@pwt-ex.com?subject=Comments'>
16: <table border="2" width="440" class="tx01">
17: <tr><td colspan="2" class="tx02"> User Feedback Form</td></tr>
18: <tr><td>To (Email):</td><td>info@pwt-ex.com</td></tr>
19: <tr><td>Subject:</td><td>User Comments</td></tr>
20: <tr><td valign=top>Comments:</td><td>
21:    <textarea name="Feedback Ref:#21-23" id="Feedback Ref:#21-23" rows="8"
22:       cols="40" wrap="yes"></textarea></td></tr>
23: <tr>
24: <td align="center"><input type="submit" value="Send" class="butSt"></td>
25: <td align="center"><input type="reset" value="Re-type" class="butSt"></td>
26: </tr>
27: </table>
28: </form>
29: </body>
30: </html>
```

This page is a form application. Line 14 gives this form a name and an identity as "mail." The processing method used in this form is called "post." Basically, this means that when the user presses the Send button defined in line 24, elements with the name attribute inside this form will be passed to the mail client as name/value pairs and appear in the mail body. The processing action

```
action='mailto:info@pwt-ex.com?subject=Comments'
```

is a `mailto` command to fill the controllable fields and deliver the mail. The only name/value pair inside the form element is the text area element `<textarea>` defined in lines 21–22. We use text area to create a user-input field for the contents of the email body. Any information inside the text area is considered as the value of the element `<textarea>`. Together with the name attribute, we have a name/value pair that will be sent to the form action once the Send button is pressed. In practice the name of the text area could also have additional reference codes for other practical (e.g., statistical) purposes.

Finally, a Re-type button (line 25) is used to clear all data and be ready for the next session. Figure 13.7 is a screen display of this page.

The `action` attribute of a form usually holds the URL of a Common Gateway Interface (CGI). This means that some applications on the server can be called and executed by using the form. Thus we can also use it to send an email via the server. This will be discussed later in this chapter. A screen shot of the mail in the Outbox of Outlook Express is shown in Fig. 13.8.

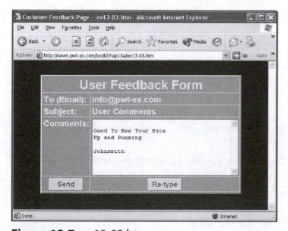

Figure 13.7 ex13-03.htm

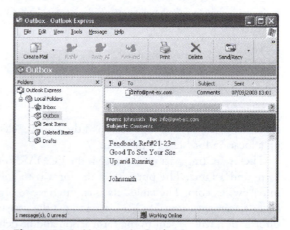

Figure 13.8 Message in Outbox

13.2.3 Signing up to a mailing list

In addition to user feedback, another popular action on the Web is to get the user's information. For example, signing up for a newsletter or joining a mailing list is a very common activity on the Internet. Many commercial sectors use the sign-up information to form a customer database for the purposes of product promotion, market research, targeted online sales, and others. As a user, signing up for the mailing list is a good way to obtain useful information.

There are a number of ways to implement a user sign-up form. For example, you can modify the example ex13-03.htm to get the email address or any other information about the user. The next example shows how to use the ECMAScript strings technique to implement a sign-up form. One advantage of using script is that XHTML statements can be formatted as a single string. This string can then be used again and be placed anywhere on the page. This technique opens up a way for code independence and hence increases the reusability of programming codes.

Consider the following page:

Example: ex13-04.htm – Signing Up For A Mailing List

```
 1: <?xml version="1.0" encoding="iso-8859-1"?>
 2: <!DOCTYPE html PUBLIC "-//W3C//DTD XHTML 1.0 Transitional//EN"
 3:     "http://www.w3.org/TR/xhtml1/DTD/xhtml1-transitional.dtd">
 4: <html xmlns="http://www.w3.org/1999/xhtml" xml:lang="en" lang="en">
 5: <head><title>Send Catalog -- ex13-04.htm</title></head>
 6: <style>
 7:   .tx01{font-size:14pt;color:#000000;background:#a0a0ff;font-weight:bold}
 8:   .butSt{background-color:#aaffaa;font-family:arial;font-weight:bold;
 9:       font-size:12pt;color:#ff0000;width:80px;height:26px}
10: </style>
11:
12: <body style="background:#ffffff;text-align:center;font-family:arial">
13: <br /><br /><div id="mailformL" name="mailformL"></div>
14:
15: <script>
16: var llSt = '<form name="mail" method="post" enctype="text/plain"'+
17: ' action="mailto:info@pwt-ex.com?subject=Email"> '+
18: '<table border="2" width="400" class="tx01"> <tr> '+
19: ' <td style="text-align:center">Sign Up For The Mailing List</td></tr>'+
20: '<tr><td height="60" valign="middle">  Email:'+
21: ' <input type="text" name="Email" class="butSt" '+
22: '    style="color:#000000;width:200px;height:26px" />  '+
23: ' <input type="submit" value="Send" class="butSt" /></td></tr>'+
24: '</table> </form>'
25:
26:   document.getElementById("mailformL").innerHTML=llSt
27: </script>
28: </body>
29: </html>
```

After the definitions of CSS style and the `<body>` element, a division element `<div>` is used in line 13 to set up a location for the sign-up form.

The interesting part of this page is the ECMAScript string in lines 16–24. This string contains an XHTML form and a table. The purpose of the form is to collect the email address and to send the information to info@pwt-ex.com. The table acts as an interface to organize the display. Inside the second row of the table, an input statement (lines 21–22) is used to get the user input. When the user presses the Send button, the input information will be sent to the form action and be delivered to the mail client.

Once you have constructed the string `llSt`, you can use the `getElementById` feature (line 26) to send this string to the location you want. Any string similar to this can be reused many times.

On a practical note, you may need to include the CSS style and any other formatting statements inside the string in order to increase code independence. If you prefer you can also replace the statement in line 26 by the write statement `document.write(llSt)` to produce screen output since innerHTML is not a W3C feature. A screen shot of this page is shown in Fig. 13.9.

In a normal case, the recipient's address is hardwired into the mailto: URL command. Can we change that at run time? In other words, can we send email to anyone we like inside a Web page?

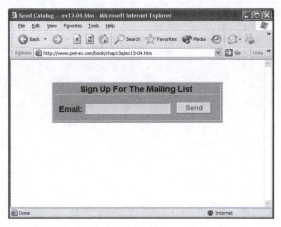

Figure 13.9 ex13-04htm

13.2.4 Sending email to someone anywhere

In order to send an email to someone within a Web page (i.e., Web Mail), you need to compose the recipient's address inside the mailto: URL command at run time. How can we do that? The basic idea is simple. You build the entire `mailto` command after the user fills in the recipient's address and before the actual delivery. By using the script function, this can be done in a simple way. Consider the following example:

```
Example: ex13-05.htm - Send Email To Someone Anywhere

 1: <?xml version="1.0" encoding="iso-8859-1"?>
 2: <!DOCTYPE html PUBLIC "-//W3C//DTD XHTML 1.0 Transitional//EN"
 3:     "http://www.w3.org/TR/xhtml1/DTD/xhtml1-transitional.dtd">
 4: <html xmlns="http://www.w3.org/1999/xhtml" xml:lang="en" lang="en">
 5: <head><title>Send Email To Someone Anywhere- ex13-05.htm</title></head>
 6: <style>
 7:   .tx01{font-size:12pt;color:#000000;background:#a0a0ff;font-weight:bold}
 8:   .butSt{background-color:#aaffaa;font-family:arial;font-weight:bold;
 9:       font-size:12pt;color:#ff0000;width:80px;height:26px}
10: </style>
11: <script>
12: function webMail()
13: {
14:     var emailTo=document.mail.To.value
15:     emailTo = "mailto:" + emailTo + "?subject="+
16:               document.mail.Subject.value
17:     this.document.mail.action = emailTo
18:     this.document.mail.submit=true
19:     return true
20:  }
21: </script>
22:
23: <body style="text-align:center;font-family:arial;background:#ffffff">
24:  <br /><form enctype="text/plain" name="mail" id="mail" method="post"
25:      action='' onSubmit="webMail()">
26:  <table border="2" width="440" class="tx01">
27:  <tr align="center"><td colspan="2">Send Email To Someone Anywhere</tr>
28:  <tr><td><input type="hidden"
29:      name="=Message Handled By Web Mail (www.pwt-ex.com)" /></td></tr>
30:  <tr><td>To (Email):</td><td>
```

```
31:    <input type="text" name="To" id="To" size="40" maxlength="40" /></td>
32:    </tr><tr><td>Subject:</td>
33:        <td><input type="text" name="Subject" id="Subject" size="40"
34:          maxlength="40" value="Web Mail" /></td></tr>
35:    <tr><td valign=top>Content:</td>
36:        <td><textarea name="Email Content" rows="8" cols="40"
37:          wrap="yes"></textarea></td></tr><tr>
38:    <td align="center"><input type="submit" value="Send" class="butSt"></td>
39:    <td align="center"><input type="reset" value="Reset" class="butSt"></td>
40:    </tr>
41:    </table>
42:    </form>
43:    </body>
44:    </html>
```

A form application is used to implement this email. The form has a name and an identity `id="mail"` (line 24). The interesting part is the empty action in line 25 and a new event handler called `onSubmit="webMail()"`. This means that the script function `webMail()` is called once the Send button (line 38) is pressed. Since you will compose the details of the `mailto` command inside the `webMail()` function, you can assign an empty action at this point.

The interface part of this page is a table defined in lines 26–41. This table is designed to get the address of the recipient, subject, and contents of the email. For example, the statement in line 31

```
<input type="text" name="To" id="To" size="40" maxlength="40" />
```

defines an input field with 40 characters for a user to type the email address of the recipient. The input address will have a name and an identity called "To." The same input structure is also used for the "subject" field in lines 33–34. Lines 36–37 define a text area with dimension 8 rows by 40 columns for the content of the email.

Once the Send button is pressed, the `onSubmit` handler will call the script function `webMail()` defined in lines 12–20. The first line of this function is to get the address of the recipient, which is stored inside the variable `document.mail.To.value`. Then the `mailto` command is composed with the `address` and `subject` fields (lines 15–16). This `mailto` command string is then assigned to the form action as shown in line 17. Finally, the form's `submit` value is set to true so that the mail can be sent accordingly.

Notice that the `document.name` access method is used instead of `getElementById` so that this `webMail()` function will work on some older versions of browsers and can be reused as a library function. A screen shot of this page is shown in Fig. 13.10. You can

Figure 13.10 ex13-05.htm

also put more addresses, each separated by a semi-colon, in the "To" field to send the email to multiple users. This is called group mail since every one of the group appears in the "To" field of the mail. If you want to send independent emails to each person in a group within a browser, you need the following techniques.

13.2.5 Sending multiple emails

One important feature in word processing is mail merging. For mail merging to work, you need a list of customer names and addresses that are stored in a list, a file, or a database. Once you have constructed a letter, you can merge the names and addresses from the list into the appropriate locations of the letter. The results can then be printed one by one. Many word processor programs also offer email merging capability so that you can send emails to a list of people or customers.

One way to send multiple emails within a browser is to use two forms. The first form is usually an interface used to get the contents of the email message. Based on the content, another form is then created on the fly and submitted as a completed email. Since the second form is represented as a script function, sending multiple emails is just an application of multiple submissions. The first form is listed as below.

```
Example: ex13-06.htm - Multiple Emails

 1: <?xml version="1.0" encoding="iso-8859-1"?>
 2: <!DOCTYPE html PUBLIC "-//W3C//DTD XHTML 1.0 Transitional//EN"
 3:     "http://www.w3.org/TR/xhtml1/DTD/xhtml1-transitional.dtd">
 4: <html xmlns="http://www.w3.org/1999/xhtml" xml:lang="en" lang="en">
 5: <head><title>Multiple Emails -- ex13-06.htm</title></head>
 6: <style>
 7:   .tx01{font-size:12pt;color:#000000;background:#a0a0ff;font-weight:bold}
 8:   .butSt{background-color:#aaffaa;font-family:arial;font-weight:bold;
 9:       font-size:12pt;color:#ff0000;width:80px;height:26px}
10: </style>
11: <script src="ex13-06.js"></script>
12: <body style="text-align:center;font-family:arial;background:#ffffff">
13: <div id="mailL"><br />
14:   <form enctype="text/plain" name="mail" id="mail" method="post"
15:       action="" onSubmit="">
16:   <table border="2" width="440" class="tx01">
17:   <tr align="center"><td colspan="2">Send Multiple Emails</tr>
18:   <tr><td>Subject:</td>
19:       <td><input type="text" name="Subject" id="Subject" size="40"
20:         maxlength="40" value="Message" /></td></tr>
21:   <tr><td valign=top>Content:</td>
22:       <td><textarea name="Content" id="Content" rows="8" cols="40"
23:         wrap="yes"></textarea></td></tr>
24:   <tr><td align="center"><input type="button" value="Send" class="butSt"
25:       onclick="mEmail()"></td><td align="center">
26:       <input type="reset" value="Reset" class="butSt"></td>
27:   </tr>
28: </table>
29: </form>
30: </div>
31: </body>
32: </html>
```

This is a form with a `subject` and a `content` field so that the user can type in anything. The entire form is embedded inside a division named `mailL` (lines 13–30). This location, and hence the form, will be replaced by a second form. The script function `mEmail()` in line 25 is activated once the Send button is pressed. For reasons of clarity and readability, the detail of this function is coded in an external file ex13-06.js. As expected, this `mEmail()` function will perform the following tasks. It can

- generate a second form on the fly;
- catch the subject and content;
- merge a list of email names and addresses; and finally
- deliver the multiple emails one by one.

The detail of the ECMAScript file ex13-06.js is listed as follows:

```
Example: ex13-06.js - The ECMAScript For Example ex13-06.htm
 1: ii=0      // Variable to control the number of Email addresses
 2: cFlag=0   // Email Content Flag, if 0 get subject and message content
 3: fFlag=0   // Finish Flag
 4: emailAdd = new Array()
 5: fName = new Array()
 6: emailAdd[1]="John@pwt-ex.com"
 7: emailAdd[2]="Peter@pwt-ex.com"
 8: emailAdd[3]="Mary@pwt-ex.com"
 9: emailAdd[4]="Tom@pwt-ex.com"
10: fName[1]="John"
11: fName[2]="Peter"
12: fName[3]="Mary"
13: fName[4]="Tom"
14:
15: function mEmail() {
16:  ii++
17:  if (ii < emailAdd.length)
18:  {
19:    if (cFlag ==0)
20:    {
21:      bodyContent=document.mail.Content.value
22:      mailSubject=document.mail.Subject.value
23:      cFlag=1
24:    }
25:  lst='<form method="post" name="mailform" ENCTYPE="text/plain" '+
26:      'onSubmit="" action="mailto:'+emailAdd[ii]+
27:      '?subject='+mailSubject+'" > '+
28:      '<textarea name="=MailServer" cols="40" rows="10">\n\nDear '+
29:      fName[ii]+'\n\n'+bodyContent+'\n\nFrom JohnSmith'
30:      '</textarea> <br /></form>'
31:   document.getElementById("mailL").innerHTML=lst
32:   document.mailform.submit()
33:   setTimeout("mEmail()",500)
34:  }
35:  else fFlag=1
36:
37:  if (fFlag==1)
38:  {
39:  fFlag =2
40:  mailList="You Have Sent Multiple Emails To: <br /><br />"
41:  for (jj=1;jj<emailAdd.length;jj++) mailList=mailList+emailAdd[jj]+"<br />"
42:   document.getElementById("mailL").innerHTML= mailList
43:  }
44:  return false
45: }
```

As an example, four artificial email addresses and names are defined in lines 6–13. In practice, these names and email addresses would normally be extracted from a list or a database. Within the mEmail() function, a counter variable ii is used to control the number of emails that you want to send. Thus if the counter value is more than the length of the array emailAdd (i.e., email address), you have sent all emails and the finish flag (fFlag=1) is set to true. If the content flag cFlag has a zero value, you need to get the subject and content fields from the interface and insert them into the multiple emails.

Again, the string technique is used to construct the multiple emails. The content of the string variable `lst` is in fact a form with `mailto` as action. As you can see in lines 26–27, the recipient's address and subject are added to the form as a concatenation of strings. A text area is then used as the final touch of the email so that the first name of the recipient, `bodyContent`, and the sender's name can be integrated together.

For each composed email, an `innerHTML` statement is used in line 31 to display it on the screen to allow a final monitoring of the multiple emails. The `setTimeout()` function will call this function once every half second, change the name and address of the recipient, and deliver the email again.

Once all the emails are delivered, a message as defined in lines 40–42 is displayed to indicate the successful completion of the application. Some screen shots are listed in Figs 13.11–13.13. If you are using Outlook Express as the mail client, you can find all four emails inside the Outbox (see Fig. 13.14).

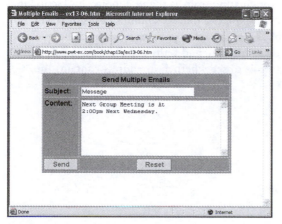

Figure 13.11 ex13-06.htm (I)

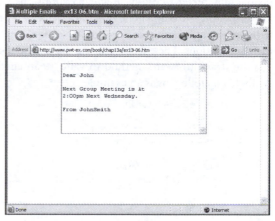

Figure 13.12 ex13-06.htm (II)

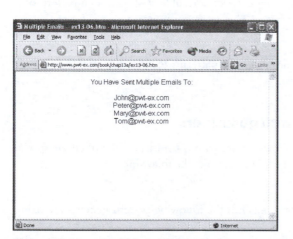

Figure 13.13 ex13-06.htm (III)

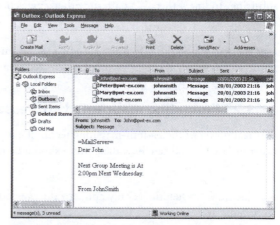

Figure 13.14 Multiple emails in Outlook Express

In addition to some passive applications such as user feedback, error reporting, and complaints, sending multiple emails within a browser is also a handy tool for the administrators and staff working in a small or medium-size corporate network with mail servers. The next section looks at a classical problem in the Internet related to emailing, i.e., verification or detection of a malformed email address.

13.3 Verifying email addresses using pattern matching

13.3.1 Pattern matching and emailing

In the early days of Web design and businesses, one of the daily problems that the network administrators faced was the increasing amount of invalid email addresses. Unlike other information, an email address has to be precise and complete so that mail can be delivered properly. Just imagine how many times you have put spaces, commas, semi-colons, and more than one "@" symbol in an email address. Before the advent of so-called fourth-generation browser software, e.g., IE4+ and NS4+, to pick up these errors and validate an email address was a difficult problem.

One effective and convenient way of validating an email address is by means of pattern matching. Some people may prefer to call it "Regular Expressions," a term originating from Perl and adopted by JScript and ECMAScript. Pattern matching has always been a popular and powerful tool for administrators of UNIX systems and every Perl programmer. In this section, we will look at some practical pattern-matching techniques and their applications. These techniques can be used to analyze the user's input and verify a malformed email address.

One straightforward method to validate an email address is to see whether an address contains the "@" symbol. The following is an example:

```
Listing: ex13-02.txt

1: <script>
2: function isEmail(valSt)
3: {
4:   var patSt = /@/
5:   return( patSt.test(valSt) )
6: }
7: </script>
```

This is a simple script function. The input argument `valSt` is a string to be searched and matched by some predefined patterns. As a special feature of scripting, anything between a double slash defines a pattern or a substring. In line 4 there is a pattern with a single character "@." The statement in line 5

```
patSt.test(valSt)
```

uses the test method to search the string `valSt` against and match the pattern stored in the variable `patSt`. It returns a false value if no "@" symbol is detected in `valSt`.

13.3.2 Eliminating malformed addresses with quantifiers

The real power of the pattern-matching technique is to validate strings with quantifiers. Quantifiers are special notation used to indicate how the pattern should be matched. For example, the following

```
/(@){2}/
```

matches "@@". Quantifiers only apply to the previous pattern. Thus the following pattern matches the string "JohnSmithh":

```
"JohnSmith{2}"
```

If you want a quantifier to apply to a string of multiple characters, you must group them together by means of braces. For example,

`"John(Smith){2}"` **matches the string** `"JohnSmithSmith"`

Table 13.1 contains some frequently used quantifiers.

Tabel 13.1 Quantifiers

Quantifier	Description
{m,n}	Must occur at least m times, but not more than n times
{n,}	Must occur at least n times
{n}	Must occur exactly n times
*	Must occur 0 or more times (same as {0,})
+	Must occur 1 or more times (same as {1,})
?	Must occur 0 or 1 time (same as {0,1})

To understand quantifiers and their applications to address validation, let's consider the pattern

```
/(@.*@)/
```

This pattern won't be matched unless a string contains more than one "@" symbol. First it starts with the "@" symbol. The period "." represents any character. Together with the quantifier "*," you have a pattern that will match any string with two "@" symbols somewhere, whether or not they are together or are separated by one or more characters.

This provides a powerful tool for searching and eliminating email addresses with more than one "@" symbol in the address string. To see how quantifiers work, let's look at the following function:

```
Listing: ex13-03.txt

1: function isEmail(valSt)
2: {
3:   var patSt = /.+@/
4:   var patSt2 = /(@.*@)/
5:   return( patSt.test(valSt) && ! patSt2.test(valSt) )
6: }
```

This function has two match patterns. The first pattern patSt defines a positive format for an email address. This means email addresses should have the "@" symbol after some characters. The second pattern patSt2 defines a negative format. This format represents some common errors that the user may make when writing an email address. The return statement in line 5 will return true only if the input string valSt matches the first pattern (patSt) and not the second one (patSt2). This function can be used to correctly identify the following types of common malformed addresses:

@pwt-ex.com	(@ cannot be the first character)
JohnSmith.pwt-ex.com	(missing the @ symbol)
John@Smith@pwt-ex.com	(more than one @ symbol)

Of course malformed addresses come in different forms. You need more match patterns to eliminate the malformed addresses. Consider the following:

/(\.\.)/	matches	JohnSmith@pwt-ex..com
/(@\.)/	matches	JohnSmith@.pwt-ex.com
/(^\.)/	matches	.JohnSmith@pwt-ex.com

As discussed, a period or full stop symbol in pattern matching matches any character. If a special character such as a period "." needs to be matched, you simply put a backslash before the special character as shown in the patterns above. A caret (or hat) symbol "^" is used to instruct the match engine to search at the beginning. The following example page illustrates how to put these patterns into action.

Example: ex13-07.htm - Validate Email Addresses (I)

```
1:  <?xml version="1.0" encoding="iso-8859-1"?>
2:  <!DOCTYPE html PUBLIC "-//W3C//DTD XHTML 1.0 Transitional//EN"
3:     "http://www.w3.org/TR/xhtml1/DTD/xhtml1-transitional.dtd">
4:  <html xmlns="http://www.w3.org/1999/xhtml" xml:lang="en" lang="en">
5:  <head><title>Validate Email Addresses (I) -- ex13-07.htm</title></head>
6:  <body style="font-family:arial;font-size:16pt;background:#000088;
7:     color:#ffff00;text-align:center">
8:  <script>
9:  function isEmail(valSt)
10:   {
11:    var patSt = /.+@/
12:    var patSt2 = /(.*@.*@)|(\.\.)|(@\.)|(^\.)/
13:    return( patSt.test(valSt) && ! patSt2.test(valSt) )
14:   }
15:
16:   emailAdd = new Array()
17:   emailAdd[1]="JohnSmith@pwt-ex.com"
18:   emailAdd[2]="John@Smith@pwt-ex.com"
19:   emailAdd[3]="JohnSmith@.pwt-ex.com"
20:   emailAdd[4]="JohnSmith@isp..com "
21:   emailAdd[5]=".JohnSmith@pwt-ex.com"
22:   emailAdd[6]="@pwt-ex.com"
23:
24:  for (ii=1;ii<emailAdd.length;ii++)
25:  {
26:  document.write(emailAdd[ii]+" is likely a "+isEmail(emailAdd[ii])+
27:     " Email address<br />")
28:  }
29:
30:  </script>
31:
32:  </body>
33:  </html>
```

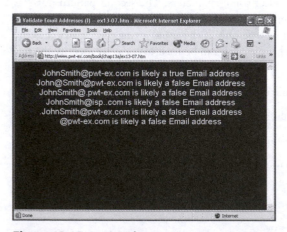

Figure 13.15 ex13-07.htm

With the detailed explanation above, this example is easy to understand. Basically, all malformed address formats are integrated into one pattern. The vertical bar "|" in line 12 is a conditional "OR" operator which allows us to have a single pattern to match a variety of malformed addresses. A screen shot of this page is given in Fig. 13.15.

To detect some malformed addresses is unfortunately only the first step in validating correct email addresses. It is not easy (if not impossible) to include all the different ways an email address can go wrong. For example, a user can accidentally put a space or a non-printable character anywhere in the email address. You need a more constructive method to accomplish this difficult task. To this end, a discussion on some special symbols and rules for pattern matching is helpful.

13.3.3 Some rules for pattern matching

As discussed earlier, pattern matching is a subject originating from the Perl language. Only a simplified version is discussed here, with the emphasis on the validation of email addresses. Let's begin with some general rules (Table 13.2); you have already seen some of them in previous sections.

Table 13.2 General rules for pattern matching

^	Matches at the beginning of the string. For example, /^@/ matches any string beginning with @
$	Matches at the end of the string. For example, /$@/ matches any string ending with @
( )	A pattern in parentheses matches the pattern inside
.	Matches any character. For example, .* matches any number of don't-care characters
[ ]	A pattern in square brackets (called a list of characters) matches any one of the characters in the list

For a character list, a hyphen may be used as a range delimiter. For example, the pattern /[a-z 0-9]/ matches any character from a to z or 0 to 9. A caret (^) at the beginning of the list causes it to match only characters that are not in the list. For example, the pattern /[^0-9]/ matches any non-digit character.

Characters that have special meaning are metacharacters and they don't match themselves. Some frequently used metacharacters are

```
^ $ * + ? . \ | ( ) [ ] { }
```

To match these characters, you put a backslash in front of them. For example, \\ matches a backslash and \$ matches a dollar sign. A backslash can also be used to turn an alphanumeric character into a metacharacter with special meaning. For example, \t matches a tab character, while \d matches any digit. Table 13.3 shows some of these commonly used backslash characters.

Table 13.3 Meaning of metacharacters

\n	Line feed
\r	Carriage return
\t	Tab
\v	Vertical tab
\f	Form feed
\d	A digit (same as [0-9])
\D	A non-digit (same as [^0-9])
\w	A word (alphanumeric) character (same as [a-zA-Z_0-9])
\W	A non-word character (same as [^a-zA-Z_0-9])
\s	A white space character (same as [\t\v\n\r\f])
\S	A non-white space character (same as [^ \t\v\n\r\f])

Parentheses around a pattern, or a part of a pattern, cause the string's portion that is matched by that part to be remembered for later use. Consider the following expressions

```
/\d+/ and /(\d+)/
```

that will match as many digits as possible. However, in the latter case, the matched substring will be remembered in a special variable called `backreference` (back reference). Back reference is defined by `\#`, where # is an integer. As an example, the following pattern expression matches a string whose first two characters are also its last two characters, but in reverse order:

```
/^(.)(.).*\2\1$/
```

One popular use of this expression is to match strings such as "/**Comment**/." Note that paired parentheses are numbered by counting the parentheses from the left. The next section shows how to use these rules to match email addresses.

13.3.4 A constructive pattern to match an email address

The basic syntax of an email address can be described by the following rules. It normally consists of:

- one or more normal characters `[a-zA-Z_0-9]` together with a combination of "_" (underscore), "." (period), and "-" (hyphen) before the "@" symbol;
- a sequence of letters, numbers, and periods which are all valid domain or IP address characters; and
- a period followed by a suffix of two–three letters of one–three digits at the end of the address.

In terms of matching patterns, the first rule can be represented by the expression

```
^\w+([\.-]?\w+)*@
```

That is, any email address should begin with a normal character `[a-zA-Z_0-9]` and then be followed by a combination of a single period or a hyphen and more normal characters before the "@" symbol. The second rule is very similar to the first one and can be matched by the expression

```
\w+([\.-]?\w+)*
```

and finally the end part by

```
(\.(([a-zA-Z]{2,3})|(\d{1,3})))+$
```

By combining all three expressions together, you will have a simple email syntax that can be used to determine a valid email address, i.e.,

```
/^\w+([\.-]?\w+)*@\w+([\.-]?\w+)*(\.(([a-zA-Z]{2,3})|(\d{1,3})))+$/
```

Consider the following page:

```
Example: ex13-08.htm - Validate Email Addresses (II)

 1: <?xml version="1.0" encoding="iso-8859-1"?>
 2: <!DOCTYPE html PUBLIC "-//W3C//DTD XHTML 1.0 Transitional//EN"
 3:     "http://www.w3.org/TR/xhtml1/DTD/xhtml1-transitional.dtd">
 4: <html xmlns="http://www.w3.org/1999/xhtml" xml:lang="en" lang="en">
 5: <head><title>Validate Email Addresses (II) -- ex13-08.htm</title></head>
 6: <body style="font-family:arial;font-size:16pt;background:#000088;
 7:    color:#ffff00;text-align:center">
 8: <script>
 9: function isEmail(valSt)
10: {
```

```
11:   patSt=/^\w+([\.-]?\w+)*@\w+([\.-]?\w+)*(\.(([a-zA-Z]{2,3})|(\d{1,3})))+$/
12:   return( patSt.test(valSt))
13: }
14:
15:   emailAdd = new Array()
16:   emailAdd[1]="JohnSmith@pwt-ex.com"
17:   emailAdd[2]="John@Smith@pwt-ex.com"
18:   emailAdd[3]="JohnSmith@.pwt-ex.com"
19:   emailAdd[4]="JohnSmith@isp..com "
20:   emailAdd[5]=".JohnSmith@pwt-ex.com"
21:   emailAdd[6]="@pwt-ex.com"
22:   emailAdd[7]="John Smith@pwt-ex.com"
23:   emailAdd[8]="JohnSmith@.i sp.com"
24:   emailAdd[9]="JohnSmith@isp;com "
25:   emailAdd[10]="JohnSmith@isp,com"
26:   emailAdd[11]="JohnSmith@isp:com"
27:   emailAdd[12]="JohnSmith@isp.u"
28:   emailAdd[13]="JohnSmith@231.198.198.1"
29:
30: for (ii=1;ii<emailAdd.length;ii++)
31: {
32: document.write(emailAdd[ii]+" is likely a "+isEmail(emailAdd[ii])+
33:   " Email address<br />")
34: }
35:
36: </script>
37: </body>
38: </html>
```

Figure 13.16 ex13-08.htm

Thanks to the constructive pattern in line 11, the isEmail() function is incredibly simple. The remaining part of this page is similar to that of example ex13-07.htm. The corresponding screen display of this page is shown in Fig. 13.16. As can be seen from Fig. 13.16, this page is capable of picking up not only the most commonly known malformed email addresses as in ex13-07.htm, but also the following common mistakes:

John Smith@pwt-ex.com   **(A space between John and Smith)**

JohnSmith@i sp.com   **(A space in the domain name)**

`JohnSmith@isp;com`	**(A semi-colon instead of a period)**
`JohnSmith@isp,com`	**(A comma instead of a period)**
`JohnSmith@isp:com`	**(A colon instead of a period)**
`JohnSmith@pwt-ex.u`	**(Last part of domain name contains only one letter)**

As an additional remark, any IP address inside a square bracket is also a valid email address. So the address JohnSmith@[231.198.198.1] is the same as JohnSmith@231.198.198.1. To include the square bracket in the match pattern, you can use the following:

```
/^\w+([\.-]?\w+)*@(\[)?\w+([\.-]?\w+)*
       (\.((([a-zA-Z]{2,3})|(\d{1,3})(\))?))+$/
```

This is a practical expression and can be used in your application. Again, this is by no means a complete or a perfect expression to detect all malformed addresses. It is virtually impossible to come up with a matching expression, or expressions, that would include all human errors in email addresses.

13.4 Controlling email with ASP and PHP server script

13.4.1 The basic ASP framework to send email

So far we have said a great deal about browsers, ECMAScript (or client-side script), and their applications on the Web. Client-side scripting is great for animating Web pages, and performing local data validation, computations, and manipulations. However the Internet, and hence its related Web technologies, is about the creation and integration of large-scale client–server applications. From this point of view, XHTML at large can be considered as a straight-through client–server application on the Internet since the server pays no attention to the page content.

If you want to build real server applications on the Web, you will need to concentrate more on the server side. In particular, server scripts and their practical usage on the Web are important. You have already encountered examples of ASP and PHP server scripts in Chapter 12. In this section, we continue to explore their applications to emailing. In section 13.5 we will discuss another server language called Perl and how to use it to send email.

Since the JScript of ASP is almost identical to ECMAScript, we begin this section with ASP. ASP is a Microsoft product and widely available on PC platforms. To use ASP to send email, you need something called the Collaboration Data Objects for NT Server (CDONTS) library. CDONTS is a component of Collaboration Data Objects (CDO) and is used to build Microsoft Windows and Internet-based messaging and collaboration applications. If you, or your ISP, run a Microsoft server system such as Microsoft NT or Windows with IIS, it is likely that you already have full ASP services installed and have the ability to send emails. Hence a server environment with CDONTS support is assumed when discussing all ASP programs.

The following page illustrates one of the simplest ways to send email by using ASP.

```
Example: ex13-09js.asp - My First Email With ASP

1: <%@language="JScript" %>
2:
3: <?xml version="1.0" encoding="iso-8859-1"?>
4: <!DOCTYPE html PUBLIC "-//W3C//DTD XHTML 1.0 Transitional//EN"
5:     "http://www.w3.org/TR/xhtml1/DTD/xhtml1-transitional.dtd">
6: <html xmlns="http://www.w3.org/1999/xhtml" xml:lang="en" lang="en">
7: <head><title>My First Email With ASP -- ex13-09js.asp</title></head>
8: <body style="font-family:arial;font-size:14pt;background:#000088">
9:
```

```
10: <%
11:  oMail = Server.CreateObject("CDONTS.NewMail");
12:  with (oMail) {
13:     To = "John@pwt-ex.com";
14:     From = "JohnSmith@pwt-ex.com";
15:     Subject = "Hello";
16:     Body = "Just want to say Hello";
17:     Send();
18:  }
19:  delete oMail;
20: %>
21:
22: <div> Mr. John Smith has Sent Email To John@pwt-ex.com</div>
23: </body>
24: </html>
```

The first line of this page is to activate ASP and to use JScript as the main server language. Lines 2–9 are the normal XHTML contents that the server will happily ignore. If you have CDONTS installed, the statement in line 11

```
oMail = Server.CreateObject("CDONTS.NewMail");
```

creates a server object called oMail by using the CDONTS.NewMail feature. Since oMail (object mail) is an object, it contains all the properties and member functions given by CDONTS.NewMail. The with statement in lines 12–18 is used to compose the email and send it out. In fact, if you prefer, you can use instead a direct call such as

```
oMail.To="John@pwt-ex.com";
oMail.From="JohnSmith@pwt-ex.com";
...
oMail.Send();
```

After the delivery of the email, a delete command (line 19) is used to terminate the object variable oMail. It is good programming practice to delete any object variables soon after finishing with them. Finally, line 22 is just a simple "feedback" message to acknowledge delivery. The structure in lines 10–20 is the basic framework for emailing with ASP.

For VBScript users, the following program fragment should help to convert this basic framework to its equivalent VBScript application:

```
Listing: ex13-04.txt - Code Fragment For VBScript

 1: <%@language="VBScript" %>
 2:
 3: <%
 4: Set oMail = Server.CreateObject("CDONTS.NewMail")
 5:
 6: With oMail
 7:     .To = "John@pwt-ex.com"
 8:     .From = "JohnSmith@pwt-ex.com"
 9:     .Subject = "Hello"
10:     .Body = "Just want to say Hello"
11:     .Send
12: End With
13:
14: Set oMail = nothing
15: %>
```

Replacing the JScript program block by this VBScript block yields a working version of ASP to send email. One common mistake when dealing with VBScript and JScript is that JScript is case sensitive whereas VBScript is not. The capital letters used in listing ex13-04.txt are purely for the purpose of improving readability and have no effect on the server. In general, we will use JScript as the default language for ASP.

Example page ex13-09js.asp is just a framework for sending mail by using ASP. A page like this has little practical value. To turn this page into a more functional one, you need to add at least an interface to get user input.

13.4.2 A general form to send email with data validation

For emailing to work, the interface part (usually an XHTML page) should contain at least the "To," "From," "Subject," and "Message" header fields so that proper email contents can be constructed from the server side. This type of page can easily be constructed as a form application. The following is an example:

```
Example: ex13-10.htm - A Page To Send Email

 1:  <?xml version="1.0" encoding="iso-8859-1"?>
 2:  <!DOCTYPE html PUBLIC "-//W3C//DTD XHTML 1.0 Transitional//EN"
 3:      "http://www.w3.org/TR/xhtml1/DTD/xhtml1-transitional.dtd">
 4:  <html xmlns="http://www.w3.org/1999/xhtml" xml:lang="en" lang="en">
 5:  <head><title> A Page To Send Email - ex13-10.htm </title></head>
 6:  <style>
 7:   .tx01{font-size:14pt;color:#ffff00;font-weight:bold}
 8:   .tx02{font-family:arial;font-size:14pt;background:#ffffff;color:#000000}
 9:   .butSt{background-color:#aaffaa;font-family:arial;font-weight:bold;
10:      font-size:14pt;color:#008800;width:80px;height:30px}
11:  </style>
12:  <script src="ex13-10.js"></script>
13:  <body style="background:#000088;font-family:arial;color:#00ee00">
14:  <div align="center" style="font-size:24pt;font-weight:bold">
15:   A Page To Send Email<br /><br />
16:   <form name="uMail" id="uMail" method="post"
17:     action="ex13-10js.asp">
18:   <table class="tx01">
19:   <tr><td>From: (Email Add.)</td>
20:     <td><input class="tx02" type="text" name="from" id="from"></td></tr>
21:    <tr><td>To: (Email Add.)</td>
22:     <td><input class="tx02" type="text" name="to" id="to"></td></tr>
23:    <tr><td>Subject:</td>
24:     <td><input class="tx02" type="text" name="subject" id="subject"></td>
25:   </tr><tr><td valign="top">Message:</td>
26:     <td><textarea name="message" id="message" class="tx02"
27:        rows="6" cols="40" wrap="yes"></textarea></td></tr><tr><td>
28:     <input class="butSt" type="button" value="Send" onclick="uChkMail()">
29:   </td><td><input class="butSt" type="reset" value="Reset"></td></tr>
30:   </table>
31:   </form>
32:   </div>
33:
34:  <script>
35:  function uChkMail()
36:  {
37:   if ( !uChkAddress("from") ) document.getElementById("from").focus()
38:   else if (!uChkAddress("to") ) document.getElementById("to").focus()
39:   else if (!uChkEmp("subject")) document.getElementById("subject").focus()
40:   else document.getElementById("uMail").submit()
41:      return true
```

```
42:  }
43:  </script>
44:
45:  </body>
46:  </html>
```

This Web page uses table and input elements to generate the necessary "To," "From," "Subject," and "Message" user input fields for emailing. Once the Send button in line 28 is clicked, an ECMAScript function uChkMail() (user check mail) is called. Sometimes, the naming convention could be useful to improve the structure and readability of your page.

The function uChkMail() is used to check valid email address and empty fields. For example, consider the statement in line 37:

```
if (!uChkAddress("from")) document.getElementById("from").focus()
```

This statement is to check whether the "from" field is a valid email address. If the user function uChkAddress("from") returns a false value, the standard function focus() will send the cursor back to the "from" field for modification and correction. The uChkEmp() function in line 39 is a function to check an empty field. You may notice that an external file ex13-10.js is declared in line 12 and the details of the above-mentioned functions are defined in this file.

```
Listing: ex13-10.js - External Program File For ex13-10.htm

 1:   function isEmail(valSt)
 2:   {
 3:    patSt=/^\w+([\.-]?\w+)*@\w+([\.-]?\w+)*(\.(([a-zA-Z]{2,3})|(\d{1,3})))+$/
 4:    return( patSt.test(valSt))
 5:   }
 6:
 7:   function uChkAddress(inAdd)
 8:   {
 9:    inVal = document.getElementById(inAdd).value
10:    if (isEmail(inVal)){
11:        return true
12:    } else {
13:        alert("Invalid Email Address! :"+inVal)
14:        return false
15:    }
16:   }
17:
18:
19:   function uChkEmp(inField)
20:   {
21:    inVal = document.getElementById(inField).value
22:    if (inVal =="") {
23:        alert("Empty "+ inField)
24:        return false
25:    } else {
26:        return true
27:    }
28:   }
```

The first function isEmail() performs a pattern-matching operation. This function will be called by the second function uChkAddress(). First, we obtain the address string by a getElementbyId() call in line 9. The address string is then tested by the isEmail function. There is a valid email address if the value of isEmail() in line 10 is true, otherwise an alert box containing an error message is displayed. The uChkEmp() function declared in lines 19–28 is to check whether the tested field is an empty field and returns the appropriate true or false value.

When all the "To," "From," and "Subject" fields are checked, a system function `submit()` is called to submit the form and "post" all data to the form action as shown in line 16 in ex13-10.htm. The form action activates the ASP program ex13-10js.asp located in the home directory of URL www.pwt-ex.com and ultimately sends the data as an email. A screen shot of this page is given in Fig. 13.17.

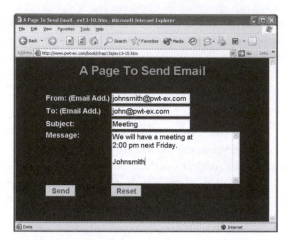

Figure 13.17 ex13-10.htm

In order to get the "To," "From," "Subject," and "Message" fields, the ASP program ex13-10js.asp needs to have a mechanism to catch them from the Web page. The ASP package contains a `Request` object and can be used to obtain any form data with a name. The ASP program is listed below.

```
Example: ex13-10js.asp - Emailing With ASP

 1: <%@language="JScript" %>
 2: <?xml version="1.0" encoding="iso-8859-1"?>
 3: <!DOCTYPE html PUBLIC "-//W3C//DTD XHTML 1.0 Transitional//EN"
 4:     "http://www.w3.org/TR/xhtml1/DTD/xhtml1-transitional.dtd">
 5: <html xmlns="http://www.w3.org/1999/xhtml" xml:lang="en" lang="en">
 6: <head><title>Emailing with ASP: ex13-10js.asp </title></head>
 7: <body style="background:#000088;font-family:arial;color:#ffff00">
 8: <div align="left" style="font-size:18pt"><br />
 9: <%
10: var vFrom=Request.Form("from");
11: var vTo=Request.Form("to");
12: var vSubject = Request.Form("subject");
13: var vBody = Request.Form("message");
14:
15: oMail = Server.CreateObject("CDONTS.NewMail");
16:
17: with (objMsg) {
18:    To = vTo;
19:    From = vFrom;
20:    Subject = vSubject;
21:    Body = vBody;
22:    Send();
23: }
24:
25: delete oMail;
26: %>
```

```
27:        Thank you! <span style="color:#ffffff"> <%=vFrom%></span><br />
28:        An Email has been sent to
29:        <span style="color:#ffffff"> <%=vTo%></span>
30: </div>
31: </body>
32: </html>
```

The form data from the interface ex13-10.htm is passed to this ASP program and can be accessed using the `Request.Form` command. For example, `Request.Form` in line 10 returns the "from" data and stores it in a new variable called `vFrom`. This way, the program captures all "To," "From," "Subject," and "Message" fields from ex13-10.htm and stores them using appropriate variables as illustrated in lines 10–13. The next step is to create the object mail `oMail` and to compose the contents of the email as shown in lines 18–21.

Finally, a simple message (lines 27–29) is used to indicate that the email has been sent. A screen shot of this page is given in Fig. 13.18.

Figure 13.18 ex13-10js.asp

13.4.3 XHTML mailing format and attachment

Most of the mailing agents such as Outlook Express can interpret HTML/XHTML language. Also, together with CSS commands, the email message can have more freedom on style, colors, font, and animated images. The following ASP program is an example used to send an animated cartoon bomb to John@pwt-ex.com.

```
Example: ex13-11js.asp – Sending Animated Images With Email

 1: <%@language="JScript" %>
 2: <?xml version="1.0" encoding="iso-8859-1"?>
 3: <!DOCTYPE html PUBLIC "-//W3C//DTD XHTML 1.0 Transitional//EN"
 4:      "http://www.w3.org/TR/xhtml1/DTD/xhtml1-transitional.dtd">
 5: <html xmlns="http://www.w3.org/1999/xhtml" xml:lang="en" lang="en">
 6: <head><title>Send Animated Image: ex13-11js.asp </title></head>
 7: <body style="background:#000088;font-family:arial;color:#ffff00">
 8: <div align="left" style="font-size:18pt"><br />
 9: <%
10: var vFrom="JohnSmith@pwt-ex.com";
11: var vTo="John@pwt-ex.com";
12: var vSubject = "A Cartoon Bomb";
13: var vBody = "<?xml version=\"1.0\" encoding=\"iso-8859-1\"?> "+
14:   "<!DOCTYPE html PUBLIC \"-//W3C//DTD XHTML 1.0 Transitional//EN\" "+
```

```
15:  " \"http://www.w3.org/TR/xhtml1/DTD/xhtml1-transitional.dtd\"> <html "+
16:  " xmlns=\"http://www.w3.org/1999/xhtml\" xml:lang=\"en\" lang=\"en\"> "+
17:  "<head><title>Emailing with ASP: ex13-11js.asp </title></head> "+
18:  "<body style=\"background:#000088;font-family:arial;color:#ffff00\"> "+
19:  "<div align=\"center\" style=\"font-size:18pt\"><br /> "+
20:  "To John With Fun <br /><br />"+
21:  "<img alt=\"pic\" src=\"bomb.gif\" /></div></body></html>"
22:
23:
24: oMail = Server.CreateObject("CDONTS.NewMail");
25:
26: with (oMail) {
27:     To = vTo;
28:     From = vFrom;
29:     Subject = vSubject;
30:     MailFormat = CdoMailFormatMime;
31:     BodyFormat = CdoBodyFormatHTML;
32:     Body = vBody;
33:     AttachURL("C:\\bomb.gif", "bomb.gif");
34:     Send();
35: }
36: delete oMail;
37: %>
38: A Cartoon Bomb has been sent to <%= vTo %>.
39: </div>
40: </body>
41: </html>
```

After the usual ASP and XHTML header (lines 1–8), this program uses variables vFrom, vTo, and vSubject to store the sender, the recipient, and the subject information of the email. The body of the mail is an XHTML page defined in lines 13–21 and used to display the message "To John With Fun" (line 20) and includes an animated image called bomb.gif (line 21).

In order to send this email, you need to add some specifications to the mail object oMail. The first specification is MailFormat=CdoMailFormatMime (line 30). This statement instructs the mailing agent to handle the mail format as MIME so that you can include images and other formats in the email. More information about this format is given later in this chapter. The second specification is given in line 31. This statement informs the mailing agent that the body of the email is in HTML/XHTML format to ensure that the email body can be interpreted and displayed properly.

To include an animated picture in the email body, you need to add the statement (line 33)

```
AttachURL("C:\\bomb.gif", "bomb.gif");
```

This statement is used to attach an image file bomb.gif from drive C into your email. Thus John@pwt-ex.com will receive an email with an animated cartoon bomb as shown in Figs 13.19 and 13.20.

Next, let's see how to include an attached file in an email. To demonstrate this, we consider a mailing list application with an attachment. This application has the following XHTML interface:

```
Example: ex13-12.htm - Email With Attachment

1: <?xml version="1.0" encoding="iso-8859-1"?>
2: <!DOCTYPE html PUBLIC "-//W3C//DTD XHTML 1.0 Transitional//EN"
3:     "http://www.w3.org/TR/xhtml1/DTD/xhtml1-transitional.dtd">
4: <html xmlns="http://www.w3.org/1999/xhtml" xml:lang="en" lang="en">
5: <head><title> Email With Attachment - ex13-12.htm</title></head>
6: <style>
7:   .tx01{font-size:14pt;color:#ffff00;font-weight:bold}
8:   .tx02{font-family:arial;font-size:14pt;background:#ffffff;color:#000000}
9:   .butSt{background-color:#aaffaa;font-family:arial;font-weight:bold;
```

Figure 13.19 ex13-11js.asp

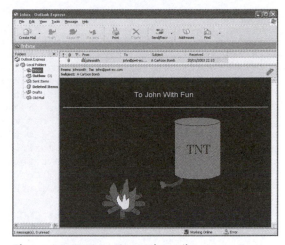

Figure 13.20 An animated email

```
10:        font-size:14pt;color:#008800;width:80px;height:30px}
11:    </style>
12:    <body style="background:#000088;font-family:arial;color:#ffff00">
13:    <div align="center" style="font-size:18pt"><br />
14:      Please Join Our Mailing List<br />
15:    <form method="post" action="ex13-12js.asp">
16:    <table class="tx01">
17:     <tr><td>Name:</td>
18:     <td><input class="tx02" type="text" name="name" id="name"></td></tr>
19:     <tr><td>Email:</td>
20:     <td><input class="tx02" type="text" name="email" id="email"></td></tr>
21:     <tr><td colspan=2>
22:      <input class="butSt" type="submit" value="Submit"></td></tr>
23:    </table>
24:    </form>
25:    </div>
26:    </body>
27:    </html>
```

This page is an application of XHTML form. The ASP program ex13-12js.asp in line 15 is activated when a user completes the form and the Submit button is pressed. This program will process the input data (name and email) and send an email to the user with an attached file. The coding of this ASP program is given below.

```
Example: ex13-12js.asp - ASP Script For ex13-12.htm

 1: <%@language="JScript" %>
 2: <?xml version="1.0" encoding="iso-8859-1"?>
 3: <!DOCTYPE html PUBLIC "-//W3C//DTD XHTML 1.0 Transitional//EN"
 4:     "http://www.w3.org/TR/xhtml1/DTD/xhtml1-transitional.dtd">
 5: <html xmlns="http://www.w3.org/1999/xhtml" xml:lang="en" lang="en">
 6: <head><title>ex13-12js.asp </title></head>
 7: <body style="background:#000088;font-family:arial;color:#ffff00">
 8: <div align="left" style="font-size:18pt"><br />
 9: <%
10: var vFrom="JohnSmith\@pwt-ex.com";
11: var vTo=Request.Form("email");
12: var vName=Request.Form("name");
13: var vSubject="Discount"
14:
```

```
15: var vBody = "<?xml version=\"1.0\" encoding=\"iso-8859-1\"?> "+
16:    "<!DOCTYPE html PUBLIC \"-//W3C//DTD XHTML 1.0 Transitional//EN\" "+
17:    " \"http://www.w3.org/TR/xhtml1/DTD/xhtml1-transitional.dtd\"> <html "+
18:    " xmlns=\"http://www.w3.org/1999/xhtml\" xml:lang=\"en\" lang=\"en\"> "+
19:    "<head><title>Emailing with ASP: ex13-10js.asp </title></head> "+
20:    "<body style=\"background:#000088;font-family:arial;color:#ffff00\"> "+
21:    "<div align=\"left\" style=\"font-size:18pt\"><br /> "+
22:    "Dear "+ vName + "<br /><br /> "+
23:    "Thank you for filling out our mailing list form. "+
24:    "As a registered customer, I would like to inform you "+
25:    "that you are entitled to a further 10% discount on all "+
26:    "brand products for the next three months.<br /><br /> "+
27:    "Sales Manager<br /> JohnSmith <br /> www.pwt-ex.com<br /> <br />"+
28:    "(PS)We have attached this month's special offer for you to consider. "
29:
30: oMail = Server.CreateObject("CDONTS.NewMail");
31: with (oMail) {
32:     To = vTo;
33:     From = vFrom;
34:     Subject = vSubject;
35:     MailFormat = CdoMailFormatMime;
36:     BodyFormat = CdoBodyFormatHTML;
37:     Body = vBody;
38:     AttachFile("C:/special.doc","special.doc");
39:     Send();
40: }
41:
42: delete oMail;
43: %>
44: <h1>Thank you!</h1>
45:     Newsletters and special discount messages will be sent to
46:     <span style="color:#ffffff"><%=vName%></span>at
47:     <span style="color:#ffffff"><%=vTo%></span>.
48: </div>
49: </body>
50: </html>
```

This program is simple. The first part is to get the name and email data from the interface and use this information to construct the necessary email fields (lines 10–13). The email body (lines 15–28) is an XHTML page and addressed to the recipient. Since the content contains XHTML language, you need to specify the `MailFormat` and `BodyFormat` as shown in lines 35 and 36. To attach a file, the following command (line 38) is used:

```
AttachFile("C:/special.doc","special.doc");
```

In this case, a Microsoft Word document called "special.doc" is attached. Figures 13.21–13.24 are some screen shots of this example in action.

Figure 13.21 ex13-12.htm

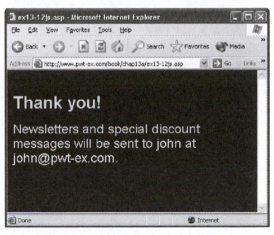

Figure 13.22 ex13-12js.asp

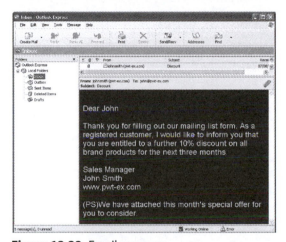

Figure 13.23 Email message

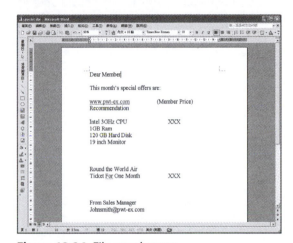

Figure 13.24 File attachment

13.4.4 Sending email with the SMTP server and check mail

Instead of using the built-in mail object of ASP, another way to send email with ASP is to contact the mail server directly. One of the most popular and reliable mail servers on systems is the SMTP mail server. As mentioned in section 13.1, you need one or more of these server identities to set up a mailing agent such as Outlook Express. Suppose the account name and identity of an SMTP server that you can use is "JohnSmith" and "smtp.pwt-ex.com" respectively. The ASP program below can be used to get the email data from an interface page and deliver the message via the SMTP server.

If you modify the XHTML interface ex13-10.htm by replacing lines 16–17 by

```
<form name="uMail" id="uMail" method="post"
      action="ex13-13.asp" >
```

and call this example ex13-13.htm, you will have an interface page to send email with the SMTP server. The corresponding ASP program ex13-13.asp is listed below:

Example: ex13-13.asp – Send Email With SMTP Server

```
 1: <%@language="JScript" %>
 2: <?xml version="1.0" encoding="iso-8859-1"?>
 3: <!DOCTYPE html PUBLIC "-//W3C//DTD XHTML 1.0 Transitional//EN"
 4:     "http://www.w3.org/TR/xhtml1/DTD/xhtml1-transitional.dtd">
 5: <html xmlns="http://www.w3.org/1999/xhtml" xml:lang="en" lang="en">
 6: <head><title> ex13-13.asp <title></head>
 7: <body style="background:#000088;font-family:arial;color:#ffff00">
 8: <div align="center" style="font-size:18pt"><br />
 9: <%
10:
11:   var vTo=Request.Form("to");
12:   var vSubject = Request.Form("subject");
13:   var vBody = Request.Form("message");
14:
15:   oSession = Server.CreateObject("CDONTS.Session");
16:   oSession.LogonSMTP("JohnSmith", "smtpmail.pwt-ex.com");
17:   oOutbox = oSession.Outbox;
18:   oMail = oOutbox.Messages.Add();
19:
20:   with (oMail){
21:     Subject = vSubject;
22:     Text = vBody;
23:     Recipients.Add(vTo, vTo, CdoTo);
24:     Attachments.Add("special.doc" , CdoFileData, "C:/special.doc");
25:     Send();
26:   }
27:
28:   delete oMail;
29:   delete oOutbox;
30:   oSession.Logoff();
31:   delete oSession;
32: %>
33:
34:   <h1>Thank you!</h1>
35:       An Email has been sent to
36:       <span style="color:#ffffff"> <%=vTo%></span>
37: </div>
38: </body>
39: </html>
```

After the fields' assignment in lines 11–13, CDONTS.Session is called to create an object oSession. In order to send email, you need to access the Outbox of oSession and add a message to it. For this to happen, you need to

- call the LogonSMTP() function to log in to an SMTP server (line 16);
- make a copy of the Outbox object oOutbox from oSession.Outbox (line 17);
- create the mail object oMail by calling the Add() function of oOutbox.Messages (line 18).

Once you have the mail object oMail, you can send email in the same way as the mail framework of ASP mentioned earlier.

When composing the contents of the email, the add() functions are used to add the recipient and attachment (lines 23 and 24). Finally the function Send() is invoked to deliver the email.

It is good programming practice to clean up the process soon after you have finished with it so that resources can be saved. Codes in lines 28–31 are used to delete all the objects and log out from the server. Finally, a simple message is used to confirm that the email has been delivered successfully.

In addition to sending email, the CDO session (CDONTS.Session) can also be used to access other mail boxes and messages. As a very simple application, the following ASP program fragment can access the inbox of an SMTP server and check the number of email messages inside.

```
Example: ex13-14.asp - Checking Email

 1: <%@ LANGUAGE="JScript" %>
 2:
 3: <%
 4: var oSession = Server.CreateObject("CDONTS.Session");
 5: oSession.LogonSMTP("JohnSmith", "www.pwt-ex.com");
 6: var oInbox = oSession.GetDefaultFolder(CdoDefaultFolderInbox);
 7: Response.Write("You Have "+ oInbox.Messages.Count +" In Your Mail Box");
 8:
 9: delete oInbox
10: oSession.Logoff();
11: delete oSession
12: %>
```

Instead of creating an Outbox object as in ex13-13.asp, this program creates an Inbox object called oInbox in line 6. Once you have this Inbox object, a direct call to the oInbox.Messages.Count property in line 7 will return the number of email messages in the box.

13.4.5 The basic PHP framework to send email

Along with ASP, another popular server scripting technology is PHP. It is a powerful, reliable, compact, and easy to use script. Most important of all, it is free. Therefore platforms such as UNIX, LINUX, Microsoft, and many others all have an implementation porting.

Basically, with PHP you don't need any additional software to send email. If you have a PHP engine up and running, you already have the ability to send email. In normal circumstances, whether your mailing agent is sendmail or SMTP, the installation of PHP includes instructions to configure them. Furthermore, PHP provides a standard command to make the process of sending email easy. This command is called mail and has the following format:

```
bool mail (string to, string subject, string message
     [, string additional_headers ])
```

The first three parameters are compulsory and used to specify the "To," "Subject," and "Message" fields. If the optional fourth string argument is presented, this string is inserted at the end of the header. This is used to add extra headers and many advanced applications are based on this structure. The function returns true if the email has been sent successfully, otherwise a false value is returned. This mail() function is generally regarded as the basic PHP framework to send email.

One simple example showing how to use mail() is listed below.

```
Example: ex13-15.php - Send Email With PHP I

 1: <?PHP echo"<?";?>xml version="1.0" encoding="iso-8859-1"<?PHP echo"?>";?>
 2: <!DOCTYPE html PUBLIC "-//W3C//DTD XHTML 1.0 Transitional//EN"
 3:     "http://www.w3.org/TR/xhtml1/DTD/xhtml1-transitional.dtd">
 4: <html xmlns="http://www.w3.org/1999/xhtml" xml:lang="en" lang="en">
 5: <head><title>Send Email With PHP I - ex13-15.php</title></head>
 6: <body style="background:#000088;text-align:center;font-family:arial">
 7: <div align="center" style="font-size:18pt;color:#ffff00"><br />
```

```
 8:  <?php
 9:  $vTo ="John@pwt-ex.com";
10:  $vSubject = "Tennis";
11:  $vBody = "Do you want to play tennis tomorrow?\n\n JohnSmith";
12:
13:  if(mail($vTo, $vSubject, $vBody))
14:     echo "Successfully sent the Email to $vTo.";
15:  else
16:     echo "Failed to send the Email to $vTo."
17:  ?>
18:  </body>
19:  </html>
```

As discussed in Chapter 12, any codes between the bracket pair `<?php` and `?>` will be processed by the PHP server engine before reaching the browser. The statements in lines 8–17 are actually PHP script. First, three PHP variables (a name with a prefix dollar sign) are used to compose the email message: `$vTo`, `$vSubject`, and `$vBody`. The contents of these variables are then used to activate the `mail()` function as shown in line 13. Upon successful delivery of the email, the `echo` statement in line 14 returns a text "Successfully sent the Email to John@pwt-ex.com" to the browser.

You can specify multiple recipients by putting a comma between each address inside the variable `vTo`. Unlike ASP or ECMAScript, the string concatenation symbol in PHP is a period ".". For example, the following PHP statement can combine a number of recipients together:

```
$vTo="JohnSmith@pwt-ex.com," . "John@pwt-ex.com," . "Mary@pwt-ex.com";
```

Another way to use the period to combine a long list of names or recipients is

```
$vTo .="JohnSmith@pwt-ex.com" . ",";
$vTo .="John@pwt-ex.com" . ",";
$vTo .="Mary@pwt-ex.com";
```

The real power of the `mail()` function lies in the fourth argument for additional headers. Even a general MIME header can be constructed and passed to the mailing agent. But first, you need to learn more about PHP by constructing a general form for emailing.

13.4.6 An emailing form with PHP

To develop a general emailing form with PHP, we follow the standard approach to divide the application into two parts – interface and form actions. The interface part is an XHTML form. This form generates the "From," "To," "Subject," "Cc," "Bcc," and "Message" headers to get user input. The form action contains a PHP program that is used to compose the email and to perform the delivery. The XHTML page is listed as follows:

```
Example: ex13-16.htm - Send Email With PHP II

 1:  <?xml version="1.0" encoding="iso-8859-1"?>
 2:  <!DOCTYPE html PUBLIC "-//W3C//DTD XHTML 1.0 Transitional//EN"
 3:      "http://www.w3.org/TR/xhtml1/DTD/xhtml1-transitional.dtd">
 4:  <html xmlns="http://www.w3.org/1999/xhtml" xml:lang="en" lang="en">
 5:  <head><title>Send Email With PHP II - ex13-16.htm</title></head>
 6:  <style>
 7:   .tx01{font-size:14pt;color:#ffff00;font-weight:bold}
 8:   .tx02{font-family:arial;font-size:14pt;background:#ffffff;color:#000000}
 9:   .butSt{background-color:#aaffaa;font-family:arial;font-weight:bold;
10:      font-size:14pt;color:#008800;width:80px;height:30px}
11:  </style>
12:  <script src="ex13-10.js"></script>
13:  <body style="background:#000088;font-family:arial;color:#00ee00">
```

```
14:    <div align="center" style="font-size:24pt;font-weight:bold">
15:    A Page To Send Email<br /><br />
16:    <form name="uMail" id="uMail" method="post"
17:       action="ex13-16.php">
18:    <table class="tx01">
19:    <tr><td>From: (Email Add.)</td>
20:      <td><input class="tx02" type="text" name="from" id="from"></td></tr>
21:     <tr><td>To: (Email Add.)</td>
22:      <td><input class="tx02" type="text" name="to" id="to"></td></tr>
23:     <tr><td>Subject:</td>
24:     <td><input class="tx02" type="text" name="subject" id="subject"></td>
25:     <tr><td>Cc: (Email Add.)</td>
26:      <td><input class="tx02" type="text" name="cc" id="cc"></td></tr>
27:     <tr><td>Bcc: (Email Add.)</td>
28:      <td><input class="tx02" type="text" name="bcc" id="bcc"></td></tr>
29:     </tr><tr><td valign="top">Message:</td>
30:      <td><textarea name="message" id="message" class="tx02"
31:         rows="6" cols="40" wrap="yes"></textarea></td></tr><tr><td>
32:        <input class="butSt" type="submit" value="Send"></td>
33:      <td><input class="butSt" type="reset" value="Reset"></td></tr>
34:     </table>
35:     </form>
36:     </div>
37:  </body>
38:  </html>
```

This page is an XHTML form that contains a number of the most frequently used email fields. The inputs "From" (lines 19–20), "To" (lines 21–22), "Subject" (lines 23–24), and "Message" (lines 29–31) are compulsory. Users have to fill in these fields to send mail with PHP. The remaining ones are optional.

For simplicity of coding, we don't want to use ECMAScript to validate email addresses and to check empty fields. For a more practical example, users should apply the techniques as demonstrated in ex13-10.htm to perform a client-side validation of the compulsory fields. The optional fields may be better handled on the server side. These fields will be composed as headers as demonstrated in this example.

Once the Send button is pressed, the form action calls the PHP program ex13-16.php (line 16–17) and passes all the input data as parameters. Unlike ASP, form data are accessed by using the `Request.Form()` function. In PHP, form data are treated just like PHP variables: all you have to do is to add a dollar sign in front of the input data name. For example, you can use the variables $from, $to, $subject, $cc, $bcc, and $message to access the values of the corresponding fields.

Consider the program code ex13-16.php:

Example: ex13-16.php – A PHP Program For ex13-16.htm

```
1:  <?PHP echo"<?";?>xml version="1.0" encoding="iso-8859-1"<?PHP echo"?>";?>
2:  <!DOCTYPE html PUBLIC "-//W3C//DTD XHTML 1.0 Transitional//EN"
3:     "http://www.w3.org/TR/xhtml1/DTD/xhtml1-transitional.dtd">
4:  <html xmlns="http://www.w3.org/1999/xhtml" xml:lang="en" lang="en">
5:  <body style="background:#000088;text-align:center;font-family:arial">
6:  <div align="left" style="font-size:18pt;color:#ffff00"><br />
7:
8:  <?php
9:
10:  function error_msg($msg)
11:  {
12:     echo "<script>alert(\"Error: $msg\");history.go(-1)</script>";
13:     exit;
14:  }
15:
```

```
16:    $vFrom =$from;
17:    $vTo =$to;
18:    $vSubject =$subject;
19:    $vBody = $message;
20:    $vCc = $cc;
21:    $vBcc = $bcc;
22:
23:    if(empty($vFrom)) error_msg("Empty From field!");
24:    if(empty($vTo)) error_msg("Empty To field!");
25:    if(empty($vSubject)) error_msg("Empty Subject!");
26:    if(empty($vBody)) error_msg("Empty Body! ");
27:
28:    $vHeaders = '';
29:    if(!empty($vFrom)) $vHeaders .= "From: $vFrom\n";
30:    if(!empty($vCc)) $vHeaders .= "Cc: $vCc\n";
31:    if(!empty($vBcc)) $vHeaders .= "Bcc: $vBcc\n";
32:
33:    if (mail($vTo,$vSubject,$vBody,$vHeaders))
34:    {
35:        echo "<br />Thank you! $vFrom <br /><br />";
36:        echo "An Email Has Been Sent To $vTo Successfully";
37:    } else {
38:        echo "<br />Sorry! $vFrom <br /><br />";
39:        echo " Unable To Send Your Email To $vTo .";
40:    }
41:
42:  ?>
43:  </div>
44:  </body>
45:  </html>
```

The main part of this program is given in lines 8–42. First, a PHP function error_msg() is developed so that errors can be handled properly. This error function generates an XHTML alert box to display the error message and to exit to the previous page via the history.go() function.

As can be seen from lines 16–21, input data from the interface act as PHP variables and assign new local variables $vFrom, $vTo, $vSubject, $vBody, $vCc, and $vBcc. This way, if you change the names of the interface, only this portion of the program needs to be changed.

Lines 23–26 are the empty string testing for the compulsory fields. Again, they are not sophisticated and used here only for demonstration purposes. The more interesting part of this program is the construction of the additional header fields in lines 28–31. First, an empty header variable $vHeader is created. If the optional field is not empty, the values are concatenated into $vHeader. Continuing in this way, you can build and add any additional header that you want.

The final part of this program (lines 33–40) is the actual delivery of the email by the function mail(). Some screen shots are shown in Figs 13.25 and 13.26.

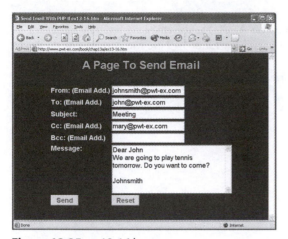

Figure 13.25 ex13-16.htm

Figure 13.26 ex13-16.php

13.4.7 MIME format and programming attachments

Email attachments with ASP are supported directly by the CDONTS module. For PHP, however, you need to program this capability yourself. For some users, this may be a challenging task since all we have is the framework function `mail()`.

The basic idea to program attachments is to read the attachment file and incorporate the data into the email body. You then send it as MIME format. The following PHP program fragment can be used to open and to read a file with PHP:

```php
$fHandle = fopen("myfile", "r");
$fData = fread($fHandle, filesize("myfile"));
```

The first statement is to open a data file "myfile" for reading and to create a file handle called `$fHandle`. By using this file handle, you can read the entire file into a variable `$fData` (file data) with the PHP function `fread()`.

To incorporate attachments into email, you need the MIME format. MIME is an important aspect of email and is a subject in its own right. The detail of MIME specifications is beyond the scope of this book. For our practical purposes, the following discussion should make the idea easy to understand and to implement.

In normal circumstances, the following simple PHP `mail()` function generates a text email:

```php
mail("John@pwt-ex.com","Hello","Hi, John \n How are you today? \n
JohnSmith","From: JohnSmith@pwt-ex.com")
```

Depending on the mailer you are using, the format of the email that contains a header and a body is similar to the listing ex13-05.txt.

```
Listing: ex13-05.txt

 1: To:      JohnSmith@pwt-ex.com
 2: From:    John@pwt-ex.com
 3: Subject: Hello
 4: Content-type: text/plain; charset="iso-8859-1"
 5: Content-transfer-encoding: 7bit
 6:
 7: Hi, John
 8: How are you today?
 9: JohnSmith
10:
```

Lines 1–5 are the headers. Apart from the "To," "From," and "Subject," the header statement in line 4 specifies the email as a plain text document by using us-ascii (i.e., US ASCII) as the character set. The statement in line 5 instructs the mailer to transfer the email with 7-bit encoding. Lines 7–9 are the contents of the body and are separated by one blank line.

For an email with an attachment, the typical MIME format would be like this:

```
Listing: ex13-06.txt

 1: To:         JohnSmith@pwt-ex.com
 2: From:       John@pwt-ex.com
 3: Subject:    Hello
 4: MIME-Version: 1.0
 5: Content-type: multipart/mixed;
 6: boundary="boundary_string"
 7:
 8: This is a MIME encoded message.
 9:
10: --boundary_string--
11: Content-type:text/plain; charset="iso-8859-1"
12: Content-transfer-encoding: 7bit
13:
14: Hi, John
15: How are you today?
16: JohnSmith
17: (PS) I have attached a document for you.
18:
19: --boundary_string--
20: Content-type:application/octet-stream;name=proposal
21: Content-transfer-encoding:base64
22:
23:    #### File Data ####
24:     ### ### ### ###
25:    #### File Data ####
26:
27: --boundary_string--
28:
```

Lines 1–9 are the headers in MIME format. After the usual email fields, the version of the MIME format is specified in line 4. The Content-type of this email is multipart/mixed so that applications, attachments, as well as text messages can be mixed together. In order to separate different contents, a boundary is defined in line 6. The boundary_string is usually a unique long (32 characters) string that is used to separate multiple contents of the email body. The remaining part of this header (lines 7–9) is some information for the mailer.

The email body consists of two parts separated by the boundary_string. The first part (lines 10–19) is a normal text message. The second part (lines 20–27) contains the data of an application. The name of the application is "proposal" and is transmitted as a stream of octet data in base 64 encoding. The actual file data appear one blank line after the encoding statement and before the next boundary_string.

In order to program attachments, you may need to generate the email in MIME format as in ex13-06.txt. First, you construct an XHTML page as the interface part.

```
Example: ex13-17.htm - Email With MIME Type

1: <?xml version="1.0" encoding="iso-8859-1"?>
2: <!DOCTYPE html PUBLIC "-//W3C//DTD XHTML 1.0 Transitional//EN"
3:    "http://www.w3.org/TR/xhtml1/DTD/xhtml1-transitional.dtd">
4: <html xmlns="http://www.w3.org/1999/xhtml" xml:lang="en" lang="en">
5: <head><title> Email With MIME Type - ex13-17.htm</title></head>
6: <style>
```

```
 7:     .tx01{font-size:14pt;color:#ffff00;font-weight:bold}
 8:     .tx02{font-family:arial;font-size:14pt;background:#ffffff;color:#000000}
 9:     .butSt{background-color:#aaffaa;font-family:arial;font-weight:bold;
10:        font-size:14pt;color:#008800;width:80px;height:30px}
11:    .butSt2{background-color:#aaffaa;font-family:arial;font-weight:bold;
12:        font-size:14pt;color:#008800;width:320px;height:30px}
13:    </style>
14:    <body style="background:#000088;font-family:arial;color:#00ee00">
15:    <div align="center" style="font-size:24pt;font-weight:bold">
16:    A Page To Send Email<br /><br />
17:    <form name="uMail" id="uMail" method="post"
18:      action="ex13-17.php">
19:    <table class="tx01">
20:    <tr><td>From: (Email Add.)</td>
21:      <td><input class="tx02" type="text" name="from" id="from"></td></tr>
22:     <tr><td>To: (Email Add.)</td>
23:      <td><input class="tx02" type="text" name="to" id="to"></td></tr>
24:     <tr><td>Subject:</td>
25:      <td><input class="tx02" type="text" name="subject" id="subject"></td>
26:      <tr><td>Attachment Name: </td>
27: <td><input class="tx02" type="text" name="attname" id="attname"></td></tr>
28:      <tr><td>Attachment File:</td>
29: <td><input type="file" class="butSt2" name="attfile" id="attfile"></td>
30:      </TR>
31:      </tr><tr><td valign="top">Message:</td>
32:      <td><textarea name="message" id="message" class="tx02"
33:         rows="6" cols="40" wrap="yes"></textarea></td></tr><tr><td>
34:         <input class="butSt" type="submit" value="Send"></td>
35:      <td><input class="butSt" type="reset" value="Reset"></td></tr>
36:      </table>
37:      </form>
38:      </div>
39: </body>
40: </html>
```

This page is a form application that is used to obtain the "From," "To," "Subject," and "Attachment Name" information from the users. The only new feature is the input statement given in lines 28–29:

```
<input type="file" class="butSt2" name="attfile" id="attfile">
```

This statement generates an open-file window so that the attachment file (attfile) can be picked up by using a mouse click. Once the Send button is pressed, the following PHP program, ex13-17.php, is called and generates the MIME format as illustrated in ex13-06.txt.

```
Example: ex13-17.php - A PHP Program For ex13-17.htm

 1: <?PHP echo"<?";?>xml version="1.0" encoding="iso-8859-1"<?PHP echo"?>";?>
 2: <!DOCTYPE html PUBLIC "-//W3C//DTD XHTML 1.0 Transitional//EN"
 3:     "http://www.w3.org/TR/xhtml1/DTD/xhtml1-transitional.dtd">
 4: <html xmlns="http://www.w3.org/1999/xhtml" xml:lang="en" lang="en">
 5: <body style="background:#000088;text-align:center;font-family:arial">
 6: <div align="left" style="font-size:18pt;color:#ffff00"><br />
 7:
 8: <?php
 9:  global $vFrom, $vTo, $vSubject, $vBody;
10:  global $vAttName, $vAtt, $vAttSize, $vHeaders;
11:
12:  $vFrom =$from;
13:  $vTo =$to;
14:  $vSubject =$subject;
```

```
15:    $vBody = $message;
16:
17:    $vAttName = $attname;
18:    $vAtt = $attfile;
19:    $vAttSize = filesize($vAtt);
20:
21:    $vHeaders="From: $vFrom\n";
22:
23:    include "ex13-17.inc";
24:
25:    if (!empty($vAttName) && ($vAttSize >0) )
26:    {
27:        myAttachment();
28:    } else {
29:      $vHeaders .= "Content-type: text/plain; charset=\"iso-8859-1\" \n";
30:      $vHeaders .= "Content-transfer-encoding: 7bit \n\n";
31:    }
32:
33:    if (mail($vTo,$vSubject,$vBody,$vHeaders))
34:    {
35:        echo "<br />Thank you! $vFrom <br /><br />";
36:        echo "An Email Has Been Sent To $vTo Successfully";
37:    } else {
38:        echo "<br />Sorry! $vFrom <br /><br />";
39:        echo " Unable To Send Your Email To $vTo .";
40:    }
41:
42: ?>
43: </div>
44: </body>
45: </html>
```

The first part of this PHP program is to get the interface data from ex13-17.htm including the "Attachment Name" and "Attachment File" in lines 17 and 18. If the attachment name is not empty and the corresponding file size is bigger than zero (line 25), you are well prepared for an attachment. The function myAttachment() is called to generate the necessary MIME format. This function is defined in the external PHP file ex13-17.inc as an included file of ex13-17.php (line 23). If you don't have an attachment, the usual text headers are generated as in lines 29–30. The final part (lines 33–40) of the program is to send the email off.

The included file ex13-17.inc is listed as follows:

```
Example: ex13-17.inc - An Include File For ex13-17.php

 1: <?php
 2:  function myAttachment()
 3:  {
 4:   global $vBody;
 5:   global $vAttName, $vAtt, $vHeaders;
 6:
 7:   $fileHandle = fopen($vAtt, "r");
 8:   $fileData = fread($fileHandle, filesize($vAtt));
 9:   $fileData = chunk_split(base64_encode($fileData));
10:
11:   $vBoundaryString = md5(uniqid(time()));
12:   $lHeaders = $vHeaders;
13:   $lHeaders .= "MIME-Version: 1.0\n";
14:   $lHeaders .= "Content-type: multipart/mixed;
15:        boundary=\"$vBoundaryString\" \n\n";
16:   $lHeaders .= "This is a MIME encoded message. \n\n";
```

```
17:
18:    $lBody = "--$vBoundaryString-- \n";
19:    $lBody .= "Content-type:text/plain; charset=\"iso-8859-1\" \n";
20:    $lBody .= "Content-transfer-encoding:7bit \n\n";
21:    $lBody .= "$vBody \n";
22:    $lBody .= "--$vBoundaryString-- \n";
23:    $lBody .= "Content-type:application/octet-stream;name=$vAttName \n";
24:    $lBody .= "Content-transfer-encoding:base64 \n\n";
25:    $lBody .= $fileData . "\n\n";
26:    $lBody .= "--$vBoundaryString--";
27:    $vBody = $lBody;
28:    $vHeaders .= $lHeaders;
29:  }
30: ?>
```

Global variables are used in this page to simplify variable passing. Soon after the variable declarations, you open the attachment file, read the data, and prepare the data into chunks of base 64 encoded streams. The streams are stored in the variable `$fileData` ready to be transmitted as an attachment.

The next step is to define the boundary string `$vBounddaryString` (line 11). In order to have a unique string, we call the UNIX time function `time()`, convert it into a unique identifier, and finally call the `md5()` function to transform it to a 32-character string. Since the `md5()` function provides 2^{128} different possibilities, there will be virtually no chance of a repeated boundary string.

The remaining task is to construct the header and the body in MIME format. A local variable `$lHeaders` is used to generate and store the header (lines 12–15). Another local variable, `$lBody`, is used to generate the email body. Since we designed one message and one attachment only, the `$lBody` has two parts separated by the boundary string `$vBoundaryString`. The first part (lines 19–21) is the email itself and the content is the user input in variable `$vBody`. The second part is the attachment and the file data are copied into `$lBody` as shown in line 25. Finally, the header and body are copied back to the global variables `$vHeader` and `$vBody`. When you have finished all the statements of this function, you then have all the required information to deliver the email with an attachment by making the function call

```
mail($vTo,$vSubject,$vBody,$vHeaders)
```

Some screen shots are shown in Figs 13.27 and 13.28.

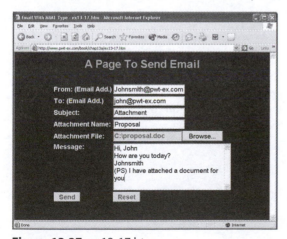

Figure 13.27 ex13-17.htm

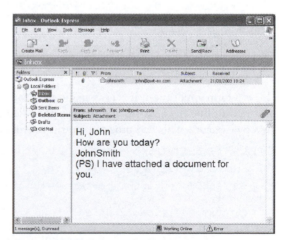

Figure 13.28 Email with attachment

13.5 Emailing and Perl

13.5.1 My first Perl script

Similar to ASP and PHP, Perl is a server language for writing script programs for the World Wide Web. It was developed in the late 1980s by Larry Wall to run initially in a UNIX environment and later adopted in many other operating systems. Perl scripts in this book will have the file extension .pl. This section is not an introduction to the language, but rather a collection of simple Perl program fragments for email applications.

Although Perl is available on PC and Microsoft systems, we will follow the original UNIX design. It's assumed that you have a general UNIX (or LINUX) environment. With the basic UNIX structure and its naming convention, you should have a directory in which XHTML documents are kept. This directory is usually called public_html under your login directory. Your ISP may have different arrangements and should be able to provide you with the information. For PC and Microsoft system users, a suitable substitution of the directory may be needed. The Perl scripts should be stored in a directory executable by the Perl interpreter. This directory may be the same as public_html (or a subdirectory called cgi-bin) and is accessible by the usual http:URL format. We also assume that the Perl interpreter is located in the directory "/usr/bin/perl." You may, of course, have a different location for the interpreter.

Perl is different from ASP and PHP for which script statements can be mixed or embedded into an XHTML page. The Web engines are happy to ignore any invalid statements. In other words, both ASP and PHP will pass everything they don't understand back to the caller. Perl, on the other hand, is a strict language in that every line of a Perl program should be a valid Perl statement.

Similar to ASP, PHP, and other server scripts, Perl can also be used to return a page of information (usually an XHTML document) to the Web browser after the browser submits a request. A typical XHTML page to call a Perl program is

```
Example: ex13-18.htm - My First Page With Perl

 1: <?xml version="1.0" encoding="iso-8859-1"?>
 2: <!DOCTYPE html PUBLIC "-//W3C//DTD XHTML 1.0 Transitional//EN"
 3:     "http://www.w3.org/TR/xhtml1/DTD/xhtml1-transitional.dtd">
 4: <html xmlns="http://www.w3.org/1999/xhtml" xml:lang="en" lang="en">
 5: <head><title>My First Perl</title></head>
 6: <body>
 7: <form method="post" action="ex13-18.pl">
 8: Please Press Button To Activate A Perl Program<br /><br />
 9: <input type="submit" value="Press Me">
10: </form>
11: </body>
12: </html>
```

This is a form application. It acts as an interface for a Perl program. When a user clicks the Press Me button as indicated in line 9, the form action activates a Perl program called ex13-18.pl located in the URL address www.pwt-ex.com. This Perl program returns the following simple XHTML page:

```
Example: ex13-18.pl - The Perl Script For ex13-18.htm

 1: #!/usr/local/bin/perl
 2: print ("Content-type:text/html\n\n");
 3: print << "mywebpage";
 4:    <?xml version="1.0" encoding="iso-8859-1"?>
 5:    <!DOCTYPE html PUBLIC "-//W3C//DTD XHTML 1.0 Transitional//EN"
 6:        "http://www.w3.org/TR/xhtml1/DTD/xhtml1-transitional.dtd">
 7:    <html xmlns="http://www.w3.org/1999/xhtml" xml:lang="en" lang="en">
 8:    <head><title>My First Perl</title></head>
 9:    <body>
```

```
10:    My First Perl Program <br >
11:    Thank you For Calling Me.
12:  </body>
13:  </html>
14: mywebpage
15:
```

The first line of the script informs the system where to find the Perl interpreter, and the second line alerts the calling browser that it is about to receive an XHTML document. The remaining part of the script makes use of a Perl facility called a `here` document. The `here` document will print everything between the statements `print<<"mywebpage"` (line 3) and `mywebpage` (line 14). This `here` document feature is useful for laying out XHTML documents to be returned by Perl scripts. If you prefer, you can replace the `here` document feature by a series of print statements. In practice, simple cut and paste of a proven and tested XHTML document can eliminate most human errors. A Web page returned in this way may be as simple or as complex as you like. Some screen shots of this example are given in Figs 13.29 and 13.30.

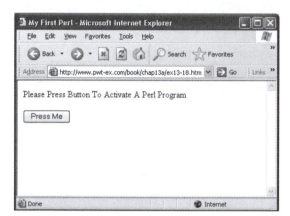

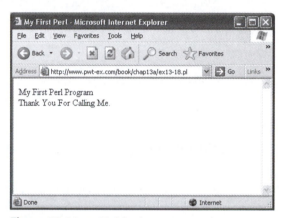

Figure 13.29 ex13-18.htm   **Figure 13.30** ex13-18.p1

Perl is a popular language on the Web. One reason is that it provides a rich set of built-in instructions for Web page editing. For example, the previous example can be rewritten as

```
Example: ex13-19.pl - My First Perl Script II

 1: #! /usr/bin/perl
 2:
 3: use warnings;
 4: use strict;
 5: use CGI qw(:standard);
 6:
 7: print (header());
 8: print (start_html("My First Perl"));
 9: print ("My First Perl Program", br(),"Thank you For Calling Me.");
10: print (end_html());
```

Perl uses the "use" directive to include modules as built-in library functions. Once you have included the module, you can call the associated functions directly. The `warnings` and `strict` modules used in lines 3 and 4 will instruct the interpreter to check valid Perl programming styles and produce warning messages.

The CGI module provides a rich set of standard functions to generate XHTML elements and related functionalities. For example, the header function in line 7 generates the HTML header. The details of the header string will depend on the Perl used, but for most Perl interpreters, this will be an XHTML header. The start_html() function returns the statement

```
<head><title>My First Perl</title></head><body>
```

The br() function generates a line break <br />. The end_html() function returns the string "</body></html>" and concludes the document. If you run this Perl program from your browser (e.g. http://www.pwt-ex.com/book/chap13a/ex13-19.p1) you will see Fig. 13.30 and the HTML/XHTML code generated by the Perl script via the "source" option of the browser. This generated XHTML page is shown in listing ex13-07.txt.

```
Listing: ex13-07.txt

 1: <?xml version="1.0" encoding="utf-8"?>
 2: <!DOCTYPE html
 3:    PUBLIC "-//W3C//DTD XHTML Basic 1.0//EN"
 4:    "http://www.w3.org/TR/xhtml-basic/xhtml-basic10.dtd">
 5: <html xmlns="http://www.w3.org/1999/xhtml" lang="en-US">
 6: <head><title>My First Perl</title></head>
 7: <body>
 8:   My First Perl Program<br />
 9:   Thank you For Calling Me.
10: </body>
11: </html>
```

13.5.2 Using Perl to get user name and email address

Before you can send email information, you need to construct a Web page to obtain the name and email address of the user. The following page is used as an interface:

```
Example: ex13-20.htm - Getting Email Input With Perl

 1: <?xml version="1.0" encoding="iso-8859-1"?>
 2: <!DOCTYPE html PUBLIC "-//W3C//DTD XHTML 1.0 Transitional//EN"
 3:      "http://www.w3.org/TR/xhtml1/DTD/xhtml1-transitional.dtd">
 4: <html xmlns="http://www.w3.org/1999/xhtml" xml:lang="en" lang="en">
 5: <head><title> Getting Email Input With Perl - ex13-20.htm</title></head>
 6: <style>
 7:   .tx01{font-size:14pt;color:#ffff00;font-weight:bold}
 8:   .tx02{font-family:arial;font-size:14pt;background:#ffffff;color:#000000}
 9:   .butSt{background-color:#aaffaa;font-family:arial;font-weight:bold;
10:      font-size:14pt;color:#008800;width:80px;height:30px}
11: </style>
12: <body style="background:#000088;font-family:arial;color:#ffff00">
13: <div align="center" style="font-size:18pt"> <br />
14:   Please Join Our Mailing List<br />
15:  <form method="post" action="ex13-20.pl">
16:  <table class="tx01">
17:   <tr><td>Name:</td>
18:    <td><input class="tx02" type="text" name="name" id="name"></td></tr>
19:   <tr><td>Email:</td>
20:    <td><input class="tx02" type="text" name="email" id="email"></td></tr>
21:   <tr><td colspan=2><input class="butSt" type="submit" value="Submit">
22:   </td></tr></table>
23:   </form>
24: </div>
25: </body>
26: </html>
```

This is a page with a simple form. Once the Submit button is clicked, the form action will call the Perl program ex13-20.pl located in the same directory. In order to obtain the data correctly from the Web page, the Perl program needs a mechanism to catch the input from this page. The corresponding Perl program is listed as follows:

```
Example: ex13-20.pl - The Perl Script For ex13-20.htm

 1: #! /usr/bin/perl
 2:
 3: use warnings;
 4: use strict;
 5: use CGI qw(:standard);
 6:
 7: my $usr_name=param("name");
 8: my $usr_email=param("email");
 9:
10: print ("Content-type/html\n\n");
11: print << "mypage";
12:    <?xml version="1.0" encoding="iso-8859-1"?>
13:    <!DOCTYPE html PUBLIC "-//W3C//DTD XHTML 1.0 Transitional//EN"
14:       "http://www.w3.org/TR/xhtml1/DTD/xhtml1-transitional.dtd">
15:    <html xmlns="http://www.w3.org/1999/xhtml" xml:lang="en" lang="en">
16:    <head><title>ex13-20.pl </title></head>
17:    <body style="background:#000088">
18:    <div style="font-family:arial;font-size:18pt;color:#ffff00">
19:       Your Name is $usr_name <br />
20:       Your Email Address is <br /> $usr_email <br />
21:    </div>
22:    </body>
23:    </html>
24: mypage
```

The only new statements in this program are lines 7 and 8. The parameter function

```
my $usr_name=param("name");
```

is used to catch the name returned by the interface page ex13-20.htm. Any input field from the form interface can be accessed by the `param()` function of Perl. The next step is to assign this user name as a variable in Perl. Variable names in Perl have a prefix dollar sign, $. The keyword my is a Perl identifier to indicate a local variable. Once the variables $usr_name and $usr_email are defined, they can be used anywhere inside the Perl program. Some screen shots of ex13-20.htm and ex13-20.pl in action are shown in Figs 13.31 and 13.32.

Figure 13.31 ex13-20.htm

Figure 13.32 ex13-20.p1

13.5.3 Mailing information to users with Perl

In this section, we will discuss two popular ways to deliver email using Perl. The first one is to use a mailing agent called `sendmail` and the second one is to use an SMTP mail server. Application `sendmail` is a popular mail program that is available in almost all UNIX environments; in fact, some books are dedicated entirely to this program. To call `sendmail`, the following program framework is frequently used:

```
Example: ex13-21.pl - An Email Framework With Perl

 1: #! /usr/bin/perl
 2: open (USRMAIL, "| /usr/lib/sendmail -oi -n -t" );
 3:
 4: print USRMAIL << "usr_message";
 5: To:John\@www.pwt-ex.com
 6: From:JohnSmith\@www.pwt-ex.com
 7: Subject:Testing
 8:
 9: Dear John:
10:
11: This is testing Email from JohnSmith@pwt-ex.com to John@pwt-ex.com
12: using Perl.
13:
14: JohnSmith
15: usr_message
16: close USRMAIL
```

The `open` statement in line 2 activates the `sendmail` program located in the `/usr/lib` directory. The parameters associated with `sendmail` are used to convert the program to a file handle (or stream) with a name `USRMAIL`. You can then use this file handle to insert a whole email message by using the `here` document feature of Perl. At the end, we terminate the stream by issuing a `close` statement.

The information in the `To:` and `From:` fields can be any acceptable email address. The slash before the "@" symbol in line 5 is a requirement in order to generate a proper "@" symbol. After that, you have the `Subject:` field and the contents of the email body. As a feature of Perl, you can of course use variables inside the email.

As a practical example, the following Perl program is constructed to email information to the requestor. This example has the same interface as ex13-20.htm, but embedded entirely in a Perl program.

```
Example: ex13-22.pl - The Perl Script for generating XHTML

 1: #! /usr/bin/perl
 2: use warnings;
 3: use strict;
 4:
 5: print "Content-type:text/html\n\n";
 6: print << "mypage";
 7: <?xml version="1.0" encoding="iso-8859-1"?>
 8: <!DOCTYPE html PUBLIC "-//W3C//DTD XHTML 1.0 Transitional//EN"
 9:     "http://www.w3.org/TR/xhtml1/DTD/xhtml1-transitional.dtd">
10: <html xmlns="http://www.w3.org/1999/xhtml" xml:lang="en" lang="en">
11: <head><title>Send Email Using Perl (I)</title></head>
12: <style>
13:   .tx01{font-size:14pt;color:#ffff00;font-weight:bold}
14:   .tx02{font-family:arial;font-size:14pt;background:#ffffff;color:#000000}
15:   .butSt{background-color:#aaffaa;font-family:arial;font-weight:bold;
16:       font-size:14pt;color:#008800;width:80px;height:30px}
17: </style>
18: <body style="background:#000088;font-family:arial;color:#ffff00">
19: <div align="center" style="font-size:18pt"><br />
20:    Please Join Our Mailing List<br />
```

```
21:   <form method="post" action="ex13-23.pl">
22:   <table class="tx01">
23:    <tr><td>Name:</td>
24:     <td><input class="tx02" type="text" name="name" id="name"></td></tr>
25:     <tr><td>Email:</td>
26:     <td><input class="tx02" type="text" name="email" id="email"></td></tr>
27:     <tr><td colspan=2><input class="butSt" type="submit" value="Submit">
28:     </td></tr></table>
29:    </form>
30:   </div>
31:   </body>
32:   </html>
33: mypage
34:
```

As you can see from this example, it is possible to develop Web pages entirely by using Perl. All you have to do is to copy the page into a here document. To capture the name and address of this page and to send email to the recipient, another Perl program is developed as follows:

```
Example: ex13-23.pl - The Perl Script For ex13-23.htm

 1: #! /usr/bin/perl
 2:
 3: use warnings;
 4: use strict;
 5: use CGI qw(:standard);
 6:
 7: my $usr_name=param("name");
 8: my $usr_email=param("email");
 9:
10:
11: print "Content-type:text/html\n\n";
12:
13: print << "mypage";
14:  <?xml version="1.0" encoding="iso-8859-1"?>
15:  <!DOCTYPE html PUBLIC "-//W3C//DTD XHTML 1.0 Transitional//EN"
16:     "http://www.w3.org/TR/xhtml1/DTD/xhtml1-transitional.dtd">
17:  <html xmlns="http://www.w3.org/1999/xhtml" xml:lang="en" lang="en">
18:  <head><title>ex13-23.pl </title></head>
19:  <body style="background:#000088">
20:  <div style="font-family:arial;font-size:18pt;color:#ffff00">
21:  <h1>Thank you!</h1>
22:      Newsletters and special discount messages will be sent to
23:      <span style="color:#ffffff">$usr_name </span>at
24:      <span style="color:#ffffff">$usr_email</span>.
25:  </div></body></html>
26: mypage
27:
28: open (USRMAIL, "| /usr/lib/sendmail -oi -n -t" );
29:
30: print USRMAIL << "usr_message";
31: To:$usr_email
32: From:JohnSmith\@www.pwt-ex.com
33: Subject:Congratulations
34:
35: Dear $usr_name:
36:
37: Thank you for filling out our mailing list form.
38: As a registered customer, I would like to inform you
```

```
39: that you are entitled to a further 10% discount on all
40: brand products for the next three months.
41:
42: Sales Manager
43: John Smith
44: www.pwt-ex.com
45:
46: usr_message
47: close USRMAIL;
```

This program contains three parts. The first part is to get the name and address from an interface such as ex13-23.htm. This interface is the same as ex13-20.htm but calls ex13-23.pl instead. The second part (lines 13–26) is a "Thank you" page to provide an instant acknowledgment. The final part is the emailing with sendmail. The variables $usr_email and $user_name in the mail content (lines 31 and 35) are used to ensure that the mailing message is a personalized one. Some screen shots of this example are given in Figs 13.33 and 13.34.

Figure 13.33 ex13-23.htm

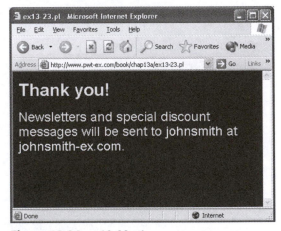

Figure 13.34 ex13-23.p1

If for any reason the sendmail program is not available, you can still use Perl to send your email if the name of your SMTP server is known. As mentioned at the beginning of this chapter, your ISP should be able to provide you with the name of the SMTP server. You need this information to set up a mail client such as Outlook Express.

First, you need to develop a Perl program to generate the "To," "From," "Subject," and "Message" information. This program can easily be constructed as follows:

Example: ex13-24.pl – SMTP Server Using Perl

```
 1: #! /usr/bin/perl
 2: print ("Content-type/html\n\n");
 3: print << "mypage";
 4:   <?xml version="1.0" encoding="iso-8859-1"?>
 5:   <!DOCTYPE html PUBLIC "-//W3C//DTD XHTML 1.0 Transitional//EN"
 6:      "http://www.w3.org/TR/xhtml1/DTD/xhtml1-transitional.dtd">
 7:   <html xmlns="http://www.w3.org/1999/xhtml" xml:lang="en" lang="en">
 8:   <head><title>ex13-24.pl</title></head>
 9:   <style>
10:     .tx01{font-size:14pt;color:#ffff00;font-weight:bold}
11:     .tx02{font-family:arial;font-size:14pt;background:#ffffff;color:#000000}
```

```
12:    .butSt{background-color:#aaffaa;font-family:arial;font-weight:bold;
13:       font-size:14pt;color:#008800;width:80px;height:30px}
14:  </style>
15:  <body style="background:#000088;font-family:arial;color:#ffff00">
16:  <div align="center"$style="font-size:18pt">
17:   Please Enter Your Name and <br />Email Address
18:   <form method="post" action=" ex13-25.pl">
19:   <table class="tx01">
20:    <tr><td>From:</td>
21:     <td><input class="tx02" type="text" name="from" id="from"></td></tr>
22:    <tr><td>To:</td>
23:     <td><input class="tx02" type="text" name="to" id="to"></td></tr>
24:    <tr><td>Subject:</td>
25:     <td><input class="tx02" type="text" name="subject" id="subject"></td>
26:    </tr><tr><td valign="top">Message:</td>
27:     <td><textarea name="message" id="message" class="tx02"
28:         rows="6" cols="40" wrap="yes"></textarea></td></tr>
29:    <tr><td><input class="butSt" type="submit" value="Submit"></td>
30:     <td><input class="butSt" type="reset" value="Reset"></td></tr>
31:   </table>
32:   </form>
33:  </div>
34:  </body>
35:  </html>
36: mypage
37:
```

Again, this is just another copy and paste example for generating XHTML using Perl. You can run this Perl page directly. The "To," "From," "Subject," and "Message" information will be sent to a Perl program called ex13-25.pl once the "Submit" button is clicked. Some screen shots of this page are given in Figs 13.35 and 13.36.

Figure 13.35 ex13-24.p1

Figure 13.36 ex13-25.p1

In order to connect an SMTP server, you need an external module called "NET::SMTP" which can be found inside a library called `libnet`. Most Perl implementations will have this package installed. For some systems, you may need to install it yourself. Suppose the identity of an SMTP server that you can use is smtp.pwt-ex.com. The following Perl program, ex13-25.pl, can be used to get the email data and deliver the message via the SMTP mail server.

Example: ex13-25.pl – Perl Script For ex13-24.pl

```perl
 1: #! /usr/bin/perl
 2:
 3: use strict;
 4: use warnings;
 5: use Net::SMTP;
 6: use CGI qw( :standard );
 7:
 8: my $from = param( "from" );
 9: my $to = param( "to" );
10: my $subject = param( "subject" );
11: my $message = param( "message" );
12:
13: print ("Content-type/html\n\n");
14: my $smtp = Net::SMTP->new ("smtp.pwt-ex.com")
15:     or die("Cannot connect to SMTP server: $!");
16:
17: $smtp->mail( "$from" );
18: $smtp->to( "$to" );
19:
20: $smtp->data();
21: $smtp->datasend( "From: $from\n" );
22: $smtp->datasend( "To: $to\n" );
23: $smtp->datasend( "Subject: $subject\n\n" );
24: $smtp->datasend( "$message\n" );
25: $smtp->dataend();
26: $smtp->quit();
27:
28: print << "mypage";
29:   <?xml version="1.0" encoding="iso-8859-1"?>
30:   <!DOCTYPE html PUBLIC "-//W3C//DTD XHTML 1.0 Transitional//EN"
31:       "http://www.w3.org/TR/xhtml1/DTD/xhtml1-transitional.dtd">
32:   <html xmlns="http://www.w3.org/1999/xhtml" xml:lang="en" lang="en">
33:   <head><title>Sending Email Using SMTP Server</title></head>
34:   <body style="background:#000088">
35:   <div style="font-family:arial;font-size:18pt;color:#ffff00">
36:         Your Email has been sent to $to
37:   </div></body></html>
38: mypage
39:
```

After the collection of data from the interface (lines 8–11), a connection to the server (line 14) is made and the object is assigned a local variable $smtp. Since $smtp is an object, you can call all its member functions directly. The first function associated with $smtp is $smtp->mail ("$from"). This function is to tell the server who is the sender of the email. The function $smtp->to("$to") identifies the recipient. The remaining series of function calls (lines 20–26) are used to create a data section and fill in the necessary To:, From:, Subject:, and Message: fields of an email. The dataend() function terminates the data section and quit() disconnects the SMTP server.

The last section of this program (lines 28–38) is just a Web page used to confirm delivery.

13.5.4 Checking emails with Perl

If you have a POP3 account somewhere on the Internet, you can use the next example to check how many emails are in your inbox. In order to gain access to your mail account, you need the following information:

- User name – Your mail account name, e.g., JohnSmith@pwt-ex.com.
- Password – The password to gain access to the account.
- Server – The name of the POP3 server or machine that holds your emails.

All this information should be available to you from your system administrator or ISP. To develop an interface to obtain the information, the following Perl program is used:

Example: ex13-26.pl – Accessing POP3 Account Using Perl

```
 1: #! /usr/bin/perl
 2: print ("Content-type/html\n\n");
 3: print << "mypage";
 4:  <?xml version="1.0" encoding="iso-8859-1"?>
 5:  <!DOCTYPE html PUBLIC "-//W3C//DTD XHTML 1.0 Transitional//EN"
 6:     "http://www.w3.org/TR/xhtml1/DTD/xhtml1-transitional.dtd">
 7:  <html xmlns="http://www.w3.org/1999/xhtml" xml:lang="en" lang="en">
 8:  <head><title>Accessing POP3 Using Perl - ex13-26.pl</title></head>
 9:  <style>
10:   .tx01{font-size:14pt;color:#ffff00;font-weight:bold}
11:   .tx02{font-family:arial;font-size:14pt;background:#ffffff;color:#000000}
12:   .butSt{background-color:#aaffaa;font-family:arial;font-weight:bold;
13:      font-size:14pt;color:#008800;width:80px;height:30px}
14:  </style>
15:  <body style="background:#000088;font-family:arial;color:#ffff00">
16:  <div align="center" style="font-size:18pt">
17:   Check Email From a<br />POP3 Server<br />
18:   <form method="post" action="ex13-27.pl">
19:   <table class="tx01">
20:    <tr><td>Username:</td><td><input class="tx02" type="text"
21:        name="username" id="username"></td></tr>
22:    <tr><td>Password:</td><td><input class="tx02" type="password"
23:        name="password" id="password"></td></tr>
24:    <tr><td>POP Server:</td><td><input class="tx02" type="text"
25:        name="server" id="server"></td></tr>
26:    <tr><td><input class="butSt" type="submit" value="Submit"></td>
27:     <td><input class="butSt" type="reset" value="Reset"></td></tr>
28:   </table>
29:   </form>
30:  </div>
31:  </body>
32:  </html>
33: mypage
34:
```

This program is easy to understand. We have used the password field in lines 22–23. If an input element with type is identified as password, the user input in this field will be masked as asterisks. The screen shot of this Perl program is given in Fig. 13.37.

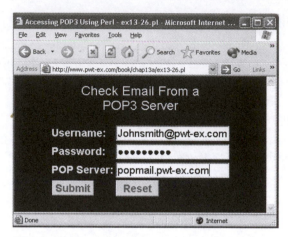

Figure 13.37 ex13-26.p1

Once the Submit button is pressed, another Perl program, ex13-27.pl, is activated. This program will perform the actual connection and check the emails from the server. The code of this program is surprisingly
simple and is listed as follows:

Example: ex13-27.pl - Perl Script For ex13-26.pl

```
 1: #!/usr/bin/perl
 2: print ("Content-type/html\n\n");
 3:
 4: use warnings;
 5:
 6: use Mail::POP3Client;
 7: use CGI qw( :standard );
 8:
 9: my $user_id = param( "username" );
10: my $password = param( "password" );
11: my $server_name = param( "server" );
12:
13: my $my_pop = new Mail::POP3Client( USER => $user_id,
14:    PASSWORD => $password, HOST => $server_name ) or
15:    die("Cannot connect: $!");
16:
17: my $email_count = $my_pop->Count();
18:
19: print << "mypage";
20:   <?xml version="1.0" encoding="iso-8859-1"?>
21:   <!DOCTYPE html PUBLIC "-//W3C//DTD XHTML 1.0 Transitional//EN"
22:      "http://www.w3.org/TR/xhtml1/DTD/xhtml1-transitional.dtd">
23:   <html xmlns="http://www.w3.org/1999/xhtml" xml:lang="en" lang="en">
24:   <head><title>Accessing POP3 Using Perl - ex13-27.pl</title></head>
25:   <body style="background:#000088">
26:   <div style="font-family:arial;font-size:18pt;color:#ffff00">
27:       $username <br />
28:       You have $email_count messages in your inbox.
29:   </div></body></html>
30: mypage
31:
32: $my_pop->Close();
33:
```

Three variables, $user_id, $password, and $server_name, as defined in lines 9–11 are used to store the corresponding input data from the interface. All this information is needed to construct the Perl command

```
my $my_pop = new Mail::POP3Client( USER => $user_id,
    PASSWORD => $password, HOST => $server_name )
```

This command opens a connection to the POP3 server via the Mail::POP3Client module and creates a new object variable called $my_pop. The expression USER=>$user_id in Perl is to assign the variable value $user_id to the identifier USER. If the creation of the object $my_pop is successful, you will have a proper connection to the mail server. In this case, a simple member function call to Count such as

```
$email_count = $my_pop->Count()
```

will return the number of emails in the inbox. This number is assigned to the variable $email_count and is used in line 28 as returned information to the user. The close function $my_pop->Close() terminates the server connection when finished. A screen shot of this program is given in Fig. 13.38.

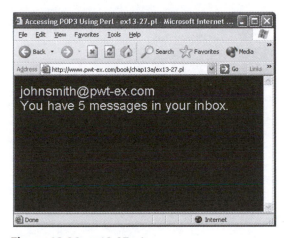

Figure 13.38 ex13-27.p1

Part IV

Server CGI techniques and databases

14 | **Using the Common Gateway Interface**

14.1 Common Gateway Interface (CGI)

14.1.1 What is CGI?

There is no doubt that World Wide Web browsers such as IE and NS are important for the entire Internet. They are among the most important software to link information and people around the world and conquer every corner of the Internet. Nowadays, the functionalities of browsers are far beyond the original design to display documents written in the HTML/XHTML language. At a minimum level we can expect a capable browser to carry out the following:

- Display documents written in the XHTML language.
- Understand CSS styles.
- Execute scripts such as ECMAScript and others.
- Implement the DOM so that events and style can be controlled using standard scripts.

Even all these functionalities cover only half of the picture, i.e., client-side activities. A basic capable browser should also act as an interface for the following server-side activities:

- Execute server programs.
- Accept server technologies such as Perl, ASP, and PHP.
- Communicate with databases in remote sites.
- Safeguard the network and perform security encryption and business transactions.

In order to perform these tasks, processing power on the server side is needed. Server technologies open a new chapter for Web applications.

As a simple example, if you have an executable program such as `myprogram` (or `myprogram.exe` for Microsoft systems) on the root directory of the server www.pwt-ex.com, you can run this program by issuing the following `http://` command in the address bar of the browser:

http://www.pwt-ex.com/myprogram

If the executable program generates an XHTML document to the calling browser via the standard input/output (I/O) channel, the browser can process and display the document. The entire process is generally regarded as the Common Gateway Interface (CGI) process.

In particular, a script or executable program is considered as a CGI script or program if

- it is inside and executable by the server;
- the execution is triggered by the browser;
- the result can be displayed on the browser window.

Based on this specification, CGI scripts and programs can be written in many languages such as Perl, ASP, PHP, and C/C++.

You already have some experience on Perl, ASP, and PHP from Chapters 12 and 13. In this chapter you will learn CGI technologies from a global point of view. We begin by executing a simple C/C++ program using the CGI process. From CGI's point of view, all ASP, PHP, and Perl can be considered as a preprocessor to produce XHTML documents. Even server software such as Apache and/or IIS can be considered as a special CGI application.

One of the central ideas of this book is to keep language features and new commands to a minimum and concentrate on applications on the Web. For each technology or language such as Perl, ASP, and PHP, a natural yet minimal approach is introduced. We will not provide a comprehensive discussion of all aspects of the language features. Alternatively, an easy to understand technological background is provided. Our main objective is to show how to apply technology to various applications and to direct them into action. This chapter provides fundamental knowledge on CGI and is a solid base for a more advanced study of server technologies and the chapters to come. Now it's time to consider the structure of the CGI.

14.1.2 The structure of CGI: how does it work?

Apart from requesting an XHTML document, the HTTP, generally, can also identify a file that contains a program or script. Depending on the settings of the server, the program may be executed when a user activates the link containing the URL. This is the CGI process. To understand how it works, you need to consider the structure and actual dialog (canonical interaction) between the browser and server.

Figure 14.1 shows a CGI application in action and the necessary calling procedure. In the figure, there is one Web client and two HTTP servers.

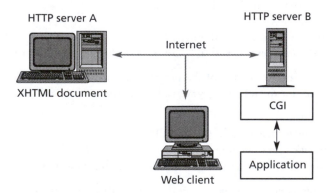

Figure 14.1 CGI structure

The Web client computer requests an XHTML document from server A and displays it on the screen. Suppose this document has a hyperlink to a program "myprogram" on server B. This program is run if the link is activated. The link can be any ordinary HTTP connection available. When the program is called, a special request is sent to server B. The message is like this:

```
Listing: ex14-01.txt - CGI Request Message To Server

1:  GET /myprogram HTTP/1.0
2:  Accept: www/source
3:  Accept: text/html
4:  Accept: image/gif
5:  Accept: image/jpg
6:  User Agent: xxxx
7:  From: xxxxxx
8:    *** a blank line ***
```

This request causes the server to locate and execute the program `myprogram`. In order to display the result via the calling browser, the program usually generates a special message through server B back to the browser. For an HTTP network such as the Internet, the response message looks like the following:

```
Listing: ex14-02.txt - CGI Response From Server

1: HTTP/1.0 200 OK
2: Server: xxx xx
3: MIME-Version: 1.0
4: Content-type: text/html
5:  *** blank line ***
6: <html><title><head> ***</head></title>
7:  *** *** ***
```

The CGI request and response are similar to the canonical client–server interaction discussed in Chapter 1. In fact, they are the standard CGI client–server interaction.

The dialog illustrates two important points:

- The first five lines specify the CGI header needed for the CGI process.
- The remaining dialog (starting from line 6) contains the document displayable by the browser.

Any program or application generating the first five lines of ex14-02.txt and returning an XHTML document generally qualifies as a CGI application. The document will appear on the client (or browser) screen. This idea is the origin of almost all server technologies on the Web, including Perl, ASP, and PHP.

Let's consider some CGI applications in the next section.

14.2 CGI applications and preprocessors

14.2.1 Example of a CGI application

From the discussion above, to develop a server technology is quite straightforward. All you have to do is to generate the CGI header (lines 1–5 of listing ex14-02.txt) and return a Web page. In fact, for a minimum CGI header the string

```
Content-type:text/html
```

with a blank line at the end will be enough. Sometimes, this string is called the "magic line" of CGI applications.

Note that the standard CGI communications between client and server require the standard I/O devices. All CGI correspondence must be echoed or printed to the standard output device such as a screen or a terminal.

To output some strings to the screen is not too difficult. In fact, you can program this with a number of computing languages. The following is a CGI example written in the ANSI/ISO C++ language. Don't worry if you are not familiar with C++: if you know how to write a "Hello World" program, you can modify the program as follows:

```
Example: ex14-01.cpp - A C++ Program For CGI

1: #include <iostream>
2: using namespace std;
3: int main()
4: {
5:    cout <<"HTTP/1.0 200 OK \n";
6:    cout <<"Server:www.pwt-ex.com\nMIME-Version:1.0\n";
7:    cout <<"Content-type: text/html\n\n";
8:
9:    cout <<"<?xml version=\"1.0\" encoding=\"iso-8859-1\"?> \n";
```

```
10:    cout <<"<!DOCTYPE html PUBLIC \"-//W3C//DTD XHTML 1.0 \n";
11:    cout <<" Transitional//EN\" \n http://www.w3.org/TR/xhtml1/DTD/ \n";
12:    cout <<" xhtml1-transitional.dtd\"> \n";
13:    cout <<"<html xmlns=\"http://www.w3.org/1999/xhtml\" \n";
14:    cout <<" xml:lang=\"en\" lang=\"en\">\n";
15:
16:    cout <<"<head><title></title></head> \n";
17:    cout <<"<body style=\"background:#000088;color:#ffff00;\n";
18:    cout <<" font-weight:bold;\n font-family:arial;font-size:22pt;";
19:    cout <<" text-align:center\"> \n";
20:    cout <<" <br /><br /> \n This page was generated by \n";
21:    cout <<" a C++ program <br /> \n";
22:    cout <<" and run as a CGI script \n</body>\n</html>\n";
23:    return 0;
24: }
```

The console output statement cout is a frequently used statement in C++ to output a string to the screen. For example, the statement in line 5

```
cout << "HTTP/1.0 200 OK \n";
```

will output the string "HTTP/1.0 200 OK" with a line break onto the screen. In fact, lines 5–7 output the entire CGI header to the screen and the rest (lines 9–22) return a simple XHTML document.

If you have a compiler capable of compiling this program, you should have an executable program on your machine. Suppose the executable program file is called ex14-01.exe.

For many systems including NT and UNIX/LINUX, CGI programs are usually stored in a default directory called cgi-bin. Other systems may have a different default directory. If the program ex14-01.exe is inside our default directory such as /book/chap14a of www.pwt-ex.com, you can run this program directly from the browser by issuing the following "http" command:

http://www.pwt-ex.com/book/chap14a/ex14-01.exe

By executing this command, the browser requests the document ex14-01.exe from the site www.pwt-ex.com and directory /book/chap14a. Since the document is an executable program, the server will run this file first. The execution result is a CGI header and an XHTML document and therefore can be displayed on the browser window.

A screen shot of this example is shown in Fig. 14.2. If you activate View and then Source from the browser menu, the source code of the page is the same as the output from the executable program ex14-01.exe (except for the CGI header). The output of the executable program is shown in Fig. 14.3.

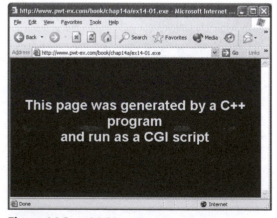

Figure 14.2 ex14-01.exe

```
HTTP/1.0 200 OK
Server:www.pwt-ex.com
MIME-Version:1.0
Content-type: text/html

<?xml version="1.0" encoding="iso-8859-1"?>
<!DOCTYPE html PUBLIC "-//W3C//DTD XHTML 1.0
  Transitional//EN"
  http://www.w3.org/TR/xhtml1/DTD/
  xhtml1-transitional.dtd">
<html xmlns="http://www.w3.org/1999/xhtml"
  xml:lang="en" lang="en">
<head><title></title></head>
<body style="background:#000088;color:#ffff00;
  font-weight:bold;
  font-family:arial;font-size:22pt;  text-align:center'
  <br /><br />
 This page was generated by
 a C++ program <br />
 and run as a CGI script
</body>
</html>
```

Figure 14.3 Source generated by program ex14-01.exe

For UNIX/LINUX systems, you may have a different name for the executable program and may need to change the program status to executable so that a browser can run the program via the Internet.

In fact, you don't need the entire CGI header to make it work. For a working CGI header, all you need is the CGI magic string

```
Content-type: text/html\n\n
```

That is, the content type plus a blank new line. If you forget to put this string in your CGI application, the result will be strange. If you delete lines 5–6 of ex14-01.cpp as in ex14-03.txt, the program will still work on all browsers.

```
Listing: ex14-03.txt - Minimum CGI Framework

 1: #include <iostream>
 2: using namespace std;
 3: int main()
 4: {
 5:
 6:
 7:    cout <<"Content-type: text/html\n\n";
 x:      xxx xxx xxx xxx
 x:      xxx xxx xxx xxx
21:    cout <<" a C++ program <br /> \n";
22:    cout <<" and run as a CGI script \n</body>\n</html>\n";
23:    return 0;
24: }
```

If you comment out line 7 and recompile the program, the behavior will be different depending on the browsers. IE6.x may still work, but others such as NS6.x and Opera will open a window to ask what you want to do with the document. For NS communicator or NS4.x, it opens a "Save As" window to help you to save the document. The reason is that if you haven't played by the rules (CGI rules), the browser will not recognize the document and the response can be different.

Many people refer to CGI software as CGI preprocessors due to the fact that documents can be processed on the server. This feature provides a powerful capability and opens up a new area of applications on the Web. Applications such as databases, e-commerce, and Web security are almost impossible without it.

Two of the very first CGI preprocessors that are free and widely available across different platforms are Perl and PHP.

14.2.2 A CGI preprocessor – the "perl" program

For Web applications, the searching and extraction power of the Perl language make it an ideal choice for handling CGI applications. In general, the Perl package contains an executable program or preprocessor called "perl" to process documents written in the Perl language (or Perl script).

Basically, the perl program takes a file or a perl file as input and outputs the CGI header and an XHTML document onto the standard screen. Since Perl already includes all the features and many more functionalities than the trivial C++ program listed in ex14-01.cpp, you no longer need to write any C++ programs.

Some advantages of using Perl are that it is

- system independent;
- easy to understand;
- a powerful alternative to C/C++ or any programming languages;
- able to call system commands and functions;
- a language with strong text-processing functions such as pattern matching.

If you have a UNIX/LINUX system up and running properly, you may already have the perl preprocessor installed. If you are using Windows XP, 2000, 9.x, and/or NT, a perl preprocessor porting or package called `ActivePerl` can be downloaded from www.activestate.com. Basically, Perl is free and available to everyone.

As one of the main objectives of this book, we will keep the language features and commands to a minimum and concentrate on applications on the Web. Following Perl practice in Chapter 13, the following format (ex14-04.txt) is used to convert an XHTML page to a Perl application.

```
Listing: ex14-04.txt - A Framework To Convert XHTML To Perl

1: #! /usr/bin/perl
2: print ("Content-type:text/html\n\n");
3:
5: print << "mypage";
6:    **** **** ****
7:        The XHTML Page
8:    **** **** ****
9: mypage
```

To use this structure, all you have to do is insert an HTML/XHTML document into lines 6–8. Consider the simple Perl script example ex14-02.pl.

```
Example: ex14-02.pl - Generating XHTML Page With Perl

1: #! /usr/bin/perl
2: print ("Content-type:text/html\n\n");
3:
4: print << "mypage";
5: <?xml version="1.0" encoding="iso-8859-1"?>
6: <!DOCTYPE html PUBLIC "-//W3C//DTD XHTML 1.0 Transitional//EN"
7: "http://www.w3.org/TR/xhtml1/DTD/xhtml1-transitional.dtd">
8: <html xmlns="http://www.w3.org/1999/xhtml" xml:lang="en" lang="en">
9: <head>
10:  <title> Generating XHTML Page With Perl - ex14-02.pl</title>
11: </head>
12: <body style="background:#000088">
13:  <table width="550" border="0" align="center">
14:  <tr>
15:   <td width="80%" align="center">
16:      <span style="font-family:arial;font-size:18pt;color:#ffff00">
17:         <b>Welcome To</b><br /></span>
18:      <span style="font-family:arial;font-size:18pt;color:#00ffff">
19:         <b>Practical Web Technologies</b></span></td>
20: <td><img alt="pic" src="logo_web.jpg" width="140" height="70" /></td></tr>
21:  <tr align="center"><td colspan="2">
22:   <img alt="pic" src="line1.gif" width="550" height="6" />
23:   <span style="font-family:arial;font-size:18pt;color:#ffff00">
24:      <br /><br /><b>A Simple XHTML Page: From Perl</b><br /></span>
25:   <span style="font-family:arial;font-size:16pt;color:#00ff00">
26:      <b>Some Text Strings and Images</b><br /><br /></span>
27:  </td></tr>
28:  </table>
29:  </body>
30: </html>
31: mypage
```

This is a Perl file to be interpreted by the perl program. After the location of the perl program (line 1), the statement in line 2 outputs the "magic" string "Content-type:text/html" and a blank new line to the standard output (screen). This is the minimum requirement to instruct the browser to listen for an HTML/XHTML document. The `print<<"mypage"` command in line 4 specifies a `here` document and is used to output all messages between lines 4 and 31 to screen.

If you have the perl program installed, you can activate it from a shell window (or MS-DOS). One such command is

```
shell> perl ex14-02.pl
```

The result of this command is shown in Fig. 14.4. If you run ex14-02.pl as a CGI application, you can use

http://www.pwt-ex.com/book/chap14a/ex14-02.pl

from the browser. In this case, the Perl file is assumed to be in the `/book/chap14a` directory. The result is shown in Fig. 14.5. The purpose of this example is not the display but to understand the nature of the perl preprocessor, the Perl source file, and the relationship with Web browsers.

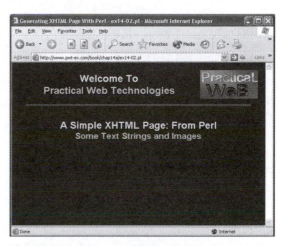

Figure 14.4 Output from Perl   **Figure 14.5** Running a Perl script

14.2.3 The PHP preprocessor

Another well-known CGI preprocessor on the Web is PHP. The PHP software is a program called "php." Perl and PHP are dedicated to device- and platform-independent CGI applications. They both work in a similar fashion in that the CGI header and an XHTML document are output to the browser via the standard output device.

Unlike Perl script, PHP returns the CGI magic string automatically to the browser together with anything that it cannot understand. This feature allows a PHP program to be embedded into existing XHTML documents. To understand how PHP works, consider a date and time example with PHP script:

```
Example: ex14-03.php – Generating XHTML With PHP

 1: <?PHP echo"<?";?>xml version="1.0" encoding="iso-8859-1"<?PHP echo"?>";?>
 2: <!DOCTYPE html PUBLIC "-//W3C//DTD XHTML 1.0 Transitional//EN"
 3:     "http://www.w3.org/TR/xhtml1/DTD/xhtml1-transitional.dtd">
 4: <html xmlns="http://www.w3.org/1999/xhtml" xml:lang="en" lang="en">
 5: <head><title>Getting Date & Time Using PHP -- ex14-03.php</title></head>
 6: <body style="background:#000088;text-align:center;font-family:arial;
 7: font-size:16pt;color:#ffff00"> Getting Today's Date Using PHP <br /><br />
 8: <?PHP $today = getdate();
 9:     $month = $today['month'];
10:     $mday = $today['mday'];
11:     $year = $today['year'];
```

```
12:     $hours = $today['hours'];
13:     $minutes = $today['minutes'];
14:     $seconds = $today['seconds'];
15: ?>
16: <script>
17:   document.write("Today Is <br /><br />")
18:   document.write( "The Current Day =<?PHP echo "$mday"; ?> <br />")
19:   document.write("The Current Month = <?PHP echo "$month"; ?> <br />")
20:   document.write("The Current Year = <?PHP echo "$year"; ?> <br /><br />")
21:   document.write("And The Time Is <br /><br />")
22:   document.write( "The Current Hours =<?PHP echo "$hours"; ?> <br />")
23:   document.write("The Current Minutes= <?PHP echo "$minutes"; ?> <br />")
24:   document.write("The Current Seconds = <?PHP echo "$seconds"; ?> <br />")
25: </script>
26: </body>
27: </html>
```

Provided you have a proper installation of PHP, you can run this PHP script with the following command:

```
shell>php ex14-03.php
```

where `shell>` is the command prompt in a console window. The result is shown in Fig. 14.6. From this figure, you can see that the first three lines are:

```
X-Powered-By:PHP/4.0.5
Content-type:text/html
xxxx a Blank Line xxxx
```

The first statement is the identity of the PHP preprocessor, while the second and third lines are the "magic" CGI header to the browser. If the following "http" command is issued from the browser

http://www.pwt-ex.com/book/chap14a/ex14-03.php

the XHTML document is rendered and displayed as in Fig. 14.7.

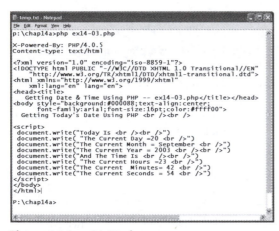

Figure 14.6 ex14-03.php

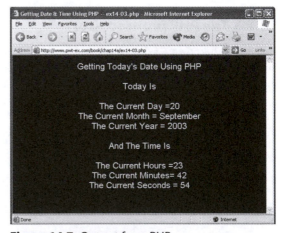

Figure 14.7 Output from PHP

Now you know how Perl and PHP work, it is time to consider how to perform CGI applications on the Web.

14.3 Using CGI with forms

14.3.1 A revision of XHTML form and related elements

Working with forms is the cornerstone of many applications on the Internet – from government departments to the private commercial sector, forms are everywhere. Just imagine how many electronic forms we all need to fill out in our daily lives. On the Web, from simple data collection, through online ordering, to database applications, forms are important tools to produce sophisticated interactive programs.

In order to use forms effectively on the Web, you need to understand the XHTML form element and its properties and methods. Also, at a professional level, a good understanding of CGI and related technologies such as Perl, PHP, and ASP is essential.

The XHTML form element `<form>` specifies a form for a user to fill out. More than one form can be specified in a single page and can be nested, i.e., forms can be inside a form. As a quick revision exercise, the form element has the following general format:

```
Listing: ex14-05.txt - Form Element

1: <form action ="url" method="xxx" style="xxx" id="xx" name="xx">
2:   ...
3:   ... Any Sensible XHTML Elements Can Be Here, In Particular The
4:   ... Interface or Input Elements
5:   ...
6:  <input type="submit" value="Submit" style="xxx" name="xxx" id="xxx" />
7: </form>
```

The `input` element in line 6 is a button-like structure. When this button is pressed, the entire form is submitted to the application or program specified by the form action in line 1. All well-defined XHTML elements associated with the form are submitted to the action.

The `action` attribute usually specifies a CGI application on the server to be run with the submitted data. If this attribute is absent, then the current document URL will be used. For example, the following action specifies a Perl script to run:

```
action="showParameter.pl"
```

The `method` attribute determines how the data, parameters, or form contents are to be submitted. In normal circumstances, two choices are available:

- get – This method causes the form contents to be appended to the URL as if they were a normal query.
- post – This method causes the form contents to be sent to the server as a data body rather than as part of the URL.

The detailed nature of these form processing methods will be discussed later in this chapter. First, let's see what kind of input or interface elements can be used inside a form.

14.3.2 Using interface elements within forms

Inside the form element `<form></form>` you can have any XHTML element except maybe another form if you have an old browser. Specifically, the `input`, `select`, and `textarea` elements are often used since they have the ability to get user input and pass information to the CGI applications. These elements sometimes refer to the interface elements due to the fact that they are designed to get user input.

In practice, the first element associated with forms is the `input` element specified by

```
<input type="xxx" class="xxx" id="xxx" name="xxx" value="xxx" />
```

The `class` attribute defines the CSS style for the element. Using a class may be more convenient than inline style since most `input` elements occur several times with consistent style settings.

The `name` attribute is important. When it is embedded within a form, the value in the name field is used to pass data or parameters back and forth from CGI applications.

The `type` attribute specifies the input types and functionality of the element, as in Table 14.1.

Table 14.1 Type attributes for the `<input>` element

Type attribute	Description and example
text	Defines a text field ready for keyboard input, e.g., `<input type="text" name="usrN" id="usrN" class="xxx" />`
password	Similar to text field. Entered characters are represented as asterisks, e.g., `<input type="password" name="passW" id="passW" class="xxx" />`

checkbox	A single toggle button; on or off. Multiple checkboxes can be defined and checked, e.g.,
	`<input type="checkbox" name="check1" id="check1" class="xxx" />`
	`<input type="checkbox" name="check2" id="check2" class="xxx" />`

radio	A single toggle button; on or off. Other toggles with the same name are grouped into "one of many" behavior, e.g., `<input type="radio" name="rad" id="rad" class="xxx" />` `<input type="radio" name="rad" id="rad" class="xxx" />`
file	The button displays a file dialog box or a select box that allows the user to select the file, e.g., `<input type="file" name="fileN" id="fileN" class="xxx" />`
button	Defines a button on the Web pages, e.g., `<input type="button" value="Click" class="xx" onclick="Fun()" />`
submit	A button that causes the current form to be packaged and sent to a remote server, e.g., `<input type="submit" value="Submit" class="xxx" />`
reset	A button that causes the various input elements in the form to be reset to their default values, e.g., `<input type="reset" value="Reset" class="xxx" /> 13`

The combination of these `input` elements creates a rich set of tools to get user input. Along with other form elements such as `textarea` and `select`, you will have an important interface to obtain information from users.

The `textarea` element creates a rectangular area for text input. A typical example is

```
<textarea row="5" col="50" name="myText" id="myText" style="xxx">
This is Textarea</textarea>
```

This command creates a text area of 5 rows and 50 columns. In this case, the initial text inside the text area is the message "This is Textarea." We used `textarea` quite often in Chapter 13 to get the contents of an email.

Another interface element used with forms is `select`. The general calling format is

```
<select name="xxx" id="xxx" size="x" style="xxx">
    <option >Option 1</option>
    <option >Option 2</option>
```

```
        ...
        <option> Option</option>
    </select>
```

If the `size` attribute is absent, it will create a button-like structure and act as a drop-down menu (similar to a combo box). If the `size` attribute is present and contains a number, e.g., 3, the select box acts like a listing box and displays three options. If you put the attribute `multiple` inside the `select` element, the select box can accept multiple choices. The option elements define the items inside the select box.

Now let's consider a simple example to use a form and submit it to CGI applications. The Web page is listed below:

```
Example: ex14-04.htm - Obtaining Form Contents

 1: <?xml version="1.0" encoding="iso-8859-1"?>
 2: <!DOCTYPE html PUBLIC "-//W3C//DTD XHTML 1.0 Transitional//EN"
 3: "http://www.w3.org/TR/xhtml1/DTD/xhtml1-transitional.dtd">
 4: <html xmlns="http://www.w3.org/1999/xhtml" xml:lang="en" lang="en">
 5: <head><title> Obtaining Form Contents - ex14-04.htm</title></head>
 6: <style>
 7:  .butSt{background:#aaffaa;width:250px;
 8:     font-family:arial;font-weight:bold;font-size:16pt;color:#880000}
 9:  .txtSt{font-family:arial;font-weight:bold;font-size:16pt;color:#ffff00}
10: </style>
11: <body style="background:#000088;color:#ffff00;font-family:arial">
12: <div style="font-size:22pt;font-weight:bold;text-align:center">
13:     Form Contents and CGI Submission</div>
14:
15: <form action="ex14-09.pl" style="text-align:center">
16:  <table class="txtSt" cellspacing="5">
17:   <tr><td>Name:</td><td>
18:    <input type="text" name="usrN" id="usrN" class="butSt" /></td></tr>
19:   <tr><td>Email:</td><td>
20:    <input type="text" name="email" id="email" class="butSt" /></td></tr>
21:   <tr><td>Password:</td><td>
22:    <input type="password" name="passW" id="passW" class="butSt" /></td>
23:  </tr></table><br />
24:
25:  <table class="txtSt" cellspacing="5"><tr>
26:   <td><input type="submit" value="Submit" class="butSt" /></td>
27:   <td><input type="reset" value="Reset" class="butSt" /></td></tr>
28:  </table>
29: </form>
30: </body>
31: </html>
```

This page contains a form defined in lines 15–29. Three `input` elements are used inside the form: namely, `usrN` (user name), `email` (email address), and `passW` (password). These text fields are used to obtain user information such as "Name," "Email," and "Password" respectively.

The form also contains a table to accommodate the Submit and Reset buttons. When the Submit button is pressed, the entire form is submitted to the CGI application ex14-09.pl declared in line 15. This Perl script is to echo the submitted contents and will be discussed later in section 14.4.1. Some screen shots of this example are shown in Figs 14.8 and 14.9.

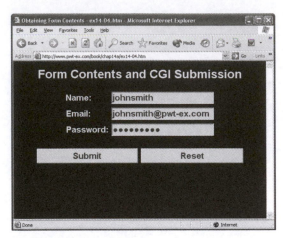

Figure 14.8 ex14-04.htm

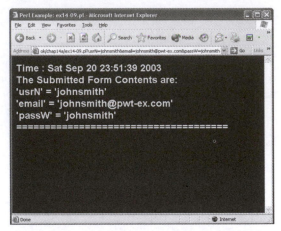

Figure 14.9 Form contents sumitted to CGI script

Next, let's consider an example to demonstrate how to use a select box with multiple selections.

14.3.3 A page with multiple select boxes

To demonstrate another use of the form element and how to submit it to a CGI application, consider an example with various select boxes. The Web page has the following listing:

Example: ex14-05.htm – Obtain Values From Multiple Select Boxes

```
 1: <?xml version="1.0" encoding="iso-8859-1"?>
 2: <!DOCTYPE html PUBLIC "-//W3C//DTD XHTML 1.0 Transitional//EN"
 3: "http://www.w3.org/TR/xhtml1/DTD/xhtml1-transitional.dtd">
 4: <html xmlns="http://www.w3.org/1999/xhtml" xml:lang="en" lang="en">
 5: <head><title> Multiple Select Boxes - ex14-05.htm</title></head>
 6: <style>
 7:  .butSt{background:#aaffaa;width:200px;
 8:     font-family:arial;font-weight:bold;font-size:16pt;color:#880000}
 9:  .txtSt{font-family:arial;font-weight:bold;font-size:16pt;color:#ffff00}
10: </style>
11: <body style="background:#000088;font-family:arial;font-size:18pt;
12:     color:#ffff00;font-weight:bold">
13: <div style="font-size:22pt;font-weight:bold;text-align:center">
14:     A Demonstration Of Form Contents and<br /> Parameter Passing</div>
15:
16: <form action="ex14-09.pl" style="text-align:center">
17:
18: <table class="txtSt" cellspacing="5"><tr><td>Name:</td>
19:  <td><input type="text" name="usrN" id="usrN" class="butSt" /></td>
20: </tr><tr><td>Email:</td><td colspan="3">
21:     <input type="text" name="email" id="email" class="butSt"
22:     style="width:510px" /></td></tr>
23: </table><br />
24:
25: <table cellspacing="20" class="txtSt"><tr><td>
26:     Which operating system are you using?</td><td>
27:     <select class="butSt" name="os" id="os">
28:      <option>Windows 9x</option><option>Windows NT</option>
```

```
29:    <option>LINUX</option><option>Mac OS</option>
30:    </select><br /></td></tr>
31: <tr><td>
32:    Which browser do you like best?</td><td>
33:    <select size="5" class="butSt" name="Browser" id="webT">
34:      <option>IE 6+</option><option>IE 5.5</option>
35:      <option>IE 5.0</option><option>NS 7+</option>
36:      <option>NS 6.x</option><option>NS 4.7</option>
37:      <option>Opera</option><option>Mozilla</option>
38:      <option>Others</option>
39:    </select></td></tr>
40: <tr><td>
41:    What kind of Web technologies do you like?<br />
42:    (You can pick multiple answers by holding <br />the Ctrl key.)</td><td>
43:    <select size="7" multiple class="butSt" name="webTech" id="webT">
44:      <option selected>XHTML</option><option>CSS</option>
45:      <option>XML & XSLT</option><option selected>ECMAScript</option>
46:      <option selected>DOM</option><option>CGI</option>
47:      <option>Database</option><option>Perl Script</option>
48:      <option>ASP</option><option>PHP</option>
49:      <option>Web Security</option>
50:    </select></td></tr>
51: </table>
52: <table class="txtSt" cellspacing="5"><tr>
53:  <td><input type="submit" value="Submit" class="butSt" /></td>
54:  <td><input type="reset" value="Reset" class="butSt" /></td></tr>
55: </table>
56: </form>
57: </body>
58: </html>
```

This is a form application to ask some questions on computers and Web technologies. In lines 16–56, we have three tables. The first table contains two input elements of text type and are used to get the name and email address of the user. The second table contains three rows. For each row, there is a select element. The first select element (lines 27–30) contains some choices of operating system. The size attribute of this <select> is absent, therefore this select box acts as a combo box and only one row is displayed. The second select element (lines 33–39) displays five rows containing a choice of Web browsers. The third select box (lines 43–50) is a select box with multiple selections and therefore multiple answers can be picked while holding down the Ctrl key. A screen shot of this example is shown in Fig. 14.10.

The page has a Submit button defined in line 53. When this button is pressed, the entire form is submitted to the form action and processed by the server program ex14-09.pl. Again, this program is a Perl script (discussed later in section 14.4.1) run by the server to display the form contents to the screen. The result is shown in Fig. 14.11.

Since the third select box in Fig. 14.10 can have multiple selections, you have multiple results associated with the name "webTech" shown in Fig. 14.11.

Before the discussion of the Perl script ex14-09.pl used in the previous two examples, let's consider a practical example regarding an online ordering form from a restaurant.

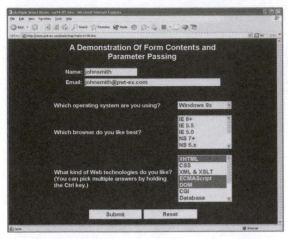

Figure 14.10 ex14-05.htm

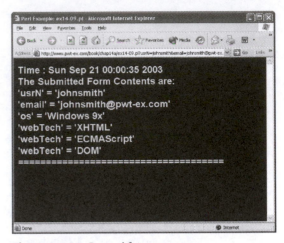

Figure 14.11 Passed form contents

14.3.4 A page to collect online orders

For small businesses such as cafés, shops, or small restaurants, the main business concern is not a large customer database, money transactions, or security on the Web. Assume you are the owner of a café. Perhaps you would like to do the following on the Internet:

- Collect "Take Away" orders.
- Notify orders so that delivery can be made.
- Keep a permanent record so that orders can be traced.

Once the orders are collected and transferred to you, your staff can collect payment at the same time the food is delivered.

This is a basic model of e-commerce and we will show you how to implement it step by step. First, getting online orders can be performed by the page below:

Example: ex14-06.htm – Collecting Online Orders

```
 1: <?xml version="1.0" encoding="iso-8859-1"?>
 2: <!DOCTYPE html PUBLIC "-//W3C//DTD XHTML 1.0 Transitional//EN"
 3: "http://www.w3.org/TR/xhtml1/DTD/xhtml1-transitional.dtd">
 4: <html xmlns="http://www.w3.org/1999/xhtml" xml:lang="en" lang="en">
 5: <head><title> Collecting Online Orders - ex14-06.htm</title></head>
 6: <style>
 7:    .butSt{background:#aaffaa;width:200px;
 8:       font-family:arial;font-weight:bold;font-size:16pt;color:#880000}
 9:    .butSt2{background:#aaffaa;width:30px;height:30px;
10:       font-family:arial;font-weight:bold;font-size:18pt;color:#880000}
11:    .txtSt{width:200px;
12:       font-family:arial;font-weight:bold;font-size:16pt;color:#ffff00}
13: </style>
14: <body style="background:#000088;font-family:arial;font-size:18pt;
15:    color:#ffff00;font-weight:bold">
16: <div style="font-size:22pt;font-weight:bold;text-align:center">
17:    Jenny's Cafe <br /> Internet Ordering & Delivery Services</div>
18:
19: <form action="ex14-09.pl" style="text-align:center">
20:
```

```
21: <table class="txtSt" cellspacing="5"><tr><td>Name:</td>
22:  <td><input type="text" name="usrN" id="usrN" class="butSt" /></td>
23:  <td>Phone Number:</td>
24:  <td><input type="text" name="phone" id="phone" class="butSt" /></td>
25: </tr><tr><td>Address:</td><td colspan="3">
26:   <input type="text" name="addr" id="addr" class="butSt"
27:   style="width:510px" /></td></tr>
28: </table><br />
29:
30: Special Offer From Today's Menu ($3.50 Each)<br />
31: All Come With Fries<br /><br />
32: <table cellspacing="5" border="0">
33: <tr><td><input type="checkbox" name="comb" id="comb" class="butSt2"
34:     value="Burger Combo" /></td>
35:  <td class="txtSt">Burger Combo</td>
36:  <td><input type="checkbox" name="seaf" id="seaf" class="butSt2"
37:     value="Sea Food Burger" /></td>
38:  <td class="txtSt">Sea Food Burger</td></tr>
39: <tr><td><input type="checkbox" name="chick" id="chick" class="butSt2"
40:     value="Chicken Burger Royal" /></td>
41:  <td class="txtSt">Chicken Burger Royal</td>
42:  <td><input type="checkbox" name="lamb" id="lamb" class="butSt2"
43:     value="Lamb Fajita" /></td>
44:  <td class="txtSt">Lamb Fajita</td></tr>
45: <tr><td><input type="checkbox" name="deli" id="deli" class="butSt2"
46:     value="Vegetarian Delight" /></td>
47:  <td class="txtSt">Vegetarian Delight</td>
48:  <td><input type="checkbox" name="supr" id="supr" class="butSt2"
49:     value="Two Jumbo Sausages" /></td>
50:  <td class="txtSt">Two Jumbo Sausages</td></tr>
51: </table><br />
52:
53: How Would You Like To Pay?<br /><br />
54: <table cellspacing="5" border="0">
55: <tr><td><input type="radio" name="rad" id="rad" class="butSt2"
56:    value="Cash" checked /></td><td class="txtSt">Cash</td>
57:  <td><input type="radio" name="rad" id="rad" class="butSt2"
58:    value="VISA" /></td><td class="txtSt">VISA</td></tr>
59: <tr><td><input type="radio" name="rad" id="rad" class="butSt2"
60:    value="Check" /></td><td class="txtSt">Check</td>
61:  <td><input type="radio" name="rad" id="rad" class="butSt2"
62:    value="Master Card" /></td><td class="txtSt">Master Card</td></tr>
63: <tr><td><input type="radio" name="rad" id="rad" class="butSt2" value=
64:    "American Express" /></td><td class="txtSt">American Express</td>
65:  <td><input type="radio" name="rad" id="rad" class="butSt2" value=
66:    "Customer Account" /></td><td class="txtSt">Customer Account</td></tr>
67: </table><br />
68:
69: <table class="txtSt" cellspacing="5"><tr>
70:  <td><input type="submit" value="Submit" class="butSt" /></td>
71:  <td><input type="reset" value="Reset" class="butSt" /></td></tr>
72: </table>
73: Payment Will Be Collected By Delivery Personnel
74: </form>
75: </body>
76: </html>
```

This page contains three parts. The first one is a table layout (lines 21–28) to collect the customer's name, telephone number, and address so that the delivery is possible. The second part defined in lines 30–51 contains the food or products that you want to offer. In this case, you have listed six special offerings from today's menu. They are listed as checkboxes so that users can select them very easily. The third part of the page defined in lines 53–67 is to collect information on the payment method. In this case, we have arranged six payment methods for customers.

Once the Submit button is pressed in line 70, the entire form contents are sent to the CGI application ex14-09.pl for processing. This Perl script outputs the "Data & Time" string as well as the online ordering. The details of this script will be discussed in section 14.4.1 since they are related to CGI techniques on passing data (we will come back to this example later in this chapter as an e-commerce example). Some screen shots of this example are shown in Figs 14.12 and14.13.

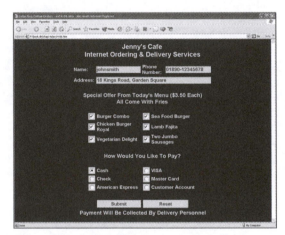

Figure 14.12 ex14-06.htm

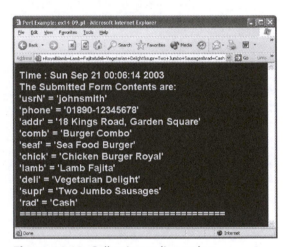

Figure 14.13 Collecting online orders

14.4   Passing data to CGI applications: name/value pairs

Passing data to CGI applications is an important subject and is the first step for all kinds of server programming. Different server technologies such as Perl, PHP, and ASP may have different command names and data-passing procedures. Fortunately, they are all based on the same structure (CGI structure) and philosophy under the HTTP.

Basically, there are two data-passing methods used in CGI applications, namely, the `get` and `post` methods. You can specify them in the `method` attribute in a form. Basically, you pass information with a name and the value of that name, i.e., a name/value pair. Since data-passing methods and name/value pairs are the secret and success of all CGI applications, we will discuss them in detail via the browser/server interaction dialog.

14.4.1 Passing form contents with the `get` method

As soon as the Submit button of a form is pressed, every element with a `name` attribute between `<form></form>` will be passed to the CGI application specified by the form action. How these parameters are passed depends on the `method` attribute of the form. Consider the following form declaration:

```
<form action="my_perl.pl" method="get">
  Enter Your Name:
  <input type="text" name="usrName" id="usrName" value="">
  Telephone Number:
```

```
    <input type="text" name="tel" id="tel" value="">
    <input type="submit" value="Submit">
</form>
```

This is a form using the `get` method. When the `method` attribute is absent, the `get` method is the default. When the user enters "JohnSmith" and "01890-1234-5678" to the form and presses the Submit button, an HTTP request (canonical client–server interaction) from the client would look something like

```
Listing: ex14-06.txt - An HTTP Message From The Client: get Method

1: GET my_perl.pl?usrName=JohnSmith&tel=01890-1234-5678
2: Accept: www/source
3: Accept: text/html
4: Accept: image/gif
5: Accept: image/jpg
6: User Agent: xxxx
7: From: xxxx
8:    *** a blank line ***
```

As we can see from this message, the form contents are assembled into a query URL to the server as (see line 1)

```
GET my_perl.pl?usrName=JohnSmith&tel=01890-1234-5678
```

The string after the first question mark "?" is called a query string. In this example, the query string passes two name/value pairs to the program my_perl.pl:

```
usrName=JohnSmith
tel=01890-1234-5678
```

The left hand side is the name and the right hand side is the value. Name/value pairs are separated by an ampersand symbol "&." Some general rules for the query string are as follows:

- Strange characters in any of the "name" or "value" string will be "escaped," i.e., encoded with the `escape()` function. This includes "=", "&," and punctuation. The space character is replaced by a "+" sign.
- For text and password entry fields, the user input will be the value of the field. If the user didn't type anything, the value will be empty but the "name=" part of the query string will still be present.
- For checkboxes and radio buttons, the `value` attribute specifies the value of a checkbox or radio button when it is checked.
- Any unchecked checkbox is disregarded completely when assembling the query string. Multiple checkboxes can have the same name (and different values), if necessary.
- Multiple radio buttons intended to have "one of many" behavior should have the same name and different values.

To see some of these rules in action, consider the example ex14-07.htm:

```
Example: ex14-07.htm - Using The get Method

 1: <?xml version="1.0" encoding="iso-8859-1"?>
 2: <!DOCTYPE html PUBLIC "-//W3C//DTD XHTML 1.0 Transitional//EN"
 3: "http://www.w3.org/TR/xhtml11/DTD/xhtml1-transitional.dtd">
 4: <html xmlns="http://www.w3.org/1999/xhtml" xml:lang="en" lang="en">
 5: <head><title> Using The get Method - ex14-07.htm</title></head>
 6: <style>
 7:    .butSt{background:#aaffaa;width:200px;
 8:       font-family:arial;font-weight:bold;font-size:16pt;color:#880000}
 9: </style>
10: <body style="background:#000088;font-family:arial;font-size:18pt;
11:    color:#ffff00;font-weight:bold">
12: <form action="ex14-07.pl" method="get">
```

```
13:
14:  Enter Your Name:<input type="text" name="usrName"
15:    id="usrName" value="" class="butSt"><br /><br />
16:  Telephone Number:<input type="text" name="tel"
17:    id="tel" value="" class="butSt"><br /><br />
18:  <input type="submit" value="Submit" class="butSt">
19:  </form>
20:
21:  </body>
22:  </html>
```

This is a simple form application and contains only two text fields. When the Submit button is clicked, the form contents are submitted to the Perl script ex14-07.pl (line 12). As a simple example, the script is constructed to output the query string and is listed below:

Example: ex14-07.pl - The Perl Script For ex14-07.htm

```
 1:  #! /usr/bin/perl
 2:
 3:  ## The magic string or CGI Application
 4:  print ("Content-type/html\n\n");
 5:
 6:  my $querySt = $ENV{ "QUERY_STRING" };
 7:
 8:  print << "myDoc";
 9:   <?xml version="1.0" encoding="iso-8859-1"?>
10:   <!DOCTYPE html PUBLIC "-//W3C//DTD XHTML 1.0 Transitional//EN"
11:   "http://www.w3.org/TR/xhtml1/DTD/xhtml1-transitional.dtd">
12:   <html xmlns="http://www.w3.org/1999/xhtml" xml:lang="en" lang="en">
13:   <head><title>Perl Example: ex14-07.pl</title></head>
14:   <body style="background:#000088;font-family:arial;font-size:18pt;
15:     color:#ffff00;font-weight:bold">
16:  myDoc
17:
18:  if ( $querySt eq "" )
19:  {
20:    print 'We have received an empty input string';
21:  } else {
22:    print 'The Query String For the get Method Is: <br /><br />',$querySt
23:  }
24:  print "</body></html>";
```

When this script is called, it returns a minimum CGI header "Content-type/html\n\n" to the browser (line 4) so that the server and the browser are linked together. Soon after that, a local variable $querySt is declared to store the environment QUERY_STRING which is the query string sent by the browser.

The rest of the program is to construct an XHTML document back to the browser. Since the query string is captured and stored in variable $querySt, a simple if statement in lines 18–23 can be used to determine whether the string is empty. If the string is not empty, the print statement in line 22 will print it out.

Some screen shots of the example are shown in Figs 14.14 and 14.15. When the get method is used, the query string is appended in the URL at the address bar (see Fig. 14.15) and passed to the program.

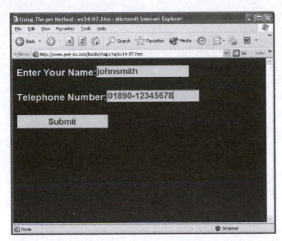

Figure 14.14 ex14-07.htm

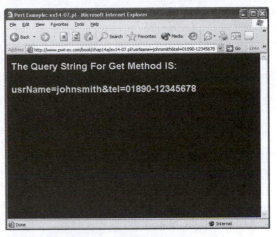

Figure 14.15 Displaying the query string

In order to have a more general and practical program, we need to get the name/value pairs from the query string one by one. Consider the following example:

Example: ex14-08.pl – The Perl Script For ex14-08.htm

```
 1: #! /usr/bin/perl
 2:
 3: ## The magic string or CGI Application
 4: print ("Content-type:text/html\n\n");
 5:
 6: my $querySt = $ENV{ "QUERY_STRING" };
 7:
 8: print << "myDoc";
 9:   <?xml version="1.0" encoding="iso-8859-1"?>
10:   <!DOCTYPE html PUBLIC "-//W3C//DTD XHTML 1.0 Transitional//EN"
11:   "http://www.w3.org/TR/xhtml1/DTD/xhtml1-transitional.dtd">
12:   <html xmlns="http://www.w3.org/1999/xhtml" xml:lang="en" lang="en">
13:   <head><title>Perl Example: ex14-08.pl</title></head>
14:   <body style="background:#000088;font-family:arial;font-size:18pt;
15:      color:#ffff00;font-weight:bold">
16: myDoc
17:
18: if ( $querySt eq "" )
19: {
20:    print 'We have received an empty input string';
21: } else {
22:    my @pairs = split ( "&", $querySt );
23:    printf "<br />The Input Form Contents are: <br />";
24:    foreach my $i (0 .. $#pairs)
25:    {
26:      my ( $name, $value ) = split ( "=", $pairs[$i] );
27:      print "'$name' = '$value'. <br />";
28:    }
29: }
30: print "</body></html>";
```

This Perl script is similar to ex14-07.pl in the sense that they both get the query string from the environment. Instead of displaying the query string entirely, this script splits the string into individual names and values.

The separation symbol for name/value pairs is "&." The statement in line 22 splits the string $querySt into a collection or array of "name=value" pairs. Now you apply the split function split() again to each element of the array @pairs using the for-loop as illustrated in lines 24–28:

```
foreach my $i (0 .. $#pairs)
{
    my ( $name, $value ) = split ( "=", $pairs[$i] );
    print "'$name' = '$value'. <br />";
}
```

The first line declares a local variable $i and sets a loop from zero to the number of items or pairs. Then for each $i, the split function performs on $pairs[$i] at the symbol "=" and assigns the split result to $name and $value.

As an example of how to use this script, you may replace line 12 of ex14-07.htm as

```
12: <form action="ex14-08.pl" method="get">
```

and call this new example ex14-08.htm. Now, this new example will display individual input fields as shown in Fig. 14.16.

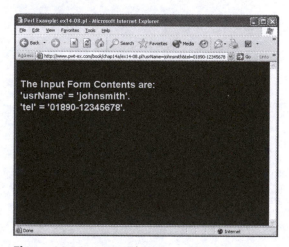

Figure 14.16 ex14-08.htm

For some short names and messages without strange characters, the Perl script ex14-08.pl is adequate to handle the input parameters. However, from the general rules of the query string we know that any special character in the name/value pairs is "escaped," i.e., encoded with the escape() function. In order to display these characters correctly, some modifications of ex14-08.pl and use of the unescape() function for decoding are necessary. The following Perl script, ex14-09.pl, is one of the modifications:

```
Example: ex14-09.pl - The Perl Script For ex14-09.htm

1: #! /usr/bin/perl
2:
3: ## Minimum Requirement For CGI Application
4: print ("Content-type:text/html\n\n");
5: my $querySt = $ENV{ "QUERY_STRING" };
6:
7: print << "myDoc";
```

```
 8:  <?xml version="1.0" encoding="iso-8859-1"?>
 9:  <!DOCTYPE html PUBLIC "-//W3C//DTD XHTML 1.0 Transitional//EN"
10:     "http://www.w3.org/TR/xhtml1/DTD/xhtml1-transitional.dtd">
11:  <html xmlns="http://www.w3.org/1999/xhtml" xml:lang="en" lang="en">
12:  <head><title>Perl Example: ex14-09.pl</title></head>
13:  <body style="background:#000088;font-family:arial;font-size:18pt;
14:     color:#ffff00;font-weight:bold">
15: myDoc
16:
17: if ( $querySt eq "" )
18: {
19:   print 'We have received an empty input string';
20: } else {
21:   my @pairs = split ( "&", $querySt );
22:   print "Time : ",scalar(localtime());
23:   printf "<br />The Submitted Form Contents are: <br />";
24:   foreach my $i (0 .. $#pairs)
25:   {
26:     ## Convert plus's to spaces
27:     $pairs[$i] =~ s/\+/ /g;
28:     my ($name, $value) = split("=",$pairs[$i]);
29:
30:     # Convert %xx from hex numbers to alphanumeric
31:     $name =~ s/%(..)/pack("c",hex($1))/ge;
32:     $value =~ s/%(..)/pack("c",hex($1))/ge;
33:   print " '$name' = '$value' <br />";
34:   }
35:   print "===================================="
36: }
37: print "</body></html>";
```

To develop a script suitable for practical purposes, we have added a time feature in line 22 to display a string of date and time. From the general rules of the query string, the spaces of the name/value pairs are replaced by the "+" sign. A matching technique is employed in line 27 to convert the "+" signs back to spaces. In order to convert the ASCII value %nn back to alphanumeric, the following statement is used:

```
$name =~ s/%(..)/pack("c",hex($1))/ge;
```

This is a replacement statement from pattern matching to replace the hex value %xx with its corresponding character. We have covered pattern matching in some detail in Chapter 13. In fact, pattern matching is a feature that originated from Perl.

If you prefer, you can ask ECMAScript to convert the %xx for you by using its unescape() function. For example, you can use the statement

```
print "'$name' = '<script>document.write(unescape('$value'))</script>'";
```

to output a normal string to the browser. In this case, ECMAScript is doing the conversion for you. To see the difference, let's replace line 12 of ex14-08.htm by

```
12: <form action="ex14-09.pl" method="get">
```

and call this new example ex14-09.htm. If you enter the following name and telephone number with some empty spaces and punctuation into the form

```
Name: Mr. John JohnSmith
Telephone Number: (01890) 1234 5678
```

you will see the difference. The results of ex14-08.htm and ex14-09.htm are shown in Figs 14.17 and 14.18.

To summarize the behavior of the get method, we have the following statement:

- The get method of the form is the default method to pass form contents to CGI applications and causes parameters to be appended to the URL as if they were a normal query.

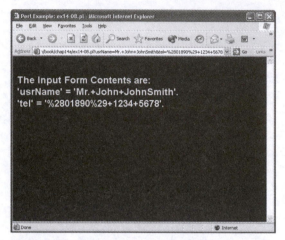

Figure 14.17 Escaped messages (ex14-08.htm)

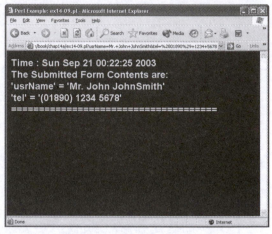

Figure 14.18 Unescaped messages (ex14-09.htm)

14.4.2 Using the `post` method

Another data-passing method often used with form is the post method. The contents of the form are encoded exactly as with the get method mentioned above. Unlike the get method, the form contents of the post method are sent in a data block as part of the client–server operation.

Consider the following "name and telephone" example fragment:

```
<form action="my_perl_2.pl" method="post">
  Enter Your Name:
  <input type="text" name="usrName" id="usrName" value="">
  Telephone Number:
  <input type="text" name="tel" id="tel" value="">
  <input type="submit" value="Submit">
</form>
```

This is a form application using the post method. When the form is filled out as

```
Enter Your Name: Mr. John JohnSmith
Telephone Number: (01890) 1234 5678
```

and submitted to the server, the following information (client–server interaction) or something similar is sent to www.pwt-ex.com by the browser:

```
Listing: ex14-07.txt - An HTTP Message From The Client: the post Method

1: POST /my_perl_2.pl HTTP/1.0
2: Accept: www/source
3: Accept: text/html
4: Accept: image/gif
5: Accept: image/jpg
6: User Agent: xxxx
7: From: xxxxxx
8: Content-type: application/x-www-form-urlencoded
```

```
 9: Content-length: 52
10:    *** a blank line ***
11: usrName=Mr.+John+JohnSmith
12: &tel=%2801890%29+1234+5678
```

Sometimes, the `post` method is also called the post-query. This post-query requests the file my_perl_2.pl from the root directory of the server (line 1). In this case, the file is a Perl script and in fact can be any CGI applications acceptable by the CGI and server.

Unlike most client–server interactions for which the content type (line 8) is usually text/html to indicate an XHTML document, the content type in this case is the MIME type specified as `application/x-www-form-urlencoded`. This means that the variable "name/value" pairs will be encoded in the same way as a URL encoding. The total length of data (lines 11–12) is 52 and stored in the content length (line 9) environment.

Bearing the client–server interaction in mind, you now have a basic picture of how CGI works and in particular how HTML/XHTML works as mentioned in Chapter 1. HTML/XHTML can be considered as a special case of CGI applications where the browser sends a simple HTTP message to get an HTML/XHTML document.

As a demonstration example, we change line 12 of ex14-09.htm to

```
12: <form action="ex14-10.pl" method="post">
```

and call this new example ex14-10.htm. This example is a form application with the `post` method. When the form is submitted, the form contents are sent to the Perl script ex14-10.pl. The main function of this script is to output the content length and the entire post-query string as illustrated in lines 9, 11, and 12 of the listing ex14-07.txt. Some screen shots are shown in Figs 14.19 and 14.20.

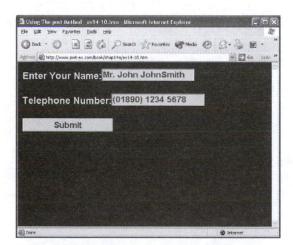

Figure 14.19 ex14-10.htm

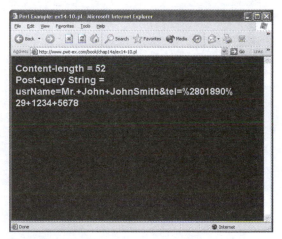

Figure 14.20 The post-query string

The listing of the Perl script ex14-10.pl is as follows:

```
Example: ex14-10.pl - The Perl Script For ex14-10.htm

1: #! /usr/bin/perl
2:
3: ## Demonstration Script On The post Method
4: ## The first thing after the Content-type is
5: ## to read the data block with CONTENT_LENGTH
6:
7: print ("Content-type/html\n\n");
8:
9: my $postQuerySt;
```

```
10: read(STDIN, $postQuerySt, $ENV{'CONTENT_LENGTH'});
11:
12: print << "myDoc";
13: <?xml version="1.0" encoding="iso-8859-1"?>
14: <!DOCTYPE html PUBLIC "-//W3C//DTD XHTML 1.0 Transitional//EN"
15: "http://www.w3.org/TR/xhtml1/DTD/xhtml1-transitional.dtd">
16: <html xmlns="http://www.w3.org/1999/xhtml" xml:lang="en" lang="en">
17: <head><title>Perl Example: ex14-10.pl</title></head>
18: <body style="background:#000088;font-family:arial;font-size:18pt;
19:   color:#ffff00;font-weight:bold">
20: myDoc
21:
22: print "Content-length = $ENV{CONTENT_LENGTH} <br />";
23: print "Post-query String = $postQuerySt";
24: print "</body></html>";
```

After the CGI header in line 7, a local variable $postQuerySt is declared to store the post-query string. To get the post-query string from the client–server interaction, you need to issue a read command to read from the standard input as illustrated in line 10. The third argument of the read command, $ENV{'CONTENT_LENGTH'}, represents the length of the string so that you have a proper reading. The content length and the post-query string are output to the screen by executing the print statements in lines 22 and 23.

To convert the encoded string back to a normal string and split the name/value pairs into individual items, let's modify the Perl script in ex14-10.pl to accept the post-query. This new Perl script is called ex14-11.pl and listed below:

```
Example: ex14-11.pl – The Perl Script For ex14-11.htm

 1: #! /usr/bin/perl
 2:
 3: ## Minimum Requirement For CGI Application
 4: print ("Content-type:text/html\n\n");
 5:
 6: my $postQuerySt;
 7: read(STDIN, $postQuerySt, $ENV{'CONTENT_LENGTH'});
 8:
 9: print << "myDoc";
10: <?xml version="1.0" encoding="iso-8859-1"?>
11: <!DOCTYPE html PUBLIC "-//W3C//DTD XHTML 1.0 Transitional//EN"
12: "http://www.w3.org/TR/xhtml1/DTD/xhtml1-transitional.dtd">
13: <html xmlns="http://www.w3.org/1999/xhtml" xml:lang="en" lang="en">
14: <head><title>Perl Example: ex14-11.pl</title></head>
15: <body style="background:#000088;font-family:arial;font-size:18pt;
16:   color:#ffff00;font-weight:bold">
17: myDoc
18:
19: if ( $postQuerySt eq "" )
20: {
21:   print 'We have received an empty input string';
22: } else {
23:   my @pairs = split ( "&", $postQuerySt );
24:   print "Time : ",scalar(localtime());
25:   printf "<br />The Submitted Form Contents are: <br />";
26:   foreach my $i (0 .. $#pairs)
27:   {
28:     ## Convert plus's to spaces
29:     $pairs[$i] =~ s/\+/ /g;
30:     my ($name, $value) = split("=",$pairs[$i]);
31:
```

```
32:      # Convert %XX from hex numbers to alphanumeric
33:      $name =~ s/%(..)/pack("c",hex($1))/ge;
34:      $value =~ s/%(..)/pack("c",hex($1))/ge;
35:    print " '$name' = '$value' <br />";
36:    }
37:    print "===================================="
38: }
39: print "</body></html>";
```

This script is similar to ex14-09.pl. The only modification is in lines 6–7 and changes the query string ($querySt) to a post-query string ($postQurySt). Line 7 is used to read the data string from the HTTP message. Once you have the data stored in the variable $postQurySt, the process for splitting the name/value pairs is the same.

Let's consider another example based on ex14-06.htm. We replace the form definition (lines 19–74) of ex14-06.htm by the form in ex14-08.txt and call this new example ex14-11.htm.

```
Listing: ex14-08.txt - Example Fragment Of ex14-11.htm

 1: <form action="ex14-11.pl" style="text-align:center" method="post">
 2:
 3: <table class="txtSt" cellspacing="5"><tr><td>Name:</td>
 4:  <td><input type="text" name="usrN" id="usrN" class="butSt" /></td>
 5:  <td>Email Address:</td>
 6:  <td><input type="text" name="email" id="email" class="butSt" /></td>
 7: </table><br />
 8:
 9: Which Operating System Do You Like Best?<br /><br />
10: <table cellspacing="5" border="0">
11: <tr><td><input type="radio" name="os" id="os" class="butSt2"
12:    value="Windows 9x" checked /></td><td class="txtSt">Windows 9x</td>
13:  <td><input type="radio" name="os" id="os" class="butSt2"
14:    value="Windows NT" /></td><td class="txtSt">Windows NT</td></tr>
15: <tr><td><input type="radio" name="os" id="os" class="butSt2"
16:    value="Mac OS" /></td><td class="txtSt">Mac OS</td>
17:  <td><input type="radio" name="os" id="os" class="butSt2"
18:    value="LINUX" /></td><td class="txtSt">LINUX</td></tr>
19: </table><br />
20:
21: Which Browser Do You Like Best?<br /><br />
22: <table cellspacing="5" border="0">
23: <tr><td><input type="radio" name="br" id="br" class="butSt2"
24:    value="IE 6+" checked /></td><td class="txtSt">IE 6</td>
25:  <td><input type="radio" name="br" id="br" class="butSt2"
26:    value="IE 5.5" /></td><td class="txtSt">IE 5.5</td></tr>
27: <tr><td><input type="radio" name="br" id="br" class="butSt2"
28:    value="NS 6+" /></td><td class="txtSt">NS 6.1</td>
29:  <td><input type="radio" name="br" id="br" class="butSt2"
30:    value="NS 4.x" /></td><td class="txtSt">NS 4.x</td></tr>
31: <tr><td><input type="radio" name="br" id="br" class="butSt2"
32:    value="Opera" /></td><td class="txtSt">Opera</td>
33:  <td><input type="radio" name="br" id="br" class="butSt2"
34:    value="Mozilla" /></td><td class="txtSt">Mozilla</td></tr>
35: </table><br />
36:
37: <table class="txtSt" cellspacing="5"><tr>
38:  <td><input type="submit" value="Submit" class="butSt" /></td>
39:  <td><input type="reset" value="Reset" class="butSt" /></td></tr>
40: </table>
41:
42: </form>
```

This fill-out form is a questionnaire trying to collect information on favorite operating system and browser from users. The user name and email fields are defined in the first table. The favorite operating system and browser questions are defined in the second and third tables respectively. They are in the format of multiple choices with radio boxes. When the form is submitted, the Perl script ex14-11.pl is called and the results are displayed. Some screen shots are shown in Figs 14.21 and14.22.

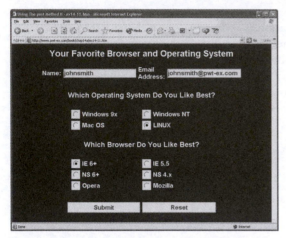

Figure 14.21 ex14-11.htm

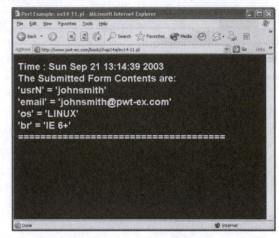

Figure 14.22 The collected results

Naturally, the next question will be: "Can we have a script to collect form contents regardless of the get or post methods?"

14.4.3 A general script for the get and post methods

If you know the name attribute of an element, the param() function of the Perl script can be used to extract the value of that element. This function applies to most XHTML elements and contains no additional restrictions. For example, suppose you have a form fragment

```
<form action="my_perl.pl" method="post">
  Enter Your Name:
  <input type="text" name="usrName" id="usrName" value="">
  Telephone Number:
  <input type="text" name="tel" id="tel" value="">
  <input type="submit" value="Submit">
</form>
```

You can gain access to the value of usrName with the following Perl statement in my_perl.pl:

```
my $username = param('usrName');
```

The param() function is a useful and widely used function and, in many cases, elegant results can be achieved. However, to use param() function, you may need to have an additional CGI module installed. Also, to include a specific name in a script would mean that you may need to change the script at the same time when you want to change the name. For example, if you want to change the form above to get an email address instead of a telephone number, you need to change param(). How can we have a Perl script work on both get and post methods and independently of parameter name?

One solution is to use detection. In Perl script the request method is stored in the environment variable $ENV{'REQUEST_METHOD'}. This variable returns "GET," if the get method is used; if this variable returns "POST," you know that the post method is in action.

Consider the following Perl script:

Example: ex14-12.pl – Combining The get And post Methods

```perl
 1: #! /usr/bin/perl
 2:
 3: ## Minimum Requirement For CGI Application
 4: print ("Content-type:text/html\n\n");
 5:
 6: my $formSt="UNKNOWN";
 7: if ($ENV{'REQUEST_METHOD'} eq "GET")
 8: {
 9:     $formSt = $ENV{'QUERY_STRING'};
10: } elsif ($ENV{'REQUEST_METHOD'} eq "POST") {
11:     read(STDIN,$formSt,$ENV{'CONTENT_LENGTH'});
12: }
13:
14: print << "myDoc";
15:   <?xml version="1.0" encoding="iso-8859-1"?>
16:   <!DOCTYPE html PUBLIC "-//W3C//DTD XHTML 1.0 Transitional//EN"
17:   "http://www.w3.org/TR/xhtml1/DTD/xhtml1-transitional.dtd">
18:   <html xmlns="http://www.w3.org/1999/xhtml" xml:lang="en" lang="en">
19:   <head><title>Perl Example: ex14-12.pl</title></head>
20:   <body style="background:#000088;font-family:arial;font-size:18pt;
21:      color:#ffff00;font-weight:bold">
22: myDoc
23:
24: if ( $formSt eq "" )
25: {
26:   print 'We have received an empty input string';
27: } else {
28:   my @pairs = split ( "&", $formSt );
29:   print "Time : ",scalar(localtime());
30:   printf "<br />The Submitted Form Contents are: <br />";
31:   foreach my $i (0 .. $#pairs)
32:   {
33:     ## Convert plus's to spaces
34:     $pairs[$i] =~ s/\+/ /g;
35:     my ($name, $value) = split("=",$pairs[$i]);
36:
37:     # Convert %XX from hex numbers to alphanumeric
38:     $name =~ s/%(..)/pack("c",hex($1))/ge;
39:     $value =~ s/%(..)/pack("c",hex($1))/ge;
40:   print " '$name' = '$value' <br />";
41:   }
42:   print "===================================="
43: }
44: print "</body></html>";
```

This script is a modification of ex14-10.pl, the only modification being the detection code in lines 6–12. If the request method equals "GET," the query string $ENV('REQUEST_STRING') is assigned to the variable $formSt (form string); if the request method is "POST," read the post-query string from the standard input and assign it to variable $formSt.

Now you have a general purpose Perl script to get form contents. This script will be used later in an e-commerce example. For further studies or if you want to program your own CGI applications with your favorite language, the following information and discussion may help.

For the `get` method, the string "GET" and the name/value pairs (query string) are stored in the environment variables "REQUEST_METHOD" and "QUERY_STRING" respectively. These settings are standard and independent of any programming language. If you are familiar with a programming language or script that can access the environment of your system, you can use it to gain access to the data passed by the XHTML form via the browser. The following listing is the pseudo code to read the query string associated with the `get` method:

```
form_method = read_env("REQUEST_METHOD");
if ( form_method eq "GET") then
 query_st = read_env("QUERY_STRING");
endif
```

The first line is to get the value of the environment variable "REQUEST_METHOD" and assign it to the variable `form_method`. If `form_method` equals "GET" then get the value of the "QUERY_STRING" and assign it to the variable `query_st`. If you are using C/C++, you can replace `read_env("REQUEST_METHOD")` by `getenv("REQUEST_METHOD")`.

For the `post` method, the string "POST" and the length of the query string are stored in the environment variables "REQUEST_METHOD" and "CONTENT_LENGTH." The query string itself is passed as a data block via the standard input (similar to keyboard input). To get the query string from the `post` method, the following pseudo code may be used:

```
form_method = read_env("REQUEST_METHOD");
if ( form_method eq "POST") then
 noChar = read_env("CONTENT_LENGTH");
 query_st = read (STDIN,noChar);
endif
```

First you get the request method from the environment "REQUEST_METHOD." If it is a "POST" method, you get the number of characters (`noChar`) of the query string from the environment "CONTENT_LENGTH." The query string can be obtained by reading `noChar`, the number of characters, from the standard input (`STDIN`) or keyboard. Next, can we pass data to a CGI application without using forms?

14.4.4 Passing parameters without forms

In fact, any XHTML element with `URL` as attribute can call CGI applications and pass data. If you want to call and pass parameters to a CGI application with these elements, all you need is to append the parameters to the URL. Indeed, the ability to append data or parameters to an arbitrary URL makes it possible to construct elements such as `<anchor>` to send data to server scripts when they are activated. This allows XHTML programmers to set up so-called "canned queries" in the document and pass parameters to CGI programs easily when other passing techniques are difficult or impossible. Canned queries are used everywhere on the Web and some people consider the `get` method as a canned query too.

From a practical point of view, one characteristic of the canned query is that the name/value pairs will appear at the address bar of your browser since the name/value pairs are appended to the URL. Almost all major sites are using them in one way or another.

For example, the following page fragment could generate a list of conferences related to "Public Health," "Cancer Treatments," and "Healthy Diet":

```
Click the topic below for a list of conferences:
```

```
<a href="http://www.pwt-ex.com/search_engine?
   year=2003&conf_topic=public_health">Public Health</a>
<a href="http://www.pwt-ex.com/search_engine?
   year=2003&conf_topic=Cancer_Treatments">Cancer Treatments</a>
<a href="http://www.pwt-ex.com/search_engine?
   year=2003&conf_topic=Healthy_Diet">Healthy Diet</a>
```

Note that the attribute href="xx...xx" defined in each anchor element should be in one line since it represents a single string. When, for example, the "Public Health" topic is clicked, the anchor action will activate the CGI application search_engine with the name/value pair parameters, i.e.,

http://www.pwt-ex.com/search_engine?year=2002&conf_topic=public_health

The CGI application search_engine in this case can be designed to handle the parameters as input and generate the appropriate list. Since you should know the CGI application that you developed, parameters can be "canned" in as name/value pairs. This is just a virtual example fragment since we haven't yet considered databases. Another practical example is given in the next section.

14.4.5 A page to log on to multiple sites

Suppose you have three offices around the world in London, New York, and Tokyo. Each office has a Web server and is protected by a password login. The Internet addresses of the Web servers are

www.pwt-ex.com (London server)

www.pwt-ex.jp (Tokyo server)

www.pwt-ex.net (New York server)

Suppose they are protected by the same password program ex14-13.pl. This program will ask for a user name (usern) and password (passw) before any server operation can be granted. Gaining access to these three computer servers is your daily business and your user name and password are

User name: johnsmith

Password: john199

Instead of typing your user name and password every time to log in to the server, you can actually develop a local Web page in your hard drive to log in to any of the servers at any time.

Consider the following page:

Example: ex14-13.htm - A Page To Log On To Multiple Sites

```
 1: <?xml version="1.0" encoding="iso-8859-1"?>
 2: <!DOCTYPE html PUBLIC "-//W3C//DTD XHTML 1.0 Transitional//EN"
 3: "http://www.w3.org/TR/xhtml1/DTD/xhtml1-transitional.dtd">
 4: <html xmlns="http://www.w3.org/1999/xhtml" xml:lang="en" lang="en">
 5: <head><title>Log On To Multiple Sites - ex14-13.htm</title></head>
 6: <style>
 7:   .butSt{width:400px;font-family:arial;font-weight:bold;
 8:   font-size:18pt;color:#ffff00}
 9: </style>
10: <body style="background:#000088;font-family:arial;font-size:18pt;
11:    color:#ffff00;font-weight:bold">
12: Connect To Multiple Offices<br /><br />
13:
14: <a href="ex14-13.pl?usern=johnsmith&passw=john199"
```

```
15:      class="butSt">Connect local (London) office</a>
16: <a href="ex14-13.pl?usern=johnsmith&passw=john199"
17:      class="butSt">Connect To Tokyo office</a>
18: <a href="ex14-13.pl?usern=johnsmith&passw=john199"
19:      class="butSt">Connect To New York office</a>
20:
21: </body>
22: </html>
```

This page contains three texts, each defined by an anchor element. The first anchor element is

```
<a href="ex14-13.pl?usern=johnsmith&passw=john199"
      class="butSt">Connect local (London) office</a>
```

This statement displays an underlined text "Connect local (London) office." When this text is clicked, the CGI application ex14-13.pl is activated with

```
usern=johnsmith&passw=john199
```

as the query string. The name/value pairs of the query string will be processed by the password program ex14-13.pl to perform the login operation. The listing of ex14-13.pl is given below:

```
Example: ex14-13.pl - The Perl Script For ex14-13.htm

 1: #! /usr/bin/perl
 2: use warnings;
 3: use strict;
 4: use CGI qw( :standard );
 5: print ("Content-type/html\n\n");
 6:
 7: my $username = param("usern");
 8: my $password = param("passw");
 9: my $matchuser=0;
10: my $matchpass=0;
11:
12: my @name = ("johnsmith","Robinson","Brown");
13: my @pass = ("john199","Mike100","Tom111");
14:
15: foreach my $ii (0..2)
16: {
17:   if($name[$ii] eq $username)
18:   {
19:       $matchuser = 1;
20:     if ($pass[$ii] eq $password)
21:     {
22:       $matchpass = 1;
23:     }
24:   }
25: }
26:
27: print << "myDoc";
28:  <?xml version="1.0" encoding="iso-8859-1"?>
29:  <!DOCTYPE html PUBLIC "-//W3C//DTD XHTML 1.0 Transitional//EN"
30:  "http://www.w3.org/TR/xhtml1/DTD/xhtml1-transitional.dtd">
31:  <html xmlns="http://www.w3.org/1999/xhtml" xml:lang="en" lang="en">
32:  <head><title>Perl Example: ex14-13.pl</title></head>
33:  <body style="background:#000088;font-family:arial;font-size:18pt;
34:    color:#ffff00;font-weight:bold">
35: myDoc
36:
```

```
37: if ($matchuser && $matchpass)
38: {
39:     print "Thank you! $username.<br />";
40:     print "You have logged on successfully.";
41: }
42: elsif ($matchuser && !$matchpass)
43: {
44:     print "Sorry! $username.<br />";
45:     print "Wrong password.";
46: }
47: else
48: {
49:     print "Sorry! Access Denied.";
50: }
51:
52: print "</body></html>"
```

After the CGI header in line 5, we use two `param()` functions to get the user name (`usern`) and password (`passw`) data from the query string of the Web page. Two local variables, `$matchuser` and `$matchpass`, are also declared. They are used to indicate whether the user name and/or password are matched. Soon after the variables, two arrays are declared which store the list of user names and their corresponding passwords. As a simple demonstration example, only three names and passwords are included. A proper password program should read the data from a file or storage media and is the subject of the next chapter. Before that, we just want to hard-code the user names and passwords as arrays.

The main operation of this password program is the for-loop in lines 16–24. The loop variable `$ii` runs from 0 through 2. That is, for each name in the array `$name[]`, a comparison test takes place against the user name variable `$username`. If they match, we set the `$matchuser` as true. The comparison test is carried on to test the password. If a match is found, the variable `$matchpass` is also set to be true. The conditions of `$matchuser` and `$matchpass` are used to determine whether you are allowed to gain access to the system. If both `$matchuser` and `$matchpass` are true, you are allowed to use the system and a welcome message is displayed. If `$matchuser` is true but not in `$matchpass`, then we have a wrong password case as illustrated in lines 42–46. If the user name is wrong, the login is denied and a message is displayed as in line 49. This script will be revisited in the next chapter to build a proper password program.

Some screen shots are shown in Figs 14.23 and 14.24.

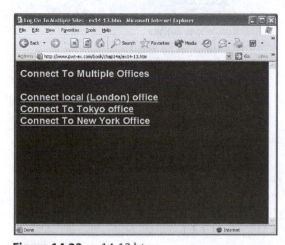

Figure 14.23 ex14-13.htm

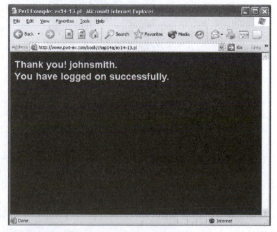

Figure 14.24 Successful logon

14.5 A simple e-commerce application for small businesses

14.5.1 A simple business model on the Internet

Many small businesses such as shops, restaurants, and cafés may already have some kind of telephone/fax ordering service. A typical telephone ordering service may include "accepting orders on the phone," "delivery in local area," and "collecting payment." For these small businesses, in addition to telephone ordering, one obvious approach to expand their businesses to reach more customers is to accept orders over the Internet.

From the customers' point of view, the major advantage of online ordering is that a full list of services/products can be seen. Pricing, additional information or descriptions, pictures of the product, and/or services can also be provided. Putting your business and accepting orders online will enhance your services and not be restricted by just one or two telephone lines.

The online business or e-commerce that we are going to design is a simple one without any money transactions over the Internet. The design involves a local computer in a shop that has access to a server on the Internet provided by an ISP (see Fig. 14.25). The server should host the shop's Web site address and be connected to the Internet all the time. Most ISPs can provide hosting services for very little charge or are virtually free. The local machine in your shop should be able to get emails from the ISP just like you check your personal emails at home through your ISP.

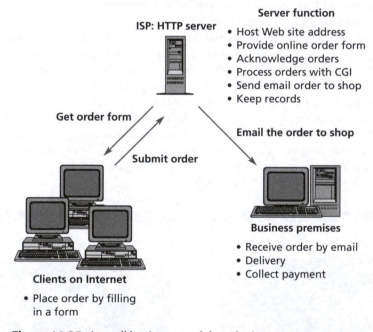

Figure 14.25 A small business model on the Internet

Basically the operation of the model is simple. You set up a Web site for your shop on the server provided by your ISP. The customers get information and an order form from your Web site. When they place an order by submitting the form back to the server, a CGI application is activated to process the form and ultimately sends the order to you by email. All you then need is to get a machine in the shop to check the email and to print the order out.

To make this work, you may need to write (or ask someone to write) a Web application that includes a page with one or more forms for online ordering and a CGI application to process the form. For a simple model like this one, the CGI application can be as simple as getting the ordered items and the ability to send email. Once you have the Web page with the CGI application uploaded to the server, you are ready to receive orders from your local machine inside the shop by email.

14.5.2 A page to receive and process online orders

As an example, suppose you are running a small café called "Jenny's Café" with a local telephone ordering and delivery service. To expand the business, you have set up a Web site address www.JennyCafe.com and an email account Jenny@JennyCafe.com allocated by an ISP. To expand the business on the Internet, you need to write an XHTML Web page to include "Today's Menu" and take orders from the customers. The page ex14-05.htm is a good example, but we want more flexibility to change the menu items and add some more easily. A modification is given below:

Example: ex14-14.htm – A Page To Receive Online Orders

```
 1: <?xml version="1.0" encoding="iso-8859-1"?>
 2: <!DOCTYPE html PUBLIC "-//W3C//DTD XHTML 1.0 Transitional//EN"
 3: "http://www.w3.org/TR/xhtml1/DTD/xhtml1-transitional.dtd">
 4: <html xmlns="http://www.w3.org/1999/xhtml" xml:lang="en" lang="en">
 5: <head><title> Receiving Online Orders - ex14-14.htm</title></head>
 6: <style>
 7:   .butSt{background:#aaffaa;width:200px;
 8:     font-family:arial;font-weight:bold;font-size:16pt;color:#880000}
 9:   .butSt2{background:#aaffaa;width:30px;height:30px;
10:     font-family:arial;font-weight:bold;font-size:18pt;color:#880000}
11:   .txtSt{width:250px;
12:     font-family:arial;font-weight:bold;font-size:16pt;color:#ffff00}
13: </style>
14: <script>
15:   noRow = 3
16:   noCol = 2
17:   menuValue = new Array("Burger Combo","Seafood Burger",
18:                         "Chicken Burger Royal","Lamb Fajita",
19:                         "Vegetarian Delight","Two Jumbo Sausages")
20:   menuPrice = new Array("3.50","4.50","3.50","4.50","3.50","4.50")
21:   currency = "\$"
22: </script>
23: <body style="background:#000088;font-family:arial;font-size:18pt;
24:   color:#ffff00;font-weight:bold">
25: <div style="font-size:22pt;font-weight:bold;text-align:center">
26:   Jenny's Cafe <br /> Internet Ordering & Delivery Services</div>
27:
28: <form action="ex14-14.pl" style="text-align:center" method="post">
29:     <div id="usrTable"></div>
30:   Special Offer From Today's Menu<br />
31:   All Come With Fries<br /><br />
32:     <div id="menuTable"></div>
33:   How Would You Like To Pay?<br /><br />
34:     <div id="payTable"></div>
35:   <table class="txtSt" cellspacing="5"><tr>
36:    <td><input type="submit" value="Submit" class="butSt" /></td>
37:    <td><input type="reset" value="Reset" class="butSt" /></td></tr>
38:   </table>
39:   Payment Will Be Collected By Delivery Personnel
```

```
40: </form>
41:
42: <script src="ex14-14.js"></script>
43: </body>
44: </html>
```

The first part of this page (lines 15–21) contains two arrays, "menuValue" and "menuPrice." They are linked to each other. For example, consider the items of each array:

```
menuValue              menuPrice
Burger Combo           3.50
Seafood Burger         4.50
...         ...
Two Jumbo Sausages     4.50
```

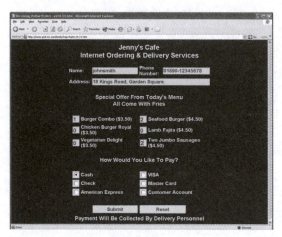

Figure 14.26 ex14-14.htm

The order of appearance is important since each price is associated with a menu item. When the form is submitted to the server, both values are needed to pass to the CGI application. Using arrays will make any changes to the menu easier. To change the online menu and prices, these arrays need to be altered and only this page needs to be uploaded again.

The second part of the page is a form application. Inside the form, there are three division elements with identities "usrTable" (user information), "menuTable" (menu information), and "payTable" (payment information). They will display three table structures with input elements generated by the ECMAScript program file ex14-14.js. The first table is a structure to obtain a customer's information such as "Name," "Phone Number," and "Address" so that delivery is possible. The second table displays the menu and obtains the customer's order. The third table structure is used to obtain the payment information. For the display of this page, see the screen shot in Fig. 14.26.

The program file ex14-14.js responsible for the generation of the table structures is listed below:

```
Example: ex14-14.js - The ECMAScript Program File For ex14-14.htm

 1:  usrSt='<table class="txtSt" cellspacing="5"><tr><td>Name:</td>'+
 2:   '<td><input type="text" name="usrN" id="usrN" class="butSt" /></td>'+
 3:   '<td>Phone Number:</td>'+
 4:   '<td><input type="text" name="phone" id="phone" class="butSt" /></td>'+
 5:   '</tr><tr><td>Address:</td><td colspan="3">'+
 6:   '<input type="text" name="addr" id="addr" class="butSt" '+
 7:   'style="width:510px" /></td></tr>'+
 8:   '</table><br />'
 9:
10: menuSt = '<table cellspacing="5" border="0">'
11:  for (ii=0;ii<noRow;ii++)
12:  {
13:    menuSt = menuSt +'<tr>'
14:   for(jj=0;jj<noCol;jj++)
15:    {
16:    menuSt = menuSt +'<td><input type="text" name="'+
17:     menuValue[(jj+ii*noCol)]+'@'+menuPrice[jj+ii*noCol]+'" id="'+
18:     menuValue[(jj+ii*noCol)]+'@'+menuPrice[jj+ii*noCol]+
```

```
19:        '" class="butSt2" value="0" /></td>'+
20:        '<td class="txtSt">'+menuValue[(jj+ii*noCol)] +
21:        ' ('+currency+menuPrice[(jj+ii*noCol)]+')</td>'
22:     }
23:     menuSt = menuSt +'</tr>'
24:  }
25:  menuSt = menuSt + '</table><br />'
26:
27:
28: paySt = '<table cellspacing="5" border="0">'+
29: '<tr><td><input type="radio" name="Payment" id="Payment" class="butSt2" '+
30: '  value="Cash" checked /></td><td class="txtSt">Cash</td>'+
31: '<td><input type="radio" name="Payment" id="Payment" class="butSt2" '+
32: '  value="VISA" /></td><td class="txtSt">VISA</td></tr>'+
33: '<tr><td><input type="radio" name="Payment" id="Payment" class="butSt2" '+
34: '  value="Check" /></td><td class="txtSt">Check</td>'+
35: '<td><input type="radio" name="Payment" id="Payment" class="butSt2" '+
36: '  value="Master Card" /></td><td class="txtSt">Master Card</td></tr>'+
37: '<tr><td><input type="radio" name="Payment" id="Payment" class="butSt2" '+
38: 'value="American Express" /></td><td class="txtSt">American Express</td>'+
39: '<td><input type="radio" name="Payment" id="Payment" class="butSt2" '+
40: 'value="Customer Account" /></td><td class="txtSt">Customer Account</td>'+
41: '</tr></table><br />'
42:
43:  document.getElementById("usrTable").innerHTML = usrSt
44:  document.getElementById("menuTable").innerHTML = menuSt
45:  document.getElementById("payTable").innerHTML = paySt
```

The table structures represented by the strings usrSt (lines 1–8) and paySt (28–41) are easy to understand. The interesting part is the table structure generated by menuSt defined in lines 10–25. The six menu items are arranged into six rows by two columns. The for-loop on the ii variable generates the rows; another for-loop handles the columns. For example, when ii=0, the first row of the table structure becomes

```
<tr><td><input type="text" name="Burger Combo@3.50"
        id="Burger Combo@3.50" class="butSt2" value="0" /></td>
    <td>Burger Combo</td>

    <td><input type="text" name="Seafood Burger@4.50"
        id="Seafood Burger@4.50" class="butSt2" value="0" /></td>
    <td>Seafood Burger</td></tr>
```

After three rows and adding the table tag names, we have a complete table structure. All three table structures are displayed by the statements in lines 43–45.

If the customer has made order 1 "Burger Combo," the value attribute associated with the text box will have value =1. When the customer presses the Submit button, the whole form data and hence the name/value pair of the "Burger Combo" are sent to the CGI application ex14-14.pl. The name/value pair of the "Burger Combo" is

```
"Burger Combo@3.50 = 1"
```

Using some simple split functions of Perl, the name/value pair can be easily split into "Burger Combo," "3.5" (price), and "1" (quantity). A confirmation of the order message is shown in Fig. 14.27.

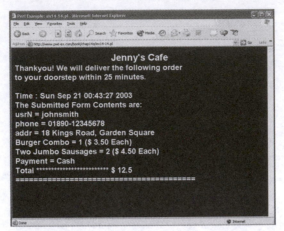

Figure 14.27 Confirmation of order

To process the submitted form, a Perl script, ex14-14.pl, is used. The first part of the script is listed below:

Example: ex14-14.pl – The Perl Script For ex14-14.htm (Part One)

```perl
 1: #! /usr/bin/perl
 2:
 3: ## Minimum Requirement For CGI Application
 4: print ("Content-type:text/html\n\n");
 5: my $formSt="UNKNOWN";
 6:
 7: if ($ENV{'REQUEST_METHOD'} eq "GET")
 8: {
 9:     $formSt = $ENV{'QUERY_STRING'};
10: } elsif ($ENV{'REQUEST_METHOD'} eq "POST") {
11:     read(STDIN,$formSt,$ENV{'CONTENT_LENGTH'});
12: }
13: my $total = 0;
14: my $outMsg = '';
15: my $price = 0.0;
16: my $name2;
17: my $name;
18: my $value;
19:
20: if ( $formSt eq "" )
21: {
22:   print 'We have received an empty input string';
23: } else {
24:   my @pairs = split ( "&", $formSt );
25:   my $tmpSt = sprintf "Time : %s",scalar(localtime());
26:
27:   $outMsg = $outMsg . $tmpSt;
28:   $outMsg = $outMsg . "<br />The Submitted Form Contents are: <br />";
29:   foreach my $i (0 .. $#pairs)
30:   {
31:   ## Convert plus's to spaces
32:     $pairs[$i] =~ s/\+/ /g;
33:     ($name2, $value) = split("=",$pairs[$i]);
34:     ($name, $price) = split("@",$name2);
35:   ## Convert %XX from hex numbers to alphanumeric
36:     $name =~ s/%(..)/pack("c",hex($1))/ge;
```

```
37:      $value =~ s/%(..)/pack("c",hex($1))/ge;
38:
39:      if ( $i <= 2)
40:      {
41:        $outMsg = $outMsg . " $name = $value <br />";
42:      } else {
43:       if ( $value != 0)
44:        {
45:         $outMsg = $outMsg . " $name = $value (\$ $price Each) <br />";
46:         $total = $total + $value * $price
47:        }
48:      }
49:    }
50:    $outMsg = $outMsg . " $name = $value <br />";
51:    $outMsg = $outMsg . " Total ********************** \$ $total<br />";
52:    $outMsg = $outMsg . "===================================== <br />";
53: }
```

This script is designed to handle both get and post methods. After the CGI header, some local variables are declared in lines 13–18, the first two of which are:

- $total   – To calculate the total payment of the order.
- $outMsg – An important string to represent all the ordering and used to confirm the order and email to the shop.

To build the $outMsg string, a number of string concatenations are performed. Line 25 is to print the date and time into a string variable $tmpSt. This string is added to $outMsg by (line 27)

```
$outMsg = $outMsg . $tmpSt
```

In Perl, a period symbol is used to combine two strings together. Since we have passed the name, price, and quantity to the script, the statements in lines 33–34 are used to split them into the variables $name, $price, and $value (quantity).

Since the first three name/value pairs are user information, the for-loop in lines 39–42 is used to add the information directly into $outMsg. For the remaining name/value pairs, we execute the following statements (lines 43–47):

```
if ( $value != 0)
{
 $outMsg = $outMsg . " $name = $value (\$ $price Each) <br />";
 $total = $total + $value * $price
}
```

That is, if the ordered quantity $value is not 0, the menu variables $name, $value, and $price are added to the string $outMsg. Then the total price of the order is calculated by $value * $price and added to $total. The final name/value pair is the payment method and is added to $outMsg at line 50. After the total price, a double line is added to the string $outMsg to represent the end of the order. The entire string $outMsg is displayed to the customer for confirmation and finally sent by email to the shop for preparation and delivery.

The second part of the script is listed below:

```
Listing: Continuation Of The Perl Script - ex14-14.pl (Part Two)
```

```
54:
55: print << "myDoc";
56:   <?xml version="1.0" encoding="iso-8859-1"?>
57:   <!DOCTYPE html PUBLIC "-//W3C//DTD XHTML 1.0 Transitional//EN"
58:   "http://www.w3.org/TR/xhtml1/DTD/xhtml1-transitional.dtd">
```

```
59:  <html xmlns="http://www.w3.org/1999/xhtml" xml:lang="en" lang="en">
60:  <head><title>Perl Example: ex14-14.pl</title></head>
61:  <body style="background:#000088;font-family:arial;font-size:18pt;
62:    color:#ffff00;font-weight:bold">
63:  <div style="text-align:center;font-size:22pt">Jenny's Cafe</div>
64:  Thank you! We will deliver the following order <br />
65:  to your doorstep within 25 minutes.<br /><br />
66:  $outMsg
67:  </body></html>
68:  myDoc
69:
70:  $outMsg =~ s/<br \/>/\\n/g;
71:  ##Send Email To The Shop
72:  open (USRMAIL, "| /usr/lib/sendmail -oi -n -t" );
73:  print USRMAIL << "usr_message";
74:  To:Jenny@JennyCafe.com
75:  From:www.JennyCafe.com
76:  Subject:Online Order
77:  $outMsg
78:  usr_message
79:  close USRMAIL;
```

The Perl script in lines 54–68 is just a `here` document to generate an XHTML page back to the customer. After the message confirming the order, the entire order is displayed at line 66.

Since the string `$outMsg` contains the XHTML element `<br />`, straightforward substitution with Perl script at line 70 will replace it with "\n" (new line). Then this new `$outMsg` is sent by email to the café with a simple call to `sendmail`. The local machine inside the café can check the emails regularly for any online orders. A screen shot of an email reaching the café is shown in Fig. 14.28.

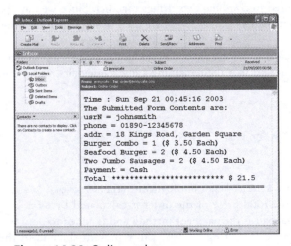

Figure 14.28 Online order

With a speed of more than 6,000 miles (9,600 kilometers) per second, email may be one of the most efficient methods of passing messages to the café. Also, by using email, hundreds of orders can be handled at the same time without any problems.

15

CGI applications using Perl script

15.1 Using server environment and system functions

15.1.1 Environment variables

We have examined some Perl scripts and their applications in Chapters 13 and 14. In this chapter, we will concentrate on how Perl can be applied to some popular interactive CGI applications including "Online Examinations and Marking," "Seat Reservations," "Search Engine," and "Database." In fact, the structure and scenario of the study is not limited to Perl script. The idea of the Common Gateway Interface or CGI, roughly speaking, is an abstraction about Web applications on a server. Perl is just a fashionable operating process to achieve that purpose. In parallel to the study and examples of this chapter, other CGI scripting languages such as PHP and ASP can also be implemented in a similar manner.

As a quick reminder of using Perl, the first line of each Perl script in this book is

```
#!/usr/bin/perl
```

This is a classical header for Perl script in the UNIX/LINUX environment. The Perl interpreter is assumed to be stored in the directory /usr/bin. If your Perl interpreter is located in another directory, you may need to change the header to reflect the location of the interpreter. If you are using a Microsoft system with IIS server and a Perl interpreter, you may use the line above as it is. For a Microsoft system with the Apache server, you may need to include the drive and location of the interpreter.

In the study of CGI applications, environment variables are an important subject. They are variables defined by the operating system for any application and program at any time. Usually, they hold information that may be useful to commands or programs running within the system.

Whether you are working in the Microsoft or UNIX/LINUX server environment, you can use Perl script to access environment variables with the statement $ENV{'variable'}. For example, the following Perl script fragment can be used to locate the window's directory in a Microsoft system:

```
#!/usr/bin/perl
print "Content-type:text/html\n\n";
print "The window directory is $ENV{windir} \n";
print "if you are using a Microsoft system";
```

If you are using a UNIX/LINUX system, the variable $ENV{'pwd'} will give you the current working directory. The entity %ENV is a collection of all environment variables.

Different systems may have different environment variable names. Furthermore, some applications such as Web server software can define their own environment variables. To see the environment variables on your server, consider the following Perl script:

```
Example: ex15-01.pl - Environment Variables With Perl

 1: #! /usr/bin/perl
 2: print ("Content-type:text/html\n\n");
 3:
 4: print << "mypage";
 5:  <?xml version="1.0" encoding="iso-8859-1"?>
 6:  <!DOCTYPE html PUBLIC "-//W3C//DTD XHTML 1.0 Transitional//EN"
 7:  "http://www.w3.org/TR/xhtml1/DTD/xhtml1-transitional.dtd">
 8:  <html xmlns="http://www.w3.org/1999/xhtml" xml:lang="en" lang="en">
 9:  <head><title>Example: ex15-01.pl</title></head>
10:   <style>.txtSt{font-size:14pt;color:#ffff00;font-family:arial}</style>
11:   <body style="background:#000088">
12: <table width="550" cellspacing="5" align="center" class="txtSt">
13: mypage
14:
15: foreach $var (sort keys %ENV)
16: {
17:    print "<tr>";
18:    print "<td>$var</td>";
19:    print "<td>$ENV{$var}<td>";
20:    print "</tr>";
21: }
22: print "    </table>";
23: print "  </body></html>";
```

After the CGI header, lines 4–13 define a here document to display part of an XHTML document. The collection of all environment variables %ENV is implemented as a hash function (or hash table). A hash function contains keys and values. For example, a typical %ENV on a system with Apache is represented internally by a hash function that looks like this:

```
%ENV = (
 DOCUMENT_ROOT       =>"/apache/htdocs"
 GATEWAY_INTERFACE =>"CGI/1.1"
 ...         ...         ...
 SERVER_SIGNATURE  =>"Apache/1.3.23 Server at www.pwt-ex.com Port 80
 )
```

The left hand side of the arrow => is the key and the right hand side contains the value. For example, the variable $ENV{'DOCUMENT_ROOT'} stores the value "/apache/htdocs." Therefore the phase (sort keys %ENV) in line 15 can be used to sort all the keys in %ENV. The statement in line 19 displays the value of the associated keys. A simple foreach loop is used to complete the XHTML table. A screen shot of the page running on the Apache system is shown in Fig. 15.1. A screen shot of the same page running on Windows XP with IIS is shown in Fig. 15.2. Note that in some earlier Windows systems, IIS is referred to as the Internet Information Server.

Another feature of Perl is the ability to call system functions. Almost any system functions can be called directly.

15.1.2 Calling system functions

In general, Perl allows you to call and run system functions, commands, and even other scripts. For example, you can run a command and send the result to the screen by

```
print 'command';
```

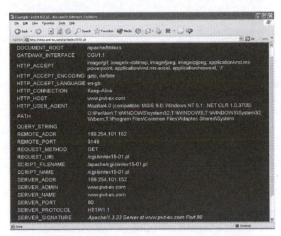

Figure 15.1 Environment variable on LINUX system with Apache

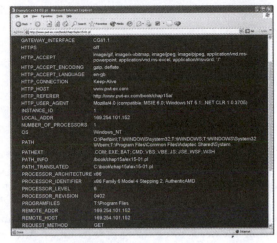

Figure 15.2 Environment variables on Windows XP systems

where the command is the name of the executable command or program to be executed by the Perl script. This feature is useful to run programs including shell commands as well as other Perl or shell scripts. For example, the following is a Perl script fragment to display the current date and time and no external function call is needed:

```
#!/usr/bin/perl
print "Content-type:text/html \n\n";
print "The Date and Time is =";
print scalar(localtime());
```

In a UNIX/LINUX system, the date function is usually located in the directory /bin/date. In this case, you can replace the last line by

```
print '/bin/date';
```

This will call the system function date and display the result in the browser window.

One of the important applications of system functions is to manipulate files. For example, you can print out the contents of a file in an UNIX/LINUX environment by

```
cat filename
```

where filename is the name of the file you want to print. For a Microsoft system, the command is type filename. The Perl statement

```
print 'cat filename';
```

will cause the contents of the file name to be sent to the browser screen. For example, suppose you have header and signature files named

```
/home/public_html/head.htm
/home/public_html/sig.htm
```

You can assign the contents of the header and signature files to variables such as $head and $sig and then use the variables in documents. Consider the following example:

```
Example: ex15-02.pl - Calling System Functions

1: #! /usr/bin/perl
2: print ("Content-type:text/html\n\n");
3: $head = 'cat /home/public_html/head.htm';
```

```
 4: $sig = 'cat /home/public_html/sig.htm';
 5:
 6: print << "mypage";
 7: $head
 8:   Thank you very much for returning the form. <br />
 9:   Your name will be added into our database and <br />
10:   we will send you our newsletter every week!
11: $sig
12:
13: mypage
```

This Perl script contains two variables, $head and $sig. The system function in line 3, 'cat/home/public_html/head.htm';, reads the contents of the file and stores it in $head. This variable is then used in line 7 to be displayed on the browser screen.

This script also contains a signature file attached at the end of the page. Using variables allows you to make changes relatively easily. In particular, if many documents refer to the same $head and $sig, only the referencing file needs to be changed or modified. After execution of the statement in line 3, the variable $head contains the following XHTML page:

```
Listing: ex15-01.txt - Web Page : head.htm

 1:  <?xml version="1.0" encoding="iso-8859-1"?>
 2:  <!DOCTYPE html PUBLIC "-//W3C//DTD XHTML 1.0 Transitional//EN"
 3:  "http://www.w3.org/TR/xhtml1/DTD/xhtml1-transitional.dtd">
 4:  <html xmlns="http://www.w3.org/1999/xhtml" xml:lang="en" lang="en">
 5:  <head><title> </title></head>
 6:  <style>.txtSt{font-size:14pt;color:#ffff00;font-family:arial}</style>
 7:  <body style="background:#000088;font-family:arial;
 8:      font-size:18pt;color:#ffff00">
 9:  <div style="text-align:center">Header Page: head.htm</div><br />
10:  <img src="line1.gif" width="500" heiht="6"><br /><br />
```

Similarly, the variable $sig contains the following XHTML page:

```
Listing: ex15-02.txt - Web Page : sig.htm

 1: <br /><br />
 2: <img src="line1.gif" width="500" height="6"><br /><br />
 3: From www.pwt-ex.com
 4: </body>
 5: </html>
```

When these two files are embedded into the Perl script as listed in ex15-02.pl, they form a completed XHTML document which is returned to the browser. In practice, you can put whatever you like in the header file representing the nature of your Web site. This is a handy technique to run a Web site with a large number of pages or directories sharing the same header and logo.

In order to use system function calls, you need to know what kind of system is on the server and what kinds of system functions are available. For example, the Perl script ex15-02.pl will return errors if run on a Microsoft server system such as Windows NT/2000/XP with IIS. For such a system to work, you may need to change the system call to

```
$head = 'type head.htm';
$sig = 'type sig.htm';
```

The command type is a proper function to display the contents of a file on Windows systems. A screen shot of this example is shown in Fig. 15.3.

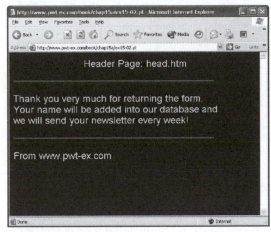

Figure 15.3 ex15-02.p1

This technique will be used to build a guest book feature later in this chapter.

15.2 Using server storage

15.2.1 Open a file for reading

Using server storage creates a permanent and reliable record for your Web activity, which in many cases is vital for many applications. For a simple page counter, database, or money transaction business, the ability to use server storage is critical.

To open a file using Perl script, the following statement is often used:

```
open (filehandle, "<filename");
```

This `open` command opens the file `filename` for reading and assigns a `filehandle` variable to control it. For different file operations, there are different file open modes. Some of the frequently used file open modes are listed in Table 15.1.

Table 15.1 File open modes

Mode	Operation	Description and example
<	Reading	Open a file for reading, e.g., `open (filehandle, "<filename");`
>	Writing	Create a file for writing. If the file already exists, discard the contents, e.g., `open (filehandle, ">filename");`
>>	Append	Open or create a file for writing. If the file exists, writing is at the end of the file, e.g., `open (filehandle, ">>filename");`
+>	Update	Create a file for update. If the file exists, discard the contents, e.g., `open (filehandle, "+>filename");`
+<	Reading & writing	Open the file for update (i.e., reading and writing). Keep the contents of the file, e.g., `open (filehandle, "+<filename");`
+>>	Update & append	Open or create a file for update. Writing is at the end of the file, e.g., `open (filehandle, "+>>filename");`

From the examples in this table, the file open mode is applied at the front of the file name. When there is no open mode specified, the reading mode is assumed as the default.

To open and display the contents of a file, the following Perl script is used:

Example: ex15-03.pl – Open A File For Reading

```
 1: #!/usr/bin/perl
 2: open(filehandle,"message.dat")
 3:   or die("Cannot open message.dat for reading");
 4:
 5: while (my $st = <filehandle>)
 6: {
 7:   print("$st");
 8: }
 9: close(filehandle);
10:
```

This Perl script opens a file called message.dat for reading. If not successful, the die statement displays a message and terminates the program. If the file operation is successful, a while-loop is used in lines 5–8 to display the contents of the file. The statement

```
$st = <filehandle>
```

reads a string from the file until a new line is encountered. The string is then assigned to the variable $st. The print statement in line 7 is a typical statement to display the string to the standard out. It is important to close any opened file at the end of the program, as illustrated in line 9.

This program is a standard application of Perl and will work on any system with a Perl interpreter. If you issue the command

```
perl ex15-03.pl
```

the result will be displayed on the console window. To convert the program to a CGI application, you may need to add the string "Content-type: text/html\n\n" to the program and construct the returned message as an XHTML document. Consider the following modification:

Example: ex15-04.pl – Open A File For Reading (CGI)

```
 1: #!/usr/bin/perl
 2: print ("Content-type:text/html\n\n");
 3:
 4: print << "mypage";
 5: <?xml version="1.0" encoding="iso-8859-1"?>
 6: <!DOCTYPE html PUBLIC "-//W3C//DTD XHTML 1.0 Transitional//EN"
 7: "http://www.w3.org/TR/xhtml1/DTD/xhtml1-transitional.dtd">
 8: <html xmlns="http://www.w3.org/1999/xhtml" xml:lang="en" lang="en">
 9: <head><title>Example: ex15-04.pl</title></head>
10: <style>.txtSt{font-size:18pt;color:#ffff00;font-family:arial}</style>
11: <body style="background:#000088" class="txtSt">
12: mypage
13:
14: open(filehandle,"message.dat")
15:   or die("Cannot open message.dat for reading");
16:
17: while (my $st = <filehandle>)
18: {
19:   print("$st <br />");
20: }
21: close(filehandle);
22:
23: print " </body></html>";
```

After the XHTML header message in lines 4–12, the only real modification of this program is that the string $st is printed with a line break element <br /> so that a line break is generated (see Fig. 15.4).

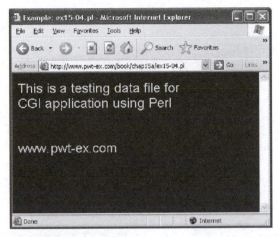

Figure 15.4 ex15-04.p1

To convert this example into a practical application, let's consider a page to read old company memos or articles.

15.2.2 A page to trace old records

Sometimes, back tracking for information such as company memos, newsletters, product support, important emails, and frequently asked questions (faq) could be an administrative nightmare for a company. A server to store all these old records and be available via a Web page could be quite handy. The next example is a simple file-based Web page to trace back records. First, we collect all faq monthly and store them in the text files on the server. The next step is to develop a page to display them.

The implementation is divided into two parts. The first part is a simple XHTML document with a select box to allow the user to pick the item he or she would like to read. The second part is a Perl script to handle the file and display it on a separate browser window.

The interface part of this example is listed below:

```
Example: ex15-05.htm - A Page To Trace Old Records

 1: <?xml version="1.0" encoding="iso-8859-1"?>
 2: <!DOCTYPE html PUBLIC "-//W3C//DTD XHTML 1.0 Transitional//EN"
 3:     "http://www.w3.org/TR/xhtml1/DTD/xhtml1-transitional.dtd">
 4: <html xmlns="http://www.w3.org/1999/xhtml" xml:lang="en" lang="en">
 5: <style> .selSt{width:380px;height:35px;background:#aaffaa;
 6: font-family:arial;font-weight:bold;font-size:16pt;color:#880000}</style>
 7: <head><title>Monthly FAQ - ex15-05.htm</title></head>
 8: <body style="background:#000088;font-family:arial;font-size:22pt;
 9:     color:#ffff00;font-weight:bold;text-align:center"><br />
10:  Monthly FAQ Available For <br />Company Staff To Read<br />
11:
12: <form action="ex15-05.pl" method="post" target="_blank">
13:  <div style="position:absolute;top:150px;left:60px;text-align:left;
14:         font-size:18pt">Monthly FAQ Available<br />
15:  <select id="monthly" name="monthlyFAQ" class="selSt">
```

```
16:    <option>November</option>
17:    <option>October</option>
18:    <option>September</option>
19:    <option>August</option>
20: </select><br /><br /><br />
21: </div>
22: <input type="submit" value="Read"
23:    style="position:absolute;top:155px;left:460px;width:100px;
24:    height:60px;font-family:arial;font-size:18pt;font-weight:bold" />
25: </form>
26: </body></html>
```

This is a simple XHTML page containing a select box (lines 15–19) with the four selections "November," "October," "September," and "August." When one of the selections is picked and the Read button is pressed, the form action defined in line 12 activates the Perl script ex15-05.pl. Since we have used the attribute `target=_blank`, the result will be displayed in another separate browser window. The function of the Perl script ex15-05.pl is to get the selection and display the corresponding file on the screen. Some screen shots of this example are shown in Figs 15.5 and 15.6.

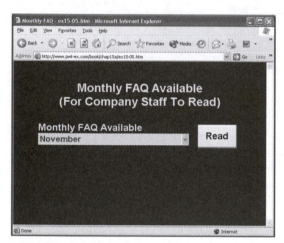

Figure 15.5 ex15-05.htm

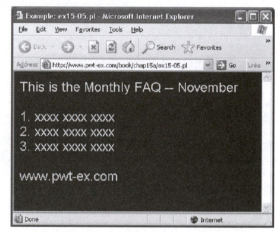

Figure 15.6 ex15-05.p1

The form action in line 12 assumes that the Web page, Perl script, and old documents are stored on the same server. If the script and document are stored on another site such as www.pwt-ex.com, you may need to use:

```
<form action="http://www.pwt-ex.com/ex15-05.pl" method="post"
target="_blank">
```

The Perl program used in this example is listed below:

```
Example: ex15-05.p1 - The Perl Script For ex15-05.htm

1: #!/usr/bin/perl
2: use CGI qw( :standard);
3: print ("Content-type:text/html\n\n");
4:
5: my $fileN = param("monthlyFAQ");
6:
7: print << "mypage";
8:    <?xml version="1.0" encoding="iso-8859-1"?>
9:    <!DOCTYPE html PUBLIC "-//W3C//DTD XHTML 1.0 Transitional//EN"
```

```
10:    "http://www.w3.org/TR/xhtml1/DTD/xhtml1-transitional.dtd">
11:    <html xmlns="http://www.w3.org/1999/xhtml" xml:lang="en" lang="en">
12:    <head><title>Example: ex15-05.pl</title></head>
13:    <style>.txtSt{font-size:18pt;color:#ffff00;font-family:arial}</style>
14:    <body style="background:#000088" class="txtSt">
15: mypage
16:
17: $fileN = $fileN . "\.txt";
18: open(filehandle,"<$fileN")
19:    or die("Cannot open file for reading");
20:
21: while (my $st = <filehandle>)
22: {
23:    print("$st<br />");
24: }
25: close(filehandle);
26:
27: print " </body></html>";
28:
```

In this script, we have used a Perl CGI module in line 2 so that parameters from the XHTML document can be accessed by using the param() function. The picked value is stored in the variable $fileN in line 5 and then used in line 17 to compose the file name by adding a file extension. The remainder of the program is to open the file and display the contents to a newly opened browser window.

This example is particularly useful for tracing text-based files. Since no XHTML statement is involved, it is economical to maintain.

15.2.3 Open a file for reading and writing

To open a file for writing, the following basic Perl script can be used:

```
Listing: ex15-03.txt - Open A File For Writing

1: #!user/bin/perl
2:  print ("Content-type:text/html\n\n");
3: open (outfile, ">file.txt")
4:     or die("Cannot Open File.. Error");
5: print (outfile "I know how to create a file using Perl script\n");
6: close(outfile);
```

Line 3 is a typical open statement to open a file for writing. If the file already exists, the contents will be destroyed. If the file is successfully opened, the open command returns a file handle. In this case, the file handle is called outfile. Using this file handle, you can employ a print command such as

```
print (outfile "Write something into the file");
```

to write something into the file.

However, in order to write something into a file and read it back, you need to open the file twice. In this case, it is a combination of both examples ex15-04.pl and ex15-05.pl. Consider the following Perl script:

```
Example: ex15-06.pl - Open A File For Reading And Writing

1: #!user/bin/perl
2: print ("Content-type:text/html\n\n");
3: open (outfile,">file.txt")
4:     or die("Cannot Open File For Writing.. Error");
5: print (outfile "I know how to create a file using Perl script\n");
6: close(outfile);
7:
```

```
 8: open (infile, "<file.txt")
 9:    or die("Cannot Open File For Reading.. Error");
10: while (my $st = <infile>)
11: {
12:   print("$st");
13: }
14: close(infile);
```

This Perl script contains two processes. The first one is to open a file called file.txt and write something into it. Soon after the writing, the file is closed by executing the statement in line 6. The file is opened again by another handle called `infile`. Using this handle, the contents of the file are read and displayed. One immediate application of file reading and writing is to build a page counter for your site.

15.2.4 Building a Web page counter

Counters are frequently used on the World Wide Web to show how many people have visited your site. Normally, a counter is implemented as an ordinary text file to store a single value representing the number of accesses to a document. Once the page is requested, the counter file is opened, increments the value by 1, and then stores the value back to the file.

You can place different counter files for different articles, documents, or even topics. A number of ISPs also provide this feature with graphical displays; we will cover this in a moment. First, let's consider a basic implementation of a page counter on the Internet.

Example: ex15-07.pl – A Page Counter With Perl

```
1: #!usr/bin/perl
2: open(filehandle,"+<counter.txt")
3:    or die("Cannot Open File - counter.txt .. Error");
4: $countNumber = <filehandle>;
5: $countNumber++;
6: seek(filehandle,0,0);  ## rewind the file to the beginning
7: print (filehandle "$countNumber");
8: close(filehandle);
```

This Perl script has only eight lines of code. Suppose you have already created a counter file called counter.txt using an editor with a number on it. The open statement in line 2 opens the file for reading and writing. If the file operation is successful, you will have a `filehandle` to control the file. Line 4 is a read statement from Perl script to read the value from the file and store it in the variable $counterNumber. After adding 1 to this variable, you may need to rewind the file to the beginning before you can actually write the new value into the file. The new command `seek(filehandle,0,0)` in Perl script is used to demonstrate how to rewind a file to the beginning. Alternatively, you can close the file and then reopen it for writing.

To apply this Perl script to a CGI application, the following page with graphical images is used:

Example: ex15-08.pl – A Page Counter With Graphical Display

```
 1: #!usr/bin/perl
 2: print "Content-type:text/html\n\n";
 3: open(filehandle,"+<counter.txt")
 4:    or die("Cannot Open File - counter.txt .. Error");
 5: $countNumber = <filehandle>;
 6: $countNumber++;
 7: seek(filehandle,0,0);
 8: print (filehandle "$countNumber");
 9: close(filehandle);
10:
11: print << "mypage";
12:   <?xml version="1.0" encoding="iso-8859-1"?>
```

```
13: <!DOCTYPE html PUBLIC "-//W3C//DTD XHTML 1.0 Transitional//EN"
14:   "http://www.w3.org/TR/xhtml1/DTD/xhtml1-transitional.dtd">
15: <html xmlns="http://www.w3.org/1999/xhtml" xml:lang="en" lang="en">
16: <head><title>Example: ex15-08.pl</title></head>
17: <style>.txtSt{font-size:18pt;color:#ffff00;font-family:arial}</style>
18: <body style="background:#000088" class="txtSt">
19: mypage
20:
21: print" <div style=\"text-align:center\">You are visitor number : ";
22: for($ii=0; $ii < length($countNumber);$ii++)
23: {
24:   $jj = substr($countNumber,$ii,1);
25:   $pic = $jj . "dc.gif";
26:   print "<img src=\"$pic\" alt=\"pic\" \/>";
27: }
28: print "</div><br /><br />";
29:
30: print "Your XHTML document can be here..<br /><br />";
31:
32: print "</body></html>";
```

Lines 3–9 are the counter implementation similar to ex15-07.pl. After the variable $countNumber and file are updated, lines 11–19 generate the header for an XHTML document. The interesting part of this script is the code in lines 22–27. This is a for-loop in Perl script to convert the number of visits to graphical display. Basically, it is used to extract the digits of the $countNumber one by one. When $ii equals 0, the command

```
$jj = substr($countNumber,0,1)
```

extracts the first character of $countNumber to variable $jj. The value of $jj is then used to compose the digit picture. For example, if $jj = 3, the value of $pic would be a string 3dc.gif and the print statement would output the XHTML image element

```
<img src="3dc.gif" />
```

to the browser. The picture 3dc.gif is a graphical image of 3 (see section 12.3.2). A screen shot of this example in action is shown in Fig. 15.7.

Figure 15.7 ex15-08.p1

When the page operates on the Internet, many users can access the Web page at the same time. This might create a danger when more than one user tries to open and alter a file at the same time. We need something to protect against file corruption or inaccuracy when handling multiple accesses.

15.2.5 Sharing files among multiple Web users

When multiple users try to access the same file, it is possible that two of them might read the current count and increment it by 1 at the same time. As a result only one new value is stored back to the file. For an example like this, the chances of experiencing difficulties due to concurrent access may not be very high since the frequency of document access is small. However, consider a seat allocation system for an airline counter in a busy airport. The concurrent access situations may be a major operational problem to be solved.

Perl does include facilities for synchronizing file accesses. A typical solution is to use the `flock()` function, which allows users to lock a file for private use. For example, you can use the statement:

```
flock(filehandle,2);
```

to lock the file immediately through the file handle. All other access to the file is denied. That is, if a script is writing, no other scripts or executable programs will be given access until that script is finished. Some Perl installations may use the command `flock(filehandle,LOCK_EX);` where the numeric value 2 is replaced by an identifier defined in some Perl modules.

To prevent the problem of inconvenient locking of the file for a long period of time, you should unlock the file soon after your file operation. The command to unlock a file is

```
flock(filehandle,8);
```

or `flock(filehandle, LOCK_UN);` for some Perl installations and additional modules.

You now have some ideas on server storage and how to use them. It is time to consider some basic CGI applications on the Web.

15.3 Basic CGI applications with Perl

15.3.1 Collect and store data online

One of the practical applications of using server storage is to collect user information online such as comments and consumer opinions. These data may be used later for statistical analysis and form one of the basic tools of marketing research.

Our next example is a page to collect users' opinions on their favorite browsers and operating systems. This page first displays an XHTML document ex15-09.htm for the user to fill. Once the form has been filled and the Send button pressed, the form will be submitted to the Perl script program ex15-09.pl for processing. After sending an acknowledgment back to the user, the Perl script opens a data file and appends the data to it.

The interface part of the example is listed below:

```
Example: ex15-09.htm - Collect And Store Data Online

  1:  <?xml version="1.0" encoding="iso-8859-1"?>
  2:  <!DOCTYPE html PUBLIC "-//W3C//DTD XHTML 1.0 Transitional//EN"
  3:       "http://www.w3.org/TR/xhtml1/DTD/xhtml1-transitional.dtd">
  4:  <html xmlns="http://www.w3.org/1999/xhtml" xml:lang="en" lang="en">
  5:  <style>
  6:    .styleSt{width:320px;height:35px;background:#aaffaa;font-family:arial;
  7:         font-weight:bold;font-size:14pt;color:#880000}
  8:    .tableSt{font-size:14pt;font-weight:bold;text-align:left}</style>
```

```
 9:    <head><title>Collecting Data Online - ex15-09.htm</title></head>
10:    <body style="background:#000088;font-family:arial;color:#ffff00">
11:
12:    <form action="ex15-09.pl" method="post">
13:    <table class="tableSt" style="position:absolute;top:30px;left:160px">
14:     <tr><td colspan="2" style="text-align:center;font-size:22pt">Your
15:         Favorite Browsers And<br />Operating Systems<br /><br /></td></tr>
16:     <tr><td>Name: </td>
17:         <td><input type="text" value="" class="styleSt" name="nameId"
18:             style="color:#000000;background:#dddddd"/></td></tr>
19:     <tr><td>Email Address:</td>
20:         <td><input type="text" value="" class="styleSt" name="emailId"
21:             style="color:#000000;background:#dddddd"/></td></tr>
22:    </table>
23:    <table class="tableSt" style="position:absolute;top:230px;left:160px">
24:     <tr><td>Internet Explorer 6.x:   </td>
25:         <td><input type="radio" class="styleSt" id="brId" name="brId"
26:             style="width:40px" value="Internet Explorer 6.x" /></td></tr>
27:     <tr><td>Internet Explorer 5.x:   </td>
28:         <td><input type="radio" class="styleSt" id="brId" name="brId"
29:             style="width:40px" value="Internet Explorer 5.x" /></td></tr>
30:     <tr><td>Netscape 6.x:   </td>
31:         <td><input type="radio" class="styleSt" id="brId" name="brId"
32:             style="width:40px" value="Netscape 6.x" /></td></tr>
33:     <tr><td>Opera:   </td>
34:         <td><input type="radio" class="styleSt" id="brId" name="brId"
35:             style="width:40px" value="Opera" /></td></tr>
36:     <tr><td>Netscape Nevigator:   </td>
37:         <td><input type="radio" class="styleSt" id="brId" name="brId"
38:             style="width:40px" value="Netscape Nevigator" /></td></tr>
39:     <tr><td>Others:   </td>
40:         <td><input type="radio" class="styleSt" id="brId" name="brId"
41:             style="width:40px" value="Others" /></td></tr>
42:    </table>
43:    <table class="tableSt" style="position:absolute;top:230px;left:450px">
44:     <tr><td>Windows XP:   </td>
45:         <td><input type="radio" class="styleSt" id="osId" name="osId"
46:             style="width:40px" value="Windows XP" /></td></tr>
47:     <tr><td>Windows 2000:   </td>
48:         <td><input type="radio" class="styleSt" id="osId" name="osId"
49:             style="width:40px" value="Windows 2000" /></td></tr>
50:     <tr><td>Windows 9.x:   </td>
51:         <td><input type="radio" class="styleSt" id="osId" name="osId"
52:             style="width:40px" value="Windows 9.x" /></td></tr>
53:     <tr><td>Windows NT:   </td>
54:         <td><input type="radio" class="styleSt" id="osId" name="osId"
55:             style="width:40px" value="Windows NT" /></td></tr>
56:     <tr><td>Linux:   </td>
57:         <td><input type="radio" class="styleSt" id="osId" name="osId"
58:             style="width:40px" value="Linux" /></td></tr>
59:     <tr><td>Mac OS:   </td>
60:         <td><input type="radio" class="styleSt" id="osId" name="osId"
61:             style="width:40px" value="Mac Os" /></td></tr>
62:    </table>
63:    <table class="tableSt" style="position:absolute;top:500px;left:210px"><tr>
64:     <td><input type="reset" class="styleSt" style="width:200px;
65:       background:#aaaaaa" value="Reset" /></td>
```

```
66:    <td><input type="submit" class="styleSt" value="Send"
67:      style="width:200px;background:#aaaaaa" /></td></tr>
68:  </table>
69:  </form>
70:  </body></html>
```

This XHTML page is a form application containing four tables. The first table defined in lines 13–22 is to get the user's name and email address. The second table in lines 23–42 generates a series of radio boxes to get the user's favorite browser. The third table in lines 43–62 again generates a series of radio boxes to obtain the user's favorite operating system. The last table (lines 63–68) in this document contains two buttons, Send and Reset. A screen shot of this interface is shown in Fig. 15.8.

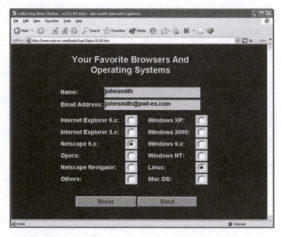

Figure 15.8 ex15-09.p1

Once the form is filled and the Send button is pressed, the form will be sent to the Perl script ex15-09.pl. The coding of this script is listed below:

```
Listing: ex15-04.txt - Perl Script ex15-09.pl For ex15-09.htm

 1: #!usr/bin/perl
 2: use CGI qw (:standard);
 3: print ("Content-type:text/html\n\n");
 4:
 5: $nameV = param("nameId");
 6: $emailV = param("emailId");
 7: $brV = param("brId");
 8: $osV = param("osId");
 9:
10: print << "mypage";
11:  <?xml version="1.0" encoding="iso-8859-1"?>
12:  <!DOCTYPE html PUBLIC "-//W3C//DTD XHTML 1.0 Transitional//EN"
13:  "http://www.w3.org/TR/xhtml1/DTD/xhtml1-transitional.dtd">
14:  <html xmlns="http://www.w3.org/1999/xhtml" xml:lang="en" lang="en">
15:  <head><title>Example: ex15-09.pl</title></head>
16:  <style>.txtSt{font-size:14pt;color:#ffff00;font-family:arial}</style>
17:
18:  <body style="background:#000088" class="txtSt">
19:    Thank You For Returning the Questionnaire<br /><br />
20:    Your information has been added into our database<br /><br />
21:
```

```
22:   <table cellspacing="15" class="txtSt">
23:    <tr><td>Name</td><td>Email</td><td>Browser</td><td>O.S.</td></tr>
24:    <tr><td>$nameV</td><td>$emailV</td><td>$brV</td><td>$osV</td></tr>
25:   </table><br />
26:   www.pwt-ex.com
27: mypage
28:
29: open(filehandle,">>user.dat")
30:   or die("Cannot Open Data File.. Error");
31: print (filehandle "$nameV,$emailV,$brV,$osV\n");
32: close(filehandle)
```

First, the `param()` function is used to capture the submitted values from the form. The values of user name, email address, browser, and operating system are stored in the variables `$nameV`, `$emailV`, `$brV`, and `$osV` respectively. The next step is to return an acknowledgment in XHTML as illustrated in lines 10–27. After the acknowledgment, the script opens a data file called user.dat for appending (line 29). The single print statement in line 31 would append all the data to the end of the file. The file is closed when all operations are completed. Some screen shots are shown in Figs 15.9 and 15.10.

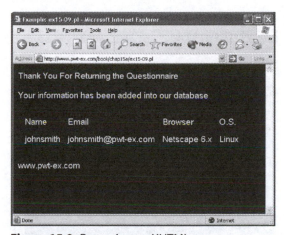

Figure 15.9 Returning an XHTML page

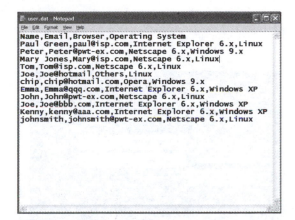

Figure 15.10 Contents of user.dat

15.3.2 Verifying user name and password

Verifying user name and password is a common security practice on the Internet. In normal circumstances, all the user names and their corresponding passwords are stored in a file on the server. Therefore, to verify user name and password for a particular user on the Internet, a CGI application is required. Since we don't have encryption at this moment, the implementation of password checking is relatively simple. Suppose you have password file called password.txt containing all the user names and passwords. To check a password for a particular user it is necessary to read this file and perform the comparison. Consider the interface part of this example:

```
Example: ex15-10.htm - Verifying Username And Password

 1: <?xml version="1.0" encoding="iso-8859-1"?>
 2: <!DOCTYPE html PUBLIC "-//W3C//DTD XHTML 1.0 Transitional//EN"
 3:     "http://www.w3.org/TR/xhtml1/DTD/xhtml1-transitional.dtd">
 4: <html xmlns="http://www.w3.org/1999/xhtml" xml:lang="en" lang="en">
 5: <head><title>Username and Password - ex15-10.htm </title></head>
 6: <style>
 7:   .butSt{background-color:#aaffaa;font-family:arial;font-weight:bold;
 8:      font-size:18pt;color:#880000;width:250px;height:35px}
```

```
 9:    .txtSt{font-family:arial;font-weight:bold; text-align:left;
10:        font-size:18pt;color:#ffff00}</style>
11: <body style="background:#000088">
12: <form action="ex15-10.pl" method="post">
13: <table style="position:absolute;left:60px;top:50px" class="txtSt">
14:  <tr><td colspan="2" style="text-align:center">
15:        Enter Your Username and<br /> Password Below<br /><br/></td></tr>
16:  <tr><td>Name:</td><td><input type="text"
17:        name="userId" id="userId" class="butSt" ></td></tr>
18:  <tr><td>Password:</td><td><input type="password"
19:        name="passId" id="passId" class="butSt"></td></tr>
20:  <tr><td><input type="submit" class="butSt" value="O.K."
21:        style="width:150px;background:#dddddd"></td></tr>
22: </table>
23: </form>
24: </body></html>
```

This is a simple interface page with two input fields. The password field in line 18 is declared with `type="password"` so that the typed characters will be covered by asterisks. A screen shot of this page is shown in Fig. 15.11.

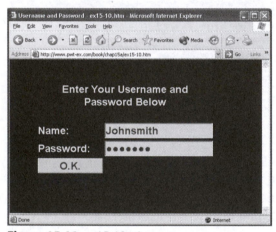

Figure 15.11 ex15-10.p1

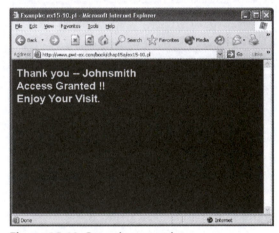

Figure 15.12 Passed accepted

When the user name and password are filled and the O.K. button is clicked, the form is sent to the Perl script ex15-10.pl for processing (Fig. 5.12). The program code of the script is listed as follows:

Example: ex15-10.pl - The Perl Script For ex15-10.htm

```
 1: #!usr/bin/perl
 2: use CGI qw (:standard);
 3: my $username = param(userId);
 4: my $password = param(passId);
 5:
 6: print "Content-type:text/html\n\n";
 7: print << "mypage";
 8:  <?xml version="1.0" encoding="iso-8859-1"?>
 9:  <!DOCTYPE html PUBLIC "-//W3C//DTD XHTML 1.0 Transitional//EN"
10:  "http://www.w3.org/TR/xhtml1/DTD/xhtml1-transitional.dtd">
11:  <html xmlns="http://www.w3.org/1999/xhtml" xml:lang="en" lang="en">
12:  <head><title>Example: ex15-10.pl</title></head>
13:  <style>.txtSt{font-size:18pt;color:#ffff00;font-family:arial}</style>
```

```
14:   <body style="background:#000088;font-weight:bold" class="txtSt">
15: mypage
16:
17: open(filehandle, "password.txt") or
18:   die "The File could not be opened .. Error.";
19:
20: while(my $st = <filehandle>)
21: {
22:     $st =~ s/\n//g;
23:     ($name, $pass) = split(/,/, $st);
24:
25:     if($name eq "$username")
26:     {
27:       $userF = 1;
28:       if ($pass eq "$password")
29:       {
30:           $passwordF = 1;
31:       }
32:     }
33:   }
34: close(filehandle);
35:
36: if ($userF && $passwordF)
37: {
38:   print ("Thank you -- $username <br /> Access Granted !!
39:           <br />Enjoy Your Visit.");
40: }
41: elsif ($userF && !$passwordF)
42: {
43:   print ("Sorry, Wrong Password !!");
44: }
45: else
46: {
47:   print ("Sorry, Access Denied !!");
48: }
49: print "</body></html>";
```

The param() functions used in lines 3 and 4 get the user name and password from the XHTML form and store them in variables $username and $password. After the document header in lines 5–15, the script opens the password file password.txt and processes the file with the following while-loop:

```
while(my $st = <filehandle>)
{
    $st =~ s/\n//g;
    ($name, $pass) = split(/,/, $st);
    if($name eq "$username")
    {
      $userF = 1;
      if ($pass eq "$password")
      {
          $passwordF = 1;
      }
    }
}
```

Inside the while-loop, each line of the file is read into the string $st. Since the string $st may contain a line break "\n" at the end, a substitution is required to remove it. The string $st is then split into $name and $pass containing the user name and password from the file. If the variable $name equals the user name from the user input, $userF is set to be true to indicate that the user name is matched. If the password is matched, the variable $passwordF is set to true.

The remaining part of the script is easy to read. Basically, if both user name and password are matched, a message is displayed to grant access. Some readers may want to use the following statement to redirect the browser to another new page:

```
print redirect('http://www.pwt-ex.com');
```

Obviously, access cannot be granted if the password is not matched. If the line break of $st is not "chopped off," you may have difficulty comparing the password.

15.3.3 Implementation of a guest book

A guest book is a common feature of many Web sites where comments are obtained from users or visitors. Visitors can write something in the guest book and share their views. Any person should be able to sign the book and view its contents at any time.

Apart from messages stored as file records on the server, a good guest book implementation should also include markup symbols for formatted display and database applications. Also a simple log file would be helpful to log all user access. The use of such a log file is common in professional programming. For example, Microsoft uses them whenever you turn on your Windows system. Our implementation of a guest book will have these features but in a much simpler form.

Consider the interface part of the example:

```
Example: ex15-11.htm - A Guest Book Using Perl

 1: <?xml version="1.0" encoding="iso-8859-1"?>
 2: <!DOCTYPE html PUBLIC "-//W3C//DTD XHTML 1.0 Transitional//EN"
 3:    "http://www.w3.org/TR/xhtml1/DTD/xhtml1-transitional.dtd">
 4: <html xmlns="http://www.w3.org/1999/xhtml" xml:lang="en" lang="en">
 5: <head><title> A Guest Book Using Perl - ex15-11.htm </title></head>
 6: <style>
 7:  .tx01{font-size:14pt;color:#000088;font-weight:bold}
 8:  .tx02{font-family:arial;font-size:14pt;background:#ffffff;color:#000000}
 9:  .butSt{background-color:#aaffaa;font-family:arial;font-weight:bold;
10:     font-size:14pt;color:#008800;width:100px;height:30px}
11: </style>
12: <body style="background:#bbbbff;font-family:arial;color:#000088">
13: <div style="font-size:18pt;text-align:center;font-weight:bold">
14:    Please Sign Our Guest Book<br />www.pwt-ex.com
15:  <form method="post" action="ex15-11a.pl">
16:  <table class="tx01">
17:  <tr><td>From:</td>
18:     <td><input class="tx02" type="text" name="from" id="from"></td></tr>
19:
20:  <tr><td valign="top">Message:</td>
21:     <td><textarea name="message" id="message" class="tx02"
22:        rows="6" cols="40" wrap="yes"></textarea></td></tr>
23:
24:  <tr><td><input class="butSt" type="submit" value="Submit"></td>
25:     <td><input class="butSt" type="reset" value="Reset"></td></tr>
26:  </table>
27:  </form><br />
28:  <a class="butSt" style="width:405px;color:#880000"
29:     href="ex15-11b.pl">
30:        Please Click Me To Read Guest Book</a>
31: </div>
32: </body>
33: </html>
```

- A "From" field for the user to type in his or her name.
- A text area so the user can write something in the guest book.
- A Submit and a Reset button.
- An anchor element to view the contents of the guest book.

A screen shot of this interface is shown in Fig. 15.13.

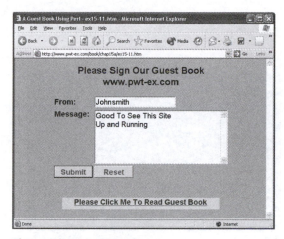

Figure 15.13 ex15-11.htm

For readability and clarity, the program code of this example is split into two parts. The first part is a Perl script ex15-11a.pl to handle all data processes once the user submits the form. The second part is also a Perl script to handle the display of the guest book contents.

For most guest books, one of the immediate features is to send a so-called "Thank you" page back to the user. The first part of ex15-11a.pl does just that and is listed below:

```
Example: ex15-11a.pl - The Perl Script For ex15-11.htm (Part One)

 1: #! /usr/bin/perl
 2: use CGI qw( :standard );
 3:
 4: my $from = param( "from" );
 5: my $message = param( "message" );
 6: my $timeV = scalar(localtime());
 7: print "Content-type:text/html\n\n";
 8:
 9: print << "mypage";
10:  <?xml version="1.0" encoding="iso-8859-1"?>
11:  <!DOCTYPE html PUBLIC "-//W3C//DTD XHTML 1.0 Transitional//EN"
12:      "http://www.w3.org/TR/xhtml1/DTD/xhtml1-transitional.dtd">
13:  <html xmlns="http://www.w3.org/1999/xhtml" xml:lang="en" lang="en">
14:  <head><title>Example - ex15-11a.pl </title></head>
15:  <body style="background:#000088">
16:  <div style="font-family:arial;font-size:18pt;color:#ffff00">
17:   Thank you -- $from <br /><br />
18:   Your Comment <br />
19:   <img src="line1.gif" height="6" width="400" /><br /><br/>
```

```
20:    $message <br/><br />
21:    <img src="line1.gif" height="6" width="400" /><br />
22:    Has Been Added Into Our Guest Book.<br /> www.pwt-ex.com
23:    </div></body></html>
24: mypage
25:
```

This Perl script gets the user name and guest book message from the interface with the `param()` function. Lines 9–24 use that information to build a simple "Thank you" page for sending back to the user. A screen shot of the page generated by this Perl script is shown in Fig. 15.14.

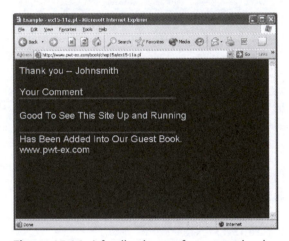

Figure 15.14 A feedback page from guest book

The second part of ex15-11a.pl below is more interesting:

```
Listing: Continuation Of The Perl Script ex15-11a.pl (Part Two)

26: open(logfile,">>log.dat")
27:  or die("Cannot Open Log File.. Error");
28:
29: print logfile "user $from access guest book at -- $timeV";
30: print logfile `cp guestbk.dat temp.dat`;
31:
32: open(filehandle,">guestbk.dat")
33:  or die("Cannot Open Data File.. Error");
34: print (filehandle " #!! #1# $message #1# #1# \n $from - $timeV #1# \n
35: ========================================!!#\n");
36: close(filehandle);
37:
38: print logfile `cat temp.dat >> guestbk.dat`;
```

In this script, a log file called log.dat is opened in lines 26–27. This file can be used to log any message that you want to have. For our simple implementation, the first thing we want to do with this file is to log the user name and time (line 29).

Another feature of our guest book is that the latest submitted message will appear at the top of the guest book file guestbk.dat. A simple way to do this is to

- copy the guest book file guestbk.dat to a temporary file called temp.dat;
- discard the contents of the guest book file and write the new message into it;
- append the contents of the temporary file temp.dat to the guest book file.

In terms of Perl programming, the tasks above can be accomplished by

```
print `cp guestbk.dat temp.dat`;
  open(filehandle,">guestbk.dat");
  print(filehandle, " XXXXX ");
print `cat >> guestbk.dat temp.dat`;
```

If you are using Microsoft systems, you may need to use the copy command instead of cp above and the type command instead of cat.

For most operating system environments, copying files from one place to another may not be totally safe. You should embed the log file handle into an operation such as (line 30)

```
print logfile `cp guestbk.dat temp.dat`;
```

Any message from the file operation, whether successful or not, will be redirected to the log file so that you can have a check afterwards.

It is almost certain that the contents of the guest book will be read and displayed by a browser. The messages may be better stored as elements of an XHTML table. For example, if $from="Johnsmith"$ and $message="Good To See This Site Up and Running"$, the print statement in lines 34–35 will generate the following record in the guest book file guestbk.dat:

```
#!! #1# Good To See This Site Up and Running #1# #1#
Johnsmith - Fri Mar 22 23:22:04 2002 #1#
===============================================!!#
```

If you perform the symbol substitutions

```
#!! replace by <tr><td>
#1# replace by <br />
!!# replace by </td></tr>
```

the record in guestbk.dat above turns out to be

```
<tr><td> <br /> Good To See This Site Up and Running <br /><br />
Johnsmith - Fri Mar 22 23:22:04 2002 <br />
===============================================</td></tr>
```

This is part of an XHTML table element and can be easily displayed by a browser. The demonstration here concentrates on ideas. It is a very simple case for formatted output. To see how the records in the guest book are displayed in a browser, consider the following Perl script:

```
Example: ex15-11b.pl - The Perl Script For ex15-11.htm

 1: #! /usr/bin/perl
 2: print "Content-type:text/html\n\n";
 3:
 4: print << "mypage";
 5: <?xml version="1.0" encoding="iso-8859-1"?>
 6: <!DOCTYPE html PUBLIC "-//W3C//DTD XHTML 1.0 Transitional//EN"
 7:    "http://www.w3.org/TR/xhtml1/DTD/xhtml1-transitional.dtd">
 8: <html xmlns="http://www.w3.org/1999/xhtml" xml:lang="en" lang="en">
 9: <head><title>Example - ex15-11b.pl </title></head>
10: <body style="background:#000088">
11: <div style="font-family:arial;font-size:18pt;color:#00ff00;
12:    text-align:center">Guest Book Message<br />
13:    =================</div><br />
14:
15: <div style="text-align:center">
16: <table style="font-family:arial;font-size:14pt;color:#ffff00;width:400px">
17: mypage
18:
```

```
19: open (infile,"<guestbk.dat")
20:    or die("Cannot Open File For Reading.. Error");
21: while (my $st = <infile>)
22: {
23:   $st =~ s/\n//g;
24:   $st =~ s/(#!!)/<tr><td>/g;
25:   $st =~ s/(!!#)/<\/td><\/tr>/g;
26:   $st =~ s/(#l#)/<br \/>/g;
27:   print("$st");
28: }
29: close(infile);
30:
31: print " </table></div></body></html>";
```

When the underlined text "Please Click Me To Read Guest Book" is clicked (see line 30 in ex15-11.htm), this script is executed. After the declaration of an XHTML table in line 16, a while-loop is used to read the entire guest book file. For each line of the file, a series of substitutions are performed in lines 23–26 to make sure that the messages are in the correct XHTML table format. After displaying all records in the file, the file is closed and the XHTML document is terminated by executing the statement in line 31. A screen shot of the display is shown in Fig. 15.15.

Figure 15.15 Displaying the record

Now you have some basic knowledge and experience of CGI techniques with Perl script, it is time to consider some practical applications.

15.4 Practical CGI applications with Perl

15.4.1 Online examinations and marking

Online examinations or testing is not a feature exclusively reserved by schools or colleges. Many marketing research firms and agencies also use this feature to get results for their clients. The online examination page that we are going to develop has the following features:

- Flexible and easy to add or change questions and answers.
- Returns results to user immediately.

- Leaves a permanent record of all results on the server.
- Provides a simple statistical file on the server for the analysis of the results.

To simplify the implementation, all questions are of multiple-choice type. The interface part is listed below:

```
Example: ex15-12.htm - Online Exam. And Marking

 1: <?xml version="1.0" encoding="iso-8859-1"?>
 2: <!DOCTYPE html PUBLIC "-//W3C//DTD XHTML 1.0 Transitional//EN"
 3:    "http://www.w3.org/TR/xhtml1/DTD/xhtml1-transitional.dtd">
 4: <html xmlns="http://www.w3.org/1999/xhtml" xml:lang="en" lang="en">
 5: <head><title> Online Exam. And Marking - ex15-12.htm</title></head>
 6: <style>
 7:   .tx01{font-size:14pt;color:#000088;font-weight:bold}
 8:   .tx02{font-family:arial;font-size:14pt;background:#ffffff;color:#000000}
 9:   .butSt{background-color:#aaffaa;font-family:arial;font-weight:bold;
10:      font-size:14pt;color:#008800;width:30px;height:30px}
11: </style>
12: <body style="background:#bbbbff;font-family:arial;color:#000088">
13: <script>
14:   var noq = 3
15:   var qq = new Array(
16:      "Which one of the following is the capital of China?",
17:         "London", "New York", "Beijing", "Hong Kong",
18:      "Which of the following is NOT a country?",
19:         "Kenya","India","Singapore","Seoul",
20:      "Which of the following is NOT a river?",
21:         "Thames","Yellow","Nile","Coco")
22: </script>
23:
24: <div style="font-size:18pt;font-weight:bold;position:absolute;
25:    top:20px;left:170px">
26:    Please Answer All Questions Below<br />ABC School
27:   <form method="post" action="ex15-12.pl">
28:    <table class="tx01" align="center">
29:     <tr><td>Name:</td>
30:      <td><input class="tx02" type="text" name="from" id="from"></td>
31:      <td>  Id. Number:</td>
32:      <td><input class="tx02" type="text" name="noId" id="noId"></td></tr>
33:    </table>
34:    <img src="line1.gif" height="6" width="600" />
35:    <div id="showq"></div>
36:   </form>
37: </div>
38: <script src="ex15-12.js"></script>
39: </body>
40: </html>
```

One of the basic methods to generate flexible online questions is to use ECMAScript. This way, the XHTML document would be quite simple and easy to read. In this page, a variable noq (i.e., number of questions) is used to represent how many questions we want to generate. Soon after that, an array is declared to store the questions and answers. To simplify the coding, the questions are arranged in a question/answers format. Only four possible choices of answer are allowed. That is, we start the array with the question and all four possible answers are attached right after it. From lines 16–21, you can clearly see that we have three questions and each question has four choices of answer. This page also contains some input fields to obtain the user name and identity number of the candidate. The generated questions are displayed in line 35. A screen shot of this page is shown in Fig. 15.16.

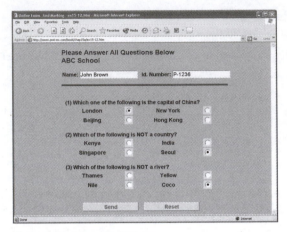

Figure 15.16 ex15-12.htm

From this figure you can see that the three questions are arranged into three big rows. Each question has four answers right under it. The four answers are formatted into two rows using radio boxes. To generate this format, the following file ex15-12.js is used:

Example: ex15-12.js – The ECMAScript Program File For ex15-12.htm

```
 1:  lst='<table class="tx01" style="position:absolute;'+
 2:     'top:160px;left:10px;width:550px">'
 3:
 4:  for (ii=0;ii<noq;ii++)
 5:  {
 6:   lst = lst + '<tr><td colspan="4"><br />('+(ii+1)+') '+
 7:       qq[ii*5]+'</td></tr>'
 8:
 9:   for (kk=0;kk<2;kk++)
10:   {
11:    lst = lst +'<tr align="center">'
12:    for (jj=1;jj<3;jj++)
13:    {
14:      lst = lst + '<td>'+qq[ii*5+kk*2+jj]+'</td><td>'+
15:      '<input class="butSt" type="radio" name="q'+(ii+1)+
16:      '" id="q'+(ii+1)+'" value="'+ qq[ii*5+kk*2+jj]+'" /></td>'
17:    }
18:    lst = lst +"</tr>"
19:   }
20:  }
21: lst = lst +'<tr><td colspan="4" style="text-align:center"><br /><br />'+
22:    '<input class = "butSt" style="width:200px" type="submit" '+
23:       'value="Send">    '+
24:    '<input class = "butSt" style="width:200px" type="reset" '+
25:       'value="Reset"></td></tr>'
26:  lst = lst +'</table>'
27:
28:  document.getElementById("showq").innerHTML=lst
```

To formulate the question/answers format, a string containing an XHTML table is constructed in this ECMAScript file. After the table declaration in line 1, a triple for-loop is employed in lines 4–20 to generate the table rows and cells. If you set ii=0 and substitute it into the for-loops, this will produce

```
<tr><td colspan="4"><br /> (1) qq[0]</td></tr>
<tr align="center">
  <td>qq[1]</td><td><input class="butSt"
    type="radio" name="q1" id="q1" value="qq[1]" /></td>
  <td>qq[2]</td><td><input class="butSt"
    type="radio" name="q1" id="q1" value="qq[2]" /></td>
</tr>
<tr align="center">
  <td>qq[3]</td><td><input class="butSt"
    type="radio" name="q1" id="q1" value="qq[3]" /></td>
  <td>qq[4]</td><td><input class="butSt"
    type="radio" name="q1" id="q1" value="qq[4]" /></td>
</tr>
```

Since the array elements $q[0]$, $q[1]$, ..., $q[4]$ store the question and the four answers for question 1, we have formatted question 1 into these table rows. Note that all radio boxes have name="q1" to represent the question identity. After the Send and Reset buttons, the table is constructed and displayed by the statement in line 28.

Once the questions are answered, the entire form is submitted to the Perl script ex15-12.pl for processing. The functions of the Perl script are as follows:

- Get the selected answer for each question.
- Compare to the correct ones and mark the examination.
- Return result to the candidate immediately.
- Open a file to store all results.
- Open another file to perform some simple statistical analyses.

The first part of the script file ex15-12.pl is listed below:

Example: ex15-12.pl - The Perl Script For ex15-12.htm (Part One)

```
 1: #! /usr/bin/perl
 2: use CGI qw( :standard );
 3:
 4: my $totQ = 3;                  ## Total number of questions
 5: my $totM = 0;                  ## Total marks
 6: my $timeV = scalar(localtime());
 7:
 8: @Ans = ("Beijing","Seoul","Coco");
 9: my $from = param( "from" );
10: my $noId = param( "noId" );
11:
12: for ($ii=0;$ii<$totQ;$ii++)
13: {
14:    $result[$ii]="Wrong";
15:    my $tmp = 'q'. ($ii+1);
16:    $qi[$ii] = param($tmp);    ## Get the answer from users
17:    $qStat[$ii]=0;             ## Set all questions answered incorrectly
18: }
19:
20: for ($ii=0; $ii< $totQ; $ii++)
21: {
22:  if ($qi[$ii] eq $Ans[$ii])
23:   {
24:     $result[$ii] = "Correct";
25:     $totM = $totM +1;
26:     $qStat[$ii]=1;
27:   }
28: }
29:
```

First, we have some Perl variables to store the total number of questions and marks. After that, the correct answers of all questions are declared inside an array named @Ans. To get the user's submitted answers, a for-loop is used in lines 12–18. For example, if you substitute $ii=0 into the for-loop, you will have the pseudo code

```
$result[0]="Wrong";
$tmp = 'q1';
$qi[0]=param($tmp);
$qStat[0]=0;
```

The first line is to create a variable to assume that the user has selected the wrong answer. The second and third lines together would get the user's selection on question 1 and store the value into variable $qi[0]. The final variable in the pseudo code $qStat[0] is used to remember how many candidates answered this question correctly.

The marking process is performed by another for-loop in lines 20–28. Again, if you substitute $ii=0 into the for-loop, you will have the pseudo code

```
if ($qi[0] eq $Ans[0]) {
    $result[0] = "Correct";
    $totM = $totM +1;
    $qStat[0]=1;
}
```

This is a simple if statement. That is, if the user answers the question correctly, the value of $result[0] is set to "Correct"; increment the total marks of this candidate $totM by 1 and set the variable $qStat[0] to indicate that this candidate answered this question correctly.

The second part of the script is to return the results to the candidate immediately. This is just a simple task to return an XHTML document to the candidate.

```
Listing: Continuation Of The Perl Script ex15-12.pl (Part Two)

30: print "Content-type:text/html\n\n";
31:
32: print << "mypage";
33:    <?xml version="1.0" encoding="iso-8859-1"?>
34:    <!DOCTYPE html PUBLIC "-//W3C//DTD XHTML 1.0 Transitional//EN"
35:        "http://www.w3.org/TR/xhtml1/DTD/xhtml1-transitional.dtd">
36:    <html xmlns="http://www.w3.org/1999/xhtml" xml:lang="en" lang="en">
37:    <head><title>Example - ex15-12.pl </title></head>
38:    <body style="background:#000088">
39:    <div style="font-family:arial;font-size:18pt;color:#ffff00">
40:      Name : $from <br />
41:      Id. Number: $noId <br />
42:      Your Test Results are as follows:<br /><br />
43:    <img src="line1.gif" height="6" width="400" /><br /><br/>
44: mypage
45:
46:    for ($ii=1; $ii <= $totQ; $ii++)
47:    {
48:      print "Question $ii = $qi[$ii-1] ($result[$ii-1]) <br />";
49:    }
50:    print "Total **** $totM out of $totQ";
51:
52: print << "endpage";
53:    <br/><br />
54:    <img src="line1.gif" height="6" width="400" /><br />
55:    Date: $timeV<br />
56:    </div></body></html>
57: endpage
58:
```

This XHTML page is quite easy to understand. After the name and identity number, the results of the examination are returned inside a for-loop in lines 46–50. Since the elements for arrays $qi[]$ and $result[]$ start from zero, an adjustment to variable $ii-1$ inside the print statement in line 48 is used. Together with the result for each question, if the candidate answers two questions correctly, a message

```
Total **** 2 out of 3
```

is displayed to represent the total marks of the examination. A screen shot of this page in action is shown in Fig. 15.17.

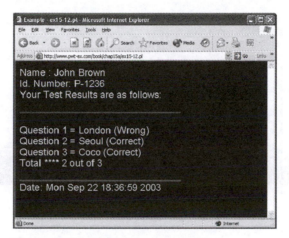

Figure 15.17 Returned exam. result

The third part of the program script opens two files. The first file is to store all the results and the second file is to store how many candidates answer each question correctly.

```
Listing: Continuation Of The Perl Script ex15-12.pl (Part Three)

59: open(outfile,">>marking.dat")
60:    or die("Cannot Open File: marking.dat");
61:    print outfile " name = $from \n Id. Number = $noId\n Date = $timeV\n\n";
62:    for ($ii=1; $ii <= $totQ; $ii++)
63:    {
64:      print outfile " Question $ii = $qi[$ii-1] ($result[$ii-1]) \n";
65:    }
66:    print outfile " Total **** $totM out of $totQ \n";
67:    print outfile "=================================================\n";
68: close(outfile);
69:
70: open(statfile,"+<markstat.dat")
71:    or die("Cannot Open File: markstat.dat");
72:
73:    for ($ii=0; $ii <= $totQ; $ii++)
74:    {
75:      $getData[$ii] = <statfile>;
76:    }
77:    seek(statfile,0,0);
78:
79:    $getData[0]++;
80:    print statfile "$getData[0]\n";
81:    for ($ii=1; $ii <= $totQ; $ii++)
```

```
82:    {
83:      $getData[$ii] = $getData[$ii] + $qStat[$ii-1];
84:      print statfile "$getData[$ii]\n";
85:    }
86: close(statfile);
87:
```

Lines 59–68 open a file called marking.dat. This file stores just about everything that is returned to the candidate. Since we have used an append mode for the file opening, the records for each examination candidate are appended together as in Fig. 15.18.

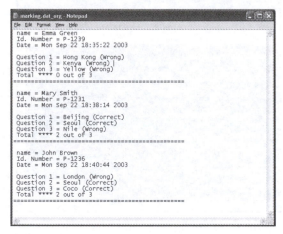

Figure 15.18 ex15-12.htm

In order to store some statistical results such as how many candidates answer each question correctly, another file called statmark.dat is used. This file has a column of zeros when started. The first line of the file represents how many candidates took part in the examination. The second line represents how many candidates answered question 1 correctly. For subsequent lines, a similar representation is used.

For the statistics file, a for-loop in lines 73–76 is used to read the data into the array $getData[]. Then you need to rewind the file in line 77 so that you can write something into the file again. After incrementing the total number of participants by 1, this value is written back to the file. Then for each question, the value of how many candidates answered it correctly is updated in line 83 by

```
$getData[$ii] = $getData[$ii] + $qStat[$ii-1];
```

These values are written back to the file markstat.dat. For example, after three candidates finished the examination as shown in Fig. 15.18, the statistics file has the values:

```
3 - Total participants
1 - One candidate answered question1 correctly
2 - Two candidates answered question2 correctly
1 - One candidate answered question3 correctly
```

Online examinations and marking are good practice for interactive Web programming with CGI. For a more practical and interactive demonstration, we consider an online seat reservation page.

15.4.2 A page to reserve your seats online

A more interactive example on the Web may be a utility to book or reserve your seats online. This kind of utility is widely used in many seat reservations for trains, theaters, and planes. It is obvious that a full commercial implementation of a seat reservation page is beyond the scope of this book. In this section, however, a cut-down version is developed.

The first thing to do is to design the data file to represent all the seats and reservations. For simplicity, we only have 12 seats and the data file is a text-based one called seat.txt. The first line of the file contains a number to represent how many seats are in the page. The data structure of the seat file looks like that given in Table 15.2.

Table 15.2 Data structure of the seat file

1:	12	< --- Number of seats
2:	0, (Empty), Tel:	< --- First seat is empty
3:	1, (Mr. Brown), Tel: 01890-12344321	< --- This seat is booked
x:	... ...	
x:	... ...	
12:	0, (Empty), Tel:	< --- Eleventh seat is empty
13:	0, (Empty), Tel:	< --- Twelfth seat is empty

In line 2, the first 0 value indicates that the seat is not yet reserved (reservation flag). Therefore, the name field next to the zero is (Empty) and the telephone field has no number. The third line demonstrates a typical reserved seat by Mr. Brown with his name and telephone number.

The basic seat reservation page that we are going to develop has two parts. The first part is a user interface to perform the following tasks:

- Read the data file and display the data as seats with numbers.
- If a seat has not been reserved by someone, the seat is represented by a checkbox.
- If a seat has been reserved, the name of the person who reserved it is displayed.
- Users can freely check the checkboxes to reserve the seat they want.

To read the data file, the following Perl script is used:

Example: ex15-13.pl - Reserve Your Seats Online (Part One)

```
 1: #! /usr/bin/perl
 2: use CGI qw( :standard );
 3: print "Content-type:text/html\n\n";
 4:
 5: my $timeV = scalar(localtime());
 6: my $noSeat=0;
 7:
 8: open(filehandle,"<seat.dir/seat.txt")
 9:    or die("Cannot Open seat.txt File.. Error");
10: my $noSeat = <filehandle>;
11: for ($ii=1;$ii <= $noSeat;$ii++)
12: {
13:    $tmp01 = <filehandle>;
14:    ($seatNote[$ii],$seatName[$ii]) = split(',',$tmp01);
15: }
16: close(filehandle);
17:
```

After opening the data file seat.txt, the first line is read into the variable $noseat in line 10. This value represents the total number of seats in the page. A simple for-loop is employed to read in all lines of the data file. For each line, the seat reservation flag and the name of the person who booked the seat are extracted into array variables $seatNote[] and $seatName[].

When information on the seats is available, you can construct an XHTML page to display it on the browser screen. The Perl script to generate the XHTML page is

Listing: Continuation Of The Perl Script ex15-13.pl (Part Two)

```
18: print << "mypage";
19: <?xml version="1.0" encoding="iso-8859-1"?>
20: <!DOCTYPE html PUBLIC "-//W3C//DTD XHTML 1.0 Transitional//EN"
21:     "http://www.w3.org/TR/xhtml1/DTD/xhtml1-transitional.dtd">
22: <html xmlns="http://www.w3.org/1999/xhtml" xml:lang="en" lang="en">
23: <head><title></title></head>
24: <style>
25:   .butSt{background:#aaffaa;font-family:arial;font-weight:bold;
26:     font-size:14pt;color:#008800;width:200px;height:30px}
27:   .chkSt{background-color:#aaffaa;font-family:arial;font-weight:bold;
28:     font-size:14pt;color:#008800;width:30px;height:30px}
29:   .txtSt{font-weight:bold;font-size:14pt;color:#ffff00}
30: </style>
31: <body style="background:#000088;font-family:arial">
32: <div class="txtSt" style="text-align:center;font-size:18pt">
33:    Reserve Your Seat Here
34:   <form action="ex15-13a.pl" method="post">
35:   <table style="width:550px" border="0" class="txtSt" align="center">
36:    <tr><td>Name: </td>
37:     <td><input type="text" id="from" name="from" class="butSt" /></td>
38:     <td>Tel: </td><td>
39:     <input type="text" id="tel" name="tel" class="butSt"></td></tr>
40:   </table><br />
41:   <img src="line1.gif" height="6" width="600" /><br /><br/>
42:   <table class="txtSt" cellspacing="30" align="center"
43:       style="width:650px;text-align:center">
44: mypage
45: $noCols = 3;
46: for($jj=0;$jj<$noCols;$jj++)
47: {
48:  print"<tr>";
49:  for ($ii=1;$ii<5;$ii++)
50:  {
51:    $tmp = $jj*4 + $ii;
52:    $tmpSt = 'ch' . $tmp;
53:    if ($seatNote[$tmp] == 0)
54:    {
55:      print "<td>Seat $tmp <br />$seatName[$tmp]<br />
56:        <input type=\"checkbox\" class=\"chkSt\" name=\"$tmpSt\"
57:        id=\"$tmpSt\" value=\"0\" /></td>";
58:    } else {
59:      print "<td style=\"color:#ffffff\">Seat $tmp <br />
60:        $seatName[$tmp]<br /><input type=\"checkbox\"
61:        style=\"visibility:hidden\" class=\"chkSt\" name=\"$tmpSt\"
62:        id=\"$tmpSt\" checked value=\"1\" /></td>";
63:    }
64:  }
65:  print "</tr>";
66: }
```

```
67:
68: print << "endpage";
69:    </table><br />
70:    <table align="center"><tr><td>
71:    <input type="submit" class="butSt" value="Submit" />   
72:    <input type="reset" class="butSt" value="Reset" /></td></tr></table>
73:    </form>
74:    <img src="line1.gif" height="6" width="600" /><br />
75:    Date: $timeV<br />
76:    </div></body></html>
77: endpage
```

This script fragment generates an XHTML page with one form and three tables inside it. The first table defined in lines 35–40 is designed to obtain the user's information. That is, the name and telephone number of the person who wants to reserve a seat. The second table defined in lines 42–69 is more interesting. The table rows and cells are generated by a double for-loop. Since we want to arrange the seats into four columns, three rows are needed. That is, the outer for-loop is responsible for generating three rows and the inner for-loop is responsible for generating four columns of seats.

For each seat, if the seat reservation note $seatNote[] equals 0 (line 53), a checkbox is generated in lines 55–57. If $seatNote[] is not 0, the name of the person who reserved it is displayed. A checkbox with visibility set to hidden is also generated so that the checkbox is not displayed. A screen shot of this script is shown in Fig. 15.19.

Figure 15.19 ex15-13.p1

From Fig. 15.19, you can see that the reserved seats are displayed with names and no checkbox is attached.

At the end of the script, a table containing Submit and Reset buttons is defined. When the Submit button is pressed, another Perl script ex15-13a.pl is activated to process the data and perform the seat reservation on the server.

The user him- or herself or some operators can fill in the form by

- entering the name and telephone number of the person who wants to reserve a seat;
- selecting some seats to reserve, such as seat 11 and seat 12.

Once the form is submitted and accepted, an acknowledgment page (Fig. 15.20) is returned by the system to indicate that the selected seats are reserved. If the user presses the Back button at this time, the page is updated with new reservations as in Fig. 15.21.

Figure 15.20 A return page

Figure 15.21 ex15-13.p1

The data file seat.txt of the seats is also updated as in Fig. 15.22.

Figure 15.22 Data file seat.txt

To see the techniques behind the display, let's consider the Perl script ex15-13a.pl. The first part of this script is responsible for reading the seat data file and collecting data including the selected seats from the user page.

Example: ex15-13a.pl – The Perl Script For ex15-13.pl (Part One)

```perl
1: #! /usr/bin/perl
2: use CGI qw( :standard );
3: print "Content-type:text/html\n\n";
4:
5: my $timeV = scalar(localtime());
6: my $noSeat=0;
7:
8: open(filehandle,"<seat.dir/seat.txt")
9:     or die("Cannot Open seat.txt File.. Error");
10: my $noSeat = <filehandle>;
11: for ($ii=1;$ii <= $noSeat;$ii++)
12: {
```

```
13:    my $tmp01 = <filehandle>;
14:    $tmp01 =~ s/\n//g;
15:    ($seatNote[$ii],$seatName[$ii],$telephone[$ii]) = split(',',$tmp01);
16: }
17: close(filehandle);
18:
19: for ($ii=1;$ii<= $noSeat;$ii++)
20: {
21:    my $tmp = 'ch'. ($ii);
22:    $checkB[$ii] = param($tmp);
23: }
24: $from = param("from");
25: $tel = param("tel");
26:
```

After opening the data file seat.txt, a for-loop in lines 11–16 is used to read in all the seat data. For each data line about the seat, a substitution is performed in line 14 to chop off the line break. Then the line is split into $seatNote, $seatName, and $telephone.

To obtain the selected checkboxes from the interface, a for-loop is employed in lines 19–23 to check all the checkboxes. If a checkbox is checked by the user, the value of the array element $checkB[] contains the value 0. The user name and telephone number are also obtained in lines 24–25. Once all this information is available, you can construct a return page back to the user. The construction is demonstrated in the following script fragment:

Listing: Continuation Of The Perl Script ex15-13a.pl (Part Two)

```
27: print << "mypage";
28:    <?xml version="1.0" encoding="iso-8859-1"?>
29:    <!DOCTYPE html PUBLIC "-//W3C//DTD XHTML 1.0 Transitional//EN"
30:       "http://www.w3.org/TR/xhtml1/DTD/xhtml1-transitional.dtd">
31:    <html xmlns="http://www.w3.org/1999/xhtml" xml:lang="en" lang="en">
32:    <head><title></title></head>
33:    <style>
34:      .butSt{background-color:#aaffaa;font-family:arial;font-weight:bold;
35:        font-size:14pt;color:#008800;width:130px;height:30px}
36:      .txtSt{font-weight:bold;font-size:14pt;color:#ffff00}
37:    </style>
38:    <body style="background:#000088;font-family:arial">
39:    <div style="font-size:18pt;color:#ffff00;text-align:center">
40:      The Following Seats Have Been <br /> Reserved For<br /><br />
41:    <img src="line1.gif" height="6" width="400" /><br /><br/>
42:    <form action="ex15-13.pl" method="post">
43:    <table class="txtSt" align="center">
44:     <tr><td>Name : </td><td>$from</td></tr>
45:     <tr><td>Tel: </td><td>$tel </td></tr>
46: mypage
47:
48:  for ($ii=1; $ii <= $noSeat; $ii++)
49:  {
50:   if (($checkB[$ii] ne '') && ($checkB[$ii] !=1))
51:   {
52:    print "<tr><td>Seat Number $ii = </td><td>(Reserved)</td></tr>";
53:     $seatNote[$ii] = 1;
54:     $seatName[$ii] = "($from)";
55:     $telephone[$ii] = "Tel: $tel";
56:   }
57:  }
58:  print "</table><br /><br />";
```

```
59:
60: print << "endpage";
61:    <input type="submit" class="butSt" value="Back" />
62:    </form>
63:    <img src="line1.gif" height="6" width="400" /><br />
64:    Date: $timeV<br />
65:    </div></body></html>
66: endpage
67:
```

All the checkboxes are represented by the array `$checkB[]`. Since the system only returns those checkboxes which are checked, a simple testing criterion in line 50

```
($checkB[$ii] ne '') ## not empty checkbox
```

can isolate all checked checkboxes. All the previous boxes checked or seats reserved by users will have the value `$checkB[]=1`. Therefore, if you add the condition as in the second half of line 50

```
$checkB[$ii] !=1
```

you can isolate the checkboxes that the current user has checked. These checkboxes are displayed and returned back to the current user by the print statement in line 52. Also, inside this for-loop, the following data are prepared (lines 53–55):

```
$seatNote[$ii] = 1;
$seatName[$ii] = "($from)";
$telephone[$ii] = "Tel: $tel";
```

These values are written into the data file seat.txt so that the file is updated. The file writing process is defined in the third part of the script as follows:

```
Listing: Continuation Of The Perl Script ex15-13a.pl (Part Three)

68:
69: open(filehandle,">seat.dir\seat.txt")
70:    or die("Cannot Open Seat.txt File.. Error");
71: flock(filehandle,2) or die("Cannot gain exclusive access.. Error.");
72: print filehandle "$noSeat";
73: for ($ii=1;$ii <= $noSeat;$ii++)
74: {
75:    print filehandle "$seatNote[$ii],$seatName[$ii],$telephone[$ii] \n";
76: }
77: flock(filehandle,8);
78: close(filehandle);
```

This script opens the data file. As soon as the file is opened, a `flock()` function is employed to gain exclusive access to the file preventing the danger of concurrent access. If exclusive access is granted, all the data including the total number of seats `$noseat`, the reservation flags array `$seatNote[]`, and the telephone number array `$telephone[]` are written into the data file. When the writing is finished, another `flock()` function is used to release the exclusive access. The updated data file seat.txt can be viewed by a simple click on the Back button.

15.4.3 A simple search engine

Search engines appear almost in every corner of the Web. Have you thought about how to develop a search engine? Even more, have you thought about how to develop a site for users to register their Web sites or pages on your search engine?

Search engines are not the exclusive property of the big players on the Web. You will find that most small groups with special interests have some kind of search engine in one form or another on their sites to communicate information to each other. For example, a small minority group in San Francisco has a Web site with a small search engine to allow users to search other similar groups and Web sites in other cities in the United States. In the next example, we will develop a small search engine to register and search Web sites on pandas.

The interface part of the search engine is a Web page generated by a Perl script.

Example: ex15-14.pl - A Search Engine With Perl

```
 1: #! /usr/bin/perl
 2: use CGI qw( :standard );
 3: print "Content-type:text/html\n\n";
 4:
 5: my $timeV = scalar(localtime());
 6:
 7: print << "mypage";
 8:   <?xml version="1.0" encoding="iso-8859-1"?>
 9:   <!DOCTYPE html PUBLIC "-//W3C//DTD XHTML 1.0 Transitional//EN"
10:       "http://www.w3.org/TR/xhtml1/DTD/xhtml1-transitional.dtd">
11:   <html xmlns="http://www.w3.org/1999/xhtml" xml:lang="en" lang="en">
12:   <head><title></title></head>
13:   <style>
14:     .butSt{background:#aaffaa;font-family:arial;font-weight:bold;
15:        font-size:14pt;color:#008800;width:200px;height:30px}
16:     .txtSt{font-weight:bold;font-size:14pt;color:#ffff00}
17:   </style>
18:   <body style="background:#000088;font-family:arial">
19:   <div class="txtSt" style="text-align:center;font-size:18pt">
20:      This Search Engine Is About Pandas<br /><br />
21:      Please Register Your Web Site About Pandas Here
22:
23:    <form action="ex15-14a.pl" method="post">
24:     <table style="width:550px" border="0" class="txtSt" align="center">
25:      <tr><td>Web Site Address (URL):
26:               e.g., www.panda.com/~Robinson/animal/panda.html</td></tr>
27:      <tr><td><input type="text" id="myUrl" name="myUrl" class="butSt"
28:               style="width:500px" /></td></tr>
29:      <tr><td>Site Description: </td></tr>
30:      <tr><td><input type="text" id="des" name="des" class="butSt"
31:               style="width:500px" /></td></tr>
32:     </table><br />
33:      <input type="submit" class="butSt" value="Submit" />   
34:      <input type="reset" class="butSt" value="Reset" />
35:    </form>
36:    <img src="line1.gif" height="6" width="600" /><br /><br/>
37:
38:    <form action="ex15-14b.pl" method="post">
39:        Search The Sites You Want<br /><br />
40:    <table style="width:550px" border="0" class="txtSt" align="center">
41:     <tr><td>Search String:</td><td>
42:       <input type="text" id="searchSt" name="searchSt" class="butSt"
43:            style="width:300px" /></td></tr>
44:    </table><br />
45:      <input type="submit" class="butSt" value="Search" />
46:    </form>
47:
48:    <img src="line1.gif" height="6" width="600" /><br />
49:    Date: $timeV<br />
50:    </div></body></html>
51: mypage
```

The Web page generated by this Perl script contains two forms. The first form defined in lines 23–35 is designed to register a page in the search engine. Once the Web site address (lines 27–28) and the description of the site (lines 30–31) are filled and the Submit button is pressed, the form is submitted to a Perl script called ex15-14a.pl (line 23) to register the site in the engine.

The purpose of the second form is to search the sites about pandas. A search string is declared in lines 42–43. When a keyword is entered and the Search button is clicked, the form is submitted to another Perl script to perform the search. To see how to register your site in the engine, some screen shots are shown in Figs 15.23 and 15.24.

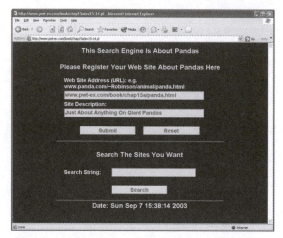

Figure 15.23 ex15-14.p1

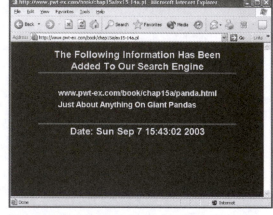

Figure 15.24 A return page for the registration

The search engine that we are going to develop is a simple text-based engine. The data file is called panda.txt and contains only two fields, namely, the description and the url of the site separated by a special symbol #1#. That is, if you fill in the url and description as

```
www.pwt-ex.com/johnsmith/animal/panda.html
Just About Anything on Giant Pandas
```

(as shown in Fig. 15.24), you will add a line at the end of the data file such as

```
Just About Anything on Giant Pandas#1#www.pwt-ex.com
johnsmith/animal/panda.html
```

Therefore the registration process is a straightforward operation to append a record to the data file panda.txt. The Perl script is listed below:

```
Example: ex15-14a.pl - The Perl Script For ex15-14.pl

 1: #!usr/bin/perl
 2: use CGI qw (:standard);
 3: print "Content-type:text/html \n\n";
 4:
 5: my $addUrl = param(myUrl);
 6: my $addDes = param(des);
 7: my $timeV = scalar(localtime());
 8:
 9: open(filehandle, ">>panda.txt") or
10:    die("The URL database could not be opened");
11: print filehandle "$addDes#1#$addUrl\n";
12: close (filehandle);
```

```
13:
14: print << "mypage";
15: <?xml version="1.0" encoding="iso-8859-1"?>
16: <!DOCTYPE html PUBLIC "-//W3C//DTD XHTML 1.0 Transitional//EN"
17:     "http://www.w3.org/TR/xhtml1/DTD/xhtml1-transitional.dtd">
18: <html xmlns="http://www.w3.org/1999/xhtml" xml:lang="en" lang="en">
19: <head><title></title></head>
20: <style>
21: .txtSt{font-family:arial;font-weight:bold;font-size:14pt;color:#ffff00}
22: </style>
23: <body class="txtSt" style="background:#000088;font-size:18pt;
24:  text-align:center" >
25:    The Following Information Has Been <br />
26:    Added To Our Search Engine
27:    <br />
28:   <img src="line1.gif" width="500" height="6" /><br /><br />
29: <table class="txtSt" border="0" cellspacing="5">
30:   <tr><td>$addUrl</td></tr>
31:   <tr><td>$addDes</td></tr>
32: </table>
33:   <br /><img src="line1.gif" height="6" width="500" /><br />
34:   Date: $timeV<br />
35: </div></body></html>
36: mypage
```

The returned url and description of the site information are stored in variables $addUrl and $addDes (lines 5–6). The open statement in line 9 opens the data file panda.txt in append mode. A simple print statement

```
print filehandle "$addDes#1#$addUrl\n";
```

would append the description and url of the site at the end of the file panda.txt. The special symbol #1# is used to separate the two fields so that you can split them in the search process. Lines 14–36 generate a return page back to the user saying that his or her site has been registered in the engine (see Fig. 15.24).

To see the search process in action, some screen shots are shown in Figs 15.25 and 15.26.

Figure 15.25 Search process

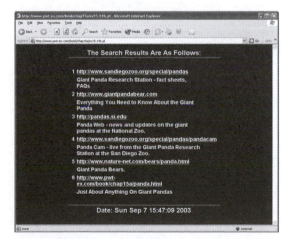

Figure 15.26 Search results

When you fill in the search string with a keyword, e.g., "Giant," all the search results about giant pandas will be shown in the returned page as in Fig. 15.26.

The details of the search process are defined in the Perl script below:

Example: ex15-14b.pl - The Perl Script For ex15-14.pl

```perl
 1: #!usr/bin/perl
 2: use CGI qw (:standard);
 3: print "Content-type:text/html \n\n";
 4:
 5: my $searchSt = param(searchSt);
 6: my $timeV = scalar(localtime());
 7:
 8: print << "mypage";
 9:   <?xml version="1.0" encoding="iso-8859-1"?>
10:   <!DOCTYPE html PUBLIC "-//W3C//DTD XHTML 1.0 Transitional//EN"
11:       "http://www.w3.org/TR/xhtml1/DTD/xhtml1-transitional.dtd">
12:   <html xmlns="http://www.w3.org/1999/xhtml" xml:lang="en" lang="en">
13:   <head><title></title></head>
14:   <style>
15:     .txtSt{font-family:arial;font-weight:bold;font-size:14pt;color:#ffff00}
16:   </style>
17:   <body class="txtSt" style="background:#000088;font-size:18pt;
18:       text-align:center" >
19:     The Search Results Are As Follows:<br />
20:     <img src="line1.gif" width="550" height="6" /><br /><br />
21:
22:   <table class="txtSt" border="0" cellspacing="5">
23: mypage
24:
25: my $count = 0;
26: open(filehandle, "<panda.txt") or
27:     die("The data file cannot be openned .. Error.");
28:
29: while(my $lst = <filehandle>)
30: {
31:   if ($lst =~ /$searchSt/i)
32:   {
33:     $count++;
34:     $lst =~ s/\n//g;
35:     my ($des, $url) = split(/#1#/, $lst);
36:     print "<tr><td valign=\"top\">$count</td><td style=\"width:450px\">
37:           <a href=\"http://$url\" style=\"color:#ffffff\">
38:           http://$url</a></td></tr>";
39:     print "<tr><td></td><td style=\"width:450px\">$des </td></tr>";
40:   }
41: }
42: if ($count ==0)
43: {
44:   print "<tr><td>Sorry ! No Result Has Been Found!</td></tr>";
45: }
46: close (filehandle);
47:
48: print << "endpage";
49: </table><br />
50:   <img src="line1.gif" height="6" width="550" /><br />
51:   Date: $timeV<br />
52: </div></body></html>
53: endpage
```

In this script the search string is captured by the variable $searchSt declared in line 5. Lines 8–23 generate the first part of the returned XHTML page. The second part of the page is more interesting. The open statement in line 26 opens the file panda.txt for reading. For each line of the data, we perform the following tasks:

- Search the entire line to match the string stored in $searchSt.
- In case a match is found:
  - Increment the count variable $count by 1.
  - Delete the line break at the end of the line.
  - Split the line into description $des and URL $url.
  - Generate table rows for $des and $url.

In terms of Perl script programming, the tasks above are implemented as a while-loop in lines 29–41. If no match is found for the entire data file, a message is returned to the user. Don't forget to close the data file after all the file operations are finished. Another here document is used in lines 48–53 to generate the final part of the returned page. Some readers familiar with Perl script may prefer to use Perl script functions to generate headers and other XHTML elements. The implementation here tries to generate a whole, readable, and easy to understand XHTML page.

15.4.4 Accessing an ODBC database with Perl script

A large number of business applications use database techniques. Among both small firms and large corporations, databases are indispensable tools to maintain, manipulate, and access records of data. There are a number of databases on the market, such as Microsoft Access, FoxPro, Borland's Paradox, Sybase, Oracle, and MySQL. Each database has its own application development language and many of them are well integrated with the database itself and incompatible with others. This has created a problem for database developers and users on the Internet.

The Open Database Connectivity (ODBC) is a product from Microsoft and is an integral part of Windows systems such as 9.x/2000/NT/XP. ODBC implements a Structured Query Language (SQL) interface for different databases. The interface takes ODBC function calls and converts them into specific functions for different databases. This feature is convenient and useful. Once a database is registered on a machine with ODBC, people all over the Internet can access the contents and records using the same kind of function calls.

As an example, we consider a Microsoft Access database file people.mdb. This database file contains one table called people. The table has four fields containing information about a group of people as given in Table 15.3.

Table 15.3 Database table: people

ID	Name	Email	Description
1	John	John@.pwt-ex.com	Male, 30 Years Old, London
2	Mary	Mary@.pwt-ex.com	Female, 22 Years Old, Paris
...	...	...	...
10	Anne	Anne@.pwt-ex.com	Female, 30 Years Old, London

To register a database on a Windows system is easy. For example, the following step-by-step procedures can be used to register the database on a Windows XP system:

- Activate the Control Panel | Administrative Tools (Fig. 15.27). Click on the Data Sources (ODBC) icon to open the "Data Source Administrator" window (Fig. 15.28).
- Click on the System DSN menu and press the Add button to open the "Create New Data Source" window (Fig. 15.29). Select Microsoft Access Drive and click Finish.

Figure 15.27 ODBC I

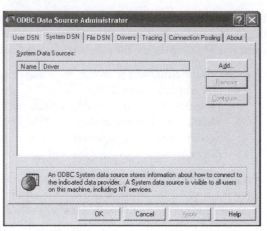

Figure 15.28 ODBC II

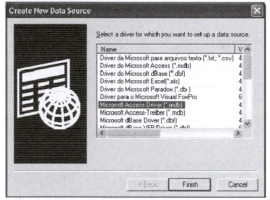

Figure 15.29 ODBC III

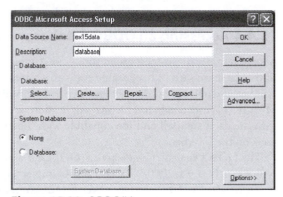

Figure 15.30 ODBC IV

- The "ODBC Microsoft Access Setup" window will appear (Fig. 15.30). Fill in the Data Source Name and Description as illustrated in Fig. 15.30. Press the Select button and upload the database file people.mdb (Fig. 15.31).
- Now click the OK button to register the database into the system (Fig. 15.32). You will have the database registered in the window. Now click the OK button to exit.

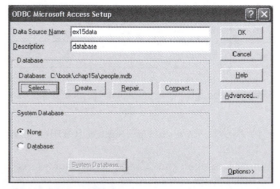

Figure 15.31 ODBC V

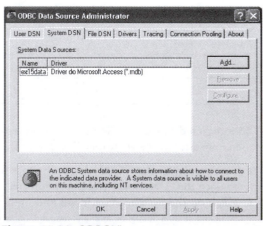

Figure 15.32 ODBC VI

When the information of the DSN and the name of the table is ready, a Web page is developed to access the database using SQL. Chapter 17 is dedicated to databases and the SQL language, but, for now, we use the following simple SQL command to display all records and data of the database:

```
SELECT * FROM PEOPLE
```

This statement can be interpreted as "select every field from a table called people." In order to send this SQL out to the ODBC database, we develop a simple XHTML page.

```
Example: ex15-15.htm - ODBC Database With Perl

 1: <?xml version="1.0" encoding="iso-8859-1"?>
 2: <!DOCTYPE html PUBLIC "-//W3C//DTD XHTML 1.0 Transitional//EN"
 3:     "http://www.w3.org/TR/xhtml1/DTD/xhtml1-transitional.dtd">
 4: <html xmlns="http://www.w3.org/1999/xhtml" xml:lang="en" lang="en">
 5: <head><title> ODBC Database With Perl - ex15-15.htm </title></head>
 6: <style>
 7:   .txt{font-family:arial;font-size:14pt;color:#000088;font-weight:bold}
 8:   .butSt{background-color:#aaffaa;font-family:arial;font-weight:bold;
 9:       font-size:14pt;color:#008800;width:520px;height:30px}
10: </style>
11: <body style="font-size:18pt;background:#bbbbff;text-align:center"
12: class="txt"> Access An ODBC DataBase <br />with Perl Script<br /><br />
13:   <img src="line1.gif" width="550" height="6" /><br />
14:
15:   <table class="txt" cellspacing="10" width="550" >
16:    <tr><td colspan="2">Remote Database Information:</td></tr>
17:    <tr valign="top"><td><img src="bullet1.gif" vspace ="3" /></td>
18:      <td>A Microsoft Access DataBase people.mdb is registered
19:         with ODBC </td></tr>
20:    <tr><td valign="top"><img src="bullet1.gif" vspace ="3" /></td>
21:      <td> Data Source Name (DSN) = ex15data</td></tr>
22:    <tr><td valign="top"><img src="bullet1.gif" vspace ="3" /></td>
23:      <td>The database contains a table called people with<br />
24:       ID, Name, Email and Description Fields</td></tr>
25:   </table>
26:
27:   <img src="line1.gif" width="550" height="6" /><br />
28:   <form action = "ex15-15.pl" method="post">
29:      Enter Your SQL Query String<br />
30:    <input type ="text" name = "querySt" size = "120"
31:      value = "select * from people" class="butSt"><br /><br />
32:    <input type = "submit" value = " Send Query" class="butSt"
33:        style="width:180px;background:#bbbbbb">
34:   </form>
35: </body>
36: </html>
```

After the page header, we have declared a table to describe the ODBC database in lines 15–25. In order to use ODBC effectively three pieces of information are needed:

- the name of the DSN (i.e., ex15data);
- the name of the database or table (i.e., people);
- the name of each field in the table (i.e., ID, Name, Email, and Description).

The final part of the page contains a form with a text box and a button. The text box is for the user to type in an SQL command. When the button is pressed, the SQL command or query will be sent to the Perl script ex15-15.pl. The purpose of this script is to connect to the database and collect results. Some screen shots of this page in action are shown in Figs 15.33 and 15.34.

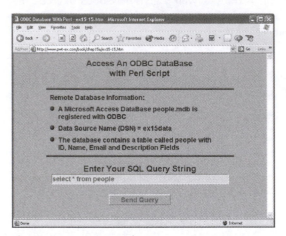

Figure 15.33 ex15-15.htm

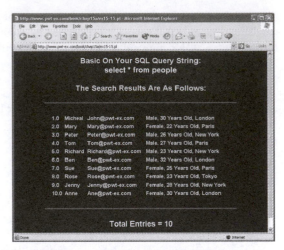

Figure 15.34 ODBC database results

The SQL query string "SELECT * FROM PEOPLE" would search and display all records of the database. If the following SQL command is used

```
SELECT Name, Email, Description FROM PEOPLE
```

you will have a returned page similar to Fig. 15.34 but without the ID column. Since SQL is not case sensitive, you can also use the command

```
Select * from people where Description like '%Female%'
```

to search and display all the female records. The SQL clause can be interpreted as

```
select all fields from the table called people
where the Description field contains a keyword Female.
```

After SQL, databases on the Web and other related technologies such as ASP and PHP are the central topics of the next two chapters; this example serves as preparation for a more detailed study of each of them. Some more screen shots on SQL in action are shown in Figs 15.35 and 15.36.

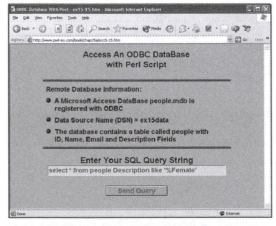

Figure 15.35 Another SQL command

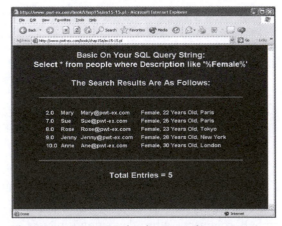

Figure 15.36 ODBC database results

To connect to the registered ODBC database and collect the results, the following Perl script fragment is used:

```
Example: ex15-15.pl - The Perl Script For ex15-15.htm (Part One)

 1: #!usr/bin/perl
 2:
 3: use Win32::ODBC;
 4: use CGI qw (:standard);
 5: print "Content-type:text/html\n\n";
 6:
 7: my $querySt = param(queryST);
 8: $dsnName = "ex15data";
 9:
10: if (!($odbcData = new Win32::ODBC($dsnName)))
11: {
12:    print "ODBC Connection .. Error..\n";
13:    exit();
14: }
15:
16: if ($odbcData->Sql($querySt))
17: {
18:    print "Error.. SQL failed..\n";
19:    $odbcData->Close();
20:    exit();
21: }
22:
```

Since ODBC is a Microsoft product and dedicated to the Windows system, an additional Perl module called Win32 is declared in line 3. After that the SQL query string is captured and stored in variable $queryST. The name of the DSN ex15data is also stored in $dsnName. To establish the connection between the script and the database, we execute the statement (see line 10)

```
$odbcData = new Win32::ODBC($dsnName)
```

This statement creates a new ODBC object with connection to $dsnName and assigns the object to variable $odbcData. If this statement doesn't return a true value, there is a failure case on the connection.

Once a proper connection is established, you can use the statement

```
$odbcData->Sql($querySt)
```

to assign the record set returned by SQL to variable $odbcData. If this process fails, you have an error on the SQL statement and the program needs to be terminated. For example, if you make a mistake by issuing the SQL command "select from peop," the error will be captured by the statements in lines 16–21.

The SQL results returned by the database are now available. The second part of the script is to construct a return page back to the user with the SQL records.

```
Listing: Continuation Of The Perl Script ex15-15.pl (Part Two)

23: print << "mypage";
24:  <?xml version="1.0" encoding="iso-8859-1"?>
25:  <!DOCTYPE html PUBLIC "-//W3C//DTD XHTML 1.0 Transitional//EN"
26:     "http://www.w3.org/TR/xhtml1/DTD/xhtml1-transitional.dtd">
27:  <html xmlns="http://www.w3.org/1999/xhtml" xml:lang="en" lang="en">
28:  <head><title></title></head>
29:  <style>
30:   .txtSt{font-family:arial;font-weight:bold;font-size:13pt;color:#ffff00}
31:  </style>
32:  <body class="txtSt" style="background:#000088;font-size:18pt;
33:      text-align:center" >
```

```
34:    Basic On Your SQL Query String:<br />
35:    <div style="color:#ffffff"> $querySt</div><br />
36:    The Search Results Are As Follows:<br /><br />
37:    <img src="line1.gif" width="600" height="6" alt="pic" /><br /><br />
38:    <table cellspacing="5" class="txtSt" width="570">
39: mypage
40:
41: $count = 0;
42: while($odbcData->FetchRow())
43: {
44:     %odbcData = $odbcData->DataHash();
45:
46:     print "<tr><td>$odbcData{ID}</td><td>$odbcData{Name}</td>
47:            <td>$odbcData{Email}</td><td>$odbcData{Description}</td></tr>";
48:     $count++;
49: }
50: $odbcData->Close();
51:
52: print << "endpage";
53:    </table><br />
54:    <img src="line1.gif" width="600" height="6" alt="pic" /><br /><br />
55:    Total Entries = $count<br /><br />
56:    </body>
57:    </html>
58: endpage
```

The first part of this script fragment is to generate an XHTML header return to the user. After that a while-loop is used to fetch each row of the SQL records. For each row, the function DataHash() is called to insert the records and individual fields into a hash table (see line 44), i.e.,

```
%odbcData = $odbcData->DataHash();
```

Therefore, the variables $odbc{ID}, $odbc{Name}, $odbc{Email}, and $odbc{Description} represent the fields of the database table people and will contain the proper values from the SQL records. The print statement in lines 46-47 formats the values into one table row with four table cells. When all the SQL records are processed, the data source of the object is closed in line 50. The remaining part of the script is to complete the ending of the XHTML page and is easy to understand.

16 | Using ASP and migrating to ASP.NET

16.1 An introduction to ASP and ASP.NET

16.1.1 What are ASP and ASP.NET?

This chapter is dedicated to Microsoft Active Server Page (ASP) and its applications on the Web. ASP is a server technology developed by Microsoft in as early as 1996 to provide CGI and many other functions in the Web server. Today, two ASP products are available, namely, ASP and ASP.NET.

Since they are both server technologies, all CGI applications discussed in the last two chapters can also be accomplished by them. What is ASP anyway?

Strictly speaking, ASP is not a language but rather an environment to develop something called an ASP page to be displayed on a browser. ASP pages usually have file extension .asp and can be written by a number of languages including

- VBScript – A scaled-down version of Visual Basic.
- JScript – Microsoft's version of JavaScript or ECMAScript.

If you have installed a script engine, you can use other languages as well. We will show you how to use Perl inside an ASP page in section 16.2.2.

The ASP package is an integral part of Microsoft's systems. If you have the server software installed on Windows 95/98 such as Personal Web Server (PWS), or Internet Information Services (IIS) on NT/2000/XP, you already have ASP configured. You can also have ASP support for your Apache Web server in a UNIX/LINUX environment by installing add-on packages. These packages are available from Apache's official site (www.apache.org). ASP is universal and a powerful tool to develop Web server applications across all Windows platforms.

In late 2001, along with the .NET technologies, Microsoft released the ASP.NET package as the next generation of software for ASP for the .NET family. ASP.NET is designed for the Windows 2000 (Professional and Server versions) and XP. It is not supported on Windows NT or 95/98 platforms. If you are using the supported systems, the software can be downloaded from Microsoft's official site: www.microsoft.com or www.asp.net.

Due possibly to the huge success and wide acceptance of ASP pages in the Web community, installing the new ASP.NET software will not disturb existing ASP already in the system. In fact, both ASP and ASP.NET software can be used by the same Web server such as IIS. This means that all your ASP applications are unaffected. After installation, one of the first things you may notice is that the ASP.NET page uses a new file extension .aspx to distinguish it from .asp used for ASP pages.

Apart from some minor differences, ASP pages are practically compatible or can be migrated to ASP.NET. In many cases, ASP pages can be converted to ASP.NET without changing any coding: all you have to do is to change the file extension from .asp to .aspx.

16.1.2 My first ASP and ASP.NET page

To develop an ASP page is easy: all you have to do is to create a text file with file extension `.asp`. Inside this file any combination of XHTML and ASP commands can be used. ASP commands are different from text or XHTML elements, in that ASP uses the delimiters `<%` and `%>` to enclose commands that will be processed by the server. You can include within the delimiters as many commands or statements as you like, provided they are logically valid and specified by your scripting language. Let's consider a simple ASP page first.

My First ASP Page ex16-01.asp is a very simple one to display a message and a time string. Consider the following page code:

```
Example: ex16-01.asp - My First ASP Page

 1: <%@ Language=VBScript%>
 2: <?xml version="1.0" encoding="iso-8859-1"?>
 3: <!DOCTYPE html PUBLIC "-//W3C//DTD XHTML 1.0 Transitional//EN"
 4:     "http://www.w3.org/TR/xhtml1/DTD/xhtml1-transitional.dtd">
 5: <html xmlns="http://www.w3.org/1999/xhtml" xml:lang="en" lang="en">
 6: <head><title> My First ASP Page - ex16-01.asp </title><head>
 7: <body style="font-family:arial;font-size:24pt;font-weight:bold">
 8:
 9:  Now is the Time: <br /> <%=Now%>
10: </body>
11: </html>
```

The first line of this page specifies that the VBScript language is used. You can change to another ASP language here. If you request the page from your browser with

```
http://www.pwt-ex.com/book/chap16a/ex16-01.asp
```

you will see a message on your browser window similar to the one below (see Fig. 16.1):

```
Now is the Time:
22/09/2003 15:35:53
```

This string was generated by the statement in line 9 and the numeric part came from the ASP command `<%= Now %>`. This is a VBScript command to generate the date and time as a string.

The statement `<%= expression %>`, in fact, is called the ASP output directive and is used to display the value of an expression. This output directive is equivalent to calling the `Write()` method from the `Response` object. That is,

`<%= Now %>` **is equivalent to** `<% Response.Write(Now) %>`

We will cover this `Response` object and many others in the coming sections. From a simple server page, to CGI and databases, ASP is a powerful technology used in countless Web applications.

As we mentioned earlier, ASP pages in many cases are compatible with ASP.NET. As a simple demonstration, if you rename file ex16-01.asp as ex16-01.aspx and request the ASP.NET page using

```
http://www.pwt-ex.com/book/chap16a/ex16-01.aspx
```

you will see the same display as in Fig. 16.1 on your browser window provided you have the ASP.NET software installed. A screen shot is shown in Fig. 16.2.

From a practical point of view, ASP is universal and popular across all Windows systems and many UNIX/LINUX platforms. This object-based language has an important role in Web development.

We begin by introducing the structure of ASP and its multiple scripting language features. Examples are provided to show how to use VBScript, JScript, and PerlScript with ASP. Then a series of ASP objects are discussed with applications on CGI and servers. You may find that using ASP objects to handle CGI applications is more convenient.

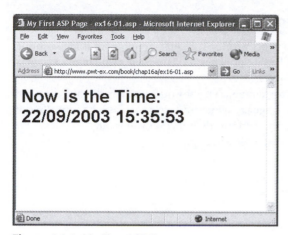

Figure 16.1 My First ASP Page

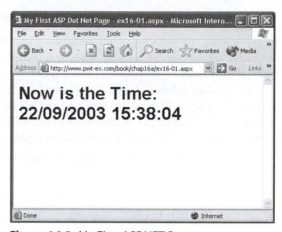

Figure 16.2 My First ASP.NET Page

Along with the CGI applications, some system resources and controls are also considered in detail, namely, drives, directories, and/or files. Databases with ASP will be discussed in Chapter 17. In fact, some of the ASP objects are dedicated to database purposes. Finally, in section 16.5, the differences between ASP and ASP.NET are discussed. We will also show you how to migrate all ASP pages in this chapter to ASP.NET.

16.2   ASP objects and their applications on the Web

16.2.1 The structure of ASP

Basically, ASP is an environment that allows you to write Web pages using a variety of scripting languages. In fact, you can use several scripting languages within a single ASP page to enhance the functionalities via scripting library scenarios. Since server scripts are read and processed on the server before being sent back to the browser, there is no client requirement for ASP. As a server page inside the server, an ASP page (or document) requires a new file extension .asp to distinguish it from the usual XHTML document.

By default, ASP uses VBScript and JScript as the processing languages. If you want to use another scripting language, you may need to install the appropriate scripting engine, which is a program that can process commands and statements written in a particular language. For every installation of ASP, VBScript and JScript are provided. We will show you how to install another scripting engine called PerlScript in the next section. A structure diagram of ASP is shown in Fig. 16.3.

To use the multiple languages feature of ASP and related objects, let's consider some examples in the discussion below.

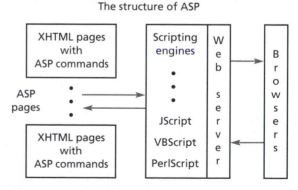

Figure 16.3 Calling an ASP page

16.2.2 Creating ASP pages with different scripting languages

In this section, we will show you how to use different languages with ASP. Simple examples of three scripting languages are introduced, namely, VBScript, JScript, and PerlScript. They all have their own language syntax and style and work in the ASP environment as family members.

Another characteristic of ASP is that it is object based. System objects will work closely with your choice of scripting languages. That means you can use your favorite language syntax and style such as VBScript, JScript (a variant of ECMAScript), or PerlScript to call ASP objects to perform the function you want.

As a simple example, consider the following ASP page written in VBScript:

```
Example: ex16-02.asp - ASP With VBScript

 1: <%@ Language=VBScript%>
 2: <?xml version="1.0" encoding="iso-8859-1"?>
 3: <!DOCTYPE html PUBLIC "-//W3C//DTD XHTML 1.0 Transitional//EN"
 4:     "http://www.w3.org/TR/xhtml1/DTD/xhtml1-transitional.dtd">
 5: <html xmlns="http://www.w3.org/1999/xhtml" xml:lang="en" lang="en">
 6: <head><title> ASP With VBScript - ex16-02.asp</title></head>
 7: <body style="font-family:arial;font-weight:bold">
 8: <% dim ii
 9: For ii=20 to 26
10: Response.Write("<div style='font-size:" & ii & "px;color:#000000'>")
11: Response.Write("style font-size = " & ii & " px -- Hello World! </div >")
12: Next
13: %>
14: </body>
15: </html>
```

The first line is to indicate that this is an ASP page using VBScript as the primary language. This means that statements inside the delimiters <% and %> (lines 8–13) will be processed by the VBScript engine installed in ASP. By default, VBScript is the primary language for ASP. Insider the delimiters, there is a for-loop in VBScript style. Consider the statement in line 10:

```
Response.Write("<div style='font-size:" & ii & "px;color:#000000'>")
```

The keyword `Response` is an object provided by ASP. With this object, you can call the member function (or method) `Write()` to output something to the browser screen. Inside the parentheses, the ampersand "&" is a VBScript symbol to concatenate two strings.

The JScript version of this example is listed below:

```
Example: ex16-03.asp - ASP With JScript

 1: <%@ Language=JScript%>
 2: <?xml version="1.0" encoding="iso-8859-1"?>
 3: <!DOCTYPE html PUBLIC "-//W3C//DTD XHTML 1.0 Transitional//EN"
 4:     "http://www.w3.org/TR/xhtml1/DTD/xhtml1-transitional.dtd">
 5: <html xmlns="http://www.w3.org/1999/xhtml" xml:lang="en" lang="en">
 6: <head><title> ASP With JScript - ex16-03.asp</title></head>
 7: <body style="font-family:arial;font-weight:bold"><br /><br />
 8: <% var ii
 9: for( ii=20;ii <=26; ii++)
10: {
11: Response.Write("<div style='font-size:" + ii + "px;color:#000000'>")
12: Response.Write("style font-size = " + ii + " px -- Hello World! </div >")
13: }
14: %>
15: </body>
16: </html>
```

The process directive in line 1 indicates that the primary language is JScript (JScript is a version of JavaScript developed by Microsoft; for this reason, JScript is very similar to ECMAScript discussed in this book). The for-loop (lines 9–13) inside the delimiters is written in JScript (or ECMAScript) style. The plus "+" symbol is used to concatenate strings. No matter what kind of language you are using, you call the same method

```
Response.Write()
```

to output something to the screen.

If you want to use another scripting language such as PerlScript on ASP, a PerlScript engine is available from ActiveState Perl (www.activestate.com). It has a Perl version with a Microsoft installer so that the installation and configuration on various Microsoft systems are fully automatic. When you install Active Perl, you will have a working version of the Perl interpreter and a PerlScript engine for ASP at the same time.

If you have a PerlScript engine already installed on your system, you can convert the example above into a PerlScript version as follows:

```
Example: ex16-04.asp - ASP With PerlScript

 1: <%@ Language=PerlScript%>
 2: <?xml version="1.0" encoding="iso-8859-1"?>
 3: <!DOCTYPE html PUBLIC "-//W3C//DTD XHTML 1.0 Transitional//EN"
 4:     "http://www.w3.org/TR/xhtml1/DTD/xhtml1-transitional.dtd">
 5: <html xmlns="http://www.w3.org/1999/xhtml" xml:lang="en" lang="en">
 6: <head><title> ASP With PerlScript - ex16-04.asp</title></head>
 7: <body style="font-family:arial;font-weight:bold"><br /><br />
 8: <%
 9: for( $ii=20; $ii <=26; $ii++)
10: {
11: $Response->Write("<div style=\"font-size:" . $ii . "px;color:#000000\">");
12: $Response->Write("style font-size =". $ii ."px -- Hello World! </div >")
13: }
14: %>
15: </body>
16: </html>
```

Again, the first line is to instruct ASP to process statements inside delimiters with PerlScript. The purpose of the for-loop is to show the calling convention when using PerlScript with ASP. Following the PerlScript syntax, all variables need to have a dollar sign in front of them. Since PerlScript uses references to call objects and functions provided by ASP, the output function is changed to $Response->Write() as illustrated in lines 11 and 12. The period symbol "." used in lines 11 and 12 is to concatenate the strings. In fact, you can put the variable $ii inside, since Perl can interpret a variable correctly even inside a string.

In ASP, the primary scripting language can call functions defined in other scripting languages. To show this feature, consider the following example:

```
Example: ex16-05.asp - Multiple Scripting Languages In ASP

 1: <?xml version="1.0" encoding="iso-8859-1"?>
 2: <!DOCTYPE html PUBLIC "-//W3C//DTD XHTML 1.0 Transitional//EN"
 3:     "http://www.w3.org/TR/xhtml1/DTD/xhtml1-transitional.dtd">
 4: <html xmlns="http://www.w3.org/1999/xhtml" xml:lang="en" lang="en">
 5: <head><title>Multiple Scripting Languages - ex16-05.asp</title></head>
 6: <body style="font-family:arial;font-weight:bold;background:#000088">
 7:
 8: <div style="text-align:center;color:#ffff00;font-size:16pt">
 9:   Time From VBScript: <%=Now()%><br />
10:   Time From JScript: <%Call outputDate()%><br /><br />
11:   From PerlScript Function:<br /><%Call outString()%>
12: </div>;
13:
```

```
14: <script language=JScript runat=server>
15: function outputDate()
16: {
17:  var x = new Date()
18:  Response.Write(x.toString())
19: }
20: </script>
21:
22: <script language=PerlScript runat=server>
23: sub outString
24: {
25:  for( $ii=20;$ii <=26; $ii++)
26:  {
27:  $Response->Write("<div style=\"font-size:". $ii ."px\">");
28:  $Response->Write("style font-size = ". $ii ."px -- Hello World!</div >");
29:  }
30: }
31: </script>
32: </body>
33: </html>
```

By default, this ASP page uses VBScript as the primary scripting language. Other scripting languages can be defined by the `<script>` element. For example, the following statement defines a script block (or an ASP script section) with JScript:

```
<script language=JScript runat=server>
... ... ...
</script>
```

Inside the script section, you can define any JScript function. The keyword `runat=server` is to instruct the ASP to run this section on the server. The block in lines 14–20 defines a JScript function called `outputDate()` to display the date and time of the system. Another script block in lines 23–30 defines a PerlScript subroutine called `outString`. This subroutine is to output some strings to the browser window.

When ASP loads this page, the ASP script section (if any) is stored and executed first. Therefore, when ASP executes the JScript statement in line 10

```
<%Call outputDate()%>
```

the JScript function `outputDate()` is already there and ready for execution. If you put any output statement inside the ASP script section, this statement will be executed and placed before the XHTML header. A screen shot is shown in Fig. 16.4.

For the rest of this chapter, we will mainly use JScript as the primary scripting language for ASP. We make this choice simply because JScript is consistent with the standard ECMAScript and acceptable by many different platforms. To learn ASP, a basic understanding of the internal objects provided by ASP installation is necessary.

Not just multiple languages can be used in ASP: with ASP objects Web applications can be developed in other dimensions. Let's consider the ASP objects and see how to build Web pages with application- and user-specific (or session) scopes in the next section.

Figure 16.4 Multiple scripting languages on ASP

16.2.3 The internal objects of ASP

Basically, ASP is a combination of XHTML, your favorite scripting language, and objects provided by you, the system, and third-party vendors. For a standard ASP installation, the system framework provides the following six built-in objects:

- Application
- Request
- Server
- ObjectContext
- Response
- Session

Built-in objects are closely integrated into every ASP page. Unlike other components, you don't even need to create them before you can use them in your scripts. For each built-in object, there are methods (or functions), collections, and properties associated with them. For example, the function `Response.Write()` used in section 16.2.2 is a function inside the `Response` object.

From a practical point of view, the best way to learn ASP is to start with one favorite scripting language such as JScript and a basic understanding of the objects associated with ASP. Basically, there are six ASP objects, as above, and the purpose of each of them is summarized as follows:

- The `Application` object is an object providing collections and utilities to share information among all users of a given application.
- The `ObjectContext` object is mainly used for transactions and enables you to commit or abort a transaction in a business application.
- The `Request` object is a widely used object in ASP. You can use it to gather the contents submitted from any type of Web form including the CGI `get` and `post` methods, and to read server variables or the contents of a digital client certificate.
- The `Response` is widely used and responsible for sending data from the server to the user. You can use this object to send information directly to the browser, redirecting the browser to other URLs and handling cookies.
- The `Server` object is to provide certain server-side functions to the users. The most important function is to create an instance of an ActiveX component with `Server.CreateObject`. For example, you can use it to open a file. Furthermore, the following statement can be used to instantiate an ActiveX Data Object (ADO) for database connection:

```
ADOConnObj = Server.CreateObject('ADODB.Connection')
```

We will discuss this application in detail in the coming sections.
- The `Session` object enables you to associate variables with a particular user section. Information or variables stored in this object are still alive when a Web application jumps from one page to another.

From ASP 3.0 and later, an additional built-in object called `ASPError` has been shipped. This object is responsible for tracking down errors during the processing of an ASP page.

For each ASP built-in object, we also have collections, methods, events, and properties associated with them. Their relationships are summarized in Table 16.1.

Table 16.1 ASP built-in objects

Object	Collections	Methods	Events	Properties
Application	Contents StaticObjects	Lock Unlock	Application	N/A
ObjectContext	N/A	SetAbort SetComplete	OnTransactionAbort OnTransactionCommit	N/A
Request	ClientCertificate Cookies Form QueryString ServerVariables	BinaryRead	N/A	TotalBytes
Server	N/A	CreateObject HTMLEncode MapPath URLEncode	N/A	ScriptTimeout
Response	Cookies	AddHeader AppendToLog BinaryWrite Clear End Flush Redirect Write	N/A	Buffer CacheControl Charset ContentType Expires ExpiresAbsolute IsClientConnected PICS Status
Session	Contents StaticObjects	Abandon	Session_OnEnd Session_OnStart	CodePage LCID SessionID Timeout

One of the best ways to study ASP objects is to learn and use the methods associated with the particular object. For example, the popular `Write()` methods of the `Response` object can be called by the following ASP statement:

```
<% Response.Write("Some Strings")%>
```

This statement will output the text "Some Strings" to the browser. If you want to redirect your ASP page to another page or location, you can use the `Redirect` method of the `Response` object as

```
<% Response.Redirect("Page2.asp") %>
```

On the whole, ASP provides a rich set of tools to build Web applications. From simple data sharing for Web pages to large, complex Web programming, these objects and their features are invaluable. We will show you how to use most of them step by step. Now, let's begin with the `Application` object.

16.2.4 Creating ASP pages with application scope

The `Application` object of ASP can be used to share information among all users. For example, if you defined a welcome message

```
<%
Application("welcome")="Welcome To Practical Web Technologies"
%>
```

your other ASP pages used by other users can obtain this text by

```
<%
Response.Write(Application("welcome"))
%>
```

In fact, the message is stored in `Application.Contents`, which is a collection of the object (see Table 16.1). Any information in `Application.Contents` can be retrieved by name. Therefore, the `Response.Write()` statement above can output the text. Not just text, but for any variables or events the entire object can be put into the `Application` object and shared among all your ASP pages. This feature is known as information with application scope.

Data or information with application scope will remain available for the live time of the application. That means they are available for all users visiting the site until after a system reboot. Unlike file storage, information with application scope is not permanent but can exist for a long period of time. This feature is particularly useful for certain kinds of applications described below. But first, let's consider the two methods provided by the `Application` object.

Since `Application` is an object designed for multiple accesses at the same time, it contains two methods (or functions), `Lock()` and `Unlock()`. You can use the `Lock()` function to lock the system and store variables or created objects to the `Contents` of the object. The `Applicaton.Contents` is a collection of the object and all information stored in it that can be retrieved later by other Web pages. In its simplest form, you can use it to build a temporary page counter to pick up a winner based on the number of visits or page hits. For this application, you don't need to create a file and it would not affect the permanent page counts. Consider the following ASP page:

```
Example: ex16-06.asp - A Page Counter Using ASP Object

 1: <%@ Language=JScript%>
 2: <?xml version="1.0" encoding="iso-8859-1"?>
 3: <!DOCTYPE html PUBLIC "-//W3C//DTD XHTML 1.0 Transitional//EN"
 4:     "http://www.w3.org/TR/xhtml1/DTD/xhtml1-transitional.dtd">
 5: <html xmlns="http://www.w3.org/1999/xhtml" xml:lang="en" lang="en">
 6: <head><title> A Page Counter Using ASP Object - ex16-06.asp</title></head>
 7: <body style="font-family:arial;font-weight:bold;background:#000088;
 8:     color:#ffff00;font-size:16pt"><br />
 9:  An Application Scope Page Counter <br />Using ASP Object<br /><br />
10: <%
11: var winNo, countN
12:    winNo = 100
13: Application.Lock()
14:    countN = Application("Hits")
15:    if ((countN > 0) && (countN < winNo))
16:      Application("Hits") = countN +1
17:    else
18:      Application("Hits") = 1
19: Application.UnLock()
20:
21:  if (countN == winNo)
22:     Response.Write("Congratulations! <br /> You Are Visitor: "+ countN +
```

```
23:       "<br />We Have A Small Gift For You. Please Contact Us.")
24:    else
25:       Response.Write("You Are Visitor No. "+ countN +"<br />")
26:    %>
27:       <br /><br />
28: </body>
29: </html>
```

For a busy site, it is likely that simultaneous access occurs at the same time. To avoid any counting confusion, the `Lock()` function in line 13 is used to lock the page for exclusive access and update. Since locking the page prevents any page updating by others, you should unlock the page as soon as you have finished the updating.

The scripting block in lines 21–25 contains a simple `if` statement. This statement is to pick up the winner when the page hits are the same as the winning number `winNo`. Some screen shots of this example in action are shown in Figs 16.5a and 16.5b.

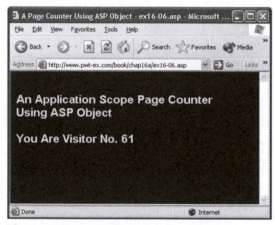

Figure 16.5a ex16-06.asp

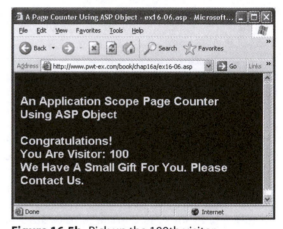

Figure 16.5b Pick up the 100th visitor

16.2.5 Building user scope applications with the `Session` object

In addition to the `Application` object, the `Session` object can be used to store information needed for a particular user session. When a user who does not already have a session requests an ASP page, the Web server automatically creates a `Session` object for him or her. Variables and information can be stored in this `Session` object dedicated to this user. This feature is usually called session scope.

You can use the same method as for the `Application` object to store messages for the `Session` object. For example, if you define the following text and store it in the Session object

```
<%
Session("welcome")="Welcome To Our On-line Shopping site"
%>
```

the string will be stored in a variable called `welcome` of the `Session` object. All visitors to this ASP page will have this message defined in an independent session. The message can be retrieved later by:

```
<%
Response.Write(Session("welcome"))
%>
```

Information stored in the `Session` object is not discarded when the user jumps between pages. When a user finishes his or her session or the `abandon` method is called, all information and objects stored in the session will be destroyed.

Also, the `Session` object provides a `SessionID` property to identify each session and user. It is a unique identifier with a long integer data type generated by the Web server. For example, the following command generates a `SessionID`:

```
<% Session.SessionID %>
```

Many Web sites use this feature to build user identity when the user visits the site. This identity is used to identify the user and give away free gifts, say. Consider the example below:

Example: ex16-07.asp - A Page To Claim Free Gift

```
 1: <%@ Language=JScript%>
 2: <?xml version="1.0" encoding="iso-8859-1"?>
 3: <!DOCTYPE html PUBLIC "-//W3C//DTD XHTML 1.0 Transitional//EN"
 4:      "http://www.w3.org/TR/xhtml1/DTD/xhtml1-transitional.dtd">
 5: <html xmlns="http://www.w3.org/1999/xhtml" xml:lang="en" lang="en">
 6: <head><title> Claim Your Free Gift - ex16-07.asp</title></head>
 7: <body style="font-family:arial;font-weight:bold;background:#000088;
 8:      color:#ffff00;font-size:16pt"><br />
 9:   ABC On-line Shopping Site<br /><br />
10:
11: <%
12:   Session("welcome")="Welcome To Our Shopping Site"
13: %>
14:
15: <%
16:   Response.Write(Session("welcome")+"<br />")
17:   Response.Write("Your Shopping ID is: "+Session.SessionID + "<br />")
18:   if (Session("gift") != "yes")
19:   {
20:   Response.Write("We Have A Free Gift For You"+"<br /><br />")
21:   Response.Write('<a href="ex16-07a.asp"'+
22:     ' style="color:#ffff00">Click Here To Claim Your Gift</a>')
23:   }
24:   else
25:     Response.Write("Your Free Gift is : "+Session("gift_detail"))
26: %>
27:
28:   <br /><br />
29: </body>
30: </html>
```

This is a simple ASP page to demonstrate the use of the `Session` object. Lines 11–13 start a session with a simple message stored in the variable `welcome`. This message is later retrieved by the `Session` statement in line 16. The `SessionID` is displayed as well. Next, there is a conditional statement to give away a free gift.

Basically, we use two more session variables `gift` and `gift_detail`. If the `gift` variable stores the string "yes" that means the user has already claimed his or her free gift and the details of the free gift are displayed (line 25). If the user has not claimed his or her free gift, the messages in lines 20–22 are displayed. In particular, the message in line 21–22:

```
Response.Write('<a href="ex16-07a.asp"'+
  ' style="color:#ffff00">Click Here To Claim Your Gift</a>')
```

uses an anchor element to activate the ASP page ex16-07a.asp to claim the gift.

Surprisingly, the ASP page ex16-07a.asp contains only six lines:

Example: ex16-07a.asp - The ASP Page For ex16-07.asp

```
1: <%@ Language=JScript%>
2: <%
3:  Session("gift")="yes"
4:  Session("gift_detail")="Monitor and Keyboard Hood"
5:  Response.Redirect("ex16-07.asp")
6: %>
```

Since this page is invisible to the user, it can be written as pure ASP code. In fact, this page has three statements only. The first statement is to assign a session variable called `gift` to the string "yes." The second statement in line 4 provides the details of the free gift. The final statement uses the `Redirect` function of the `Response` object to redirect the user back to the original page ex16-07.asp. Some screen shots of this example are shown in Figs 16.6a and 16.6b.

Figure 16.6a ex16-07.asp

Figure 16.6b Claim your free gift

This example has session scope and every user or activation will be assigned a `SessionID`. Unless you have many gifts, you may also need to ask the user to fill out a claim form in order to make a claim.

16.3 CGI applications with ASP

Although the `Request` object of ASP has only one function, it contains a number of collections, dedicated for CGI applications. The concept of a collection is similar to that of an array. It is a place to store strings, numbers, objects, and other variables with values. Unlike arrays, you can access the data of a collection through either indices or names. The first collection of the `Request` object that we are going to introduce is the `ServerVariables` collection.

16.3.1 Using server variables

Server variables are environment features from the server providing critical information if you want to develop server-specific applications. Some frequently used server variables are:

- GATEWAY_INTERFACE
- HTTP_HOST
- QUERY_STRING
- REQUEST_METHOD
- SERVER_NAME
- SERVER_PROTOCOL
- SERVER_SOFTWARE
- URL

The Request object from the ASP package contains a collection called ServerVariables (see Table 16.1) that can be directly used to get the data stored in a particular variable. For example, to get the version of the gateway interface, you can use the following command in your ASP page:

```
Request.ServerVariables("GATEWAY_INTERFACE")
```

Since ServerVariables is implemented as a collection in ASP, you can access the data through names referencing. To get the server variables above, you can use the following ASP page:

Example: ex16-08.asp - Some Server Variables

```
 1: <%@ LANGUAGE="JScript" %>
 2: <?xml version="1.0" encoding="iso-8859-1"?>
 3: <!DOCTYPE html PUBLIC "-//W3C//DTD XHTML 1.0 Transitional//EN"
 4:     "http://www.w3.org/TR/xhtml1/DTD/xhtml1-transitional.dtd">
 5: <html xmlns="http://www.w3.org/1999/xhtml" xml:lang="en" lang="en">
 6: <head><title> Server Variables - ex16-08.asp</title></head>
 7: <body style="background:#000088;font-family:arial;color:#ffff00">
 8: <div style="font-size:22pt;text-align:center;color:#00ff00">
 9:    Some Server Variables</div>
10: <table style="font-size:14pt" cellspacing="15" align="center" >
11:  <tr><th>Variable</th><th>Value</th></tr>
12:  <%
13:  Response.Write('<tr><td>GATEWAY_INTERFACE</td><td>' +
14:      Request.ServerVariables("GATEWAY_INTERFACE") + '</td></tr>')
15:  Response.Write('<tr><td>HTTP_HOST</td><td>' +
16:      Request.ServerVariables("HTTP_HOST") + '</td></tr>')
17:  Response.Write('<tr><td>QUERY_STRING</td><td>' +
18:      Request.ServerVariables("QUERY_STRING") + '</td></tr>')
19:  Response.Write('<tr><td>REQUEST_METHOD</td><td>' +
20:      Request.ServerVariables("REQUEST_METHOD") + '</td></tr>')
21:  Response.Write('<tr><td>SERVER_NAME</td><td>' +
22:      Request.ServerVariables("SERVER_NAME") + '</td></tr>')
23:  Response.Write('<tr><td>SERVER_PROTOCOL</td><td>' +
24:      Request.ServerVariables("SERVER_PROTOCOL") + '</td></tr>')
25:  Response.Write('<tr><td>SERVER_SOFTWARE</td><td>' +
26:      Request.ServerVariables("SERVER_SOFTWARE") + '</td></tr>')
27:  Response.Write('<tr><td>URL</td><td>' +
28:      Request.ServerVariables("URL") + '</td></tr>')
29:  %>
30:  </table>
31: </body>
32: </html>
```

In this example, the ASP section is defined in lines 12–29. This section contains direct function calls to Request.ServerVariables() for each of the server variables above.

Figure 16.7 ex16-08.asp

After all the statements in the scripting section are processed, a complete XHTML page is returned back to the browser. From the browser's point of view, the returned page is a pure XHTML page. A screen shot of this example on Windows XP with IIS using the IE6 browser is shown in Fig. 16.7.

If you need to develop an ASP page dedicated to server software such as Microsoft IIS 4.0, you may need to perform detection on the server variable `SERVER_SOFTWARE`.

There are more than 40 server variables available from the `ServerVariables` collection. An iteration method is used to find them all later in this section. Some frequently used server variables are listed in Table 16.2.

Table 16.2 Server environment variables

Variable	Description
ALL_HTTP	All HTTP headers sent by the client
CONTENT_LENGTH	The length of the content as given by the client
CONTENT_TYPE	The data type of the content
GATEWAY_INTERFACE	The revision of the CGI specification used by the server
HTTP_\<HeaderName>	The value stored in the header `HeaderName`
INSTANCE_ID	The ID for the IIS instance in textual format
INSTANCE_META_PATH	The metabase path for the instance of IIS that responds to the request
LOCAL_ADDR	Returns the server address on which the request came in
LOGON_USER	The Windows NT account that the user is logged into
PATH_INFO	Extra path information as given by the client
PATH_TRANSLATED	A translated version of `PATH_INFO` that takes the path and performs any necessary virtual-to-physical mapping
QUERY_STRING	Query information stored in the string following the question mark (?) in the HTTP request
REMOTE_ADDR	The IP address of the remote host making the request
REMOTE_HOST	The name of the host making the request
REMOTE_USER	Unmapped user name string sent in by the user
REQUEST_METHOD	The method used to make the request. For HTTP, this is `get`, `head`, `post`, and so on
SCRIPT_NAME	A virtual path to the script being executed. This is used for self-referencing URLs
SERVER_NAME	The server's hostname, DNS alias, or IP address as it would appear in self-referencing URLs

Table 16.2 Continued

SERVER_PORT	The port number to which the request was sent
SERVER_PORT_SECURE	A string that contains either 0 or 1. If the request is being handled on the secure port, then this will be 1. Otherwise, it will be 0
SERVER_PROTOCOL	The name and version of the request information protocol. The format is protocol/version
SERVER_SOFTWARE	The name and version of the server software that answers the request and runs the gateway. The format is name/version
URL	Gives the base portion of the URL

16.3.2 Passing form data to ASP pages with `QueryString`

Most of the server and CGI applications are related to forms. Therefore passing form information to ASP pages is important before any real application can be constructed. The `Request` object of ASP provides two collections, namely, `QueryString` and `Form` dedicated to retrieving form data from ASP pages. The first collection `QueryString` is responsible for obtaining form data when a `get` method is used. To understand how `QueryString` works, let's consider the following XHTML form document:

Example: ex16-09.htm - Passing Form Data To ASP With QueryString

```
 1: <?xml version="1.0" encoding="iso-8859-1"?>
 2: <!DOCTYPE html PUBLIC "-//W3C//DTD XHTML 1.0 Transitional//EN"
 3:      "http://www.w3.org/TR/xhtml1/DTD/xhtml1-transitional.dtd">
 4: <html xmlns="http://www.w3.org/1999/xhtml" xml:lang="en" lang="en">
 5: <head><title> Passing Form Data To ASP - ex16-09.htm</title></head>
 6: <style>
 7:  .butSt{background:#aaffaa;width:250px;
 8:     font-family:arial;font-weight:bold;font-size:16pt;color:#880000}
 9:  .txtSt{font-family:arial;font-weight:bold;font-size:16pt;color:#ffff00}
10: </style>
11: <body style="font-family:arial;font-weight:bold;font-size:18pt;
12:     background:#000088;color:#ffff00"><br />
13:  Passing Form Data To ASP With QueryString<br /><br />
14: <form name="myForm" action="ex16-09.asp" method="get">
15: <table class="txtSt">
16:   <tr><td>Name:</td><td>
17:     <input type="text" name="name" class="butSt"></td></tr>
18:   <tr><td>Email Address:</td><td>
19:     <input type="text" name="email" class="butSt"></td></tr>
20:   <tr><td>Telephone:</td><td>
21:    <input type="text" name="phone" class="butSt"></td></tr>
22:   <tr><td><input type=reset value="Clear" class="butSt"></td><td>
23:     <input type=submit value="Submit" class="butSt"></td></tr>
24: </table>
25: </form>
26: </body>
27: </html>
```

This XHTML page contains a form with three fields, namely "name," "email," and "phone." They are all defined as text boxes in lines 17, 19, and 21 respectively. Suppose you have filled the form with data

```
Name:              Johnsmith
Email Address:     johnsmith@pwt-ex.com
Telephone:         01890-12345678
```

From line 14, this form uses the `get` method to submit the data. This means that once the Submit button is pressed, the form will activate the ASP page ex16-09.asp with the following URL request:

```
http://www.pwt-ex.com/ex16-09.asp?name=Johnsmith&
      email=johnsmith@pwt-ex.com& phone=01890-12345678
```

The string after the question mark "?" is called the query string from the CGI. This query string contains the name/value pairs input by the user and attached at the end of the ASP page. Using ASP, the entire query string is automatically stored in the `QueryString` collection of the `Request` object. To retrieve, for example, the name, you can use the following statement:

```
<% Request.QuseryString("name") %>
```

To complete the example, the ASP page ex16-09.asp is listed below:

```
Example: ex16-09.asp - The ASP Page For ex16-09.htm

 1: <%@ LANGUAGE="JScript" %>
 2: <?xml version="1.0" encoding="iso-8859-1"?>
 3: <!DOCTYPE html PUBLIC "-//W3C//DTD XHTML 1.0 Transitional//EN"
 4:     "http://www.w3.org/TR/xhtml1/DTD/xhtml1-transitional.dtd">
 5: <html xmlns="http://www.w3.org/1999/xhtml" xml:lang="en" lang="en">
 6: <head><title>ASP Page: ex16-09.asp </title></head>
 7: <body style="font-family:arial;font-weight:bold;font-size:18pt;
 8:     background:#000088;color:#ffff00"><br />
 9:    You Have Entered The Following Data:<br /><br />
10:
11:    Name = <%=Request.QueryString("name")%><br />
12:    Email = <%=Request.QueryString("email")%><br />
13:    Phone = <%=Request.QueryString("phone")%><br />
14: </body>
15: </html>
```

To extract the form data from the CGI query string, all you have to do is to call the function `Request.QueryString()` three times as illustrated in lines 11–13. Some screen shots of this example are shown in Figs 16.8–16.9.

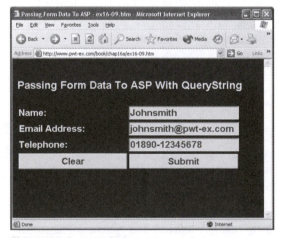

Figure 16.8 ex16-09.htm

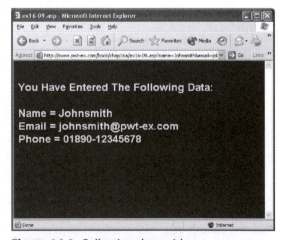

Figure 16.9 Collecting data with `QueryString`

You can see that the query string appears in the address bar of Fig. 16.9. In fact, any query string submitted to an ASP page in name/value format is intercepted and stored in the `QueryString` collection. This process pays no attention as to whether a form is used or not. For example, you can replace the entire form (lines 14–25) of ex16-09.htm by one statement:

```
<a href="http://www.pwt-ex.com/ex16-09.asp?name=Johnsmith&
email=johnsmith@pwt-ex.com&phone=01890-12345678">Click Me</a>
```

In this case, you don't need to complete the form in order to pass data. This statement is the so-called canned query. The main characteristic is that the name/value pairs are hardwired into the URL. When the underlined text is clicked, the entire URL is submitted to the ASP page ex16-09.asp. The query string will be captured by the `QueryString` collection. Therefore you have the same result as illustrated in Fig. 16.9. One popular use of canned query is to pass data automatically. For example, you can put user name and password in a query string and submit them in order to log into some sites and/or database applications.

16.3.3 Capture checkbox values with the `Form` collection

The `Request` object also has a collection called `Form` to handle all form information submitted by the `post` method. The usage of the `Form` collection is similar to the `QueryString` collection. Suppose you have form data called email defined in the following XHTML fragment:

```
<form name="myForm" action="ex16-08.asp" method="post">
    Enter Your Email Address: <input type="text" name="name">
    Enter Your Name: <input type="text" name="email">
    Enter Your Phone Number: <input type="text" name="phone">
    <input type="submit" value="Submit">
</form>
```

This is an XHTML form using the `post` method. Once the Submit button is clicked, the form data, i.e., name, email, and phone, can be accessed using the following ASP statements:

```
Name = <%=Request.Form("name")%>
Email = <%=Request.Form("email")%>
Phone = <%=Request.Form("phone")%>
```

All you have to do is to replace the keyword `Request.QueryString` with `Request.Form` for the CGI `post` method.

The characteristics of using `QueryString` are as follows:

- `Form` data are passed to an application through the environment variable `QUERY_STRING`.
- `QueryString` can be used for canned query.

One of the main criticisms of `QueryString` is that you may run the risk of losing data if your Web server cannot handle long (or very long) strings. Since `QueryString` data appear on the address bar of browsers, some Web servers tend to restrict the size of the URL string. Any `QueryString` longer than the allowed length will be truncated. This may be a nasty bug for your Web applications.

On the other hand, the CGI `post` application passes data using the HTTP request body. This means that you can send a virtually unlimited number of characters to a server. Also, by using HTTP to hide the submitted data, you have a minimum level of data security for some applications. Based on these reasons, a popular application of the `Form` collection is to handle data from XHTML input boxes. We will show you how to use the `Form` collection to capture checkbox data below.

In fact, you have already encountered a number of checkbox applications in previous chapters. Together with radio and select boxes, they are a fundamental resource for building interactive Web pages. In the next example, we will show you how to control them using the ASP `Form` collection objects.

Checkboxes are composite structures and often have multiple values. To handle structures like this, you will find that an ASP object is easier to operate. For example, if you want to use a property or function of an object, you just append the function or property name at the end of the object with a period. To demonstrate this characteristic, consider the XHTML part of the following example:

```
Example: ex16-10.htm - Using CheckBoxes With ASP

 1: <?xml version="1.0" encoding="iso-8859-1"?>
 2: <!DOCTYPE html PUBLIC "-//W3C//DTD XHTML 1.0 Transitional//EN"
 3:     "http://www.w3.org/TR/xhtml1/DTD/xhtml1-transitional.dtd">
 4: <html xmlns="http://www.w3.org/1999/xhtml" xml:lang="en" lang="en">
 5: <head><title> Using CheckBoxes With ASP - ex16-10.htm</title></head>
 6: <style>
 7:  .butSt{background:#aaffaa;width:250px;
 8:     font-family:arial;font-weight:bold;font-size:16pt;color:#880000}
 9:  .chkSt{background:#aaffaa;width:30px;height:30px;
10:     font-family:arial;font-weight:bold;font-size:16pt;color:#880000}
11:  .txtSt{font-family:arial;font-weight:bold;font-size:16pt;color:#ffff00}
12: </style>
13: <body style="font-family:arial;font-weight:bold;font-size:18pt;
14:    background:#000088;color:#ffff00"><br />
15:
16: <form name="statForm" action="ex16-10.asp" method="post">
17:  <div style="position:absolute;top:40px;left:60px;">
18:        Which Operating Systems Have You Used? </div><br />
19:  <div style="position:absolute;top:100px;left:100px;">
20:     <input name="os" type="checkbox" value="Windows XP" class="chkSt" />
21:        Windows XP<br />
22:     <input name="os" type="checkbox" value="Windows 2000" class="chkSt" />
23:        Windows 2000<br />
24:     <input name="os" type="checkbox" value="Windows 9x" class="chkSt" />
25:        Windows 9x<br />
26:     <input name="os" type="checkbox" value="LINUX" class="chkSt" />
27:        LINUX<br /> </div>
28:  <div style="position:absolute;top:100px;left:340px;">
29:     <input name="os" type="checkbox" value="Mac OS" class="chkSt" />
30:        Mac OS<br />
31:     <input name="os" type="checkbox" value="IRIS" class="chkSt" />
32:        IRIS<br />
33:     <input name="os" type="checkbox" value="Solaris" class="chkSt" />
34:        Solaris<br />
35:     <input name="os" type="checkbox" value="Sun OS" class="chkSt" />
36:        Sun OS<br /> </div>
37:  <div style="position:absolute;top:260px;left:60px;">
38:     <input type="submit" value="Submit" class="butSt">
39:     <input type="reset" value="Clear" class="butSt">
40:  </div>
41: </form>
42: </body>
43: </html>
```

This is a classic form application from XHTML. Inside the form defined in lines 16–41, there are four divisions. They all have position properties set up in the CCS style so that they are set in some particular location of the browser window. For example, the second division (lines 19–27) is a block containing four checkboxes located at (100px, 100px) in (top, left) format. Right next to these checkboxes, another four check boxes are generated. A screen shot of this page is shown in Fig. 16.10.

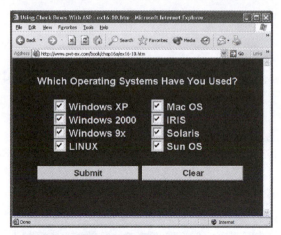

Figure 16.10 ex16-10.htm

Once the Submit button is pressed, the form will be sent to the ASP page below:

Example: ex16-10.asp - The ASP Page For ex16-10.htm

```
 1: <%@ LANGUAGE="JScript" %>
 2: <?xml version="1.0" encoding="iso-8859-1"?>
 3: <!DOCTYPE html PUBLIC "-//W3C//DTD XHTML 1.0 Transitional//EN"
 4:     "http://www.w3.org/TR/xhtml1/DTD/xhtml1-transitional.dtd">
 5: <html xmlns="http://www.w3.org/1999/xhtml" xml:lang="en" lang="en">
 6: <head><title>ex16-10.asp</title></head>
 7: <body style="font-family:arial;font-weight:bold;font-size:18pt;
 8:     background:#000088;color:#ffff00"><br />
 9: <%
10:  if (Request.Form("os").Count ==0)
11:  {
12:    Response.Write("You Have Used No Operating System Before!<br />" +
13:    " I Don't Believe You!")
14:  }
15:  else if (Request.Form("os").Count==1)
16:  {
17:   Response.Write("You Only Use This Operating System?<br /> ")
18:   Response.Write (Request.Form("os")(1) + "<br />")
19:   Response.Write("Try to Use More.")
20:  } else
21:  {
22:   var i
23:   Response.Write("You've Used All These Operating Systems? <br /><br />")
24:   for (i = 1; i <= Request.Form("os").Count; i++) {
25:      Response.Write (Request.Form("os")(i) + "<BR>")
26:    }
27:   Response.Write("<br />" + "Very Good...")
28:  }
29: %>
30: </body>
31: </html>
```

When the `Request` object is applied to `Form("os")`, you have an object like

```
Request.Form("os")
```

containing data from all checkboxes with name "os." To find out how much data are actually inside the object, you can use

```
Request.Form("os").Count
```

Therefore, you can use this property to construct a conditional statement in lines 10–14 to detect if no checkbox has been checked. Furthermore, if the first check box is checked by a user, the property

```
Request.Form("os")(1)
```

will return the value defined by the first checkbox. This feature can be used to construct a for-loop in lines 24–26 to display all the operating systems picked by the user. A screen shot is shown in Fig. 16.11.

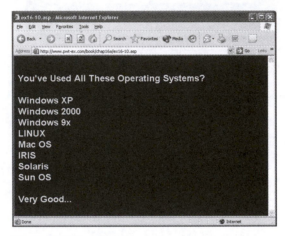

Figure 16.11 ex16-10.asp

`Count` is a method available for most ASP collections. Therefore the `QueryString` collection can also have this feature.

Up to now, we have only used a collection in the same way as an array. In fact, a collection is more powerful than a traditional array. To understand more about the ASP collection structure, an iterating method is introduced to display all name/value pairs stored in ASP collections.

16.3.4 Using iteration methods on ASP collections

If you take a look at ASP objects (Table 16.1), you will find that most of them support a data type called collection. Collection is an important structure for CGI programming using ASP and hence essential for Web applications.

In fact, the `ServerVariables` of the `Request` object is a collection in ASP containing a large number of variables. A collection is a place to store strings, numbers, objects, and other variables with values. The concept of a collection is similar to that of an array and you can retrieve data from it. Unlike an array, the position of a collection may vary from time to time when the collection is modified. Also, ASP provides a `Count` property for a collection. The statement

```
Request.ServerVariables.Count
```

returns the total number of items in the `ServerVariables` collection. You can access elements in a collection by its name or its position (or index). For example, the following two statements return the same results:

```
Request.ServerVariables("REQUEST_METHOD")
Request.ServerVariables(35)
```

Using position, you can loop through all server variables. For example, the following JScript for-loop can display all data in the `ServerVariables` collection:

```
<%
 endNo = Request.ServerVariables.Count
 for (ii=0;ii<endNo;ii++)
 {
  Response.Write(Request.ServerVariables(ii))
 }
%>
```

Basically, a collection is a structure that can provide name/value referencing. If your ASP scripting language supports `for–each` statements, you can use it to iterate through a collection to get all name/value pairs. For example, you can use the following VBScript fragment to find name/value pairs of server variables:

```
<%
 for each key in Request.ServerVariables
        Response.Write key & " = "
   if Request.ServerVariables(key) = "" then
        Response.Write " "
   else
        Response.Write Request.ServerVariables(key) & "<br />"
   end if
  next
%>
```

In this case, the variable `key` contains the server variable names one by one and the function `Request.ServerVariables(key)` returns the data associated with `key`.

If you are using JScript, you can use the `Enumerator` object to iterate through an ASP collection. Basically, the `Enumerator` object provides the following three functions to move around a collection:

`atEnd()`	–	Indicates whether there are any more items in the collection.
`moveNext()`	–	Sets the next item in the collection as the current item.
`item()`	–	Gets the name of the current item.

For example, the JScript fragment below demonstrates how to use this `Enumerator` object:

```
enObj = new Enumerator(Request.ServerVariables)
while (!enObj.atEnd(enObj))
{
   key = enObj.item()
   Response.Write( key +' = ' +
     Request.ServerVariables(key) + ' <br />')
   enObj.moveNext()
}
```

The first line is to create an object using the `Enumerator()` function on a collection. This new object `enObj` contains all data from `ServerVaraibles`. The while-loop, basically, is a detector to see whether the current item is the end item. If not, the name is output to a variable called `key`. Since the variable `key` represents the name of the server variable, it can be used to make the call `Request.Server Variables(key)` to obtain the data. A call to `enObj.moveNext()` will move to the next item. When the while-loop is completed, all the name/value pairs are displayed.

To see this example fragment into action, consider the ASP page below:

```
Example: ex16-11.asp - Display All Server Variables

1: <%@ LANGUAGE="JScript" %>
2: <?xml version="1.0" encoding="iso-8859-1"?>
3: <!DOCTYPE html PUBLIC "-//W3C//DTD XHTML 1.0 Transitional//EN"
```

```
 4:        "http://www.w3.org/TR/xhtml1/DTD/xhtml1-transitional.dtd">
 5: <html xmlns="http://www.w3.org/1999/xhtml" xml:lang="en" lang="en">
 6: <head><title> Display All Server Variables - ex16-11.asp</title><head>
 7: <body style="background:#000088;font-family:arial;color:#ffff00">
 8: <div style="font-size:22pt;text-align:center;color:#00ff00">
 9:    Display All Server Variables</div>
10:  <table style="font-size:14pt" align="center" border="1">
11:   <tr><th>Variable</th><th>Value</th></tr>
12:   <% var enObj, ii
13:       enObj = new Enumerator(Request.ServerVariables)
14:       while (!enObj.atEnd(enObj))
15:       {
16:        ii = enObj.item()
17:        Response.Write('<tr><td>' + ii + '</td><td>' +
18:          Request.ServerVariables(ii) + '</td></tr>')
19:        enObj.moveNext()
20:       }
21:   %>
22:  </table>
23: </body>
24: </html>
```

This ASP page iterates through the server variable collection and displays all name/value pairs as a table. The scripting block defined in lines 12–21 is inline with the JScript fragment mentioned above. All server variables including names and data are displayed as a table.

This example can also be applied to all CGI applications. For example, instead of a `QueryString` collection, you can get the submitted results of example ex16-09.htm by the `post` method as follows:

- Copy example ex16-09.htm to a new example ex16-12.htm.
- Replace line 14

  ```
  <form name="myForm" action="ex16-09.asp" method="get">
  ```

  by the new line

  ```
  <form name="myForm" action="ex16-12.asp" method="post">
  ```

This new example uses the CGI `post` method to call the ASP program ex16-12.asp.

The ASP collection `Request.Form()` contains all the CGI name/value pairs submitted by a form using the `post` method. To get and display all submitted name/value pairs, you can develop the ASP program ex16-12.asp by replacing the ASP statements in lines 8–22 in ex16-11.asp by

```
Example: ex16-12.asp - Iterating All Name/Value Pairs For ASP Collection

 8: <div style="font-size:22pt;text-align:center;color:#00ff00">
 9:    CGI Name/Value Pairs <div><br />
10:  <table style="font-size:14pt" align="center" border="1">
11:   <tr><th>Variable</th><th>Value</th></tr>
12:   <% var var enObj,ii
13:       enObj = new Enumerator(Request.Form)
14:       while (!enObj.atEnd(enObj))
15:       {
16:       ii = enObj.item()
17:       Response.Write('<tr><td>' + ii + '</td><td>' +
18:         Request.Form(ii) + '</td></tr>')
19:       enObj.moveNext()
20:      }
21:   %>
22:  </table>
```

This example is a general method to capture all data submitted by a CGI `post` method. In fact, we simply replaced one statement, i.e., to change the `ServerVariables` collection to `Request.Form` collection. A screen shot to display all submitted data from ex16-12.htm is shown in Fig. 16.12.

Iteration methods can be applied to any ASP collections and therefore are a general technique for all ASP objects with collections.

Since `QueryString` is an ASP collection for the CGI `get` method, you can use an iteration method to get all CGI name/value pairs related to the query string. Basically, all you have to do is to replace the `Request.Form` with `Request.QueryString`.

We have introduced a number of CGI applications in the last two chapters. You can try applying ASP techniques to these CGI applications to achieve the same or

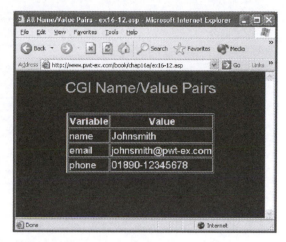

Figure 16.12 ex16-12.asp

similar results. Instead of the Perl script page, you now have ASP page support.

Apart from the internal objects, the ASP package for PWS and IIS also included some server-side ActiveX components. These components provide objects that greatly enhance the capability of ASP on Web applications. Two of them are:

- `Scripting.FileSystemObject` – Provides methods for accessing files and directories on the server's storage system.
- ActiveX Data Object (ADO) – Provides an object library for database access and manipulation.

These components and objects are discussed in the coming sections 16.4.1 and 16.4.2.

16.4 Controlling system storage and resources with ASP

16.4.1 Using `FileSystemObject`

One of the great strengths of ASP is to use and handle files and directories. Any ASP study will not be complete without a section dealing with these features.

To understand the whole picture of file and directory handling with ASP, you need to start with the object `FileSystemObject` and objects associated with it. Basically `FileSystemObject` is an ActiveX object providing access to a computer's file system. Under `FileSystemObject`, you have four objects to handle all aspects of files and directories (or folders), namely, `TextStream`, `File`, `Drive`, and `Folder`. The structure of `FileSystemObject` is described in Fig. 16.13.

`FileSystemObject` contains methods and functions controlling file and directory handling. Most of these methods return objects or collections for further functionalities and properties. The entire object provides a complete source to handle files and directories with ASP. Some frequently used methods in `FileSystemObject` are listed in Table 16.3 and references can be found in Microsoft's official site (msdn.microsoft.com).

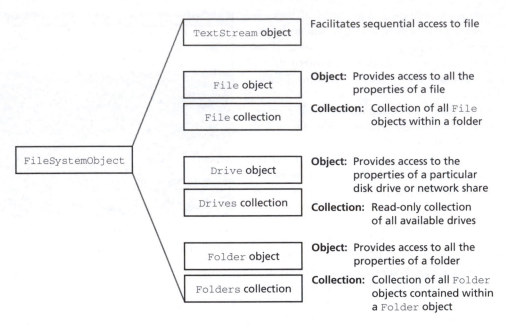

Figure 16.13 The structure of `FileSystemObject`

Table 16.3 Frequently used methods in `FileSystemObject`

`CopyFile()`	`DriveExists()`	`GetDriveName()`	`GetSpecialFolder()`
`CopyFolder()`	`FileExists()`	`GetExtensionName()`	`GetTempName`
`CreateFolder()`	`FolderExists()`	`GetFile()`	`MoveFile()`
`CreateTextFile()`	`GetAbsolutePathName()`	`GetFileName()`	`MoveFolder()`
`DeleteFile()`	`GetBaseName()`	`GetFolder()`	`OpenTextFile()`
`DeleteFolder()`	`GetDrive()`	`GetParentFolderName()`	

Perhaps the most popular method to open a file using `FileSystemObject` is `OpenTextFile()`. This method has the format:

```
streamobject = object.OpenTextFile(filename, iomode, create)
```

where

`streamobject` **is always the name of a** `TextStream` **object**

`object` **is always the name of a** `FileSystemObject`

`filename` **a string expression to identify the file to open**

`iomode` 1 = **reading**, 2 = **writing**, 8 = **appending**

`create` true = **create** false = **not create**

When you open a file with `OpenTextFile()`, this function returns a `TextStream` object. In this case, all methods (including reading and writing) associated with the `TextStream` object can be used to read and write to the file.

Consider the following example:

```
Example: ex16-13.asp - Creating And Writing To File

 1: <%@ Language=JScript%>
 2: <?xml version="1.0" encoding="iso-8859-1"?>
 3: <!DOCTYPE html PUBLIC "-//W3C//DTD XHTML 1.0 Transitional//EN"
 4:     "http://www.w3.org/TR/xhtml1/DTD/xhtml1-transitional.dtd">
 5: <html xmlns="http://www.w3.org/1999/xhtml" xml:lang="en" lang="en">
 6: <head><title> Creating and Writing To File - ex16-13.asp</title><head>
 7: <body style="font-family:arial;font-weight:bold;background:#000088;
 8:    color:#ffff00;font-size:16pt"><br />
 9:    Creating And Writing To File : c:\testfile.txt <br /><br />
10:
11: <%
12: var fs,dataStream,retString, ForWriting, ii
13: ForWriting = 2
14:
15: fs = new ActiveXObject("Scripting.FileSystemObject")
16: dataStream = fs.OpenTextFile("c:\\testfile.txt",ForWriting,true)
17:
18: for(ii=1;ii<10;ii++)
19: {
20:    dataStream.WriteLine("This is a test string "+ii+
21:       " from file: c:\\testfile.txt");
22: }
23:
24: dataStream.Close()
25: %>
26:
27: <br /><br />
28: </body>
29: </html>
```

For some historic reasons, variable `ForWriting` is often used to represent writing to file (value = 2). In line 15, an instance of `ActiveXObject` is assigned to `FileSystemObject` with variable `fs`. This variable is used to activate the `OpenTextFile()` method and then creates the file as a `TextStream` object called `dataStream`. The simple for-loop in lines 18–22 employs the `WriteLine()` method of `TextStream` to output nine lines to the created text file. The `Close()` method flushes the buffer and closes the file.

Now you have a file called testfile on your C drive. You may need another ASP page to read all the data inside the file and display the data on your page.

```
Example: ex16-14.asp - Reading A File Into An ASP Page

 1: <%@ Language=JScript%>
 2: <?xml version="1.0" encoding="iso-8859-1"?>
 3: <!DOCTYPE html PUBLIC "-//W3C//DTD XHTML 1.0 Transitional//EN"
 4:     "http://www.w3.org/TR/xhtml1/DTD/xhtml1-transitional.dtd">
 5: <html xmlns="http://www.w3.org/1999/xhtml" xml:lang="en" lang="en">
 6: <head><title> Reading A File - ex16-14.asp</title><head>
 7: <body style="font-family:arial;font-weight:bold;background:#000088;
 8:    color:#ffff00;font-size:16pt"><br />
 9:    Open And Read A File : testfile.txt <br /><br />
10:
11: <%
```

```
12: var fs,dataStream,retString, ForReading, ii
13: ForReading = 1
14: fs = new ActiveXObject("Scripting.FileSystemObject")
15: dataStream = fs.OpenTextFile("c:\\testfile.txt",ForReading,false)
16: while(dataStream.AtEndOfStream !=true)
17: {
18:   retString = dataStream.ReadLine()
19:   Response.Write(retString+"<br />")
20: }
21: dataStream.Close()
22: %>
23:
24: <br /><br />
25: </body>
26: </html>
```

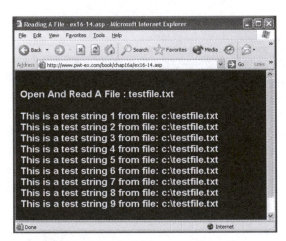

Figure 16.14 ex16-14.asp

This page opens the same text file (c:\testfile.txt) as in the previous example for reading. The variable ForReading in line 13 has the value 1 to specify iomode. Once iomode is defined, you can open the text file using the OpenTextFile() method associated with Scripting.FileSystemObject. The method returns a TextStream object named dataStream.

In order to read all data in the file, the AtEndOfStream property of TextStream is used. The following while-loop (lines 16–20) will guarantee that all data of the text file are read and displayed to the ASP page. The ReadLine() method from the TextStream object reads a text line to variable retString. A simple call to Response.Write() would display the string. Don't forget to close your file with a call to Close(). A screen shot of this example is shown in Fig. 16.14.

Some of the methods and properties of the TextStream object are summarized in Table 16.4.

Table 16.4 Methods of the TextStream object

Close()	ReadLine()	Write()
Read()	Skip()	WriteBlankLines()
ReadAll()	SkipLine()	WriteLine()

Properties of the TextSream object

AtEndOfLine	AtEndOfStream	Column	Line

These methods and properties provide a fundamental framework to use server storage for CGI applications. One of the classic applications of file storage is to build a guest book. Let's develop a guest book using ASP objects.

16.4.2 A guest book using ASP objects

As an application of ASP to file storage, let's consider how to develop a guest book using ASP and related objects. You may find that the ReadAll() method from the TextStream object is a powerful feature to read an entire file in one step.

The following is the interface part of the guest book:

Example: ex16-15.htm - A Guest Book Using ASP

```
 1: <?xml version="1.0" encoding="iso-8859-1"?>
 2: <!DOCTYPE html PUBLIC "-//W3C//DTD XHTML 1.0 Transitional//EN"
 3:    "http://www.w3.org/TR/xhtml1/DTD/xhtml1-transitional.dtd">
 4: <html xmlns="http://www.w3.org/1999/xhtml" xml:lang="en" lang="en">
 5: <head><title> A Guest Book Using ASP - ex16-15.htm</title><head>
 6: <style>
 7:   .tx01{font-size:14pt;color:#000088;font-weight:bold}
 8:   .tx02{font-family:arial;font-size:14pt;background:#ffffff;color:#000000}
 9:   .butSt{background-color:#aaffaa;font-family:arial;font-weight:bold;
10:      font-size:14pt;color:#008800;width:100px;height:30px}
11: </style>
12: <body style="background:#bbbbff;font-family:arial;color:#000088">
13: <div style="font-size:18pt;text-align:center;font-weight:bold">
14:   Please Sign Our Guest Book<br />www.pwt-ex.com
15: <form method="post" action="ex16-15a.asp">
16: <table class="tx01">
17: <tr><td>From:</td>
18:   <td><input class="tx02" type="text" name="from" id="from"></td></tr>
19:
20: <tr><td valign="top">Message:</td>
21:   <td><textarea name="message" id="message" class="tx02"
22:       rows="6" cols="40" wrap="yes"></textarea></td></tr>
23:
24: <tr><td><input class="butSt" type="submit" value="Submit"></td>
25:   <td><input class="butSt" type="reset" value="Reset"></td></tr>
26: </table>
27: </form><br />
28: <a class="butSt" style="width:405px;color:#880000"
29:  href="ex16-15b.asp" target="_blank">
30:    Please Click Me To Read Guest Book</a>
31: </div>
32: </body>
33: </html>
```

This XHTML page is very similar to example ex15-11.htm. It generates a text box (line 18) for the user to type his or her name and a text area (lines 21–22) to type in the guest book message. A screen shot of this page is shown in Fig. 16.15.

When the Submit button is pressed, the form will be sent to the ASP program ex16-15a.asp specified in line 15. This ASP program is responsible for capturing the user name and guest book message and saving them into the text file guestbook.txt located in the C directory. Since ASP is a Microsoft product, a Microsoft

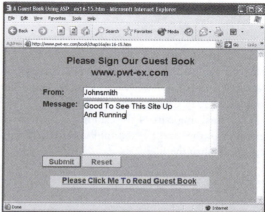

Figure 16.15 ex16-15.htm

system convention is used here. If you run ASP on other systems, you should use the files and path of the appropriate convention. The ASP page ex16-15a.asp is listed below:

```
Example: ex16-15a.asp - ASP Page For ex16-15.htm

 1: <%@ Language=JScript%>
 2: <%
 3: message = Request.Form("message")
 4: from = Request.Form("from")
 5: tt = new Date()
 6: ttime = tt.toLocaleString()
 7: tmpSt1 = "<br />"+message+"<br /><br />"
 8: tmpSt2 ="==============================================<br />"
 9:
10: var fs,dataStream, ForReading, ForWriting
11: ForReading = 1, ForWriting = 2
12:
13: fs = new ActiveXObject("Scripting.FileSystemObject");
14: dataStream = fs.OpenTextFile("c:\\guestbook.txt", ForReading)
15: lst = dataStream.ReadAll()
16: dataStream.Close()
17:
18: dataStream = fs.OpenTextFile("c:\\guestbook.txt",ForWriting,true)
19: dataStream.WriteLine()
20: dataStream.WriteLine(tmpSt1)
21: dataStream.WriteLine()
22: dataStream.WriteBlankLines(2)
23: dataStream.Write(from + " : "+ttime+"<br />")
24: dataStream.WriteLine()
25: dataStream.WriteLine(tmpSt2)
26: dataStream.WriteLine()
27: dataStream.WriteLine(lst)
28: dataStream.Close()
29:
30: Response.Redirect("ex16-15.htm")
31: %>
```

Traditionally, ASP is an embedded programming language for HTML/XHTML. You can integrate ASP commands inside any XHTML files. The demonstration here is to show that you can also use it as a core program. Lines 3–4 are used to get the user name and guest message from the XHTML page. Lines 6–9 set up the local time string and prepare the guest book message to be saved into the text file guestbook.txt.

After opening the guest book file, the statement in line 15

```
lst = dataStream.ReadAll()
```

reads the entire contents of the file into a string lst. The purpose of reading the entire file into a string is so that you can add the new guest book message at the front and store it back to the guest bookfile. The ReadAll() method is an efficient feature and is faster than calling system functions as illustrated in the guest book example in Chapter 15.

The remaining part of the example is to construct the saving format for the guest book file. For this, some functions of the TextStream objects are used. For example, you can use the following function to write two blank lines into the file:

```
dataStreamBlankLines(2)
```

In the interface page ex16-15.htm, users can also read the guest book by pressing the underlined text of the anchor element defined in lines 28–30. This anchor element activates another ASP page, ex16-15b.asp, to display the contents of the guest book in a new browser window. The coding of this ASP page is listed below:

```
Example: ex16-15b.asp - Reading The Guest Book

 1: <%@ Language=JScript%>
 2: <?xml version="1.0" encoding="iso-8859-1"?>
 3: <!DOCTYPE html PUBLIC "-//W3C//DTD XHTML 1.0 Transitional//EN"
 4:      "http://www.w3.org/TR/xhtml1/DTD/xhtml1-transitional.dtd">
 5: <html xmlns="http://www.w3.org/1999/xhtml" xml:lang="en" lang="en">
 6: <head><title>ex16-15b.asp</title><head>
 7: <body style="font-family:arial;font-weight:bold;background:#000088;
 8:    color:#ffff00;font-size:16pt"><br />
 9:    Guest Book Messages: From www.pwt-ex.com <br /><br />
10:    <img src="line1.gif" width="600" height="5" /><br /><br />
11:
12: <%
13:    var fs,dataStream, ForReading
14:    ForReading = 1
15:
16:    fs = new ActiveXObject("Scripting.FileSystemObject")
17:    dataStream = fs.OpenTextFile("c:\\guestbook.txt", ForReading)
18:    lst = dataStream.ReadAll()
19:
20:    Response.Write(lst)
21: %>
22:
23: <br /><br />
24: </body>
25: </html>
```

This page is very similar to ex16-14.asp and is easy to understand. A screen shot of the result is illustrated in Fig. 16.16.

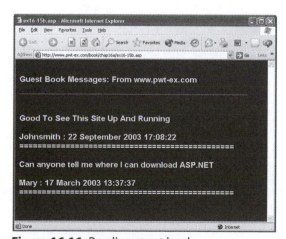

Figure 16.16 Reading guest book

It's now time to consider other functionalities of ASP objects related to files and directories. As a reminder, the ASP JScript language is more or less the same as ECMAScript introduced in Part II of this book. They have the same structure, function names, and calling formats. For some historic reasons, the name JScript is used for server-side scripting and ECMAScript is usually used for client-side scripting.

16.4.3 A page to locate and show properties of files

The ASP `File` objects and collections (see Table 16.3) provide a rich set of functions and properties for file operations. In particular, the properties of the `File` object contain useful information on a file. You can, for example, use them to build an application to locate a file anywhere in the file system and display the file information. Some of the frequently used properties of the `File` object are listed in Table 16.5.

Table 16.5 Properties of the ASP `File` object

Attributes	DateLastAccessed	ParentFolder	ShortPath
DateCreated	Drive	Path	Size
DateLastModified	Name	ShortName	Type

Before you can display the file information and properties, you may need to locate the file first. In fact, you can use the following XHTML input element to find and locate a file anywhere:

```
<input type="file" ...>
```

This element is used to build the simple file locator page ex16-16.htm below:

```
Example: ex16-16.htm - Finding Information On A File

 1:  <?xml version="1.0" encoding="iso-8859-1"?>
 2:  <!DOCTYPE html PUBLIC "-//W3C//DTD XHTML 1.0 Transitional//EN"
 3:      "http://www.w3.org/TR/xhtml1/DTD/xhtml1-transitional.dtd">
 4:  <html xmlns="http://www.w3.org/1999/xhtml" xml:lang="en" lang="en">
 5:  <head><title>File Information - ex16-16.htm</title></head>
 6:  <style>
 7:  .butSt{background-color:#aaffaa;font-family:arial;font-weight:bold;
 8:      font-size:14pt;color:#008800;width:150px;height:35px}
 9:  </style>
10:  <body style="background:#000088;font-family:arial;font-size:20pt;
11:      color:#ffff00;font-weight:bold;text-align:center">
12:    Finding The Details Of A File<br />
13:
14:  <img src="line1.gif" width="550" height="6" alt="pic" />
15:  <div style="font-size:14pt">
16:    Type the file including full path or <br />
17:    browse your file system with the Browse button.
18:  </div> <br /><br />
19:
20:  <form action="ex16-16.asp" method="post">
21:    <table align="center">
22:     <tr><td><input type="text" readonly class="butSt"
23:           style="color:#000088" value="File Name" /></td><td>
24:        <input type="file" name="fileId"
25:           class="butSt" style="width:350px" /><br /></td></tr>
26:     <tr><td><input type="submit" class="butSt" value="Details" /></td>
27:        <td><input type="reset" class="butSt" value="Reset" /></td></tr>
28:    </table>
29:  </form>
30:  </body>
31:  </html>
```

The purpose of this page is to get a file name either by user input or by browsing the file system. The `file` input type defined in line 24 generates a button named "Browser" automatically (see Fig. 16.17). If this button is pressed, a "Choose file" window is generated (Fig. 16.18). With this "Choose file" window, you can browse the whole file system on your machine.

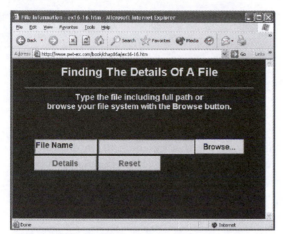

Figure 16.17 ex16-15.htm

Figure 16.18 "Choose file" window

Once you have picked your file and the Details button is pressed, the file name together with the full path is submitted to the following ASP page ex16-16.asp for processing:

Example: ex16-16.asp – ASP Page For ex16-16.htm

```
 1: <%@ LANGUAGE="JScript" %>
 2: <?xml version="1.0" encoding="iso-8859-1"?>
 3: <!DOCTYPE html PUBLIC "-//W3C//DTD XHTML 1.0 Transitional//EN"
 4:     "http://www.w3.org/TR/xhtml1/DTD/xhtml1-transitional.dtd">
 5: <html xmlns="http://www.w3.org/1999/xhtml" xml:lang="en" lang="en">
 6: <body style="background:#000088;font-family:arial;font-size:16pt;
 7:     color:#ffff00;font-weight:bold;text-align:left">
 8: Details of a File - Using the File Object <br /><br />
 9:
10: <%
11: var fileId, fs, fileInfo
12: fileId = Request.Form('fileId')
13: Response.Write("The Details of the File Properties are: <br />")
14:
15: if (String(fileId) != '') {
16:     fs = new ActiveXObject("Scripting.FileSystemObject")
17:     fileInfo = fs.GetFile(fileId)
18:
19:     Response.Write('Name: <span style="color:#00ff00">' +
20:         fileInfo.Name + '</span><BR>');
21:     Response.Write('Size: <span style="color:#00ff00">' +
22:         fileInfo.Size + ' bytes </span><BR>');
23:     Response.Write('Type: <span style="color:#00ff00">' +
24:         fileInfo.Type + ' </span><BR>');
25:     Response.Write('Path: <span style="color:#00ff00">'+
26:         fileInfo.Path + ' </span><BR>');
27:     Response.Write('Created: <span style="color:#00ff00">' +
28:         fileInfo.DateCreated +' </span><BR>');
29:     Response.Write('LastModified: <span style="color:#00ff00">' +
```

```
30:         fileInfo.DateLastModified + ' </span><BR>')
31:    Response.Write('LastAccessed: <span style="color:#00ff00">' +
32:         fileInfo.DateLastAccessed+ ' </span><BR>')
33: }
34: else
35: {
36:    Response.Write("Error.. File Identity.. ")
37: }
38: %>
39: </body>
40: </html>
```

This ASP program creates an instance of `FileSystemObject` as variable `fs`. This `fs` can be used to activate the `GetFile()` function in line 17:

```
fileInfo = fs.GetFile(fileId)
```

The `GetFile()` function returns a `File` object corresponding to the file in a specific path. In this case, the `File` object `fileInfo` contains all information of the file represented by `fileId`. The remaining part of the page is a series of output statements to display:

`fileInfo.Name`	–	Name of the file
`fileInfo.Size`	–	Size of the file
`fileInfo.Type`	–	Type of the file
`fileInfo.Path`	–	Path of the file
`fileInfo.DateCreated`	–	The date when the file was created
`fileInfo.DateLastModified`	–	The date when the file was last modified
`fileInfo.DateLastAccessed`	–	The date when the file was last accessed

Note that all this file information concerns properties of the `File` object. Once `fileId` is specified, the `File` object `fileInfo` returned by the `GetFile()` method contains all these properties.

If `fileId` is not defined, the statements in lines 34–37 output an error message to the user. For example, if you press the Details button without a file name, you will have an undefined `fileId`. Some screen shots of this page are shown in Figs 16.19 and 16.20.

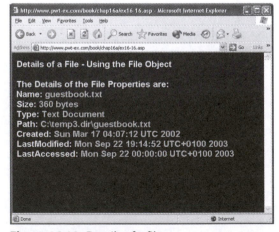

Figure 16.19 Details of a file

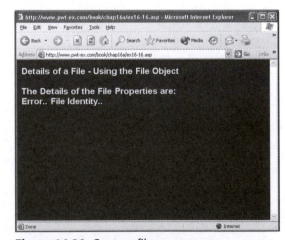

Figure 16.20 Capture file error

16.4.4 Obtaining drive information with the `Drive` object

The `Drive` object and collection are special ASP structures to provide information about drives installed on a machine with Microsoft systems. The `Drive` object contains the properties in Table 16.6.

Table 16.6 Properties of the `Drive` object

AvailableSpace	FileSystem	Path	ShareName
DriveLetter	FreeSpace	RootFolder	TotalSize
DriveType	IsReady	SerialNumber	VolumeName

In fact, the `Drive` object and collection are derived from the `Drives` property of `FileSystemObject`. Before you can use these properties, you need to create the `Drive` collection and object from the `Drives` property of `FileSystemObject`. For example, the following ASP statements can be used to create the `Drive` collection:

```
fs= new ActiveXObject('Scripting.FileSystemObject')
driveCol = new Enumerator(fs.Drives)
```

The first line creates a `FilesSystemObject` called `fs`. Then the `Enumerator` object is used on the property of `fs.Drives` to generate a collection called `driveCol`. This `driveCol` is a `Drive` collection and each item inside this collection is a `Drive` object representing a drive.

To understand how to get all drives on your system, consider the following example:

```
Example: ex16-17.asp - Finding All Drives Using The Drive Object Of ASP

 1: <%@ Language=JScript%>
 2: <?xml version="1.0" encoding="iso-8859-1"?>
 3: <!DOCTYPE html PUBLIC "-//W3C//DTD XHTML 1.0 Transitional//EN"
 4:     "http://www.w3.org/TR/xhtml1/DTD/xhtml1-transitional.dtd">
 5: <html xmlns="http://www.w3.org/1999/xhtml" xml:lang="en" lang="en">
 6: <head><title> Finding All Drives - ex16-17.asp</title></head>
 7: <body style="font-family:arial;font-weight:bold;background:#000088;
 8:    color:#ffff00;font-size:16pt"><br />
 9:    The Following Drives Are Found In Your System <br /><br />
10: <%
11: var fs, driveCol, enumDrive, driveObj
12: fs= new ActiveXObject('Scripting.FileSystemObject')
13: driveCol = fs.Drives
14: enumDrive = new Enumerator(driveCol)
15: while(enumDrive.atEnd() != true)
16: {
17:    driveObj = enumDrive.item()
18:    Response.Write("Drive: "+ driveObj.DriveLetter + "<br />")
19:    enumDrive.moveNext()
20: }
21: %>
22:
23: <br /><br />
24: </body>
25: </html>
```

Once the `Drive` collection (`driveCol`) is specified in line 13, we know that each item inside the collection is a `Drive` object containing information on a specific drive. The statement in line 14 is to turn the collection into an `Enumerator` object (i.e., `enumDrive`). A simple while-loop applied to `enumDrive` will get all the `Drive` objects available. Inside the while-loop, we have two statements:

```
driveObj = enumDrive.item()
Response.Write("Drive: "+ driveObj.DriveLetter + "<br />")
```

The first statement is to get the `Drive` object from the items of the collection, i.e., `driveCol.Item()`. When the `Drive` object `driveObj` is defined, the property

```
DriveObj.DriveLetter
```

can be used to get the drive letters such as C, D, E, …, from a machine with a Microsoft system. In fact, not just the `DriveLetter`, but all `Drive` object properties mentioned in Table 16.6 can be applied.

For a more general application on drives and their properties, let's consider an example that can locate drives on your system and display information on them interactively. In order to store all the drive letters in the system, you may want to use a select box as an interface. Our example will store all the available drives into a select box. If one of the drives is picked, information about that drive will be displayed accordingly. For this example, only one ASP page is developed. This page will call itself to display the drive information.

The first part of this ASP page is listed below:

Example: ex16-18.asp - Display Drives Information Interactively (Part One)

```
 1: <%@ Language=JScript%>
 2: <?xml version="1.0" encoding="iso-8859-1"?>
 3: <!DOCTYPE html PUBLIC "-//W3C//DTD XHTML 1.0 Transitional//EN"
 4:     "http://www.w3.org/TR/xhtml1/DTD/xhtml1-transitional.dtd">
 5: <html xmlns="http://www.w3.org/1999/xhtml" xml:lang="en" lang="en">
 6: <head><title> Display Drives Information - ex16-18.asp</title></head>
 7: <style>
 8:  .butSt{background-color:#aaffaa;font-family:arial;font-weight:bold;
 9:     font-size:14pt;color:#008800;width:200px;height:30px}
10: </style>
11: <body style="font-family:arial;font-weight:bold;background:#000088;
12:    color:#ffff00;font-size:16pt"><br />
13:    The Following Drives Are Found In Your System <br /><br />
14:    Please select a drive letter and<br />
15:    press the Drive Information button <br /><br />
16: <form method="post" action="ex16-18.asp">
17: <select name="driveLetter" class="butSt">
18: <%
19:    var fs, driveCol, enumDrive, driveObj
20:    fs = Server.CreateObject('Scripting.FileSystemObject')
21:    driveCol = fs.Drives
22:    enumDrive = new Enumerator(driveCol)
23:    while(enumDrive.atEnd() != true)
24:    {
25:       driveObj = enumDrive.item()
26:       Response.Write('<option value="'+ driveObj +'"> Drive ' +
27:          driveObj.DriveLetter + '</option>')
28:       enumDrive.moveNext()
29:    }
30: %>
31: </select>     
32: <input type="submit" name="submit" value="Drive Information" class="butSt">
33: </form>
```

This ASP page is, in fact, a form application defined in lines 16–33. Inside the form, there is a select box; all options in the select box are generated by the ASP code. The while-loop in lines 23–29 would iterate over the drive object. For each `Drive` object, the corresponding drive letter is displayed by the statement (lines 26–27)

```
Response.Write('<option value="'+ driveObj +'"> Drive ' +
    driveObj.DriveLetter + '</option>')
```

This statement generates an option element in XHTML. Since ASP code is processed before any XHTML code, the result will be a complete select box with the available drive letters as options. A screen shot of this ASP fragment is shown in Fig. 16.21.

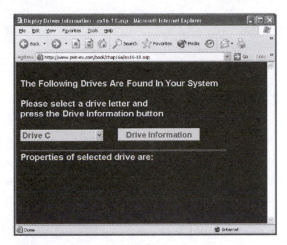

Figure 16.21 ex16-18.asp

When the Drive Information button (line 32) is pressed, this form is submitted to the ASP itself. This page will also capture the drive letter and display the information on the drive. In order to do this, you need the second half of the ASP page below:

```
Listing: Continuation Of The ASP Page ex16-18.asp (Part Two)

35: <img src="line1.gif" width="500" height="6" alt="pic" /><br />
36: <b>Properties of selected drive are:</b><br /><br />
37: <%
38: var typeArr, strLetter, strDriveType
39: typeArr = new Array("","Removable","Fixed","Network",
40:                      "CD-ROM","RAM Drive")
41: strLetter = Request.Form('driveLetter')
42:
43: if (String(strLetter) != "undefined")
44: {
45:   driveObj = driveCol.Item(strLetter)
46:   Response.Write('Drive letter = ' + driveObj.DriveLetter + '<br />')
47:
48:   if ( driveObj.DriveType >0 && driveObj.DriveType < 6)
49:   {
50:     strDriveType = typeArr[driveObj.DriveType]
51:   }else {
52:     strDriveType = 'Unknown'
53:   }
54:   Response.Write('Drive type = ' + strDriveType + '<br />')
55:
56:   if (!driveObj.IsReady)
57:   {
58:      Response.Write('Drive ' + strLetter + ' is not ready.')
59:   }else{
60:     Response.Write('File system = ' + driveObj.FileSystem + '<br />')
61:     Response.Write('Available space= ' +driveObj.AvailableSpace +'<br />')
```

```
62:         Response.Write('Free space = ' + driveObj.FreeSpace + '<br />')
63:         Response.Write('Total size = ' + driveObj.TotalSize + '<br />')
64:         Response.Write('Path = ' + driveObj.Path + '<br />');
65:         Response.Write('Root folder = ' + driveObj.RootFolder + '<br />')
66:         Response.Write('Serial number = ' + driveObj.SerialNumber + '<br />')
67:         Response.Write('Share name = ' + driveObj.ShareName + '<br />')
68:         Response.Write('Volume name = ' + driveObj.VolumeName + '<br />')
69:     }
70: }
71: %>
72:
73: <br /><br />
74: </body>
75: </html>
```

In this ASP page fragment, an array `typeArr` is defined to store the name of the drive type. After the drive letter displays in line 46, the conditional statements in lines 48–54 use this array to display the name of the drive type. In general `driveObj.DriveType` is a number with the following meanings

1 – Removable drive	2 – Fixed drive	3 – Network drives
4 – CD-ROM drive	5 – RAM drive	`Others` – Unknown drives

The array `typeArr` is an efficient way to convert the number into a string. After the drive type, the remaining part of the page is easy to understand. Basically, if the drive is "Ready," a series of `Response.Write()` functions are called to display the corresponding information of the drive. A screen shot of the result is shown in Fig. 16.22.

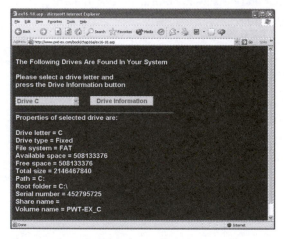

Figure 16.22 Drive information

16.4.5 A simple folder explorer using ASP

Now you have some experience of handling files and drives with ASP and related objects, it's time to use some of the skills to develop a simple folder explorer to browse through your system. To build a folder explorer, you need to use the methods and properties of the `Folder` object associated with `FileSystemObject`. Some of the methods and properties of the `Folder` object are listed in Table 16.7.

Table 16.7 Properties of the `Folder` object

Attributes	Drive	ParentFolder	Size
DateCreated	Files	Path	SubFolders
DateLastAccessed	IsRootFolder	ShortName	Type
DateLastModified	Name	ShortPath	

Methods of the `Folder` object

Copy()	Delete()	Move()	OpenAsTextStream()

The folder explorer that we are going to develop will search and display all available drives on your system. Once you double click one of the drives, the ASP page will search and display all available folders of the selected drive on a sized selected box. If you double click one of the folders, all sub-folders will be searched and displayed. The entire folder path of the selected folder is also displayed as a string. A screen shot of the folder explorer is shown in Fig. 16.23. When you double click the folder "C:\mysql," all sub-folders of `mysql` are displayed (see Fig. 16.24). MySQL is a popular and free database package with source code available and we will discuss it in Chapter 17.

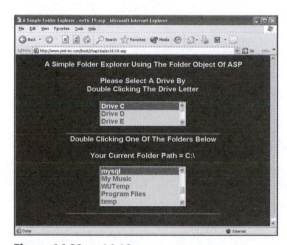

Figure 16.23 ex16-19.asp

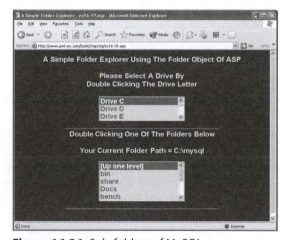

Figure 16.24 Sub-folders of MySQL

The first function of this example is to search and display all available drives in the system and therefore it is quite similar to example ex16-18.asp. In this example, we have added the following two features:

- All select boxes are sized so that some rows are displayed when the page is activated.
- There is no Submit button in the example. You can double click the selections inside the select box.

The first part of the example is listed below:

```
Example: ex16-19.asp - A Simple "Folder" Explorer Using ASP (Part One)

1: <%@ Language=JScript%>
2: <?xml version="1.0" encoding="iso-8859-1"?>
3: <!DOCTYPE html PUBLIC "-//W3C//DTD XHTML 1.0 Transitional//EN"
4:     "http://www.w3.org/TR/xhtml1/DTD/xhtml1-transitional.dtd">
5: <html xmlns="http://www.w3.org/1999/xhtml" xml:lang="en" lang="en">
```

```
 6: <head><title> A Simple Folder Explorer - ex16-19.asp</title></head>
 7: <style>
 8:   .butSt{background-color:#aaffaa;font-family:arial;font-weight:bold;
 9:      font-size:14pt;color:#008800;width:250px}
10: </style>
11: <body style="font-family:arial;font-weight:bold;background:#000088;
12:   color:#ffff00;font-size:16pt;text-align:center" >
13:   A Simple Folder Explorer Using The Folder Object Of ASP<br /><br />
14:   Please Select A Drive By<br />
15:   Double Clicking The Drive Letter <br /><br />
16:
17: <form action="ex16-19.asp" name="myForm" method="post">
18: <select name="driveLetter" size="3" class="butSt"
19:    ondblclick="document.myForm.submit()">
20: <%
21: var strDr,fs,enumDr,driveObj
22: strDr = Request.Form('driveLetter')
23: fs= new ActiveXObject('Scripting.FileSystemObject')
24: enumDr = new Enumerator(fs.Drives)
25: while (enumDr.atEnd() != true)
26: {
27:    driveObj = enumDr.item()
28:    Response.Write('<option ')
29:    if (driveObj.DriveLetter == strDr)
30:    {
31:       Response.Write(' selected ')
32:    }
33:    Response.Write('value="'+ driveObj.DriveLetter +'"> Drive '+
34:       driveObj.DriveLetter + '</option>')
35:    enumDr.moveNext()
36: }
37: %>
38: </select>
39: </form>
40: <img src="line1.gif" width="450" height="6" alt="pic" /><br />
```

This ASP page fragment contains a form with a select box called `driveLetter`. This select box has a size = "3" in line 18 so that it will display three rows. If you take a closer look at the select box, you will find the following statement attached at the end of it:

```
ondblclick="document.myForm.submit()"
```

This is an ECMAScript statement and will be executed by the browser (not the server). If you double click any of the options, this statement will activate the `submit()` function and submit the form "myForm." The effect is the same as the Submit button. The remaining part of the ASP fragment is very similar to example ex16-18.asp and can be understood easily.

If one of the drives is clicked twice, the drive is selected. If the drive is ready, all the sub-folders of the drives are displayed. In some cases, the selected drive may not be ready, e.g., if it is a floppy drive with no floppy disk inside. We need to detect this situation and return an appropriate message.

Also, before the details of all folders are listed in another selected box, you may need to handle some parameter passing from the page to itself. Basically, if no previous selected folder is defined, the folder path is naturally set to be the selected drive. If the folder path is already defined, it should be used as the folder path.

The following second part of the page fragment is designed to handle these tasks.

```
Listing: Continuation Of The ASP Page ex16-19.asp (Part Two)
41:  Double Click One Of The Folders Below <br /><br />
42:  <%
43: var strDr, driveObj, strFolder,strFolderName,folderObj,subFolerObj,lst
44: strDr=String(strDr)
45: if (strDr != 'undefined')
46: {
47:  driveObj = fs.GetDrive(strDr)
48:  if (!driveObj.IsReady)
49:  {
50:     Response.Write('Drive is not available.<br />')
51:  }
52:  else
53:  {
54:     strFolder = String(Request.Form('folderPath'))
55:     if (strFolder == 'undefined')
56:        folderObj = driveObj.RootFolder
57:  else
58:  {
59:     strFolderName = String(Request.Form('folderName'))
60:     if (strFolderName != 'undefined')
61:     {
62:        if (strFolderName == '[Up one level]')
63:           strFolder = strFolder + '\\..'
64:        else
65:           strFolder = strFolder + '\\' + strFolderName
66:     }
67:     folderObj = fs.GetFolder(strFolder)
68:  }
69:  Response.Write('Your Current Folder Path = '+ folderObj.Path +'<br />')
70:
```

The variable strDr in line 44 stores the drive letter of the selected drive. It is used to get the Drive object so that whether this selected drive is ready can be detected in line 48. If the drive is not ready, no sub-folder is available and a message is output in line 50. If the drive is ready, you may need to test whether the folder path is defined or not. If it is undefined, the RootFolder is used as the folder path stored in the variable folderObj (line 56), otherwise a string concatenation technique is used to build the folder path from the submitted data. Finally, the folder path is displayed by the statement in line 69.

The final part of the example is designed to handle the search and to display all sub-folders to a sized select box. When any of the sub-folders is double clicked, the page is submitted to the ASP program again to search and display all sub-folders. This part of the program is listed below:

```
Listing: Continuation Of The ASP Page ex16-19.asp (Part Three)
71: lst = '<form action="ex16-19.asp" name="formFolder" method="post"> '+
72: '<input type="hidden" name="driveLetter" value="'+ driveObj.DriveLetter+'">'+
73: '<input type="hidden" name="folderPath" value="'+ folderObj.Path+'">' +
74: '<select name="folderName" size="5" class="butSt"'+
75: ' ondblclick="document.formFolder.submit()" >'
76: Response.Write(lst)
77:
78:    if (!folderObj.IsRootFolder)
79:    {
80:       Response.Write('<option selected>[Up one level]</option>');
81:    }
```

```
82:
83:    var enumFolders = new Enumerator(folderObj.SubFolders);
84:    while ( enumFolders.atEnd() != true )
85:    {
86:     SubFolderObj = enumFolders.item()
87:     Response.Write('<option>' + SubFolderObj.Name +'</option>')
88:     enumFolders.moveNext()
89:    }
90:    Response.Write('</select>')
91:    Response.Write('</form>')
92:  }
93: }
94: %>
95: <img src="line1.gif" width="450" height="6" alt="pic" /><br /><br />
96: </body>
97: </html>
```

In this page fragment, we use a string technique to generate a form with a select box. For example, if you have picked drive C and folder `mysql` then lines 71–76 would generate the following XHTML code to the browser:

```
<form action="ex16-19.asp" name="formFolder" method="post">
    <input type="hidden" name="driveLetter" value="C">
    <input type="hidden" name="folderPath" value="mysql">
    <select name="folderName" size="5" class="butSt"
        ondblclick="document.formFolder.submit()" >
```

The double click statement is used to submit the form when any of the sub-folders is double clicked. The remainder of the program code is used to complete this select box by filling in the options. First, if the folder is not the root folder, the following option element is added (line 80):

```
<option selected>[Up one level]</option>
```

This option can be used to move the folder one level up so that you can have two-way browsing. When the `Enumerator` object applies on `folderObj.SubFolders` (line 83), all the available sub-folders are returned. A simple while-loop (lines 84–89) can be used to get all the sub-folder information.

Another important topic on ASP is to use ADO for database programming. This subject will be discussed in the next chapter as an application of databases. Now, however, let's see how to migrate ASP pages to ASP.NET.

16.5 Migrating ASP to ASP.NET

16.5.1 A brief word on compatibility of ASP and ASP.NET

As we mentioned in section 16.1, ASP.NET was developed for the Microsoft .NET family and for the future of Windows platforms. The front end design of ASP.NET is to help preserve the applications and investment of traditional ASP technology. Many ASP pages can be converted to ASP.NET without the need to change anything. There are some fundamental differences between ASP and ASP.NET, as follows.

One of the major differences is that ASP is an interpreted environment. Languages used in ASP are interpreted by the script engine and then the results are sent to the browser. Although transparent to most users, ASP.NET on the other hand is a compiled environment. All supporting languages such as C#, JScript, and VB.NET are compiled languages. This arrangement provides a fundamental framework for the .NET family to use the components of each other easily. This feature is known as the Common Language Runtime in .NET technology. Because of that, ASP.NET is not an upgrade of ASP: the software is completely new and had to be rewritten entirely. Also because of that, it is impossible to maintain 100% compatibility with ASP.

For example, we have demonstrated in ex16-05.asp how to include multiple languages in one ASP page. This feature is useful for using functions defined in other scripting libraries or engines. Due to the compiled nature and strong discipline, ASP.NET supports only one language on one page. You can, however, use multiple pages in a single application and one language on each page. Technically, this feature enables you to integrate and take advantage of multiple languages.

As a logical evolution of ASP, ASP.NET provides syntax compatibility with existing ASP pages. In other words, a large number of ASP pages (simple ones) can be converted into ASP.NET by changing the file extension to .aspx. For more complex applications, some modifications may be required. In this situation, usually only a few minor changes may be required to fix the problem.

Now, let's see how many examples in this chapter can be converted into ASP.NET directly by just changing the file extension. The results are listed in Table 16.8.

Table 16.8 Convert ASP pages to ASP.NET

ASP examples	ASP.NET	ASP examples	ASP.NET
ex16-01.asp	Yes	ex16-11.asp	Yes
ex16-02.asp	Yes	ex16-12.asp	Yes
ex16-03.asp	Yes	ex16-13.asp	Yes
ex16-04.asp	No	ex16-14.asp	Yes
ex16-05.asp	No	ex16-15.asp	Yes
ex16-06.asp	Yes	ex16-16.asp	Yes
ex16-07.asp	Yes	ex16-17.asp	Yes
ex16-08.asp	Yes	ex16-18.asp	Yes
ex16-09.asp	Yes	ex16-19.asp	Yes
ex16-10.asp	No		

Please note that when you rename the ASP file .asp to .aspx, don't forget to change the corresponding statements in the related XHTML files.

We will explain why some of the examples cannot be converted to ASP.NET directly in section 16.5.2 and provide some guidelines for migration to ASP.NET.

16.5.2 Migrating ASP to ASP.NET with examples

As we mentioned earlier, one of the important differences between ASP and ASP.NET is that ASP.NET is a compiled environment. Therefore most of the compatibility and migration issues are concentrated on the differences between a compiled language and an interpreted language.

A compiled language usually has a strong discipline and can provide an overall description of the program structure. This is important when developing complex programs. The first thing to establish a strong discipline in programming is to request programmers to declare all variables.

In order to support the compiled nature of the .NET technology, ASP.NET employs a variable declaration checking scheme. All ASP.NET variables in C#, Visual Basic, and JScript must be defined before they can be used.

As a simple example, let's rename ex16-03.asp as ex16-20.aspx so that it is an ASP.NET page. From Table 16.8, you can see that this example works well in ASP.NET. However, the page no longer works if you comment out the variable "ii" in line 8 as illustrated in the following example:

```
Example: ex16-20.aspx - An ASP Example Not Working In ASP.NET

 1: <%@ Language=JScript%>
 2: <?xml version="1.0" encoding="iso-8859-1"?>
 3: <!DOCTYPE html PUBLIC "-//W3C//DTD XHTML 1.0 Transitional//EN"
 4:     "http://www.w3.org/TR/xhtml1/DTD/xhtml1-transitional.dtd">
 5: <html xmlns="http://www.w3.org/1999/xhtml" xml:lang="en" lang="en">
 6: <head><title> A Not Working ASP In ASP.NET - ex16-20.aspx</title><head>
 7: <body style="font-family:arial;font-weight:bold"><br /><br />
 8: <% //var ii
 9: for( ii=20;ii <=26; ii++)
10: {
11: Response.Write("<div style='font-size:" + ii + "px;color:#000000'>")
12: Response.Write("style font-size = " + ii + " px -- Hello World! </div >")
13: }
14: %>
15: </body>
16: </html>
```

If you request this ASP.NET page using IE6.x with the command:

http://www.pwt-ex.com/book/chap16a/ex16-20.aspx

you will get an error page as illustrated in Fig. 16.25.

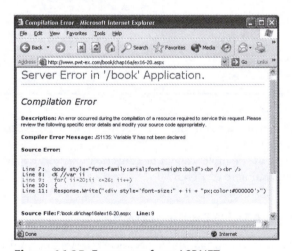

Figure 16.25 Error page from ASP.NET

From this figure, you can see that the IE6.x browser is clever enough to locate the following compilation error:

Compiler Error Message: JS1135: Variable 'ii' has not been declared

The error code is JScript 1135 (JS1135), meaning that the variable "ii" is not declared before use. The source of the error is located at line 9 and displayed in red.

Therefore, if you want your ASP page to work in ASP.NET, the first thing is to declare all variables before using them such as:

var ii, jj, kk, enObj, str, folderInfo, subFolder — Using JScript

dim ii, jj, kk, enObj, str, folderInfo, subFolder — Using VBScript

Another major difference comes from the CGI application. In ASP, when you request data from a query string or a form using the functions

```
Request.QueryString()
Request.Form()
```

you will have an array or a collection of strings. In ASP.NET, these two functions only return a single string containing all the options.

For example, the following code fragment defines three checkboxes:

```
<form action="ex16-21.xxx" method="post">
        Which Operating Systems You Are Using?
  <input name="os" type="checkbox" value="Windows XP" />Windows XP<br />
  <input name="os" type="checkbox" value="Windows 2000" />Windows 2000<br />
  <input name="os" type="checkbox" value="Windows 9x" />Windows 9x<br />
  <input type="submit" value="Submit" class="butSt">
</form>
```

Suppose you have checked all the boxes and pressed the Submit button; the data are then passed to the program ex16-21.xxx. If this program is an ASP page, you can access the data by

`Request.Form("os").Count` – to get the number of items in the collection

`Request.Form("os")(1)` – to get the first item, i.e., "Windows XP"

`Request.Form("os")(2)` – to get the second item, i.e., "Windows 2000"

If the program ex16-21.xxx is an ASP.NET page, the three functions above will generate errors, because `Request.Form("os")` returns a single string such as

`Request.Form("os")` – returns "Windows XP, Windows 2000, Windows 9x"

In order to gain access to the data individually, you may need to employ some explicit methods such as `GetValues()` to get array access. For example, you may use

`Request.Form.GetValues("os").Length` – to get the number of items

`Response.Write(Request.Form.GetValues("os")[0]` – to get "Windows XP"

`Response.Write(Request.Form.GetValues("os")[1]` – to get "Windows 2000"

Please note that ASP.NET array elements start from 0.

Now you know why example ex16-10.asp does not work by simply changing its name to ASP.NET format. In order to make it work, the first step is to rename the files:

ex16-10.htm   to   ex16-21.htm

ex16-10.asp   to   ex16-21.aspx

The second step is to modify the XHTML file ex16-21.htm as follows:

```
Example: ex16-21.htm - Getting Form Data With ASP.NET

 1: <?xml version="1.0" encoding="iso-8859-1"?>
 2: <!DOCTYPE html PUBLIC "-//W3C//DTD XHTML 1.0 Transitional//EN"
 3:     "http://www.w3.org/TR/xhtml1/DTD/xhtml1-transitional.dtd">
 4: <html xmlns="http://www.w3.org/1999/xhtml" xml:lang="en" lang="en">
 5: <head><title> Getting Form Data With ASP.NET - ex16-21.htm</title><head>
 6: <style>
 7:  .butSt{background:#aaffaa;width:250px;
 8:     font-family:arial;font-weight:bold;font-size:16pt;color:#880000}
 9:  .chkSt{background:#aaffaa;width:30px;height:30px;
10:     font-family:arial;font-weight:bold;font-size:16pt;color:#880000}
```

```
11:   .txtSt{font-family:arial;font-weight:bold;font-size:16pt;color:#ffff00}
12: </style>
13: <body style="font-family:arial;font-weight:bold;font-size:18pt;
14:   background:#000088;color:#ffff00"><br />
15:
16: <form name="statForm" action="ex16-21.aspx" method="post">
17:   <div style="position:absolute;top:40px;left:60px;">
18:       Which Operating Systems Have You Used? </div><br />
19:   <div style="position:absolute;top:100px;left:100px;">
20:     <input name="os" type="checkbox" value="Windows XP" class="chkSt" />
21:         Windows XP<br />
22:     <input name="os" type="checkbox" value="Windows 2000" class="chkSt" />
23:         Windows 2000<br />
24:     <input name="os" type="checkbox" value="Windows 9x" class="chkSt" />
25:         Windows 9x<br />
26:     <input name="os" type="checkbox" value="LINUX" class="chkSt" />
27:         LINUX<br /> </div>
28:   <div style="position:absolute;top:100px;left:340px;">
29:     <input name="os" type="checkbox" value="Mac OS" class="chkSt" />
30:         Mac OS<br />
31:     <input name="os" type="checkbox" value="IRIS" class="chkSt" />
32:         IRIS<br />
33:     <input name="os" type="checkbox" value="Solaris" class="chkSt" />
34:         Solaris<br />
35:     <input name="os" type="checkbox" value="Sun OS" class="chkSt" />
36:         Sun OS<br /> </div>
37:   <div style="position:absolute;top:260px;left:60px;">
38:     <input type="submit" value="Submit" class="butSt">
39:     <input type="reset" value="Clear" class="butSt">
40:   </div>
41: </form>
42: </body>
43: </html>
```

This is a simple XHTML page to define a series of checkboxes. In fact, this page is the same as ex16-10.htm except for lines 5 and 16. When this form is submitted, the form action defined in line 16 calls the ASP.NET program ex16-21.aspx. This program will process the form data using ASP.NET commands. The program code of ex16-21.aspx is listed below:

```
Example: ex16-21.aspx - ASP.NET Program Code

 1: <%@ LANGUAGE="JScript" %>
 2: <?xml version="1.0" encoding="iso-8859-1"?>
 3: <!DOCTYPE html PUBLIC "-//W3C//DTD XHTML 1.0 Transitional//EN"
 4:     "http://www.w3.org/TR/xhtml1/DTD/xhtml1-transitional.dtd">
 5: <html xmlns="http://www.w3.org/1999/xhtml" xml:lang="en" lang="en">
 6: <head><title>ex16-21.aspx</title></head>
 7: <body style="font-family:arial;font-weight:bold;font-size:18pt;
 8:     background:#000088;color:#ffff00"><br />
 9: <%
10:  var ii, tmpSt =""
11:  tmpSt = Request.Form.GetValues("os")
12:
13:  if (!tmpSt)
14:  {
15:    Response.Write("You Have Used No Operating System Before!<br />" +
16:    " I Don't Believe You!")
17:  }
18:  else if (Request.Form.GetValues("os").Length ==1)
19:  {
20:     Response.Write("You Only Use This Operating System?<br /> ")
21:     Response.Write (Request.Form.GetValues("os")[0] + "<br />")
```

```
22:      Response.Write("Try to Use More.")
23:    }
24:    else
25:    {
26:     Response.Write("You've Used All These Operating Systems? <br /><br />")
27:     for (ii=0; ii < Request.Form.GetValues("os").Length;ii++)
28:     {
29:        Response.Write(Request.Form.GetValues("os")[ii] + '<br />')
30:     }
31:     Response.Write("<br />" + "Very Good...")
32:    }
33: %>
34: </body>
35: </html>
```

First, we declare the variables ii and $tmpSt$ in line 10. The $tmpSt$ variable is used to obtain the input data from the submitted form. If you check all the boxes, $tmpSt$ will contain a string with all your selections. If $tmpSt$ is empty (line 13), the message in lines 15–16 is displayed to indicate you haven't checked any box. If you just check one box (line 18), the ASP.NET statement in line 21

```
Request.Form.GetValues("os")[0]
```

is used to obtain only the selected item. If you have selected more than one item, the following for-loop will print out all the selections on the browser window:

```
for (ii=0; ii < Request.Form.GetValues("os").Length;ii++)
{
    Response.Write(Request.Form.GetValues("os")[ii] + '<br />')
}
```

Please note that the coding in this example concentrates on the idea of migrating ASP pages to ASP.NET. In real applications, the length of the array should not be inside a loop in order to increase efficiency. Some screen shots are shown in Figs 16.26 and 16.27.

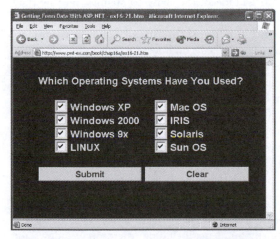

Figure 16.26 Getting form data with ASP.NET I

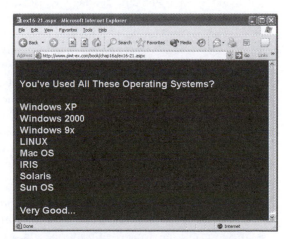

Figure 16.27 Getting form data with ASP.NET II

Now you have some ideas on how to migrate ASP pages into ASP.NET. In fact, using the guidelines in this subsection, even some of the ASP database applications can be easily converted to ASP.NET. Databases and their applications will be discussed in the next chapter.

As a final remark, you may ask why the examples ex16-04.asp and ex16-05.asp in Table 16.8 are not working. The answer is simple: they both use Perl script. By default Perl is not supported in ASP.NET. Also the multiple language feature on a single page is not supported by ASP.NET.

17 Programming databases and MySQL

17.1 An introduction to SQL databases

17.1.1 What is an SQL database?

Over the last decade, computing technologies have made permanent changes in the way business is conducted in offices around the world. Whether you are running a large corporation or just the owner of a small business, orders placed by customers in foreign countries can now be instantly processed by a few mouse clicks on the Internet. By traveling at a speed well beyond 6,000 miles (9,600 km) per second with a good connection, emails and millions of Web sites on the Internet are now an integral part of the so-called global economy.

Also, thanks to relational database management systems (RDBMS) and the Structured Query Language (SQL), database systems have become indispensable structures for almost all corporations, large or small. We can say that information is now stored on databases in every conceivable business environment. Apart from some word processing skills, a basic knowledge of databases and SQL is a requirement for most office staff nowadays. With the Internet and World Wide Web, we are all riding the wave of the so-called online age: online banking, shopping, and trading are just some examples. Indeed, for many companies, putting their databases online is vital for their business expansion and to get into the international global market.

In this chapter, an introduction to databases on the Internet is presented. In particular, a database product called MySQL is used for most examples and demonstrations. Some details on how to install and use it on the Internet are given. Along with SQL, information on other database products such as Microsoft Access and Oracle is also provided. They are the so-called SQL-based databases or simply SQL databases since they can be controlled and accessed by SQL. This capability is the main characteristic of all RDBMS dominating the database market and applications. From Microsoft Access and FoxPro, to Borland's Paradox and to Sybase, Informix, Oracle, and MySQL – all these database products use SQL.

Compared to others, MySQL from MySQL AB (see www.mysql.com) is a relatively new arrival in the database race. The decision to use MySQL for examples and demonstrations in this chapter is based on the following reasons:

- It is a mature implementation of the SQL standard, easy to use, and can be used with Web applications in mind. For example, PHP has built-in support for MySQL access.
- It is available on virtually all platforms and operating environments including Microsoft Windows and UNIX/LINUX systems.
- It is free with source code available.

This chapter is an introduction to database programming on the Web. Some dedicated pages or utilities are developed to access and control MySQL on the Internet. Together with server scripting techniques, Open Database Connectivity (ODBC) and Database Interface (DBI) technologies are also discussed in detail. To understand and program databases on the Web, let's begin with the characteristics of SQL databases.

17.1.2 The characteristics of SQL databases

Roughly speaking, a database that can be controlled and accessed by the SQL commands and language is called an SQL database. The following is a sample SQL command (see example ex15-15.htm):

```
SELECT * FROM people;
```

This command, basically, would select and display all the fields from a table called people. SQL commands are not case sensitive. In order to distinguish between system commands and user-defined names, we generally use capital letters for system keywords and lower case for defined names. Consider the SQL command above; it pays no attention to what kind of database is involved. Once the database involved has been set up on a remote server or on the Internet, whether it is a Microsoft Access, FoxPro, Oracle, or MySQL database, the same command can be used to access the data.

SQL is a standard language from the American National Standards Institute (ANSI) used to manipulate and retrieve data from databases. SQL provides a complete set of languages to enable a programmer or database administrator to do all sorts of things, such as query a database for information, update the contents, or even change the structure of a database. You will learn more about SQL databases and statements in the coming sections.

Another characteristic of SQL databases is the use of tables. All information in an SQL database or relational database is represented explicitly as values in tables. One database can have multiple tables with names and related to each other. Using a table structure, all information in the database is guaranteed to be accessible by using a combination of the table name, primary key value, and column (or field) name. For example, suppose you have created a database called personnel with MySQL. Inside this database, a table called people may look as in Table 17.1.

Table 17.1 An MySQL table: people

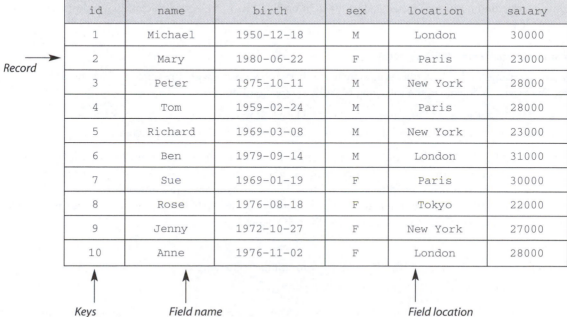

id	name	birth	sex	location	salary
1	Michael	1950-12-18	M	London	30000
2	Mary	1980-06-22	F	Paris	23000
3	Peter	1975-10-11	M	New York	28000
4	Tom	1959-02-24	M	Paris	28000
5	Richard	1969-03-08	M	New York	23000
6	Ben	1979-09-14	M	London	31000
7	Sue	1969-01-19	F	Paris	30000
8	Rose	1976-08-18	F	Tokyo	22000
9	Jenny	1972-10-27	F	New York	27000
10	Anne	1976-11-02	F	London	28000

Record (label pointing to row 2)

Keys   *Field name*   *Field location*

In this case, the first column id is the primary key of the table providing a unique numbered reference to the record. The 10 rows are the records in the table. To retrieve the first five records, a user would issue the SQL command

```
SELECT * FROM people WHERE id < 6;
```

To retrieve a specific record, e.g., Mary, a user may use

```
SELECT * FROM people WHERE name="Mary";
```

Don't worry too much about the syntax and exact explanation at this moment; more details and explanations will be given later in this chapter. The important point at this stage is that every element inside the database can be accessed using the table structure.

Before we continue the discussion of SQL, let's install and set up a database product called MySQL on our system.

17.2 Using MySQL

17.2.1 Installing and configuring MySQL

By supporting more than 10 different operating systems, MySQL has become one of the most popular free database packages available. From Microsoft Windows, LINUX, and Solaris, to SGI Iris, it is very likely that you will find a distribution directly suitable for your machine and operating environment. Also, since all source codes related to the product are freely available, you will have total freedom to modify the product to suit your own needs.

Once you know the machine and operating system, you can download the MySQL package from the official Web site: www.mysql.com. If you don't want to compile the product yourself, the binary distribution is recommended.

Since MySQL is designed to work on TCP/IP networking (or Internet), the package comes with two parts. The server part should be installed on a server and the client MySQL should be run on machines connecting to the server. Client and server can be the same machine running at the same time. To handle MySQL, some information on how to install and configure it on Red Hat LINUX and Microsoft Windows XP systems is provided.

Installation for UNIX/LINUX systems

If you are using the LINUX operating system or other UNIX system with a resource package module (RPM), you may want to download the following MySQL binary distribution:

- MySQL–VERSION.i386.rpm   –   The MySQL server
- MySQL–client-VERSION.i386.rpm   –   The standard MySQL client programs

where VERSION should be replaced by the version number of the installation. For example, MySQL-3.23.44-1.i386.rpm is the MySQL package with version number 3.23.44-1. For more information on the latest versions and platforms, the official site of MySQL www.mysql.com is recommended.

These two files contain the standard minimal installation of the MySQL package. To perform the installation, execute the following command in a LINUX shell window:

```
shell> rpm -i MySQL-VERSION.i386.rpm MySQL-client-VERSION.i386.rpm
```

If you just want to install the MySQL client, you can run the command

```
shell> rpm -i MySQL-client-VERSION.i386.rpm
```

After installing the RPM files, the MySQL server program `mysqld` daemon should be up and running and you should now be able to start using MySQL.

Installation for Microsoft Windows systems

Compared to UNIX/LINUX systems, installation and configuration on Windows are less automatic. For example, since MySQL is designed for networking, you may need to have PWS, IIS, or other Web server software on your Windows 9.x/NT/ 2000 or XP system to make it work. For our system, Windows XP with the Apache server is used. To install MySQL on a system, you can download the following file from the official MySQL site:

mysql-VERSION-win.zip

where the VERSION is the version number. Again, you may download the latest version for your installation. The MySQL used in this chapter is mysql-3.23.43-win.zip. The actual installation process is quite simple. All you have to do is to unzip the package into an empty directory and run the setup.exe program.

By default, the MySQL package is installed in "C:\mysql." If you want to install MySQL elsewhere, it is recommended that you install it in "C:\mysql" first and then move it. If you move MySQL to another location, you may need to set up some configuration files or variables to tell the system where MySQL is located.

Table 17.2 MySQL installation layout

Directory	Contents of directory
bin	Client programs and the `mysqld` server
data	Log files, databases
include	Include (header) files
lib	Libraries
Docs	MySQL documents
examples	Configuration files and test examples
scripts	`mysql_install_db`
share/mysql	Error message files
sql-bench	Benchmarks

After installation, you will have the directories in Table 17.2 set up by MySQL. They are all under the installation directory of your choice. Suppose you have installed MySQL in "C:\mysql." Inside the bin directory, you will find two server and one standard client program:

mysqld	–	MySQL server program mainly for Windows 9.x with PWS
mysqld-nt	–	MySQL server program mainly for Windows NT, 2000, and XP with IIS.
mysql	–	Standard MySQL client program used to access MySQL server

To start the server program `mysqld` on Windows 9.x, you should run it inside a DOS window. That is,

```
C:\mysql\bin> mysqld
```

This will start `mysqld` in the background. You can kill the server program by executing

```
C:\mysql\bin> mysqladmin -u root shutdown
```

If you are using Windows NT/2000/XP, the server program is `mysqld-nt`. Normally you should install this program as a service. Go to the `bin` directory and install the server program once using

```
C:\mysql\bin>mysqld-nt --install
```

After you have installed the server as a service, you can start and stop the service by the two commands below:

```
C:\> NET START mysql
C:\> NET STOP mysql
```

Whether you are using UNIX/LINUX or Microsoft Windows, the important thing is to get the server program running. Once a server program is running somewhere on a remote site, you can use the standard MySQL client program `mysql` to gain access to the server and start your database application.

For example, if you have a MySQL server running in your local machine, you can start MySQL by

```
C:\> mysql
```

This program connects you to the local server so that you can start your MySQL database application. If MySQL is installed on a remote server called www.pwt-ex.com and you have a user name and a password to access its databases, you can make the connection by

```
C:\>mysql -h www.pwt-ex.com -u johnsmith -p
Enter Password: ********
```

where www.pwt-ex.com is the address of the site. The directive `-p` instructs MySQL to display the "Enter Password" prompt for you to enter your password.

If you are using UNIX/LINUX systems, the prompt `C:\>` should be replaced by your shell prompt `shell>` from a shell window. From now on, we generally use the `shell>` prompt to represent a DOS window or a shell window in the UNIX/LINUX environment.

MySQL is a database system designed for TCP/IP networking (or Internet). The client program `mysql` is a console application with browsing functionalities providing an effective tool to control your databases. Of course, MySQL databases can also be accessed and controlled by SQL via browsers. This is the main topic of this chapter.

If the connection is successful, you will see some introductory information followed by a

```
mysql>
```

prompt. When you see this prompt, your MySQL is ready for action. Typing `help` will show the commands available from the `mysql` monitor. A screen shot of MySQL running on Windows XP is displayed in Fig. 17.1.

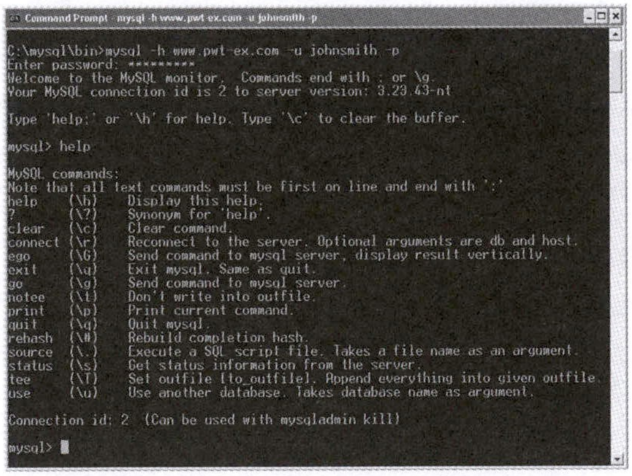

Figure 17.1 MySQL welcome message

A simple `quit` command from the client terminates the connection. A simple way to see whether you have connected to the server is to enter a query string at the `mysql>` prompt. For example, you can use the following commands to create a new database called personnel and view any database in MySQL:

```
Example: ex17-01.sql - Creating Database On MySQL

1:   mysql>CREATE DATABASE personnel;
2:   mysql>SHOW DATABASES;
```

You may issue the command SHOW database; (line 2) to see all the MySQL databases available to you. To delete a database in MySQL, you can use the DROP command, e.g., DROP DATABASE personnel. A screen shot of example ex17-01.sql in action is shown in Fig. 17.2.

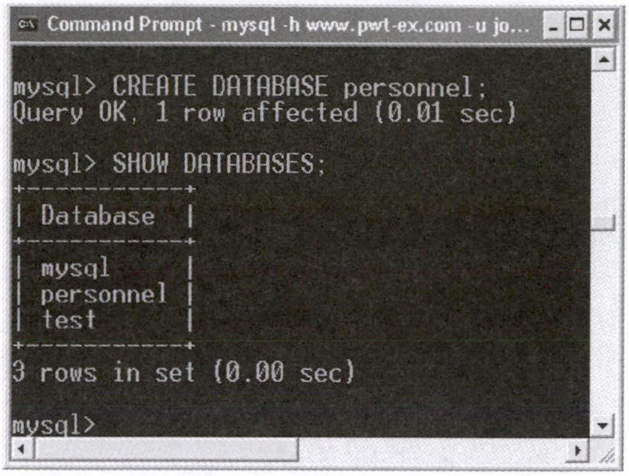

Some readers may find that the client/server dialog of MySQL is similar to Oracle's. You can use this mysql program to do just about everything you want with your databases. Indeed this client program and the client/server dialog have been the center of all database applications for many years. In this chapter, we will transform this client and client/server dialog into Web applications using Web pages and browsers. More precisely, we will show you how to program MySQL on the Web using different Web technologies.

Figure 17.2 Show database

In addition to database functionalities, MySQL also offers security. All user accounts and passwords are handled entirely by MySQL to a high standard of protection. This feature, in many cases, can be used to compensate some of the security black holes of Windows systems.

17.2.2 Setting up user accounts, passwords, and security

MySQL is a database package with networking (or Internet) in mind. Without security anyone with the client program mysql can gain access to your databases. Also, just like all other database systems, MySQL at some point may store important information about you, your colleagues, and/or your company business that you don't want to share with others. Therefore, it is recommended that security measures be imposed as soon as MySQL is up and running. At a minimum level, every user should have a user account and be protected by a password.

When MySQL is installed on a system, it will create a root account and maybe some anonymous (no user name) accounts automatically. All user accounts, passwords, and security are stored in a database called mysql (see Fig. 17.2). The root account has the absolute power to change everything inside the database system. Therefore, your first tasks would be to:

- Set up a password for the root account.
- Delete all anonymous accounts (if any).

To set up a password to the root, the following commands can be used from the mysql prompt:

```
Example: ex17-02.sql - Adding Password To Root Account

1:   shell> mysql -u root mysql
2:   mysql> USE mysql
3:   mysql> UPDATE user SET Password=PASSWORD('my_password')
4:      -> WHERE user='root';
5:   mysql> FLUSH PRIVILEGES;
```

The first line connects to the MySQL server as the root. If the connection is successful, the mysql> prompt appears. The second line is to use the mysql database as the current database. Line 3 is an SQL statement to update the user table and set up a password "my_password" to the root account. The password is encrypted by the PASSWORD() function. Note that you can split a long command into two lines such as lines 3–4. By executing the FLUSH PRIVILEGES; statement the change has immediate effect.

To remove any empty account, you can use the DELETE command:

Example: ex17-03.sql - Deleting Anonymous Accounts

```
1:  mysql> DELETE FROM user WHERE User= "";
2:  mysql> FLUSH PRIVILEGES;
```

Once you have done this, your MySQL is protected by the password. The following local and remote access will be denied:

```
shell> mysql
shell> mysql -u root mysql
shell> mysql -h www.pwt-ex.com
```

If you have a machine with the client program mysql, you can access the remote server (www.pwtex.com) using the new password as

```
Shell> mysql -h www.pwt-ex.com -u root -p
Enter Password: ****
```

Now you have the power to add new users to MySQL. For example, to add a new user, you can use

Example: ex17-04.sql - Creating New Account With Default Privileges

```
1:  mysql> INSERT INTO user (Host,User,Password)
2:      -> VALUES ('%','johnsmith',PASSWORD('john'));
3:  mysql> INSERT INTO user (Host,User,Password)
4:      -> VALUES ('localhost','johnsmith',PASSWORD('john'));
```

This statement will add two records to the user table from the database mysql. This database controls all administrations of MySQL. The first record is

```
Host = '%'
User = 'johnsmith'
Password=PASSWORD('john')
```

This will set up a new account for johnsmith with default privileges. By using Host='%', he can connect to the server from anywhere using the user name johnsmith and password john. The second statement (lines 3–4) is used to set up the same privileges on the server machine (localhost) for johnsmith so that he can use the server machine to connect. To set up an account for johnsmith with all privileges, you can use

Example: ex17-05.sql - Creating New Account With All Privileges

```
1:  mysql>DELETE FROM user WHERE user='johnsmith';
2:  mysql> INSERT INTO user VALUES ('%','johnsmith',PASSWORD('johnsmith'),
3:      ->'Y','Y','Y','Y','Y','Y','Y','Y','Y','Y','Y','Y','Y','Y');
```

The statement in line 1 is to delete any existing user johnsmith before new settings can be made. The 14 Ys set all privileges as true. MySQL also allows you to set privileges on individual databases. For example, you can use the GRANT command to grant certain SQL keywords or statements to johnsmith.

Example: ex17-06.sql - Granting Privileges To Existing Account

```
1:  mysql> GRANT SELECT,INSERT,UPDATE,DELETE,DROP,LOAD DATA LOCAL INFILE
2:      -> ON personnel.* TO johnsmith@'%' IDENTIFIED BY 'johnsmith'
```

This statement only allows user johnsmith to use SELECT, INSERT, UPDATE, DELETE, CREATE, DROP and LOAD DATA commands on database personnel when he connects from a remote client. Now, let's create some databases and tables on MySQL for our programming purposes.

17.2.3 Creating tables for databases

Tables are important for all SQL databases (or relational databases); a database without a table (empty database) is not very useful. In this section, a simple method is introduced to create a table in MySQL. This table is called people and will use the information given in Table 17.1. In order to use memory effectively, the data type of each field (or column) of the table people is defined as:

- id   –   Positive integer
- name   –   Character string (max. 30 characters)
- birth   –   Date format, yyyy-mm-dd
- sex   –   Character (one character)
- location   –   Character string (max. 30 characters)
- salary   –   Integer

Also, the id field should be the primary key for MySQL to identify each record. Therefore id cannot be null and should be incremented by 1 automatically. In terms of SQL statements, this table can be created by the CREATE statement below:

```
Example: ex17-07.sql - Creating A Table Called people

 1: mysql> CREATE TABLE people (
 2:    ->    id INTEGER UNSIGNED NOT NULL AUTO_INCREMENT,
 3:    ->    name VARCHAR(30),
 4:    ->    birth DATE,
 5:    ->    sex CHAR(1),
 6:    ->    location VARCHAR(30),
 7:    ->    salary INTEGER,
 8:    ->    PRIMARY KEY (id)
 9:    -> );
10: Query OK, 0 rows affected (0.00 sec)
11:
12: mysql>
13: mysql> DESCRIBE people;
14: +----------+------------------+------+-----+---------+----------------+
15: | Field    | Type             | Null | Key | Default | Extra          |
16: +----------+------------------+------+-----+---------+----------------+
17: | id       | int(10) unsigned |      | PRI | NULL    | auto_increment |
18: | name     | varchar(30)      | YES  |     | NULL    |                |
19: | birth    | date             | YES  |     | NULL    |                |
20: | sex      | char(1)          | YES  |     | NULL    |                |
21: | location | varchar(30)      | YES  |     | NULL    |                |
22: | salary   | int(11)          | YES  |     | NULL    |                |
23: +----------+------------------+------+-----+---------+----------------+
24: 6 rows in set (0.01 sec)
```

This example shows the client–server dialog of a typical MySQL session. Lines 1–9 are the CREATE statement input by you to create the table people. Note that you may need to issue the SQL command "USE personnel" to get into the database first. Line 10 is the message returned by MySQL. To see the existence and internal data type of people, DESCRIBE people; can be used.

Before you can input data into this table, you need to construct the data first. One simple way to construct table data in MySQL is to use a text file. You can use your favorite text editor to type the data field. The following is a simple example:

```
Listing: 17-01.txt - Text Data File (people.dat)

     NULL    Michael  1950-12-18    M   London    30000
     NULL    Mary     1980-06-22    F   Paris     23000
     ...     ...      ...           ... ...       ...
     NULL    Anne              1976-11-02   F    London 28000
```

The format of the text file is that each record should occupy one line. Fields are separated by a tab and the id field is NULL so that MySQL can insert the index automatically. When the data are saved into a text file called people, you can use the statement LOAD DATA INFILE to read them into the table. Consider the following example:

```
Example: ex17-08.sql - Loading A File Into Database Table

 1: mysql>  LOAD DATA INFILE 'people.dat'
 2:     ->    INTO TABLE people
 3:     ->    LINES TERMINATED BY '\n';
 4: Query OK, 10 rows affected (0.00 sec)
 5: Records: 10  Deleted: 0  Skipped: 0  Warnings: 10
 6:
 7: mysql> SELECT * FROM people;
 8: +----+---------+------------+------+----------+--------+
 9: | id | name    | birth      | sex  | location | salary |
10: +----+---------+------------+------+----------+--------+
11: | 1  | Michael | 1950-12-18 | M    | London   | 30000  |
12: | 2  | Mary    | 1980-06-22 | F    | Paris    | 23000  |
13: | 3  | Peter   | 1975-10-11 | M    | New York | 28000  |
14: | 4  | Tom     | 1959-02-24 | M    | Paris    | 28000  |
15: | 5  | Richard | 1969-03-08 | M    | New York | 23000  |
16: | 6  | Ben     | 1979-09-14 | M    | London   | 31000  |
17: | 7  | Sue     | 1969-01-19 | F    | Paris    | 30000  |
18: | 8  | Rose    | 1976-08-18 | F    | Tokyo    | 22000  |
19: | 9  | Jenny   | 1972-10-27 | F    | New York | 27000  |
20: | 10 | Anne    | 1976-11-02 | F    | London   | 28000  |
21: +----+---------+------------+------+----------+--------+
22: 10 rows in set (0.01 sec)
```

The LOAD DATA INFILE in line 1 can load any text file into a table. Since records in the text file are separated by a new line "\n," you need an additional instruction, LINES TERMINATED BY '\n', to read the file properly. Again, this example shows the client–server interaction in MySQL.

The MySQL client program mysql basically can do everything related to your databases. However, mysql is a console (text mode) program and not all machines have it. Can we access MySQL databases using a Web browser over the Internet?

There are a number of ways to put an SQL database onto the Internet and accessible by a Web browser. One popular way is to use ODBC described below.

17.3 Database programming with ODBC

17.3.1 The structure of ODBC

Open Database Connectivity (ODBC) is a product from Microsoft to provide a unified interface for different database types. ODBC has existed since the early days of Windows and become the *de facto* standard for database applications across different vendors and platforms. The unique feature of ODBC is that none of its functions are vendor specific. Once you have registered your database with ODBC, you can access your remote data with browsers. Whether you have an Access, dBase, FoxPro, Oracle, or MySQL database, you can control it with the same type of programming and coding.

The first step to use ODBC is to register your databases with the ODBC administrator. This administrator is an interface between your Web applications and the actual databases. Your Web pages can open a connection to the desired database via the DSN of ODBC and perform your SQL query.

The ODBC interface works by providing different drivers for different types of database. Depending on your system, some popular ODBC drivers for Windows systems are: dBase, Access, Excel, FoxPro, and Oracle. ODBC drivers are usually provided by vendors and configured automatically when you install the corresponding database products. For example, if you install Microsoft Office, you will install the ODBC drivers for Access and Excel at the same time. A diagram describing ODBC in action is shown in Fig. 17.3.

The structure of ODBC

```
┌──────────┐   ┌───┐   ┌───┐   MySQL
│ Web pages│   │ B │   │ O │   ────────→  ▭
│    or    │   │ r │   │ D │   ←────────
│applications│ │ o │   │ B │
└──────────┘   │ w │   │ C │   MS Access
     •         │ s │   │   │   ────────→  ▭
     •         │ e │   │   │   ←────────
     •         │ r │   │   │
┌──────────┐   │ s │   │   │   Oracle
│ Web pages│   │   │   │   │   ────────→  ▭
│    or    │   │   │   │   │   ←────────
│applications│ │   │   │   │
└──────────┘   └───┘   └───┘   Remote SQL
                                databases
```

Figure 17.3 ODBC database, browsers, and applications

ODBC drivers are controlled by the ODBC driver manager and administrated by the ODBC administrator. For Windows systems, the driver manager is a dynamic link library (DLL) provided by Microsoft to determine which driver to load based on the DSN. For other systems such as UNIX/LINUX, ODBC managers are also available.

To use MySQL on the Web, you need to register MySQL databases with ODBC first.

17.3.2 Registering MySQL databases on the Web with ODBC

The driver to handle MySQL databases is called MyODBC and available from the official site of MySQL. Basically, there are two versions of MyODBC: one is for Windows and the other is for UNIX/LINUX operating systems.

For example, to install MyODBC on Windows NT/2000/XP, you can use the file

myodbc-2.50.39-nt.zip

Unzip the file into an empty directory and run the set-up program setup.exe. You will see a `Setup` dialog window as in Fig. 17.4. If you press the Continue button, the `Install Drivers` dialog box will appear with MySQL driver (see Fig. 17.5). Highlight this driver and click the OK button. Once MyODBC is installed, you are ready to register your remote MySQL databases with ODBC.

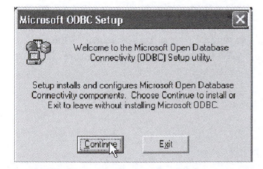

Figure 17.4 MyODBC installation

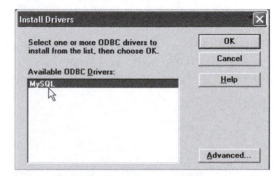

Figure 17.5 MySQL driver for ODBC

Assume that you have MySQL database personnel located on a server called www.pwt-ex.com. The procedure to register this database on a client machine running Windows XP is as follows:

- Activate the Start | Control Panel and click on "Administrative Tools" from XP (Fig. 17.6).

- Click the "Data Source (ODBC)" icon to open the "ODBC Data Source Administrator" window (see Fig. 17.7).

Figure 17.6 MyODBC installation

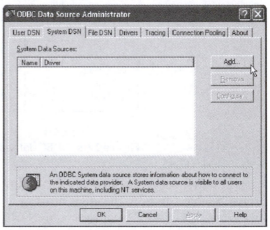

Figure 17.7 System DSN

- Click on the "System DSN" Menu and press the Add button.

- The "Create New Data Source" window is shown. Highlight the "MySQL" option and click the Finish button (Fig. 17.8).

- The "MySQL Driver" default configuration screen appears (Fig. 17.9). For a basic configuration with `hostname`, `username` and `password`, fill in the following fields and click the "OK" button (Fig. 17.09):

```
Windows DSN name:            personnel
MySQL host(name or IP):      www.pwt-ex.com
MySql database name:         personnel
User:                        johnsmith
Password:                    ********
```

The values in these fields will be used as the defaults when you attempt to make a connection. Registering a database in system DSN would allow your colleagues to use it. If you want some privacy, you can register your database in user DSN.

You now have a remote MySQL database called personnel registered in your local machine. One way to test your MyODBC driver and MySQL system is to develop a Web page to access the remote database with browsers.

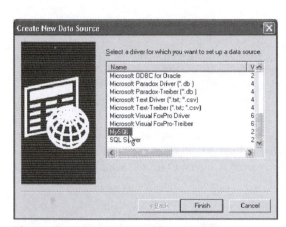

Figure 17.8 Create a new data source

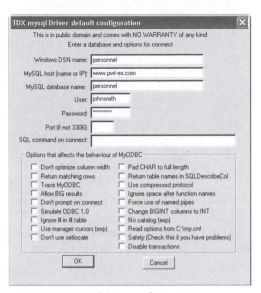

Figure 17.9 MySQL driver configuration

17.3.3 A page to access ODBC databases

At the end of Chapter 15, we used Perl script to develop a Web page to get information from a Microsoft Access database. The example ex15-15.pl uses the Win32::ODBC Perl module to gain access to the remote database registered on your local machine. With some simple modifications, this page can be used to establish a more general page to access database on the Web. In order to accept multiple line input for SQL statements, the first modification is to use `textarea` for user input. The XHTML coding for this page is listed below:

```
Example: ex17-09.htm - A Page To Access ODBC Databases

 1: <?xml version="1.0" encoding="iso-8859-1"?>
 2: <!DOCTYPE html PUBLIC "-//W3C//DTD XHTML 1.0 Transitional//EN"
 3:    "http://www.w3.org/TR/xhtml1/DTD/xhtml1-transitional.dtd">
 4: <html xmlns="http://www.w3.org/1999/xhtml" xml:lang="en" lang="en">
 5: <head><title> Access ODBC Databases - ex17-09.htm</title></head>
 6: <style>
 7:   .txt{font-family:arial;font-size:14pt;color:#000088;font-weight:bold}
 8:   .butSt{background-color:#aaffaa;font-family:arial;font-weight:bold;
 9:      font-size:14pt;color:#008800;width:520px;height:30px}
10:   .textareaSt{background-color:#aaffaa;font-family:arial;font-weight:bold;
11:      font-size:14pt;color:#008800;width:580px;height:200px}
12: </style>
13:
14: <body style="font-size:18pt;background:#bbbbff;
15:    text-align:center" class="txt">
16:  Accessing MySQL Database(s) via ODBC<br />with Perl Script<br />
17:
18:  <img src="line1.gif" width="550" height="6" />
19:  <table class="txt" align="center" cellspacing="10" width="550" >
20:   <tr><td colspan="2">Remote Database Information:</td></tr>
21:   <tr valign="top"><td><img src="bullet1.gif" vspace ="3" /></td>
22:      <td>The remote database type is MySQL</td></tr>
23:   <tr><td valign="top"><img src="bullet1.gif" vspace ="3" /></td>
24:      <td>The name of the database is called personnel</td></tr>
25:   <tr><td valign="top"><img src="bullet1.gif" vspace ="3" /></td>
```

```
26:      <td>The database contains a table called people<br /></td></tr>
27:  </table>
28:  <img src="line1.gif" width="550" height="6" /><br />
29:
30:  <form action = "ex17-09.pl" method="post">
31:     Enter Your SQL Query String<br />
32:   <textarea rows="5" cols="30" name = "querySt" class="textareaSt">
33:      SELECT * FROM people;</textarea><br /><br />
34:   <input type = "submit" value = "Send Query" class="butSt"
35:       style="width:180px;background:#bbbbbb">
36:  </form>
37:  </body>
38:  </html>
```

This is a simple page to get the SQL query string such as SELECT * FROM people;. After the introductory text, the main part of this page is the XHTML form declared in lines 30–36. The textarea element inside the form (lines 32–33) generates a text box for the user to enter an SQL query. Once the Send Query button is pressed, the following form action (line 30)

```
<form action="ex17-09.pl" method="post">
```

will activate the CGI program ex17-09.pl in the same directory as the Web page ex17-09.htm. The purpose of this Perl program is to process the SQL query in the text area and return results to the user. A screen shot of this page is shown in Fig. 17.10.

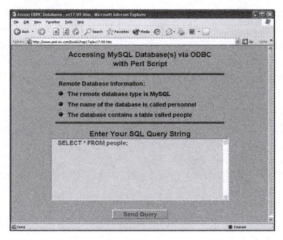

Figure 17.10 ex17-09.htm

The CGI program ex17-09.pl is a Perl implementation to access databases via ODBC. As long as you have a remote database somewhere on the Internet and registered on your local machine with ODBC, you can use this example to gain access to it. The first part of the program is listed as follows:

```
Example: ex17-09.pl - ODBC Database With Perl (Part One)

1: #! /usr/bin/perl
2:
3: use Win32::ODBC;
4: use CGI qw (:standard);
5: print "Content-type:text/html\n\n";
6:
7: my $querySt = param(querySt);
8: $querySt =~ s/\n/ /g;
```

```
 9: ($querySt,$tmp1) = split(/;/,$querySt);
10: $querySt = $querySt . ";";
11:
12: $dsnName = "personnel";
13:
14: if (!($odbcData = new Win32::ODBC($dsnName)))
15: {
16:    print "ODBC Connection .. Error..\n";
17:    exit();
18: }
19:
20: if ($odbcData->Sql($querySt))
21: {
22:    print "Error.. SQL failed..\n";
23:    $odbcData->Close();
24:    exit();
25: }
```

This is an ODBC application and therefore you need to include the Win32::ODBC module in the program (line 3) to make it work. The SQL query string is captured by the usual Perl function `param()` and stored in the variable `$querySt`.

Since the query string `$querySt` represents the user input from `textarea`, it may contain non-printable characters to prevent the execution of the SQL query. For example, if you spread the SQL statement over multiple lines, each line will have a `newline` character attached at the end. In this case, the SQL query may stop after the first line. To prevent this situation and accept multiple line input, we use the following three simple treatments (see lines 8–10):

```
$querySt =~ s/\n/ /g;
($querySt,$tmp1) = split(/;/,$querySt);
$querySt = $querySt . ";";
```

The first line is to replace all `newline` characters by a space so that the multiple line SQL query can be executed. Since all SQL statements are terminated by a semi-colon, the second line is used to extract the query string up to the first appearance of a semi-colon. The SQL statement is stored in `$querySt` and the remaining part in `$tmp1`. All characters after the first semi-colon will be ignored. After the second statement, the query string will have no semi-colon. The third statement is to add the semi-colon at the end of the query string. This will guarantee that the program will still work if you forget to put a semi-colon at the end of your query.

This program is hardwiring an ODBC connection to a MySQL database called personnel. If you want to use other databases or have more than one database, you can modify the data source name `$dsnName` in line 12 to suit your needs.

The command below (line 14) is to make the connection between your browser and the database:

```
if (!($odbcData = new Win32::ODBC($dsnName)))
```

If you have a successful connection, the variable `$odbcData` object can be used to execute the SQL query by the statement (see line 20)

```
if ($odbcData->Sql($querySt))
```

If this SQL query is successful, the variable `$odbcData` will contain the query data. Next, you need to develop a Web page to display the query result in XHTML format. Consider the second half of the program:

```
Listing: Continuation Of Perl Script ex17-09.pl (Part Two)

26:
27: print << "mypage";
28:  <?xml version="1.0" encoding="iso-8859-1"?>
29:  <!DOCTYPE html PUBLIC "-//W3C//DTD XHTML 1.0 Transitional//EN"
30:      "http://www.w3.org/TR/xhtml1/DTD/xhtml1-transitional.dtd">
```

```
31:    <html xmlns="http://www.w3.org/1999/xhtml" xml:lang="en" lang="en">
32:    <head><title>Example ex17-09.pl</title></head>
33:    <style>
34:      .bodySt {font-family:arial;font-weight:bold;background:#000088;
35:          font-size:18pt;color:#ffff00;text-align:center}
36:      .txtSt{font-family:arial;font-weight:bold;font-size:13pt;color:#ffff00}
37:    </style>
38:    <body class="bodySt" >
39:    Based On Your SQL Query String:<br />
40:
41:    <div style="font-size:14pt" align="center">
42:     <table><tr><td class="txtSt" style="color:#ffffff;width:500px;
43:            text-align:center;font-size:14pt"><br />
44:        $queryySt </br><br /></td></tr>
45:    </table>
46:      Query O.K. And The Returned Results Are As Follows:<br />
47:    </div>
48:   <img src="line1.gif" width="600" height="6" alt="pic" />
49:      <br /><br />
50:      <table cellspacing="5" class="txtSt" align="center" width="570">
51:   mypage
52:
53: $count = 0;
54: while($odbcData->FetchRow())
55: {
56:     %odbcData = $odbcData->DataHash();
57:      @keys = keys(%odbcData);
58:
59:    if ($count ==0)
60:    {
61:      print "<tr>";
62:      for ($ii = 0; $ii < @keys; $ii++)
63:      {
64:        print "<td style=\"color:#00ff00;font-size:16pt\">$keys[$ii]</td>";
65:      }
66:      print "</tr>";
67:    }
68:
69:    print "<tr>";
70:    for ($ii = 0; $ii < @keys; $ii++)
71:    {
72:      print "<td>$odbcData{$keys[$ii]}</td>";
73:    }
74:    print "</tr>";
75:     $count++;
76: }
77: $odbcData->Close();
78:
79: print << "endpage";
80:    </table>
81:   <img src="line1.gif" width="600" height="6" alt="pic" />
82:   <br /><br />Total Entries = $count<br /><br />
83: </body>
84: </html>
85: endpage
```

This part is a Web page returned by the Perl program when the SQL query is successful. In this case, the variable $odbcData contains the SQL query results. In order to display the contents in $odbcData effectively, an XHTML table is used. The while-loop in lines 54–76 fetches the database and processes the records one by one. A hash function in lines 56–57 is used to convert each row (or record) of the database to members of a hash element called @keys. Inside @keys, the array $keys[] stores the field names of the database table and $odbcData($keys[]) stores the values of the associated field. The first member of @keys looks like this:

```
$keys[0] = location      $odbcData($keys[0]) = London
$keys[1] = salary        $odbcData($keys[1]) = 30000
   ...        ...          ...        ...
$keys[5] = name          $odbcData($keys[5]) = Michael
```

These are the field name/value pairs. Therefore the first for-loop in lines 62–65 displays the field names $keys[n]. This for-loop only needs to be executed once since we only want to display the names once. The second for-loop in lines 70–73 outputs the elements $odbcData($keys[n]). For each n, the variable $odbcData($keys[n]) stores the field data of the table. When we run through all the rows, the entire SQL query data are returned to the browser. At this point, a Close statement in line 77 is needed to close the ODBC connection.

If you enter the SQL query SELECT * FROM people; as shown in Fig. 17.10, all records of the table people are displayed on the browser screen. A screen shot is shown in Fig. 17.11.

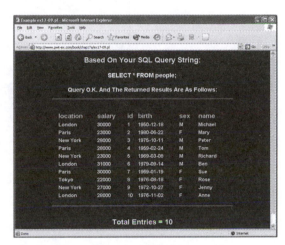

Figure 17.11 SQL query result

17.3.4 A page to access multiple database types

Suppose you are running a successful business with four offices located in New York, London, Paris, and Tokyo. The sales records for each office are stored in databases as in Table 17.3.

Table 17.3 Multiple database types

Location	Database type	Database name	Table name
New York	MySQL	sale_usa	sales
London	MySQL	sale_uk	sales
Paris	MS Access	sale_fr	sales
Tokyo	MS Access	sale_jp	sales

The first thing in developing a Web page to access all these databases is to register them on your local machine with ODBC. After registration, a screen shot of the "Data Source Administrator" window on a Windows XP machine will appear as in Fig. 17.12.

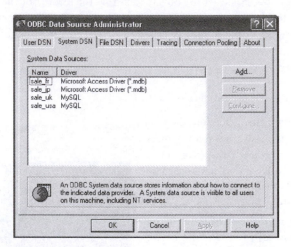

Figure 17.12 "Data Source Administrator" window

Note that the database type and name from Table 17.3 are shown in the name and driver fields inside the ODBC administrator.

One of the efficient ways to implement this example is to use a select box. With a select box, you can change the database and perform an SQL query easily. Consider the following page:

Example: ex17-10.htm - Access Multiple Database Types With ODBC

```
 1:   <?xml version="1.0" encoding="iso-8859-1"?>
 2:   <!DOCTYPE html PUBLIC "-//W3C//DTD XHTML 1.0 Transitional//EN"
 3:      "http://www.w3.org/TR/xhtml1/DTD/xhtml1-transitional.dtd">
 4:   <html xmlns="http://www.w3.org/1999/xhtml" xml:lang="en" lang="en">
 5:   <head><title> Access Multiple Database - ex17-10.htm</title></head>
 6:   <style>
 7:   .txt{font-family:arial;font-size:16pt;color:#000088;font-weight:bold}
 8:   .butSt{background-color:#aaffaa;font-family:arial;font-weight:bold;
 9:      font-size:14pt;color:#008800;width:520px;height:30px}
10:   .textareaSt{background-color:#aaffaa;font-family:arial;font-weight:bold;
11:      font-size:14pt;color:#008800;width:580px;height:150px}
12:   </style>
13:   <body style="font-size:18pt;background:#bbbbff;
14:      text-align:center" class="txt">
15:    Multiple Database Types with ODBC<br /><br />
16:    <img src="line1.gif" width="550" height="6" /><br />
17:
18:   <form action = "ex17-10.pl" method="post">
19:    <div class="txt" style="width:550px;height:150px" >
20:      Remote Databases Information:<br /><br />
21:      <select class="butSt" style="width:440px" name="database" >
22:      <option value="sale_usa">Sales In
23:         New York: Table: sales (MySQL)</option>
24:      <option value="sale_uk">Sales In
25:         London: Table: sales (MySQL)</option>
26:      <option value="sale_fr">Sales In
```

```
27:              Paris: Table: sales (MS Access)</option>
28:          <option value="sale_jp">Sales In
29:             Tokyo: Table: sales (MS Access)</option>
30:        </select>
31:      </div><br />
32:      <img src="line1.gif" width="550" height="6" /><br />
33:         Enter Your SQL Query String<br />
34:      <textarea rows="8" cols="30" name = "querySt" class="textareaSt">
35:         SELECT * FROM sales;</textarea><br /><br />
36:      <input type = "submit" value = "Send Query" class="butSt"
37:         style="width:180px;background:#bbbbbb">
38:      </form>
39:   </body>
40: </html>
```

This is a form application and the main part of this example is the select box defined in lines 21–30. Consider the first option value of the select box:

```
<option value="sale_usa">Sales In New York: Table: sales (MySQL)</option>
```

The message in the middle tells us that the database is a MySQL type representing company sales in New York. The table inside the database is called sales. Once this option is picked and submitted to the Perl script ex17-10.pl, the string sale_usa is returned as the value of the select box. This sale_usa is one of the DSNs registered on ODBC so that it can be used to access the corresponding database. A screen shot of this example is shown in Fig. 17.13.

Once you have the information on the selected database, the script program ex17-10.pl becomes very similar to ex17-09.pl. Basically, all you have to do is to change the DSN (i.e., $dsnName) to the value returned by the select box. That means you only need to change lines 1–25 of ex17-09.pl and call it ex17-10.pl. The first 25 lines of ex17-10.pl are listed below:

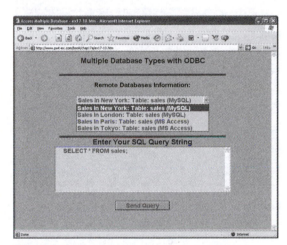

Figure 17.13 Accessing multiple databases

```
Example: ex17-10.pl – The Perl Script For ex17-10.htm

 1: #!o:/perl/bin/perl
 2:
 3: use Win32::ODBC;
 4: use CGI qw (:standard);
 5: print "Content-type:text/html\n\n";
 6:
 7: my $dataB = param("database");
 8: my $querySt = param(querySt);
 9: $querySt =~ s/\n/ /g;
10: ($querySt,$tmp1) = split(/;/,$querySt);
11: $querySt = $querySt . ";";
12:
13: $dsnName = $dataB;
14: if (!($odbcData = new Win32::ODBC($dsnName)))
15: {
16:    print "ODBC Connection .. Error..\n";
17:    exit();
18: }
```

```
19:
20: if ($odbcData->Sql($querySt))
21: {
22:     print "Error.. SQL failed..\n";
23:     $odbcData->Close();
24:     exit();
25: }
```

Every time the Send Query button is pressed, the value of the select box is passed to the variable $dataB defined in line 7. This variable is then assigned to the DSN variable $dsnName in line 13. Once this $dsnName is fixed, we can consider that the entire application involves only one database. All the ODBC connections, SQL processing, and displays are the same as in ex17-09.pl. Thus the remaining program codes of this example are the same as in ex17-09.pl. Some screen shots of this example in action are shown in Figs 17.14 and 17.15.

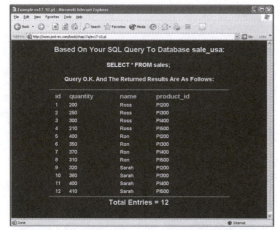

Figure 17.14 Getting data from a MySQL database

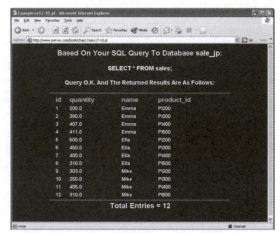

Figure 17.15 Getting data from an MS Access database

From the viewpoint of ODBC, databases from MySQL and Access are the same.

ODBC does provide a good tool to access different databases on the Web. However, it also relies heavily on the Windows coding. From line 3 of ex17-09.pl and ex17-10.pl, you can see that it includes the module

```
use Win32::ODBC;
```

in the Perl processor; Win32::ODBC only works on Win32 systems. As a Web programmer, you may be asked to write a page or a program to access some databases in an environment other than Windows or without ODBC. Can we access databases without ODBC?

For a truly platform-independent database interface, the so-called Database Interface is a popular candidate on the Web.

17.4 Database programming with Database Interface (DBI)

17.4.1 What is DBI?

Compared to ODBC, DBI is a relatively new technology to handle platform-independent database applications. To understand DBI, let's quote a statement from its founder:

> *DBI is a database access Application Programming Interface (API) for the Perl Language. The DBI API Specification defines a set of functions, variables and conventions that provide a consistent database interface independent of the actual database being used.*

> *Tim Bunce*, www.perl.com

From functional and structural points of view, DBI is similar to ODBC. It is also a database interface allowing users to access multiple database types transparently. Whether you are using Oracle, Informix, Sybase, MySQL, or whatever, you don't need to know the underlying vendor-specific codes. The API defined by DBI will work on all database types provided the corresponding DBI driver modules are included in your Perl program.

Similar to the Perl package and MySQL database, DBI is free with open source code. In many cases it is included in the distribution with Perl so that installation and configuration are automatic. At the time of writing, the driver modules (DBD) in Table 17.4 are available and supported by DBI.

Table 17.4 DBI driver modules

DBD::ADO	DBD::Informix	DBD::PrimeBase
DBD::ASAny	DBD::Ingres	DBD::RAM
DBD::Adabas	DBD::InterBase	DBD::SearchServer
DBD::Altera	DBD::LDAP	DBD::Solid
DBD::CSV	DBD::MySQL	DBD::Sprite
DBD::DB2	DBD::ODBC	DBD::Sybase
DBD::Empress	DBD::Oracle	DBD::Unify
DBD::Illustra	DBD::Pg	DBD::XBase

If you don't have DBI installed on your system or you need some of the driver modules, you can download them from Perl's official site: www.perl.com.

From this table, you can see that DBI supports a large number of database types including MySQL and ODBC. This means that you can also access your Microsoft Access and SQL server databases using the DBD::ODBC module. The important feature of DBI is that whether you are using Microsoft or UNIX/LINUX systems, the program codes are the same.

Also, the action of DBI is more straightforward and there is no need for any additional layer or administrator to handle database registrations.

17.4.2 The structure of DBI

DBI is designed to save you time and from programming the details of the database vendor libraries. It has a very simple interface to get the SQL queries you want and to handle the results returned by the database. The main function of DBI is to locate and load the corresponding DBI drivers or DBD (database driver) modules. The DBD modules have vendor libraries designed to talk to the real databases. You can say that DBI works simply because of DBD modules. In effect, there is one DBD module for every different database.

In a Web page or application, when you make a query through the DBI, it sends the query to the appropriate DBD module. When it gets the results back, it passes them to DBI so that you can process them. Figure 17.16 shows how DBI works.

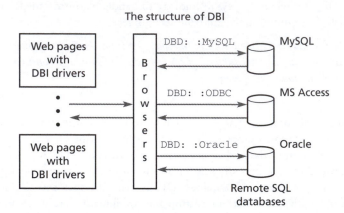

The structure of DBI

Figure 17.16 Database Interface (DBI) driver in action

Since there is no additional layer between your Web page and the actual database, you don't need to perform any database registration before you can use them. All you need is to load and activate the associated DBD module. Because of that, DBI works for almost any operating system and is a truly platform-independent technology for handling databases on the Web.

17.4.3 Using DBI and `DBD::MySQL`

To use DBI with a particular database, you need to install the DBI and the associated driver module (DBD) into the Perl processor. For example, if you are using Active Perl (a Perl package) on a Windows system, you can use the following PPM interactive shell to install DBI and `DBD::mysql`:

```
C:/Perl/bin/> ppm
PPM> install DBI
PPM> install DBD::mysql
```

This will fetch the modules via the HTTP (Internet) and install them. For this procedure to work, you will need to have a connection to the Internet. If the above procedure doesn't work, you may need to upgrade to the latest version of Active Perl.

If you are using UNIX/LINUX such as Red Hat LINUX, the installation (version 7.1 or later) comes with MySQL and `DBD::mysql`. You need to ensure that the following RPMs are installed:

```
shell> mysql
mysql> perl-DBI
mysql> perl-DBD::MySQL
```

If you want to install DBI at source code level, information on installation and configuration can be found on the official site www.Perl.com/CPAN.

Basically, a Web interface for SQL databases can be developed by the following procedures:

- Get the user SQL query string.
- Connect to the remote database server.
- Execute the SQL query string.
- Interpret the returned results.

To get the user SQL query string is simple. All you have to do is to write a Web page similar to example ex17-08.htm. In order to save some coding time, you can take example ex17-09.htm and replace line 16 by

```
Accessing MySQL Database(s) via DBI<br />and DBS::MySQL<br /><br />
```

This line changes the information to indicate that DBI and the DBD::MySQL module are used. Another line you need to change is line 30:

```
<form action = "ex17-11.pl" method="post">
```

This form element will activate another Perl program, i.e., ex17-11.pl, to perform the SQL processing. We call this new page ex17-11.htm.

To connect to the remote database server and execute the SQL statement, we need the first part of the program ex17-11.pl listed below:

```
Example: ex17-11.pl - The Perl Script For ex17-11.htm (Part One)

 1: #! /usr/bin/perl
 2:
 3: use DBI;
 4: use CGI qw (:standard);
 5: print "Content-type:text/html\n\n";
 6:
 7: my $querySt = param(querySt);
 8:
 9: if(!($dbh = DBI->connect('dbi:mysql:personnel:www.pwt-ex.com',
10:             'johnsmith', 'johnsmith')))
11: {
12:   print "Connection Error ..";
13:   exit();
14: }
15:
16: if (!($sth = $dbh->prepare($querySt)))
17: {
18:   print "SQL Statement Preparation Error ..";
19:   exit();
20: }
21:
22: if (!($sth->execute()))
23: {
24:   print "SQL Statement Error ..";
25:   exit();
26: }
```

In order to use DBI, the statement "use DBI;" is used in line 3. Once this DBI module is included in the Perl program, the function DBI->connect() can be used to connect to the database server. The calling format for this function is (see lines 9–10)

```
DBI->connect('dbi:mysql:personnel:www.pwt-ex.com','johnsmith','johnsmith')
```

This function uses the DBI driver dbi:mysql to connect to the remote site www.pwt-ex.com and access the MySQL database called personnel. The connection is made with user name johnsmith and password johnsmith.

If the connection is successful, this function will return a database handle represented by the variable $dbh. If the connection fails, the statement in lines 12–13 will be executed to display the message "Connection Error..."

The prepare() function in line 16

```
prepare($statement)
```

prepares an SQL statement for execution by the registered database engine. This function returns a statement handle ($sth), which you can use to invoke the execute method to perform the SQL query, i.e.,

```
$sth->execute()
```

If the SQL query is not successfully processed, the statements in lines 24–25 are used to return a message to the user and terminate the program. If the query is successful, all the rows (or records) affected by the execute method are returned. The next step is to get these rows and display them in the browser window. Consider the second part of the program ex17-11.pl:

```
Listing: Continuation Of The Perl Script ex17-11.pl (Part Two)

27:
28: print << "mypage";
29:   <?xml version="1.0" encoding="iso-8859-1"?>
30:   <!DOCTYPE html PUBLIC "-//W3C//DTD XHTML 1.0 Transitional//EN"
31:       "http://www.w3.org/TR/xhtml1/DTD/xhtml1-transitional.dtd">
32:   <html xmlns="http://www.w3.org/1999/xhtml" xml:lang="en" lang="en">
33:   <head><title></title></head>
34:   <style>
35:     .txtSt{font-family:arial;font-weight:bold;font-size:13pt;color:#ffff00}
36:   </style>
37:   <body class="txtSt" style="background:#000088;font-size:18pt;
38:         text-align:center" >
39:     Based On Your SQL Query String:<br />
40:     <div style="font-size:14pt" align="center">
41:     <table><tr>
42:       <td class="txtSt" style="color:#ffffff;width:500px;
43:         text-align:center;font-size:14pt"><br />
44:       $querySt </br><br /></td></tr>
45:     </table>
46:       Query O.K. And The Returned Results Are As Follows:<br /><br />
47:     </div>
48:     <img src="line1.gif" width="600"
49:         height="6" alt="pic" /><br />
50:     <table cellspacing="5" class="txtSt" align="center" width="570">
51:   mypage
52:
53:   my @data;
54:   my $count =0;
55:
56:   $colNames = $sth->{NAME};
57:   print "<tr>";
58:   for ($ii = 0; $ii < length($colNames); $ii++)
59:   {
60:     print "<td style=\"color:#00ff00;font-size:16pt\">$colNames->[$ii]</td>";
61:   }
62:   print "</tr>";
63:
```

Soon after the XHTML page fragment in lines 28–51, an array variable @data is declared to store the database records. Before this array @data is populated with database data, we want to display the name of each field first. To get the field name of each column, you can use the following (line 56):

```
$sth->{NAME};
```

This statement returns an array reference of field names. Armed with this information, the for-loop in lines 58–61 displays each field name correctly.

To populate the array @data with database data, let's consider the third part of the program below:

Listing: Continuation Of The Perl Script ex17-11.pl (Part Three)

```
64: while (@data = $sth->fetchrow_array())
65: {
66:   print "<tr>";
67:   for ($ii=0;$ii<@data;$ii++)
68:   {
69:     print "<td>$data[$ii]</td>";
70:   }
71:   print "</tr>";
72:
73:   $count++
74: }
75:
76: if ($count == 0)
77: {
78:     print "<tr><td style=\"color:#00ff00;font-size:16pt\">
79:     No record is matched `xxxx'.</td></tr>";
80: }
81:
82: $sth->finish;
83: $dbh->disconnect;
84:
85: print << "endpage";
86:     </table><br />
87:     <img src="line1.gif" width="600"
88:         height="6" alt="pic" /><br />
89:     Total Entries = $count<br /><br />
90:     </body>
91:     </html>
92: endpage
```

To get one row of data, you can use the fetchrow_array() function as

```
@data = $sth->fetchrow_array()
```

This function fetches one row of data and assigns them to the array element @data. The for-loop used in lines 67–70:

```
for ($ii=0;$ii<@data;$ii++)
{
 print "<td>$data[$ii]</td>";
}
```

displays the data $data[$ii] inside an XHTML table. The counting variable $count is then incremented by 1 in line 73. If you apply a while-loop on top of this for-loop, you will display all returned database records. If the counting variable $count is zero, an error message is displayed to show that no record is matched.

Soon after all the data are displayed, the finish statement is called:

```
$sth->finish;
```

This statement terminates the SQL query and frees up the database handle $sth and any system resources associated with it. The disconnect method used in line 83 disconnects the database handle from the database. The rest of the program is used to complete the XHTML page and return to the user. To call this program ex17-11.pl, you can make a copy of example ex17-09.htm and call it ex17-11.htm. The next step is to modify the form action to call this Perl script. As a result the new example ex17-11.htm will execute ex17-11.pl instead of ex17-09.pl to get the database records. Some screen shots of this example in action are shown in Figs 17.17 and 17.18.

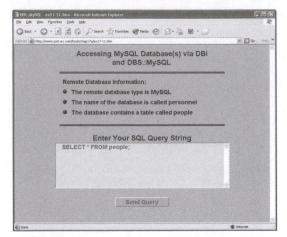

Figure 17.17 ex17-11.htm

Figure 17.18 SQL query result

Since the DBD::MySQL module can only be used to access MySQL database systems, the next question is: "How can we use DBI to access ODBC databases such as Microsoft Access and SQL server?"

To answer this question, let's consider an example to use the DBI driver module DBD::ODBC. You will find that to change from DBI::MySQL to DBI::ODBC is surprisingly easy.

17.4.4 Using ODBC with module DBD::ODBC

To develop a DBI example to use ODBC databases, we first make a copy of ex17-11.htm and call it ex17-12.htm. The next step is to modify lines 16 and 30 as below:

```
16: Accessing MySQL Database(s) via DBI<br />and DBD::ODBC<br /><br />
30: <form action = "ex17-12.pl" method="post">
```

The first line is a message to let the user know that you are using the DBD::ODBC module to access databases on ODBC. The second line activates the Perl program ex17-12.pl to perform the SQL query. To convert example ex17-11.pl to ex17-12.pl, all you have to do is to change one line (i.e., line 9) for DBI::ODBC access. The first 14 lines of ex17-12.pl are listed as follows:

```
Example: ex17-12.pl - The Perl Script Fragment For ex17-12.htm

 1: #! /usr/bin/perl
 2:
 3: use DBI;
 4: use CGI qw (:standard);
 5: print "Content-type:text/html\n\n";
 6:
 7: my $querySt = param(querySt);
 8:
 9: if(!($dbh = DBI->connect('dbi:ODBC:personnel', 'johnsmith', 'johnsmith')))
10: {
11:   print "Connection Error ..";
12:   exit();
13: }
14:
```

Basically, the modification in line 9 is to change the name from MySQL to ODBC. Since we have registered the MySQL database personnel on ODBC, the connection is legal and will be executed. That's it: we now have an interface to handle ODBC through DBI. If you put in a multiline SQL string such as

```
SELECT *
FROM people
WHERE salary > 25000;
```

all employees whose salary is more than 25,000 will be displayed. Some screen shots are shown in Figs 17.19 and 17.20.

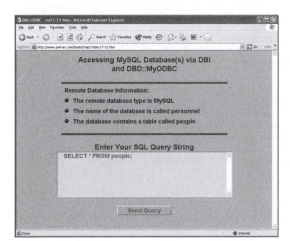

Figure 17.19 ex17-12.htm

Figure 17.20 SQL query result

There are a number of differences between Win32::ODBC and the `DBI::ODBC` module. Basically, Win32::ODBC provides more low-level functions to control your databases. That means you may need to do things yourself. On the other hand, the structure of `DBI::ODBC` is closer to high-level programming with fewer callable functions. Functions in `DBI::ODBC` are compatible with all other DBI modules.

Now we have a number of programs using Perl to control databases on the Web, let's consider other technologies and programming techniques to control MySQL, namely, ADO and ASP from Microsoft.

17.5 Accessing databases with ADO and ASP

17.5.1 What is ADO?

ActiveX Data Objects, or ADO for short, is a Microsoft product providing database access at the programming level. It is a series of objects closely related to ASP discussed in the last chapter. ADO can be used to simplify the tasks for adding database functionalities to your Web pages. Any scripting language supported by ASP can be used to call ADO functions. In this section, we will show you how to use JScript (a version of ECMAScript) to program ADO databases. Then the same program will be translated into PerlScript in ASP format. Note that PerlScript is a scripting language that can be used in ASP and is different from the general programming language Perl.

ADO is part of a larger structure called Universal Data Access (UDA) constructed by Microsoft. A structural diagram of UDA is shown in Fig. 17.21.

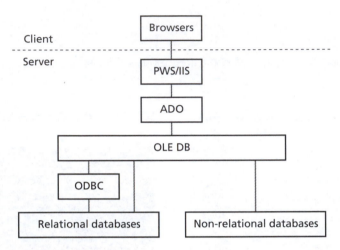

Figure 17.21 The structure of Universal Data Access (UDA)

Basically, you don't need to install ADO explicitly. As part of the Microsoft Data Access Component, ADO will be installed automatically with Microsoft server products. This means that if you have installed the IIS or PWS, you already have ADO ready for action.

In fact, ADO is a DLL and the current version is msado15.dll. It is usually located inside the "Program Files" directory. You can use the `Find` feature of your Windows system or issue the command `dir msado*.dll /s` in a DOS window to locate the library.

ADO works by connecting to any relational databases through Open Database Connectivity (ODBC) or the Object Linking and Embedding Database (OLE DB).

Once you have a database on ODBC, you can concentrate on ADO programming. ADO provides seven objects for us to access and manipulate databases at the programming level. We will introduce two of them, namely, the "Connection Object" and the "Recordset Object," in this section.

17.5.2 Accessing databases with `Connection` and `Recordset` objects

The `Connection` object of ADO represents a unique session with a data source. You can use it to establish and manage connections between your applications and ODBC databases. The `Connection` object contains a number of methods and properties. We are particularly interested in the following methods:

- `Open()`   – Opens a connection to a data source.
- `Close()`   – Closes a connection to a data source.
- `Execute()`   – Executes the specified database query and SQL statement.

For example, the following ADO statements open the ODBC database personnel:

```
Conn = new ActiveXObject("ADODB.Connection")
Conn.Open("personnel")
```

To establish a database connection with ADO, you first create an instance of the `Connection` object. In this case, the instance is called `Conn`. With this `Conn`, you can activate the `Open()` method to open the ODBC database personnel.

This database contains one table called people and the SQL statement below is often used to extract all the data inside the table people:

```
SELECT * FROM people
```

To execute this SQL statement, you can use

```
RS = Conn.Execute("SELECT * FROM people")
```

Although the `Connection` object simplifies the task of connecting to an ODBC database and execution of a SQL query, it has limitations. In particular, you cannot (or at least it is not convenient to) create scripts with the `Connection` object to retrieve, display, and manipulate data and related information. This is the job of another ADO object called `Recordset`. In fact, the `execute` command above from the `Connection` object returns a `Recordset` object (`RS`) about all data inside the table people.

The `Recordset` object, as its name implies, contains properties and features that you can use to display all database fields and a set of database rows, or records. For example, you can use the count property of the `Recordset` below to count and display all fields about the table people:

```
count = RS.Fields.Count;
for ( ii = 0; ii < count; ii++ )
{
 Response.Write( RS.Fields(ii).Name )
 Response.Write("<br />");
}
```

The name property associated with `RS.Fields(ii).Name` returns the name of the field of the table. The value property of the fields will return the data value associated with the field.

For a real example, let's consider the database example ex15-15.htm and convert it to ASP. First, we use the same XHTML interface by copying ex15-15.htm to ex17-13.htm and changing the following two lines:

```
12: Access An ODBC DataBase <br />with ASP<br /><br />
28: <form action = "ex17-13.asp" method="post">
```

Line 28 simply changes the form action to call the ASP page ex17-13.asp. The listing of this ASP page is follows:

```
Example: ex17-13.asp - Using ADO

 1: <%@Language=JScript%>
 2: <?xml version="1.0" encoding="iso-8859-1"?>
 3: <!DOCTYPE html PUBLIC "-//W3C//DTD XHTML 1.0 Transitional//EN"
 4:     "http://www.w3.org/TR/xhtml1/DTD/xhtml1-transitional.dtd">
 5: <html xmlns="http://www.w3.org/1999/xhtml" xml:lang="en" lang="en">
 6: <head><title>Example ex17-13.asp</title></head>
 7: <style>
 8:  .txtSt{font-family:arial;font-weight:bold;font-size:13pt;color:#ffff00}
 9: </style>
10: <% querySt = Request.Form("querySt") %>
11: <body class="txtSt" style="background:#000088;font-size:18pt;
12:       text-align:center" >
13:   Based On Your SQL Query String:<br />
14:   <div style="color:#ffffff"><%= querySt %></div><br />
15:   The Search Results Are As Follows:<br /><br />
16:   <img src="line1.gif" width="600" height="6" alt="pic" /><br />
17:   <table cellspacing="5" class="txtSt" width="570">
18:
19: <%
20:   Conn = new ActiveXObject("ADODB.Connection")
21:   Conn.Open("personnel" )
```

```
22:   RS = Conn.Execute(querySt)
23:
24:   count = RS.Fields.Count
25:   Response.Write("<tr>")
26:   for ( ii = 0; ii < count; ii++ )
27:   {
28:   Response.Write("<td style='color:#00ff00'>"+RS.Fields(ii).Name+"</td>" )
29:   }
30:   Response.Write("</tr>")
31:
32:   rowCount = 0
33:   while ( ! RS.EOF )
34:   {
35:    Response.Write("<tr>")
36:    for ( ii = 0; ii < count; ii++ )
37:    {
38:    Response.Write("<td style='color:#ffff00'>"+RS.Fields(ii).Value+"</td>")
39:    }
40:    Response.Write("</tr>")
41:    RS.MoveNext()
42:    rowCount++
43:   }
44:
45:    RS.Close()
46:    Conn.Close()
47: %>
48:
49: </table>
50: <img src="line1.gif" width="600" height="6" alt="pic" /><br />
51: Total Entries = <%= rowCount%> <br /><br />
52: </body>
53: </html>
```

First, the query string submitted from the XHTML page is captured by the `Request.Form` object (line 10). The ADO statements in lines 20–22 open the database personnel and execute the SQL statement `querySt`. The for-loop in lines 26–29 uses the count property of the `Recordset` object to count and display all field names. All the coding here is in line with the discussion above.

In order to display all the rows (or database data), you can use the following while-loop against the end of file of the `Recordset` (lines 33–43):

```
while ( ! RS.EOF )
{
 Response.Write("<tr>")
 for ( ii = 0; ii < count; ii++ )
 {
   Response.Write( "<td>"+RS.Fields(ii).Value+"</td>" )
 }
 Response.Write("</tr>")
 RS.MoveNext()
 rowCount++
}
```

`RS.EOF` is a property of the `Recordset` object to represent the end of the record. This while-loop will loop through all rows of the table. Inside the while-loop, there is a simple for-loop to construct and display all field data as a single table row in XHTML format. The statement

```
RS.MoveNext()
```

will move to the next row of data so that the while-loop can continue the row iteration. Since the `Recordset` object is considered as a file, you need to close it in line 45 along with closure of the `Connection` object. Some screen shots of this example are shown in Figs 17.22 and 17.23.

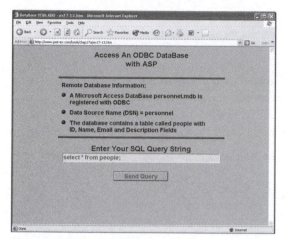

Figure 17.22 ex17-13.htm

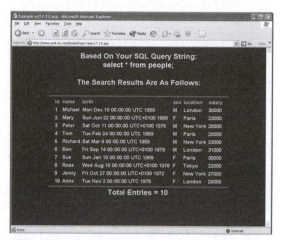

Figure 17.23 ODBC with ASP

17.5.3 Using ASP PerlScript to call ADO functions

ASP is a language-independent package where multiple scripting languages are accepted. We have shown in Chapter 16 that VBScript, JScript, and PerlScript can co-exist on the same ASP page. In this section, we will show you how to use PerlScript to call ADO functions to perform database functionalities. PerlScript is an ASP scripting language engine running on a PC with Microsoft windows. PerlScript is free and available from Active Perl (www.active.com). When you install the Active Perl language for a Microsoft system, you will have already installed the PerlScript engine for ASP.

Again, only the `Connection` and `Recordset` objects associated with ADO are considered. To open the database and execute an SQL query statement, you can use the following PerlScript:

```
<%
$Conn = $Server->CreateObject("ADODB.Connection");
$Conn->Open( "personnel" );
$RS = $Conn->Execute("SELECT * FROM people");
%>
```

You may already have noticed that these statements are very similar to the JScript version in previous example ex17-13.asp. PerlScript is designed to work with ASP and contains all the advantage of being a Perl-compliant language. That's why all the variables above have a dollar sign in front of them. Unlike JScript, PerlScript uses reference to call ADO functions. For example, the arrow symbol

```
$Conn->Open( "personnel" );
```

indicates that the object variable `$Conn` calls the `Open()` function using a reference method. When the SQL query string `SELECT * FROM people` is executed, the query results are returned to the variable `$RS`. This variable is actually an object of `Recordset` type. All the properties of the `Recordset` object can be applied to format the result. For example, the following code can be used to display all the names of the fields as an XHTML table row:

```
$count = $RS->Fields->{Count};
$Response->Write("<tr>");
for ( $i = 0; $i < $count; $i++ )
{
  $Response->Write("<td>");
  $Response->Write($RS->Fields($i)->Name);
  $Response->Write("</td>");
};
$Response->Write("</tr>");
```

Now you can use ASP and PerlScript to program databases. As a quick example, you can use the same XHTML interface by copying ex17-13.htm to ex17-14.htm and changing the following two lines:

```
12: Access An ODBC DataBase <br />Using PerlScript with ADO<br /><br />
28: <form action ="http://www.pwt-ex.com/chap17a/ex17-14.asp" method="post">
```

The statement in line 28 changes the form action to call the ASP page ex17-14.asp. The listing of this ASP page is as follows:

```
Example: ex17-14.asp - Using ASP PerlScript To Call ADO Functions

 1: <%@Language=PerlScript%>
 2: <?xml version="1.0" encoding="iso-8859-1"?>
 3: <!DOCTYPE html PUBLIC "-//W3C//DTD XHTML 1.0 Transitional//EN"
 4:     "http://www.w3.org/TR/xhtml1/DTD/xhtml1-transitional.dtd">
 5: <html xmlns="http://www.w3.org/1999/xhtml" xml:lang="en" lang="en">
 6: <head><title>Example ex17-14.asp</title></head>
 7: <style>
 8:   .txtSt{font-family:arial;font-weight:bold;font-size:13pt;color:#ffff00}
 9: </style>
10: <% $querySt = $Request->Form("querySt"); %>
11: <body class="txtSt" style="background:#000088;font-size:18pt;
12:        text-align:center" >
13:   Based On Your SQL Query String:<br />
14:   <div style="color:#ffffff"><%= $querySt%></div><br />
15:   The Search Results Are As Follows:<br /><br />
16:   <img src="line1.gif" width="600" height="6" alt="pic" /><br />
17:   <table cellspacing="5" class="txtSt" width="570">
18:
19: <%
20: $Conn = $Server->CreateObject("ADODB.Connection");
21: $Conn->Open( "personnel" );
22: $RS = $Conn->Execute( $querySt);
23:
24: $count = $RS->Fields->{Count};
25:
26: $Response->Write("<tr>");
27: for ( $i = 0; $i < $count; $i++ )
28: {
29:   $Response->Write("<td style='color:#00ff00'>");
30:   $Response->Write($RS->Fields($i)->Name);
31:   $Response->Write("</td>");
32: };
33: $Response->Write("</tr>");
34:
35: $rowCount =0;
36: while ( ! $RS->{EOF} )
37: {
38:   $Response->Write("<tr>");
39:   for ( $i = 0; $i < $count; $i++ )
```

```
40:    {
41:       $Response->Write("<td style='color:#ffff00'>");
42:       $Response->Write($RS->Fields($i)->{Value});
43:       $Response->Write("</td>");
44:    };
45:    $Response->Write("</tr>");
46:    $RS->MoveNext();
47:    $rowCount++;
48: };
49:
50: $RS->Close();
51: $Conn->Close();
52: %>
53:
54: </table><br />
55: <img src="line1.gif" width="600" height="6" alt="pic" /><br />
56: Total Entries = <%= $rowCount %> <br /><br />
57: </body>
58: </html>
```

Basically, this ASP page is a direct translation of example ex17-13.asp into the PerlScript language. All structure and function names are the same. Lines 20–22 open the ODBC database called personnel and execute the query statement SELECT * FROM people. The for-loop in lines 27–32 uses the count property of the Recordset object to display all the names of the database fields. Finally, the while-loop in lines 36–48 iterates over all the rows returned by the query. For each row, a for-loop is used to format the database data

```
$RS->Fields($i)->{Value}
```

as a table row in XHTML format.

18 Application of SQL and PHP to databases

By finishing Chapter 17, you should now have some experience of database programming on the Web and some general database pages ready for action. In fact, all the programs introduced in the previous chapter are SQL test programs. They are handy and practical because they allow you or users to send SQL statements to databases performing all kinds of database-related actions. In order to use these programs effectively, you may need to have a basic knowledge SQL and its statements, but a solid understanding of SQL is far more important than that. From a practical point of view, knowledge of SQL is considered as the single important key for designing successful database applications on the Web. For example, as a Web programmer for an online banking corporation, say, you cannot expect your front end users to understand SQL; all SQL actions should be transparent to users.

The first part of this chapter is dedicated to a background study of SQL. Some frequently used SQL statements and aggregate functions are introduced. You can use any database programs developed in the previous chapter to run and test the SQL performance. By default, we assume the MySQL database is installed. SQL is a database-independent language and therefore can be applied to any SQL-based database application. Once you have aquired some knowledge of SQL, the second half of the chapter concentrates on how to use it to design some database applications for front end users. For this part, PHP is used as the action scripting language. PHP was designed with databases in mind and the built-in support for MySQL and ODBC makes it an ideal choice for database applications. When working with databases, PHP is a very effective tool. First, let's consider some SQL statements to create databases and tables.

18.1 Creating databases and tables with SQL

18.1.1 Designing databases with tables

In this section, we will show you how to use MySQL databases to design tables on the Web. Some information regarding the data type differences among Microsoft Access, Oracle, and MySQL is also provided. In general the MySQL package is assumed to be installed on a remote machine called www.pwt-ex.com. Inside the MySQL server, we also assume a database called personnel and a table called people in early sections of this chapter.

You can refer to section 17.2 of Chapter 17 to see how to install MySQL, connect to the MySQL server, and create databases. Once you have registered a database such as personnel on your local machine, you can control it using the Web pages developed in Chapter 17. In particular, we use ex17-12.htm and ex17-12.pl to demonstrate and evaluate SQL statements. As a starting point, this example is referred to as ex18-01.htm and ex18-01.pl here.

The page ex18-01.htm is a basic Web page using Perl to establish communications between you and the MySQL databases installed on www.pwt-ex.com. Although the implementation is simple, it is a database application on the Web using ODBC. For example, you can enter the

```
SHOW DATABASES;
```

statement to see all databases on www.pwt-ex.com available to you. Some screen shots to see this in action are shown in Figs 18.1 and 18.2.

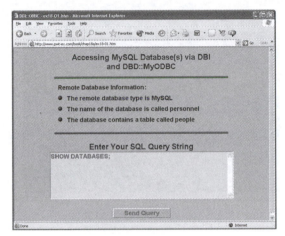

Figure 18.1 SHOW DATABASES;

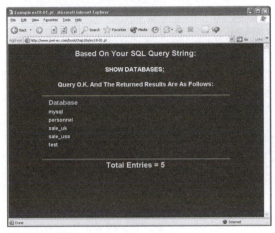

Figure 18.2 Returned databases

In general, we will use the examples ex18-01.htm and ex18-01.pl as our SQL test programs. In fact, you can use any SQL test program including the MySQL client mysql> to test and evaluate the examples. If your SQL test program can display something similar to Fig. 18.2, you should have no problems in evaluating all the examples in the first three sections of this chapter.

Although MySQL commands are not case sensitive, the user-defined names are. To avoid confusion and improve readability, capital letters are used for all system keywords and lower case for defined names.

Since you can have a number of databases in MySQL, if you are using the MySQL client mysql>, you must select your active database before starting your query or operation. To select a database, the keyword USE is used. For example, the following USE command selects personnel as the current database:

```
USE personnel;
```

Since ODBC and DBI already have registered the default database, the statement above is not necessary.

The real contents of a database are tables. Before any data can get into a database, you will need to know how to create a table to store them. One simple way to create a table is to use the CREATE TABLE statement. Before a more formal syntax or definition of this statement is given, consider a simple example as follows:

```
Example: ex18-01.sql - Creating A Table Called expense

1: CREATE TABLE expense (
2:    name CHAR(30),
3:    amount INTEGER,
4:    account INTEGER
5: );
```

This is a multiline example. You can spread your SQL command or statement over multiple lines and type them into the Web page. Once a semi-colon is encountered, the system will execute the entire SQL statement as a single command.

This example creates a table called `expense` with three fields, i.e., `name`, `amount`, and `account`. The name is a string of 30 characters. The amount and account are of integer type.

The `SHOW TABLES;` statement can be used to display all tables in the database `personnel`. If you enter this command in the SQL test program, you will see that the table `expense` exists as shown in Fig. 18.3. You can use the `DESCRIBE expense;` statement to see the internal structure of the table (Fig. 18.4).

Figure 18.3 Show all tables   **Figure 18.4** Show data types of a table

Figure 18.4 shows the structure or data types of the table `expense`. In many cases, this command is an effective way to examine the table that you created or a table that you don't know much about. To remove the table from the database, the `DROP TABLE` command can be used. For example, the following command removes the table `people` from the database:

```
DROP TABLE people;
```

After removing this table, let's see how to re-create it. In general, the SQL statement to create a table is

```
CREATE TABLE table_name
(
  field1 datatype,
  field2 datatype,
  ... ...
  fieldn datatype
);
```

The fields represent the names for each column of the table. Unfortunately, definitions for data types may be different among database vendors. SQL itself has no direct specifications or implementation on data types. Some of the frequently used data types on Access, Oracle, and MySQL are listed in Table 18.1.

Table 18.1 Data types used in Access, Oracle, and MySQL

Access	Oracle	MySQL	Description
`TEXT`	`CHAR(N)`	`CHAR(N)` `VARCHAR(N)`	`CHAR(N)` is a fixed length string with `N` characters `VARCHAR(N)` is a string with variable length (max. `N` characters)
`INTEGER`	`NUMBER`	`SMALLINT` `INT(N)`	The range of `SMALLINT` is `-32768` to `32767`. The range of `INT(N)` is from `-2147483648` to `2147483647`
`SINGLE`	`NUMBER`	`SINGLE`	Single-precision floating point number. Allowable values are `-3.402823466E+38` to `-1.175494351E-38`
`DOUBLE`	`NUMBER`	`DOUBLE`	Double-precision floating point number. Allowable values are `-1.7976931348623157E+308` to `1.7976931348623157E+308`
`DATE/TIME`	`DATE`	`DATE` `DATETIME`	The `DATE` format is `'0000-00-00'`. The `DATETIME` format is `'0000-00-00 00:00:00'`
`MEMO`	`LONG`	`LONGTEXT`	A `BLOCK` or `TEXT` column with a maximum length of 4294967295 (2^{32} – 1) characters

From this table, we can see that the data types in MySQL are more disciplined and that other systems are more flexible. For example, the data type `NUMBER` in Oracle systems can represent numeric, positive, or negative fixed or floating point data.

To design a table suitable for your needs is extremely important to the success of your application. It is recommended that you should always start from the name and proper data type for your fields. Also keep a record of your design with comments.

For example, to describe the staff of a company, you might start with a table called `people`. The first field of this table is usually a positive small integer called `id` to uniquely identify each employee of the company. This `id` cannot be empty and should be automatically incremented by 1. You may also want to have `name`, `birth`, `sex`, `location`, and `salary` fields inside the table. Table 18.2 is a simple design.

Table 18.2 Data type of the table `people`

Field name	Structure (data type)	Comments
`id`	`SMALLINT UNSIGNED NOT NULL AUTO_INCREMENT`	Automatic increment by 1 and cannot be `NULL` This field is the primary key
`name`	`VARCHAR(30)`	Name of the person
`birth`	`DATE`	Birthday of the person
`sex`	`CHAR(1)`	Female (`F`) or male (`M`)
`location`	`VARCHAR(30)`	Traveling location
`salary`	`INT(6)`	Annual salary

Put all your data requirements into data types and describe them by SQL keywords. Since data types are not the same among database vendors, you may need to consult your database manual for further information. Based on this information, you can define the table `people` with the SQL statements below:

Example: ex18-02.sql - Creating A Database Table Called people

```
1:   CREATE TABLE people (
2:      id SMALLINT UNSIGNED NOT NULL AUTO_INCREMENT,
3:      name VARCHAR(30),
4:      birth DATE,
5:      sex CHAR(1),
6:      location VARCHAR(30),
7:      salary INT(6),
8:      PRIMARY KEY (id)
9:   );
```

This is a long SQL statement split into multiple line input. The result and data types of this table are shown in the screen shots in Figs 18.5 and 18.6.

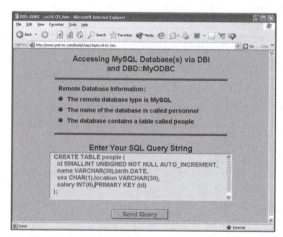

Figure 18.5 ex18-02.sq1

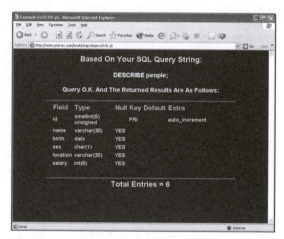

Figure 18.6 Data types of table `people`

Now you have a database table, the next question is: "How can we load data into the table?"

18.1.2 Input/output data from database tables

Different database products may have different ways to load data into a table. For example, Access has a number of visualization tools for data loading. Whether your tables were created with Microsoft Word or Excel, Access supports all of them. Apart from proprietary utilities to convert databases and tables from other vendors, most database products support text files for import and export. That means you can load or dump text files from and to tables. We will introduce a text file method to load data into a MySQL table in this section.

By using the MySQL function `LOAD DATA`, a text file can be read into a table provided:

- Each line of the file represents a record of the table.
- Field data are in the right order as described in the table and are separated by a tab.

Suppose you have created a text file called people.dat with your favorite editor in the exact format as described above. A section of the text file is

```
Listing: 18-01.txt - Text Data File (people.dat)
    NULL          Michael          1950-12-18   M       London 30000
    NULL          Mary             1980-06-22   F       Paris  23000
    ...           ...              ...          ...     ...    ...          ...
    NULL          Anne             1976-11-02   F       London 28000
```

You can use the statement

```
LOAD DATA INFILE "people.dat" INTO TABLE people;
```

to load the file into the table. If the fields of the data file were delimited by commas, you can use the following statement to read it in:

```
Example: ex18-03.sql - Load Data Into A File

1: LOAD DATA INFILE 'people.dat'
2: INTO TABLE people
3: FIELDS TERMINATED BY ',';
```

The LOAD DATA INFILE is a useful feature in MySQL. It can be used to read files obtained from external sources. For example, a database file in dBASE format will have fields separated by commas and enclosed in double quotes. To read such a file, you can issue the command

```
Example: ex18-04.sql - Load Data Into A File With Delimiter

1: LOAD DATA INFILE 'people.dat'
2: INTO TABLE people
3: FIELDS TERMINATED BY ','
4: ENCLOSED BY '"'
5: LINES TERMINATED BY '\n';
```

For Microsoft systems, every line of a text file contains a carriage return and a line feed to represent the end of a line. That is, if you create the data file people.dat on a Windows platform, you should use the following statement to read the file in:

```
Example: ex18-05.sql - Loading A File With DOS/Windows Format

1:  LOAD DATA INFILE 'people.dat'
2:  INTO TABLE people
3:  LINES TERMINATED BY '\r\n';
```

Type this statement into the page as in Fig. 18.7. The result is shown in Fig. 18.8.

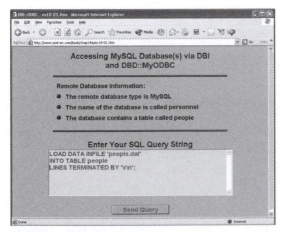

Figure 18.7 Load data

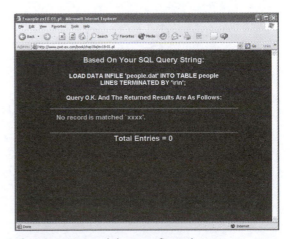

Figure 18.8 Load data confirmed

If the execution of the query is successful, a confirmation message is displayed at the top of the returned page. Since this query has no returned data, the total entries field is zero.

The complement of LOAD DATA is to output data into a text file. Outputting data into a text file is not just a good way to communicate with other databases; the data can be used as a backup or for further processing too. To output data from a table into a text file, the statement SELECT*INTO OUTFILE is used. For example,

```
Example: ex18-06.sql - Output A Text File

1:   SELECT * INTO OUTFILE 'data.txt'
2:   FROM people;
```

This statement will output all data from the table people into a text file called data.txt. If you want fields to be separated by a comma or a line terminated by a new line, you can use the following example:

```
Example: ex18-07.sql - Output A Text File With Format

1:   SELECT * INTO OUTFILE 'data.txt'
2:   FIELDS TERMINATED BY ','
3:   LINES TERMINATED BY '\n'
4:   FROM people;
```

If you are using a Windows system, you may need to add the carriage return together with the new line symbol (i.e., "\r\n").

```
Example: ex18-08.sql - Output A Text File In DOS/Windows Format

1: SELECT * INTO OUTFILE 'data.txt'
2: FIELDS TERMINATED BY ','
3: LINES TERMINATED BY '\r\n'
4: FROM people;
```

MySQL also has a script mode or batch mode to simplify statement typing. For example, suppose you have created the database personnel with MySQL and have no table in it. You can type the following commands into a file called personnel.txt:

```
Example: ex18-09.sql - Batch Mode File For MySQL

1:   USE personnel;
2:   CREATE TABLE people (
3:     id SMALLINT UNSIGNED NOT NULL AUTO_INCREMENT,
4:     name VARCHAR(30),
5:     birth DATE,
6:     sex CHAR(1),
7:     location VARCHAR(30),
8:     salary int(6),
9:     PRIMARY KEY (id)
10:  );
11:  LOAD DATA INFILE "people.dat" INTO TABLE people
12:  LINES TERMINATED BY '\r\n';
```

To execute this file, you type the following command from a shell or DOS window:

```
shell> mysql < personnel.txt
```

If you need to supply a user name and password for connection to a server, you can use the command

```
shell> mysql -h www.pwt-ex.com -u johnsmith -p < personnel.txt
Enter Password: ****
```

The client program `mysql` in this case will log in to the remote server with user name and password. If everything is all right, it will execute the statements inside the script file.

Getting input/output text files from tables is a popular technique to establish a dialog among different databases. The text files, in many cases, are convenient for further data processing.

18.1.3 Manipulating table data with SQL

Once the data are in the table, you can use the following SQL statements to manipulate them:

- The `INSERT` statement – To insert a record to the table.
- The `UPDATE` statement – To change a record.
- The `DELETE` statement – To delete a record from the table.

There are two versions of the `INSERT` statement.

- `INSERT INTO table_name (field1, field2, ..., fieldN)`
  `VALUES (value1, value2, ..., valueN)`

- `INSERT INTO table_name (field1, field2, ..., fieldN)`
  `SELECT (field1, field2, ..., fieldN)`
  `FROM table_name2`
  `WHERE search_condition`

The `INSERT...VALUE` statement enters one record at a time into a table. It is designed for small operations to manipulate a table. For example, if you want to add another person called "Jack" into the `people` table, you can enter

```
Example: ex18-10.sql - Insert A Record

1:   INSERT INTO people
2:   VALUES
3:   (NULL,'Jack','1968-07-08','M','Tokyo',32000);
```

The insertion result is shown in Figs 18.9 and 18.10.

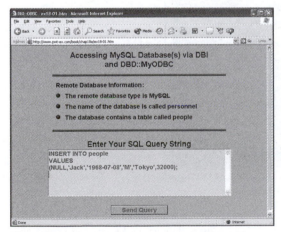

Figure 18.9 Insert data

Figure 18.10 Insertion results

When using the SELECT...VALUE statement, the data type, size, and location of the inserted fields must match the corresponding fields declared in the table. Unless you use programming techniques to generate this SQL statement, the limitation is that you can only add one record at a time. Also, this statement cannot be used to build a table from other tables.

To copy information from one table into another or to build a new table from information in an existing one is common practice in SQL. For this purpose the INSERT...SELECT statement can be used. Suppose you want to create a table to project a salary increase of 7% for all your staff next year. You may use the following SQL statements:

```
Example: ex18-11.sql - Populate A Table From An Existing Table

 1:   CREATE TABLE salary (
 2:     name VARCHAR(30),
 3:     sex CHAR(1),
 4:     salary INT(6),
 5:     new_salary INT(6)
 6:   );
 7:
 8:   INSERT INTO salary
 9:   SELECT name, sex, salary, (salary * 1.07) as new_salary
10:   FROM people;
11:
```

This example contains two SQL statements. You need to enter the statements one by one into the Web page. The first SQL statement defined in lines 1–6 is to create a new table called salary. Once this table is created, you can call the second statement to fill it. The first three fields, name, sex, and salary are selected from the existing table people. The SQL clause

```
(salary * 1.07) as new_salary
```

generates the fourth field called new_salary and is a 7% rise on the previous field salary. A screen shot is shown in Fig. 18.11.

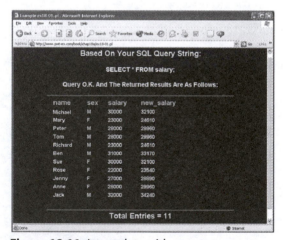

Figure 18.11 Insert data with Select

To change the values of existing records, the SQL statement UPDATE is used. The general format or syntax is

```
UPDATE table_name
SET field1 = value1, field2=value2, ... , fieldN=valueN
WHERE search_condition
```

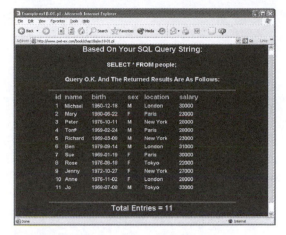

Figure 18.12 Updated table

A simple application for UPDATE is to change the data of a table. For example, the following statements change the names and salary of Jack (Fig. 18.12):

```
Example: ex18-12.sql - Update The Contents Of A Table

1:  UPDATE people
2:  SET name='Jo', salary='33000'
3:  WHERE name='Jack';
```

As another example, let's use UPDATE to construct a new salary table. The salary table can also be generated by the following three steps:

Step 1: Create a new table called salary from the fields name, sex, and salary of the table people.

Step 2: Alter the table by adding a new field called new_salary.

Step 3: Update the new_salary fields by (salary*1.07).

In terms of SQL, these three steps can be accomplished by the following three SQL statements:

```
Example: ex18-13.sql – Using ALTER TABLE And UPDATE

1:  CREATE TABLE salary
2:  SELECT name, sex, salary
3:  FROM people;
4:
5:  ALTER TABLE salary ADD new_salary INT(6);
6:
7:  UPDATE salary
8:  set new_salary = salary * 1.07;
```

The first statement (lines 1–3) creates a table salary. The three fields name, sex, and salary are copied to the new table from an existing table people and carry the same data type. Creating a table this way provides a handy method to populate the data fields or to back up a table.

To add a column or field to the new table, the second statement (line 5) is used. The command

```
ALTER TABLE salary ADD new_salary INT(6);
```

will alter the table structure by adding a new field called new_salary with data type INT(6). In addition to the ADD keyword, you can also use the MODIFY keyword to modify the data type of an existing field.

For the last step, you can use the UPDATE statement to populate the new_salary field. For example, you can use:

```
UPDATE salary
set new_salary = salary * 1.07;
```

to generate the data for new_salary as the salary field increased by 7%.

As your experience with SQL grows, you will find these statements particularly useful for preparing and backing up your tables for database applications.

Finally, to remove a record from a table, you can use the keyword DELETE. For example,

```
Example: ex18-14.sql - Delete Table Element

1:   DELETE FROM salary
2:   WHERE new_salary < 25000;
```

This example will delete all the entries (if any) from the table salary where the salary is less than 25,000 (Fig. 18.13).

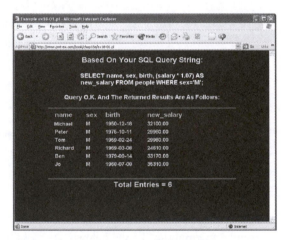

Figure 18.13 Delete data from table

Now you have some experience on SQL tables with data, it's time to consider some SQL queries. Most of the SQL queries introduced in section 18.2 are core queries to the user. Behind the XHTML interface or scripting, they are the driving force for many database applications on the Web.

18.2   Basic SQL query statements

18.2.1 Using the SELECT statement and logical operators

One way or another, most of the database applications on the Web (or Internet) are SQL based. This may include all kinds of online banking, search engines, and shopping. For most of them, a user-friendly interface is designed to hide the fact that they are actually using the SQL query.

The most frequently used SQL command is the SELECT statement, which generates a table and returns data to the user. For example, we have frequently used

```
SELECT * FROM people;
```

in our previous examples to display all data from the table `people`. The general syntax of `SELECT` consists of three parts:

```
SELECT field1, field2, field3, ..., fieldN
FROM table1, table2, ..., tableK
WHERE search_condition;
```

The first part begins with keyword `SELECT` and is used to build the fields of a table. The keyword `FROM` is to tell the database system where to find the fields. The keyword `WHERE` provides a search condition so that you can search for the data you require.

For some simple use of the `SELECT` statement, let's consider the database and table `people` that we created in sections 18.1.2 and 18.1.3.

The following `SELECT` statement returns all data from the table `people` whose salary is more than 25,000:

```
SELECT * FROM people WHERE salary > 25000;
```

The asterisk after `SELECT` means that you are selecting all data. You can also combine multiple search conditions together in your SQL statement. For example, to locate all females whose salary is more than 25,000 you can use

```
Example: ex18-15.sql - Logical AND

1:  SELECT *
2:  FROM people
3:  WHERE salary > 25000 AND sex='F';
```

To find out who is responsible for the business in Tokyo or Paris, you can use the logical `OR` keyword. For example,

```
Example: ex18-16.sql - Logical OR

1:  SELECT *
2:  FROM people
3:  WHERE location='Tokyo' OR location='Paris';
```

SQL is a flexible language. For example, you can also compare the date of birth within the `WHERE` keyword, such as

```
Example: ex18-17.sql - Flexible Comparison

1:  SELECT *
2:  FROM people
3:  WHERE birth >='1960-1-1';
```

This statement will select the people who were born after January 1, 1960. The results of these three examples are shown in Figs 18.14–18.16 respectively.

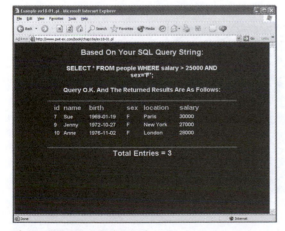

Figure 18.14 SQL logical AND

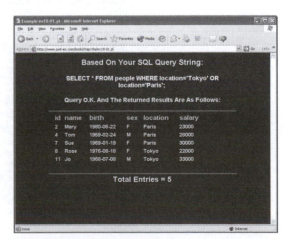

Figure 18.15 SQL logical OR

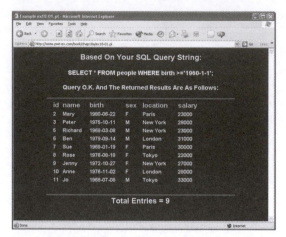

Figure 18.16 SQL flexible comparison

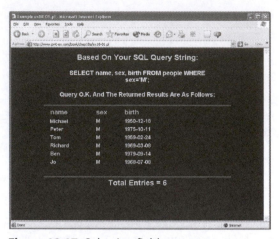

Figure 18.17 Selecting fields

To select particular columns, you need to replace the asterisk by the names of fields separated by commas. For example, to get the name, sex, and date of birth of all male staff, you can use the SQL statement in ex18-18.sql below:

```
Example: ex18-18.sql - Selecting Fields

1:   SELECT name, sex, birth
2:   FROM people
3:   WHERE sex='M';
```

The result is shown in Fig. 18.17. Also, new fields can be generated from existing ones and added to the table. For example, the following adds a new field to the table:

```
Example: ex18-19.sql - Adding A New Field

1:   SELECT name, sex, birth, (salary * 1.07) AS new_salary
2:   FROM people
3:   WHERE sex='M';
```

The result of this example is shown in Fig. 18.18.

Figure 18.18 Adding a new field

SQL is flexible. You can rewrite line 1 of ex18-19.sql as

```
SELECT name, sex, birth, (salary * 1.07) new_salary
SELECT name, sex, birth, salary * 1.07 new_salary
```

and still produce the same result.

18.2.2 Sorting and multiple sorting of records

Sometimes, it is more convenient to examine the query result if the output is sorted by order. To sort a result, you can use the ORDER BY clause as in the example below:

```
Example: ex18-20.sql - SQL Sorting

1:   SELECT name, sex, birth
2:   FROM people
3:   WHERE sex='M'
4:   ORDER BY birth;
```

This example returns a result ordered by birthday (see Fig. 18.19).

Figure 18.19 Ordering by birthday   **Figure 18.20** Sorting with descending order

By default, the ORDER BY clause sorts the results in ascending order. To sort in reverse order, the keyword DESC can be used (see Fig. 18.20).

```
Example: ex18-21.sql - SQL Sorting With Descending Order

1:   SELECT name, sex, location, birth
2:   FROM people
3:   WHERE sex='M'
4:   ORDER BY birth DESC;
```

You can also perform sorting on multiple fields. For example, if you want to group the people by location and then sort staff within each group by birth dates, you can issue the query

```
Example: ex18-22.sql - Multiple Sorting

1:   SELECT name, sex, location, birth
2:   FROM people
3:   WHERE sex='M'
4:   ORDER BY location, birth DESC;
```

This statement sorts the data in the `location` field and then orders the data in the field `birth` within `location`. A screen shot is shown in Fig. 18.21.

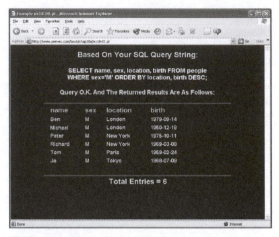

Figure 18.21 Multiple sorting

From this example, you can see that the data in the `location` field are sorted in ascending order. The data in the `birth` field are sorted in descending order and bounded or grouped by `location`.

18.2.3 Building new fields with expressions

For a database and table to store information about your employees, it may be more convenient to include age as a field. However if you put a data value into the `age` field, you may need to change it every year. Thus in practice, the `age` field in many cases will be implemented at run time.

If you want to find out the age of an employee, you can use the following steps:

Step 1: Get the current year minus the year of birth as age.

Step 2: Get the current month and date (mm-dd) and compare to the month and date of birth.

Step 3: If the current month and date is less than the month and date of birth decrease the age by 1.

In terms of SQL statements, the year difference (step1) can be expressed as

```
LEFT(CURRENT_DATE,4) - LEFT(birth,4)
```

This is an arithmetic expression and the result is a number. The entire date format used in MySQL is yyyy-mm-dd, where the `LEFT()` function can be used to extract the first four characters from a string. The result is the difference of the current year and the year of birth.

In order to perform steps 2 and 3, you need a logical expression from SQL.

As you might expect, the `RIGHT()` function can extract the month and date (mm-dd). For example, the following expression can be used to extract the five characters from the month and date string of birth:

```
RIGHT(birth,5)
```

To perform the comparison described in step 3, the following logical expression or comparison is used:

```
RIGH(CURRENT_DATE,5) < RIGHT(birth,5)
```

SQL will return the value 1 if this expression is true and 0 otherwise. Now you can perform query with age as follows:

```
Example: ex18-23.sql - Calculating Age

1:   SELECT name, sex, location, salary,
2:    ((LEFT(CURRENT_DATE,4) - LEFT(birth,4)) -
3:     (RIGHT(CURRENT_DATE,5) < RIGHT(birth,5)))
4:   AS age
5:   FROM people
6:   ORDER BY age;
```

Soon after the name, sex, location, and salary fields, a simple mathematical expression (lines 2–3) is used to declare a new field called age. Since age is generated at run time, it will not store or affect the actual data of the database. A screen shot of this example is shown in Fig. 18.22.

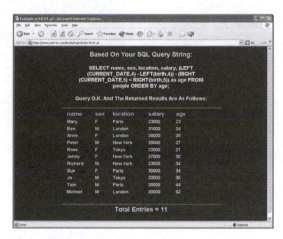

Figure 18.22 Calculating age

18.2.4 The LIKE operator and wildcards

In some cases, you may want to query or search for a partial pattern. For example, the following example uses the LIKE operator to search for any employee whose name begins with "J":

```
Example: ex18-24.sql - Using The LIKE operator

1:   SELECT *
2:   FROM people
3:   WHERE name LIKE 'J%';
```

The LIKE operator together with the percentage symbol "%" causes the system to return all names begin with letter "J." A screen shot is shown in Fig. 18.23. When used inside a LIKE expression, the percentage symbol works as a wildcard. If you change line 3 to

```
WHERE location LIKE '%York%';
```

this SQL query will return all the records where the location field contains the word "York." When dealing with data query, references to data are always case sensitive. For example, the following query will return nothing since there is no "york" in the table:

```
WHERE location LIKE '%york%';
```

Another wildcard often used in SQL query is the underscore "_." The underscore is the single-character wild-card and will accept any single character for the query. For example, it can be used to find every employee who was born in the 1960s, like this:

Example: ex18-25.sql - The Underscore Wildcard

```
1:    SELECT *
2:    FROM people
3:    WHERE birth LIKE '%196_%';
```

The result is shown in Fig. 18.24.

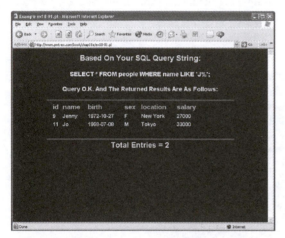

Figure 18.23 The `LIKE` operator

Figure 18.24 The underscore wildcard

18.2.5 Concatenation of fields

Some SQL implementations use the double pipe symbol "||" to concatenate two strings. In MySQL, the functions `CONCAT()` and `CONCAT_WS()` are used. The calling format for `CONCAT()` is

```
CONCAT(str1,str2,...)
```

This function returns the concatenated string from the argument strings, and returns `NULL` if any argument is null. Any numeric argument is converted to the equivalent string form. Some calling examples are

```
select CONCAT('Web','Technologies');
```
 – Return the string "WebTechnologies"

```
select CONCAT('Web',NULL,'Database');
```
 – Return the string NULL

```
select CONCAT(1234,5678);
```
 – Return the string "12345678"

Another concatenation function in MySQL is `CONCAT_WS()`. The first argument of this function is the separator for the rest of the arguments. The calling format for this function is

```
CONCAT_WS(separator, str1, str2,...)
```

The separator can be a string as well as the rest of the arguments. The separator is added between the strings to be concatenated. Some examples are

```
select CONCAT_WS(",","name","sex","birth");
```
 – Return the string "name,sex,birth"

```
select CONCAT_WS("#","name","salary");
```
 – Return the string "name#salary"

```
select CONCAT_WS("#","name",NULL,"salary");
```
 – Return the string "name#salary"

The CONCAT_WS() function ignores any null data. To put this function in use, consider the example

Example: ex18-26.sql - Concatenate Fields

```
1:   SELECT name,sex,birth,
2:   CONCAT_WS(',',salary, (salary * 1.07))
3:   AS salary_projection
4:   FROM people;
```

This example displays the fields name, sex, birth, and a new field called salary_projection. This new field is a concatenation of salary and (salary * 1.07). A screen shot is shown in Fig. 18.25.

You can also use this function to populate another table.

Example: ex18-27.sql - Concatenate Fields II

```
1:   CREATE TABLE information
2:   SELECT name,
3:   CONCAT_WS(',',sex,birth,salary)
4:   AS description
5:   FROM people;
```

This example first creates a table called information. Then a SELECT statement with the CONCAT_WS() function is used to populate the new table from the existing table people. The table information now contains two fields, name and description. If you issue the SELECT * FROM information; statement, you will have the result shown in Fig. 18.26.

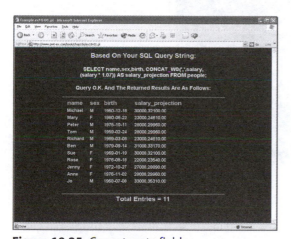

Figure 18.25 Concatenate fields

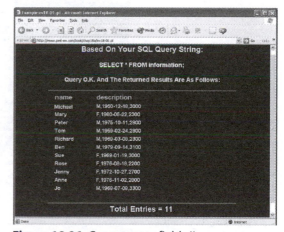

Figure 18.26 Concatenate fields II

18.3 Built-in SQL functions and multiple tables

18.3.1 Using aggregate functions

Aggregate functions are functions that work on the data of a column. Sometimes they are referred as group functions in SQL. These functions, in many cases, increase your ability to handle and manipulate information for analysis purposes. Some frequently used aggregate functions are:

- COUNT()   –   Returns the number of rows.
- SUM()   –   Returns the sum of all values.
- AVG()   –   Computes the average of a column.

All these functions can be called while satisfying the condition in the WHERE clause. For example, you can use the following statement to find out how many female employees there are in the people table:

```
Example: ex18-28.sql - Using Counting Function

1:   SELECT COUNT(*)
2:   FROM people
3:   WHERE sex='F';
```

How do you get the number of female and male employees at the same time? The answer to this question is that you can perform a grouping inside the sex field. This way you will have two groups, "F" and "M." A simple counting on sex will return the results you want. In terms of SQL statements, we have

```
Example: ex18-29.sql - Using Group By

1:   SELECT sex, COUNT(*)
2:   FROM people
3:   GROUP BY sex;
```

The use of GROUP BY in line 3 will group together all records for each sex. Applying the function COUNT() along with sex returns the count for females and males. A screen shot of example ex18-28.sql is shown in Fig. 18.27.

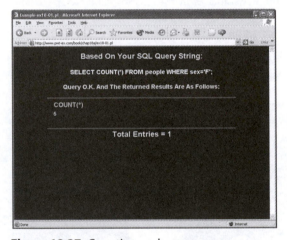

Figure 18.27 Counting and GROUP BY

When COUNT() and GROUP BY work together, you have a powerful tool to solve some frequently asked query problems. For example, in the business sector, a similar statement to ex18-30.sql is often used to find out

- the orders generated or business carried out by each salesperson;
- the selling situation of each product.

Similar to SQL sorting, you can also perform multiple GROUP BY. Consider the following example:

```
Example: ex18-30.sql - Using Multiple Group By

1:   SELECT location, sex, COUNT(*)
2:   FROM people
3:   GROUP BY location, sex;
```

This example would group the location first and then the sex. A simple `COUNT()` on sex returns the number of female and male employees for each city. A screen shot is shown in Fig. 18.28.

In addition to the `COUNT()` function, the `SUM()` function can be used to sum all the values in a column. For example, the SQL statement below will display total salary expenditure:

```
Example: ex18-31.sql - Using The Sum Function

1:   SELECT SUM(salary)
2:   AS total_salary
3:   FROM people;
```

The `SUM()` function can also work with `GROUP BY`. For example, if you add the `SUM(salary)` keyword into ex18-30.sql, you will have the SQL statement as in ex18-32.sql.

```
Example: ex18-32.sql - Using SUM() With GROUP BY

1:   SELECT location, sex, COUNT(*), SUM(salary)
2:   FROM people
3:   GROUP BY location, sex;
```

This example generates an expenditure table on each city and for each female and male group. A screen shot is shown in Fig. 18.29.

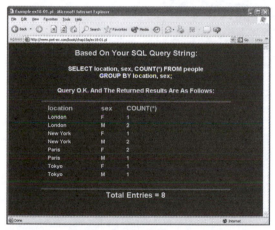

Figure 18.28 Using `GROUP BY`

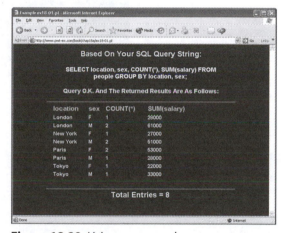

Figure 18.29 Using `SUM()` and `GROUP BY`

The average function `AVG()` returns the average value from a column. The use of `AVG()` is similar to `SUM()`. For example, the function `AVG(salary)` can be added into ex18-33.sql to calculate the average salary at the same time.

```
Example: ex18-33.sql - Using The Average Function AVG()

1:   SELECT location, sex, COUNT(*), SUM(salary), AVG(salary)
2:   FROM people
3:   GROUP BY location, sex;
```

By default, the `AVG()` function returns a floating point number with four decimal places. To control the decimal output, you can use the SQL function

`ROUND(X,D)` – Returns the argument `X`, rounded to a number with `D` decimal places.

In many cases, we can use the following example to control the decimal output of `AVG(salary)`:

```
Example: ex18-34.sql - Controlling Decimal Output

1:   SELECT location, sex, COUNT(*),
2:       SUM(salary) AS sum_salary,
3:       ROUND(AVG(salary),2) AS avg_salary
4:   FROM people
5:   GROUP BY location, sex;
```

A screen shot of this example is shown in Fig. 18.30.

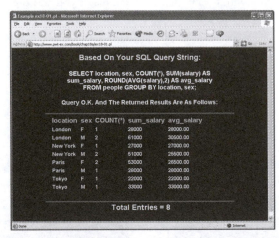

Figure 18.30 Conrtrolling decimal output with `AVG()`

18.3.2 Handling multiple tables

One of the most powerful features of an SQL database is its capability to gather and handle data from multiple tables. If you have two tables with fields such as

```
Table1 - Field1, Field2, Field3
Table2 - Field1, Field2
```

you can access the `Field2` of `Table1` by `Table1.Field2`. Putting a period between the table name and field name provides a method of identifying table data.

If you have the proper privileges, you can gather and access tables from other databases. For example, suppose you have two databases and tables as follows:

```
Database1 - Table1, Table2
Database2 - Table1, Table2, Table3
```

If the current database is `Database1`, you can access `Table3` in `Database2` by `Database2.Table3`.

Suppose you have created another database called `company` and registered it with the ODBC or DBI. Inside this database, you have two tables, namely, `product` and `sales`. The tables can be created by the following SQL statements:

```
Example: ex18-35.sql - Creating Tables product And sales

Creating Table product
1:   # Creating And Loading Data For Table product
2:   CREATE TABLE product (
3:   product_id VARCHAR(30),
```

```
4:    description VARCHAR(50),
5:    unit_cost int(6)
6:    );
7:    LOAD DATA LOCAL INFILE "product.dat" INTO
8:    TABLE product LINES TERMINATED BY '\n';
```

```
Creating Table sales
```

```
1:    # Creating And Loading Data For Table sales
2:    CREATE TABLE sales (
3:    quantity int(6),
4:    name_id VARCHAR(30),
5:    product_id VARCHAR(30)
6:    );
7:    LOAD DATA LOCAL INFILE "sales.dat" INTO
8:    TABLE sales LINES TERMINATED BY '\n';
```

The contents of the tables `product` and `sales` are shown in Figs 18.31 and 18.32.

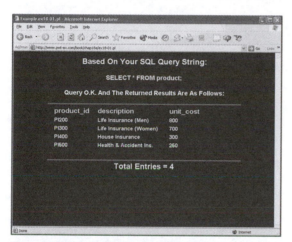

Figure 18.31 Contents of table `product`

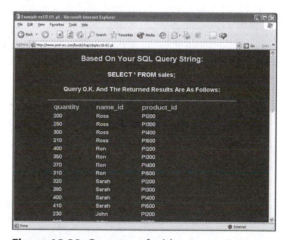

Figure 18.32 Contents of table `sales`

One of the common disasters for database applications is the loss of tables. One popular solution is to back up the tables into another database such as BACKUP. For example, to import table `people` from database BACKUP into your current database, you can use the statement CREATE TABLE people SELECT * FROM BACKUP.people to restore the table.

Another application of this important technique is that you can import, for instance, the names of personnel conducting sales from another database. Consider the following SQL statements:

```
Example: ex18-36.sql - Import Table From Another Database
```

```
1:    CREATE TABLE people
2:      SELECT *
3:    FROM BACKUP.sales_person;
```

Now, the table `people` contains the names of the personnel conducting the sales (see Fig. 18.33). Together with the tables `product` and `sales`, you have three related tables. From Figs 18.31 and 18.32, you can see that the `product_id` fields of tables `product` and `sales` are the same. Also, the `name` field of the table `people` (i.e., `people.name`) is the same as `sales.name_id`.

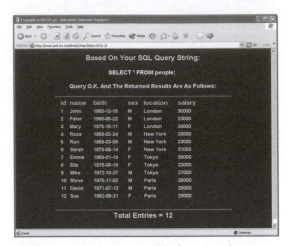

Figure 18.33 Importing table from another database

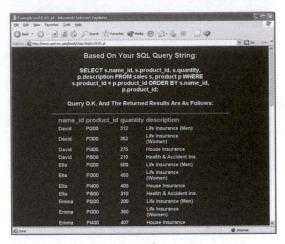

Figure 18.34 Sorting results

Since `sales` and `product` are related, you can display the `sales` table with an additional column to describe the information of the `product`. Consider the example below:

Example: ex18-37.sql - Adding A Field From Other Table

```
1:    SELECT
2:      s.name_id,
3:      s.product_id,
4:      s.quantity,
5:      p.description
6:    FROM sales s, product p
7:    WHERE
8:       s.product_id = p.product_id
9:    ORDER BY
10:      s.name_id, p.product_id;
```

In this example, we also use an alias technique to simplify field identification. In line 6, a single character `s` is used to represent the table `sales` and the character `p` for the table `product`. The `s` and `p` characters are attached to the `SELECT` arguments in lines 2–5. The entire statement can be interpreted as follows: select the fields

`s.name_id`	–	The `name_id` field from sales
`s.product_id`	–	The `product_id` field from sales
`s.quantity`	–	The `quantity` field from sales
`p.description`	–	The `description` field from product

from `sales` and `product` where the `product_id` acts as the common column of the tables. In order to have a more readable result, sorting is applied on the `s.name_id` and then the `p.product_id`. A screen shot is shown in Fig. 18.34.

From this figure, you can clearly see how many insurance products each salesperson has sold in a year. With some modifications, this example can be used to calculate the business income generated by each salesperson. Try the example below:

Example: ex18-38.sql - Adding A Field From Another Table

```
1:  SELECT
2:    s.name_id, s.product_id, s.quantity,
3:    s.quantity * p.unit_cost AS buss_income
4:  FROM sales s, product p
5:  WHERE
6:    s.product_id = p.product_id
7:  ORDER BY
8:    s.name_id, p.product_id;
```

The new field `buss_income` in line 3 is generated by `quantity` from `sales` multiplied by `unit_cost` from the table `product`. If you apply the `SUM()` function, you can calculate the total business income generated by each salesperson and their commission.

Example: ex18-39.sql - Calculating Business Income And Commission

```
1:  SELECT
2:    s.name_id AS name,
3:    SUM(s.quantity * p.unit_cost) AS buss_income,
4:    SUM(s.quantity * p.unit_cost *0.05) AS commission
5:  FROM sales s, product p
6:  WHERE
7:    s.product_id = p.product_id
8:  GROUP BY
9:    s.name_id;
```

This statement generates three columns: name, `buss_income`, and commission. The commission is 5% of the business income. Since we have used the `SUM()` function and `GROUP BY` keyword, the total business income and commission of each salesperson are calculated automatically. The result is shown in Fig. 18.35.

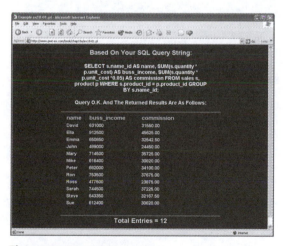

Figure 18.35 ex18-39.sq1

Sometimes, it may be more useful to see the business income and commission for each location or region rather than individual salesperson. Since `location` is a field inside the table `people`, you need to include this table into the SQL statement. Consider the example below:

Example: ex18-40.sql - Calculating Business Income And Commission

```
1:  SELECT pe.location AS region,
2:    SUM(s.quantity * p.unit_cost) AS buss_income,
3:    SUM(s.quantity * p.unit_cost *0.05) AS commission
```

```
 4:   FROM
 5:     sales s, product p, people pe
 6:   WHERE
 7:     s.product_id = p.product_id AND
 8:     s.name_id = pe.name
 9:   GROUP BY pe.location;
10:
```

This example joins all three tables together by the FROM keyword in line 4. These tables relate to each other. The product_id columns of tables sales and product are the same and the name column of people is the same as the name_id column of product. By linking these tables together, we can perform the calculation of business income and commission for each location of London, New York, Paris, and Tokyo. A screen shot of this example is shown in Fig. 18.36.

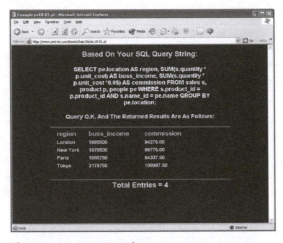

Figure 18.36 ex18-40.htm

18.3.3 Joining tables and sub-queries

When dealing with multiple tables, we are working with so-called joined tables. Basically, there are five kinds of table joins frequently used in SQL statements:

- Cross-Join (Inner-Join)
- Equi-Join
- Nonequi-Join
- Right-Outer-Join
- Left-Outer-Join

In order to demonstrate all these table joins, let's create another table called provider in our database company. This table contains information about the insurance provider for each insurance product that the company sells. You can create the provider table by

Example: ex18-41.sql - Creating and Loading Data For The Table provider

```
1:   #Creating The Table provider
2:   CREATE TABLE provider (
3:    product_id VARCHAR(30),
4:    provider VARCHAR(50)
5:   );
6:   #Loading Data For The Table provider
7:   LOAD DATA INFILE "provider.dat" INTO
8:   TABLE provider LINES TERMINATED BY '\n';
```

The details of these two tables (i.e., `product` and `provider`) are shown in Figs 18.37 and 18.38.

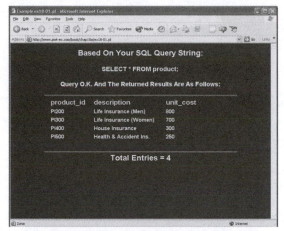

Figure 18.37 The `product` table

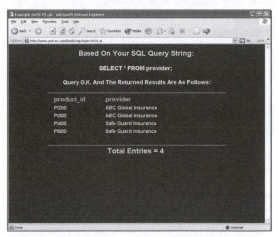

Figure 18.38 The `provider` table

The `Cross-Join`, or sometimes called the `Inner-Join`, of these two tables is the simplest and can be done by the following `SELECT` statement:

```
SELECT * FROM product, provider
```

This statement will perform an insertion of all records from the table `product` to every record of `provider`. The result is a table with 16 records. A screen shot of this table join is shown in Fig. 18.39.

The `Cross-Join` process is the base for the next two table joins. For example, if you use an equals sign in a `WHERE` clause as follows, you will have `Equi-Join`:

```
Example: ex18-42.sql - Equi-Join Of Two Tables

1:  SELECT * FROM product pp, provider pd
2:  WHERE pp.product_id = pd.product_id;
```

The `WHERE` clause searches for any match of `product_id` in both tables. This process will pick up to four records. This join is called `Equi-Join` because the objective is to match the values of a field in one table to the corresponding values in a second table. The result is just like merging Figs 18.38 and 18.39 together. A screen shot is shown in Fig. 18.40.

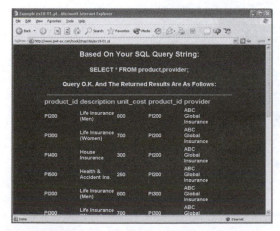

Figure 18.39 `Cross-Join` of tables

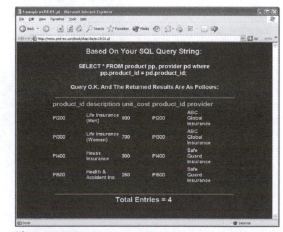

Figure 18.40 `Equi-Join`

`Equi-Join` is one of the most popular table joins used in SQL. It can merge two tables together and perform further SQL action by putting logical AND/OR operators in the WHERE clause.

The counterpart of `Equi-Join` is `Nonequi-Join`. This uses everything but an equals sign in the WHERE clause to join fields of two tables. For example, the following SQL statement performs `Nonequi-Join` of two tables:

```
Example: ex18-43.sql - Nonequi-Join Of Two Tables

1:  SELECT * FROM product pp, provider pd
2:  WHERE pp.product_id > pd.product_id
```

This SQL statement will pick up the records in Fig. 18.39 where the `product_id` of table `product` is bigger than the `product_id` of table `provider`.

All three table joins above can be classified as inner joins. They are all based on the cross-join of two tables. An inner join is where the records of the tables are combined with each other and therefore they produce a new table with records equal to the product of the number of fields in each table. Also, the inner join uses this new table to determine the result of the WHERE clause. In some cases, this will cause some inefficiency in the use of memory or storage. Imagine you were asked by a bank to perform some SQL queries on two tables with 500,000 records each. The inner join of these two tables will produce $(500,000)^2$ records.

The counterpart of the inner join is the outer join. An outer join groups two tables in a different way. Based on this grouping, there are two kinds of outer joins, namely, `Left-Outer-Join` and `Right-Outer-Join`. For example, the SQL statement below performs `Left-Outer-Join` of two tables:

```
Example: ex18-44.sql - Left-Outer-Join Of Two Tables

1:  SELECT *
2:  FROM
3:      product pp
4:  LEFT OUTER JOIN
5:      provider pd
6:  ON pd.product_id="PI200";
```

This SQL statement performs `Left-Outer-Join` from table `product` to table `provider`. Line 6 is used to specify that the entire table `product` is joined to the `provider` table where the `product_id` of `provider` is PI200. The result is similar to inserting the entire `product` table into one record of another table. All other unrelated records are disregarded. A screen shot of this table join is shown in Fig. 18.41.

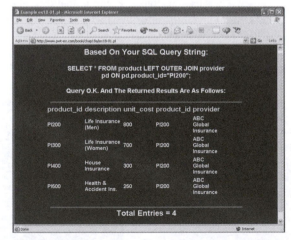

Figure 18.41 `Left-Outer-Join`

The SQL statement below performs `Right-Outer-Join` of two tables:

Example: ex18-45.sql - Right-Outer-Join Of Two Tables

```
1:   SELECT *
2:   FROM
3:      product pp
4:   RIGHT OUTER JOIN
5:      provider pd
6:   ON pd.product_id="PI200";
```

This SQL statement also performs an insertion of the table `product` into the table `provider` where the `product_id` of `provider` is PI200. The difference is that in `Right-Outer-Join`, all records of the right hand side records are kept. A screen shot of this example is shown in Fig. 18.42.

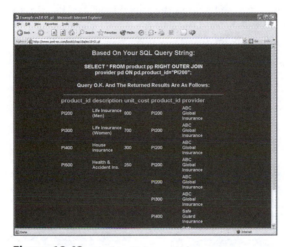

Figure 18.42 `Right-Outer-Join`

If you have some large (or very large) tables, you should seriously consider use of `Outer-Join` .

Another popular use of table joins is to detect consistency in a table. Suppose someone in your company has made a mistake entering a new product in the `product` table with an existing `product_id` (PI300) such as in Table 19.3.

Table 19.3 Inconsistent data in a table

product_id	description	unit_cost
PI200	Life Insurance (Men)	800
PI300	Life Insurance (Women)	700
PI400	House Insurance	300
PI500	Health & Accident Ins.	250
PI300	Home Contents	120

724 Applications of SQL and PHP to databases

This kind of mistake occurs quite often and the result could be quite serious: all your invoices to customers and commissions to working staff could be wrong. If you have a large number of products, this kind of error may be difficult to find.

This mistake can be spotted if you join the product table to itself. For example, you can issue the statement below:

Example: ex18-46.sql - Detecting Data Inconsistency I

```
1:   SELECT *
2:   FROM
3:     product p1, product p2
4:   WHERE
5:     p1.product_id = p2.product_id;
```

In line 5, we have used Equi-Join on product_id of table product to itself. Any inconsistency of product_id within the table product will show up in the joined table (see Fig. 18.43)

Better still, you can add more search conditions to the WHERE clause to clarify the search result. For example, you can issue the SQL statement below:

Example: ex18-47.sql - Detecting Data Inconsistency II

```
1:   SELECT *
2:   FROM
3:     product p1, product p2
4:   WHERE
5:     p1.product_id = p2.product_id AND
6:     p1.unit_cost <> p2.unit_cost;
```

By adding one more search condition such as that in line 6 you can greatly reduce the number of returned records. Now, you can clearly see from Fig. 18.44 that one product_id is corresponding to two unit_costs. It is clearly a mistake and should be dealt with quickly.

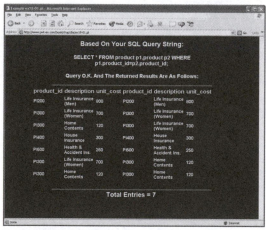

Figure 18.43 Data inconsistency I

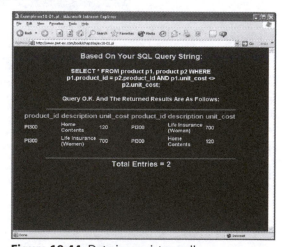

Figure 18.44 Data inconsistency II

In some cases, you may want to submit a query result in another query. This is called the sub-query. The general syntax for a sub-query is:

```
SELECT * FROM tableA
WHERE tableA.somefield =
(
  SELECT some_other_field FROM tableB
  WHERE some_other_field = some_value
)
```

The second query statement is nested inside the first query. Sometimes a sub-query is also known as an embedded select statement. To apply sub-query in practice, let's consider the example below.

Suppose you want to find out all the sales information for Women's Life Insurance. To do that, you may want to find out all the instances of Women's Life Insurance from the `product` table

```
SELECT product_id
FROM product
WHERE description LIKE '%women'
```

and submit the result in the query below:

```
SELECT ss.*, pd.description
FROM sales ss, product pd
Where product_id = (The query result above is here)
```

In terms of sub-query, you may use the following SQL statement:

```
Example: ex18-48.sql - Sub-Query

1:   SELECT ss.* pd.description
2:   FROM sales ss, product pd
3:   WHERE
4:    ss.product_id =
5:   (SELECT product_id
6:   FROM product
7:   WHERE description LIKE '%women')
```

However, at the time of writing, the current version of MySQL (version 3.x) doesn't support sub-query, though there is a plan to support sub-query in version 4.1 and later (see www.mysql.com). In this situation, sub-query can be implemented by using multiple tables.

The idea is quite simple. You can store or put all the nested query results into a table (or temporary table). The main query can then be performed on the two tables. For example, you can store all the Women's Life Insurance results in a table called `tptable` by

```
Example: ex18-49.sql - Sub-Query By Multiple Tables (Part One)

1:   CREATE TABLE tptable
2:   (
3:     product_id VARCHAR(30),
4:     description VARCHAR(30)
5:   );
6:
7:   INSERT INTO tptable
8:   SELECT product_id, description FROM product
9:   WHERE
10:    description LIKE '%Women%';
```

Lines 1–5 are used to create the table `tptable`. The INSERT...SELECT statement in lines 7–10 is used to search for any Women's Life Insurance. The result is stored in the `tptable` table. Once you have the `tptable` table, you can perform the query below to find the sales situation:

```
Listing: Continuation Of The SQL File: ex18-49.sql (Part Two)

11:   SELECT ss.*, tb.description
12:   FROM sales ss,tptablE tb
13:   WHERE ss.product_id = tb.product_id;
```

A screen shot of this example is shown in Fig. 18.45.

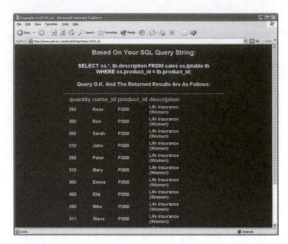

Figure 18.45 Multiple table for sub-query

18.4 Designing database applications with PHP (I)

18.4.1 Using PHP on databases

Starting out as a Personal Home Page tool in 1995, PHP is now a widely used scripting language on the Web. It is believed that more than 5 million sites use PHP as their scripting language on the Internet (see www.php.net).

As a CGI scripting language, PHP can do everything that other CGI programs can do. Also, like ASP, PHP is an HTML/XHTML embedding language so that PHP statements can be integrated within XHTML pages. Perhaps the most important reason for its success is the support of a wide range of databases. PHP has built-in functions directly supporting the databases listed in Table 18.4.

Table 18.4 Databases directly supported by PHP

Adabas D	Informix	MySQL	Sybase
dBase	Ingres	ODBC	Velocis
Empress	InterBase	Oracle (OCI7 and OCI8)	Unix dbm
FilePro (read-only)	FrontBase	Ovrimos	
Hyperwave	mSQL	PostgreSQL	
IBM DB2	Direct MS-SQL	Solid	

Supporting databases has become the most significant feature of PHP. For each of the database types in the table, there are built-in PHP functions dedicated to controlling and accessing them. For example, there are more than 40 functions directly related to MySQL. All MySQL-supported functions have "mysql" as a prefix. Some frequently used PHP functions for MySQL are listed in Table 18.5.

Table 18.5 PHP functions for the MySQL database

`mysql_affected_rows`	–	Get number of affected rows in previous MySQL operation
`mysql_change_user`	–	Change logged-in user of the active connection
`mysql_close`	–	Close MySQL connection
`mysql_connect`	–	Open a connection to a MySQL server
`mysql_create_db`	–	Create a MySQL database
`mysql_data_seek`	–	Move internal result pointer
`mysql_db_name`	–	Get result data
`mysql_db_query`	–	Send a MySQL query
`mysql_drop_db`	–	Drop (delete) a MySQL database
`mysql_fetch_array`	–	Fetch a result row as an associative array, a numeric array, or both
`mysql_fetch_assoc`	–	Fetch a result row as an associative array
`mysql_fetch_field`	–	Get column information from a result and return as an object
`mysql_fetch_lengths`	–	Get the length of each output in a result
`mysql_fetch_object`	–	Fetch a result row as an object
`mysql_fetch_row`	–	Get a result row as an enumerated array
`mysql_field_flags`	–	Get the flags associated with the specified field in a result
`mysql_field_name`	–	Get the name of the specified field in a result
`mysql_field_len`	–	Return the length of the specified field
`mysql_field_seek`	–	Set result pointer to a specified field offset
`mysql_field_table`	–	Get name of the table the specified field is in
`mysql_field_type`	–	Get the type of the specified field in a result
`mysql_free_result`	–	Free result memory
`mysql_insert_id`	–	Get the id generated from the previous `INSERT` operation
`mysql_list_dbs`	–	List databases available on a MySQL server
`mysql_list_fields`	–	List MySQL result fields
`mysql_list_tables`	–	List tables in a MySQL database
`mysql_num_fields`	–	Get number of fields in result
`mysql_num_rows`	–	Get number of rows in result
`mysql_pconnect`	–	Open a persistent connection to a MySQL Server
`mysql_query`	–	Send a MySQL query
`mysql_result`	–	Get result data
`mysql_select_db`	–	Select a MySQL database
`mysql_tablename`	–	Get table name of field
`mysql_get_client_info`	–	Get MySQL client info
`mysql_get_host_info`	–	Get MySQL host info
`mysql_get_proto_info`	–	Get MySQL protocol info
`mysql_get_server_info`	–	Get MySQL server info

For a complete listing of the database-supported functions and others, see the documentation that comes with your PHP package or visit the official PHP site on www.php.net.

With PHP, you don't need to install add-on packages. In a proper PHP installation, you can expect that everything will be ready for you to perform database actions. For example, you can use the following PHP program fragment to connect to the MySQL in www.pwt-ex.com:

```
Listing: ex18-03.txt - PHP Page Fragment To Connect MySQL

1:  <?php
2:     $host="www.pwt-ex.com";
3:     $user="johnsmith";
```

```
4:      $password="johnsmith";
5:      mysql_connect($host,$user,$password);
6:      mysql_select_db("personnel");
7:      $result = mysql_query("SELECT * FROM people");
8: ?>
```

In this PHP fragment, we have used three MySQL-related functions:

- `mysql_connect()` – Connect to the MySQL database (line 5).
- `mysql_select_db()` – Select the particular database against the SQL query (line 6).
- `mysql_query()` – Perform the SQL query and return the results (line 7).

Based on this program fragment, you can develop an SQL testing page using PHP.

18.4.2 An SQL test page using PHP

A general SQL test page is important for almost any database programming on the Web. It is a fundamental tool to see whether you have a healthy database connection and have used the functions or technologies correctly. In many cases, it helps to spot errors and perform evaluations of quality with different database types. If you can read and understand a good SQL test program for a particular technology, you should be able to design database applications with the style, syntax, and layout of that particular technology.

To develop an SQL test program using PHP, consider a new example ex18-50.htm which is the same as ex18-01.htm but with line 15 replaced by

```
15: Accessing MySQL Database(s) <br />Using PHP Built-in Functions<br />
```

This line indicates that you are using the PHP server page. Another line you need to change is line 30:

```
30: <form action = "ex18-50.php" method="post">
```

This form element will activate another the PHP program ex18-50.php to perform the SQL query. The first part of the PHP page is listed below:

Example: ex18-50.php - The PHP Script For ex18-50.htm (Part One)

```
 1: <?PHP echo"<?";?>xml version="1.0" encoding="iso-8859-1"<?PHP echo"?>";?>
 2: <!DOCTYPE html PUBLIC "-//W3C//DTD XHTML 1.0 Transitional//EN"
 3:     "http://www.w3.org/TR/xhtml1/DTD/xhtml1-transitional.dtd">
 4: <html xmlns="http://www.w3.org/1999/xhtml" xml:lang="en" lang="en">
 5: <style>
 6:   .txtSt{font-family:arial;font-weight:bold;font-size:13pt;color:#ffff00}
 7: </style>
 8: <body class="txtSt" style="background:#000088;font-size:18pt;
 9:      text-align:center" >
10:   Based On Your SQL Query String:<br />
11:   <div style="font-size:14pt" align="center">
12:   <table><tr>
13:     <td class="txtSt" style="color:#ffffff;width:500px;
14:       text-align:center;font-size:14pt"><br />
15:     <?php echo($querySt); ?> </br><br /></td></tr>
16:   </table>
17:       The Returned Results Are As Follows:<br /><br />
18:   </div>
19:   <img src="line1.gif" width="600"
20:       height="6" alt="pic" /><br />
21: <?php
22:   $host="www.pwt-ex.com";
23:   $user="johnsmith";
```

```
24:     $password="johnsmith";
25:
26:     mysql_connect($host,$user,$password);
27:     mysql_select_db("personnel");
28:     $querySt = stripSlashes($querySt) ;
29:     $result = mysql_query($querySt);
```

This PHP program fragment is easy to read. The PHP statements in lines 21–24 obtain the necessary parameters for connecting to a database. The MySQL functions in lines 26–29 perform connection to the database and store the results. In order to display the results on the browser window, we need the second half of the PHP program below:

```
Listing: Continuation Of The PHP Script ex18-50.php (Part Two)

30:
31:     if ($result == 0):
32:       echo("SQL Query Error..");
33:     elseif (mysql_num_rows($result) == 0):
34:       echo("SQL Query executed successfully!<br />");
35:     else :
36:     echo('<table cellspacing="5" class="txtSt" align="center" width="570">');
37:       echo('<tr>');
38:       $num_field = mysql_num_fields($result);
39:       for ($ii = 0; $ii < $num_field; $ii++)
40:       {
41:     echo("<td style='color:#00ff00'>".mysql_field_name($result,$ii)."</td>");
42:       }
43:       echo('</tr>');
44:
45:       $count = mysql_num_rows($result);
46:       for ($ii = 0; $ii < $count; $ii++)
47:       {
48:           echo("<tr>");
49:           $row_array = mysql_fetch_row($result);
50:           for ($jj = 0; $jj < $num_field; $jj++)
51:           {
52:           echo("<td>" . $row_array[$jj] . "</td>");
53:           }
54:           echo("</tr>");
55:       }
56:       echo('</table>');
57:     endif
58: ?>
59:
60:   <img src="line1.gif" width="600"
61:       height="6" alt="pic" /><br /><br />
62:   Total Entries = <?php echo($count); ?><br />
63: </body>
64: </html>
```

If the query result $result is zero, you will have an SQL query error. You may need to double-check your SQL query statement and/or connection to the database. If the query result is not zero and the number of returned rows is zero (lines 33–34), that means the SQL query has been executed successfully but not returned anything. For example, if you insert some data into the database, the database may not return anything to you. If the database returns some rows to you, the coding in lines 36–56 will generate a table to display all the rows. Since PHP has a built-in function called mysql_field_name() to control the fields, a simple for-loop with this function (see lines 39–42) is used to display all the field names. A double for-loop as illustrated in lines 46–55 outputs all the rows and field data to the browser window. A screen shot of this example is shown in Fig. 18.46.

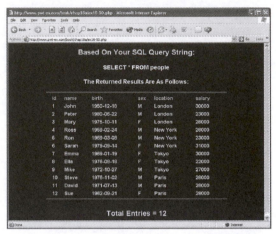

Figure 18.46 An SQL testing program with PHP

Now it is time to design some database applications on the Web using PHP.

18.4.3 A page to explore all MySQL databases and tables

In this section, we are going to develop a PHP page that can walk through any MySQL installation and databases on the Internet with their associated tables. This page will display three text fields, Host, User, and Password. These fields are used to connect to the MySQL on the remote site. All the available databases will be displayed in a select box. Once you have picked a particular database and clicked the button, all the tables associated with the database will be displayed in another select box. For an application like this, we use a single page with PHP built-in functions to hide all the details from the end users.

The first part of the PHP page is listed below:

```
Example: ex18-51.php - Exploring All MySQL Databases And Tables (Part One)

 1: <?PHP echo"<?";?>xml version="1.0" encoding="iso-8859-1"<?PHP echo"?>";?>
 2: <!DOCTYPE html PUBLIC "-//W3C//DTD XHTML 1.0 Transitional//EN"
 3:     "http://www.w3.org/TR/xhtml1/DTD/xhtml1-transitional.dtd">
 4: <html xmlns="http://www.w3.org/1999/xhtml" xml:lang="en" lang="en">
 5: <head><title> Exploring All MySQL Databases - ex18-51.php</title></head>
 6: <style>
 7:   .butSt{background-color:#aaffaa;font-family:arial;font-weight:bold;
 8:       font-size:14pt;color:#008800;width:240px;height:30px}
 9:   .butSt2{background-color:#aaffaa;font-family:arial;font-weight:bold;
10:       font-size:14pt;color:#008800;width:250px;height:120px}
11: </style>
12: <body style="background:#000088;text-align:center;font-family:arial;
13:       font-size:16pt;color:#ffff00">
14: <div style="font-size:16pt;color:#ffff00">
15:   Exploring MySQL Databases and Tables<br /><br />
16:
17: <?php
18:       global $database,$host,$user,$password;
```

```
19:  ?>
20:
21:  <form action="ex18-51.php" method="post">
22:    <table style="font-size:14pt;font-weight:bold">
23:      <tr><td>Host Name: </td><td><input type="text" name="host"
24:             value="<?PHP echo($host)?>" class="butSt" /></td></tr>
25:       <tr><td>User Name: </td><td><input type="text" name="user"
26:             value="<?PHP echo($user)?>" class="butSt" /></td></tr>
27:        <tr><td>Password: </td><td><input type="password" name="password"
28:             value="<?PHP echo($password)?>" class="butSt" /></td></tr>
29:  </table>
30:
```

After the global variable declarations in line 18, this page fragment contains a form with three fields. They are used to get the user input on host name, user name, and password so that a proper connection to the specified MySQL can be made. We have used a PHP echo() function on the value of each field to capture the data whenever the program is activated.

The next task of the page is to make the connection, search for all available databases, and store them in a select box. Once you have picked a particular database and clicked the Find Databases/Tables button (see Fig. 18.47), all the tables associated with the selected database will be displayed in another select box. The second part of the page is listed as follows:

```
Listing: Continuation Of The PHP Script ex18-51.php (Part Two)

31:  <table cellspacing="20" style="font-size:12pt;font-weight:bold"><tr>
32:    <td>
33:      Select Your MySQL Databases Here And Click
34:      The Button Below To Find All Tables<br /><br />
35:      <input type="submit" value="Find Databases/Tables" class="butST"
36:        style="background:#bbbbbb" /><br /><br />
37:
38:      <select name="database" size="1" class="butSt" >
39:      <?php
40:        mysql_connect($host, $user, $password);
41:        $db_table = mysql_list_dbs();
42:
43:        for ($i = 0; $i < mysql_num_rows($db_table); $i++)
44:        {
45:          $dbs = mysql_tablename($db_table, $i);
46:          if ($database == $dbs)
47:            echo("<option selected>" . $dbs);
48:          else
49:            echo("<option>" . $dbs);
50:        }
51:      ?>
52:    </select>
53:    </td><td>
54:      All The Tables Of Your Selected Database Are Here:<br /><br />
55:      <select name="tables" size="4" class="butSt2" >
56:      <?php
57:        $db_table = mysql_list_tables($database);
58:        for ($i = 0; $i < mysql_num_rows($db_table); $i++)
59:        {
60:            echo("<option>" . mysql_tablename($db_table, $i));
61:        }
62:      ?>
63:    </select>
64:    </td></tr>
```

```
65:    </table>
66:    </form>
67:    </body>
68:    </html>
```

The page fragment contains an execution button in lines 35–36. Also, we have two select boxes. Inside the first box (lines 38–52), some PHP functions are called to make the database connection (line 40), get the database listing (line 41), and populate the select box with the names of the databases using a for-loop. The `selected` keyword used in line 47 is to specify the selected database so that it will not disappear or scroll away from the select box.

Once you have selected your database and clicked the Find Databases/Tables button, the statement in line 57 will get all the tables from that database and display them in another select box using a for-loop in lines 58–61.

A page like this is handy to locate any MySQL databases and tables anywhere on the Internet. Some screen shots are shown in Figs 18.47 and 18.48.

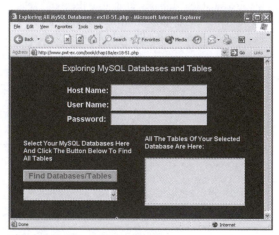

Figure 18.47 ex18-51.php

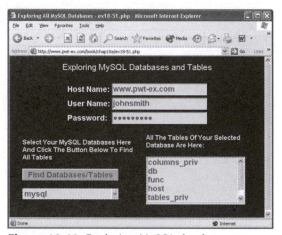

Figure 18.48 Exploring MySQL databases and tables

18.5   Designing database applications with PHP (II)

18.5.1 Deleting records from a table

From the SQL discussion earlier in section 18.2, you learned that the following SQL statement can be used to remove a record from a table:

```
DELETE FROM ... WHERE ...
```

To integrate this statement into a Web page, let's develop a PHP page to delete records from a MySQL table. This page will display all records and each record has an underlined text `DELETE` attached to it. To delete a record, all you have to do is to click on the underlined text. The new record will be updated automatically. The coding of the page is listed below:

```
Example: ex18-52.php – Deleting Records From A Table

1: <?PHP echo"<?";?>xml version="1.0" encoding="iso-8859-1"<?PHP echo"?>";?>
2: <!DOCTYPE html PUBLIC "-//W3C//DTD XHTML 1.0 Transitional//EN"
3:      "http://www.w3.org/TR/xhtml1/DTD/xhtml1-transitional.dtd">
4: <html xmlns="http://www.w3.org/1999/xhtml" xml:lang="en" lang="en">
```

```
 5: <head><title> Deleting Records From A Table - ex18-52.php</title></head>
 6: <body style="background:#000088;text-align:center;font-family:arial;
 7:     font-size:14pt;color:#ffff00">
 8: <div style="font-size:16pt;color:#ffff00;font-weight:bold">
 9:   Deleting Records From A Table<br /><br /></div>
10:   Click the DELETE keyword to delete a record<br/><br />
11:   <img src="line1.gif" width="600"
12:       height="6" alt="pic" /><br /><br />
13: <?php
14:   $db = mysql_connect("www.pwt-ex.com", "johnsmith","johnsmith");
15:   mysql_select_db("personnel",$db);
16:
17:   if ($delete =="yes")
18:   {
19:     $sql = "DELETE FROM people WHERE id=$id";
20:     $result = mysql_query($sql);
21:   } else {
22:      $delete = no;
23:   }
24:   $result = mysql_query("SELECT * FROM people",$db);
25:   while ($myrow = mysql_fetch_array($result))
26:   {
27:    printf("%s, %s, %s, %s, %s --- ",$myrow["name"], $myrow["sex"],
28:           $myrow["location"], $myrow["birth"], $myrow["salary"]);
29:
30:    printf("<a href=\"%s?id=%s&delete=yes\" style=\"color:#00ff00\">
31:        (DELETE)</a><br />",$PHP_SELF, $myrow["id"]);
32:   }
33: ?><br /><br />
34:   <img src="line1.gif" width="600"
35:       height="6" alt="pic" /><br /><br />
36: </body>
37: </html>
```

The first two statements (lines 14–15) inside the PHP scripting block are used to connect to MySQL and select test as the active database. If the DELETE underlined text is pressed, the statements in lines 19–20 execute the SQL delete statement to remove the record according to its id. After the deletion, there is a while-loop in lines 25–32 to display the updated records. The print functions printf() used in the page are C/C++ style. Then can print out a string according to the format setting. The first printf() in lines 27–28 will print out five strings and each %s will be substituted by the corresponding string variable. For example, the first record will be printed out like this:

```
Jenny, F, New York, 1972-10-27, 27000 ---
```

The second print function printf() will output the following string attached to the end of the text above:

```
<a href="$PHP_SELF?id=01&delete=yes"
    style=\"color:#00ff00\">(DELETE)</a><br />
```

This is an anchor element with an underlined text (DELETE). If this text is clicked on, the same page is called with query string id=01&delete=yes. The id parameter is used to identify the record to be deleted. A screen shot of this example is shown in Fig. 18.49.

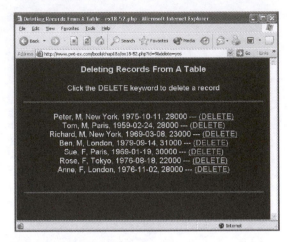

Figure 18.49 ex18-52.php

18.5.2 A page to insert and update records

No matter what kind of database application you are designing, in addition to deletion, inserting and updating a record are also the most basic techniques you may need. As a demonstration, we are going to develop a PHP page which can perform delete, insert, and update operations on a table called `test` inside the `company` database. The `test` table is a copy of the table `people` so that it contains all the fields of `people`. The page will display all records in a select box so that it can hold a reasonably large number of records without destroying the view of the browser window. When one of the records is clicked twice (double click), the data of the record will be displayed in a series of text boxes so that manipulation can be made. We have three buttons to control the captured data:

- Delete – Delete the record from the table.
- Insert – Insert the data into the table as a new record.
- Update – Send the data back to update the record.

The basic skills behind this page are the following two SQL statements:

```
UPDATE test SET name='$name',sex='$sex',location='$location',
      birth='$birth', salary='$salary' WHERE id=$id;

INSERT INTO test (id,name,sex,location,birth,salary)
      VALUES (NULL,'$name','$sex','$location','$birth','$salary');
```

Once you have the data `$name`, `$sex`, `$location`, `$birth`, and `$salary` specified, these two statements can be used to manipulate the records of the table. To hide the SQL statements from the users, you need to write a PHP page, the first part of which is listed as follows:

Example: ex18-53.php – A Page To Insert And Update Records (Part One)

```
 1: <?PHP echo"<?";?>xml version="1.0" encoding="iso-8859-1"<?PHP echo"?>";?>
 2: <!DOCTYPE html PUBLIC "-//W3C//DTD XHTML 1.0 Transitional//EN"
 3:     "http://www.w3.org/TR/xhtml1/DTD/xhtml1-transitional.dtd">
 4: <html xmlns="http://www.w3.org/1999/xhtml" xml:lang="en" lang="en">
 5: <head><title>Manipulating Records - ex18-53.php</title></head>
 6: <style>
 7:   .txtSt{font-family:arial;font-weight:bold;font-size:14pt;color:#ffff00}
 8:   .butSt2{background-color:#aaffaa;font-family:arial;font-weight:bold;
 9:       font-size:14pt;color:#008800;width:550px}
10:   .butSt{background-color:#aaffaa;font-family:arial;font-weight:bold;
```

```
11:      font-size:14pt;color:#008800;width:150px}
12: </style>
13: <body style="background:#000088;text-align:center;font-family:arial;
14:      font-size:14pt;color:#ffff00">
15: <div style="font-size:16pt;color:#ffff00;font-weight:bold">
16:    Manipulating Database Records<br />
17:    Select The Item By Double Clicking The Record Below <br /><br /></div>
18:  <img src="line1.gif" width="600"
19:      height="6" alt="pic" /><br /><br />
20: <?php
21: $db = mysql_connect("www.pwt-ex.com", "johnsmith","johnsmith");
22: mysql_select_db("personnel",$db);
23:
24: global $id,$delete,$update,$insert,$sel_id,
25:         $name,$sex,$location,$birth,$salary;
26:
27:    if ($sel_id)
28:    {
29:      $id = $sel_id;
30:      $sel_id = false;
31:    }
32:
33:    if ($update)
34:    {
35:      $sql = "UPDATE people SET name='$name',sex='$sex',
36:       location='$location',birth='$birth', salary='$salary' WHERE id=$id";
37:      $result = mysql_query($sql);
38:      $update = false;
39:    }
40:     if ($insert)
41:     {
42:       $sql = "INSERT INTO people (id,name,sex,location,birth,salary)
43:             VALUES (NULL,'$name','$sex','$location','$birth','$salary')";
44:      $result = mysql_query($sql);
45:      $insert = false;
46:     }
47:
48:    if ($delete)
49:    {
50:      $sql = "DELETE FROM people WHERE id=$id";
51:      $result = mysql_query($sql);
52:      $delete = false;
53:    }
```

This PHP page fragment is mainly for controlling the SQL operations. Lines 21–22 are used to connect to the MySQL and select the database company. To control the SQL operations, we have used a series of if statements in this example. The first if statement (lines 27–31) means the user has double clicked one of the records inside a select box. If one of the records is selected, the id field of the record is passed to the variable $id in line 29. This $id variable is used to extract the record data from the table and display them in a series of text boxes for editing.

When the Update button is pressed, the if statement in lines 33–39 is activated. In this case, the SQL update statement is executed by the statement in lines 35–36 and consequently updates the record inside the table. When the Insert button is clicked, the SQL insert statement defined in line 42 is executed to insert the record at the end of the table. If the Delete button is pressed, the statements in lines 49–53 are executed to delete the record from the table.

When all the buttons are defined as illustrated in this page fragment, you need to display all records of the table in a select box waiting for a double click. The PHP coding for this task is listed in the page fragment below:

Listing: Continuation Of The PHP Script ex18-53.php (Part Two)

```
54:
55:    $result = mysql_query("SELECT * FROM people ORDER BY id",$db);
56:
57:    echo("<form name=\"myForm\" method=\"post\" action=\"$PHP_SELF\">
58:           <select class=\"butSt2\" size=\"10\" name=\"sel_id\"
59:             ondblclick=\"document.myForm.submit()\" >");
60:
61:    while ($myrow = mysql_fetch_array($result))
62:    {
63:      if ($myrow["id"] == $id)
64:      {
65:       printf("<option selected value=\"%s\" />%s, %s, %s, %s, %s <br />",
66:         $myrow["id"], $myrow["name"], $myrow["sex"], $myrow["location"],
67:         $myrow["birth"], $myrow["salary"]);
68:      } else {
69:       printf("<option value=\"%s\" />%s, %s, %s, %s, %s <br />",
70:         $myrow["id"], $myrow["name"], $myrow["sex"], $myrow["location"],
71:         $myrow["birth"], $myrow["salary"]);
72:      }
73:    }
74:    echo("</select></form>");
75: ?>
76:  <img src="line1.gif" width="600"
77:        height="6" alt="pic" /><br /><br />
```

To display all records of the table `test` in a select box, you may need to issue an SQL statement to get all the records as in line 55. Then a form and a select box are generated in lines 57–74. We have used the variable $PHP_SELF in the form action so that this example will call itself when the form is submitted. Inside the select box, the following double click handler is used:

```
ondblclick="document.myForm.submit()"
```

If any item of the select box is double clicked, the form will be submitted. To populate the select box, we have used a while-loop on the rows ($myrow) of the table. Each row is displayed as an XHTML option element. When the row identity equals the selected or double-clicked record, the keyword selected is added to the option statement (line 65) so that the double-clicked record is kept active in the select box. When all records of the table have been generated, the statement in line 74 terminates the box and the form. A graphical line (lines 76–77) is then generated to separate the browser window.

If one of the records of the select box is double clicked, the record is extracted in a series of text boxes so that editing can be easily done. To demonstrate this part, the following page fragment is constructed:

Listing: Continuation Of The PHP Script ex18-53.php (Part Three)

```
78:    <form method="post" action="<?php echo $PHP_SELF?>">
79: <?php
80:    if ($id)
81:    {
82:       $sql = "SELECT * FROM people WHERE id=$id";
83:       $result = mysql_query($sql);
84:       $myrow = mysql_fetch_array($result);
85:       $name = $myrow["name"];
86:       $sex = $myrow["sex"];
87:       $location = $myrow["location"];
88:       $birth = $myrow["birth"];
```

```
89:      $salary = $myrow["salary"];
90:
91:   }
92: ?>
93:    <input type=hidden name="id" value="<?php echo $id ?>">
94:    <table class="txtSt" cellspacing="10">
95:     <tr><td>Name:</td><td><input class="butSt" type="Text"
96:          name="name" value="<?php echo $name ?>"> </td>
97:       <td>Sex:</td><td><input class="butSt" type="Text"
98:          name="sex" value="<?php echo $sex ?>"></td></tr>
99:     <tr><td>Location:</td><td><input class="butSt" type="Text"
100:          name="location" value="<?php echo $location ?>"> </td>
101:        <td>Birth:</td><td><input class="butSt" type="Text"
102:          name="birth" value="<?php echo $birth ?>"></td></tr>
103:     <tr><td>Salary:</td><td><input class="butSt" type="Text"
104:          name="salary" value="<?php echo $salary ?>"></td>
105:        <td>Current ID :</td><td><?php echo $id ?></td><tr>
106:    </table>
107:    <input class="butSt" type="submit" name="update" value="Update">
108:         
109:    <input class="butSt" type="submit" name="insert "value="Insert">
110:         
111:    <input class="butSt" type="submit" name="delete" value="Delete">
112:    </form>
113: </body>
114: </html>
```

If one of the records is selected by a double click, the `id` field is stored in the variable `$id`. This data can be used to execute the SQL statement to extract the row from the table (line 82):

```
SELECT * FROM test WHERE id=$id;
```

The field data of this row are then stored in variables `$name`, `$sex`, `$location`, `$birth`, and `$salary`. When these variables are defined, an XHTML table (lines 94–106) is constructed to display them in a series of text boxes. Since text boxes are editable, modifications can be made easily. Finally, three buttons are defined in lines 107–111, namely, Update, Insert, and Delete buttons with submit type. Each button has a name so that the corresponding variable can be recognized when pressed. For example, when the Update button is pressed, the form is submitted to the page with variable `$update` defined. In this case, the SQL statements in lines 35–37 update the record. Some screen shots of this example are shown in Figs 18.50 and 18.51.

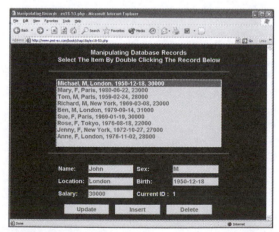

Figure 18.50 ex18-53.php

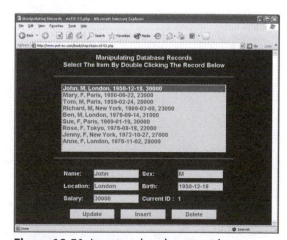

Figure 18.51 Insert and update records

18.5.3 A page to walk through records with navigation buttons

Another interesting PHP function related to MySQL is the data seek function `msql_data_seek()`. This function has the following general calling format:

```
int msql_data_seek (int query_identifier, int row_number)
```

This function moves the internal row pointer of the `query_identifier` to point to the specified row number. Therefore, the next call to any fetch function such as `msql_fetch_row()` would return that row.

Even in this simple form, the function can be called and used to fetch the rows in reverse order. Consider the following simple example:

```
Example: ex18-54.php - A Page To Fetch The Rows In Reverse Order

 1:  <?PHP echo"<?";?>xml version="1.0" encoding="iso-8859-1"<?PHP echo"?>";?>
 2:  <!DOCTYPE html PUBLIC "-//W3C//DTD XHTML 1.0 Transitional//EN"
 3:      "http://www.w3.org/TR/xhtml1/DTD/xhtml1-transitional.dtd">
 4:  <html xmlns="http://www.w3.org/1999/xhtml" xml:lang="en" lang="en">
 5:  <head><title>Fetch In Reverse Order - ex18-54.php</title></head>
 6:  <body style="background:#000088;text-align:center;font-family:arial;
 7:      font-size:14pt;color:#ffff00">
 8:  <div style="font-size:16pt;color:#ffff00;font-weight:bold">
 9:    Displaying Database Records<br />
10:    In Reverse Order Using PHP Functions<br /><br /></div>
11:  <img src="line1.gif" width="600"
12:      height="6" alt="pic" /><br /><br />
13:  <?php
14:  $db = mysql_connect("www.pwt-ex.com", "johnsmith","johnsmith");
15:  mysql_select_db("personnel",$db);
16:  $query = "SELECT * FROM people";
17:  $result = mysql_query ($query)
18:     or die ("SQL Query Error..");
19:
20:  for ($ii = mysql_num_rows ($result) - 1; $ii >=0; $ii--)
21:  {
22:    if (!mysql_data_seek ($result, $ii))
23:    {
24:       echo "Error on Seeking Row $ii <br />";
25:       continue;
26:    }
27:
28:    if(!($row = mysql_fetch_array ($result)))
29:       continue;
30:
31:    printf("%s, %s, %s, %s, %s <br />",
32:    $row['name'], $row['sex'], $row['location'],
33:    $row['birth'], $row['salary']);
34:  }
35:
36:  mysql_free_result ($result);
37:  ?>
38:
39:  <br /><img src="line1.gif" width="600"
40:      height="6" alt="pic" /><br /><br />
41:  </body>
42:  </html>
```

This example displays all records in reverse order. The for-loop in lines 20–34 begins from the last row of the table and the function:

```
mysql_data_seek ($result, $ii)
```

moves the internal pointer to the row represented by `$ii`. The fetch function `mysql_fetch_array()` in line 28 obtains the data of that row, which are displayed by the print function in lines 31–33.

As a practical example, let's consider a page that can display the database records one by one using navigation buttons. This technique is a popular choice for many online recruitment agencies or dating agencies to display their database records to clients. Usually, details of the record with a photo are displayed on the browser window one by one and controlled by a Next or Previous button (navigation buttons).

For obvious reasons, our implementation can only be a simple one; no fancy searching interface is constructed. A simple SQL query is employed on a table called `people`. The records are displayed with navigation buttons. The details of the staff including photos are displayed on the browser window. Only the photos of the first four people are provided. You can use the Next or Previous buttons to walk through all returned records. Some screen shots of this example are shown in Figs 18.52 and 18.53.

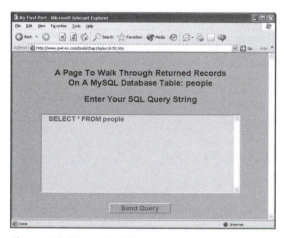

Figure 18.52 ex18-55.htm

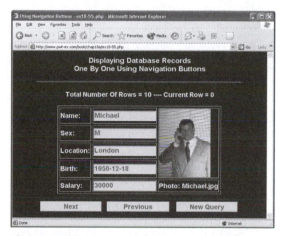

Figure 18.53 Viewing records with navigation buttons

As you can see from Fig. 18.52, the interface part is a simple XHTML page. The page is listed as follows:

```
Example: ex18-55.htm - Walk Through Records With Navigation Buttons

 1: <?xml version="1.0" encoding="iso-8859-1"?>
 2: <!DOCTYPE html PUBLIC "-//W3C//DTD XHTML 1.0 Transitional//EN"
 3:     "http://www.w3.org/TR/xhtml1/DTD/xhtml1-transitional.dtd">
 4: <html xmlns="http://www.w3.org/1999/xhtml" xml:lang="en" lang="en">
 5: <head><title>Using Navigation Buttons - ex18-55.htm</title></head>
 6: <style>
 7:   .txt{font-family:arial;font-size:14pt;color:#000088;font-weight:bold}
 8:   .butSt{background-color:#aaffaa;font-family:arial;font-weight:bold;
 9:      font-size:14pt;color:#008800;width:520px;height:30px}
10:   .textareaSt{background-color:#aaffaa;font-family:arial;font-weight:bold;
11:      font-size:14pt;color:#008800;width:580px;height:230px}
12: </style>
13: <body style="font-size:18pt;background:#bbbbff;
14:      text-align:center" class="txt"><br />
```

```
15:    A Page To Walk Through Returned Records<br />
16:    On A MySQL Database Table: people <br />
17:
18:  <form action = "ex18-55.php" method="post">
19:    Enter Your SQL Query String<br /><br />
20:  <textarea rows="8" cols="30" name = "queryS" class="textareaSt">
21:    SELECT * FROM people</textarea><br /><br />
22:  <input type = "submit" value = "Send Query" class="butSt"
23:    style="width:180px;background:#bbbbbb">
24:  </form>
25: </body>
26: </html>
```

The first part of this PHP page is to design some navigation functionalities to be used by some navigation buttons. To start, the page will display the first record (record 0). When you press the Next button, the current record will be incremented by 1. Similarly, the current record is decreased by 1 if you press the Previous button. If you press the New Query button, the PHP page will redirect you to the XHTML page ex18-55.htm so that a new query can be entered.

The first part of this PHP program is listed below:

```
Example: ex18-55.php - The PHP Script For ex18-55.htm (Part One)

 1: <?PHP echo"<?";?>xml version="1.0" encoding="iso-8859-1"<?PHP echo"?>";?>
 2: <!DOCTYPE html PUBLIC "-//W3C//DTD XHTML 1.0 Transitional//EN"
 3:      "http://www.w3.org/TR/xhtml1/DTD/xhtml1-transitional.dtd">
 4: <html xmlns="http://www.w3.org/1999/xhtml" xml:lang="en" lang="en">
 5: <head><title>Using Navigation Buttons - ex18-55.php</title></head>
 6: <style>
 7:  .txtSt{font-family:arial;font-size:14pt;color:#ffff00;font-weight:bold}
 8:  .butSt{background-color:#aaffaa;font-family:arial;font-weight:bold;
 9:     font-size:14pt;color:#008800;width:180px;height:30px}
10: </style>
11: <body style="background:#000088;text-align:center;font-family:arial;
12:      font-size:14pt;color:#ffff00;font-weight:bold">
13: <div style="font-size:16pt;color:#ffff00;font-weight:bold">
14:    Displaying Database Records<br />
15:    One By One Using Navigation Buttons<br /><br /></div>
16:  <img src="line1.gif" width="600"
17:      height="6" alt="pic" /><br /><br />
18:
19: <form method="post" action="<?php echo $PHP_SELF?>">
20: <?php
21:  global $query,$queryS,$next,$previous,$currentRow,$endRow,$result;
22:  if ($queryS)
23:  {
24:   $currentRow = 0;
25:   $query = $queryS;
26:   $queryS = false;
27:  }
28:  if ($next)
29:  {
30:   $currentRow++;
31:   if ($currentRow > ($endRow-1)) $currentRow = 0;
32:   $next = false;
33:  }
34:  if ($previous)
35:  {
```

```
36:      $currentRow--;
37:      if ( $currentRow < 0)
38:         $currentRow = $endRow -1;
39:.     $previous = false;
40:   }
41:
```

This page contains three `if` statements. When an SQL statement is submitted to this page, the variable `$querySt` has the true value (line 22). In this case, we set the current row `$currentRow` equals to 0 and assign the query statement to PHP variable `$query`.

If you press the Next button, the `if` statement in lines 28–33 is executed. The current row is incremented by 1 to reflect the current row situation. If the current row is beyond the last row, the first record (i.e., record 0) is set. Similarly, if the Previous button is clicked, the current row is decreased by 1. If the row number is a negative value, the end row is assigned in line 38.

The second part of the PHP program is responsible for obtaining the detailed data of the current row. Based on the discussion in example ex18-54.php, the coding is listed below:

```
Listing: Continuation Of The PHP Script ex18-55.php (Part Two)

42:   $db = mysql_connect("www.pwt-ex.com", "johnsmith","johnsmith");
43:   mysql_select_db("personnel",$db);
44:   $result = mysql_query ($query)
45:      or die ("SQL Query Error..");
46:   $endRow = mysql_num_rows ($result);
47:
48:   echo("Total Number Of Rows = $endRow ----
49:         Current Row = $currentRow<br />");
50:
51:   if (!mysql_data_seek ($result, $currentRow))
52:   {
53:      echo "Error on Seeking Row $currentRow <br />";
54:   }
55:
56:   $myrow = mysql_fetch_array($result);
57:   $name = $myrow["name"];
58:   $sex = $myrow["sex"];
59:   $location = $myrow["location"];
60:   $birth = $myrow["birth"];
61:   $salary = $myrow["salary"];
62:   mysql_free_result ($result);
63:   $photo = $name . ".jpg";
64: ?>
```

After connecting to the MySQL database and execution of the query in lines 42–45, the total number of rows returned by the query is captured in the variable `$endRow`. This value together with the current row is displayed by the echo statement in lines 48–49. In order to obtain the data of the current row, the function

```
mysql_data_seek ($result, $currentRow)
```

is used to move the internal pointer to the row represented by `$currentRow`. The `mysql_fetch_array()` function in line 56 obtains the data of the current row. The remaining coding of this page fragment is to store the data into variables:

- `$name`   — Store the name of the staff.
- `$sex`   — Sex of the staff.
- `$location` — Location information of the staff.
- `$birth`   — Birthday of the staff.

- $salary   – Salary of the staff.
- $photo   – The file name of the photo (the file name is the name of the staff with .jpg as extension as illustrated in line 63).

Now we have everything necessary for us to develop the final part of the page to display and navigate the records. The coding of this page fragment is listed as follows:

```
Listing: Continuation Of The PHP Script ex18-55.php (Part Three)
65: <form method="post" action="<?php echo $PHP_SELF?>">
66:   <input type=hidden name="query" value="<?php echo $query ?>">
67:   <input type=hidden name="currentRow" value="<?php echo $currentRow ?>">
68:   <input type=hidden name="endRow" value="<?php echo $endRow ?>"> <br />
69:   <table class="txtSt" cellspacing="5" border="1">
70:    <tr><td>Name:</td>
71:       <td><input class="butSt" type="Text" readonly
72:          name="name" value="<?php echo $name ?>"> </td>
73:       <td rowspan="4"><img src="<?php echo($photo);?>" alt="pic"
74:          width="150" height="200" /></td></tr>
75:    <tr><td>Sex:</td>
76:       <td><input class="butSt" type="Text" readonly
77:          name="sex" value="<?php echo $sex ?>"></td></tr>
78:    <tr><td>Location:</td>
79:       <td><input class="butSt" type="Text" readonly
80:          name="location" value="<?php echo $location ?>"> </td></tr>
81:    <tr><td>Birth:</td>
82:       <td><input class="butSt" type="Text" readonly
83:          name="birth" value="<?php echo $birth ?>"></td></tr>
84:    <tr><td>Salary:</td>
85:       <td><input class="butSt" type="Text" readonly
86:          name="salary" value="<?php echo $salary ?>"></td>
87:       <td>Photo: <?php echo($photo);?></td></tr>
88:   </table><br />
89:   <input class="butSt" type="submit" name="next" value="Next">  
90:   <input class="butSt" type="submit" name="previous" value="Previous">
91:       
92:   <input class="butSt" type="button" name="new_query" value="New Query"
93:     onclick="document.location='ex18-55.htm'">
94: </form>
95: </body>
96: </html>
```

Since this PHP page can call itself, we need to generate some hidden input elements as in lines 66–68 to pass the $query, $endRow, and $currentRow parameters to the page. To display the detailed row information, a table with five rows is used in lines 69–88. The name, sex, location, birth, and salary information are displayed here. Along with the name field, an image element is used in lines 73–74 to display the photo. The size of the photo will cover four table rows.

Finally, three buttons are declared in lines 89–93. Each button is defined as submit type with a name. This name can be used to activate the corresponding PHP variable to perform actions. For example, if you press the Next button declared in line 89, the variable $next will have the true value and then the statements in lines 28–33 in ex18-55.php will be executed. The Next and Previous buttons are known as the navigation buttons in databases. They allow you to walk through records.

Part V

Web security, e-commerce, and other topics

19 Security technologies on the Web

19.1 Basic data security

19.1.1 Cryptography: encryption and decryption

Even in the ancient world, people were fully aware of the importance of data security. Important messages were usually disguised or hidden from anyone for whom they were not intended. For example, messages were often encrypted with substitution methods or written in special ink visible only under heat. These are the ancestors of the encryption, or more precisely cryptographic, technologies today.

In general, any technique that can transform a readable document (or plain text) into unreadable gibberish is called encryption. The data after the encryption are known as ciphertext (or cipher). Under this definition, almost any text transformation methods including compression are considered as encryption. For example, the following message can be encrypted by transformation into other fonts:

SECRET MESSAGE – Courier

ΣΕΧΡΕΤ ΜΕΣΣΑΓΕ – Symbol

❑❀❖❑❒ ✗❒❑❑❀❏❒ – MS Outlook

or into other representations such as hexadecimal:

534543524554 4D455353414745 – hex representation

If you were an emperor in ancient Rome, say, you might also perform a character shift by two (or sometimes three) on top of the first substitution above. That is, changing "A" to "C" and "B" to "D." In this case, even the readable message "SECRET MESSAGE" turns out to be "UGETGV OGUUCIG."

By today's standards these encryption measures are simple to attack because they all have a pattern to follow. However, if you add these simple additional measures (or personal touches) on top of the advanced encryption and cryptography covered in this chapter, you may create major headaches even for some cryptography experts.

As a symmetric process to encryption, decryption is a process to convert the ciphertext back to plain text. Cryptography is the technology of using mathematical formulas or algorithms to encrypt and decrypt data. In cryptographic terms, the tools for encryption and decryption are often considered as keys. For example, if you use a changing font for encryption/decryption, the key would be the name of the font. If you rotate (or shift) the alphabet for encryption/decryption, the rotation number is the key.

19.1.2 Digital keys and passwords

In our digital world of cryptography, a key is usually a value that works with an algorithm to encrypt and decrypt data. Usually, keys are big numbers measured in bits; bigger keys (in bits) will result in stronger security. Data security is measured in the time and resources it would require to recover the plain text when under attack. It is believed that even ordinary public-key encryption (discussed later) is difficult to crack. If you were to have a billion computers doing a billion instructions each a second, you wouldn't be able to recover the plain text before the end of the universe. Of course, this is measured in terms of raw computing power. Even with human intelligence and tools, to attack a ciphertext is not easy. This is the main reason why everything from simple email transmissions to missile launch sequences (or passwords) is guarded with digital keys.

When dealing with computers, most people are familiar with passwords as unique strings (digital key) used to restrict access to computer resources. Passwords are used in almost every aspect related to computers and are an important subject for cryptography. Basically, to generate a password, a one-way function (or hash function) is used. This function has the following mathematical characteristics:

- For all x, the function y or $f(x)$ is easy to compute.
- For virtually all y, it is extremely difficult to find an x such that $f(x) = y$.

Using this kind of function to generate a password is common practice in security. As a good starting point, a password algorithm known as "Message Digest" or "Finger Print" and its applications are introduced in section 19.2. "Message Digest" is a standard known as the Internet Engineering Task Force (IETF) RFC 1321 standard. This algorithm is an important part of many encryption, decryption, and digital signature techniques discussed in this chapter.

As a simple example, the standard "Message Digest" (MD) function md5() on "johnsmith" and "john" produces the following results:

```
md5("johnsmith") = cd4388c0c62e65ac8b99e3ec49fd9409
md5("john") = 527bd5b5d689e2c32ae974c6229ff785
```

The numeric value represents the digest of the original message or string. Virtually no two different strings produce the same numeric value. It is difficult to reproduce the original text from the numeric result and therefore this is a powerful one-way function. As you may remember, the passwords of the MySQL package can be protected by the MD function.

Even a good technology cannot prevent or protect careless errors. To prevent a brute-force (or "Try Them All") attack by hackers, it is recommended that the original text should be long enough and include both characters and numbers to discourage intruders. Don't forget that it only needs from 1 to 99,999 comparisons to build a lookup table to decode all five-digit passwords. Since MD can take input of variable length, some organizations use the numeric value of the md5() function as the original text and run it through several times to generate an encrypted password.

A good secret key (or password) and an advanced cryptographic algorithm can make it so difficult for intruders to decode a message (or ciphertext) that it isn't worth the effort to try. They may try to steal your secret key using human intelligence instead.

Using one key (or password) is classified as conventional cryptography. If you want to send an encrypted message to someone, you may have to reveal the secrecy of your password so that your message can be properly decoded by the person you trust. This can create some key distribution problems and compromise data security.

Also, with one key, it is not easy to perform data integrity and verification. For example, how does someone know that an important message was really sent by you? As a simple example, if you send a message to the bank, how does the bank manager determine that the message was really sent by you? How does the bank know the message sent by you hasn't been attacked by a hacker to transfer money to his or her account? To provide a solution to these problems public-key cryptography is used.

19.1.3 Public-key cryptography, digital signatures, and data verification

Public-key cryptography solves the key distribution problem by defining an algorithm to generate two keys. Each key can be used to encrypt a message. If key A is used to encrypt a message, then the other must be used to decrypt it. This arrangement makes it possible to publish one key to the general public for encrypting messages to you. You can keep the other key (private key) secret permanently to decrypt messages intended for you. Anyone may encrypt a message using your public key and send it to you. Only the owner of the private key is able to decode it.

Public-key techniques are very popular – there is even a standard for it, IETF RFC 2440, known as Open Pretty Good Privacy (OpenPGP). For the practical nature of this book, only ideas, methods, and application examples are provided to show how to secure your data transmission on the Web. In general, for any public-key software package or algorithm, the process for encryption and decryption is as follows:

- Obtain two keys from the public-key algorithm or software packages.
- Publish one key to the general public and keep the other key as a secret (or private) key.
- People can send you emails, files, or messages encrypted by your public key.
- Only you or the owner of the private key would be able to decode the encrypted messages.

Now you may feel more comfortable about sending a message to the bank since public-key technology provides pretty good privacy protection. There is still concern at the bank to verify that the message was really from you. The solution is called a digital signature. You can perform a digital signature by encrypting some information with your private key. If the bank or other person can decrypt the information encrypted by your private key, the information must have been sent by you. The digital signature verification process as follows:

- Encrypt your message with some of your personal information with your private key as signature.
- Encrypt the entire message with someone's public key.
- Send the encrypted message to the receiver.
- The receiver uses his or her private key to decrypt the message.
- If the receiver can decrypt the signature using your public key, the message must have been sent by you.

Another question is how you verify that the messages you send to the bank haven't been modified or replaced by an intruder. The answer lies in the MD technique mentioned above. Since the MD function can produce a summary of a long message, you can obtain a digest (a numeric value) of your message to the bank and create a signature good only for this particular message. The process is as follows:

- Obtain the MD (a numeric value) for the entire message that you want to send.
- Encrypt this digest with your own private key as the digital signature.
- Encrypt the message and the digital signature with the receiver's public key.
- Send the entire encrypted message to the intended receiver.
- The receiver uses his or her private key to decrypt the message.
- The receiver uses your public key to decrypt your digital signature to get the digest of the message.
- The receiver uses the MD function to obtain a digest of the message you sent. If the two digests match, the message is intact.

For some public-key or OpenPGP implementations, when you sign a message with a digital signature, it also contains a unique sequence of numbers to protect against:

- interception and reuse of the signature by an intruder at a later date;
- fraudulent claims from you that you didn't send the message (non-repudiation).

All these processes will be discussed below at an understandable level and practical examples will also be provided. Let's start encryption and protection with passwords.

19.2 Data protection begins with passwords

19.2.1 A simple page to use an encrypted password

One of the best and most effective ways to protect against unauthorized access to your Web site is to use a password. As we mentioned in section 19.1, MD is a powerful tool to generate encrypted passwords and in fact is a standard in the Internet community known as IETF RFC 1321. The MD function has gone through five versions. Many implementations use the function name md5() to represent the version number. Different Web technologies may have slightly different names for this function, but all produce the same result. For example, the md5() function in PHP and Perl may have different names, but produce the following numeric values:

PHP script:

```
md5("johnsmith") = cd4388c0c62e65ac8b99e3ec49fd9409
md5("john") = 527bd5b5d689e2c32ae974c6229ff785
```

Perl script:

```
md5_hex("johnsmith") = cd4388c0c62e65ac8b99e3ec49fd9409
md5_hex("john") = 527bd5b5d689e2c32ae974c6229ff785
```

For a Web programmer or designer, a page to generate an encrypted password using an MD string, in many cases, is handy. Consider the following simple Web page using Perl script:

```
Example: ex19-01.pl - Generating Encrypted Password

 1: #!/usr/bin/perl
 2: use CGI qw (:standard);
 3: use Digest::MD5 qw(md5 md5_hex md5_base64);
 4:
 5: print ("Content-type:text/html\n\n");
 6: my $passId = param("passId");
 7: my $enc_passId = md5_hex($passId);
 8:
 9: print << "mypage";
10: <?xml version="1.0" encoding="iso-8859-1"?>
11: <!DOCTYPE html PUBLIC "-//W3C//DTD XHTML 1.0 Transitional//EN"
12: "http://www.w3.org/TR/xhtml1/DTD/xhtml1-transitional.dtd">
13: <html xmlns="http://www.w3.org/1999/xhtml" xml:lang="en" lang="en">
14: <head><title>Generating Encrypted Password - ex19-01.pl</title></head>
15: <style>
16: .butSt{background-color:#aaaaaa;font-family:arial;font-weight:bold;
17:     font-size:18pt;color:#880000;width:150px;height:35px}
18: .butSt2{background-color:#aaffaa;font-family:arial;font-weight:bold;
19:     font-size:18pt;color:#880000;width:250px;height:35px}
20: .txtSt{font-family:arial;font-weight:bold; text-align:left;
21:     font-size:18pt;color:#ffff00}
22: </style>
23:
24: <body style="background:#000088;text-align:center" class="txtSt">
25: A Simple Page To Generate<br />
26: Encrypted Password Using Perl Script<br /><br />
27:
28: <form action="ex19-01.pl" method="post">
29: <table class="txtSt"><tr>
30:  <td>Password:</td>
31:  <td><input type="text" name="passId" id="passId" class="butSt2" /></td>
32: </tr><tr>
33:   <td><input type="submit" value="Generate" class="butSt" /></td>
```

```
34:    <td><input type="reset" value="Clear" class="butSt" /></td></tr>
35:    </table>
36:    </form><br /><br />
37: mypage
38:
39: print "You Have Submitted the Password <br /> $passId <br /><br />";
40: print "The Encrypted Password is below:<br /> $enc_passId <br /><br />";
41: print " </body></html>"
```

In order to use MD, the Perl module `Digest` is included in line 3. In this module, three versions of the `md()` functions are introduced:

- `md5()` – Generates `Digest` string in binary format.
- `md5_hex()` – Generates `Digest` string in hexadecimal format.
- `md5_base64()` – Generates `Digest` string in base 64 format.

This page contains a form to submit to itself. First, a text field is displayed to allow the user to fill in a password. Once the Generate button defined in line 33 is clicked, the input password is captured by the variable `$passId` in line 6. Based on this password, an encrypted password is obtained by a call to the function (line 7)

```
$enc_passId = md5_hex($passId);
```

Now the encrypted password is stored in the variable `$enc_passId` in hexadecimal format. Both the original and encrypted passwords are displayed by two print functions in lines 39–40.

This is a simple Web page to generate an encrypted password. In many cases a page like this is useful when you want to add some secret coding to your Web pages. A simple cut and paste of the generated numeric value to your code or program will guarantee no typing errors. A screen shot of this example is shown in Fig. 19.1.

MD is an important tool and often considered as the foundation of advanced cryptography. Before we continue to discuss how to use MD to protect Web pages, let's consider an example to generate an MD string or encrypted password using PHP. Consider the following PHP page:

Figure 19.1 ex19-01.pl

```
Example: ex19-02.php - To Generate Encrypted Password Using PHP

 1: <?PHP echo"<?";?>xml version="1.0" encoding="iso-8859-1"<?PHP echo"?>";?>
 2: <!DOCTYPE html PUBLIC "-//W3C//DTD XHTML 1.0 Transitional//EN"
 3: "http://www.w3.org/TR/xhtml1/DTD/xhtml1-transitional.dtd">
 4: <html xmlns="http://www.w3.org/1999/xhtml" xml:lang="en" lang="en">
 5: <head><title>Encrypted Password Using PHP - ex19-02.php</title></head>
 6: <style>
 7: .butSt{background-color:#aaaaaa;font-family:arial;font-weight:bold;
 8:     font-size:18pt;color:#880000;width:150px;height:35px}
 9: .butSt2{background-color:#aaffaa;font-family:arial;font-weight:bold;
10:     font-size:18pt;color:#880000;width:250px;height:35px}
11: .txtSt{font-family:arial;font-weight:bold; text-align:left;
12:     font-size:18pt;color:#ffff00}
13: </style>
14:
15: <body style="background:#000088;text-align:center" class="txtSt">
```

```
16:    A Simple Page To Generate<br />
17:    Encrypted Password Using PHP<br /><br />
18:
19:    <form action="ex19-02.php" method="post">
20:    <table class="txtSt"><tr>
21:      <td>Password:</td>
22:      <td><input type="text" name="passId" id="passId" class="butSt2" /></td>
23:    </tr><tr>
24:      <td><input type="submit" value="Generate" class="butSt" /></td>
25:      <td><input type="reset" value="Clear" class="butSt" /></td></tr>
26:    </table>
27:    </form><br /><br />
28:
29:    <?php
30:    global $passId,$enc_passId;
31:    if ($passId)
32:    {
33:     $enc_passId = md5($passId);
34:     echo "You Have Submitted the Password <br /> $passId <br /><br />";
35:     echo "The Encrypted Password is below:<br /> $enc_passId <br /><br />";
36:     echo " </body></html>";
37:    }
38:    ?>
```

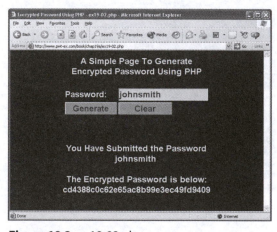

Figure 19.2 ex19-02.php

The first part of this PHP program (lines 1–27) is in fact an XHTML page to obtain an original password. This page will submit to itself for processing when the Generate button is clicked. The processing code is defined in the PHP block in lines 29–38.

When the password variable $passId is defined, the MD function md5() is called in line 33 to obtain the encrypted password of $passId. Both the original and encrypted passwords are displayed by the two echo statements in lines 34 and 35. A screen shot of this example is shown in Fig. 19.2.

A straightforward application of an encrypted password is to protect access to Web pages. From now on, we will assume that the Web server is a secure machine and the Web pages are in a secure environment.

19.2.2 A Web page protected by a password

If you have a personal Web site or page that you don't want to share with the general public, your best bet may be to protect it with an encrypted password. Also, it has become increasingly popular for some companies to load information into Web pages protected by an encrypted password to make sure that it remains strictly confidential.

Provided the page is in a secure server, the following example can be used to offer protection against unauthorized access.

```
Example: ex19-03.pl - A Web Page Protected By A Password

 1: #!/usr/bin/perl
 2: use CGI qw (:standard);
 3: use Digest::MD5 qw(md5 md5_hex md5_base64);
 4:
 5: print ("Content-type:text/html\n\n");
 6:
```

```
 7: print << "mypage";
 8: <?xml version="1.0" encoding="iso-8859-1"?>
 9: <!DOCTYPE html PUBLIC "-//W3C//DTD XHTML 1.0 Transitional//EN"
10: "http://www.w3.org/TR/xhtml1/DTD/xhtml1-transitional.dtd">
11: <html xmlns="http://www.w3.org/1999/xhtml" xml:lang="en" lang="en">
12: <head><title>A Page Protected By Password - ex19-03.pl</title></head>
13: <style>
14: .butSt{background-color:#aaaaaa;font-family:arial;font-weight:bold;
15:     font-size:18pt;color:#880000;width:150px;height:35px}
16: .butSt2{background-color:#aaffaa;font-family:arial;font-weight:bold;
17:     font-size:18pt;color:#880000;width:250px;height:35px}
18: .txtSt{font-family:arial;font-weight:bold; text-align:left;
19:     font-size:18pt;color:#ffff00}
20: </style>
21: <body style="background:#000088" class="txtSt">
22: mypage
23:
24: my $enc_passId = md5_hex(param("passId"));
25: my $passSt = 'cd4388c0c62e65ac8b99e3ec49fd9409';
26:
27: if ($enc_passId eq $passSt)
28: {
29:   print "Access Granted";
30: }
31: else
32: {
33:  $llst = 'This is a private page for<br /> members only<br /><br />' .
34:   ' <form action="ex19-03.pl" method="post">'.
35:   ' <table class="txtSt"><tr>' .
36:   '    <td>Password:</td>' .
37:   ' <td><input type="text" name="passId" id="passId" ' .
38:   '     class="butSt2" /></td> </tr><tr>' .
39:   '    <td><input type="submit" value="Submit" class="butSt" /></td>' .
40:   '    <td><input type="reset" value="Clear" class="butSt" /></td></tr>' .
41:   ' </table>' .
42:   ' </form> ';
43:  print "$llst";
44: }
45:
46: print " </body></html>"
```

This is a simple page using Perl script. When first loaded, it displays a dialog field asking for password input. The password is then submitted to the same page for processing. If the input password matches, a message Access Granted is displayed. Otherwise, the same dialog field is displayed again asking for the password. The dialog field is defined by a Perl string $llst in lines 33–42.

After the necessary set-up codes in lines 1–22, the main statements are (lines 24 and 25)

```
my $enc_passId = md5_hex(param("passId"));
my $passSt = 'cd4388c0c62e65ac8b99e3ec49fd9409';
```

whichs declare two variables. The first variable stores the digest of the input password and the second variable contains the numeric string. If these two variables are the same, the print statement in line 29 is executed. Otherwise, the Perl string $llst is output to the browser window asking for the password again. Since the code, in this form, is hardwired as in lines 24–25, only the password "johnsmith" can gain access to this page.

This example is a framework to protect a Web page at the entry level. You can put in any instruction you like or jump to another page code in lines 28–30 to suit your needs. Since Perl script is executed inside a Web server, all the Perl statements are transparent to end users. Therefore, the password string $passSt and other information are protected to some degree against unauthorized access.

One characteristic of this example is that you can easily change the password string $passSt using the generation program ex19-01.pl. Another advantage of using MD is that it is difficult for an intruder to guess the original password even if he or she can spy on this page and knows the password string

```
$passSt= 'cd4388c0c62e65ac8b99e3ec49fd9409'
```

This means that your original password is not compromised even if this page is stolen and you don't need to change your password for other applications. The intruder may need to take the risk of stealing again in order to gain access to other pages. The original password for this password string is of course "johnsmith". Some screen shots of this example are shown in Figs 19.3 and 19.4.

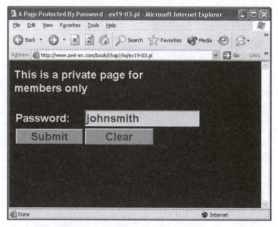

Figure 19.3 ex19-03.p1   **Figure 19.4** Access granted

In order to allow a group of people to have their own passwords and gain access to the same Web resources, you may need to use file storage to store passwords.

19.2.3 Using encrypted passwords in a file

To demonstrate how to use file storage for encrypted passwords, we revisit example ex15-10.htm in Chapter 15. This example shows how to use a password file in the Web server for a group of people. The original password file password.txt contains the user name and password pair. The contents of this file are:

```
Listing: ex19-01.txt - Contents Of The Password File: password.txt

1:    Paul,paul123
2:    JohnSmith,johnsmith
3:    Peter,p2341
4:    Mary,mary2001
5:    Tom,tom213
6:    Joe,joe900
7:    chip,c2309
8:    Emma,emma234
9:    John,jkl12
```

Since this password file is not protected, it may be a disaster if it is stolen by a hacker. To protect this file, you can run through all passwords with the encrypted password program ex19-01.pl. The new password file with MD encrypted passwords is called password2.txt and is listed below:

```
Listing: ex19-02.txt - Contents Of The Password File: password2.txt

1:    Paul,2e69f107d4be5f743461cb66d55d5e6e
2:    JohnSmith,cd4388c0c62e65ac8b99e3ec49fd9409
3:    Peter,15c1c83a0ec7f06f4e63aa8224902efc
4:    Mary,980a37df7f08b2a6299329518f5f37ed
5:    Tom,9a453212fc8bca35646312f0b7b5106a
6:    Joe,15a04b72d7535ebc143cc6d729044ed7
7:    chip,6df39694a5db6f6ed331e53f07a99e56
8:    Emma,31d8c49fb2e6d2fdb28460db4d2751be
9:    John,6e4e8727006525d13c12dbe4d2b51abf
```

The next step is to develop an XHTML page as in ex19-04.htm to collect the user name and password so that a comparison can be made against the password file.

```
Example: ex19-04.htm - Using Encrypted Passwords In A File

 1: <?xml version="1.0" encoding="iso-8859-1"?>
 2: <!DOCTYPE html PUBLIC "-//W3C//DTD XHTML 1.0 Transitional//EN"
 3:     "http://www.w3.org/TR/xhtml1/DTD/xhtml1-transitional.dtd">
 4: <html xmlns="http://www.w3.org/1999/xhtml" xml:lang="en" lang="en">
 5: <head><title>Encrypted Passwords In A File - ex19-04.htm</title></head>
 6: <style>
 7:   .butSt{background-color:#aaffaa;font-family:arial;font-weight:bold;
 8:      font-size:18pt;color:#880000;width:250px;height:35px}
 9:   .txtSt{font-family:arial;font-weight:bold; text-align:left;
10:      font-size:18pt;color:#ffff00}</style>
11: <body style="background:#000088">
12: <form action="ex19-04.pl" method="post">
13:   <table style="position:absolute;left:60px;top:50px" class="txtSt">
14:   <tr><td colspan="2" style="text-align:center">
15:      Enter Your Username and<br /> Password Below<br /><br/></td></tr>
16:   <tr><td>Name:</td><td><input type="text"
17:         name="userId" id="userId" class="butSt" ></td></tr>
18:   <tr><td>Password:</td><td><input type="password"
19:         name="passId" id="passId" class="butSt"></td></tr>
20:   <tr><td><input type="submit" class="butSt" value="Submit"
21:         style="width:150px;background:#dddddd"></td></tr>
22:   </table>
23: </form>
24: </body>
25: </html>
```

This interface page is a form to obtain the user name and password from the user. The page will be submitted to the Perl script program ex19-04.pl for processing. The processing program will perform the following tasks:

- Capture the user name and password input pair from ex19-04.htm.
- Open the password file password2.txt.
- Compare the user name/password pair against the pairs in the password file.
- If a match is found, a welcome message will be displayed, otherwise the message "Access Denied" is displayed.

This Perl script program is similar to ex15-10.pl but with encrypted password protection. The details of the Perl script are listed below:

```
Example: ex19-04.pl - The Perl Script For ex19-04.htm

1: #!usr/bin/perl
2: use CGI qw (:standard);
3: use Digest::MD5 qw(md5 md5_hex md5_base64);
4: my $username = param(userId);
```

```
 5: my $password = md5_hex(param(passId));
 6:
 7: print "Content-type:text/html\n\n";
 8: print << "mypage";
 9: <?xml version="1.0" encoding="iso-8859-1"?>
10: <!DOCTYPE html PUBLIC "-//W3C//DTD XHTML 1.0 Transitional//EN"
11: "http://www.w3.org/TR/xhtml1/DTD/xhtml1-transitional.dtd">
12: <html xmlns="http://www.w3.org/1999/xhtml" xml:lang="en" lang="en">
13: <head><title>Encrypted Passwords In A File - ex19-04.pl</title></head>
14: <style>.txtSt{font-size:18pt;color:#ffff00;font-family:arial}</style>
15: <body style="background:#000088;font-weight:bold" class="txtSt">
16: mypage
17:
18:
19: open(filehandle, "password2.txt") or
20: die "The File could not be opened .. Error.";
21:
22: while(my $st = <filehandle>)
23: {
24:    $st =~ s/\n//g;
25:    ($name, $pass) = split(/,/, $st);
26:
27:    if($name eq "$username")
28:    {
29:      $userF = 1;
30:      if ($pass eq "$password")
31:      {
32:         $passwordF = 1;
33:      }
34:    }
35: }
36: close(filehandle);
37:
38: if ($userF && $passwordF)
39: {
40:   print ("Thank you -- $username <br /> Access Granted !!
41:          <br />Enjoy Your Visit.");
42: }
43: elsif ($userF && !$passwordF)
44: {
45:   print ("Sorry, Wrong Password !!");
46: }
47: else
48: {
49:   print ("Sorry, Access Denied !!");
50: }
51: print "</body></html>";
```

The user name and password from the interface ex19-04.htm are captured by the variables $username and $password defined in lines 4–5. Since the md5_hex() function is used, the value stored in the variable $password is encrypted. The Perl statement in lines 19–20 is to open the password file password2.txt.

When the file is opened successfully, a while-loop (lines 22–35) is employed to read through all the user name/password contents as variable pairs $name/$pass. If the $username equals $name then we have a match on user name. In this case, the value of the user name flag $userF is set to 1. If the input password $password equals the password in the file $pass, a match is found on password. In this case, the value of the password flag $passwordF is set to 1.

To interpret the results of the comparison, a series of `if` statements (lines 38–50) are used. If both user name and password are matched, the print statement in lines 40–41 will be executed and hence a welcome message is displayed. If the user name is matched but not the password, the "Wrong Password" message is output. If the user name is not matched, the "Access Denied" message defined in line 49 is displayed.

Some screen shots of this example are shown in Figs 19.5 and 19.6.

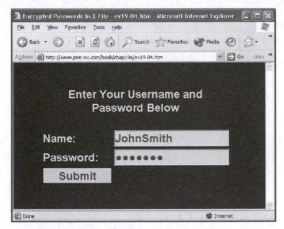

Figure 19.5 ex19-04.htm

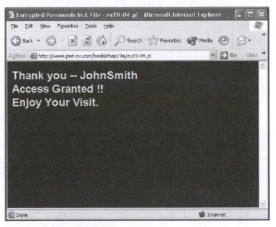

Figure 19.6 Access granted

19.3 Putting encrypted passwords in databases

19.3.1 Creating an encrypted password table in MySQL

If your Web site has a large number of members, storing encrypted passwords in a file may not be efficient and may be difficult to maintain. In this case, a good alternative is to consider putting all passwords into a database. Since we already have some experience on the database package MySQL, we will set up a password table in MySQL and use it to protect a page.

In fact, putting user or member passwords into a database can have all the benefits of a database application. For example, the following features can be easily added or implemented as SQL statements:

- Search password for a particular user.
- Set up new member accounts with password.
- Update or change password.

We will show you in this section how to develop Web pages to demonstrate all these functionalities. First, you need to create a password table to be used in MySQL. For obvious reasons, our password table in MySQL is a simple one and contains three fields only.

- `id` – A number to store the identity or index of each row.
- `name` – Character string (max. 30 characters) to store the user name.
- `password` – Character string (max. 60 characters) to store the encrypted password.

You can add more fields to have more features if you want. For example, you can add a field for the expiry date so that the password in your page can be monitored by the date and time.

As an example, the data in ex19-02.txt are used to build the password table. First, you need to modify the data as in ex19-03.txt:

```
Listing: ex19-03.txt - Password Data File For MySQL: password3.txt

1:    NULL,Paul,2e69f107d4be5f743461cb66d55d5e6e
2:    NULL,JohnSmith,cd4388c0c62e65ac8b99e3ec49fd9409
3:    NULL,Peter,15c1c83a0ec7f06f4e63aa8224902efc
4:    NULL,Mary,980a37df7f08b2a6299329518f5f37ed
5:    NULL,Tom,9a453212fc8bca35646312f0b7b5106a
6:    NULL,Joe,15a04b72d7535ebc143cc6d729044ed7
7:    NULL,chip,6df39694a5db6f6ed331e53f07a99e56
8:    NULL,Emma,31d8c49fb2e6d2fdb28460db4d2751be
9:    NULL,John,6e4e8727006525d13c12dbe4d2b51abf
```

The next step is to create the password table in MySQL. You can do this by typing the following SQL statements with the MySQL client program mysql>. A dialog is shown below:

```
Listing: ex19-04.txt - Creating The Table password

1:   mysql> CREATE TABLE password (
2:       -> id SMALLINT UNSIGNED NOT NULL AUTO_INCREMENT,
3:       -> name VARCHAR(30),
4:       -> password VARCHAR(60),
5:       -> PRIMARY KEY (id)
6:       -> );
7:   Query OK, 0 rows affected (0.00 sec)
```

This table contains two fields, name and password. The maximum lengths for the name and password fields are 30 and 60 characters respectively. Once you have the table, you can load the data file password3.txt into this password table by the LOAD DATA statement. A dialog with the MySQL client is shown as follows:

```
Listing: ex19-05.txt - Load Data password3.txt Into Table password

1:   mysql> LOAD DATA INFILE 'password3.txt'
2:       -> INTO TABLE password
3:       -> FIELDS TERMINATED BY ','
4:       -> LINES TERMINATED BY '\r\n';
5:   Query OK, 9 rows affected (0.00 sec)
6:   Records: 9 Deleted: 0 Skipped: 0 Warnings: 9
```

You can verify the password data in the table by issuing the command

```
SELECT * FROM password;
```

using the mysql client program. If the data have been loaded successfully, you will see the dialog as illustrated in ex19-06.txt. You can also verify this result by using the program we developed in the last chapter if you prefer.

```
Listing: ex19-06.txt - The Details Of The Password Table

 1:   mysql> SELECT * FROM password;
 2:   +----+-----------+----------------------------------+
 3:   | id | name      | password                         |
 4:   +----+-----------+----------------------------------+
 5:   |  1 | Paul      | 2e69f107d4be5f743461cb66d55d5e6e |
 6:   |  2 | JohnSmith | cd4388c0c62e65ac8b99e3ec49fd9409 |
 7:   |  3 | Peter     | 15c1c83a0ec7f06f4e63aa8224902efc |
 8:   |  4 | Mary      | 980a37df7f08b2a6299329518f5f37ed |
 9:   |  5 | Tom       | 9a453212fc8bca35646312f0b7b5106a |
10:   |  6 | Joe       | 15a04b72d7535ebc143cc6d729044ed7 |
11:   |  7 | chip      | 6df39694a5db6f6ed331e53f07a99e56 |
12:   |  8 | Emma      | 31d8c49fb2e6d2fdb28460db4d2751be |
13:   |  9 | John      | 6e4e8727006525d13c12dbe4d2b51abf |
14:   +----+-----------+----------------------------------+
15:   9 rows in set (0.00 sec)
```

One straight application of this password table is to use it to build a page to allow users or members to sign on to the Web site.

19.3.2 A page for members to sign on

Now you have everything ready to build a Web page to use this password table to allow members to sign on with their passwords. As a quick reminder, the information you need to build a MySQL database application is:

- Host name (MySQL): `www.pwt-ex.com`
- User name (MySQL): `johnsmith`
- Password (MySQL): `johnsmith`
- Database name: `company`
- Table name: `password`

For this database page, we would like to use PHP for the development. The first part of this example is responsible for generating two text fields for the user to enter the user name and password. The program code is listed below:

Example: ex19-05.php – Putting Encrypted Password In Database (Part One)

```
 1: <?PHP echo"<?";?>xml version="1.0" encoding="iso-8859-1"<?PHP echo"?>";?>
 2: <!DOCTYPE html PUBLIC "-//W3C//DTD XHTML 1.0 Transitional//EN"
 3:     "http://www.w3.org/TR/xhtml1/DTD/xhtml1-transitional.dtd">
 4: <html xmlns="http://www.w3.org/1999/xhtml" xml:lang="en" lang="en">
 5: <head><title>Encrypted Password in Database - ex19-05.php</title></head>
 6: <style>
 7:   .butSt{background-color:#aaffaa;font-family:arial;font-weight:bold;
 8:       font-size:18pt;color:#880000;width:250px;height:35px}
 9:   .butSt2{background-color:#aaaaaa;font-family:arial;font-weight:bold;
10:       font-size:18pt;color:#880000;width:150px;height:35px}
11:   .txtSt{font-family:arial;font-weight:bold; text-align:left;
12:       font-size:18pt;color:#ffff00}</style>
13: <body style="background:#000088" class="txtSt">
14:
15: <?php
16: global $llst, $userId, $passId;
17:
18: $llst = 'Thank you For Visiting This Site !<br /> ' .
19: 'Enter Your User Name and Password<br /><br />' .
20: '<form action="ex19-05.php" method="post">'.
21: '<table class="txtSt"><tr>' .
22: '   <td>Username:</td><td>' .
23: '<input type="text" name="userId" id="userId" class="butSt" /></td>' .
24: ' </tr><tr>' .
25: '   <td>Password:</td><td>' .
26: '<input type="password" name="passId" id="passId" class="butSt" /></td>' .
27: '   </tr><tr><td colspan="2" style="text-align:center"><br />' .
28: '   <input type="submit" value="Submit" class="butSt2" />' .
29: '   <input type="reset" value="Clear" class="butSt2" /></td></tr>' .
30: ' </table>' .
31: ' </form> ';
```

This PHP page fragment is, in fact, a string defined in lines 18–31. The string variable `$llst` contains a series of XHTML elements to define a form and two text input boxes. When you execute the following PHP echo or print statement

```
echo "$llst";  or print   "$llst";
```

the two text input boxes defined in lines 22–26 will be displayed and provide a mechanism for the user to enter user name and password. Also, when you press the Submit button, the form action will submit the form to this PHP page.

The second part of this example is responsible for all database operations and password comparisons. First, it will contact the MySQL database, locate the table name, and search for the password for the user that matched the user name. Once the password has been extracted from the database, a simple comparison against the user input password is performed. The comparison is done using the MD string so that some degree of security is achieved. This part of the example is listed as follows:

```
Listing: Continuation Of The PHP Script ex19-05.php (Part Two)

32:
33:   if ($passId && $userId)
34:   {
35:     $passId = md5($passId);
36:
37:     $db = mysql_connect("www.pwt-ex.com", "johnsmith","johnsmith");
38:     mysql_select_db("password",$db);
39:
40:     $query = "SELECT * FROM password WHERE name='$userId'";
41:     $result = mysql_query ($query) or die ("SQL Query Error..");
42:
43:     $row = mysql_fetch_array ($result);
44:
45:     if ($passId == $row['password'])
46:     {
47:     echo"Thank You $userId! <br /> Enjoy Your Visit<br /><br />";
48:     }
49:   else
50:   {
51:      echo "$llst";
52:   }
53:   mysql_free_result ($result);
54:   }
55:   else
56:   {
57:      echo "$llst";
58:   }
59:   ?>
60:   </body>
61:   </html>
```

First, we perform a test in line 33 to see whether the user has filled in both the user name and password fields. If one of the fields is not filled, the echo statement in line 57 is executed and hence the user has to input again. If both the user name and password are not empty, the statement in line 35 is used to obtain the MD string of the input password.

Once this encrypted password is ready, the `mysql_connnect()` function is called to contact the database. When the connection is successfully made and the desired database is selected, the following SQL statement is executed in line 40:

```
SELECT * FROM password WHERE name='$userId'
```

Since the variable `$userId` contains the input user name, this SQL statement will return the record (name and password) where the name equals `$userId`. The `mysql_fetch_array()` function in line 43 extracts the records and puts them into an array variable called `$row`. A simple comparison of `$passId` against the variable `$row['password']` as illustrated in line 45 can therefore determine whether we have a match on the encrypted password. If there is a match, a simple welcome message is displayed. If the two passwords are different, the echo statement in line 51 will display the user name and password text boxes for the user to try again.

This example is a framework to demonstrate how to put encrypted passwords into a database. In real applications, you should put your Web page elements or statements inside the block in lines 46–48. Some screen shots of this example are shown in Figs 19.7 and 19.8.

Figure 19.7 ex19-05.php

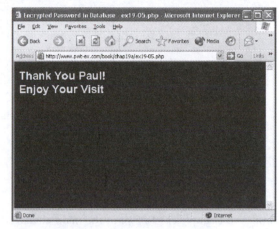

Figure 19.8 Sign-on successful

The unencrypted password for Paul, in this case, is paul123 and is listed in ex19-01.txt of section 19.2.3. Using the database, you can develop pages to set up new accounts easily.

19.3.3 Set up new password accounts

Before your Web site can have more members, you probably need to include a sign-up feature in your page to allow someone to join your community. One of the simplest forms for this feature may be a small page or area to allow the user to enter his or her user name and password. You can find all kinds of sign-up utilities on a large number of Web sites, in particular the commercial sites that can provide services and charges on the Internet.

In this section, we are going to develop a sign-up utility to allow someone to join a membership. This page displays two boxes, one for the user name and the other for the password. The password will be encrypted using the MD string. Both the user name and password are then inserted into the password table that we develop in ex19-06.txt. Also, we will add a feature to the utility such that if the user name has been used by someone else, the utility will let you know and ask you to sign up again with a new user name.

The implementation style is similar to ex19-05.php. The first part of this example is responsible for generating the user name and password fields and is listed below:

```
Example: ex19-06.php - Set Up New Password Accounts (Part One)

 1: <?PHP echo"<?";?>xml version="1.0" encoding="iso-8859-1"<?PHP echo"?>";?>
 2: <!DOCTYPE html PUBLIC "-//W3C//DTD XHTML 1.0 Transitional//EN"
 3:     "http://www.w3.org/TR/xhtml1/DTD/xhtml1-transitional.dtd">
 4: <html xmlns="http://www.w3.org/1999/xhtml" xml:lang="en" lang="en">
 5: <head><title>Set Up New Password Accounts - ex19-06.php</title></head>
 6: <style>
 7:    .butSt{background-color:#aaffaa;font-family:arial;font-weight:bold;
 8:       font-size:18pt;color:#880000;width:250px;height:35px}
 9:    .butSt2{background-color:#aaaaaa;font-family:arial;font-weight:bold;
10:       font-size:18pt;color:#880000;width:150px;height:35px}
```

```
11:    .txtSt{font-family:arial;font-weight:bold; text-align:left;
12:       font-size:18pt;color:#ffff00}</style>
13: <body style="background:#000088" class="txtSt">
14:
15: <?php
16: global $llst, $userId, $passId, $db, $query,$result,$row;
17:
18:  $llst = 'Welcome To ABC Site<br />Please Enter ' .
19:  ' Your User Name And <br />Password To Join <br /><br />' .
20:  ' <form action="ex19-06.php" method="post">'.
21:  ' <table class="txtSt"><tr>' .
22:  '    <td>Username:</td><td>' .
23:  ' <input type="text" name="userId" id="userId" class="butSt" /></td>' .
24:  ' </tr><tr>' .
25:  '    <td>Password:</td><td>' .
26:  ' <input type="password" name="passId" id="passId" class="butSt" />' .
27:  '    </td></tr><tr><td colspan="2" style="text-align:center"><br />' .
28:  '    <input type="submit" value="Submit" class="butSt2" />' .
29:  '    <input type="reset" value="Clear" class="butSt2" /></td></tr>' .
30:  ' </table>' .
31:  ' </form> ';
32:
```

Similar to example ex19-05.php, the main characteristic of this PHP program fragment is the string `$llst` defined in lines 18–31. This string contains a form and all the input fields to allow a user to enter his or her user name and password. A simple echo or print function can be used to display this string and hence the input fields anywhere on the page.

The second part of this example concerns processing. Basically, you need to capture the input user name and password and encrypt the password into MD string. Once you have the information at hand, you can contact the MySQL database and perform a data update with the following SQL statement:

```
INSERT INTO password (id,name,password)
    VALUES (NULL,'$userId','$passId');
```

In order to prevent data or user name duplication, we also perform a detection to see whether the user name has already been stored in the database before the insert statement above. If the sign-in user name has been used by someone else, a message is output and no insertion take place in the database.

The PHP program fragment for this part is listed below:

```
Listing: Continuation Of The PHP Script ex19-06.php (Part Two)

33:  if ($passId && $userId)
34:  {
35:   $passId = md5($passId);
36:
37:   $db = mysql_connect("www.pwt-ex.com", "johnsmith","johnsmith");
38:   mysql_select_db("password",$db);
39:
40:   $query = "SELECT * FROM password WHERE name='$userId'";
41:   $result = mysql_query ($query) or die ("SQL Query Error..");
42:   $row = mysql_fetch_array ($result);
43:   if ($userId != $row['name'])
44:   {
45:    $sql = "INSERT INTO password (id,name,password)
46:           VALUES (NULL,'$userId','$passId')";
47:    $result = mysql_query($sql) or die ("SQL Query Error..");
48:
49:    echo "A New Account Has Been Set Up <br /><br />";
```

```
50:     echo "Username = $userId <br />";
51:     echo "Encrypted Password = <br />$passId <br />";
52:   }
53:   else
54:   {
55:    echo "The User Name You Picked <br />Has Been " .
56:         "Used By Someone.<br /> Please Try Again! <br />";
57:   }
58: }
59: else
60: {
61:    echo "$llst";
62:  }
63:  ?>
64: <br /><img src="line1.gif" width="500" height="6" alt="pic" />
65: <br /><br />
66: </body>
67: </html>
```

When the user has filled in all the fields and pressed the Submit button, the variables $userId and $passId are defined to contain the user name and password respectively. If not all the fields are filled, the echo statement in line 61 is executed and hence the user can enter his or her selected user name and password.

The input password is encrypted by the md5() function in line 35. After the connection to the database in lines 37–38, the following SQL statement is run to search inside the database for any existence of the user name (see line 40):

```
SELECT * FROM password WHERE name='$userId';
```

If the user name exists inside the database then the echo statement in lines 55–56 is called. This echo statement displays a message to let the user knows that the input user name has already been used by someone else. He or she should try to sign in again. If the user name is a new one, the SQL insert statement is executed to add the user name and encrypted password to the database as a new record (see lines 45–46):

```
INSERT INTO password (id,name,password)
       VALUES (NULL,'$userId','$passId');
```

The echo statements in lines 49–51 output a message to let the user know that a new account has been set up successfully for him or her. Some screen shots of this example are shown in Figs 19.9 and 19.10.

Figure 19.9 ex19-06.php

Figure 19.10 Set up a new account

The MD string or `md5()` function is a one-way function. To use it on an encrypted password provides strong protection against attack. The original password text is safe in a strong sense. It is virtually infeasible to calculate the original text provided the intruder doesn't know the length of your password. The disadvantage is that not even the network administrator of the Web site knows the original password string. If you lose or forget your password, the administrator of the Web site usually has to destroy the encrypted password before a new one can be issued.

19.3.4 A page to change your account's password

One of the common practices in computing to improve data security is to change passwords regularly. On the Web, this basic security measure still has not been implemented on a large scale. Although a large number of Web sites still haven't provided utilities to allow members to change their account passwords, in fact to develop a page to allow a user to change his or her password online is simple. Usually all you have to do is to set up some text fields for the user to enter:

- User name
- Current password
- New password
- Confirm password

When the user name and current password match the information in the database and the new password is the same as the confirm password, you have consistent data. Once the data are consistent or well defined, a simple SQL update statement can be employed to update the data inside the database.

On the other hand, if either the user name or current password does not match the data in the database, or the new password is not the same as the confirm password, you have inconsistent data and all the update operations should stop. Now, let's consider the first part of the example below:

```
Example: ex19-07.php - A Page To Change Password (Part One)

 1: <?PHP echo"<?";?>xml version="1.0" encoding="iso-8859-1"<?PHP echo"?>";?>
 2: <!DOCTYPE html PUBLIC "-//W3C//DTD XHTML 1.0 Transitional//EN"
 3:     "http://www.w3.org/TR/xhtml1/DTD/xhtml1-transitional.dtd">
 4: <html xmlns="http://www.w3.org/1999/xhtml" xml:lang="en" lang="en">
 5: <head><title>A Page To Change Password - ex19-07.php</title></head>
 6: <style>
 7:   .butSt{background-color:#aaffaa;font-family:arial;font-weight:bold;
 8:       font-size:18pt;color:#880000;width:250px;height:35px}
 9:   .butSt2{background-color:#aaaaaa;font-family:arial;font-weight:bold;
10:       font-size:18pt;color:#880000;width:150px;height:35px}
11:   .txtSt{font-family:arial;font-weight:bold; text-align:left;
12:       font-size:18pt;color:#ffff00}</style>
13: <body style="background:#000088" class="txtSt">
14:
15: <?php
16: global $id, $llst,$userId,$passId,$newId,$confId,$db,$query,$result,$row;
17:
18:  $llst = 'Change Your Password<br /> ' .
19:    ' Please Enter All Information Below:<br /><br />' .
20:    ' <form action="ex19-07.php" method="post">'.
21:    ' <table class="txtSt"><tr>' .
22:    '    <td>Username:</td><td>' .
23:    ' <input type="text" name="userId" id="userId" class="butSt" /></td>' .
24:    ' </tr><tr>' .
25:    '    <td>Current Password:</td><td>' .
26:    ' <input type="password" name="passId" id="passId" class="butSt" />' .
27:    ' </td></tr> ' .
28:    '    <td>New Password:</td><td>' .
29:    ' <input type="password" name="newId" id="newId" class="butSt" />' .
30:    ' </td></tr> ' .
```

```
31:     '    <td>Confirm Your Password:</td><td>' .
32:     ' <input type="password" name="confId" id="confId" class="butSt" />' .
33:     ' </td></tr> ' .
34:     '<tr><td colspan="2" style="text-align:center"><br />' .
35:     '  <input type="submit" value="Submit" class="butSt2" />' .
36:     '  <input type="reset" value="Clear" class="butSt2" /></td></tr>' .
37:     ' </table>' .
38:     ' </form> ';
39:
```

Again, the main feature of this PHP program fragment is the string $llst defined in lines 18–38. This string contains XHTML coding to generate four input text fields Username, Current Password, New Password, and Confirm Password. Note that the string $llst contains the definition only and you will need to use PHP echo() or print() functions to display the fields on browsers.

The second part of the example is to control the action and is listed as follows:

Listing: Continuation Of The PHP Script ex19-07.php (Part Two)

```
40: if ($passId && $userId && $newId && $confId)
41: {
42:   $passId = md5($passId);
43:
44:   $db = mysql_connect("www.pwt-ex.com", "johnsmith","johnsmith");
45:   mysql_select_db("password",$db);
46:
47:   $query = "SELECT * FROM password WHERE name='$userId'";
48:   $result = mysql_query ($query) or die ("SQL Query Error..");
49:   $row = mysql_fetch_array ($result);
50:   $id = $row['id'];
51:
52:   if (($userId == $row['name']) && ($passId == $row['password']) &&
53:       ($newId == $confId))
54:   {
55:    $newId = md5($newId);
56:    $sql = "UPDATE password SET name='$userId',
57:    password='$newId' WHERE id='$id'";
58:    $result = mysql_query($sql) or die ("SQL Query Error..");
59:    echo "Thank you! $userId <br /><br />";
60:    echo "Your Password Has Been Updated <br />";
61:    echo "Encrypted Password Is <br />$passId <br />";
62:   }
63:   else
64:   {
65:   echo "Your Information Is Not Consistent: <br />" .
66:        "Please Check The Following:<br /><br />" .
67:        "  Spelling Of Your Username <br />" .
68:        "  Double Check Your Current Password <br />" .
69:        "  Your New Password May Not Match Your<br />" .
70:        "  Confirm Password <br /><br />" .
71:        "Please Try Again!<br />";
72:   }
73: }
74: else
75: {
76:    echo "$llst";
77: }
78: ?>
79: <br /><img src="line1.gif" width="500" height="6" alt="pic" />
80: <br /><br />
81: </body>
82: </html>
```

This program fragment begins with a detection to see whether all four fields are filled with data. If not, the echo statement in line 76 will generate the fields again. If all the fields are filled, the program starts a process (lines 42–51) to contact the database and extract the user name and encrypted password information, which is stored in variables `$row['name']` and `$row['password']` respectively. Now, we want to perform a data consistency test as below:

- The input user name matches the user name in the database.
- The input password (encrypted) matches the password in the database.
- The new password is the same as the confirm password.

These tasks can be performed as a single `if` statement as illustrated in lines 52–53. If the data fail the consistency test, the echo statement in lines 65–71 is executed to suggest a possible reason. If the data are well defined, the following simple SQL update statement

```
UPDATE password SET name='$userId',
     password='$newId' WHERE id='$id';
```

is executed to update the record in the database. Before this update statement, don't forget to encrypt the new password as illustrated in line 55. Some screen shots of this example in action are shown in Figs 19.11–19.13.

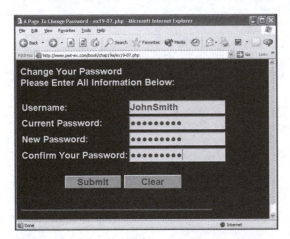

Figure 19.11 ex19-07.php

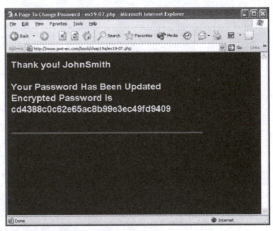

Figure 19.12 Change password successful

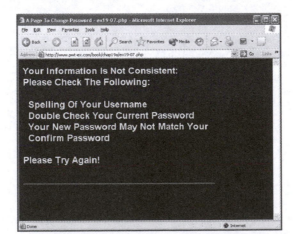

Figure 19.13 Input data not consistent

19.4   MD and digital signatures

The MD algorithm (or process) is a basic tool in advanced cryptography and security, and can be used to encrypt a password. More importantly it can produce the so-called digital signature in many applications related to the Internet and Web. If you want to sign a document or file just like you sign a paper document so that no one can alter it afterward, you need to use MD. The basic idea is simple and can proceeds as follows:

- Run your document or file through the MD or `md5()` function. This would produce a fixed length MD string similar to the encrypted password representing the signature of the document.
- Send your document and the signature to the intended recipient by email or other transmission method.
- The recipient can run the `md5()` function on the document or file you sent to obtain the MD string to see whether there is a match with the signature. If the signature you sent matches the MD string, the document is considered as genuine.

Due to the practical nature of this book, we will not cover the details of the MD (or MD5) algorithm as it is described in the IETF standard known as RFC 1321. A copy of this report can be found on the companion Web site. Also, if you perform a decent Internet search for the MD5 algorithm or a tutorial on it, you will find thousands and thousands of references and comments to this RFC 1321 report, the algorithm, and implementations in all kinds of computing languages.

In this section, we will show you how to use the standard C code implementation of the algorithm included in the RFC 1321 specification to build an MD5 utility. This utility will be used for digital signature and other applications.

19.4.1 Building a utility from the MD standard programs

The MD5 standard specification includes a C implementation of the algorithm with the following program files:

global.h — **Contains all constants and generic types**

md5.h — **Header file for md5.c**

md5.c — **The primary program to implement the MD5 algorithm**

mddriver.c — **A driver program to use md5.c (utility)**

If you have a C/C++ compiler such as Borland C/C++, Microsoft C/C++, or UNIX/Linux C/C++, you can compile this md5.c program and build a utility to use any time and anywhere you like. Since the md5.c program is not designed as an executable program, the standard also provides a driver program called mddriver.c so that an executable program can be built. This driver program is the utility we want to build.

For example, if you are using the Microsoft C/C++ compiler, you can build the utility by using the command

```
cl -D MD=5 mddriver.c md5.c
```

This command performs the following:

- Compiles the C programs mddriver.c and md5.c into object files mddriver.obj and md5.obj.
- Uses the object files to build the executable program mddriver.exe.
- Since the standard programs can be used to compile MD4 or even MD2, uses the directive `-D MD=5` to define a macro in mddriver.c to make sure that MD5 (version 5) is wanted.

If you are using UNIX/LINUX with a `gcc` or `cc` compiler, you can compile the utility with the following command:

```
gcc -o mddriver -D MD=5 mddriver.c md5.c
```

This command will define the macros `MD=5` and compile the C programs. Instead of the traditional executable file name a.out, this command will name the executable file as mddriver.

After the compilation, you should have an executable file called mddriver.exe or mddriver if you are using UNIX/LINUX in your local directory. The compiling process using the Microsoft C/C++ compiler is captured and shown in Fig. 19.14.

```
H:\bk_pwt.dir\chap19a>cl -D MD=5 mddriver.c md5.c
Microsoft (R) 32-bit C/C++ Optimizing Compiler Version 12.00.8168 for 80x86
Copyright (C) Microsoft Corp 1984-1998. All rights reserved.

mddriver.c
md5.c
Generating Code...
Microsoft (R) Incremental Linker Version 6.00.8168
Copyright (C) Microsoft Corp 1992-1998. All rights reserved.

/out:mddriver.exe
mddriver.obj
md5.obj

H:\bk_pwt.dir\chap19a>
```

Figure 19.14 Compiling MD5 programs

According to the RFC 1321 specification, you can test the program by activating the test suite of the driver using the command `mddriver` such as

```
mddriver -x
```

If you can see the following messages on your screen, you have a working MD5 utility:

```
Listing: ex19-07.txt - Testing For Message Digest

 1:    MD5 test suite:
 2:    MD5 ("") = d41d8cd98f00b204e9800998ecf8427e
 3:    MD5 ("a") = 0cc175b9c0f1b6a831c399e269772661
 4:    MD5 ("abc") = 900150983cd24fb0d6963f7d28e17f72
 5:    MD5 ("message digest") = f96b697d7cb7938d525a2f31aaf161d0
 6:    MD5 ("abcdefghijklmnopqrstuvwxyz") = c3fcd3d76192e4007dfb496cca67e13b
 7:    MD5 ("ABCDEFGHIJKLMNOPQRSTUVWXYZabcdefghijklmnopqrstuvwxyz0123456789")
 8:       = d174ab98d277d9f5a5611c2c9f419d9f
 9:    MD5 ("12345678901234567890123456789012345678901234567890123456789012345678901234567890
10:       12345678901234567890") = 57edf4a22be3c955ac49da2e2107b67a
```

Now you have a utility that can produce an MD5 string. The utility `mddriver` also includes a `-s` directive to generate an MD5 string for an arbitrary input text. For example, you can use the command to generate an MD5 string of `johnsmith`:

```
mddriver -sjohnsmith
```

You will see the following output on your screen:

```
MD5 ("johnsmith") = cd4388c0c62e65ac8b99e3ec49fd9409
```

You can compare this result with the Perl and PHP scripts used in examples ex19-01.pl and ex19-02.php. Don't put any empty space between your text and the directive `-s`. If you do, the utility will generate an MD5 string based on your text with an empty space. This would generate a completely different result.

19.4.2 Using the MD utility for digital signatures

One of the popular uses of the MD5 string is to obtain the digital signature of a document or file. If you run the MD utility `mddriver` without any directive, it will assume the input is a file and try to produce an MD string of the file.

For example, assume you have written a letter with your favorite editor to your personal banker as shown in example ex19-08.txt. This letter is stored as a text file called banker.txt.

```
Listing: ex19-08.txt - An Example Letter To A Banker (banker.txt)

 1:    Dear My Personal Banker
 2:
 3:    I would like to transfer US$500
 4:    to the following account:
 5:
 6:    Account Name: ABC Online-Shopping
 7:    Account Number: 1234-5678
 8:
 9:    Regards
10:    John Smith
```

When you use the MD utility and issue the command

```
mddriver banker.txt
```

you will have the MD5 string

```
MD5 (banker.txt) = d22d9c9b366a6a0935b087b58f98fbbe
```

This MD5 string can be used as a signature of your letter. When you send your letter and the signature to the banker separately, your banker will be able to use mddriver or other MD5 program to verify whether the letter has been altered in any way.

If, say, someone has altered the account name and number as

```
Account Name: CBA Online-Shopping
Account Number: 8765-4321
```

the MD5 string from the banker would turn out to be

```
MD5 (banker.txt) = 7f5858de974e8fff1dbbd9456c4a6e38
```

Therefore, your banker knows that the letter has been altered. The original letter and the altered one are shown in Figs 19.15 and 19.16.

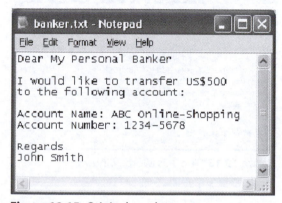

Figure 19.15 Original text letter

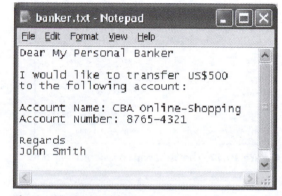

Figure 19.16 Modified text letter

The MD5 string is really a digest of a document or file and can be used as a signature on almost all file formats.

Since the letter above was written in plain text, it is not wise to send the signature together with the letter by email. If you do, an intruder can intercept your letter and alter both the contents and the signature at the same time.

To provide a solution to this problem, encryption of the letter is needed. Before we discuss public-key protection, let's consider a very simple example using WinZip. This is a compression program widely used in the computing community. Although the password protection and encryption provided by WinZip is not very sophisticated, the compression offered by the program does provide an efficient non-pattern-based encryption. Suppose you need to write an important letter (see ex19-09.txt) to your company boss about the tendering value for an airport security project. This letter is stored as a text file called tender.txt.

```
Listing: ex19-09.txt - An Important Business Letter (tender.txt)

 1:    Dear Mr. Johnsmith
 2:
 3:    After a careful evaluation, the following is the
 4:    tender value recommended by our team:
 5:
 6:    Project Name: MMV-Airport Security
 7:    Recommended Project Value: US$:xxxxxxx
 8:
 9:    Good Luck!
10:
11:    Regards
12:    John
```

To compress this file with a password using WinZip, all you have to do is to activate WinZip and press the Add icon. The "Add With Password" dialog box will appear as in Fig. 19.17. When you click the password button, the Password dialog window will appear (see Fig. 19.18). After you have typed in a password (e.g., john) and clicked the OK button, you will be asked to confirm your password. Then the text file tender.txt is compressed and protected by a password.

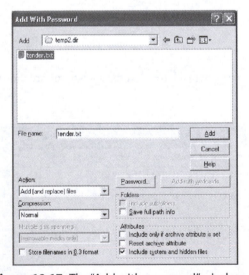

Figure 19.17 The "Add with password" window

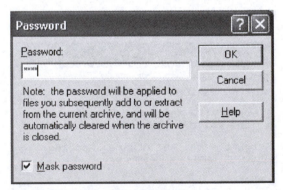

Figure 19.18 The "Password" window

Now, you can run the MD utility to obtain a signature of this zip file, e.g., tender.zip, and the MD5 string is

```
MD5 (tender.zip) = e25dfe5856aa8f0691c3f0b5c65c46b3
```

When you have this signature to hand, you can write an email to your company boss to include the digital signature and the WinZip file tender.zip as an attachment. An example of this email is shown in Fig. 19.19. The digital signature can guarantee that no one has altered the zip file. Even a simple use of the digital signature with WinZip protection can reduce the chances of being attacked by intruders to a certain degree.

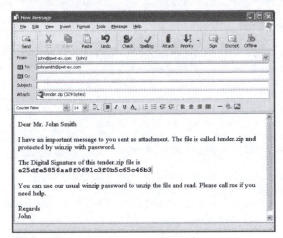

Figure 19.19 The "Password" window

If you have some advanced digital key encryption/decryption programs such as IDEA, DES, and/or the IETF standard CAST5, you can use them to provide better data protection.

19.4.3 A page to protect downloads from viruses and alterations

Another use of the MD driver on the Web is to protect downloaded files from viruses and alterations. The idea is simple. Suppose you have the following files on your site or page ready for someone to download:

- An executable file   –   mddriver.exe
- A Microsoft Word file   –   intro.doc
- A text file   –   rfc1231.txt
- A JPG image file   –   logo_web.jpg

You can run WinZip to zip all these files with or without a password depending on your requirements. The next step is to obtain the MD5 signature of each zip file using the MD utility `mddriver` developed in section 19.4.1. The result is listed in Table 19.1.

Table 19.1 Digital signatures of some downloaded files

Original file	Zip file	MD5 digital signature of the zip file
mddriver.exe	mddriver.zip	fb069dda063efc5a040599a966d27a56
intro.doc	intro.zip	76cdb2bad9582d23c1f6f4d868218d6c
rfc1321.txt	rfc1321.zip	911170e036041597737b7b2905f96c96
Logo_web.jpg	Logo_web.zip	4e75d83462537a10c795e048dd2f241f

Now you can develop a simple page to allow the download operation on the files. Consider the example page below:

```
Example: ex19-08.htm - Protect Downloaded Files Against Viruses And Alterations

 1:  <?xml version="1.0" encoding="iso-8859-1"?>
 2:  <!DOCTYPE html PUBLIC "-//W3C//DTD XHTML 1.0 Transitional//EN"
 3:      "http://www.w3.org/TR/xhtml1/DTD/xhtml1-transitional.dtd">
 4:  <html xmlns="http://www.w3.org/1999/xhtml" xml:lang="en" lang="en">
 5:  <head><title>Protect Download Files - ex19-08.htm</title></head>
 6:  <style>
 7:   .txtSt{font-family:arial;font-weight:bold; text-align:left;
 8:       font-size:18pt;color:#ffff00}</style>
 9:  <body style="background:#000088;text-align:center" class="txtSt">
10:  A Page To Protect Downloaded Files<br />
11:  From Viruses And Alterations<br /><br />
12:
13:  <div class="txtSt">
14:   You are welcome to download the following files.<br />
15:   Please check the MD5 signature (or MD5 CheckSum) <br />
16:   against Viruses and Alterations: <br /><br /></div>
17:
18:  <table class="txtSt" cellspacing="10">
19:  <tr><td>File Name</td><td>MD5 Signature</td></tr>
20:  <tr><td><a href="mddriver.zip" style="color:#00ff00">mddriver.zip</a>
21:      </td><td>fb069dda063efc5a040599a966d27a56</td></tr>
22:  <tr><td><a href="intro.zip" style="color:#00ff00">intro.zip</a>
23:      </td><td>76cdb2bad9582d23c1f6f4d868218d6c</td></tr>
24:  <tr><td><a href="rfc1321.zip" style="color:#00ff00">rfc1321.zip</a>
25:      </td><td>911170e036041597737b7b2905f96c96</td></tr>
26:  <tr><td><a href="logo_web.zip" style="color:#00ff00">logo_web.zip</a>
27:      </td><td>4e75d83462537a10c795e048dd2f241f</td></tr>
28:  </table>
29:  </body>
30:  </html>
```

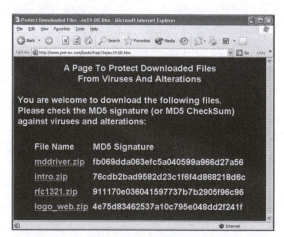

Figure 19.20 Protection against viruses and alterations

This is a simple page to list all the zip files for downloading. The MD5 strings of the zip files are displayed along with the file. A screen shot of this example is shown in Fig. 19.20.

The user can double click any file to download it. Once the file is on the hard disk, the user can obtain an MD5 string of the file with any MD5 utility. If the string generated by the user matches the MD5 string listed in the page, the file is intact. Any modification of the zip file by a virus or alteration will result in a different MD5 string. An MD5 string on a file is also called the MD5 check sum among the Internet community.

This technique is used on many Web sites on the Internet including the standard cryptography implementation site GNU Privacy Guard (www.gnupg.org).

For some real encryption/decryption against intruders, we need something called public-key cryptography, which is discussed below.

19.5   Data security with public-key technology

19.5.1 Conventional and public-key cryptography

Conventional encryption methods only use one key for encryption and decryption. The sender encrypts the message or document with this key and sends it to the receiver. In order to decrypt this document, the receiver has to have the same key.

The advantage of the algorithms in these methods is that they are fast, efficient, and computationally safe. Some popular implementations are:

- IDEA [IDEA]
- Blowfish (128-bit key, 16 rounds)
- DES (DES-EDE)
- CAST5 (128-bit key, known as RFC 2144)

For further information, the description and algorithm of the first three are available from the "Cypto C-Source" Web site (www.cc.jyu.fi/~paasivir/crypt/source.html). The CAST5 algorithm is DES-like and is an IETF standard known as RFC 2144.

For conventional methods to work, the key must be provided to the receiver in such a way that others won't be able to obtain it. If somebody else does have the key, this entire security will be compromised. Due to the secrecy nature of the key, these encryption/decryption methods are called secret-key (or symmetric) cryptography.

The use of the so-called public keys can solve this major problem. Instead of using only one key, public-key cryptography is a concept where two keys are involved. One key is a public key that can be widely published and can be obtained by anyone. Many people suggest that a public-key server should be involved. The other key is a secret (or private) key and should be kept secret permanently. It is computationally infeasible (or difficult) to derive the secret key from the public one. When you encrypt a message with one key, the other key must be used to decrypt the message.

An additional use of public-key technology is in digital signatures. In this case, the role of the private and public keys is reversed. If a sender encrypts a document using his or her private key, everyone can decrypt and read the document by using the sender's public key. Since only the sender of the document has the secret key, he or she must have sent the document. This digital signature can also be used to prevent repudiation: the sender cannot claim that he or she did not actually send the message. In common practice, the private key is used to encrypt an MD of the document as the signature from the sender.

In general, the idea of public-key technology is based on prime number factorization. An internationally recognized public/private-key algorithm is named RSA after its creators (Ron Rivest, Adi Shamir, and Len Adleman). A brief discussion of this algorithm will be introduced shortly.

19.5.2 Hybrid cryptography

In many cases, conventional encryption/decryption with one key can provide more efficient and safer protection against intruders. Therefore, most advanced cryptographic systems nowadays offer hybrid methods to take advantage of both methods. Most implementations of hybrid cryptography would involve the following:

- Use conventional methods to encrypt a message.
- Use a public-key method to encrypt the digital key from the conventional method.
- Send the encrypted message and encrypted digital key to the recipient.
- Get the recipient to use his or her private key to decrypt the digital key.
- Then get the recipient to use the decrypted digital key to decrypt the message.

Using hybrid methods, you can solve the key distribution problem and get stronger protection against intruders than with secret-key cryptography. All techniques related to digital signatures can also apply to hybrid methods.

The first commercial product of public-key technology and hybrid methods is Pretty Good Privacy (PGP) developed by Philip Zimmermann. Based on this product, an IETF standard known as RFC 2440 (or OpenPGP) was established in November 1998. Complying with the standard, a freely available implementation of OpenPGP was developed by GNU called Gnu Privacy Guard (GnuPG).

A quick tour of GnuPG with examples is provided in section 19.6 so that we can put public-key security into practice. For now, let's consider a basic public-key algorithm.

19.5.3 A brief discussion on the RSA public-key algorithm

A well-known public-key algorithm is called RSA after its creators Ron Rivest, Adi Shamir, and Len Adleman, the founders of RSA Data Security Inc. Basically, the algorithm can be used to generate two keys for encryption and decryption. One key is called public and the other, obviously, is called private. The algorithm can be briefly described in the following four steps:

Step 1: Find the prime numbers p and q and their product pq

- Search for two, large random, and distinct primes p and q.
- The values of $p-1$ and $q-1$ should not have a large common divisor.
- Compute the product pq.

Step 2: Compute the encryption (e) and decryption (d) exponents

- Calculate the encryption exponent e such that

   $$e < pq$$

   and e is relatively prime to $p-1$ and $q-1$.

- Calculate decryption exponent d such that

   $$d = e^{-1} \bmod \mathrm{lcm}(p-1, q-1)$$

   i.e., the inverse of e modulo the least common multiple of ($p-1$, $q-1$). The least common multiple $\mathrm{lcm}(p-1, q-1)$ is the smallest number divisible by $p-1$ and $q-1$.

Step 3: Output the public and private keys

- Output the values of e and pq as the public key.
- Output the values of d and pq as the private key.

Step 4: Perform encryption and decryption

- Encryption: given a message m, the ciphertext c can be computed using the public key by

   $$c = m^e \bmod pq$$

   where e and pg are the information in the public key.

- Decryption: given a ciphertext c, the plain text m can be computed using the private key by

   $$m = c^d \bmod pq$$

   where d and pq are the information in the private key.

This algorithm is widely used in many systems, both private and public, to provide data security and digital signatures on an insecure transmission environment such as the Internet. From a practical point of view, any implementation of this algorithm should consist of three parts: keys generation, encryption, and decryption. There are a number of program codes and libraries related to this algorithm available on the Internet and a good place to find and download them is the site www.cc.jyu.fi/~paasivir/crypt/source.html.

A practical implementation of public-key and hybrid technologies is called Gnu Privacy Guard (GnuPG). We will provide a quick tour in the next section on how to use it to protect data against attack.

19.6   A quick tour of GnuPG

19.6.1 Installation of GnuPG

GnuPG is a free software package available to everyone on the Internet. It is a standard implementation of the IETF standard RFC 2440 on public-key and hybrid cryptography. GnuPG is a complicated program offering a large number of command-line arguments. The main program is called `gpg`. This program contains more than 30 commands and more than 30 options. We will cover some of the most popular uses of the program from a practical point of view. Examples related to GnuPG will have the file extension `.gpg` in this chapter.

First, you can download the software package from the official site www.gnupg.org. GnuPG has a number of versions dedicated to different platforms and operating systems. If you want to start from scratch, you may download the following source code version and compile the software yourself:

gnupg-xxxx.tar.gz

In particular, if you are using UNIX/LINUX systems, you are encouraged to compile and install the software yourself. The xxxx represents the version number of the package. At the time of writing, the latest version (that we used here) is gnupg-1.0.6.tar.gz. The compilation and installation of the software for a typical Red Hat LINUX system are summarized as the following steps:

- Unpack the package by executing the following commands:

  gunzip gnupg-1.0.6.tar.gz   –   To extract the tar file gnupg-1.0.6.tar

  tar -xzvf gnupg-1.0.6.tar   –   To extract all files into the `gnupg-1.0.6` directory

- Go to this directory `gnupg-1.0.6` and issue the command

      ./configure

  After all the checking, all the necessary files to build the software are generated.
- Now build the package by typing the command

      make

  Finally, install the software by typing the command `make install`.

If you want to build the software to use on Microsoft Windows systems, the details are in the readme.w32 file.

It is strongly recommended that you double check whether you have unmodified software before you install it on your system. One simple way to check the integrity of the software is to use the MD5 string. According to the official GnuPG site, the MD5 string of the file gnupg-1.0.6.tar.gz is

    md5(gnupg-1.0.6.tar.gz)=7c319a9e5e70ad9bc3bf0d7b5008a508

You can use the MD5 utility in section 19.4.1 to verify the integrity of the software. If you don't want to start GnuPG from the source code, you can download the binary version for your machine. For Microsoft Windows systems, the binary version and MD5 string are

    gnupg-w32-1.0.6.zip
    md5(gnupg-w32-1.0.6.zip)=1dbf36a54b20026562e22a76d3ae06aa

To install this binary version for Microsoft Windows is simple. All you need is to unzip the package and store everything in the directory `c:\gnupg`. To install GnuPG into another directory, you may need to add a string to the Windows Registry. In this case, you may want to read the readme.w32 file for more details.

When you have successfully installed the software on your system, you can start to use it for data security and protection.

19.6.2 Generating and deleting public/private-key pairs

In order to use GnuPG effectively, you are advised to consult the handbook, manual, guide, and/or documentataion related to the software. The following is a quick discussion with demonstration examples on how to use GnuPG on data security. For our practical purposes, information and examples on key generation, deletion, encryption, and decryption are provided.

The first thing in using public-key security software such as GnuPG is to generate some keys. For security reasons, it is recommended that you should

- only generate keys on a machine where you have complete control and direct access;
- never generate keys over a network.

When you are ready, you can generate the public/private keys by opening a shell window (or DOS window) and issuing the command

```
gpg --gen-key
```

When you use this command, you will be asked a number of questions one by one so that the key pair (public/secret keys) can be generated successfully. For most questions, you can press the Enter key to accept the default. The questions and the information that GnuPG requires are as follows:

- Which algorithm is used to generate the key pair? (The default is DSA/ElGamal.)
- What key length do you want to use? (The default is 1024 bits.)
- The life of the key pair. (The default never expires.)
- What is your real name? (You need to type a name, e.g., johnsmith, for this question.)
- What is your email address? (You should enter your email address, e.g., johnsmith@pwt-ex.com.)
- Enter a comment. (You can type anything for this question, e.g., gnupg.)
- Enter a passphrase. (Passphrase should be a phrase and is used to protect your secret key, e.g., have a nice day.)
- Confirm your passphrase. (Retype your passphrase.)

At this point, you will be offered a chance to change the information before the key pair is generated. If you enter OK, the key pair will be generated. Since key pair generating is an important process, we will walk through the process together in the next example. A computer dialog is generated and shown in ex19-09.gpg. In the example, the user input corresponding to the questions is illustrated in a bold face.

```
Example: ex19-09.gpg - Generating Public/Secret - Key Pair Dialog

 1: shell> gpg --gen-key
 2: gpg (GnuPG) 1.0.6; Copyright (C) 2001 Free Software Foundation, Inc.
 3: This program comes with ABSOLUTELY NO WARRANTY.
 4: This is free software, and you are welcome to redistribute it
 5: under certain conditions. See the file COPYING for details.
 6:
 7: Please select what kind of key you want:
 8:    (1) DSA and ElGamal (default)
 9:    (2) DSA (sign only)
10:    (4) ElGamal (sign and encrypt)
11: Your selection? (Just Press Enter Key Here)
```

```
12:
13: DSA keypair will have 1024 bits.
14: About to generate a new ELG-E keypair.
15:               minimum keysize is 768 bits
16:               default keysize is 1024 bits
17:     highest suggested keysize is 2048 bits
18: What keysize do you want? (1024) (Just Press Enter Key Here)
19:
20: Requested keysize is 1024 bits
21: Please specify how long the key should be valid.
22:          0 = key does not expire
23:       <n>  = key expires in n days
24:       <n>w = key expires in n weeks
25:       <n>m = key expires in n months
26:       <n>y = key expires in n years
27: Key is valid for? (0) (Just Press Enter Key Here)
28:
29: Key does not expire at all
30:
31: Is this correct (y/n)? y
32:
33: You need a User-ID to identify your key; the software constructs the user
id
34: from Real Name, Comment and Email Address in this form:
35:     "Heinrich Heine (Der Dichter) <heinrichh@duesseldorf.de>"
36:
37: Real name: johnsmith
38:
39: Email address: johnsmith@pwt-ex.com
40:
41: Comment: gnupg
42:
43: You selected this USER-ID:
44:     "johnsmith (gnupg) <johnsmith@pwt-ex.com>"
45:
46: Change (N)ame, (C)omment, (E)mail or (O)kay/(Q)uit? O
47:
48: You need a Passphrase to protect your secret key.
49:
50: Enter passphrase:  have a nice day     (You cannot see this string)
51: Repeat passphrase: have a nice day     (You cannot see this string)
52:
53: We need to generate a lot of random bytes. It is a good idea to perform
54: some other action (type on the keyboard, move the mouse, utilize the
55: disks) during the prime generation; this gives the random number
56: generator a better chance to gain enough entropy.
57: +++++++++++++++++++.+++++.+++++.++++++++++..+++++..++++
58: ++++++..++++++++++++++++++.++++++++++++++++++++++.++
59: +++++++++++++++++++++++++>+++++..+++++.>.+++++..
60: +++.....>+++++................................+++++
61: Not enough random bytes available. Please do some other work to give
62: the OS a chance to collect more entropy! (Need 245 more bytes)
63: We need to generate a lot of random bytes. It is a good idea to perform
64: some other action (type on the keyboard, move the mouse, utilize the
65: disks) during the prime generation; this gives the random number
66: generator a better chance to gain enough entropy.
67: +++++.++++++++++.+++++.++++++++++++++.++++++++
68: ++++++++++++++.++++++++++++++++++++++++++....+++
```

```
69: ++.+++++++++++++++++++++++++++++..+++++>+++++...............
70: ..............+++++^^^
71:
72: public and secret key created and signed.
```

In this example, suppose you want to generate the keys using the name `johnsmith` (line 37) and email address `johnsmith@pwt-ex.com` (line 39). A public and a secret key for johnsmith@pwt-ex.com (email address) are generated. In fact, GnuPG has two key rings: one is called the public-key ring containing all public keys in the system; the other is called the secret-key ring. Key rings are used to maintain and/or perform administration on keys.

For example, if you want to delete the key pair of `johnsmith`, you need to delete the secret key from the secret-key ring first and then delete the public key from the public-key ring. The commands to delete the key pair are

```
gpg --delete-secret-key johnsmith@pwt-ex.com
gpg --delete-key johnsmith@pwt-ex.com
```

The email address is often used to identify the user in GnuPG. A processing dialog is shown in the following example listing:

```
Example: ex19-10.gpg - Deleting Secret And Public Keys

 1: shell> gpg --delete-secret-key johnsmith@pwt-ex.com
 2: gpg (GnuPG) 1.0.6; Copyright (C) 2001 Free Software Foundation, Inc.
 3: This program comes with ABSOLUTELY NO WARRANTY.
 4: This is free software, and you are welcome to redistribute it
 5: under certain conditions. See the file COPYING for details.
 6:
 7: sec 1024D/40158CCA 2002-01-21 johnsmith (gnupg) <johnsmith@pwt-ex.com>
 8:
 9: Delete this key from the keyring? y
10: This is a secret key! - really delete? y
11:
12: shell> gpg --delete-key johnsmith@pwt-ex.com
13: gpg (GnuPG) 1.0.6; Copyright (C) 2001 Free Software Foundation, Inc.
14: This program comes with ABSOLUTELY NO WARRANTY.
15: This is free software, and you are welcome to redistribute it
16: under certain conditions. See the file COPYING for details.
17:
18: pub 1024D/40158CCA 2002-01-21 johnsmith (gnupg) <johnsmith@pwt-ex.com>
19:
20: Delete this key from the keyring? y
21: shell>
```

To help safeguard the private keys, the software saves the private key in an encrypted format protected by a symmetric (or conventional) encryption. The key for this symmetric encryption is the `passphrase` that you supply (see lines 50–51 of ex19-09.gpg). You will need this `passphrase` every time you want to use your private key.

In order for someone to be able to use the public key, you need to export and send your public key to him or her.

19.6.3 Exporting and importing public keys

Suppose you (johnsmith) have a business partner called Mary Anderson. You can export your public key with the command:

```
gpg --armor --output johnsmith_key --export johnsmith@pwt-ex.com
```

where the command arguments have the following meanings:

--armor	–	**Output the key as ASCII code**
--output	–	**Output the key into a file**
--export	–	**Export who's key**

This command has no returned message on the screen. In this case, the public key of johnsmith is output to the file johnsmith_key in ASCII code. The 1,024-bit public key is shown in example ex19-11.gpg.

```
Example: ex19-11.gpg - The Public-Key Of johnsmith (file: johnsmith_key)

 1: -----BEGIN PGP PUBLIC KEY BLOCK-----
 2: Version: GnuPG v1.0.6 (MingW32)
 3: Comment: For info see http://www.gnupg.org
 4:
 5: mQGiBDxM9lwRBADzsn+FPdjXVc91L3+6UkZRVlyW58tmRvueQMGwPjXOEM5JwgBd
 6: Nw6sRM+cNYhQQBgL0jgvAr9/2lmekt4PO85c7AkdI2kNnHnOYNiBs5fk30B5V67m
 7: RKPQkd5XsTf1RqlSAxsbj4S9GSfk/lxQQZ8vFHxi6P/0yEZV7R3rUbZLnwCg7wH8
 8: /Bf4cUVtFYXuaBf/PWsDdgkEAMffDDQ97zFzduefkAli7awpIaYHt4l2MaRQI/w/
 9: 1PgCs5enfXzaMF4GLnWX1qOfuP2uBqZdNH21IMLV7kvDYwfgsLsKuDoLTvS0CXpq
10: Ul+lrmFlqS6N2TQxn1panptDtBfzuI/oj7IyWXTL0YBomvZgXb30wPcdcnZWDDyt
11: Ffm6A/4//wHsF2G6ofYRXuVOO+nENeCgjXqvTBRdxtxK+0drSCRK44gvwFJljjjx
12: KCAd/WbjTiJMNuvECGwydRbqYg43wy69x9o863Q8D8XTVTsDMvSs9phbieiujamV
13: n4THaFd/VBYx6lfDBOI13ycKF3eOQmgm31DhbqMlgUfXnGgDcrQlam9obnNtaXRo
14: IChnbnVwZykgPGPpvaG5zbWl0aEBpc3AuY29t Poh XBBMRAgAXBQI8TPZcBQsHCgME
15: AxUDAgMWAgECF4AACgkQhZgOLDGFvG8jsQCgyXipE6ptHzxlBIqsVaqP1FGtjsoA
16: n2UVNBmkZlKLgN7yIcMmq4GyJpS0uQENBDxM9l8QBAD9HrpogezBIeBZDdVxAHcd
17: Q5QBcvEaz/HivzYtrnVlg/LNAVVzSZcm8ZisZRKM2r6vHlp+mWQK+8h64in664k+
18: MPhEEqYgbelmR0BxKxtpQkbSksgAD39ABZoNMgc+W661u7vkMwoDCxu6U89HWwPC
19: +Ofgr3jV3Z1hfmzoTbA2xwADBQP/feWgpn4WZ02Ywf6BRBv0EDZwOmHmF4R5Lhnd
20: aOkdtYlGgmrdR9AC5ZN6MaUwBHLLfkw4sC4l3Ygb72tfn+NlKdS38j3I36pFCuOI
21: bVMjF1HGCF3x5BOi8jYJcpZAcryYD4oiG3K+2Iehat4o3JscPtl5LIUn3rkOUzAl
22: kFWnJVGIRgQYEQIABgUCPEz2XwAKCRCFmA4sMYW8bx9TAKCuk+UeV7tGhNSF/8as
23: QZ+4rECOUQCg3/I0PTR16r4kVS1NgUhRmkYzyMo=
24: =dOU0
25: -----END PGP PUBLIC KEY BLOCK-----
```

You can then send the public-key file johnsmith_key to Mary by email so that she can send you encrypted messages. Similarly, Mary can email her public key to you. Suppose Mary's public-key file is called mary_key. You can import Mary's public key into your key ring by

```
gpg --import mary_key
```

A process dialog is shown in example ex19-12.gpg.

```
Example: ex19-12.gpg - Importing A Public Key

 1: shell> gpg --import mary_key
 2: gpg: key 94E6A35F: public key imported
 3: gpg: Total number processed: 1
 4: gpg:                 imported: 1
```

You can see all your public keys in your key ring by

```
gpg -list-keys
```

As an example, all public keys of `johnsmith` are shown in ex19-13.gpg.

```
Example: ex19-13.gpg - List All Public Keys

 1: shell> gpg --list-keys
 2: /gnupg/pubring.gpg
 3: ------------------
 4: pub 1024D/3185BC6F 2003-01-22 johnsmith (gnupg) <johnsmith@pwt-ex.com>
 5: sub 1024g/BA36A672 2003-01-22
 6:
 7: pub 1024D/94E6A35F 2003-01-19 mary <mary@pwt-ex.com>
 8: sub 1024g/29E0ACFD 2003-01-19
```

All newly imported keys should be validated before use. This process can be done by extracting the fingerprint of the public key. For example, you can extract the fingerprint of Mary's public key and telephone her to verify the key. To extract the fingerprint, you can use the following edit-key command:

```
gpg --edit-key mary@pwt-ex.com
```

This command will show the public key of `mary@pwt-ex.com` and display a command prompt

```
command>
```

waiting for further input. If you put the subcommand `frp`, the program will display a fingerprint of Mary's key. The fingerprint of Mary's public key is a numeric string in hexadecimal values similar to a message digest string (see line 14 of ex19-14.gpg). In fact, sometimes the MD string is called the fingerprint. This fingerprint can be verified with Mary for consistency by telephone or other means. After the verification process, you can validate the key by signing it with the subcommand `sign`.

A processing dialog is shown in ex19-14.gpg below:

```
Example: ex19-14.gpg - Validate And Signing An Imported Key

 1: shell>gpg --edit-key mary@pwt-ex.com
 2: gpg (GnuPG) 1.0.6; Copyright (C) 2001 Free Software Foundation, Inc.
 3: This program comes with ABSOLUTELY NO WARRANTY.
 4: This is free software, and you are welcome to redistribute it
 5: under certain conditions. See the file COPYING for details.
 6:
 7:
 8: pub 1024D/94E6A35F created: 2002-01-19 expires: never trust: -/q
 9: sub 1024g/29E0ACFD created: 2002-01-19 expires: never
10: (1). mary <mary@pwt-ex.com>
11:
12: Command> fpr
13: pub 1024D/94E6A35F 2002-01-19 mary <mary@pwt-ex.com>
14:      Fingerprint: BD6E 8F98 0423 B31F B4F6 3E7A 75B8 A3A9 94E6 A35F
15:
16: Command> sign
17:
18: pub 1024D/94E6A35F created: 2002-01-19 expires: never trust: -/q
19:      Fingerprint: BD6E 8F98 0423 B31F B4F6 3E7A 75B8 A3A9 94E6 A35F
20:
21:     mary <mary@pwt-ex.com>
22:
23: Are you really sure that you want to sign this key
24: with your key: "johnsmith (gnupg) <johnsmith@pwt-ex.com>"
25:
26: Really sign? y
```

```
27:
28: You need a passphrase to unlock the secret key for
29: user: "johnsmith (gnupg) <johnsmith@pwt-ex.com>"
30: 1024-bit DSA key, ID 3185BC6F, created 2002-01-22
31:
32: Enter passphrase: have a nice day
33: Command> quit
34: Save Changes? y
35: shell>
```

Now we have everything ready for some encryption and decryption actions using GnuPG.

19.6.4 Encryption and decryption using GnuPG

Compared to other activities, encryption and decryption are relatively easy. For example, you (or `johnsmith`) can use GnuPG to encrypt and send the following important message to Mary:

```
Listing: ex19-10.txt - Sample Important File: mymesg.txt

1: Dear Mary
2:
3: The company board would like to invite
4: you to take part in the take over
5: meeting at 2:pm this Friday.
6:
7: Regards
8:
9: John Smith
```

To encrypt this text file with Mary's public key, all you have to do is to activate the command

```
shell>gpg --output mymesg.gpg --armor --encrypt
            --recipient mary@pwt-ex.com mymesg.txt
```

This command will encrypt the file mymesg.txt using the public key of `mary@pwt-ex.com` and produce an ASCII output file called mymesg.gpg. This encrypted file is similar to the listing below:

```
Example: ex19-15.gpg - The Encrypted Message File: mymesg.gpg

 1: -----BEGIN PGP MESSAGE-----
 2: Version: GnuPG v1.0.6 (MingW32)
 3: Comment: For info see http://www.gnupg.org
 4:
 5: hQEOA6/tk02bPMnrEAP/UG512Mzu+e0HTkbi8JNroH8pkj3gBiXZR4PapT5e2zr9
 6: x5+9FpSWgxrq4ojeOiML1dI74r9QdwB1tAig10uqC81tm9fWgNxsJ77cmfMUExgm
 7: CtmxG7GESUZ3KprbSWMSzObClmSIlVkJOz9Kkz8eqBTVO3UgFsrXpYqyEFNyNEME
 8: AJy5LnMCeWHPvKUrqT+09d52Vmonuj5kTyLkbH+3OwHCmqP/GZOeDOTtI7rC0kRy
 9: NJxgoeqnkgDRCPB+FppJBrgUJ4TQKEKeMvAIPqdCxTpHkNiXQQUeXwWY65XRE/f2
10: VfnoGEwxE1xEDWsqGaSfuKqglfqj3KsNBz4bODEYLLdY0rkB1Yh3TWOzFp3IZaAO
11: Ub9J4zvRH8qU0yjU7nEqj/b5jyEwoeFxWHWxOXlVLRGkUQ9v/F+D0GlbCxpen37w
12: hJNFcNquA2HynPk1JOHlZFclxQVm4KsW8ciYcbIE1A6LOxyrBSxnUvi5q0TisNTm
13: BmCAuq5cUTrCdJuUSPW11YQOrt9exyoc2lxJehBsVDz8qZQFVXCYQuy3oKtWcGit
14: CA/7DGcnNXAT4Opu2v6xT7bnDBYUAMCyBjyelA==
15: =a15z
16: -----END PGP MESSAGE-----
17:
```

You can then email this file as an attachment to Mary and only Mary or the owner of Mary's private key can decrypt it. When Mary receives the file, she can decrypt it using her private key as:

```
shell> gpg --output message --decrypt mymesg.gpg
```

In this case, the encrypted file mymesg.gpg is going to be decrypted by Mary's private key and the result output to a file called message. Since private keys in GnuPG are protected by passphrases, Mary may need to provide her passphrase to complete the decryption.

A typical processing dialog is shown below:

```
Example: ex19-16.gpg - Decryption Using GnuPG

 1: shell>gpg --output message --decrypt mymesg.gpg
 2:
 3: You need a passphrase to unlock the secret key for
 4: user: "mary Anderson (business partner) <mary@pwt-ex.com>"
 5: 1024-bit ELG-E key, ID 9B3CC9EB,created 2002-01-22 (main key ID 1D5BBD53)
 6:
 7: Enter passphrase: have a nice day
 8:
 9: gpg: encrypted with 1024-bit ELG-E key, ID 9B3CC9EB, created 2002-01-22
10: "mary Anderson (business partner) <mary@pwt-ex.com>"
11:
12: shell>
```

In addition to public-key cryptography, GnuPG can also offer symmetric encryption/decryption as well. For example, you can activate symmetric encryption on GnuPG by

```
gpg -output en_mesg.gpg -armor -symmetric mymesg.txt
```

This command uses a symmetric method to encrypt the message file mymesg.txt and produce the encrypted result in en_mesg.gpg. Since you are using a symmetric method, GnuPG in this case would ask you to input a key (i.e., passphrase) for encryption. You also need the same key for decryption, when you activate the decryption command

```
gpg -output message --decrypt en_mesg.gpg
```

A typical processing dialog is shown in ex19-17.gpg below:

```
Example: ex19-17.gpg - Symmetric Encryption And Decryption Using GnuPG

 1: shell> gpg --output en_mesg.gpg --symmetric mymesg.txt
 2:
 3: Enter passphrase: see you later
 4: Repeat passphrase: see you later
 5: shell>
 6:
 7: shell> gpg --output message --decrypt en_mesg.gpg
 8: Enter passphrase: see you later
 9: shell>
```

In many practical cases, the passphrase is an MD5 string generated by the MD utility such as

```
MD5 ("see you later") = a3e6d94880ba5f0d09b0dce37e65439f
```

to provide more protection against brute-force attack. In this case, the attacker has to crack the MD5 string instead of a nice phrase.

All commands and options related to GnuPG can be displayed on your screen if you activate the program with the help option:

```
gpg --help
```

Finally, there are a number of user interfaces for GnuPG on different platforms and operating systems available on the Internet. Some of them are integrated with email systems such as Outlook Express and some of them are embedded into Windows systems. Once again, a good reference can be found on the official GnuPG site: www.gnupg.org.

20 Practical e-commerce and SSL security

20.1 An introduction to e-commerce

20.1.1 What is e-commerce and why?

A company that performs any online activity is generally considered an e-commerce company. Online activity means any business operation conducted over a network 24 hours a day and 7 days a week all year round. Under this definition, all kinds of business activities on the Web such as

- buying, selling, and trading
- service provision
- banking
- entertainment

are characterized as e-commerce or e-business. Although e-commerce is a relatively new term even from our computer dictionary, it was widely used by many big corporations decades ago. In particular, the banking industry used Electronic Funds Transfer (EFT) to transfer money between accounts and/or banks long before the creation of the Internet. Also, many big companies and government organizations use the so-called Electronic Data Interchange (EDI) sharing information among divisions and/or departments. Business over a small network environment has become very active only since the easy availability of databases and computers.

Before the advent of the Internet, e-commerce or any online business was expensive. Usually some dedicated underground wiring or channels using microwave technologies were involved to provide a direct link among the dedicated organizations. The physical link and data transmission format were usually proprietary and therefore established an essential secure environment for the business activity. These kinds of business still exist and are active today. In fact, many people consider this kind of e-commerce as business over a secure channel or network.

The Internet opened the flood gates for affordable networking. Twenty-four hours a day and 7 days a week, connecting people all over the globe is no longer a problem. All of a sudden, we have a global economy reaching every corner of the world. For example, a luxury home or house auction in South Africa can instantly attract hundreds of buyers from Europe and North America. All buying, selling, and other transactions can be completed within minutes. It is believed that total Internet money transactions will be more than a trillion dollas by the time this book is published. This is the power of bringing people and business together.

On the other hand, with the same network type and data transmission protocol, e-commerce on the Internet operates in an insecure environment. In general, from a security point of view, the Internet is a place where anybody can be everybody. Again, all of a sudden, online fraud occurs everywhere.

For example, if someone has ordered some goods from your Web site on the Internet, do you trust his or her identity? Do you trust his or her credit card number? Even if you can get the money from the credit card company, how do you know you are not charging someone else illegally? In fact, online security is a big issue for us all, not just businesses.

This chapter discusses e-commerce and related security concerns. It is not intended to cover all topics. From a practical point of view, the first half of this chapter is dedicated to how e-commerce models are characterized and implemented depending on their business nature. The core technologies for successful implementations are also discussed. As an example, an e-commerce activity known as online bargain hunting is demonstrated with database techniques.

In the second half of the chapter, online security is our main concern. In order to provide a secure business transaction in an insecure network or environment, a number of technologies are introduced. In particular the Public-Key Infrastructure (PKI) with digital keys, certificates, the Certification Authority (CA), and the Secure Sockets Layer (SSL) are introduced in some detail. A quick tour of the SSL software package OpenSSL is also presented. At the end, we will use all you have learned to build a secure Web site to provide secure communications to Web users.

For a successful implementation of e-c ommerce, the nature of the business is essential. Different businesses may have different structures, requirements, and hence business models. A general discussion of some popular e-commerce models and requirements is presented in the next section.

20.1.2 Some common e-commerce models

Since no one knows exactly how many different types of business there are on the Internet, it is impossible to provide a full account of all e-commerce. Also, only the owner of the business fully understands the operations and nature of his or her business. Even a full account of one e-commerce model may not be easy. For some small or medium-sized businesses based on some popular implementations on the Web, we have the following business models for e-commerce that target individuals:

- Online shopping-cart model
- Online auction model
- Online personal services model
- Online finance model
- Online entertainment model

If your business belongs to one of these categories, chances are that you may already have set up or very much want to set up your business on the Web.

For individual customers, the models above may cover a substantial number of services a customer may want or need on the Web. For example, if you want to buy something, you may want to go to a site with a shopping cart. An auction site is the place if you want to hunt for a bargain. Whether accepting payment or not, any business providing services to individuals on the Internet belongs to the personal services model. One well-known business of this type is your ISP. It provides Internet access and charges for it. Other popular service provider examples are:

- Personal dating services
- Recruitment services
- Travel services
- Products and services hunting

Almost all banking and online financial activities belong to the finance model. Apart from Internet banks, most ordinary banks offer online banking facilities to their customers as well. Many companies and financial institutes are also providing online loans to customers. Watching a movie, listening to online music, playing a game, or other enjoyable activities on the Internet are all characterized as online entertainment.

Each model targets different kinds of clients and may require different technologies to support it. Almost all of them require database knowledge and techniques. This is because they need to handle customers on a reasonable (if not large) scale if they want their businesses to be successful. For example, almost all service providers (ISPs or entertainment) on the Web require good accounting practices so that charges can be made. Unless your business is very small and customer records and concerns are not essential, chances are that you need database applications.

We have already implemented an elementary online shopping cart in Chapter 7. This shopping cart will be visited again by adding database management and security in this chapter. An online bargain hunting shop is implemented in section 20.3 with a database. Using database management and an online product catalog, updates or changes can be made easily to target bargain hunters. Although still quite simple when compared to commercial standards, it is a first step toward practical e-commerce.

If you want to charge your customer for online services or shopping, a mechanism to get payment information is vital. Usually this can be implemented as a login page or checkout facility using a password and a payment form.

20.2   A general login page for e-commerce

20.2.1 Designing the customer profile with credit card information

All businesses need good customers. Building mutual trust between you as a merchant and the customers is the number one priority for your business. This is particularly true when you want to trade online since you cannot see your customer face to face. There are no closed circuit TVs or security personnel to help you. In fact, we have reached an age where even thieves engage in online business!

More online security and secured sites with SSL will be discussed later in this chapter. At a minimum level, any e-commerce site should implement a good database system to handle information and records of customers. Records should be protected by the user's password in encrypted form. In particular, credit card information should be verified and checked against the listing of stolen cards. If possible, you should back up your business with a good insurance policy against online theft. Most important of all, Web pages regarding sensitive material such as credit card information or transactions should be protected by a secure environment, transmission, and protocol such as secured HTTP (or HTTPS). For obvious reasons we can only show you a simple example of how to design and set up a customer profile to store the information (including credit card information) you may need for your business. This example can be used as a starting point for a variety of e-commerce sites.

To design a customer profile is simple. All you need is to write down the customer's information you want to store. Too much or too little information would be inappropriate. For most online businesses, the following information may be considered as sufficient:

- Name
- Gender
- Age
- Address
- Email address
- Telephone number

- User_id
- Password
- Credit card number
- Card type
- Expiry date

To set up the information above as a database table, consider the following example in MySQL:

```
Example: ex20-01.sql - SQL Statement To Create Customer Profile Table

 1: mysql> CREATE DATABASE buss_db;
 2: Query OK, 1 row affected (0.05 sec)
 3:
 4: mysql> USE buss_db;
 5: Database changed
 6: mysql> CREATE TABLE cust_profile
 7:     -> (
 8:     ->     name VARCHAR(50) NOT NULL,
 9:     ->     gender VARCHAR(10) NOT NULL,
10:     ->     age VARCHAR(10) NOT NULL,
```

```
11:     ->        address01 VARCHAR(60) NOT NULL,
12:     ->        address02 VARCHAR(60) DEFAULT NULL,
13:     ->        city VARCHAR(20) NOT NULL,
14:     ->        country VARCHAR(20) NOT NULL,
15:     ->        post_code VARCHAR(20) NOT NULL,
16:     ->        email_add VARCHAR(20) NOT NULL,
17:     ->        phone_number VARCHAR(20) NOT NULL,
18:     ->
19:     ->        user_id VARCHAR(20) NOT NULL,
20:     ->        password VARCHAR(60) NOT NULL,
21:     ->        card_no VARCHAR(20) NOT NULL,
22:     ->        card_type VARCHAR(20) NOT NULL,
23:     ->        expiry_date VARCHAR(20) NOT NULL,
24:     ->     PRIMARY KEY(user_id)
25:     -> );
26: Query OK, 0 rows affected (0.01 sec)
```

The SQL statement in line 1 is to create a database for the business called `buss_db`. The statement in line 4 uses the newly created `buss_db` as the current database. Line 6 creates a customer profile table called `cust_profile` with a detailed description as in the profile mentioned earlier. The response from MySQL in line 26 indicates that the table is successfully created.

Since we want to use Message Digest (MD) encryption to protect the password, the length of the password field (line 20) is longer than expected. The following example shows the internal representation of the table.

```
Example: ex20-02.sql - SQL Statement To Create Customer Profile Table

 1: mysql> DESCRIBE cust_profile;
 2: +--------------+-------------+------+-----+---------+-------+
 3: | Field        | Type        | Null | Key | Default | Extra |
 4: +--------------+-------------+------+-----+---------+-------+
 5: | name         | varchar(50) |      |     |         |       |
 6: | gender       | varchar(10) |      |     |         |       |
 7: | age          | varchar(10) |      |     |         |       |
 8: | address01    | varchar(60) |      |     |         |       |
 9: | address02    | varchar(60) | YES  |     | NULL    |       |
10: | city         | varchar(20) |      |     |         |       |
11: | country      | varchar(20) |      |     |         |       |
12: | post_code    | varchar(20) |      |     |         |       |
13: | email_add    | varchar(20) |      |     |         |       |
14: | phone_number | varchar(20) |      |     |         |       |
15: | user_id      | varchar(20) |      | PRI |         |       |
16: | password     | varchar(60) |      |     |         |       |
17: | card_no      | varchar(20) |      |     |         |       |
18: | card_type    | varchar(20) |      |     |         |       |
19: | expiry_date  | varchar(20) |      |     |         |       |
20: +--------------+-------------+------+-----+---------+-------+
21: 15 rows in set (0.01 sec)
```

This example contains only one statement, DESCRIBE. This DESCRIBE command in line 1 displays a detailed account of all fields inside the table `cust_profile`. In this case, the `user_id` field is the primary key as illustrated in line 15.

You may now want to develop a page to allow your customer to become a member.

20.2.2 Register new member to user profile

In fact, the user information in the example above can be grouped into four sections:

- General information
- Login information
- Credit card information
- Contact information

Grouping the information is good practice to target the sensitive data so that security measures or priorities can be set. The general information contains the details of the customer including the name, gender, age, address, and email address. The login information is the user name and password that the user needs to log in to the system and perform online shopping. The credit card information is used to collect payment from the customer; it should contain the card number, card type, and expiry date. Finally, the contact information is usually the phone number of the customer which is useful for home delivery or other contact purposes.

To develop an example to register new members is quite straightforward. As you might expect, the first thing is to write an XHTML page such as ex20-03.htm to obtain all the general, login, credit card, and contact information about a user. Once the Register button is pressed, all information is sent to the associated database and table stored as a record.

A screen shot of the page is shown in Fig. 20.1.

From this figure, you can see that the information is grouped into four sections. At a minimum level, it should increase the clarity and readability for users. Another immediate advantage of grouping information

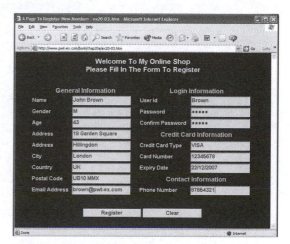

Figure 20.1 ex20-03.htm

is that once the form is submitted to a processing program, the information in a particular section can be easily checked and proper action taken accordingly. We will show you how to perform this shortly.

One of the simplest ways to implement this page is to use text boxes arranged by an XHTML table. For this example, it is natural to use one table with 10 rows and four columns. The coding is listed as follows:

```
Example: ex20-03.htm - Register Member Into User Profile

 1: <?xml version="1.0" encoding="iso-8859-1"?>
 2: <!DOCTYPE html PUBLIC "-//W3C//DTD XHTML 1.0 Transitional//EN"
 3:     "http://www.w3.org/TR/xhtml1/DTD/xhtml1-transitional.dtd">
 4: <html xmlns="http://www.w3.org/1999/xhtml" xml:lang="en" lang="en">
 5: <head><title>A Page To Register New Members - ex20-03.htm</title></head>
 6: <style>
 7:    .butSt{background-color:#aaffaa;font-family:arial;font-weight:bold;
 8:        font-size:12pt;color:#880000;width:180px;height:28px}
 9:    .txtSt{font-family:arial;font-weight:bold; text-align:left;
10:        font-size:12pt;color:#ffff00}
11:    .txtSt2{font-family:arial;font-weight:bold; text-align:center;
12:        font-size:14pt;color:#00ff00}
13: </style>
14: <body style="background:#000088;text-align:center" class="txtSt">
15: <div class="txtSt" style="font-size:16pt;text-align:center">
16:    Welcome To My Online Shop <br />
17:    Please Fill In The Form To Register</div><br /><br />
18:
19: <form method="post" action="ex20-03.php">
20: <table border="0" width="90%" class="txtSt">
```

```
21:    <tr><td colspan="2" class="txtSt2">General Information</td>
22:        <td colspan="2" class="txtSt2">Login Information</td></tr>
23:    <tr><td >Name</td><td>
24:      <input type="text" name="name" class="butSt">   </td>
25:      <td >User Id</td>
26:      <td ><input type="text" name="user_id" class="butSt"></td></tr>
27:    <tr><td >Gender</td>
28:      <td><input type="text" name="gender" class="butSt"></td>
29:      <td >Password</td>
30:      <td ><input type="password" name="pass_id" class="butSt"></td></tr>
31:    <tr><td >Age</td>
32:      <td><input type="text" name="age" class="butSt"></td>
33:      <td >Confirm Password</td>
34:      <td ><input type="password" name="con_pass_id" class="butSt"></td></tr>
35:    <tr><td >Address</td>
36:      <td><input type="text" name="add01" class="butSt"></td>
37:      <td colspan="2" class="txtSt2">Credit Card Information</td></tr>
38:    <tr><td >Address</td>
39:      <td><input type="text" name="add02" class="butSt"></td>
40:      <td >Credit Card Type</td>
41:      <td ><input type="text" name="card_type" class="butSt"></td></tr>
42:    <tr><td >City</td>
43:      <td><input type="text" name="city" class="butSt"></td>
44:      <td >Card Number</td>
45:      <td ><input type="text" name="card_no" class="butSt"></td></tr>
46:    <tr><td >Country</td>
47:      <td><input type="text" name="country" class="butSt"></td>
48:      <td >Expiry Date</td>
49:      <td ><input type="text" name="expiry_date" class="butSt"></td></tr>
50:    <tr><td >Postal Code</td>
51:      <td><input type="text" name="post_code" class="butSt"></td>
52:      <td colspan="2" class="txtSt2">Contact Information</td></tr>
53:    <tr><td >Email Address</td>
54:      <td><input type="text" name="email" class="butSt"></td>
55:      <td >Phone Number</td>
56:      <td ><input type="text" name="phone_no" class="butSt"></td></tr>
57:    </table><br /><br />
58:    <input type="submit" value="Register" class="butSt">
59:    <input type="reset" value="Clear" class="butSt">
60:  </form>
61:  </body>
62:  </html>
```

Since this page was implemented as a table with four columns, there may be some confusion on the text box layout. However, if you read the page with the picture of Fig. 20.1 in mind, you should have no difficulty reading the code. It is common practice to draw the picture first before any implementation coding is done.

Alternatively, you can use multiple tables. For example, you can use two or three tables where each of them contains one section of information. With CSS position capability, you can place all tables together to build the page. This way, you can improve both the program readability and clarity of layout. You can add some more features to enhance the user input. One common practice in the industry is to use select boxes on some commonly known fields. For example, you can use a select box to replace the gender field. The select box contains the male, female options for the user to pick so that no typing is needed. Another improvement may be to change the age field to an age group with a select box. As your experience grows, new ideas will come more easily.

When the Register button is pressed, the PHP program ex20-03.php is activated (see line 19). This program is the processing engine for the example and will perform the following tasks:

- Check if all fields in the general information area have been filled.
- Check if all fields in the login information area have been filled.
- Check if all fields in the credit card information area have been filled.
- Check if all fields in the contact information area have been filled.
- Check if the password matches the confirm password.

If any one of these checks fails, a message window is displayed to ask the user to complete the specific part of the form. When all the checks return a true value, the program will perform the following:

- Connect to the desired database.
- Store the information as a new record in the customer profile table cust_profile.

If an error occurs at this stage, it is likely that the user's identity field user_id has already been used by someone already on the database. Recall that user_id is the primary key of the database and should be uniquely defined. If the database is updated successfully, you have registered a new member into your online shop. As soon as the member starts his or her online shopping, you can generate revenue for your business. The PHP program is listed below:

```
Example: ex20-03.php - The PHP Script For ex20-03.htm

 1: <?PHP echo"<?";?>xml version="1.0" encoding="iso-8859-1"<?PHP echo"?>";?>
 2: <!DOCTYPE html PUBLIC "-//W3C//DTD XHTML 1.0 Transitional//EN"
 3:   "http://www.w3.org/TR/xhtml1/DTD/xhtml1-transitional.dtd">
 4: <html xmlns="http://www.w3.org/1999/xhtml" xml:lang="en" lang="en">
 5: <head><title>Example: ex14-03.pl</title></head>
 6: <body style="background:#000088;text-align:center;
 7:   font-family:arial;font-size:16pt;color:#ffff00">
 8: <?php
 9: if ( (trim($name)=="")    || (trim($gender)=="") || (trim($email)=="") ||
10:      (trim($age)=="")     || (trim($add01)=="") ||
11:      (trim($add02)=="")   || (trim($city)=="") ||
12:      (trim($country)=="") || (trim($post_code)==""))
13: {
14:    echo "Error.. General Information is not completed!";
15:    exit();
16: }
17: else if ( (trim($user_id)=="") || (trim($pass_id)=="") ||
18:           (trim($con_pass_id)=="") )
19: {
20:    echo "Error.. Login Information is not completed!";
21:    exit();
22: }
23: else if ( (trim($card_type)=="") || (trim($card_no)=="") ||
24:           (trim($expiry_date)=="") )
25: {
26:    echo "Error.. Credit Card Information is not completed!";
27:    exit();
28: }
29: else if (trim($phone_no)=="")
30: {
31:    echo "Error.. Contact Information is not completed!";
32:    exit();
33: }
34: else if ($pass_id != $con_pass_id) {
35:    echo "Error.. Two Passwords are not matched!";
```

```
36:    exit();
37: }
38: else
39: {
40:    $pass_id = md5($pass_id);
41:    $db = mysql_connect("www.pwt-ex.com", "johnsmith","johnsmith");
42:    mysql_select_db("buss_db",$db);
43:
44:    $sql = "INSERT INTO cust_profile
45:           (name,gender,age,address01,address02,city,country,
46:           post_code,email_add,phone_number,
47:           user_id,password,card_no,card_type,expiry_date)
48:        VALUES
49:           ('$name','$gender','$age','$add01','$add02','$city','$country',
50:            '$post_code','$email','$phone_no',
51:            '$user_id','$pass_id','$card_no','$card_type','$expiry_date')";
52:
53:    $result = mysql_query($sql);
54:
55:    if (!$result)
56:    {
57:        echo "Registration Failed..Someone has used the userID";
58:        exit() ;
59:    }
60:    echo "Registration Successful! <br /> Enjoy Your Shopping";
61:    exit();
62: }
63: ?>
64: </body>
65: </html>
```

This is a PHP page embedded into XHTML. The first part of this program is a series of conditional statements to perform checking on user input. The first `if` statement (lines 9–16) is used to test whether the user has filled in all the fields on the general information area. If any one variable in the general information area is empty, a message is output (see line 14) and the program terminated. Another three `if` statements covering lines 17–33 are used to test the login, credit card, and contact areas. In normal circumstances, you may also need to test whether the password `$pass_id` is the same as the confirm password (lines 34–37). This is a good practice to prevent password errors such as typing an unintended string.

Figure 20.2 Register new member

The second part of the page is for database manipulation. Line 40 is to encrypt the password with an MD string. The next line is to make the connection to the database and the following line is to select `buss_db` (business database) as the current database. The variable `$sql` in lines 44–51 stores an SQL statement to insert all user input into table `cust_profile` (customer profile) as a new record. This SQL statement will be executed at line 53. If the returned result is not a true value, you have an error on creating the record. One of the common reasons for this is that the user name `user_id` has already been used by someone else. In this case, a message is printed at line 57 and the program terminated. If the execution of the `mysql_query()` function is successful, you have registered a new member into your database. A simple message is then output as illustrated at line 60. A screen shot is shown in Fig. 20.2.

Note that this program demonstrates a simple, yet general PHP page for e-commerce to register members into the user profile. We concentrate only on the concept and structure of the page. For some real applications, you may need to add protection code if the database connection should fail. Also, you may want to tell your customers that the security of the shopping site is good and protected by the SSL or Secure Electronic Transfer (SET) from a trusted organization such as a bank. A practical demonstration of how to set up a secure site with Apache and OpenSSL is provided later in section 20.5. This secure site can be used to provide security so that you and your customers know that virtually no one can decode the transmitted information between your site and customers.

Line 61 should be replaced by a jump to the URL address of your main page. In many cases, the main page is your e-commerce site such as online services or shopping-cart implementation. In addition to this new member page, you should also develop a general page to allow members to log in and start shopping.

To make sure the information is inserted into the customer profile, you can issue the following simple SQL command

```
SELECT * FROM cust_profile;
```

on the `mysql` prompt. The result is shown in the following example.

```
Example: ex20-04.sql -Verify New Member In Database
 1: mysql> SELECT * FROM cust_profile;
 2: +------------+--------+-----+-----------------+------------+--------+
 3: | name       | gender | age | address01       | address02  | city   |
 4: +------------+--------+-----+-----------------+------------+--------+
 5: | John Brown | M      |  43 | 18 Garden Square | Hillingdon | London |
 6: +------------+--------+-----+-----------------+------------+--------+
 7:
 8: +---------+-----------+-----------------+--------------+---------+
 9: | country | post_code | email_add       | phone_number | user_id |
10: +---------+-----------+-----------------+--------------+---------+
11: | UK      | UB10 MMX  | brown@pwt-ex.com | 87654321     | john    |
12: +---------+-----------+-----------------+--------------+---------+
13:
14: +----------------------------------+---------+-----------+-------------+
15: | password                         | card_no | card_type | expiry_date |
16: +----------------------------------+---------+-----------+-------------+
17: | 527bd5b5d689e2c32ae974c6229ff785 | 12345678 | VISA     | 22/12/2007  |
18: +----------------------------------+---------+-----------+-------------+
19:
20: 1 row in set (0.00 sec)
```

After the SQL statement in line 1, you should see a long table on your MySQL screen. We split the table into three rows in ex20-04.sql for display purposes. As you can see from this example, the user information is stored in the fields in table `cust_profile`. The user password is encrypted by an MD string.

20.2.3 A login page for e-commerce

Once you have the customer database ready, to construct a general login page for your e-commerce site is a straightforward process. All you have to do is to develop a page to get the user name and password of your members. They are then compared to the data stored in the user profile database. If there is a match, the user is allowed to begin his or her online shopping. In many cases, you may also want to add a button to incorporate example ex20-03.htm to allow a new user to join as a member.

We use the PHP language to implement this example and the first part of the page is listed below:

```
Example: ex20-05.php - A Login Page For E-Commerce (Part One)

 1: <?PHP echo"<?";?>xml version="1.0" encoding="iso-8859-1"<?PHP echo"?>";?>
 2: <!DOCTYPE html PUBLIC "-//W3C//DTD XHTML 1.0 Transitional//EN"
 3:     "http://www.w3.org/TR/xhtml1/DTD/xhtml1-transitional.dtd">
 4: <html xmlns="http://www.w3.org/1999/xhtml" xml:lang="en" lang="en">
 5: <head><title> A Login Page For E-Commerce - ex20-05.php</title></head>
 6: <style>
 7:   .butSt{background-color:#aaffaa;font-family:arial;font-weight:bold;
 8:       font-size:18pt;color:#880000;width:250px;height:35px}
 9:   .butSt2{background-color:#aaaaaa;font-family:arial;font-weight:bold;
10:       font-size:18pt;color:#880000;width:180px;height:35px}
11:   .txtSt{font-family:arial;font-weight:bold; text-align:left;
12:       font-size:18pt;color:#ffff00}</style>
13: <body style="background:#000088;text-align:center" class="txtSt">
14:
15: <?php
16: global $llst, $userId, $passId;
17:
18: $llst = 'Welcome To ABC Online Shopping<br /> ' .
19:   ' This Is A Member Only Site<br /><br /> ' .
20:   ' Enter User Name and Password To Log In<br />' .
21:   ' <form action="ex20-05.php" method="post">'.
22:   ' <table class="txtSt">' .
23:   ' <tr><td>Username:</td><td>' .
24:   ' <input type="text" name="userId" id="userId" class="butSt" />' .
25:   ' </td></tr>' .
26:   ' <tr><td>Password:</td><td>' .
27:   ' <input type="password" name="passId" id="passId" class="butSt" />' .
28:   ' </td></tr> ' .
29:   ' <tr><td colspan="2" style="text-align:center"><br />' .
30:   ' <input type="submit" value="Login" class="butSt2" />' .
31:   ' <input type="button" value="Join Member" class="butSt2" '.
32:   ' onclick="location.href=\'ex20-03.htm\'" /> </td></tr>' .
33:   ' </table>' .
34:   ' </form> ';
35:
```

This part of the page is simple. We use a PHP string `$llst` to store an XHTML message so that it can be displayed anywhere at any time. The message string contains two text fields (lines 23–24 and 26–27) to allow the user to enter his or her user name and password. The string also has two buttons defined in lines 30–32. If the Login button is clicked, the page is submitted to itself for further processing. If the Join Member button is clicked, the command in line 32

```
onclick="location.href=\'ex20-03.htm\'"
```

will activate the page ex20-03.htm so that the user can sign in as a new member. The second part of the page is to process the input data and compare it to the values in the database.

```
Listing: Continuation Of The PHP Script ex20-05.php (Part Two)

36: if ($passId && $userId)
37: {
38:   $passId = md5($passId);
39:
40:   $db = mysql_connect("www.pwt-ex.com", "johnsmith","johnsmith");
41:   mysql_select_db("buss_db",$db);
42:
43:   $query = "SELECT * FROM cust_profile WHERE user_id='$userId'";
44:   $result = mysql_query ($query) or die ("SQL Query Error..");
```

```
45:
46:  $row = mysql_fetch_array ($result);
47:
48:  if (($passId == $row['password']) && ($userId == $row['user_id']))
49:  {
50:    echo"Thankyou $userId! <br /> Enjoy Your Shopping!<br /><br />";
51:  }
52:  else
53:  {
54:    echo "$llst";
55:    if ($userId == $row['user_id'])
56:    {
57:      echo "<br />Sorry! Wrong Password.. Please Try Again..<br />";
58:      $passId = false;
59:    }
60:  }
61:  mysql_free_result ($result);
62: }
63: else
64: {
65:    echo "$llst";
66: }
67: ?>
68: <br /><img src="line1.gif" width="500" height="6" alt="pic" />
69: <br /><br />
70: </body>
71: </html>
```

The main purpose of this page is to obtain the user name and password from the user and compare them against the values in the database. Lines 40–41 are used to make the connection to the database so that the SQL statement can be performed. The SQL statement that we want to execute is

```
"SELECT * FROM cust_profile WHERE user_id='$userId'";
```

This statement will get all the information in the database that matches the user name. If the execution of this SQL is successful, the user's information is stored in variable `$row` as illustrated in line 46. Now you can compare the user name and password. If both match the values in the database (line 48), a simple welcome message is displayed. If the input password is not the same as the value in the database, you have a wrong password case. In this situation, the XHTML string `$llst` together with a wrong password message is displayed (see lines 54–59). Note that the password comparison is performed using MD strings. Some screen shots are shown in Figs 20.3 and 20.4.

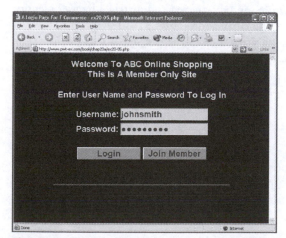

Figure 20.3 ex20-05.php

Figure 20.4 Wrong password case

In fact, a large number of online entertainment sites and/or service providers have a page similar to this so that user's information can be stored and more importantly regular (or monthly) charges can be made. If you have an e-commerce main page, you can activate it in line 50 so that your customer can start his or her online services and/or shopping trip. As a practical example, let's consider how to use this page to implement a shopping cart for an online bargain hunting shop below.

20.3   Implementation of an online bargain hunting shop

20.3.1 Getting user information with cookies and a database

There are a number of ways to implement a shopping-cart feature for an online shop. In fact, you developed an elementary implementation in Chapter 7. To simply our approach, we are going to use all the ECMAScript functions developed in section 7.4 and included in the libraries

> `cookie.js` and `online.js`

These two libraries provide all ECMAScript functions that we need to handle cookies. In order to make the shopping cart in Chapter 7 more practical and more suitable for our online bargain shop, the following database features are added:

- Obtain user information from the database and pass them to the shopping cart of the shop.
- Develop an online shopping catalog with a database table so that changes can be made rapidly and easily.

Other features of the shopping cart parallel the examples in Chapter 7.

One of the beauties of using database features is that once you have done all the design and programming, you can add more items or change prices, product descriptions, and even product pictures easily. In many cases, you don't need to touch your XHTML coding or pages at all!

As we mentioned in Chapter 7, most shopping cart implementations use cookies. In normal circumstances, two sets of cookies are used. One set of cookies is to identify the customer so that charges can be made, the second set of cookies is, obviously, to remember the shopping items in the shopping cart. Usually, the user information cookies are

- User name
- Email address
- Shopping identity

In terms of our user profile in section 20.2.1, this information can be extracted and matched by user identity (`userId`), encrypted password (i.e., MD string of `passId`), and email address (`email_add`).

To use the login example in section 20.2.3 for our shopping site is simple. The first step is to copy the example ex20-05.php to ex20-06.php. The second step is to replace the code after line 14 by the following:

```
Example: ex20-06.php - Program Fragment For User Login

15: <?php
16: global $llst, $userId, $passId;
17:
18: $llst = 'Welcome To ABC Online Bargain Hunting<br /> ' .
19:   ' This Is A Member Only Site<br /><br /> ' .
20:   ' Enter User Name and Password To Log In<br />' .
21:   ' <form action="ex20-06.php" method="post">'.
22:   ' <table class="txtSt">' .
23:   ' <tr><td>Username:</td><td>' .
24:   '  <input type="text" name="userId" id="userId" class="butSt" />' .
25:   '  </td></tr>' .
```

```
26:     ' <tr><td>Password:</td><td>' .
27:     '  <input type="password" name="passId" id="passId" class="butSt" />' .
28:     '  </td></tr> ' .
29:     ' <tr><td colspan="2" style="text-align:center"><br />' .
30:     '  <input type="submit" value="Login" class="butSt2" />' .
31:     '  <input type="button" value="Join Member" class="butSt2" '.
32:     '     onclick="location.href=\'ex20-03.htm\'" /> </td></tr>' .
33:     ' </table>' .
34:     ' </form> ';
35:
36: if ($passId && $userId)
37: {
38:  $passId = md5($passId);
39:
40:  $db = mysql_connect("www.pwt-ex.com", "johnsmith","johnsmith");
41:  mysql_select_db("buss_db",$db);
42:
43:  $query = "SELECT * FROM cust_profile WHERE user_id='$userId'";
44:  $result = mysql_query ($query) or die ("SQL Query Error..");
45:
46:  $row = mysql_fetch_array ($result);
47:
48:  if (($passId == $row['password']) && ($userId == $row['user_id']))
49:  {
50:    echo"Thankyou $userId! <br /> Enjoy Your Shopping!<br /><br />";
51:    global $userName, $shoppingId, $Id;
52:    $userName = $userId;
53:    $shoppingId = $row['password'];
54:    $emailId = $row['email_add'];
55:    echo('<script>window.location="ex20-07.php?name=' . $userName .
56:          '&id=' . $shoppingId . '&em='. $emailId .'"</script>');
57:  }
58:  else
59:  {
60:    echo "$llst";
61:    if ($userId == $row['user_id'])
62:    {
63:      echo "<br />Sorry! Wrong Password.. Please Try Again..<br />";
64:      $passId = false;
65:    }
66:  }
67:  mysql_free_result ($result);
68: }
69: else
70: {
71:    echo "$llst";
72: }
73: ?>
74: <br /><img src="line1.gif" width="500" height="6" alt="pic" />
75: <br /><br />
76: </body>
77: </html>
```

This page is almost identical to the page ex20-05.php. The only differences are at line 21 and in the program block in lines 48–57. Inside this program block is the case when the user name and password match the information in the database. The user name, password, and email address from the database are assigned to the variables $userName, $shoppingId, and $emailId respectively.

Suppose you log in with

User name = johnsmith **and Password** = johnsmith

then the statement in lines 55–56 turns out to be

```
<script>window.location="ex20-07.php?
  name=johnsmith&
  id=cd4388c0c62e65ac8b99e3ec49fd9409&
  em=$johnsmith@pwt-ex.com"
</script>
```

This statement will activate our main shopping-cart page with name, identity (id), and email (em) as the query string. The query string is passed to the page ex20-07.php as variables. This process is similar to the get method used in an XHTML form. The information is passed to the shopping-cart program and can later be used to identify the user and make charges using the credit card information in the database.

Now let's consider how to use a database to construct an online catalog for our e-commerce site.

20.3.2 Designing an online catalog with a database

If you don't have a database package such as Microsoft Access, MySQL, etc., you can still build and develop your shopping catalog using plain XHTML coding. For example, if you only have a handful of products that you want to sell on the Internet, it may be even easier to hard-code them using XHTML tables similar to the examples in Chapter 7. It is fair to say that as long as you can handle the administrative work of your commercial site, you may be better off without using a database.

On the other hand, if you have a large number of products to sell on the Web, you may need a database approach. Also, if your products change every one or two weeks just like an online bargain hunting shop, you need to consider the use of a database to help you.

Putting items into a database will greatly reduce the administrative and maintenance work. If you are working or want to work for a Web design company, chances are that your company will demand database skills from you.

To use a database for an online catalog is no different from the database applications on people or personnel in Part IV of this book. The basic idea is that product items are stored in the database as records of a table. An XHTML page is then developed to extract the records and display them on the browser window. To simplify the implementation, we only consider the following fields in the database:

- Product identity (product_id)
- Product image (product_img)
- Product description (description)
- Product price (price)

Suppose you want to set up an online big bargain shop dedicated to members or customers. The shop sells different products at a good discount every week. For this week (e.g., week112), you are selling blank CDs with big savings on quantities. Three products are selected, namely, CD-R, CD-RW, and DVD-R. First, you need to use the SQL statement in ex20-01.txt to create the table for the products.

```
Listing: ex20-01.txt - Building Catalog With MySQL

1: CREATE TABLE week112
2: (
3:   product_id VARCHAR(20) NOT NULL,
4:   product_img VARCHAR(20) NOT NULL,
5:   description VARCHAR(50) NOT NULL,
6:   price VARCHAR(10) NOT NULL,
7:   PRIMARY KEY(product_id)
8: );
```

With the MySQL knowledge in Chapters 18 and 19, this SQL statement is easy to understand. The next step is to generate some product data and load them into a table. As a simple example, the product data file week112.dat is listed below:

```
Listing: ex20-02.txt - Data File For E-Commerce (File: week112.dat)

1:    50 CD-R, cdr.gif, 50 CD-R Disc <br /> 1x-16x 74min, 5.50
2:    50 CD-RW, cdrw.gif, 50 CD-RW Disc <br />4x-10x 74min , 7.00
3:    25 DVD-R, dvdr.gif, 25 DVD-R <br />4.7GB , 55.00
```

The first column is the product identity to identify the items. The second column contains the image files of the product. They are used to display a picture of the product in the catalog. The third column is a description of the product. The new line code <br /> is used to insert a new line when you display the description on a browser window. The final column contains the prices of each product.

Now, you can load the data file week112.dat into the table using the usual LOAD DATA statement below:

```
LOAD DATA INFILE 'week112.dat'
INTO TABLE week112
FIELDS TERMINATED BY ','
LINES TERMINATED BY '\n';
```

Please note that, if you are using MySQL in Microsoft systems, the last statement above should be replaced by

```
LINES TERMINATED BY '\r\n';
```

because every text string in Microsoft systems is terminated by a carriage return ("\r") followed by a new line ("\n"). After the data loading, you can use the following SELECT command to examine the table:

```
SELECT * FROM week112;
```

You should see the table with the data as in ex20-03.txt.

```
Listing: ex20-03.txt - Building Catalog With MySQL

1: +------------+------------+---------------------------------+-------+
2: | product_id | product_img | description                     | price |
3: +------------+------------+---------------------------------+-------+
4: | 50 CD-R    | cdr.gif    | 50 CD-R Disc <br /> 1x-16x 74min | 5.50  |
5: | 50 CD-RW   | cdrw.gif   | 50 CD-RW Disc<br /> 4x-10x 74min | 7.00  |
6: | 25 DVD-R   | dvdr.gif   | 25 DVD-R <br />4.7GB | 55.00     |       |
7: +------------+------------+---------------------------------+-------+
```

20.3.3 Building the shopping-cart page

From the demonstration examples in section 7.4, we know that as long as you can put the product identity, name, price, and picture into ECMAScript arrays such as

```
<script>
goodsId= Array("50 CD-R","50 CD-RW","25 DVD-R");
goodsName=Array("50 CD-R Disc <br /> 1x-16x 74min",
                "50 CD-RW Disc<br /> 4x-10x 74min",
                "25 DVD-R <br />4.7GB");
goodsPrice=Array("5.50","7.00","55.00");
goodsPic=Array("cdr.gif","cdrw.gif","dvdr.gif");
</script>
```

you can use the examples in ex07-19.htm to ex07-22.htm directly to build a shopping cart. More precisely, you can use the functions defined in the ECMAScript files cookie.js and online.js.

The implementations in section 7.5 are independent of any selling products and their descriptions. That is, if you can use the database table in section 20.3.2 and fill up the ECMAScript arrays above, you can modify the examples in section 7.5 (i.e., ex07-19.htm to ex07-20.htm) to develop the shopping cart for the shop.

Basically, the implementation of our shopping-cart page is to extract the product information from the database table `week112` to fill up the arrays above. Let's consider the first part of the page:

```
Example: ex20-07.php - Main Page For The Shopping Cart (Part One)

 1: <?PHP echo"<?";?>xml version="1.0" encoding="iso-8859-1"<?PHP echo"?>";?>
 2: <!DOCTYPE html PUBLIC "-//W3C//DTD XHTML 1.0 Transitional//EN"
 3:     "http://www.w3.org/TR/xhtml1/DTD/xhtml1-transitional.dtd">
 4: <html xmlns="http://www.w3.org/1999/xhtml" xml:lang="en" lang="en">
 5: <head><title>Shopping Cart - ex20-07.php </title></head>
 6: <style>
 7:   .tx01{background-color:#000088;font-family:arial;
 8:       font-size:14pt;color:#ffff00;text-align:left}
 9:   .tx02{font-size:22pt;color:#00ffff}
10:   .butStyle{background-color:#aaffaa;font-family:arial;
11:       font-size:14pt;color:#008800;width:170px;height:35px}
12:   .chBut{background-color:#aaffaa;font-family:arial;
13:       font-size:18pt;color:#008800;width:50px;height:25px}
14: </style>
15: <body class="tx01" style="text-align:center">
16: <span class="tx02">Today's Special Buy</span><br /><br/>
17: <img src="line1.gif" width="600" height="6" /><br /><br />
18:
19: <script src="cookie.js"></script>
20: <script src="online.js"></script>
```

This PHP page is simple. The main feature is to include the two ECMAScript files cookie.js and online.js into the program (see lines 19–20). These two program files provide all functions that are needed to handle cookies. For a full detailed explanation of these files, see section 7.5.2.

The next step is essential for the entire page. The following tasks are performed:

- Connect to the database table `buss_product` and obtain the product information.
- Use the product information to build the following ECMAScript arrays:
  - `goodsId = Array("xxx","xxx",..,"xx");`
  - `goodsName = Array("xxx","xxx",..,"xx");`
  - `goodsPrice= Array("xxx","xxx",..,"xx");`
  - `goodsPic = Array("xxx","xxx",..,"xx");`

Each array represents one column in the catalog. For example, the elements in the `goodsPic` array store the image files of the products and will be displayed as images. Let's consider the PHP program coding for this part:

```
Listing: Continuation Of The PHP Script ex20-07.php (Part Two)

21: <script>
22:   var goodsLength;
23:
24: <?php
25:     $host="www.pwt-ex.com";
26:     $user="johnsmith";
27:     $password="johnsmith";
28:     $databaseName = "buss_db";
29:     $tableName = "week112";
30:
31:     mysql_connect($host,$user,$password);
32:     mysql_select_db($databaseName);
```

```
33:    $querySt = "SELECT * FROM " . $tableName;
34:    $result = mysql_query($querySt);
35:    global $gId, $gNa, $gPr;
36:
37:    if ($result == 0)
38:      echo("SQL Query Error..");
39:    else
40:    {
41:     $gId = "goodsId=Array(";
42:     $gNa = "goodsName=Array(";
43:     $gPr = "goodsPrice=Array(";
44:     $gPic = "goodsPic=Array(";
45:     $count = mysql_num_rows($result);
46:     for ($ii = 0; $ii < $count-1; $ii++)
47:     {
48:         $row = mysql_fetch_array ($result);
49:         $gId = $gId . '"' . $row['product_id'] . '",';
50:         $gNa = $gNa . '"' . $row['description'] . '",';
51:         $gPr = $gPr . '"' . $row['price'] . '",';
52:         $gPic = $gPic . '"' . $row['product_img'] . '",';
53:     }
54:         $row = mysql_fetch_array ($result);
55:         $gId = $gId . '"' . $row['product_id'] . '");';
56:         $gNa = $gNa . '"' . $row['description'] . '");';
57:         $gPr = $gPr . '"' . $row['price'] . '");';
58:         $gPic = $gPic . '"' . $row['product_img'] . '");';
59:    }
60:    echo($gId);
61:    echo($gNa);
62:    echo($gPr);
63:    echo($gPic);
64: ?>
65:
```

Since PHP is a server script, it can be used to generate ECMAScript and executed by the calling browser. First, lines 25–32 are used to connect to the database buss_db and table week112. After execution of the SQL statement, the information on the products is stored in the variable $result as illustrated in line 34. The next step is to define four variables, $gId (goods identity), $gNa (goods name), $gPr (goods price), and $gPic (goods picture). These variables are used to build the desired ECMAScript arrays. The actual building process is no more than a series of string concatenation operations. Lines 41–44 are used to build the starting string. The for-loop in lines 46–53 simply fetches each row of the database table and fills the arrays with product items. Lines 54–58 are used to put the finishing touches to the arrays. The contents of the variables are listed below:

```
$gId -- goodsId= Array("50 CD-R","50 CD-RW","25 DVD-R");
$gNa -- goodsName=Array("50 CD-R Disc <br /> 1x-16x 74min",
                        "50 CD-RW Disc<br /> 4x-10x 74min",
                        "25 DVD-R <br />4.7GB");
$gPr -- goodsPrice=Array("5.50","7.00","55.00");
$gPic -- goodsPic=Array("cdr.gif","cdrw.gif","dvdr.gif");
```

The echo statements in lines 60–63 output the variables to the browser and ultimately define the arrays using ECMAScript.

Now, if you want to change the prices of the products, you can change the data inside the table week112 using SQL statements without even touching any XHTML coding.

For the next bargain week, all you have to do is to design the week113 data file (e.g., week113.dat) similar to ex20-02.txt and to generate a new table as in ex20-03.txt. Don't forget to change the database table name $tableName in line 29 of ex20-07.php so that the page can recognize the changes to the data.

Now we have the shopping items under control. Our next task is to identify the individual who is doing the shopping. For this purpose, you need to capture the user information submitted from the login page ex20-06.php and store the customer information as cookies. Consider the third part of ex20-07.php below:

```
Listing: Continuation Of The PHP Script ex20-07.php (Part Three)
66:   userInfo=Array("UserName","Email Address","ShoppingId","Date&Time")
67:
68:   userInfoLength = userInfo.length
69:   goodsLength=goodsName.length
70:   function initialAll()
71:   {
72:    expDate = new Date
73:    expDate.setTime(expDate.getTime()+(1000 * 60 * 60 * 24*365))
74:  <?php
75:    echo(' setCookie("UserName","' . $name .'",expDate);');
76:    echo(' setCookie("Email Address","' . $em .'",expDate);');
77:    echo(' setCookie("ShoppingId","' . $id .'",expDate);');
78:  ?>
79:
80:   }
81:  </script>
82:
```

The main feature of this page is the ECMAScript function initialAll() defined in lines 70–81. Inside this function, a small PHP code is used to capture the user name ($name), email address ($em), and shopping identity ($id) from the login page.

Suppose you log in with

User name = johnsmith **and Password =** johnsmith

The initialAll() function turns out to be

```
function initialAll()
{
 expDate = new Date
 expDate.setTime(expDate.getTime()+(1000 * 60 * 60 * 24*365))
 setCookie("UserName","johnsmith",expDate);
 setCookie("Email Address","johnsmith@pwt-ext.com",expDate);
 setCookie("ShoppingId","cd4388c0c62e65ac8b99e3ec49fd9409",expDate);
}
```

Obviously, the shopping identity (ShoppingId) of the user is actually the MD string returned from the login page representing the password johnsmith. If this function is called, it will set the user name, email address, and shopping identity information as cookies.

You now have everything you need to develop an interface page to show the online catalog. Consider the fourth part coding of the example:

```
Listing: Continuation of Example ex20-07.php (Part Four)
83:  <script>
84:    initialAll()
85:    userName = getCookie("UserName")
86:    outMsg="For: "+userName+" (Half Price!)"
87:    document.write(outMsg)
88:  </script><br /><br />
```

```
89:
90: <script>
91:  tableSt ='<table cellspacing="10" align="center" class="tx01">'+
92:          '<tr align="center">'
93:  tableSt += '<td>Picture </td><td>Description</td>'+
94:              '<td>Price </td><td>Add To <br /> Shopping Cart</td></tr> '
95:
96: for (ii = 0; ii< goodsLength; ii++)
97: {
98:  tableSt += '<tr align="center">' +
99:      '<td><img src="'+goodsPic[ii]+'" width="70" height="60" /></td>'+
100:       '<td>'+goodsName[ii]+'</td><td>'+goodsPrice[ii]+'</td> '+
101:       '<td><input style="height:35px;width:35px" '+
102:             'type="checkbox" id="'+ goodsId[ii]+'" /></td></tr> '
103:  }
104:  tableSt +='</table><br />'
105:  document.write(tableSt)
106: </script>
107:
108: <img src="line1.gif" width="600" height="6" /><br /><br />
109: <input type="button" value="Checkout" class="butStyle"
110:       onclick="orderItem();location.href='ex20-08.htm'" />
111: <input type="button" value="Reset Boxes" class="butStyle"
112:       onclick="resetBoxes()" />
113:
114: </body>
115: </html>
```

The first part of this code fragment (lines 83–88) is to call the function `initialAll()` to set up the user information as cookies. Then a welcome message to the user is displayed.

To build the catalog, a single XHTML table which is defined as an ECMAScript string called `tableSt` is used. Lines 91–94 define a table row for the headings of the catalog which include the "Picture," "Description," "Price," and "Add to Shopping Cart."

The for-loop in lines 96–103 simply fills the rows of the table with product information. Note that product information is now stored in the ECMAScript arrays `goodsPic[]`, `goodsName[]`, `goodsPrice[]`. Also, we have used a checkbox to indicate whether the product is added to the shopping cart. For commercial applications, you may want to enhance this facility by adding buttons, quantities, and many other features including all kinds of cookie administration as illustrated in Chapter 7. A checkbox is considered to be a simple solution for our demonstration purposes as the user can always see what he or she has ordered at any time just by taking a look at the box. Line 104 puts the finishing touch to the table and the next line is to output the table to the browser window.

When the user has picked something and is satisfied with what he or she wants to buy, a Checkout button (lines 109–110) is ready for him or her to proceed. Once this button is clicked, the ECMAScript function `orderItem()` is called. This function is located in the script file online.js. The main purpose of this function is to set all the selected items as cookies on the user's machine. Therefore we have all the cookies about the user and products ready. Now control is transferred to the checkout page as illustrated by the script statement `location.href='ex20-08.htm'` at the end of line 110.

Some screen shots of this example are shown in Figs 20.5 and 20.6.

Another feature of this example is the use of PHP to control the database and ECMAScript to implement the cookie part. The bridge is performed by some ECMAScript arrays such as `goodsName`, `goodsId`, etc. No matter what kind of server database technologies you are using, the program will work fine if your database can fill up the arrays consistently. This feature would enhance the portability and reusability of your program code in some ways. Also, as a good Web engineer, you should be able to integrate or mount two technologies together at any time if necessary.

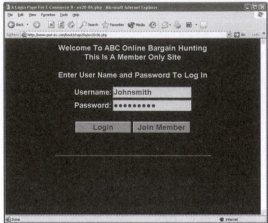

Figure 20.5 ex20-06.php

Figure 20.6 ex20-07.php

Now it's time to take a look at the checkout facilities of our shop.

20.3.4 A checkout facility

For obvious reasons our checkout facility can only be a simple one. Even a minimal checkout should include the following functionalities:

- Display all selected items from the cookies so that the customer knows the items, price, delivery terms, and other information.
- Include a Cancel button so that cancellation can be made at the last minute.
- Include a Confirm button to confirm the order.
- If the Confirm button is clicked, a permanent record of the order should be saved on the server so that charges can be made later using the member's credit card information.
- Delete all cookies as soon as possible.

Since ECMAScript is used to implement cookies, the main page of this checkout facility is coded by XHTML. The first part of the page is listed below:

```
Example: ex20-08.htm – A Checkout Page (Part One)

1: <?xml version="1.0" encoding="iso-8859-1"?>
2: <!DOCTYPE html PUBLIC "-//W3C//DTD XHTML 1.0 Transitional//EN"
3:     "http://www.w3.org/TR/xhtml1/DTD/xhtml1-transitional.dtd">
4: <html xmlns="http://www.w3.org/1999/xhtml" xml:lang="en" lang="en">
5: <head><title> Checkout Page – ex20-08.htm</title></head>
6: <style>
7:   .tx01{background-color:#000088;font-family:arial;font-size:14pt;
8:       font-weight:bold;color:#ffff00;text-align:left}
9:   .tx02{font-size:18pt;color:#00ffff}
10:   .butStyle{background-color:#aaffaa;font-family:arial;font-weight:bold;
11:       font-size:12pt;color:#008800;width:160px;height:28px}
12: </style>
13: <body class="tx01" style="text-align:center">
14: <span class="tx02">Order Confirmation</span><br />
15: <img src="line1.gif" width="480" height="6" /><br /><br />
16: <script src="cookie.js"></script>
17: <script src="online.js"></script>
```

```
18: <script>
19:   var cookieN = new Array()
20:   var cookieV = new Array()
21:   var cookieL
22:   function showSelectedItem()
23:   {
24:    var localMsg="<table class='tx01'>"
25:    var cookieTable=""
26:    if (document.cookie !="")
27:    {
28:     var cookieItem = document.cookie.split("; ")
29:     cookieL = cookieItem.length
30:     for (i=0; i< cookieItem.length; i++)
31:     {
32:       cookieN[i] = cookieItem[i].split("=")[0]
33:       cookieV[i] = unescape(cookieItem[i].split("=")[1])
34:
35:       localMsg += "<tr><td width='150' align='left'>"+
36:                     cookieN[i]+"</td>"+
37:                   "<td width='300' align='left'>"+
38:                     cookieV[i]+"</td></tr>"
39:     }
40:     cookieTable="<div align='center'>"+localMsg+"</table></div>"
41:     document.write(cookieTable)
42:    }else
43:     document.write("There Is No Selected Item")
44:   }
45: showSelectedItem()
46: </script><br />
47: <img src="line1.gif" width="480" height="6" />
48: <div class="tx01" style="color:#00ff00;text-align:center">
49:     Delivery Term: Within 7 Days</div><br />
50:
```

To display all selected items (or cookies) on the browser window, a script function called `showSelectItem()` is developed in lines 22–44. If there is no cookie on the local machine, the message in line 43 is displayed. If the cookie string is not empty (see line 26), we want to build a simple table to display all of them. Since cookies are stored as a string separated by semi-colons (";"), the function in line 28

```
cookieItem = document.cookie.split("; ")
```

is used to separate them one by one into collection `cookieItem`. Each `cookieItem` contains a name/value pair with an equals ("=") sign. To separate them further, the following split functions are used (see lines 32–33) to store the name/value pair into two arrays:

```
cookieN[i] = cookieItem[i].split("=")[0]
cookieV[i] = unescape(cookieItem[i].split("=")[1])
```

These two arrays are then used to build the contents of an XHTML table as illustrated in lines 35–38. At the end the `cookieTable` is built and output to the browser in line 41.

The `showSelectedItem()` function is called in line 45 so that the user can see all the selected items on the screen. At the end of this code fragment, the delivery terms are also displayed (see lines 48–49).

To implement the Confirm and Cancel buttons for our checkout, consider the following example code:

```
Listing: Continuation of Example ex20-08.htm (Part Two)

51: <form method="post" action="ex20-09.php">
52: <script>
53:   var lst = '<input type="hidden" name="itemL" value="'+cookieL+'" />'
54:   for (ii = 0; ii < cookieL; ii++)
```

```
55:    {
56:        lst += '<input type="hidden" name=selItem[]'+
57:                ' value="'+ cookieN[ii]+' = ' + cookieV[ii] +'" />'
58:    }
59:    document.write(lst);
60: </script>
61: <input type="button" value="Confirm Order" class="butStyle"
62:    onclick="delAllCookies();submit()" />
63: <input type="button" value="Cancel Order" class="butStyle"
64:    onclick="delAllCookies();location.href='ex20-10.htm'" /><br />
65: </form>
66: </body>
67: </html>
```

This is a form application containing two buttons. The contents of the form are built by a for-loop (lines 54–58) making a series of input elements with cookie names and values. The type of each input element is hidden so that it will not display to the user. Also, we use an array called selItem[] as the name of the input element so that the entire array will be passed to the form action program.

The purpose of this arrangement is that when the Confirm Order button in line 61 is clicked, these input elements are submitted as data to an order confirmation page. Inside this confirmation page, the selected items will be saved as permanent records. Any server script with file-handling capabilities such as Perl, ASP (or ASP.NET), and PHP can do that. In this example, we use a PHP script ex20-09.php to perform the file operation.

Since we want to delete all cookies as soon as possible, the delAllCookies() function is called before the form submission in line 62. If the Cancel Order button is clicked, all cookies will be deleted and perform a jump to the cancellation page ex20-10.htm as illustrated in line 64.

First, consider the order confirmation page ex20-09.php below:

Example: ex20-09.php – The Order Confirmation Page

```
1: <?PHP echo"<?";?>xml version="1.0" encoding="iso-8859-1"<?PHP echo"?>";?>
2: <!DOCTYPE html PUBLIC "-//W3C//DTD XHTML 1.0 Transitional//EN"
3:     "http://www.w3.org/TR/xhtml1/DTD/xhtml1-transitional.dtd">
4: <html xmlns="http://www.w3.org/1999/xhtml" xml:lang="en" lang="en">
5: <head><title>Online Shopping Confirmation -– ex20-09.php</title></head>
6: <style>
7:    .tx01{background-color:#000088;font-family:arial;font-size:13pt;
8:        font-weight:bold;color:#ffff00;text-align:left}
9:    .tx02{font-size:18pt;color:#00ffff}
10: </style>
11: <body class="tx01" style="text-align:center"><br /><br />
12:
13:    <span class="tx02">Order Confirmed. <br />Thank you ! <br /><br /><br />
14:    We Will Deliver Your <br />Order Within 7 Days</span><br />
15:
16: <?php
17:    $filename = "ordering.txt";
18:    $fd = fopen ($filename, "a");
19:
20:    for ($ii=0; $ii < $itemL ; $ii++)
21:    {
22:        $llst = $selItem[$ii] . "\n";
23:        fwrite ($fd, $llst);
24:    }
25:        fwrite($fd,"=====================================\n");
26:        fclose ($fd);
27: ?>
28: </body>
29: </html>
```

This is a simple PHP page to perform file operations. Recall that example ex20-08.htm submitted one variable `$itemL` (i.e., item length) and one array `$selItem[]` (i.e., selected items) to this program through the form action. The array stores all items ordered by the customer and needs to be saved into a file as a permanent record. In order to do that, the PHP program block in lines 16–27 is implemented.

First, you can assign a file name to the variable `$filename`. The next step is to open the file with append mode so that a new purchase order is appended at the end of the file. The for-loop in lines 20–24 is to write the elements of the array `$selItem[]` into the file one by one.

The purpose of using a new string variable `$llst` in line 22 is to add a new line symbol ("\n") at the end of the element `$selItem[]` so that the string `$llst` contains a new line character. When this string is written into a file by the statement in line 23, it will occupy one line. If you are using Microsoft systems, you should use the following:

```
$llst = $selItem[$ii] . "\r\n";
```

When all ordered items have been written to the file, the file is closed with a separation line as illustrated in lines 25–26. Since file operations are transparent to the end user, a simple message is displayed in lines 13–14 to confirm the order. A screen shot of example ex20-08.htm is shown in Fig. 20.7. The permanent record of the online order file (i.e., ordering.txt) is shown in Fig. 20.8.

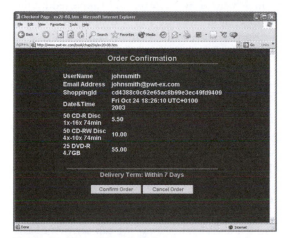

Figure 20.7 ex20-08.htm   **Figure 20.8** The contents of the file ordering.txt

When used with the user profile, the ordering.txt file should be able to provide charging information for your customer.

Finally, if the Cancel Order button is clicked, a cancel page (ex20-10.htm) is activated. This is a very simple XHTML page. For completeness of the example, this page is listed as follows:

```
Example: ex20-10.htm - The Order Cancellation Page

 1: <?xml version="1.0" encoding="iso-8859-1"?>
 2: <!DOCTYPE html PUBLIC "-//W3C//DTD XHTML 1.0 Transitional//EN"
 3:     "http://www.w3.org/TR/xhtml1/DTD/xhtml1-transitional.dtd">
 4: <html xmlns="http://www.w3.org/1999/xhtml" xml:lang="en" lang="en">
 5: <head><title> Order Cancellation Page - ex08-10.htm</title></head>
 6: <style>
 7:   .tx01{background-color:#000088;font-family:arial;font-size:13pt;
 8:       font-weight:bold;color:#ffff00;text-align:left}
 9:   .tx02{font-size:18pt;color:#00ffff}
10: </style>
```

```
11: <body class="tx01" style="text-align:center"><br /><br />
12:   <span class="tx02">Your Order ! <br /><br /><br />
13:    Has Been Cancelled.</span><br /><br />
14: <img src="line1.gif" width="500" height="6" alt="pic" /><br />
15: </body>
16: </html>
```

Now it's time to discuss some serious security measures on the Web that can provide security and transparency between your customers and your e-commerce site(s).

20.4 Secure Sockets Layer (SSL) and OpenSSL

20.4.1 What is SSL and how does it work?

SSL is a communications protocol layer which may be placed between your TCP/IP and HTTP suites. In effect, it can intercept your Web traffic and provide security between the browser and server. The encryption or cryptography used in SSL guarantees secure communications in an insecure environment. More importantly, all security operations are transparent to both ends.

The first practical SSL protocol known as SSL v2.0 was implemented by Netscape and supported by the NS 1.x/2.x and IE 3.x browsers. This version of SSL is mainly vendor specific and with limited features. Although not a standard, the next version of SSL (SSL v3.0) attracted much more attention and is widely supported by the Web community.

Perhaps not many ordinary Web users notice that most browsers and browser families including IE, NS, and Opera support security in a strong cryptography sense. For example, they all support 128-bit encryption (RSA key exchange) for SSL v1.0/v2.0, and the successor Transport Layer Security (TLS v1.0) from the IETF. All of them also extend the cryptographic support to a wider area beyond HTTP (Web) covering NNTP (news), POP, and SMTP (email). They provide security by means of encryption/decryption, generating private/public keys and responding to certificate (in the SSL sense) requests.

In addition to gaining support from browsers, more importantly, an open source implementation called OpenSSL is freely available from the Open Source Initiative (OSI). This software package can be integrated into server software such as Apache with little effort. Therefore, secure Web servers or add-on transmission packages are no longer costly proprietary products. In fact, the latest implementation of OpenSSL matches almost all cryptography standards including both SSL v2.0/v3.0 and TLS v1.0. Now, we can say that SSL is there, free, and widely available to us all.

In fact, OpenSSL is a cryptography toolkit. More precisely, it is a collection of functions organized in a library structure controlled by a command-line program called openssl. The package implements the SSL v2.0/v3.0 and TLS v1.0 network protocols and many other related cryptography standards required by them. At a minimum level, it can be used to generate a certificate (in the SSL sense) identifying yourself. This certificate can then be imported into your favorite browser such as IE, NS, or Opera. We will show you how to install OpenSSL and how to use it for security purposes later in section 20.4.2. In section 20.5, we will show you how to set up a secure Web site that people can surf with HTTPS. Examples related to SSL will have the extension .ssl in this chapter.

Before the engineering work, let's consider how SSL works to provide a secure environment for Web communication.

Basically, SSL establishes mutual trust between browser and server. This mutual trust is controlled by the SSL Record Protocol with handshake sequences. The handshake contains the following three layers:

- SSL Handshake Protocol
- SSL Change Cipher Specification
- SSL Alert Protocol

These sequences are used to establish an SSL session. When this session is identified and established, secure connection and transmission take place. In normal circumstances, there will be some certificate exchange and an agreed cipher suite will be used for the transmission. This means that both the client and server will have the chance to identify themselves and request authentication of each other via certificate requests. When this initial handshake is established, an agreed cipher (encryption) is used to protect the privacy of the transmission. If something goes wrong during the entire connection or SSL session, the SSL Alert Protocol is used to convey SSL error messages between client and server. A typical SSL session is shown in Fig. 20.9.

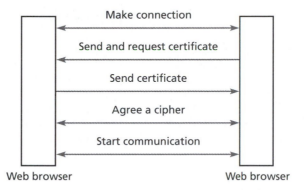

Figure 20.9 A typical SSL session between browser and server

To make this work, the key is the certificate administration. A certificate in SSL is a special piece of information associated with a public key and the real identity of the object concerned, which includes the individual, server, or other entity. Any SSL implementation should be able to generate certificates for you and/or your applications. The public key can be used to decrypt the message you send to the receiver. In order to increase the credibility of the certificate, the certificate should be signed by a trusted organization known as a Certification Authority (CA). Once the certificate is signed, it can be imported into your favorite browser to identify you as the client. A signed certificate can also be installed into a Web server for authentication purposes. We will show you how to generate these certificates by examples later in this section.

Once the Web server is equipped with SSL security and changed into a secure server, the secure Web server can be surfed by https such as:

```
https://www.pwt-ex.com
```

or using the following URL with anchor element:

```
<a href="https://www.pwt-ex.com"> This is a secure link</a>
```

When your browser enters the secure mode with SSL, you will see an alert window. The alert windows for IE, NS, and Opera are shown in Figs 20.10–20.12.

Before you can activate OpenSSL and make it work for you, it is necessary to install the package on your system first.

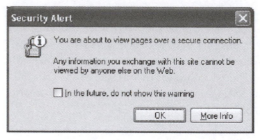

Figure 20.10 IE6.x "Seucurity Alert" window

Figure 20.11 NS6.x alert window

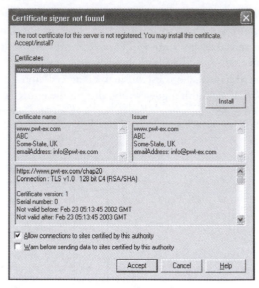

Figure 20.12 Opera security alert

20.4.2 Installation of OpenSSL

OpenSSL is a software package from the Open Source Initiative (OSI), which means that you can use it for commercial or non-commercial purposes. You can download a copy of the software from the official site www.openssl.org. The version and tar that we are using is

```
openssl-0.9.6c.tar.gz
```

Unlike many other software packages, this file contains everything you need to install OpenSSL for the following platforms:

- UNIX/LINUX
- Windows
- OpenVMS
- MacOS

The OpenSSL software team has done a very good job in encapsulating all these environments into one distribution. If you are using UNIX/LINUX, you can use the following commands to extract the files and subdirectories into your machine:

```
gzip -d openssl-0.9.6c.tar.gz
tar -xvf openssl-0.9.6c.tar
```

These two commands will extract all the files and associated subdirectories into a directory called `openssl-0.9.6c`. Sometimes, you can use one process command

```
tar -zxvf openssl-0.9.6c.tar.gz
```

to do the job. For Windows users, you can use WinZip to extract all files to the destination directory in one process.

In order to build the package, you will also need the following additional packages up and running:

- Perl 5
- An ANSI C compiler such as `gcc` or `cc` with development environment (e.g., make, libraries, and header files)

Suppose you are using a UNIX/LINUX system and you are already inside the OpenSSL file directory (e.g., `openssl-0.9.6c`). You can use the following two commands to build and install the package on your system temporarily:

```
$./config
$make
```

This will build the OpenSSL libraries `libcrypto.a` and `libssl.a` and the OpenSSL command-line program `openssl`. The command-line program is stored in the subdirectory called `apps`. When the package is built, you should test it before installing it on your system permanently. You can test the libraries by

```
$make test
```

OpenSSL is a complicated software package; even the testing printout is well over two full pages. Basically, the test is to see whether the built libraries can generate RSA keys and perform client–server authentication. If everything is in working order, you will see "passed all tests" at the end of the screen output. In this case, you can perform the following command to install the package:

```
$make install
```

Among other things, this will create the following subdirectories under the target directory `openssl-0.9.6c`:

`certs`	–	**Initially empty, this is the default location for certificate files**
`private`	–	**Initially empty, this is the default location for private-key files**
`bin`	–	**Contains the** `openssl` **binary and a few other utility programs**
`include/openssl`	–	**Contains the header files needed if you want to compile programs with** `libcrypto` **or** `libssl.library`
`lib`	–	**Contains the OpenSSL library files themselves**

For most users, the command-line program `openssl` and the certificates are the essential tools to make SSL work. For programmers, the header files in the `include/openssl` directory and the libraries are important components for building SSL applications.

If you are using Windows systems, a default subdirectory or folder called `ms` under the folder `openssl-0.9.6c` is available for you to build OpenSSL there. To compile OpenSSL under Windows, a Perl package for Win32 is required. Such a package is available from (www.activestate.com/ActivePerl). Also, you may need at least one of the following compilers:

- Visual C++ (VC++)
- Borland C
- GNU C (Mingw32 or Cygwin32)

We will describe how to compile OpenSSL using Visual C++ only. First, run the Perl program to configure OpenSSL for VC++:

```
perl Configure VC-WIN32
```

The next step is to build the `makefile` dedicated for Visual C++ by the following command:

```
ms\do_ms
```

This command runs the batch file `do_ms.bat` under the `ms` directory and subsequently builds all make files for Visual C++. Now you can compile the software using `nmake` as

```
nmake -f ms\ntdll.mak
```

Again, we assume all commands were typed under the openssl-0.9.6c directory. If all goes well it will build all Dynamic Linked Libraries (DLLs) and executables in the out32dll directory. Now, you can run OpenSSL inside out32dll or put this directory into your path. For example, you can test the libraries and software by

```
cd out32dll
..\ms\test
```

Let's consider some examples of how to use OpenSSL for security purposes. The first application of OpenSSL is to generate some digital keys and certificates.

20.4.3 Generating digital keys and certificates

If you install OpenSSL correctly, most SSL applications can be performed by the command-line program openssl. This program is a command-line tool for using the various cryptography functions of OpenSSL's crypto libraries from a console window. Even at a basic level, it can be used for

- Creation of RSA, DH, and DSA digital keys and administration
- Creation of X.509 certificates, Certificate Signing Request (CSR), and signing the certificates
- Calculation of MD
- Encryption and decryption with ciphers
- SSL/TLS client and server tests

We will go through some major functionalities with you step by step. In particular, we will concentrate on the creation and application of certificates. Once certificates are created and signed by a CA, they can be imported into browsers such as IE and NS so that user authentication can be performed. Certificates can also put into a Web server so that secure HTTP (or HTTPS) can be established.

The openssl program offers well over 100 commands and options. Many of them are characterized into three categories:

- Standard commands
- MD commands
- Cipher commands

Each category contains a rich set of operational commands. Some of them are complicated with a large number of arguments and options. There is a help utility in openssl, though. If the program openssl doesn't understand a command or statement, a command summary is displayed to provide help. A session of the command summary is shown in ex20-11.ssl below:

```
Example: ex20-11.ssl - The Command Summary Of OpenSSL

 1: [openssl-0.9.6c]$ openssl help
 2:
 3: Standard commands
 4: asn1parse       ca              ciphers         crl             crl2pkcs7
 5: dgst            dh              dhparam         dsa             dsaparam
 6: enc             errstr          gendh           gendsa          genrsa
 7: nseq            passwd          pkcs12          pkcs7           pkcs8
 8: rand            req             rsa             rsautl          s_client
 9: s_server        s_time          sess_id         smime           speed
10: spkac           verify          version         x509
11:
12: Message Digest commands (see the `dgst' command for more details)
13: md2             md4             md5             mdc2            rmd160
14: sha             sha1
15:
16: Cipher commands (see the `enc' command for more details)
```

```
17: base64          bf              bf-cbc          bf-cfb          bf-ecb
18: bf-ofb          cast            cast-cbc        cast5-cbc       cast5-cfb
19: cast5-ecb       cast5-ofb       des             des-cbc         des-cfb
20: des-ecb         des-ede         des-ede-cbc     des-ede-cfb     des-ede-ofb
21: des-ede3        des-ede3-cbc    des-ede3-cfb    des-ede3-ofb    des-ofb
22: des3            desx            idea            idea-cbc        idea-cfb
23: idea-ecb        idea-ofb        rc2             rc2-40-cbc      rc2-64-cbc
24: rc2-cbc         rc2-cfb         rc2-ecb         rc2-ofb         rc4
25: rc4-40          rc5             rc5-cbc         rc5-cfb         rc5-ecb
26: rc5-ofb
```

As for many cryptography studies, a natural starting point is the MD string. From example ex20-11.ssl, you can see a rich set of MD functions under the dgst (digest string) command. The general calling syntax for this dgst command is

```
openssl dgst
    [-md5|-md4|-md2|-sha1|-sha|-mdc2|-ripemd160|-dss1]
    [-c] [-d] [-hex] [-binary] [-out filename] [-sign filename]
    [-verify filename] [-prverify filename] [-signature filename]
    [file...]
```

One of the best ways to show you how to use it is by examples. Like most openssl commands, this dgst command is designed to work with files. If you have a file called johnsmith.txt that contains only one word, johnsmith, you can obtain the MD string (e.g., md5) of johnsmith by

```
openssl dgst -md5 johnsmith.txt
```

This statement will digest the contents of the file johnsmith.txt and output the md5 string to the screen. To output the md5 string to a file, you can use

```
openssl dgst -out out.txt -md5 johnsmith.txt
```

Also, if openssl cannot understand the arguments or options, it will display a help screen to display a summary on the arguments and options. A session on how to use dgst is shown in the next example.

```
Example: ex20-12.ssl - Using Message Digest With OpenSSL

 1: [openssl-0.9.6c]$ openssl dgst -md5 johnsmith.txt
 2: MD5(johnsmith.txt)= cd4388c0c62e65ac8b99e3ec49fd9409
 3:
 4: openssl-0.9.6c>openssl dgst -h
 5: unknown option '-h'
 6: options are
 7: -c               to output the digest with separating colons
 8: -d               to output debug info
 9: -hex             output as hex dump
10: -binary          output in binary form
11: -sign    file    sign digest using private key in file
12: -verify file     verify a signature using public key in file
13: -prverify file   verify a signature using private key in file
14: -signature file  signature to verify
15: -binary          output in binary form
16: -md5 to use the md5 message digest algorithm (default)
17: -md4 to use the md4 message digest algorithm
18: -md2 to use the md2 message digest algorithm
19: -sha1 to use the sha1 message digest algorithm
20: -sha to use the sha message digest algorithm
21: -mdc2 to use the mdc2 message digest algorithm
22: -ripemd160 to use the ripemd160 message digest algorithm
```

If you have a private key, you can use it to sign your message together with the MD with the -sign option in line 11. Also, before you can generate certificates, you need to generate private keys. Let's consider how to generate private keys using openssl.

You can generate private keys using openssl genrsa or openssl gendsa depending on what kind of keys you want to use. For example, if you want to generate an RSA private key, you can use the following command:

```
openssl genrsa -des3 -out johnsmith.key 1024
```

The option -des3 (see line 22 of ex20-11.ssl) specifies the encryption method used for the private key. It means that the generated private key is encrypted by the des3 method with a passphrase.

The program openssl will ask you to input the passphrase. Once the passphrase has been input, the private key is output to the file johnsmith.key. A dialog session to see this command in action is shown in ex20-13.ssl.

```
Example: ex20-13.ssl - Generate RSA Private Key Using OpenSSL

 1: [openssl-0.9.6c]$ openssl genrsa -des3 -out johnsmith.key 1024
 2: Loading 'screen' into random state - done
 3: warning, not much extra random data, consider using the -rand option
 4: Generating RSA private key, 1024 bit long modulus
 5: .....++++++
 6: ..............................++++++
 7: e is 65537 (0x10001)
 8: Enter PEM pass phrase: johnsmith <--------------------- (Will Not Display)
 9: Verifying password - Enter PEM pass phrase: johnsmith <-(Will Not Display)
10:
11: [openssl-0.9.6c]$ more johnsmith.key
12: -----BEGIN RSA PRIVATE KEY-----
13: Proc-Type: 4,ENCRYPTED
14: DEK-Info: DES-EDE3-CBC,929A7CE14A2FF8E5
15:
16: IQ/sgRGNgg1MDqiUh3aour+rxnphWcbGVkTgana0BPzAa38p88QYZdHT1tccr29p
17: 2joCWOEYobe7TQrnUcBHfJQDctEy9Wn6sosnyI0tfow1nhVo3pzJNcPByf5KSI7X
18: ax6RrBD11jU04bzli2P4WlfbdpvFoLfX+4f8X3U5nbOVF3nAI/gso18BNs0WaIwt
19: tdzoQgolFbO8FhYteZh8pjXwpTzGGdwb2rDvHOHWzUzD5BU5K9Gma3jPBqdPSp4O
20: TxQ5yT4RxCGGSKSvNNdwQjLstRFW8YZLgYtYUYMdP+wi5ObyGN/kNxwCr1SKfsdk
21: X4md+FXJPGu3zzit+ksX1LI5YGG8NdIL/OWxEeHSRqx63xTjlsv3Jn2AJJXsh0OY
22: DenhjhWHpCPh4xwWBm4r0UmDXIkDJmU1YlgYqO7S6Py1mXUqriUNu7gp8QnmDQ55
23: 9vcm/Y8p5icxypwLhLlIBJoHh0czZoBBrhr7NvZ+ktrQ+KbGjgOYnLIy1m5GdR9E
24: 5iMOgp/xWqc59KbtcXSrSpaG5cO1NltHMeFny2Pb37qyxDnl4XqVQG21AZB5Wtzr
25: zit/jQ+8LVrA1Mv5Ct4kQy4+EDjFu9EpSNXGFayLtxyRnNUoUgZdDKJo/xy9bi27
26: Br7T/z2V16AwZv9dQUoMSpOQHA51mETeFyMWrysSFI9VJLH0zr+L7J3oFpFk/LM1
27: DcEhGOmkRMeGBrDPqhxZ0jQ0/ihgxxoTG5Ccpjn1VVU7lXBfsiI7CKwAbXXAfLig
28: 6nlPzd6L1AY0CVzvwNE/kaqgjZKRKzfqeiQ9wjNSH2ZmQvlprHVosw==
29: -----END RSA PRIVATE KEY-----
30:
```

The more command in line 11 is a general system command of UNIX/LINUX to display the contents of a file. Lines 13–14 indicate that the key is protected by the DES-EDE3-CBC (des3) encryption method with a passphrase. You can see the details of your private key by

```
Openssl rsa -noout -text -in johnsmith.key
```

This statement displays a detailed report about the private key johnsmith.key on the screen. If you just want to store the unprotected private key, you can issue the command

```
openssl rsa -in johnsmith.key -out johnsmith.unprotected
```

After asking for the `passphrase` of johnsmith.key, the unprotected private key is output into the file johnsmith.unprotected.

To generate a certificate, you need to go through the following two processes:

- Generate a Certificate Signing Request (CSR).
- Get the CSR signed by a CA or yourself.

The CSR is, basically, a digital form to identify you. Usually, you generate a CSR with your private key. For example, `johnsmith` can use his private key johnsmith.key to generate a CSR form using the following command:

```
openssl req -new -key johnsmith.key -out johnsmith.csr
```

This command generates a new CSR form in the local directory using the default configuration file openssl.cnf and its location. If the OpenSSL configuration file openssl.cnf is in another directory, you should include the `-config` option such as:

```
openssl req -new -key johnsmith.key -out johnsmith.csr -config ./openssl.cnf
```

This statement uses the OpenSSL configuration file openssl.cnf in the local directory.

In order to identify yourself, the `openssl` program will ask you a series of questions. You can answer most of them just by hitting the return key. A typical session dialog is shown in ex20-14.ssl.

```
Example: ex20-14.ssl - Generate A Certificate Signing Request

 1: [openssl-0.9.6c]$ openssl req -new -key johnsmith.key
 2:                       -out johnsmith.csr -config ./openssl.cnf
 3: Using configuration from ./openssl.cnf
 4: Enter PEM pass phrase: johnsmith <------------------- (Will Not Display)
 5: You are about to be asked to enter information that will be incorporated
 6: into your certificate request.
 7: What you are about to enter is what is called a Distinguished
 8: Name or a DN.
 9:
10: There are quite a few fields but you can leave some blank
11: For some fields there will be a default value,
12: If you enter '.', the field will be left blank.
13: -----
14: Country Name (2 letter code) [AU]:UK
15: State or Province Name (full name) [Some-State]: (Just Press Return)
16: Locality Name (eg, city) []:(Just Press Return)
17: Organization Name (eg, company) [Internet Widgits Pty Ltd]:ABC
18: Organizational Unit Name (eg, section) []:www.pwt-ex.com
19: Common Name (eg, YOUR name) []:johnsmith
20: Email Address []:johnsmith@pwt-ex.com
21:
22: Please enter the following 'extra' attributes
23: to be sent with your certificate request
24: A challenge password []:johnsmith
25: An optional company name []: (Just Press Return)
26:
27: [openssl-0.9.6c]$
```

Now, you have a CSR in your system. The next step is to send this CSR file johnsmith.csr to a CA for signing. The result is then a real certificate that can be used for applications or imported to your browser. There are a number of commercial CAs on the Internet ready to sign your CSR. Two popular ones are:

- Verisign at http://digitalid.verisign.com
- Thawte Consulting at http://www.thawte.com

Usually, you may need to fill in a form on their Web site and post your CSR. They will digitally sign your CSR and return a signed certificate to you. The signed certificate is normally a file with a file extension .crt such as johnsmith.crt.

For testing or very lightweight applications, you can sign the CSR yourself. For example, you can sign the CSR form johnsmith.csr by using your own private key as follows:

```
openssl x509 -req -in johnsmith.csr -out johnsmith.crt
     -signkey johnsmith.key -days 365
```

This command signs this CSR file using the signing key johnsmith.key and outputs the signed certificate using the X509 standard format. The final certificate is output to a file called johnsmith.crt. The certificate itself is an encrypted file similar to the key file johnsmith.key listed in ex20-13.ssl. To convert the file into meaningful text, you can use the command

```
openssl x509 -noout -text -in johnsmith.crt
```

A dialog session to use the two statements above is shown in ex20-15.ssl.

```
Example: ex20-15.ssl - Signing CSR With Your Own Private Key

 1: [openssl-0.9.6c]$ openssl x509 -req -in johnsmith.csr
 2:                        -out johnsmith.crt
 3:                        -signkey johnsmith.key -days 365
 4: Loading 'screen' into random state - done
 5: Signature ok
 6: subject=/C=UK/ST=Some-State/O=ABC/OU=www.pwt-ex.com/CN=johnsmith/
 7:          Email=johnsmith@pwt-ex.com
 8: Getting Private key
 9: Enter PEM pass phrase: johnsmith <----------------- (Will Not Display)
10:
11: [openssl-0.9.6c]$ openssl x509 -noout -text -in johnsmith.crt
12: Certificate:
13:     Data:
14:         Version: 1 (0x0)
15:         Serial Number: 0 (0x0)
16:         Signature Algorithm: md5WithRSAEncryption
17:         Issuer: C=UK, ST=Some-State, O=ABC, OU=www.pwt-ex.com,
18:                 CN=johnsmith/Email=johnsmith@pwt-ex.com
19:         Validity
20:             Not Before: Feb 20 05:28:39 2002 GMT
21:             Not After : Feb 20 05:28:39 2003 GMT
22:         Subject: C=UK, ST=Some-State, O=ABC, OU=www.pwt-ex.com,
23:                  CN=johnsmith/Email=johnsmith@pwt-ex.com
24:         Subject Public Key Info:
25:             Public Key Algorithm: rsaEncryption
26:             RSA Public Key: (1024 bit)
27:                 Modulus (1024 bit):
28:                     00:c8:70:e5:e4:a8:1b:fc:27:37:22:2c:55:0f:8d:
29:                     70:f4:ec:30:10:c5:03:79:e7:8c:fe:35:a5:29:30:
30:                     c4:ce:3b:a8:23:27:da:56:83:51:96:8f:f7:3a:8d:
31:                     c5:32:7c:9e:5e:dc:3f:15:09:da:13:c3:e4:26:4d:
32:                     83:8e:87:a7:d1:9e:b2:e2:06:b1:d0:f5:d3:e1:10:
33:                     d0:c2:45:d7:7b:68:9f:a9:fd:46:3d:d8:3a:db:c2:
34:                     26:9d:d6:99:e6:df:51:19:01:a0:82:38:28:e8:2f:
35:                     be:cf:30:af:aa:8a:30:76:1e:6f:4a:d7:b5:09:1b:
36:                     25:b9:d3:f1:08:ac:b1:14:2f
37:                 Exponent: 65537 (0x10001)
38:     Signature Algorithm: md5WithRSAEncryption
39:         3d:31:21:bd:66:a4:f3:80:28:68:06:d5:94:95:31:4a:c7:db:
```

```
40:          2a:b7:f3:fd:c7:e0:d0:67:dd:02:b4:da:c7:c6:65:5a:f8:3c:
41:          10:a7:b1:64:ca:40:88:07:db:10:43:18:60:18:1e:ac:9f:b5:
42:          c5:b8:93:cf:64:27:66:25:12:a0:bc:a2:41:57:8d:42:48:56:
43:          f0:7c:e2:dd:33:f9:0c:ee:26:79:ba:96:bb:b7:d2:fb:39:dc:
44:          06:a0:6f:39:ae:cb:e3:4f:c7:0d:f3:49:be:e3:b6:b6:53:2e:
45:          a1:0f:e8:e8:03:60:14:ea:24:cb:d1:d4:10:9f:52:d3:83:8c:
46:          7a:8b
```

The command in lines 1–3 is used to generate the signed certificate johnsmith.crt. In order to get the private key, the `openssl` program will ask you to input the `passphrase` in line 9. The command in line 11 is used to generate meaningful text output from the certificate.

From this example, you can see that a certificate contains the following sections:

- A validity section to specify the life of the certificate (lines 19–21).
- A public-key section to store the public key (lines 24–37).
- A signature section (lines 38–46).

The information above is vital for any secure communications using certificate exchange. For some real applications, the certificate must be signed by a CA. With OpenSSL, we can create our own CA and sign certificates.

20.4.4 Signing certificates as a CA with OpenSSL

To manipulate the CA, you may need to deal with the command

```
openssl ca ...
```

This command is one of the most complicated commands in OpenSSL. The full syntax and options are listed below:

```
openssl ca [-verbose] [-config filename] [-name section] [-gencrl]
  [-revoke file] [-subj arg] [-crldays days] [-crlhours hours]
  [-crlexts section] [-startdate date] [-enddate date] [-days arg]
  [-md arg] [-policy arg] [-keyfile arg] [-key arg] [-passin arg]
  [-cert file] [-in file] [-out file] [-notext] [-outdir dir] [-infiles]
  [-spkac file] [-ss_cert file] [-preserveDN] [-noemailDN] [-batch]
  [-msie_hack] [-extensions section] [-extfile section]
```

Together with some strange arrangement of the configuration file `openssl`, it doesn't allow one to use this "openssl ca" easily. For this reason, the distribution of OpenSSL includes a Perl script file called CA.pl in the `apps` directory to help.

Basically, this Perl script is to create the right environment so that using the command "openssl ca" is a lot easier. In its simplest form, the following command will create a CA certificate and private key:

```
CA.pl -newca
```

The CA's signed certificate (cacert.pem) and private key (cakey.pem) are stored in the directories `apps/demoCA` and `apps/demoCA/private` respectively. A dialog session is shown in ex20-16.ssl.

```
Example: ex20-16.ssl - Generating CA's Certificate And Private Key

  1: [openssl-0.9.6c/apps]$ CA.pl -newca
  2: CA certificate filename (or enter to create) (Just Press Return)
  3:
  4: Making CA certificate ...
  5: Using configuration from ./openssl.cnf
  6: Loading 'screen' into random state - done
  7: Generating a 1024 bit RSA private key
  8: ...................................++++++
```

```
 9: ...............++++++
10: writing new private key to './demoCA/private/cakey.pem'
11: Enter PEM pass phrase: myca <----------------------- (Will Not Display)
12: Verifying password - Enter PEM pass phrase: myca <--- (Will Not Display)
13: -----
14: There are quite a few fields but you can leave some blank
15: For some fields there will be a default value,
16: If you enter '.', the field will be left blank.
17: -----
18: Country Name (2 letter code) [AU]:UK
19: State or Province Name (full name) [Some-State]: <--- (Just Press Return)
20: Locality Name (eg, city) []:<----------------------- (Just Press Return)
21: Organization Name (eg, company) [Internet Widgits Pty Ltd]:MyCA
22: Organizational Unit Name (eg, section) []:<---------- (Just Press Return)
23: Common Name (eg, YOUR name) []:<-------------------- (Just Press Return)
24: Email Address []:<---------------------------------- (Just Press Return)
25:
```

If you are using a PC with Microsoft systems, you may need to use the following command in line 1:

```
C:\openssl-0.9.6c\out32dll>perl ..\apps\CA.pl -newca
```

Note that you may also need to delete the existing cacert.pem and cakey.pem files to make this example work. Now, you can use this new CA's certificate and private key to sign the CSR form. One of the simplest ways to do this is to rename the johnsmith.csr file as newreq.pem and then call the CA.pl script as

```
CA.pl -sign
```

This command will sign the CSR file newreq.pem using the default CA created in ex20-16.ssl. The signed certificate is called newcert.pem. This file can be renamed to johnsmith.crt later as a real certificate. A dialog session is shown in example ex20-17.ssl.

```
Example: ex20-17.ssl - Signing Certificate With Your Own CA
 1: [openssl-0.9.6c/apps]$ mv johnsmith.csr newreq.pem
 2:
 3: [openssl-0.9.6c/apps]$ CA.pl -sign
 4: Using configuration from ./openssl.cnf
 5: Loading 'screen' into random state - done
 6: Enter PEM pass phrase: myca <----------------------- (Will Not Display)
 7: Check that the request matches the signature
 8: Signature ok
 9: The Subjects Distinguished Name is as follows
10: countryName            :PRINTABLE:'UK'
11: stateOrProvinceName    :PRINTABLE:'Some-State'
12: organizationName       :PRINTABLE:'ABC'
13: organizationalUnitName :PRINTABLE:'www.pwt-ex.com'
14: commonName             :PRINTABLE:'johnsmith'
15: emailAddress           :IA5STRING:'johnsmith@pwt-ex.com'
16: Certificate is to be certified until Oct 2 05:40:44 2004 GMT (365 days)
17: Sign the certificate? [y/n]:y
18:
19: 1 out of 1 certificate requests certified, commit? [y/n]y
20: Write out database with 1 new entries
21: Data Base Updated
22: Signed certificate is in newcert.pem
```

Now let's see how certificates can be imported into browsers.

20.4.5 Importing certificates into browsers

By installing a certificate in a browser, you have given your favorite browser the capability to identify you. This is important when your browser communicates with a Web server in secure mode. Your browser can respond to the request of the server by sending the certificate over. This process is called client authentication. Together with server authentication, mutual trust can be built and security serves its purposes.

By default the structure of the certificate used in OpenSSL is called X509. This is an authentication certificate scheme recommended by the International Telecommunication Union (ITU-T) and supported by the SSL/TLS standard. The default format for X509 certificates used by OpenSSL is the base 64 Privacy Enhanced Mail (PEM) encoding. This is why a number of authors and articles use the file extension .pem for certificates generated by OpenSSL. Unfortunately, this PEM format is not very popular (at least not in this form) among browsers. For example, PEM is not accepted by both IE and NS as an import or export certificate. Some browsers such as IE do support the PEM format in a binary form known as DER.

Another widely accepted standard format for certificates is called PKCS#12. It is a structure to store private keys and certificates securely. Some advantages of this format are:

- It is supported by most Web browsers including IE, NS, Opera, and others.
- By integrating private keys and certificates together, only one file is needed for import and export.
- It is probably the only way to access the private keys of other certificates.

With OpenSSL, to generate a PKCS#12 file from the standard PEM files is not difficult. For example, you can generate the PKCS#12 file johnsmith.p12 corresponding to the johnsmith.key and johnsmith.crt by the following command:

```
openssl pkcs12 -export -in johnsmith.crt -inkey johnsmith.key
    -certfile cacert.pem -name "johnsmith" -out johnsmith.p12
```

This command takes johnsmith.crt, johnsmith.key, and cacert.pem as the input argument. The output file is johnsmith.p12 in PKCS#12 format. A dialog session of this process is shown in ex20-18.ssl.

```
Example: ex20-18.ssl - Creating PKCS#12 Certificates

1: openssl-0.9.6c\apps>openssl pkcs12 -export -in johnsmith.crt
2:                         -inkey johnsmith.key -certfile newcert.pem
3:                         -name "johnsmith" -out johnsmith.p12
4:
5: Loading 'screen' into random state - done
6: Enter PEM pass phrase:johnsmith <-------------------- (Will Not Display)
7: Enter Export Password: anything <-------------------- (Will Not Display)
8: Verifying password - Enter Export Password: anything <-(Will Not Display)
9:
```

Now you have a certificate in PKCS#12 format and ready to be imported into the IE browser. If you are using IE5.x or IE6.x, you can use the following step-by-step procedure to import the certificate johnsmith.p12 into the browser:

- Activate the IE browser.
- From the menu, choose Tools | Internet Options | Contents | Certificate.
- Click the Certificate button to activate the "Certificates window" (Fig. 20.13).
- Click the Import button to launch the Certificate Import Wizard and then click the Next button to import the file (Fig. 20.14). You may use the Browser button if you like.

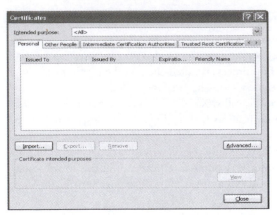

Figure 20.13 "Certificates" window

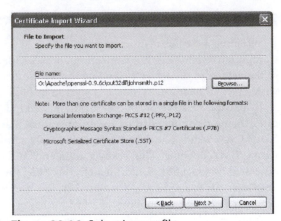

Figure 20.14 Select import file

- When you click the Next button of Fig. 20.14, a "Password" window appears to ask for a password for the private key (Fig. 20.15). Also, you have the chance to increase security by checking the strong private-key protection.
- The Next button will activate the "Certificate Store" window (Fig. 20.16). If you want to change the Certificate Store, you can do so by clicking the Browse button.

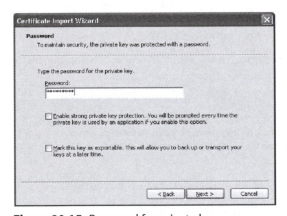

Figure 20.15 Password for private key

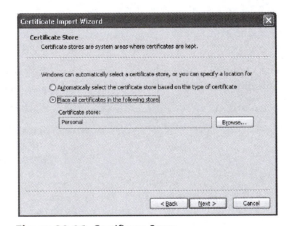

Figure 20.16 Certificate Store

- Next, you will see a summary of your import certificate (Fig. 20.17). When you click the Finish button, an import successful message is displayed. The certificate appears inside the "Certificates" window (Fig. 20.18).

If you are using NS6.x, you can use the following steps to import the certificate johnsmith.p12:

- Activate the NS6.x Web browser.
- From the menu choose Edit | Preferences (see Fig. 20.19).
- Inside the Privacy & Security menu, select the "Certificates" option and click the "Manage Certificates" option (Fig. 20.20).
- Now press the Restore button and select the file johnsmith.p12 into NS6.x (Fig. 20.21). You will notice that there is only one default file type in Fig. 20.21, i.e., PKCS#12.
- After inputting some passwords (Fig. 20.22), the file johnsmith.p12 will be restored in the certificate window as illustrated in Fig. 20.23.
- If you press the View button, you will see a summary of the certificate (Fig. 20.24).

Figure 20.17 Certificate summary

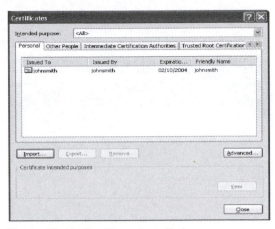

Figure 20.18 Certificate installed

Figure 20.19 Certificate menu

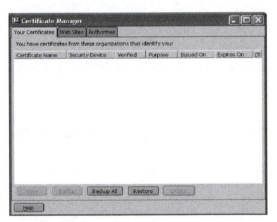

Figure 20.20 Restore certificate

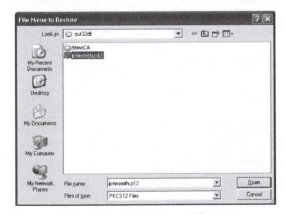

Figure 20.21 Select PKCS#12 certificate

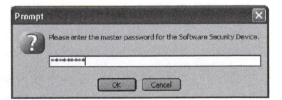

Figure 20.22 Type in password

Figure 20.23 Restore certificate   **Figure 20.24** View certificate

For other browsers, client certificates can be handled in a similar manner. Now let's consider how to set up a secure Web server or a secure site.

20.5 Building a secure Web site with HTTPS

The basic idea to set up a secure Web site is to integrate the SSL with the Web server software. The SSL provides handshake and encrypted information exchange between the browser and server. As a result, secure Web communications are accomplished. The HyperText Transfer Protocol (HTTP) over a secure channel, or more precisely HTTP over SSL, becomes a new standard known as HTTPS.

As we mentioned in previous sections, one of the important tasks for secure communications is the handshake between the browser and server via authentication and certificate exchange. If you can import certificates into your browser for client authentication, you have completed half of the story. Together with server authentication, mutual trust is built so that cipher suit (encryption method) exchange is employed to perform the desired secure Web communications.

In fact, in many secure Web communications, client authentication is optional depending on the settings of the server software: you can turn off the client authentication requirement. In this case, there will be no client certificate request from the server. However, server authentication is a compulsory requirement for standard HTTPS on the Web.

Apart from the security issue, the main difference between HTTP and HTTPS is that they use different ports. By default, an ordinary Web server uses port 80, but a secure Web server listens via port 443. For example, the following protocols are used to contact a normal and a secure Web site:

> http://www.pwt-ex.com – – – ordinary Web communications using port 80
>
> https://www.pwt-ex.com – – – secure Web communications using port 443

For a capable Web server, it is possible to set up a Web site listening to the two protocols above. In this case, all security operations are almost completely transparent to the end users. We will show you how to do this in the final section of this chapter. Before that, we would like to demonstrate how to build a secure Web site in the first place.

20.5.1 Basic requirements to build a secure Web site

In normal circumstances, a secure Web site is a machine running Web server software with SSL functionalities. In this case Web communications can be secured by SSL encryption. Since secure Web sites involve SSL, the basic requirements to build one include the following:

- Web server software.
- An SSL software implementation or package.
- A software patch to integrate the above two together.

In terms of a real example, we will show you how to build a secure Web site using the following software packages:

- Apache (available from www.apache.org)
- OpenSSL (available from www.openssl.org)
- Mod_SSL (available from www. modssl.org)

The main reason for selecting these packages is that they are popular and freely available with source code. That means you can build the final software from scratch and use it for both commercial and non-commercial applications. Also, it seems that the only free solution to provide secure Web communications on a PC with Windows systems is the Apache, OpenSSL, and Mod_SSL combination.

We covered how to compile and set up OpenSSL in section 20.4.2. Apache is important server software and is very popular and widely used by the Web community, including both UNIX/LINUX and Windows. We have covered Apache to some degree on a number of occasions in this book.

The only new software here is Mod_SSL (or mod_ssl from the official site). This is a software patch or, more accurately, an Apache interface to OpenSSL. The software can be downloaded from the official site www.modssl.org. The mod_ssl package is based on particular versions of Apache. For example,

```
mod_ssl-x.x.x-y.y.y.tar.gz
```

represents the mod_ssl software version x.x.x and is designed for Apache software of version y.y.y. The mod_ssl package we are going to use is mod_ssl-2.8.7-1.3.23.tar.gz and is dedicated to Apache version 1.3.23. Therefore, if you are using other versions of Apache, you may need to download the module suitable for your requirement. Also, to make mod_ssl work, you need the source code of Apache so that they can be compiled together. The Apache package we are going to use is

apache_1.3.23.tar.gz or

apache_1.3.23-win32-x86-src.msi

The Microsoft Installer (msi) version is for the Windows environment. Both these Apache packages are available from www.apache.org. When you extract or unpack the Apache, OpenSSL, and Mod_SSL package files, you should have the following subdirectories:

- apache_1.3.23
- mod_ssl-2.8.6-1.3.23
- openssl-0.9.6c

We assume that the OpenSSL package has already been installed on your system and the directory openssl-0.9.6c is located side by side with the others. Now, let's proceed to perform the integration of Apache and OpenSSL.

20.5.2 Integrating Apache and OpenSSL using Mod_SSL

In this section, we will show you how to integrate Apache and OpenSSL together using Mod_SSL. By default, the Mod_SSL (Apache interface to OpenSSL) package supports the UNIX/LINUX platform or platforms of a similar type. Therefore, to integrate Apache and OpenSSL on a UNIX/LINUX machine is much simpler. Believe it or not, the entire compilation, installation, and configuration process can be done in just a couple of lines as illustrated in example ex20-19.ssl.

```
Example: ex20-19.ssl - Integrating Apache And OpenSSL With Mod_SSL

 1: $ cd mod_ssl-2.8.7-1.3.23
 2: $ ./configure \
 3:    --with-apache=../apache_1.3.23 \
 4:    --with-ssl=../openssl-0.9.6c \
 5:    --prefix=/usr/local/apache
 6: $ cd ..
 7: $ cd apache_1.3.23
 8: $ make
 9: $ make certificate
10: $ make install
```

Line 1 is to go to the Mod_SSL directory `mod_ssl-2.8.7-1.3.23`. Inside this directory, run the configure program with parameters (see lines 2–5)

```
--with-apache=../apache_1.3.23
--with-ssl=../openssl-0.9.6c
--prefix=/usr/local/apache
```

The first parameter is to set the name and location of the Apache source directory and the second parameter sets the name and location of the OpenSSL source directory. The prefix parameter is to tell Mod_SSL where to find the installed Apache executables, libraries, and binaries. In this case, we have assumed that the installed Apache software is located in the directory `/usr/local/apache`. If your default directory for Apache is not `/usr/local/apache`, you may need to change the prefix parameter.

The main function of the configure program is to set up and prepare an SSL-aware Apache ready for recompilation. Lines 6–7 are to go to the Apache source directory `apache_1.3.23`. By issuing the `make` command in line 8, the Apache software is recompiled with SSL features.

Before the Apache software can be used for server authentication, you need to generate a certificate and import it into the server. The `make` command in line 9 will do just that. More precisely, the `make` command is to generate a private key together with a server certificate and install them into the configuration file httpd.conf of Apache. Finally, the `make` statement in line 10 is to install the new Apache package in the target install directory `/usr/local/apache`.

In order to make this new Apache server work, you need to activate it with SSL. This can be done by the following command if you are using UNIX/LINUX systems:

```
$ /usr/local/apache/bin/httpd -DSSL
```

If your newly created secure site is called www.pwt-ex.com, you can test it with the following command:

https://www.pwt-ex.com

You will see an alert window (Fig. 20.25) to tell you that you are about to enter into a secure Web communication. If you click the OK button, you will see a welcome message form Mod_SSL as illustrated in Fig. 20.26.

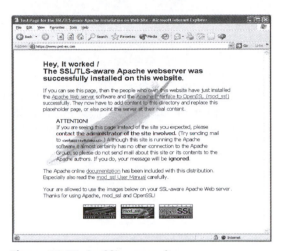

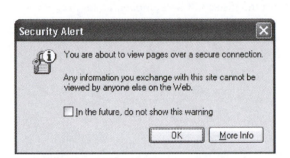

Figure 20.25 "Security Alert" window   **Figure 20.26** An SSL-aware site

If you are using a Microsoft Windows system, you may need to do this from scratch by yourself. Don't worry, we will show you how to get it done step by step. The first step is to get the following packages:

apache_1.3.23-win32-x86-src.msi

mod_ssl-2.8.7–1.3.23.tar.gz

openssl-0.9.6c.tar.gz

If you have a Microsoft installer, you can install the Apache package apache_1.3.23-win32-x86-src.msi by double clicking on this file. If you don't have an installer, a copy can be downloaded from the official download center of www.microsoft.com. Next, you can use the WinZip utility to unzip and extract files from the other two packages. Suppose all three packages are located in the following drive and directories:

```
o:\apache_1.3.23
o:\mod_ssl-2.8.6-1.3.23
o:\openssl-0.9.6c
```

In this case, we have assumed the default drive is `o:\`. Do ensure that all three source directories are side by side, otherwise you may need to change the following three compilation and configuration steps.

Step 1: Configure and build the OpenSSL package This step is similar to the one we used to compile OpenSSL in section 20.4.2. In order to compile and configure OpenSSL, you need Perl and a Visual C/C++ compiler up and running on your system. The entire building process is illustrated in the following example:

```
Example: ex20-20.ssl - Configure And Build The OpenSSL Package

 1: cd openssl-0.9.6c
 2: perl Configure VC-WIN32 --prefix=o:/openssl
 3: ms\do_ms
 4: nmake /f ms\ntdll.mak
 5: md  o:\openssl
 6: md  o:\openssl\bin
 7: md  o:\openssl\lib
 8: md  o:\openssl\include
 9: md  o:\openssl\include\openssl
10: copy /b inc32\*            o:\openssl\include\openssl
11: copy /b out32dll\ssleay32.lib  o:\openssl\lib
```

```
12: copy /b out32dll\libeay32.lib    o:\openssl\lib
13: copy /b out32dll\ssleay32.dll    o:\openssl\bin
14: copy /b out32dll\libeay32.dll    o:\openssl\bin
15: copy /b out32dll\openssl.exe     o:\openssl\bin
16: cd ..
```

The first four lines are used to compile the package with the Visual C/C++ compiler. Note that we have defined an installed directory for the OpenSSL by the parameter "-- prefix = o:/openssl" in line 2. This directory will be used by the compilation of Apache. Before that, you need to create the following directories for the OpenSSL executables, libraries, and binaries (see lines 5–9):

```
o:\openssl
o:\openssl\bin
o:\openssl\lib
o:\openssl\include
o:\openssl\include\openssl
```

By default, all executables, libraries, and binaries of the win32 version of OpenSSL are stored in the `out32dll` directory; a series of copy procedures are employed to copy them into the target directories (see lines 10–15). Make sure that the directory `o:\openssl\bin` is in your path.

Step 2: Configure Mod_SSL for Apache Now you can configure the `mod_ssl` package for Apache. The configuration process is illustrated in the following example:

```
Example: ex20-21.ssl - Configure Mod_SSL For Apache

1: cd mod_ssl-2.8.7-1.3.23
2: configure.bat --with-apache=..\apache_1.3.23 --with-ssl=o:\openssl
3: cd ..
```

Then you will be asked to proceed as in step 3 to recompile the Apache software.

Step 3: Building the SSL-aware Apache The actual compilation procedure is incredibly simple as illustrated in the following example:

```
Example: ex20-22.ssl - Building The SSL-aware Apache

1: cd apache_1.3.23\src
2: nmake /f Makefile.win
3: nmake /f Makefile.win installr
```

Line 1 is to go to the Apache source code directory. Then by calling the Visual C/C++ `nmake` utility in line 2, the Apache software will be compiled. Another call to the `nmake` utility in line 3 is to install the package into the directory `o:\apache`.

Now you should have the SSL-aware Apache installed. However, you cannot use SSL features such as HTTPS. The reason is that you still need to configure Apache yourself.

20.5.3 Configuring Apache to use SSL

As an example, the information in this section is dedicated to Windows users. However, the general techniques to configure the Apache server apply to us all. After installation of Apache, you should have the main program apache.exe and the following directories under `o:\apache`:

```
bin    cgi-bin   conf   htdocs    icons    include
lib    libexec   logs   modules   openssl  proxy
```

Among other things, you still need to configure Apache by

- creating a certificate and importing it to Apache;
- changing the port setting from 80 to 443 so that secure Web communications can be listened to properly.

Before any configuration, we strongly recommend that you do some testing to make sure you have the Apache software properly built. The first test would be to activate the program apache.exe with a command-line option such as

```
apache -h
```

If you can see all the options as listed in ex20-23.ssl, the program is working.

```
Example: ex20-23.ssl - Testing Apache - apache -h

 1: O:\Apache>apache -h
 2: Usage: apache [-D name] [-d directory] [-f file] [-n service]
 3:               [-C "directive"] [-c "directive"] [-k signal]
 4:               [-v] [-V] [-h] [-l] [-L] [-S] [-t] [-T]
 5: -D name : define a name for use in <IfDefine name> directives
 6: -d directory : specify an alternate initial ServerRoot
 7: -f file : specify an alternate ServerConfigFile
 8: -C "directive" : process directive before reading config files
 9: -c "directive" : process directive after reading config files
10: -v              : show version number
11: -V              : show compile settings
12: -h              : list available command line options (this page)
13: -l              : list compiled-in modules
14: -L              : list available configuration directives
15: -S              : show parsed settings (currently only vhost settings)
16: -t              : run syntax check for config files (with docroot check)
17: -T              : run syntax check for config files (without docroot check)
18: -n name         : name the Apache service for -k options below;
19: -k stop|shutdown : tell running Apache to shutdown
20: -k restart      : tell running Apache to do a graceful restart
21: -k start        : tell Apache to start
22: -k install   | -I : install an Apache service
23: -k config       : reconfigure an installed Apache service
24: -k uninstall | -u : uninstall an Apache service
25: -W service      : after -k config|install; Apache starts after 'service'
26: -w              : holds the window open for 30 seconds for fatal errors.
```

Next, you should also perform a test of server capability to make sure that everything is fine before the configuration. Apache with SSL can be run on Windows 98, ME, NT, 2000, and XP. As recommended by the Apache authority, Apache will run better if installed as a service (net service) on Windows NT, 2000, and XP. To install and start Apache as a service on Windows XP, the following commands are used:

```
apache -k install
net start apache
```

If your system already has Apache running, you may need to stop it first by

```
net stop apache
```

Once you have Apache up and running, you can use your favorite browser to test it. Try the following:

http://localhost

Figure 20.27 http://localhost

You may want to change the address of localhost to some sites you know. If you can see something similar to Fig. 20.27, your Apache is properly installed.

From Fig. 20.27, you may also think that you have properly set up SSL/LTS-aware Apache. No, you haven't, at least not yet! The reason is that you have used the http:// protocol which has no SSL involved. Also, Apache is still listening to port 80. Nonetheless, you know that the new Apache is working properly and you can concentrate on its configuration.

Now, back up a copy of the Apache configuration file httpd.conf from the directory apache\conf. Edit this file with your favorite editor and perform the following configuration steps:

Step 1: Configure the port

- Locate the string "Port 80" and comment it out as "#Port 80."
- Locate the string "Listen" and change it to "Listen 443."
- Locate the string "ServerName" and change it to the real server name of your system, e.g., "ServerName www.pwt-ex.com."

Although the SSL feature is still not functioning, you should be able to call your site www.pwt-ex.com using the port 443. Try the following command on a browser:

    http://www.pwt-ex.com:443

If you can see a page like that in Fig. 20.27, the configuration of port 443 is OK. Now you can generate a certificate for Apache.

Step 2: Generating a certificate for the Apache server Now, go to the subdirectory `openssl` and make sure you have the `OpenSSL` main program openssl there. Open a DOS window and perform the following commands from the default directory of Apache (i.e., `o:\apache`) to generate a certificate for our server:

```
Example: ex20-24.ssl - Generating A Certificate For Apache Server

1: cd openssl
2: openssl  req -new -out server.csr -config ./openssl.cnf
3: openssl  rsa -in privkey.pem -out server.key
4: openssl  x509 -in server.csr -out server.crt -req
5:          -signkey server.key -days 365
```

The first line is to get into the `openssl` directory. Line 2 is used to generate a CSR with a private key called private.pem. This certificate will be used to identify your Apache server. Therefore, when `openssl` asks for a common name, you should input the real hostname of the server such as www.pwt-ex.com. This is necessary because when a browser requests a secure connection such as

    https://www.pwt-ex.com

the server will send this certificate to the browser. The browser will complain if the common name of the certificate does not match the server's URL.

Line 3 is to remove the `passphrase` from the private key privkey.pem and generate a server.key. This server.key is used to sign the CSR server.csr and output the signed certificate as server.crt (lines 4–5). This process is the same as that given in ex20-15.ssl.

Note that the self-signed certificate should be used on a temporary basis or for testing purposes. In a real application, you should replace the self-signed certificate by a real one signed by a CA or at least signed by a CA created by you (see ex20-17.ssl).

Now, let's create an `apache/conf/ssl` directory and move both the files server.key and server.cert into it. Once you have the server key and certificate, you can insert them into a virtual host of Apache as

```
SSLCertificateFile          conf/ssl/server.crt
SSLCertificateKeyFile       conf/ssl/server.key
```

for certificate exchange. More details will be presented later. Now you may want to generate the certificate as a DER-encoded form so that your users can import it into their browsers. To generate a DER-encoded certificate, you can use

```
openssl x509 -in server.crt -out server.der.crt -outform DER
```

You can now send this server.der.crt file to your staff, users, or members so that they can import the certificate into the certificate storage of their browser.

Step 3: Configuring Apache to use SSL To use SSL in Windows, the first thing is to copy the dynamic libraries `ssleay32.dll` and `libeay32.dll` from the apache\openssl\lib directory to WINDOWS\system32. If you are using NT, the directory should be WINNT\system32. Next, you copy all necessary files such as executables, libraries, and binaries to make `openssl` work in the Apache directory (e.g., `o:\apache`).

Edit the Apache configuration file httpd.conf and locate the string

```
LoadModule ssl_module modules/mod_ssl.so
```

If this statement is commented, you can uncomment it by removing all the hash symbols in front of it. In this case Apache can load the SSL module `ssl_module`. Make sure that the module `mod_ssl.so` is located inside the directory `apache/modules`.

In order to make the SSL module function, you also need to locate the string

```
AddModule mod_ssl.c
```

and uncomment it. Finally, you need to set up an Apache virtual host to use the secure site. An example is given below. You can simply copy the following fragment to the end of the configuration file.

```
Example: ex20-25.ssl - Setting Configuration

 1: SSLMutex sem
 2: SSLRandomSeed startup builtin
 3: SSLSessionCache none
 4:
 5: SSLLog logs/SSL.log
 6: SSLLogLevel info
 7:
 8: <VirtualHost www.pwt-ex.com:443>
 9:    SSLEngine On
10:    SSLCertificateFile conf/ssl/server.crt
11:    SSLCertificateKeyFile conf/ssl/server.key
12: </VirtualHost>
```

Lines 1–6 are the standard routines to initialize SSL so that the SSL powered by OpenSSL is ready for action. If anything goes wrong, you can debug via the log file SSL.log located in the `apache/logs` directory. Since the error and log file systems of Apache and Mod_SSL are so good, some online SSL authors may even refuse to answer any of your questions if you haven't read the log file first.

Now you have a new Apache configuration file httpd.conf. The next step is to save this file and relaunch Apache to use the new settings. Open a DOS window and issue the following commands:

```
net stop apache
apache -k uninstall
apache -k install
net start apache
```

The first two commands are used to stop the Apache service and then uninstall it from the system. The third command is to install the Apache server again with new configuration settings. The final command is to start Apache as a service. You may want to test it by issuing the secure HTTP below:

https://www.pwt-ex.com

You should see a page exactly the same as that in Fig. 20.27. From this page, if you click on the underlined text "documentation," a full documentation of Apache is displayed (see Fig. 20.28). If you click on the underlined text "mod_ssl User Manual," the user manual of Mod_SSL is displayed (see Fig. 20.29).

Figure 20.28 Apache manual

Figure 20.29 Mod_SSL manual

As we mentioned on a number of occasions, one of the differences between HTTP and HTTPS is the use of ports. They use different ports and therefore are not compatible by default. For example, suppose the site www.pwt-ex.com is configured as a secure site. If you use the following command on a browser:

http://www.pwt-ex.com

and if the system does not crash, you will get an error message. The reason is because you are using port 80 to talk to a server which can only listen via port 443.

With the elegance of Apache's virtual hosts, however, it is possible and quite easy to set up a Web site listening to both port 80 and 443.

20.5.4 Configuring Apache for secure and insecure connections

As mentioned in section 20.5.3, you should back up a copy of the configuration file httpd.conf before any modification is made. Suppose the file httpd.conf is configured for a secure situation. In order to modify it to accept both secure and insecure connections, you need to change it back to the insecure case first. Edit the file httpd.conf with your favorite editor and perform the following two steps:

Step 1: Configure the port:

- Locate the string "#Port 80" and uncomment it as "Port 80" so that Apache can use port 80.
- Locate the string "Listen 443" and change it to "Listen 80."

Step 2: Delete the secure virtual host setting.

- Locate the secure virtual host settings as in example ex20-25.ssl.
- Delete the entire virtual host settings.

Now your Apache server is set to handle insecure connections. HTTP is working via port 80. To add secure connections to this httpd.conf file, all you need is to create a virtual host that can activate SSL and listen to port 443. You can do that by copying the following code fragment to the end of the configuration file:

```
Example: ex20-26.ssl - Virtual Host Listens To Port 443

 1: SSLMutex sem
 2: SSLRandomSeed startup builtin
 3: SSLSessionCache none
 4:
 5: SSLLog logs/SSL.log
 6: SSLLogLevel info
 7:
 8: <IfDefine HAVE_SSL>
 9: Listen 443
10:    <VirtualHost www.pwt-ex.com:443>
11:       SSLEngine On
12:       SSLCertificateFile conf/ssl/server.crt
13:       SSLCertificateKeyFile conf/ssl/server.key
14:    </VirtualHost>
15: </IfDefine>
```

Yes! That's it. By changing everything back to port 80 this means that all normal communications with HTTP will be handled in usual way. That is, Apache is listening to port 80 by default and searching the http:// document from the DocumentRoot setting in the early part of httpd.conf. Now, if you activate the following command from your browser

http://www.pwt-ex.com

the Apache server, in this case, will search for the default document such as index.html from the DocumentRoot (e.g., o:\apache\htdocs) directory and return it to the browser. Note that we have used the root directory as the default URL rather than the usual http://www.pwt-ex.com/book/chap20a settings.

The if-define directive <IfDefine HAVE_SSL> in lines 8–15 means that if HAVE_SSL is defined, Apache will listen to port 443. If the browser requests the virtual host www.pwt-ex.com in secure mode (i.e., www.pwt-ex.com:443), the certificate and key will be available from the location specified in lines 12–13. Now, when you issue the command

https://www.pwt-ex.com

the Apache server will use this secure virtual host to handle security and connection. Since this virtual host has the same name as the `ServerName` setting, Apache will search the default document (e.g., index.html) from the same directory as specified by HTTP.

In order to use the new settings of this httpd.conf file, you may need to relaunch Apache using the following commands:

```
net stop apache
apache -k uninstall
apache -k install -D SSL -D HAVE_SSL
net start apache
```

The third command above is to install Apache with the variables `SSL` and `HAVE_SSL` defined so that the `if-define` directive can take effect. Virtual host is a powerful feature of Apache and you can use it to set up different sites at different or the same locations. Each virtual host has its own settings and is treated as an independent site. For more details, the Apache manual or documentation is recommended. Now, let's consider some examples of how to use secure communications on the Web.

20.5.5 Some examples to use the secure site

To use the site you have built in the previous section is easy. All you have to do is to put all your Web pages (both secure and insecure) into the directory specified by the variable `DocumentRoot` of Apache. In our case, the directory is o:\apache\htdocs.

To call a page in secure mode, all you need is to change the "http" to "https" in all URL situations. For example, you can use "https" in the anchor or button element as

```
<a href="https://www.pwt-ex.com/abc.htm">Secure Connection</a>
<input onclick='location.href="https://www.pwt-ex.com/abc.htm"'
       type="button" value="Secure Connection" />
```

For the button case, when the Secure Connection button is clicked, the `onclick` event will activate the following statement:

https://www.pwt-ex.com/abc.htm

In this case, the browser is requesting the abc.htm page from the Web site www.pwt-ex.com using secure mode.

As a simple test example, let's consider writing some donation pages for a charity organization. For security reasons, and also the privacy of the donors, we are going to develop a page using both secure and insecure (normal) channels for the donation. Consider the simple XHTML page below:

```
Example: ex20-27.htm - A Page To Get Donation For Charity

 1: <?xml version="1.0" encoding="iso-8859-1"?>
 2: <!DOCTYPE html PUBLIC "-//W3C//DTD XHTML 1.0 Transitional//EN"
 3:     "http://www.w3.org/TR/xhtml1/DTD/xhtml1-transitional.dtd">
 4: <html xmlns="http://www.w3.org/1999/xhtml" xml:lang="en" lang="en">
 5: <head><title>Secure & Normal Web Connection - ex20-27.htm</title></head>
 6: <style>
 7:   .tx01{background-color:#000088;font-family:arial;font-size:22pt;
 8:       font-weight:bold;color:#ffff00;text-align:left}
 9:   .tx03{font-size:18pt;color:#00ff00}
10:   .butSt{background-color:#aaffaa;font-family:arial;font-weight:bold;
11:       font-size:14pt;color:#880000;width:250px;height:35px}
12: </style>
13: <body class="tx01" style="text-align:center">
14:   Welcome To ABC Charity Site<br /><br />
15: <div class="tx03">
```

```
16:    Your Privacy Is Our Top Priority <br />
17:    You Have A Choice To Use <br />
18:    Secure Or Normal<br />
19:    Channel To Make Your Donation.
20: </div><br />
21:    <input type="button" class="butSt" value="Secure Connection" onclick=
22:       'location.href="https://www.pwt-ex.com/ex20-28.htm"' /><br /><br />
23:    <input type="button" class="butSt" value="Normal Connection"
24:    onclick='location.href="http://www.pwt-ex.com/ex20-28.htm"' /><br />
25: </body>
26: </html>
```

This is a simple XHTML page containing two buttons offering both secure and normal communications for the charity donors. When the first button (lines 21–22) is clicked, the following command is activated:

https://www.pwt-ex.com/ex20-28.htm

This command requests the document ex20-28.htm from the server www.pwt-ex.com over a secure channel. On entering an insecure environment from a secure environment, the browser would normal display a security alert window before any security action. Some screen shots of this are shown in Figs 20.30 and 20.31.

Figure 20.30 ex20-27.htm

Figure 20.31 Alert window

When the OK button in Fig. 20.31 is clicked, the XHTML page ex20-28.htm is displayed with SSL protection (see Fig. 20.32). This ex20-28.htm page is also a very simple page to display the following message for the donor to fill in:

```
Name              Telephone
Address           Amount
```

When the donor completes all the fields and presses the Back button, example ex20-27.htm is activated with the normal HTTP channel. On leaving a secure environment and entering an insecure area, an alert window will also be displayed by the browser (see Figs 20.32 and 20.33).

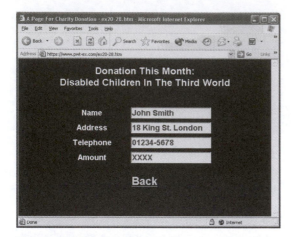

Figure 20.32 ex20-28.htm

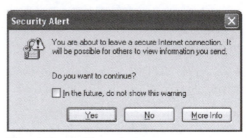

Figure 20.33 Alert window

For completeness of the example, the listing of ex20-28.htm is shown as follows:

Example: ex20-28.htm - A Simple Page To Accept Donation

```
 1: <?xml version="1.0" encoding="iso-8859-1"?>
 2: <!DOCTYPE html PUBLIC "-//W3C//DTD XHTML 1.0 Transitional//EN"
 3:     "http://www.w3.org/TR/xhtml1/DTD/xhtml1-transitional.dtd">
 4: <html xmlns="http://www.w3.org/1999/xhtml" xml:lang="en" lang="en">
 5: <head><title>A Page For Charity Donation - ex20-28.htm</title></head>
 6: <style>
 7: .butSt{background-color:#aaffaa;font-family:arial;font-weight:bold;
 8:     font-size:14pt;color:#880000;width:200px;height:28px}
 9: .txtSt{font-family:arial;font-weight:bold; text-align:center;
10:     font-size:14pt;color:#ffff00}
11: .txtSt2{font-family:arial;font-weight:bold; text-align:center;
12:     font-size:20pt;color:#00ff00}
13: </style>
14: <body style="background:#000088;text-align:center" class="txtSt">
15: <div class="txtSt" style="font-size:18pt;text-align:center">
16:    Donation This Month:<br />
17:    Disabled Children In The Third World
18:    </div><br /><br />
19:
20: <table border="0" width="400" class="txtSt">
21: <tr><td >Name</td><td>
22:     <input type="text" name="name" class="butSt"></td><tr>
23: <tr><td >Address</td><td>
24:     <input type="text" name="add" class="butSt"></td><tr>
25: <tr><td >Telephone</td><td>
26:     <input type="text" name="phone" class="butSt"></td><tr>
27: <tr><td >Amount</td><td>
28:     <input type="text" name="amount" class="butSt"></td><tr>
29: </table><br />
30: <a href="ex20-27.htm" class="txtSt2">Back</a></body></html>
```

This page should be easy to understand. The main purpose of this example is to show how both secure and normal Web communications can be set up together.

Secure Web pages are very popular in the business community. For example, most e-commerce sites have some links or connections in secure mode. Our next example is to modify the "General Login" page developed in section 20.2.3 with SSL security.

In order to save some typing time, we perform the following:

- Copy the general login page ex20-05.php into ex20-29.php.
- Copy the "Join Member" pages ex20-03.htm and ex20-03.php to ex20-30.htm and ex20-30.php.

Make sure all these pages are in the default directory of the secure Web site. For Apache servers, whether you are using UNIX/LINUX or Windows, the default directory is usually called htdocs.

Now you can edit the PHP page ex20-29.php, locate the string variable $llst, and change it to the following:

```
Listing: ex20-04.txt - Code Fragment Of ex20-29.php

 1: $llst = 'Welcome To ABC Online Bargain Hunting<br /> ' .
 2:   ' This Is A Member Only Site<br /><br /> ' .
 3:   ' Enter User Name and Password To Log In<br />' .
 4:   ' <form action="ex20-29.php" method="post">'.
 5:   ' <table class="txtSt">' .
 6:   ' <tr><td>Username:</td><td>' .
 7:   '  <input type="text" name="userId" id="userId" class="butSt" />' .
 8:   '  </td></tr>' .
 9:   ' <tr><td>Password:</td><td>' .
10:   '  <input type="password" name="passId" id="passId" class="butSt" />' .
11:   '  </td></tr> ' .
12:   ' <tr><td colspan="2" style="text-align:center"><br />' .
13:   '  <input type="submit" value="Login" class="butSt2" />' .
14:   '  <input type="button" value="Join Member" class="butSt2" '.
15:   '   onclick="location.href=\'https://www.pwt-ex.com/ex20-30.htm\'" />' .
16:   '  </td></tr></table>' .
17:   ' </form> ';
```

If you compare this code fragment with the code listing in ex20-05.php, you will find that we have changed only two lines (i.e., lines 4 and 15). When the Join Member button is pressed, this page will call

https://www.pwt-ex.com/ex20-30.htm

In this situation, you are calling the join member page ex20-30.htm in secure mode. That's it – nothing more. When you issue the command

http://www.pwt-ex.com/ex20-29.php

you will see the page as in Fig. 20.34. When the Join Member button is pressed, an alert window is launched (see Fig. 20.35).

Figure 20.34 ex20-29.php

Figure 20.35 Alert window

When you press the OK button and if the server's certificate is not a trusted certificate in your browser, you will see a further security alert window as in Fig. 20.36. This window will tell you that the server certificate is not in your trust list and ask whether you want to proceed. If you press the Yes button, the ex20-30.htm page will be displayed in secure mode (see Fig. 20.37).

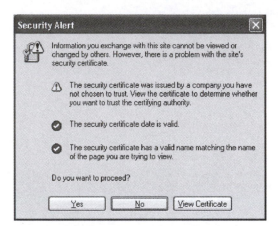

Figure 20.36 Further security alert

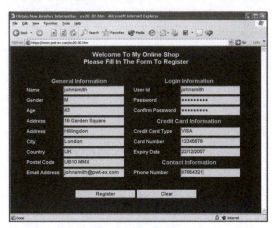

Figure 20.37 ex20-30.htm

Alternatively, if you press the View Certificate button, the details of the certificate are as displayed as in Fig. 20.38. You can see the certificate is issued to and by the same person. Now, you have a chance to install the certificate into trust storage. If you press the Install Certificate button, the "Certificate Import Wizard" is launched. Next, you will be asked whether you want to store the certificate in a location depending on its type (see Fig. 20.39).

Figure 20.38 View the certificate

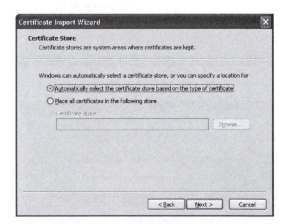

Figure 20.39 Store the certificate

Next, the system will select the storage for your certificate and ask for confirmation (see Fig. 20.40). If you say yes by pressing the Yes button, the server certificate is stored in the root store. If you go to Tools | Internet Options | Content | Certificate from your IE browser and click on the Trusted Root Certification Authority tag, you will see the imported certificate as illustrated in Fig. 20.41.

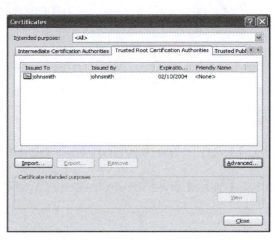

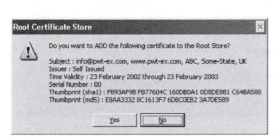

Figure 20.40 Confirm the storage

Figure 20.41 Certificates in trusted root certification authority

21 Mobile Internet and WML

21.1 An introduction to Mobile Internet

21.1.1 What are Mobile Internet and WAP?

By now, most of us are familiar with XHTML, the Web, and have considerable experience on the Internet. Some of you may also have rich experience in online business or e-commerce. Writing business Web pages and building practical Web sites are part (or will be, if not yet) of our daily lives. There is no doubt that business on the Internet is a fast-growing business. At the same time, have you noticed that another information technology (IT) is going to revolutionize our way of life and how we work, play, and communicate? That is, the mobile or wireless revolution!

If you compare the number of mobile phones that people own around the world to the number of computers, you will find an unbalanced result. In terms of applications, the time people spend on mobile phones is far more than on their computers. Also, in many parts of the world, it is already difficult to find a family without a mobile phone. For personal security and many other reasons, you may find it hard to live without one. Together with the Color Screen Phone (CSP), Personal Data Assistant (PDA), and other wireless devices, the entire mobile business or m-business has become a huge success in a relatively short time.

Now, mobile business is far beyond the functionality of a traditional phone. The industry can offer uncompromising information services and online business to its mobile users and is in many ways similar to the Web community. We call it the Mobile Internet.

In fact, the structure and style of the Mobile Internet is similar to the Web community. From a functional point of view, they have the one-to-one correspondence shown in Table 21.1.

Table 21.1 The Web and WAP community

Web community	Mobile Internet (WAP) community
Internet	Mobile Internet
TCP/IP protocol	Wireless Application Protocol (WAP)
XHTML language	Wireless Markup Language (WML)
ECMAScript	Wireless Markup Language Script (WMLScript)
Web site	WAP site (or WML site)
Web page	WAP page (or WML page)
Browser	Micro-browser (or WAP browser)
W3C authority	WAP Forum (www.wapforum.org)

Similar to the Web situation, mobile phones are equipped with a browser that is much smaller than IE or NS and is therefore called a micro-browser. The micro-browser can request a Wireless Application Protocol (WAP) page from a WAP site on the Mobile Internet. WAP pages are usually written in a language called Wireless Markup Language (WML) which is similar to XML. The WAP standard and languages are maintained by an industry association called the WAP Forum (www.wapforum.org). To describe WAP, nothing is more accurate than the description used in the official site of the WAP Forum:

The de facto worldwide standard for providing Internet communications and advanced telephony services on digital mobile phones, pagers, personal digital assistants (PDA) and other wireless terminals.

(www.wapforum.org)

WAP is a global standard and driving force for Mobile Internet applications. Since the markup language used in WAP is WML, we generally refer to WAP sites and pages in the same way as to WML.

21.1.2 How does the Mobile Internet work?

Basically, WAP provides browsing capabilities on the Mobile Internet similar to the Web. The main difference is that WAP is designed to accommodate the following drawbacks from a small device such as a mobile phone:

- Limited memory
- Small screen
- Low bandwidth
- Unreliable and high latency connections

Based on WAP, the WAP Forum created the new markup language called WML. People can use this language to write WAP pages and display them on a mobile phone with a micro-browser. The WML language is similar to XML but with a restrictive syntax. WML (or WAP) pages usually have a file extension .wml and are stored on a WAP site. A mobile phone or other wireless device with a micro-browser can request a WML page via the WAP gateway and display it. The usual architecture of the Mobile Internet is shown in Fig. 21.01.

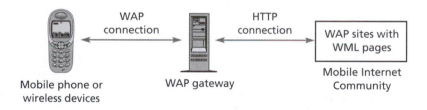

Figure 21.1 Mobile Internet architecture

A typical Mobile Internet session or operation can be summarized as:

- The micro-browser asks the WAP gateway for a WML page at a specific URL.
- The WAP gateway transfers the request to the Web server for the WML page located in the URL.
- The Web server returns the wml deck (WML page) to the WAP gateway.
- The WAP gateway compiles and sends a binary form of wml (byte code) to the micro-browser.
- The micro-browser processes the returned information and displays it.

Don't worry too much about the technical terms at this moment. We will guide you through all the processes and provide a comprehensive background for the Mobile Internet.

In particular, we focus on writing WML pages using WML v1.x and WML v2.x specifications so that pages can be displayed on almost all wireless devices. The version 1.x of WML is widely accepted and used by the mobile industry including almost all mobile phones and devices.

In addition to backward compatibility, WML v2.x has adopted a special version of XHTML known as XHTML-Basic as its default language. This new feature greatly enhances the integration of the WAP and Web communities. XHTML-Basic also includes a special version of the WAP Cascading Style Sheet (WCSS) so that styles can be defined in a WAP sense. XHTML-Basic requires more processing power and memory from your devices; it is targeted for high-end mobile devices such as the CSP, PDA, and smart phones (e.g., PDA + mobile phone).

The connection between the WAP gateway and the Mobile Internet community is actually an ordinary HTTP connection (i.e., Web). In fact the usual Web server can be modified to deliver WML pages to the micro-browser through the WAP gateway. We will show you how to do this in section 20.2.2.

Since the WAP gateway can request documents from Web servers, all CGI techniques that we have learned can be applied. As long as the server returns WML pages to the WAP gateway, the Mobile Internet session is considered as valid. In this case, all server scripts such as Perl, ASP, PHP, and database techniques are all in the same system.

The main function of the WAP gateway is to compile the WML page into byte code. The process is similar to the idea of Java. The byte code is then transmitted to the mobile phone or wireless device. The micro-browser is actually a byte code interpreter to display the byte code on the screen (small screen). Now, let's develop some WML (or Mobile Internet) pages.

21.1.3 My very first Mobile Internet pages

Without knowing all the details, our first Mobile Internet page is a very simple one. It is a WML page to display "Hello World" on your mobile phone screen. Consider the following coding:

```
Example: ex21-01.wml - My First Mobile Internet Page

 1: <?xml version="1.0"?>
 2: <!DOCTYPE wml PUBLIC "-//WAPFORUM//DTD WML 1.3//EN"
 3: "http://www.wapforum.org/DTD/wml_1.3.xml">
 4: <wml>
 5:  <card id="card1" title="Welcome Message">
 6:     <p>Hello World! <br />
 7:         I know how to write<br />
 8:         WML pages too!</p>
 9:  </card>
10: </wml>
```

The first three lines of the page define the heading for every WML page. In particular, the statement in line 3

http://www.wapforum.org/DTD/wml_1.3.xml

specifies that we are using the WML v1.3 standard defined by the WAP authority, i.e., the WAP Forum (www.wapforum.org).

The element <wml> in line 4 defines the beginning of the page. Inside this page, we have only one card specified by the element <card> in lines 5–9. The title of this card is "Welcome Message." The title of the card will be displayed at the top of your mobile screen. The contents of this card (lines 6–8) are some messages to be displayed on your mobile screen. They are, in fact, elements of XHTML and can be understood easily.

This page illustrates one important thing about WML: the contents of a WML page are formed by a series of cards. That is why WML applications are also known as a card deck.

If you put this page into a server capable of delivering WAP pages, you can use your mobile phone to browse the page with the URL

http://www.pwt-ex.com/ex21-01.wml

provided the site www.pwt-ex.com can deliver WML pages. A screen shot of this page on your mobile may look like that in Fig. 21.2.

Figure 21.2 My first WML page

Figure 21.3 Mobile Internet image

Using WML, your mobile phone can display images too. Consider the following WML page:

```
Example: ex21-02.wml - My First Mobile Internet Image

 1: <?xml version = "1.0"?>
 2: <!DOCTYPE wml PUBLIC "-//WAPFORUM//DTD WML 1.3//EN"
 3: "http://www.wapforum.org/DTD/wml_1.3.xml">
 4: <wml>
 5:  <card id = "index" title = "Mobile Internet">
 6:  <p align="center">
 7:     IMAGE<br />
 8:     <img src="logo.wbmp" alt="pic" />
 9:  </p>
10:  </card>
11: </wml>
```

This is another simple WML page containing one card and one paragraph <p>. Inside the paragraph, there is one word "IMAGE" and an image element

```
<img src="logo.wbmp" alt="pic" />
```

The usage of this element is almost identical to the image element <img> used in XHTML. The only difference is that in WML version 1 only one image format is supported. That is the Wireless BMP (or WBMP) with the file extension .wbmp. This example is shown in Fig. 21.3.

As you may ask, how can we develop WML or Mobile Internet pages effectively if we need to use our mobile phone to see the page all the time? Can we have some tools to simulate the micro-browser? Yes! The simulation tool is called the Mobile Internet Toolkit.

21.2 Mobile Internet pages with WML I

21.2.1 Using the Mobile Internet Toolkit

It is believed that the first Mobile Internet Toolkit (MIT) was developed by big mobile phone companies to promote their products and take advantages of the Internet capabilities. Most of the MIT packages are free and available to anyone who wants to develop Mobile Internet applications (i.e., Mobile Internet pages). One of the original and successful packages is the Nokia MIT available from

www.nokia.com   or   www.forum.nokia.com

Nokia's MIT package used in this book is called "NokiaToolkit3_0.zip" and is a complete development suite for Mobile Internet applications. It also comes with mobile handset simulation software. You can pick the mobile phone handset you like and start to develop your WML pages for it.

When you activate the software, you will see a main window and the Nokia Mobile Browser appear on your screen. A mobile browser is in fact a simulation of a mobile phone. All WML pages developed by the MIT package can be displayed on this mobile browser.

If you have a WML page such as our example ex21-01.wml stored on your computer, you can use File | Open to locate and import it into the toolkit. In this case, the toolkit will open an editor window to display it (see Figs 21.4 and 21.5).

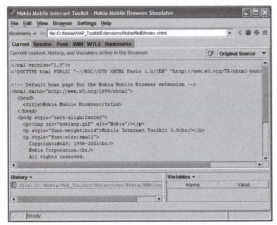

Figure 21.4 Nokia's mobile toolkit main window

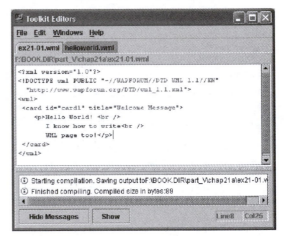

Figure 21.5 Editor window

From the editor window, you can modify any loaded WML page that you like. When you press the Show button, the WML page will be compiled, producing the byte code. The compilation process is shown in the lower window of Fig. 21.5. For this example, the compilation result (byte code) contains only 89 bytes.

As a result, the page is displayed in the mobile browser as illustrated in Fig. 21.6a. If you have a mobile phone simulator installed, you can see the WML page appear on it as demonstrated in Fig. 21.6b.

If you have your WML page uploaded onto a Web server, you can enter the URL address from the main window (see Fig. 21.4) to browse it. You can also go to File | New | WML Deck to open a new editor window to type your WML page.

Figure 21.6a Nokia Mobile Browser

Figure 21.6b Microsoft phone simulator

The main difference between a mobile browser and a phone simulator is that the phone simulator is a real simulation of the actual phone. For example, if the phone doesn't support some features of WML v1.x or v2.x, it will not display any such features. At the time of writing, still not many mobile phones support full WMLv2.0. The mobile browser on the other hand supports all WML features.

Whether you are using a browser, phone simulator, or real phone, they all have a common feature called navigation keys. Usually, you have "Up," "Down," and "Select" keys on your mobile handset, used to scroll the tiny screen so that more information can be displayed. The select key is used to make your selection or decision. Depending on your device, you may also have two soft keys called "Left" and "Right." They are called soft keys because they can be controlled and assigned by software programming using WML.

If you don't want the complete development suite, you can download a "Simulation Application" package such as

Nokia_SimApp2.0Install.exe

This package (SimApp2.0) displays the Nokia Mobile Browser or the phone simulator of your choice. The result is the same as that shown in Fig. 21.6a or 21.6b.

Another interesting MIT package is from Microsoft and called the Microsoft Mobile Internet Toolkit. This package is available from the download center of www.microsoft.com. You may need Windows NT, 2000, or XP Professional and the Microsoft .NET framework to make it work. When your system has the .NET framework installed, you can download the following packages from the Microsoft download center:

- Microsoft Mobile Internet Toolkit, e.g., mobileit.exe
- Microsoft Mobile Explorer, e.g., mme30.exe

Figure 21.6c Microsoft Mobile Explorer

Once you have installed these packages, you can use the toolkit or the Mobile Explorer to start your development. For example, if you have a WML page on your local machine or on a Web server, you can locate the page file from the Mobile Explorer to display the page. A screen shot of example ex21-01.wml on the Mobile Explorer is shown in Fig. 21.6c.

The Mobile Explorer supports WML as well as HTML and therefore provides more features than most mobile phones or devices and the standard. On the other hand, if you want to develop real applications for real devices, Nokia's package is one of the popular choices. As a professional Web or WAP programmer, understanding the limitations of devices and backward compatibility is vital.

In general, we will use a Nokia mobile phone (similar to Fig. 21.6b) to display the results of many WML v1.x examples. Depending on the features of your mobile device, sometimes the key-in procedure and display arrangement may not be the same even from the same manufacturer. For some WML v2.0 functions or features not found in most mobile devices, we will use the Nokia Mobile Browser to display the results.

Before we concentrate on writing WML pages, let's consider how to configure a Web server to deliver a WML page.

21.2.2 Setting up a Web server to deliver WML pages

To configure a Web server to deliver WML pages is easy. All you have to do is to modify the configuration settings so that the content types used on WML pages are supported. The main settings you may need to consider are

```
MIME Types
```

Depending on your wireless device and applications, in most cases, you only need to modify the MIME type settings. In other words, the Web server only needs to know how to recognize the MIME type of the WML pages, i.e., all the file extensions of WML pages. The file extensions used for WML pages are listed in Table 21.2.

Table 21.2 File electronics used on WML applications

`text/vnd.wap.wml`	`wml`	WML source
`application/vnd.wap.wmlc`	`wmlc`	WML compiled
`text/vnd.wap.wmlscript`	`wmls`	WMLScript source
`application/vnd.wap.wmlscriptc`	`wmlsc`	WMLScript compiled
`image/vnd.wap.wbmp`	`wbmp`	Wirless bitmaps
`text/html`	`xhtml`	XHTML source
`text/css`	`css`	CSS source
`text/x-vcard`	`vcf`	Electronic Business Card (VCARD)
`text/x-vCalendar`	`vcs`	Electronic Calendar Event (VCAL)
`text/vnd.wap.si`	`si`	Service Indication (SI) source
`application/vnd.wap.sic`	`sic`	Service Indication (SI) encoded
`text/vnd.wap.sl`	`sl`	Service Loading (SL) source
`application/vnd.wap.slc`	`slc`	Service Loading (SL) encoded
`text/vnd.wap.co`	`co`	Cache Operation (CO) source
`application/vnd.wap.coc`	`coc`	Cache Operation (CO) encoded

In fact, you don't need to add any of these types to your Web server. To make matters clear, let's consider an example. Suppose you are using the Apache Web server and only want to support WML v1.x pages. You can perform the following tasks to configure Apache:

- Edit the Apache configuration file httpd.conf.
- Locate the strings

    ```
    #
    # AddType allows you to tweak mime.types without actually editing them, or to
    # make certain files into certain types.
    #
    AddType application/x-tar .tgz
    ```

- Add the following statements right after the strings above:

    ```
    AddType text/vnd.wap.wml .wml
    AddType application/vnd.wap.wmlc .wmlc
    AddType text/vnd.wap.wmlscript .wmls
    AddType application/vnd.wap.wmlscriptc .wmlsc
    AddType image/vnd.wap.wbmp .wbmp
    ```

Now, your Apache server recognizes all file extensions used in the WML v1.x specification. If you want your Apache to support WML v2.0 or XHTML-Basic, you should add one more line:

```
AddType text/html                              .xhtml
```

Don't forget to relaunch Apache so that the new settings can take effect. If you are using the UNIX/LINUX system, you can relaunch Apache by the command "httpd." If you are using Windows, you may need to stop the Apache service and start it again by

```
net stop apache
net start apache
```

Now we can write another simple WML page to test our Web site www.pwt-ex.com with new settings. Consider the following WML page:

```
Example: ex21-03.wml - Contents Of Chapter 21

 1: <?xml version="1.0"?>
 2: <!DOCTYPE wml PUBLIC "-//WAPFORUM//DTD WML 1.3//EN"
 3: "http://www.wapforum.org/DTD/wml_1.3.xml">
 4: <wml>
 5:  <card id="Card1" title="www.pwt-ex.com">
 6:    <p>CHAPTER 21<br />
 7:        <b>21.1 Mobile Internet</b><br />
 8:        <b>21.2 WML Pages</b><br />
 9:        <b>21.3 WMLScript</b><br />
10:        <b>21.4 XHTML-Basic</b><br />
11:        <b>21.5 Practical Examples</b></p>
12:  </card>
13: </wml>
14:
```

This is a simple WML page with only one card. Inside this card, six messages are displayed, all of which are formatted by XHTML elements and easy to understand.

If you activate Nokia's Simulator Application "SimApp2.0," you will see the mobile browser on the screen. In addition, you will also have a small `SimApp` icon on your system tray. If you right click on the icon and select "Open File or URL...," you will activate the "Open File or URL..." window on screen. Now type the following in the input field as illustrated in Fig. 21.7.

http://www.pwt-ex.com/ex21-03.wml

If you click the OK button, you will see this WML page rendered on the mobile browser (see Fig. 21.8).

Figure 21.7 The "Open File or URL..." window

Figure 21.8 ex21-03.wml on the Nokia Mobile Browser

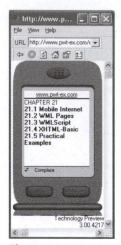

Figure 21.9 ex21-03.wml on Microsoft Mobile Explorer

Don't forget to put the WML page ex21-03.wml in the default directory (e.g., `htdocs`) of Apache.

If you are using Microsoft Mobile Explorer (MME), you can enter "http://www.pwt-ex.com/ex21-03.wml" at the URL bar to see the page. A screen shot is shown in Fig. 21.9.

Once your mobile browser can see WML pages via "http://," you will have configured your Web server correctly. Your page should now be available for wireless devices such as mobile phones.

To configure the Microsoft IIS to support WML pages is also easy. For example, if you are using XP Professional, you can activate the IIS window by Start | Control Panel|Administrative Tools|Internet Information Services. Inside the IIS window, if you expand the Web Sites node, you will see the URL of our default Web site www.pwt-ex.com (see Fig. 21.10). Now, perform the following actions:

- Right click on the Web site www.pwt-ex.com and select the "property" option to activate the property window.
- From the menu of the property window, select "HTTP Headers" (see Fig. 21.10).
- Click the file types and press the New Types button to open a "File Type" window (see Fig. 21.11).

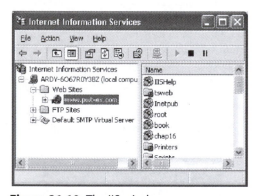

Figure 21.10 The IIS window

Figure 21.11 The file type window

- In the "File Type" window, enter the file extension and the MIME as illustrated in Fig. 21.11. Click the OK button to register the file type.
- Open another "File Type" window to register another WML file type until all file types have been registered (see Figs 21.12 and 21.13).

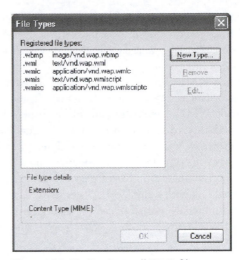

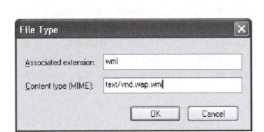

Figure 21.12 Select the HTTP headers   **Figure 21.13** Register all WML file types

Now your IIS Web server can deliver and support WML pages, let's start to write some Mobile Internet pages using WML.

21.2.3 The basic elements of WML

WML is a markup language based on XML. In fact, many people consider WML as a special implementation of XML with XHTML style and elements. WML is used to create WML pages (or Mobile Internet pages) that can be displayed on a WAP browser.

A WAP browser or micro-browser is a small piece of software usually installed on wireless devices and makes minimal demands on hardware, memory, and CPU power. Wireless devices with a micro-browser can display information written in WML.

A structural diagram of WML is shown in Fig. 21.14.

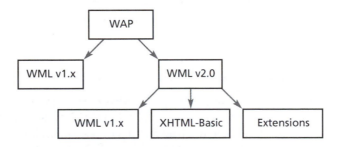

Figure 21.14 Development diagram of WML

WML was created by the industry association WAP Forum and has gone through two versions. Pages written by WML v1.x (version 1) are called decks, which are constructed as a set of cards using the `<card>` element. Together with some extensions, WML version 2 has adopted a special version of XHTML called XHTML-Basic as a default language to strengthen the capability of Web browsing. For backward compatibility, WML v2.0 also includes previous versions.

Since most mobile or wireless devices are still using WML v1.x, we will show you how to write version 1 WML pages in sections 21.3.1 to 21.3.4. XHTML-Basic will be discussed in section 21.3.5. If you want to develop all-singing and dancing Mobile Internet pages that work on all devices, WML v1.x may be your best (if not only) option.

On a WML page, after the WML header, the contents are defined by a series of cards. Each card is specified by the element `<card>` in XML syntax. Inside each card, you can have all kinds of ways of designing or formatting WML elements to control the display. In normal circumstances, only one card can be displayed at a time. Each card can be considered as a new page connected together by a link. Instead of having a large number of WML pages sitting on Web servers, related WML pages are implemented as cards so that the WAP gateway can compile them all together and send them to your mobile phone. Technically, this process is the same as sending a number of pages to your mobile device at the same time. Unless you want to activate an external link with other WML pages, cards can be navigated on your mobile. This feature is particularly useful to accommodate a small screen for small devices such as mobile phones.

A typical framework for a WML page is shown in the next example:

```
Example: ex21-04.wml - An Example Framework For WML Pages

 1: <?xml version="1.0"?>
 2: <!DOCTYPE wml PUBLIC "-//WAPFORUM//DTD WML 1.3//EN"
 3: "http://www.wapforum.org/DTD/wml_1.3.xml">
 4: <wml>
 5:   <card id = "card1" title = "Card1 Title">
 6:   <p>
 7:     This is card1 <br />
 8:     WML Formatting Elements Are Here.
 9:   </p>
10:   </card>
11:
12:   <card id = "card2" title = "Card2 Title">
13:   <p>
14:     This is card2 <br />
15:     WML Formatting Elements Are Here.
16:   </p>
17:   </card>
18: </wml>
```

This example defines a WML page with two cards. However, an example like this is not very useful because, first, there is no link between `card1` and `card2` – only `card1` is displayed; and second, there are no formatting features or elements defined in the page.

21.2.4 The text formatting and table elements in WML

In order to make this page a bit more interesting, we need to add some formatting power to it. Unlike most of the markup languages or technologies on the Web such as HTML/XHTML, ASP, Perl, PHP, etc., the text formatting power of WML is very primitive. In most cases, you cannot even control the font face and size as you want. Some frequently used formatting elements in WML are listed in Table 21.3.

As we can see from the table, the elements are identical to XHTML. Bear in mind that the formatting elements used in WML are a special subset of XHTML. Also, not all mobile devices are capable of displaying all features of the formatting elements.

Table 21.3 WML elements

WML element	Purpose	WML element	Purpose
`<b>`	Defines bold text	` `	Defines a line break
`<big>`	Defines big text	`<p>`	Defines a paragraph
`<em>`	Defines emphasized text	`<a>`	Defines an anchor (link)
`<i>`	Defines italic text	`<img>`	Defines an image
`<small>`	Defines small text	`<table>`	Defines a table
`<strong>`	Defines strong text	`<td>`	Defines a table cell (table data)
`<u>`	Defines underlined text	`<tr>`	Defines a table row

When you design your WML pages, knowing your target clients and the capabilities of the devices is important. Consider the following text formatting example (ex21-05.wml):

```
Example: ex21-05.wml - Text Formatting Using WML

 1: <?xml version="1.0"?>
 2: <!DOCTYPE wml PUBLIC "-//WAPFORUM//DTD WML 1.3//EN"
 3: "http://www.wapforum.org/DTD/wml_1.3.xml">
 4: <wml>
 5: <card title="Text Formatting">
 6:     <p align="center"> Center Text </p>
 7:     <p align="right"> Right Text    </p>
 8:     <p>          Normal Text <br />
 9:      <em>       Emphasized Text  </em>     <br />
10:      <strong> Strong Text        </strong><br />
11:      <b>        Bold Text        </b>      <br />
12:      <i>        Italic Text      </i>      <br />
13:      <u>        Underline Text   </u>      <br />
14:      <big>      Big Text         </big>    <br />
15:      <small>    Small Text       </small>
16:     </p>
17: </card>
18: </wml>
```

This WML page contains a number of text formatting features. For example, a string or message can be placed at the center, right, and left as illustrated in lines 6–8. Some other formatting elements are demonstrated in the rest of the example code. Since most screens of mobile devices are small, we don't have the luxury of control over the font face or font size (not until WML v2.0 and XHTML-Basic).

Also, CSS or more precisely the Wireless CSS is not supported in WML v1.x. We cannot use any CSS properties (at least not yet!). Instead, in order to place a string at the center of the screen, the "align" attribute is used in association with the paragraph element `<p>`. A screen shot of this example is shown in Fig. 21.15. Since not many mobile devices have the capability to display all text format features, we use the Nokia Mobile Browser to demonstrate the result.

The table element is an important formatting tool in XHTML and widely used in this book. The next example is to show you how to use the table element on a WML page. Consider the following example code:

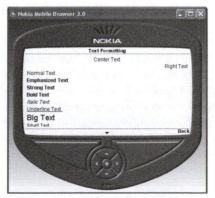

Figure 21.15 WML text formatting (ex21-05.wml)

```
Example: ex21-06.wml - Text Formatting Using WML
 1: <?xml version="1.0"?>
 2: <!DOCTYPE wml PUBLIC "-//WAPFORUM//DTD WML 1.3//EN"
 3: "http://www.wapforum.org/DTD/wml_1.3.xml">
 4: <wml>
 5: <card id="card1" title="WML Table" newcontext = "true">
 6: <p align="center">WAP Phone Prices
 7: <table columns="2">
 8:    <tr><td>Color Screen Phone </td><td> 80</td></tr>
 9:    <tr><td>Multi-function Phone </td><td> 50</td></tr>
10:    <tr><td>WAP Phone</td><td> 30</td></tr>
11: </table>
12: </p>
13: </card>
14: </wml>
```

This is a WML page to display a price list for WAP phones. The price listing is formatted by a table element with three rows and two columns. In order to format a table correctly and effectively, you may need to specify the number of columns at the beginning of the table element as illustrated in line 7. If the number of columns doesn't match the number of <td> elements in any one row (e.g., <tr>), an error will occur. A screen shot of this example is shown in Fig. 21.16.

Figure 21.16 WML table
(ex21-06.wml)

21.2.5 Displaying images on the Mobile Internet

To display an image on a WML page is easy: all you have to do is to define it with an image element <img>. However, due to the restrictions of wireless devices such as memory and CPU power, WML v1.x supports only one image format called Wireless BMP (or WBMP). Your favorite Web browser such as IE or NS may not support it. A WBMP file is specified by the WAP authority as the standard image format to be displayed on a wireless device. This format is in fact a black & white, uncompressed, simple BMP file.

You don't need to write programs for WBMP images. There is free software on the Internet that will allow you to convert an existing image file to WBMP format. Some of the software will even allow you to convert a large number of different image formats into WBMP.

The Nokia MIT also has a utility to convert other images instantly into WBMP format. For example, you can go to File | Open from the toolkit window and then select the JPEG image file dvd.jpg into the utility and save it as dvd.wbmp on your machine (see Fig. 21.17).

Now you can develop a WML page to offer, say, entry to a lucky draw for a DVD player. Consider the example below:

```
Example: ex21-07.wml - Using WBMP Image

 1: <?xml version = "1.0"?>
 2: <!DOCTYPE wml PUBLIC "-//WAPFORUM//DTD WML 1.3//EN"
 3: "http://www.wapforum.org/DTD/wml_1.3.xml">
 4: <wml>
 5:  <card id = "Index" title = "Free Draw Today">
 6:   <p align="center">
 7:     A DVD Player.<br />
 8:     <img src="dvd.wbmp" alt="pic" />
 9:   </p>
10: </card>
11: </wml>
```

By Web browser standards, the WBMP image is a little short of impressive. However, when displayed on a mobile phone, it looks fine (see Fig. 21.18). Remember that until the full acceptance of WML version 2, WBMP may be the only available choice to display images across all mobile devices.

Figure 21.17 The pic2wbmp utility

Figure 21.18 ex21-07.wml

21.3 Mobile Internet pages with WML II

21.3.1 Controlling WML cards

As we mentioned earlier, every WML page is similar to a deck of cards. Some people may refer to WML pages as deck or card applications. Cards can be considered as a tiny page displayed on your mobile device. In fact, for some mobile phones, the internal operations in the Options menu are implemented as cards.

Although the WAP gateway compiles all the cards and sends them to your mobile phone, the micro-browser only displays one card at a time. Therefore navigation among cards is an important characteristic of WML pages.

In general, all WML v1.x pages consist of cards. Each card is defined by the following format:

```
<card id="CardId" title="CardTitle" >
   Some WML Formatting Elements
</card>
```

You can have as many cards as you like (in theory). The id attribute is used to identify the individual card so that navigating among cards is possible. One simple way to navigate among cards is to use the anchor element. Consider the following example:

```
Example: ex21-08.wml - Navigating Among Cards

 1: <?xml version="1.0"?>
 2: <!DOCTYPE wml PUBLIC "-//WAPFORUM//DTD WML 1.3//EN"
 3: "http://www.wapforum.org/DTD/wml_1.3.xml">
 4: <wml>
 5: <card id="Index" title="Mobile Shopping">
 6:  <p>
 7:    <a href="#Card2">Buy A New Phone?</a> <br />
 8:    <a href="http://www.pwt-ex.com/ex21-07.wml#Index">Free Draw?</a><br />
 9: </p>
10: </card>
11:
12: <card id="Card2" title="MM128 Color Phone">
13:  <p>
14:    Large Color Screen<br />
15:    Full WML Features <br />
16:    Price xx (50% Discount)<br />
17:    Call 0800-12345678
18:  </p>
19: </card>
20: </wml>
```

This is a WML page with two cards. The identity of the first card is "Index" and that of the second card is "Card2." You can use the following anchor element to jump from the first card to the second one (see line 7):

```
<a href="#Card2">Buy A New Phone?</a>
```

As usual, your mobile device will underline the text between the <a> tags. When you select the underlined text using the navigation keys on your mobile, the href action will jump to the "Card2" identified by the id value. Line 8 is another example of using the anchor element to jump to another WML page and card on that page.

In fact, this page is a product promotion to sell color screen mobile phones. The second card contains some details of the phone. Suppose your device has some navigation keys such as "Up," "Down," "Left," "Right," and "Select." If you press the Select button on your mobile phone or device, you will see "Card2" on your screen. Some screen shots are shown in Figs 21.19 and 21.20.

Figure 21.19 ex21-08.wml

Figure 21.20 The Card2 of ex21-08.wml

Now you can navigate from one card to another using the anchor element, you may want to add a jump from "Card2" to the previous one by using another anchor element. Another way to do this is to use the element <do> to trigger a task. For example, consider the following example ex21-09.wml:

```
Example: ex21-09.wml - The Use Of <do> Element
 1:  <?xml version="1.0"?>
 2:  <!DOCTYPE wml PUBLIC "-//WAPFORUM//DTD WML 1.3//EN"
 3:  "http://www.wapforum.org/DTD/wml_1.3.xml">
 4:  <wml>
 5:  <card id="Index" title="Mobile Shopping">
 6:   <p>
 7:    <a href="#Card2">Buy A New Phone?</a> <br />
 8:    <a href="http://www.pwt-ex.com/ex21-07.wml#Index">Free Draw?</a><br />
 9:   </p>
10:  </card>
11:
12:  <card id="Card2" title="MM128 Color Phone">
13:  <do type="accept" label="Back"> <prev/> </do>
14:   <p>
15:       Large Color Screen<br />
16:       Full WML Features <br />
17:       Price xx (50% Discount)<br />
18:       Call 0800-12345678
19:   </p>
20:  </card>
21:  </wml>
```

This page is basically the same as ex21-08.wml but with a do statement added in line 13:

```
<do type="accept" label="Back"> <prev/> </do>
```

This is a do element with `type="accept"` and `label="Back"`. As a result, this will force your mobile device to accept `"Back"` as a new option assigned to a soft key. For some mobile phones, you can find the "Back" option in the Options menu (see Fig. 21.20). Some mobile devices may display this "Back" option at the bottom right corner of screen. When this option is selected, the element `<prev />` will bring you back to the previous card.

As a more practical example, let's consider a WML page to report the weather in some cities. Our weather report page is a simple one containing four cities: London, New York, Tokyo, and Paris. You can pick one city and jump to the weather report for that city. Each weather report has a Back button so that you can go back to the main page. Some screen shots of this example are shown in Figs 21.21 and 21.22.

Figure 21.21 ex21-10.wml

Figure 21.22 Weather report

Sometimes, a WML page like this is quite handy. You can check the weather anywhere in the world with your mobile device. Furthermore, the page can also be used as a warning page for holiday makers and travelers. For example, if there is a violent storm about to hit a city, you would not recommend that people travel there. Even better, you could modify this page to become a last-minute "Travel Warning" page by putting on it all cities with severe weather conditions.

The coding of this page is listed below:

Example: ex21-10.wml – A WML Page For Weather Report

```
 1: <?xml version="1.0"?>
 2: <!DOCTYPE wml PUBLIC "-//WAPFORUM//DTD WML 1.3//EN"
 3: "http://www.wapforum.org/DTD/wml_1.3.xml">
 4: <wml>
 5:   <card id="Index" title="City Weather">
 6:      <p>
 7:       <a href="#London">London</a>
 8:       <a href="#NewYork">New York</a>
 9:       <a href="#Tokyo">Tokyo</a>
10:       <a href="#Paris">Paris</a>
11:     </p>
12:   </card>
13:
14:   <card id="London" title="London Weather">
15:       <do type="accept" label="Back"> <prev/> </do>
16:       <p>
17:          Rainy Day<br/>Temp: Max. 8C, Min. 1C <br />
18:          Air Pollution (Med)
19:       </p>
20:   </card>
21:   <card id="NewYork" title="New York Weather">
22:     <do type="accept" label="Back"> <prev/> </do>
23:     <p>
24:          Sunny Day<br/>temp: Max. 4C, Min. -4C <br />
25:          Air Pollution (Med)
26:     </p>
27:   </card>
28:   <card id="Tokyo" title="Tokyo Weather">
29:     <do type="accept" label="Back"> <prev/> </do>
30:     <p>
31:          Sunny Day<br/>Temp: Max. 7C, Min. 0C <br />
32:          Air Pollution (Med)
33:     </p>
34:   </card>
35:   <card id="Paris" title="Paris Weather">
36:     <do type="accept" label="Back"> <prev/> </do>
37:     <p>
38:          Very Windy<br/>Temp: Max. 4C, Min. -3C <br />
39:          Air Pollution (Med)
40:     </p>
41:   </card>
42: </wml>
```

With the explanations above, this page is easy to read. Although the screen of a mobile device is black and white and usually small, it doesn't mean we cannot do something interesting. Let's see how to animate a WBMP picture using WML cards.

21.3.2 Creating animated pictures (WBMP) on WML pages

The idea of how to animate a WBMP image is straightforward. The whole process can be summarized in two steps:

Step 1: Use one card to store one image using the usual `<img>` element.

Step 2: Install a timer on each card so that it will switch from one card to another.

A typical and simple code fragment to perform these steps is illustrated as follows:

```
<card id="image1" ontimer="#image2">
    <timer value="10" />
    <p align="center">
       <img src="img01.wbmp" alt="img01" />
    </p></card>
<card id="image2">
    <p align="center">
      <img src="img02.wbmp" alt="img02" />
    </p></card>
```

The first line of this code fragment defines a card with identity `image1`. Along with the identity, we have installed a timer using the attribute `ontimer="#image2"`. It says that once the time is up, jump to the card with `id="#image2"`. The second line of this code fragment defines the value of the timer and in this case it is 1 second. By switching a series of cards and images, we have animated effects even on a tiny mobile screen.

As a practical example, we consider an animated WBMP sequence to deliver email. This example can be used to notify a user when a new email has arrived.

Example: ex21-11.wml – An Animated WBMP Image To Deliver Email

```
 1: <?xml version="1.0"?>
 2: <!DOCTYPE wml PUBLIC "-//WAPFORUM//DTD WML 1.3//EN"
 3: "http://www.wapforum.org/DTD/wml_1.3.xml">
 4: <wml>
 5:   <card id="image1" ontimer="#image2" title="WML Email">
 6:       <timer value="10" />
 7:       <p align="center">
 8:          <img src="img1.wbmp" alt="img1" />
 9:       </p></card>
10:   <card id="image2" ontimer="#image3" title="WML Email">
11:       <timer value="5" />
12:       <p align="center">
13:         <img src="img2.wbmp" alt="img2" />
14:       </p></card>
15:   <card id="image3" ontimer="#image4" title="WML Email">
16:       <timer value="5" />
17:       <p align="center">
18:         <img src="img3.wbmp" alt="img3" />
19:       </p></card>
20:   <card id="image4" ontimer="#image5" title="WML Email">
21:       <timer value="5" />
22:       <p align="center">
23:         <img src="img4.wbmp" alt="img4" />
24:       </p></card>
25:   <card id="image5" ontimer="#image6" title="WML Email">
26:       <timer value="10" />
27:       <p align="center">
28:         <img src="img5.wbmp" alt="img5" />
29:       </p></card>
30:   <card id="image6" ontimer="#card2" title="WML Email">
31:       <timer value="10" />
```

```
32:          <p align="center">
33:            <img src="img6.wbmp" alt="img6" />
34:          </p></card>
35:
36:     <card id="card2" title="WML Email" ontimer="#image1">
37:          <timer value="15" />
38:          <p align="center">
39:            You Have Email<br /><br />
40:            <a href="#card3">Save Email</a>
41:          </p></card>
42:     <card id="card3" title="WML Email">
43:          <p align="center"><br />
44:            Email Saved!<br />
45:          </p></card>
46: </wml>
```

This page contains six WBMP images from img1.wbmp to img6.wmp. They are hardwired into a series of WML cards with identities from `image1` to `image6` (see lines 5–34). Each card has a timer installed so that control will switch from one card to another forming an animated sequence.

After the animated image, there is a card called `card2` (lines 36-41) to output a text message to let you know you have a new email. Inside this card, there is also an action text (line 40) defined by an anchor element <a> so that you have a choice whether to save the email. If the action text "Save Email" is not pressed within the timer limit, the animated sequence will start again. If the action text is activated, control jumps to the next card to display "Email Saved."

Some screen shots of this example are shown in Figs 21.23–21.25.

Figure 21.23 Animated WBMP image I

Figure 21.24 Animated WBMP image II

Figure 21.25 Animated WBMP image III

21.3.3 Obtaining user input with text boxes

Now we have some experience of the structure and style of WML, it's time to learn more about how to use them in real applications.

Similar to XHTML, WML also contains input elements to allow a user to enter information. For example, the following input element is used to define a text box:

```
<input name="MyText" value="" maxlength="20" />
```

This element defines a text box called "MyText" with a maximum length of 20 characters. Unlike XHTML, the `type` attribute is not used to define a text box here. The `value` attribute is used to predefine a string for the text box value.

The `name` attribute is important if you want to gain access to the value of this text box. For example, if you give the name of the box as "MyText," you can access the value of the box or the input information by using the variable

```
$MyText
```

By putting a dollar sign in front of the name, you can use it anywhere on the page. Consider a simple example to send short email messages below:

```
Example: ex21-12.wml - Obtain User Input With Text Boxes

 1: <?xml version="1.0"?>
 2: <!DOCTYPE wml PUBLIC "-//WAPFORUM//DTD WML 1.3//EN"
 3: "http://www.wapforum.org/DTD/wml_1.3.xml">
 4: <wml>
 5:  <card id="index" title="Short Email" newcontext = "true">
 6:   <p>
 7:     From: <input name="From" value="jo@pwt-ex.com" maxlength="20"/>
 8:     To:   <input name="To"   value="" maxlength="20"/>
 9:     Msg:  <input name="Msg"  value="" maxlength="40"/>
10:     <a href="#Card2">Send</a>
11:   </p>
12:  </card>
13:  <card id="Card2" title="Sent Email">
14:   <p>
15:     From: $From <br/>
16:     To: $To <br/>
17:     Mg: $Msg<br />
18:   </p>
19:  </card>
20: </wml>
```

This example can be used as an interface to send short email messages to someone on the Internet. The page contains two cards. The first card has three input boxes (lines 7–8) and one anchor element (line 9). The first two input fields (lines 7–8) specify the email address of the sender and receiver. You can put a default address into the "From" field so that you don't need to enter the information. The third input field (line 9) is where you can enter your message.

In fact, when you define three text boxes as in lines 7–9, you create three WML variables, namely, $From, $To, and $Msg. They are used to store the data corresponding to the "From," "To," and "Msg" boxes.

Once the information has been filled in and the Send button is selected, Card2 is activated to display the variables and hence the input result. Some screen shots are shown in Figs 21.26–21.28.

Figure 21.26 Filling in the receiver's address

Figure 21.27 Filling in the email message

Figure 21.28 The results of the input data

The Send button in Fig. 21.27 was created by an anchor element in line 10. When you press this button, Card2 is activated to display the input data.

Unlike your computer, most mobile devices don't have the luxury of a full-size keyboard and therefore entering lots of information using the handset may be an uncomfortable task. Another popular feature for Mobile Internet pages is the select element <select>.

21.3.4 Single and multiple selections

Similar to XHTML, select boxes on a WML page are defined by the select element. The options inside the selection are specified by the option element `<option>`. The only difference is that the value of the selected item is stored in the variable defined as the name of the select element. Consider the following example:

```
Example: ex21-13.wml - Using Select Element In WML

 1: <?xml version="1.0"?>
 2: <!DOCTYPE wml PUBLIC "-//WAPFORUM//DTD WML 1.3//EN"
 3: "http://www.wapforum.org/DTD/wml_1.3.xml">
 4: <wml>
 5:  <card id="index" title="Occupation Info" newcontext = "true">
 6:   <p>Please Select One:
 7:     <select name="Occupation">
 8:      <option value="Student">Student</option>
 9:      <option value="Engineer">Engineer</option>
10:      <option value="Programmer">Programmer</option>
11:      <option value="Others">Others</option>
12:     </select>
13:     <a href="#Card2">Send</a>
14:   </p>
15:  </card>
16:
17:  <card id="Card2" title="Your Occupation">
18:  <do type="accept" label="Back"><prev /></do>
19:   <p>
20:      ==> $Occupation <br/>
21:   </p>
22:  </card>
23: </wml>
```

Again, this page contains two cards. The first card contains a select element `<select>` and four options. The select element creates a selection framework and the four options form the selectable items. In this case, you can pick one item as your occupation. Your selection is stored in the variable $Occupation which is specified in the name attribute. After you have picked the item and pressed the Send button, Card2 is activated and your selection is output to the screen. Some screen shots are shown in Figs 21.29–21.31.

Figure 21.29 Activate the selection

Figure 21.30 Making the selection

Figure 21.31 Displaying the selected result

If your device has a tiny screen, you may see a form similar to Fig. 21.29. The first option "Student" (see line 8) appears in the brackets. When you activate the selection, your device will open another window to display all selectable items or options as illustrated in Fig. 21.30. You may use your navigation keys to select your choice. Your choice will appear in the bracket area in Fig. 21.29. When you press the "Send" underlined text, Card2 is activated and your new selection will appear on your screen as in Fig. 21.31.

This arrangement may look strange, but it is useful for displaying a number of select elements on a tiny screen. By ignoring all other selectable items on the main card, more select boxes can be allocated to one screen for particular information.

If your device has a bigger screen (compared to a mobile phone) such as a PDA or smart phone, this example ex21-13.wml may have the display as in Figs 21.32–21.34.

Figure 21.32 Display all selections

Figure 21.33 Making the selection

Figure 21.34 Displaying the selected result

As you can see from Fig. 21.32, all options are displayed when the page is loaded. In other words, WML is a language for Mobile Internet pages, but it doesn't specify every detail on how individual devices should act or behave.

Another frequently used input element on the Mobile Internet is the multiple select. If you operate a shop on the Mobile Internet, you will be delighted when your customers buy more than one or all of the items you offer. Consider the following example:

Example: ex21-14.wml Multiple Selections Using WML

```
 1: <?xml version="1.0"?>
 2: <!DOCTYPE wml PUBLIC "-//WAPFORUM//DTD WML 1.3//EN"
 3: "http://www.wapforum.org/DTD/wml_1.3.xml">
 4: <wml>
 5:  <card id="index" title="Shopping By Phone" newcontext = "true">
 6:    <p>Product Catalog:
 7:     <select name="buy" multiple="true">
 8:      <option value="PDA">Color PDA(100)</option>
 9:      <option value="DVD">DVD Player(100)</option>
10:      <option value="Cam">Digital Camera(60)</option>
11:      <option value="pho">Smart Phone(120)</option>
12:     </select>
13:     <a href="#Card2">Send</a>
14:   </p>
15:  </card>
16:  <card id="Card2" title="Thank you">
17:  <do type="accept" label="Back"><prev /></do>
18:   <p>You have picked:<br/>
19:        $buy <br/>
20:   </p>
21:  </card>
22: </wml>
```

This is a "Shopping By Phone" example. The product catalog has four items to sell. They are arranged by a select element in lines 7–12. The `multiple` attribute used in line 7 indicates that this is a multiple select box and therefore more than one choice can be made. After some selections have been made, the Send button will call `Card2` to display the result. Some screen shots are shown in Figs 21.35–21.37.

Figure 21.35 Display product catalog

Figure 21.36 Making the multiple selection

Figure 21.37 Displaying the selected result

For a mobile phone with a tiny screen, the opening window (Fig. 21.35) may not show any of the multiple choices. The multiple options are shown in another window instead (see Fig. 21.36) so that you can mark or unmark the items. When Done is pressed, you will return to Fig. 21.35 with all the choices. If you press the Send button, your multiple selections will be displayed as in Fig. 21.37. If you have a large-screen mobile phone, your display may be different.

While WML v1.x functions well and is a global standard for mobile applications, the WAP Forum has released a major specification called version 2 of WML dedicated to the next generation of WAP and wireless devices.

21.3.5 WML v2.x and XHTML-Basic

The technology is advancing daily. It is believed that the next generation of mobile phone or wireless devices will no longer be restricted by the processing power, memory, and screen size architecture. Mobile devices such as large color screen phones, PDAs, and smart phones (PDA + mobile phone) are already on the market. We can see that higher user demand and functionalities are inevitable. In fact, according to the WAP Forum, the future of WAP lies in its close alignment with the Internet standard and community such as the Web. This is why the WAP Forum and the World Wide Web Consortium (W3C) have joined together to define the next Mobile Internet standard called WML v2.x. In fact, the WAP Forum has adopted the XHTML-Basic standard from W3C as the basis for WML and WAP 2.0.

According to W3C, XHTML-Basic is a special version of XHTML to define a document type which is rich enough to format pages across different classes of device such as desktop computers, PDAs, TVs, and mobile handsets. Essentially, XHTML-Basic is an adaptation of XHTML 1.0 containing every element of it except those not appropriate for devices with small screens such as frames. Also, WML version 2 supports a subset of CSS1 called Wireless CSS (or WCSS) as an extension of XHTML-Basic so that WML pages can use styles. In order to maintain services and support for millions of mobile devices around the world, WML v2.x also includes full support for WML v1.x.

To have XHTML capability on mobile devices is great. However, when designing Mobile Internet pages, certain differences between mobile devices and PCs need to be considered. Apart from the physical differences such as screen size and power, the main issue is that a Mobile Internet page is designed for people with mobility. A typical WML page should offer *brief*, *exact*, and *quick* information to the client rather than to the browser. Based on this, the following are some guidelines for designing Mobile Internet pages with XHTML-Basic:

- Try to avoid messages longer than the display.
- Try to keep the length of your page to a minimum (four or five lines).
- Try to avoid excessive use of colors on one page.
- Always target your mobile device and test it before uploading it to the server.

It is true that XHTML-Basic can deliver the full features of a Web page. However, it would upset most (if not all) of your mobile users. Don't forget that most mobile device users are paying the cost per minute. Try your best to reduce your clients' airtime costs.

Instead of providing a full account of what elements are available on XHTML-Basic, we will provide a simple table of elements and features not supported by XHTML-Basic or WML2.x, as in Table 21.4.

Table 21.4 Elements and features not supported by XHTML-Basic

Element	Features not supported
`<body>`	`bgcolor`,`text`, or `link`
`<frame>`	Frames are not supported
Text related	`<center>`,`<font>`,`<s>`,`<tt>`,`<b>`,`<big>`,`<i>`,`<small>`, and `<u>`
Form related	`<button>` or `<input type="button" ..>`
Table related	`align`,`cellpadding`,`cellspacing`,`width`,`height`, and `border`
`<img>`	`align`,`border`,`usemap`,`hspace`, and `vspace`
`<script>`	Scripts are not supported

As we can see from this table, most of the XHTML pages developed in this book are characterized as XHTML-Basic standard. To develop an XHTML-Basic page is easy. Consider the example below:

```
Example: ex21-15.xhtml - XHTML-Basic Used On WAP

 1: <?xml version="1.0"?>
 2: <!DOCTYPE html PUBLIC "-//W3C//DTD XHTML Basic 1.0//EN"
 3: "http://www.w3.org/TR/xhtml-basic/xhtml-basic10.dtd" >
 4: <html xmlns="http://www.w3.org/1999/xhtml">
 5: <head>
 6:    <title>XHTML-Basic</title>
 7: </head>
 8: <body style="font-family:arial">
 9:
10: <h1 style="text-align:center">Header Demo</h1>
11: <div class="h">
12:    <h1>Heading H1 &lt;h1&gt;</h1>
13:    <h2>Heading H2 &lt;h2&gt;</h2>
14:    <h3>Heading H3 &lt;h3&gt;</h3>
15:    <h4>Heading H4 &lt;h4&gt;</h4>
16:    <h5>Heading H5 &lt;h5&gt;</h5>
17: </div>
18:
19: <h1 style="text-align:center">Table Demo &lt;table&gt;</h1>
20: <table>
21:  <tr><td>Name</td><td>Phone No.</td>
22:      <td>Name</td><td>Phone No.</td></tr>
23:  <tr><td>Tom</td><td>1892-5312</td>
24:      <td>Mary</td><td>1891-3344</td></tr>
25:  <tr><td>John</td><td>1892-1234</td>
26:      <td>Anna</td><td>1891-3456</td></tr>
```

```
27:   <tr><td>Peter</td><td>1892-5432</td>
28:       <td>Susan</td><td>1891-2133</td></tr>
29:  </table><br />
30:
31:  <h1 style="text-align:center">Image Demo &lt;img&gt;</h1>
32:    <img src="logo01.gif" alt="pic" />
33:  <br /><br />
34:
35:  </body>
36:  </html>
```

This is a simple page to demonstrate some frequently used features of XHTML-Basic. Three basic features are illustrated: the text formatting (lines 10–17), table (lines 20–29), and the use of image (lines 31–33). All features are identical to XHTML. Some screen shots of this example are shown in Figs 21.38–21.40.

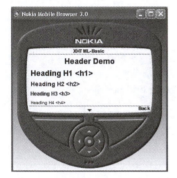

Figure 21.38 Header element demo

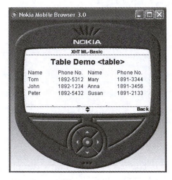

Figure 21.39 Table element demo

Figure 21.40 Image demo

The inline style of the page is not a part of the XHTML-Basic standard. In fact, the WAP Forum includes the inline style as an XHTML-extension and is a part of WML v2.0.

Now we know that we are fully prepared for the next generation of wireless devices and the markup language (XHTML-Basic) for them.

For the Web environment, ECMAScript is a powerful tool and the engine on the Web browser for client-side functions and data processing. For the WAP environment, the counterpart is called Wireless Markup Language Script (or WMLScript).

21.4   Using WMLScript with WML pages

21.4.1 What is WMLScript and how does it work?

Basically, WMLScript is a client-side script language based on ECMAScript and dedicated for low-bandwidth devices such as a mobile phone. Many people may refer to WMLScript as the ECMAScript dialect for wireless applications. Unlike ECMAScript, WMLScript functions or statements are not defined inside a WML page. Instead, all WMLScript language or statements are stored in another file with file extension `.wmls` (Wireless Markup Language Script).

When your WML page calls a WMLScript function, you call the reference of the function by URL. When a function of WMLScript is called, the script is compiled into byte code by the WAP gateway and then sent to the micro-browser for interpretation.

Apart from the difference above, WMLScript shares the same structure and style of ECMAScript including variables, function declarations, and many standard library functions. In fact, the programming techniques of the two are basically the same and interchangeable.

First, consider the simple WML page below:

Example: ex21-16.wml- My First WMLScript

```
 1: <?xml version="1.0"?>
 2: <!DOCTYPE wml PUBLIC "-//WAPFORUM//DTD WML 1.3//EN"
 3: "http://www.wapforum.org/DTD/wml_1.3.xml">
 4: <wml>
 5: <card id="Line" title="First WMLScript">
 6:  <onevent type="onenterforward">
 7:      <go href="ex21-16.wmls#hello()" />
 8:  </onevent>
 9:      <p> $message </p>
10:  </card>
11: </wml>
```

This is a WML page (not WMLScript) containing only one card. Inside this card, an event with type `onenterforward` (lines 6–8) is defined so that when the card is loaded, the following action is activated:

```
<go href="ex21-16.wmls#hello()" />
```

This `go` represents the calling format for WMLScript and its function. In this case, the `go` action will jump to the WMLScript file ex21-16.wmls and execute the function `hello()`. As you might expect, the `hello()` function is used to construct a string and store it in the variable `$message`. When this WML page is refreshed, the statement in line 9 displays the message on the screen.

The details of the WMLScript and `hello()` function are listed below:

Example: ex21-16.wmls – WMLScript File For ex21-16.wml

```
1: extern function hello()
2: {
3:   WMLBrowser.setVar( "message",
4:       "Hello World! \n I know WMLScript now." );
5:   WMLBrowser.refresh();
6: }
```

This WMLScript contains one function called `hello()`. The function is declared as `extern` (external) so that it can be called by other cards and applications. The first statement inside the `hello()` function is

```
WMLBrowser.setVar( "message",
    "Hello World! \n I know WMLScript now." );
```

In fact, this is a function called `setVar()` from the `WMLBrowser` object. The purpose of this function is to set a value to a variable. In this case, the entire string in line 4 is stored in the variable `message`. Therefore, the statement in line 9 of ex21-16.wml can be used to print out the "Hello World!..." message. The new line symbol "\n" in line 4 is to generate a line break so that multiple lines can be generated in one string.

Another statement in the `hello()` function is

```
WMLBrowser.refresh();
```

This `refresh()` function from the `WMLBrowser` object is to refresh the WML page ex21-16.wml so that the message is displayed. A screen shot is shown in Fig. 21.41.

Figure 21.41 My First WMLScript

This example demonstrates two important points. First, apart from the user-defined function `hello()`, standard WMLScript functions are methods of objects. In this case, the two functions

```
WMLBrowser.setVar()
WMLBrowser.refresh()
```

are methods of the standard `WMLBrowser` object. The second important point is that the main purpose of WMLScript is to perform computations and process the data for the main page. Soon after the computations, control is usually transferred back to the main page. Now let's consider some more WMLScript and functions.

21.4.2 The standard WMLScript libraries and functions

Compared to ECMAScript, WMLScript is smaller. The main components of the entire WMLScript are implemented as six standard objects (or libraries):

- `WMLBrowser` – Contains functions that can be used to access browser variables.
- `Dialogs` – Provides functions to display alert, confirm, and prompt dialog windows.
- `Lang` – Contains a set of functions that are closely related to the WMLScript core such as parsing a string to integer etc.
- `Float` – Contains a set of mathematical functions, mostly about rounding of numbers.
- `String` – Contains functions quite similar to the ones found in the JavaScript `string` object.
- `URL` – Contains a set of functions for handling relative and absolute URLs.

For obvious reasons, only the first three objects are discussed here. The first three libraries and functions should provide a good foundation for us to start WMLScript programming.

The first important library in WMLScript is the `WMLBrowser` library (or object). It provides an essential set of functions to navigate among cards and set global variables for them. A summary of the frequently used functions in the `WMLBrowser` object is listed in Table 21.5.

Table 21.5 Frequently used functions in the `WMLBrowser` object

Function name	Description and example
`getCurrentCard()`	Returns the (relative) URL of the current card, e.g., `var k = WMLBrowser.getCurrentCard();`
`getVar()`	Returns the value of a variable, e.g., `var k = WMLBrowser.getVar("DVDPrice");`
`go()`	Goes to a new card, specified by the new URL, e.g., `var k = WMLBrowser.go(card4);`
`newContext()`	Clears all variables, e.g., `var k = WMLBrowser.newContext();`
`prev()`	The browser goes back to the previous card, e.g., `var k = WMLBrowser.prev();`
`refresh()`	Refreshes the current card, e.g., `var k = WMLBrowser.refresh();`
`setvar()`	Sets the value of a variable, e.g., `var k = WMLBrowser.setVar("DVDPrice", 104);`

As your Mobile Internet experience grows, you will find that the functions in this object are the most often used. Consider an example to use `getCurrentCard()`, `setVar()`, and `go()` as follows:

```
Example: ex21-17.wml - Using The Functions In WMLBrowser Object

 1: <?xml version="1.0"?>
 2: <!DOCTYPE wml PUBLIC "-//WAPFORUM//DTD WML 1.3//EN"
 3: "http://www.wapforum.org/DTD/wml_1.3.xml">
 4: <wml>
 5:  <card id="card1" title="WMLScript">
 6:  <p>
 7:    Run WMLScript to get the name of this card. <br />
 8:    <anchor><go href="ex21-17.wmls#getCard()" />Run</anchor>
 9:  </p>
10:
11:  </card>
12:  <card id="card2" title="WMLScript">
13:  <p>
14:    The Current Card is ex21-17.wml#card2 and the previous card is
15:    $curCard
16:  </p>
17:  </card>
18: </wml>
```

This example will return the identity (or name) of a card. When the action text "Run" defined in line 8 is clicked, the user-defined function `getCard()` in ex21-17.wmls is called. This function will use the standard function `WMLBrowser.getCard()` to find the identity of the current card and return the identity as variable `%curCard` in another card with `id="card2"`.

The WMLScript source file ex21-17.wmls is listed below:

```
Example: ex21-17.wmls - WMLScript File For ex21-17.wml

 1: extern function getCard()
 2: {
 3:   var temp0 = WMLBrowser.getCurrentCard();
 4:   var temp1 = WMLBrowser.setVar("curCard",temp0);
 5:   var temp2 = WMLBrowser.go("#card2");
 6: }
 7:
```

This file contains three statements only. The first statement in line 3 is to get the identity of the card and store it in variable `temp0`. The second statement (line 4) is to set up a variable `curCard` to carry the identity of the card. The final statement is to go back to `card2` so that the value in variable `curCard` is displayed. Some screen shots are shown in Figs 21.42 and 21.43.

Figure 21.42 Getting current card I

Figure 21.43 Getting current card II

The next library is the `Dialogs` object. This object provides a valuable set of functions to generate dialog boxes on the mobile screen. They are valuable tools to get user input. Basically, there are three dialog boxes defined in this object and listed in Table 21.6.

Table 21.6 Frequently used functions in the `Dialogs` objects

Function name	Description and examples
`alert()`	Displays a message and waits for a confirmation, e.g., `var k = Dialogs.alert("The input must be numeric!");`
`confirm()`	Displays a message, waits for an answer, and returns a Boolean value depending on the input, e.g., `var k = Dialogs.confirm("Exit?","Yes","No");`

`prompt()`	Displays a question, waits for an input, and then returns the user's answer,
	e.g., `var k = Dialogs.prompt("Enter a number:","0");`
	`         k = "7"  (if you entered the value 7)`
	`         k = "0"  (if you did not enter a value)`

Although these three dialog functions are simple, they provide an important tool to get user input. For example, if you want a simple solution to get a number from the user and perform some calculation, you may have no choice but to use the `prompt()` function. The examples provided in the table show you how to use them.

The third library we would like to introduce is the `Lang` object. This object provides some simple, yet important functions dedicated to the WMLScript language and is therefore called the `Lang` (language) object.

For example, when you ask your mobile user to input a value, the value is usually represented as a string. Before any calculation can be performed, this string may need to be converted into a number (an integer or a floating point number). Also, if you want to terminate the WMLScript, you may want to use the `abort()` or `exit()` function inside this `Lang` object.

Some frequently used functions in the `Lang` object are listed in Table 21.7.

Table 21.7 Frequently used functions in the `Lang` objects

Function name	Description and examples
`abort()`	Aborts WMLScript and returns a message to the caller of the script, e.g., `Lang.abort("Error.. Program Abort.. ");`
`exit()`	Exits WMLScript and returns a message to the caller of the script, e.g., `Lang.exit("Done !");`

`isFloat()`	Returns true if a specified value can be converted into a floating point number and false if not, e.g., `var a = Lang.isFloat("6.5"); -- true`
	`        var b = Lang.isFloat(" -9.45e2"); -- true`
	`        var c = Lang.isFloat("@432"); -- false`
	`        var c = Lang.isFloat("hello"); -- false`

`isInt()`	Returns true if a specified value can be converted into an integer and false if not, e.g., `var a = Lang.isInt("-576"); -- true` `       var b = Lang.isInt("6.5"); -- false`

`parseFloat()`	Returns a floating-point value defined by a string,
	e.g., `var a = Lang.parseFloat("99.99"); -- (a=99.99)`
	`       var b = Lang.parseFloat("-.3 C"); -- (b=-0.3)`
	`       var c = Lang.parseFloat("100 pt"); -- (c=100)`

`parseInt()`	Returns an integer defined by a string, e.g., `var a = Lang.parseInt("2345"); -- (a=2345)` `var b = Lang.parseInt("200 dollar"); -- (b=200)`

These functions are simple to use and the examples in the table provide a good starting point. From the selection of functions, we can see that the WAP Forum has done a good job in providing a fundamental programming framework for mobile devices.

Now let's consider some applications of WMLScript in m-business.

21.4.3 My first WMLScript on m-business

Many people regard business on mobile devices (m-business), including shopping and trading, as the next generation for business in parallel with or even replacing e-commerce in the Web sense. Whether m-business will merge with e-commerce or not, m-business is certainly an attractive subject. We can see that more and more funds are being pumped into research and development by the big mobile companies driven by customer demand.

Compared to e-commerce, m-business is relatively simple, but more precise, focussed, and decision driven. According to some successful m-business companies and agents, m-business is huge by any standards. Imagine how many people around the world would say yes to the following message on their mobile phones:

```
Send 12 beautiful roses
and a box of chocolates
to your mother on
mother's day (next week)
for xx dollars?
```

If you can make an agreement with the mobile company to charge the customer's account for this service, you will be in business – even better if all you need from your customer is the telephone number of his or her mother instead of the address.

Whether we are in business or not, to write a WML page to display the above message on a mobile phone should not be a problem. To write WMLScript to get the telephone input is also not difficult. Consider the following example:

```
Example: ex21-18.wml – Using WMLScript On M-Business

 1: <?xml version="1.0"?>
 2: <!DOCTYPE wml PUBLIC "-//WAPFORUM//DTD WML 1.3//EN"
 3: "http://www.wapforum.org/DTD/wml_1.3.xml">
 4: <wml>
 5:   <card id="index" title="Mother's Day Offer" newcontext = "true">
 6:     <p>
 7:        12 Roses + A box of chocolates to your mum for xx dollars?
 8:        <anchor><go href="ex21-18.wmls#phone()" />YES</anchor>
 9:     </p>
10:   </card>
11:   <card id="card2" title="Thankyou">
12:    <p>12 Roses + A box of chocolates will arrive
13:        address (Tel: $phone) on mother's day.<br />
14:        XX will be charged to your account.
15:    </p>
16:   </card>
17: </wml>
```

This m-business page displays an attractive text on the mobile screen. While many people are still searching the Internet for a perfect gift for Mother's Day, this text will arrive on your phone to provide convenience. A brief, focussed message will trigger the action. When the user presses the "YES" text, the WMLScript function phone() will be activated to get the telephone number so that delivery can be made. The telephone number is sent back to card2 for confirmation.

The details of the WMLScript are listed below:

```
Example: ex21-18.wmls - WMLScript File For ex21-18.wml

1: extern function phone()
2: {
3:   var temp0=Dialogs.prompt("Your Mother's Phone No.:","");
4:   WMLBrowser.setVar("phone",temp0);
5:   WMLBrowser.go( "#card2" );
6: }
```

In this WMLScript, three standard functions are used:

- `Dialogs.prompt()`
- `WMLBrowser.setVar()`
- `WMLBrowser.go()`

The process again is simple. First, get the user input by a dialog prompt; perform some calculations on the data if you want, then create a variable to be sent back to the main page.

Some screen shots of this example are shown in Figs 21.44–21.46.

Figure 21.44 M-business with WMLScript I

Figure 21.45 M-business with WMLScript II

Figure 21.46 M-business with WMLScript III

For a more general framework for m-business, we will develop an interface for m-business using WMLScript.

21.4.4 Using WMLScript for m-business

For a more general page or interface for m-business, the page should have the capability to perform some calculations. For example, suppose you are offering a special purchase to your mobile users; you would certainly like each of your customers to buy more than one. In this case, to calculate the total charges is essential for the business. Consider the example below:

```
Example: ex21-19.wml - M-Business Page With Calculation

1: <?xml version="1.0"?>
2: <!DOCTYPE wml PUBLIC "-//WAPFORUM//DTD WML 1.3//EN"
3: "http://www.wapforum.org/DTD/wml_1.3.xml">
4: <wml>
5: <card id="index" title="Special Offer" newcontext = "true">
6:   <p>
7:     MA288: A color screen smart phone
8:     (Only <b>120</b>)<br /><br />
```

```
 9:     <anchor><go href="ex21-19.wmls#qty()" />Buy</anchor>
10:   </p>
11:  </card>
12:
13:  <card id="card2" title="Thank you">
14:   <p><b>$count</b>x MA288 ordered <br />
15:      Total: <b> $total </b> will be charged to your account.
16:   </p>
17:   </card>
18: </wml>
```

This example offers a color screen smart phone called MA288. When the user clicks the Buy button (or action text), the statement in line 9 is activated to call the WMLScript function `qty()` in ex21-19.wmls. This `qty()` function uses the function `Dialogs.prompt()` to get the user input. The input is a value to represent the quantity he or she wants to buy. The quantity and the total price are then returned to the second card (card2) to confirm the purchase. Also, charges will be made from the mobile account.

The details of the WMLScript function `qty()` are listed below:

Example: ex21-19.wmls - WMLScript File For ex21-19.wml

```
 1: extern function qty()
 2: {
 3:    var temp0=Dialogs.prompt("How many MA288 do you want?","");
 4:
 5:    var temp1 = Lang.parseInt(temp0);
 6:    WMLBrowser.setVar("count",temp1);
 7:
 8:    var temp2 = temp1 * 120;
 9:    WMLBrowser.setVar("total",temp2);
10:
11:    WMLBrowser.go( "#card2" );
12: }
```

Line 3 is to get the user input. The input result is stored in the variable `temp0`. By default, `temp0` is a variable of string type. The statement in line 5 is used to convert the string into an integer and store it in `temp1`. This `temp1` variable is then assigned to a variable called `count` by

```
WMLBrowser.setVar("count",temp1);
```

Therefore the variable `count` can carry the value back to the main page. Lines 8–9 are used to calculate the total cost for the ordering and assign it to a variable called `total`. At the end, the function

```
WMLBrowser.go( "#card2" );
```

will pass control back to `card2` of the main page. A combination of this process can be used to form a effective interface for m-business. Some screen shots of this example are shown in Figs 21.47–21.49.

Figure 21.47 ex21-19.wml special offer

Figure 21.48 Getting user imput for quality

Figure 21.49 Confirmation of the order

Now, let's ask the big question: "Can we use CGI and database techniques on WML pages?" The answer to this question is "Yes."

21.5   WML applications with CGI and databases

21.5.1 Using Perl script to generate WML pages

From the structure of WAP and WML (see Fig. 21.1), we know that the communications between the WAP gateway and the WAP sites are using the standard HTTP. There is no reason why we cannot use CGI techniques on these WAP sites to deliver a WML page to the WAP gateway. In fact, in this section, we are going to do just that.

We will show you how to construct Perl and PHP scripts to deliver WML pages to a mobile device. Also, by opening up the CGI techniques to WML pages, a new chapter of applications can be created. All the skills that you have learned from this book are applicable to mobile devices. We will also show you how to connect to a MySQL database and build database applications at the end of this chapter. First, let's see how to develop a Perl script on a server that can deliver a WML page to the WAP gateway.

Like almost all server scripting languages, a Perl page is resident inside a server. When it is called, the server will execute all the Perl statements before sending the resulting page to the browser. To use Perl on the microbrowser of mobile devices, all you have to do is to instruct Perl to output all the necessary headers in WML.

Yes! The whole process is as simple as that. One thing you may need to change is the "Content-type" for WML.

As a reminder, when you send a Web page to a browser such as IE or NS using Perl, you need to send the magic string

```
Print "Content-type: text/html\n\n";
```

along with the Web page headers. For the WAP gateway, the magic string is

```
print "Content-type: text/vnd.wap.wml\n\n";
```

After this magic string, you can construct the usual WML headers by Perl and send them off. A typical code fragment in Perl is

```
print "<?xml version=\"1.0\"?>\n";
print "<!DOCTYPE wml PUBLIC \"-//WAPFORUM// DTD WML 1.3//EN\"
      \"http://www.wapforum.org/DTD/wml_1.3.xml\">\n";
print "<wml>\n";
```

Consider a simple "Hello World" example as follows:

```
Example: ex21-20.pl - Using Perl On WML Pages

 1: #! /usr/bin/perl
 2: print "Content-type: text/vnd.wap.wml\n\n";
 3:
 4: print "<?xml version=\"1.0\"?>\n";
 5: print "<!DOCTYPE wml PUBLIC \"-//WAPFORUM//DTD WML 1.3//EN\"
 6:         \"http://www.wapforum.org/DTD/wml_1.3.xml\">\n";
 7: print "<wml>\n";
 8: print "  <card id=\"card1\" title=\"Perl Script\">\n";
 9: print "    <p>Hello World! </p>\n";
10: print "  </card>\n";
11: print "</wml>\n";
```

This is a simple "Hello World!" WML page generated by Perl script. After the Perl heading and the magic string in lines 1–2, we use a series of print statements in Perl to generate a WML page. As for all Perl programs, you may need to use

\" – to generate the double quote " inside a print statement

\n – to generate a new line

As you may say, there are too many print statements in the page. Can we use the `here` document feature of Perl? Yes! You can. Consider the following example:

```
Example: ex21-21.pl - Using Perl On WML Pages II

1: #! /usr/bin/perl
2: print "Content-type: text/vnd.wap.wml\n\n";
3:
4: print << "myWMLDoc";
5:  <?xml version="1.0"?>
6:  <!DOCTYPE wml PUBLIC "-//WAPFORUM//DTD WML 1.3//EN"
7:       "http://www.wapforum.org/DTD/wml_1.3.xml">
8:  <wml>
9:  <card id="card1" title="Perl Script">
10:   <p>
11:     Hello, I know how to write
12:     Perl script to generate WML pages for
13:     mobile devices.
14:   </p>
15:  </card>
16: </wml>
17:
18: myWMLDoc
```

After the Perl heading and the magic string, the `here` document is defined in line 4. From line 5 to the end of the `here` document, you are free to write any WML statements. As a simple example, our WML page contains only one card to display one message.

If you activate this page using your mobile device as

```
http://www.pwt-ex.com/chap21a/ex21-21.pl
```

you will see Fig. 21.50 on your mobile screen. This page can also be called within a WML page using the `go` element such as `<go href="">`.

You have now established a bridge to integrate Perl and WML together. All CGI techniques mentioned in Part IV related to Perl can also be applied to WML pages.

As a practical example, the following is a Perl program to build a WAP counter to count the number of visits to a WAP site.

Figure 21.50 Perl script and WML

21.5.2 Building a WAP page counter using Perl

To build a WAP page counter to count the number of visitors is straightforward. Basically, you need to open a counter file (a text file) and perform the following tasks:

- Open the counter file and read the data when the page is called.
- Increment the data by 1.
- Store the data back to the file.
- Generate the WML page to display the data.

In Chapter 15, we learned that a page counter can be built using Perl by the following code fragment (see ex15-07.pl):

```perl
#!usr/bin/perl
open(filehandle,"+<counter.txt");
$countNumber = <filehandle>;
$countNumber++;
seek(filehandle,0,0); ## rewind the file to the beginning
print (filehandle "$countNumber");
close(filehandle);
```

Now to generate a WML page to display the count data $countNumber is easy. An implementation is shown in the example below:

```
Example: ex21-22.pl – Building A WAP Page Counter With Perl

 1: #!usr/bin/perl
 2: open(filehandle,"+<counter.txt");
 3: $countNumber = <filehandle>;
 4: $countNumber++;
 5: seek(filehandle,0,0); ## rewind the file to the beginning
 6: print (filehandle "$countNumber");
 7: close(filehandle);
 8:
 9: print "Content-type: text/vnd.wap.wml\n\n";
10: print << "myWMLDoc";
11: <?xml version="1.0"?>
12: <!DOCTYPE wml PUBLIC "-//WAPFORUM//DTD WML 1.3//EN"
13:        "http://www.wapforum.org/DTD/wml_1.3.xml">
14: <wml>
15: <card id="card1" title="$countNumber Visitor">
16:    <p>
17:       ABC WAP Site <br />
18:       All Bargain Holidays Are Here!
19:    </p>
20: </card>
21: </wml>
22:
23: myWMLDoc
```

Every time this page is called, the data ($countNumber) inside the text file counter.txt are read (see lines 2–3). After adding 1 to the variable $countNumber, the data are stored back to the text file so that we have an up-to-date counter.

The rest of the program is to generate a WML page to include the counter data `$countNumber`. This WML page contains only one card and the counting data are output in title field of `card1` (line 15) so that they will appear at the top of the mobile screen. A screen shot of this example is shown in Fig. 21.51.

Another popular server scripting language is PHP. To generate a WML page using PHP is simple: all you need is to output WML statements using PHP echo or print functions. We will show you more than that. The following is a discussion of how to develop Mobile Internet applications with PHP.

Figure 21.51 A WAP page counter using Perl

21.5.3 WAP and/or Web browser detection with PHP

If you are running an online shop for the Web community, one simple and straightforward way to expand your business to the WAP community is to write some WML pages to introduce your business to that community or mobile phone users. In order to save the resources of the business and utilize existing facilities, the first thing you may want is a page to detect the environment of the users and redirect them to the appropriate pages (WAP or Web).

There are a number of ways to detect the browser type (WAP or Web). Many people perform the detection by searching the environment variable HTTP_USER_AGENT to see whether it contains any substring of the word "Mozilla." Consider the following example:

```
Example: ex21-23.php - WAP And WEB Browser Detection I

 1: <?PHP
 2:   $webredirect = "http://www.pwt-ex.com/chap21a/web.htm"; // A Web Page
 3:   $wapredirect = "http://www.pwt-ex.com/chap21a/wap.wml"; // A WML Page
 4:
 5:   if(strpos(strtoupper($HTTP_USER_AGENT),"ZILLA") > 0)
 6:   {
 7:     header("Location: ".$webredirect);
 8:   }
 9:   else
10:   {
11:     header("Location: ".$wapredirect);
12:   }
13: ?>
```

This PHP program appears clear and tightly written. Lines 2–3 define the two redirections to the Web and WAP pages depending on the browser type.

The `if` statement in line 5 performs the comparison. First, the program converts the environment variable $HTTP_USER_AGENT to upper case and then searches for the position of a substring "ZILLA." Comparison with "ZILLA" instead of the whole word "MOZILLA" is a good move to eliminate a zero value so that only a bigger than 0 condition is needed at the end of line 5.

Finally, the two header redirections are employed to redirect the user to the appropriate Web or WAP page.

From a practical point of view, this program is poorly written, since most micro-browsers are not Mozilla based. In addition, not all Web browsers in the market are Mozilla type. The program will have more value if the comparison is performed on the variable $HTTP_ACCEPT and looks for the MIME type. Consider the example below:

Example: ex21-24.php - WAP And WEB Browser Detection II

```
1: <?PHP
2: $webredirect = "http://www.pwt-ex.com/chap21a/web.htm"; // A Web Page
3: $wapredirect = "http://www.pwt-ex.com/chap21a/wap.wml"; // A WML Page
4:
5: if(strpos(strtoupper($HTTP_ACCEPT),"VND.WAP.WML") > 0)
6: {
7:   header("Location: ".$wapredirect);
8: }
9: else
10: {
11:   header("Location: ".$webredirect);
12: }
13: ?>
```

In this PHP program, the comparison in line 5 is looking for a match with the MIME type of the WAP page. If the browser accepts the WAP type, it should have no problem displaying WML pages. Some screen shots of this example are shown in Figs 21.52 and 21.53.

Figure 21.52 WAP and Web browser detection I

Figure 21.53 WAP and Web browser detection II

This example works simply because the WAP gateway passes the HTTP_ACCEPT value to the program. Not all gateways are designed to pass this value to your site. In this case, you may need to do it the hard way. That is, to tackle the HTTP_USER_AGENT string directly to determine the actual identity of the phone. Before that, consider a simple PHP page:

Example: ex21-25.php - WAP Browser Detection

```
1: <?
2: header("Content-type: text/vnd.wap.wml");
3: echo("<?xml version=\"1.0\"?>\n");
4: echo("<!DOCTYPE wml PUBLIC \"-//WAPFORUM//DTD WML 1.3//EN\"
5:     \"http://www.wapforum.org/DTD/wml_1.3.xml\">\n\n");
6: ?>
7: <wml>
8:   <card id="init" title="Client Info">
9:   <p>
10:     <?
11:       echo("HTTP_USER_AGENT" . $HTTP_USER_AGENT ."<br />");
12:     ?>
13:   </p>
14:   </card>
15: </wml>
```

This PHP program generates a WML page. The first statement (line 2) sends out the "Content-type" of a WML page. Lines 3–5 generate a complete WML page header so that cards and other WML elements can be defined.

In fact, this is a simple PHP script to print out the HTTP_USER_AGENT string to show the identity of the mobile phone (or device). The PHP echo statement in line 11 gets the string value and outputs it as ordinary WML text. If you run this program on Nokia's 7110 and 3330 phones, you will see Fig. 21.54 and Fig. 21.55 respectively.

Figure 21.54 Mobile phone identity I

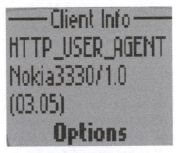

Figure 21.55 Mobile phone identity II

From these figures, we can see that the HTTP_USER_AGENT variable for these Nokia phones carries the Nokia trademark. Therefore, this trademark can be used to detect the identity of the phone and the micro-browser type. At a minimum level, we can use it to detect the browser on Nokia phones. Consider the example below:

Example: ex21-26.php - More WAP Browser Detection

```
 1: <?PHP
 2:    $webredirect = "http://www.pwt-ex.com/chap21a/web.htm"; // A Web Page
 3:    $wapredirect = "http://www.pwt-ex.com/chap21a/wap.wml"; // A WML Page
 4:
 5:    if(strpos(strtoupper($HTTP_ACCEPT),"VND.WAP.WML") > 0)
 6:    {
 7:      header("Location: ".$wapredirect);
 8:    }
 9:    else
10:    {
11:      $browser=substr(trim($HTTP_USER_AGENT),0,4);
12:      if( $browser=="Noki" ||
13:          $browser=="Eric" ||
14:          $browser=="UP.B" )
15:      {
16:        header("Location: ".$wapredirect);
17:      }
18:      else
19:      {
20:        header("Location: ".$webredirect);
21:      }
22:    }
23: ?>
```

This example is a modification of ex21-25.php to add detection on some mobile phones. Line 11 is used to extract the first four characters of the variable HTTP_USER_AGENT. This string is used to compare with the following strings:

- Noki – Nokia phones
- Eric – Ericsson (or Sony Ericsson) phones
- UP.B – Motorola phones (most Motorola phones use UP.Browser)

If the gateway fails to deliver the HTTP_ACCEPT string and the browser type is picked up by these three types of phones, a redirection to a WAP page is activated in line 16. Otherwise, we assume that the redirection is to a Web page. You should put more phone detections inside the if statement defined in lines 12–14. More information on mobile company trademarks and HTTP_USER_AGENT strings can be found on the site http://allnetdevices.com.

To be able to distinguish a WAP or Web browser is not just for redirection. The technique provides a fundamental framework for programmers to target specific devices. For example, a rich set of functions and features for mobile phones recommended by the WAP Forum is known as the Wireless Telephony Application Interface (WTAI) standard (www.wapforum.org). The WTAI specifications are dedicated to controlling your mobile phone with programming techniques. Functions recommended by the WTAI can be used if a WTAI-compliant micro-browser is detected.

As a simple example, consider the following WML go element:

```
<go href="wtai://wp/mc;12345678">Tom Tel:(12345678)</go>
<go href="wtai://wp/mc;22334455">Anna Tel:(12345678)</go>
```

If you develop a WML page with these lines, you can click on the underlined text and make a phone call to the people you want.

Have you thought about sending an email using your mobile phone? A WML page to send a short email message sometimes is quite handy since you can use it anywhere at any time. Also, the email message will be waiting in the recipient's inbox whenever he or she is available in the office or at home. That is, an email message will never get a "Busy Tone."

21.5.4 Emailing with your mobile phone: mobile email

The basic idea of sending email messages using a WAP or WML page is simple. First, you create a WML page with some text boxes to obtain the "To" and "Message" fields. The data are then sent to a server script such as Perl or PHP. Finally, all you have to do is to construct the server script to deliver the email for you.

Before we consider a WML page to deliver mobile email, we need to know how to pass variables from a WML page to CGI script. One simple way to do this is to use the query string. As a reminder, the following anchor <a> element can pass data from a WML or XHTML page to CGI script:

```
<a href="http://www.pwt-ex.com/chap21a/exAA-BB.php?var1=
    data1&var2=data2">Activate a PHP Script </a>
```

In normal circumstances, when the CGI script, e.g., exAA-BB.php, is called, it contains the following two name/variable pairs:

```
$var1 = data1
$var2 = data2
```

For some reason, a number of mobile phones, WAP gateways, and/or micro-browsers accept only one name/value pair of the query string. In this case, we may need to consolidate all the "From," "Subject," "To," and "Message"' fields of an email into one name/value pair as

```
<a href="http://www.pwt-ex.com/chap21a/mobile_email.php?
  QST=$from;$subject;$to;$message">Send Mobile Email</a>
```

It is only a simple process to separate the query string QST into variables using PHP. In this case, the delimiter is a simple semi-colon ";." Consider the mobile email example below:

```
Example: ex21-27.wml - Mobile Email Using WML

 1: <?xml version="1.0"?>
 2: <!DOCTYPE wml PUBLIC "-//WAPFORUM//DTD WML 1.3//EN"
 3: "http://www.wapforum.org/DTD/wml_1.3.xml">
 4: <wml>
 5:  <card id="index" title="Mobile Email" newcontext = "true">
 6:  <p>
 7:   From:    <input name="Fr" value="jo@www.pwt-ex.com" maxlength="30" />
 8:   Subject: <input name="Su" value="Mobile Email" maxlength="20" />
 9:   To:      <input name="To" value="info@www.pwt-ex.com" maxlength="30" />
10:   Msg:     <input name="Mg" value="Mobile Email" maxlength="80" />
11:   <a href =
12:     "http://www.pwt-ex.com/chap21a/ex21-27.php?QST=$Fr;:;$Su;:;$To;:;$Mg">
13:    Send</a>
14:  </p>
15:  </card>
16: </wml>
```

Only 16 lines of code are needed to do this job. This WML page contains only one card with four text input fields. They are the usual email headers From, Subject, To, and Message corresponding to the text boxes defined in lines 7, 8, 9, and 10. Once these boxes are filled in and the Send button is clicked, the anchor <a> statement in lines 11–13 is called. The following action (see line 12)

http://www.pwt-ex.com/chap21a/ex21-27.php?QST=$Fr;:;$Su;:;$To;:;$Mg

would activate the PHP program ex21-27.php with a query string containing all the email input data separated by a special delimiter ;:;.

The function of the PHP program ex21-27.php is simple. First, it will capture the query string and then separate and store it into variables $From, $Subject, $To, and $Body. After that a simple call to the PHP mail function

```
mail($To,$Subject,$Body,$Headers);
```

would deliver the email to the recipient. Since the email originated from a mobile phone (or device), we generally call it mobile email.

The program code of the PHP script ex21-27.php is listed below:

```
Example: ex21-27.php - The PHP Script For ex21-27.wml

 1: <?
 2:   header("Content-type: text/vnd.wap.wml");
 3:   echo("<?xml version=\"1.0\"?>\n");
 4:   echo("<!DOCTYPE wml PUBLIC \"-//WAPFORUM//DTD WML 1.3//EN\"
 5:     \"http://www.wapforum.org/DTD/wml_1.3.xml\">\n\n");
 6: ?>
 7: <wml>
 8: <card id="PHPScript" title="Mobile Email">
 9: <p>
10:
11:   <?php
12:   list ($From, $Subject, $To, $Body) = split (';:;', $QST);
13:   $Headers = "From: " . $From;
14:
15:   if (mail($To,$Subject,$Body,$Headers))
16:   {
17:     echo ("The Mobile Email Has Been Sent To: " . $To);
```

```
18:    } else {
19:       echo ("Sorry!<br />");
20:       echo ("Unable To Send Your Mobile Email To: " . $To);
21:    }
22: ?>
23:
24: </p>
25: </card>
26: </wml>
```

This PHP program is also easy to understand. Lines 1–6 are used to define the necessary headers for a WML page using PHP. After that, we define a WML card called "Mobile Email." Inside this card, a block of PHP statements are used to deliver the email.

First, the following PHP `list` command is used to extract the email data from the query string `$QST` into the `$From`, `$Subject`, `$To`, and `$Body` variables (line 12):

```
list ($From, $Subject, $To, $Body) = split (';:;', $QST);
```

Note that the delimiter used in ex21-27.wml must match the delimiter inside the `split()` function.

Since the normal PHP mail function `mail()` doesn't have a "From" field, the header variable `$Header` in line 13 is used to construct the address of the sender. Finally, a simple call to the `mail()` function would deliver the email. Depending on the returned value of the `mail()` function, a message is displayed to show the result of the delivery.

In this example, Jo sends an email message to John Smith on his mobile phone. The process is shown in Figs 21.56–21.58. When John Smith arrives his office, an email message is waiting for him on his machine as illustrated in Fig. 21.59.

Figure 21.56 Mobile email I

Figure 21.57 Mobile email II

Figure 21.58 Mobile email III

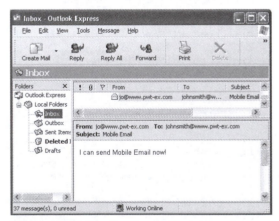

Figure 21.59 Email arrives in the inbox of Outlook Express

Databases are important tools for many commercial and non-commercial applications. As the final section of this chapter, let's consider how to implement an m-business "Last Minute Offer" with a database.

21.5.5 M-business with a database

Databases and their applications are big subjects and have occupied a significant area in this book. In this section, we will only show you how to apply database (MySQL) techniques to implement an m-business.

The m-business we are going to build is called "Last Minute Offer" targeting mobile phone customers. Suppose the company has an online business (Web type) with a good customer database. The new m-business is offering a special discount on a single product for a very short period of time to its members with a mobile device. The site is members only and they will need a user name and password to log in. The user name and password will be checked against the values in the customer database.

For our step-by-step demonstration, we will implement this m-business in two modules. The first module is to implement a WAP framework of the site. This framework, basically, has the following functions:

- Display the site "Last Minute Offer."
- Obtain the user name and password of a member.
- Check the user name and password against the data inside a customer database.
- Allow only a valid customer to log in.

Due to the small-screen nature of most mobile phones, the interface of the m-business is a simple one. Consider the following WML page:

```
Example: ex21-28.wml – WML Interface For An M-Business

 1: <?xml version="1.0"?>
 2: <!DOCTYPE wml PUBLIC "-//WAPFORUM//DTD WML 1.3//EN"
 3: "http://www.wapforum.org/DTD/wml_1.3.xml">
 4: <wml>
 5: <card id="index" title="Company Name" newcontext = "true">
 6: <p>Members Only Site
 7:  Name:       <input name="userId" value="johnsmith" />
 8:  Password:  <input name="passId" value="johnsmith" />
 9:  <a href="http://www.pwt-ex.com/chap21a/ex21-28.php?QST=$userId;:;$passId">
10:   login</a>
11: </p>
12: </card>
13: </wml>
```

This is a simple WML page with one card and two text boxes. The text boxes are used to obtain the user name and password. When the underlined text "login" is clicked on, the PHP program ex21-28.php is called with the following query string as input (see line 9):

```
ex21-28.php?QST=$userId;:;$passId
```

Again, the user name and password are consolidated as one query argument. A simple `split()` function can be used to split them in the PHP program.

The PHP program ex21-28.php is the main processing engine for this example. This program is, in fact, a database application to perform the following tasks:

- Obtain the input user name $userId and password $passId.
- Connect to the MySQL database buss_db and the customer profile table cust_profile.
- Execute an SQL statement to locate the $userId and obtain the related data.
- Compare the password in the database against the variable $passId for a match.

This PHP program is listed below:

Example: ex21–28.php– The PHP Script For ex21–28.wml

```
 1: <?
 2:   header("Content-type: text/vnd.wap.wml");
 3:   echo("<?xml version=\"1.0\"?>\n");
 4:   echo("<!DOCTYPE wml PUBLIC \"-//WAPFORUM//DTD WML 1.3//EN\"
 5:      \"http://www.wapforum.org/DTD/wml_1.3.xml\">\n\n");
 6: ?>
 7: <wml>
 8: <card id="card1" title="Company Name">
 9: <p>
10: <?php
11:
12:   list ($userId,$passId) = split (';:;', $QST);
13:
14:   if ($passId && $userId)
15:   {
16:     $passId = md5($passId);
17:
18:     $db = mysql_connect("www.pwt-ex.com", "johnsmith","johnsmith");
19:     mysql_select_db("buss_db",$db);
20:
21:     $query = "SELECT * FROM cust_profile WHERE user_Id='$userId'";
22:     $result = mysql_query ($query) or die ("SQL Query Error..");
23:
24:     $row = mysql_fetch_array ($result);
25:
26:     if ($passId == $row['password'])
27:     {
28:         echo("Thank you! <br /> Enjoy Your Visit");
29:     }
30:     else
31:     {
32:       echo "Sorry! Wrong Password <br />";
33:     }
34:     mysql_free_result ($result);
35:   }
36:   else
37:   {
38:     echo "Sorry! Access Denied <br />";
39:   }
40: ?>
41: </p>
42: </card>
43: </wml>
```

The first six lines are used to construct the necessary WML header using PHP. The rest of the program contains one card and one PHP program block (lines 10–40).

First, the user name and password are extracted from the query string $QST in line 12. Lines 18–19 are used to make the connection to the database buss_db and the customer profile table cust_profile. The next two statements (lines 21–22) are used to execute the SQL statement

```
SELECT * FROM cust_profile WHERE user_Id='$userId'
```

so that the database information matches the $userId stored in array variable $result. By calling the function mysql_fetch_array() in line 24, the password data from the database are stored in the variable $row['password']. This value can then be used to compare to the $passId (line 26). If there is a match, we know that the user is a member of the site: if there is no match, we have a wrong password case. Please note that the passwords are compared as MD encrypted strings. Some screen shots of this example are shown in Figs 21.60 and 21.61.

Figure 21.60 A login page using WML I

Figure 20.61 Login successful

Now we can implement the second module to change this framework into an m-business site. First, we would like to change the company name to "Last Minute Offer." Instead of the "Thank you" message as in Fig. 21.61, a stunning special offer is needed to attract the customers. For this example, we use the following business message:

```
500x DVD Players
40 Dollars Each
Buy One?
```

Right under this message, you may also need to construct Yes and No buttons. This message and the buttons can be implemented as the following PHP strings:

```
$llst = "500x DVD Players <br /> 40 Dollars Each<br />Buy One?<br />";
$yes = "<a href=\"http://www.pwt-ex.com/chap21a/ex21-29.php?QST=yes;:;"
            .$userId.";:;" .$passId."\">Yes</a>";
$no = "<a href=\"http://www.pwt-ex.com/chap21a/ex21-29.wml\">No</a>";
```

For example, when you execute the echo function echo($yes) in a WML page, you will see an underlined text "Yes." This text is in fact an anchor element <a> to link to the program ex21-29.php and ultimately trigger the purchase.

First, let's see the interface part of this m-business page. The page is very similar to ex21-28.wml and is listed below:

```
Example: ex21-29.wml - Implement The M-Businss "Last Minute Offer"

 1: <?xml version="1.0"?>
 2: <!DOCTYPE wml PUBLIC "-//WAPFORUM//DTD WML 1.3//EN"
 3: "http://www.wapforum.org/DTD/wml_1.3.xml">
 4: <wml>
 5: <card id="index" title="Last Minute Offer" newcontext = "true">
 6: <p>Members Only Site <br />
 7:    Name: <input name="userId" value="johnsmith" />
 8:    Password: <input name="passId" value="johnsmith" />
 9:    <a href=
10:    "http://www.pwt-ex.com/chap21a/ex21-29.php?QST=no;:;$userId;:;$passId">
11:    login</a>
12: </p>
13: </card>
14: </wml>
```

If you compare this page with ex21-28.wml, you will find that the only major difference is in line 10. That is, the query string QST has one more argument. The first argument of QST contains the word "no." This is used to indicate that the user hasn't bought anything yet.

In order to accommodate the business, we need to convert the example ex21-28.php program to ex21-29.php and make some major changes. Apart from the special offer message to attract customers, you may also need to perform some file operations to store the order permanently. Consider the program code as follows:

```
Example: ex21-29.php - The PHP Script For ex21-29.wml

 1: <?
 2:   header("Content-type: text/vnd.wap.wml");
 3:   echo("<?xml version=\"1.0\"?>\n");
 4:   echo("<!DOCTYPE wml PUBLIC \"-//WAPFORUM//DTD WML 1.3//EN\"
 5:       \"http://www.wapforum.org/DTD/wml_1.3.xml\">\n\n");
 6: ?>
 7: <wml>
 8: <card id="card1" title="Last Minute Offer">
 9: <p>
10:   <?php
11:
12:   list ($bu,$userId,$passId) = split (';:;', $QST);
13:
14:   $llst = "500x DVD Players <br /> 40 Dollars Each<br />Buy One?<br />";
15:   $buyone = "One DVD Player -- 40 Dollars";
16:
17:   $yes = "<a href=\"http://www.pwt-ex.com/chap21a/ex21-29.php?QST=yes;:;"
18:                 .$userId.";:;" .$passId."\">Yes</a>";
19:   $no = "<a href=\"http://www.pwt-ex.com/chap21a/ex21-29.wml\">No</a>";
20:
21:   if ($passId && $userId)
22:   {
23:    $passId = md5($passId);
24:
25:    $db = mysql_connect("www.pwt-ex.com", "johnsmith","johnsmith");
26:    mysql_select_db("password",$db);
27:
28:    $query = "SELECT * FROM password WHERE name='$userId'";
29:    $result = mysql_query ($query) or die ("SQL Query Error..");
30:
31:    $row = mysql_fetch_array ($result);
32:
33:    if ($passId == $row['password'])
34:    {
35:      if ($bu =="no")
36:      {
37:        echo($llst);
38:        echo($yes . " ------ ". $no);
39:      }
40:      if ($bu =="yes")
41:      {
42:        $today = getdate();
43:        $timeSt = $today['mday'] ." ". $today['month'] ." ".
44:                  $today['year'] ." ". $today['hours'] .":".
45:                  $today['minutes'].":". $today['seconds'];
46:
47:        $ordSt = "Ordered by: ".$userId .
48:                  "\r\n -- Password Check OK --\r\n".
49:                  $timeSt ."\r\n". $buyone ."\r\n";
```

```
50:
51:            $filename ="mobileorder.txt";
52:            $fd = fopen($filename,"a");
53:            fwrite($fd,$ordSt);
54:            fwrite($fd,"\r\n==============================\r\n");
55:            fclose($fd);
56:
57:          echo("Thank you and Confirmed!<br/>Delivery Within 7 Days<br />");
58:            }
59:      }
60:    else
61:    {
62:      echo "Sorry! Wrong Password <br />";
63:      }
64:    mysql_free_result ($result);
65:    }
66:    else
67:    {
68:        echo "Sorry! Access Denied <br />";
69:    }
70:    ?>
71: </p>
72: </card>
73: </wml>
```

The first part of this program is to construct the strings

    $llst   –   Special offer (or discount) string (line 14)

    $yes   –   The Yes button (line 17)

    $no   –   The No button (line 19)

    $buyone –   When the "Yes" button is clicked, this string will be written into a file as a permanent record (line 15)

The major part of this program is in lines 35–58. When this program is called by ex21-29.wml, the variable $bu carries a "no" value to indicate that no purchase has been made. In this case, line 37 is used to display the special offer message stored in variable $llst. The next line is to display the Yes and No buttons together waiting for a user input.

When the user presses the Yes button, the anchor element <a> in lines 17–18 turns out to be

```
<a href="http://www.pwt-ex.com/chap21a/ex21-29.php?
    QST=yes;:;$userId;:;$passId">Yes</a>"
```

Therefore the same program ex21-29.php is called with a "yes" value stored in the variable $bu. This situation will lead to the execution of the PHP program block defined in lines 40–58. The tasks of this program block are:

- Build the data and time string $timeSt (lines 42–45) so that the purchase order has a time stamp.
- Build the ordering string $ordSt. This order string contains the following detailed information:
  - Who makes the order.
  - When the order was made.
  - Password checking status.
  - Details of the special offer.

When this information is ready, the following simple file operation would write the purchase order into the file mobileorder.txt as a permanent record:

```
$filename ="mobileorder.txt";
$fd = fopen($filename,"a");
fwrite($fd,$ordSt);
fwrite($fd,"\r\n===============================\r\n");
fclose($fd);
```

Together with the information in the database, the records in the file can then be used for delivery and making charges. Some screen shots of this example are shown in Figs 21.62–21.64. Some of the records inside the file mobileorder.txt are shown in Fig. 21.65.

Figure 21.62 The login page for M-Business

Figure 21.63 Login successful

Figure 21.64 Confirmation message for the order

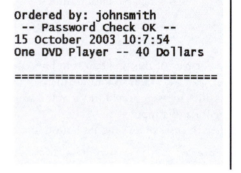

Figure 21.65 The permanent purchase record

Glossary

Active Perl A popular software implementation of the Perl Language from Active State. It supports Windows platforms as well as Solaris and LINUX.

Active Server Page (ASP) A specification from Microsoft to write server script. When a browser requests an ASP page, the Web server generates a page with HTML/XHTML code and sends it back to the browser. By convention, ASP files end with `.asp` as the file extension.

ActiveX A set of technologies developed by Microsoft based on Object Linking and Embedding (OLE) and Component Object Model (COM). ActiveX allows special features such as calling and embedding an application within another among Microsoft products.

ActiveX Data Objects (ADO) A high-level interface from Microsoft for data objects. ADO is used to provide a consistent way of accessing data regardless of how the data are structured.

American National Standards Institute (ANSI) Founded in 1918, ANSI is a voluntary organization composed of over 1,300 members that creates standards for the computer industry.

America Online (AOL) A commercial organization offers subscribers a connection to the Internet. *See also* Internet service provider.

American Standard Code for Information Interchange (ASCII) An 8-bit character set defining alphanumeric characters. For example, the ASCII code for character A is 65. ASCII is widely used to represent English characters on computers.

Animated GIF (GIF89a) A type of GIF image that contains several images in a single GIF file. By cycling through each image, animation is achieved. It has become extremely popular on the Web because it is small and supported by nearly all Web browsers. By convention, animated GIF files usually end with a `.gif` file extension.

Apache A public domain Web server package developed by a group of volunteers. Apache is free with sophisticated features and excellent performance. It is used to host more than 50% of all Web sites in the world.

Applet An applet is a small program designed to run within another application. Once applets are downloaded from the Web they can be executed quickly by the user's browser.

Application layer The interface layer that establishes communication rights to other applications and can initiate a connection between two applications.

Application Programming Interface (API) A set of routines or functions that are available to developers and applications to provide specific services used by a system.

ASP.NET A Microsoft server-side Web technology to develop Web pages. Unlike ASP, an ASP.NET page is compiled into an intermediate language by a .NET common language run-time-compliant compiler and then to a native machine code to run. By convention ASP.NET files end with `.aspx` as the file extension.

Asynchronous Communications without a regular time basis allowing transmission at unequal rates.

Audio Video Interleaved (AVI) A standard system from Microsoft for integrating sound and vision for Windows into a single file for computer storage. By convention AVI files usually end with `.avi` as the file extension.

Bandwidth The amount of data that can be transmitted through a medium in a fixed amount of time. For digital devices, the bandwidth is usually expressed in bits per second (bps) or bytes per second. For analog devices, the bandwidth is expressed in cycles per second, or hertz (Hz).

Binary digit (Bit) The most basic unit used by computers. A single bit can hold only one of two values, 0 or 1. More meaningful values are obtained by combining consecutive bits into larger units.

Bit rate The rate that bits are transmitted over a network, usually expressed in seconds.

Bitmap (BMP) The standard graphics and image format used in the Windows environment. By convention, BMP files usually end with a `.bmp` file extension.

Broadcast The simultaneous transmission of the same data to all nodes connected to a network.

Browser *See* Web browser.

Browser–server interaction The dialog and operations between a Web server and browser.

Buffer A memory area used for handling input and output.

Bytecode The compiled format for Java source programs. Once a Java program has been converted to bytecode, it can be transferred across a network and executed by JVM or JRE. By convention, Java bytecode files end with a `.class` file extension.

Cascading Style Sheet (CSS) A feature added to HTML/XHTML that provides more control over how pages are displayed. With CSS, designers and users can create structural style sheets that define how elements appear. These style sheets can then be used again and applied to any Web page.

Certificate (or digital certificate) An attachment to an electronic message used for security purposes. The common purpose of a digital certificate is to verify the identity of the sender.

Certification Authority (CA) A trusted third-party organization or company that issues digital certificates. The CA guarantees that the identity of the party in the certificate is genuine.

Character DATA (CDATA) For HTML/XHTML documents, this means "don't interpret these characters."

Client A computer or device on a network that calls another computer for resources.

Client script Sometimes called client-side script. Client scripts are usually embedded into an HTML/XHTML document and run by the Web browser to generate special or dynamic features. ECMAScript is the standard for developing client script. *See also* Server script.

Collaboration Data Objects (CDO) A high-level set of COM objects that allow easy access to email systems embedded in Microsoft Windows products.

Collaboration Data Objects for NT Server (CDONTS) A library of functions interfacing with a Simple Mail Transfer Protocol (SMTP) server to handle email.

Common Gateway Interface (CGI) A specification for transferring information between a program on a Web server and a Web client.

Common Gateway Interface application (CGI application) Any program on a Web server accepting and returning data that conform to the CGI specification. CGI applications can be written by many programming languages such as C/C++, Perl, ASP, and PHP. CGI scripts are CGI applications.

Common Gateway Interface script (CGI script) The scripts on a Web server that can generate HTML/XHTML code back to a browser. Perl, ASP, and PHP are languages that can be used to write CGI scripts.

Component Object Model (COM) A specification developed by Microsoft for building software components that can be assembled into programs or add functionality to existing programs running on Microsoft Windows platforms.

Connection A link between two or more computers, processes, applications, devices, networks, and so on. Connections may be logical, physical, or both.

Connection oriented A type of network service in which the Transport Layer Protocol sends acknowledgments to the sender regarding incoming data. Data will be retransmitted if necessary.

Console window An application of the operating system that allows you to type commands and communicate with the operating system using the keyboard.

Cookie A message from a Web server computer, sent to and stored by the browser on your computer. The message is then sent back to the server each time the browser requests a page from the server.

Coordinated Universal Time (UTC) The time scale based on the Earth's inconsistent rotation rate and highly accurate atomic time. When atomic time and Earth time approach a 1 second difference, a leap second is introduced into UTC.

Cryptography A general term for the encryption and decryption methods used for data transmission and protection.

Data Source Name (DSN) A piece of information that links an embedded database query to a specific database on a server.

Database Interface (DBI) Perl's abstract database interface which supports any database product with a database driver.

Database management systems (DBMS) The software that allows you to construct, modify, and maintain a database. DBMS provide the link between user and data.

Database server A computer system used to process database queries.

Document Object Model (DOM) The standard specification from W3C for how objects in a Web page (text, images, headers, links, etc.) are represented. The DOM defines what attributes are associated with each object, and how the objects and attributes can be manipulated.

Document Type Definition (DTD) This states the syntax of tags, elements, and attributes to ensure that all documents are formatted the same way.

Domain Name System (DNS) An Internet service that translates names into IP addresses. Every time you use a name such as www.pwt-ex.com on the Internet, DNS is used to translate it to an IP address.

Dynamic Extensible Hyper Text Markup Lanaguage (DXHTML) An XHTML page with dynamic features such as moving objects, interaction with users, and automation. There is no formal standard and specification for DXHTML.

Dynamic Hyper Text Markup Lanaguage (DHTML) An HTML page with dynamic features such as moving objects, interaction with users, and automation. There is no formal standard and specification for DHTML.

ECMAScript (ECMA262) A standard scripting language developed by ECMA and based on JavaScript. ECMAScript is supported by all major browsers such as IE, NS, and Opera.

E-commerce Conducting business online. This includes, for example, buying and selling products on the Internet.

Electronic Data Interchange (EDI) The transfer of data between different companies using networks, such as the Internet. ANSI has approved a set of EDI standards known as the X12 standards.

Electronic Funds Transfer (EFT) At the point of sale, this is a system which takes money straight out of your bank account when you pay for something with your plastic card.

Element For HTML, element refers to the name you usually put inside a tag (e.g., < . . . >). All elements in XHTML should have an end tag (e.g., < / . . . >).

Email Electronic messages transmitted on a network. It is a general term for electronic mail or Internet mail.

European Computer Manufacturers Association (ECMA) An organization that sets computer standards in Europe.

Event Any input and/or interaction caused by the user, which could be keystrokes, button clicks, or the position of the mouse pointer.

Event handler A routine inside an application to be triggered by an event such as a mouse click.

Event listener A routine inside an application to listen to any event generated by the user.

Extensible Hyper Text Markup Language (XHTML) A language similar to HTML with XML syntax. XHTML is recommended by the W3C authority for creating documents on the World Wide Web.

Extensible Markup Language (XML) A specification developed by the W3C for Web pages. It allows designers to create their own customized elements.

Extensible Style Language Transformation (XSLT) The language used in XSL style sheets to transform XML documents into other documents such as HTML, XHTML, and XML.

File server A computer or device on a network dedicated to storing files and providing file services to users.

File Transfer Protocol (FTP) The protocol used on the Internet for sending and receiving files.

Gateway A networking device that translates protocols of one type of network into those of another network.

Gnu Privacy Guard (GnuPG) A freely available software package provides a complete implementation of the Open Pretty Good Privacy (OpenPGP) standard (IEFT RFC 2440).

Graphical User Interface (GUI) A program interface that uses the graphics capabilities of the computer to make the program easier to use.

Graphics Interchange Format (GIF) A bitmap graphics format from CompuServe to transfer images between different computers. A GIF picture is limited to 256 colors and is more effective for scanned images such as drawings and illustrations. By convention, GIF files usually end with a `.gif` file extension.

Greenwich Mean Time (GMT) The internationally accepted standard time. GMT is the local time in Greenwich. For example, the time zone of the Philippines is 0000 GMT (+ 8) = 8.00 am. That is, 8 hours ahead of GMT time.

Hexadecimal A base 16 number system consisting of 16 unique symbols: 0, 1, 2, 3, 4, 5, 6, 7, 8, 9, A, B, C, D, E, and F. For example, hexadecimal F represents the value 15 in decimal and FF is 255 in decimal.

Host *See* Web server.

Hyper Text Markup Language (HTML) A language originally developed by Tim Berners-Lee and later adopted as a standard to create documents on the World Wide Web.

Hyper Text Transfer Protocol (HTTP) The underlying protocol defining how messages are formatted and transmitted on the Web, and what actions Web servers and browsers should take in respond to various commands.

Hyperlink A feature that allows an element in an electronic document to be linked to another place in the same or another document.

Integrated Service Digital Network (ISDN) A set of standards for integrating multiple services such as voice, data, video, etc.

Internet Sometimes called the TCP/IP network, this is the vast collection of interconnected networks that all use the TCP/IP suite.

Internet Engineering Task Force (IETF) The main standards organization for the Internet concerned with Internet architecture and operations. It is open to anyone who is interested.

Internet Explorer (IE) The Web browser developed by Microsoft for Windows platforms. IE is the most popular browser used on the Web.

Internet Information Services (IIS) Microsoft's Web server that runs on Windows platforms. IIS comes bundled with Windows NT, 2000 Professional, and XP Professional.

Internet Service Provider (ISP) A company that provides services and access to the Internet.

IP address (or IP number) A unique number consisting of four parts separated by dots, e.g., 165.113.223.2 Each part can have values from 0 to 255. For the TCP/IP network (or Internet), IP addresses can be used to uniquely identify a computer on the network.

ITU Telecommunications Standardization Sector (ITU-T) ITU-T is a permanent part of the International Telecommunication Union (ITU) and is responsible for studying technical, operating and tariff questions and issuing recommendations on them with a view to standardizing telecommunications on a worldwide basis.

J2SDK A Java development environment from Sun Microsystems used to develop Java applications. It converts Java source file to bytecode to be executed by the JVM and JRE.

Java A high-level programming language developed by Sun Microsystems. Java is an object-oriented language similar to C++, but simplified to eliminate language features that cause common programming errors. By convention, Java program files end with a `.java` file extension.

Java applet Refers to the applet written in the Java language. By convention, Java program files end with a `.class` file extension.

Java Media Framework (JMF) A package developed by Sun Microsystems for programmers to develop multimedia applications using the Java language.

Java Player An application written in the Java language and developed by Sun Microsystems to handle (including playback) multimedia files such as sound, video, and movie. Java Player can be used to capture live video. It is supported on all major platforms such as Windows, MacOS, and UNIX/LINUX.

Java Runtime Environment (JRE) A run time environment developed by Sun Microsystems to convert Java bytecode into machine language and execute it locally.

Java Vitural Machine (JVM) An abstract computing machine, or virtual machine, JVM is a platform-independent execution environment that converts Java bytecode into machine language and executes it locally.

JavaScript A scripting language developed by Netscape to enable Web authors to design interactive Web pages. JavaScript can be embedded in and interact with HTML/XHTML source code. JavaScript is not Java – they are different.

Joint Photographic Expert Group (JPEG or JPG) JPEG is a lossy compression technique for color images. Image files in JPEG or JPG format are only about a tiny fraction (5%) of their original size. It is popular to transfer them on the Internet. By convention, JPEG files usually end with a `.jpeg` or `.jpg` file extension.

JScript Microsoft's implementation of ECMAScript (ECMA262), an international standard based on JavaScript.

Leased line A dedicated communication line between two points. It is usually used by organizations to connect computers over a dedicated network medium or telephone circuit.

LINUX An implementation of UNIX that runs on PCs and many other platforms. It was developed mainly by Linus Torvalds. LINUX is freely distributable with open source code.

Local Area Network (LAN) A network of computers and devices that spans a relatively small area. With LAN many users can share devices.

Mail agent An electronic mail program that helps end users manage messages. Microsoft's Outlook Express is a mail agent.

Mail client A front end email application used to compose, send, and receive electronic mail (email).

Mail exchanger A system used to relay mail into a network.

Markup language (ML) A language that has codes for indicating layout and styling such as bold face, italics, and paragraphs within a text file. Widely used markup languages include Standard General Markup Language (SGML), Hyper Text Markup Language (HTML), and Extensible Hyper Text Markup Language (XHTML).

Medium Access Unit (MAU) A device for the central connection of devices operating on a network.

Metacharacter A specific character within a text file that signals the need for special handling; in HTML angle brackets (<), ampersand (&), hash sign (#), and semi-colon (;) are metacharacters.

Micro-browser A browser in a handheld wireless device (e.g., mobile phone) that can be used to locate and display Wireless Markup Language (WML) pages on the Mobile Internet.

Microsoft Outlook Express A mail client application developed by Microsoft.

Mobile business (m-business) Conducting business on handheld wireless devices.

Mobile Internet A system of interconnected networks that allows a handheld wireless device (e.g., mobile phone) to use the network resources.

Mobile Internet Toolkit (MIT) A software package used to develop Wireless Markup Language (WML) pages on the Mobile Internet.

Modem (modulator–demodulator) A device that converts digital signals into analog signals and vice versa. Used for conversion of signals for transmission over telephone lines.

Mouse event A general term referring to operations and actions related to the pointing device (mouse).

Moving Picture Expert Group (MPEG or MPG) A working group of the International Organization for Standardization (ISO) to set standards for digital audio and video compression. MPEG or MPG compression formats are widely used in compact discs (CDs), video compact discs (VCDs), and digital video discs (DVDs). By convention, MPEG files usually end with an `.mpeg` or `.mpg` file extension.

MPEG Layer 3 Format (MP3) One of three coding schemes (Layer 1, Layer 2, and Layer 3) for the compression of audio or sound signals. By removing all signals the human ear can't detect, it compresses more than 10 times that of layer 2.

Multimedia The use of computers to present text, graphics, sound, video, movies, and animation in a unifying way. Nearly all PCs are now capable of multimedia features up to a certain level depending on the power of the computer's video adapter and CPU.

Multipurpose Internet Mail Extension (MIME) A specification for formatting non-ASCII messages so that graphics, audio, and video can be sent over the Internet.

Musical Instrument Digital Interface (MIDI or MID) A standard adopted by the electronic music industry for controlling devices, such as synthesizers and sound cards, that emit music. By convention MIDI files usually end with a `.midi` or `.mid` file extension.

MySQL A popular Structured Query Language (SQL) database server from MySQL AB. MySQL is free, distributable, open source software and available on all major platforms including Windows, Solaris, and LINUX.

Name resolution The process of mapping names or nodes to an IP address. The Domain Name System (DNS) is one system that does this.

.NET Microsoft's framework for Web-based services and component software. The design of .NET is to transform the Internet into a single computing experience regardless of programming languages or operating systems.

Netscape browser (NS) The Web browser developed by Netscape Communications. It runs on all the major platforms such as Windows, MacOS, and UNIX/LINUX.

Network News Transfer Protocol (NNTP) The protocol used to post, distribute, and retrieve USENET messages. The official specification is RFC 977.

Network service An operating system process that operates continuously and unattended to perform a service over a network. The TCP/IP network uses several network services to establish communications processes and provide server facilities.

Node For the TCP/IP network, a term refering to network devices. For Web pages, node represents a branch of elements in the sense of the Document Object Model (DOM).

Object Linking and Embedding (OLE) A technique used in the Microsoft Windows GUI. Object is a piece of information in an application. Embedding is the act of copying the object from one application to another. Linking provides an invisible link between the copied object and its original.

Object Linking and Embedding Database (OLE DB) Refers to a database system with OLE capabilities.

Open Database Connectivity (ODBC) A standard database access method developed by Microsoft. The goal of ODBC is to make it possible to access data from any database products regardless of manufacturer.

Open Pretty Good Privacy (Open PGP) An encryption standard based on Pretty Good Privacy (PGP) widely used on email. Open PGP is defined by the OpenPGP Working Group of the Internet Engineering Task Force (IETF) standard RFC 2440.

Open Source Initiative (OSI) An international organization to promote open source software that is completely free, and distributable with source code. Some famous products of OSI on the Web are Apache, Perl, and `sendmail`.

Opera: A popular Web browser from Opera Software. Opera is small, fast, and available for all major platforms including Windows, Solaris, and LINUX.

Packet In the TCP/IP network, a term referring to the data passing between the Internet layer and the data link layer. Also a generic term used to refer to data transferred through a network.

Parsed Character Data (PC DATA) For HTML/XHTML documents, the entities or texts that should be expanded by applications such as a Web browser and processed as HTML/XHTML texts and commands.

PerlScript The script engine from Active Perl to allow the Perl language to be used in Active Server Page (ASP).

Personal Data Assistant (PDA) A handheld device that combines computing, telephone/fax, Internet, and networking features.

Personal Web Server (PWS) The Web server software from Microsoft used mainly on Windows 9.x platforms.

PHP Hypertext Preprocessor (PHP) PHP is a server-side, HTML embedded scripting language used to create dynamic Web pages. PHP has built-in support for database applications on the Web. By convention, PHP files end with a `.php` file extension.

Plugin (or Plug-in) A piece of hardware or a software module that adds a specific feature or service to a larger system. On the Web, plugins are used to enhance the functionalities of Web browsers such as playing back video files.

Port A number used to identify TCP/IP applications. Generally a port is an entry or exit point.

Post Office Protocol (POP) A protocol used to retrieve email from a mail server. There are two versions of POP. The first, called POP2, requires SMTP to send messages. The POP3 version can be used with or without SMTP.

Practical Extraction and Report Language (Perl) Perl is a programming language developed by Larry Wall, especially designed for processing text. Because of its strong text processing abilities, Perl has become one of the most popular languages for writing CGI scripts. By convention, Perl files end with a `.pl` file extension.

Pretty Good Privacy (PGP) A method developed by Phil Zimmermann to encrypt or disguise computer information so that it can be securely transmitted over a network.

Private key The digital key that is kept secret in a public-key cryptographic structure. *See also* Public-key cryptography.

Protocol Rules governing the behavior or method of operation.

Public key The digital key mode available to the public in a public-key cryptographic structure. *See also* Public-key cryptography.

Public-key cryptography A cryptographic technique that uses two digital keys, a public key known to everyone and a private or secret key to keep secret. When, say, John wants to send a secure message to Mary, he uses Mary's public key to encrypt the message. Only Mary or the owner of the corresponding secret key can decrypt the message.

Public-Key Infrastructure (PKI) A system of digital certificates, Certification Authorities, and other registration authorities that verify and authenticate the validity of each party involved in an Internet transaction.

Real-Time Transport Protocol (RTP) An Internet protocol on top of the User Datagram Protocol (UDP) for transmitting real-time data such as audio and video. RTP itself does not guarantee real-time delivery of data, nor to arrive at all. It is used primarily for broadcasting messages over a network.

RealPlayer Formerly known as RealAudio, this is a browser plugin that lets you listen to or view sound or video as it is downloaded to your computer.

Relational database management system (RDBMS) A database management system that can handle several different database files at the same time, allowing the user to link the files of related data.

Remote Procedure Call (RPC) A TCP/IP feature that provides a routine to call a server, which returns output and status codes to the client.

Request For Comments (RFC) Publications from the Internet Engineering Task Force (IETF) which detail the Internet's standards.

Resource package module (RPM) A software management package. RPM allows you to install, uninstall, upgrade, and maintain a database of installed software packages on your system.

Router A device that connects LANs to the Internet and routes traffic between them.

Script Similar to a macro or batch file, a script is a list of commands or simple functions that can be executed without user interaction. Scripts are popular on the Web to create dynamic features. *See also* Client script and Server script.

Scripting language The programming language you can use to write scripts. ECMAScript (for client script), VBScript, ASP, PHP, and Perl are some of the scripting languages on the Web.

Search engine A program that searches documents for specified keywords and returns a list of the documents where the keywords were found. A search engine is an important tool for distributing and searching Web sites.

Secure Electronic Transfer (SET) A standard used by major credit card companies to set up secure credit card transactions on the Internet. SET allows your credit card number to go direct to the credit card company without being seen by the merchant.

Secure Sockets Layer (SSL) A protocol developed by Netscape to set up a public-key cryptography connection on the Web. SSL allows a Web browser to locate and display a Web page in secure mode. The Web browser and server, in this case, are performing encryption/decryption using public-key technologies online.

Server A computer or device on a network that manages network resources. Usually, servers are set up on a network to provide services to clients. *See also*, File server, Database server, and Web server.

Server script Scripts to be run by a server. Most server scripts are CGI script and used to generate HTML/XHTML documents and return them to a browser. Perl, ASP, and PHP are languages used to write server scripts.

Simple Mail Transfer Protocol (SMTP) A protocol for sending email messages between servers. Most email systems that send mail over the Internet use SMTP to send messages from one server to another.

Socket In the TCP/IP network, an addressable point that consists of an IP address and a TCP or UDP port number that provides applications with access to TCP/IP.

Socket address The complete designation of a TCP/IP node consisting of a 32-bit IP address and a 16-bit port number.

SQL database The database systems that use the SQL language.

Standard Generalized Markup Language (SGML) A specification from the International Organization for Standardization (ISO) for organizing and tagging elements of a document. SGML specifies the rules for tagging elements and contains no particular formatting features.

Structured Query Language (SQL) A standardized query language for requesting information from a database. It is defined by ANSI and the resulting file of data should be transferable to other databases.

Synchronous The transfer of data between two devices on a network at a timed rate (as opposed to asynchronously).

Tag For HTML/XHTML, tag is a command (e.g., < . . .>) inserted in a document that specifies how the document, or a portion of the document, should be formatted.

TCP/IP network The network using the TCP and IP suite. TCP guarantees data transmission; IP deals with packets and address. TCP/IP networks are generally called Internet.

Traffic A general term used to describe the amount of data on a network.

Transmission Control Protocol (TCP) One of the main protocols in TCP/IP networks. TCP enables two hosts to establish a connection and exchange data. It guarantees delivery of data and also that packets will be delivered in the same order in which they were sent. Data will be retransmitted if necessary.

Transport Layer Security (TLS) Based on Netscape's SSL 3.0, TLS is an extension of SSL.

Uniform Resource Identifier (URI) The generic term for all types of global names and addresses that refer to objects on the Web. A URL is one kind of URI.

Uniform Resource Locator (URL) The global address of documents and other resources on the Web. For example, http://www.pwt-ex.com/ex01-01.htm and ftp://www.pwt-ex.com/ex01-01.htm are two URLs to identify the same file on the Web.

Universal Data Access (UDA) A high-level specification developed by Microsoft for accessing data objects regardless of their structure.

UNIX An operating system written by Ken Thompson of Bell Labs and used for mainframes and minicomputers. It is now available for personal computers (PCs).

USENET A world-wide network of systems (part of the Internet) with thousands of newsgroups. Users can post messages and read messages among newsgroups.

User agent A device that interprets HTML or other Web documents. The most commonly used user agents are Web browsers on computer screens.

User Datagram Protocol (UDP) A connectionless protocol that, like TCP, runs on top of IP networks. Unlike TCP/IP or Internet, UDP does not perform retransmission of data. It is used primarily for broadcasting messages over a network where the loss of some video data is not very important.

VBScript A scripting language developed by Microsoft and supported by Microsoft's IE browser family. VBScript is a simplified version of the Visual Basic programming language.

WAP Cascading Style Sheet (WCSS) A specification from WAP. It specifies a subset of CSS2 with WAP specific extensions. WCSS can be used to style XML, XHTML-Basic, and WML 2.0 documents.

Waveform (WAV) The sound file format developed jointly by Microsoft and IBM and supported by all Windows platforms. By convention, Waveform files are usually end with a .wav file extension.

Web A community of Internet servers that support HTML/XHTML formatted documents. The documents or Web pages support a feature that links to other documents, as well as graphics, audio, and video files.

Web browser A software application used to locate and display Web pages on the Internet.

Web client A computer or device running a Web browser to request network resources.

Web page A document on the Web. Every Web page is identified by a unique address called the uniform resource locator (URL).

Web server A machine running server software such as Apache or IIS, assigned an IP address, and connected to the Internet so that it can provide documents on the Web. A Web server is sometimes called a host computer.

Web site A Web server with a global unique URL.

Web site address Refers to the IP address (such as 165.181.109.11) of the host computer or the name (such as www.pwt-ex.com) that can be translated into an IP address.

Wide Area Network (WAN) A system of LANs networked together.

Windows Media Player (WMP) An application developed by Microsoft to handle (including playback) multimedia files such as sound, video, and movies. WMP is mainly used on Windows platforms and can capture live video.

Wireless Application Protocol (WAP) A protocol that defines the development and operating environment for handheld wireless devices such as mobile phones, pagers, and PDAs. WAP uses a lighter version of the TCP/IP suite for transmission between devices.

Wireless Application Protocol Forum (WAP Forum) The authority that create standards for wireless devices and applications. The Wireless Markup Language (WML) specification was set by the WAP Forum.

Wireless Markup Language (WML) The standard language used to develop documents especially for small and low-bandwidth devices such as mobile phones with limited processing power and a small screen.

Wireless Markup Language page (WML page) A document written in the Wireless Markup Language (WML). A WML page can be located and displayed by a handheld wireless device with a micro-browser.

Wireless Markup Language Script (WMLScript) A specification that can be used to write scripts and work with Wireless Markup Language (WML) pages.

Wireless Telephony Application Interface (WTAI) A specification from the WAP Forum describing standard telephony-specific extensions including Wireless Markup Language (WML) and Wireless Markup Language Script (WMLScript).

World Wide Web *See* Web.

World Wide Web Consortium (W3C) Founded by Tim Berners-Lee in 1994, this is an international consortium of companies to set standards on the Web.

WYSIWYG Stands for "what you see is what you get" and refers to programs that show on a screen exactly what will appear when a document is printed.

XHTML-Basic A simplified version of XHTML used in version 2 of the Wireless Markup Language (WML 2.0).

XML Schema Definition (XSD) A specification from W3C for Extensible Markup Language (XML) definition and including both structural and data type standards.

XML Style Sheet Language (XSL) A standard specification by W3C for separating style from content. With XSL and XSLT, an XML document can be transformed into other document formats such as HTML for display on browsers.

Index

DATE DUE

NOV 1 9 2004		
APR 1 2 2007		

GAYLORD   #3522PI   Printed in USA